THE HINDU WORLD

A well-chosen spread of articles by a galaxy of outstanding scholars on the main topics within the Hindu traditions—it all adds up to the most exciting as well as informative guide yet.

(John Brockington, Professor of Sanskrit, The University of Edinburgh)

The Hindu World is the most authoritative and up-to-date single volume on Hinduism available today. In twenty-four chapters, written by leading international scholars, it provides a comprehensive and critical guide to the various literatures, traditions, and practices of Hinduism. Ideally tailored as an introduction to key topics in Hinduism and for use as a definitive reference source, the book offers fresh insights into many aspects of Hindu life that are organized under six headings: Oral Teachings and Textual Traditions, Theistic and Devotional Movements, Cosmic Order and Human Goals, Social Action and Social Structure, Vitality in Persons and in Places, and Linguistic and Philosophic Analysis.

The Hindu World contains new research that defines the current study of Hinduism. It reflects upon the impact of recent poststructuralist approaches while emphasizing Hinduism's classical heritage and everyday customs in ways that will be familiar to Hindus themselves. Exploring the enormous diversity of Hinduism's multidimensional culture while considering its status as a category for analysis, the book achieves a distinctive creative balance between scholarly "outsider" perspectives, and the beliefs and values of practicing Hindus.

Contributors: Surinder M. Bhardwaj, Francis X. Clooney, Madhav M. Deshpande, Kathleen M. Erndl, James L. Fitzgerald, Gavin Flood, Robert P. Goldman, Sally J. Sutherland Goldman, John A. Grimes, Alf Hiltebeitel, Barbara A. Holdrege, Walter O. Kaelber, R. S. Khare, Dermot Killingley, Randy Kloetzli, Klaus K. Klostermaier, Julius Lipner, James Lochtefeld, David N. Lorenzen, Mary McGee, McKim Marriott, Vasudha Narayanan, Laurie L. Patton, Velcheru Narayana Rao, Hartmut Scharfe, Tony K. Stewart, Herman W. Tull, and Susan S. Wadley.

Sushil Mittal is Assistant Professor of Religion at James Madison University in Harrisonburg, Virginia. He is founding editor of the *International Journal of Hindu Studies*. **Gene Thursby** is Associate Professor of Religion at the University of Florida in Gainesville, Florida. He is author of *The Sikhs* (1992), and a member of the editorial boards of the *International Journal of Hindu Studies* and *Nova Religio*.

THE ROUTLEDGE WORLDS

The Routledge Worlds are widely acclaimed one or two volume thematic surveys of key historical periods and cultures. Each is made up of specially written, original pieces by an international team of the leading experts in the field. The Routledge Worlds are ideal reference works that bring their subjects to life and provide both a comprehensive overview and a real flavour of the newest research in the area.

THE GREEK WORLD
Edited by Anton Powell

THE ROMAN WORLD
Edited by John Wacher

THE BIBLICAL WORLD
Edited by John Barton

THE EARLY CHRISTIAN WORLD
Edited by Philip F. Esler

THE CELTIC WORLD
Edited by Miranda Green

THE MEDIEVAL WORLD
Edited by Peter Linehan and Janet L. Nelson

THE REFORMATION WORLD
Edited by Andrew Pettegree

THE ENLIGHTENMENT WORLD
Edited by Martin Fitzpatrick, Peter Jones, Christa Knellwolf and Iain McCalman

THE HINDU WORLD
Edited by Sushil Mittal and Gene Thursby

Forthcoming

THE EGYPTIAN WORLD
Edited by Toby Wilkinson

THE BABYLONIAN WORLD
Edited by Gwendolyn Leick

THE VIKING WORLD
Edited by Stefan Brink and Neil Price

THE RENAISSANCE WORLD
Edited by John Jeffries Martin

THE HINDU WORLD

Edited by

Sushil Mittal and Gene Thursby

Routledge
Taylor & Francis Group
NEW YORK AND LONDON

First published 2004 in the USA and Canada
by Routledge
29 West 35th Street, New York, NY 10001

Simultaneously published in the UK
by Routledge
2 Park Square, Milton Park, Abingdon, Oxfordshire OX14 4RN

Routledge is an imprint of the Taylor & Francis Group

Typeset in Times New Roman by
Newgen Imaging Systems (P) Ltd, Chennai, India
Printed and bound in Great Britain by
Cromwell Press, Trowbridge, Wiltshire

Library of Congress Cataloging in Publication Data
A catalog record for this book has been requested

British Library Cataloguing in Publication Data
A catalogue record for this book is available from the British Library

ISBN 0–415–21527–7 (hbk)

FOR ANKUR AND ADITI

CONTENTS

PART IV: COSMIC ORDER AND HUMAN GOALS

PART V: SOCIAL ACTION AND SOCIAL STRUCTURE

PART VI: VITALITY IN PERSONS AND IN PLACES

PART VII: LINGUISTIC AND PHILOSOPHIC ANALYSIS

NOTE ON TRANSLITERATION

We have, in general, adhered to the standard transliteration system for each of the Indic languages. Although Indic languages make no distinction between uppercase and lowercase letters, we use capitals to indicate proper names and titles; all other Indic terms, with the exception of those used as adjectives, are italicized and not capitalized. Terms that have been anglicized in form or have come into English usage are nevertheless given in their standard transliterated forms, with diacritics (e.g. *karma*, *paṇḍita*, and *yoga*). Modern place-names are given in their current transliterated forms, but without diacritics. If references to such places are made in a literary or historical context, however, they are given in their standard transliterated forms, with diacritics. Modern proper names are given in their current transliterated forms, but without diacritics. All premodern proper names, however, are in their standard transliterated forms with diacritics.

CONTRIBUTORS

Surinder M. Bhardwaj is Professor in the Department of Geography, Kent State University.

Francis X. Clooney, S.J., is Professor in the Department of Theology, Boston College.

Madhav M. Deshpande is Professor in the Department of Asian Languages and Cultures, University of Michigan.

Kathleen M. Erndl is Associate Professor in the Department of Religion, Florida State University.

James L. Fitzgerald is Professor in the Department of Religious Studies, University of Tennessee.

Gavin Flood is Professor in the Department of Religious Studies, University of Stirling.

Robert P. Goldman is Professor in the Department of South and Southeast Asian Studies, University of California, Berkeley.

Sally J. Sutherland Goldman is Lecturer in the Department of South and Southeast Asian Studies, University of California, Berkeley.

John A. Grimes is at Kodaikanal International School, Tamilnadu, India.

Alf Hiltebeitel is Professor in the Department of Religion, George Washington University.

Barbara A. Holdrege is Associate Professor in the Department of Religious Studies, University of California, Santa Barbara.

Walter O. Kaelber is Professor in the Department of Philosophy and Religion, Wagner College.

R. S. Khare is Professor in the Department of Anthropology, University of Virginia.

Dermot Killingley, now retired, was Reader in the Department of Religious Studies, University of Newcastle upon Tyne.

Randy Kloetzli is an Independent Scholar.

Klaus K. Klostermaier is Professor Emeritus in the Department of Religion, University of Manitoba.

Julius Lipner is Professor in the Faculty of Divinity, University of Cambridge.

James G. Lochtefeld is Associate Professor in the Department of Religion, Carthage College.

David N. Lorenzen is Professor in the Centro de Estudios de Asia y Africa, El Colegio de México.

Mary McGee is Dean of Students in the School of General Studies, Columbia University.

McKim Marriott is Professor Emeritus in the Department of Anthropology and in Social Sciences College, University of Chicago.

Sushil Mittal is Assistant Professor in the Department of Philosophy and Religion, James Madison University.

Vasudha Narayanan is Professor in the Department of Religion, University of Florida.

Laurie L. Patton is Professor in the Department of Religion, Emory University.

Velcheru Narayana Rao is Professor in the Department of Languages and Cultures of Asia, University of Wisconsin-Madison.

Hartmut Scharfe is Professor Emeritus in the Department of East Asian Languages and Cultures, University of California, Los Angeles.

Tony K. Stewart is Professor in the Department of Philosophy and Religion, North Carolina State University.

Gene Thursby is Associate Professor in the Department of Religion, University of Florida.

Herman W. Tull is Lecturer in the Department of Classics, Princeton University.

Susan S. Wadley is Professor in the Department of Anthropology, Syracuse University.

BHŪMIKĀ

Sushil Mittal and Gene Thursby

The Hindu World is a contribution to a series of books on great cultures of the world. Compare *The Greek World* (1995) edited by Anton Powell, an earlier volume in the series and another large book like this one that brings together previously unpublished work by authors who are engaged in academic teaching and research. We follow Powell in organizing the work of our contributors by general themes that function as plausible entry points for inquiry into the Hindu world but do not pretend to reveal a deep structure or irreducible essence of the "world" that is retrieved, reconstructed, and represented from a number of perspectives. However, we depart from Powell's procedure by assigning to each of our contributors a single noun or adjective derived from the Sanskrit language as the topic for their chapter. Where he proposed to bring together "some of the most influential new approaches used by analysts of Greek history" we propose to show that even a limited lexicon can open into a distinctive "world" of human possibilities generated in a culture that deserves to be designated as classical.

The "classical" world of Hindu culture could be regarded as an ideal type—a simplified model, a schematization, or an approximation that serves as a learning resource for intermediate students and general readers as well as a point of departure for further empirical studies. We understand it to include a range of roles and functions, teachings and texts, ideas and images, and places in the Indian subcontinent, each invested with authority and power and each contributing to a characteristic configuration of a major civilization and its modes of signification and significance. Among the several languages of the subcontinent, Sanskrit has enjoyed a disproportionately large share of cultural prestige, and so our point of departure for representing what is "classical" in Hindu culture is a set of key terms derived from Sanskrit that do not find ready equivalents in other linguistic and cultural systems. We invite you to enter into the Hindu world and explore it from the vantage points provided by these terms which serve as titles for the individual chapters of this book.

WHAT IS A HINDU WORLD?

The introductory chapter by Julius Lipner gives careful attention to the heatedly argued question whether the terms "Hindu" and "Hinduism" serve or rather subvert serious scholarship. Perhaps Powell's title *The Greek World* could pass without question, whatever a reader's attitudes toward things Hellenic or Hellenizing or Hellenistic, but *The Hindu World* as a title runs counter to currently influential modes of scholarly discourse. Poststructuralist or postmodern assumptions now in the ascendant are politically sensitive and insistently nominalist. They tend to problematize generalizations as signs of unwarranted reification and can be expected to generate resistance to the definite article and singular designation of our title. How is it possible, it will be asked, for a thoughtful person to write under the title *The Hindu World*? The introductory chapter by Lipner invites the reader to consider the issues involved in the use of the terms "Hindu" and "Hinduism" and attempts "to provide grounds, in nonessentializing terms, for describing Hinduism under its own rubric. Some such effort is called for in the world of scholarship if we are to justify a range of ongoing activities" (34n23).

Readers may know Lipner already from his fine book *Hindus: Their Religious Beliefs and Practices* (1998a [1994]). The banyan tree model that he introduced there he develops further here and utilizes it to commend a polycentric approach that appreciates diversity within the Hindu world and the range of interpretive practices represented among the contributors to this volume. Although it will be helpful to keep in mind Lipner's introduction while moving through this book, it is intended as the first rather than last word. After all, basic terms of inquiry in the social sciences and humanities, as Gananath Obeyesekere reminded us in *The Work of Culture* (1990), are perennially contended, never settled. Readers are invited to compare Lipner's polycentric approach to "Hindu" and "Hinduism" with other perspectives (some of them addressed in his chapter) represented in two recent handbooks: *The Study of Hinduism* (2003) edited by Arvind Sharma and *The Blackwell Companion to Hinduism* (2003) edited by Gavin Flood.

Lipner poses questions about how to formulate and frame the activities of inquiry—in which one may engage with a full range of intellectual passions—and these are *opening* questions that invite repeated consideration in order to appreciate the rich diversity within and among South Asian traditional communities. Here is an example. Lipner states the case for the heuristic advantage of acknowledging the normative status of the Veda in the Hindu world but leaves open several interpretive options such as how to understand where, when, and by what means the Veda was produced. Who were the agents or intermediaries in its early transmission? What is the range and extent of its various manifestations? What might qualify as a veritable or virtual Veda? Could it be mediated by a language other than Vedic Sanskrit? Other than by language?

Questions at the level of whether (and if so then how and when) the Veda can be dated, and the chronological placement of other formative features of the Hindu world, should not be expected to generate general agreement. Nevertheless, difficult questions of this kind are taken up again and again from different vantage points, in diverse thematic settings, and with a variety of interpretive frameworks at several points throughout this book. Readers in turn will understand that questions that have established distinctive communities and that set the ground rules for discussion or that attempt to reach and reflect the most profound features of reality have been at the center of debates within the Hindu world for centuries. Such questions get treated by this book's authors in ways appropriate to their assigned topics and as informed by their best insights, their own tradition of scholarship, and evidence currently available.

TEACHINGS, TEXTS, AND THEISTIC TRADITIONS

Veda, Itihāsa/epic (the *Mahābhārata*, including the *Bhagavad Gītā*, and the *Rāmāyaṇa* of Vālmīki), and Purāṇa comprise a vast and internally diverse corpus of oral teaching, some of it long kept secret within a few human lineages and restricted initiatory traditions, some of it esoteric and difficult to understand, and much of it still undergoing the process of being reduced to writing and then reconstructed in critical editions produced by scholars. Laurie L. Patton opens her chapter by placing the Veda in the ritual context of sacrificial action. She goes on to introduce the various strata of Veda, belief and action systems, and efforts within the tradition to systematize its teachings. Like Veda, it is difficult to know where the *Mahābhārata*—one of the world's greatest and longest epics—begins and ends. James L. Fitzgerald terms it "a tradition of religious epic" and a "library" that extends over a vast range of time as well as of textual and cultural space. Hindus "classically" have assumed that multiple lifetimes get generated by unresolved actions productive of repeated rebirths and that gives the epic convention of starting *in medias res* a multidimensional twist—every situation and sentient life-form is endowed (and pregnant) with ranges of significance that could threaten to outstrip the imagination. This gives rise to mighty reversals and paradoxes. The frame story or boxed story—the story within a story—is a highly developed narrative convention in the Hindu world, too. Fitzgerald guides the reader through the text, describes difficulties in the project of producing a critical edition, and reflects on gender identities and relations in the epic.

The *Rāmāyaṇa*, a relatively shorter epic rendered in Sanskrit and non-Sanskrit versions, contains one of the world's most widely known stories. Robert P. Goldman and Sally J. Sutherland Goldman offer an apt liquid image, for indeed the epic tale of righteous kingship has "saturated" most of Asia. The theme of the ordeal of love—destined, found, threatened, interrupted, regained, and then again in jeopardy—is developed in the *Rāmāyaṇa* in a way that lends itself to ritual performance and immediately connects with the energies of everyday life, too. In recent years, each of the two great epics has been serialized via television, and the main characters in the *Rāmāyaṇa* have been implicated in one of the most intractable land disputes in modern India. Although the extensive corpus of Purāṇa literature is less well known outside India than the great epics and may be regarded as less authoritative than Veda, Velcheru Narayana Rao makes a case for the "complementarity" of Veda and Purāṇa in Hindu culture (the first restricted to high-caste males and the second available to all, including low-caste males and women) and for Purāṇa as a distinct literary genre that maps out a widely influential Hindu cosmography of vast extent in space and time.

These oral teachings continue to be recited and enacted in ritual dramas today and to a large extent are now available in print media as textual sources. They evidence a rich archaic background of poet-seer, bardic, priestly, martial, courtly, and popular sources. They take for granted a great range of extrahuman, transhuman, and superhuman realities from among which a few have generated widely supported devotional and textual traditions. Gavin Flood makes clear the multiple and complex features of Śiva who is known by devotees as the great divine being—*mahādeva*—and the extraordinary range of textual sources relevant to the task. Kathleen M. Erndl introduces the theme of feminine manifestations of the divine and those who are devoted to one or more of them—*śākta*—by establishing a background in terms of relevant scholarly resources and basic concepts, then giving close attention to representation of the goddess in the popular text the *Devī Māhātmya* as well as the identification of the *śakti* or power of the goddess with specific sacred sites in the subcontinent. Francis X. Clooney and Tony K. Stewart similarly introduce the complex figure of Viṣṇu, his multiple *avatāra* or earthly descent manifestations, and then select two Vaiṣṇava subtraditions for close attention: the Śrīvaiṣṇava of Tamilnadu in the south and the Gauḍīya of Bengal in the northeast. Finally, David N. Lorenzen approaches some of the same material from a different angle by focus on *bhakti* which includes personal devotion that may be directed to (and through) a saintly person or personal form of divinity. The conserving and the revolutionary potential of intense devotion, including aniconic or iconoclastic devotionalism, are acknowledged by Lorenzen. Apparently poles apart from the esoteric and hierarchical exclusivism of Veda, Hindu *bhakti* movements energized regional languages and empowered conventionally low-status people, extending the range and variety of the Hindu world.

SOCIETY AND SACRED INTERSECTIONS

There are four categories or life-ideals (*caturvarga* or *puruṣārtha*) that usually are said to provide the framework for classical Hindu society. *Dharma*, the first of the four, functions as a kind of master trope and normative center to which nearly all major Hindu ideas, ideals, and practices repeatedly refer. Barbara A. Holdrege characterizes it as "an encompassing category that incorporates and at the same time transcends" other distinctions. She connects it back to Vedic *ṛta*, traces it through a long process of development, and discusses its elaboration into "a pivotal category of Hindu identity" as *varṇāśramadharma* which envisions a compartmentalized society composed of endogamous human lineages, social hierarchies based on ascribed status by birth, and a ritually guided life plan for high-status males. That life plan finds an approved place for investment in activities and things that produce wealth and power (*artha*); in human reproduction, erotics, and aesthetic enjoyment (*kāma*); and liberation from endless action and rebirth (*mokṣa*). In the course of his analysis of *artha*, Hartmut Scharfe indicates ways in which the first three (termed *trivarga* when linked to the exclusion of *mokṣa*) may be involved in what he calls "a revolving hierarchy" and constitute a cluster of competing yet mutually overlapping norms. Dermot Killingley carries his analysis of *kāma* through ascending levels of meaning from a root sense as "desire" and its various refinements right up through ritual, sacred, and cosmic levels as a world-generating cause of bondage and impulse toward release—a source of seemingly endless suffering and delight. Where Killingley arouses the mind with the troubling thought that the entire cosmos "may be the unplanned result of an act which was prompted by *kāma*," Klaus K. Klostermaier marshals resources to enable us to consider a variety of ways that an ultimate resolution of this plight has been conceived in the Hindu world—by disciplined practice, study, other forms of action, devotion, wisdom—as a human possibility.

The dramatic cosmography of the Hindu world, with its overwhelming variety of kinds and levels, is pervaded by threads of significance carried by notions of action and consequences. Herman W. Tull describes some of the most influential ways in which the "ubiquitous" notion of *karman* winds through the Hindu world like an attractive, dangerous, and yet unifying creeper vine. In turn the institution of a series of life-cycle rites or *saṃskāra*s has been relied upon ritually to control and reduce unwanted traces and consequences of former actions, whether they occur here in this life or originate before or beyond it. Mary McGee provides a lively account of rites of the life-cycle, starting with the hinge on which they turn: the act of marriage which links families and leads to new generations. Traditionally the making of marriage alliances and other forms of social interaction have been guided by Hindu assumptions about separate human subcommunities reckoned in terms of strands of characteristics that function something like genetic material. McKim Marriott, a scholar long associated with a project that seeks to understand the Hindu world through Hindu categories, contributes a dense and discerning chapter on birth-status and human types under the aspect of *varṇa* and *jāti*. These are at once structural and dynamic categories, and their dynamic potential is made more evident by the traditional ideal of an orderly human procession through distinctive stages of life or *āśrama*, a norm entailed in *dharma*, *karma*, and *saṃskāra* but also one that merits the separate treatment given here by Walter O. Kaelber.

Sources of energy and modes of vitality are universal human concerns that have been given distinctive expressions in the Hindu world, especially in the ways that food is understood, theorized, and shared. As R. S. Khare makes evident, food is at the point of departure for some of the most profound and powerful human classification systems. Not only are humans "made of food," so are societies, cultures, and civilizations. Until recently India was primarily a peasant civilization with a wide agricultural base and linked across regions by networks established in marriage and kinship, by genealogical record-keeping, by patterns of disposition of the dead, and by the impulse to visit great temples and other sacred sites. The role of the settled agricultural community—the village or *grāma*—is presented by Susan S. Wadley. She is an anthropologist who has a long association with a village in North India that has been intensively studied for two generations. Vasudha Narayanan, a religious studies scholar with a background in South India, adds an analysis of *ālaya*, great and small temple complexes, some of which comprise major settlements or the equivalent of small cities supporting ritual activities, the preservation and transmission of traditional learning, and visits by pilgrims. James G. Lochtefeld and Surinder M. Bhardwaj expand this theme to take in an even wider range of traditionally acknowledged and attractive pilgrimage centers or *tīrtha*s. These have functioned for centuries as ways in which people in the Hindu world have experienced and expressed their distinctive identities and allegiances and also have sought to transform or to surpass them toward something greater.

LANGUAGE AND PHILOSOPHY

Whether one takes a social constructionist approach to the human enterprise of "constructing" and maintaining a social and cultural world or instead accepts social and cultural worlds as "givens," language is a primary medium of expressing, if not generating, them. Worldview and ethos, patterns of belief and of action, are found to make sense and are given meaning through language. Traditional South Asia as it centers in the subcontinent of India has been a rich source of linguistic diversity. How India's languages—*bhāṣā*s—have carried the concerns and institutions of the Hindu world is explored by

Madhav M. Deshpande. Then John A. Grimes takes up one of the most important terms in the Sanskrit lexicon—*darśana*—which refers to the intuition, insight, or illuminative vision that may have its source in intense thought, deep reflection, or the immediate sight of a sacred or holy object. The word also serves as the label for the whole range of intellectual activity to which the term "philosophy" may refer in modern English. The topic is extensive and can be managed only by schematic treatment here. If available space will not allow a longer treatment of *darśana*, neither does it allow more than a respectful but brief exploration of the companion concept of time—*kāla*—which is surely as formidable and dominant a category for the Hindu world as it was for Augustine in the West. A classical problem for the Hindu world, at a level perhaps more profound than for the high-speed modern urban person, is to fathom the mysteries of time. Randy Kloetzli and Alf Hiltebeitel illumine ways in which that great (t)rope strings us along so many yesterdays, todays, and tomorrows. Their chapter brings the book to a close and prepares the reader to circle around through it again and again with increasing discernment.

WELCOME TO THE HINDU WORLD

Although *The Hindu World* can serve as a general reference work, some previous study of India will help the reader to obtain maximum benefit from the book. It will be particularly useful to intermediate and advanced students engaged in regional and area studies of South Asia as well as in academic fields that range from anthropology, history, languages and linguistics, sociology and political science, to religious studies. Students who are pursuing a course of study in the world's religions, for instance, will recognize that several of our contributing authors have written substantial and sound introductory textbooks on Hindus and Hinduism. Along with Julius Lipner's commendable and previously mentioned *Hindus* (1994), the student may refer to Klaus K. Klostermaier's *A Survey of Hinduism* (1994 [1989]) and Gavin Flood's *An Introduction to Hinduism* (1996), as well as the chapter by Vasudha Narayanan in Willard G. Oxtoby, ed., *World Religions: Eastern Traditions* (2002 [1996]). *The Hindu World* extends the treatment of several topics that are introduced in those textbooks and can serve to complement them in college and university courses of study.

Our deep appreciation goes to the authors of the book's chapters and to an even larger number of outside readers. All of them are professional scholars with expertise in the languages and cultures of South Asia. Many of them have been contributors to the *International Journal of Hindu Studies* (1997–) for which Sushil Mittal is the founding editor. The Journal has helped to foster an international community of inquiry and to establish Hindu studies as a recognized area of scholarly research. Without the hard work and goodwill of these many contributors, this volume would not have been possible. Nevertheless the editors alone are responsible for the final result that you have in hand.

PART I

INTRODUCING THE HINDU WORLD

CHAPTER ONE

ON HINDUISM AND HINDUISMS: THE WAY OF THE BANYAN

Julius Lipner

THE NATURE OF OUR TASK

The purpose of this chapter is not to attempt some comprehensive account of what Hinduism is. The remaining chapters of this book will give a clearer picture of that. My task is one of orientation: to attempt a constructive critique of what various commentators have considered Hinduism to be, and to suggest what I believe to be a fruitful *approach* to the totality we call "Hinduism." I cannot, of course, claim that the approach outlined in this chapter is the only fruitful way of understanding Hinduism. Such a vast, multifaceted record of the way in which many millions of human beings, over many centuries, have shaped their lives, both as individuals and as groups, demands for its understanding an open-ended methodology that accommodates a variety of disciplines and points of view. What we call Hinduism today has always included, under its broad canopy, features of life that may be described not only as religious but also as social, political, economic, rational, aesthetic, environmental, and so on. And just as there is not only one way culturally of expressing what it is to be human, so also the sheer complexity, the multi-layeredness of the Hindu phenomenon allows one to be Hindu in a variety of ways.

Still, there are some approaches to our subject that are more fruitful than others. I shall argue that the one outlined here has particular advantages and that there are other approaches that are unhelpful: they do not seem to square with how the majority of people we have called Hindus over the ages have behaved or with what they have claimed their basic values and purposes in life to be. As my thesis unfolds, I hope the reader will be placed in an advantageous position to follow the various topics pursued in the rest of this book. One needs to face the right way if one is to reach one's goal.

But first we may ask: is there such a thing as "Hinduism" at all? And if so, what kind of "thing" is it? What are the pitfalls of using the term "Hinduism" unwarily? A historical perspective of the task at hand will provide a useful starting point.

THE ISSUE: ITS HISTORY AND POLITICS

The English word "Hinduism" is of fairly recent coinage, not much more than a couple of centuries old (see Sweetman 2000). It is not a translation of some early Indian term purporting to give a self-description of Indian religion or culture. It is a Western invention, created for a specific purpose. But it was not entirely plucked out of thin air. Part of this name—the "Hindu" element—is derived from the name of the great river, the Indus, which runs along the northwest of the subcontinent with its tributaries. The word "Indus" itself seems to have been derived from the description which ancient inhabitants of this region, the so-called Āryans, gave to this riverine system, recorded at least as long ago as the second millennium BCE. This area is historically important for our purposes because along its banks (or former banks) there are sites where civilization in the Indian subcontinent had an early flowering, in the technical sense of "civilization," with urban centers and their civic, sociopolitical, and communicational infrastructure, together with various forms of architectural, commercial, artistic, and ritual expression. We have archaeological records of this civilization known as the Indus Valley or Harāppan from about 3000 BCE. The precise ethnic and cultural relationship between the "Āryans" from whose description of the river we have derived the present name, on the one hand, and the great civilization mentioned above, on the other, is part of the issue we are considering.

In their multidialect language which they described as *saṃskṛta* (meaning "refined, polished," and which has been anglicized as "Sanskrit"), the former peoples called the rivers of the northwest, especially its main artery, *sindhu* (*sindhavaḥ* in the plural). Subsequent invaders or immigrants from beyond the northwest, for example, the Persians (*c.*550 BCE), the Greeks (from the early fourth century BCE), and the Muslims (eighth to ninth century CE onwards), used the element "ind" from *sindhu* in their names for the land and/or the peoples to the east of this river. Thus the Greeks spoke of *Indikoi* ("Indians"), while Arabic-speaking Muslims referred to the land as *al-Hind*. Gradually, after the arrival of the British, who assumed prominence in the subcontinent from the middle of the eighteenth century, the terms "*Ind*ia" and "H*ind*u"/"H*ind*uism" became current.[1]

In Sanskrit, which progressively became the language of cultural self-expression of the male-orientated elite, the "Āryans" referred to their geographical heartland as Āryāvarta, which in time was more or less supplanted by Bhārata. The variant "Bhārat" is the name by which Indians often refer to their country, and it is the Indian word that appears on the country's postage stamps. Āryāvarta means "land of the Āryans," while Bhārata alluded to the territory over which the Bhārata clan, a preeminent lineage in ancient India, held sway. Today "Bhārat(a)" stands for the political entity that is India.[2]

There is a vigorous ideological debate current as to who the Āryans originally were and where their homeland was. *Ārya* means "noble" in Sanskrit, so, by way of self-description, the Āryans were the noble ones, those whose language and lifestyle were superior to the culture of non-Āryans. It is not difficult to see then that any debate about the Āryans' ethnicity can have strong political overtones. Were these "noble" people(s) whose developing language and culture gradually dominated civilized India, *indigenous* inhabitants historically, namely, in some sense "locals" or native, or did they come from elsewhere? In other words, is "traditional" Indian civilization, with its reputation today of being artistically highly developed, linguistically sophisticated, mythologically rich, and philosophically and theologically profound, rooted originally in the soil—or not? The political implications are not hard to see.

Members of one group argue that the Āryans were indigenous, that they constituted or were part of the first, older Indus civilization, rather than supplanting it by some form of intrusion. They are not happy with the view that the Āryans were originally from outside the subcontinent whose culture took over from the Indus culture and created a substantial part of the infrastructure we call Hinduism today. They are not hospitable to "outside" influences affecting in any significant way what they regard as the "core" or essentials of "the Hindu way of life." The main reason seems to be that they wish to draw lines of exclusion between what they regard as their own cultural domain and that of others, especially Muslims and Christians (mediated by British colonial rule), who entered India in significant numbers for long periods of hegemonic rule (about six hundred years where the Muslims are concerned, and two hundred years in the case of the British). We note that a particular view of Hinduism prevails here: that "it" is a kind of block-reality with discernible essentials or an identifiable core. This perception can then be manipulated for certain ends, for example, for determining who is a true son or daughter of the soil and for prescribing what the outsider must do to be accepted. Some of these ideologues even argue that the heartland of the Indus civilization was the original home of the Āryans who then spread to other parts of the world.

Members of another group also favor the conclusion that the Āryans were indigenous, but interestingly for other reasons. If it can be agreed that so-called Āryan culture originated in the subcontinent, then subsequent distinctive socioeconomic discriminations which have been embedded within the system for nearly three millennia and which were from early times reckoned to be congenital—they are referring to the phenomenon of "caste"—have in fact no real historical ethnic basis. If the Hindu caste structure was originally superimposed from within the system, then it can be removed from within the system in favor of modern perceptions of a more egalitarian way of life. In short, Hindus can clean up their own act without violating the essential integrity of their cultural roots. These are two tendentious positions which for separate sets of reasons favor the indigeneity or nativeness of Āryan ethnicity and culture.

But there is a third position which is argued almost exclusively on archaeological grounds. Let us call it "the Archaeological Stance." This position is dismissive of the arguments of the so-called historical linguists whose case rests mainly on the way they perceive speech patterns to migrate, based on comparative philological analysis. According to these language experts or comparative philologists, there is strong evidence for an Āryan incursion—here "Āryan" refers primarily to modes of speech and culture—from beyond the northwest into the Indus Valley during the later phases of the Indus civilization (*c.*1500–1200 BCE) (see e.g. Witzel 1995).

It is these language specialists who have had the main influence hitherto in shaping the received scenario of Āryan presence in India (to which we shall return presently). The Archaeological Stance disregards the claims of these linguists as unsubstantiated and misguided. According to this view, the Indus civilization, whose early phases began in about 4000 BCE, was a development of the wheat-/barley-based agriculture that was part of a broad interaction zone from the Oxus Valley in North Afghanistan to the Indus Valley. This kind of agriculture was itself linked to the general agricultural growth between the Balkans and Baluchistan, traceable to about 7000 BCE.

However, as it matured, the so-called Indus civilization developed more or less independently. Its core area was not sites along the Indus river system (as maintained in the inherited scenario), but the now dried up river valley in the Bahawalpur region of present-day Pakistan. This region was originally watered by the Sarasvatī River (which is mentioned often in the *Ṛg Veda*, one of the earliest segments of the canonical Hindu scriptures, the Vedas). But as the river began to dry up, there was a steady shifting of sites eastwards into inner India. Thus the "Āryans" who composed the Vedas were in fact Indus Valley peoples, users of the Indo-Āryan language family, and with a long history of 3,000 years already behind them (before this, it is admitted that they may have come originally as wheat/barley agriculturists from pockets in West Asia). The Vedas could have developed autonomously in the fold of the various phases of the Indus civilization whose longevity eventually allowed it to spread massively towards the south and east and may well have formed the core of this civilization's religiocultural beliefs and hence of Hinduism as we know it subsequently. This view seeks seriously to challenge the very basis of the received scenario.

We can now give a fairly sophisticated version of the received scenario about the origins of the Āryan presence in the northwest (or Punjab region) of the subcontinent: towards the middle of the second millennium BCE, the great Indus civilization, which was linguistically and culturally non-Āryan and which had spread widely over and beyond the northwestern landmass of the Indian subcontinent, was in a process of marked fragmentation and decline. Probably by a "trickle" or "knock-on" effect over many previous generations, people(s) whose culture may be described as "Āryan" had penetrated the Indus region from places more or less distant, east of the great river. These people(s) seem to have incorporated aspects of early European ancestry and ways of life and in the course of time mingled to greater or lesser degree through intermarriage and otherwise with the inhabitants of the Indus civilization. In time—over centuries—their developing language and culture spread hegemonically, though unevenly, over the entire subcontinent.[3] The gradual penetration and dispersion of the so-called Āryans on this scenario may well make it possible to accommodate the apparently unbroken archaeological sequence (as emphasized by the Archaeological Stance) of the rise, decline, and aftermath of the Indus civilization.[4]

This received view is ideologically attractive to another group of people who wish to depict the cultural tradition called Hinduism as a culture of synthesis and, by implication, of basic patterns of tolerance. Hinduism for them has derived from a converging of ideas and practices and from a mingling of peoples. The culture that subsequently held sway, however objectionably it may have done so in certain circumstances, for example, by discriminations of caste and androcentrism, was nevertheless the result of syntheses of various kinds. "Hinduism," therefore, was not built on purist foundations but on compromise. And, notwithstanding the frailties of history, the tradition today too must be able to act hospitably towards immigrants and their ideas. The real nobility of Hinduism, its "Āryanness," is its essentially tolerant nature. This is the position of cultural "inclusivists" or "pluralists."

CONSTRUCTING HINDUISM

But, we may ask, is there no *evidence* to decide the issue, to tell us what exactly "Āryan" stands for and how "Hinduism" began? As we know, "evidence" that is supposed to decide racial and cultural roots and the origins of ideas and practices is usually loaded with *interpretation*, and the "evidence" in this case, which is mainly linguistic, anthropological, and archaeological, is still fragmentary. It is constantly being added to, revisited, and reinterpreted. It is not our purpose to review the evidence here, and it is certainly not the case that all those concerned with this question are ideologically enslaved. Nevertheless, it is my view that a dispassionate inquiry into the evidence available supports *some* version of the received scenario, though important adjustments in our understanding of the mingling of the "old" and "new" inhabitants of northwestern India during the first few millennia BCE (and perhaps earlier) with regard to the diffusion of speech patterns and other cultural traits will have to be made (for a reasonably up-to-date scholarly review of the data largely but not exclusively in favor of the received scenario, see Erdosy 1995c; for an impassioned defense of a version of the Archaeological Stance, see D. Chakrabarti 1995, 1997).

However, that is not quite the point of our discussion. The point is that "Hinduism" is a *construct*, the result of interpreting the evidence and of being continually open to fresh interpretations and evidence. Indeed, this is why there can be a number of fruitful approaches to Hinduism. But this does not mean that the evidence we have is by nature so pliable that "any interpretation goes, so long as it makes sense." In fact, there are plenty of hard features to Hinduism: particular beliefs, practices, myths, symbols, artifacts, and so on, which are generally agreed to be incontestably Hindu. A large number of these will be discussed in this book, and they are more or less vital, recognizable components in the constructions we shape.

Thus it is necessary to enter into a dialectical relationship with the evidence, to hold an ongoing conversation with it. It is a process of asking appropriate questions of what we regard as the evidence and of being prepared to be interrogated by the evidence in turn. The nature of the questions we ask will be regulated by the epistemological principles and code of conduct generally agreed by those with professional expertise in the relevant discipline(s). There is a need for constant vigilance that we are not guided by ulterior motives or unsustainable prejudices in our formulations. In short, one must attempt to keep ideology at bay and draw *responsible* conclusions, mindful that the evidence may be provisional or reconfigurable. But this is not to say that we cannot make firm judgments and progress in our understanding of what Hinduism is, that we cannot learn from mistakes of the past (for a stimulating analysis of ways in which Hinduism was ideologically constructed in the West in the eighteenth and nineteenth centuries, often as part of the colonial project, see Inden 1990). An important aim of this book is precisely to give some idea of what we can say more or less confidently about Hinduism as a religiocultural phenomenon, based on the available evidence and on increasingly sophisticated methodologies of cross-cultural understanding.

We, therefore, return to the idea that the word "Hinduism" (originally spelt "Hindooism") refers to a construct, to a certain configuration of data. It is an abstract term (note the "-ism"), implying a tendency to generalization, obliquely derived from the Sanskrit term "*sindhu*." It is about two hundred years old, though the English word "Hindu" (originally spelt "Hindoo") seems to have been in use well over a century earlier.[5] But this does not mean that these words (and their Western equivalents) were invariably employed, in the course of their history, with the same set of preconceptions by Western writers. Let us inquire into this briefly.

To begin with, certainly the early uses of the words had no uniformly "imperialist" presuppositions, if by "imperialist" one refers to a ruling power's desire to acquire a new polity outside its home territory. With reference to the usage of "Hindu/-oo," European imperialist aspirations were hardly developed in the early seventeenth century, when Westerners were in India mainly to trade or preach the Christian gospel, nor were they more than germinal, if that, in the third quarter of the eighteenth century (when "Hinduism/-ooism" came into use). Full-fledged imperialist connotations of "Hinduism" began to appear with the consolidation of British rule in India in the first half of the nineteenth century. It is therefore not the case, as books that comment on the history of this term sometimes imply or state, that "Hindu/Hinduism" had imperialistic connotations from the beginning. It may have acquired these connotations in some contexts but has now lost them in modern parlance.

Nevertheless, it was not long before these Western terms were used to designate beliefs and practices of the majority of India's population in a way that we would describe today as "Orientalist," where "Orientalist" refers to Western ways (beginning roughly in the late eighteenth century) of "dominating, restructuring, and having authority over the Orient" (Said 1978: 3), namely, of institutionalizing psychological, political, social, religious, and other structures for expressing superiority over the "East." Because of colonialism and its vested interests, Orientalism has had a long and vigorous history with regard to India, and the term "Hinduism" has been a major carrier of this project (see Inden 1990 for examples). Even today, though we are being increasingly alerted methodologically to Orientalist strategies, words such as "Hinduism" continue to be invested with Orientalist connotations not only in the media but also in scholarly works.

Further, early Western uses of "Hinduism" were not confined only to what we would regard today as *religious* data. This is because words used by careful early Western observers to characterize beliefs and practices of inhabitants in India we would now call Hindu and which functioned as precursors of the Western designation "Hindu" (for example, "Gentoo/Gentile," "Vaiṣṇava," "Śaiva," "Brāhmaṇ," "Banian," and so on) described not only what their users considered to be sacred but also cultural practices we might not regard as religious today, for example, caste relationships and occupations (see Sweetman 2000: chapter 4). This led to early Western uses of "Hindu" having cultural connotations broader than the merely religious, a usage in fact that reflects Hindus' own early and subsequent description of themselves as "Hindu" (see below). Some contemporary scholars of Hinduism (e.g. Lipner 1998a, 2000) wish to emphasize this wider connotation in current usage.

Indeed, early Western studies of religious practices and beliefs of India we would now describe as "Hindu" were generally aware that such behavior did not constitute a single, monolithic faith. On the contrary, these studies were keen to point to significant doctrinal and other variations, even to the extent of declaring that these variations amounted to the existence of *different (but related) religions*. Thus as early as the seventeenth century, Roberto de Nobili, a Jesuit missionary in South India, could write that the people he studied "have one public way of life but many religions." And already in 1846, the noted British Indologist, Horace Hayman Wilson, declared, in the opening sentence of his *Sketch of the Religious Sects of the Hindus*, that "the Hindu religion is a term, that has been hitherto employed in a collective sense, to designate a faith and worship of an almost endlessly diversified description" (1).[6] These are not blunt references to the nature of Hindu religion, and they indicate that, in the past, Western understandings of religious Hinduism were not always unnuanced. This goes against the view generally held today that a methodologically sensitive approach to the study of Hindu religion has been only a recent development.

In fact, as we have seen, Western observers of the past were aware that religious Hinduism was a diversified phenomenon, and this has provided some precedent for the views of those contemporary scholars (such as Lipner 1996, 1998a; Stietencron 1986, 1989) who maintain that traditional Hinduism in its religious aspects is appropriately conceptualized as *a group* of related religions rather than as one, homogenized faith.

Thus we see that from both past and current Western usage, the terms "Hinduism" and "Hindu" are susceptible of methodological sensitivity and pliable application; as such, they can be both linguistically and cognitively useful. It need not be the case then, as Wilfred Cantwell Smith (1962) and Robert Frykenberg (1989), for example, believe, that the term "Hinduism" is hopelessly vitiated as a semantic tool.

According to Smith, "The term 'Hinduism' is . . . a particularly false conceptualization, one that is conspicuously incompatible with any adequate understanding of the religious outlook of Hindus. . . . ['Hinduism' is] a notion that cannot but be inadequate. To use this term at all is inescapably a gross oversimplification. . . . The concept of religion and the religions . . . in principle ought to be dropped altogether" (1962: 63, 144, 153), while for his part Frykenberg has declared that the concept " 'Hinduism' (if not the word 'Hindu') is a concept so *soft* and *slippery,* so opaque and vague, that its use all but brings critical analysis to a halt and intellectual discourse to the verge of paralysis (if not futility)" (1989: 33; emphasis in original).[7]

I have argued that we *are* capable of acquiring a historical perspective of the term and of using it in a critically informed way. It can be welcomed to stay, so long as this is a procedurally nuanced welcome. Smith's and Frykenberg's strictures are premature and also impractical.[8] We need functional terms for everyday use—handy "abbreviations," pragmatic descriptions, to refer to broad realities for the job at hand. It is such terms that enable us to devise readings, publications, and so on, which can be described generically as "Hindu" or "Buddhist" or whatever, leaving us free to specify as precisely as we wish how we propose to deal with these subjects subsequently. And it is part of the task of introductions such as this one to prepare the ground for this kind of exercise.

HINDUS ON "HINDU": QUESTIONS OF METHOD AND IDENTITY

On describing

We come now to Hindu descriptions of what is "Hindu." But first, I am keen to undermine the distinction between "insider" and "outsider" descriptions, which often crops up, explicitly or implicitly, in studies like ours.

There is a view that only "insiders" or adherents are suitably placed to describe the culture they practice or the faith they hold. After all, the argument goes, since it is *their* experience they are describing, only they can describe it. No doubt—but as it stands, this is a poor argument. For the question is, what exactly is being described? If the adherent is describing his or her own *personal* experience, then of course, in an obvious sense, he or she has privileged access to it. But even this can be problematic. For the description based on "privileged access" may be uninformed, selective, or misinterpreted. This is why we often need expert analysis, perhaps psychological, sociological, or historical, to help us decode our own experiences. Consider how often we need help in understanding the motivations and forces that shape our descriptions of our own personal experiences. To begin with, therefore, "privileged access" to personal experience is not always an uncontroversial matter.

But narrating one's personal experience is not really the point at issue, for it does not amount to an authoritative description of some *collective* experience over space and time, which is what a culture or faith comprises. Even within the agreed boundaries of some culture or religion, one individual's personal experience may be significantly different from another's. And who's to say that this particular adherent is entitled to speak on behalf of the group? How often it is the case that a member of some group claims to represent the experience of the group only to be repudiated by other members of that group, on the grounds that the claimant has superimposed or valorized his or her own particular experiences or interpretations at the expense of the others! And even if it *were* agreed that some particular individual was entitled to represent the group, the description of a collective experience must be sufficiently *critically detached* from each individual's particular experience so as to represent what is shared in such a way that each individual of the collective recognizes his or her own experience in the representation. But to adopt this stance of critical distance is to begin to adopt the stance of the *observer* or so-called outsider parallel to the "objective" stance of the scholar. At which point the insider is becoming an outsider, and the argument is being turned inside out.

But conversely, one may say, can the outsider take steps to adopt the stance of an insider, so that "outsider" and "insider" approaches may meet, so to speak, in the middle? Not only is this possible, but in different contexts of life, as outsiders, we are able to adopt—more or less—the stance of an insider. It happens by what has been called *empathy,* namely, training one's cognitive faculties, especially the imagination, to enter, as far as possible, the perspective of the other (Lipner 1998b). We do this when we learn to enter, say, Shakespeare's world, by studying the vocabulary and sociocultural circumstances of the times and using our intuition on this basis to insert ourselves into the relevant context. We do this when we are guided by sensitive expertise, either by the written or spoken word, or with the help of external images, or by some combination of these, to understand the minds of people of another gender or race or way of life, perhaps far removed in time and space from our own. (Consider, for example, the part played by a good biography or history in this process. Such accounts will have made judicious use of first person reports, of the multivocal witness of the times. They will also have made good use of the relevant contemporary heuristic critical devices available, such as gender- and culture-sensitive critiques.) We *can* succeed in this project, more or less. Our degree of success will depend on the quality of guidance and the cognitive and imaginative effort we ourselves are prepared to contribute.

Thus to say, without qualification, that only Hindus can understand or explain what Hinduism is or what it is to be Hindu is to miss the point. The methodological problems both Hindus and non-Hindus encounter in trying to explain or understand Hinduism can, with due care, be resolved in such a way—by adopting the critical method of observation and empathy mentioned here—that there is significant common ground between them. In other words, entering into *The Hindu World* in a manner that can be personally enriching and educationally instructive is a viable project.

Traditional senses of identity

How then have Hindus sought to identify or describe themselves and their own traditions? I have pointed out already that the term "Hindu" (not to mention "Hinduism") is not very old and that it seems to acquire some currency in Western circles from about the early seventeenth century. In Indian usage it has an even more murky past in that its history is still obscure. It has been pointed out that the term was used in Indian texts in medieval (and late medieval) times (usually in a context demarcating Hindus from Muslims) (O'Connell 1973; Wagle 1989).[9] An earlier reference—but not much earlier—occurs in the medieval Hindi poems of the North Indian saint, Kabīr (fifteenth century), who himself eludes neat classification in terms of the modern category, "Hindu." Thus, there is a tradition that when he died both Muslims and "Hindus" wished to claim his body for disposal according to the rites of their own faiths.

In poems attributed to Kabīr we find (S. Kumar 1984: 21, 31):

'Gorakh! Gorakh!'
cries the Jogī
'Rām! Rām!'
says the Hindu.
'Allāh is One'
proclaims the Muslim.
But . . .
My Lord pervades all.

The god of Hindus resides in a temple;
The god of Muslims resides in a mosque.
Who resides there
Where there are no temples
Nor mosques?

Note that "Hindu" is not a straightforward category here: there is a marking off from those who are Muslims, but a distinction is also made between "Hindu" and "Jogī/Yogī," though the latter appellation today would fall under "Hindu." This indicates not only how malleable the term "Hindu" has been even among Indians themselves but also that it was used as a self-ascriptive marker by Hindus to separate themselves from others who did not share their way of life. Here the term tended to be appropriated with an exclusivistic function.

More traditionally, however, Hindus affirmed identity and marked exclusion in other ways, for example, by referring to differences of doctrinal belief (by such designations as "Śrīvaiṣṇava," "Prābhākara," "Pāśupata," "Bauddha"), or to specific practices or insignia ("Kānphaṭā/splitear," "Kapālika/skullbearer"), or to occupation ("Sairaṃdhrī," namely, a maidservant), or to personal names ("Rādhā," "Rāma," "Madhva"), or to family descent ("Yādava," "Kaunteya," "Jānakī"), or to particular achievements or qualities ("Savyasācī/ambidextrous," "Vṛkodara/wolfbelly," "Nīlakaṇṭha/darkthroat"), or to birth group ("Brāhmaṇ," "Khatrī," "Baniyā"), or to ancestral village, or to race ("Yavana," "Mleccha"), and so on. It is important to note that individuals or groups were accustomed to being referred to by more than one designation concurrently, as context demanded. Thus within the space of a day or a single episode, an individual could be referred to by different designations—for example, "scorcher of the foe" in battle, "ruler of my heart" in the home, "bigfoot" by way of jest or insult, and "Mura" matter-of-factly—depending on the intention of the speaker. In other words, Hindus traditionally functioned in terms of *multiple-identity appellations*, and this reflected the complex and multilayered social world in which they lived. Even today, this is a feature of Hindu social relations, though with a somewhat reduced scope (for instance, formally designating individuals in terms of particular achievements is no longer common practice). This "polycentric" dynamic, namely, having multicentered identities, generated, and still generates, a fluid sense of identity and encourages continuous oscillation from one identity context to another, as and when need arises. We shall return to this distinctive trait of polycentrism in Hinduism later.

Modern tendencies

However, there is no doubt that in some respects, for example, in some political and religious contexts, the term "Hindu" has become a catchall category, used to homogenize identity with a view to making broad, often tendentious, distinctions. This goes against the sense of fluid identity mentioned here. In other words, the terms "Hindu" and "Hinduism" are being used increasingly to forge ways of speaking and thinking that go against traditional practices, both personally and collectively. This has been an important modern development in the history of these terms and needs further elucidation.

We noted earlier that there is no Indian equivalent of the Western term "Hinduism." But there is an Indian word, sometimes wrongly translated "Hinduism," which is a Sanskritic construction grammatically and which is not more than about one-hundred-and-fifty years old. It has become an important term, in fact, a slogan, in contemporary debate about Hindu identity, with repercussions for a particular approach to Hinduism. The word is *hindu-tva,* which is best translated by "Hindu-ness," to mean the defining characteristic(s) of what is "Hindu."

To understand the history of *hindutva* we must go back to a famous Bengali novel of the late nineteenth century. This novel, called *Ānandamaṭh* by Bankimchandra Chatterji (1838–94), was first published in book form in 1882 and soon became one of the sources for the development of Hindu nationalist consciousness, especially in Bengal which pioneered the movement to free India from colonial rule.

The novel is set in Bengal early in the last third of the eighteenth century. It tells of the patriotic activities of the leaders of an Order of Bengali freedom fighters called *santān*s (pronounced "shontaans," which means "children"). The *santān*s are children of their motherland, which is identified with the nurturing yet avenging mother goddess. Thus the dominant symbolism is uncompromisingly Hindu. In the novel, the children fight directly to overthrow local corrupt Muslim rule, but it is not hard to see that the Muslims are a screen for the author's disenchantment with the British colonial regime and for national opposition to this regime.

In one passage, the author writes, "In particular, everyone was angry with the Muslims for the lawlessness and indiscipline of their rule. Because the Hindu code of life (*hindu-dharma*) had disappeared, many Hindus were keen to establish a sense of Hindu identity (*hindutva*)" (Chatterji 1882: chapter 1 of part 3). This is a very early and significant use of the term "*hindutva*," and it occurs in a passage affirming Hindu identity over and against that of Muslims. It is also a "universalizing" use of the term. Hindus are spoken of as a uniform collective, without adverting to internal distinctions. I am not claiming that Bankim invented the modern use of *hindutva,* but in what became an important nationalist text, its occurrence, for whatever reason, reflects/reinforces the term's main import in nationalist discourse subsequently: standardizing Hindu identity in terms of something vague called "the Hindu code/way of life" in opposition to "the other" (especially the Muslim other).

The term continued its hard-nosed career, acquiring more strident political overtones in the course of time. A watershed in this development was its use in the political-cultural writings of Vinayak Damodar Savarkar (1883–1966), the seminal ideologue of most right-wing groups in India today. He "fought in countless speeches and publications for a violent liberation of India under the Hindu banner from everything foreign, and a complete restoration of Hindu ideas and Hindu society" (Klostermaier 1994: 463). In his important tract, "Essentials of Hindutva," Savarkar wrote:

> A Hindu . . . is . . . [one] who feels attachment to the land that extends from *sindhu* to *sindhu* [sea] as the land of his forefathers—as his Fatherland; who inherits the blood of the great race . . . which[,] assimilating all that was incorporated and ennobling all that was assimilated[,] has grown into and come to be known as the Hindu people; and who, as a consequence of the foregoing attributes, has inherited and claims as his own . . . the Hindu civilization, as represented in a common history, common heroes, a common literature, a common art, a common law and a common jurisprudence, common fairs and festivals, rites and rituals, ceremonies and sacraments.
>
> (1964: 64)

Thus for Savarkar and his followers, one's appropriation of *hindutva* must be accommodated to a view that is racial, territorial, quite androcentric (note the contrast here between Savarkar's use of "fatherland" and Bankim's idea of "motherland" in *Ānandamaṭh*), culturally conformist (there is great stress on the word "common" in the extract), and exclusivist of "the other." Approaches to Hinduism predicated on these assumptions must have the same ideological, essentializing characteristics.

Savarkar was responding in his own way to the British, and more widely Western, construct of the nation-state and national identity of the times. It was also a reaction to processes of thought embedded in the colonial agenda in India to distance its regime from the subject peoples both epistemically and racially, that is, "You are so different from us that there cannot be a real meeting of minds and hearts." This agenda was well established by the time of Savarkar's youth. The development of the concept of *hindutva* is important for understanding recent antipathies in Indian Hindu politics, where once again the Muslim in particular has taken on the role of the demonized other, and the conformist expectations of Hindu religious culture that goes with them (see Basu, Datta, Sarkar, Sarkar, and Sen 1993). As I shall point out, this bureaucratic, centralizing strategy tends to be at odds with the historical realities represented by traditional Hindu beliefs and practices.

Here it will be instructive to consider another modern concept often associated with *hindutva*, though it need not have the same sinister political implications. It is also an essentializing and standardizing notion, popular with, though not exclusive to, the urban middle classes. This is the notion of *sanātana-dharma*: "the eternal order or way of life."

Though the roots of this phrase go back about two thousand years (it occurs in the plural form in Sanskrit, *kuladharmāḥ sanātanāḥ,* in the sense of "the enduring rules of the family or community," in the influential text, the *Bhagavad Gītā* [1.40]), in its modern form it has become increasingly popular in the last two centuries or so as "a programmatic expression of traditionalist self-assertion" (Halbfass 1988: 343). It functions as a defensive, and at times defiant, marker of opposition to culturally alienating influences, even though the lifestyle it recommends may be susceptible to these influences in a number of ways.

The claim is invariably made that this way of life arises in some way from the ancient Vedic scriptures, though the program recommended may vary from group to group of *sanātanī*s. Some Sanātanīs/-nists may sit lightly to hereditary caste-distinctions, others may try to justify them; some may seek to reinstate a form of Vedic ritual, while others may argue that this has become obsolete; some may practice religious devotionalism, while others may advocate a form of Veda-based monism: there are many permutations. What these groups have in common is that their concept of *sanātana-dharma*, like the concept of *hindutva,* is a modern construct, devised to cope with the encroachments of "the foreign other," in the name of some claim based on the "essentials" of Vedic teaching. Nevertheless, though modern in their revisionist intent, in their various implementations these concepts may well retain strong links with Hindu beliefs and practices of the past.

Indeed, both these modern defensive constructs are popular in the Hindu diaspora, not least among young Hindus who live in the West and seek to affirm their Indian roots. But the way these concepts tend to function in the lives of their adherents in the diaspora may differ in important respects from the way they do so in the "homeland." In the former context, there is often a greater emphasis on formulating a uniform Hindu identity, as an act of self-esteem and self-preservation, in the face of alien cultural pressures from an overwhelming host-majority. A concomitant strategy may be to affirm a universalistic understanding of Hinduism in either descriptive or prescriptive terms, namely, this is what all Hindus do/believe or should do/believe. Antipathy towards the cultural-other may not be a priority. It is not uncommon to find that these programmatic accounts are governed by sometimes not-so-subtle attempts to idealize Hinduism as a faith or culture by way of features perceived to be attractive to the host community or derived from some notion of prevailing wisdom.

We can exemplify this by referring to a book produced by the Vishva Hindu Parishad (World Council of Hindus) in the United Kingdom. The Vishva Hindu Parishad was founded in India in 1964 to defend, uphold, and propagate Hindu commitment in a militant way (see McKean 1996b: especially chapter 4; see also Hellman 1993). In India today, the Vishva Hindu Parishad is actively embroiled in right-wing politics, but Parishad offshoots in other parts of the world may not necessarily reflect the political agenda of their Indian progenitor. In the diaspora, the priority often seems to be not proactive involvement in local politics but the formulation of a self-affirming and uniform Hindu identity or construct of Hinduism to meet the challenge of cultural alienation or religious aggression.

In the book, entitled *Explaining Hindu Dharma: A Guide for Teachers* (Prinja 1996), we are told:

> There are a variety of religious sects or traditions in Hinduism. However, in spite of this diversity, there is a certain unity among all the various doctrines and schools of

> thought because their basic principles are based on the "eternal laws of nature" which can be rightly defined as Sanatana (eternal) Dharma (laws of nature). . . . The Vedas are now recognized by many scholars as the most ancient literature in the world. The term "Sanatana" is often used to highlight this quality of being ancient and eternal [7]. . . . Hinduism allows use of various terms, names, symbols and images to allow people to discover God in whichever way they want to. This freedom of thought and form of worship is unique to Hinduism [13]. . . . In Hindu history no example of imposing Hinduism by coercion or conversion can be found [54]. . . . In spite of . . . external diversity, there is an inner unity among all Hindus. This unity is based on the following five main commonalities: *Common race. . . . Common Dharma* . . . The founders of various sects or "-isms" did not intend to disunite Hindus, they were simply explaining Hinduism according to the need of the time. *Common motherland. . . . Common language. . . . Common philosophy* [60; emphasis in original] . . . . Initially all the four Varnas [caste-orders] were equal [70]. . . . In India the oppression of women increased during the Moghul [Muslim] rule. Women were put on a pedestal in Hinduism but at the same time their "freedom" was curtailed for the sake of protection [72]. . . . In Hinduism, there is no conflict between science and religion [153]. . . . Erotic rituals are against the basic fundamentals of Hinduism [161]. . . . Hindu sages have always asserted that political leaders should not advocate or work for the good of one particular denomination or sector of people. What matters is the welfare of society as a whole [175]. . . . There is no room for feelings of superiority or prejudice in Hindu philosophy [176].

In this extract, which contains assertions representative of the book as a whole, the ideals of *sanātana-dharma* and *hindutva* have been conflated in a conception of Hinduism which claims to unify a wide, accommodating diversity and preserve ancient, unchanging values through a lifestyle that allows Hindus to meet modern challenges of science and society in a wholesome, unproblematic way. Hardly any indication is given that the authors have seriously considered the possibility that many aspects of Hindu belief and practice observable today are the product of either resolved or indeed continuingly unresolved contestation or negotiation. It is a construct of Hinduism that is, to say the least, ahistorical, seamless, and optimistic.

One way, then, of summing up our discussion so far is to say that one can speak of "Hinduisms" rather than of "Hinduism" and of the Hinduism of the scholar as well as of the Hinduism of the propagandist. It would be important to discern between the two so as to make an appropriate response. Both forms of Hinduism are, of course, distributed alike between Westerners and Hindus, and, to complicate matters, both forms of Hinduism can on occasion be found nesting in the same place.

The "uniqueness" of Hinduism

I have argued that, all things considered, we need not dispense with the term "Hinduism." It can be used with methodological sensitivity. There is a further caveat we must consider, only hinted at so far, before we discuss our own approach to Hinduism.

In his important book already alluded to, *The Meaning and End of Religion,* Wilfred Cantwell Smith contends that abstract (Western) designations for religious ways of life, such as "Hindu*ism*" and "Christian*ity*," tend to "re-ify," to make a "thing" of that which they designate (1962: e.g. chapters 2–3).[10] The impression is given that their intended referents—the religions in question—exist as some kind of social reality with a discernible essence, on the basis of which one can make generalizations and homogenize and overlook or downplay important internal distinctions on which identities and lifestyles are predicated. So we must do away with this tendency to reify, of "mentally making religion into a thing, gradually coming to conceive [of] it as an objective systematic entity" (W. C. Smith 1962: 51).[11] Smith's solution is drastic: abandon the abstract terms themselves rather than recontextualize our ways of using them. We must replace them by the language of (religious) "faith" on the one hand, evoking the personal, subjective dimension of religion, and of "the cumulative tradition" on the other, denoting the observable, public dimension of ritual, rites of passage, beliefs, doctrines, places of worship, and so on (W. C. Smith 1962: especially chapters 5–7). How exactly this linguistic transition is to be effected has never been clarified; one suspects that these new patterns of speech would soon find ways of slipping back into the bad, old methodologically unenlightened ways. After all, the new way calls for dismantling entrenched terminology—a gargantuan task—and replacing this with new locutions. But why not short circuit the process by recharging the old terminology with a greater procedural alertness in the first place? This is my point. We can agree that Hinduism is not a "thing" in the sense rejected by Smith, but the answer is not to abandon such terms as "Hinduism." Let us keep the baby but get rid of the bathwater. Designations like "Hinduism" can and do perform a useful role: as artfully imprecise names, they provide a terminological canopy for legitimating ongoing debate about the nature of the phenomena they address, which in itself implies that they are being used in a methodologically instructive manner.

Nevertheless Smith has a point. It has become all too easy to use these abstractions to affirm one, and only one, form of life as superior—in the context of, say, living as a Christian or being a Hindu. The implication is that there is a preferred way—*the* way—of expressing commitment to a religious or cultural tradition, and it lurks in such monolithic questions as "What is *the* Hindu understanding of the social role of women?," or "What is *the* Christian view of homosexuality?," or "What is *the* Muslim view of a just society?"—as if there is only one in each case. This approach fails to take note of the inherent plurality of religious and cultural forms of life, which thrive on adaptation, the inventive response to life's challenges, contextuality, and multiple forms of transmission and interpretation of tradition. To stress uniformity here at the expense of creative expression is to seek to endorse the status quo and the vested interests of its authority structures. It is also to discriminate against or marginalize those who may be seeking legitimate change or reform.

The deployment of power that seeks to shape the image of a tradition need not be overtly political. It can be expressed through forms of social or conceptual engineering: perhaps a tendentious appeal to the "superiority" of an imagined construct or goal which places potential rivals at a disadvantage. This can be done by hierarchizing religious or cultural commitment. In his well-known and still widely read book, *The Hindu View of Life*, first published in 1927, the distinguished philosopher and former president of India, Sarvepalli Radhakrishnan (1888–1975), valorizes a monistic form of religious Hinduism called Advaita Vedānta, as the high point of "*the* Hindu view of life." The goal of Advaita, as endorsed by Radhakrishnan, is for the individual to experience his or her essential (spiritual) identity with the supreme reality, *brahman*. Thus forms of religious commitment are graded with this end in view:

> Hinduism accepts all religious notions as facts and arranges them in the order of their more or less intrinsic significance. The bewildering polytheism of the masses and the uncompromising monotheism of the classes are for the Hindu the expressions of one and the same force at different levels. Hinduism insists on our working steadily upwards and improving our knowledge of God. "The worshippers of the Absolute are the highest in rank; second to them are the worshippers of the personal God; then come the worshippers of the incarnations like Rāma, Kṛṣṇa, Buddha; below them are those who worship ancestors, deities and sages, and lowest of all are the worshippers of the petty forces and spirits."
>
> (Radhakrishnan 1980: 24)

Here Radhakrishnan's approach to Hinduism is reductive (it identifies Hinduism with forms of religious rather than wider cultural commitment), essentializing (ultimately Advaita or nonduality is the core of Hinduism), and hierarchically assimilative (non-monistic forms of Hindu religiosity are graded and progressively assimilated to the Advaitic goal). Most Hindus, however, are theists or religious dualists of one sort or another. I submit that they would reject "the order of . . . intrinsic significance" espoused by Radhakrishnan, which would place their faith in an inherently inferior position to Advaita which resides at the summit of the scale. Radhakrishnan's position remains unsubstantiated, epistemologically, metaphysically, and indeed phenomenologically; we could not recommend an approach to Hinduism based on such a priori assumptions.

But after having been actively involved as agents from the earliest stages in the various constructions of the term "Hinduism" (by way of collaboration in such Western projects as the translation of texts, religious encounter and confrontation, and political contestation),[12] Hindus have now appropriated the term themselves. The reasons for this, as we have suggested, are numerous: historical revision, political negotiation (or manipulation), social or religious consolidation, indeed, epistemological or ideological recognition. This has been a very long and multivocal process beginning with the Hindu savant Rammohan Roy early in the nineteenth century; there is every indication that it will continue for the foreseeable future.[13]

But the model of religion in this process of appropriation, of course, has been Christianity. It was against the backdrop of Christianity that Western observers, scholars, administrators, and missionaries entered into their numerous conceptual transactions with Hindus. By the late eighteenth century, as this process consolidated its effects in the deployment of British influence and power, the norm for an authentic religious identity was a discernible system of axial, corporate belief. As we have seen, to a large extent the diversified phenomenon of Hinduism did not (and does not) conform to this norm. This led to strategies legitimating colonial rule as a "civilizing," indeed, sacralizing process. As the nineteenth century developed, colonial rule in the subcontinent increasingly ascribed to itself the task of being engaged in a "noble mission" to remake its subjects, if not in the exalted image of their masters, then at least in some semblance of humanity.

But though there are many things in Hindu religion which overlap with Christian paradigms, there are also many differences. In important respects, Hindu ways of being religious do not conform to Christian molds. There will be many examples of this in this book.

The repeated attempts of observers, both Western and Hindu, through the centuries to point to exceptional features of Hinduism in contrast to Abrahamic models, are, as we have seen, an indication of this. This simply makes Hinduism distinctive, not inferior or beyond the pale. It enriches our understanding of human diversity, of the implications of being religious in a world of cultural heterogeneity, and it broadens the scope of what it means to be authentically human. In the process, it ruptures hidebound or stereotypical notions of religious commitment.

I have indicated that "Hindu" and "Hinduism" can be used as religious terms only if they have certain wider cultural ramifications. In this respect, they are not religious in the way "Christian" or "Muslim" are religious.[14] We are now ready to inquire into the cultural context, that is, into the cultural distinctiveness of the complex and somewhat evasive nexus of symbols and markers that we tend to designate "Hinduism."

A BANYAN MODEL

We have now considered two of the three leading questions raised at the beginning of this chapter: "Is there such a thing as 'Hinduism'?" and "What are the pitfalls of using the term 'Hinduism' unwarily?" We can now move on to the third: "What kind of 'thing' is Hinduism?" or, to put it differently, "What is the basis of our own approach to the phenomenon we call 'Hinduism'?"

In recent work (Lipner 1996, 1998a), I have likened Hinduism to the massive banyan tree that is a chief attraction of the botanical gardens on the outskirts of Kolkata (formerly Calcutta), capital of the Indian state of West Bengal. This is not meant to be an exact comparison but only a basis for constructing a model of Hinduism that bears functional resemblances to this particular tree. The Kolkata banyan is very old—it has a history of well over two hundred years—and in the way of ancient banyans has put out aerial roots from its branches which have reached the ground and resemble trunks themselves. For some reason there appears to be no central axis, so that the Kolkata banyan looks like a grove of interconnected trees. In fact, there are more than a thousand trunks with a canopy of about four acres (Hawkins 1986: 39). The effect is that of a three-dimensional lattice that is multicentered; each of the thicker "trunks" seems to sustain a microsystem of lesser trunks with their branches, and the whole comes across as an arboreal grid that is one, yet many.

This is a promising model for the view of Hinduism that I propose: an interconnected, polycentric phenomenon in the flux of growth, change, and decay—but there is a difference. As a single organic system, the banyan can display only a limited diversity of its botanic structure (fruits, foliage, and so on); furthermore, dubious (perhaps parasitic) growths can be identified for what they are by accredited scientific means. There are ways of telling botanically whether something is "banyan" (*ficus benghalensis*) or not. This is where the resemblance with the model of Hinduism I am proposing breaks down. On the one hand, I wish to retain the rhetoric of an organic unity in the Hindu banyan, on the other, I wish to allow for a wider range of diversity of its constituent features than in its botanic counterpart (with regard to rites, rituals, doctrines, and so on). Further, in terms of social scientific discourse, there seem to be no clear ways of discerning on occasion where the Hindu banyan ends and non-Hindu characteristics take over, that is, whether something can with confidence be described as "Hindu" or not. There are problem cases. But none of this is to say that we cannot characterize a great many things (individuals, events, artifacts, systems of thought, modes of speech, and behavior), over a wide spectrum of time and space, as clearly "Hindu."

So when speaking about Hinduism, everything is not up in the air. As I have indicated, we know where and from when to start looking, namely, in the Indian subcontinent, at least from the time of the appearance of the so-called Āryan culture as we recognize it today, that is, from about 1200 BCE. In order to build our case, let us now look illustratively at some of the salient features of this culture as it developed religiously and in other ways.

Polycentrism

We can start with a body of texts that are generally agreed to be unambiguously Hindu. These are the Vedas (or Veda, in the cumulative sense of "the knowledge," from the Sanskrit *vid* to know), the earliest canonical scriptures of the tradition. I am using the term "text" here in the sense of a concatenation of signifiers (words, gestures, and so on) committed to some form of recognizable, transmittable expression in the public domain. In this sense, "text" does not need to have a written form, and indeed from the time of their origins in the subcontinent (*c.*1200 BCE), the Vedas existed for centuries primarily as an oral, verbal tradition. In due course, it became convenient to commit them to writing, and today they can be consulted and studied in the form of books. As we have noted, "Veda" means "knowledge," and from the time the ancient tradition we call "Hinduism" began to coalesce, these voluminous, multilayered, many-stranded texts composed in Sanskrit, which became the language of religiocultural hegemony in Hindu tradition, were perceived as the normative repository of religiously effective wisdom. They were "scripture."

Using the Veda as our starting point may surprise scholars of Hinduism both by its apparent predictability and by the procedural objection it may be seen to raise. But predictability is no bad thing if it can be put to good use and procedural objections can be duly addressed. Let us consider the latter.

To start with the Veda, it may be objected, is to start with a focus of Hinduism that is both "elitist" and "orthodox" in important ways and hence insufficiently comprehensive. But this objection is misplaced. For our purposes, there is great heuristic advantage in this particular starting point. For by their normative scriptural status, the Vedas have exerted from earliest times to the present enormous influence on all strata of Hinduism as a sociocultural phenomenon. This cuts across such (admittedly contentious) distinctions as "elite" and "popular," "orthodox" and "heterodox," and "great tradition" and "little tradition(s)," not to mention gendered divides (let us call these and similar distinctions collectively, "the index of polarities"). This influence can be valorized in positive and negative terms, of course, or as engendering proactive or reactive consequences: the Vedas have been influential as much for the way their religious and social paradigms have been actively appropriated by various groups as for the way other groups have devised means and ends to reject them. Nevertheless, their wide-ranging hegemony is indisputable and has been the subject of numerous studies in the various disciplines of the social sciences and humanities.[15] So it will be useful to begin with the Vedas if we can approach them in such a way as to reveal what appears to be a fundamental characteristic of the Hindu banyan.

For the present we do not need to be apprised of the actual religious content of the Vedas. Suffice it to say that they are a large body of Sanskrit utterances, arranged in the course of time in four collections which were in canonical formation from about 1200 BCE to about the beginning of the Common Era and ratified as the source of saving knowledge—as in effect the foundation of one's accredited way of life or *dharma*—by (the male members of) what was emerging as the most powerful socioreligious stratum of traditional Hindu society, the Brāhmaṇ or priestly order. Though the Brāhmaṇs, who became an increasingly heterogeneous group, granted direct access to Vedic power in important ways to other (male) strata of Hindu society who were described as having the ritual status of being "twice-born," they retained overall control of this power; in this sense, the Vedas remained a Brāhmaṇical preserve. Excluded from direct access to the salvific efficacy of the Vedas were women in general and increasingly larger sections of the male population who were not regarded as twice-born. Further, there was a growing consensus even among the Brāhmaṇs that the purport of the Vedas was not always easy to interpret or decode.

In consequence, a widespread tendency arose to regard other texts—some in Sanskrit, others in the vernacular—as more accessible, alternative Vedas: alternative, but not mutually exclusive with respect to their legitimating Vedic source. In fact, they were perceived as entering into an organic relationship with the Vedas (and often with each other), so as to adapt, refract, reissue, and disseminate in more accessible and popular ways the salvific power incorporated in the Vedas. To this end, they were called "Veda" too. These alternative Vedas include such diverse examples as the epic narrative, the *Mahābhārata,* the so-called "Tamil Veda(s)," and the Purāṇas in corporate form.

The *Mahābhārata* is a sprawling narrative in Sanskrit meter in eighteen books and many thousands of verses,[16] believed by scholars to have been produced more or less in the form available to us, from about 400 BCE to 400 CE. In effect, the *Mahābhārata* is a multivocal discourse in classical context on the nature of the complexity of *dharma* or righteous conduct. Because of its range of heroic and other characters and vivid anecdotal style, it has held enormous sway in providing both proactive and reactive guidelines for the meaning of *dharma* in virtually every echelon of Hindu society, overriding in the process the index of polarities mentioned earlier. One of the well-known descriptions of the *Mahābhārata* is "fifth Veda"; indeed, it makes no bones about pronouncing itself a Veda equal to the traditional Vedas (see 1.56.14f of the Pune edition). It fulfills this function of spiritual enablement not only in its Sanskrit form but through its many vernacular and other adaptations over the centuries in various parts of the subcontinent and beyond, right up to the present day. These latter-day adaptations include the medium of theatre, film, and television.[17] What precisely "Veda" means functionally in this context, I shall return to later.

The "Tamil Veda(s)" are a large body of Tamil devotional hymns to the supreme being in both Śaiva and Vaiṣṇava traditions produced in southern India from about sixth to ninth centuries CE. It is claimed not that they supersede the Vedas but that they reveal their true meaning in an accessible manner (primarily for Tamil speakers, of course). This is why they are called Veda. But since they have arisen out of Tamil culture, they are a regional form of "revelation." The implication is that there may be other instances of such regional revelation, mediating, in their own context, the purport of the Vedas. We shall return to this and another example later.

The Purāṇas are more or less large collections of data in Sanskrit about a great many aspects of so-called orthodox as well as heterodox forms of life, ranging in time over most of the last two millennia. There is a great deal of religious material in the Purāṇas concerning different deities and facets of their worship as well as various kinds of treatment of *dharma.* Collectively, the Purāṇas are also called "the fifth Veda" because of the wealth of information they contain enabling humans to live a good life and achieve their spiritual end (on the assumption that they have been properly interpreted, of course).

I have given but the briefest description of these three examples for two reasons: first, to indicate how influential they can be both at the local and the transregional levels, and, second, to clarify the functional meaning of "Veda" in this context. Thus "Veda" here does not have some extraneous or metaphorical meaning analogous to the use of "Bible" in such statements as "The Highway Code is the Bible of motorists in England" or "Buy this book: it will become the Bible of the PC user." In the latter context, "Bible" is being used merely to symbolize an authoritative source of knowledge in a particular field of human endeavor, not to signify that this source is the fount of religious salvation in the way the real Bible (or a part of it) is perceived to be by Jews and Christians.

But in the case of the alternative Vedas, it is being claimed that these sources really do mediate in some way the salvific efficacy of the "original" Vedas. Without doing away with the Vedas, they relocate them contextually and make them more accessible and efficacious. They exist in a kind of organic relationship with the Vedas salvifically, and if more than one such alternative Veda is recognized, an interactive grid of these "Vedas" (together with the original Vedas) is set up whereby the foci or centers of this grid empower and validate each other. (Even if only one alternative Veda is recognized in a particular context, the original and the alternative Veda exist in dynamic tension in the way that will now be described.) The original Veda continues to be legitimated and reinvented in terms of its related foci, while the alternative Vedas derive their authority by virtue of their functional mediation. So "Veda" is being used here in its intrinsic meaning. Each alternative Veda functions simultaneously as a self-reflexive microsystem of textual activity with its own ambience of commentarial tradition and particular forms of worship and ritual and as an exocentric impulse in interactive tension with the original Veda (and the other member[s] of the grid).

This is a form of intertextuality that is both decentering and re-integrative: by virtue of its decentering tendency it can accommodate an indefinite number of members simultaneously in the nexus; in so far as it is re-integrative it is capable of sustaining itself. The dynamic of the whole permits individual members to be subtracted from or added to the grid in more or less contingent fashion. "Vedas" can drop out of or enter the system by force of historical circumstance without impairing either the critical mass or the modality of the whole. This is one way in which polycentrism as a characteristic of the Hindu banyan expresses itself, and it is a way of tenacious survival and adaptive propagation.

Note that we are speaking here of a characteristic of Hinduism that is by and large *functional.* With regard to the mode of polycentrism described earlier, namely, the Vedification of text, the way is left open for deploying different strategies to legitimate the process. One strategy for rationalizing Vedification has been in terms of the distinction between what we may call general and special revelation. Mariasusai Dhavamony (1971: 4–5) has noted that some passages of the scriptures (or Āgamas) of a school of devotional Hinduism called Śaiva Siddhānta seem to repudiate the authority of the Vedas, while there are others which endorse it by the claim that the devotion they propound reveals the true import of the Vedas. How to resolve this paradox? Dhavamony quotes Tirumūlar, one of the contributors to the *Tirumuṟai* (tenth-century Tamil texts but often with much older material, which form another portion of the Śaiva Siddhānta canon and which are also referred to as a "Tamil Veda"), to the effect that "the Vedas and the Āgamas are both true and both are the word of God," the regulative difference being that the former are restricted to twice-born castes, while the latter are open to all castes. Thus by invoking the distinction of general and special revelation from the viewpoint of caste, the Āgamas have been Vedified and the apparent conflict between Vedic and Āgamic content is theoretically, if not exegetically, resolved.

Another strategy has made use of the concept of "completing" the (Vedic) revelation. Friedhelm Hardy (1979) traces how the so-called Tamil Veda of the early medieval Vaiṣṇava poet saints has been incorporated into the scriptures of the Śrīvaiṣṇava school as consummating, and for some even supplanting, the traditional Veda, and in another example of Vedification, that of "progressive revelation," the late fifteenth-century theologian Vallabha declares: "In the early part [of the Veda] Kṛṣṇa appears as the sacrifice, in the later [Upaniṣadic portion] he appears as *brahman*; [in the *Bhagavad Gītā*] he is the *avatārin* [god in human form], but in the *Bhāgavata Purāṇa,* Kṛṣṇa appears clearly [as himself]" (*Tattvārthadīpanibandha* 38). Here Vallabha endorses his form of devotion to Kṛṣṇa, derived from the *Bhāgavata Purāṇa* (*c.* ninth century CE), by placing this text at the summit of a hierarchy of revealed texts starting with the traditional Veda. These are all examples of the way, irrespective of the legitimating strategies, polycentric Vedic lattices are established, in order to multiply, adapt, and perpetuate Vedic authority as part of a textured expansion of influence. Let us give another example with a regional emphasis.

Kunal Chakrabarti (2001: chapter 5) has shown that similar strategies have been implemented in the medieval Sanskrit Purāṇas of the Bengal area to draw non-Āryan Tantric practices into the Vedic fold during the process of the region's "Brāhmaṇization." Here too, he claims, somewhat sweepingly, "There is no direct continuity from the *Veda*s to the *Tantra*s" (K. Chakrabarti 2001: 188). Yet in the *Mahābhāgavata Purāṇa*, the goddess speaks as follows: "The *Āgama* [here the Tantras] and the *Veda* are my two arms with which I sustain the whole universe. . . . If, out of ignorance, one violates either of these two, he is sure to slip away from my hands. . . . Both the *Veda*s and the *Āgama*s lead to welfare. . . . Wise people should practice *dharma* by accepting these two as identical" (cited in K. Chakrabarti 2001: 189). He gives other examples where relations of equivalence are posited in some way or other between Veda and Tantra. For their part, once this process was under way, the Tantras too opted for a strategy of convergence. "The *Kulārṇavatantra* claims that the *Tantra*s are the essence of the *Veda*s which were churned out from the Vedic ocean by Śiva with the stick of his intuitive wisdom. . . . In the *Niruttaratantra*, the *Tantra*s have simply been described as the fifth *Veda*" (K. Chakrabarti 2001: 188). Again, in the *Bṛhaddharma Purāṇa*, "The goddess tells Śiva that he is the presiding deity of the *Āgama*s and [that] Hari is the presiding deity of the *Veda*s. But Śiva was appointed first and Hari later" (K. Chakrabarti 2001: 189). K. Chakrabarti argues that these are transparent attempts to muffle sectarian rivalries between traditions that started out without a clear associative history, to strengthen their affiliation, and to "smother the boundaries of their individual identities" (2001: 190). As noted earlier, we are speaking here of a form of survival and propagation, the very opposite of divide and rule in that it represents a multifaceted attempt to transcend and overcome the divides signified by the index of polarities. In this particular mode, Hindu polycentrism is not a monomorphic enactment. Rather, the many rationalizing strategies it accommodates show it to be an effective way of nuanced self-diffusion.

But there are a number of other modes by which the polycentric functionality of the Hindu banyan disperses itself. Let us consider some of these.

Our next example has to do with a well-rehearsed method of configuring space and time, with special reference to the modality of pilgrimage in Hinduism. Here is a salient illustration. It is well known that the city of Varanasi ("Kāśī" is its Sanskritic name), towards mid-northeastern India, has long been one of the holiest pilgrimage sites (*tīrtha*) for Hindus. The river Ganges at Kāśī is believed to be particularly effective with regard to its religiously purificatory role. But the subcontinent is a large place, and Kāśī has a definite location. As in the case of the Veda, this has led to the rise of "alternative" Kāśīs related in a similar fashion to the "original" Kāśī. Diana Eck has described this as follows:

> A place such as Kāshī is important, even supreme, without being unique. . . . To celebrate one god or one *tīrtha* need not mean to celebrate only one. Far from standing alone, Kāshī, like a crystal, gathers and refracts the light of other pilgrimage places. Not only are other *tīrtha*s said to be present in Kāshī, but Kāshī is present elsewhere. In the Himālayas . . . on the way to the headwaters of the Ganges, the pilgrim will come to a place called the "Northern Kāshī". . . . This kind of "transposition of place" is a common phenomenon in Indian sacred topography. . . . *[T]he affirmation is that the place itself, with its sacred power, is present in more than one place.* In addition to the northern Kāshī, there is a southern Kāshī and a Shiva Kāshī in the Tamil South. . . . In a similar way, the River Ganges is a prototype for other sacred waters, and her presence is seen in countless rivers and invoked into ritual waters all over India.[18]
>
> (1982: 39–41; emphasis added)

This system of interactive nodes or centers does not seem to occur so pervasively and efficaciously in the cultural transactions of the other major world religions. Thus, from the point of view of our example of a privileged pilgrimage site, there is, by contrast, but one Mecca to which the *hajjī* must travel, one Rome to which the pilgrim must come, one Jerusalem, one Wailing Wall, to which the faithful must defer. But in the Hindu world the symbiotic, multipolar dispersals of potency or *śakti* of which we speak exist in dense and far-flung matrices over a wide spectrum of speech and behavior patterns, transcending the index of polarities while dispersing the ones and redintegrating the manys.[19]

It is part of our case that polycentrism does not extend only to instances we may describe conventionally as religious. Indeed, we have already adduced enough evidence, I think, to indicate that the phenomenon characterizes a *mentalité*, a way of constructing the world. The following examples might serve to underscore this point.

Both David Shulman (1985) and Ronald Inden (1990) have written on patterns of kingship in medieval Hindu polity. Adverting to Shulman elsewhere, I have noted: "Painting a 'synthetic portrait of the medieval South Indian state,' Shulman (1985: 21) contends that in this state 'no single center exists. . . . The state has no real boundaries. Instead, [one] would gradually become aware of a varied, shifting series of centers of different kinds and functions, connected with various interlocking networks' " (Lipner 1996: 122–23). The analysis is complex, but its purport is to show how these centers validate and energize one another in a system of social, religious, and political interaction, expressing yet another though related modality of the polycentric phenomenon. The point is that this polity is not monoaxial with a more or less pyramidically progressive and arterial devolution—and reclamation—of power, to and from its far-flung termini (a standard prototype of "despotic" rule). Rather, Shulman's analysis reveals a dense multidimensional matrix of symbiotic, shifting centers of authority, interacting at different levels by negotiating, absorbing, and reemitting shared provenances of power.

Surprisingly, Inden does not mention Shulman, yet his own treatment of Hindu statecraft in medieval central India complements that of Shulman, taking it further and more explicitly in the direction of our own thesis. Inden demonstrates how it was customary for rulers in the region to legitimate their kingly authority by strategies of transposition, that is, by superimposing the features of a sacred topography located elsewhere geographically, upon counterparts in their own territory (rather as in the case of Kāśī described earlier), in order to affirm the divine validation of their own rule:

> Mount Kailāsa was [symbolically] the chief mountain among the Himalayas, in the sense that it was the place where India was fashioned at the beginning of a cosmic cycle. . . . The foremost pilgrimage places of the Vaishnavas and Śaivas . . . were both situated there. At these sites, the highest forms of these contending high gods were to be found. . . . Kailāsa and the Gaṅgā were, thus, both the epistemological and ontological centre of India. . . . So when Krishna I and his successors built and extended the Kailāsa temple at Ellora they were not simply doing obeisance to some distant and awe-inspiring model of a sacred place; they were *claiming to make that place, as constituted by them, [re]appear [in their own territories] in the Sahyadris or Vindhyas, [namely,] in the mountains of the Deccan homologous with the Himalayas.*
>
> (1990: 257; emphasis added)

And,

> When we consider that all rivers were said ultimately to originate from the Gaṅgā, when we take into account the fact that some of the *Purāṇas* refer to the Godavari and the Krishna, the rivers constituting the imperial domains of the Rashtrakutas [in middle-eastern India], as Gaṅgās of the south, when we remember that the Rashtrakutas were talking about these topographical features [namely, Mount Kailāsa and the Gaṅgā] *not simply as physical places, but as the domains of purposive agents interacting with time, country, universal king and cosmic overlord to make and remake a divinized polity*, it all makes good sense.
>
> (Inden 1990: 259; emphasis added)

In other words, it was characteristic for these rulers to justify their political goals in terms of what I have described earlier as polycentric modalities.

In modern India, it seems that such political strategies have fallen into desuetude. After all, the protracted imposition of subject status gave rise to protestations of power among the Indian elite that reflected the political structures of their colonial masters. For the first half-century of independence, India has struggled to maintain a centralized nation-state. But, as we know, recently this polity has been fragmenting, and perhaps we are beginning to see regional and other forms of coalition emerging which will begin to replicate polycentric dispersions of this currently centralized authority. The situation is unclear, particularly in the face of what appear to be counteracting forces of political and cultural universalization. Will the new instruments of these homogenizing forces, namely, *hindutva* and some interpretations of *sanātana-dharma*, evolve some form of polycentric dynamic after all? Events await development and further analysis.

CONCLUSION

Much remains to be said, but space is limited. Modalities of polycentrism seem to be detectable in a host of other contexts. We could speak of the polycentrism of Hindu conceptions of deity, discernible from early Vedic times. Even some of the pioneering Western Orientalists of a bygone age saw that the "gods" or *deva*s of the early portion of the Vedas, the Saṃhitās, could not be described straightforwardly as comprising a "polytheistic" pantheon but existed in a nexus of relationships which made the particular focus of attention the supreme god of the moment, the implication here being that each of these foci refracted an energizing power that underlay them all (the "one"). Friedrich Max Müller (1823–1900) invented the awkward term "henotheism" for this phenomenon, though his explanation for it (see Neufeldt 1980) reflects the procrustean tendencies of his times. So-called Hindu polytheism of today could be seen as a derivation of Vedic theism in polycentric terms, where particular deities exist with others in a concatenation of various (sometimes tiered) reciprocities. The particular theologies of these reciprocities in the different later schools may vary, just as the legitimating strategies of Vedification vary, but the mutuality they consider is, to begin with, polycentric, not "polytheistic" in the classical sense of this expression. In fact, quite perceptively latter-day Hindu theism has been described as "polymorphous monotheism" rather than as polytheism. But these ideas are still work-in-progress and require further treatment.

Similar claims might be made for the deployment of the concept of *avatāra*s or (multiple) descents of transcendent realities; for the conception of Word (*vāc*, *śabda*) in some philosophies as a refractive yet re-integrative process of the manifestation of horizontal and hierarchical forms of intelligible being in the world; for the notion of a divinized and feminized *mūlaprakṛti,* in the sense of a "root" goddess, who displays in pluriform yet assimilative and recombinative ways (see K. Chakrabarti 2001: chapter 5, where he argues that the role of the pluriform goddess in the Purāṇas of medieval Bengal was to legitimate Brāhmaṇization by enfolding heterodox practices); for the distinctive technique of legitimation for social and religious ends, in the replication of myth; for that particular understanding of *dharma* as the law of right living according to which the individual's/the group's sociomoral status is continually being determined by response to a web of concurrent pulls discernible through such categories as *strīdharma* (woman's *dharma*), *varṇadharma* (the *dharma* of caste-order), *jātidharma* (the *dharma* of one's birth group), *kuladharma* (the *dharma* of one's family/clan), and so on.[20] Such polycentric exemplification can be multiplied almost indefinitely and extended over a range of contexts.[21]

I observed earlier that the phenomenon I have described in this chapter perpetuates propagation and survival. But it is more than just that: in so far as it is an open-ended process, it endorses the ingenuity of adaptation and improvisation, encourages integration across the index of polarities (in this sense it has a leveling impulse: for example, the little tradition can have its Veda or ratified *tīrtha* or goddess, as well as the great tradition), and legitimates particularity in the context of a wider "identity."[22]

In an earlier article, I spoke of polycentrism as follows:

> I do not wish to dwell exclusively on a radical de-centring, in conceptual or behavioural structures, as distinctive of [Hinduness]. . . . A radical de-centring *tout court,* semantic or otherwise, is an evanescent process with nowhere to go. . . . In my analysis, any process of de-centring is part of a larger process, within the same framework of discourse, of continuous re-centring among a set of interactive polarities in dynamic tension. This allows for forms of "progress," of identity-in-difference, in which both *theoria* and *praxis* have the scope to develop in terms of constructed (and where necessary, alterable) teleologies. The Hindu phenomena we have considered are not semantic black holes, susceptible merely of some radical deferral of meaning in which sense and reference are systematically swallowed up in deconstructive chaos. On the contrary, . . . they are conductors both of the elusiveness and re-purchase of meaning in a continuous equilibrating tension.
>
> (Lipner 1996: 125)

I am not claiming that what I have called polycentrism does not exist in some form elsewhere. There may well be evidence of this complex phenomenon in other cultures and faiths. What I am claiming is that as a way of ordering the world, microcosmically and macrocosmically, it has been sufficiently pervasive historically in the seething totality we are pleased to call "Hinduism" so as to make it *a* leading, if not *the* leading characteristic of this tradition, and that as such this makes Hinduism distinctive.[23] That is a bold claim. But I hope I have done enough to indicate, not least by collating and reconfiguring evidence drawn from a wider scholarship (not only textual but also sociological and anthropological), that it merits serious scrutiny and collaborative research.

What the future holds in store is uncertain. As I have hinted earlier, homogenizing forces have made an appearance in a post-independence "secular" India (where "secular" has a meaning all its own) amid the rampant pressures of a crushing globalization.[24] It may be that the history of Hinduism is about to take a sharp turn. Whether this would be for the better or for the worse remains unclear. On the other hand, it could be that these homogenizing forces themselves develop polycentric modalities of their own. In that case, the momentum of history may yet triumph, and an enduring tradition that I have sought to describe in fluid rather than in essentializing terms may continue to survive, adapt, and reform itself in humanly and humanely creative ways.

NOTES

1 The word "Hindoo" was in use by the early seventeenth century, and "Hindooism" by at least the 1780s (Sweetman 2000).

2 Another term sometimes used by Indians in a way politically synonymous with "Bhārat" is "Hindusthān," namely, "land of the Hindus," though "Hindusthān" can have more specific meanings referring to territory in nonpeninsular India. On Āryāvarta and related concepts, see Killingley 1997a.

3 Thus this does not mean that everyone spoke the same language or displayed identical cultural traits. Within the context of dominant Āryan linguistic and cultural patterns, there was room for sometimes substantial variation (e.g. in the south of the subcontinent).

4 How the various views delineated here will be able to come to terms with what seem to be recent finds of much earlier urban centers discovered (underwater) off the Gulf of Cambay remains to be seen. Such finds appear to be in the earliest stages of discovery and assessment.

5 As we shall see, the term "*hindu*," as an Indian word, was in regular use perhaps a couple of centuries before that.

6 He then goes on to give short summaries of dozens of popular sects "of some of the provinces" under the administration of the Bengal government.

7 Frykenberg (1989: 31) seems to argue that a concept must be definitionally "crisp or precise" to have a useful life, but this overlooks the epistemological complexity of concept-formation and concept-deployment, not least in social-scientific contexts. In such contexts, many concepts are necessarily open-ended interpretatively and methodologically malleable, as indices of historical multivocality and theoretical contestation.

8 But to be fair to Smith, it was his objections, first raised over forty years ago, that appreciably helped sharpen awareness of the methodological issues involved in our use of such terms as "religion" and the abstract designations, "Hinduism," "Buddhism," "Christianity," and so on.

9 But see Sen (1998) for a nuanced treatment of Hindu-Muslim relations, in which such boundaries were regularly breached, in post-Caitanya (namely, post-sixteenth century) contexts of eastern India.

10 Here Smith seems to reduce "Hinduism" to a religious way of life, which does not fully accord with our own position.

11 This must not be confused with the "objective" stance mentioned earlier, which gave rise to the academic study of religion in the West, of distancing oneself qua observer from personal religious experience or commitment (including one's own), irrespective of cultural context.

12 A well-documented procedure: see, for example, C. Bayly (1996); Kopf (1969, 1979); Raychaudhuri (1988).

13 On the thought of Rammohan Roy, who pioneered Hindu interaction with the West, see Crawford (1987); Killingley (1977, 1993). Killingley notes, "Rammohun was probably the first Hindu to use the word *Hinduism*" (1993: 61; emphasis in original), and in a footnote adds that Rammohan used the word in 1816.

14 Or even "Buddhist" for that matter. On the one hand, Buddhism in its numerous modes derives from a historical founder, on the other, there are no claims to unity on the basis of belief in a single scriptural canon or transcendent reality such as God, and so on.

15 For a careful analysis, first of some of the dyads mentioned earlier (in terms of the models of "Sanskritization" and great-little traditions), and then of the way Vedic paradigms have exerted hegemony in acculturating a whole region, see K. Chakrabarti (2001: chapters 3ff.).

16 Traditionally numbered as one hundred thousand, but in the so-called Pune critical edition about seventy-five thousand verses long.

17 Folk enactments have been a form of expressing *Mahābhārata* teachings for centuries; for a treatnent of a televisual adaptation, see Lipner (2001). For detailed scholarly information on the Sanskrit epics, see Brockington's (1998) monumental work.

18 Not only among Hindus in India. On page 277 in Lipner (1998a), I have cited an instance of "inducting" the spiritual power of the Ganges into the waters of a Mauritius lake, with a consequent expansion of the Ganges's sphere of polycentric influence. Among the Hindus of Mauritius, this lake is known as Gaṅgā Talāb.

19 In his fascinating study of the many potential "lives" of Hindu holy places and icons, Richard Davis points out the contrast between Muslim and Hindu perceptions of the temple of Somanātha, in the south of the Gujarat peninsula. He writes: "When confronting the polycentric Indian [=Hindu] political and religious order...[early] Muslim chroniclers *wished and needed to identify a center, the Indian equivalent of Mecca or the caliphal Baghdad.* They chose to promote Somanātha to this preeminent position in their own accounts, and turned Maḥmūd's [eleventh century CE] victory over Somanātha into a synecdoche for the conquest of India" (R. Davis 1997: 94; emphasis added). Thus, the conquest of Somanātha meant the conquest of

Hindudom, presumably analogous to the way the conquest of Mecca would imply the subjugation of Islamic religiopolitical order.

20 See Lipner (1998a: chapter 8), for a detailed analysis of *dharma* in terms of this model in the context of the famous dicing incident of the *Mahābhārata* (Book 2, chapters 43–65, in the Pune edition).

21 It is perhaps germane to our argument to quote from an obituary of the distinguished Indian photographer, Raghubir Singh, who died in 1999: "Beyond showing the rich palette of India's landscape and peoples, many of his pictures also reveal *an Indian way of seeing*, in that *they simultaneously capture several equally important knots of activity* in the manner of old miniatures, rather than leading the viewer's eye to some primary focal point" (Kaufman 1999; emphasis added).

22 But there is an ambivalence lodged here in that it also permits manipulation for vested interests.

23 What I have attempted is to provide grounds, in nonessentializing terms, for describing Hinduism under its own rubric. Some such effort is called for in the world of scholarship if we are to justify a range of ongoing activities, namely, the planning and undertaking of study and research from the point of view of various disciplines under a recognizable focus, the pursuit of interreligious dialogue across identifiable traditions, engaging in projects of transcultural understanding, the production and publication of books on "Hinduism" or aspects thereof, and so on. No doubt such attempts must leave room for the provisionality, on occasion, of the naming process, but their undertaking is anything but an idle semantic exercise, for to abandon it is to leave the subject unrecognized and hence voiceless.

24 "Secular" in the Indian Constitution does not mean "opposed to religion"; it permits the expression and propagation of religious belief (provided that the human and civic rights of others are not violated in the process) in such a way that no single religious tradition, even that of a majority, is constitutionally privileged (for a treatment of the term in the context of the Indian nation-state and Indian history, see Larson 1995).

PART II

ORAL TEACHINGS AND TEXTUAL TRADITIONS

CHAPTER TWO

VEDA AND UPANIṢAD

Laurie L. Patton

THE VEDAS

It is sunrise; a group of men are standing above a rounded firepit and chanting poetic rhythms. Near the firepit, outside a boundary, the sound of women pounding rice is interspersed with the hymns. Every few verses end with the sound "*svāhā*." The men pour an amount of *ghī* or clarified butter from a wooden bowl, and the fire flares up suddenly. Next to the firepit is a long glistening pole wrapped in yellow, rubbed in an oily substance. The entire scene is a medley of light: the sunrise, the fire, the golden butter, and the yellow pole. The priests are reciting hymns to Agni, the fire god, comparing him to the sun, which is rising now and casting light all around. Their hymns are also likening him to the color of the butter being cast into the pit, making a spectacle of sparks and smoke. Later the rice that the women have pounded will be shaped into balls of rice-offerings, making the arena a place of eating as well as offering for the priests and for the community as a whole.

When did this scene occur? It could have occurred in 1500 BCE, a time when the Vedic corpus of *mantras* was used in sacrifice, or it could have occurred in Spring 2000, in western Maharashtra, in a revival of Vedic sacrifice which attempts to follow the ancient texts exactly. The span of 3,500 years of tradition has compelled many (most recently on Internet Web sites concerned with Hinduism, but in many scholarly and popular publications before that) to define the Vedas as the core of Hindu practice and identity. Because the Vedic tradition is an elite tradition, this is not an uncontroversial statement. Popular *bhakti* or devotional movements have rejected Vedic knowledge and practices and prompted the untouchable saint Tukārāma to declare that he who gives himself over to study of the Vedas "gets tangled up and dies therein." In the light of Tukārāma, and other Hindu men and women like him, it is perhaps more accurate to say that the Vedic tradition remains a kind of prestigious and ancient touchstone around which Hindu religious arguments revolve.

This touchstone called the "Vedas" emerged as a series of practices involving oral compositions and a set of sacrifices involving fire. While oral texts and the practice of fire sacrifice probably existed for several centuries, if not millennia, before 1500 BCE, the scholarly consensus is that the Vedic practices emerged as we know them around this time in Western India and moved eastward along the Gangetic plain. They were the property of people who called themselves *ārya* (nobility) and distinguished themselves linguistically from the *dāsa* (enslaved ones) and the *mleccha* ("those who speak indistinctly," foreigners).

At present much debate exists about the origins of the Āryans themselves (see Bryant 2001; Patton and Bryant 2004). Much of nineteenth-century European scholarship posited an "invasion" of an early group, springing from an Indo-European homeland who migrated through the Caucasus, Iran, and into the Hindu Kush, around 2000–1500 BCE. However, recent archaeological evidence suggests that the story is far more complex and does not involve an invasion at all. Rather, the Āryans might have cohabited and mingled with their counterparts, the inhabitants of the Indus Valley civilization (covering what is now present-day Pakistan and parts of Western India), for several centuries, before the great towns and cities of the Indus Valley civilization fell into decay around 1700 BCE. Archaeological evidence also suggests that Indus Valley towns and ways of life lasted in smaller scale far beyond that time of the demise of its great cities and that the Āryans were present in the more central parts of India far earlier than had been previously thought. In light of this picture of ancient developments, some scholars argue that the Indus Valley and the Vedic civilizations were a single civilization. While the debate is still raging, suffice it to say that the Vedic world emerged in a complex and gradual way, involving both migration from outside as well as indigenous growth from within.

How would the Āryan women pounding rice and the men pouring butter have understood themselves as a people? What distinguished the Āryans from other groups and the Vedas from other texts? First, the Āryans worked with chariots, horses, and weapons of war which included iron. Second, their social organization was broadly tribal in nature and focused on cattle as a form of wealth and status. Third, their method of worship revolved around an elaborate system of sacrifice involving vegetable and animal offerings, in which the power of speech played a central role.

TEXTS AND CONTEXTS

The Vedas

This power of speech is where the Vedas come clearly into focus. The word "*veda*" means knowledge; historically, this knowledge took the form of word and chant. Four kinds of knowledge are specified as the property of Brāhmaṇ priests, the hereditary keepers of tradition: the *Ṛg Veda* or knowledge of the verses, the *Sāma Veda* or knowledge of the chants, the *Yajur Veda* or knowledge of the ritual directions, and the *Atharva Veda* or knowledge of the *atharvāṇa*s, the procedures for everyday life (also called "magical" formulae). These four divisions reflect a division of labor amongst the priestly elite as to who was to do what, and it meant that knowledge itself was organized around the performance of *yajña* or sacrifice. For the Vedic Āryans *yajña* is the central action that was meant to motivate and sustain the entire universe. The Vedas are the words and chants accompanying the actions and served to augment and vitalize the actions into having cosmic power. Without the sacrifice, the sun would not rise in the morning; nor would the cattle grow and multiply; nor would the crops flourish throughout the year. The possibility of long and healthy life for humans and the worship of the fathers or ancestors after death would not be present.

As early to contemporary Vedic commentators have observed, the women pounding rice in the scene described earlier would not have understood the meaning of the words of the Veda. This knowledge, aside from being a kind of fourfold division of labor of the sacrifice, was also hereditary through the male line and learned entirely orally. The different collections of hymns in the *Ṛg Veda* are called *maṇḍala*s and are essentially "family" collections which reflect the idea that this knowledge was passed down father to son or teacher to student. Moreover, the method of keeping the knowledge oral was highly advanced science of memorization. Later the Vedic texts were divided into *saṃhitāpāṭha* or the words combined in euphonic combination (*sandhi*); *padapāṭha*, in which the words are separated and stand on their own; and *kramapāṭha* or syllabic separation which showed the ways in which each syllable was to be memorized and repeated in a regular pattern and accompanied by bodily movement.

To this day, when one attends a performance of a Vedic sacrifice, one sees students sitting near the Vedic fires, learning the *kramapāṭha* system and moving their heads and hands and wrists in accordance with the rhythm. In the twentieth century, this learning is augmented by books; this was not the case during the Vedic (both early and late) period of early India, from about 1500 to 300 BCE. The *Ṛg Veda* alone consists of some 10,000 verses, and the recitation of such a work involved mental feat of great magnitude indeed. But the sheer human effort of this memorization occurred in very everyday contexts—fathers teaching sons, teachers instructing students in small villages across the Gangetic plain.

The Brāhmaṇas and the Sūtras

Enough ambiguity existed in Vedic compositions to leave room for an expansive interpretive tradition. The Brāhmaṇas and the Sūtras are groups of texts which form distinct chronological layers after the composition of the Vedas and are concerned with both the etiology and the performance of sacrifice. We might formulate the problems of these texts in the following way: what are the outgrowths and results of such a sacrificial system, both in practice and in the idealized textual representation? The authors of the prose Brāhmaṇas developed an elaborate ritual philosophy in which the central questions were metapractical as well as metaphysical.[1] They ask, "What is the origin of this sacrificial practice, and why does it work the way it does?" Etiological narrative is mixed with ritual instruction, and the progression of thought is associative rather than strictly logical along the lines of later classical Hindu philosophy. Each Veda has its Brāhmaṇa—or putting it in a general way, each form of knowledge had its own ritual elaboration and explanation. (The *Ṛg Veda* has the *Kauṣītaki* and *Aitareya Brāhmaṇa*s; the *Yajur Veda* has the *Śatapaṭha* and *Jaiminīya Brāhmaṇa*s, and so on. We will see this system expanded into the Upaniṣads, to be discussed later.)

The Vedic schools also produced the basic shortened formulae or Sūtras of how to perform these sacrifices (although some would argue that even these, too, are idealized types and not recipes or descriptions of the actual procedures) (Thite 1996).[2] The manuals for the public sacrifices are the Śrautasūtras and contain ritual directions as well as *viniyoga*s or applications of Vedic *mantra*s. The manuals for the more domestic rites, prescribed for those living in villages around the central arena, are contained in the Gṛhyasūtras. These are a very valuable source of information for the kinds of rituals that would inform "everyday life," such as the birth of a child, the funeral for a Brāhmaṇ, getting rid of an enemy, a rival co-wife, and getting lost in the woods. They too contain ritual instructions as well as which Vedic *mantras* to use in which situation. The role of women becomes more prominent in these rituals. In the Gṛhyasūtras, we see the beginning of an emphasis on personal learning and self-sufficiency, in which the actual sacrificial arena becomes less and less important and the internalization of *mantra* on the part of the mobile priest becomes far more the modus operandi of the Vedic virtuoso.

Finally, in the late Vedic period, there emerged the Vidhāna literature, those which consist entirely of *viniyogas* outside the sacrificial situation entirely. These texts imply that the Brāhmaṇ himself, through the mere utterance of *mantras*, can change any and all situations in which he might find himself in. These Vidhāna texts are, in a way, a natural extension of the Gṛhyasūtras, and yet the domestic ritual itself is less present and the focus is on the use of the Vedic text alone as having magical powers. This is the *svādhyāya* or self-study of which Timothy Lubin (2003), Charles Malamoud (1977), and others have written so persuasively. It creates a kind of Vedic universe in which mental agility alone can account for Vedic knowledge, and the prestige of the Veda becomes embodied not in sacrificial action but in the verbal and imaginative skill of the reciter and performer.

All of these texts and schools can be geographically located in some important ways and saw particular growth across the Gangetic plain. Most of the early Vedic schools flourished in the Western part of India, beginning in the Gandhāran region and expanding into the Kuru-Pañcāla and Kosala (later written Kośala)-Videha regions, with areas south and west of these regions also participating. During the late Vedic period Kuru-Pañcāla was clearly the center of Vedic theology and speculation, with the Videha region acting as a kind of outlying area. Later, the regions of Aṅga in the southeast and the Vindhya Mountains in central India also supported the composition of Vedic texts. Thanks to recent scholarship, each of the Vedic schools have been tentatively located in particular geographical regions: the Taittirīya school, which housed the school of the Kṛṣṇa Yajur Veda, in the northwest regions of Kuru-Pañcāla; the Śukla Yajur Veda school in the central region of Kosala-Videha; and the Kauṣītaki school more broadly to the south between the Satvan and Matsya kingdoms just to the north of the Vindhya Mountains.[3]

THE DETAILS OF SACRIFICIAL PERFORMANCE

What did the act of sacrifice look like to the men and women at the sunrise performance? Each sacrificial arena consisted of a large rectangle, about the size of a small soccer field. One half of the arena was divided into three main fires, each symbolically representing a different power and a different function. Ideally, the fire itself originated from the home of the *āhitāgni* or household keeper of the fire, who lived near the sacrificial arena, kept miniature versions of the fires in his home, and recited *mantras* with his wife to keep them burning throughout the day. (Villages in Andhra Pradesh still reflect this arrangement and have been documented, thanks to the work of David Knipe [1997] and others.) In the larger public arena, the *gārhapatya* fire represents the fire of the home and hearth, the *āhavanīya* fire, the source of priestly power, and the *dakṣiṇā* fire, the southern fire that protects against the demons who might emerge from that inauspicious direction. In some sacrifices involving *soma*, the sacred drink imbibed by both the priests and the gods, the middle of the rectangular field is the *soma*-cart, a large platform on wheels which hauls the stocks from which the *soma* is made. At the far end is the *mahāvedi*, the round firepit into which clarified butter and other offerings are given at various pivotal points in the sacrifice itself. Between these main fire altars are various smaller altars which serve particular functions such as the crushing of the *soma* and various stations of the priests whose role is to recite Vedic verses at different parts of the sacrifice.

Just as the Vedas themselves represent a kind of division of labor, so too the priests' labor are divided into various kinds like any other well-organized "central office," and one might think of the sacrificial arena as a kind of central office of the universe itself. Priests took up their roles at different places within the performance arena, and each form of labor is weighted with a kind of cosmic, mythical significance. The *hotṛ* is in charge of the *Ṛg Veda* or poetic formulae; the *adhvaryu* priest is an expert in the *Yajur Veda* and in charge of overseeing the actual movements of all of the subpriests and moves all about as a kind of "master of ceremonies." The *udgātṛ* priest is in charge of the musical elements and said to be mythically descended from the Gandharvas or heavenly musicians. His Veda, not surprisingly, is the *Sāma Veda* or the Veda of chants. The Brāhmaṇ priest, associated with the *Atharva Veda*, is in charge of the entire sacrifice, and his role is to sit in silence on a stool at the center, observing the proceedings and being consulted in moments of ritual error or confusion. Silence in the Veda tends to signify either great insight or great defeat, and of course, in this case of the Brāhmaṇ, insight is indicated.

Another, separate ritual role is reserved for the sponsor of the Vedic sacrifice, called the *yajamāna*, and his wife, the *patnī*. The two provide the economic resources for the entire thing to be performed. The *yajamāna* holds a special seat during the proceedings and, at various moments at the beginning and the end, performs an inaugurating function for certain rituals. His wife, too, is present at various moments of the sacrifice such as the *pravargya* or secret ceremony before the *soma* sacrifice. At times she is covered with a parasol, and at other times she participates in offerings. She represents fertility and a kind of cosmic sexuality, and her public role is to be noted as a major exception to the general role of women during the sacrificial performances. In recent sacrificial revivals, she is honored as a sacred person in her own right.

The basic structure of the Vedic sacrifice is that of the *haviryajña*s, which primarily include vegetable offerings in the forms of gruel and rice cakes and dairy offerings such as *ghī* and curds. Animal sacrifices are also *haviryajña*s, but tend to be viewed as more elaborate rituals in their own right, called *paśubandha*s. Time was measured by these regular *haviryajña*s, and even the villagers mentioned in the morning scene described earlier would have recognized the proceedings of the priests at important transitions of the day and of the seasons. The *agnihotra* marked the morning and the evening of each day; the *darśapūrṇamāsa* was the new and full moon offering; and the seasonal sacrifices marking spring, rainy season, and autumn were called the *cāturmāsyāni* or four-month offerings.

Relatedly, the *soma* sacrifice is also a basic form of structural organization in the Vedic ritual and involves the crushing and offering of *soma* in the morning, mid-day, and evening. Each *soma* sacrifice consists of several offerings, either vegetable or animal, and each offering is dedicated to a particular deity and accompanied by *mantra*s that are devoted to that deity. These rites are the basic offerings around which the larger procedures such as the kingly coronation (*rājasūya*) and the horse sacrifice, designed to conquer land (*aśvamedha*), are built. These larger sacrifices usually involve other, special rites, frequently of a contestual nature. The *aśvamedha* involves a dialogue between Brāhmaṇs and Śūdras or servants. The *mahāvrata* or equinox rite involves a mock battle over the sun, in the form of a white disk.

In fact, many scholars have argued that contest per se is the essence of the Vedic worldview: each sacrifice was a kind of Brāhmaṇical "potlatch" ceremony in which wealth was displayed, and members of competing Āryan tribes engaged in verbal battles in which the very life of the contestants was at stake.[4] They conjecture that these performances created an escalating scale of violence from which the authors of the more contemplative works, the Upaniṣads, departed in favor of a more internalized view of sacrifice. Whatever level of violence was actually and metaphorically present, it is clear that these acts of sacrifice were also bargaining chips for political power in a system of small tribes and tribal alliances and continued to remain so as the sacrificial system moved into the period of more consolidated kingdoms along the Gaṅgā River around 500 BCE.

Whatever the actual nature of the sacrifices, it is abundantly clear from the texts themselves that several rituals provided "prototypes" (*vikṛti*) for other variant rituals (*prakṛti*), which could be constructed around them. Many of the basic ritual structures could remain in place, while the oblations, the *mantra*s recited, and the deities propitiated might change. The Brāhmaṇas and the Sūtras also make provision for the fact that some rituals can be "embedded" within other rituals, and thus the variation on the same basic ritual observance can be quite large indeed.

While there exist solemn and sacred divisions of priestly knowledge and priestly labor in this solemn sacrificial tradition, in recent revivals one is struck by an overall atmosphere of festivity and lightheartedness during the proceedings themselves. As it is performed today, a *yajña* involves the economic systems of an entire village—the woodcutters for the fires, the rice growers for the offerings of balls of rice, the bamboo splitters for the boundaries and decorations of the entire sacrificial arena itself.[5] It is a kind of village *melā* or festival, in which even those who do not participate become joyful observers. To draw close to the arena in which sacred sounds or acts are being performed is to draw close to a source of auspiciousness. Frederick Smith (2000, 2001) has called this phenomenon the contemporary "Hinduization" of Vedic sacrifice and argues that forms of worship from the "Classical period" of Hinduism such as the *pūjā* or worship of images, both statues and drawings, are regularly enacted around the periphery of the sacrificial arena. In addition, in the twentieth century, impromptu classes attended by local villagers and taught by Brāhmaṇ priests are conducted around the peripheries of the performance.

Aside from the twentieth century additions, what gods would our second-millennium villagers have worshiped in the Vedic sacrifice proper, and what is the theology behind them? The *Ṛg Veda* is our best source for poetic theology, containing, as they do, stories and fragments of stories about their divine exploits. As one might expect, the Vedic gods are also divided into relative divisions of labor. Agni, the fire god, and Soma, the god of the sacrificial drink, are the priestly gods who are in charge of transporting the sacrifice to the heavens (Agni) and inspiring the poet who praises (Soma). With these priestly gods, we see the Vedic world at its most philosophically playful: the texts constantly move between the abstract and the concrete. At times Agni is the actual fire, and at others he is clearly the god of fire, and this constant oscillation between the two states is part of the genius of Vedic poetry. Soma, too, is both a deity of eloquence and the sacred drink that is crushed and when imbibed causes eloquence (see Maṇḍala 9 of the *Ṛg Veda* for hymns dedicated to Soma).

The warrior god, Indra, is far more human in his incarnations. His feats include cosmic heroism; he freed the cows from their cave in heaven and thereby allowed them to roam freely about the world (*Ṛg Veda* 3.31). In so far as cows are also symbolic of light in the *Ṛg Veda*, he thereby allowed the light to roam freely about the world. He also slew the serpent Vṛtra, whose huge body had dammed up the rivers and stopped the waters from flowing (*Ṛg Veda* 1.32). Indra is an appetitive god and is frequently caught in exploits with sage's wives. Yet the element of mystery is not entirely absent from Indra, either; perceiving Indra in disguise or being able to tell his voice from far away are parts of the ways that the ancient sages showed their prowess (*Ṛg Veda* 8.14, 2.12). Some of the more well-known deities of the third class, the agricultural class, are the Aśvins, the twin deities who heal, cause safe childbirth, restore beauty, and prolong life (*Ṛg Veda* 1.92, 1.116).

The Vedic world is also filled with other deities, identified with but not limited to the natural world. Sūrya, the sun god, is the most prominent of these deities and is depicted as the deity who rides a chariot across the skies and whose cyclical journey is identified with the calendar year (*Ṛg Veda* 1.50). The power of Sūrya is lurking behind many Vedic verses referring to light and to time. Vāyu, the wind god, helps the worshiper send an oblation; Rātrī, the goddess of night, takes messages from one Vedic character to the other (*Ṛg Veda* 10.127). Uṣas, the goddess of dawn, reveals herself to the world like a loving wife reveals herself to her husband (*Ṛg Veda* 1.92). Pūṣan, the pathfinder, allows us to find our way when we are lost in the woods (*Ṛg Veda* 1.42, 6.55). Yama presides as the god of death and the underworld, where the dead man visits after his soul has left this world (*Ṛg Veda* 10.14, 10.16).

In addition, the sages (*ṛṣi*) and fathers (*pitṛ*) play an important role in the Vedic cosmos: many would argue that they, rather the gods, are the real actors in the *yajña*. The *ṛṣi*s are frequently the heroes of Vedic hymns and the utterers of them. In no sense can they be called "original" authors, as we might call William Wordsworth or John Keats in the European tradition, however. Rather they perceive the hymns, through both sight and sound; the hymns themselves are thought to be self-existent before the creation of the world, and the sage's job is not to create but to receive and transmit them appropriately. Thus, the families who own the different *maṇḍala*s or cycles of the *Ṛg Veda* are seen as guardians of them, not their originators. Moreover, the sages were said to be present at the original sacrifice that created the world: in this sense, they have the same, if not greater, role in creation than the Vedic gods. The fathers, on the other hand, are the receivers of the sacrifice along with the gods. The fathers are seen as the ancestors of the sacrificer who makes the offering: in certain texts they are viewed as the successful sacrificer who has gone onto gain the status of a deity in his next life by virtue of offering so many sacrifices in his previous one.

The style of these Vedic hymns is frequently enigmatic, built on a set of metaphorical constructions which contain two or more realities. As mentioned before, Agni is both the fire and the fire god, the power of fire itself. Cows frequently represent light and the free passage, the passage of sunlight throughout the world. They also represent wealth and gold. Sometimes metaphoric constructions make explicit comparisons, such as the comparison of the voices of priests to the voices of frogs in the spring (*Ṛg Veda* 7.103). Another hymn compares the labor of the poet reciting *mantra*s to the labor of a carpenter or a physician or a miller with grinding stones (*Ṛg Veda* 9.112). Equally frequently, the enigmas can take the form of explicit riddles, such as those in *Ṛg Veda* 1.164.34–35:

> I ask you about the farthest end of the earth. I ask you about the navel of the universe. I ask you about the semen of the stallion bursting with seed; I ask you about the final abode of speech.
>
> This altar is the farthest end of the earth; this sacrifice is the navel of the universe. This *soma* is the semen of the stallion bursting with seed; this Brāhmaṇ priest is the final abode of speech.

These enigmas are assumed to be part of the verbal contest in the center of the sacrificial performance, mentioned earlier. Finally, enigmas can take the shape of explicit paradox such as "With the sacrifice the gods sacrificed to the sacrifice" (*Ṛg Veda* 10.90.16), in which the poets create a kind of verbal Möbius strip in which nothing can exist independently. Elements of the universe do not engage in a form of linear creation, rather they engage in acts of mutual creation that serve as challenges to reciter and to hearer in the sacrificial arena.

The fate of the Vedic schools, given their widespread geographical range, is itself a matter of puzzlement and interest. Schools of interpretation of Vedic meaning, such as the *aitihāsika* or legendary school, the *nirukta* or etymological school, and the *yajñika* or ritual school, are also mentioned even in late Vedic and early epic texts. Some schools of philosophical interpretation based on the Veda also flourished. Mīmāṃsā is one such school—meaning "intensive investigation," Mīmāṃsā originated in the *sūtra*s or small aphorisms of Jaimini in the fourth century BCE. Mīmāṃsā thinkers were concerned with the right procedures of sacrifice so that they could fulfill their dharmic obligations; thus it could be called a kind of ritual philosophy. They divided the Vedic compositions into those statements which helped them to perform *dharma* and those statements which were "ancillary" aids to that purpose. The Vedas also produced kinds of Vedāṅgas or limbs other than the Vedic schools described here. The *jyotirśāstra*, or science of astrology, and the *dhanurveda*, or knowledge of archery, are two such limbs which made it more broadly into Indian culture.

While these schools are very important kinds of continuities in the Vedic traditions, there were discontinuities as well. During the second century BCE and continuing into the first few centuries CE, a great sea change occurred, in which practices of sacrifice became less and less important and the honoring of images emerged into the foreground. Perhaps because of interaction with Buddhist and Jaina ideas and practices, the Vedic way of life became rather more of a prestigious remnant than a dominant set of ideas and practices. Certainly, in the Gupta and medieval periods, ideas about sacrifice continued in the scholarly commentarial traditions, including Mīmāṃsā. And while Vedic worlds and deities were stock-in-trade backdrop to the Purāṇas, the theological texts of the medieval period, such Vedic references were only that—backdrop. In the medieval period, the philosopher Madhva, from the Dvaita school of thought, also composed an important commentary on the Veda. Less well-known commentators such as Skandasvāmin also turned their attention to Vedic texts exclusively. The most well known is Sāyaṇa, the fourteenth-century commentator who supervised a massive gloss on the *Ṛg Veda* and other Vedic texts, according to Vedānta tradition. Sāyaṇa's small industry was based in fourteenth-century Vijayanagara kingdom.

Finally, the colonial period also ushered in an interest in the Veda that was highly determined by conversations between local elite Brāhmaṇ rulers, missionaries, and British administrators. This conversation involved the so-called "discovery" of the Vedas by

British colonial translators; the creation of a false Veda as an authoritative text by British missionaries; the "critical edition" of the Veda by a German scholar working in England, Friedrich Max Müller, in the mid-eighteenth century; and the critique of the Vedas by Hindu reformers such as Dayānanda Sarasvatī, Rammohan Roy, Vivekānanda, and others. Some of that critique involved dissolving the "idolatrous content" and others involved a stress on personal experience rather than textual fidelity. Other activists such as Aurobindo were less critical of the Vedas but strove to see in them mystical readings that could rival any Western religious texts.

By the mid-twentieth century the Vedas were "owned" by several groups: the traditional *paṇḍita*s and priests who recited them at weddings, small sacrifices, and other life-cycle occasions; European and American philologists who parsed and analyzed them for historical purposes; Indian scholars who used both traditional Indian and Western exegetical methods; theosophists who saw in them a transcultural, transhistorical meaning. This situation continues to be the case in the early twenty-first century, with the addition of a small but visible group of Vedic revivalists, whose purpose is to reenact Vedic sacrifices with as much fidelity to the Śrautasūtras as possible.[6] While Vedic sacrifices have continually been performed in various parts of India, these performers are explicitly attempting to make the performances relevant to twenty-first century concerns. Indian educators inspired by Hindu nationalist concerns are also focusing on Vedic content in school curricula, emphasizing the Vedic texts as a form of intellectual achievement that has been overlooked by colonial educational system.

THE UPANIṢADS

Let us turn to another scene that might have occurred a few hundred years later, in say 800 BCE. It is sunrise, and the learning is happening in a wilderness area, of forest, outside of the village where the smoke of the Vedic sacrifices is still rising. Maitreyī is asking a question of her husband and teacher, Yājñavalkya. Yājñavalkya is making a long trip and about to divide his wealth between his two wives. Maitreyī responds by saying, "What is the point in getting something that will not make me immortal? Tell me instead all that you know." Developing personal wisdom, inner knowledge of the meaning of immortality, in addition to and at times in substituting for, external wealth, and even the external acts of sacrifice make up the scenes of the Upaniṣads.

Why did this conversation take place, and why was it memorized and handed down orally as part of Vedic lore? During the middle-late Vedic periods, during which many of these oral texts were composed, new interactions between both Kṣatriyas and Brāhmaṇs led to new conversations about the nature and meaning of the sacrifice. Maitreyī is told by Yājñavalkya, for instance, that priestly power, royal power, the worlds of the Vedic cosmogony, and the gods, the beings, and the whole (*sarvam*), all of these are venerated not for themselves but for the self. The self is not only the motivating force behind these externals; rather they are these externals. And thus the self, Yājñavalkya concludes to Maitreyī, must be identified with the whole—in fact, must be the whole. Then duality disappears, for when the whole has become one's very self, then who is there to perceive and by what means? (*Bṛhadāraṇyaka Upaniṣad* 2.4.1–12). The whole here has also been referred to in most other Upaniṣads as *brahman*, the force that unites the entire universe.

The Upaniṣads were part of the "branches" of the Vedas, and they grew up in the following way: as each of the schools grew, each text or new area of inquiry was added to the Vedic schools. As mentioned earlier, the Brāhmaṇas were a kind of ritual elaboration that showed the value and origins of each of the sacrificial practices. The Sūtras, both public and domestic, were condensed manuals of operation. In addition to the Sūtras, however, there were also parts of the Brāhmaṇas' ritual philosophy which were to be taught in the forest, as Maitreyī was being taught in the scene described before. Because these teachings were meant to be uttered beyond the bounds of traditional sacrificial society, they were eventually called Āraṇyakas or forest teachings. Some of these compositions (such as the *Bṛhadāraṇyaka Upaniṣad*) were also called, adjectivally, Upaniṣad or "esoteric teaching." Others of these collections came to be called "Upaniṣads" in their own right, separate from the Āraṇyakas. The *Ṛg Veda* produced the *Aitareya* and *Kauṣītaki Upaniṣads*; the *Kṛṣṇa Yajur Veda* led to the *Taittirīya*, *Śvetāśvatara*, and *Kaṭha Upaniṣads*; the *Śukla Yajur Veda* produced the *Bṛhadāraṇyaka* and *Īśā Upaniṣads*; the *Sāma Veda* engendered the *Chāndogya* and *Kena Upaniṣads*, as well as the *Jaiminīya Upaniṣad Brāhmaṇa*; and the *Atharva Veda* gave rise to the *Muṇḍaka*, *Praśna*, and *Māṇḍūkya Upaniṣads*.

How might we describe the religious world reflected in these texts and in conversations such as the one between Maitreyī and Yājñavalkya? The Upaniṣads departed from the basic elaboration of these ritual themes. Rather, they used sacrifice as a reference point, a metaphor, for the focus upon and realization of the self (*ātman*) and the identity of the self with the all-important force that animates the world (*brahman*). Some scholars have called this process "the internalization of the sacrifice." It is important to note that this is not "rejection of the sacrifice in favor of philosophy" as some earlier scholars have characterized the Upaniṣadic move.

Moreover, Maitreyī and Yājñavalkya shared a geographical imagination. While Upaniṣadic perspectives differ from each other, all draw from a common stock of stories, dialogues, and metaphorical constructions involving famous kings and teachers from a broad geographical spread, covering the Gangetic plain from Kuru-Pañcāla in the west to Kosala-Videha in the east. This Upaniṣadic way of life expressed a radically different social and political reality from the heyday of Vedic society. There is a strong presence of movement across kingdoms and a high level of trade amongst kingdoms. In addition, kings (Kṣatriyas) are as strong as Brāhmaṇs in their theological prowess and concerns. However, while this strong presence has led some early historians to hypothesize that the Kṣatriyas may have been the authors of the Upaniṣads, it is fairer to say that the mutual relationship between the Brāhmaṇs and the Kṣatriyas took on a new vibrancy as kings played a new role in the emerging urban landscape. As Patrick Olivelle (1993) and others have argued, the consolidation of kingdoms led to their being a kind of town/wilderness split which fostered such institutions as celibacy and asceticism.[7]

This system could be supported by the more established kingdoms, as the Āryan tribes were no longer simply constantly on the move and concerned about their own tribal survival. We have references to mercantile centers and kingdoms, such as Videha and Kāśi (*Bṛhadāraṇyaka Upaniṣad* 2.1.1, 3.8.2; *Kauṣītaki Upaniṣad* 4.1). Even the Upaniṣadic schools were gathered around small communities of at least one, and usually several, teacher and their families as well as students. Philosophical ideas for which the Upaniṣads are so famous are linked to crafts, such as pottery and weaving; and luxuries, such as garlands and perfumes, become major images. Courtly images, such as food and drink and singing and music, are crucial for the new Upaniṣadic perspective (*Chāndogya Upaniṣad* 8.2.1–10). One of the Upaniṣads describes the world of *brahman* like a court palace with watchmen, doorkeepers, throne and couch, rivers, trees, and courtyard (*Kauṣītaki Upaniṣad* 1.3–5).

The Upaniṣads also reflect a basic chronology of themes and structure. The earliest Upaniṣads probably originated around 600–500 BCE and were composed in prose. They focused on many common topics such as the nature of *brahman*; the nature of sacrificial speak and the verses; the various forms of breath; the homologization of parts of the body to the powers in the universe. The teaching of the five fires as the essence of the major parts of the cosmos (e.g. fire as man, woman, and the three worlds) is especially distinctive in these early prose compositions. The later Upaniṣads are composed in verse and developed the theme of *brahman* into a theistic, rather than monistic, point of view. They also focus on the idea of liberation through meditation. The final prose Upaniṣads also focus on these themes and derive from the first centuries CE.

What did this internalization of the sacrifice look like? Each Upaniṣad had a different method for teaching this knowledge, but all used the basic imageries of the sacrifice to show the ways in which bodily processes and processes of awareness allowed the student to conceive of the sacrifice as going on inside his body. A close examination of one particular passage will show how this process works: In the *Bṛhadāraṇyaka Upaniṣad* 3.1.8–10, Aśvala the Hotṛ priest (presumably trained in sacrifice and sacrificial recitation) asks Yājñavalkya the teacher about what will happen "today at the sacrifice." Notice that, already, someone who is a sacrificer is asking someone else about the inner meaning of the sacrifice. When Aśvala asks how many oblations there will be, Yājñavalkya responds that each oblation has its own modality and is therefore connected to the world that has its own modality. The oblations that flare will win the world of the gods, for the world shines that way. The oblations that overflow (*atinedante*) will go to the world of the ancestors, for that world is "over above" (*ati*). The oblations that lie down (*adhiśerate*) will go to this human world, for that world is here below (*adha*). This imagery continues a basic cosmology which one sees in earlier Vedic texts of the worlds of the gods, the fathers, and the ancestors. However, it attributes, through etymologies, different modes of being to each of the offerings and each of the worlds.

Aśvala then asks Yājñavalkya how many deities will be used by the Brāhmaṇ priest to protect the sacrifice that day. And Yājñavalkya departs from other Vedic texts, such as the *Bṛhaddevatā* or the *Sarvānukramaṇī*, whose main point is to number the deities in an appropriate fashion. He answers, instead, "One, the mind." He argues that this is possible because the mind is without limit and the All-Gods are without limit, and the world which one gains by it is also limitless. Thus the deities become identified with mind itself—and by implication, the Brāhmaṇ priest, the controller of the sacrifice, can earn his authority through the machinations of his own mind. Finally, in discussing the hymns that are used in the sacrifice, Aśvala asks what these hymns are with respect to the "self-body" (*ātman*). Yājñavalkya replied that the hymn recited before the sacrifice is the out-breath, the hymn that accompanies the sacrifice, the in-breath, and the hymn of praise, the inter-breath.

In this short story, then, each of the basic sacrificial procedures, present from the earliest ritual texts, becomes homologized with the individual breathing body. We see this in many other parts of the *Bṛhadāraṇyaka* and other Upaniṣads. The sacrificial fires are seen as part of the inner workings of the body; the role of the *adhvaryu* priest is identified with the eyes, and the process of sight itself, and this sight can see the nature of the whole world (*Bṛhadāraṇyaka Upaniṣad* 3.1.5). In other passages, it is not only the cosmology of the sacrifice that is given to the body but also the cosmology of the entire world and its topography. For instance, rivers of the world are identified as the rivers contained within the body (*Bṛhadāraṇyaka Upaniṣad* 1.1.1; *Śvetāśvatara Upaniṣad* 1.4.5), the eye of the world is also the sight of the body (*Chāndogya Upaniṣad* 1.7.4), and so on.

What then becomes of the Vedic deities? Are these powerful tools of the early Vedic imagination harnessed in another way? Yes and no. Many of the deities are still quite active and involved—such as Indra, who is engaged in much questioning and dialogue throughout most of both the earlier and later Upaniṣadic texts. However, while the activity of sacrifice is still presumed, the Upaniṣads use the deities themselves as aids to a certain kind of knowledge, a special kind of wisdom that only the meditator has access to. Thus, the world of the gods is only one world that can be gained; the possibility of nonreturning altogether is anew and quite intriguing prospect. The object of that knowledge is no longer the gods per se but that new force called *brahman*.

How might have Maitreyī thought and argued about the nature of *brahman*, this key to the universe? First, it was thought of as the power behind the sacrifice, and as the Upaniṣadic thought developed, it was described as the power behind every living thing and every element in the universe. *Brahman* was "the whole" (*Bṛhadāraṇyaka Upaniṣad* 2.5) and transcended even the gods. It also existed beyond all known things in this world and yet was also present within them. It was set apart from beings, and yet dwelling within beings at the same time. This basic identification between the selves of beings and *brahman* leads to the famous Upaniṣadic equation that the self (*ātman*) is the same as the power behind the universe (*brahman*). As the sage Yājñavalkya puts it: "The self within all is this self of yours." Occasionally, as we see from Yājñavalkya's words, the larger *brahman* is also spoken of as the *ātman* or "self" of the universe, and thus the poetic nineteenth-century translation, "the world-soul." The *Bṛhadāraṇyaka* puts it eloquently: "This self is the honey of all beings, and all beings are the honey of this self. The radiant and immortal person in the self and the radiant and immortal person connected with the body [here, also referred to as *ātman*]—they are both one's self. It is the immortal; it is *brahman*, it is the whole" (2.5.9).

Brahman is also spoken of as a formulation of truth—a truth which is to be attained by wise men and women who have practiced meditation and focused on the forest teachings for a very long time. *Brahman* is the highest object of the teachings on hidden connections—an object rooted in austerity and the knowledge of the self (*Śvetāśvatara Upaniṣad* 1.9). The imagery here is not simply that of a truth to be attained but an abode in its own right. *Brahman* is almost like a "truth realm." For instance, *Chāndogya Upaniṣad* 3.11 states of *brahman*: "There, surely, it has never set, nor ever risen. By this truth, O gods, let me not be stripped of the formulation of *brahman*." The text goes on to say that when someone knows this teaching, for that person the sun neither rises nor sets—for him it is always day.

Similarly, other Upaniṣads also describe *brahman* as a stainless realm (*Praśna Upaniṣad* 1.16) in its own right—a world of unending peace, an ancient formulation which is heard in the heavenly abodes (*Śvetāśvatara Upaniṣad* 2.4). Other delightfully worldly images are also used to describe *brahman*, such as a divine fort (*Muṇḍaka Upaniṣad* 2.2.7), a wheel (*Bṛhadāraṇyaka Upaniṣad* 2.5.19; *Śvetāśvatara Upaniṣad* 2.4), and a kind of clay which has been smeared but now is clean (*Śvetāśvatara Upaniṣad* 2.14). The meditator, in turn, is a person whose body is the "bottom slab with the syllable *oṃ* the upper drill" (*Śvetāśvatara Upaniṣad* 1.14) who seeks *brahman* "like oil in sesame seeds and butter in curds" (1.15).

Finally, true to the sages' understanding of their work as "hidden teachings" and "hidden connections," the Upaniṣads are filled with metaphors which hint at, but can never directly state, the true nature of *brahman*. Here, we can cite many dialogues within the earlier Upaniṣads which use the themes of invisibility and negation. The famous dialogue between Uddālaka and his son Śvetaketu shows the son and pupil dividing the seeds of a fruit into smaller and smaller units until he cannot see anything left. Uddālaka explains, "You are that" (*tat tvam asi*). In other words, Śvetaketu and his inner self (*ātman*) are also identified with that invisible force that makes the seed grow (*brahman*). *Brahman* is like that, says his teaching. Moreover, many of the famous dialogues argue that the best way to describe *brahman* is through negation, "Not this, and not that." It is important to note that this Upaniṣadic approach is not simply a mystical *via negativa*, as has been often described. Rather, the dialogues show that *brahman* is a practical process of reduction from something to nothing, until one ends with a paradox, about which one can say very little. Maitreyī begins with this process when she questions her husband, and it is assumed that she, like all other Upaniṣadic sages, will internalize the wisdom and become a teacher in her own right.

But what would Maitreyī have expected after she arrived at this point of knowledge? What would her expectations of the afterlife have been? We see emerging in the Upaniṣads a theory of death and birth which is strikingly different that the Vedic sacrificial fear of "re-death" (*punarmṛtyu*). The Upaniṣads contain the earliest records of what we have come to call *saṃsāra*, or the endless cycle of birth and death, as well as *mokṣa*, or the path that leads away from *saṃsāra*. The story of Jabālā is instructive on this point. Jabālā is ashamed that his native learning, gleaned at his father's knee, is not sufficient in the court to which he travels. He must learn an entirely new set of metaphors, in which each section of life (man, woman, semen, food) is said to be identical with the sacrificial fire. While these are not unusual for many sections of the Upaniṣads, the subsequent section is startlingly new. Those whose conduct is good, but who choose to offer sacrifices in the village, will go on the path of the moon and be reborn accordingly. Those who choose the path of the forest and the knowledge of *brahman* will go on the path of the sun and leave this life altogether. And those whose conduct is reprehensible will be reborn into a lesser, probably repugnant, womb.

Why is this a new way of thinking? To be sure, the language of paths which are good to go on is an old and very familiar Vedic trope; we see it in the hymn to the horse as he is being sacrificed in *Ṛg Veda*. Here, however, the familiar Vedic idea of going on a path after life is transformed into nothing less than a new theory of the afterlife—a theory which has informed Hindu ideas ever since. The later texts of Patañjali's *Yogasūtra* (*c*. second century BCE) pick up on these ideas and make them into a strict and methodical philosophical system. Much of the Vedānta worldview is premised upon this and other basic understandings of the "paths" of the Upaniṣads.

Some scholars have viewed the Upaniṣads as the beginnings of Hindu philosophy and figures such as Yājñavalkya and Maitreyī as protophilosophers. It is important to point out that this would be a misleading characterization. The later books of the Vedas and the Brāhmaṇas contain philosophical elements about the nature of the universe, and the

Upaniṣads really draw their inspiration from these sources. Moreover, some of the books, such as the sixth chapter of the *Chāndogya Upaniṣad*, contain a number of rituals and prescriptions that resemble some of the domestic manuals of the Gṛhyasūtras or the later "magical" texts of the Vidhānas. (Some have even postulated that this book is a kind of "proto"-Gṛhyasūtra.) These contain very touching vignettes of the relationships between students and teachers, men and women, rituals to instill intelligence in a newly born child, and rituals for making love or to seduce a reluctant lover. Therefore, it is hard to place a definitive "genre" marking upon them such as "philosophy" rather than ritual or even poetry.

What has been the Upaniṣads' role in Hindu history? It is hard to overestimate it; certainly, in the Vedāntic tradition, which makes up the world of so many Hindus today, they are the foundations of spirituality and practice. Although there were many commentators before him, the eighth-century philosopher Śaṃkara was the great systematizer of Upaniṣadic thought and elevating the linkage between *brahman* and *ātman* to the level of a metaphysical principle. For Śaṃkara's reading of the Upaniṣads, it was not only that *brahman* was ultimate reality but also that all else was *māyā* or cognitive error. Realizing the nature of this error was the first step to realizing *brahman*. Moreover, Vedānta philosophy called itself Uttara Mīmāṃsā (literally, later, or even ultimate, investigation), the school of thought which superseded the Pūrva Mīmāṃsā (literally, earlier investigation) or ritual philosophy of the Vedic schools. In the colonial period, they emerged as documents which could provide the answer to the missionaries' claim that the Hindus had no scripture per se—or certainly no scripture which could provide the kind of spiritual insight that the Bible could. Indeed, nineteenth-century Hindu reformers, such as Rammohan Roy and Vivekānanda, championed the Upaniṣads as the core of a Hindu spirituality which could rival any Christian notions. The Upaniṣads became a core of "resistant spirituality" in the best sense. What is more, the Upaniṣads influenced many Western thinkers as the font of wisdom, just as the translations into European languages were beginning to emerge. Today Vedānta philosophy is the bedrock of twenty-first-century middle-class Hinduism, having been made famous by Hindu mystical leaders such as Rāmakṛṣṇa and social reformers such as Vivekānanda. And each of these schools of thought begins with a close reading of the Upaniṣads.

CONCLUSION

It is hard to know whether the women pounding rice as they listened to the sunrise *mantra*s had any idea that they were participating in a tradition that would last over three thousand years beyond their recent crop of rice. These women's situation, and Maitreyī's as she argues with Yājñavalkya, point to the complexity of these Vedic and Upaniṣadic compositions of early India. The Vedic women would have known of the great authority of that chanted sound, and Upaniṣadic Maitreyī would have known of the great intellectual tradition in which she was participating with her husband.

Among the twice-born classes, the Vedas and Upaniṣads have astounding foundational longevity. They contain poetic brilliance, unique philosophical insight, and incomparable ritual complexity. Among intellectual elites throughout those classes, they have been recited, read, and reinterpreted with a spirit of innovation and fidelity to tradition. They have also been used as symbols of the unity of India, the cradle of Hindu thought, and have emerged on the stage of world literature in the last century.

Yet the Vedic women would have also known that they could not then have had access to the meanings of the *mantra*s and that their contributions of rice were as close as they could get to the traditions of sacrifice. Maitreyī, too, would have been as anxious, if not more so, as to how she would be cared for if her husband did not return from his journey, than about the nature of *brahman*. If the Hindu world extends from villager to Brāhmaṇ priest, then Vedic and Upaniṣadic traditions oscillate between being at the very core of the Hindu world and being at its radical periphery. Thus, perhaps, is the fate of all great intellectual traditions.

NOTES

My translations in this chapter follow K. F. Geldner, Wendy Doniger [O'Flaherty], and Patrick Olivelle.

1 This idea was developed in an East Asian context by Kasulis (1992). However, it can be appropriately applied to the concerns of Mīmāṃsā, whose concerns are about the efficacy of ritual as a means of instruction in *dharma* or correct religious role.

2 Thite's is a very provocative thesis based on very detailed knowledge of the prescriptive texts and years of observation of Vedic sacrificial procedures, their timing, and the resources required for them.

3 The most definitive geographical reading of these schools has been two recent articles by Witzel (1987b, 1989). Most of the work rests on a careful analysis of references to persons, places, flora, and fauna within each of the texts.

4 Although this idea is as old as the writings of nineteenth-century Indologists such as Bergaigne (1963), Heesterman has put it into the most succinct terms (for a basic explanation, see his 1985).

5 We can also infer that there was some greater involvement in the community during early Indian times from Buddhist texts like the *Dīghanikāya* (*Kūṭadanta Sutta* 5.18), where servants and workmen performing their tasks for the sacrifice are mentioned.

6 In my own fieldwork I have interviewed the major sponsor of the sacrifices, Ranganath Krishna Selukar, and his wife and family, from the period of 1993 through 1999. He speaks particularly of placing his performances in the tradition of the leader and mystic Jñāneśvara. In addition, smaller performances of *sattra*, as well as the sacrifice of the *āhitāgni*s or householder sacrificers, speak of the spiritual teachings of their *yoga* teachers being translated into this new and ancient form of sacrificial practice (also see Lubin 2001). F. Smith's many years of ethnographic work in this area also confirms this view. Along with Knipe, Smith's *The Vedic Sacrifice in Transition* (1987) is an excellent beginning in this area, and the field awaits further work.

7 Anthropologists such as Susan Wadley have also focused on this idea of *grāma* even in contemporary work.

CHAPTER THREE

MAHĀBHĀRATA

James L. Fitzgerald

The *Mahābhārata* is a tradition of religious epic that has lived in numerous different cultural niches—some oral, some written, some Sanskrit, some vernacular—in South and Southeast Asia for over two thousand years. From its very beginnings the *Mahābhārata* has played a fundamental role as a sacred "scripture" in defining the Hindu world. Countless times it has been, and still is, dramatized by actors, puppets, and dancers for the entertainment or edification of audiences or as part of rituals or festivals (Hiltebeitel 1988–91; Sax 1991a). It has been declaimed in Sanskrit in temples and has been repeatedly translated into the vernaculars of South Asia. Some parts of it have been and are often chanted in congregational liturgies, in Sanskrit or a vernacular, sometimes with audiences chanting refrains. Lessons have often been drawn from it by learned expositors before live audiences (*pravacana*), and it has often been the object of devoted private reading and study. In the 1990s it was broadcast serially throughout India on television, and vast portions of the population of India watched it regularly and eagerly. In spite of the tremendous extent and variety of this tradition, or rather because of it, the description of the *Mahābhārata* in this chapter is based only on the most accessible, and the single most important, subtradition of the larger phenomenon, the written Sanskrit text of the epic.

The written Sanskrit *Mahābhārata* was fixed and promulgated in Northern India between about 300 and 450 CE, that is, about the time of the Gupta empire, and that text became, de facto, an almost normative redaction for written copies of the Sanskrit text (Bigger 1998: 13–19; Fitzgerald 1985: 126–28). The prior history of this Gupta text of the Sanskrit *Mahābhārata* has been a regular subject of inquiry and debate in Western-based scholarship on the epic for over one hundred and fifty years (see Brockington 1998: 130–58). There is broad agreement that the particular precursors of this text, that is, some kind of "Bhārata" epic, came into existence and began developing sometime after 400 BCE. There is also broad agreement, though not unanimity (see Hiltebeitel 1999c), that the *Mahābhārata* has antecedents of some kind in older Indo-Āryan, oral bardic literature and perhaps even in more ancient Indo-European bardic songs about warriors and wars. Relying upon Franklin Edgerton's (1939) penetrating study of the different forms of the *Mahābhārata*'s minority verse form (the *triṣṭubh*, which makes up about 11 percent of the almost 160,500 lines of verse in the epic), Mary Carroll Smith (1992: xiii–xiv) argued that the eight thousand lines of older, Vedic-style *triṣṭubh*s in the *Mahābhārata* constitute the core of the original epic and reflect an ancient, non-Brāhmaṇized warrior society with close thematic ties to Homer and to *Beowulf*. This thesis has yet to be studied closely. A number of scholars have studied the oral poetry of the *Mahābhārata* and shown the persistence in it of formulas and techniques common in extemporizing oral bardic traditions known in the nineteenth and twentieth centuries (see Grintser 1974; J. Smith 1999). On the basis of the work of Pavel Grintser and comparative studies of ancient and modern epic literatures, Yaroslav Vassilkov, sometimes working in collaboration with S. Neveleva, has provided a very interesting comprehensive overview of the *Mahābhārata* and its development in terms of a threefold typology of archaic epics, classical epics, and religious didactic epics. "The Mbh [*Mahābhārata*] went through the stage of the classical heroic epic and was partly transformed into a religious didactic épopée. But during this process, the Indian epic paradoxically retained some features typical of the epic folklore at the archaic stage" (Vassilkov 1995: 255). Vassilkov sees in this extended process of thematic absorption and synthesis "the true uniqueness of the Mbh. There is no other epic in the world which combines in the same way the features of all three main historical stages of development: archaic, classical and late" (1995: 255).

There is, however, no scholarly consensus on something that is a necessary prerequisite for the mounting of seriously detailed historical arguments—namely, an agreed upon reading of the Gupta text and a classification of the text's elements based on that reading. Many scholars have made substantial contributions to developing a consistent reading of this Gupta text, but there is as yet no generally focused discussion on these issues. Madeleine Biardeau (1968–78) developed a comprehensive ideological reading of the epic, and Georg von Simson (1984, 1994) presented a reading based on naturalistic, mainly planetary, interpretations of the main characters of the epic, carrying forward similar themes from the nineteenth century. The recent work of the Nārāyaṇīya project under the lead of Peter Schreiner (1997) has carried out an excellent comprehensive study of one important part of the *Mahābhārata*, a study that provides some important models for the systematic analysis of this and other bodies of "anonymous" Sanskrit literature, in addition to its many concrete contributions. A large-scale treatment of the *Mahābhārata* quite different from that presented here was recently published by Alf Hiltebeitel (2001a; Fitzgerald forthcoming).

What follows is based on a new reading of the Gupta text as a whole (as represented in the Pune edition) in the light of much prior scholarship. This reading revives and refurbishes some aspects of the "Brahmin Renaissance" arguments of a century ago, of which one of the main proponents was Haraprasad Shastri (1910), who was unconvincingly rebutted by Romila Thapar (1973: 197–203) and G. M. Bongard-Levin (1985: 100). Because it uses historical hypotheses as a key to reading the epic narrative, this telling of the *Mahābhārata* story must be deferred until the categories and themes that animate it have been presented. To synopsize the story of the *Mahābhārata in abstracto* oversimplifies it to the point of boredom or transforms it into Oriental curiosity. This new reading is fundamentally informed by the historical hypothesis that two of the most important arguments governing the text's basic formation were: the covertly anti-Mauryan (especially anti-Aśokan) argument that proper rule should be *brāhmaṇya*, that is, based on reverence for unique Brāhmaṇ priority in the determination of social, political, and cultural matters; and the argument (against the Śuṅga and Kaṇva examples) that governance and its intrinsic violence are inappropriate for men of the most refined natures and sensibilities, that is, Brāhmaṇs. The Pāṇḍava narrative of the *Mahābhārata*—the central narrative that is focused on the five Pāṇḍava brothers—and some of its important supplemental narratives and teachings pit Brāhmaṇ agents along with divine or semidivine

Kṣatriya agents against much of the stratum of the world's rulers (Kṣatriyas), who are portrayed as largely corrupt. The *Mahābhārata* tells an apocalyptic (which signifies here the literal sense of the Greek *apo-kaluptein*, "uncover," the "uncovering" of the hidden divine and *not* simply "eschatological destruction") story of the destruction of this corrupt stratum of society by an alliance of the Brāhmaṇ and divine agencies and the consequent establishing of the small band of semidivine Kṣatriyas (the Pāṇḍavas) as the new and proper rulers of the earth. This nexus of ideas and arguments makes most sense when viewed as a derivative reflection of political, social, and cultural events in northern India beginning at the start of the fourth century BCE, especially the rise and success of Veda-and-Brāhmaṇ-rejecting religions, such as Jainism and Buddhism, and the rise of the "Śūdra" Nanda empire at Pāṭaliputra (*c.*340 BCE), its giving way to the Mauryan dynasty (in either 317 or 314 BCE) and the overthrow of Mauryans by the Brāhmaṇ general Puṣyamitra Śuṅga in 187 or 185 BCE.

In this view, the *Mahābhārata* developed as a Brāhmaṇ-inspired response to the tremendous damage (as seen from the point of view of some Brāhmaṇs between approximately 300 and 100 BCE) wrought by the rise of the empires at Pāṭaliputra and the "heathen" (*nāstika*, Jainism and Buddhism, particularly) religions these empires promoted (see Fitzgerald 2004). But, though its basic inspiration was reactionary and conservative, the *Mahābhārata* was an intensely creative response to the perceived crisis. At the time of its initial development as the Pāṇḍava epic (sometime between 300 and 100 BCE) it synthesized older Vedic religious ideas with newer developments (some of the ethics and worldview of *yoga*, especially the ideal of "harmlessness," *ahiṃsā*), and in later centuries subsequent redactors wove together meaningfully many of the new religious ideas (such as elements of Śaivism, the worship of the goddess, *bhakti*, the theory of the *yuga*s, and others) that emerged into prominence in India between the time of that original development and the time it became more or less fixed (sometime between 300 and 450 CE). The *Mahābhārata*'s main narrative laid down some of the fundamental history that grounded "Hinduism," and it contained within it the first canonical library of "Hinduism" (as opposed to the earlier canonical library of Brāhmaṇism, the four Vedas). The text was put forward as "the fifth Veda," "the Veda for women and Śūdras"; it was the utterance of the inspired seer Vyāsa intended to serve as a comprehensive, Brāhmaṇ-inspired basis for living a good life in a good society in a good polity (see Fitzgerald 1985).

The good polity envisioned and promoted in the *Mahābhārata* is protected within and without by a king who wields the rod of force (*daṇḍa*, which refers to his imposition of punishment and to his army). He is energetic, self-restrained (*niyata*), and subjects himself to the guidance of Brāhmaṇs, whom he supports materially and preserves from all harm. A principal way the king preserves Brāhmaṇs from harm is by ensuring the good society, one in which there are four different orders (*varṇa*) of people making four different kinds of contribution to the whole. The good society is characterized fundamentally by the existence of Brāhmaṇs, "men of *brahman*," the unseen, fundamental reality of the universe that is acoustically manifest in the hymns of the Vedas, first seen and heard by the ancient seers. These "Brāhmaṇs" have learned the *brahman* (in the form of the hymns of the Vedas) by hearing it from the mouth of the previous generation, and they put it to use to guarantee prosperity and general well being to the members of society in this life and after death. The good society has another special kind of men, Kṣatriyas, "men of *kṣatra*" (armed force). Kṣatriyas are warriors and rulers, whose main obligation is the protection (*rakṣaṇa*) of society. In addition to these two specially charged orders of society, there are the ordinary "people," the Vaiśyas, who are the basic economic producers of society. All three of these orders are eligible to use the *mantras* (effective ritual formulas) of the Brāhmaṇs' Vedas for rites of divine worship (*yajña*). A fourth order, Śūdras, is not eligible to use the Brāhmaṇs' religious services directly (but see *Mahābhārata* 12.60.36ff.). Their contribution to the general social function is obedient service to the three higher orders. In the good society, the king is responsible for keeping all members of the orders engaged in their own particular lawful kinds of work (their *svadharma*, i.e. the particular work by which a person of one or another order accumulates "merit" for the next life). The opposite condition is one in which some or many in society fail to engage in their proper work, doing instead the work of other kinds of people. Not only do such people fail to perform their lawful work (their *dharma*), the orders of society become indistinct, break down as separate groups, and cease to exist in fact. One of the worst forms of this *saṃkara* (mixture) so dreaded by Brāhmaṇ thinkers has non-Brāhmaṇs or untrained Brāhmaṇs purporting to teach the Vedas or perform Vedic rites and has many Brāhmaṇs taking up soldiering, commerce, or even agriculture out of economic necessity. The outcome of this *saṃkara* is the disappearance of Brāhmaṇs as a distinct group making a good and valuable contribution to the social welfare. The good life was available to the three upper orders of society, for they had the right to use the Vedic rites of worship and perform other special acts that would accumulate merit (one of the basic meanings of the word "*dharma*" in the *Mahābhārata*) and bring them benefits in the future in this life and guarantee them a good life after death (most often envisioned as life in a heavenly world, sometimes as a good rebirth). The rhetoric of the *Mahābhārata* is often aimed at Kṣatriyas, and the good life for them involved gaining glory and riches, dying heroically of wounds in battle, and going to a high heaven.

The library of "Hinduism" contained in the *Mahābhārata* recorded authoritative examples and teachings on a diverse set of philosophical and religious themes ranging from making pilgrimages to the performance of Vedic rituals to rules for renouncers. It described visions of Viṣṇu and Nārāyaṇa; of Śiva; of Yama (the lord of the dead) and his alter ego, Dharma; and of Śrī; of death herself (Mṛtyu); of the rod of force (*daṇḍa*); and of other marvelous divinities. It told many stories of gods, Brāhmaṇs, and kings and taught geography, the calculations of time, and the general history of the universe. And it included various hymns in praise of Viṣṇu, Śiva, and even one or two other gods (Agni and Sūrya).

The history told by the *Mahābhārata* recorded a divinely led, tremendously violent purge of the armed men (the *kṣatra*) of the world because many of these Kṣatriyas had abandoned the ideals of good polity and good society, completely ignored the right and lawful ways of behaving (*dharma*), and tyrannized and abused all the creatures of the earth. The *Mahābhārata* is a story of *avatāra* in the original sense of that term, *avatāraṇa*—a "taking down," a relieving of a burden that oppressed the earth (Hacker 1978a). (Only later did this term come to signify the "descent" of a deity for such a rescue mission.) These wicked Kṣatriyas were in fact the most recent incarnations of the demons (*asura*) defeated by the gods in their last war. The elimination of these demonic Kṣatriyas by good Kṣatriyas was planned by the supreme god Viṣṇu-Nārāyaṇa and Indra (the ancient Vedic god of the monsoon thunderstorm) in concert with the other gods (see *Mahābhārata* 1.58.30–59.6), and the campaign was led on earth by the five Pāṇḍavas (the "sons of Pāṇḍu" in the lunar Kṣatriya lineage of the Kaurava Bharatas): Yudhiṣṭhira, Bhīma, Arjuna, and the twins Nakula and Sahadeva. The mother of the first three was Kuntī, who had also had a premarital son named Vasuṣeṇa (later called Karṇa) by Sūrya, the sun god, before her marriage to Pāṇḍu; the twins' mother was Mādrī.

THE FIVE PĀṆḌAVAS: WAR-PARTY OF THE GODS

At one level of the epic the five Pāṇḍavas function as a single symbolic entity to represent the god Indra on the earth, using violence in the interests of gods and Brāhmaṇs. Explained as five instances of Indra at one key point (in *Mahābhārata* 1.189), the five brothers were all married to the Pāñcāla princess Draupadī, a secret incarnation of the chthonic goddess Śrī (royal splendor), the consort and emblem of the richness, majesty, and authority of the good and successful king. Born up in the heights of the northern "snowy mountains" (Himavat, the Himālayas) not far from the heavenly worlds, the Pāṇḍavas were escorted down to the Bhārata capital Hāstinapura on the plains of the Gaṅgā by Brāhmaṇs soon after Pāṇḍu died, while they were still very young. Down on the plains, aided by three "dark," "obscure," or "secret" (*kṛṣṇa*) holy agents whose true identities or interests were not publicly known—Kṛṣṇa Vāsudeva, the incarnation of Viṣṇu-Nārāyaṇa; Kṛṣṇā Draupadī, the incarnation of Śrī; and Kṛṣṇa Dvaipāyana Vyāsa, the actual father of Pāṇḍu and grandfather of the Pāṇḍavas and representative of the world's Vedic Brāhmaṇs—the Pāṇḍavas led an action to purge from the earth the demon-infested *kṣatra*. The fivefold Pāṇḍava Indra came down from the mountains as the overt, public agent of this divine purge ("*pāṇḍu*" means "white, light, bright" and connotes "overt" and "public" over against the "black, covert" characters of the three Kṛṣṇas) and directly challenged and eventually eradicated the demonic Kṣatriyas of the world, represented principally by the Pāṇḍavas' paternal first cousins, the wicked sons of Pāṇḍu's blind brother Dhṛtarāṣṭra—the hundred wicked Dhārtarāṣṭras led by their eldest Duryodhana. The Pāṇḍavas accomplished this with the aid of their divine or quasi-divine covert backers, that is, with the gentle wisdom and advice of their grandfather Kṛṣṇa Vyāsa, with desire and fury stimulated by their wife Kṛṣṇā Draupadī and the abuse of her by demonic Kṣatriyas, and with the guidance and manipulation of their cousin and friend Kṛṣṇa Vāsudeva.

At the same time, each of the five Pāṇḍavas has another symbolic identity in the epic: While nominally sons of the Bharata Pāṇḍu, the five were actually the physical sons of the gods Dharma, Wind, Indra, and the Aśvin twins, respectively. As the work of Georges Dumézil (1968) has shown, these gods, and thus the Pāṇḍavas who represent them, symbolize the three functions of ancient Indo-European culture—creating and preserving well being: through control of the unseen powers of the world, through physical force and violence, and through nurture, healing, and abundant generation. These functions are rightly associated in general with the ideas of the characteristic work contributions of the three upper orders of Indian Āryan society—Brāhmaṇs, Kṣatriyas, and Vaiśyas—and the five Pāṇḍavas, though they are fundamentally all Kṣatriyas, simultaneously present, through their different paternities, a microcosm of the complete Āryan society. So Yudhiṣṭhira, the eldest Pāṇḍava and the son of God Dharma (the epic deity who has replaced the Vedic gods Mitra and Varuṇa in the position of the first function) is characterized by the main concerns of *dharma* of the day (some of which pulled in opposite directions at the time of the epic's composition: he was punctilious about lawful duties but also generous; he was a dutiful military leader and thus a lord of death, but he was inclined toward kindness; as a king responsible for the wealth and success of his people, he was forced by concerns of *artha* [success] and *nīti* [policy] to be a duplicitous liar, but he was a man who loved truth), and he had a strong predilection for the Brāhmaṇ order of society and some of its aspirations for beatitude. Bhīma, the second Pāṇḍava and the son of the god Wind (Vāyu), represents the tremendous energy of physical force—he was a large, impulsive man with great appetites who embodied the sheer physical power and violence of the Kṣatriya order of society. And Bhīma fulfilled most clearly the responsibility of Kṣatriyas to be protectors, as he was the Pāṇḍava most solicitous of the comfort and safety of their wife Draupadī, and the one who was the champion of them all in situations of general danger. The twins Nakula and Sahadeva manifest the abundance and multiplicity of the function of fertility and growth that characterizes the Vaiśya order of society, whose work tending animals they sometimes performed. These four Pāṇḍavas, representing the three functions embodied in the three ancient orders of good noble (*ārya*) society, stand together as a representation of that whole complex society over against its king, represented in this mythic theme by Arjuna, the son of Indra, the violent leader of the gods. As an image of the king, Arjuna unites the attributes of all three other functions within himself and is ultimately responsible for all three of the others. This "bright one" in particular (as does "*pāṇḍu*," so does "*arjuna*" mean "white, light, bright") had special relationships with two of the "dark ones," Kṛṣṇā Draupadī and Kṛṣṇa Vāsudeva: It was by Arjuna's prowess that Draupadī became the Pāṇḍavas' wife; Arjuna later also married Kṛṣṇa's sister Subhadrā, and Kṛṣṇa was Arjuna's special friend and charioteer during the war. (Georg von Simson [1984: 197] sees Arjuna and Kṛṣṇa as representations of the bright moon and the dark [new] moon.) There is yet another sacred theme encoded in Kṛṣṇa and Arjuna—they together share a covert identity as incarnations of Nārāyaṇa and Nara, god and man, who live in the mountains at Badarī, near where the Gaṅgā descends to earth, performing asceticism. They come to earth from time to time, taking up weapons to defend the gods. The multiple encoding of the epic's main characters is possible because the general themes that the different encodings represent are basically concentric.

DEMONIC KṢATRA

This purge, this *avatāraṇa* of the earth's burden, was called for because the earth was suffering grievously under the onslaught of loutish and malicious Kṣatriyas, and the last effective method of handling them—the regular elimination of them by the enraged Bhārgava Brāhmaṇ Rāma Jāmadagnya—was no longer available (as Rāma had been stopped by his troubled Brāhmaṇ forbears and banished by the Brāhmaṇ patriarch Kaśyapa for eliminating the earth's kings). After the most recent of the recurring wars between the gods and the demons, the defeated demons had incarnated themselves on earth as new Kṣatriyas in the vacuum left by Rāma's repeated slaughters (see below); they neglected *dharma* and abused Brāhmaṇs and other beings constantly. The *Mahābhārata* contains numerous accounts of Kṣatriyas abusing Brāhmaṇs that illustrate and extend this indictment, and these stories chronicle different Brāhmaṇ responses to these Kṣatriya provocations. On the one extreme is the response of the seer Vasiṣṭha, who, when persecuted by King Kalmāṣapāda (see *Mahābhārata* 1.165–68), tried several times unsuccessfully to commit suicide. Then there was the response of the young Bhārgava Brāhmaṇ Aurva, who in enduring rage at the persecution of the Bhārgavas by the Kārtavīryas (a Kṣatriya line descended from Kṛtavīrya), took up asceticism to destroy the entire world.

And finally, at the opposite extreme from Vasiṣṭha, there is another Bhārgava Brāhmaṇ, Rāma Jāmadagnya, who slew all the earth's Kṣatriyas twenty-one times over when a vendetta arose between him and other descendents of Kṛtavīrya after King Arjuna Kārtavīrya stole the calf of Rāma's father's cow. Rāma killed the Kārtavīrya King Arjuna in revenge, Arjuna's sons killed Rāma's father, Rāma retaliated against them, and for thousands of years after, Rāma's mission was to kill every Kṣatriya everywhere. New generations of Kṣatriyas were produced after each slaughter when Brāhmaṇs impregnated the widows of the dead Kṣatriyas in order to regenerate the *kṣatra* (see *Mahābhārata* 3.115–17, 12.48–49). But after twenty-one genocidal slaughters Rāma was halted and banished in order to save some remnant of Kṣatriyas.

(The story of Rāma Jāmadagnya is much more than one more Brāhmaṇ-abuse story in the epic. It is told four times in the *Mahābhārata* at strategically important locations—twice at length—and Rāma Jāmadagnya's slaughter is mentioned or alluded to numerous other times across most of the text's length. V. S. Sukthankar [1936] took these facts and numerous other stories and references to Rāma's Bhārgava kinsmen in the epic to be indicative of a massive Brāhmaṇ redaction done by a historical clan of Bhārgava Brāhmaṇs. He saw this redaction to be what transformed an older warrior epic—the *Bhārata*—into the sprawling Dharmaśāstra represented by the received text of the *Mahābhārata*. Decades later Robert Goldman [1972, 1977, 1978] studied the Bhārgava corpus of the epic closely and argued Sukthankar's case in greater detail. Adalbert Gail's 1977 study of Rāma Jāmadagnya offered new insights, and recent reexaminations of this material from new perspectives by Christopher Minkowski [1991], Lynn Thomas [1996], Alf Hiltebeitel [1999c], and James Fitzgerald [2002b] have developed a completely different approach to Rāma Jāmadagnya in the *Mahābhārata* that necessitates a reassessment of the Sukthankar-Goldman theses.)

In the setting of the *Mahābhārata*'s narrative, the new generation of demon Kṣatriyas prowled the earth, led by the incarnation of the demon Kali (strife) as Duryodhana Bharata, the Pāṇḍavas' first cousin. Duryodhana was destined to provoke a different, more satisfying resolution of the continuing problem of Kṣatriyas' neglect of *dharma* (see *Mahābhārata* 3.239.15–240.28, 11.8.24–26). He and his ninety-nine brothers (who were incarnations of Rākṣasa monsters) were aborted initially as a grotesque fetal mass their mother had carried for two years. Vyāsa divided the mass and had their gestation finished in pots filled with *ghī*, which resulted eventually in one hundred thoroughly wicked (*duṣṭātman*) young men, the Dhārtarāṣṭras, "sons of Dhṛtarāṣṭra" (Dhṛtarāṣṭra was Pāṇḍu's blind brother; the mother of these incarnate demons was Gāndhārī, who voluntarily covered her eyes at the time of her betrothal to Dhṛtarāṣṭra, so as not to be superior to her husband). In time Duryodhana became fast friends with a foundling child of a charioteer-bard of the Bhārata court, a young man named Vasuṣeṇa. (He was later known as Karṇa, a name signifying the terrible act of his cutting off of his body the golden armor and earrings that had formed part of his body at birth. This boy was in fact the inadvertent, premarital child of Kuntī and Sūrya, the sun.) Vasuṣeṇa, Karṇa, was the most intense, resolute, and loyal of Duryodhana's allies and the destined enemy of Arjuna.

The one hundred Dhārtarāṣṭras formed the core group of the Kṣatriyas targeted by the *avatāra* mission of the gods, and while Duryodhana was unmistakably the leader of this party, Karṇa, embodying some of the sun, was the main warrior at the center of this group (Bhīṣma, an incarnation of the god Sky, Dyaus, claimed that place first, but he was older and wiser and less intense and single-minded than was Karṇa). At one basic level of the *Mahābhārata* narrative, this story is another telling of the war between the gods and the demons (see below), and in the *Mahābhārata* retelling, Karṇa is the water-restricting Vṛtra to Arjuna's Indra (Indra was an ancient embodiment of the monsoon rains).

THE TAPAS (HEAT, FIRE, PAIN) AT THE CENTER OF THE MAHĀBHĀRATA

The violence of the purge of the Kṣatriyas that is the core of the *Mahābhārata* narrative is shocking in its intensity, its extent, and its thoroughness. This purge has its roots in a kind of genocidal hatred (the *Mahābhārata* is replete with accounts of frequently interrupted genocide—is itself narrated at a rite [ultimately interrupted] to kill all the world's snakes!—and it grows immediately out of the genocidal rampage against all the world's Kṣatriyas by the Brāhmaṇ Rāma Jāmadagnya, which too was interrupted and subjected to repeated criticism within the *Mahābhārata* [Fitzgerald 2002b]), but the *Mahābhārata* has repudiated rage that is simply genocidal (Hiltebeitel 1999c: 166; Minkowski 1991: 399–400) and assimilated its violence to the philosophy of kingship described briefly above and to an account of the history of that kingship (see *Mahābhārata* 12.59.94–140, the story of King Pṛthu, for the basic statement of that history). The rage depicted in the *Mahābhārata* and the philosophy of kingship in which that rage eventually came to rest both answered important historical events in northern India in the last half of the first millennium BCE, events that called the violent Rāma Jāmadagnya story into being as well as its more sophisticated cousin, the Pāṇḍava *avatāraṇa* story (see Fitzgerald 2002a; Malinar 1996; von Simson 1984: 220–23; Sutton 1997). The events involved are those transformations of the "second urbanization" of India (see Erdosy 1995a,b) and the rise of the imperial state of Pāṭaliputra, the Mauryans' elevation of Jainism and Buddhism to eminence at the expense of Brāhmaṇism, and the emperor Aśoka's "Dharma campaign," which, implicit criticism in the *Mahābhārata* seems to suggest, was viewed by at least some Brāhmaṇs as arrogant and hypocritical. We know definitely from his inscriptions that Aśoka, who was a lay follower of the Buddha, did not subordinate himself to Brāhmaṇ guidance and even insulted Brāhmaṇism by treating it as just one more religious elite among many elites that were all eligible for imperial support if they adopted the tolerant and pluralistic view of religions the emperor advocated (see Major Rock Edict Twelve, Thapar 1973: 255). It is likely that Aśoka's "insubordinate" attitude toward Brāhmaṇs was merely the most prominent rejection of Brāhmaṇ philosophy by a ruler of the era, for the *Mahābhārata* has numerous stories depicting the failures of Kṣatriyas to respect the dignity, special position, and special contributions Brāhmaṇs saw themselves making to society. Also, the Brāhmaṇs had significant competition from the Jaina, Buddhist, and other new religious elites of the time, and any support the Mauryans and other kings offered those other groups cost Brāhmaṇs in terms of treasure and honor both.

But the creation and development in the *Mahābhārata* of these accounts of violent apocalyptic redress of an unacceptable political and social situation set in motion fundamental philosophical and ethical conflicts that had basically lain dormant before. The more universal and subject-centered philosophies of *yoga* and the concomitantly more socially sensitive ethics of kindness, generosity, patience, and harmlessness that had developed with increasing momentum through the middle of the millennium (Bodewitz 1999; Schmidt 1968, 1997) had always been in tension with the older ritual- and duty-centered notions of *dharma*. But the violently revanchist action imagined in the *Mahābhārata* narrative brought the contradictions between these perspectives out into the open fully and deeply, and the *Mahābhārata* is at one level the record of a tremendous struggle in which its authors try to resolve what some of them think of as necessary violence with what many others regard to be the superior ethic of harmlessness (see Lath 1990). There is a tremendous ambivalence and contradiction regarding *dharma* in the *Mahābhārata*, an ambivalence that turns up in the narrative at many places, and nowhere as much as in the several appearances of the god Dharma in the epic narrative (who is an alter ego of Yama, the lord of the dead) and in the character of Dharma's primary representative in the story, his son, the eldest Pāṇḍava, Yudhiṣṭhira. This tension was basically irresolvable and was one of the fundamental sources of the epic's tremendous creativity (Fitzgerald 2004).

Over time the intellectuals in and around this tradition worked out, in the *Mahābhārata*, a number of ways to try to dispel the contradiction: a renewed emphasis upon the different ethics of Brāhmaṇs as opposed to Kṣatriyas was one theme developed; another was the *karmayoga* doctrine, by which a person performed his proper duties, his *svadharma*, and escaped the lasting consequences (and rewards) of those deeds and gained the beatitude of *yoga* by doing those deeds with a *yoga*-transformed mind, that is, without any desire, simply as duty; the amalgamation of the *karmayoga* theme with ideas of *bhakti*, "devotion to god" (this is the main teaching of the *Mahābhārata*'s *Bhagavad Gītā*, *Mahābhārata* 6.23–40), allowing the assignment of all responsibility for violence to god, was yet another. Toward similar ends, the horror of the violent purge was sometimes explained through conceptual structures that removed human agents from responsibility for it: at one point the Bhārata war, war in general, is said to be the fury of Rudra—the essential being of each and every human—using himself to destroy himself when the tide of evil among people has become too great (*Mahābhārata* 12.74.17–21). Often the whole affair is represented as a tremendous, all-consuming sacrificial fire, in which the offered victims—the warriors—go to heaven with the upward rising flames and smoke: a sacrifice presided over by Dharma, that is, Yama the king of Dharma (*dharmarāja*) armed with his "rod" (*daṇḍa*) (L. Thomas 1994). At other times this paroxysm of violence is represented as a general purge of the world by Śiva (e.g. *Mahābhārata* 12.74.17), who is the deity who seems to represent general destruction and who presides over violence that seems to erupt from the deepest anger and is the most intense (such as the night raid on the sleeping warriors of Book 10 of the *Mahābhārata*; see Johnson 1998). At other times the whole business is laid to fate or time (e.g. *Mahābhārata* 12.34.2–12). At other times the destruction depicted in the epic is said to be a cosmic dissolution (*pralaya*) that occurs at regular intervals in the cosmic cycles of time as part of the natural degeneration of existent being over time (see González-Reimann 2002; Madeline Biardeau [1968–78]) has seen this theme as one of the major keys to unlocking the structure of the *Mahābhārata* in terms of the ideas of cosmic cycles of destruction and recreation, the descent of Viṣṇu to rejuvenate *dharma* at these junctures, and the call to human participation in the action of god.) The violence and destruction of the *Mahābhārata* narrative is tied to principles the authors deliberately and strongly affirmed, chiefly the king's *daṇḍa*, his "rod of force." Thus the repugnant elements of the story could not simply be dispensed with in favor of *ahiṃsā*. And because the violence was ultimately affirmed in the face of the enduring sense that *ahiṃsā* was the supremely right way to live (i.e. the supreme *dharma*), a dynamically creative tension lived at the heart of the *Mahābhārata* for a very long time.

THE CAMPAIGN OF THE PARTY OF THE GODS AGAINST THE DEMON HORDE

The main narrative of the *Mahābhārata* is the Pāṇḍava narrative, which cryptically tells the "secret of the gods," the holy, paradigmatic story of the gods' *avatāraṇa* (the "off-lifting") of the earth's burden of oppressive men of arms (unworthy Kṣatriyas). The theme of *avatāraṇa* told in the *Mahābhārata* has been assimilated to the ancient theme of the gods warring against their elder brothers, the demons (*asura*), and thus the Pāṇḍava narrative is also one more retelling of the war between the gods and the demons, particularly the fight between Indra and the water-choking *asura* Vṛtra.

The account of this thrilling narrative moves out of its preparatory phases around chapter 100 of the epic's *Book of the Beginning* and relates the births of the sons of Dhṛtarāṣṭra in the Bhārata capital of Hāstinapura and the births of Pāṇḍu's five sons far up in the Himālayan northland on Mount Gandhamādana. Pāṇḍu died shortly after the birth of his sons, and the seers of this holy area led the boys down to their ancestral capital on the Gaṅgā and put them in the charge of their father's brother, Dhṛtarāṣṭra. The slopes of the Himālayas are not far from the lower heavens, and this descent of the semidivine Pāṇḍavas to the Bhārata court where they joined their demonic cousin-brothers is the actual beginning of the symbolic struggle between the gods' party and the demons, as told through the loosely encrypted Pāṇḍava narrative. Shortly after the Pāṇḍavas' arrival in Hāstinapura, the Pāṇḍavas began attacking the Dhārtarāṣṭras with boisterous juvenile mischief, and Duryodhana and his brothers responded maliciously. The hostilities became more serious a few years later as the young men's training came to an end, and a public display of their martial skills ended with open antagonism and an aborted confrontation between Arjuna and Karṇa.

From this point onward the malicious rivalry between the two phratries was deadly serious, and the prospect of a death match between Arjuna and Karṇa is one of the themes that dominates the horizon of the narrative. The party of the gods, the Pāṇḍavas, was sent away from the ancestral court to the town of Vāraṇāvata on a transparent pretext. There the Pāṇḍavas eluded a Dhārtarāṣṭra fire trap by hiding in a hole in the ground beneath the burning house, and then they fled into the forest and hid there for some time, disguised as Brāhmaṇ ascetics, while all the world believed them dead. Next, still disguised as Brāhmaṇs, they hid for a while in the town of Ekacakrā. While hiding out during this time, the Pāṇḍavas were aided by the mysterious (*kṛṣṇa*) agent of Brāhmaṇism Vyāsa, who first set them up in Ekacakrā and then later counseled them to leave to seek the Pāñcāla princess Draupadī as their wife. The party of the gods emerged from this period of retreat and weakness in the face of its enemies with a tremendous flash of brilliance and force, when Arjuna alone passed the martial test to win the princess Draupadī, and he and Bhīma then fended off the assault of the gathered Kṣatriyas (who attacked Arjuna, outraged because it seemed a Brāhmaṇ would marry the princess Draupadī). This burst of unexpected brilliance culminated in all five Pāṇḍavas, that is, the one composite Indra, wedding Draupadī, the incarnation of Śrī, while announcing their true identities to King Drupada and the rest of the world. (Because of a superficial misunderstanding, their mother Kuntī had unwittingly commanded all her five sons to share Draupadī equally, an irreversible pronouncement that in fact fulfilled five requests for a husband which Draupadī had made to Śiva in an earlier birth [*Mahābhārata* 1.157].)

Much of the ensuing Pāṇḍava narrative has the same oscillating rhythm of the heroes emerging from absence, obscurity, weakness, or retreat (which is typically hallowed by some kind of association with gods or Brāhmaṇs or both) to a brilliant display of strength in the arena of martial achievement and then withdrawing once again. There is a kind of chiaroscuro quality to this narrative of Pāṇḍavas and Kṛṣṇas, a play of light against dark which suggests that ceaseless alternation of the moon between brilliance and obscurity that was so fundamental to Brāhmaṇ religion in ancient India. And these oscillations give the narrative a recurrently apocalyptic quality, wherein hidden divine agency is disclosed (the key notion of "apocalypse"), often with some form of violence or profound deviation from normal or expected behavior. On another level, this waxing and waning of the Pāṇḍavas is part of a larger pattern that is symbolic of the divine Pāṇḍavas' surge forward in attack against their demonic enemies (their initial descent from the Himālayas), their pressing their enemies hard (their youthful success and popularity in Hāstinapura) until they were repulsed and driven into retreat (Vāraṇāvata, the fire, the hiding disguised as Brāhmaṇs) only to counterattack powerfully (the winning of Draupadī, which was followed [see below] by the establishment of "Indra's Station" [Indraprastha], Yudhiṣṭhira's building a magnificent assembly hall there, and his royal consecration as a king of kings), and on and on to the victorious Pāṇḍavas' final departure from their seat of power as they embark upon the suicidal "great journey" to heaven at the end of the entire story, where they confront, and join with, the Dhārtarāṣṭras once again. The alternating movement of the story corresponds to the general pattern of accounts of Indra's battle with Vṛtra, particularly the major version of it that is told in the *Mahābhārata* as "Indra's victory" in Book 5 (in this account Indra is even temporarily swallowed by Vṛtra—an extreme form of the *Mahābhārata*'s fundamental theme of Indra's waning before his waxing). And as various versions of Indra's battle with the demons shows, he is typically aided by Brāhmaṇs (when Indra was swallowed by Vṛtra, the gods made the demon yawn so Indra could escape) and by Viṣṇu (in our "Indra's victory" paradigm Viṣṇu counseled the gods to lull Vṛtra with a deceitful truce and Viṣṇu then assisted Indra by, completely unexpectedly, entering into a handful of foam which then became Indra's deadly weapon against the demon) and typically has a very difficult time that is marked by setbacks (his being swallowed) and retreats (the false truce) before his final victory. New to the Pāṇḍava narrative's symbolic version of this ancient battle is the assistance given to Indra by Śrī (i.e. in the Pāṇḍava narrative, the energizing of the Pāṇḍavas by Draupadī).

With the Pāṇḍavas' "rebirth" by their wedding to Draupadī the Dhārtarāṣṭras were dispirited, and again they contemplated measures to get rid of or suppress the Pāṇḍavas. Cooler heads prevailed, and the Pāṇḍavas were given an undeveloped half of the kingdom to the west, on the Yamunā River, where they built a marvelous city "like a new heaven" that was called "Indra's Station." Here Yudhiṣṭhira, waxing powerfully, decided to build a splendid palace, and when that was done he launched a royal consecration sacrifice, Rājasūya, to become the ruler of the entire world. This rite required that he actually subdue the entire world, something Yudhiṣṭhira did with the help of Kṛṣṇa Vāsudeva and his own brothers. All the major kings of the world then gathered at "Indra's Station" to witness Yudhiṣṭhira's consecration as the universal sovereign.

The splendor of Yudhiṣṭhira's consecration rankled Duryodhana deeply, so the demonic phratry struck again with a scheme to bring the Pāṇḍavas down. Yudhiṣṭhira was invited to engage in a friendly dicing match with Duryodhana at Hāstinapura, a challenge the king was bound to accept (van Buitenen 1972). Yudhiṣṭhira, however, was not as skilled at the game as Duryodhana's stand-in, Śakuni (Duryodhana's mother's brother), and the Pāṇḍava king lost round after round until he had wagered and lost each of his brothers and then himself and then Draupadī. (Collating the results of previous research on ancient Indian dicing, David Shulman [1992] argues that this episode appropriately leads to war because dicing [*devana*] is inherently connected to "fate" [*daiva*], "the very essence" of which is "negativity, in the sense of destructive, dis-integrating, crooked and unbalancing forces" [359]. *Daiva* is "the individual's situation within" . . . "a cosmic structure with inherently violent and destructive components" [Shulman 1992: 359, 358].) Draupadī, who was menstruating and dressed only in the single garment women wore in the women's apartments, was then dragged by her hair into the men's hall of assembly. The Dhārtarāṣṭras had a high time abusing Draupadī, as she would now be their servant, while her husbands hung their heads in shame and virtual silence. Duḥśāsana even tried to strip Draupadī bare, but she was miraculously spared that indignity. Draupadī then challenged the proceedings, demanding to know if Yudhiṣṭhira had already gambled himself away before wagering her. Before the elders could fully respond to her challenge, the presiding elder, the blind Dhṛtarāṣṭra, in dread of doom, called the whole match off and restored to Yudhiṣṭhira all he had lost.

This dispensation drew the Pāṇḍavas back from the abject humiliation visited upon them by Yudhiṣṭhira's helplessness with the dice. But the Pāṇḍavas' resurgence was short-lived. Duryodhana soon challenged Yudhiṣṭhira to one last throw by which the loser would spend twelve years out in the wilderness followed by one year of complete incognito. Yudhiṣṭhira lost that last throw as well, and, in the familiar rhythm of the epic, he and his brothers and Draupadī departed for the obscurity of the wilderness.

This party of the gods, this embodiment of Indra with Śrī, temporarily set back once again, dwelled outside the city in the forest and wilds for twelve years. The group diminished significantly when Arjuna left the others for several years. Arjuna journeyed up into the mountains, toward heaven to visit various gods in order to gain more powerful weapons for the battle against the demonic enemy. In the course of this journey he was tested by Śiva, who then gave him the secret of the terrifically destructive Brahmā-head or Pāśupata weapon. He received different special weapons from the gods Yama, Varuṇa, and Kubera—gods who stand guard over the earthly realms of the south, west, and north, respectively. Indra, his father, the god who guards the east, invited him to heaven and there gave Arjuna his, Indra's, special weapon, the lightning bolt. Arjuna stayed in heaven, sitting on his father's throne, for five years, and in this time he learned music and dancing from a Gandharva. In the meantime the other Pāṇḍavas, guided and protected by the Brāhmaṇ Lomaśa, moved east across far northern India (skirting the Gaṅgā Valley proper, crossing its tributaries to the north), stopping at various potent "bathing-shrines" (*tīrtha*) where men of powerful deeds or even gods had performed great rites of sacrifice (King Gaya, Viśvakarman, Rāma Jāmadagnya). At some of these places Yudhiṣṭhira performed sacrifices or asceticism and experienced spiritual exaltation (see *Mahābhārata* 3.114). The party also visited the retreats (*āśrama*) of Agastya on a northern tributary of the Mahānadī, Vibhāṇḍaka Kāśyapa on the Kauśikī, and Rāma Jāmadagnya on Mount

Mahendra in Kaliṅga, near where the Vaitaraṇī empties into the ocean (in present-day Orissa). In these retreats the party of Indra heard tales of the Kṣatriya abuse of Brāhmaṇs, abuse that was always redressed by surprising displays of Brāhmaṇ power. Rāma Jāmadagnya, who had virtually exterminated the world's Kṣatriyas repeatedly and who was ill-disposed toward Kṣatriyas in general, received the Pāṇḍavas' worship and, remarkably, extended a blessing to the Kṣatriya Yudhiṣṭhira. The party then rapidly traveled through southern peninsular lands and then back north and west to Śurpāraka (a site on the western ocean on the opposite side of the subcontinent from Kaliṅga), a place also associated with Rāma Jāmadagnya in the period after his vendetta had been halted. The party traveled a little farther north to Prabhāsa, near where the Sarasvatī, at that time, emptied into the ocean, and Kṛṣṇa and his brother Rāma met them there and lamented their shrunken condition and predicted their eventual triumph. From here the party headed east up the Sarasvatī to Kurukṣetra, visiting retreats, hearing more stories of Brāhmaṇ power and accounts of the great deeds and rites of mighty kings, some of them ancestors of the Pāṇḍavas. Next they turned north and went far up, braving many dangers and difficulties, past the Himālayas into the Gandhamādana, near the heavens, where they had been born. There they stayed at the hermitage of Nārāyaṇa and Nara on the bank of the Gaṅgā on Mount Kailāsa. Then they journeyed to "White Mountain" (Śveta) to await Arjuna's descent from heaven. Arjuna came down, met them, and showed them the weapons he had acquired. After three more years the Indra represented by the Pāṇḍavas—strengthened and enhanced by their immersions and their meetings and now doubly fortified with the new divine weapons of the son of Indra—descended to the plains and lived out the twelve years in the forests near the Sarasvatī River, not too far from the Bhārata kingdom.

During the last year or two of this exile, the demonic party attacked the divine party while it was down and out. Duryodhana, egged on by Karṇa, launched a cattle roundup in the forest near the Pāṇḍava encampment. On the main narrative level, the real purpose of the Dhārtarāṣṭras was to see the Pāṇḍavas' hardship and to gloat. But the outing ended up badly for Duryodhana—he happened into a battle with Gandharvas and had to be rescued by the Pāṇḍavas. Duryodhana was so shamed by this he wished to fast to death and was dissuaded only after the world's demons summoned him to the nether realms with a rite, informed him of his secret identity and the hidden nature of the struggle with the Pāṇḍavas, and predicted to him his victory over them. Heartened, Duryodhana returned to Hāstinapura and wished to perform a royal consecration of his own. The priests informed him he could do no such thing while Yudhiṣṭhira lived and while his father lived, but they urged him to perform the grand "Vaiṣṇava" rite with a ploughshare wrought of molten gold, a rite to rival the Rājasūya. Duryodhana performed this rite, and kings from all over the earth came with tribute and offered him felicitations.

The Pāṇḍavas then went into hiding for the agreed upon thirteenth year. They and Draupadī donned symbolically significant disguises, entered Virāṭa's capital city in the kingdom of the Matsyas (fishes), and disappeared altogether from public view. Draupadī passed herself off as a low-caste hairdresser-maid, separated from her husbands (see Hiltebeitel 1981). Arjuna pretended to be a eunuch and lived in the harem, teaching dancing to the women of the palace (see Hiltebeitel 1980). Yudhiṣṭhira posed as a master of dicing named Kaṅka (named after the *kaṅka* bird, the death-dealing, carrion-eating bird that stalks fish deceptively [a composite of the crane, heron, and stork; the tallest and most imposing of the carrion-feeders on battlefields; see Fitzgerald 1998]). The demonic

Kaurava party again attacked the weakened and withdrawn Pāṇḍavas, though this time the attack was unwitting, as it was actually directed against the Matsyas. The Pāṇḍavas just made it through the year of darkness without being discovered, and when they reemerged into the light, their allies gathered at Upaplavya in Virāṭa's kingdom to mount a campaign to recover their lost glory and their half of the Bhārata kingdom (i.e. to elevate the war against the demons into an all out effort), and Duryodhana's allies gathered at Hāstinapura to resist that campaign. The Dhārtarāṣṭras refused to yield back the Pāṇḍavas' half of the kingdom through negotiations, and war seemed inevitable. Final embassies were undertaken to avert war, Yudhiṣṭhira, conflicted and inconsistent, as ever, offered to settle for just five villages of their former kingdom, but Duryodhana and his supporters were belligerent. Eighteen armies then gathered on Kurukṣetra, the "altar of Prajāpati, the Progenitor," seven allied to the Pāṇḍavas and eleven aligned with the Dhārtarāṣṭra Kauravas. As the armies faced each other on the field, Arjuna lost the will to face his own kinsmen in battle and proposed the Pāṇḍavas back down. He spoke only to Kṛṣṇa, who was serving as his charioteer and who then lectured him on the rightness of the war, on the ultimate religious superiority of doing one's lawful duty (*dharma*) over renouncing one's duty, on the fact that doing one's duty can be a form of devotion to god that completely transforms one's soul and delivers one to absolute and eternal beatitude. Kṛṣṇa told Arjuna, the son of Indra and the leading Indra of the Pāṇḍava Indra-aggregate, that he himself, Kṛṣṇa, was Viṣṇu-Nārāyaṇa incarnate, and he showed the awestruck Arjuna his form as all-destroying time, here on earth to relieve the earth's burden. This sermon and demonstration (corresponding to the infusion of energy that Viṣṇu often furnished Indra at the critical point in his battles against Vṛtra and analogous demons; see *Mahābhārata* 5.10.1–38) transformed Arjuna, restoring his usual intensity and steely resolve. Yudhiṣṭhira then dutifully walked across the battlefield and took leave of his elders on the other side one by one.

The hostilities commenced and raged for eighteen days and through the night of the eighteenth day. The battle was a horrific, genocidal bloodletting in which the initiative swung back and forth between the parties of the gods and the demons. Most remarkable in this battle, on the level of the human narrative, were the transgressions committed by the Pāṇḍavas—they committed four virtual parricides, and they regularly engaged in crooked behavior, usually at the behest of Kṛṣṇa Vāsudeva. Linking up with earlier themes of ambiguous sexual identities in the epic, Arjuna felled the grandfather Bhīṣma on the tenth day of battle as he, Arjuna, screened himself behind Śikhaṇḍin, a prince against whom Bhīṣma would not fight, as he had once been a woman. The Kaurava army was led next by the teacher of all the boys, Droṇa, and the five days he led the Kaurava forces saw a number of painful and troubling deeds and killings—Abhimanyu, Arjuna's young son by his second wife, Subhadrā (Kṛṣṇa's sister), was killed very dramatically; at Kṛṣṇa's command Arjuna shot off the arm of his distant Bharata cousin Bhūriśravas as that pious man was poised to kill his ancient family rival Sātyaki (a Vṛṣṇi favorite of Kṛṣṇa and Arjuna); Arjuna hunted down Jayadratha (a man who briefly kidnapped Draupadī during the period of the Pāṇḍavas' forest exile) and severed his head with such force that it landed in the lap of Jayadratha's old father, whence it bounced to earth, killing the old man by virtue of a curse he himself had uttered against anyone who might make his son's head fall to earth; Kṛṣṇa manipulated Ghaṭotkaca, Bhīmasena's son by his second wife, the night-monster (*rākṣasī*) Hiḍimbā, to fight Karṇa during the night battle after the fourteenth day and force

Karṇa to discharge his one infallible weapon. But the fifteenth day saw worse, as Yudhiṣṭhira, the man whose truthfulness his teacher Droṇa trusted implicitly, lied outright to his teacher Droṇa, telling the master that his son Aśvatthāman was dead, in order to demoralize him (which it did). Draupadī's brother, the Pāṇḍavas' military commander-in-chief Dhṛṣṭadyumna, then swooped down upon Droṇa, who has sat down and was meditating in *prāya* (the fast to death), and Dhṛṣṭadyumna decapitated him.

The secret elder brother of the Pāṇḍavas, Karṇa, became the leader of the Kaurava army next. As Bhīma steadily slaughtered the century of Dhṛtarāṣṭra's sons, the battle was funneling down to the final confrontations of Bhīma with Duḥśāsana (whose blood Bhīma had sworn to drink when that Kaurava grotesquely abused Draupadī at the time of the dicing match), of Arjuna with Karṇa, and of Bhīma with Duryodhana. On the seventeenth day of battle Bhīma fulfilled his vow against Duḥśāsana. And Karṇa rode out to face Arjuna, with the skilled horseman Śalya as his charioteer for the battle. But Śalya, the brother of Mādrī (the mother of the Pāṇḍava twins), who was fighting for the Kauravas only because of a chance misunderstanding, had made an arrangement with the duplicitous Yudhiṣṭhira to work at demoralizing Karṇa. Śalya lived up to his agreement by berating Karṇa and praising Arjuna. Due to earlier curses in Karṇa's ill-starred life, his ability to defend himself against Arjuna evaporated and then a wheel of his chariot mired in mud. At Kṛṣṇa's urging, Arjuna refused to yield Karṇa free time to extricate his chariot's wheel, and the son of Indra, the god of the rains, killed the son of the rain-parching sun as he struggled to free his chariot's wheel from the wet earth.

Duryodhana consecrated Śalya as his commander-in-chief after Karṇa's death, but the war was now almost finished. Yudhiṣṭhira, who suborned Śalya's treachery against Karṇa in the first place (*Mahābhārata* 5.8), claimed Śalya as his to kill, and around noon on the eighteenth day he did kill his uncle. Fighting continued for some time after this, until Sahadeva Pāṇḍava beheaded Duryodhana's uncle and mentor, Śakuni. The Kaurava army was now almost entirely gone, and Duryodhana fled the field. All the great warriors on the Kaurava side were now dead with the exception of Duryodhana, Aśvatthāman, Kṛpa, and Kṛtavarman. After the killing of Śalya and Śakuni the narrative spiraled down to Bhīma's club duel with Duryodhana, Aśvatthāman's "attack upon the sleeping enemy" (the *sauptika* attack, the "night raid" that killed King Drupada Pāñcāla's progeny, including the five sons of Draupadī), and the concluding face-off between Aśvatthāman and Arjuna.

When Duryodhana despaired and left the battlefield he fled on foot to a nearby lake, and, using magic (*māyā*), he solidified some of the lake's water and entered into it, having resolved to live there in suspended animation. But after a time the Pāṇḍavas discovered his location and confronted him. He and Yudhiṣṭhira angrily debated the ethics of the general situation, and Yudhiṣṭhira, once again revealing his fundamentally divided nature, offered to let Duryodhana retain the kingship if he could defeat any one of the Pāṇḍavas in a duel. Duryodhana emerged from the lake defiantly, donned golden armor, and told the Pāṇḍavas to pick one of their number to fight him with a club. The entire party then moved back to Kurukṣetra because it was a much more auspicious place than any other for a warrior to die. The Pāṇḍavas chose Bhīmasena as their champion, but Kṛṣṇa voiced a doubt whether even Bhīma could defeat Duryodhana in a club duel. After many accusations and insults the two fought, and each knocked the other down. Kṛṣṇa told Arjuna that Bhīma could win only if he fought unfairly. Taking that cue, Arjuna slapped his left thigh, signaling Bhīma to strike an unfair blow below the navel, and Bhīma soon hurled his club at Duryodhana's thigh, smashing it and winning the duel. Still in a vengeful rage, Bhīma insulted Duryodhana by placing his left foot upon the fallen king's head. Everyone disapproved of that, and Yudhiṣṭhira made his brother stop. Duryodhana then excoriated Kṛṣṇa for his conduct during the war, and a shower of flowers fell upon him from the heavens as he lay pathetically upon the ground. Kṛṣṇa justified as necessary all the unfair tactics he had recommended to the Pāṇḍavas. Kṛṣṇa then recommended that the Pāṇḍavas and Sātyaki spend the night on the bank of the Oghavatī River outside their own camp.

In the meantime the trio of Kaurava survivors had returned to where Duryodhana lay broken and dying of his wounds. Duryodhana, who had not yet given up, consecrated Aśvatthāman as his next commander-in-chief. Aśvatthāman still seethed with rage over Dhṛṣṭadyumna's killing of his father Droṇa. His final desperate assaults were the subject of the Tenth Book of the *Mahābhārata*, *The Book of the Attack upon the Sleeping Enemy* (Johnson 1998). After this consecration, Aśvatthāman, accompanied by Kṛpa and Kṛtavarman, went to the gate of the Pāṇḍava camp that night. While his companions slept, Aśvatthāman observed an owl fall upon a flock of crows sleeping in the large fig tree above him. Aśvatthāman resolved to fall similarly upon the Pāṇḍavas while they slept. As he approached the gate of the Pāṇḍava camp, Aśvatthāman saw there a huge and horrific being, and he attacked it vigorously but in vain. He prayed for the help of Mahādeva (Śiva), recited a hymn to that god, and offered the elements of his own body as an offering to him. The god appeared to him, blessed his intention, gave him a sword, and entered into his body. Aśvatthāman set Kṛpa and Kṛtavarman to guard the camp's gate, and he entered, found the Pāṇḍavas absent, and proceeded to kill Dhṛṣṭadyumna (the killer of Aśvatthāman's father) using only his bare hands (depriving him of the warrior's death on a blade). He then killed Drupada's other son, Śikhaṇḍin, and Drupada's grandsons, the five sons of Draupadī, and all of their attendants. Meanwhile Kṛpa and Kṛtavarman set fire to the camp. Aśvatthāman and his companions then went back to Duryodhana and informed him of what they had done. Duryodhana praised Aśvatthāman and then died. The three surviving Kauravas then went their separate ways.

The Pāṇḍavas chased Aśvatthāman and caught up with him at the hermitage of Vyāsa along the Gaṅgā River. Aśvatthāman charged a blade of grass with the formula that made it "the head of Brahmā" and hurled the dart "that there be no Pāṇḍavas." Arjuna shot a counterweapon capable of neutralizing Aśvatthāman's shot. The seers Vyāsa and Nārada then positioned themselves between the two weapons, which were blazing against each other in one huge fireball. Then Arjuna, with great difficulty, was persuaded to withdraw his weapon; he did so, exhorting the seers to protect them all against Aśvatthāman's. But Aśvatthāman, whose soul was not clean, could not withdraw his without it rebounding and killing him, so Vyāsa proposed that Aśvatthāman be spared if he would spare the Pāṇḍavas and hand over the jewel on his head. Aśvatthāman agreed, but as the weapon had to do some harm if not recalled, he directed it into the wombs of the Pāṇḍava women, and it killed Parikṣit in the womb of Uttarā, Abhimanyu's widow. Kṛṣṇa predicted that though the fetus would die, the dead baby would be revived and live a long life. He then sentenced Aśvatthāman to wander the earth for 3,000 years shrouded with miasma.

Just as Indra was, in some accounts, plagued with evil for killing Vṛtra (who was sometimes conceived of as a Brāhmaṇ)—evil which caused the god to retreat and hide until it was fully expiated—so the immediate aftermath of the Bhārata war was dominated by a sense of horror and malaise, which especially troubled and impeded the victorious Pāṇḍava king, Yudhiṣṭhira. Yudhiṣṭhira's sense of the war's wrongfulness persisted to the end of the text, in spite of the fact that everyone else, from his wife to Kṛṣṇa Vāsudeva, told him the war was right and good; in spite of the fact that the dying patriarch Bhīṣma lectured him at length on all aspects of the good law (the duties and responsibilities of kings, which have rightful violence at their center; the ambiguities of righteousness in abnormal circumstances; and the absolute perspective of a beatitude that ultimately transcends the oppositions of good versus bad, right versus wrong, pleasant versus unpleasant, and so on); in spite of the fact that he performed a grand horse sacrifice, Aśvamedha, as expiation for the putative wrong of the war. These debates and instructions and the account of this horse sacrifice are told at some length after the massive and grotesque narrative of the battle; they form a deliberate tale of pacification (*praśamana, śānti*) that aims to neutralize the inevitable miasma of the war.

In the years that followed the war, Dhṛtarāṣṭra and his queen Gāndhārī and Kuntī, the mother of the Pāṇḍavas, lived a life of asceticism in a forest retreat and died with yogic calm in a forest fire. Thirty-six years after the war the clan of Kṛṣṇa Vāsudeva erupted in a drunken brawl, and they all slaughtered each other; Kṛṣṇa's soul dissolved back into the supreme god Viṣṇu (Kṛṣṇa had been born when a part of Viṣṇu took birth in the womb of Kṛṣṇa's mother). When they learned of this, the Pāṇḍavas believed it was time for them to leave this world too, and they embarked upon the "great journey," which involved walking north toward the polar mountain—that is, toward the heavenly worlds around the upper slopes of that mountain—until one's body dropped dead. One-by-one Draupadī and the younger Pāṇḍavas died along the way until Yudhiṣṭhira was left alone with a dog that had followed him all the way. Yudhiṣṭhira made it to the gate of heaven and there refused the order to drive the dog back, at which point the dog revealed itself to be an incarnate form of the god Dharma who had come to test Yudhiṣṭhira's virtue. Once in heaven Yudhiṣṭhira faced one final test of his virtue: He saw only the Dhārtarāṣṭras in heaven, and he was told that his brothers were in hell. He insisted on joining his brothers in hell, if that were the case. It was then revealed that they were really in heaven, that this illusion had been one final test. So ends the *Mahābhārata*.

THE WRITTEN SANSKRIT TEXT OF THE MAHĀBHĀRATA AND THE PUNE EDITION

As was said at the outset, this chapter is based upon the single most important resource for entering into and charting the extensive *Mahābhārata* tradition, the written Sanskrit text of the *Mahābhārata*. The single most important and useful version of this text is the attempted critical edition carried out and published at the Bhandarkar Oriental Research Institute in Pune between 1919 and 1966.

The first printed edition of the *Mahābhārata* was carried out in Calcutta between 1834 and 1839 and presented a northern Indian version of the epic. This was followed by the publishing in Bombay in 1862–63 of a somewhat different northern version, one established by Nīlakaṇṭha, a Marathi Brāhmaṇ working in Varanasi in the latter part of the seventeenth century (Brockington 1998: 130), who also wrote an extensive commentary on the text. As the Calcutta Sanskrit scholar Mohan Ganguli worked on a translation of the entire northern recension (under the patronage of Pratap Chandra Roy, between 1884 and 1896), there was scholarly awareness of a longer southern recension of the *Mahābhārata* (published in Kumbokonam in Tamilnadu, 1906–10), and Western scholars began discussing and calling for a critical edition of the manuscript tradition.

The process of preparing a critical edition of the *Mahābhārata* was begun at the Bhandarkar Oriental Research Institute in Pune in 1919 and went under the general direction of V. S. Sukthankar (who had studied philology in Berlin) in 1925. Publication of the complete, critically established text and apparatus was carried out between 1933 and 1966 by Sukthankar and his successors S. K. Belvalkar and P. L. Vaidya and their associate editors. Hundreds of relatively young *Mahābhārata* manuscripts (the oldest manuscript of known date was a barely four-hundred-year-old manuscript from Nepal; Dunham 1985: 6–7; Sukthankar 1933: lix) were surveyed, many were collated, and dozens were chosen to form the basis for editing the eighteen *parvan*s of the epic one by one. This heuristic process revealed literally thousands upon thousands of variations among the manuscripts in the reading of individual lines, in the order of verses and chapters, and in the inclusion and omission of particular passages and episodes. This fact was not surprising. It fits with all our general knowledge of oral epic narrative traditions, of the great vitality of Indian bardic traditions, and of the decentralized nature of Indian cultural institutions. But this process also revealed the striking fact that in the midst of all this variation, there was a remarkable degree of close agreement in readings line after line, in the order of verses, and in the contents of the *parvan*s, agreement that can be explained only by postulating the existence of a normative written text at some point in the past and in some significant measure (see Bigger 1998: 13–19; Fitzgerald 1985: 137n5).

But the manuscript tradition proved to have been too fluid and too dynamic to allow the editors to recover the archetype (see Dunham 1985: 11–12, 15–18; Sukthankar 1933: lxxxvi). Emerging from and existing in the larger, energetic, multichannel *Mahābhārata* tradition, the Sanskrit manuscript tradition was too permeable and characterized by too much circulation of too many of its exemplars (and consequently, too much interpenetration of its subtraditions) to allow an accurate genealogical tree of the great variety manifest in the manuscripts. Fully cognizant of these problems, Sukthankar and his colleagues did their best to approximate the archetype while admitting that actually recovering it was an unattainable goal. Their attempt and the edition they produced generated immediate controversy on different fronts. Scholars sympathetic to their ends were skeptical of their efforts; other scholars thought the effort to edit the tradition critically was fundamentally misguided; and some people were upset that certain motifs and passages of the text familiar to them were relegated by the Pune editors to the obscurity of the apparatus to the edition. For all the problems that remain with its survey of the manuscript tradition (Dunham 1985; Grünendahl 1993) and in spite of the enduring controversies, the Pune edition has been an immense scholarly advance in the study of the written Sanskrit *Mahābhārata* tradition and is today the starting point of all serious investigation of this part of the *Mahābhārata* tradition. In the 1990s the Japanese scholar Muneo Tokunaga (1996) led an immense effort that resulted in the digitization of the Pune text. John Smith (1999–2001) reworked the Tokunaga text, significantly improving the method of transcription employed, correcting the remaining typographical errors, and including all lines and passages relegated to the Pune apparatus (but not including individual variant readings of words and syllables). The searchable computer files of the Pune text offer tremendous new advantages for the study of the *Mahābhārata*.

Sukthankar and his colleagues made a great advance in the charting of the manuscript tradition of the written Sanskrit text. The apparatus of their edition includes the variant readings contained in all the manuscripts consulted and the text and variants of the numerous passages found in some manuscripts that were judged not to have been part of the putative archetype. Also, the approximation of the archetype which the Pune editors labored hard to produce is, for all its artificiality (it is a reconstruction, it never was any person's or community's actual text), a reasonable and defensible editorial result, and the study of Indian civilization is the richer for it. One of the very greatest values of the labors of the Pune editors in doing this reconstruction is their recovery of many "difficult readings" (*lectiones difficiliores*) that had been dropped or "corrected" in many of the manuscript traditions because these readings were obscure or regarded as mistaken. On the other hand, a great danger the Pune edition occasions is the possibility that its established text will be printed and distributed without its intrinsically important but cumbersome apparatus, a possibility, thus, that the Pune edition could efface much of the variegated development of the *Mahābhārata* textual tradition.

The Pune text gives us an approximation of what must have been a very prestigious and important written Sanskrit text that eclipsed prior versions of the *Mahābhārata* both oral and written, though probably it did not eliminate them altogether. The critically established text is in part a "lowest common denominator," and while Sukthankar was right to posit that everything in this "Gupta archetype" (not his designation) was faithfully transmitted everywhere (thus everything not found everywhere derives from some source outside the Gupta archetype), that putative fact does not mean that any and all textual elements not deriving from the Gupta archetype are posterior developments. In all likelihood there were prestigious written redactions of a Sanskrit *Mahābhārata* prior to that of the Gupta era as well as major and minor oral traditions. Many elements of such traditions not included in the "official" Gupta era redaction no doubt found their way into many, or even all, of the particular manuscript traditions through the normal processes of conflation.

WOMEN IN THE MAHĀBHĀRATA

The basic premise of the *Mahābhārata* as a myth of *avatāra* (in the original sense of that word; see Hacker 1978a and above) describes the action of men motivated by the need of women or femininely construed entities (especially the earth). This widely familiar narrative structure occurs and recurs often in the epic text in ways large and small, and much of what men actually say and do in the epic is accurately represented by it. But at the same time, this Indian setting of this familiar theme is strikingly different from its most famous instances in Western literature. There is in the *Mahābhārata* a much more thorough and dynamic presence of energetic women and female powers that will remind Western readers more of Irish epic literature than Homer's *Iliad*. The *Mahābhārata* spends a great deal of time recounting the generation and birth of its heroes, and its heroes are named as often with matronyms as with patronyms. The wives and mothers of these men—especially Gāndhārī, Kuntī, and Draupadī—figure prominently and often potently in the main and subordinate narratives of the epic, even when serving functions described by the "familiar theme." And furthermore, the premises of the "familiar theme" are regularly complicated or break down completely in the *Mahābhārata*, as men prove themselves too weak or corrupt to defend or contend for a woman, and a woman is left to fend for herself or she rescues or trumps the men involved (examples given below). Finally, the importance of this sexual charge in the epic narrative is underscored by the surprising degree to which the sex that is in-between male and female (generally referred to as the "third nature" or, most commonly, "nonmale," *napuṃsaka*) is represented and developed in it.

The familiar structure of the *avatāra* theme represents dramatically what Manu, in the same general era during which the *Mahābhārata* was developing, prescribed as the duty of men toward women, *rakṣaṇa* ("guarding, protecting from harm, preserving, keeping in the desired state": "When she is a girl, her father guards her; when she is a young woman, her husband guards her; when she is an old woman, her sons guard her. A woman should never be on her own"; *Manusmṛti* 9.3), and this structure and this idea occur and recur often in the *Mahābhārata*. The *Mahābhārata*, presenting one part of the "secret understanding of the gods" (1.58.3), depicts the earth pleading with Brahmā and the gods of his celestial court for relief from the hordes of demons that oppressively crawl all over her (1.58.30ff., 11.8.20ff.). The gods agreed to descend and help her. Shortly after, Śrī (not the earth herself, but the representation of her as the alluring and empowering consort of the good king; see Gonda 1954: 176–231) was born from the ground demarcated for King Drupada's sacrifice (the "altar," *vedi*) at the same rite that gave birth to her brother, Dhṛṣṭadyumna (the chief executive military officer of the Pāṇḍavas in the war), from the fire. As soon as she was born, a bodiless voice announced: "This most splendid of all women, this dark one (*kṛṣṇā*, which is actually her proper name) will tend to lead the *kṣatra* to destruction. She with her lovely figure (*sumadhyamā*) will in time do the business of the gods. Because of her a tremendous danger for Kṣatriyas will develop" (*Mahābhārata* 1.155.44–45). In the epic narrative the Pāṇḍavas flourished when they married Draupadī; and when the demonic Kṣatriyas abused her, a war to the death became all but certain. (Additionally, the motif of the goddess Śrī's leaving a wicked king or a king fallen on hard times is a commonplace of the epic, and there is a collection of stories and sermons focused upon Śrī's shuttling between the gods and the demons at *Mahābhārata* 12.215–21. In *Mahābhārata* 12.124 Dhṛtarāṣṭra repeats a version of one of these histories to Duryodhana when the latter feels humiliated by the splendor of Yudhiṣṭhira's royal consecration.)

The structure of this basic premise is sustained in the epic narrative in many other ways: for example, *The Book of the Women* (Book 11) movingly describes the terrific destruction and human loss caused by the great war, and it does so through an interesting, extended portrayal of the bereaved women prowling the battlefield, looking for the bodies and heads of the men who died doing their duty of *rakṣaṇa* (at the human level of events, the Kauravas were defending their continued possession of land—their portion of the earth—and rights against the Pāṇḍavas who were quasi-interlopers). This important and detailed scene not only exemplifies the basic premise of the epic, it amplifies and extends it by emphasizing the Kaurava women's accustomed material comfort and their general fragility. This scene contributes to the glorification of the warriors' deeds by highlighting the need they claimed to serve and affectingly portraying sorrow at their loss.

But the *Mahābhārata* also shows protection breaking down at times and women forced to act on their own and fend for themselves. Śakuntalā, effectively an orphan, was seduced and impregnated by King Duḥṣanta, and she had to sue the king herself with great energy and eloquence to secure his honoring his promises to her (see *Mahābhārata* 1.62–69; Śakuntalā's son was Bharata, the eponymous progenitor of the heroes of the epic). Damayantī was deserted in the wilderness by her mad husband Nala and worked hard and resourcefully to save herself (see *Mahābhārata* 3.60ff.). The Mādra princess Sāvitrī engaged the lord of the dead (Yama) in a battle of wits with which she revived her dead husband and restored his family and her own to health and prosperity (see *Mahābhārata* 3.277–83). And most importantly Draupadī, "like a boat upon the ocean," saved herself and her husbands during the dicing match (see above). One of the historical premises of the *Mahābhārata* is that proper Kṣatriya protection had failed or broken down, that the earth had been overrun by wicked men of arms. The contrived scene of Draupadī's brutal abuse at the dicing match, with its unbelievable passivity on the part of the Pāṇḍavas, seems intended to mirror this argument and highlight the role of femininely construed power in the rectification of the situation. The tremendous brutality of Bhīma's vengeance—culminating in his drinking Duḥśāsana's blood on the seventeenth day of the battle—is an amplification of the familiar theme that corresponds to the inversion of that theme at the time of the gambling.

RELIGION IN THE MAHĀBHĀRATA

The *Mahābhārata* was called into existence by a crisis perceived by the Brāhmaṇ elite of ancient India—a crisis threatening its very existence because of unprecedented competition for patronage and support in the context of the new political and economic institution of the Mauryan empire. The Pāṇḍava epic was a religiously energized political response to this situation that launched a reinvigorated Brāhmaṇ vision of the ideal polity and society. It was "religiously energized" in the sense that many members of this elite were genuinely invested in the notions that the Vedas they possessed were a transcendent sacred entity that really did protect and prosper society in one way or another, "by feeding and pleasing the 'gods'." But this Brāhmaṇ counter-revolution was creative as well as reactionary, and it succeeded—it laid the foundation of what we today retrospectively identify as "Hinduism." Because many in the Brāhmaṇ tradition had participated in the creation and promotion of much of the religious perspective of *yoga* and the ethics of harmlessness between 700 and 200 BCE, the reaction of the *Mahābhārata* carried many of these ideas along with it. Because the Brāhmaṇ elite was diffuse, rural, and had no institutions of central authority, it created a tradition that was naturally open to absorbing and disseminating ideas and motives from a wide range of geographic locations and from various non-Brāhmaṇ groups of society. Nicholas Sutton (2002) has recently provided a comprehensive treatment of this entire subject.

The most important and most powerful new developments in the *Mahābhārata*—from the point of view of those Indian people who held Brāhmaṇs in some esteem, or at least reverence, and whose religious ideas were conditioned by Brāhmaṇs—were the abundant and open way that the *Mahābhārata* presented a wonderful new theism coupled with a moving new devotionalism. Second, the *Mahābhārata* presented a new scenario of holiness in the Brāhmaṇically sanctioned world, one that highlighted a Brāhmaṇ elite in the process of withdrawal into a way of life relatively more irenic and isolated, dedicated to nonviolence (*ahiṃsā*), asceticism, *yoga* meditation, and sometimes complete renunciation (this theme is developed in several essays in Heesterman 1985). A form of this ideal of holiness was then generalized to all members of society when it was articulated as the doctrine of *karmayoga*, performing one's *dharma* with the inner desirelessness of *yoga*.

Regarding the first development: The *Mahābhārata* portrays a world in which tremendous gods—Brahmā, Śiva, Viṣṇu, and, as Alf Hiltebeitel and Madeleine Biardeau have pointed out, some early representations of the goddess—are active, and it does so at length and with dramatic detail. Scholars of ancient Indian religions are well aware of the rich theism contained in the Vedic texts, but in ancient India those texts became esoteric and socially restricted. And their expressions of wonder and worship were short bursts of praise, their myths short and obscure narratives, and they came to be surrounded by the obscure sets of correspondences that concerned men who were ritual technicians rather than seers or poets. The *Mahābhārata* was a tremendous departure from that esoteric priestly tradition. The *Mahābhārata* contains many direct representations of the transcendent power and majesty of many different gods: right near the beginning of the *Mahābhārata* (at 1.3.60–70) is a wonderful imitation of a Ṛg Vedic hymn to the Aśvins (said falsely in the *Mahābhārata* to be from the *Ṛg Veda*). Shortly after this, in the *Mahābhārata*'s next episode, the seer Bhṛgu wrongly curses the god Agni to eat omnivorously, that is, indiscriminately, and the god, reprimanding the sage, gives a nice characterization of one attribute of transcendence characteristic of some gods as he says of himself: "With my power I make myself many and exist in many bodies—in *agnihotra*s, in *sattra*s, and in various rites and ceremonies. And what is offered into me according to the prescriptions declared in the Vedas refreshes the gods and the ancestors" (*Mahābhārata* 1.7.6–7).

These are old ideas, in India as well as elsewhere, but they were not widely circulated in India with Brāhmaṇic authority before the *Mahābhārata*. (Also, I mention both of these because both contain direct mentions of the primary Vedas.) The image of the gods and the *asura*s pulling back and forth with the snake Vāsuki to twirl the Mandara Mountain and churn the ocean, creating the sun and the moon and other good things as well as the elixir of immortality, is momentous even as it is lightly humorous. Śiva's sudden attack upon Arjuna in the mountain wilderness, his testing Arjuna, and Arjuna's devoted surrender to him inspire awe, fear, and worship. The image of the wide, nurturing Goddess Earth covered and burdened with thugs terrorizing and slaughtering innocents (*Mahābhārata* 1.58) arouses far-reaching compassion and rage, and when she travels up to the heaven of Brahmā, her sorry plight represents all vicious injustice and terrestrial long-suffering as it moves all the gods to action. Brahmā's benevolence and majesty and the roiling energy of the other celestials around him gives way to Viṣṇu's far greater majesty, when all the gods must travel up even higher for an audience with him. Viṣṇu's earthly incarnation, Kṛṣṇa Vāsudeva, is breathtaking when Śiśupāla's insults finally trigger his rage; he is awesome when Duryodhana thinks he can contain him, but Kṛṣṇa shows all things in and radiating from himself; and Kṛṣṇa is both breathtaking and awesome in the climactic demonstration of himself as all-devouring time to Arjuna just before the war commences. This list could go on at some length reciting affecting images of truly awesome and marvelous beings (Śiva-Rudra, Nārāyaṇa, Śrī, Mṛtyu [death], Yama [the lord of the dead, the king of Dharma], Kubera, Gandharvas, Apsarases, Yakṣas, and so on; even Kāla [time]). Like the Vedas, the *Mahābhārata* has gathered textual representations of all the gods into a single, compendious whole. Unlike the primary Veda, the *Mahābhārata* made all of this available openly and widely—a virtue to modern sensibilities as, evidently, it was to some in ancient India.

But as potent and moving as many of these images and related stories are, even more powerful, I suspect, was the fusion of divine action to the main human focus of the *Mahābhārata*, the horrific war that stands as a tremendous inferno at its center. It was a war of human kings to all appearances, but the audience knew it was really a purge of demonic thugs led by the gods, and it demonstrated the power and influence of gods in the affairs of human beings. Finally, the war itself is something of a divinity.

Simultaneously fascinating and repelling, war holds out the promise of resolving one's earthly life—it leads to death or glory, heaven or victory. "As moths speeding full tilt to their demise fly right into a fire," so have men rushed to the war (*Bhagavad Gītā* 11.29), soon to enter the flaming, fanged mouth of god (11.25, 11.27, 11.30). Kurukṣetra is the "the creator's sacrificial altar" (as it is sometimes called, see *Mahābhārata* 3.81.178, 3.129.22, 9.52.20), the war is a sacrificial offering to the gods (see Hiltebeitel 1990), battle is the digesting fire by which the gods absorb their food. And in this nightmarish conflagration there is a moral and spiritual collapse into god as well as a material one: the deeds of Kṛṣṇa Vāsudeva in the war are often immoral from the perspective of men who understand themselves to be noble, who do not wish any ignoble advantage in battle, not even to save their lives or win the war. But the party of the gods wins only because of Kṛṣṇa's baffling deeds and counsel that ignores the rules of warfare (*dharma*) and even truthfulness. This advice and behavior makes Kṛṣṇa Vāsudeva just the sort of baffling, unheard of and unimagined new kind of being that Sheldon Pollock (1991: 34–43) sees emerging as the essence of the regular incarnations of Viṣṇu who periodically descend into the world to reenergize *dharma* (the later and familiar sense of the word "*avatāra*"). So from the human point of view the collapse into the conflagration of the war looks more like the end of the world, when God Agni reduces everything to its elements, likely at the command of the great god Śiva. The war is the mouth of god eagerly devouring the whole world and everyone in it (*Bhagavad Gītā* 11.30). The vast war narrated across more than 40,000 lines of text, the central and most imposing fact of the *Mahābhārata*, is also the most exhilarating, awesome, and consistently moving (frightening, horrifying) reality of the *Mahābhārata*. The quasidivine Bhārata war is one of the principal mysteries presented in the text, and this fact, coupled with Kṛṣṇa's baffling behavior (he later comes to be known commonly as *mohana*, "causing confusion, or consternation, mystifying") and the immorality of the Pāṇḍavas in order to win the war, has barred this Veda from most homes, except for the *Bhagavad Gītā*, which assimilates Kṛṣṇa and the war and teaches a doctrine fusing devotion to Kṛṣṇa to the *yoga* of the *karmayoga*.

CHAPTER FOUR

RĀMĀYAṆA

Robert P. Goldman and
Sally J. Sutherland Goldman

Although it is little known to the average, educated Westerner, the *Vālmīki Rāmāyaṇa* is arguably one of the three or four most important and most widely influential texts ever written. For the impact this poem and the countless other works it has inspired upon the religions, the arts, and the social and political thought of much of Asia has been and continues to be both profound and widespread. Indeed, the influence of the *Rāmāyaṇa* is in many ways comparable to that only of such monumental texts as the Bible and the Qur'ān.

But where these other two great religious documents have, like the *Rāmāyaṇa*, made themselves at home in many different cultures, each of them has done so within the confines of a single greater religious tradition, the Judeo-Christian and the Islamic, respectively. In contrast, the *Rāmāyaṇa*, over the past two-and-a-half millennia, has established itself as a central cultural document of most of the major Hindu, Jaina, Buddhist, and Islamic cultures of South and Southeast Asia.

In short, it is hardly an exaggeration to say that in terms of its diversity, longevity, and ability to transcend boundaries of language, culture, religion, social class, gender, and politics, the *Rāmāyaṇa*—by which we mean the collectivity of the oral, literary, folk, performative, and artistic representations of the ancient Hindu tale of Rāma and Sītā that have permeated, indeed saturated, the cultures of South, Southeast, and to some extent Central, West, and East Asia beginning with the first millennium BCE—is among the most popular, versatile, and influential stories the world has known. In the following pages we will attempt to trace a few of the outlines of the extraordinary trajectory of this vast and complex polymorphic set of texts (to use the broadest possible reading of that term), as its components have impacted the lives, beliefs, aesthetics, politics, social relations, and general culture of diverse nations and communities spanning nearly three millennia of human history and stretching over immense areas of Asia from Iran to the Philippines and from Sri Lanka to Mongolia.

THE RĀMĀYAṆA OF VĀLMĪKI

We will begin with a discussion of what we believe to be the oldest surviving version of the Rāma story, the monumental Sanskrit epic poem, the *Rāmāyaṇa* (the Adventures of Rāma), attributed to the legendary poet-sage Vālmīki. This epic appears to have been largely composed during the first half of the first millennium BCE (R. Goldman 1984: 14–23). The precise dating of the poem is, however, difficult, and scholarly opinion on the matter varies considerably (Brockington 1984: 1, 1998: 377–79). It is also apparent that some portions of the text, as it has come down to us, were composed later than others (Brockington 1984: 312, 315). Moreover, indigenous traditions of India regard the poem to be a work of the Tretā Yuga, the second of the four great cyclical ages of cosmic time, since its author is a contemporary of the epic hero, who is said to have lived in that age. This would, in the traditionalist reckoning, date the epic many hundreds of thousands of years before the modern era. Then, too, a corollary of Yuga theory is that the cosmic ages constantly recur and that events of a given *yuga* will recur with some variations when that same era comes around again. By this reckoning, Rāma reappears and—with some variations—undergoes his adventures, trials, and triumphs in each of the endlessly recurring Tretā Yugas.

As it has come down to us, the *Vālmīki Rāmāyaṇa* is a lengthy, originally orally composed, narrative poem of roughly 25,000 verses in generally simple, but sometimes moderately ornate, Sanskrit couplets divided into seven large books or *kāṇḍa*s. For the purposes of comparison, then, the poem is approximately twice the length of Homer's *Iliad* and *Odyssey* combined. Because of the popularity of the work and its central cultural and religious significance, it is likely that the poem was subject to a long and complex history of oral transmission before and during the period in which it came to be frequently copied and recopied over the centuries in all of the regions and scripts of India. As a result there has evolved a complex recensional history of the poem during which it, like its sister epic the *Mahābhārata*, came to be transmitted in two major regional recensions, the northern and southern, each of which has a number of subregional variants. These in turn are subdivided into groups of manuscripts composed in the various scripts of the subcontinent (Bhatt and Shah 1960–75, 1: xiii–xxix). The textual variations that characterize the two major recensions are significant, with only about one-third of the total text identical in the two versions. Despite this textual variation and the fact that the two larger versions sometimes breakup one or two of the *kāṇḍa*s differently, the general configuration of the narrative is quite similar in all recensions and has generally been regarded by scholars as the departure point for the sometimes quite different treatments of the tale in other, later *Rāmāyaṇa* versions.

It will be helpful, we believe, to summarize the plot of the *Vālmīki Rāmāyaṇa* as a starting point to a discussion of the social, cultural, aesthetic, and theological significance of the poem in the development of the larger *Rāmāyaṇa* tradition and of Hindu civilization in general.

THE STORY

Unlike the Homeric epics, but somewhat similarly to the *Mahābhārata*, the poem begins with a framing narrative whose purpose is to provide a history of its conception, composition, and early dissemination. The sage Vālmīki is introduced in conversation with the divine seer Nārada. Questioned by the former as to the existence of a truly exemplary man in the current era, Nārada responds with a terse biography of Rāma, the current ruler of the kingdom of Kosala, whose capital is the city of Ayodhyā. After fulsome praise of Rāma's physical and moral perfection, the sage relates his career from the eve of his first, abortive consecration, through his exile and sufferings and the war in Laṅkā, to his ultimate accession to his ancestral throne and the utopian era that this inaugurates. This brief narrative essentially encompasses, in much abbreviated form, the substance of Books 2 to 6 of the larger epic.

Reflecting on Nārada's edifying tale, Vālmīki wanders into the woodlands surrounding his *āśrama* for his daily ablutions. There his blissful contemplation of nature is rudely interrupted as he witnesses the cruel death of one of a pair of mating cranes at the hands of a tribal hunter. Stunned by what he sees as an act of unrighteousness and deeply moved by the grief of the surviving bird, the sage curses the hunter for his wanton act. The form of this particular curse, however, turns out to be more interesting than its substance, for it issues from the sage's lips as a perfectly formed metrical unit, a verse, consisting of four equal quarters of eight syllables each whose prosody makes it ideal for singing to the accompaniment of stringed and percussion instruments. Puzzled by these strange events, Vālmīki returns to his *āśrama* to ponder them. There he is visited by the great creator divinity Lord Brahmā who tells him that he need not be perplexed, for it was through the inspiration of the god that the sage has been able to transform his sorrow (*śoka*) for the suffering of the grieving crane into an entirely new aesthetic medium: *śloka* or true poetry. Brahmā then reveals his purpose, commissioning Vālmīki to employ his newfound poetic inspiration to compose a monumental poem about the career of Rāma, a brief account of which he had heard earlier that morning from Nārada, and granting him the divine vision to be able to know the events of that remarkable career intimately. The sage composes the epic, filling it with all of the poetic moods (*rasa*), and teaches it to his disciples, notably the twins Lava and Kuśa, who perform it throughout the land to the plaudits of all who hear them. Eventually the fame of these singers of tales—who are in actuality the sons of Rāma—reaches the ears of King Rāma himself, and he calls them to his court where he becomes both the audience and subject of the narrative. It is at this point that the epic story proper begins.

This charming and interesting preamble (*upodghāta*) to the poem is important because it is the source of the widely established tradition that regards Vālmīki as not just a great poet but in fact as the *ādikavi* or first poet and his immortal composition as therefore the *ādikāvya* or first poem, the source and inspiration for all later poetic composition. This reputation, in many ways richly deserved, is significant for a larger study of the *Rāmāyaṇa* tradition, in that it accounts in large measure for the enormous prestige the *Rāmāyaṇa* has enjoyed over the centuries, even among those who do not, and in fact cannot, read its Sanskrit. It also firmly establishes the tradition that Vālmīki's is the original formal or literary rendering of the *Rāmakathā* or the story of Rāma and the direct or indirect source of all subsequent versions.

The epic narrative proper begins with a description of the rich and powerful kingdom of Kosala, the ancestral domain of the Solar dynasty, the noble race of kings who trace their lineage back to the very sun god himself. As the tale begins, the kingdom is being ruled from its prosperous, fortified capital city of Ayodhyā by the Solar dynast Daśaratha. The aged monarch is represented as possessing everything a man could desire in terms of wealth, virtue, power, and fame with the critical and potentially tragic exception of a son to carry on his ancient line. On the advice of his ministers and with the assistance of the sage Ṛśyaśṛṅga, the king performs sacrifices with the aim of remedying this lack. Out of the sacrificial fire emerges a divine personage bearing a vessel filled with porridge which, the king is instructed, is to be fed to his three wives so that they may conceive and bear him sons.

While the king's *putrakāmeṣṭi* or rite for the production of a son is in progress, the gods, assembled to receive their shares of the oblation, address the creator Brahmā, complaining to him that a terrible demon, a *rākṣasa* named Rāvaṇa, taking advantage of Brahmā's boon of invulnerability at the hands of all supernatural beings, has begun to oppress the whole world. Learning from the creator that, in his arrogance, Rāvaṇa had omitted the mention of mere mortals from the list of those who could not harm him, the gods appeal to Lord Viṣṇu, asking him to divide himself into four parts and take birth as the four heroic sons of Daśaratha in order to encompass the destruction of the demon king. Viṣṇu accepts this mission, and Brahmā instructs the gods to father countless semidivine apes and monkeys to serve as his allies.

This episode—found in all surviving recensions and manuscripts—is of considerable significance to our understanding of the theological importance of the *Rāmāyaṇa*, as it establishes the poem early on as one of the central texts of the emerging Vaiṣṇava corpus and identifies Rāma (along with his three brothers) as, like Kṛṣṇa Vāsudeva, one of the principal *avatāra*s or incarnations of Viṣṇu and, in the course of time, one of the major objects of Hindu devotionalism. We shall return to the discussion of Rāma's divinity below when we consider the history of *Rāmāyaṇa* scholarship.

Unlike the later narratives of the life of Kṛṣṇa and some relatively modern retellings of the Rāma story, Vālmīki's poem pays little attention to the childhood of its hero, moving swiftly from the narrative of his birth to that of his coming of age. As the idealized prince and his brothers approach manhood, the tranquility of the Kosalan court is shattered by the arrival of the frightening and irascible sage Viśvāmitra who demands that the aged king lend him his beloved son to defend the sage's *āśrama* from the depredations of some *rākṣasa*s who have been interfering with his sacrificial rites. The fond king is reluctant to part with Rāma but is at last persuaded under the threat of a curse, and Rāma, together with Lakṣmaṇa, his inseparable companion and younger brother, is committed to the care of the sage. The three setoff on what amounts to a kind of initiatory journey, during the course of which Rāma receives instruction in mythological lore from the sage, rids the woodlands of a terrible demoness, is initiated in the secret lore of divine weapons, and, finally, fulfills his mission by ridding the Viśvāmitra's *āśrama* of its predatory *rākṣasa*s.

In the wake of Rāma's success Viśvāmitra reveals to him a further purpose of their journey. He informs him that King Janaka of the nearby city of Mithilā is holding a contest of strength and martial vigor for the hand of his adoptive daughter, a princess of rare beauty whom he had found as an infant in the ploughed furrow of a sacrificial ground and accordingly named Sītā, "furrow." The test, which no warrior has yet passed, is the lifting and wielding of an immensely heavy and powerful bow that had been entrusted to the king's care by its owner, the mighty lord Śiva himself.

Although still a mere youth, Rāma easily passes the test, lifting and, in fact, breaking the mighty bow. He thus wins the hand of Sītā in marriage, while his brothers wed other girls of Janaka's household. On the return journey the wedding party is accosted by Rāma Jāmadagnya (Paraśurāma), the dreaded Brāhmaṇ nemesis of the warrior class. To the horror of Daśaratha and his attendants, the Brāhmaṇ-warrior expresses his contempt for what he considers the defective bow of Śiva that Rāma has so easily broken and challenges him to test his mettle with the more powerful weapon of Viṣṇu that he himself carries. Rāma seizes and masters the bow using it to cutoff the heavenly path of the irascible Brāhmaṇ.

This odd confrontation of the two Rāmas is interesting, since both are regarded as *avatāras* or incarnations of the lord Viṣṇu. Here the younger Rāma literally displaces the elder and comes into his own more fully as the incarnation of his age. It similarly serves as the final element in the opening book's *bildungsroman* of Rāma as an epic hero who has overcome the oedipal dread of the patriarchal Brāhmaṇ to emerge as a fully formed hero in his own right.

The happy couple, Rāma and Sītā, returns to Ayodhyā deeply absorbed in their mutual love. This brings to a close the first book of the epic, the *Bālakāṇḍa*.

The action of the second book, the *Ayodhyākāṇḍa*, opens some years later and concerns itself centrally with a political intrigue in the women's apartments of King Daśaratha's household and its cataclysmic consequences. The old king, feeling the burden of his years, decides that the time is propitious for him to withdraw from the life of a householder and monarch and consecrate his eldest and most deeply beloved son, Rāma, as *yuvarāja* or prince regent. He determines that the moment is particularly opportune since his next oldest son, Prince Bharata, the son of his favorite queen Kaikeyī, is temporarily away from the capital on a visit to his mother's family. The immediate consecration of Rāma is announced to the general rejoicing of the populace. However, when the news reaches the ears of Kaikeyī's lifelong servant-woman, the hunchback Mantharā, she rushes to her mistress to report what she sees as a calamity. The naive queen is at first delighted at the good fortune of Rāma, but Mantharā soon persuades Kaikeyī that the accession of Rāma and the attendant elevation of his mother, Kausalyā, to the status of queen-mother can only spell disaster for her and her son. At length persuaded, the simple-minded Kaikeyī skillfully employs her feminine wiles and takes advantage of the sexual thralldom of the aged king to force Daśaratha to grant her two thus far unfulfilled and unspecified boons he had once promised her as a reward for her assistance. Using the boons she forces the king, for whom the keeping of his given word is sacred, to agree to the exile of Rāma to the wilderness as a penniless wanderer for fourteen years and to the succession of her own son Bharata in his place. The blow to Daśaratha is a crushing one.

Most noteworthy at this juncture is the way in which Rāma distinguishes himself by the stoicism and calm fortitude with which he accepts the sudden reversal of his fortunes. His only concern is to maintain the truth of his father's word despite the advice to refuse his father's command on the part of his impetuous brother Lakṣmaṇa and his own mother. Rāma takes his leave of his family. His mother is desolate, but Sītā, arguing passionately that a wife's place is at her husband's side through thick and thin, rejects Rāma's arguments that she should remain behind in safety and comfort. In this way, Sītā establishes herself firmly in the popular imagination as the archetype of the *pativratā*, the unconditionally devoted Hindu wife, just as Rāma has now proven himself to be the idealized son, deferring unconditionally to patriarchal authority and the all-powerful code of *dharma*.

Divesting themselves of their wealth and finery, Rāma, Sītā, and the ever-faithful Lakṣmaṇa set out for the wilderness, followed by virtually the entire population of the city. Slipping away from their devoted followers, they cross the Gaṅgā and enter the idyllic woodlands of Mount Citrakūṭa. In the meanwhile, Daśaratha, his heart broken, dies grieving for his beloved son.

Bharata, alerted to the catastrophe at Ayodhyā through prophetic dreams, returns home in haste to find his father dead, his brother banished, and the kingdom without a ruler. Rebuking his mother for what she has done and refusing the royal consecration pressed upon him by the court Brāhmaṇs, he organizes a grand expedition to bring Rāma back to take up his rightful place as king. The brothers meet but cannot come to any immediate resolution of the succession issue. Both refuse the throne, Rāma on the grounds that he must adhere strictly to his father's words, and Bharata on the grounds that Rāma should, by virtue of his age and qualities, be the king in any case. At length a compromise is reached whereby Bharata will rule the kingdom as Rāma's regent for the specified period of the latter's exile, placing Rāma's sandals on the throne as a symbol of the latter's true sovereignty. At the end of the fourteen years, Rāma is to return and take up his long delayed consecration as king. Bharata returns to a village outside Ayodhyā to await his brother's return. Rāma and his party, however, eager to avoid further such encounters, plunge deeper into the wilderness. This brings the *Ayodhyākāṇḍa* to a close.

The third book of the epic, the *Araṇyakāṇḍa*, finds the hero wandering with his wife and brother Lakṣmaṇa amongst the hermitages of the sages of the Daṇḍaka Forest. The ascetics appeal to Rāma to protect them from the savage *rākṣasa*s that haunt the region. Rāma agrees, despite Sītā's uneasiness at her husband's involvement in the world of violent conflict. After several hostile encounters with monstrous demons who foreshadow the central moment of the book and the poem by attempting to abduct Sītā, the threesome settles into a peaceful, rustic life near the banks of the Godāvarī River. This sylvan idyll, however, is soon interrupted by the arrival of a promiscuous *rākṣasa* woman, Śūrpaṇakhā, sister of the demon-king Rāvaṇa. Attempting first to seduce the brothers and then devour Sītā, she is teased and ultimately disfigured by the heroes. She reports her humiliation first to the local *rākṣasa* garrison, whose warriors are then annihilated in combat by Rāma, and ultimately to Rāvaṇa himself. Śūrpaṇakhā's report fills the *rākṣasa* overlord with hatred for Rāma and passion for his beautiful wife, Sītā. He forms a plan to lure Rāma and Lakṣmaṇa away from the *āśrama* with the assistance of a *rākṣasa* named Mārīca who takes the form of a golden deer. Sītā, seeing the enchanting animal covets it, and she sends Rāma to catch it for her. Mārīca draws Rāma off to a great distance and, when he is finally struck down by Rāma's arrow, cries out for assistance in Rāma's voice. Sītā, hearing what she thinks to be her husband's desperate cries, urges Lakṣmaṇa to go to his aid. The latter, knowing that Rāma cannot really be in danger and heedful of his brother's instructions not to leave Sītā unguarded, attempts to reason with her. But Sītā, in her alarm, accuses Lakṣmaṇa of harboring a desire to eliminate Rāma in order to possess her for himself. Cut to the quick Lakṣmaṇa disobeys Rāma's orders and rushes off into the forest.

Rāvaṇa, who has been lurking nearby, then takes on the form of a venerable forest ascetic and presents himself at Sītā's hut on the pretext of asking for alms. His conversation soon takes a decidedly nonascetic turn. Rāvaṇa reveals himself in his true form, seizes the princess, and carries her off through the sky in his flying chariot. Attracted by the commotion, the vulture-king Jaṭāyus, an old friend of Daśaratha, attempts to come to Sītā's aid, but he is overpowered and mortally wounded by Rāvaṇa. Rāvaṇa then carries Sītā off through the air to his island kingdom of Laṅkā.

Rāma and Lakṣmaṇa return from the forest to find Sītā missing. They search for her in desolation and at length come upon the dying Jaṭāyus, who informs them of her abduction but who dies before he can tell them where she has been taken or by whom.

Rāma wanders mournfully in search of his wife, giving vent to a terrifying outburst of anger in an almost mad display of grief and rage. Soon he and Lakṣmaṇa encounter the monstrous *rākṣasa* Kabandha, who, when killed and cremated by the princes, reveals himself to be a divine being. Kabandha directs them to the mountain Ṛśyamūka, where he says they will find the monkey-lord Sugrīva, who will assist them in their search. The brothers proceed to lake Pampā, near Ṛśyamūka, bringing the *Araṇyakāṇḍa* to a close.

The fourth book, the *Kiṣkindhākāṇḍa*, opens with Sugrīva, the exiled lord of the monkeys, dispatching his loyal minister Hanumān to find out the intentions of the two princes who are wandering in the guise of ascetics. Rāma and Sugrīva meet and exchange their sad histories. Like Rāma, the monkey-king claims that he has been wrongfully driven from his kingdom and robbed of his wife. He tells Rāma of how, mistakenly thinking his powerful elder brother Vālin to have been killed in a battle with a demon, he took over both the kingdom and his brother's wife. When Vālin returns, he drives his brother Sugrīva out of the kingdom and takes his wife in turn.

Rāma and Sugrīva form a pact of mutual assistance, with Rāma agreeing to kill Vālin and replace Sugrīva on the throne in exchange for Sugrīva's assistance in finding and recovering Sītā. Rāma instructs Sugrīva to engage his brother in single combat and, true to his word, strikes down Vālin from ambush, justifying this questionable action in the face of the complaints of the dying monkey. This episode has remained one of the more vexed ethical problems in the story until the present day.

After some delay, Sugrīva marshals vast numbers of his monkey troops and organizes them into four great search parties, each of which is dispatched to scour one of the four cardinal points of the compass. The southern party, led by Vālin's son Aṅgada, eventually makes its way to the southern slopes of the Vindhya Mountains, where, in despair at the failure of their mission and the daunting immensity of the southern ocean, the monkeys vow to fast themselves to death. Their vow is interrupted by the vulture Sampāti, the older brother of Jaṭāyus, who approaching to devour them ends by informing them that he has seen Sītā being carried across the ocean to the *rākṣasa*s' island kingdom of Laṅkā. Resolved to send one of their number as a spy to scout for the abducted princess, the monkey leaders each declare the distance he can leap. Only Hanumān, son of the wind god, sits silent. When it has been made clear that none of the other monkeys has the power to leap the mighty ocean, the task falls to him. As he prepares to make his flight, the *Kiṣkindhākāṇḍa* draws to a close.

The fifth book of the epic, the *Sundarakāṇḍa*, opens with a lengthy account of Hanumān's prodigious leap and his long and frustrating search of the *rākṣasa* king's city and palace grounds. The poet depicts the forlorn princess in captivity and her confrontations with her monstrous suitor Rāvaṇa. Eventually, Hanumān discovers Sītā in a park attached to the harem. He reveals himself to her, reassuring her with his accurate description of Rāma and his presentation of Rāma's signet ring. He offers to carry her back, but she refuses, stating her preference of being rescued by her husband himself. Hanumān then takes his leave of Sītā and begins a rampage of destruction in the palace parklands, during which he encounters and kills many of the *rākṣasa* warriors sent to capture him. At length he is captured by Rāvaṇa's son Indrajit. Dragged before the *rākṣasa* king, the monkey rebukes him for his lawless conduct and urges him to restore Sītā to Rāma or face the most severe consequences. Rāvaṇa orders that Hanumān be paraded through the town with his tail set ablaze. But the monkey slips his bonds and, leaping from rooftop to rooftop, sets the city ablaze.

Taking leave once more of Sītā, Hanumān leaps back across the ocean, to the delight of the waiting monkeys. In high spirits they march back to the monkey capital of Kiṣkindhā to report the discovery of Sītā to Rāma, Lakṣmaṇa, and Sugrīva. This brings the *Sundarakāṇḍa* to a close.

The sixth book, called the *Yuddhakāṇḍa* (or in some versions the *Laṅkākāṇḍa*), is the longest of Vālmīki's poem and deals with the great battle before the gates of Rāvaṇa's gilded citadel. Rāma and his forces march to the shore of the ocean, where, after Rāma subdues the turbulent ocean divinity, the monkeys construct a great causeway by means of which the army crosses to Laṅkā. There they are joined by Rāvaṇa's younger brother Vibhīṣaṇa who has defected after Rāvaṇa has brutally rejected his advice to return Sītā. Rāma and his forces lay siege to Laṅkā, and a protracted and gory battle rages for many days with triumphs and disasters on both sides. Rāma and Lakṣmaṇa encounter and ultimately destroy such fearsome warriors as Indrajit, Rāvaṇa's son and master of supernatural weaponry, and the demon king's gargantuan brother, the monstrous Kumbhakarṇa. Nonetheless, their victory does not come easily. At one point both of the brothers are immobilized and nearly killed by the magical serpent arrows of Indrajit and are revived only in the eleventh hour by the arrival of the divine bird Garuḍa, the celestial mount of Viṣṇu and the sworn enemy of all serpents. When the redoubtable Indrajit uses his supernatural weaponry to strike down virtually the entire monkey host, Hanumān once more saves the day by flying to the Himālayas to carry back a mountain on which healing herbs are growing. This episode remains in popular art and the popular imagination as one of the central iconic moments of the epic tale and in the cultus of Hanumān. At length, after a terrific battle, Rāma is finally successful in slaying the ten-headed demon-king.

But now, after his long sought and costly victory, Rāma is far from demonstrating the expected joy at the recovery of his abducted wife. Instead, he speaks harshly to Sītā, repudiating her as one who has lived in the house of another man and claiming that he has fought the battle only for the sake of his own honor. He dismisses her, telling her to go with whomever she wishes. It is only when Sītā subjects herself to an ordeal by fire, and thus publicly demonstrates her fidelity to her lord, that Rāma agrees to take her back, stating that he had known all along of her loyalty but needed to demonstrate it to others. The couple then returns to Ayodhyā, where at long last Rāma, having carried out to the letter his father's orders, is consecrated as king. This brings to an end the sixth book.

The last book of the poem, the *Uttarakāṇḍa*, serves both as an epilogue to the epic narrative and a prologue to the careers of some of its secondary characters. Thus it provides a lengthy biography of Rāvaṇa, relating his birth, his conquests, his penances, his boons, and the curses that will lead ultimately to his undoing. Similarly, but much more succinctly, it provides an account of the childhood and early deeds of Hanumān. Returning to the central characters, the book describes Rāma's formal dismissal of his monkey and *rākṣasa* allies and the well-deserved pleasures of his life with Sītā. The felicity of the royal couple is, however, soon shattered when Rāma's spies bring him reports of gossip among the citizens of Ayodhyā concerning the chastity of the queen during the year in which she lived in captivity in the house of Rāvaṇa and the propriety of Rāma's having taken her back into his household. Acting to protect the honor of his house and his moral authority as a ruler, Rāma commands Lakṣmaṇa to take Sītā, now pregnant, to the forest on the pretext of an excursion and abandon her to her fate. The forlorn queen takes refuge in the *āśrama* of none other than the sage Vālmīki, author of the poem, where she gives birth to

Rāma's twin sons, Lava and Kuśa. These two, as was narrated in the *upodghāta* of the *Bālakāṇḍa*, will become principal performers of the epic poem. The *kāṇḍa* continues with a variety of exemplary epic and Purāṇic narratives of great kings and supernatural beings. At one point, Rāma dispatches his brother Śatrughna to aid the sages of the Yamunā region by slaying the oppressive demon Lavaṇa. Śatrughna accomplishes this feat and establishes himself in the city of Mathurā. At another point, Rāma is confronted by a Brāhmaṇ grieving for the untimely death of his son. Realizing that such an untoward event could occur only if there were irregularity in his otherwise perfect kingdom, Rāma scours his realm until he finds the source of this disharmony in the form of a lowly Śūdra engaged in the austerities normally reserved for his betters. Rāma unhesitatingly slays the offending Śūdra, thus restoring harmony to the kingdom and the Brāhmaṇ's son to life.

At length Rāma decides to perform an *aśvamedha*, the great horse sacrifice of the ancient Hindu kings. In the course of the ritual, Kuśa and Lava, acting on the instructions of their *guru* Vālmīki, proceed to Ayodhyā to sing the *Rāmāyaṇa* at the gateway of Rāma's sacrificial enclosure. Rāma is amazed and delighted by the poem, and upon inquiry discovers that its singers are in fact his own sons and that its author has been sheltering his beloved Sītā. He sends for Sītā, bidding her to declare her fidelity under oath once again in the assembly. Sītā appears with Vālmīki who, as an irreproachably truthful seer, attests to her innocence. Rāma declares that he has always been convinced of Sītā's fidelity but repudiated her for fear of public censure. He acknowledges his sons and expresses his desire to be reconciled with his wife. Sītā, however, calls upon her mother, the earth goddess, to witness her devotion to her husband and to once more receive her if she has been pure in thought and deed. The goddess emerges from the earth on a celestial throne and, taking her daughter in her arms, descends once more into the depths. Rāma is filled with rage at this turn of events and threatens to tear up the earth and destroy it, if Sītā is not returned to him. He is, however, pacified through the intercession of Brahmā, the creator god, who reminds him that he is in fact the supreme divinity Viṣṇu and assures him that he will be blissfully reunited with his beloved wife in heaven. Bereft of Sītā, Rāma rules his kingdom joylessly for many years. At last, Yama, the god of death himself, comes to Rāma to remind him that the purpose of his earthly existence has been accomplished and that it is time for him to return to the heavenly realm. Acting on the advice of Bharata, whom he is prepared to consecrate in his place, Rāma divides his territory into the kingdoms of northern and southern Kosala, establishing his sons in these realms respectively. Then, surrounded by all the inhabitants of Ayodhyā, Rāma immerses himself in the waters of the Sarayū River and ascends to heaven in his divine form, thus bringing the *kāṇḍa* and the epic to an end.

LEVELS OF SIGNIFICANCE IN VĀLMĪKI'S RĀMĀYAṆA

The Rāmāyaṇa as an aesthetic creation

As will be evident from a reading of the earlier synopsis, the *Vālmīki Rāmāyaṇa* works powerfully on a number of critical levels. One of these, which we have already discussed, is the literary and aesthetic. This poem, uniquely among all versions of the Rāma story, is regarded as the original and the archetype of human poetry. In its claim to have originated the genre of poetic composition through the transmutation of raw emotion into aesthetic delight by means of literary composition and artistic performance, the poem lies at the heart of the important and well-known philosophy of aesthetics, which we recognize under the rubric of *rasa* or aesthetic relish, derived from the sublimation of human emotion. The prologue to the epic contains one of the earliest if not the earliest listing of the *rasa*s first systematized by Bharata in his *Nāṭyaśāstra*. The prestige of the work as the "great source for all poetry" has, moreover, carried over to a number of major retellings in important regional languages of South Asia. Thus works such as the *Irāmāvatāram* of Kampan̲, the *Rāmcaritmānas* of Tulasidāsa, and the *Rāmāyaṇa* of Kṛttibāsa are frequently regarded as the outstanding and even foundational literary compositions in their respective languages, here Tamil, Avadhi, and Bengali, respectively.

The Rāmāyaṇa as a social text

A second critical level on which the *Rāmāyaṇa* operates powerfully is the social. The poet has skillfully crafted his central characters, and the situations in which they find themselves, to be monovalent examples of idealized positive and negative role models in Hindu society. Thus Rāma is the ideal son, elder brother, husband, monarch, and general exemplar of a favored Hindu norm of masculinity. He is handsome, energetic, brave, compassionate, stoic, and wholly committed to the governing principles of *dharma* by which society, and indeed the entire cosmos, is supposed to be regulated. These traits emerge most clearly in a number of focal episodes in the epic narrative. Particularly noteworthy here is Rāma's calm acceptance of the cruel and unjust exile (*Rāmāyaṇa* 2.16),[1] which he must undergo as a result of Kaikeyī's manipulation of King Daśaratha (2.9–10). At no point does Rāma betray either dejection at his loss of the kingship or even anger at the wickedness of his stepmother. His sole concern is his deference to his father's orders and his preservation of the king's reputation for truthfulness. This easy renunciation and seeming indifference to worldly power and pleasures are among the characteristic traits of the spiritual hero as described in Hindu literary and religious texts from a very early period.

One of the main concerns of the epic poet in the creation of the character of Rāma is a focus on the maintenance of the integrity and harmony of the Hindu joint family. The poet is everywhere eager to portray his hero as ready to sacrifice his personal good for that of the family. In this the *Rāmāyaṇa* contrasts very starkly with its sister epic the *Mahābhārata*, where conflicting interests lead inexorably to the rupture and annihilation of the central ruling house. Although depicted as a supremely competent warrior, Rāma is shown as always willing to take the path of peace, deferring to Bharata (*Rāmāyaṇa* 2.16, 2.99), accepting Vibhīṣaṇa (6.12), and even, it appears, being willing to make peace with the demonic Rāvaṇa should he somehow abandon his evil ways (6.12.21). This, too, contrasts strongly with the implacable enmity and bloodthirsty vengefulness of the warrior heroes of the *Mahābhārata*.

Similarly, figures such as Lakṣmaṇa, Sītā, Kausalyā, and Hanumān represent, respectively, the idealized deferential younger brother, the single-mindedly devoted wife, the virtuous mother, and the perfect servant-devotee. On the other hand, the epic's plethora of monstrously perverse characters, notably the licentious and violent Rāvaṇa himself, represents in uncomplicated form the radical opposite of those models of restraint, decorum, chastity, and deference that the epic idealizes so powerfully. The complex ambiguities, conflicting loyalties, and shades of gray that so characterize the central figures of the *Mahābhārata* are almost nowhere to be seen in Vālmīki's work. In this way, the *Vālmīki Rāmāyaṇa* and many of its subsequent reworkings stand out as among traditional South Asia's most powerful and widely disseminated instruments for the formation of and reinforcement of characteristic social and cultural norms.

Central to Vālmīki's social vision is the powerful valorization of the late Vedic conception of *varṇāsramadharma*. This is the set of the normative rules laid out most clearly in the Dharmaśāstras or law texts. According to these, society is to be ordered by means of a strict social and ritual hierarchy in which each of the four *varṇa*s or social classes knows and maintains its traditional place, status, and duties and each individual, at least those of the higher *varṇa*s, is expected to pass through a prescribed series of life stages. This is the rigid top-down system of the four *varṇa*s: Brāhmaṇ, Kṣatriya, Vaiśya, and Śūdra. Each of these adheres to its immemorial function and defers to the classes above it. In this system, Brāhmaṇs are to be especially respected and feared as the equals or even superiors of the gods themselves. This seminal concern of the Brāhmaṇical literature is nowhere more powerfully illustrated than in the *Bālakāṇḍa*'s extensive treatment of the history of the sage Viśvāmitra and his conflicts with and triumphs over kings, sages, and divinities in the course of his struggle to transform himself from a Kṣatriya to a Brāhmaṇ (*Rāmāyaṇa* 1.50–64). The question of the traditional *āśrama*s or life stages (student, householder, hermit, renunciant) is not explicitly taken up in any elaborate way in the epic but can be seen implicitly in such episodes as that in which King Daśaratha in his old age wishes to renounce the throne in favor of his son (*Rāmāyaṇa* 2.1).

A particularly significant aspect of the social message of the *Vālmīki Rāmāyaṇa* is the way in which the epic poet and his characters deal with the issues of gender and sexuality. In a number of ways, the *Rāmāyaṇa* has become a touchstone in traditional India for the assertion and reinforcement of the power of patriarchal attitudes. Sītā's idealization as the perfect woman and the perfect wife rests centrally on her unwavering subordination to the wishes and interests of her husband. Although she is shown occasionally to question Rāma's decisions, she does so only when his initial decision is at variance with the demands of the normative subordination of women. This, of course, is most clearly seen in the famous episode where Sītā refuses to accede to Rāma's plan to leave her behind when he goes into exile (*Rāmāyaṇa* 2.24). Sītā's lengthy meditations and soliloquies during her captivity (*Rāmāyaṇa* 5.23–24, 5.26), as well as her sharp rebukes of her demonic suitor (5.19–20), focus largely on the issue of gender subordination and the representation of the wife virtually as a form of property of the husband (S. Goldman 2001). In this way Sītā stands in sharp contrast to a figure such as Draupadī, heroine of the *Mahābhārata*, who, aside from having five husbands, is far more outspoken in defense of her rights and privileges as a woman (Sutherland 1989).

Surely, the most critical gender related issue in the *Rāmāyaṇa* in terms of its impact on the lives of the people of South Asia is Rāma's treatment of Sītā after she has been freed from the clutches of the demon-king. The issue is clearly of great importance to Vālmīki, since he highlights it twice in the poem, once during the course of Sītā's *agniparīkṣā* or trial by fire (*Rāmāyaṇa* 6.104–6), and again when she is banished on the strength of vulgar rumors about her conduct in the house of Rāvaṇa (7.44–47). It is noteworthy that the poet constantly stresses the fact that Rāma, for all his harsh treatment of his wife, never for a moment in fact doubts her absolute fidelity. His brutal treatment of Sītā on both occasions, it is stressed, derives from his concern for the loss of honor and prestige that unchecked rumors about the queen's chastity would bring in their train. The Sītātyāga or "abandonment of Sītā" is a somewhat controversial episode and is not present in all versions of the story. Nonetheless it has sent a powerful message.

If Sītā represents the idealization of feminity in Hindu India—chaste, demure, dependent, and soft-spoken—the epic poet has, as in the case of his male characters, given us several striking counterexamples. On the one hand, there is the somewhat ambiguous characterization of Kaikeyī, essentially a good-hearted and devoted, if somewhat simple-minded, mother to her son Bharata, who allows herself to be led away from the path of wifely devotion by her twisted alter ego, the scheming hunchbacked serving maid, Mantharā (Sutherland 1992). Kaikeyī, although she becomes the representation of the proverbial "shrewish wife" in popular imagination (Aklujkar 1999), is quietly rehabilitated by the poet and appears to blend back in with the other mothers at the court of Ayodhyā after the exile of Rāma.

On the other hand, in his characterization of the voracious and voraciously sexual *rākṣasa* women, notably Tāḍakā and Śūrpaṇakhā, the poet has given us dramatic examples of traditional South Asia's nightmare image of feminity run amok. The treatment of Śūrpaṇakhā is in radical contrast to that of Sītā, for whereas the latter is dependent, submissive, generally compliant, and fiercely chaste, the former is independent, outspoken, and, above all, sexually aggressive. The sexual liaison she proposes between Rāma and herself in the *Araṇyakāṇḍa* is treated by the poet and his heroes as ludicrously incongruous and as a source of both amusement and violent retribution (*Rāmāyaṇa* 3.16–17). This attitude contrasts very notably with the parallel situation in the *Mahābhārata* where, with the sanction of his mother and brothers, the Pāṇḍava hero Bhīma enjoys just such a sexual idyll with the *rākṣasa*-woman Hiḍimbā (*Mahābhārata* 1.139–43).[2]

For all its powerful assertion of patriarchal authority and the subordination of women in almost every respect to males, the *Rāmāyaṇa* of Vālmīki puts forward a somewhat gentler vision of masculinity than is to be found in some parallel documents of ancient Hindu culture. Thus, for example, where the warrior heroes of the *Mahābhārata* tend to exemplify a certain brutal, boastful, and vengeful hypermasculinity, Rāma, as noted above, is represented as having his Kṣatriya pride and martial prowess tempered by compassion and concern for the rules of family and society.

Although it is less given to prescriptive passages than the *Mahābhārata* and the Dharmaśāstras, the *Vālmīki Rāmāyaṇa* functions like these works also as a sort of treatise on the political constitution of the early Hindu state. At several points in the narrative it is suggested that kingship is regarded as partaking of divinity (Pollock 1991: 15–54). Additionally, much of the narrative revolves around the critical issues of royal legitimacy and succession. This is true not only in the realm of the Solar dynasty of Kosala but also among the monkeys of Kiṣkindhā and even the *rākṣasa*s of Laṅkā. The *Ayodhyākāṇḍa* in particular sheds interesting light on the ancient conception of kingship, illustrating a situation where King Daśaratha appears to have to engage in at least ceremonial consultation with his citizens and advisors before naming Rāma as his successor (*Rāmāyaṇa* 2.1.34–2.2).

Perhaps the most enduring legacy of the *Vālmīki Rāmāyaṇa* for the political life of South Asia has been its positing of the possibility of a utopian kingdom under the authority of a perfectly righteous ruler for whom Rāma would be the archetype. This conception is brought forward especially in the *Bālakāṇḍa* and *Uttarakāṇḍa* with their descriptions of Rāma's kingdom as being free from crime, disease, poverty, natural disasters, social strife, and so on, and is clearly illustrated in the episode of Rāma's slaying of the Śūdra ascetic mentioned earlier. Such a conception has had significant implications both for the redefinition of the Hindu state in late medieval India and for a powerful vision of the construction of a post-independence Indian utopia in the modern era. There is some evidence that Hindu monarchs of the medieval period confronted with the threat of the alien forces of Islam turned increasingly to the *Rāmāyaṇa* as a source for the revalorization of a specific notion of divine Hindu kingship (Pollock 1993).

In more modern times, political leaders ranging from Mahātmā Gandhi to Rajiv Gandhi and the ideologues of the resurgent Hindu right have frequently raised the slogan of "Rāmrājya," the idealized integral Hindu polity, as a mobilizing strategy. The ideological and emotional force derived from this aspect of the *Rāmāyaṇa* is such that it is no accident that the leaders of the Bharatiya Janata party identified the issue of the "Rāmajanmabhūmi"—the campaign to erect a temple dedicated to Rāma in place of an existing mosque at the site traditionally believed to be his birthplace—as the one that would vault them into positions of power.

The *Rāmāyaṇa* has also played a role in the area of ethics in traditional India. As the ideal man and ideal monarch, Rāma is everywhere held up as the paragon of ethical behavior, scrupulously following all the rules put forward by the culture of *dharma*. In this he is, again, often in contrast with the parallel epic heroes of the *Mahābhārata*, who frequently engage in unethical and even vicious behavior in the name of achieving higher goals of righteousness (R. Goldman 1997). Rāma makes a particularly interesting and enlightening contrast with his fellow *avatāra*, Kṛṣṇa, who, as he is represented in texts such as the *Harivaṃśa*, *Mahābhārata*, *Bhāgavata Purāṇa*, and the like, blithely transcends the rules of sexual, social, and ethical propriety. Rāma is, of course, most starkly to be contrasted with the great antihero of the *Rāmāyaṇa*, Rāvaṇa, giving rise to such popular moralizing prescriptions as "You should always try to behave like Rāma, never like Rāvaṇa."

Rāma's ethical conduct is so heavily stressed that those few instances in which it has been called into question, whether in Vālmīki's text or by later authors, have tended to loom large in the popular consciousness. The two episodes most often cited in this regard are Rāma's killing of the monkey-king Vālin from ambush in the *Kiṣkindhākāṇḍa* (*Rāmāyaṇa* 4.17–19) and the abandonment and exile of his blameless, pregnant wife Sītā (7.44) (R. Goldman 1997). The former incident is the subject of lively debate between Vālin and Rāma in the text itself, in which the stricken monkey sharply castigates Rāma for what he sees as a gross violation of the rules of combat. Rāma rejects Vālin's criticism on a number of grounds, and his arguments succeed in satisfying the monkey that he had indeed acted in accordance with *dharma*. Nonetheless, the issue has continued to haunt the imagination of *Rāmāyaṇa* commentators and audiences to the present day, as evidenced in such documents as the popular *Rāmāyaṇaśaṅkāvalī*s in which contemporary preachers and authors respond to "doubts" or questions on the part of the faithful.

The ethical issue raised by the abandonment of Sītā is not explicitly engaged in Vālmīki's text. The only hint the poet gives us of the controversial nature of Rāma's decision is the fact that Rāma forbids his brothers, on pain of suffering dire consequences, from questioning or criticizing it (*Rāmāyaṇa* 7.44.18). Nonetheless, this seemingly cruel and unjust treatment of the devoted and virtuous Sītā has disturbed readers of the text from ancient times down to the present. The great poet-playwright, Bhavabhūti, in his eighth-century drama the *Uttararāmacarita*, has several of his characters, most notably Rāma himself, roundly condemn the cruelty of his treatment of Sītā (R. Goldman 1997: 201). Later authors such as the immensely influential Tulasīdāsa confront the issue with a magisterial silence, excising the entire episode from their renderings of the Rāma story. This issue grew heated once again during the production of the popular Indian television serialization of the tale, the *Ramayan* of Ramanand Sagar. The question of whether or not to include the epilogue representing the rejection of Sītā led to political conflict, labor unrest, and litigation that pitted a sweeper caste identifying itself with Vālmīki against high-caste Hindu groups (Jain 1988: 81). The controversy was only resolved through a very delicate rendering of the episode on the part of Sagar, who, treating it from a kind of feminist perspective, makes Sītā, and not Rāma, the author of her own banishment (Tully 1991: 132–33).

The Rāmāyaṇa as a religious text

Perhaps the most dramatic impact the *Rāmāyaṇa* has had on Hindu culture and civilization, particularly in the medieval and modern periods, lies in the area of religion. As noted earlier, the received text of the *Vālmīki Rāmāyaṇa* in all versions and recensions identifies Rāma as an *avatāra* of the supreme divinity Viṣṇu at various points in the poem. The history of this identification has been, as we shall discuss next, a matter of some scholarly dispute. However, it is fair to say that for the overwhelming majority of Hindus, the main thrust of the epic story is the exemplary narrative of god's birth and career as a man engaged in the central avatāric mission of the salvation of the virtuous, the destruction of evildoers, and the reestablishment of *dharma* as the governing principle of the cosmos. The identification of Rāma with Viṣṇu, like that of Kṛṣṇa in the *Mahābhārata*, is both textually and theologically complex. The theological complexity derives from the fact that one of the features of the principal human *avatāra*s is the ambiguity with which the incarnation is represented as both man and god and yet neither clearly one nor the other and the fact that the nature of the incarnate divinity is often represented as occluded even to himself (R. Goldman 1995). The liminal status of the *avatāra* is particularly pronounced in the case of Rāma, since by the terms of Rāvaṇa's boon, the demon cannot be destroyed by a simple god (Pollock 1991: 15–43). Although Vālmīki's poem seems thoroughly suffused with the notion of Rāma's divinity, the work only sporadically takes on an intensely devotional tone, focusing more centrally on the narrative, aesthetic, and exemplary aspects of the story. In this, it contrasts with the many later renderings of the tale, some of which, notably for example, the *Rāmcaritmānas* of Tulasīdāsa, are deeply and thoroughly permeated with an intense spirit of Rāma-*bhakti* or devotion to Rāma as a personal savior.

Although there seems to be only scanty evidence for the large-scale cultic worship of Rāma as a temple divinity prior to around the ninth century CE (Pollock 1993), the practice became widespread in the centuries following that time. Rāma temples sprang up throughout India, and Rāma and Sītā emerged as the central sectarian divinities of a wide variety of religious traditions, ranging from the Viśiṣṭādvaita schools of Rāmānuja and his followers based largely on Vālmīki, through the mainstream North Indian devotional tradition textually grounded in Tulasīdāsa, to the esoteric gender-bending beliefs and praxis of the *rasik sādhus* of Ayodhya (van der Veer 1988), who canonize the obscure and esoteric

Bhuśuṇḍi Rāmāyaṇa (Keislar 1998). Rāma has, as noted earlier, also become a central icon of Hindu religious and political revivalism, especially in the north. Certainly by the time of the composition of the early Mahapurāṇas, Rāma has become virtually universally accepted as one of the standard Vaiṣṇava Purāṇic group of the ten *avatāra*s of Viṣṇu (Brockington 1984: 233–41). Some of the later Vaiṣṇava Purāṇas show a more complex sense of the Rāma-*avatāra*, regarding Daśaratha's four sons, whom Vālmīki already recognizes as partial incarnations of Viṣṇu (*Rāmāyaṇa* 1.17.6–9), as corresponding to the four manifestations (*vyūha*) of Viṣṇu as they are represented in the Pañcarātra school of Vaiṣṇava theology (Brockington 1984: 236).

In addition to the towering figure as Rāma as god-become-man, two other major characters in the epic story have acquired significant religious identities of their own. The first of these, of course, is Sītā. Since Rāma is generally acknowledged to be one of the principal incarnations of Viṣṇu, it follows that his wife Sītā must be a corresponding manifestation of Viṣṇu's consort, the goddess Śrī or Lakṣmī, although this is not made as clearly explicit in Vālmīki's poem as is Rāma's identification with Viṣṇu. As such, Sītā, along with Rāma, becomes a focal object of worship as she is part of the divine couple or *yugal sarkar* central to some forms of Vaiṣṇava temple worship. In some religious traditions, such as those of the *rasik sādhu*s (van der Veer 1988) and the Śrīvaiṣṇavas, Sītā may be foregrounded as an object of devotion or approached in her motherly aspect as the principal intercessor between the worshiper and the lord (Mumme 1991). In some Śākta traditions, particularly in eastern India, Sītā emerges clearly as the dominant member of the divine couple, and it is her power as the goddess that enables Rāma to defeat his demonic foes. In some cases, she is actually called upon to rescue him from them (W. L. Smith 1988).

The second of these figures is the semidivine monkey-hero Hanumān, the partial incarnation of the Vedic wind-god Vāyu. This fascinating figure achieves enormous status in the Vaiṣṇava tradition in his role as the *paramarāmabhakta* or supreme exemplar of devotion to Lord Rāma. As such, he is extolled in many versions of the Rāma story and is a regular figure in plastic representations of the story and its major characters. But the popularity of Hanumān is such that it extends well beyond the cult of Rāma and the celebration of the *Rāmakathā*. He is widely worshiped as a divinity in his own right in connections that are either utterly separate from the *Rāmāyaṇa* story or at best only tangentially connected to it. As such, he has taken on many roles as a divine intercessor. He is the patron divinity of the *akhāṛā*, the wrestlers' pit of North and western India, the highest recourse for those afflicted with spirit possession, a much invoked aid in connection with fertility and even a stalwart defender of the Republic of India against the perceived threat of Pakistan. Indeed, it has been asserted that of all the manifold divinities in worship among the diverse communities of Hindu India, Hanumān, whose shrines seem to appear on every street corner, is the most widely worshiped of all (Goldman and Goldman 1994; Ludvik 1994; Lutgendorf 1997).

THE RĀMĀYAṆA IN INDIA AND BEYOND

In the more than two thousand years since the composition of the *Vālmīki Rāmāyaṇa*, the Rāma story has undergone a truly extraordinary number of reworkings at the hands of authors composing in every major language and belonging to every significant indigenous religious tradition of the vast, rich, and diverse cultural domains throughout Asia. In one form or another, the text has been widely available and continually in use by countless hundreds of millions of people for as long or longer than virtually any non-Indian text still known and imbibed by a mass audience.

The almost staggering profusion of *Rāmāyaṇa* versions in the high literary, folk, and—more recently—popular genres of the region is, first and foremost, a consequence of the tremendous importance that many traditional cultures of Asia have placed upon the story. These versions have been multiplied many times in Sanskrit, Prakrit, and the regional languages of India and beyond at every chronological stage in their development. The epic, moreover, along with its characters and central themes has been appropriated by virtually every religious, philosophical, and sectarian tradition in the long history of the cultures of South and Southeast Asia. All of this serves as a demonstration that the text was seen as being of absolutely seminal importance, so much so that regional and sectarian audiences needed to have versions available to them that they could understand and which adapted the epic story to the various and changing needs of all segments of the society.

From as far back as the tools of textual criticism can take us, the monumental Sanskrit poem had already been differentiated into a number of regional recensions and subrecensions written down in virtually every area and script of India. In addition, the epic story was reworked numerous times for inclusion into other Sanskrit texts, such as the *Mahābhārata*, many Purāṇas, and numerous religious and philosophical texts. Versions of this sort are the *Rāmopākhyāna* of the *Mahābhārata*, the *Ānandarāmāyaṇa*, the *Adhyātmarāmāyaṇa*, the *Yogavāsiṣṭha*, and the like (Brockington 1984: 233–41). The Rāma story, moreover, became a favorite theme of the poets and playwrights of classical Sanskrit. Numerous Sanskrit literary works explore particular aspects of the complex Rāma story, and although some of these are now lost or known only as fragments (Raghavan 1961), poetic masterpieces, such as the *Raghuvaṃśa* of Kālidāsa, the *Bhaṭṭikāvya*, and the *Rāmāyaṇacampū*, and important Sanskrit dramas, such as the *Pratimānāṭaka* of Bhāsa and the *Mahāvīracarita* and *Uttararāmacarita* of Bhavabhūti, are still read and deeply enjoyed by those conversant with Sanskrit.

Nor are the versions of the *Rāmāyaṇa* restricted to the cultural universe of Hindu India. Despite, or perhaps because of, the fact that the epic's hero, Rāma, came very early onto be regarded as one of the principal *avatāra*s of the great Hindu divinity Viṣṇu, a central figure of devotional Hinduism, his story was of such importance and popularity that even non-Hindu groups, such as the Buddhists and the Jainas, rapidly learned the value of adapting the *Rāmāyaṇa* to serve the propagation of their own religious systems.

The Rāma story was appropriated early by the Buddhists. Thus the historical Buddha is often said to have been born in a branch of the Ikṣvāku dynasty whose greatest hero was Rāma. The Rāma story in its various parts figures significantly in the important Jātaka tales, which provide a transmigrational biography of the previous births of the Bodhisattva, the future Buddha. One of them, the *Daśaratha Jātaka*, recounts a version of the epic story that completely excises its central avatāric narrative of the rapacious demon king and his abduction of Sītā, focusing instead on Rāma Paṇḍita's legendary self-control as an exemplary illustration of this cardinal Buddhist virtue. In another, the *Sāma Jātaka*, the *Ayodhyākāṇḍa* episode in which the banishment of Rāma is attributed to a curse laid upon his father for having, in his youth, accidentally slain the son of a blind ascetic couple, is reworked with a different cast of characters. In this reading, Rāma is in fact one of the earlier incarnations of the Bodhisattva. Moreover, Vālmīki's poem is known to and admired by the first century CE Buddhist poet Aśvaghoṣa who not only alludes to the *Rāmāyaṇa*'s representation of Vālmīki as the first poet but also clearly uses his creation as the model for his poetic biography of the Buddha, the *Buddhacarita*.

Jaina authors especially make the Rāma legend their own, regarding Rāma not, of course, as an *avatāra* of godhead but as one of the thirty-two *śalākāpuruṣa*s or exemplary Jaina laymen and the hero of numerous Jaina Rāmāyaṇas such as the *Paumacariya* in both Sanskrit and Prakrit (Narasimhachar 1939). Here even the martial character of the epic warrior-hero, the scourge of the demonic *rākṣasa*s, must give way before the Jaina imperative of *ahiṃsā*, noninjury, to all living beings. Thus the Hindu *avatāra*'s central and most defining act, the slaughter of his ten-headed nemesis, Rāvaṇa, is, in Jaina versions of the tale, assigned to his loyal younger brother Lakṣmaṇa.

In the regional languages of India, the influence of the *Rāmāyaṇa* has been even more profound. In virtually all of the major literary languages of India, there exists a significant and immensely popular version of the epic that is regarded as marking the very beginning of that language's literary tradition. Such, for example, is the popularity and prestige of poems, such as Kṛttibāsa' Bengali *Rāmāyaṇa*, Kampa<u>n</u>'s Tamil *Irāmāvatāram*, and the massively popular devotional rendering of the sixteenth-century epic in the Old Avadhi dialect of Hindi, the *Rāmcaritmānas* of the scholar-poet Tulasīdāsa, widely revered among the three hundred million inhabitants of the "Hindi Belt" of North India.

Even these powerful and hegemonic regional versions of the *Rāmāyaṇa* do not exhaust the diversity of the poem. Each region has, in addition to this kind of major literary *nachdichtung,* many other versions, performative and literary, oral and written. In this category may be noted the various Rāmalīlās of North India, the Jātra plays of Bengal, and the many folk versions and dance-dramas of the *Rāmāyaṇa* story known from every region of the subcontinent. One recent author has noted and described some fifty different literary Rāmāyaṇas from the eastern states of Bengal, Assam, and Orissa alone, each with a different religious, aesthetic, or ethical thrust (W. L. Smith 1988). In addition, the Rāma story has virtually saturated the plastic arts of South Asia in innumerable temple sculptures and reliefs, court paintings and folk painting, and even the ubiquitous commercial "calendar" art.

A text of such massive diffusion that has permeated the "high" and folk traditions of textual composition as well as the visual arts of both pan-Indian and regional cultures for nearly three millennia can hardly have failed to make a profound impression on the popular culture of modern cosmopolitan India. The nature of this impression can be judged by an examination of the media of popular culture in both their elite forms and those that are consumed by a mass audience. A survey of modern Indian literature from the time of the nineteenth-century Bengali poet Michael Madhusudan Dutt down to Salman Rushdie reveals that the Rāma story and its themes and characters appear to continually haunt the imagination of the modern writer in the colonial and postcolonial period. A survey of Indian cinema yields similar results. For not only have the producers of the popular Hindi musicals exploited various aspects of the story but also the story of Rāma has formed a rich source for the makers of the popular "mythologicals," such as Homi Wadia's *Hanuman Chalisa* and the Telugu *Sampoorna Ramayana*. Even the art films of such auteurs as Aravindan in his *Kancana Sita* and the "avant garde" Akshara Theater's production of *Ramayana* have based their works on the epic tale.

Nowhere, perhaps, has the immense popularity of the *Rāmāyaṇa* been demonstrated more clearly and dramatically than by the extraordinary success of the lengthy serialization of the epic created for Doordarshan, the Indian government television network, by the filmmaker Ramanand Sagar. This production was originally broadcast throughout India in weekly half-hour episodes and has since been widely marketed there and throughout the world in the form of video cassettes and DVDs. Newspaper and eyewitness accounts describe how the showings would empty the bustling streets and *bāzārs* of the country, leaving an impression of desolation as people, often having bathed and dressed as for worship, would gather in front of television screens to watch the unfolding of the ancient and well-known story with rapt attention. The tremendous political and cultural aspects of this phenomenal success have already been the subject of a considerable body of journalistic and scholarly analysis. Indeed as recent events—many of them tragic—have demonstrated, the influence of the *Rāmāyaṇa* on the hearts and minds of the Indian people—far from waning with time—has grown both more powerful and more apparent in recent years.

But the cultural saturation of the Rāma story is by no means confined to the Indian subcontinent. As is well known to students of Southeast Asia, the *Rāmāyaṇa* has achieved a position of productive cultural centrality in virtually all of the countries of this far-flung and highly diverse region. In Buddhist Thailand the *Rāmakien* becomes a sort of foundational epic for the Ayutthayan dynasty (1409–1767 CE) which names its descendants after the epic hero (Rāma I, II, and so on). At least six or seven poetic or dramatic versions of the story, many of which are attributed to the various king Rāmas, are widely known and performed (H. Sarkar 1983). In Laos the *Phra Lak Phra Lam* and the *Gvāy Dvoraḥbī* give eloquent testimony to the localization and naturalization (to use Sachchidanand Sahai's phrase) of the epic in a variety of milieus (Sahai 1976). In Islamic Malaysia and Indonesia, as is well known, the Rāma story in the form of texts such as the *Hikayat Seri Rāma*, the Javanese *Rāmāyaṇa Kakawin*, the widespread and diverse styles of *wayang* or shadow puppet theater, and the temple sculptures of such complexes as Prambanan have established the story of Rāma there regarded as the model of an Islamic prince, as one of the region's principal cultural artifacts and acculturative devices (Sweeney 1972, 1980). The *Rāmāyaṇa* tradition is well attested in Burma with the performance tradition of the *Yāma-pwe*. Moreover, it has deeply saturated traditional Cambodian culture in a wide variety of forms, including various literary renderings of the Rāma story, such as the *Rāmakerti* from around the sixteenth century CE (Pou 1977), and the famous reliefs at Angkor Wat (Han and Zaw 1980). In Sri Lanka the literary rendering of the story attributed to the sixth-century CE monarch Kumāradāsa, the *Jānakīharaṇa*, is thought to be the earliest Sanskrit work to be found in that country (Godakumbura 1980). Even as far as the Philippines we find texts such as the *Maharadia Lawana*, current among the Maranao ethnic group from perhaps the seventeenth century, which have kept the story, derived here no doubt from Malay sources, alive (Francisco 1980).

But the *Rāmāyaṇa* story has spread in other directions as well. It has traveled to the West where there are a number of poorly studied Persian versions of the tale and notably to the North and East. J. W. de Jong (1983) and others have studied and translated the Tibetan manuscripts of the *Rāmāyaṇa* found at Tun-huang, while the Mongolian scholar T. S. Damdinsuren (1980) has discovered and studied four versions of varying length in Mongolian as well as three Tibetan versions. Khotanese versions have been found at

Tun-huang as well. Mongolian versions appear to have come from Tibet, and their influence can in turn be found as far north into Central Asia, as a Kalmuk folk version of the epic has been preserved in manuscript form in the Siberian branch of the Russian Academy of Sciences (Chandra 1980: 651–52).

Although the presence and the destiny of the *Rāmāyaṇa* story in East Asia is harder to trace than in some other areas of the continent where its influence is pervasive, it is no less real and may, in some ways, be more interesting. There can be little doubt that some versions, particularly those found in the Jātakas and other Buddhist sources, would have been known to Chinese scholars from the early centuries CE. K'ang-seng-hui, for example, is said to have translated Jātaka tales into Chinese in 251 CE, and other versions followed in the ensuing centuries as the passion for the translation of Indic Buddhist texts into Chinese grew into a virtual cottage industry. It is also well known, as mentioned earlier, that Tibetan and Khotanese texts of the *Rāmāyaṇa* were kept in the cave library at Tun-huang along with the *pien-wen* manuscripts of early Chinese literary texts (Dudbridge 1970: 160–61). Indeed, it has been a subject of extensive scholarly debate as to whether, and to what extent, the character of the hero of the famous sixteenth-century novel *Hsi-yu chi* (The Divine Monkey), Sun Wu-k'ung, and his antecedents in Chinese literature may have been inspired by Hanumān, the monkey divinity and hero of the *Rāmāyaṇa* tradition, who shares many of his characteristics and exploits.

From China, it is hardly surprising to note, versions of the Rāma legend made their way in time to Japan. The Japanese Sanskrit scholar Minoru Hara has studied two interesting texts derived from Chinese Buddhist sources. The first is an abridgement of the Rāma legend found in the twelfth-century collection of popular tales, the *Hobutsushu* of Tairano Yasuyori that appears to derive from a Chinese canonical *Liu-po-lo-mi-ching* (otherwise known as *Liu-tu-tsi-ching* or *Rokudojikkyo*, the Six Pāramitāsūtra). The second, a rendering of the *Rāmāyaṇa* episode in which Daśaratha is cursed for accidentally killing a blind ascetic couple's son, is from a tenth-century collection of tales, the *Sambo-ekotoba* of Minamotono Tamenori, derived, no doubt, from the canonical version of the *Sāma Jātaka*. In addition to these Buddhist canonical sources, which inspired, it would seem, popular literary authors, Hara hypothesizes that the Rāma story may have made its way into popular or courtly circulation directly from the oral versions narrated by Hindu savants, such as Bharadvāja Bodhisena, who were known to have visited Japan from the eighth century onwards (Hara 1983). In East Asia, as in the rest of the continent, the *Rāmāyaṇa* story has been fully localized and naturalized and is rarely regarded as belonging to an exotic or alien culture.

LITERARY AND SCHOLARLY TREATMENT OF THE RĀMĀYAṆA IN INDIA AND BEYOND

It is hardly surprising that a text that has had so diverse and profound an impact on the civilization of India for so long a period should have given rise to numerous additional works and representations in the spheres of literary and artistic production, the performing arts, folklore, philosophical and religious discourse, and scholarly and commentarial analysis both in India and in the West. No doubt the oldest and most sustained surviving corpus of scholarly analysis of the *Vālmīki Rāmāyaṇa* is that contained in the substantial body of Sanskrit commentaries the work inspired in India. These, of which some forty-five survive in whole or part (Bhatt and Shah 1960–75, 7: 655–56), were composed largely between the twelfth and eighteenth centuries CE (R. Goldman 1984: 115–17; Lefeber 1994: 17–28). They vary considerably in their density and in the textual and substantive issues they address, ranging from the very sparse gloss attributed to Rāmānuja, to thoroughgoing analytical treatises like the *Dharmākūtam* of Tryambakarāya Makhin. However, they collectively present us with a diverse and learned set of readings of the poem by a series of scholars for whom it was of more than purely intellectual interest and who, one may say, more closely approximate the "intended audience" of the epic than any other readers who have left us written records of their responses to it. As such, these commentaries constitute a critical resource for our own understanding of the poem and of its receptive history. It is a pity that these works have not, for the most part, been taken seriously or even read in many cases by modern Western and Indian students of the epic.

It must be noted by way of background to the contributions of the Sanskrit commentaries that they are rarely if ever works of the sort of disinterested or objective scholarship that was unquestioningly associated with European and European-style Orientalism in the pre-Saidian era. Most of the works—when they are more than mere glosses—are the products of scholars associated with one or another school of Śrīvaiṣṇavism, for which religious system the *Vālmīki Rāmāyaṇa* is *the* foundational text. From this it follows that the vast majority of surviving Sanskrit commentaries on the text, and virtually all of the significantly analytical ones, are associated with one or another of the manuscript traditions of the southern recension or with the mixed recensional versions recorded in the Devanagari script and affiliated largely with the southern text. As such, several of the surviving commentaries, notably those of Maheśvaratīrtha, Nāgeśa Bhaṭṭa, Govindarāja, Mādhavayogin, and Satyatīrtha, concern themselves to a greater or lesser extent with the numerous theological issues that present themselves during a reading of the poem, particularly from a Vaiṣṇava perspective. These commentators are by no means in any kind of agreement as to these issues and often debate and quarrel with the interpretations of their predecessors, whom they may quote with approbation or revile in the strongest possible terms.

But this said, it must be acknowledged that the Sanskrit commentaries are important repositories of scholarly information and interpretation. Their authors draw on vast, even encyclopedic knowledge of the śāstraic literature to shed considerable light on the innumerable grammatical, lexical, rhetorical, and textual problems that a work such as the *Vālmīki Rāmāyaṇa* inevitably presents. In the textual area, particularly, it is noteworthy that the commentators pay careful attention to the textual variants available to them and earlier commentators and make interesting judgments as to the spuriousness and authenticity of individual verses and passages. In addition, they provide much useful information about the realia, flora, fauna, architecture, technology, and social and religious customs, which they associate with the epic period. While it must be acknowledged that the commentators cannot be regarded as a univocal or infallible resource, coming as they do many centuries later than the composition of the *Rāmāyaṇa* text and frequently disagreeing among themselves, they are at least tacitly aware of the speculative nature of much *Rāmāyaṇa* exegesis and remain an essential source for contemporary *Rāmāyaṇa* scholarship.

The antiquity of the *Rāmāyaṇa* and its centrality to Hindu and larger Indian civilization over the millennia early on attracted the attention of European savants interested in

Sanskrit and the culture of which it was the principal medium. The text of Vālmīki was edited by William Carey and Joshua Marshman in the opening years of the nineteenth century (1806–10), and scholarly interest in the text and its message gained force and momentum steadily through the nineteenth and twentieth century. Early European scholarship on the *Rāmāyaṇa*, in many ways like that stimulated by the *Mahābhārata*, concerned itself with the issues of the sources and historicity of the story. Some scholars such as Albrecht Weber (1872) viewed the poem as derivative of what he saw as earlier texts, notably the *Daśaratha Jātaka* and even the Homeric epics. Others saw the work as kind of extended allegory referring to historical, natural, or mythological events. Thus Christian Lassen (1866–74, 1) interpreted the epic as a coded reminiscence of the Āryan subjugation of the Dravidian south, while J. Talboys Wheeler (1867–81, 2: 1–406) saw in it the conquest of the Buddhist civilization of Ceylon (Sri Lanka). Victor Henry (1904: 162–67) read the text as the reflection of ancient solar mythology, while Hermann Jacobi (1893: 120–39) saw in it a revision of the Ṛg Vedic myth of Indra and Vṛtra. A. Weber (1872), likewise, additionally read the epic story as a myth alluding to the cycle of agricultural growth. In fact, the *Rāmāyaṇa*, like the *Mahābhārata*, presented itself as a fertile field for the popular theories of textual interpretation of the nineteenth century (Brockington 1998: 48–52; R. Goldman 1984: 14–29).

Rāmāyaṇa studies in the twentieth century underwent an explosive growth during the course of which Vālmīki's epic and the many other retellings the Rāma story from virtually all parts of Asia have been studied and subjected to analyses that take into account the diverse linguistic, textual, historical, literary, rhetorical, religious, political, social, and psychological aspects of the *Rāmāyaṇa* tradition in its various settings. It would be impossible within the scope of this discussion to even begin to scratch the surface of the enormous body of *Rāmāyaṇa* scholarship in dozens of languages that has appeared in print (Brockington 1998; Krishnamoorty 1991; Stientencron, Gietz, Malinar, Kollmann, Schreiner, and Brockington 1992). However, a few central questions and issues concerning the text of Vālmīki have tended to stand out in the discussions of scholars and continue to inspire learned debate. These issues center around the distinction—also important in *Mahābhārata* studies—between the so-called synthetic and analytic interpretations of the text. One such issue concerns the textual history of the poem itself. Jacobi (1893: 55–59) argued that the first and last books of the epic as we know it are later additions to a central core consisting of what are now Books 2 to 6. Similarly, he argued that the central portions of the fifth book or the *Sundarakāṇḍa*, the episodes that deal with Hanumān's exploits in Laṅkā, are later than the older portions of that book. These assertions have stimulated a lively and still ongoing debate about the epic's textual history (Brockington 1998: 377–97; R. Goldman 1984: 60–81; Goldman and Goldman 1996: 87–91). This discussion has, of course, involved controversy about the date of the text as well (Brockington 1998: 379–83; R. Goldman 1984: 14–23).

One particularly controversial issue associated with this type of analysis concerns the question of whether or not earliest strata of Vālmīki's text recognizes Rāma as an *avatāra* of the supreme divinity Viṣṇu. Some early European scholars argued that textual evidence supported the view that the oldest portions of the poem do not regard the hero in this way (Jacobi 1893: 61, 65; Muir 1967, 4: 441–81), while some more recent authorities have taken an opposite view (Pollock 1991: 15–55). The issue is still a matter of debate among *Rāmāyaṇa* scholars (Brockington 1998: 464–72). Interest in issues such as these and many others relevant to a deeper understanding of the *Vālmīki Rāmāyaṇa* has been reignited in recent years by the completion of the critical edition of the text by scholars at the Oriental Institute at Baroda (Bhatt and Shah 1960–75) and by the appearance of a translation of the critical text accompanied by elaborate introductions and copious annotations in which these and other scholarly issues are discussed (R. Goldman 1984–96).

Contemporary scholarship on the *Rāmāyaṇa* ranges widely over the intellectual spectrum with many interesting studies being undertaken in the field from such diverse disciplinary perspectives as feminist and gender studies (S. Goldman 2001), psychological analysis (R. Goldman 1978), performance studies (Blackburn 1996; Schechner 1985), religious (Lutgendorf 1991b), political (Pollock 1993), folkloric (Ramanujan 1991b; Singh and Datta 1993), and so on. The diversity of disciplinary approaches to the study of the *Rāmāyaṇa* in all its many manifestations has given rise over the past few decades to numerous monographs and anthologies concerned with the manifold aspects of the tradition (Iyengar 1983; Richman 1991; Singh and Datta 1993; Thiel-Horstmann 1991). So rich is the *Rāmāyaṇa* in implications for the study of all aspects of traditional and modern South Asia that it is likely that scholarly interest in this great textual tradition will continue in the coming decades and develop in as yet unanticipated dimensions.

CONCLUSION

In conclusion, it is safe to say that no full or deeply nuanced understanding of the cultures and societies of South and Southeast Asia can be achieved without at least a basic familiarity with the plot, characters, and central themes of the Rāma story first introduced to a broad audience by the legendary poet-sage Vālmīki in his immortal epic, the Rāmāyaṇa. The destiny of this extraordinary work and its unparalleled influence on the arts, cultures, societies, and religions of the region from the middle of the first millennium BCE down to the present day have amply validated Lord Brahmā's prophecy concerning the longevity of the poem:

yāvat sthāsyanti girayaḥ saritaśca mahītale |
tāvat rāmāyaṇakathā lokeṣu pracariṣyati || 1.2.35

As long as the mountains and rivers shall endure upon the earth,
so long will the story of the *Rāmāyaṇa* be current throughout the worlds.

NOTES

1 All *Rāmāyaṇa* references are to the critical edition published in Baroda.
2 The *Mahābhārata* reference is to the critical edition published in Pune.

CHAPTER FIVE

PURĀṆA

Velcheru Narayana Rao

Purāṇa is a general term used to refer to a large number of religious texts, most of them composed in Sanskrit, which defy ready description, classification, authorship, or dating. Despite this obvious difficulty, efforts to assign authorship, classify, date, and describe them have been made both within the Hindu tradition and outside the tradition by modern scholars. This chapter is an effort to present the indigenous concepts of the Purāṇa and to provide a brief overview of modern scholarship on the Purāṇas.

INDIGENOUS CONCEPTS OF THE PURĀṆA

Traditionally, Vyāsa is believed to be the author of all Purāṇas. The son of Parāśara, Vyāsa, also known as Kṛṣṇa Dvaipāyana, was born an adult and had direct access to perfect knowledge of everything past, present, and future. Vyāsa was also the editor of the Veda, which he had divided into four parts: *Ṛg*, *Yajur*, *Sāma*, and *Atharva*. Authorship by such a superhuman person elevates the Purāṇas to an infallible status and endows them with a coherent meaning. The disparate texts themselves include a variety of contents, which in fact are not organized coherently. However, the idea that such a powerful personality as Vyāsa is the single author of these many texts encourages the readers/listeners trained in the culture to see a coherent meaning throughout despite apparent inconsistencies. Tradition also speaks of the Purāṇa as a broad genre, including the epic texts. While it is generally stated that there are eighteen Purāṇas and eighteen more Upapurāṇas or minor Purāṇas, the fact is that there are a lot more than thirty-six texts. It is difficult to list all the names under which the various texts are known in different parts of India or to arrive at a firm textual boundary to each text. Such textual flexibility of the Purāṇas was accepted in the tradition with no anxiety. No one seriously concerned themselves with minor variations between one version of a text and the other or for that matter even when the variations were huge, as is well known in the case of *Skanda Purāṇa*.

In contrast, the Vedas, included in the class of *śruti* (revealed texts), are considered fixed, unalterable, and beyond translation. They were rarely put into writing but were memorized with meticulous care to their word order, accent, and stress. The Hindu tradition speaks of the Purāṇas as texts that expand on the Vedas and considers them compliments of each other. The Purāṇas renew themselves and adapt to the changing times by including new material and new meanings, while the Vedas keep the religion unified and authorized under their inflexible verbal power. This allowed Hinduism a flexibility unavailable for the religions of the book, such as Christianity or Islam, which depend upon one single source, the Bible or the Qur'ān, for both divine word and meaning.

The interdependence of the Purāṇas and the Veda is best stated in the following frequently quoted verses, which occur in many Purāṇas (for instance, in *Vāyu* 1.200) and the *Mahābhārata* as well (Rocher 1986: 15, 15n10): "The Brāhmaṇ who learns his four Vedas along with their Upaniṣads and ancillary texts does not become a learned man until he learns the Purāṇas. The Veda has to be expanded with the aid of the epics and the Purāṇas. The Veda itself fears a man of little learning lest he should hurt it."

The complementarity of the Vedas and the Purāṇas is crucial for an understanding of the text culture of Brāhmaṇic Hinduism. It is as if the two inseparable components of language—the sound of an utterance and its meaning, the signifier and the signified—have been split apart and located in two separate groups of texts perceived as one unit. The Veda is considered to be *śabdapradhāna*, that which is important for its sound, and therefore untranslatable and unchangeable. The Purāṇa is *arthapradhāna,* that which is important for its meaning. This classification allows the Purāṇas to be told in many different ways as long their meaning is kept unaltered. Their meaning is authorized by Vyāsa, but the actual text in which Purāṇas are written may vary depending on the choice of the *paurāṇika*. Such freedom in reworking the texts gave modern scholars the impression that the Purāṇas are loose and disorganized, where any *paṇḍita* with a modicum of Sanskrit changed and added sections as he pleased. Despite these allegations, the Purāṇas are a genre with well-recognized stylistic features, understood and respected by the *paurāṇika*s and the listening public. The popularity of these texts, as evidenced by a huge number of manuscript copies disseminated all over India and the adaptations and translations into many regional languages, attests to the widespread community approval of these texts. The Purāṇas were also rewritten in many languages with alterations and embellishments appropriate to the language into which they were rewritten. The fifteenth-century rewriting of the *Bhāgavata Purāṇa* by the Telugu poet Bammera Potana illustrates the transformations a Sanskrit Purāṇa could undergo when it is retold in a regional language (Shulman 1993).

WHAT THE PURĀṆAS SAY ABOUT THEMSELVES

As highly intertextual and self-conscious texts, the Purāṇas themselves are a useful source to learn about the Purāṇas. The *Viṣṇu* (3.6.15ff.), *Agni* (271.11ff.), *Vāyu* (61.55ff.), and *Brahmāṇḍa* (2.35.63ff.) *Purāṇa*s say that Vyāsa composed a *Purāṇa Saṃhitā* (Rocher 1986: 45–46). He gave it to his disciple Romaharṣaṇa, who in turn gave it to his six disciples Sumati Ātreya, Akṛtavraṇa Kāśyapa, Agnivarcas Bhāradvāja, Mitrāyu Vāsiṣṭha, Sāvarṇi Saumadatti, and Suśarman Śāṃśapāyana. The *Matsya Purāṇa* (53.4) says that in the beginning there was only one Purāṇa of one hundred *crore* (ten million) verses, and it still exists in the world of gods. For the benefit of the humans, Viṣṇu assumes the form of Vyāsa in every Dvāpara Yuga and proclaims it in a shorter version of four hundred thousand verses in eighteen texts (Rocher 1986: 47).

In a culture where the Purāṇas and the Veda are always linked together and the Veda is considered the highest authority, it is interesting to see how the Purāṇas relate themselves to the Veda. In several Purāṇas there is a statement which says that the Purāṇas were created earlier than the Veda (for instance, *Brahmāṇḍa* 1.40–41, *Matsya* 3.3–4, *Vāyu* 1.54). R. C. Hazra (1962) suggests that this blatantly anachronistic statement makes perfect sense if we take the word "*purāṇa*" not to mean the Purāṇa texts as we know them but in its etymological meaning, that is, ancient stories and legends, for such stories were told during Vedic sacrifices. He brings in evidence for his suggestion from the *Atharva Veda*, the earliest text to mention the word "*purāṇa*," which says that chants, songs, meters, and *purāṇa* are leftovers (*ucchiṣṭa*) from the sacrifice along with the sacrificial formulas (Hazra 1962: 241). However, the *Bhāgavata Purāṇa* (3.12) says that Brahmā uttered the four Vedas first, one after the other, with each of his four mouths and afterwards spoke the Purāṇas with all four of his mouths in unison (Anantaramayya 1984: 17).

THE PURĀṆA AS A DISTINCT GENRE: FIVE DISTINGUISHING MARKS OF A PURĀṆA

Amarasiṃha, the fifth-century lexicographer defined the Purāṇa as one that has five marks (*purāṇam pañcalakṣaṇam*), and his commentators add an explanation as to what constitutes the five marks, *lakṣaṇa*s. These are: *sarga*, the story of the creation of the universe; *pratisarga*, the secondary creation or recreation of the universe after its dissolution; *vaṃśa*, genealogies of the gods, the sun, the moon, and other beings; *manvantara*, the period of time when a particular Manu from among the fourteen Manus in every *kalpa* (see below) is in charge; and *vaṃśānucarita*, the history of the kings in the ruling dynasty during the particular *manvantara* in question. The significance of the *pañcalakṣaṇa* is generally misunderstood among modern scholars who thought they were the five main topics that a Purāṇa should cover and were puzzled why such important subjects do not occupy much space in some of the Purāṇas and were nowhere to be found in others. Vans Kennedy (1831: 153n) was the first to observe that these five *lakṣaṇa*s are by no means the principal subject of the Purāṇas. P. V. Kane agrees that these five topics occupy less than 3 percent of the extant Mahāpurāṇas, but their significance according to him consists in marking the Purāṇas as distinct from the epics. Apparently the line of demarcation between these two genres was rather thin before fifth century (Kane 1930–62, 5.2: 840–41). An entirely different interpretation is suggested by Stephan Levitt (1976), who says that the standard understanding of the phrase "*pañcalakṣaṇa*" in Amarasiṃha's dictionary was due to a misunderstanding and that it meant "having five different descriptions," *itihāsa*, *ānvīkṣikī*, *daṇḍanīti*, *ākhyāyikā*, and *purāṇa* itself. I suggest that the five *lakṣaṇa*s serve to indicate the time and place within which the events recorded in the Purāṇa texts occur, and so there is no reason why they should occupy a major portion of the Purāṇa text. The significance of the *pañcalakṣaṇa*s is that they ideologically transform whatever content is incorporated into the Purāṇas into a Brāhmaṇic scheme of time and place (Narayana Rao 1993: 87–89; see also Bailey 1995: 12–14).

PURĀṆIC TIME AND SPACE

Events included in a Purāṇa are assumed to have happened at a particular point in a downward spiraling, circular, repetitive time frame. Purāṇic time is divided into four *yuga*s,

Kṛta, Tretā, Dvāpara, and Kali. Each of these ages is smaller than the preceding until finally the shortest age, Kali, ends in a dissolution (*pralaya*) of the universe leaving room for a new cycle to begin. Purāṇic time is measured in divine years, where each divine year is equal to 360 human years and each divine day is equal to a human year of 360 days. The four *yuga*s: Kṛta, Tretā, Dvāpara, and Kali each last for 4,000, 3,000, 2,000, and 1,000 divine years, respectively, and each of these ages have a transition time before the next one begins, lasting respectively for 800, 600, 400, and 200 divine years. Together the cycle of four *yuga*s—a *mahāyuga*—lasts for a period of 12,000 divine years. A thousand such *mahāyuga*s is a *kalpa*, which is a fabulous total of 4,320 million human years.

The decreasing number of years of each *yuga* in a four-*yuga* cycle also symbolizes a decrease in the virtues and excellence of human beings. A story from the *Varāha Purāṇa* (32.2–5) popularly retold is that Dharma, in the form of a bull, walks on all four legs in the Kṛta Yuga, on three legs in the Tretā, on two legs in the Dvāpara, and on one leg in the present age of Kali. Kṛta is the best of the ages, when human beings live long lives of honesty and happiness in harmony with divine law, the all-pervasive *dharma*. During the Tretā Yuga human beings need laws prescribing social behavior and a king to maintain the laws. Dvāpara is characterized by a confusion of social and religious conventions. Vyāsa is born to arrange the Vedic hymns into four Vedas and compose the Purāṇas. The Kali Yuga represents the lowest level to which humans deteriorate, where men and women lose their moral standards, Brāhmaṇs fall from their level of purity and acquire Śūdra habits. Śūdras, in turn, attain kingship and pretend to be Kṣatriyas. Atheists, such as Buddhists and Jainas, emerge and misdirect people onto wrong paths. The *yuga* ends with Viṣṇu incarnating himself to dissolve all creation, after which a new cycle begins all over. This concept of circular, spiraling, and deteriorating time created by the Purāṇas is their single most important contribution to Hindu civilization. Hindus still calculate their ritual calendar based on Purāṇic time.

The concept of space in the Purāṇas is equally complex. Space is conceived as the egg of Brahmā (*brahmāṇḍa*), made up of seven concentric spheres. Seven successively higher heavens where the gods and immortal beings live are situated above the earth, and seven lower worlds where demons live are below. The earth, on which human beings live, is located in the middle. On earth the central location is Jambūdvīpa, surrounded concentrically by six other circular lands separated by seven seas: one each of salt water, milk, *ghī*, curds, liquor, sugar cane juice, and fresh water. Holy Mount Meru rises in the center of Jambūdvīpa. Four lesser mountains support Meru from the four directions: Mandara from the east, Gandhamādana from the south, Vipula from the west, and Supārśva from the north. A godly city sits on top of Meru where Brahmā, Viṣṇu, and Śiva dwell, worshiped by mortals and lesser gods. On the sides of the great mountain in the four major and the four intermediate directions lie the cities of the lesser gods. The chiefs of those directions are: Indra in the east, Agni in the southeast, Yama in the south, Nirṛti in the southwest, Varuṇa in the west, Vāyu in the northwest, Soma in the north, and Īśāna in the northeast. The river Gaṅgā falls from the heavens and passes through the lands of Jambūdvīpa. One of these lands is Bhāratavarṣa, the ancient name for the land of India, home of the Bhāratas, named for the legendary progenitor of the Indian people. Bhāratavarṣa is where proper rituals are performed, and therefore it is called *karmabhūmi,* the land of ritual. Apparently this is where Purāṇic time of the four *yuga*s, dissolution and recreation, operates. "The Purāṇic picture of space is complex, highly organized and symmetrical. Envisioned is a three-dimensional *maṇḍala* with the land of Bhārata near the center. . . . The whole is an imaginative vision of the shape of the cosmos which clearly locates the land of India in the center of the universe" (Dimmitt and van Buitenen 1978: 28–29).

Hindu ritual performance is oriented to time and space based on the Purāṇic concepts. For instance, a Brāhmaṇ householder performing a ritual in India is likely to say that he is performing the ritual in the first quarter of the *yuga* of Kali, during the reign of Manu Vaivasvata. He will mention the particular name of the year in the sixty-year cycle and the fortnight, light (when the moon is waxing) or dark (when the moon is waning) as the case may be, and mention the name of the day according to the Purāṇic calendar. He will then continue by mentioning his location in terms of Purāṇic space in the land of Jambūdvīpa, in the area called Bhāratavarṣa, and in the country called Bharatakhaṇḍa (if he is in the south, he will orient himself as being south of Mount Meru), and finally he will conclude the chant by saying that he is performing the ritual in his own house with his wife and children.

THE NUMBER OF PURĀṆAS AND THEIR CLASSIFICATION

As mentioned earlier, tradition accepts that there are eighteen Purāṇas. The fact, however, is that there are many more, so many that the number one comes up with depends on how one counts. A verse in the oral tradition about the Purāṇas serves as a mnemonic device to list the eighteen Purāṇas.

bha-dvayam ma-dvayam caiva
bra-trayam va-catuṣṭayam
a-nā-pa-liṅ-ga-kū-skāni
purāṇāni pracakṣyate

Two begin with a "bha," and two more with a "ma."
Three begin with a "bra," four with a "va,"
and one each with "a" "nā," "pa', "liṅ," "ga," "kū," and "ska."
That's how the names of the Purāṇas go, they say.

The Purāṇas listed in this verse with their first syllable are: *Bhāgavata*, *Bhaviṣya*, *Matsya*, *Mārkaṇḍeya*, *Brahma*, *Brahmavaivarta*, *Brahmāṇḍa*, *Viṣṇu*, *Varāha*, *Vāmana*, *Vāyu*, *Agni*, *Nārada*, *Padma*, *Liṅga*, *Garuḍa*, *Kūrma*, *and Skanda.*

These eighteen are considered *mahā*- or great Purāṇas, and a further list of eighteen are called *upa*- or minor Purāṇas. The convention of listing eighteen Purāṇas in each group is well established, even though there are discrepancies as to which Purāṇas are included. Some Purāṇas themselves include such a list, and Ludo Rocher observes that *Vāyu Purāṇa* begins a list of eighteen but enumerates only sixteen; it introduces *Ādi Purāṇa* to the list but omits *Liṅga Purāṇa* and, according to one reading, also *Agni*. The *Bṛhaddharma Purāṇa* announces eighteen but only lists seventeen and, furthermore, considers *Nārada* and *Vāmana Purāṇas*, which are normally considered Mahāpurāṇas, as Upapurāṇas (Rocher 1986: 32). As may be expected, we find no uniformly accepted list of eighteen Upapurāṇas either.

Classifying texts into *mahā* and *upa* appears to be a convenient device to organize the texts in a schematic order. The prefix *mahā*- does not necessarily give the text a greater authority, nor the prefix *upa-* relegate the text to a lower order. Since the name Purāṇa itself elevates the text to a level of infallibility, the question whether a particular text is called a Mahāpurāṇa or an Upapurāṇa does not appear to be relevant to determine its status. The relative status of these texts, actually, seems to be highly contextual, depending on the area and community in which the text is presented. For instance, James Nye (1985) notes vastly divergent opinions in the Purāṇa texts: we find statements saying that the Upapurāṇas are only appendixes (*khila*) or a subvariety (*upabheda*) of the Mahāpurāṇas, while the *Parāśara Purāṇa* goes to the other extreme to state that the Upapurāṇas are greater than the Mahāpurāṇas. Furthermore, there are many highly respected texts called Māhātmyas such as *Gayā Māhātmya* which describe the religious power of a location, temple, or a river. Some of these texts are found as independent Purāṇa texts, and some as parts of a Purāṇa such as *Skanda Purāṇa*. Finally, one finds some Upapurāṇas claiming the status of Mahāpurāṇas. *Narasiṃha Purāṇa* appears in the list of Mahāpurāṇas in *Padma* and *Bhaviṣya Purāṇa*s, while *Devībhāgavata Purāṇa* asserts that it is the real *Bhāgavata Purāṇa* and the other *Bhāgavata Purāṇa* is merely an Upapurāṇa. V. R. Ramachandra Dikshitar (1951: xiv) considers that the classification of *mahā* and *upa* is a later development, and Rocher suggests that "the distinction between mahāpurāṇas and upapurāṇas is not as historically important as it is generally made to be" (1986: 68).

DIALOGICAL STRUCTURE OF THE PURĀṆAS: THE PURĀṆA ETHOS

The Purāṇas are framed in a dialogical structure. They are invariably set as a conversation between an interlocutor and a respondent. For instance, in the *Nārada Purāṇa*, Romaharṣaṇa tells Śaunaka and other *ṛṣi*s the story that was originally told to Nārada by Sanaka. In the *Brahma Purāṇa*, many *ṛṣi*s attend a twelve-year *sattra yāga*, where *sūta* Romaharṣaṇa arrives. The *ṛṣi*s ask him: "How did this world come to happen, the moving and the stable beings, the gods, the antigods, the *gandharva*s, the *yakṣa*s, the snakes, and the demons?" (*Brahma Purāṇa* 1.18). In answer to that question, the *sūta* narrates the *Brahma Purāṇa*. Similarly, in the *Varāha Purāṇa*, *sūta* is the narrator of an original story narrated by Viṣṇu to Pṛthivī, the goddess of the earth, when she asks Viṣṇu to tell her how he, in the form of a boar, Varāha, saved her from the demon. Again in the *Viṣṇu Purāṇa*, *sūta* narrates what Parāśara (Vyāsa) said when Maitreya asks him: "I am interested in knowing from you how the world has come into existence and how it will be in the future" (1.4). The atmosphere of a Purāṇa narrative is set in such questions, which are answered by an all-knowing sage. The readers/listeners perceive the answers as being given for the benefit of the world. In this framework, which creates an elevated tone and authenticity, the topics discussed acquire an aura of infallibility.

The topics covered in the Purāṇas, as described by Hazra, include:

> glorifications of one or more of the sectarian deities like Brahmā, Viṣṇu, Śiva, . . . numerous chapters on new myths, and legends, and multifarious topics concerning religion and society, for instance, duties of the different castes and orders of life, sacraments, customs in general, eatables and non-eatables, duties of women, funeral rites and ceremonies, impurity on birth and death, sins, penances and expiations, purification of

things, names and descriptions of hells, results of good and bad deeds . . ., pacification of unfavourable planets, donations of various types, dedication of wells, tanks, and gardens, worship, devotional vows . . ., places of pilgrimage, consecration of temples and images of gods, initiation, and various mystic rites and practices.

(1962: 246–47)

SŪTA, THE TELLER OF STORIES

Sūta is ubiquitous as the teller of the Purāṇa stories. He is called Romaharṣaṇa because he made his listeners' hair (*roman*/*loman*) stand on end with his engaging narrative skill. *Skanda Purāṇa* says that Romaharṣaṇa's own hair stood on its end when he heard the stories from Vyāsa (Kane 1930–62, 5.2: 862). It is well known that *sūta* Ugraśravas, the son of Romaharṣaṇa (or Lomaharṣaṇa), narrated the story of the *Mahābhārata* to Śaunaka and other sages in the forest. Other references to *sūta* seem to relate to a caste of people who have a high position as senior confidants of the king and are very learned even though they do not have the right to study the Veda. Manu (*Manusmṛti* 10.11.17) clearly states that *sūta* is of a mixed-caste origin from a Kṣatriya father and Brāhmaṇ mother. Amarasiṃha's dictionary lists the word "*sūta*" twice. It is defined, first, as a charioteer (*Nāmaliṅgānuśāsana* 517) and, the second time, as a son born of a Brāhmaṇ woman by a Kṣatriya father (662). The appearance of *sūta* in the *Mahābhārata* and the Purāṇas has given rise to a speculation among modern scholars whether the Purāṇas were originally non-Brāhmaṇ oral texts later appropriated by Brāhmaṇs. But Kane (1930–62, 5.2: 862) quotes Kauṭilya's *Arthaśāstra* (3.7.29) to distinguish *sūta* of the Purāṇas from the mixed-caste *sūta*. (However, according to Kangle [1960–65, 2: 215n], the text of the *Arthaśāstra* is difficult to construe.) R. N. Dandekar (1985) states that the narrator Sūta of the Purāṇas and the *Mahābhārata* is the name of a person and should not be confused with the word that indicates a caste of charioteers. Rocher quotes two parallel passages from the *Vāyu* and the *Padma Purāṇa*s which state that *sūta*'s special duty is to preserve the genealogies of gods, sages, and glorious kings displayed in the epics and the Purāṇas and, after some discussion, concludes that the status of *sūta* cannot be ascertained definitively. "Either one tries the synchronic approach: the mixed caste element explains how the *sūta* could simultaneously fulfill a kṣatriya function, that of a charioteer and equerry, and a purely brahmanic role, that of bard and singer. Or one looks for a diachronic explanation: the *sūta* as the son of a kṣatriya father and a brahman mother is a later application of the term only, and it was not that of the Vāyu and Padma texts . . ." (Rocher 1986: 56).

PURĀṆAS IN THE POPULAR UNDERSTANDING OF THE HINDUS

It is generally stated that the Purāṇas are meant for the benefit of women and Śūdras who are not eligible to receive instruction from the Vedas. However, the popularity of the Purāṇas suggests that these texts were read/listened to by all Hindus, including the highest caste Brāhmaṇs. Scholars prided themselves on having mastered all the Purāṇas, and poets listed the Purāṇas as an important item in their education. The Purāṇas were read/performed in temples and other religious locations. A class of *paurāṇika* performers made it their profession to perform these texts, and they were patronized by kings, local chiefs, elders of society, and temple authorities. For the average listener, the Purāṇas tell the stories of gods, goddesses, demons, and devotees and the stories of why sacred places became sacred. They also contain instructions for various rituals and pilgrimages to holy places. As a repertoire of stories, the Purāṇas are unrivaled. The worldviews that are most characteristic of Hindus are almost completely derived from the teachings of the Purāṇas. Their views of the creation, protection, and dissolution of the universe, the gods who are responsible for these activities, their views of time and space, cosmological perceptions, ideas of good and evil, *karma* and rebirth, the sacred and profane—are all derived from the Purāṇas. The most popular stories known to every Hindu about gods and demons are from the Purāṇas, even though no one, other than Purāṇa scholars, cares to remember which Purāṇas tell what story. All the Purāṇas merge in the memory of the average Hindu into one single group of texts. It is from the Purāṇas that Hindus know that Lord Nārāyaṇa sleeps on the milky ocean, on the thousand-hooded snake, Ādiśeṣa, and that his consort Lakṣmī, the goddess of prosperity, sits by his side serving him. From Viṣṇu's navel rises a lotus out of which emanates the four-faced god, Brahmā, who creates the world. The Vedas come out of his four mouths, and his consort, Sarasvatī, is the goddess of speech. Nārāyaṇa as Viṣṇu takes *avatāra*s, which include the fish, tortoise, boar, man-lion, dwarf, Rāma, Kṛṣṇa, and Buddha, with a final *avatāra* of Kalkin yet to come. Again, it is from the Purāṇas that the Hindus know all the stories about Śiva, who lives in the cremation ground or alternately on the peaks of the Himālayas, wears snakes as ornaments, and is naked except for the skin of an elephant around his loins. His vehicle is a bull and his consort is Pārvatī, the daughter of the Himālayas. The Purāṇas also tell the stories of the great goddess Devī, mother of the universe, fierce to her enemies and compassionate to her devotees. Essentially, all Hindu religious, political, social, cultural, and even literary education is derived from the Purāṇas.

Internal contradictions among the Purāṇas, however, do not seem to be an issue in the popular mind. During their performances, *paurāṇika*s interpret the apparent contradictions to the satisfaction of their listeners. To quote Janamanci Seshadrisarma, a famous *paurāṇika* of the early twentieth century: "The intentions of the Purāṇas are deep and not easily available on the surface. Every action is properly directed in them with appropriate results. The deities described in them are made to suit the specific eligibility of each person, but not every Purāṇa is meant for everybody. The path for liberation for each person is different, and therefore the teaching of the Purāṇas appears self contradictory" (1931: 15).

THREE KINDS OF PURĀṆAS

According to the Hindu worldview, all things in creation are made up of three qualities or *guṇa*s: *sattva*, a light, gentle, and enlightening quality; *rajas*, a fierce, dynamic and aggressive quality; and *tamas*, a dark, dull, and vegetative quality. Even the Purāṇa texts have not escaped this classification. According to the *Padma Purāṇa*, the classification is as follows: The *sāttvika* Purāṇas are *Viṣṇu*, *Nārada*, *Bhāgavata*, *Garuḍa*, *Padma*, and *Varāha*. The *rājasika* Purāṇas are *Matsya*, *Kūrma*, *Liṅga*, *Brahmāṇḍa*, *Brahmavaivarta*, *Bhaviṣya*, *Mārkaṇḍeya*, *Vāmana*, and *Brahma*. The *tāmasika* Purāṇas are *Matsya*, *Kūrma*, *Liṅga*, *Śiva*, *Skanda*, and *Agni*. The *sāttvika* Purāṇas are supposed to lead to liberation, the *rājasika* ones to heaven, and the *tāmasika* ones to hell. It is interesting indeed to note that texts supposed to be authored by such a great sage as Vyāsa could lead one to hell. Division of the Purāṇas into these three classes is apparently based on the gods favored in each Purāṇa and motivated by sectarian passions of the Vaiṣṇavas. It is well known that Hinduism passed through some rather rough periods of sectarian conflict, and obviously the Purāṇas reflect that situation. It would, however, be risky to interpret the sectarian statements of the Purāṇas as their essential meaning because such statements represent highly contextualized connotations. Rocher has aptly stated that the sectarianism of the Purāṇas should not be interpreted "as exclusivism in favor of one god to the detriment of others" (1986: 23). The same Purāṇa may make a passionately sectarian statement in favor of one god on one page and a few pages later may make an equally passionate statement in favor of another god (Rocher 1986: 21–22). Such apparent contradictions, however, become irrelevant when one realizes that no Purāṇa text is ever read from cover to cover and that a Purāṇa performer chooses sections and interprets them appropriately to the occasion and the audience. This also underscores the fact that part of the problem modern readers face in interpreting the Purāṇas is that protocols of reading have changed, and we read every page and every line subjecting them to a uniform valence based on one-dimensional textual linearity. More on this later.

THE PURĀṆAS AND THE BHAKTI TRADITION

Bhakti marked a significant shift in the religious traditions of India, and the Purāṇas reflect this change. As a term, "*bhakti*" is more a cover word for a variety of personal relationships to a deity rather than a single definitive theological concept. Broadly speaking, the *Bhagavad Gītā*'s concept of *bhakti*, which is also stated in the *Viṣṇu Purāṇa*, presents god as accessible to living beings through a discipline of personal worship and surrender. In contrast to this, the seventh-century Āḻvārs of Tamilnadu sang and preached a different mode of *bhakti* where human emotions of passionate erotic love and affection are accepted as modes of worship. Experiencing god through such a passionate personal relationship is superior to the knowledge one can gain through the study of philosophical texts, the performance of ritual practices, and the chanting of the Veda. Furthermore, people of all classes and stations in life, from kings to commoners, from learned Brāhmaṇs to illiterate outcastes, men and women—all have equal access to god through this *bhakti*. In fact, the lower the station of a person in life, the easier it is for him or her to reach god. This is clearly a subversive concept in a society based on Brāhmaṇic ritual superiority and social hierarchies. The *bhakti* of the Āḻvārs gradually undergoes a Brāhmaṇic reformation when it is incorporated into the *Bhāgavata Purāṇa* and becomes a part of the Purāṇic religious complex.

THE BHĀGAVATA PURĀṆA

The bulk of the *Bhāgavata Purāṇa* represents what was first told by Vyāsa's son, Śuka, to King Parikṣit, son of Abhimanyu of the Pāṇḍava line. The context of narration is especially poignant. King Parikṣit was cursed by Sage Śṛṅgī to die within seven days from the bite of the deadly snake, Takṣaka. The reason for the curse was that the king playfully hung a dead snake around the neck of Śṛṅgī's father, when the latter was deeply lost in meditation and did not respond to the king's inquiries. King Parikṣit, realizing that the end is near, asks Sage Śuka what a man nearing his death should do. Basically, Śuka's answer to this question is the core of the *Bhāgavata Purāṇa*. Stories from the *Bhāgavata Purāṇa* have become independently popular and have been retold in many languages and genres.

To get acquainted with the message of the *Bhāgavata Purāṇa*, let us visit a few of these stories beginning with the story of Prahlāda. Prahlāda, antigod Hiraṇyakaśipu's son, rejects his father's beliefs and sings of God Viṣṇu, until his father angrily demands that he show him where Viṣṇu lives. Prahlāda replies that Viṣṇu is everywhere, he is omnipresent. Hiraṇyakaśipu points to a pillar in the assembly hall and sarcastically asks if Viṣṇu is also present in the pillar and then furiously kicks it. Viṣṇu emerges from the pillar as a half-man, half-lion and claws Hiraṇyakaśipu to death. Another story relates how the elephant-king Gajendra, who is caught by a mighty crocodile, cries to Viṣṇu for help. Viṣṇu appears and kills the crocodile with his discus. The story of Rukmiṇī tells of how she fell in love with Kṛṣṇa, whom her elder brother Rukmi hated. When Rukmi arranges a marriage for Rukmiṇī with another man, the distressed Rukmiṇī sends word to Kṛṣṇa to come and take her away. Kṛṣṇa appears on the wedding day and takes Rukmiṇī away on his chariot, defeating her brother's army, which chases after him. All these stories celebrate the superiority of personal devotion to god even at the expense of social status and normal family relations between father and son, brother and sister, husband and wife.

The narratives of the *Bhāgavata Purāṇa* create an opportunity to celebrate god. The style in which the stories are told is aimed not so much at informing the readers, as is the case with the other Purāṇas, but of reminding them of what they already know, thus creating an atmosphere in which they can remember god's name. At the beginning of each of these stories King Parikṣit asks Sage Śuka to tell him of a particular event in Kṛṣṇa's life, such as his birth or wedding, and then immediately says how wonderful it would be to hear these stories one more time. Listeners/readers of the *Bhāgavata Purāṇa* feel exactly like the king. They already know these stories but want to adore god one more time.

Acceptance of the *bhakti* stories, so different from what the earlier texts preach, left their mark on the Purāṇa itself. The emotional/devotional nature of the stories gives the Purāṇa a lyrical quality. The *Bhāgavata Purāṇa* is written in a language both more beautiful and at the same more archaic than the other Purāṇas. The archaism of this Purāṇa, as J. A. B. van Buitenen (1966: 38) notes, serves to legitimize the late text and gain for it a degree of ancientness. In fact, the *Bhāgavata Purāṇa* itself makes us aware that it is a different kind of Purāṇa in that it lists ten *lakṣaṇa*s instead of the usual five that are supposed to mark a Purāṇa (Rocher 1986: 27).

The most popular part of the *Bhāgavata Purāṇa* is the tenth chapter, which narrates the love-games Kṛṣṇa plays in Vṛndāvana with his cowherd girls. Kṛṣṇa's love-games inspired a number of poems in many regions of India among which the *Gītā Govinda* is the most well known. Scholars have noted that Rādhā, the most important of Kṛṣṇa's cowherd girls, does not have a place in the *Bhāgavata Purāṇa* stories. Scholars attribute this absence to the South Indian origin of the text, whereas Rādhā stories originate from North India. In addition to being South Indian in origin, it is also claimed that the *Bhāgavata Purāṇa* was a late composition attributed to a certain Vopadeva.

THE SKANDA PURĀṆA

The *Skanda Purāṇa* is in sharp contrast with the *Bhāgavata Purāṇa*. If the *Bhāgavata* expounds the value of *bhakti* as an experience of total devotion to the deity and rejects the value of ritual practice, *Skanda* emphasizes rituals and the power of sacred places. This Purāṇa is largely a collection of stories describing the power of holy places and temples (Sthalapurāṇas). As such, this Purāṇa apparently continued to grow as new temples and holy sites came under the influence of Brāhmaṇic Hinduism. This also explains the popularity of the *Skanda Purāṇa* as well as its segmentary nature because each holy place promoted its own story under the rubric of this Purāṇa. Additions to the *Skanda Purāṇa* are so numerous, with some as recent as the sixteenth century, that even the native tradition regards this Purāṇa as a "scrap-bag" (Doniger 1993: 59). The expansive *Skanda Purāṇa* is available in two versions, one made up of *khaṇḍa*s and the other made up of *saṃhitā*s—each of which contains a number of sub-*khaṇḍa*s. The stories in the *Skanda Purāṇa* cover the major Brāhmaṇic holy places in virtually the entire subcontinent. For instance, *Kedārakhaṇḍa* and *Badrī Māhātmya* cover the Himālayan region, *Kāśīkhaṇḍa* and *Ayodhyā Māhātmya* describe the holy places in Uttar Pradesh, *Āvantyakhaṇḍa* tells of the holy places in Malva, Rajasthan, and parts of Gujarat, *Revakhaṇḍa* relates to the holy places in the Narmadā Valley, *Nāgarakhaṇḍa* and *Prabhasakhaṇḍa* cover the sacred places in Gujarat and other parts of western India, *Puruṣottamakṣetra Māhātmya* tells the story of Puri in Orissa, *Veṅkaṭācala Māhātmya* and *Setu Māhātmya* describe Tirupati in Andhra Pradesh and Ramesvaram in Tamilnadu.

One of the notable sections of the *Skanda Purāṇa* is the *Kāśīkhaṇḍa*, which tells the story of Kāśī (Banaras). Once, the Vindhya Mountain grew higher and higher in competition with the Himālayas, and it obstructed the sun and the moon from traveling across the sky. Time stopped since the sun and the moon stood still. Śiva intervened and asked Agastya to take care of the problem. The sage and his wife, Lopāmudrā, traveled south towards the mountain. Seeing the great sage and his wife, the mighty Vindhya bowed to them in respect. Agastya walked across and asked the mountain to stay bent until his return, which he never did. This was how the power of the mighty Vindhya Mountain was subdued. However, Agastya, a long-time resident of Kāśī, missed his city and remembered it by describing its beauty in detail to his wife. It is in this context that the *Kāśīkhaṇḍa* lists all the sacred places along the Gaṅgā and serves like a guide to the city, including stories and descriptions for each of its shrines.

THE OTHER PURĀṆAS: AGNI AND BHAVIṢYA

Each Purāṇa is interesting in its own way (see Rocher 1986: 133–254 for a full survey of the Purāṇas), but I will briefly focus on two because they are very different from the rest. The *Agni Purāṇa* is extraordinary in that it includes discourses on the science of politics and statecraft, administrative branches of the state, qualifications of the king, his duties, the role of his ministers and other officers, the army, and so on. It includes information on trees and water resources, medicine, and anatomy. Furthermore, it has elaborate chapters on metrics, poetics, and lexicography. In a way this is an encyclopedic Purāṇa.

The name *Bhaviṣya Purāṇa* is a contradiction in terms, since *purāṇa* means "old" and *bhaviṣya*, "future." Cast in a frame of telling events that will take place, this Purāṇa, to summarize Hazra (1975: 169), tells the stories of Adam, Noah, Nādir Shāh, and Jalāluddīn Akbar. It tells the story of Pṛthvīrāja and Jayacandra and goes on to include information about Varāhamihira, Śaṃkarācārya, Rāmānuja, Nimbārka, Madhva, and Jayadeva. It includes the grammarian Bhaṭṭojidīkṣita, Kabīr, and Nānak. It even describes British rule in India and mentions Calcutta and the parliament. Evidently, the text was composed after all the events that it purports to predict took place, which makes it a new and innovative mode of writing history.

COUNTER-PURĀṆAS

Prominent opposition to the Purāṇic worldview came from the Jainas. The Jainas were great storytellers and competed with the Brāhmaṇs in precisely the same narratives, which the Brāhmaṇic religion used for spreading its message. In contrast to the Brāhmaṇic Purāṇas, which are composed by anonymous authors under the cover name of Vyāsa and run into many redactions, the Jaina Purāṇas are all written by historically identifiable authors, and their texts are relatively more fixed and datable. The Jainas used Maharashtri, Prakrit, Apabhramsa, and Kannada, in addition to Sanskrit, and apparently succeeded in bringing their versions to the people more successfully than the Brāhmaṇs. It is possible that the medieval retellings of the Brāhmaṇic Purāṇas by Brāhmaṇic poets in regional languages was motivated by the desire of the Brāhmaṇs to counter the popular reach of the Jaina versions. To the Jainas goes the credit of questioning the truth-value of the Brāhmaṇic Purāṇa stories, continuously offering critical and rational alternatives to them.

The Jaina Purāṇas essentially narrate the lives of the sixty-three great men (*triṣaṣṭiśalākāpuruṣa*) of the Jaina tradition through which the Jainas will learn the work of *karma* according to the Jaina worldview. While this is the larger goal, there is also an unmistakable interest on the part of the Jainas to create a counter-Purāṇa to the major Brāhmaṇic epic narrative. The Jaina *Rāmāyaṇa* and the Jaina *Harivaṃśa* are primary among such attempts. The Jaina narrative of the *Rāmāyaṇa* is told in Vimalasūri's *Paumacariya*. These texts were not always called Purāṇas. They were also called Caritras, life stories. According to John Cort (1993: 187), the Digambara Jainas called their texts Purāṇas, while the Śvetāmbara Jainas called their texts Caritras, although in some cases both terms were applied to the same work.

PURĀṆAS FROM BELOW

Following the established convention of calling narratives that are not fixed in writing or not written in a standard language, folk narratives, A. K. Ramanujan (1993b: 101–20) identified several folk mythologies and folk Purāṇas. However, there is also a genre of Purāṇa texts relating the origin myths of non-Brāhmaṇ castes, which are often, if not always, written in Sanskrit. We can call these Purāṇas of the lower castes, who have moved up in society or had attempted to do so. It is well known in Indian social history that one of the strategies of upward mobility for a low caste is to create a Sanskrit text and invent a mythology associating itself with Vyāsa. Rocher (1986: 72) reports a number of caste Purāṇas from Gujarat. In addition, there is a text called the *Bhāvanarṣi Purāṇa* which relates the origin of weavers, another called the *Viśvakarma Purāṇa* which tells the story of the goldsmiths. The *Kanyakā Purāṇa* tells the origin myth of the unity of trading castes, and the *Jāmba Purāṇa* conveys the caste story of leatherworkers. All these Purāṇas are known in the Telugu-speaking area of Andhra Pradesh, and, except for the *Jāmba Purāṇa*, all these texts are written in Sanskrit. The *Jāmba Purāṇa*, sung among the Mādiga caste of leatherworkers, is interesting because it borrows the name Purāṇa but is actually a Telugu oral narrative, a genre often studied by anthropologists and folklorists rather than by Purāṇa scholars. The regional nature of these Purāṇas is both an asset and a problem in coming to a comprehensive understanding of the nature of these texts. An asset because the texts of these Purāṇas are relatively few and do not create major problems in determining their path of transmission, and a hardship because of the vast areas one has to cover to collect these regional texts.

Unlike the Brāhmaṇic Purāṇas, which are written with a view to establishing a Brāhmaṇic ideology, these Purāṇas question Brāhmaṇic superiority and attempt to upset it. The lower-caste Purāṇas, if written in Sanskrit, closely follow the general style of the Brāhmaṇic Purāṇas. The differences are ideological and political rather than textual. Among these Purāṇas, the Purāṇa of the goldsmiths, the *Viśvakarma Purāṇa*, attacks the Brāhmaṇs for usurping a ritual superiority assigned by god to the Viśvabrāhmaṇs, the goldsmiths. The *Kanyakā Purāṇa*, the Purāṇa of the Komaṭis (merchant caste), does not oppose the Brāhmaṇs but shows that the Komaṭi caste is as pure as the Brāhmaṇs. The well-known *Basava Purāṇa* may be studied in this context, even though it is not strictly a caste Purāṇa but a Purāṇa of Vīraśaivites who were virulently anti-Brāhmaṇic. The *Basava Purāṇa*, written in Telugu and Kananda, tells the stories of the militant followers of Basveśvara, the twelfth-century leader of the Śaivite movement in Karnataka. It also narrates a number of stories of Śaiva devotees from the earlier *Periya Purāṇa*, written by Cēkkiḻār in Tamil (Narayana Rao 1990).

COLONIAL SCHOLARSHIP OF THE PURĀṆAS

The early Western scholars of the colonial period, eager to gather religious and cultural information and knowledge about the Hindus, encountered the Purāṇa texts and were clearly bewildered by their variety, complexity, and multiplicity. As early as 1784, Warren Hastings commissioned Radhakanta Sarma to prepare a summary of the Purāṇas (Rocher 1986: 2). Vans Kennedy, an Englishman in the military service, and Horace Hayman Wilson spent most of their lives studying this vast body of texts. Wilson employed a small army of native Sanskrit *paṇḍitas* to produce detailed indices of the contents of all the Purāṇas. He trained native young men to translate these indices into English and then examined the original and the translation "and corrected [them] wherever necessary" (Wilson 1839: 64). In 1840, Wilson published a translation of the *Viṣṇu Purāṇa* with a scholarly introduction. However, Purāṇa studies did not hold a sustained interest for him because they were not, in their present form, ancient texts such as the Vedas. "They preserve, no doubt, many ancient notions and traditions; but they have been so mixed-up with foreign matter, intended to favour the popularity of particular forms of worship or articles of faith, that they cannot be unreservedly recognised as genuine representations of what we have reason to believe the Puráṇas originally were" (Wilson 1961: lvi). Attention to the

Purāṇas was revived when Vincent A. Smith demonstrated that the *Vaṃśānucarita* of the *Matsya Purāṇa* was basically an accurate record of the ancient Āndhra dynasty. Frederick Eden Pargiter energetically established the historical validity of the Purāṇas, followed by R. Morton Smith (Rocher 1986: 115–25). Only then did the Purāṇas become valuable because they were believed to be useful in reconstructing the ancient history of India.

However, the general attitude of suspecting the Purāṇa texts as reliable records continued. More bewildering than anything to the colonial scholar was the very nature of their existence as texts. As serious classical scholars trained in Latin and Greek, the colonial scholars expected the Purāṇas to be concrete written texts with the usual corruptions that result from centuries of use. Little were they prepared to encounter a tradition whose concept of text is very different from their own, where texts interact with their oral discourses and where *paurāṇika*s move through these texts with unfathomable conventions, and whose practices appeared to Western eyes to be verging on forgery, interpolation, and textual manipulation. Lack of communication between the two groups of scholars—the Western Indologists and the native *paṇḍita*s—developed into irresolvable suspicion of each others' methods. As for the colonial scholar, ancient India was great, it was only contemporary India that was rotten. This belief led to their perception that the texts deteriorated in the hands of ignorant transmitters. The ancient texts were magnificent, but the Purāṇas we have at hand are corrupted.

The Austrian scholar Maurice Winternitz carries this line of thinking and reports the general view of colonial scholarship. According to his survey, the language of the Purāṇas was sloppy and grammatically flawed, and their content was wildly confusing and full of meaningless exaggerations. For him the extant texts represent an inferior class of literature, belonging to the "lower, uneducated priesthood," who transmitted the Purāṇas.

> Still many old sagas of kings and many very late genealogical verses (anuvaṃśaślokas) and song stanzas (gāthās) of the original bard-poetry have been preserved to us in the later texts which we have received. And fortunately the compilers of the Purāṇas who worked haphazardly did not disdain what was good and have included in their texts some dialogues reminiscent of the Upaniṣads in form and content as well as individual legends and texts of profound thought-content taken from the ancient ascetic poetry. . . . Even in the desert of the Purāṇa-literature there is no lack of oases.
>
> (Winternitz 1963–83, 1: 507)

However, prejudices of this nature did not last for long as a more sophisticated and nuanced modern scholarship developed.

MODERN SCHOLARSHIP ON THE PURĀṆAS

After two hundred years of active and persistent application of Western methods and progressive training of Indian scholars in Western text-criticism, a highly sophisticated field of Purāṇa study has emerged which should be called modern rather than Western or Indian, since it includes Indian as well as European scholars. An international group of philological scholars have rigorously applied principles of text-criticism to a number of manuscripts and made strenuous and laudable efforts to refine the methods of producing critical editions of the Purāṇas, including the *Mahābhārata* and the *Rāmāyaṇa*. Scholars from different countries—Australia, England, France, Germany, India, Italy, and the Netherlands, to name some, participate in active debate and discussion in this enterprise.

The idea of producing critical editions has exercised the minds of Indologists for a long time. Winternitz first expressed the need for a critical edition of the *Mahābhārata* at the 11th International Congress of Orientalists in Paris in 1897. In 1908, Heinrich Lüders submitted an eighteen-page prospectus of the *Mahābhārata*, drawing upon twenty-nine manuscripts. However, nothing came of this until 1920 when Ramakrishna Gopal Bhandarkar began to work on a critical edition of the *Mahābhārata* in Pune. At the completion of this renowned critical edition, Haraprasad Shastri expressed a fervent hope that similar editions should be produced for all the Purāṇas. Serious work on the Purāṇas began when the All-India Kashiraj Trust was formed under the patronage and guidance of Vibhuti Narayan Singh, the Mahārājā of Kāśī, which, in addition to producing critical editions of the Purāṇas, also published the journal *Purāṇam*.

The standards of philological method require that all the available manuscripts of a particular Purāṇa be gathered together and closely examined for variations. Following strictly established practices of text-criticism, the Ur-text of a Purāṇa is theoretically possible to reconstruct. This model assumes that there was a single author for each of the Purāṇas who produced a single text which was then transmitted throughout a wide area over a long period of time during which the text acquired scribal errors, textual attritions, not to mention deliberate interpolations by motivated anonymous authors.

Controversies regarding critical editions led to a range of opinions regarding the feasibility and usefulness of such editions. On one end were scholars who wanted to adopt the Western methods to reconstruct as pristine a text as possible, if not exactly the Ur-text of the Purāṇa from which all the other texts of the Purāṇa in question took off. On the other end were scholars who argued that the very idea of a critical edition was wrong and that texts should be read as they are, in their localities and communities.

Madeleine Biardeau (1968) opposes the methods of producing critical editions of the Purāṇas and the methods adopted by V. S. Sukthankar in his critical edition of the *Mahābhārata* as well. Following her teacher Sylvain Lévi, Biardeau questions the validity of making critical editions of texts which are primarily oral and local. She draws a sharp distinction between the connotations of an oral tradition in the West and in India and observes that in the West the written word is valued more highly than the oral tradition, whereas in India it is the oral word (*śruti*) that is respected as the highest authority. Furthermore, she asserts that the Purāṇas derive their acceptance from the local Brāhmaṇ communities who use the texts. To erase the pivotal importance of the locally authorized text in favor of a constructed text because the latter is perceived to be closer to the oldest possible version is to distort the reality. She points to her experience with the Śrīvaiṣṇavite Brāhmaṇs of Simhachalam temple in Andhra Pradesh, who insisted that a certain version of the Narasiṃha and Prahlāda story they tell was, for them, authoritative. They claimed that their version was from the *Skanda Purāṇa*, while at the same time they had no difficulty admitting that it differed from what appears in the extant version of this Purāṇa. Biardeau maintains that "any locally accepted version is authoritative in its own right" (1968: 122–23) and should prevail over the version of the so-called critical editions which are assumed to be older and therefore closer to Vyāsa's text. Biardeau's method raises a different problem in that it leads to a plethora of texts from different regions under one name with no unity. To resolve this problem, she suggests that their unity is to be found in the meaning of the stories and "not in their particular contents or historical bearing" (1968: 123). She also suggests "the manuscript evidence be checked and strengthened through consultations with the people who, even now, have a first hand knowledge of the . . . purāṇas" (Biardeau 1968: 123).

V. M. Bedekar of the All-India Kashiraj Trust responds to Biardeau's critique by defending Sukthankar's methods, strongly insisting that once a tradition is committed to writing, it is open to textual criticism—irrespective of the fact whether it is oral or written in its origin. He does not deny that local Brāhmaṇs hold the power of authorizing their version, but that in itself does not cause a problem for the editors of critical editions, since the latter are not competing for authority, rather they are only producing an edition which presents the text—in Sukthankar's words (1933: cii), which Bedekar (1969: 225) quotes—"in all its variety, all its fullness" (for a survey of the debate, see Coburn 1980).

Anand Swarup Gupta, also of the All-India Kashiraj Trust, who undertook the preparation of critical editions of the *Vāmana*, *Kūrma*, and *Varāha Purāṇa*s, steers clear of most of the debate but firmly rejects the Western methods, including those adopted by Sukthankar. Gupta questions the assertion that additions made to the Purāṇas over time should be considered "spurious." Gupta prefers to view them as a natural growth of the texts and wanted to "keep them in line with the current religious and social ideas of their times in order to preserve the encyclopaedic nature of the Purāṇas and keep them up-to-date" (1971: xxxi). His project was to reconstruct a single text of a Purāṇa based on all the available manuscripts collected from different regions of the country. "Such single critical text must be a conflated text by its very nature, but this defect is more than compensated by giving the readings and variants of all the available versions in the critical apparatus (in the form of the critical footnotes of a critical edition)" (A. S. Gupta 1971: xxxii).

Rocher (1986: 99), too, rejects critical editions saying that in so far as the Purāṇa tradition is purely oral, of which only parts were accidentally committed to writing, producing critical editions based on the standard rules of textual criticism makes little sense. Elsewhere, he says: "I too have been trained in classical philology in Europe. I too have learned how to prepare critical editions, comparing manuscripts and reconstructing *the* original text—the archetype. But I am prepared to forget all that when it comes to the Purāṇas" (Rocher 1983: 72; emphasis in original).

In contrast to Rocher, however, R. Adriaensen, H. Bakker, and H. Isaacson (1998) strongly believe in the written text of the Purāṇas. In their view there is "no reason to assume any but a written transmission of the Purāṇa, although it is certainly the case that at times a transmitter's memory of other similar texts may have had some influence" (Adriaensen, Bakker, and Isaacson 1998: 38). They categorically state that the oral character of the Purāṇas was exaggerated. They follow the strict philological approach of starting with the oldest available text of the *Skanda Purāṇa* from which they aim to produce an edition that accurately presents the readings of available manuscripts and a constituted text that is superior, as a whole, to that found in any of the individual manuscripts (Adriaensen, Bakker, and Isaacson 1998: 40). They published their first volume of *Skanda Purāṇa* in 1998, and their work is still in progress. Earlier, in 1995, Greg Bailey (1995: 3–73) had articulated a wholly different approach of working with Purāṇa texts in his *Gaṇeśapurāṇa*. Adopting a structuralist methodology, Bailey argued that every single Purāṇa text is a coherent whole and every redaction of it is equally systematic. In response,

Adriaensen, Bakker, and Isaacson affirm that "It is through philological research based on manuscripts that this selection on the one hand and substitution on the other, as well as the intrinsic criteria by which they operated—i.e. the general generic principles of Purāṇa literature—can be brought to light. No structuralistic analysis, taking printed texts for granted, will ever delve so deep" (1998: 17; see also the Preface by Heinrich von Stietencron of the Tübingen Purāṇa Project in Bailey 1995: ix–xi). Apparently, the debate concerning the production of critical editions of the Purāṇas is not over yet.

DATING THE PURĀṆAS

Modernity is inseparably connected with historicity, and as such, there is no wonder that a text without a date causes anxiety to a modern mind. Traditional ideas that connect the Purāṇa with the Veda and therefore consider them dating from the beginning of time while also presenting a gradual development of the texts in the hands of Vyāsa, his disciples, and other *paurāṇika*s sharply clash with the modern positivistic need for a date on a linear time line. Purāṇas as religious texts created by a superior authority in a cyclic time and Purāṇas as empirically verifiable, man-made texts in historical time belong to two different world-views, and a reconciliation of the two is impossible. Still, scholars made valiant efforts to fix a date for each of the Purāṇas. The early colonial scholars tended to give the Purāṇas a relatively late date, while Indian scholars tried to push them as far back as possible. For Wilson, the Purāṇas belong to the late period when Hinduism was developing a sectarian character, worshiping Śiva or Viṣṇu, and therefore cannot be older than Śaṃkara, Rāmānuja, Madhva, and Vallabha. Gradually, a consensus seems to have emerged that there is a great deal of ancient material in the Purāṇas along with very modern material and that composite, ever-changing texts such as these are impossible to date as whole texts (Rocher 1986: 100–03). Cornelia Dimmitt and J. A. B. van Buitenen (1978) suggest an innovative idea of dating the Purāṇa material by correlating different sections of the Purāṇas with phases of Hindu tradition as known from other literature. They speculate that

> The oldest material in the Purāṇas is contemporaneous with the Vedas, but was recited either in a different milieu than the brahminic ritual or by persons other than the brahmin priests. This alternate milieu would be the source of the *smṛti* tradition that gave rise eventually to both epic and Purāṇic collections. Thus the Purāṇas, which share many stories from the epics, the *Mahābhārata* in particular, do not derive from that epic, but from the same body of oral tradition, or *smṛti*, whose origins may be as old as the period of the Vedas.
>
> (Dimmitt and van Buitenen 1978: 5–6)

Dimmitt and van Buitenen go on to suggest that some of the Purāṇa material was collected about 1000 BCE, the period after the *Mahābhārata* war, and again during the Gupta period, that is, fourth to sixth century. More new material continued to be added to the Purāṇas well after the sixth century, and there is no final closing date for the Purāṇas (Dimmitt and van Buitenen 1978: 5–6). Rocher says that despite insurmountable difficulties in dating individual Purāṇas, scholars still assign specific dates to them. He reports dates set by others in his very erudite and informative book, *The Purāṇas* (Rocher 1986), stating at the same time that it is not possible to set a specific date for any Purāṇa as a whole.

THE ABSENT PAURĀṆIKA

Prevailing ideas about critical editions fall on one or the other side of the oral/written divide. For Rocher, the Purāṇas were oral texts that were accidentally written down. For Adriaensen, Bakker, and Isaacson, they were basically written texts. The fact however is that they were both. The orality of Indian languages, unlike that of Western languages, allows for what I call oral literacy. The *paurāṇika* performer prided himself in his scholarship and distinguished himself from the nonliterate performer who sang oral narratives which have no written authority. Every Purāṇa says in writing that it was orally told by *sūta* who himself heard it from an earlier telling by Vyāsa or some such authority. Nowhere in the long line of transmission of the Purāṇa recorded in writing in each Purāṇa text is the act of writing mentioned (except in the case of the *Mahābhārata* where Gaṇeśa serves as the scribe for Vyāsa). Curiously, then, an authentic Purāṇa happens to be a written text, which claims in that very writing that it is not a written text. Scholars agree that no Purāṇa is ever performed in its entirety as it is written. A typical *paurāṇika*, a *paṇḍita* who is well versed in the Purāṇa tradition and would be known by different regional language names throughout India, chooses a section of a Purāṇa for a discourse, reads out a portion of the text in Sanskrit or the regional language, and comments on it, incorporating material from other similar texts and expanding on their relevance to that specific place and point in time. The erudition of the *paurāṇika* allows him to move across many Purāṇas with his memory as the only authority to determine which text he has borrowed from. When such a *paurāṇika* serves also as a producer of Purāṇa texts, he feels justified in incorporating material that he has quoted from other texts into the one he is producing. The style in which Purāṇas were composed, a simple Sanskrit meter called *anuṣṭubh,* easily allows for moving substantial portions of one Purāṇa text to another Purāṇa text. Vyāsa was the author of all the Purāṇas, but the actual producers of the texts were the *paurāṇika*s who made these texts and renewed them as context required. Literally thousands of such producers of texts over a period of hundreds of years worked quietly without seeking any individual recognition under the imagined direction of the legendary sage Vyāsa. The creativity that went into the making and remaking of the Purāṇas is quite remarkable.

Elsewhere I draw a distinction between the recorded text and the received text in India (Narayana Rao 1995). What is recorded on palm leaf, and later on paper, is not the entire text, it is only a part of it. It acquires its fullness in performance, at which time it is appropriately recreated by the *paurāṇika*, who is trained in reading the Purāṇas and interpreting them. His knowledge, which was not written down, would be crucial in determining the received text. The recorded Purāṇa text tells only part of the story. When the *paurāṇika*s who knew the received text disappeared, scholars were left with only the recorded text, which has become our sole text. Simply reading the recorded text in a linear order, without the training in performing it, scholars found a number of irresolvable contradictions and discontinuities, not to mention a plethora of scribal errors. But if the early scholars had actually studied the Purāṇa in performance and learned how the trained performer constructed and presented a Purāṇa in each performance, we would have an entirely different kind of Purāṇa scholarship today. Instead of suspecting the *paṇḍita*s, the agents of transmission of this tradition from generation to generation, if the early scholars had striven to understand the nature of this text culture, a whole different way of asking questions would have emerged.

The *paurāṇikas* who knew this text culture had been initially marginalized and eventually disappeared from the scholarly scene. So much so that the entire scholarship of the Purāṇas has been conducted viewing these texts as artifacts with little direct interaction with the users of these texts and their textual practices. The textual activities of this culture—production, transmission, performance, and reproduction, which includes the training of the *paurāṇikas*, the principles and methods of text creation they employed, and the rules governing such activities—need to be properly understood. In the absence of such an understanding, texts collected from their original locations and stacked in the air-conditioned rooms of libraries and studied in isolation could only give a distorted picture. The Purāṇa culture where hundreds and even thousands of *paurāṇikas* served as silent authors without claiming individual recognition—all speaking in the voice of the revered Vyāsa over such a long period of time in the history of India awaits to be properly understood.

PART III

THEISTIC AND DEVOTIONAL MOVEMENTS

CHAPTER SIX

ŚAIVA

Gavin Flood

Śaiva traditions are those whose focus is the deity Śiva, and a Śaiva is a Hindu who follows the teachings of Śiva (*śivaśāsana*). These teachings are thought to have been revealed in sacred scriptures and propagated through the generations in traditions of ritual observance and theology. Many Śaivas have also worshiped the goddess, Śiva's consort and power (*śakti*), as the esoteric heart of their religion, and it is often impossible to meaningfully distinguish between Śaiva and Śākta traditions. Every culture creates its own forms (Castoriadis 1997: 84), and in the following pages I shall discuss the forms that Śaiva traditions produced and hope to convey something of the Śaiva religious *imaginaire*. This *imaginaire* is distinctive within the Indic traditions and relates to wider cultural and political history, both insofar as it has corroborated and upheld the values and goals of mainstream, orthodox society and in the ways it has challenged those norms. On the one hand, the Śaiva imagination has been in line with the instituting power of particular regions, on the other, it has brought to life a world that undermines that power through its promotion of a vision of the self that transcends social institutions and political stability. It is this ambiguity that shares many of the wider goals of collective life while eroding those goals through promoting a subjectivity external to them, which is a characteristic of Śaiva traditions. It is in this truly creative dynamic in which Śaiva values are embedded in social institutions, such as caste and kingship, while simultaneously undermining those values that the genius of the tradition resides. It is perhaps not a coincidence that this ambiguity is reflected in the ultimate imaginary signification of the tradition, Śiva himself, as the erotic ascetic (O'Flaherty 1981), as family man and vagabond, as form and formless, and as transcendence and immanence.

In this chapter I will focus on early Śaiva traditions, and although I will briefly discuss the fifteenth-century Kerala tradition, I will not venture much past the eleventh century. In effect, largely due to limitations of space, I will not deal with developments of Śaivism during most of the last millennium, which includes the Nātha tradition, the traditions of later North India, and the Siddha or Cittar tradition in Tamilnadu, nor the Śaiva Vedānta of the Śaṃkarācāryas and their monastic institution (*maṭha*). I can only justify this exclusion on the grounds that the important doctrinal foundations and practices are established during the earlier period and the later traditions are rooted in these earlier forms. But it is to the indigenous understanding of what a Śaiva tradition is that we must turn first.

THE IDEA OF A ŚAIVA TRADITION

The Śaiva understanding of tradition has been to see it in terms of a "stream" (*strotas*) or line of transmission of texts and practices flowing through the generations from teacher to disciple. Another term used is Śaiva "*āmnāya*," a classification associating traditions of scripture with the four directions or a classification of five emanating from the five mouths of Śiva (Dyczkowski 1988: 66–85; Padoux 1994: 35–40). Such a tradition is transmitted through textual commentary and exegesis and through the lineage of teachers, the *guru santāna* or *santati*. Another term used in Śākta or Kula texts is "*ovallī*," initiatory lineages (six in number), which are "currents of consciousness" (*jñānapravāha*) flowing from a transcendent source through the founder of the particular lineage. The source of such a stream or torrent of transmission in the case of the *āmnāya* is believed to be Śiva. From him the teachings are generally transmitted to the goddess, and from her through a series of divine and semidivine intermediaries to the human world, for the kind of knowledge revealed through revelation is adapted to the abilities of beings to receive it (*Mālinīvijayottara Tantra* 1.24). For example, the ninth- or tenth-century root text of the Kashmiri Śaiva tradition, the *Mālinīvijayottara Tantra* (1.7), declares itself to be derived from the "mouth of the supreme lord" (*parameśamukha*), from where it is transmitted through a series of intermediaries, namely, the lord Pareśa, to the goddess (Devī), thence to her son Kumāra, who in turn transmits the teachings to Brahmā's four sons who transmit it to the human world (*Mālinīvijayottara Tantra* 1.2–4, 14). The tenth-century Kashmiri theologian Abhinavagupta, likewise, traces the *guru* lineage of the esoteric "family" (*kula*) tradition to the four mythical figures, lords Khagendra, Kūrma, Meṣa, and Macchanda, and thence to Śiva (*Tantrāloka* 29.29–32; Dyczkowski 1988: 62, 68–69; Goudriaan and Gupta 1981: 5). Similarly, the sage Vasugupta, having received a system of teachings from numerous perfected male and female beings (*siddha* and *yoginī*) who made his heart pure, received teachings from Śiva who revealed in a dream that they were inscribed upon a stone on the Mahādeva Mountain (namely, the *Śivasūtra*) (*Śivasūtravimarśinī* p. 1). During this transmission process, the teachings are believed to become condensed and accessible to the limited understanding of the receivers.

Other examples could be cited, but the point is that tradition in Śaivism is derived from a divine source and is understood in cosmological terms. Indeed, Śaivism could be said to be a cosmological religion in which tradition is not a human construction but is given through a process of transformation through levels of a hierarchical cosmos to the human world. It is the *guru* who is the embodiment of this tradition and who is the channel of divine grace (*anugraha*) to the community of disciples. The *guru* lineage or *santāna* is therefore an expression of Śiva's power (*śakti*) (*Śivasūtravimarśinī* p. 60), and the *guru*, at least in monistic Śaivism, is identified with Śiva as one who liberates beings through bestowing initiation (*dīkṣā*) and giving power to *mantra* (*mantravīrya*) (*Spandanirṇaya* pp. 52–53). Even in dualistic Śaivism, Śiva enters the *guru* for the purposes of initiation. The *guru* becomes the embodiment of tradition, reveals the supreme, liberating truth (*tattva*) to the disciple (*Śivasūtravimarśinī* p. 59), and reveals the structure of the hierarchical cosmos. The *Mālinīvijayottara Tantra* defines the *guru* in these terms: "He who knows the meaning of all the levels of the cosmos (*sarvatattvāni*) is the *guru* equal to me (*matsamaḥ*) [i.e. Śiva], who has taught the illumination of the power of *mantra* (*mantravīryaprakāśaḥ*). Men who are touched, spoken to, and seen by him with a delighted mind (*prītacetasā*) are released from sin (*pāpa*) even in seven lifetimes" (3.10–11). Because of this emphasis on tradition as a stream flowing through the generations from a divine source into the *guru*, the distinctions between Śaiva and Śākta traditions become blurred. Some texts such as the *Yoginīhṛdaya*, which forms part of the root text of the Śrīvidyā cult, are clearly Śākta in orientation. What has become known as "Kashmir" Śaivism, a nondualistic tradition developing from at least the ninth century, identifies Śiva with undifferentiated consciousness and also identifies this condition with a form of the goddess Kālī called Kālasaṃkarṣiṇī (see p. 129). The more esoteric the Śaiva traditions are, the more there is a tendency to focus upon the goddess.

The implications of this for understanding not only Śaiva traditions but also the wider field of Hindu traditions are great. First, this understanding of tradition and the emphasis on the *guru* indicates strong decentralizing processes. While the texts of revelation are important, it is above all the revelation as the living tradition of the *guru* lineage that animates the tradition and through which the grace of Śiva is believed to flow. Here text becomes performance and the texts' teachings embodied in the human *guru*. Second, this structure, which places such great emphasis on the teacher-disciple relationship, allows for a kind of particularism or individualism which is yet impersonal, insofar as tradition is designed to transcend personality or limited sense of ego (*ahaṃkāra*). It is in this relationship that the transmission of tradition (and the grace of Śiva) occurs. The boundaries of the Śaiva and Śākta traditions are therefore sufficient to ensure transmission through the generations, yet are also porous in allowing the influence of other, related traditions. This can be seen by Śaiva theologians quoting from a range of sources and borrowing from different traditions. Abhinavagupta, for example, was initiated into a number of Śaiva systems, and the Kashmiri theologian Utpalācārya quotes with approval a text of the Vaiṣṇava Pāñcarātra tradition, the *Jayākhya Saṃhitā* (*Spandapradīpikā* pp. 6–7). This is not to say, of course, that the Śaiva theologians regarded all revelation as equal; they did not. Rather, each new revelation incorporated the earlier within it at a lower level, and so, while a text of a different tradition might be quoted with approval, it is generally only regarded as a truth emanating from the level of the cosmos from which it derives. Later esoteric teachings transcend the previous revelation.

While these traditions maintain a hierarchical structure in the classification of revelation, as we will see, we nevertheless have in the Śaiva understanding of tradition an example of the decentralizing strategies of what we call "Hinduism," which should make us skeptical of the usefulness of the category in a historical context. While Śaiva authors were keen to make totalizing claims about the universal truth of their teachings, the model of tradition shared by all Śaiva schools is inherently pluralistic in the idea of the *guru* lineage while simultaneously being hierarchical in its assumption of a graded cosmos or ontology and a graded teaching. These initiatory lineages have been extremely important in the history of Śaivism and have mostly been associated with groups of texts called Tantra. But there has also been a more general temple Śaivism associated with Smārta Brāhmaṇism. As Alexis Sanderson (1988: 660–64) has shown, the term "*śaiva*" is technically restricted to an initiate into one of the Śaiva systems, while the term "*maheśvara*" has been used for a Brāhmaṇ worshiper of Śiva within the Smārta domain. It is Sanderson's (1985, 1986, 1988) general mapping of these systems in the early medieval period that I follow here, although a more complete mapping of the traditions by him, which will revolutionize our understanding of Śaivism and the history of Hindu traditions more generally, will have to wait (Sanderson Nd). But before we trace this history, a few remarks on the earliest indications of reverence for Śiva and the development of Śaiva traditions are necessary.

EARLY AND PURĀṆIC ŚAIVISM

Some scholars maintain that the worship of Śiva goes back many thousands of years in the subcontinent to the Indus Valley civilization, where steatite seals have been found suggestive of a deity akin to Śiva. The famous "Paśupati" seal shows a seated, perhaps ithyphallic, horned figure surrounded by animals. John Marshall (1931, 1: 52) has claimed that this is a prototype of Śiva as the *yogin* and Paśupati, the lord of animals. But it is not clear from the seals that this is a proto-Śiva figure, and Asko Parpola (1994: 248–50) has convincingly suggested that the seal is in fact a seated bull, almost identical to figures of seated bulls found on early Elamite seals of about 3000–2750 BCE. It may be, of course, that elements of Śiva's later iconography—such as the crescent moon in his hair—can be traced to this period, but unless the Indus Valley script is deciphered, these seals can only be suggestive. There are early textual references to Rudra, arguably a forerunner of Śiva, one of whose epithets is "auspicious" (*śiva*), in the *Ṛg Veda*. Here three hymns are addressed to Rudra, the "roarer." He is clothed in an animal skin, brown with a black belly and a red back. Even at this time he is an ambiguous deity who is like a ferocious beast destroying families and livestock, yet who is also a benevolent healer of disease (*Ṛg Veda* 1.43, 1.114, 2.33). A famous hymn in the *Ṛg Veda*, the hundred names of Rudra (*śatarudriya*), speaks further of this ambiguous nature, a hymn which is referred to in the *Śiva Purāṇa* and is still recited in Śiva temples today (Gonda 1980).

But it is only with the *Śvetāśvatara Upaniṣad*, composed some time prior to the *Bhagavad Gītā*, that a theism focused upon Rudra-Śiva begins to emerge in the literature. This text is important in marking a link between the earlier monistic Upaniṣads and the later theistic traditions. Here Rudra is elevated from the feral deity on the edges of society to the status of the supreme being as the cause of the cosmos, the magician (*māyin*) who produces the world through his power (*śakti*), yet who transcends his creation. He is the lord who, by his grace (*prasāda*), liberates the soul from its journey from body to body due to its actions. The seeds of Śaiva theology are here, and indeed the terms "*guru*" and "*bhakti*" occur for the first time in the text (*Śvetāśvatara Upaniṣad* 6.23), although more than likely this passage is a later interpolation. But, certainly, the seeds of devotion are implicit in the text's theism.

The formation of Śaiva traditions as we understand them begins to occur during the period from 200 to 100 BCE. Apart from the *Śvetāśvatara*, we have references to a Śaiva devotee, a Śiva Bhāgavata, in the grammarian Patañjali's commentary on the Pāṇini grammar (*Aṣṭādhyāyī* 5.2.76). He describes him as a figure clad in animal skins and carrying an iron lance as a symbol of his god, and there are references to early Śaiva ascetics in the *Mahābhārata* (Bhandarkar 1982: 165). There are also suggestions of Śiva worship on the coins of Greek, Śāka, and Parthian kings who ruled North India during this period, bearing a bull, a later symbol of Śiva. While little can be inferred from this, it is probable that adoption of Śaiva traditions of some form accompanied the general "Indianization" of the foreign, barbarian (*mleccha*) rulers (La Vallée-Poussin 1930: 239–41).

During the Gupta dynasty (*c.*320–50 BCE) the Purāṇas developed along with Smārta Brāhmaṇ forms of worship (on this, see Bühnemann 1988). The Śaiva Purāṇas, most notably the *Liṅga* and *Śiva Purāṇa*s, contain standard material on genealogy, caste responsibilities, and cosmology, along with specifically Śaiva topics of installing the symbol (*liṅga*) of Śiva in temples, descriptions of the forms of Śiva, and material on early Śaiva sects. The follower of the Purāṇic religion, the Maheśvara referred to by Śaṃkara (*Brahmasūtrabhāṣya* 2.2.37), would at death, having led a life of devotion and responsible enactment of social duties, be transported to Śiva's heaven (*śivaloka*) at the top of the world egg (*brahmāṇḍa*) and so be liberated. This is the Śaiva equivalent of the Vaiṣṇava heaven (*vaikuṇṭha*) where the Purāṇic Vaiṣṇava would go at death. Fully orthoprax, the Maheśvara adhered to the Smārta observance of social duties, the *varṇāśramadharma*, performed Vedic domestic rites and Purāṇic *pūjā*, making vegetarian offerings to orthodox forms of Śiva and using Vedic *mantra*s. He followed the Brāhmaṇical path in an ordered universe in which his place in the cosmos at death was assured, as had been his social position in life (Sanderson Nd).

In contrast to the Brāhmaṇ householder who followed the Purāṇic Smārta injunctions, a number of other Śaiva groups are listed in the Purāṇas which are on the edges of orthopraxy and are even condemned by some texts. These Śaiva sects are classified in quite complex ways in the Purāṇas and other medieval sources—there are references in Śaṃkara's and Rāmānuja's commentaries on the *Brahmasūtra* and in Yāmuna, among others—but four groups in particular emerge as important. These are the Pāśupata, Lakulīśa, Śaiva, and Kāpālika sects. There are variant names for some of these, and they are also subdivided (Dyczkowski 1988: 16–19; Lorenzen 1991a: 1–12). While the Purāṇas mention these sects and the later Purāṇas contain material that is derived from the non-Vedic revelation of the Tantras, they are often hostile to the non-Purāṇic Śaiva traditions, partly in reaction to the Tantric tradition's hostility towards the Vedic; the *Kūrma Purāṇa* (1.14.30, 1.20.69), for instance, condemns the Pāśupata system as heretical (see Dyczkowski 1988: 10–11). A picture therefore emerges of a Purāṇic Śaiva tradition, revering the Vedas with orthoprax social attitudes, and being confronted by renunicate Śaiva traditions, at first by the Pāśupata sect who threatened Purāṇic tradition but later by more extreme groups. These alternative Śaiva sects ranged from ascetics who regarded themselves as being within the Vedic-fold, namely, the Pāśupatas and Saiddhāntikas, to groups who consciously placed themselves outside of that sphere such as the Kāpālikas. It is to these non-Purāṇic groups that I wish to pay some attention, as it is these groups who have formed the majority Śaiva traditions and who are still extant in the subcontinent.

NON-PURĀṆIC ŚAIVISM

Sanderson has shown that we can make a broad distinction between the Vedic Purāṇic devotee of Śiva, on the one hand, and the non-Purāṇic Śaiva initiate, on the other. These latter had undergone an initiation (*dīkṣā*) into the cults of their affiliation for the purpose of liberation in this life (*mukti*) and/or obtaining magical power to experience pleasure in higher worlds (*bhukti*). Within this group a distinction can be made between those Śaivas who follow the outer or higher path (*atimārga*) and those who follow the path of *mantra*s (*mantramārga*). The followers of the *atimārga* sought only liberation, while the followers of the *mantramārga* sought not only liberation but also power and pleasure in higher worlds (Sanderson 1988: 664–90). Among the groups of the *atimārga* two are particularly important, the Pāśupatas and, a subbranch, the Lākulas, from whom another important sect, the Kālamukhas, developed.

The Pāśupatas are the oldest named Śaiva group, dating probably from around the second century BCE. They are referred to in the *Mahābhārata* (*Śāntiparvan* 349.64), but the earliest surviving text of the group is the *Pāśupatasūtra*, pre-tenth century, with a commentary by Kauṇḍinya. This text was regarded as revelation by the Pāśupatas. The myth behind it is that Śiva entered the corpse of a young Brāhmaṇ that had been cast into a cremation ground and reanimated it as Lakulīśa (the lord of the staff), who then gave out the teachings contained in the text to his four disciples.

These teachings present the Pāśupata as an ascetic somewhat on the edges of orthoprax society, even though such an ascetic had to be a Brāhmaṇ male who should not speak with low castes nor with women (*Pāśupatasūtra* 1.13). But whereas an ordinary, Vedic Brāhmaṇ would pursue the social norms of adherence to duties regarding caste and stage of life (*varṇāśramadharma*), the Pāśupata had transcended these responsibilities to a higher or perfected (*siddha*) fifth stage beyond the Vedic fourth stage of renunciation. To achieve this perfection the ascetic undertook a vow or observance (*vrata*) in three developmental stages. First, the Pāśupata should live within the environs of a Śaiva temple, bear the mark (*liṅga*) of a Pāśupata ascetic, namely, the ashes in which he bathes thrice daily, and worship Śiva with song, dance, laughter, and *mantra* repetition. Living on alms, the aspirant (*sādhaka*) undertakes the development of virtues, such as not stealing, celibacy, and not harming creatures by straining water, and so on (*Pāśupatasūtra* 1.2–11 and commentary). He thereby gradually purifies himself and enters the second stage of his practice in which he discards external signs of his observance, leaves the temple, and undertakes various forms of antisocial behavior. These include pretending to be asleep in public places, making his limbs tremble as though he were paralyzed, limping, acting as if mad, and making lewd gestures to young women (*Pāśupatasūtra* 3.12–17). Such practices, the text claims, are doors to the acquisition of merit, for in behaving in this way the ascetic will attract verbal and physical abuse, whereby his sin (*pāpa*) will be passed over to his abusers and their merit (*sukṛta*) passed over to him (*Pāśupatasūtra* 3.8–9). In the third stage of the practice the *sādhaka* withdraws from the public eye to a deserted house or cave, lives off alms, and devotes himself to meditation upon the five sacred *mantra*s of Śiva along with the syllable *oṃ* (*Pāśupatasūtra* 5.21–24). Through this he unites his soul with Śiva and gains uninterrupted union for a period of six months (*Pāśupatasūtra* 5.9–12). Finally, the ascetic withdraws to become a resident in a cremation ground (*śmaśānavāsī*), where he lives on whatever is available (*Pāśupatasūtra* 5.30–32) and dies reaching union with Śiva (*rudrasāyujya*) and the end of sorrow through his grace (*Pāśupatasūtra* 5.33, 5.40).

There were more extreme forms of Pāśupata religion. The Lākula ascetic imitated the terrible form of his God Rudra, carrying a cranium begging bowl, a skull-topped staff, a garland of human bones, ash covered, with matted hair or shaved head (Sanderson 1988: 665–66). This kind of Śaiva had taken the "great vow" (*mahāvrata*) or penance for killing a Brāhmaṇ in the Dharmaśāstras, namely, living beyond the pale of Vedic society and carrying the skull of his victim for twelve years (*Manusmṛti* 11.73). This practice is reinforced by a myth in which Śiva as the terrible Bhairava decapitates Brahmā's fifth head with his left-hand thumb because Brahmā had attempted incest with his daughter. The skull sticks to Bhairava's hand, and he wanders as the beggar Bhikṣāṭana until he reaches Varanasi where the skull falls at Kapālamocana, a site of pilgrimage (*tīrtha*) (Eck 1982: 119). The Lākula sect gave rise to a further subsect, the Kālamukhas, who were especially dominant in Karṇāṭakā during the eleventh to thirteenth centuries. Indeed they were an important group here, attracting donations and political patronage for Kālamukha temples and monastic centers (*maṭha*) (Lorenzen 1991a: 97–140). The Kālamukhas in turn probably gave rise to the important Liṅgāyata or Vīraśaiva tradition, still extant in Karnataka and famous for their devotional poetry (Ramanujan 1973).

With these groups of the higher path we have the beginnings of a tendency away from orthodox forms of religion and adherence to the Vedic social order. Although Brāhmaṇs within the Vedic order, the Pāśupatas believed their teachings to transcend that order. They went beyond the four stages on life's way (*āśrama*) into a fifth stage beyond the fourth Vedic order, they also saw themselves as being within that order. Similarly, the Kālamukhas in seemingly rejecting the Vedic world, vividly symbolized by their great vow as a consequence of Brāhmaṇicide, were yet at the center of the social order in Karṇāṭakā, supported by kings with well-funded centers of practice and learning. The relationship between these groups and the established hierarchy is therefore complex and cannot be seen in terms of a simple rejection of Vedic values by a heterodox or excluded community. The issue of the relation of these groups to the wider society and to Vedic orthopraxy becomes even more sharply delineated with the traditions of the *mantramārga*, all of which revered a body of scripture distinct from the Veda, known as the Tantras.

THE TANTRAS

The Tantras are a vast body of literature in Sanskrit, composed mostly between the eighth and eleventh centuries BCE, claiming to have the status of revelation and to supercede the Vedas. Some Tantras acknowledged the Vedas, while others rejected them. The Tantras were composed in a number of traditions where they are sometimes known by the name of Āgama in the Śaiva Siddhānta and Saṃhitā in the Vaiṣṇava Tantric tradition or Pāñcarātra. There are also a very few Jaina Tantras, a vast body of Buddhist Tantras, mostly preserved in Tibetan and Chinese translations, and Tantras to the sun, none of which have survived (Sanderson 1988: 660–61). As the Buddhist Tantras were translated into Tibetan, so some of the Śaiva Tantras were translated into Tamil and are used as the basis for temple rituals in South India to this day. All of the Śaiva traditions of the *mantramārga* accept the Tantras, or rather different groups of Tantras, as their textual basis, although some Śaiva traditions have been more closely aligned to orthoprax, Brāhmaṇical practice than others.

While there are specific traditions and the language of the Tantras is often obscure, partly because these texts would have been accompanied by a living, oral tradition and partly because they regarded themselves as secret and heavily symbolic, they nevertheless share common features. They are concerned with practice (*sādhana*) involving ritual and *yoga* undertaken after initiation (*dīkṣā*) by a *guru* but also contain sections on temple building, architecture, and occasional rites such as funerals. Indeed, each Tantra of the Śaiva Siddhānta theoretically rests on the four "feet" (*pāda*) of doctrine (the *vidyāpāda* or *jñānapāda*), *yoga*, ritual (*kriyāpāda*), and behavior (*cāryapāda*), although most texts do not follow this rather artificial scheme. The majority of the Tantric corpus is concerned with ritual of some kind, and the texts follow a common ritual structure, as we shall see, for the purposes of attaining liberation and, above all, magical power and pleasure in higher worlds. These rituals involve the enacting of elaborate hierarchical cosmologies and are concerned with the divinization of the body, with divine energy or power (*śakti*), and with possession (*āveśa*) and exorcism.

We do not yet have a full picture of the groups of ascetics and the social context in which the Tantras originated, although Sanderson's work (1985, 1988, Nd) on manuscript sources will clarify the picture. The Tantras probably originated with groups of ascetics similar to the Lākula Pāśupatas, on the edges of Brāhmaṇical society who were supported by low castes, although the low-caste origins of Tantra is contentious as the Tantras are linked to courtly circles and royal power (Sanderson Nd). Cremation ground asceticism is a very old tradition in the subcontinent, and meditation on death is an important feature in the meditation practice of early Buddhist monks (see, e.g. Norman 1971). The Tantras became more popular, and Tantric images and ideas become pervasive in later Hindu traditions. Although generally distancing themselves from the Tantras, the Purāṇas nevertheless absorb Tantric elements (Dyczkowski 1988: 8; Hazra 1975), and Tantric ideas and practices became absorbed by the eleventh century into mainstream, Brāhmaṇical society and courtly circles. The divine power (*śakti*) of the goddess becomes identified with the power of the king in different regions such as Vijayanagara. But it is in Kashmir, above all, where we see this process of the Brāhmaṇization of Tantric ideology and practice. This history has been traced by Sanderson through the sequences of texts and the divisions of the Śaiva Tantric canon. It is to this canon and the traditions it expresses that we now turn.

The path of *mantra*s can be divided into the texts and teachings of the Śaiva Siddhānta, on the one hand, and the teachings of Bhairava of non-Siddhānta groups, on the other. While the former, although accepting twenty-eight "dualist" Tantras, adhered to Vedic social practice and made generally vegetarian offerings to a milder form of Śiva known as Sadāśiva, the latter accepted a large body of texts which were often hostile to Vedic orthopraxy. This distinction between orthoprax and heteroprax Śaivism is identified in the sources, as Sanderson has shown, as a distinction between traditions of the right (*dakṣiṇa*), namely, the Śaiva Siddhānta, and traditions of the left (*vāma*), namely, the non-Saiddhāntika traditions (Sanderson 1995: 18). While the Śaiva Siddhānta is a dualistic tradition, maintaining a distinction between the soul and the lord, the non-Saiddhāntika groups, especially the tradition known as the Trika, are nondualistic, claiming that the self and Śiva are identical. This dualistic and nondualistic distinction also applies to the ritual realm where the Śaiva Siddhānta accepted the Vedic distinction between purity and impurity, remaining within the Vedic rules of purity, whereas the non-Saiddhāntika rejected this distinction (Sanderson 1995: 17).

These Śaiva Tantric traditions not only permeated the subcontinent but became royal religions, along with Buddhism, in Southeast Asia and beyond to Java and Bali during the medieval period. Here kings modeled themselves on South Asian kings, Sanskrit became the sacred language, and Brāhmaṇ priests officiated at rites of royal consecration. In Java, for example, there are early Śaiva inscriptions (732 BCE), and eighth-century Śaiva temples seemed to have followed ritual patterns found in the subcontinent of bathing the Śiva-*liṅga* (Dumarçay 1986). In Bali Śaiva temple priests still perform daily rites in which the priest symbolically becomes Śiva through uttering the five-syllabled *mantra* "*namaḥ śivāya*" (homage to Śiva) (Goudriaan and Hookyaas 1971). There are important Tantric Buddhist texts of Indonesia such as the *Kuñjarakarṇadharmakathana* depicting Śaiva elements but in a Buddhist context (Nihom 1994: 119–41).

THE ŚAIVA SIDDHĀNTA

The Śaiva Siddhānta forms the fundamental Śaiva system, providing the template for ritual and theology of all other Śaiva groups within the path of *mantras*. The tradition may have originated in Kashmir, where it developed a sophisticated theology propagated by theologians, such as Sadyojyoti, Bhaṭṭa Nārāyaṇakaṇṭha, and his son Bhaṭṭa Rāmakaṇṭha (*c.*950–1000 CE). It spread to the south where the Sanskrit scriptures are complemented with Tamil texts. Here the gnostic, ritual system becomes infused with an emotional devotionalism (*bhakti*) characteristic of southern Śaiva Siddhānta, through the Tamil poetry of the Śaiva saints or Nāyaṉārs. Ritual and devotion are accompanied here by theology in works by Bhojadeva (eleventh century) and Aghoraśiva (twelfth century) (Gengnagel 1996).

The Śaiva Siddhānta is dualistic (*dvaita*), maintaining a distinction between the self and Śiva and claiming that there are three distinct ontological categories, the lord (*pati*), the self (*paśu*), and the bond (*pāśa*). The lord or Śiva in his form as five-faced Sadāśiva performs the five acts (*pañcakṛtya*) of creation, maintenance, and destruction of the universe, concealing himself and revealing himself to devotees (*Tattvaprakāśa* 1.7). The self or "beast" (*paśu*) is eternally distinct from Śiva and bound within the cosmos or "bond" (*pāśa*) in the cycle of birth and death by impurity (*mala*), action (*karma*), and the material substratum of the cosmos (*māyā*). Śiva performs the five acts for his play (*krīḍā*) and for the liberation of beings (*Tattvaprakāśa* 6.1). This liberation is attained with the grace (*anugraha*) of Śiva through initiation (*dīkṣā*) by a teacher in whose body Śiva has become established (*ācāryamūrtiṣṭha*) (Hulin 1980: 115–17; *Tattvaprakāśa* 1.15). Through initiation and the subsequent actions of daily and occasional rituals performed throughout his life, the impurity, which is a substance (*dravya*) covering the soul, is gradually removed, and the aspirant finally achieves liberation at death through the descent of Śiva's grace (*śaktipāta*). Once liberated, the soul does not merge with Śiva, because of their ontological distinction, but becomes equal to Śiva (*śivatulya*), possessing all of Śiva's powers of omniscience and omnipotence but remaining eternally distinct (R. Davis 1991: 83–111; Sanderson 1995: 39–40).

There were two initiations which the Śaiva Siddhāntin would undergo, the lesser initiation (*samayadīkṣā*) into the cult ritual and scriptures and the liberating initiation (*nirvāṇadīkṣā*) ensuring the soul's final release (Brunner 1975). While initiation was open to all classes, it was not open to women who could only participate in Śaiva worship vicariously through the actions of their husbands and so at death rise up to Śiva's abode (Sanderson 1995: 35–36). The daily ritual acts of the Saiddhāntika were performed at the junctures of the day (dawn, midday, sunset) and involved the standard Tantric ritual structure of the purification of the body through its symbolic destruction (*bhūtaśuddhi*), the creation of a divine body through imposing *mantras* upon it (*nyāsa*), mental or inner worship (*antarayāga*) in which offerings are made mentally to the deity, in this case, Sadāśiva, and external worship in which external *pūjā* is performed. In the Śaiva Siddhānta, the form of Sadāśiva worshiped is consortless, possessing five faces with three eyes and ten arms, holding a trident, and covered in a tiger skin (*Netra Tantra* 9.19c–25) and, in the *Īśānaśivagurudevapaddhati*, is represented as a beautiful 16-year-old youth (3.14.5d), although there is some variation in the objects held in his ten hands (3.1–11). This ritual structure is standard, found in both primary scriptures and in ritual manuals such as Īśānaśivagurudeva's and Somaśambhu's *Paddhati*s (twelfth century). The ritual structure in these texts is also found outside the Siddhānta, showing that some degree of ritual invariance occurs across the Tantric traditions in spite of divergent theologies and deities (Brunner-Lachaux 1963–98, 3: xxi–xxii; Flood 2002; Padoux 1990: 330–38; Sanderson 1988: 660–704).

But while the ritual of the Śaiva Siddhāntin is very closely aligned with the normative, Vedic rites of the Smārta Brāhmaṇs (Sanderson 1995: 27–38) and the Saiddhāntika followed a straightforward path of fulfilling *dharma* along with performing ritual enjoined by his initiation, there was another path that could be followed. This was the path of power and the enjoyment of pleasure in higher worlds that required a distinct consecration (*sādhakābhiṣeka*) after the *nirvāṇadīkṣā* (Brunner 1975). In contrast to one who simply desired liberation at death (*mumukṣu*), one desiring powers (*bubhukṣu*), technically referred to as a *sādhaka*, could take on supererogatory rituals. While this distinction between the *mumukṣu* and the *bubhukṣu* does not directly map on to the distinction between the Śaiva Siddhānta followers of the right and the non-Saiddhāntika groups of the left because the *sādhaka* path was an option also within the Siddhānta, it is nevertheless the case that the non-Saiddhāntika traditions are more concerned with attaining power in this sense. Indeed, the obtaining of various forms of magical power through the practice of *yoga* and the performance of rituals for a desired end (*kāmya*) are integral to the Tantras. The *Svacchanda Tantra*, for example, describes rituals for the Sādhaka to attain the goals of causing the death of enemies (*maraṇa*), ruining his enemies (*uccāṭana*), the subjugation of women (*vaśikaraṇa*), the power of attraction (*ākarṣaṇa*), and the tranquilizing of supernatural forces (*śānti*) (9.46; on these powers, see Goudriaan 1978: 251–412) through the worship of a particular ferocious form of the god Svacchanda called Koṭarākṣa or Aghorahṛdaya (9.2). For example, the destruction of enemies and subjugation of a desired woman are achieved through establishing their names in a magical diagram (*yantra*), visualizing the enemy or desired person, and repeating certain *mantra*s (*Svacchanda Tantra* 9.65c–70). These kind of rites are an important part of the Tantras of the left often associated with the cremation ground traditions.

NON-SAIDDHĀNTIKA ŚAIVISM

In contrast to the orthoprax Śaiva Siddhānta, the second major division of the path of *mantra*s comprises the Bhairava Tantras and their various subdivisions. These texts are concerned with the Śaivas who worshiped a ferocious form of Śiva called Bhairava and which originated in ascetic groups living in cremation grounds. These groups are generally known as Kāpālikas, the "skull-men," so-called because, like the Lākula Pāśupata, they carried a skull-topped staff (*khaṭvāṅga*) and cranium beginning bowl. Unlike the respectable Brāhmaṇ householder of the Śaiva Siddhānta or Smārta tradition, the Kāpālika ascetic imitated his ferocious deity, covered himself in the ashes from the cremation ground, and propitiated his gods with the impure substances of blood, meat, alcohol, and sexual fluids from intercourse unconstrained by caste restrictions (Sanderson 1985: 200–202). He thereby flaunted impurity rules and went against Vedic injunctions. His aim was power through evoking deities in the rites associated with his particular system, especially ferocious goddesses. In Hindu drama the Kāpālika was often lampooned, but his continued existence, although in small numbers, into the present in the form of the Aghorī ascetics of Varanasi bears witness to the power of this tradition (Parry 1994: 251–64).

Within this broad purview of Kāpālika Śaivism or the Śaivism of the left, a number of distinct traditions developed during the early medieval period, especially the Kaula, Krama, and Trika traditions, which form part of the Kula ensemble. These originated in cremation ground asceticism but became incorporated into householder life. As Sanderson has clearly demonstrated, while for the Krama and Kaula there was no conformity to Vedic ritual purity, for the Trika there was some conformity for the householder, although transcendence of Vedic orthopraxy remained at the tradition's esoteric heart where transcendence is achieved through transgression (Sanderson 1995: 21–23). But in order to understand the distance of these Śaiva groups from the Siddhānta let us look at the Krama tradition first.

The Krama or "gradation" tradition existed in Kashmir where it is known about through the works of the author Abhinavagupta (*c*.975–1025 CE) and the anonymous *Mahānayaprakāśa* which can be dated between the late tenth and thirteenth centuries. In contrast to the Śaiva Siddhānta in which Sadāśiva is worshiped without a consort, in the Krama system the goddess is worshiped without a male consort as a form of Kālī (Kālasaṃkarṣiṇī), surrounded by a retinue of twelve identical forms (Sanderson 1986: 197–98). Within the Krama system these forms are identified with emanations of pure consciousness, and Abhinavagupta describes the process of the projection of pure consciousness into apparent manifestation as objects of knowledge and its contraction back into itself. The expansion (*vikāsa*) of the cosmos in manifestation is the contraction (*saṃkoca*) of consciousness, while conversely the contraction of manifestation becomes the expansion of consciousness (*Tantrasāra* pp. 29–30; see also Silburn 1975: 134–90, 193–94). The explanation of existence is to be found in these goddesses who are the impulse (*udyoga*) for experience, its manifestation (*avabhāsana*), the tasting of it (*carvaṇa*), and finally its destruction (*vilāpana*) (*Spandanirṇaya* p. 6). In consonance with this idealism, the Krama denied the Vedic distinction between purity and impurity in its rituals.

Closely associated with the Krama are the Trika and Kaula traditions which merge at the higher levels of their initiatory hierarchy. The Trika is a particularly important form of Śaivism which came to dominate Kashmir and is generally understood as "Kashmir" Śaivism. This form of Śaivism was absorbed into the householder life in Kashmir and developed a sophisticated theology that became known as the Recognition school (*pratyabhijñā*). It was strongly influential on the Śaivism of the south and on the goddess tradition of the Śrīvidyā. The root text of the tradition is the *Mālinīvijayottara Tantra*, around which text Abhinavagupta centered his monumental exposition, the *Tantrāloka*, and two other works, the *Tantrasāra* and his commentary on the text, *Mālinīślokavārttika*. Abhinavagupta claimed that the text is the essence of the nondualist Tantras, although Sanderson (1992: 291–306) has argued that the text itself is in fact dualistic in its orientation. Sanderson (1995: 22) observes that Abhinavagupta's basing his teaching on this text shows his desire to ground his idealism in a text that had wide circulation and appeal. This idealism comprised the central claim that all manifestation, including the self, is identical with the pure consciousness (*saṃvit*, *caitanya*) of Śiva and to therefore qualify the Saiddhāntika distinction between lord, self, and bond. Liberation is not becoming equal to

Śiva, as the Siddhānta believed, but the realization of the nondistinction between self and Śiva or Kālī as absolute consciousness.

To show that this realization is the overall goal of practice (*sādhana*), Abhinavagupta adopted the Trika pantheon of three goddesses, Parā, Parāparā, and Aparā, from where the tradition derives its name, showing that they are all manifestations of consciousness. Consciousness is at the esoteric heart of the Trika which Abhinavagupta identified with the Krama goddess Kālasaṃkarṣiṇī, and this rejection of dualism at a theological level is reflected in the rejection of the dualism of purity and impurity at a ritual level. Abhinavagupta distinguished between two ritual systems, the normative rite of the Trika householder (the *tantraprakriyā*) and the optional esoteric rites which flaunted Vedic purity rules (the *kulaprakriyā*). The former was enjoined on the Trika initiate and involved the worship and internalization of a ritual diagram in the form of a trident (*triśūlābjamaṇḍala*) whose prongs were identified with the three goddesses stemming from pure consciousness of the fourth goddess Kālasaṃkarṣiṇī (Sanderson 1986). This normative Trika rite followed the pattern of Saiddhāntika daily worship. But for the suitable person (*adhikārin*) the supererogatory rite of the *kulaprakriyā* was possible in order to achieve gradual perfection (*siddhikrama*) which would otherwise take thousands of years with floods of *mantra*s (*Tantrāloka* 29.1–3). This rite involved making offerings of meat, wine, and sex (*Tantrāloka* 29.97–98), ritually anathema to the orthoprax Brāhmaṇ, with a partner or "messenger" (*dūtī*) who was regarded as the *sādhaka*'s "door" (*dvāra*) to realizing the wonder (*camatkāra*) of pure consciousness (*Tantrāloka* 29.115b–17). The *sādhaka* and his ritual partner thereby recapitulated the union (*yāmala*) of Śiva and his female power, Śakti, and the pleasure of their union reflected the universal joy (*jagadānanda*) of liberation. The deities in these esoteric levels of the Trika and Krama demanded to be appeased by impure substances, such as offerings which included drops of the five substances, urine, semen, menstrual blood, feces, and phlegm, along with other substances polluting to the Brāhmaṇ, such as garlic and onions (Sanderson 1995: 82). The Trika goddesses were so powerful that they must be placated with offerings of blood and alcohol, only after which could ordinary offerings of flowers and incense be made (*Tantrāloka* 26.51c–53b, cited in Sanderson 1995: 81). The secret Kula rites were available only to the Trika initiate who would also maintain outward, Vedic responsibilities. Thus Abhinavagupta could say that the Trika initiate should be internally a Kaula (that is, a practitioner of the secret rite) and externally a Śaiva and Vedic in his social practice (*Tantrālokaviveka* vol. 3, pp. 27, 277–78, cited in Sanderson 1985: 205).

The Trika was very successful in Kashmir and its theologians succeeded in making their interpretation of the scriptures predominant. With Muslim invasion in the eleventh century the tradition became greatly eroded, but there is still a Śaiva householder tradition in Kashmir (Madan 1987) and until recently a living representative of the Recognition school in Svāmī Lakshman Joo. But while the Trika and Krama schools were important within ascetic and intellectual circles, the majority of Śaivas followed less demanding forms of religion in the popular cults of Śiva.

POPULAR ŚAIVISM

Alongside the Trika was the popular worship of Śiva in the Kashmir Valley as Svacchandabhairava. His cult, expressed in the *Svacchandabhairava Tantra*, has continued to the present and is closely connected with the cult of the lord of the eye (Netranātha) found in the *Netra Tantra*. Both of these texts show concerns with special rites of protection, exorcism, and rites for a desired goal (*kāmya*), such as the destruction of enemies or seduction of a desired person. While both the Netra and Svacchanda cults conformed to the ritual purity of the Śaiva Siddhānta, the latter contained the worship of impure forms of the deity. The majority of all Śaivas were probably followers of these cults rather than the more esoteric and demanding Trika and Krama (Sanderson 1995: 22–23). Although popular, these texts present quite complex systems of visualization (Brunner 1974), and their deities as emanations of Netranātha tend to be ferocious, a characteristic of the Kāpālika cults. The *Netra Tantra*, although the text itself has connections with royalty, also bears witness to popular possession and exorcism rites which were probably pervasive among lower social levels. Indeed, one of the main tasks of the orthoprax Brāhmaṇ was to prevent possession. These "demons" (*bhūta*) and powerful female deities or "mothers" (*mātṛ*) enter through the "hole" (*chidra*) of the shadow of impure men and women whose behavior is bad (*durācāra*) and who have neglected their ritual obligations, so causing the evil eye (*dṛṣṭipāta*) to fall upon them (*Netra Tantra* 19.34, 19.45–46).

The classification of possessing beings in the sources is a fascinating example of the way in which cosmological taxonomies link in to Śaiva cosmological structures. The *Netra Tantra* and the Kashmiri Śaiva theologian Kṣemarāja's commentary list several classes of being who possess and who must be appeased through different ritual offerings. These beings include a class of female deities called "mothers" (*mātṛ*), the "removers" (*vināyaka*), "demon-grabbers" (*bhūtagraha*), and others (*Netra Tantra* 19.55–80 and commentary), who are classified in a broader scheme depending upon their motives for possession. Thus there are those desirous of meat offerings (*balikāma*), those desirous of sexual pleasure (*bhoktukāma*), and those desiring to harm and kill (*hantukāma*) (*Netratantroddyota* p. 168). These malevolent powers are within the cosmic hierarchy assumed by the Śaiva systems. They exist within a family (*kula*) of powers with a deity at the head and are indeed particles or fragments (*aṃśa*) of that higher being. Through appeasing the lord of the family of the possessor, the possessor leaves the possessed person (*Netra Tantra* 19.80b–81a). For example, if possessed by the Vināyakas, one worships their Lord Vighneśa (i.e. Gaṇeśa), offering him sweetmeat, meat, and plenty of alcohol (*Netra Tantra* 19.63–65). Or if possessed by the innumerable *mātṛ*s who desire to do harm, then one should perform worship (*prapūjayet*) for the great mothers (*mahāmātṛ*), namely, the famous seven or eight goddesses Brahmī, Maheśvarī, and so on, from whose wombs they have originated (*Netra Tantra* 19.55–56). The lower beings in the hierarchy are emanations or particles of the higher. Once the higher being is appeased with offerings of flowers, rice, and the four kinds of meat from domestic and wild, aquatic, and flying animals (*Netratantroddyota* 9.59–61a), then also are the lower manifestations.

While the *Netra Tantra* is from the north, similar concerns are shown in the Śaiva Siddhānta ritual treatise, probably composed in Kerala, the *Īśānaśivagurudevapaddhati*. This is the only Saiddhāntika text that I am aware of that deals with possession and exorcism and contains a typology of supernatural beings, although the Kerala medical text, the *Tantrasārasaṃgraha* (12.9–11), knows the same typology. The text has eighteen types of powers who can possess (*Īśānaśivagurudevapaddhati* 2.42.1), although the typology is different from that of the northern text. Īśānaśivagurudeva does classify them broadly into those desiring sexual pleasure (*ratikāma*) and those wanting to kill (*hantukāma*). These beings are everywhere, in rivers, gardens, mountains, lakes, empty places, cremation grounds, and temples (*Īśānaśivagurudevapaddhati* 2.42.3b–4). The text goes on to describe the kinds of people these beings attack, usually people on the social margins or in vulnerable situations; for example, children, those alone in the night, those whose wealth has been lost, those wishing to die, and those separated from their loved ones. But especially vulnerable are women when naked, who have bathed after menstruation, and who are filled with passion, intoxicated, pregnant, or prostitutes (*Īśānaśivagurudevapaddhati* 2.42.5b–8). That is, possession happens to those who are or are potentially outside of social control, as women's sexuality was perceived to be by the male-oriented Śaiva Brāhmaṇism. Indeed, women's sexuality was a threat to Brāhmaṇical order because, according to the *Pāśupatasūtra* (9, commentary p. 66), it is beyond the control of the scriptures. The *Īśānaśivagurudevapaddhati* also makes clear that possession is caste related. Thus there are demons who specifically possess Brāhmaṇs (*brahmarākṣasa*), warriors (*kṣatriyagraha*), and so on (*Īśānaśivagurudevapaddhati* 2.42.26–29), and one of the symptoms of possession is somebody from one caste taking on the roles or pretending to perform the duties of another.

There are specific cures or rituals to enact a cure prescribed in the text. For example, the exorcist should nail the tuft of the possessed person to a tree and the *bhūta* will then go (*Īśānaśivagurudevapaddhati* 2.43.3), or he should make an ersatz body of the possessor and pierce it with sharp sticks (2.43.11–12), and so on. All of these rites involve the use of *mantra*s, ritual diagrams, and offerings such as the substitute blood (*raktatoya*) so common in Kerala rites (*Īśānaśivagurudevapaddhati* 2.43.28–30). The construction and use of *mantra*s is a striking feature of this tradition, and for exorcising especially powerful beings, the text gives distorted or garbled *mantra*s (*Īśānaśivagurudevapaddhati* 2.43.83). In dealing with local, possessing deities, the text also thereby expresses the concerns of those in lower social strata. Not only do the texts articulate the dominant ideology, they also express divergent voices which can be heard in the places dealing with possession and which can be read in terms of social protest (Lewis 1971).

The Śaiva cults of possession and exorcism are an important aspect of the tradition, which show links between religion, healing, and social comment. Possession is linked to the diagnosis of disease and the prescription of *mantra*s; the *mantravāda* in Kerala, for example, is related to the Āyurveda. Indeed, it is these aspects of tradition which, while being local in origin, have traveled to other areas. The Śaiva exorcist deity Khaḍgarāvaṇa, for example, in the text of the *Kumāra Tantra*, while originating in the north, became popular in Tibet and Southeast Asia (Filliozat 1937). Where these topics are dealt with we move away from the ordered world of temple and domestic ritual into a world of the lower levels of the supernatural order and so of lower levels of the social order. But although the *Īśānaśivagurudevapaddhati* is concerned with possession and exorcism, most of the text is devoted to the more usual concerns of the Śaiva Siddhānta, its temple ritual and deities.

THE SOUTHERN ŚAIVA SIDDHĀNTA

By the eleventh century, Śaiva Siddhānta had faded in Kashmir but developed in Tamilnadu, where it exists to the present time. Here in the south the dualist tradition merged with the Tamil devotionalism of the sixty-three Śaiva saints, the Nāyaṉārs.

Śaivism took on a distinctive flavor, and the Sanskritic ritualism and theology of the northern tradition combined with Tamil poetry and devotion to produce a distinctively southern Śaiva religious *imaginaire*. This devotional poetry is still sung in temples throughout South India. It was in the south that Śaivism had royal patronage in the Cōḻa dynasty (*c.*870–1280 CE), with the great Śaiva temples at Cidambaram, Tanjavur, Darasuram, and Gangaikondacolapuram thriving, and the famous Cōḻa bronzes developed. At Cidambaram, for example, wealthy donors' inscriptions made in the temple walls show how the temple supported and legitimized royal power in the region (Younger 1995: 125–58). This power was not centralized as in a modern state but pervaded through a segmented hierarchy, whose basic unit was the locality or *nāṭu* (Stein 1980). But even here where Śaivism became aligned with an ideology of royal power and the king was thought to embody the power (*śakti*) of the lord, Śaivism not only upheld Vedic norms but simultaneously undermined them in a devotionalism where the devotee transcends his birth to fall in love with his lord. It is these two aspects of Śaiva Siddhānta in the south that I wish to briefly examine.

Tamilnadu developed an extensive temple culture in which large, regional temples became not only places of worship but also centers of political power and great centers of learning. In Tamilnadu a distinctive sense of the sacredness of place and temple buildings develops (Shulman 1980). Perhaps this is nowhere seen more vividly than in the temple-city of Cidambaram, the "sky of consciousness," where Śiva is installed, not as in all other Śiva temples in the aniconic form of the *liṅga*, but as the dancing Śiva (Naṭarāja). Here he is installed along with a bronze icon of his consort Śivakāmasundarī and, in contrast to fixed icons, is paraded on festival occasions (D. Smith 1996: 10). Like other Śaiva temples, Cidambaram had a group of texts associated with it, extolling its virtues and narrating its mythology, namely, the twelfth-century *Cidambara Māhātmya* along with four Sthalapurānas, a Tamil translation of the former text, and Umāpati Śivācārya's hymn of praise to Naṭarāja (D. Smith 1996: 8–9). Through these texts and the popular imagination, Cidambaram became incorporated into the sacred geography of Tamilnadu.

Although the Śaiva Siddhānta has been the predominant form of theology and ritual in southern Śaivism and Cidambaram was an important center for this theology, the temple and its rites are not sectarian in a strict sense. Indeed, the community of Brāhmaṇs who perform six daily rituals to Naṭarāja claim that they follow Vedic practice rather than Tantric or Āgamic. They thereby differentiate themselves from the hereditary priests at other Śaiva Siddhānta temples, the *arccakaṉs*, who follow the Tantric or Āgamic rites of the texts we have discussed. The Dīkṣitas (Tamil Dīṭcitars), as they are called, are an endogamous community, who perform rites accompanied by Smārta Brāhmaṇs or Aiyars who are qualified to perform recitation of the Vedas (Younger 1995: 13–24). These rites are quite elaborate and involve the performance of *pūjā* to a crystal *liṅga* transported out from the inner sanctum of the bronze Naṭarāja to an outer porch where ablutions are made over it (*abhiṣeka*). It is then returned to the inner shrine, and *pūjā* to the icon of Naṭarāja himself is performed, involving the offering of lights (*dīpa*), sound, and, at certain times of the day, food (*naivedya*). During one of the evening *pūjās* low-caste singers, the *ōtuvār*s, sing Tamil devotional hymns before the icon, as they do elsewhere throughout Tamilnadu.

While Tamil Śaivism is strongly associated with royal power and the upholding of orthoprax values, as we can see at Cidambaram, it simultaneously undermines those values through its emphasis on popular devotion. We can see this in the context when a caste of singers, the *ōtuvār*s, sing hymns to the icon of Śiva and during the great festival when the icons of Naṭarāja and his consort are paraded through the streets by Vēḷāḷas, outside of Brāhmaṇical control (Younger 1995: 60–63). In one sense festival transgression of formal boundaries can serve to reinforce those boundaries, but in another sense the carnival disrupts hierarchy and in it we can hear voices otherwise occluded. Indeed, it is these voices that are articulated in much of the devotional poetry of the Nāyaṉārs, which partly developed against the oppression of the lower castes in the feudalism of the southern kingdoms.

The Nāyaṉārs were often low caste themselves, composing love songs to Śiva in his icons at different temples. In the love or *bhakti* presented in these Tamil sources, what is important is the direct, unmediated relationship between the devotee and the lord in which the devotee can become mad (*piccu*, *unmatta*) with devotion. The texts of the Nāyaṉārs are incorporated into the canon of the southern Śaiva Siddhānta, the *Tirumuṟai*, which also contains Śaiva Siddhānta *śāstra*s in Tamil (Peterson 1989: 52–59; Zvelebil 1975). Among the Nāyaṉārs represented, the most famous is Māṇikkavācakar dated by tradition to the fifth century, who composed the "sacred verses" (*Tiruvācakam*) and whose twenty-verse hymn, the *Tiruvempāvai*, is still recited in temples today. Māṇikkavācakar is the most revered saint of Tamil Śaivism. He was a court official in Madurai but retired to a life of meditation at Cidamabram, where, tradition maintains, he entered the inner sanctum never to return and merged with his god (Younger 1995: 194–201). Other texts are also recited by the *ōtuvār*s, particularly the later *Tēvāram* (Peterson 1989). The following is an example from the Nāyaṉār Appar, who expresses a devotional sentiment specific to a place, to the particular temple in which Śiva dwells (Peterson 1989: 210):

> When I think of the skullbearer
> who wears a wreath of flowers in his hair,
> the Lord with the white moon who likes to live
> in Veṇṇi's ancient city,
> a flood of ambrosia
> wells up in my tongue.

This kind of devotionalism, so typical of the *bhakti* movement, spread from Tamilnadu to neighboring Karnataka where the Liṅgāyata or Vīraśaiva sect was founded by Basava (*c.*1106–67 CE), although there was some continuity with the Kālamukha sect (see pp. 123–25). As in Tamilnadu, this form of Śaivism is highly devotional, and the *bhakti* movement instigated by Basava was against asceticism (as would have been practiced by the Kālamukhas), against caste, and against formal, temple worship, preferring instead an immediate relationship between devotee and lord symbolized by a small *liṅga* worn around the neck. As in Tamilnadu, beautiful devotional poetry was composed in Kannada to Śiva and his forms (Ramanujan 1973). The fusion of *bhakti* with Tantric ritual that occurred in the Tamil Śaiva Siddhānta and Liṅgāyatas of Karnataka provided a rich mix that gave expression to both a popular religiosity and to formal, Brāhmaṇical Tantric ritual. There is a fusion of the two in that the personal religion of *bhakti* becomes formalized and incorporated into temple ritual structure.

Śaiva Siddhānta temple ritual found its way into Kerala where the Nambūdiri Brāhmaṇs, akin to the Tamil *arccakaṉs*, developed a distinctive form of temple Tantrism based on a fifteenth-century *Tantrasamuccaya* by Cēnnāsu Nārāyaṇam Nampūtirippāṭu, although some families use the *Īśānaśivagurudevapaddhati* (Freeman 1999). This tradition is not strictly Śaiva but a synthesis of traditions focusing on the temple worship of Śiva, Viṣṇu, Gaṇeśa, Devī, and low-caste regional goddesses.

In the Śaiva Siddhānta of the south and in the related Kerala Tantrism, we see traditions which formally align themselves with adherence to Vedic worship and social mores (*varṇāśramadharma*) but which in practice perform worship according to the Tantras. The southern tradition absorbed lower-caste devotion and succeeded in all but eradicating the ascetical traditions of Buddhism and Jainism from the region and successfully aligned the Tantric tradition with the Vedic. This alignment is achieved in ritual where the Śaiva Siddhānta and Kerala traditions absorb Vedic elements into the Tantric ritual structure that then forms a common pattern in both temple and private cults. Having taken this survey of Śaiva history so far, it is to the patterns of Śaiva practice that we must now turn.

ŚAIVA TEMPLE RITUAL

While personal *yoga* and private ritual for both liberation and power must not be forgotten in Śaiva traditions, it is the ritual life of the temple that provides its wider social coherence. The Śaiva Siddhānta is the basic ritual and theological structure to which the other Tantric traditions respond and build. Many of the Śaiva Siddhānta Tantras and manuals are concerned with temple ritual such as the *Rauravottarāgama*, while others such as the *Mṛgendra* are not concerned with temples but with personal practice under the direction of a teacher. The *Rauravottara* describes various styles of temple and the rites for the installation of the temple and of deities within it (*pratiṣṭhā*). The deities of the directions (*dinmūrti*) are first established and then others may be installed in the vicinity of the central shrine, namely, the gods Gaṇeśa, Dakṣiṇāmūrti, Viṣṇu, Brahmā, and Durgā. Finally, the *liṅga* is installed as the central icon of Śiva. The *liṅga* is regarded as the highest, undifferentiated (*niṣkala*) form of Śiva in contrast to the anthropomorphic form which is differentiated (*sakala*). The *liṅga* with a face or faces is a mixture of both (*sakalaniṣkala*) (R. Davis 1991: 121–22).

There are different kinds of *liṅga* for different kinds of temple, and an elaborate typology is offered in the *Rauravottara* (chapter 15). Abhinavagupta offers an esoteric interpretation of the *liṅga* as being unmanifest (*avyakta*) where it is equated with absolute consciousness or the "supreme heart of tranquility" (*viśrāntihṛdayam param*), manifest-unmanifest (*vyaktāvyakta*) when identified with the body, and manifest (*vyakta*) as an outer symbol (*Tantrāloka* 5.117a). It is with the outer symbol and its worship that the Śaiva Siddhānta is mainly concerned. Having made the icon of wood, metal, or stone, the eyes are opened, and the icon is purified by being immersed in water, the altar (*vedikā*) constructed, firepits (*kuṇḍa*) placed around it, the deity invoked in the icon, the icon bathed (*abhiṣeka*), priests honored, and Brāhmaṇs fed (Bhatt 1982: cxii). Daily rites are thereafter performed, involving bathing the icon, its decoration, the offering of vegetarian food (*naivedya*) to the accompaniment of ringing bells, the vision (*darśana*) of the deity for devotees, and the offering of light (*dīpa*).

PRIVATE YOGA

While it is often not meaningful to draw a hard distinction between private ritual and *yoga*, there are nevertheless practices beyond the basic daily ritual structure that can be undertaken. Many dualistic Tantras have sections on *yoga* (the *yogapāda*), often virtually identical to the Yoga of Patañjali, and some Śaiva Siddhānta texts are devoted to *yoga* such as Jñānaprakāśa's *Śivayogaratna* (Michaël 1975). But in nondualistic Śaivism there is a particular emphasis on various kinds of *yoga* practice beyond the ritual obligations of the initiate. These practices are categorized into four methods or ways (*upāya*): the "non-means" or the pathless path (*anupāya*), the divine means (*śāmbhavopāya*), the way of energy (*śāktopāya*), and the individual means (*āṇavopāya*) (see Dyczkowski 1987: 163–218). This structure, the oldest description of which is in the *Mālinīvijayottara Tantra* (2.21–23) where they are called "immersions" or "possessions" (*samāveśa*), was used by the monistic Śaivas Abhinavagupta and Kṣemarāja as a lens through which to view the earlier tradition. Thus Kṣemarāja uses the scheme as a way of organizing the *Śivasūtra*. The classification of the three *upāya*s relates to the three perceived human and divine faculties of desire or will (*icchā*), cognition (*jñāna*), and action (*kriyā*). Thus the *śāmbhavopāya* is linked to desire or will as the sudden upsurge of emotion and instinct that shatters thought construction, thereby enabling the adept to perceive the nonduality of consciousness. This can be achieved through extreme situations of fear or through inducing pain by scratching the arm with a sharp instrument (*Vijñānabhairava* 93), through the arising of sexual desire (41, 73), and so on. Abhinavagupta even says that thought-shattering energy (*vīrya*) can arise in the heart upon seeing a loved one unexpectedly (*Parātrīśikāvivaraṇa* p. 16). In fact, any emotional situation is potentially transformative.

While the *Mālinīvijayottara Tantra* (2.25a) says that the ways are identical as to goal but differ as to method, Abhinavagupta and his commentator Jayaratha claim that the *upāya*s form a graded hierarchy (*upāyayogakramatā*) (*Tantrāloka* 13.157), with the individual means at the bottom and the nonmeans at the top. But Abhinavagupta also observes elsewhere that because of his extreme monism, there cannot really be any hierarchical gradation; any hierarchy (*uttaratva*) contains the delusion of dualism (*Parātrīśikāvivaraṇa* p. 8). This idea is reflected in the last method, which is no method. The *anupāya* is the realization of the nonduality of self and Śiva that is a sudden realization because the path and the goal are the same. This realization without any method (other than the *guru* who is not a method) is understood as an intense descent of power (*śaktipāta*) and realization that consciousness was never bound. From this nondual perspective, the very idea of a path, which implies a journey from one place to another, is erroneous. Even the idea of a descent of power is problematic in this context. Abhinavagupta writes in an eloquent passage:

> The supreme lord is the essence of his own light and our own self. By what means then is he to be achieved? Due to his own light he cannot be known. Due to his eternity his essence cannot be attained. Due to the nonexistence of a covering, there cannot be the cessation of a covering (of consciousness). What then is the means? If it is distinct then it cannot be accomplished. Therefore the totality is a single reality of consciousness only, undivided by time, unlimited by space, unclouded by constraints, unobstructed by forms, unsignified by word, and unmanifested by means of knowledge.
>
> (*Tantrasāra* pp. 8–9)

Because there is only the reality of pure consciousness in this tradition, a practice cannot lead to a goal that implies a distinction between self and object of attainment. The web of paths (*upāyajāla*) cannot illumine Śiva (*Tantrasāra* p. 9). The monistic Śaivism of Kashmir regarded this as its highest truth. If there is one reality only, then there can be no distinction between knower (*vedaka*) and object of knowledge (*vedya*) and nothing which is impure (*Śivasūtravimarśinī* p. 8). Abhinavagupta is certainly aware of this problem. If the lord is equidistant from all points, then does it make sense to also claim that he crowns a hierarchy? But while the tradition claimed this nondual awareness to be the supreme realization, the tradition nevertheless cultivated an elaborate ritual structure and sought to defeat its opponents, the dualist Saiddhāntikas and the Buddhists, in theology.

ŚAIVA THEOLOGY

Śaivism developed a sophisticated theology articulated in commentaries on its sacred texts. The Śaiva Siddhānta's most important theologians in its early years were Sadyojyoti (eighth century), Bhaṭṭa Rāmakaṇṭha (*c.*950–1000 CE), and Bhojadeva (eleventh century). These theologians through their textual hermeneutics argued for a dualism regarding the self and lord which the nondualist theologians of the Pratyabhijñā attempted to refute. There was rigorous debate between these two theologies, although the monists succeeded in supplanting the Siddhānta in Kashmir. Debate focused particularly on two issues: the first was the nature of the self, the second was the nature of matter, both of which had consequences for practice.

For the Saiddhāntikas the self is quite distinct from the lord and from matter. The self is, in fact, trapped or bound by matter from which it must break free through its own efforts but ultimately through the grace of Śiva, whereupon it will achieve equality with him and not be reborn again. In his *Nareśvaraparīkṣa*, Sadyojyoti argues against his theological rivals to establish this position regarding the self. The self is the knower and actor who experiences the fruits of his action (*Nareśvaraparīkṣa* 1.2) and is constituted by cognition itself. The self knows sense objects (he uses the typical Sanskrit expression "such as blue and so on") as distinct and does not perceive an undifferentiated field (*Nareśvaraparīkṣa* 1.13). He thereby argues against the monists from a pragmatic perspective of common experience as well as against the Buddhist view that there is no self but only a series of momentary perceptions. Sadyojyoti also goes on to argue, against the Mīmāṃsā, for the authorship of the Veda by the lord, arguing that the Veda is a sound, which is a product and so must be produced from one whose knowledge transcends the human, for it takes effort for us to understand it (*Nareśvaraparīkṣa* 3.76). This view of the self as distinct is constantly refuted by the nondualists of the Pratyabhijñā who systematically present a nondual interpretation of sacred scripture and argue their position in independent treatises. Perhaps the best introduction to this theology is Kṣemarāja's *Pratyabhijñāhṛdaya*, a commentary on his own verses arguing against other theological positions.

Apart from the nature of the self and its relation to the divine, the second major area of disagreement between the Śaiva Siddhānta and the Pratyabhijñā was over the status of matter or rather the substrate of matter, *māyā*. Both regard *māyā* as that which constitutes the cosmos. In the higher levels or pure creation of the cosmic hierarchy comprising a number of levels or *tattva*s, it is called, by the Saiddhāntikas, *mahāmāyā* or the "drop" (*bindu*), while in the lower or impure creation it is called *māyā*. For the Siddhānta *māyā* is an eternal substance (*dravya*) as real as the self and the lord, upon whom the lord acts through his regent Ananta and other higher beings (the Vidyeśvaras) to create the cosmos. *Māyā* is thus the material cause of the universe (*upadānakāraṇa*), whereas Śiva is only the efficient cause (*nimittakāraṇa*). For the Pratyabhijñā, by contrast, *māyā* is not a substance but a manifestation of pure consciousness or indeed identical with pure consciousness. The consequences of these doctrines were the theological justification of their practices. For the Siddhānta liberation is the removal of impure substance from the self which, because it is a substance, can only be done through action (i.e. ritual action). For the Pratyabhijñā liberation is not the removal of substance but the recognition of the self's identity with the absolute and so is the highest knowledge and not action (see Sanderson 1992: 283–87).

The methods whereby these doctrines were established were generally through commentary on sacred texts. The doctrinal neutrality of some texts was such that they lent themselves to both dualistic and monistic interpretations. Much of the language of these texts is in bad Sanskrit, and the commentators, such as Kṣemarāja on the *Svacchanda Tantra* and Bhaṭṭa Rāmakaṇṭha on the *Kiraṇa Tantra*, excused this "language of the lord" (*aiśa*) as a kind of disruption of language due to its sacredness (Goodall 1998: lxv–lxxi). Through their commentaries the Śaiva theologians clarified the doctrines of their own schools by drawing upon a full apparatus of techniques open to Hindu philosophical analysis. For example, as Sanderson (1995: 59–65) and Eivind Kahrs (1998) have shown, Abhinavagupta and Kṣemarāja use a method called *nirvacana*, an interpretive device whereby the name of a thing is analyzed into its component parts to reveal its true nature. Through this method Kṣemarāja interprets the names of deities and their *mantra*s in an esoteric sense, thereby linking language and metaphysics. For example, Kahrs (1998: 86–89) cites Kṣemarāja's analysis of the term "Bhairava" in his commentary on the *Svacchanda Tantra* to embrace a variety of meanings, such as he who is the inner nature of *yogin*s, who destroys transmigratory existence, and so on. In this way monistic doctrines could be injected into the text if they were not there already.

CONCLUSION

This survey of Śaiva history, practice, and doctrine shows the diversity of the traditions. Yet it also shows a distinctive religious *imaginaire* that sets Śaivism apart from other Hindu traditions. I have focused on what I would regard as the most important developments, but this treatment is not of course exhaustive or even comprehensive. For example, there is a fascinating history of groups of *yogī*s known as Nāthas or Siddhas, which has been strongly influenced by Śaivism, and a rich history of Śaiva tradition in Southeast Asia (see White 1996). Until the last thirty years or so Śaivism was often only given cursory treatment in the history of Hinduism. This was partly due to scholarly ignorance of these traditions and partly due to not taking seriously their major sources, namely, the Tantras. The situation has changed with groups of scholars working on this material, particularly in Pondichery, Oxford, Paris, and Rome. In Pondichery the Centre d'Indologie has continued to edit and publish Tantras of the Śaiva Siddhānta, and scholarly interest in Śaivism exists at many major centers of learning. The study of Śaivism has contributed to our wider understanding of Hindu traditions in showing the importance of non-Vedic, Tantric tradition and the incoherence of the term "Hinduism" in a historical context.

As regards Śaivism itself, the Śaiva Siddhānta still provides the ritual template of temple worship in the south and is a form of Śaivism that has come to America in a new form as the Church of the Śaiva Siddhānta. The nondualistic Śaiva traditions have been eroded over time, although the Pratyabhijñā still has some followers and has become a tradition in the West, where it has influenced a number of contemporary groups, particularly Siddha Yoga and the Nityānanda Institute of Svāmī Cetanānanda. The image of Śiva is now deeply embedded as a cross-cultural icon. It remains to be seen the extent to which traditional forms of Śaivism will be eroded in India and to what extent it will be transformed in the global, new religious context.

CHAPTER SEVEN

ŚĀKTA

Kathleen M. Erndl

Worship of goddesses or divine feminine manifestations is surely one of the oldest religious expressions on the Indian subcontinent, though as a sectarian or textual movement it became integrated into the more orthodox Sanskritic tradition at a relatively late period. Śākta, that which pertains to Śakti, the power of the universe conceived of as a goddess, is often considered to be the third major Hindu sectarian tradition, after Vaiṣṇava (worship of Viṣṇu) and Śaiva (worship of Śiva) traditions, but it is much more difficult to delineate than either of those. For one thing, all Hindus worship goddesses as part and parcel of a nonsectarian polytheism. For another, goddesses and concepts of *śakti* saturate the Vaiṣṇava and Śaiva traditions. It is a common saying that all Brāhmaṇs are Śākta because of their daily recitation of the preeminent Gāyatrī-*mantra*, the prayer to the sun which is personified as the goddess Sāvitrī or Gāyatrī, the wife of Brahmā and mother of the Veda. If one defines as Śākta those who worship goddesses, from the Brāhmaṇ priest who recites his daily Gāyatrī to the men and women of even the lowest castes who propitiate their village and family goddesses, then Śāktas are to be found everywhere. But there is also a sense in which Śāktas are difficult to find, either in scholarly literature or as a label of self-identification among practitioners. In scholarly literature Śāktism is often ignored, subordinated to Vaiṣṇavism or even more commonly to Śaivism, or conflated with Tantrism. It is often misunderstood, especially by Western scholars, even to the point where in a recent world religions textbook, a scholar of Hinduism declares—erroneously—that Śāktism cannot be considered a *mārga* or path to liberation because it is concerned only with obtaining worldly benefits for the worshiper, not liberation from the realm of *saṃsāra* (Hein 1993). Because of Śākta association with unorthodox Tantric practices and non-Vedic or tribal cultures, some goddess worshipers are hesitant to label themselves Śākta and practice their tradition in secret or under the guise of Śaivism. As a Bengali saying goes, one should be "Vaiṣṇava in public, Śaiva in private, and Śākta in secret."

DEFINING ŚĀKTISM

What exactly is Śāktism? Śāktism is sometimes considered to be synonymous with Tantrism or to be an offshoot of Śaivism, but in fact it is neither, though it overlaps with both. Some preliminary definitions of Śāktism and Tantrism are offered here and elaborated at various points throughout this chapter, keeping in mind that Śāktism has many forms, both regional and with respect to philosophical elaboration and ritual practice, and that it overlaps in many areas with other Hindu traditions.

Briefly Śāktism is the worship of *śakti*, the primordial power underlying the universe, personified as a female deity who is the supreme being, the totality of all existence. As such, it stresses the dynamic quality of the deity as both deluding and saving power. This goddess takes on many different forms, usually subsumed under the categories *saumya* (gentle, beneficent), such as Pārvatī, Ambā, or Śrī, and *raudra* (fierce, horrific), such as Durgā, Kālī, or Caṇḍī. Śāktism has many different forms, encompassing esoteric Tantric practices as well as the more exoteric devotional (*bhakti*) practices found in popular cults throughout India.

Narendra Nath Bhattacharyya (1973: 73) distinguishes between "dependent" Śāktism, the cult of the female principle under the garb of Vaiṣṇavism, Śaivism, Buddhism, or Jainism, and an "independent" Śāktism, the cult of the female deity as supreme being in her own right. Pushpendra Kumar simply states that "Śāktism is the worship of *Śakti* or the female principle, the primary factor in the creation and reproduction of the universe" (1974: 1). June McDaniel (2004), in her massive study of varieties of Bengali Śāktism, delineates three major strands of Śāktism: the folk/tribal strand, which involves possession, shamanism, and animism; the Tantric/yogic strand, which involves meditation, visualization, and spiritual disciplines; and the devotional/*bhakti* strand, which involves love of a particular form of the goddess and her worship. Each of these has several subtypes, and, in practice, they are found in combined form.

Śāktism is sufficiently distinctive that it must be considered a movement of its own, not an offshoot of Śaivism, although in later times and in certain regions such as Bengal the cult of Śakti has been closely associated with the cult of Śiva. Similarly, the glorification of Rādhā or Lakṣmī within certain forms of Vaiṣṇavism reflects Śākta influence. In earlier Śākta texts such as the *Devī Māhātmya*, to be considered in more detail later, the goddess is associated more with Viṣṇu, as in her epithets Nārāyaṇī and Viṣṇumāyā, than with Śiva, who is mentioned only once in the role of messenger. The same text shows that the goddess can be represented as the personified *śakti* or creative power of the male gods collectively, without being represented as a consort. Furthermore, she can produce her own *śakti*s or concentrated manifestations of power without a male counterpart.

Śāktism is a worldview oriented towards *śakti*, while Tantrism is an amalgam of yogic and ritual practices with an aim towards gaining power and liberation. André Padoux characterizes Tantrism as "a practical way to attain supernatural powers and liberation in this life through the use of specific and complex techniques based on a particular ideology, that of a cosmic reintegration by means of which the adept is established in a position of power, freed from worldly fetters, while remaining in this world and dominating it by a union with (or proximity to) a godhead who is the supreme power itself" (1987: 274). Teun Goudriaan lists at least eighteen features, the combination of which, rather than any single one, distinguishes Tantric from non-Tantric Hinduism. These features include the use of verbal formulas (*mantra*), mystical diagrams (*yantra*, *maṇḍala*, *cakra*), visualization of images, coded language, the intentional reversal of accepted social norms, the necessity of initiation by a *guru*, mystical physiology in which the body is a microcosm of the universe, the recognition of both mundane aims and spiritual emancipation as goals for the practitioner, and the importance of female manifestations called Śaktis (Goudriaan 1979: 7–9). Of particular note are the so-called "five *m*'s" (*pañcamakāra*) peculiar to Tantric practice, which are meat (*māṃsa*), fish (*matsya*), wine (*madya*), parched grain (*mudrā*), and sexual intercourse (*maithuna*). There are two ways of using these, the "left-hand path" (*vāmācāra*), in which the initiate uses the actual items in *sādhana* (spiritual practice), and the "right-hand path" (*dakṣiṇācāra*), in which pure substitutes or mental visualizations are used.

Goudriaan states that Śāktism and Tantrism are not the same but that although Tantric elements are found in all Indian religions, they are most prevalent in Śāktism. He defines Śāktism as the worship of *śakti*, "the universal and all-embracing dynamis [*sic*] which manifests itself in human experience as a female divinity," adding that an inactive male partner is inseparably connected with her and that she functions as his power of action and movement (Goudriaan 1979: 7). Goudriaan is accurate in his insistence upon a male partner in most Tantric forms of Śāktism, but it should be pointed out that there are also Śākta texts and cults, especially in village and folk contexts, in which a goddess is worshiped as the supreme being with little or no importance placed on a male counterpart.

SCHOLARSHIP

Śākta traditions have been studied from a variety of academic perspectives which can be grouped into four main categories: historical surveys, thematic or contextual studies, studies of specific goddesses, and textual translations and analyses.

The first approach, that of the broad historical survey, tends to view Śāktism as a continuous developing tradition, beginning with the prehistoric archaeological artifacts of the Indus Valley civilization, pausing to consider the goddesses of the Vedas, and then moving through the epics and the Purāṇas up through the Tantras and devotional poetry to the modern period. Indian, predominantly Bengali, writers have produced most of these studies. The most prominent are Narendra Nath Bhattacharyya's *History of the Śākta Religion* (1973) and *The Indian Mother Goddess* (1977). Others include a volume edited by D. C. Sircar (1967b) and the works of Pushpendra Kumar (1974), Ernest Payne (1933), and Sukumar Sen (1983). Pupul Jayakar in *The Earth Mother* (1990) uses archaeology, art history, and folk arts to study the development of Śāktism in India; and Tracy Pintchman's *The Rise of the Goddess in the Hindu Tradition* (1994) treats the early development of Śākta concepts.

The second approach, that of specific localities and contexts, usually involves social science methodology, such as sociology, psychology, or anthropology, or history of religions methodology. Rather than looking at long-term historical developments, this approach focuses on specific persons, places, and events, using fieldwork, interview, and biography. Some examples of work in this category are Kathleen Erndl's *Victory to the Mother* (1993), which focuses on religious experience in Northwest India; Stanley Kurtz's *All the Mothers are One* (1992), which is a psychological study that explores the influence of early childhood on Śākta belief; and William Sax's *Mountain Goddess* (1991b), which shows the effect of goddess worship on social interaction. These works tend to focus on present-day beliefs and practices, rather than on the past.

The third approach, studies of specific goddesses, involves literary, mythic, and iconographic analysis. Goddesses are studied as subjects in themselves. Two standard sources on multiple goddesses are David Kinsley's *Hindu Goddesses* (1986) and John Hawley's and Donna Wulff's *Devī: Goddesses of India* (1996). Kinsley's (1997) book on the ten

Mahāvidyās is a valuable contribution toward the understanding of these little-studied Tantric goddesses. In addition, there are works on most of the individual Hindu goddesses. Lynn Foulston's *At the Feet of the Goddess* (2002) follows a combination of the second and third approaches, focusing on specific village goddess in two regions of India, Orissa, and Tamilnadu.

The fourth approach, translations and interpretations of Śākta texts, follows the traditional Indological focus on sacred texts. The pioneer in this area, with a particular focus on Śākta Tantrism, was John Woodroffe (1969, 1974), who did his scholarship in the first quarter of the twentieth century. The *Devī Māhātmya* has been studied by Vasudeva Agrawala (1963) and Thomas Coburn (1984, 1991). The *Devībhāgavata Purāṇa* has been studied by C. Mackenzie Brown (1990). Douglas Brooks focuses on a single Śrīvidyā text in *The Secret of the Three Cities* (1990) and broadens his scope to include a wider variety of sources in *Auspicious Wisdom* (1992). Bengali devotional Śākta poetry by Ramprasad Sen and others is the subject of work by Malcolm McLean (1998) and Rachel McDermott (2001a,b).

These works with their various approaches all make valuable contributions to the study of Śākta traditions in their historical, cultural, literary, and philosophical contexts. A recent work which incorporates all of the approaches mentioned here and at the same time takes a self-critical and reflexive stance *vis-a-vis* the scholarly study of Hindu goddesses, especially in regard to gender issues, is a collection of essays entitled *Is the Goddess a Feminist?: The Politics of South Asian Goddesses*, edited by Alf Hiltebeitel and Kathleen Erndl (2000). The relationship between Śāktism, goddesses, and women has emerged as a concern recently not only among scholars of Hinduism but also among Hindu intellectuals, grass-roots activists, artists, and cultural critics. This relationship will be considered briefly in the final section of this chapter.

GENERAL ŚĀKTA CONCEPTS

Although, as stated earlier, Śāktism is not a systematic, uniform philosophical system, it will be useful here to discuss briefly some key concepts associated with Śāktism generally. That is not to say that all Śākta texts and practitioners subscribe to such views or articulate them but that they are frequently imbedded in texts, songs, stories, and rituals connected with goddess worship.

Implicit in Śākta theology is a kind of monism in which matter and spirit are not ultimately distinct but are a continuity subsumed within *śakti*, the dynamic feminine creative principle. This is not the monism of Advaita Vedānta which denies the reality of the material world but a monism in which the material world is identical with the divine which is conceived of as being feminine. Śaiva and Vaiṣṇava theologies associated with the male deities Śiva and Viṣṇu both recognize *śakti* as the active aspect of the divine, the complement to the inactive aspect. Śākta theology, on the other hand, understands *śakti*, identified with Mahādevī, the great goddess, to be the ultimate reality itself and the totality of all being. Even when the goddess is joined with a male consort, as she is with Śiva in many of the Tantric traditions, if it is *śakti* which is emphasized theologically, devotionally, or ritually, then the tradition may reasonably be called Śākta. In some cases it is difficult to make a clear-cut distinction. For example, Kashmiri Śaivism places a strong philosophical emphasis on *śakti*, and many of its practitioners have a strong devotional attachment to a form of the goddess. Conversely, the Śrīvidyā school, which is unambiguously Śākta in its cultic orientation, has borrowed much of its philosophical terminology from Kashmiri Śaivism (D. Brooks 1990: 74–75). Even some Vaiṣṇava schools have strong Śākta elements. For example, the *Lakṣmī Tantra*, belonging formally to the Vaiṣṇava Pāñcarātra school, reads much more like a Śākta text, with Lakṣmī taking over from Viṣṇu the creation and preservation of the universe. Again, it is the degree of emphasis and importance placed on *śakti*, resulting in cosmogonic, ritual, and/or soteriological preeminence of a goddess. Wendell Beane has rightly stated that *śakti* is the "irreducible (*sui generis*) ground for understanding both the non-Sanskritic, popular, and exoteric and the Sanskritic, philosophical, and esoteric" aspects of the worship of the divine feminine (1977: 41). All names and forms of goddesses, gentle (*saumya*) and fierce (*raudra* or *ghora*), are manifestations of the one supreme being. What this means in the context of specific Śākta texts or practice traditions is that one primary form becomes paramount while the others become ancillary. For example, in the Śrīvidyā tradition, the primary form of the goddess is the lovely and gentle Lalitā, also known as Tripurasundarī. In Bengali or Assamese Śāktism, which has subsequently spread throughout India, especially in its popular forms, the primary goddess is a form of either Durgā or Kālī.

Although Śākta theology, as will be discussed next, shares many terms and concepts with the formal philosophical systems of dualistic Sāṃkhya and nondualistic Advaita Vedānta, it differs from them in its relentless exaltation of the material world. Espousing a kind of "divine materialism," it is more thoroughly world-affirming than either Sāṃkhya or Advaita Vedānta. The goddess is often identified with *prakṛti*, sometimes translated as nature, the matter-energy composed of three *guṇa*s or qualities that is the basis of all creation. In the classical Sāṃkhya system and in the Yoga system of Patañjali which is based upon it, *prakṛti* is viewed as dynamic and creative but unconscious and unintelligent and thus the source of bondage in *saṃsāra*. It has a somewhat negative connotation, being seen as the web of matter in which the spirit, *puruṣa*, is entrapped. Liberation in Sāṃkhya-Yoga terms is the isolation (*kaivalya*) of *puruṣa*, which literally means "the male," from the feminine *prakṛti*. This formulation is similar to the Greek, and subsequently Christian, identification of the male with spirit and the female with matter, resulting in the inevitable devaluation of both the material world and the feminine. Śāktism turns this concept of *prakṛti* on its head, giving it not only ontological and cosmogonic status but also soteriological status by identifying it with the great goddess who pervades the phenomenal world as *bhuktimuktipradāyinī*, the "grantor of both material enjoyment and liberation."[1] As *prakṛti*, the goddess contains within herself the three *guṇa*s, *tamas*, *rajas*, and *sattva*, personified as her three major manifestations, Mahālakṣmī, Mahākālī, and Mahāsarasvatī, respectively. From the Śākta point of view, *prakṛti* is conscious and *puruṣa* and *prakṛti* are ultimately the same; or rather *prakṛti* contains within her *puruṣa*.

Similarly, the goddess is identified with *māyā*, one of her major epithets being Mahāmāyā. This term is most closely associated with the Advaita Vedānta school, where it refers to the illusion or ignorance that prevents one from seeing things as they really are. According to the Advaitins, *brahman*, the nonmaterial absolute which is neuter in gender, is the only real entity; it is only by overcoming *māyā*, which has no reality in any case, that one can attain liberation. The Śākta idea of *māyā*, as seen for example in the first episode of the *Devī Māhātmya* discussed next, retains some of this negative connotation, but as the material world is real, not illusory as in Advaita, *māyā* is part of a divine process. Another shade of meaning which *māyā* takes on, in the Purāṇas and elsewhere, is power or creative energy, and it is this sense which is prevalent in Śāktism, though the idea of the goddess as "deluding power" is there as well. However, as the power of the goddess that animates the world, *māyā* is a necessary part of existence and thus is considered her blessing.

In some contexts, for example, in the *Devībhāgavata Purāṇa*, the goddess is equated with *brahman* (see C. M. Brown 1990). This is not surprising, as *brahman* from the time of the Upaniṣads has been the most commonly accepted term for the ultimate reality.[2] *Brahman* has been described in two ways: *nirguṇa* (beyond all qualities) and *saguṇa* (having qualities). As *nirguṇa* it is the basis of all existence yet defies description; as *saguṇa* it manifests in the form of various deities. Some texts, despite their elaborate descriptions of the goddess's feminine *saguṇa* manifestation, state that ultimately she is beyond the distinction of male and female, that she is the *nirguṇa brahman*.[3] Śāktism, like Advaita Vedānta, is monistic, though perhaps less systematically so. The difference between them, though, is that Advaita sees only *brahman* as real, the material world being ultimately unreal. Śāktism, on the other hand, recognizes the world as real and maintains that it is ultimately identical to *brahman*.

The general thrust of Śākta theology, then, is to affirm the reality, power, and life force that pervade the material world. Matter itself, while always changing, is sacred and not different from spirit. The goddess is the totality of all existence. Thus, as a reflection of how things really are, she takes on both gentle and fierce forms. Creation and destruction, life and death, are seen as two sides of reality. The goddess encompasses both. That is perhaps why popular temple Śāktism is typically associated with vows and fulfilling the wishes of devotees, an aspect of the tradition which has led some observers to characterize it as more "material" than "spiritual" (see, e.g. Bhardwaj 1971; Hein 1993). In Śāktism, however, the two categories collapse; the material world is a manifestation of the goddess, so desire for material benefits does not contradict feelings of devotion (*bhakti*) or the ultimate goal of liberation.

ANTECEDENTS TO ŚĀKTISM

While the focus of this chapter is on the classical forms of Śāktism, it will be useful to look briefly at some of its antecedents which developed into the mature conception. Worship of the divine feminine in various forms is one of the most ancient religious expressions in India, as it was in the ancient Near East and elsewhere in the world.

Some scholars, Bhattacharyya preeminent among them, hold that Śāktism had its origins in the Indus Valley civilization (2500–1500 BCE) or even earlier in the Zhob Valley and Kullī cultures (third millennium BCE) rather than in the Vedic or Brāhmaṇic tradition which was imported into the subcontinent during the second millennium BCE by waves of Āryan immigrants. Bhattacharyya has stated:

> In its present form Śāktism is essentially a medieval religion, but it is a direct offshoot of the primitive Mother Goddess cult which was so prominent a feature of the religion of the agricultural peoples who based their social system on the principle of mother-right. The origin of the anomalous position of the male principle in the Śākta religion can presumably be traced to the anomalous position of the males in a matriarchal society.
>
> (1973: 1, see also 1977: 1–34, 253–77)

While few scholars are willing to embrace the matriarchy thesis, many are satisfied to assume the pre-Āryan origins of Hindu goddess worship. The evidence for such a position lies in the preponderance of female images (presumed, probably correctly, to be goddess figures) in the archaeological record of the pre-Āryan cultures and the relative paucity of female deities in the *Ṛg Veda*, the closest thing we have to a record of the ancient Indo-Āryan religion. The general argument, stated with various degrees of refinement, is that the pre-Āryans, being concerned mainly with agriculture, worshiped female and to a lesser extent male earth deities who represented fertility, regeneration, and the processes of life and death. The Āryans, on the other hand, being nomadic cattle herders and warriors, worshiped primarily male sky deities. When the Āryans settled in India, the argument continues, they took up agriculture and gradually assimilated the indigenous culture(s). Thus the various philosophical movements and cults that came to be called Hinduism are a synthesis of Āryan and non-Āryan elements.[4] This picture of prehistoric Indian religion, however elegant it may be, is greatly oversimplified. Few, if any, scholars deny that goddess worship is an indigenous Indian religious expression, but some such as Kinsley (1986: 212–20) are more cautious about postulating continuity between the Indus Valley civilization and later non-Āryan cultures, let alone with goddess worship in classical Hinduism, simply because the evidence is too scanty and inconclusive.

The worship of goddesses in particular is integrated rather late into the elite Sanskritic tradition. Vedic imagery is predominantly masculine, the major deities invoked are male, and most goddesses who figure in the Vedic hymns do so in a minor way. Goddesses are not absent, however, and there are some powerful examples of feminine imagery. One is Vāc, the goddess of speech, who is extolled as a creative force and mother of the Vedas. The *Vāgāṃbhṛnīsūkta* (*Ṛg Veda* 10.125), a hymn to Vāc, figures prominently in later Śākta practice, being recited as an appendage to the *Devī Māhātmya*. Uṣas, associated with the dawn, is an auspicious goddess often likened to a cow. Pṛthivī, the earth, in the *Ṛg Veda* is almost always coupled with Dyaus, the sky god, though in the later *Atharva Veda*, she appears more as a deity in her own right. Sarasvatī, the personification of a mighty river, Nirṛti, associated with death and bad luck, and Rātrī, the night, are other goddesses. All of these goddesses have similarities with later Hindu goddesses, but there is no overarching concept of a great goddess. While there is little evidence to suggest the Vedic origins of a goddess cult, there is a foreshadowing of the concept of *śakti* in the Vedas, especially in relation to Vāc, and even more definite indications of the concept in the Upaniṣads. For example, the *Kena Upaniṣad* (3.12) introduces Umā Haimavatī as the *guru* of the gods and the personified knowledge of *brahman*; and the *Muṇḍuka Upaniṣad* (1.24) speaks of two of Agni's tongues as Kālī and Karālī.

The period of the epics, the *Mahābhārata* and the *Rāmāyaṇa* (*c.*400 BCE–400 CE), is one of transition in the integration of goddesses into the Hindu pantheon. Goddesses figure strongly in the narratives, but as supporting characters, not as major deities. Here we find goddesses portrayed as wives of the gods, but there is little emphasis on their soteriological, cosmogonic, or ontological significance. Pārvatī, daughter of the Himālaya, is the wife of Śiva. Sarasvatī, now identified as the goddess of wisdom, is the wife of the creator Brahmā. Sītā, the heroine of the *Rāmāyaṇa*, is the wife of King Rāma and exemplifies all the wifely duties. Lakṣmī is the celestial consort of Viṣṇu and, especially as Śrī, the splendor and sovereignty of kings. The worship of the goddess as a supreme being has not yet been legitimated and absorbed into the Sanskritic tradition.

It is during the Purāṇic period (400 CE onward) that goddesses as significant individual deities and the concept of the goddess become prominent in Sanskrit literature. Goddesses who are paired with gods as their consorts are portrayed as instrumental in their partners' activities or even dominant over them.[5] Furthermore, there is a growing tendency to conceive of an independent cosmic goddess (Devī) or great goddess (Mahādevī) who contains within her all goddesses and is the supreme being. By the period between 400 and 800 CE, a full-blown cult of such a mother goddess had arisen in Āryan India. In succeeding centuries the movement spread, both influencing and absorbing various ritual, mythic, and symbolic elements of tribal and local female deities. According to Agrawala (1963: xii), the following strands compose goddess worship: the Vedic tradition with its notions of *vāc* and *trayīvidyā* (triple knowledge); the philosophical traditions of Sāṃkhya and Vedānta with their concepts of *prakṛti*, *māyā*, and *brahman*; Purāṇic mythology in which Lakṣmī, Sarasvatī, and Durgā are conceived as the three *śakti*s of Viṣṇu, Brahmā, and Śiva, respectively, and the Purāṇic cult of the seven (little) mothers (*saptamātṛkā*); and prevailing local and tribal cults. The goddess not only incorporates within her all feminine qualities but masculine qualities as well. As Kinsley (1978: 498) points out, in taking over the roles of the creator, preserver, and destroyer from Brahmā, Viṣṇu, and Śiva, respectively, she makes the male gods superfluous.

DEVĪ MĀHĀTMYA: A KEY ŚĀKTA SCRIPTURE

The most important Śākta scripture on both the esoteric and exoteric levels, the *Devī Māhātmya* is the earliest Sanskrit text that presents a sustained image of the goddess as the supreme being who creates, preserves, and destroys the universe. The *Devī Māhātmya*, which means glorification or greatness of the goddess, is an example of the *māhātmya* genre of Sanskrit literature which extols the virtues and activities of a sacred place, being, or object. The text comprises chapters 81–93 of the *Mārkaṇḍeya Purāṇa*, a text usually dated to the fourth century, but the *Devī Māhātmya* portion was most likely added later, during the sixth century. Furthermore, it has an independent life of its own, appearing in numerous editions and serving as a mythological, theological, and ritual text among Śāktas and non-Śāktas throughout India. As a mythological and theological text, it is an important source of lore and wisdom about the goddess in her various manifestations. As a ritual text, it is considered to be a potent collection of *mantra*s, which, when recited as a whole or in part, has a power far beyond their verbal narrative meaning.

The *Devī Māhātmya* represents a major focal point in the process of Sanskritization of various indigenous local goddess cults. On one hand, it can be seen as a synthesis of goddess cults that existed at the time of its composition; these goddesses become identified in the text as aspects of one great goddess, the Devī or Mahādevī. Here the goddess's exploits appear in a Vedic context. The demons have displaced the gods of the Vedic pantheon and have deprived them of their portions of the sacrifice. By defeating the demons, she restores the cosmic order that has been thus threatened. Furthermore, the language of the text shows Vedic resonance, with epithets, such as Svāhā and Svadhā, associated with the oblations of the fire sacrifice, juxtaposed with epithets, such as Ambikā and Caṇḍikā, revealing the motherly and destructive aspects of the goddess, respectively. On the other hand, the *Devī Māhātmya* itself later becomes a vehicle of Sanskritization in which other local goddesses become identified with the goddess who is extolled in it.

Both the oldest and most popular text in the Śākta tradition, the *Devī Māhātmya*, as Coburn (1984, 1991) demonstrates, is the first time a well-integrated theology and mythology of the goddess as supreme being presented in the Sanskrit language, "crystallizing" earlier myths and images of goddesses. The interpretation of the story given here is largely dependent on Coburn's work.

The structure of the *Devī Māhātmya* is simple and elegant, a frame story enclosing three episodes illustrating the greatness of the goddess. As the text is part of the *Mārkaṇḍeya Purāṇa*, the sage Mārkaṇḍeya himself introduces the story by saying that it explains the birth of Sāvarṇi Manu and how he came to be the ruler of the eighth "Manu interval" (*manvantara*) or cosmic cycle. The frame story begins with a king named Suratha whose enemies have deprived him of his sovereignty and a merchant named Samādhi whose family has cheated him out of his riches. They meet in the forest and go to the hermitage of Ṛṣi Medhas, who tells them that Mahāmāyā (the "great illusion," an epithet of the goddess) is the cause of the world's delusion and that she is also responsible for the creation of the world and for granting liberation from it. In answer to their inquiries about the identity of this great goddess, the sage narrates her deeds, saying that although she is eternal, she manifests in various ways.

The first episode of the *Devī Māhātmya* opens before the creation of the world when the entire earth is covered with water upon which the serpent Śeṣa floats. The great god Viṣṇu is sleeping atop Śeṣa when the creator Brahmā, seated upon a lotus, emerges from Viṣṇu's navel and sees two demons, Madhu and Kaiṭabha, who have been born from the dirt of Viṣṇu's ears. When the two demons start to attack Brahmā, he sings a hymn of praise to the goddess as Yoganidrā, the sleep of the yogic state of absorption, beseeching her to depart from Viṣṇu's body, thus allowing him to awaken and slay the demons. It is clear in this cosmogonic myth that the goddess is the personification of sleep. She is also called Tāmasī, the dark, sluggish force. In the divine economy of this myth, she is primary in that her departure as *tamas* (sleep, inactivity) is necessary in order for Viṣṇu as the force of *sattva* (preservation of purity and harmony) to prevail over the demons, so that Brahmā as the dynamic force *rajas* can create the world. In his hymn Brahmā also calls her the creator, preserver, and destroyer of the universe, as well as *prakṛti*, Mahādevī (great goddess), and Mahāsurī (great demoness). These epithets imply that she is the actual force behind all the activities of the gods, indeed, all the activities of the universe. After Brahmā praises her, she emerges from Viṣṇu's body, and he slays the demons after a five-thousand-year battle.

By the time of the *Devī Māhātmya*'s composition, the myth of Viṣṇu's killing Madhu and Kaiṭabha was well known and had been included in the *Mahābhārata* (3.194.8–30); Madhusūdana, killer of Madhu, is a common epithet of Viṣṇu throughout the *Mahābhārata*. The main difference the *Devī Māhātmya* version introduces is that Viṣṇu's capacity to act is shown to be derived from the goddess, to be contingent upon the withdrawal of *yoganidrā* from his body. The epithet used for the goddess in the Madhu-Kaiṭabha myth is Mahāmāyā, the great illusion; for she deludes the two demons into thinking they can overpower and outwit the divine. In the same way, she deludes human beings, here represented by the king and the merchant for whose benefit the story is told, and it is through her alone that they must seek a way out of this delusion. Thus the story is a creation myth, but one that also points to the path of human salvation. It has soteriological as well as cosmogonic significance.

The second episode of the *Devī Māhātmya* centers on the goddess's killing of Mahiṣāsura, the buffalo demon. Here the dynamic of the text moves from the cosmogonic orientation of the first episode to the more routine, periodic activity of preserving and maintaining order in the created universe. The demon Mahiṣa has usurped the powers of the gods so that they no longer receive their proper shares of the (Vedic) sacrifice, leaving them powerless to kill themselves. They approach Viṣṇu and Śiva for help, and all the gods together, through their anger, emit a great brilliance (*tejas*), which fuses together "like a flaming mountain whose flames pervaded the entire sky" (*Devī Māhātmya* 2.11). This heap of brilliance becomes a beautiful woman, each part of her body formed from the brilliance of a particular god. Each god then gives her a weapon, ornament, or other emblem: Śiva gives her a trident, Kṛṣṇa a discus, Himālaya a lion as her vehicle, and so on. The goddess, her eyes burning with anger, proceeds to demolish Mahiṣa's armies, while her lion devours the dead bodies. Finally she faces Mahiṣa himself, who in the course of the battle takes on successively the forms of a buffalo, a lion, a man holding a sword, an elephant, and again a buffalo. Pausing to guzzle wine and filling the sky with her eerie laughter, the goddess places her foot on the buffalo demon's neck and pierces it with her trident. As the demon in his original form tries to emerge from the buffalo's mouth, the goddess cutoff his head with a flourish. The gods praise her lavishly in a lengthy hymn, extolling her as the supreme protector and boon giver; she has saved the world from ruin and has even been gracious to the defeated demons, who achieve a heavenly state after being purified by her weapons. The gods ask her to return whenever they remember her. She agrees and then disappears.

The image of the goddess as a warrior seated on a lion, her most sustained image in the *Devī Māhātmya*, is difficult to trace in earlier Sanskrit literature, although it was probably common in folk traditions. Her creation from the powers of the various gods is undoubtedly connected with royal traditions, as is evident from the almost identical description of the creation of a king from the collective powers of the gods found in the *Manusmṛti* (7.1–11). It is not surprising that the goddess would be portrayed according to a kingly model, for in this text she is the supreme ruler and protector, her paramountcy obvious in her ability to accomplish what the male deities could not.

The killing of the buffalo demon is the myth most widely associated with the goddess in post-*Devī Māhātmya* times, but, unlike the Madhu-Kaiṭabha theme of the first episode, there are few references to it in literature which predates the *Devī Māhātmya*. In the *Mahābhārata* (3.221) it is Skanda, the son of Śiva, who kills Mahiṣāsura. Although the goddess Durgā is called the killer of Mahiṣa in the *Durgā Stava* of the *Mahābhārata*, that is considered to be an interpolation in the text which dates to a period later than the *Devī Māhātmya*. On the basis of textual evidence alone, it could be presumed that the story of Devī or Durgā killing the buffalo demon was adapted from the Skanda myth. However, the artistic motif of a goddess slaying a buffalo is of considerable antiquity, predating literary references. The earliest such iconographic representation is in terracotta plaques discovered at Nagar near Uniyara in Tonk district, Rajasthan, dating between the first century BCE and the first century CE (see Sircar 1967a). The image of a lion-riding goddess killing a buffalo demon may well have pre-Āryan or non-Āryan origins, though in the

Devī Māhātmya it is placed in the Vedic context of restoring the proper portions of sacrifice to the gods and thus upholding and preserving the cosmic order.

The third episode moves from the celestial toward the terrestrial plane, as it takes place in the Himālayas, the borderland between the realm of the gods and the realm of humans. It is the longest of the three episodes, containing several subepisodes within it, and from a narrative point of view, it is the most complicated. It is also the most syncretic in that it introduces numerous individual goddesses, such as Kālī and Cāmuṇḍā, who are integrated into the one great goddess.

The story resumes after an indeterminate length of time when once again the gods are in trouble because the three worlds and the shares of sacrifice have been snatched from them by demons, this time by the brothers Śumbha and Niśumbha. Remembering the goddess's promise to return when needed, the gods go to the Himālayas to invoke her as the "extremely gentle and extremely fierce" (*Devī Māhātmya* 5.11). Viṣṇumāyā, the goddess who exists in all beings in the form of such diverse qualities as consciousness, intelligence, sleep, hunger, shadow, *śakti*, desire, patience, production, modesty, faith, beauty, *lakṣmī*, conduct, memory, mercy, satisfaction, mother, and mistake (*Devī Māhātmya* 5.13–32). As the gods were engaged in their praise, Pārvatī, who had approached that spot to bathe in the Gaṅgā, asked them who they were praising. Immediately, the beautiful Ambikā (also called Śivā or Kauśikī) emerged from Pārvatī's bodily sheath, saying that it was she whom the gods were invoking. Here the text states that Ambikā was created from Pārvatī's bodily sheath (*kośa*); therefore she is known as Kauśikī. The text further states that when Ambikā emerged, Pārvatī became black (*kālī*) and is therefore known as Kālikā. From this point on, Pārvatī-Kālikā plays no further part, and Ambikā-Kauśikā takes over the action.

Seeing the beautiful Ambikā, Caṇḍa and Muṇḍa, the servants of the demons Śumbha and Niśumbha, describe her to their masters. Śumbha sends them to Ambikā with the message that she should choose either him or his brother as her husband. The goddess refuses, saying that she had long ago made a vow that she would marry only the one who defeated her in battle. Hearing this reply, Śumbha and Niśumbha send out their general Dhūmralocana (smoky-eyed) to capture her alive, but she slays him. Caṇḍa and Muṇḍa and their armies attack her, and a bloody battle ensues, with the goddess's lion devouring the demon's bloody remains. From her forehead, the goddess produces a *śakti*, the goddess Kālī, who kills Caṇḍa and Muṇḍa, thus gaining the appellation Cāmuṇḍā. Although, strictly speaking, such an etymology is linguistically impossible, the text employs narrative and alliteration to identify two previously separate goddesses, Kālī and Cāmuṇḍā.

As the battle continues, *śakti*s emerge from the bodies of seven male gods who, up until this point, have not been figured in the action but who presumably have been nonparticipant observers. Not consorts but the feminine powers or essences of the gods, these *śakti*s are the famous "seven mothers" (*saptamātṛkā*) who figure widely in Hindu myth and iconography. In this text, they are designated by the names Brahmāṇī (from Brahmā), Māheśvarī (from Maheśvara or Śiva), Kaumarī (from Kumāra or Skanda), Vaiṣṇavī (from Viṣṇu), Vārāhī (from Varāha or Viṣṇu's boar incarnation), Narasiṃhī (from Narasiṃha or Viṣṇu's man-lion incarnation), and Aindrī (from Indra). In addition to these seven and to Kālī whom the goddess has already produced, the goddess emits one more *śakti* called Śivadūtī because she enlists Śiva as a messenger to challenge the demons to further battle. In a dramatic scene, the demon Raktabīja (blood-drop) appears on the battlefield. This demon's claim to fame is that every drop of his blood that falls on the ground gives rise to another demon. Kālī saves the situation by lapping up all his blood with her long tongue, thus destroying him.

With the help of the seven mothers, the goddess kills Niśumbha and the whole army, leaving Śumbha standing alone. When Śumbha taunts her that she is receiving help from so many other women, she says to him, "I am one. Where in this world is there another besides me? Look, O evil one, as these manifestations of mine enter back into me" (*Devī Māhātmya* 10.3). Then all the *śakti*s disappear into the body of the goddess, and she alone defeats Śumbha. The third episode concludes with the gods singing to the goddess a lengthy hymn of praise, the famous *Nārāyaṇī Stuti*, which reinforces her theological supremacy as the creator, preserver, and destroyer of the universe. The goddess then appears before them and, in a manner reminiscent of Kṛṣṇa in the *Bhagavad Gītā*, says that whenever evil threatens the world, she will reappear in the form of various incarnations (*avatāra*).

The relationship of the goddess to male deities, especially Viṣṇu and Śiva, in this text is noteworthy, especially as it differs significantly from that found in later texts, especially the Tantras. In the *Devī Māhātmya*, the goddess seems to have a particularly strong connection with Viṣṇu, both in his cosmic form and as his Kṛṣṇa incarnation. The Madhu-Kaiṭabha myth in the first episode connects her with Viṣṇu/Nārāyaṇa, as do epithets such as Viṣṇumāyā and Nārāyaṇī found throughout the text. The goddess's slaying of the demons Śumbha and Niśumbha in the third episode has an interesting connection with the legend of Kṛṣṇa Gopāla. During the narration of the episode itself, there is no mention of any possible connection, but in a later chapter when Devī is recounting her future incarnations she says: "When the twenty-eighth Yuga has arrived in the Vaivāsvata Manu period, two other great *asura*s named Śumbha and Niśumbha will be born. Then born from the womb of Yaśodā in the house of the cowherd king Nanda, dwelling on the Vindhya Mountains, I shall destroy those two *asuras*" (*Devī Māhātmya* 11.38–39). Though not mentioned as such in the *Devī Māhātmya*, Nanda and Yaśodā are known in the mythology of Kṛṣṇa as his cowherding foster parents who raised him from birth in order to protect him from his murderous uncle, King Kaṃsa. The *Harivaṃśa*, a sequel to the *Mahābhārata* roughly contemporaneous with the *Devī Māhātmya*, recounts that Viṣṇu went to the underworld and requested the goddess Nidrā (sleep) to be born to Yaśodā. She would be switched at birth with Kṛṣṇa, the eighth child of Devakī. Later, she would go to the Vindhya Mountains and kill the demons Śumbha and Niśumbha (*Harivaṃśa* 47.23–37). This story is connected with the common South Indian designation of Durgā and other goddesses as the sister of Viṣṇu and with the North Indian Vraja tradition of Yogamāyā, Yoganidrā, and other goddesses as the sister of Kṛṣṇa. There is a temple, for example, to Yogamāyā or Jogamāyā in Meherauli, South Delhi, which the priests say is dedicated to Kṛṣṇa's sister who escaped being murdered by King Kaṃsa.

Śiva, who is closely identified with the goddess in later mythology such as that of the *śaktipīṭha*s and in the Tantras, in the *Devī Māhātmya* has a very low profile. In the first episode, he is completely absent. In the second episode, he figures only as one of the many gods who help to produce Devī. In the third episode, Pārvatī, who in other texts is the wife of Śiva, appears, but after Kauśikī (also called alternately Ambikā or Caṇḍikā) emerges from her body, she plays no further part in the action. Furthermore, Pārvatī, whose name means "one who is of the mountain," seems to have been brought into the story not because of her association with Śiva—nowhere is he said to be her husband—but because of her association with the mountain Himālaya. Śiva appears only one other time in this episode and in a subordinate role at that, when Devī's *śakti*, Śivadūtī (the one whose messenger is Śiva), dispatches him as a messenger to Śumbha and Niśumbha.

Although in the *Devī Māhātmya* the goddess is more closely associated with Viṣṇu than with Śiva, the purpose of the text seems not to associate her with any particular male god but to show her as the ultimate reality who is both immanent and transcendent, the grantor of both material pleasures and liberation from *saṃsāra*. None of the many goddesses who appears in the story is portrayed as the consort of a male deity. Even the seven mothers who emanate as *śakti*s from the bodies of the gods are their powers of activity, female alter egos, not their wives. Furthermore, the ability to produce a *śakti* is not limited to the male gods. The goddess is able to produce her own *śakti*s, such as Kālī and Śivadūtī. Likewise, even though the seven mothers have emerged from the bodies of the male gods, the goddess reabsorbs them into her own body which is their ultimate origin. Thus, one does not find in the *Devī Māhātmya* two related conceptions which are widely found in later Śākta and Tantric texts, namely, that of the divine as the male-female polarity Śiva-Śakti and the gendered duality of *śakti* as feminine and its possessor (*śaktimān*) as masculine. Rather, one finds a celebration of a holistic goddess who, as the supreme being, is both the embodiment and possessor of *śakti*.

Ritual significance of the Devī Māhātmya

Besides being included as part of a Purāṇa and having importance from a mythological and theological point of view, the *Devī Māhātmya* has an important liturgical life of its own. As well as being a written document, in subsequent times it has been transmitted orally through ritual recitation. It is the ritual recitation of the text which makes it arguably one of the most well-known and widely distributed Sanskrit texts in India.

Though it is not certain when historically the ritual recitation of the text became a common practice, the ritual significance of such practice is pointed out in the text itself, when in the twelfth chapter the goddess says that those who recite or listen to her *Māhātmya* with devotion on the eighth, ninth, or fourteenth day of the lunar fortnight at the time of offering an animal sacrifice, during a fire sacrifice, or during the autumn goddess worship (Navarātrī) will have all their afflictions removed and all their wishes fulfilled. In the thirteenth and final chapter, the king Suratha and the merchant Samādhi, having heard all the exploits of the goddess, set out to attain her *darśana*, her sacred vision. Seated on a riverbank, they chant her praises (*māhātmya*) as the gods had done and make an earthen image of her, worshiping it with flowers, incense, fire, sprinkled water, and blood from their own bodies. After three years the goddess appears and grants them boons. The king regains his kingdom and will be reborn in the future as Sāvarṇi Manu, the universal ruler, while the merchant gains the knowledge that cuts the bonds of attachment and leads to liberation.

In the ritual setting, the text is usually called *Durgāsaptaśatī*, *Durgāpāṭha*, or *Caṇḍīpāṭha*. Today the text is widely published in various editions in Sanskrit with translation, commentary, and ritual instructions in the regional Indian languages. Although it actually contains somewhat fewer than six hundred verses (*śloka*), editions of the text using the *saptaśatī* pattern make up for the difference by counting stage directions and splitting some of the verses, thus breaking the text into seven hundred *mantra*s or ritual utterances.[6] These *mantra*s are believed to please the goddess when recited and to have efficacy beyond their verbal meanings. P. V. Kane (1930–62, 5.1: 155n) points out that the *Durgāsaptaśatī* is in some ways treated as if it were a Vedic hymn, being lifted from its *smṛti* context as part of a Purāṇa and functioning as *śruti* in a ritual context. In editions intended for recitation, each important division of the text is preceded by a *viniyoga* verse that specifies the *ṛṣi* (seer), deity, meter, and purpose of its recitation, just as is the case for Vedic hymns. In addition, numerous Tantric features accompany the recitation of the text. These include the Devī's nine-syllable *mantra* (*oṃ aiṃ hrīṃ klīṃ cāmuṇḍāyai vicce*), *nyāsa* (blessing and depositing deities on each part of the body through the recitation of *mantras*), and special protective recitations, such as the *kavaca* (armor), *argala* (bolt for fastening), and *kīlaka* (pin, the inner syllable of a *mantra*). A *dhyānam* (meditation verse) describing the iconography of different manifestations of the goddess is recited before each chapter. The *Durgāsaptaśatī* can be recited by the worshiper or by a Brāhmaṇ recitant (*pāṭhaka* or *vācaka*) hired for the occasion. Usually it is done on all nine days of the Navarātrī festival, followed by a fire sacrifice (*havan*) on the tenth day or on a selected day during the festival. It can also be recited at any other time, particularly in fulfillment of a vow. Ritual editions of the text contain instructions for its recitation as well as for more elaborate and time-consuming *śatacaṇḍī* and *lakṣacaṇḍī*, hundred- and thousand-fold recitations. Some Śākta temples are well known for recitation of the *Devī Māhātmya*, for example the Vindhyācala temple in Mirzapur district, Uttar Pradesh (Humes 1996).

The *Devī Māhātmya* takes on further ritual and theological significance by its division into three episodes (*carita*), presided over by one of the three cosmic forms of the Devī, each of whom is associated with one of the three *guṇas* (natures or qualities). Thus, the first episode, the killing of the "ear-wax demons" Madhu and Kaiṭabha, is that of Mahākālī, who is black and has the nature of *tamas* (lethargy, inertia). The second, the killing of the buffalo-demon Mahiṣa, is that of Mahālakṣmī, who is red and has the nature of *rajas* (activity, passion). The third, the killing of Śumbha and Niśumbha, is that of Mahāsarasvatī, who is white and has the nature of *sattva* (purity). Mahālakṣmī, however, is also the original form, the first cause who is endowed with all three *guṇas*. This scheme has been elaborated in the *Rahasya Traya*, a short text which is undoubtedly later than the *Devī Māhātmya* but which Hindu commentators treat as an integral part of the text to be recited after the three episodes. The *Rahasya Traya* serves as an esoteric interpretation of the *Devī Māhātmya*, elaborating on the cosmogonic and ritual-soteriological framework of goddess worship. The *Pradhānika Rahasya*, like the first episode of the *Devī Māhātmya*, stresses the cosmogonic importance of the goddess. It is an account of the primal Mahālakṣmī's creation of Mahākālī and Mahāsarasvatī and their subsequent creation of the male and female deities who go on to create the universe. The *Vaikṛtika Rahasya*, like the second episode of the *Devī Māhātmya*, comes closer to the mundane realm with a description of the iconographic forms of the three cosmic manifestations (Mahālakṣmī, Mahākālī, and Mahāsarasvatī), their activities, and the methods of worshiping them. The *Mūrti Rahasya*, like the third episode of the *Devī Māhātmya*, comes even closer to areas of human concern with a discussion of the immanent, earthly incarnations of the goddess.

The *Devī Māhātmya* has been chosen here as a representative Śākta text because of its widespread popularity, and the Sanskrit version of the story as found in the *Mārkaṇḍeya Purāṇa* has been summarized because it is the most well known throughout India. However, it should be kept in mind that other versions of the stories told in the *Devī Māhātmya* are found not only in other Sanskrit texts such as the Purāṇas but in regional languages throughout India.

Later Śākta texts, such as the *Devībhāgavata Purāṇa*, *Kālikā Purāṇa*, and *Mahābhāgavata Purāṇa*, have been important, especially in eastern India, in elaborating and disseminating philosophical and mythological traditions of the great goddess.

ŚĀKTA TANTRISM: ŚRĪVIDYĀ

A comprehensive review of Tantrism is outside the scope of this chapter, for, as is clear from earlier discussion, not all Tantrics are Śākta and not all Śākta are Tantrics. The major general features of Tantrism have been discussed earlier. Schools of Śākta Tantrism fall into two broad categories, Kālīkula and Śrīkula. Kālīkula emphasizes narrative traditions and spiritual practices (*sādhana*) connected with fierce (*ghora* or *raudra*) forms of the goddess, such as Kālī, Tārā, Caṇḍī, or sometimes Durgā. This form of Śākta Tantrism is found primarily in Bengal, Assam, and Orissa and more widely throughout North India. These traditions are only loosely, if at all, connected with a developed canon of textual traditions and tend to be more reliant on folk and popular traditions, oral transmission by *guru*s, solitary practice through visions and personal experience, and informal networks of practitioners. In the Śrīkula traditions, emphasis is on the gentle, beneficent, and motherly (*saumya* or *aghora*) forms of the goddess. The Śrīvidyā school of Śākta Tantrism belongs to the Śrīkula category. It has been found in South India since the seventh century and is still practiced there today, and in Kashmir it has been closely associated with the school of Kashmir Śaivism. D. Brooks, in choosing the Śrīvidyā tradition of South India as an exemplary Śākta Tantric tradition to study, states:

> Śrīvidyā is among the few cults of Hindu Tantrism—whether they be Śiva-centered, Viṣṇu-centered, or Śakti-centered—in which a comparison of textual ideologies and prescriptions with living interpretations and practices is theoretically possible. Others lack either texts or a tradition of living interpreters. Of the two areas . . . in which Śrīvidyā has flourished most visibly, Kashmir and south India, only the latter remains a vital tradition . . . . South Indian Śrīvidyā creates its distinctive tradition principally in two ways. First, by adopting and then expanding the Kashmiri canon and second, by assimilating the ethics and ideologies of south Indian brahman culture.[7]
>
> (1992: xv)

Śrīvidyā is thus perhaps more in tune with Sanskritic Hindu orthodoxy than some other forms of Tantrism, while at the same time elaborating a highly esoteric and in some ways alternative worldview and religious praxis.

In Śrīvidyā the supreme Devī is worshiped in a beautiful form under the names Lalitā, Śrī, or Tripurasundarī. She is the active and dynamic aspect of the supreme reality, the Śakti, who, while maintaining preeminence on the cult, is in eternal union with her consort Śiva, who represents the sentient and eternal reality. As D. Brooks states:

> Śrīvidyā conforms to a basic theological structure common to Hindu Tantrism: the initially unified Absolute becomes a dyadic divinity composed of masculine and feminine complements; the binary godhead creates from its union a universe composed of triadic structures. Creation is understood as a process of self-expansion (*prapañca*)

in which the universe is considered identical to *and* different from the Absolute. Put differently, the Absolute creates a *reflection (vimarśa) projecting its own inherent self-illumination (prakāśa).*

(1992: 60; emphasis in original)

According to Bhāskararāya, the preeminent theologian of Śrīvidyā, the goddess has three main manifestations, each of which partakes equally in the illuminative and reflective aspects. These are the physical (*sthūla*), which is the iconic Lalitā Tripurasundarī; the subtle (*sūkṣma*), which is the Śrīvidyā-*mantra*; and the supreme (*parā*), which is the diagrammatic *śrīcakra* or *yantra* form.

The physical or "gross" form of the goddess is her anthropomorphic iconic form. Known by such names as Lalitā (lovely, playful one), Tripurasundarī (beautiful of the three worlds), Mahātripurasundarī, and Rājarājeśvarī (queen of kings), she is the supreme form of the goddess in gentle, benign form, though she encompasses all forms within herself and is thus capable of taking on horrific forms, as in the story of destruction of the demon Bhaṇḍa by her. Sometimes she is called Śrīdevī, but she is different from the Vaiṣṇava Śrī who is ever subordinate to Viṣṇu. Widely known outside the initiate circles of Śrīvidyā, she is identified with popular goddesses enshrined in South Indian temples, especially Kāmakṣī of Kancipuram. She is worshiped with traditional *pūjā*s and the recitation of texts such as the popular *Lalitāsahasranāma* (Thousand Names of Lalitā). In this text and others, she is elaborately described: seated on a lion throne like a great queen, shining like a thousand suns, dressed in red, and bearing in her four hands the noose of desire, the elephant goad or wrath and worldly knowledge, the arrows of the five essences, and the sugarcane bow of the mind, her luster envelops the twelve *siddhi*s. She bathes the universe in her rosy complexion, she has many fragrant flowers in her hair and wears a crown of jewels. She bears the auspicious mark of marriage between her eyes and is modest in demeanor; her thin waist is burdened by heavy breasts. The lord of desire or Śiva in the form of Kāmeśvara drowns in the fullness of her smile. She is attended by Viṣṇu, Brahmā, and Indra, as well as by Lakṣmī and Sarasvatī who fan her with honor. "Three characteristics unify Lalitā's mythic and iconic symbolism: She is royal, auspicious, and subsuming. All three characteristics are manifestation of her most essential attribute: power (*śakti*)" (D. Brooks 1992: 64).

The subtle aspect of the goddess is her fifteen (or, according to some authorities, sixteen) syllable *mantra*, the Śrīvidyā, which, when recited by a properly initiated practitioner, results in the attainment of all desires, the conquering of all worlds, achievement of unity with Śiva, breaking through the illusion of Viṣṇu, and obtaining the supreme *brahman*. Her *mantra* is her essence in sound form and is considered to be superior to all other *mantra*s of all other deities. That is not only because the deity is superior but also because the *mantra* consists only of pure seed-syllables (*bījākṣara*)—*ka e ī la hrīṃ ha sa ka ha la hrīṃ sa ka la hrīṃ*—which have no verbal or grammatical meaning. The *mantra* does not praise a deity or make a request, as do many other *mantra*s, including the famous Gāyatrī-*mantra*; instead, it is a pure expression of the divine's highest nature, a form of the absolute *brahman*. D. Brooks writes:

The mantra's power stems from the combination of its inherent capacity as an emanation of the goddess with the acquisition of grace and diligent self-effort. Since the mantra is a concentrated form of the divine power it has the capacity to bring about events that defy all normal and conventional modes of understanding. The guru, as

> embodiment of both Śiva and Śakti, is the primary source for bringing out the mantra's latent power. The student not only depends on the teacher for the mantra's esoteric meaning but to empower the sounds themselves.
>
> (1992: 112)

The *śrīcakra* is the transcendent aspect of the goddess Lalitā. It is a *yantra*, a two-dimensional geometrical figure which represents the essence of the deity. It is formed by five downward-pointing triangles representing Śakti which intersect with four upward-pointing triangles representing Śiva. Through the intersection of these nine triangles are formed forty-three triangles. This is surrounded by concentric circles with eight and then sixteen lotus petals. The figure is surrounded by a square of three lines with openings in the middle of each side. There is a dot in the center of the entire diagram which represents the unity of Śiva and Śakti. From the point of view of Śrīvidyā, meditation upon it in conjunction with the *mantra* is the culmination of spiritual practice for the initiated adept, for whom it functions on three levels: as a map of creation's divine essences projected visually; as divine power which can become accessible to those who obtain esoteric knowledge about its use; and as the real presence (*sadbhava*) of the divine, "worthy of worship, admiration, and even fear because of its potential to transform one's relationship with the sacred" (D. Brooks 1992: 118).

A striking visual icon, the *śrīcakra* in recent times has been publicly displayed and worshiped esoterically in Hindu temples, has appeared as an illustration in popular ritual manuals, and has migrated to New Age literature to the point where it may be the most widely recognized Hindu emblem, even in the West. This phenomenon highlights the fluid relationship between the most esoteric doctrines and practices and popular religiosity.

SACRED GEOGRAPHY: THE ŚAKTIPĪṬHAS

The idea of the goddess as a dynamic force inherent in matter is given expression in the myth and ritual of the *śaktipīṭha*s or *śāktapīṭha*s (places of power). The image of the earth itself and, more particularly, the land of India as a goddess is ancient and pervasive in the Hindu tradition. Similarly, the idea that certain features, such as mountains, rivers, lakes, and caves are a manifestation of the sacred is also one of great antiquity. While these geographical hierophanies are often associated with a particular deity or saint, it is the place itself that is sacred. In Hinduism there developed an elaborate system of pilgrimage to *tīrtha*s, literally, river fords, places where one can "cross over" from the human to the divine realm. Important Śākta places of pilgrimage are called *pīṭha*s which form an elaborate scheme which became a hallmark of Śāktism, though it may have Buddhist antecedents.

At some point the worship of the goddess became associated with a formal system of *pīṭha*s (seats, abodes) enshrining parts of her body which served to account for the unified identity of the goddess amidst a multiplicity of forms and local traditions. The earliest reference to *pīṭhas* is in the *Hevajra Tantra*, a seventh-century Buddhist text, which lists four: Jālandhara (in the Punjab hills), Oḍiyāṇa or Uḍḍiyāṇa (in the Swat Valley), Pūrṇagiri (location unknown), and Kāmarūpa (in Assam). A system of four *pīṭha*s is common to both Hindu and Buddhist Tantric texts and may have some connection with the legends that the Buddha's body was divided at his death and enshrined in *stūpa*s. There is also a Tantric Buddhist tradition that the Indian subcontinent is the *vajra* body of the Buddha, divided into twenty-four limbs or *pīṭha*s (Stablein 1978).

The mythical source for the *pīṭha* scheme is the story of the goddess Satī and the destruction of her father Dakṣa's sacrifice by her husband Śiva. This story is found in germ form in the Brāhmaṇas and in more elaborate form in most of the Purāṇas with numerous variations. The most extensive work on *śaktipīṭha*s has been done by Sircar, who has painstakingly traced the development of this myth. The following is extracted from his classic account:

> The earliest form of the legend of *Dakṣa-yajña-nāśa* is probably to be traced in the *Mahābhārata* (XII, chapters 282–83; cf. *Brahma Purāṇa*, ch. 39) and a slightly modified form of the same story is found in many of the Purāṇas (*Matsya*, ch. 12; *Padma*, *Sṛṣṭikhaṇḍa*, ch. 5; *Kūrma*, I, ch. 15; *Brahmāṇḍa*, ch. 31, etc.) as well as in the *Kumārasambhava* (I, 21) of Kālidāsa who flourished in the fourth and fifth centuries and adorned the court of the Gupta Vikramādityas. According to this modified version of the legend, the mother-goddess, who was the wife of Śiva, was in the form of Satī one of the daughters of Dakṣa Prajāpatī. Dakṣa was celebrating a great sacrifice for which neither Satī nor Śiva was invited. Satī, however, went to her father's sacrifice uninvited, but was greatly insulted by Dakṣa. As a result of this ill-treatment, Satī is said to have died by *yoga* or of a broken heart, or, as Kālidāsa says, she put herself into the fire and perished. . . . When the news of Satī's death reached her husband, Śiva is said to have become furious and hastened to the scene with his numerous attendants. The sacrifice of Prajāpatī Dakṣa was completely destroyed. Śiva, according to some of the sources, decapitated Dakṣa who was afterwards restored to life and thenceforward acknowledged the superiority of Śiva to all gods.
>
> (Sircar 1973: 5–6)

It is clear that these earlier versions of the story are told from a Śaiva sectarian point of view in order to establish the superiority of Śiva. Later versions, however, take on a distinctly Śākta slant as the narrative centers on Satī rather than Śiva. Sircar continues:

> In still later times, probably about the earlier part of the medieval period, a new legend was engrafted to the old story simply for the sake of explaining the origin of the Pīṭhas. According to certain later Purāṇas and Tantras (*Devībhāgavata*, VII, ch. 30; *Kālikā Purāṇa*, ch. 18, etc.), Śiva became inconsolable at the death of his beloved wife Satī, and, after the destruction of Dakṣa's sacrifice, he wandered over the earth in a mad dance with Satī's dead body on his shoulder (or, head). The gods now became anxious to free Śiva from his infatuation and made a conspiracy to deprive him of his wife's dead body. Thereupon Brahman, Viṣṇu and Śani entered the dead body by *yoga* and disposed of it gradually and bit by bit. The places where pieces of Satī's dead body fell are said to have become Pīṭhas, i.e. holy seats or resorts of the mother-goddess, in all of which she is represented to be constantly living in some form together with a Bhairava, i.e. a form of her husband Śiva. According to a modified version of this story, it was Viṣṇu who, while following Śiva, cut Satī's dead body on Śiva's shoulder or head piece by piece by his arrows or his discus.
>
> (1973: 6–7)

According to various schemes, there are 4, 7, 8, 42, 51, or 108 of these *pīṭhas*, the lists reflecting the local traditions, sectarian loyalties, and perhaps literary license of the writers. The scheme has also passed into local and regional oral traditions, with goddess temples all over India being counted among the *śaktipīṭhas* whether there is any textual basis for doing so. It is clear that the myth serves both to emphasize the importance of Satī over Śiva, as is graphically portrayed by his placing her on his head, and to integrate various local goddess shrines into the body of the goddess. As an example of universalization by division, the myth is an inversion of the *Devī Māhātmya* story in which the goddess is put together limb by limb through the efforts of the gods.[8] Here she is dismembered limb by limb and distributed throughout the landscape. The places where her limbs fell are alive with her presence and thus infused with *śakti*.

Sources vary as to which part of Satī fell where, although the *yoni* or female generative organ is invariably placed at Kāmarūpa in Assam which is considered the *ādipīṭha* (original or primordial seat). This is considered to be the most important Śākta and Tantric site in India and is the central focus of the *Kālikā Purāṇa* and the *Yoni Tantra*. The main shrine at Kāmarūpa, on a hill near the modern city of Gauhati, houses the goddess under the name of Kāmākhyā, who is often identified with the Mahāvidyā Ṣodaśī. A natural spring from an underground river keeps moist the *yoni* stone which is the main image of the temple. Pilgrims collect sacred water from this spring. The temple is closed for three days annually to celebrate the menses of the goddess, opening on the fourth day for the festival of Ambuvācī. Also on the hillside are shrines to each of the other ten Mahāvidyās and to other goddesses. Other famous *śaktipīṭhas*, according to the *Pīṭhanirṇaya*, which lists fifty-one, are Kālīpīṭha (Kalighat in Calcutta) where the right toe fell, Hingulā (Hing Laj in Baluchistan) where the *brahmarandhra* (top of the head) fell, and Jvālā Mukhī (in Kangra district, Himachal Pradesh) where the tongue fell.

Dismemberment is an extremely archaic motif in the history of religions, being found in Southeast Asia, Oceania, North and South America, and the ancient Middle East. Mircea Eliade (1969: 347–48) writes that the *pīṭha* system in India is an example of the coalescence among the fertility cults of the great goddess and popular *yoga*, for the *pīṭhas* were places of pilgrimage for Śākta and Tantrics. He adds that most of them were aniconic altars that had acquired rank as holy places by virtue of the fact that ascetics and *yogīs* had meditated and attained special powers (*siddhi*) there. Sircar speculates that the earliest *pīṭhas* were associated with the phallus (*liṅga*) of a male god and the female organs (*yoni*) and breasts of a goddess. Hills and mountains were regarded as self-born *liṅgas*, tanks and pools as *yonis*, and a pair of hills as breasts. Water coming out of the springs in these hills would be regarded as the goddess's milk. These male and female hierophanies, he theorizes, were worshiped by the pre-Āryans (Sircar 1973: 7–8). Whatever their origins, it is clear that the *pīṭhas* express a worldview in which the earth is considered sacred and the deity manifests herself in living earthly forms.

The theory and practice of the *śaktipīṭhas* in many ways sum up the wide sweep of Śākta influences and developments, from the archaic mother goddess cults, to devotional, mythological, and ritual traditions in classical Hinduism, to philosophical speculations on the nature of reality and paths to liberation, to esoteric Tantric conceptualizations and practices.

THE GODDESS AND EXPERIENCE

Of all the world's religions, Hinduism has the most elaborate *living* goddess traditions. Hindu conceptions of female deities and the overarching great goddess stem from the supreme cosmic power, Śakti, from whom all creation emerges and by whom it is sustained. The worship of the goddess, of the divine as female, has a long history in India and continues to become even more popular today. By virtue of their common feminine nature, women are in some contexts regarded as special manifestations of the goddess, sharing in her powers. Thus, the goddess can perhaps be viewed as a mythic model for Hindu women. Western religious traditions, on the other hand, while not totally devoid of feminine imagery, lack any true parallel to the Hindu goddess. This perceived deficiency has inspired some Western religious feminists to recover and revive goddesses and feminine images of the divine from the ancient past. Nevertheless, some feminists and scholars of religion have argued that the existence of the Hindu goddess has not appeared outwardly to have benefited women's position in Indian society.

The question of the relationship between Indian (primarily Hindu, but extending also to Buddhist and Jaina) goddesses and women is multifaceted and complex, frequently leading to contradictory answers, depending upon how the question is framed and who is doing the asking—and answering. Some observers stress the essentially patriarchal structure of Hindu society and argue that goddesses serve only to uphold or at best provide temporary relief from that structure. Others argue that male and female in Hindu culture are hierarchically related, though in a complex complementarity that defies Western notions of patriarchy and feminism. Still others suggest that Hindu goddesses provide a model and inspiration for women and men to transcend deeply engrained cultural norms. Yet another perspective is that some goddesses or modes of Śākta practice (e.g. the powerful Durgā or Tantra with its female *gurus* and exaltation of women) are liberating for women, while others (the obedient wife Sītā or the male-dominated exoteric temple worship) are oppressive. Finally, some contend that the relationship between goddesses and women is multivalent, context specific, and constantly changing (see Hiltebeitel and Erndl 2000 for these and other perspectives).

From a religious perspective, the one factor which cuts across gender, regional, caste, and philosophical differences is the importance of personal religious experience for the devotee and the self-transformation which results from interacting with her. Whether a devotee is offering coconuts to a village deity, making a pilgrimage to a famous goddess temple to fulfill a vow, consulting a goddess-possessed woman about a personal problem, or engaging in a complex visual meditation, it is the immediacy and tangibility of the goddess which is most important. To illustrate this point, I conclude this chapter with two short pieces from different regions of India—without further commentary or interpretation—in order to provide a taste of the flavor of that experience.

The first is the story of Dhyānū Bhagat, told in the Hindi and Punjabi languages, which is part of the oral tradition of popular Śākta traditions in northwest India (Erndl 1993: 46):[9]

> There once was a devotee of the Goddess named Dhyānū Bhagat who lived at the same time as the Mughal Emperor Akbar [sixteenth century]. Once he was leading a group of pilgrims to the temple of Jvālā Mukhī where the Goddess appears in the form of a flame. As the group was passing through Delhi, Akbar summoned Dhyānū

to the court, demanding to know who this goddess was and why he worshiped her. Dhyānū replied that she is the all-powerful Goddess who grants wishes to her devotees.

In order to test Dhyānū, Akbar ordered the head of his horse to be cut off and told Dhyānū to have his goddess join the horse's head back to its body.

Dhyānū went to Jvālā Mukhī where he prayed day and night to the Goddess, but he got no answer. Finally, in desperation, he cut off his own head and offered it to the Goddess. At that point, the Goddess appeared before him in full splendor, seated on her lion. She joined his head back to his body and also joined the horse's head back to its body. Then she offered him a boon. He asked that in the future, devotees not be required to go to such extreme lengths to prove their devotion. So, she granted him the boon that from then on, she would accept the offering of a coconut to be equal to that of a head. That is why people today offer coconuts to the Goddess.

The second example of personal experience of the goddess is a poem by the most famous Śākta devotional poet, Ramprasad Sen of Bengal, who lived in the eighteenth century (McDermott 2001b: 70–71):

The world's a shoreless ocean;
there's no crossing it.
But I bank on Your feet and the treasure of Your company—
rescue me, Tāriṇī,
in my distress.

I see the waves
  the bottomless waters
and shiver in terror:
I might drown and die!
Be merciful,
save Your servant,
Harbor me now
  in Your boat
    Your feet.

The tempest storms without lull,
so too shaking my body.
I'm repeating Your name
  Tārā! the essence of the world.
Fulfill my desire.

Prasād says:
Time has passed
I haven't worshiped Kālī
and life is gone, unfruitful.
So free me from these worldly bonds.

Mother Tāriṇī,
without You
to whom shall I give my burden?

(Used by permission of Oxford University Press, Inc.)

NOTES

1 Some scholars have argued for the pre-Vedic and non-Āryan origins of the Sāṃkhya system that the concept of *prakṛti* evolved out of an ancient Mother Earth cult (for this view, see Bhattacharyya 1973: 16–17, 87–90). Bhattacharyya further argues that the original Sāṃkhya, as opposed to the classical formulation by Īśvarakṛṣṇa, stemmed from a matriarchal society.
2 The ideas in this paragraph follow Kinsley (1986: 136–37).
3 This idea is especially prevalent in the *Devībhāgavata Purāṇa*, as discussed in C. M. Brown 1990 (see also D. Brooks 1990, 1992).
4 Of course, this theory assumes that the Āryans did migrate into India and would have to be thrown out completely if there is any truth to claims about a Sarasvatī civilization or other indigenous Āryan culture on the Indian subcontinent. Evaluation of indigenous Āryan theories is beyond the scope of this chapter (for an even-handed consideration of the evidence, see Bryant 2001).
5 This theme is developed in O'Flaherty (1982).
6 The significance of the number seven hundred is most likely that it is the number of *śloka*s found in the highly popular text the *Bhagavad Gītā*.
7 Most of the material on Śrīvidyā which follows is heavily reliant on this work and on D. Brooks 1990.
8 This idea was expressed by Eck (1986).
9 The story is found in numerous popular religious pamphlets and in oral versions throughout northwest India and as far east as the Vindhyācala temple in Mirzapur, Uttar Pradesh.

CHAPTER EIGHT

VAIṢṆAVA

Francis X. Clooney and Tony K. Stewart

WHAT CONSTITUTES VAIṢṆAVA TRADITION

In the most general sense, to be Vaiṣṇava means simply to worship the deity Viṣṇu or one of his many alternate forms, such as Rāma or Kṛṣṇa. In the early centuries prior to the common era, Viṣṇu, who was often recognized by the epithets Nārāyaṇa and in other associations such as Vāsudeva-Kṛṣṇa and Saṃkarṣaṇa-Balarāma, became refuge for increasing numbers. Sometime during the early centuries of the millennium, he began to be attended by a consort, the goddess Lakṣmī or Śrī, an association that has continued to the present.[1] Evidence is textual from a variety of sources stretching back to the Vedas and their commentaries and the Upaniṣads, but, by the Gupta period, the most compelling citations are plastic, sculpture, and architecture ranging from one end of the Indian subcontinent to the other. By the early centuries of the Common Era, sedentary ruling clans departed from the more mobile worship afforded in traditional Vedic ritual by patronizing temples in honor of Viṣṇu, structures that were made of durable, permanent materials. Appropriate to this permanent setting, Viṣṇu was from the earliest times associated with protection and sustenance, while his consort Śrī complemented this strength by nurturing the general weal, from hearth and health to the creation of wealth. This temple-based worship of images of Viṣṇu suggested the first stirrings of a "cult," what tradition would call by the general name of Bhāgavata, but in the early stages by the more specific name of Pāñcarātra. Their texts were Āgamas, that is, dealing with rituals of serving the image, their titles often bearing the name and classification of Tantra; they were esoteric practical manuals and, much like their Vedic forebears, of limited access to an increasingly specialized and hereditary group of Brāhmaṇ priests. Systematic theological speculation would come a little later. Today there are South Indian priests, called Vaikhānasa, who still carry out these rituals that derive from the oldest Vaiṣṇava texts, the *Vaikhānasasūtra* that predate Baudhāyana, rituals that appear in form and function to be consistent with the fundamentals first formulated in the ancient texts of the *Pāñcarātra Āgama*. Followers are certain, and scholars seem generally to concur, that the Vaikhānasa practices represent the contemporary mode of an unbroken tradition. Its singular endurance stretches over several millennia and testifies to the centrality of Vaiṣṇava practice in the religious life of South Asia, its basic features continually revalorized, speaking to the needs of each new generation with a direct and immediate relevance. Some of that immediacy can be traced to two distinctive characteristics: the individual's unique participation in the reality understood to have been generated and organized by Viṣṇu, and the ability of the tradition to accommodate change by a system of constant renewal that reorders the world according to contemporary exigencies. Other Hindu traditions have demonstrated much this same ability to absorb and incorporate local traditions, but part of what demarcates the Vaiṣṇava approach is a unique rational justification. While somewhat vague, indeed inconsistent in its articulation at first, this justification is eventually consolidated in the form of a widely generalized *avatāra* theory, the theology of divine descent, an umbrella concept that eventually accounts for all the myriad manifestations of Viṣṇu.

Avatāra: the response of god to devotees

In its simplest form, the word "*avatāra*" derives from the Sanskrit root *tṛ* and the prefix *ava*, meaning to "descend" or "alight"—in this case, the descent from the heavens to earth—with the more general sense of simply "appearing." The term is often translated into English as "incarnation," but scholars of the tradition have over the centuries increasingly demurred because it is problematic to argue that the descent of god to earth involves gross or carnal matter, the key element of flesh associated with worldly existence. God can only be purity and truth, generally termed "*sattva*"; the adjudication of this basic ontological issue was central to the development of the traditional four schools noted later. While theologians will differ on how much of this descent qualifies as docetism, dependent as that is on the concept of how substantive the body of god is understood to be, the reality of that descent is never questioned. Yet, ironically, the world, indeed the entirety of the universe, is understood to exist within Viṣṇu so that devotees live with the awareness of inhabiting the body of their lord, an awareness that sanctifies the act of living itself, making the experience deeply personal and immediate. To be Vaiṣṇava is somehow to participate in the divine order, in divinity itself. Perhaps the most elegant and succinct statement of this can be found in the text of the *Bhagavad Gītā*, eighteen chapters in the sixth book of the *Mahābhārata*, although equivalent explanations can be found throughout the literatures of the Vaiṣṇavas. And its elegance is no doubt partially dependent on its generality, for the *Bhagavad Gītā* is not a precise theological document but a statement of principle that requires elaboration in all parts of the tradition. Here we find a general explanation of the nature of devotion, *bhakti*, and what it means to be a *bhakta*, a devotee.

The word "*bhakti*" comes from the Sanskrit root *bhaj*, which means "to apportion" or "to share with or in," and the logic works something like this. The world is created by Viṣṇu-Nārāyaṇa—or, in this particular case, working under the name and personality of Kṛṣṇa—and as his creation, it is automatically perfect and balanced and well proportioned. The natural order of this perfect creation is apportioned according to role and function to its minutest part and is then governed by rules established by god, Bhagavān, or, literally, "he who possesses or governs the parts." A devotee who worships Bhagavān finds through that devotion his or her own proper place in that divine order and participates in it (*Bhagavad Gītā* 6, 9). In this sense, the devotee lives in god, in the way of god, both figuratively and literally, and that participation becomes its own reward, eventually resulting in a permanent place in the service of Viṣṇu or Kṛṣṇa or Rāma or some other form as one is personally inclined.

Problems arise when humans fail to observe the order as planned—and that, of course, is part of the human condition, an inability to discipline itself because of the frailties borne of basic desires, of greed and anger and lust, to mention the most common. Because of the abject failure of humans to conform to Viṣṇu's divine plan, the world gradually loses its center and destabilizes, its moral order compromised. When that happens Bhagavān hears the cries of his devotees' agony, their plea for compassion for themselves and their fellow beings, and so he makes ready to descend (*Bhagavad Gītā* 4.7–8). But—and this is where the tradition demonstrates an uncanny knack for adapting itself to the local environment—Bhagavān will descend in a form and shape and with a message appropriate to each and every era and locale (*Bhagavad Gītā* 4.11). When he does so, the goal is to reestablish order, *dharma*, in a new image that serves to correct the excesses of the moment. Not only does Bhagavān assume different shapes but also the ordering *dharma* itself shifts, sometimes dramatically and sometimes subtly, to address the pressing needs of his followers, remaking *dharma*, which is often erroneously depicted as eternal and unchanging, as contextual and relative according to his own personal will. Consequently, through this mechanism of divine descent, Bhagavān can be seen and worshiped in myriad forms that relay instruction for survival in a constantly shifting world.

Traditional avatāra theory

Traditionally the *avatāra* system articulated six, then ten, and eventually a seemingly limitless host of descents, each one subordinate to Viṣṇu-Nārāyaṇa. Not surprisingly it is at this juncture that theology asserts itself as a rational justification of these acts of inclusion and expansion. Perhaps the first systematic assertion of this cosmological emanation is the doctrine of "separate manifestation" (*vyuha*), that linked the early aggregates as Vāsudeva, Saṃkarṣaṇa, Pradyumna, and Aniruddha, the *caturvyuha*. Another early system, finally explained formally in the *Manusmṛti*, proposes a descent for each age of a Manu (4,320,000 human years), the *manvantara-avatāra*s who were the progenitors and sovereigns of humanity in each of the fourteen ages. But a parallel development articulated a different serial descent, the first references of which can be found in the *Ṛg Veda* (namely, the "three steps" of Viṣṇu) and expanded in the Taittirīya recensions of the *Śatapatha Brāhmaṇa*. Following these initials claims, other texts began to assert other forms which have been standardized over the last one and one-half millennia. In the most common Purāṇic versions, the theoriomorphic forms of Matsya the "fish," Kūrma the "tortoise," Varāha the "boar," and Narasiṃha the "half-man, half-lion," were understood to have appeared in the first age of the world, the Kṛta or Satya. In the next age, the Tretā, Viṣṇu assumed more recognizably human dimensions, as Vāmana the "dwarf," he of the "three steps," and Paraśurāma or "Rāma of the axe." Signaling the close of that Tretā Yuga was Rāma, hero of the *Rāmāyaṇa*. The following Dvāpara Yuga was brought to a close by Kṛṣṇa, advisor and guide to heroes in the *Mahābhārata* and whose own childhood and adolescent exploits were recorded later so lovingly in the *Bhāgavata Purāṇa*. The Buddha was also incorporated, signifying the close ties to that tradition, although the ostensible motivation for his appearance—to encourage the demonic and wicked to turn away from the truth—suggests the ambivalent nature of this connection. Finally, Viṣṇu is said ready to come at some indeterminate future date in the last and final degraded age, the Kali. This final form is signified by the image of Kalkin the "white horse." While some groups within the tradition today argue that the time for descent is passed, it is through this open-ended invitation that other contemporary practitioners of Vaiṣṇavism can place their own images of divinity such as the figure of Satya Pīr—who adorns himself with both Hindu and Muslim accoutrements signaling an intention to synthesize a new dharmic life that accommodates Hindus to Muslims—to historical figures such as Kṛṣṇa Caitanya (1486–1533), the inspiration of the Gauḍīya Vaiṣṇava tradition. This open-ended set of ten has been labeled the *līlā-avatāra*s, descents of divine play, while a subset is popularly called the four *yuga-avatāra*s, one for each of the four Purāṇic ages. Even though the different sets appear to be inconsistent, the principle behind the doctrine of descent remains coherent.

In its earliest form, the theory of divine descent imagined a supreme godhead that manifested subordinate forms on earth, but as the tradition matured, followers of particularly popular forms, especially those of Rāma and Kṛṣṇa, argued that they were not subordinate at all. Eventually the manifestations of Viṣṇu were conceived to range from the descent of the god himself, *svayaṃ bhagavān*, to replicas classified as the traditional *avatāra*s, to lesser parts of divinity on earth (portions, *kalā*; minor parts, *aṃśa*; parts of parts, *aṃśāṃśa*; and so forth), until divinity was even seen to be present in the possession and inspiration of great men and even women, a momentary descent (*āveśa*) that derives from learning to live within the moral order created by the lord. The result was that all Vaiṣṇavas were understood to be in some sense partaking of divinity by living the proper life—and that notion even stretched to include those beyond the formal system, hence the appearance of individuals such as Mahātmā Gandhi and even Martin Luther King in popular Vaiṣṇava art of the late twentieth century. While the terms for these various manifestations vary from one theological system to another within the tradition, the basic concept remains constant. Binding them together is the overriding motivation of compassion (*karuṇā*, *dayā*), an interest that undoubtedly received at least some impetus from the prominence of Buddhist groups in the period of early Vaiṣṇava formation. The emphasis on compassion as the motivation for Bhagavān's presence is matched by the devotee's correlative emphasis on love of the divine, producing a symbiotic relationship between lord and devotee, so much so that some later poets speak of a lord who cannot live without his followers, a divinity whose very existence is dependent on their love. In these general terms, all of Vaiṣṇavism can be understood then as an attempt to stabilize the world in which they live, motivated by compassion for the plight of humanity that seems inevitably to diverge from moral rectitude, the proper response to which is to inculcate love for god; everything else will fall into place if that be accomplished.

Forms of god, forms of practice

Because the foundations of Vaiṣṇava practice are centered on stabilizing the contemporary world whose needs change continually, the tradition has an inherent tolerance of diversity in practice and theology. But this does not mean that anything goes as long as one calls it worship of Viṣṇu; rather, there are principles that must be observed in articulating each new theological and practical perspective. While it is impossible to delineate all of the factors that go into this process of creating an acceptable Vaiṣṇava vision, perhaps the most common characteristic is the impulse to recognize Bhagavān in all of his forms and, by extension, to recognize the validity of communities of practitioners who opt for a different priorities and devotional foci. It is perhaps a rational response after the initial recognition of divinity and what that meant for practitioners to begin to focus on the classification of forms of divinity, the work of these forms, their accessibility, and the proper ways of approaching each image, although in such general terms it might be better to see that tendency as a technique of differentiation as the numbers of schools began to proliferate. Nārāyaṇa-Viṣṇu or Vāsudeva is, for instance, seen to function as a sovereign and majestic overlord, usually depicted with multiple arms, holding weapons, such as club and disc, by which he curbs the excesses of the patrons of moral disorder, that is, *adharma*, while also holding contrasting benign emblems of his compassionate and loving nature, the lotus and conch. When a devotee chooses this form (there are actually twenty-four permutations, depending on the order of implements in the arms), he or she does not ignore the others but relegates them hierarchically to a different position of priority. For some the human form is more desirable and approachable, so Rāma replaces Nārāyaṇa as a sovereign ruler, but as a two-armed accessible figure. Likewise, Kṛṣṇa, especially in his adolescent form that celebrates young love, requires a different orientation that does not eliminate Viṣṇu's other roles and functions but subordinates them to preferred or less preferred rank and accessibility. Today devotees often talk of these images of divinity as interchangeable: Viṣṇu is Kṛṣṇa is Rāma, and so on, so that when a devotee of Kṛṣṇa hears the name Rāma he hears Kṛṣṇa, and vice-versa. Historians of religions refer to this process as homologizing, but, in this particular case, it is not a simple equation or substitution; rather, each practitioner will come to understand that his or her chosen form of divinity is the complete godhead and that all other forms are but manifestations of it, in each case creating a new hierarchy of subordinated divine images and the graded activities that support it. While this attitude could conceivably produce a theoretically infinite set of variations, like so many other features of Indic culture, the tradition has recognized that the varieties tend to group together as a finite set of options, of perspectives that one might take to recognize difference while maintaining a standard of consistency and purpose. Historically these took shape as the four schools of Vaiṣṇava thought, *sampradāya*s, the oldest of which is now some nine hundred plus years in the making.

Sampradāyas: systematic formulations of devotion

The four schools were founded by the historical figures of Rāmānuja (eleventh century), Madhva or Ānandatīrtha (eleventh century), Nimbārka (thirteenth century), and Vallabha (fifteenth to sixteenth century). Looking back from a contemporary perspective, to qualify as a *sampradāya* seems to have meant that each leader mapped a formal intellectual justification of belief and practice, that is, a systematic theology that supported focused ritual practices ranging from the large public rituals oriented around temple culture to the individual practices of both laity and professional practitioners, including especially ascetics; ritual schools such as the Vaikhānasa, devoid of a systematic theology, tend not to warrant the classification of *sampradāya* within the tradition itself. It is significant that as the earliest *sampradāya*s were formed, the philosophical foundation included a commentary on the *Brahmasūtra*, the touchstone of Vedāntic thinking. By the seventeenth century, that commentary seems to have become a desideratum, as argued by members of the Vallabha *sampradāya* who brought suit against the upstart Gauḍīyas, claiming in a celebrated court case argued before the Mahārājā of Jaipur that the latter were not qualified to conduct the service of the image in a temple in Vraja because they did not have a commentary on the *Brahmasūtra* and were therefore not officially a *sampradāya* (a few weeks later one was produced thereby legitimating them in the court). While nowhere officially stated, clearly Vedānta set the terms of discourse that Vaiṣṇavas felt compelled to address in order to differentiate themselves to a greater or lesser degree from the classical formulation of monism or nondualism (Advaita), which was anathema to the dualistic devotional conception of a theistic ultimate. Beyond the *Brahmasūtra*, this formal differentiation began with Rāmānuja's *Viśiṣṭādvaita* or qualified nondualism, following Nāthamuni several centuries earlier. In each case the intellectual dimension was forged in a series of Sanskrit *śāstra*s, texts that explored basic questions of ontology, epistemology, cosmology, and, of course, soteriology. But the inspiration for these rational justifications of belief and practice came from a far different source, the devotional literatures in the vernacular, especially poetry that glorified god and the love that connected him to the devotee. Knowing the divine through direct and unmediated experience validated the truths that had to be articulated rationally; it was an emotional *bhakti* that inspired its intellectual defense.[2] Based on extant textual evidence, the earliest impulse to the vernacular came from the south, the product of the Āḻvār poets writing in Tamil at least as early as the seventh century, and references to Kṛṣṇa and Viṣṇu go back much further. This impulse to vernacular expression has become the hallmark of Vaiṣṇava devotion, spurring many of the works that have become classics, such as Tulasīdāsa's Hindi *Rāmāyaṇa* or the poetry of Caṇḍīdāsa, Vidyāpati, and Govindadāsa in Bengali, and has even become a vehicle for serious theology, a traditional preserve of Sanskrit. The effect of this parallel development of emotional and intellectual *bhakti*, with parallel developments in vernacular and Sanskrit literature, can be illustrated by looking at two examples of Vaiṣṇavism prominent in the subcontinent today. Śrīvaiṣṇavism and Gauḍīya Vaiṣṇavism. The Śrīvaiṣṇavism of Rāmānuja's school is the southernmost and oldest anchor of contemporary traditions and is seen here from a largely theological and ethical perspective. This will be contrasted with the Gauḍīya Vaiṣṇava or Caitanya movement of Bengal and Vraja, a northeastern development that comes after the founding of the four *sampradāya*s but which has claimed for itself the status of a fifth *sampradāya*, replete with all of the requisite pragmatic and philosophical justifications, but viewed here from the perspective of vernacular expression and individual praxis.

ŚRĪVAIṢṆAVISM

The Śrīvaiṣṇava community's sense of itself

The Śrīvaiṣṇava tradition traces its origins back to the primordial gracious initiative of Lord Viṣṇu and thus to the beginning of the world; more immediately, it also claims verification in the oldest literature in the Sanskrit and Tamil languages, most clearly and famously in the seventh- to ninth-century songs of the poet saints known as the Āḻvārs. Śrīvaiṣṇavism is an intensely textual tradition which self-consciously defines itself in terms of its canon, scriptural sources read in the context of their later commentaries and elaborations. One could fairly well describe the self-understanding of the community simply by recounting what great Śrīvaiṣṇava teachers, ancient and modern, have said in the course of their commentaries and more systematic presentations of scriptural teachings. But here we have opted instead to introduce a contemporary but nonetheless deeply traditional view of Śrīvaiṣṇavism, a small volume by R. Ramaswami Ramanujadasar simply and aptly entitled *Śrīvaiṣṇavam* (1984). This respected treatise is meant to catechize Śrīvaiṣṇavas in the basics of their own faith. Written in the Tamil language, it is clearly intended for the community and not for a wider academic audience. As such, it gives us a good sense of how the Śrīvaiṣṇava tradition sees itself.[3]

After general characterizations (such as those with which we began this essay) and particular emphasis on the importance of Śrī as the eternal consort of Viṣṇu and mediator of all grace, Ramanujadasar reviews the history of the Vaiṣṇava religion by drawing on common Sanskrit sources, such as the Upaniṣads, the *Bhagavad Gītā*, the *Nārāyaṇīya* section of the *Mahābhārata*, and so on. He emphasizes Śrīvaiṣṇavism's unbroken lineage, the prominence of Vaiṣṇava beliefs in the oldest Hindu texts, and its superiority vis-a-vis other schools of thought. Śrīvaiṣṇavism stands firmly in the center of the religious traditions of ancient India; it is original, authentic, and an eminently effective guide to life.

Since certain truths are necessary for salvation, Ramanujadasar accordingly expounds the basic Vaiṣṇava theological positions: the dependent relationship of conscious beings and nonconscious beings on the lord; the lord's role as material as well as efficient cause of the world; and the various ways in which the lord relates to the world, that is, as transcendent, in evolved cosmological forms (*vyuha*), in divine descents (*avatāra*), in consecrated temple images (*arcā*), and within each self.

Ramanujadasar then identifies and explains the five steps in the project of salvation: the lord himself is the highest object of knowing and loving; human nature is oriented to the lord; reaching the lord is the human goal; complete surrender is the means to that goal; and obstacles to the goal, such as lust and pride, can be overcome by clear knowledge and simple surrender. He also offers a detailed description of key practices, customs, and observances distinctive to the Śrīvaiṣṇava tradition: for example, the purifications and preparations (*saṃskāra*) which define the mature Śrīvaiṣṇava, including insignia to be worn, names appropriately taken, prayers and rites to be learned (including the three sacred *mantra*s which encapsulate the faith), the daily routine, and practices of worship. In addition, he mentions specific rules regarding eating, special rules regarding the behavior of women (since the list is in general conceived of as pertaining to men), and a list of prohibited actions.

Finally, Ramanujadasar surveys texts distinctive to the Śrīvaiṣṇava tradition and makes clear that although Sanskrit texts are important, Śrīvaiṣṇavism is distinguished by its focus on South Indian, Tamil-language texts. Most important are the Tamil-language devotional songs of the Āḻvārs gathered in the *Divyaprabandham* canon. These texts express the true spirit of religion and the array of interior virtues, which a lover of the lord must ultimately have; they complement and even surpass the Sanskrit texts, which the community also reverences. Foremost among the twelve Āḻvārs is Caṭakōpaṉ (popularly known as Nammāḻvār, "our Āḻvār"), author of the 1,102 verses of *Tiruvāymoḻi*, a set of one hundred songs in which were found all the defining tenets of Śrīvaiṣṇavism. To know *Tiruvāymoḻi* well is to be informed by its values and so to acquire the wisdom which characterizes the tradition as a whole (see Clooney 1996: chapters 3–4).

Śrīvaiṣṇavism as a public and argumentative tradition

Despite emphasis on tradition and the internal cohesion of the tradition, Śrīvaiṣṇava theologians also insist on formulating the community's positions as truth claims that surpass other and often conflicting views of the nature of god, humans, and the world. They were prepared to argue accordingly. Śrīvaiṣṇavism is the original and true religion, revealed by god at the very origin of the universe, and its worldview is the best that is accessible to reason as well as the worldview affirmed by scripture. The tradition is not relativistic regarding positions it holds to be true and never concluded that its views were merely local beliefs; rather, they were understood to be universally cogent and liable to intellectual affirmation by all honest, reasoning persons.

As we have seen, the Śrīvaiṣṇavas shared standard Vedānta doctrines articulated in texts like the Upaniṣads, the Vedānta commentaries, and the *Bhagavad Gītā* and particularly in the Viśiṣṭādvaita Vedānta tradition of interpretation. Rāmānuja (1017–1137), the leading Śrīvaiṣṇava theologian, explained and defended the Śrīvaiṣṇava interpretation of those texts and doctrines as correct and compelling even for persons outside the community who were nonetheless still willing to reason honestly. In his key writings, such as the *Śrībhāṣya* commentary on the *Brahmasūtra* of Bādarāyaṇa, the *Gītābhāṣya*, and the *Vedārthasaṃgraha*, Rāmānuja argued against materialism, reductive ritualism, various Buddhist and Jaina teachings, nontheistic and extreme nondualist views of the meaning of the Upaniṣads, and even other theistic sects whose members worshiped god by other names, for instance, as Śiva. Even in his most argumentative moments Rāmānuja put the highest priority on spiritual values and appreciated the necessity of divine grace, but he did not hesitate to assert the truth of his tradition's positions. He gives no hint of the view that Śrīvaiṣṇavas have one truth, other Vaiṣṇavas other truths, Buddhists and Jainas still other truths. All Vaiṣṇavas adhere to the same truth; there is no other truth.

Several generations after Rāmānuja, Vedāntadeśika (1270–1369) likewise presented in a clear light the argumentative and intellectually assertive side of Śrīvaiṣṇavism. For instance, his *Paramatabhaṅga* lines up and refutes a number of opposing views, arranged according to the quantity and gravity of error—divergence from Vaiṣṇava tenets—in their positions. His *Nyāyasiddhāñjana* vigorously defends correct views on seven important topics: the dependent nature of material reality; the eternal but dependent individual self; the supreme lord; the lord's eternal spiritual and material abode; the nature of understanding and of objective knowledge; and the reality of intellectual qualities. In each section, right views are defended by rational and scriptural arguments, and wrong views discounted on the same basis.[4]

These philosophical and theological attitudes and projects are carried forward in other Vaiṣṇava traditions as well, by renowned teachers such as Madhva and Vallabha. In all these cases, despite significant differences, there is consistency in doctrine and in the tradition's claim to present and defend the truth. Since Śrīvaiṣṇavism and other Vaiṣṇavisms thus claim their beliefs to be universally valid, we can see on this basis that there is a reality to "Vaiṣṇavism" broader than any particular regional or cultural instantiations of the tradition.[5]

Continuity and change in Śrīvaiṣṇavism: three examples

To explore further the nature of Śrīvaiṣṇavism, we make several comments on the tension between continuity and adaptation in the tradition, for it discovered itself, so to speak, at those moments when it had to identify the limits of its practices and beliefs.

First there is continuity. The Śrīvaiṣṇava tradition is very mindful of its lineage back to Rāmānuja in the Sanskrit Vedānta tradition and to the Tamil heritage of the Āḻvārs. It sees both of these as rooted ultimately in the lord's divine intention and gracious communication. Śrīvaiṣṇavas have enormous respect for their great learned and spiritual teachers (*ācārya*), whose lives and lineage, recounted in ancient accounts such as the *Divyasūricaritam* and *Guruparamparāprabhāvam*, are thought to pass down the original truth to new generations. The nature of this respect is captured nicely in the preface to the recently published *Ācāryavaipavam*, a compendium containing brief accounts of the lives and deeds of great teachers from Nāthamuni (tenth century) to the present time. The author of the preface, S. V. S. Raghavan (Krishnamacaryar Swami 1992), writes:

> The truth of Viśiṣṭādvaita was originated by the lord himself, who taught it to the lady, and she taught it to Viśvakṣena, who taught it to Nammāḻvār. Nammāḻvār taught it to Nāthamuni. In the Dvāpara Yuga, the great *ṛṣi* Vyāsa taught the meanings of the Upaniṣads succinctly in *sūtra* form. Great *ṛṣi*s like Brahmānandi, Taṅkar, Dramiḍa, Bodhāyana, and Guhadeva composed commentaries. Bodhayana composed a very succinct commentary known as the *Vṛtti* [the Explanation]. Following this closely, Rāmānuja composed his *Śrībhāṣya* [the Holy Commentary on the *Brahmasūtra*]. Lord Deśika composed a work entitled *Sampradāyaparisuddhi* [the Purification of the Tradition], a *maṇipravāḷa*[6] work which insured that authentic teachers in our tradition would take for their foundation the meaning of our settled positions and all would teach with one mind. For it is well known from the Upaniṣads and the texts supporting them that the specific meanings of the teachings pertaining to the self according to our tradition of teachers must be ascertained first. Therefore we must know the succession of teachers related to our teachings on the self.[7]

It is a matter of extraordinary importance for Śrīvaiṣṇavas to see themselves as part of this unbroken tradition and to assess current developments and problems in light of their fidelity to what has always been taught in the tradition. Novelty is not a virtue.

Tensions between Vedic and Sanskritic/elitist values and Tamil and popular devotional values were resolved by compromises in which the old and new were shown to be complementary truths. In the context of continuity, however, there is also change, at which the Śrīvaiṣṇava tradition has shown itself to be adept. To illustrate this we introduce three cases where early Śrīvaiṣṇavas strove for equilibrium: the balancing of the Tamil language tradition with a Sanskrit language heritage; the maintenance of caste structures along with the transformation of their meaning; and the simultaneous displacement and enhancement of eroticism.

Even in its earlier textual sources, Śrīvaiṣṇavism has been distinguished by a commitment to a Tamil tradition (cultural, linguistic and literary, psychological, religious, and spiritual), which did not entail abandoning the Sanskrit tradition. The community was formed in light of the religion and poetry of the Āḻvārs, in so powerful an engagement that it was impossible merely to glean selected ideas for incorporation into the established Brāhmaṇical system. Room had to be made for Tamil compositions, sensitivities, and values. The task for the teachers was to draw primarily and deeply on the Tamil heritage while continuing to adhere to Brāhmaṇical and Sanskritic tradition. For this purpose they had to foster a creative relation between the two language heritages, honoring the one without sacrificing the other (see Hart 1975; Ramanujan and Cutler 1983).

The argument about the value of non-Sanskrit compositions is worked out most clearly in relation to *Tiruvāymoḻi*. The most important of the Tamil Vaiṣṇava works, it also occasioned the clearest and sharpest battles about whether the community could legitimately appeal to sources from outside the established Brāhmaṇical canon. We can see the cautious yet radical attitude of the Śrīvaiṣṇavas at work in the defense of *Tiruvāymoḻi* put forward by Naññīyar, who wrote the first introduction to the work in the twelfth century CE.

Naññīyar raised directly the question of the authority of the Tamil hymns with respect to the Sanskrit tradition by taking up a series of eight objections against taking the vernacular Tamil tradition seriously: the songs of *Tiruvāymoḻi* are written in an inferior language, which ought not to be used for sacred purposes; they are learned and transmitted by low-caste men and even by women; they were composed by a low-caste male; composed in the Tamil vernacular, the songs are known only in the Tamil region of India; in that region, however, even people from outside the Vedic tradition honor the songs; the songs speak of things that are not to be approved such as sexual desire; and they also downgrade traditional ideals highly praised in the Sanskrit tradition, such as autonomy (*aiśvarya*) and isolation (*kaivalya*).

Naññīyar refutes these objections by turning each alleged flaw into a virtue. For example, since divine inspiration is the source of the songs, the author's low-caste status is not a detriment but a benefit, making it all the more clear that the lord takes the lead. Moreover, if the lord inspires the Āḻvār, it is obviously on that basis that people of all backgrounds come to enjoy them. It is the content of these songs and their excellent style that explain their wide attraction beyond traditional boundaries; even people in other parts of India who do not know Tamil wish they did, just to be able to hear the songs. The songs do not exclude traditional values but hierarchize them properly in relation to the lord's initiatives. The ancient Sanskrit texts teach what the lord has in mind, but *Tiruvāymoḻi* excels in expressing most clearly and perfectly the nature of god while still inspiring and increasing devotion.

Naññīyar did not conclude that Sanskrit revelation should be replaced by Tamil revelation, nor that a Tamil-Sanskrit mix should replace both. Rather, he and other Śrīvaiṣṇava teachers defended the theory of a "twofold Vedānta," the view that the fullness of revelation is expressed equally in the two languages, even if according to the differing strengths of each. Sanskrit should be read and Tamil should be read to know the mind of the lord expressed in the two languages. Although an outside observer might stress differences—between the Upaniṣads and the Tamil songs, for example—the Śrīvaiṣṇava community was actually more daring in its decision to assert that the seemingly divergent Sanskrit and Tamil canons are equal, parallel expressions of a single revelation of the lord, human nature, and the way that humans reach god.[8]

A second issue about which Śrīvaiṣṇavas argued was the religious meaning of "caste"—here, birth status (*jāti*) interpreted as religious class (*varṇa*)—and its social implications. If love of god and surrender to god are the sufficient and necessary requirements for liberation, is caste, along with all its religious implications irrelevant at best and in fact odious? Here too the Śrīvaiṣṇavas sought a balanced position, neither rejecting caste nor subordinating devotion to it.

All the Śrīvaiṣṇava teachers seemed to agree that considerations of caste could not be allowed to lead to the exclusion of low-caste or outcaste persons, but they disagreed over whether or not caste distinctions should nevertheless be maintained. Teachers in the Teṉkalai (southern) school of Tamil Vaiṣṇavism, connected closely with the great temple at Srirangam, argued that caste distinctions within the community were at best secondary. As Patricia Mumme (1988: 163) has shown, these teachers maintained that service to fellow devotees, regardless of their birth or conduct, is the defining manifestation of the soul's dependent nature, more important even than submission to the lord alone and certainly far more decisive than caste rules. This service of all is most pleasing to the lord. Piḷḷailōkācārya, a key Teṉkalai teacher, charged that investigating caste identity is as repugnant as examining the materials out of which a consecrated temple image is made (Mumme 1988: 164). Some teachers such as Aḻakiyamaṇavāḷa Perumāḷ, the brother of Piḷḷailōkācārya and the author of the *Ācārya Hṛdayam*, may have argued for the abolition of the distinctions of birth status and religious class altogether.

By contrast, the Vaṭakalai (northern) school of Śrīvaiṣṇavism held that although devotion to the lord was primary and all devotees were to be respected, distinctions based on birth status and religious class, plus the accompanying purity rules, and so on, were not abrogated by the new values. Vedāntadeśika argued that both scripture and reason support a continued observance of caste distinctions and duties; all devotees are dear in the lord's eyes and in the eyes of other devotees, but it pleases the lord that differences in caste continue to be observed. Some devotees are Brāhmaṇs, some are Śūdras, some are outcastes, and this differentiation is not to be overlooked.

Both Teṉkalai and Vaṭakalai Śrīvaiṣṇavas gave a higher priority to devotion than to caste; they disagreed on how firmly the strictures of caste were to be maintained and perhaps on whether a situation might be expected in which those strictures disappeared entirely. Most pertinent to this chapter is to notice that these Vaiṣṇavas were able to disagree with one another while continuing to respect one another as Vaiṣṇavas. Even if the differences of attitude toward caste contributed to the separation of the Teṉkalai and Vaṭakalai communities, such differences did not lead either group to deny to the other the title "Vaiṣṇava." This combination of intellectual commitment (such that argument is possible) and mutual inclusion (such that intellectual differences do not entirely separate Vaiṣṇavas from one another) is a distinguishing feature of Vaiṣṇavism as a coherent religious tradition throughout its long history.

A third example of the Śrīvaiṣṇava tradition's struggle to maintain continuity while incorporating new values lies in its treatment of eroticism. The charge seems to have been forcefully made, as was suggested in Nañjīyar's arguments given above, that the language of eroticism was largely out of bounds in Brāhmaṇical circles, particularly the austere Vedāntic traditions adopted by the Śrīvaiṣṇavas, and that obviously erotic words and images in the Āḻvār poetry caused some initial upset in orthodox circles. But to eradicate the language of eroticism would have conflicted with the Śrīvaiṣṇava instinct to conserve and honor its entire heritage. Since the Āḻvārs' poetry included a strongly erotic tone, especially with respect to the desire for the lord, eroticism could not be merely dismissed as inappropriate, and a compromise had to be worked out.

Dealing broadly with the issue of the Śrīvaiṣṇava resignification of the erotic tradition of the loves of Kṛṣṇa, Nancy Nayar (1997) suggests that despite the characteristic moral conservativism of the Śrīvaiṣṇava community, it actually preserved and extended the erotic tradition. The teachers took seriously the mythic scenario according to which Kṛṣṇa departs from the cowherd women and is no longer present (for them or for later devotees) by way of easy accessibility, but they then accentuate the new possibility of intimacy with the lord and his consort Lakṣmī in temple encounters. Erotic proximity is displaced and then intensified as temple experience:

> The highly emotional nature of the religiosity of the Āḻvārs is its central and most original feature. While this same emotionalism is not to be found in the Ācāryas' portrayals of Kṛṣṇa and the *gopī*s, it is nonetheless present, but now contained, in their stanzas in praise of God's iconic presence in the temple. . . . When addressing the iconic-incarnation, the poets are personally and passionately involved with the Lord fully and substantially present before them: they "drink in with their eyes" the lovely Lord; they ask Him to rain down upon them "the waters of compassion"; their minds "drink in His golden garment"; they ask to be able to enjoy Him thoroughly; they beg that His face may remain in them forever; they exclaim: "How can the person who sees You bear to see anything else?"; they let their eyes "feast" on the beautiful Lord present right before them.[9]
>
> (Nayar 1997: 208)

It is remarkable that the teachers transpose the eroticism connected with Kṛṣṇa and the cowherd women onto the transcendent Lord Viṣṇu and his consort Śrī Lakṣmī, the eternal husband and wife. What is seemingly lost in the realm of ordinary life is intensified in temple worship; "mere eroticism" is suspect, but the eroticization of temple worship and encounters with Viṣṇu and Lakṣmī is commended.

The influential thirteenth-century commentator Nampiḷḷai dealt with the issue of eroticism when introducing *Tiruvāymoḻi* 1.4, sung in the voice of a young woman separated from her lover (and the first of more than twenty-five songs in the woman's voice). According to Nampiḷḷai, Vaiṣṇavas could neither merely take the erotic for granted nor merely exclude it. He illustrated the balance involved by an anecdote. There was a man who wanted to learn *Tiruvāymoḻi*, but his mind was not fully open to the teachings he heard. He enjoyed the exposition of the first songs in *Tiruvāymoḻi*, but when the fourth was introduced, he was scandalized by the language of erotic love, as if the lord and humans could be lovers. He decided that this song was nothing but lust, so he walked out, refusing to listen any more. Nampiḷḷai comments that it was the man's bad fortune that his mind was so narrow; he missed the real substance of the truth one must learn in order to know the lord and oneself, a truth articulated in the erotic imagery.[10] Such songs express the Āḻvār's interior experience and are not to be dismissed or skipped. Not only is *Tiruvāymoḻi* not scandalous, but also its erotic language actually fulfills the mandates and values of the Upaniṣadic tradition: the language of knowledge and the language of passion are both required. Devotees were thus challenged to accept an unusual synthesis of erotic and ascetic words and images[11]—a synthesis recognized and accepted in other Vaiṣṇava traditions as well.

Here, too, we see the Śrīvaiṣṇava tradition's desire to maintain its theological coherence while reinterpreting some of its basic concepts and practices—such as relate to language, caste, eroticism—so as to incorporate new religious impulses. Deep respect for the Brāhmaṇical and Sanskritic traditions was coupled with a stubborn insistence that the lord could speak, and humans praise, in other languages and styles; caste structures are worthy of respect but cannot be allowed to divide the community or exclude devotees; the language and experiences of passion are important enough that even the most austere formulations of Vaiṣṇava values must accommodate modes of expression that tap into the deepest human desires and longings.

Śrīvaiṣṇavism in the West

Even in the modern world Śrīvaiṣṇavism has continued to prize the truth of its most ancient traditions and to foster formation in keeping with familiar communal values. Accordingly, it remains reluctant to accommodate itself to a changing and increasingly secular world. It is quite noticeable that books like *Śrīvaiṣṇavam* say nothing in particular about the modern world, changing religious values, the secularization of large Indian cities, the myriad challenges surely facing pious Śrīvaiṣṇavas who work in banks or commercial firms or government offices, whose children attend large schools with diversified student bodies and faculties. We do not find modern Śrīvaiṣṇava treatises that discuss contemporary ethical issues—for example, proper Vaiṣṇava positions regarding new medical technologies, human rights, economic justice—and we do not get the sense that the Śrīvaiṣṇava tradition feels required to do anything more than reaffirm its traditional wisdom on how to be a good human being, a Vaiṣṇava; such persons, properly trained in virtue, will be able to venture forth and return safely, living rightly before god and with one another, as their ancestors have for millennia. People properly educated in the tradition do not need books on ethics.

But this emphasis on personal formation in religious values and general disinterest in intellectual adjustment to modernity do not mean that Śrīvaiṣṇavism lacks the ambition to root itself in new environs. Vasudha Narayanan (1992) has studied the process of adaptation of the Śrīvaiṣṇava tradition to the North American context, using the Śrīveṅkateśvara temple near Pittsburgh as an example. This popular and well-established temple demonstrates extreme fidelity to tradition; in architecture, ritual, and custom it replicates the great Veṅkateśvara temple at Tirupati in India and indeed was built so that Śrīvaiṣṇava beliefs and practices could remain intact in the new, American context.

To be sure, there is little indication that living in pluralistic America and in a majority Christian culture has instigated new developments in Śrīvaiṣṇava theology or stimulated Śrīvaiṣṇavas to reflect on the meaning of religious pluralism, the nature of American secularism, or the challenge to redefine oneself in terms of a public discourse that draws upon multiple traditions. Yet, as Narayanan indicates, the community has accommodated itself to the American context in numerous ways. The Śrīveṅkateśvara temple uses the more flexible Pāñcarātra form of ritual as well as the stricter Vaikhānasa ritual used at Tirupati; both Tamil as well as Sanskrit scriptures are recited; the calendar of rituals is adjusted, wherever possible, to fit the American weekend and the American calendar of holidays (e.g. Thanksgiving, the 4th of July, Labor Day, and so on); devotional songs released by the temple celebrate the Penn Hills location of the temple as a holy place, just as holy places are celebrated in South India; the temple offers some non-Śrīvaiṣṇava rituals to accommodate other Hindus; as would not be normally the case in India, there is an image of the elephant-headed Gaṇeśa in the temple; and the temple's publications include inclusive articles that stress the symbolic and inviting nature of Hindu imagery and worship.[12] While it is too early to tell whether life in a country like the United States will more deeply affect Śrīvaiṣṇava beliefs and practices, especially among newer generations born in America, there is reason to believe that "American Śrīvaiṣṇavism" will continue to find ways of establishing itself fruitfully in a country very different from South India. And such has been the experience of the Gauḍīya Vaiṣṇavas, a group that represents one of the latest developments in Vaiṣṇava tradition.

VAIṢṆAVISM IN BENGAL: THE GAUḌIYA TRADITION

Thus far we have considered the development of Vaiṣṇavism as a theologically self-conscious tradition according to its general Sanskrit background and in its Tamil instantiation as the Śrīvaiṣṇava tradition. In the Bengali context of northeast India, a tradition that received its inspiration centuries after the Śrīvaiṣṇavas depends heavily on many of the same perspectives, yet by contrast will demonstrate that Vaiṣṇavism is itself an elastic term. Vaiṣṇavism in this context describes both a particular Hindu tradition or traditions, which flourished in various parts of India, but also maintains a continuity and elasticity in these various contexts: there are many Vaiṣṇava traditions, but we can also legitimately speak of Vaiṣṇavism—which is instantiated as "Śrīvaiṣṇavism," "Gauḍīya Vaiṣṇavism," and so forth.

A new vernacular impetus for devotion

When the devotional forms of Vaiṣṇavism moved from South India to north, as most scholars are inclined to trace it (Hardy 1983), the tradition witnessed but small and incremental changes in modes of worship until the fifteenth and sixteenth centuries, when the northern vernacular languages suddenly found their voice. Among the first compositions in the vernaculars were the devotional epics—the *Mahābhārata* and the *Rāmāyaṇa*—and Tulasīdāsa's Hindi retelling of the latter, the *Rāmcaritmanas*, has in the centuries that followed become a favorite of all ages. But the most common form of devotional expression to grow from this period was the local lyric verse or *pada*. Many of the great religious figures of the period indicate at least an awareness of the Tamil verse compositions of the Āḻvārs, and more than one North Indian *guru* has circulated Yamunācārya's Sanskrit *Stotraratna* and other devotional eulogies. But perhaps more than any other it was the lyric retelling of the love of Rādhā and Kṛṣṇa portrayed in Jayadeva's Sanskrit *Gītā Govinda*—itself an elegant poetic rendering of the poignant passages of the tenth book of the *Bhāgavata Purāṇa*—that inspired local poets (see B. Miller 1977). One such poet, Vidyāpati, wrote in a language sufficiently transparent across northern dialects that his poetry is claimed by numerous variants of both Hindi and Bengali as one of their earliest literary ancestors—and that poetry sets a precedent that eventually defined the genre of the *pada*. The *pada* was seldom recited but sung, and in its singing comes the impetus for the major ritual structures of North Indian Vaiṣṇavism: *bhajana* and the more versatile *kīrtana*, singing the praises of the lord, Kṛṣṇa or Rāma. Today the poetry of Sūradāsa, Mīrābāī, Caṇḍīdāsa, Govindadāsa, Jñānadāsa, Ravidāsa, Rāmadāsa, and others dominates the literary histories of these local religious traditions.

This form of praise allows the devotee to celebrate the love of and the love for the deity directly, with no need for mediation, for example, by a priest. Like vernacular language itself, *kīrtana* and the more focused *nāmakīrtana* or *nāmajapa* (which simply repeats the names of god in cycles of auspicious numbers) require no special ritual space. That feature of this *bhakti* has important ramifications, since it frees the devotee from dependence on the institution of the temple, making the ritual form available to anyone. While temple worship or *pūjā* continued to be desirable, it was no longer the exclusive or even dominant mode of devotional expression; even the images used in temples were small mobile images identical to those often installed in home shrines (which bear a striking resemblance to the processional images of temples in the south).[13]

Rather, the mediation of religious experience through the vernacular inevitably decentered and dispersed practice into local forms, and that shift follows a logic of its own making that disperses centralized authority and practice: forms of Vaiṣṇava practice were often analogous or structurally similar but highly variable from region to region.

The shift to vernacular-based theology and ritual had the immediate effect of placing the burden of religious responsibility on the individual in a way never previously encountered but certainly anticipated (if not begun) in the modified karmic system of the *Bhagavad Gītā*. Accompanying that responsibility—each individual suddenly holding the opportunity for salvation in his or her own hands in an immediate way—is a new interest in "intention." While following the ritual prescriptions of *japa* and so forth were considered to be sufficient to guarantee a positive result—one of the mechanistic features of a traditional orthopraxy—a devotee's seriousness and intention were constantly gauged and tested to determine the quality of the devotion; in short, the devotee was increasingly expected to "mean it" when worshiping.[14] This, in turn, led to a kind of introspection of motive and close analysis of the individual's personal devotional proclivities that required a new kind of formalization, but it was also a necessary result of a devotional approach that hinged on the inculcation of emotion (the domain of individual) as the base for religious experience.

The system of this generalized North Indian Vaiṣṇava *bhakti* depended then and now on a complex "phenomenology of repetition" to achieve its goal, and the panoply of practices uniformly reflects this binding theme. Nearly all of the North Indian groups systematized their approaches (often in Sanskrit) after the initial impulse of devotion was manifested (in the vernacular), but it was the Gauḍīya Vaiṣṇavas perhaps more than others who excelled in the logic of this new systemization. For the Gauḍīyas, the inspiration and exemplar of this new way of doing Vaiṣṇavism was Kṛṣṇa Caitanya, né Viśvambhara Miśra (1476–1533), a Bengali from Nadīyā who was believed to be god himself, *svayaṃ bhagavān*, but also a unique fusing of two persons, Kṛṣṇa the adolescent cowherd and his lover, Rādhā.[15] Gauḍīya Vaiṣṇava practice derived directly from the example of this god among men, and as the vernacular expression captured the emotional content of this new kind of *bhakti*, he instructed several intellectually precocious followers to systematize and propagate the devotion he taught, giving it a grounding in the traditional *śāstra*s and fixing its features in the language of the great tradition, Sanskrit. Not insignificantly, two of these six men—Gopāla Bhaṭṭa and Raghunātha Bhaṭṭa—came from the south and fixed the ritual dimension of temple-based worship. The youngest of the six, Jīva Gosvāmī, was the leading metaphysician, while Sanātana and Raghunātha Dāsa added more devotionally oriented works. Most notable among the group was Rūpa Gosvāmī, a former secretary to the Muslim ruler of Bengal, Ḥusain Shāh (r. 1492–1519), and who became the group's leading theoretician of the nature of devotion.

Rūpa Gosvāmī's aesthetics of devotion

According to Rūpa Gosvāmī (*Bhaktirasāmṛtasindhu* 1.2.90–92, 1.2.238–45), to become a Vaiṣṇava—a feat accomplished with a simple initiation and the reception of one's personal *mantra*—one had only to practice a few basic ritual prescriptions. While the full set of injunctions numbered sixty-four, five are declared most efficacious, and by that evaluation understood to subsume hierarchically the other fifty-nine. They are: chanting the name (*nāma*) of Kṛṣṇa in *kīrtana*; remembering (*smaraṇa*) and savoring the narratives of the *Bhāgavata Purāṇa*, which reveal Kṛṣṇa's exploits; reverently and lovingly serving the image of Kṛṣṇa in the temple (*pūjā*); living in the company of holy men or *sādhus*; and living in the realm or *maṇḍala* of Mathura.[16] These acts are ritual injunctions (*vaidhī*), and in the first—chanting the name—resides the motivating power of the rest. *Smaraṇa* became the impulse behind the writing of many texts, *pūjā* promoting temple construction, and the association of devotees leading to formal communities. The desire to live in Vraja led to the reclamation of its sacred geography by the Gosvāmī theologians and by followers of other religious traditions, most notably those of Vallabha, while leading to pilgrimage routes that at one time connected northern and southern sites in India, but eventually became effectively self-contained in Kṛṣṇa's realm of Vraja and Caitanya's realm of Bengal. To follow these seemingly simple activities is to repeat them, and when one repeats them often enough a change comes about in the devotee. The seeds of love are sown, the devotee inculcates a devotion for Kṛṣṇa, and that love grows by imagining oneself increasingly to inhabit a world that is dictated by the presence of Kṛṣṇa, physically, mentally, emotionally. Through a constant exposure to the various relationships enjoyed by those around Kṛṣṇa, the devotee gradually comes to understand his or her own proclivities, how best to love god, a love tailored to one's own personality, an approach with obvious roots in southern Vaiṣṇavism. To be true to that realization is gradually to come to "mean" the love one experiences, that is, the love must be made emotionally profound and "real," and that is the program of the new *bhakti*. To pursue that love to its conclusion is to imbue the mechanical ritual acts (*vaidhī bhakti*) with passion (*rāga*), a process that once started is uncontrollable, although it can be directed; eventually that passion will take a life of its own. Rūpa calls this new phase *rāgānugā bhakti*, the "following of passion," which is all-consuming. As the experience matures, the mechanical rituals continue as a reflex, while the passion of devotion is pursued through more sophisticated forms of ritual practice (*sādhana*), many of which are yogically based and that help the devotee find his or her true identity as an eternal servitor (*nitya parikara*) of Kṛṣṇa.

According to Rūpa, the devotee seeks to discover the kind of love that matches one's own emotional makeup through a series of repetitive exercises starting with *nāmajapa* and culminating in meditative reconstructions of the idyll of Vraja and those who people it in the company of Kṛṣṇa. These emotions of love, adapted from Bharata's aesthetics of *rasa* and detailed in the *Bhaktirasāmṛtasindhu*, are grouped into five basic types called *sthāyibhāvas*: *śānta* or the quiescent mode denotes a feeling of tranquillity and awesomeness at such great distance from the personality of god that many within the Gauḍīya and other North Indian traditions do not even consider this an emotion appropriate for worship, if it is an emotion at all (it is often loosely indicated as a forerunner of the Vedāntic merging of the self with *brahman* and therefore anathema). *Dāsya* or servitude, however, does indicate an approach that acknowledges Kṛṣṇa as the celestial sovereign in a distant and vertical remove from the servile devotee, whose existence is exclusively dominated by perpetual service. The *sakhyabhāva*, however, breaks down this distance between devotee and lord by treating Kṛṣṇa as a friend and companion, although Kṛṣṇa continues to dominate the relationship. The love experienced by a parent, called *vātsalya*, is a powerful relationship that makes Kṛṣṇa the recipient of the nurturing and indulgent love appropriately bestowed on children. And, finally, the highest form of love for Gauḍīya Vaiṣṇavas is *śṛṅgāra* or erotic love, and it is this love that becomes the topic of most of the Gauḍīya literature. The focus is on the adolescent Kṛṣṇa, the mischievous cowherd lover, who pursues and is pursued by the young women of Vraja, the *gopīs*.

While his exploits with these women are inexhaustible, more than any other it is the loveplay with Rādhā that captures the Gauḍīya Vaiṣṇava imagination. As the purest form of eroticism, her love automatically subsumes within it all other possible forms, which is to say that *śṛṅgāra* includes within it all other *bhāva*s as well as its own erotically charged connection. Because Rādhā's *śṛṅgāra* includes all other emotions, it is the most complete and therefore the most satisfying love for Kṛṣṇa. It intrigues him with its waywardness (*vāmatā*, literally, "left-ness" or crookedness) precisely because he cannot predict or control it. Because it is most satisfying and complete, Rādhā's love then is the ideal, and its development becomes the aspiration of devotees. That unselfish and pure love is called *prema*. It is here, in the pursuit of Rādhā's *prema*, that the Gauḍīya Vaiṣṇava tradition reveals the complexity of its interpretation and demonstrates how seemingly insignificant hermeneutical differences can lead to a multitude of divergent practices.

Nearly all of the Vaiṣṇava traditions of North India choose one or more of the basic emotional conditions (*bhāva*) to develop as the ideal form for loving Kṛṣṇa, although they will hierarchize them differently, but the common point is to create an experience of that love, which allows the devotee to savor it in a clear and unsullied way, a way that is ultimately abstracted and freed from its earthly distractions, making it pure and divine. The savoring experience is metaphorically described as "tasting the *rasa*" of it, accomplished by the devotee who approaches it in a manner modeled on Bharata's cultivated esthete, the "man with heart" (*sahṛdaya*). *Rasa* is literally the "juice" or "sap," which is characteristic of something good, sweet, alive, and nurturing; and as the refined experience of emotion abstracted form its commonplace, it is analogous to the nectar of immortality (*amṛta*), for to taste it is to experience the ultimate love for Kṛṣṇa while providing for Kṛṣṇa the ultimate pleasure in return. To taste *rasa* is to experience the divine, and that ultimately constitutes a salvation. In that the northern traditions are more or less uniform; where they differ is how to cultivate this love in a practical way.

For the Gauḍīya Vaiṣṇavas, it was Kṛṣṇa Caitanya who revealed how this was possible, for he was not only believed to be god, *svayaṃ bhagavān*, but also a unique combined form of Kṛṣṇa in eternal union and separation from Rādhā, an androgyne, which bound together the principles of devotion: the object of love, Kṛṣṇa, "king of *rasa*," and the embodiment of the devotion that satisfied him, Rādhā, the "great love." As hagiographer Kṛṣṇadāsa Kavirāja described it in the Bengali *Caitanya Caritāmṛta* (2.8.229–42) when Caitanya revealed his divinity to adept devotee Rāmānanda Rāya:

> Then, smiling, Prabhu [Caitanya] showed to him his true form: Rasarāja [Kṛṣṇa] and Mahābhāva [Rādhā], the two in one form. And when he saw this, Rāmānanda was faint with joy; he could not control his body and fell to the earth. Prabhu with a touch

> of his hand brought him back to consciousness; and seeing him as a *saṃnyāsin* [renunciant], [Rāya] was astonished. Embracing him Prabhu comforted him. "Except for you, no one has seen this form. It is because of your perception of the metaphysical principle (*tattva*) of the *rasa* of my play (*līlā*) that I have shown this form to you. The golden-colored body is not mine but is the touch of the body of Rādhā; she touches no one except the son of Gopendra. I experience in my heart and soul everything she feels; then I taste the *rasa* of the sweetness of myself. None of my acts are secret to you. Even though I have hidden them, by the power of your *prema* you understand the secret meaning of everything.
>
> (2.8.233–40)

The point of this androgynous descent of god was to allow Kṛṣṇa to taste the experience of Rādhā herself, who as the ultimate lover of Kṛṣṇa suffered a love even greater than any Kṛṣṇa could imagine, for the object of her love was god, and Kṛṣṇa as god was excluded from that experience. Only by becoming Rādhā while remaining himself could he know it. But given the seeming completeness and exclusivity of this pair's love as manifested by Caitanya, it was not altogether clear what role a devotee might have in promoting it.

Those who followed the Gosvāmī theologians appointed by Caitanya to develop the systematic statement of *bhakti* and its practice developed sophisticated techniques for yogic meditation wherein the repetitive sixty-four *vaidhī* injunctions provided a foundation upon which the devotee could cultivate the imagination to the point of entering Kṛṣṇa's presence, not just here on earth but eventually in Goloka, Kṛṣṇa's intimate heaven. The techniques were arduous, with long exercises devoted to the construction of interior landscapes replete with the sacred geography of Vraja. In meditation the adept learned to people these landscapes with the characters described in the *Bhāgavata Purāṇa*, well known of course because of the constant telling and retelling of the *līlā*s. As the devotee was increasingly driven by the passion of *rāgānugā*, he would discover that the stories played out in this mental theater were not always scripted but spontaneous. Eventually the spontaneity was so consuming that he found himself personally swept up in the thick of the drama (see Haberman 1988). To participate in these activities of Rādhā and Kṛṣṇa and the myriad of other characters required a perfected body or *siddha deha*, and in this body he could move freely in the eternal realm of Vraja. Rūpa and the other Gosvāmīs identified themselves with servants of Rādhā, called *mañjari*s, and in these roles aided the trysts but never became the object of Kṛṣṇa's personal advances. Others within the tradition, however, understood themselves to participate in the identities of direct players in the Vraja *līlā*s, so much so that Purī-based theologian Kavikarṇapūra composed the *Gauragaṇoddeśadīpikā* to enumerate more than two hundred of these identities among the followers of Caitanya. Among these and later generations, different *guru*-lineages would promote different interpretations of this basic principle of participation, and, as might be expected given the focus of the tradition on the erotic, there were those who chose not just to make it a mental construction.

Alternative developments to the mainstream

One group among the many that coalesced around Caitanya from his earliest period in Navadvīpa—led by such poets as Narahari Sarkāra, Vāsudeva Ghoṣa, and Locana Dāsa—saw

Caitanya not in terms of Kṛṣṇa but as divinity in his own right. Certainly on the model of Kṛṣṇa, but identifying the object of their worship as Caitanya or Gaura, the "golden one," they composed hundreds of lyrics praising his features and desiring his love (see Bandyopadhyaya 1979), much to the disgust of more conservative groups, as evidenced by the invective in Vṛndāvana Dāsa's hagiography of Caitanya, the *Caitanya Bhāgavata*. Somewhat later, and certainly following the model reported about Rāmānanda Rāya's mode of ritual practice in Purī, another group saw Caitanya not just as the embodiment of Rādhā and Kṛṣṇa but also as the exemplar for all humanity, that is, they believed that what Caitanya revealed to Rāmānanda by way of the dual incarnation was in fact to be found in every human being. And if it was to be found, it had to be pursued physically, for Caitanya's dual incarnation could only exist on earth in a physical form, the magic of the physical universe (*māyā*) enabling this subterfuge to allow Kṛṣṇa to taste Rādhā's love. The approach was styled "*sahajiyā*" or the "way of physical nature" (see Bose 1930; Dimock 1966). The pivotal text for this loosely organized Tāntrika tradition was Ākiñcana Dāsa's *Vivarta Vilāsa*, which served as an impromptu commentary on the mainstream *Caitanya Caritāmṛta* of Kṛṣṇadāsa noted above, and the *pada*s of a host of poets, many of which are ascribed to the popular Vaiṣṇava poet Caṇḍīdāsa, although of obviously later provenance. And while over the next few centuries many would fight this connection and attempt to disavow it, the roots unmistakably lead to the very center of the mainstream interpretation—the androgynous dual incarnation and the debate over the identity of Kṛṣṇa's *gopī* lovers as either *svakīyā* (belonging to Kṛṣṇa) or *parakīyā* (belonging to another, i.e. married, the favored interpretation and basis for choosing a ritual partner). In the extremes of this innovation, the realization of the masculine and feminine principles within each human moves from a mental to a physical practice, and the practitioner seeks a suitable female partner for a disciplined yogic-based sexual intercourse. The practice seems to have been common enough in the seventeenth and eighteenth centuries to be well known but began to move underground as pressures within and from outside the community mounted to curb the practices.

In the nineteenth century, and coinciding with the newly available printing press, the Gauḍīya Vaiṣṇava community was transformed once again by individuals who sought to purify the tradition of its more "unsavory" elements, such as the Sahajiyās and related groups, while offering a newly packaged form of the religion. Kedarnath Datta served the British Rāj in the subexecutive and subjudicial branch of the Indian Civil Service while studying Sanskrit in his spare time in order to read Vaiṣṇava *śāstra*s (see Marvin 1996). While stationed in Purī in the 1870s, he became frustrated with the dearth of reliable printed editions of important Vaiṣṇava works and dedicated himself at that point to the production of texts as part of a larger commitment to reform the Vaiṣṇava tradition. Adapting and adopting organizational strategies from years of government service, Kedarnath proselytized an ever-widening community in ways analogous to the ways circuit judges visited different regions. Using the rhetoric of the commercial trading companies—no doubt borne of his long contact with a Kartābhajā *guru* and the commercial impulse behind much of administrative life in the Rāj—Kedarnath, who had by this time gained the title of Bhaktivinoda, organized his growing community into more than five hundred "markets of the name" (*nāmahaṭṭa*), reemphasizing the recitation of the name as the currency of salvation. Working both independently and through the growing institution Viśva Vaiṣṇava Sabhā, he published prolifically, including a journal *Sajjana Toṣaṇī*, that forged his distinctive style of "modern" urban Vaiṣṇavism. With an eye to reclaiming some of Gauḍīya

Vaiṣṇavism's luster, he began reclamation projects near Caitanya's birthplace, but claiming Māyāpura, not Navadvīpa, as the center. Theologically his group was conservative, as evidenced by the elevation of Caitanya's connection with his second wife Viṣṇuprīyā as a more appropriate model for male-female interaction (as opposed to Kṛṣṇa's more rambunctious play with the wives of others). And ritually, the sixty-four *vaidhī* injunctions were promoted for the general public, with other practices reserved exclusively for the advanced adept. Eventually his organization established itself in Calcutta as the Gauḍīya Maṭha, with a publication and social service agenda that endures to this day. Bhaktivinoda successfully imitated the first generation of followers that had surrounded Caitanya, by fixing the texts to create a newly defined canon, to reclaim a sacred geography, and to purge the perceived excesses of ritual practice. This tradition, with deep roots among the *bhadralok* and burgeoning middle classes and its sprawling urban network, became in the early twentieth century the de facto measure of Vaiṣṇava orthodoxy in Bengal. And it was out of this lineage that the tradition was exported to the West.

ISKCON as one form of Gauḍīya Vaiṣṇavism in the West

Gauḍīya Vaiṣṇavism is extending itself, in part through the immigration of Vaiṣṇavas to the West, but also through other movements, for example, with the International Society for Krishna Consciousness. Thomas Hopkins (1989) has shown how ISKCON's success in adaptation in Western countries was prepared for already by an openness that developed in nineteenth- and twentieth-century Gauḍīya Vaiṣṇavism, particularly as encouraged by several Gauḍīya Vaiṣṇava teachers, for example, Bhaktivinoda Ṭhākura (Kedarnath Datta; 1838–1914), noted earlier, and his son Bhaktisiddhānta Sarasvatī (1874–1937). Bhaktisiddhānta continued his work, for example, by subordinating caste boundaries to the primary power and force of devotion and opening the community to wider membership. He also commissioned disciples to travel to the West, among them Bhaktivedānta Svāmī (1896–1977), familiarly known as Prabhupāda, a non-Brāhmaṇ born with the name of De, who brought Vaiṣṇavism to New York in 1965 and started the community which came to be known as ISKCON.

By the time Bhaktivedānta reached New York to begin this work, he was already well versed in methods of adaptation; he was already accustomed to publicizing and promoting the Vaiṣṇava faith in the English language, since he had started his English-language magazine, *Back to Godhead*, in 1944 in Calcutta. While readily admitting a variety of factors which together contributed to Bhaktivedānta's improbable success, T. Hopkins observes that

> The major factor in this success . . . was the legacy that Bhaktivedanta brought with him from Bengal, the century of effort by Kedarnath Dutt and Bhaktisiddhanta to relate the Vaisnava devotional path to the modern world. Not only did they provide the vision of a universal religion, but they had worked through many of the difficult practical questions: How Vaisnava teachings can be presented to the widest possible audience, how they can be explained to the Western mentality, how new devotees can be brought into the Caitanya movement, and how the movement can be stabilized to ensure its continuity. Almost every apparent innovation that Bhaktivedanta made can be traced back to this work of his predecessors.[17]
>
> (1989: 50; see also C. Brooks 1998; Klostermaier 1998)

Just as difficult issues related to language, caste, and emotion were resolved early on Śrīvaiṣṇavism, this form of Gauḍīya Vaiṣṇavism too had to find within itself resources for its adaptation to the Western context. The growth of ISKCON as a form of Gauḍīya Vaiṣṇavism in the Western world has included numerous small adjustments based on the need to adjust a traditional Hindu religious community, monastic and lay, to a culture as different and varied as that of the United States. Converts had to find ways of shaping fresh religious identities, without entirely abandoning the older cultural and religious sensitivities they had grown up with.

Tamal Kṛṣṇa Gosvāmī (1946–2002), a senior ISKCON teacher, wrote about the ways in which Bhaktivedānta presented a form of Gauḍīya Vaiṣṇavism that was extremely orthodox, even accentuating the conservative tendency promoted by Bhaktivinoda a century earlier; his message was uncompromising in its truth claims. Bhaktivedānta remained thoroughly committed to scriptures such as the *Bhagavad Gītā* and *Bhāgavata Purāṇa* as the foundations of his teaching even in America; he also situated himself firmly in the Gauḍīya tradition, tracing his lineage back to Caitanya and ultimately to Lord Kṛṣṇa. In Bhaktivedānta's writings we find few explicit alterations in basic Vaiṣṇava doctrines, although he does emphasize forms of devotional love that are considered by the larger tradition to be of a much lower order. Likewise there is no direct grappling with the ideas and beliefs of Americans of other religious traditions. Nothing suggests that Bhaktivedānta saw learning about other religions as part of the presentation of his message; it sufficed to teach essential Vaiṣṇava truths, ideally as they had been taught through the history of Vaiṣṇavism—but in this case heavily modified for a Western audience. Yet, he was also welcoming to people unfamiliar with the tradition, alert to the need to attract listeners and win them over by couching his message in terms that did not seem merely alien or entirely wedded to the idioms of Hindu culture. Following the example of Bhaktivinoda and Bhaktisiddānta, he energetically presented a socially inclusive form of Vaiṣṇavism unrestricted by traditional Indian caste boundaries. He sought to make sense of his tradition in a new context, relying not on conceptual innovation—something Vaiṣṇavas seem rarely to have ambitioned—but on adjustments in style and social practice, which would make settled values more accessible to newcomers. And evidence of this success of overcoming traditional Hindu expectations regarding the propriety of conversion can be found in the way that ISKCON devotees are now incorporated into the religious life of pilgrimage centers in India, occasionally somewhat grudgingly, but accepted nonetheless.

CONCLUSION

In the preceding sections we have proposed that Vaiṣṇavism is a coherent religious and theological tradition, which can be justly spoken of in the singular. Even today, Vaiṣṇavism remains an integral tradition with great continuity in its beliefs about god and the world and human destiny. Nonetheless, this one Vaiṣṇavism flourishes in rich regional traditions which, although they remain meaningfully Vaiṣṇava, are yet possessed of rich distinguishing features. We can therefore also speak of "Vaiṣṇavisms" as well as "Vaiṣṇavism." In this essay we have illustrated this unity-in-diversity not in a comprehensive fashion but by pointing to two instances of local Vaiṣṇavisms, that is, the Śrīvaiṣṇava tradition of Tamilnadu and the Gauḍīya Vaiṣṇava tradition of Bengal.

Regarding each we have argued that these traditions are local and specific, yet genuinely Vaiṣṇava; we have noted too that each is adapting itself to the modern world in ways which are adjustments consonant with the oldest Vaiṣṇava sources. By extension, and in important work which would necessarily supplement and complete the observations offered here, other Vaiṣṇava traditions rooted in various geographical and language regions of India will likewise attest to the continuities and differences which make up Vaiṣṇavism as an object of study and a living religious tradition.

NOTES

1 Among the classic scholarly works on this early material, see Gonda (1954); Jaiswal (1981).

2 The intellectual/emotional *bhakti* distinction is best described by Hardy (1983).

3 It is a fairly recent publication, dated 1984, representative of traditional Śrīvaiṣṇava positions and published by the Society for the Wisdom of the Āḻvārs, a respected Vaiṣṇava organization in Chennai (Madras). As its title suggests, *Śrīvaiṣṇavam* is self-consciously comprehensive in its coverage of the traditional views and practices of the Śrīvaiṣṇava community; detailed in describing specific practices; written in Tamil, it was written for Śrīvaiṣṇavas, not for scholars of religion (for an overview of some more recent English-language writings on Śrīvaiṣṇavism, see Clooney 1993).

4 In the section of the *Nyāyasiddhāñjana* entitled "The Definition of 'Lord' " (*Īśvarapariccheda*), Deśika takes up the standard discourse about God, a well-known topic debated in various Brāhmaṇical Hindu contexts and in Buddhist and Jaina contexts long before Deśika. He asserts the truth of Vaiṣṇava positions gleaned from scripture, now defended also as the most reasonable of positions, against a series of opposing positions introduced by way of various objections. He confidently refutes the nondualist Vedānta and other strands of Vedānta difference-and-non-difference, Buddhism, Jainism, and Śaivism. What Vaiṣṇavas believe is true, and it can be shown rationally, to the satisfaction of reasonable persons not biased by secondary issues, to stand as superior to alternative views put forward by other traditions.

5 Another way to put this point is to say that in terms of theology and practice, Vaiṣṇavas generally do not think of themselves as "Hindus" but as believers in a tradition, which is very much more specific and yet also more universal. One should think and act in a certain way to be a Śrīvaiṣṇava, but one does not have to be culturally a Hindu or even an Indian, as we shall see in the following section "Continuity and change in Śrīvaiṣṇavism: three examples."

6 *Maṇipravāḷa* discourse includes numerous Sanskrit words within sentences following Tamil syntax.

7 First page of preface by Raghavan (no page number given) in *Ācāryavaipavam*.

8 In practice, of course, various individual Śrīvaiṣṇavas and communities prefer either the Tamil or the Sanskrit tradition, with a correspondingly diminished role accorded to the other, and the two schools of Śrīvaiṣṇavism are in part distinguished by a greater (in the "northern" [Vaṭakalai] school) and lesser (in the "southern" [Teṉkalai] school) focus on the Sanskrit tradition. But this bilingual commitment, though not without its difficulties in practice, represents a conscious, intentional choice on the part of the Śrīvaiṣṇavas to preserve the Sanskrit tradition while accepting Tamil sources from outside it. Vaiṣṇavism found a way to grow, yet without suffering discontinuity.

9 We will see in the section "Vaiṣṇavism in Bengal: the Gauḍiya tradition" some similar issues related to the Gauḍiya Vaiṣṇava tradition of Bengal; see for example the other essays in the same issue of the *Journal of Vaiṣṇava Studies* (5, 4, 1997), which is focused on the theme, "Kṛṣṇa and the Gopīs."

10 As recorded in Vaṭakkutiruvīttippiḷḷai's comment on *Tiruvāymoḻi* 1.4?

11 Another specific instance of this is the acceptance and orthodox reading of the passionate erotic songs of Āṇṭāḷ. See also Thiruvengadathan (1985) on the images of bathing in old Tamil poetry, its reuse in the songs of Āṇṭāḷ, and further reinterpretation, as symbolic of the experience of *brahman*, in the Śrīvaiṣṇava commentaries.

12 One might also examine the use of the internet as a means of the dissemination of Śrīvaiṣṇava learning, both for discussion of contemporary issues and for the retrieval and dissemination of knowledge about the tradition. For example, web pages include online versions of the songs of the Āḻvārs and even some of Vedāntadeśika's works. Other sites include essays on the Śrīvaiṣṇava tradition, pictures of the Āḻvārs and *ācāryas*, the 108 sacred places praised in song by the Āḻvārs, and pictures of Viṣṇu and Śrī as iconically manifest in these sacred places. These websites serve both to inculcate devotion to Viṣṇu and Śrī and to educate members of the tradition; they also serve to preserve the Śrīvaiṣṇava community and tradition from the generic melting pot of diaspora Hinduism. The use of the web by other Hindu communities in the West can of course also be documented, and one might even argue that the web is helping to strengthen specifically Hindu identity.

13 It would be wrong to argue that this decoupling of most Vaiṣṇava ritual from the institution of the temple resulted from the dramatic shift in patronage of temples as Muslims of various origins assumed control of the political sphere across most of North India and in that political conquest displaced many of the Hindu *rājās* who would be expected to support such institutions. That view would confuse the effect with the cause, ignoring the major shift in praxis, which dictated this move. The historical record makes clear that temples were not only maintained but actually grew in number during the extended period of Muslim suzerainty; many of these temples were in fact encouraged if not directly patronized by various Muslim rulers. The temple-razing activity of the last and most infamous Mughal ruler, Aurangzēb ʿĀlamgīr, has in recent political parlance served as a metonym for all Muslim rule in India, an unfortunate rhetorical strategy that is historically misleading: there were conflicts earlier, but not predictably. The temple-based worship of the Vaiṣṇavas posed no threat to the Muslim ruling elites, and, if anything, many of them saw in the Vaiṣṇava approach to divinity a religious impulse that was theologically resonant with both Sūnni and Ṣūfī understandings of god, as is evidenced by such Muslim-Vaiṣṇava figures as Satya Pīr in Bengal. The public street processions of *saṃkīrtana* were on occasion contentious; the beating of drums and the right to process being the preserve of the ruler, not to mention the recurring complaints of "disturbing the peace" levied by non-Vaiṣṇavas. But there is little evidence to support the idea that in order to survive, North Indian Vaiṣṇavism had to retreat and go underground, in order to develop devotional practices that could essentially be invisible except to those within the community.

14 Here the parallel with Protestant Christianity is intriguing but does not provide an adequate explanation for the impulse behind this development.

15 This is described by Kṛṣṇadāsa Kavirāja, the author of the *Caitanya Caritāmṛta* (Dimock 1999).

16 The sixty-four acts are summarized in 1.2.73–95 (*Bhaktirasāmṛtasindhu*) and individually detailed in 1.2.96–245.

17 In another essay, a conversation with Steven J. Rosen, C. Brooks (1992) recounts the earlier and largely unsuccessful effort of another disciple of Bhaktisiddhānta, Bon Mahārāja, to bring Vaiṣṇavism to the West in the 1930s. His effort was to influence the influential, well-educated leaders of society, but, despite his efforts, there never developed a community with deeper and more flourishing roots.

CHAPTER NINE

BHAKTI

David N. Lorenzen

For over two thousand years the primary meaning of the word "*bhakti*" has been "personal devotion to a god or saintly person." The noun *bhakti* is derived from a Sanskrit verb whose root sense is "to distribute" or "to share." In a religious context, this sense is used to indicate the sharing of portions of a sacrificial offering. This meaning has been expanded to encompass such ideas as "to participate in," "to experience," "to feel," "to honor," and "to adore." Another related noun, *bhajana*, usually means either "worship" or "a song of worship." Finally, the noun *bhakta* or *bhagata* indicates "a devotee" who worships some god or saintly person.

In its very general sense of "devotion," *bhakti* is obviously an integral part of any religion and not just Hinduism. Starting in the first or second century of the Common Era, however, in India *bhakti* gradually became associated with a specific set of gods and religious beliefs and practices. Today *bhakti* is the single most important element of both Hindu and Sikh religious traditions, so much so that both can be included within a more general category of *bhakti* traditions. This tradition is divided into four general currents based on the specific god or set of gods chosen for worship. Some worship forms of the god Śiva and his family members; some worship forms of the god Viṣṇu and his *avatāra*s and associates; some worship forms of the goddess or Devī; and some, most notably the Sikhs and the Kabīr *panthī*s, worship a more abstract, formless god often called Sat Nām (true name), Sat Puruṣa (true spirit), or Rām (not identified directly with the *avatāra* Rāma). These latter groups that worship a formless god are often called "*nirguṇī*" movements, since they worship a god who is without attributes (*nirguṇa*). The other three groups that worship anthropomorphic or theriomorphic forms of god are similarly called "*saguṇī*" movements, since they worship a god who has attributes (*saguṇa*).

The Sikhs, Kabīr *panthī*s, and related *nirguṇī* movements often use the vocabulary of Vaiṣṇava *bhakti*, but since they reject anthropomorphic forms of Viṣṇu and his *avatāra*s, they cannot logically be grouped with the Vaiṣṇavas (although Kabīr *panthī*s do sometimes identify themselves as Vaiṣṇavas). In addition, the social ideology of the *nirguṇī* movements, notably their theoretical rejection of the caste system (*varṇadharma*), however qualified this may be in practice, clearly differentiates them from *saguṇī* Vaiṣṇava movements, since most *saguṇī* movements defend this system.

This *nirguṇī/saguṇī* distinction has a long scholarly tradition behind it and has proved quite useful, particularly to categorize religious movements in North India. In this chapter, however, we will introduce a rather different distinction that serves a similar purpose, but one that emphasizes the differences in social ideology between *bhakti* movements rather than their metaphysical preferences for a god with or without attributes. Those movements that generally support the hierarchical caste system, traditionally called *varṇāśramadharma*, will be called *varṇadharmī* movements, while those that generally reject this system will be called *avarṇadharmī* movements.

Besides highlighting a practical social difference rather than a theoretical theological difference, this *varṇadharmī/avarṇadharmī* distinction also enables us to include two influential *saguṇī* movements together with other mostly *nirguṇī* movements. These two *saguṇī* movements are the loosely organized followers of the poet-saint Mīrābāī and the better defined movement of the Liṅgāyatas or Vīraśaivas. As a word of caution, it should be noted that even in key *avarṇadharmī* movements, such as the Kabīr Panth and Sikhism, caste practices are in practice often present. Nonetheless, on a theoretical level caste is rejected. On the other hand, in *varṇadharmī* movements, such as those of the followers of Vallabhācārya and Caitanya, individual poets may sometimes express anticaste sentiments or else avoid any discussion of caste and social norms whatsoever. The movements as a whole, however, accept *varṇāśramadharma* as a valid institution.

Recently, several scholars have claimed that Hinduism is essentially an invention of early nineteenth-century British administrators and scholars who were the first to imagine that the many sects and cults of indigenous origin in India all belonged to a single religion. Before this date, they assert, the word "Hindu" had only an ethnogeographical sense. Since the Vaiṣṇava current was already dominant among Indian sects and cults by the early nineteenth century, the Hinduism that the British supposedly invented was primarily Vaiṣṇava *bhakti* combined, in a somewhat uneasy alliance, with monistic (*advaita*) Vedānta metaphysics. In this view, the Hindus themselves only took up this idea of belonging to a unitary religion in the later half of the nineteenth century, when intellectual leaders such as Hariścandra argued that *bhakti*, above all Vaiṣṇava *bhakti*, should be regarded as the central element of Hinduism (Dalmia 1999: 425–29).

At best this view is an immense exaggeration. Hinduism has always been divided up into a vast array of currents, doctrines, cults, and sects. Nineteenth-century British scholars, the so-called Orientalists, did play an important role in clarifying what all these components had in common, while nineteenth-century Indian intellectuals did try to foment a greater consciousness among different sorts of Hindus that they belonged to a common religion. Nonetheless, there exists ample evidence that outside observers—including Christian missionaries and Muslim scholars—had identified Hindu religion as an internally diverse but single religious system as far back as the tenth century, while the Hindus themselves were quite conscious of their own religious unity in diversity at least as early as the fourteenth century and probably long before (Lorenzen 1999b).

Looked at historically, we can say that something approaching modern Hinduism, in which *bhakti* occupies a central role, took shape in the early centuries of the Common Era. The chief features of this *bhakti*-based Hinduism were: an elaborate set of myths about the gods Viṣṇu, Śiva, Devī, and their godly associates and demon enemies; an equally elaborate iconography of the many anthropomorphic forms and incarnations of these gods and demons; a generally simple and individualistic style of worshiping (*pūjā*) images of these gods located in temples and shrines, both public and private; a number of seasonal and calendrical public festivals, some celebrated almost everywhere and some centered in specific cultural regions or individual localities; a set of life-cycle rites going back, at least in part, to the early Vedic period; a highly diversified set of metaphysical schools (*darśana*), each claiming to be ultimately based on Vedic texts (*śruti*), that discuss such topics as the nature of the real (*brahman*), *karma*, transmigration (*saṃsāra*), and salvation (*mokṣa*); and a religiously legitimated social, legal, and political system (*dharma*) based on caste (*jāti*) and class (*varṇa*).

In this chapter, we will first look at the rise of devotion to Śiva, Viṣṇu, and Devī through the lens of the many key Sanskrit texts starting from the *Śvetāsvatara Upaniṣad* and the *Bhagavad Gītā* through several Purāṇas. Then we will look at the attempts to make *bhakti* into a more systematic doctrine in the so-called *Bhaktisūtra* and the compositions of Rāmānuja. Finally, we will discuss the poets who wrote songs, stories, and verses to these gods in vernacular languages and became, in several cases, the reputed founders of influential sectarian movements.[1]

THE ŚVETĀSVATARA UPANIṢAD

Taking the term "*bhakti*" in the wide sense of any sort of religious devotion to any god, even the earliest Vedic texts, starting from the *Ṛg Veda*, can be said manifest *bhakti* to gods such as Indra, Varuṇa, Agni, Rudra, and Viṣṇu. Some scholars may object that Vedic texts leave out the key element of a deeply personal relationship between the worshiper and his or her chosen god. But there are in fact many quite personal hymns in Vedic texts, and there are also many quite emotionally austere songs and verses composed by later *bhakti* poets, particularly by those associated with *nirguṇa bhakti*. What is missing in early Vedic texts is not *bhakti* in this wide generic sense but the association of *bhakti* with Purāṇic mythology, with the key ideas of Hindu metaphysics such as *brahman*, *dharma*, *karma*, *saṃsāra*, and *mokṣa*, and with the social ideology of caste and class (*varṇadharma*).

The early text that best prefigures the essential features and associations of later *bhakti* is the *Śvetāsvatara Upaniṣad*. This is one of the latest of the early Upaniṣads and is unusual among these texts for its advocacy of a monotheistic metaphysics. The date of this text is unknown, but it was probably written some time after 500 BCE. The object of devotion in the *Śvetāsvatara Upaniṣad* is the god Rudra, an early form of Śiva. The text several times uses the word "*śiva*" (benign or auspicious) as an epithet of the god. Rudra is also often described as *eka* (the one, the sole, or the unique), a word that shows the innovative monotheism of the text. Its many citations of verses about Rudra from the *Ṛg Veda* and other earlier Vedic texts, however, suggests that the author was also attempting to ground devotion to the god in the sacred prestige of this much earlier collection of hymns.

The ideas and language of the *Śvetāsvatara Upaniṣad* are in fact highly composite. The text begins with the traditional Upaniṣadic theme of the cause and nature of the impersonal ground of being, *brahman*, but soon modulates into a description of a "unique" god (*īśa* or *deva*). As in most early Upaniṣads, the text stresses the role of *knowing* or *understanding* the ultimately real as a means of salvation. The person who "knows" this *brahman*, here loosely equated with god, is said to "be freed from all fetters." Then the text turns to a brief description of the postures and the breath and mind control of yoga, a meditation discipline that was likely first developed in roughly this period. This description is followed by a chapter full of Vedic quotes about Rudra, again stressing the role of *knowing* god as a means to immortality and infinite peace.

In the final chapter of the *Śvetāsvatara Upaniṣad*, the ideas and language acquire a clearly devotional emphasis quite similar to those of the *Bhagavad Gītā*, notwithstanding the elevation of quite different god to monotheistic status in the two texts. The *Śvetāsvatara Upaniṣad*'s doctrine of *bhakti* is less systematic than that of the *Bhagavad Gītā*, but the relation between the worshiper and the god is described in similar terms. The worshiper is said to "take refuge" (*śaraṇam aham prapadye*) in god, using an expression already found in earlier texts but also one that later becomes a key element not only in the *Bhagavad Gītā* but also in the devotional doctrines of the great theologian Rāmānuja (1017–1137 CE) and his disciples. The worshipers are advised to "worship" (*upāsya*) the "adorable god" (*īḍyam devam*), who is the lord (*īṣa*) and the protector (*gopa*) of men. This god is said to be: "The creator of all, omniscient, his own source, the knower, the creator of time, . . . the cause of transmigration (*saṃsāra*), of liberation (*mokṣa*), of maintenance, of bondage" (*Śvetāsvatara Upaniṣad* 6.16). At the very end of the *Śvetāsvatara*, the word "*bhakti*" itself appears, its only occurrence in the early Upaniṣads: "The topics explained here become visible to a great soul who has the highest *bhakti* for god and who reveres his *guru* like his god" (6.23).

THE BHAGAVAD GĪTĀ

The real foundation text of *bhakti* is the *Bhagavad Gītā*. This "Song to the Lord" forms part of the great *Mahābhārata* epic. The *Bhagavad Gītā* was probably written by several authors over a considerable period, although some scholars insist that it must be the creation of a single great poet (Basham 1989: 82–97). In either case, the *Bhagavad Gītā* must have been established in its present form by about the beginning of the Common Era or a century or two earlier.

The god Viṣṇu appears in the *Bhagavad Gītā* as the *avatāra* Kṛṣṇa, the advisor and charioteer of the warrior Arjuna. When Arjuna hesitates before the final battle, uncertain about whether it is right for him to fight and kill his own relatives, Kṛṣṇa delivers an eloquent discourse to remove Arjuna's doubts and urges him to fight. In the course of this sermon, Kṛṣṇa expounds three disciplines (*yoga*) leading to salvation: the discipline of acts (*karmayoga*), the discipline of knowledge (*jñānayoga*), and the discipline of devotion (*bhaktiyoga*). The *Bhagavad Gītā* never clearly specifies if these different disciplines are meant to be practiced at the same time or successively or if they represent separate alternatives. The text does explicitly recommend a combination of *bhakti* with dispassionate action ("without thought about its fruits"). It is clear, however, that the authors of the final text regarded the discipline of devotion as the easiest and most efficacious path to salvation for the people who live in the present age of the degenerate Kali Yuga.

The *Bhagavad Gītā* begins with a description of the disciplines of knowledge and work. Already in the fourth of its eighteen chapters, however, it introduces a key component of *bhakti*, the doctrine of the *avatāra*s of Viṣṇu. It is not clear how developed this doctrine was when the text was written. In the *Bhagavad Gītā*, in contrast to the later Purāṇas, no *avatāra*s apart from Kṛṣṇa are mentioned by name, and neither the term "*avatāra*" itself nor the corresponding verb (*ava-tṛ*) appears in the text. Nonetheless, the key passage, often cited in later texts, sets out the essence of the doctrine. Kṛṣṇa says to Arjuna:

> Both you and I have passed through many births, O Arjuna. I know all of them, but you do not. Even before I am born my soul (*ātman*) is imperishable, and I am the lord of all beings. I take on my material nature and am born through my own supernatural power (*ātmāmāyā*). Whenever there is a decrease of *dharma*, O Bhārata, and an increase of its opposite, then I become incarnate. I am born in age after age in order to protect good persons, destroy evil-doers, and reestablish *dharma*.
>
> (*Bhagavad Gītā* 4.5–8)

There is, however, another reason why Viṣṇu comes to earth in these visible forms. Mortal men need a concrete and easily conceptualized object of devotion. According to the *Bhagavad Gītā*, god in his transcendent, divine form is impossible to imagine without god's own direct intervention. Kṛṣṇa says: "Those whose minds are directed to the unmanifest suffer greater anguish, for it is difficult for embodied beings to obtain the unmanifest goal" (*Bhagavad Gītā* 12.5). In place of this arduous discipline, Kṛṣṇa tells Arjuna: "Direct the mind to me alone. Let your intellect enter into me. From then on you will reside in me" (*Bhagavad Gītā* 12.8). In fact, devotion combined with a renunciation of the fruit of one's action is all that is needed for final liberation. After Kṛṣṇa gives Arjuna a vision of his awe-inspiring divine form, Kṛṣṇa says: "He who acts for me, who considers me above all, who is devoted to me and free from attachment, who has no hatred against any living beings, he will go to me" (*Bhagavad Gītā* 11.55).

Another great advantage of *bhakti* is that it makes liberation available to all men and women and not just to upper-class males. The ideas of the *Bhagavad Gītā* about class and caste however are complex, and the text can be read in different ways. Clearly the division of humans into the four hierarchical classes (*varṇa*) known as Brāhmaṇs, Kṣatriyas, Vaiśyas, and Śūdras is regarded as a social institution created by god himself. Kṛṣṇa says: "I created the set of four classes according to the divisions of qualities (*guṇa*) and acts (*karman*)" (*Bhagavad Gītā* 4.13). In other words, each class is associated with a particular set of skills and dispositions and a particular sort of appropriate behavior and occupation. Toward the end of the text, the characteristics of each class are specified. For instance, Kṛṣṇa says this about the Vaiśyas and Śūdras: "Agriculture, cow herding, and commerce are the acts appropriate to the nature of the Vaiśyas. Acts whose essence is service are appropriate to the nature of the Śūdras" (*Bhagavad Gītā* 18. 44).

But are these four classes based on the innate aptitudes of each individual or are they fixed by one's birth in a specific family? Some modern Hindu apologists such as Sarvepalli Radhakrishnan (1960: 364–68) have tried to argue that the divisions are based on each individual's aptitudes, but this reading is unlikely to have been the original intention of the text. For instance, the first chapter of the *Bhagavad Gītā* contains several verses that describe the evils that arise through the mixture (*saṃkara*) of the different *varṇa*s. One verse states: "Through the misdeeds of those who destroy the family by mixing together the classes, the eternal laws of caste (*jāti*) and of family are destroyed" (*Bhagavad Gītā* 1.43). What this "mixing together" means is never clearly specified, but it seems to imply both following inappropriate occupations and making interclass marriages or liaisons. Finally, there is a well-known verse that directly repudiates the idea that class should be based on individual aptitudes: "It is better to perform one's own duty (*svadharma*) badly than to perform another's duty well. It is better to die performing one's own duty, for another's duty is dangerous" (*Bhagavad Gītā* 3.35).

At the same time that the *Bhagavad Gītā* offers this defense of the social system of these four hereditary and hierarchically arranged classes, however, it never directly connects birth in any specific class or caste with the moral or immoral actions one has committed in past lives, in spite of the fact that the text fully accepts that human beings are reborn time and again and that liberation consists of escaping from this cycle of birth and death. More important, Kṛṣṇa offers such liberation *even* to sinners, women, and low-class persons by means of the easy discipline of *bhakti*: "Those who come to me for refuge—even if they are born in sin or are women, Vaiśyas, or Śūdras—they will reach the highest goal. What then [need one say about] meritorious Brāhmaṇs and devoted royal sages?" (*Bhagavad Gītā* 9.32–33). In other words, the *Bhagavad Gītā* apparently fully accepts the existence of a class and gender hierarchy based on birth but also refrains from explicitly tying these births to the *karma* of previous lives and in the end permits liberation through devotion to everyone.

What this social and religious ideology represents in historical terms is uncertain. The *Bhagavad Gītā* and its doctrine of *bhakti* is obviously more socially liberal than traditional Sanskrit law books such as the *Mānavadharmaśāstra*, since these texts generally accept a rigid caste and gender hierarchy based on the *karma* of past lives and specify in detail the many privileges of high caste and male status and the burdens of low caste and female status. On the other hand, the *Bhagavad Gītā* is generally less socially liberal than the beliefs and practices of many Buddhist and Jaina traditions that represented the alternative to Brāhmaṇic religion in the period when the *Bhagavad Gītā* was composed and edited. The logical conclusion is that the authors of the *Bhagavad Gītā* were attempting to elaborate a religious and social ideology that could appeal to a wide segment of the population while still preserving most of the traditional customs and norms of class, gender, and caste.

THE DEVĪ MĀHĀTMYA

The *Devī Māhātmya* (The Greatness of the Goddess), also called the *Durgā Saptaśatī* (Seven Hundred Verses about Durgā), was probably composed in about the first part of the sixth century (Coburn 1991). Like the *Bhagavad Gītā*, the text has achieved great popularity independent of the larger work in which it is imbedded, the *Mārkaṇḍeya Purāṇa.* Whereas the *Bhagavad Gītā* is a religious and theological discourse situated within the epic story of the *Mahābhārata* war, the *Durgā Māhātmya* is a set of three myths about the Devī situated within a larger collection of myths. As a result, the *Durgā Māhātmya* is more a direct manifestation of *bhakti* than a religious discussion about what *bhakti* means and does.

In the *Devī Māhātmya* the sage Medhas tells three stories about the goddess. In the first story the demons Madhu and Kaiṭabha are said to arise out of the dirt in Viṣṇu's ear while he is sleeping under the influence of the goddess in her form as Yoganidrā (sleep of *yoga*). Brahmā then praises the goddess and asks her to release Viṣṇu from his sleep. She does so, and Viṣṇu cuts off the heads of the demons with his discus. The second story is about goddess's own battle with the buffalo-demon Mahiṣāsura. When the army of the gods led by Indra is defeated by Mahiṣāsura, the gods go to Viṣṇu and Śiva to ask their help. Viṣṇu and Śiva become angry, and a fiery energy comes forth from them and from all the other gods and takes the form of the goddess. The gods then give her weapons, ornaments, and a lion mount. In this form she defeats Mahiṣāsura and his army. The third story is about the goddess's battle with the army of demons led by Śumbha and his brother Niśumbha. They too defeat Indra and the gods. The gods however remember the goddess, and she comes to their aid. The supreme goddess, here usually called Ambikā or Caṇḍikā, first emerges from the body of the goddess Pārvatī. Śumbha hears about her beauty and asks her to marry him. She challenges him to a battle. During the battle various secondary forms of the goddess, starting with the terrifying Kālī, come forth from her body. When all the demons except Śumbha have been killed, the secondary forms of the goddess are reabsorbed into the body of Ambikā, and she destroys him as well.

In the first story the goddess has a secondary role as the cause of Viṣṇu's sleep. In the second her role is more central, but she remains an emanation of the many male gods. In the last story, she herself creates female emanations who do most of her work. This progression to ever more exalted status parallels the historical evolution and synthesis of the unique goddess out of the individual goddesses who serve as consorts and helpers of the male gods. In other words, the same movement toward a monotheistic concept of god found in the *Śvetāsvatara Upaniṣad* and the *Bhagavad Gītā* also informs the *Devī Māhātmya*, except that here the supreme deity is female. Although monotheism is perhaps not a strict logical necessity for *bhakti*-based religion, there has obviously been a strong tendency to move in this direction among the followers of Śiva, Viṣṇu, and Devī. Each god becomes the supreme deity of whom the other gods and goddesses are merely secondary emanations or helpers.

Neither the *Śvetāsvatara Upaniṣad* nor the *Bhagavad Gītā* has much to say about the ritual practices associated with *bhakti*. Both do describe the basic posture and meditative techniques of *yoga*, but these are preliminary or secondary to *bhakti*. The *Bhagavad Gītā* does have a famous verse that mentions flower offerings. Kṛṣṇa says: "If a pious soul with *bhakti* offers me a leaf, a flower, a fruit or water, if it is offered with *bhakti* I will accept it" (9.26). Kṛṣṇa also instructs the devotee to study and listen to the text itself: "Any man who studies this sacred dialogue of ours . . . and listens to it with faith and without anger will become liberated and reach the auspicious worlds of those who acted with merit" (*Bhagavad Gītā* 18.70–71). In the *Devī Māhātmya,* the goddess insists on the recitation of the text itself and specifies in somewhat more detail how and when she should be worshiped. She specifies that "my *Māhātmya*" should be recited "with *bhakti*" on the "eighth, fourteenth and ninth days" of each lunar fortnight and especially at the "great offering" (*mahāpūjā*) held every year in the autumn, an early reference to the important fall festival now known as Durgā-*pūjā* (*Devī Māhātmya* 12.4, 12.12). The goddess also recommends that she be worshiped with offerings of flowers and the like but makes this secondary to recitation of the *Māhātmya*: "I am pleased by excellent [offerings] of animals, flowers, guest-offerings (*arghya*), incense, perfumes, and lamps; by daily feeding, oblations, and consecrations given to Brāhmaṇs; and by [making] various other gifts and favors during the year. But I am equally pleased with him who listens to [the story of my] virtuous deeds. When it is heard, it removes sins and bestows good health" (12.21–22).

The mention of offerings of animals (*paśu*) is worth noting. Animal sacrifice, particularly of buffaloes, has traditionally been an important part of goddess worship. The killing of Mahiṣāsura, the buffalo demon, is precisely the divine archetype of such sacrifices. Worshipers of Viṣṇu and his *avatāra*s, on the other hand, mostly reject animal sacrifice and often insist on a vegetarian diet. Since *bhakti* has come to be associated primarily with the worship of Viṣṇu and since *bhakti* in all its forms embodies a rejection of the complex sacrificial rites of Vedic religion, it is often assumed that *bhakti* religion necessarily rejects the violence of animal sacrifice. The *Devī Māhātmya* clearly shows that this is not always true.

THE BHĀGAVATA PURĀṆA

Among the texts that preach *bhakti* to Viṣṇu, the *Bhāgavata Purāṇa* has probably been even more influential than the *Bhagavad Gītā*. Various historical clues suggest that it was composed in South India sometime around the ninth century (Hopkins 1966: 4–6). This text is most famous for its narration of the birth, childhood, and adolescence of Viṣṇu's *avatāra* Kṛṣṇa in its long tenth chapter. Other books tell the stories of the sage Nārada, the aftermath of the *Mahābhārata* war, the creation of the universe, the appearance of Viṣṇu's boar *avatāra*, of Dakṣa's sacrifice and Satī, the sage Dhruva, the king Pṛthu, the royal sage Bharata, the Brāhmaṇ Ajamīḷha, the conflict between the god Indra and the demon Vṛtra, the pious demon Prahlāda, and Viṣṇu's dwarf *avatāra*.

Interspersed throughout all this narrative material are many discursive passages that discuss social, philosophical, and religious topics, such as the system of the four classes and stages of life (*varṇāśramadharma*), the nature of ultimate reality, and the relative value of the three disciplines (*yoga*) of knowledge (*jñāna*), good works (*karman*), and *bhakti*. As in the *Bhagavad Gītā*, *bhakti* is extolled as the best and easiest path to liberation. Most of the *bhakti*-related themes in the *Bhāgavata Purāṇa* are in fact already anticipated or prefigured in the *Bhagavad Gītā*, although there are also important changes of emphasis.

One such change of emphasis is a more clearcut devaluation of all other paths to liberation, including Vedic learning, Sāṃkhya and Yoga, religious penance, sacrifices, oblations, and all manner of ritual activities. Compared to association with good persons (*satsaṅga*), an essential part of *bhakti*, the lord says, none of these other practices can win me over: "Neither Yoga nor Sāṃkhya nor *dharma* nor Vedic study (*svādhyāya*), penance, or renunciation nor the merit of sacred rites nor gifts to *guru*s nor vows, sacrifice, Vedic hymns (*chanda*), pilgrimages, or moral restraints can influence me in the way that association with good persons, an association that supersedes all others, holds me" (*Bhāgavata Purāṇa* 11.12.1–2).

The *Bhāgavata Purāṇa* still regards the Vedas as sacred, but when Vedic learning and rites conflict with *bhakti* they become obstacles to liberation. As in the *Bhagavad Gītā,* the discipline of *bhakti* is preferred over those of knowledge and action. The lord says:

> I have announced three disciplines for the sake of causing men to attain the highest good. These are knowledge, *karma*, and *bhakti*. There are no other means anywhere. The discipline of knowledge is for those who are disgusted with actions and have renounced them. The discipline of *karma* is for those whose minds are not disgusted with actions and desire [their fruits]. For the man who has spontaneously has faith in your stories, who is neither disgusted with nor attached to actions, for him the discipline of *bhakti* gives success.
>
> (*Bhāgavata Purāṇa* 11.20.6–8)

The *Bhāgavata Purāṇa* is particularly emphatic about the power and convenience of *bhakti* in the present Kali Yuga when human intelligence, morality, health, sanity, economic well being have declined to a vile minimum and will only get worse in future. In these terrible conditions, *bhakti* has become the ideal path to liberation for men and women belonging to all classes and castes, even when they almost inevitably lack intelligence, are immoral, unhealthy, mentally unbalanced, or economically distressed. These ideas obviously build on the earlier cited verse of the *Bhagavad Gītā* that offers liberation to all those who go to Kṛṣṇa for refuge "even if they are born in sin or are women, Vaiśyas, or Śūdras" (9.32). In the *Bhāgavata Purāṇa*, however, *bhakti* becomes a more radical doctrine.

Among the people who need to discover *bhakti* to Viṣṇu before they can find liberation are women. The archetypal models of the women who find liberation through *bhakti* to Viṣṇu are the young women who herd cows in the fields of Vṛndāvana near the Yamunā River. These are the famous *gopī*s or milkmaids who fall in love with the adolescent Kṛṣṇa. They are so overwhelmed by their passion for Kṛṣṇa that they are willing to betray their own husbands to be with him. Since Kṛṣṇa is really an *avatāra* of Lord Viṣṇu, their adulterous passion is transmuted into divine *bhakti*, and they become liberated devotees: "Their sins were removed by the fierce pain of their unbearable separation from their lover. Their good fortune was preserved by their delight in an imagined embrace with Kṛṣṇa. They were united with the supreme soul himself, even as they regarded him as their lover. Their bonds to this world were destroyed immediately and they left aside their material bodies" (*Bhāgavata Purāṇa* 10.29.10–11).

The discipline of devotion can also save those who are born in low castes and classes. The *Bhāgavata Purāṇa* is filled with passages that claim that even Śūdras and untouchables achieve liberation by means of *bhakti* to Viṣṇu. For instance, it claims that impure people of a variety of foreign and local ethnic groups, such as Kirātas, Hūṇas, Āndhras, Pulindas, Pulkasas, Ābhīras, Kaṅkas, Yavanas, and Khasas, provided that they

> depend on his refuge are purified. . . . By hearing or reciting his name, . . . even a dog-eater becomes eligible for the Soma sacrifice. Amazingly, a dog-eater becomes venerable if your name is on the tip of his tongue. . . . Even a Pulkasa is freed from *saṃsāra* by just once hearing his name. . . . I regard a dog-eater whose mind, speech, efforts, wealth, and life are dedicated to him to be better a Brāhmaṇ endowed with the twelve virtues who turns his face away from the lotus feet of Viṣṇu. . . . Antevasāyins are purified by hearing about you, singing about you, and meditating on you. . . . *Bhakti* dedicated to me purifies even dog-eaters of [the stigma of their] birth.
> (*Bhāgavata Purāṇa* 2.4.18, 3.33.6–7, 6.16.44, 7.9.10, 10.10.43, 11.14.21)

Most impressive is a long list of famous demons, animals, women, and low-caste men, including Vṛtrāsura, Prahlāda, the vulture Jaṭāyu, the monkey Hanumān, the *gopī*s of Vṛndāvana, and many others, who are said to have all attained Viṣṇu, though they had not studied the Vedas, through their *bhakti*-grounded association with the good (*satsaṅga*) alone (*Bhāgavata Purāṇa* 11.12.3–13). In the *Bhāgavata Purāṇa*, even those who hate or fear Viṣṇu-Kṛṣṇa can achieve liberation through the fact that their minds are fixed on him. Kṛṣṇa's uncle Kaṃsa, who heard a prophesy that he would be killed by Kṛṣṇa, attained to him through fear. Śiśupāla, an old enemy of Kṛṣṇa and former suitor of Kṛṣṇa's wife Rukminī, attained to him through hatred (*Bhāgavata Purāṇa* 7.1.30).

These passages should not be understood to suggest that the *Bhāgavata Purāṇa* intends to attack the ideology of the traditional social system based on four classes, each ascribed by birth, and four life stages (*varṇāśramadharma*). The text contains two lengthy defenses of an idealized conception of this class system (*Bhāgavata Purāṇa* 7.11.1–35, 11.17.1–49), and numerous briefer passages reinforce the same arguments. As is true of the *Bhagavad Gītā* and most other *bhakti* texts composed in Sanskrit, one of the principal aims of the *Bhāgavata Purāṇa* was evidently to propound a religious doctrine that defended the traditional ideology of classes and life stages at the same time that it opened up the hope of liberation to wide segments of the population including women and low-caste people.

According to the *Bhāgavata Purāṇa*, the ease and wide availability of *bhakti* as a means of liberation is a special feature of the Kali Yuga. The miserable age in which we live—despite the enormous decline in human morality, health, and well being—becomes, thanks to *bhakti*, the best of all ages in which humans can be born: "What one attains in the Kṛta Yuga by meditating on Viṣṇu, in the Tretā Yuga by sacrificing with oblations, in the Dvāpara Yuga by worshiping, that is attained in the Kali Yuga merely by praising Viṣṇu" (*Bhāgavata Purāṇa* 12.3.52).

But how should people practice *bhakti*? Here the *Bhāgavata Purāṇa* advocates a number of simple observances similar to those mentioned briefly in the *Devī Māhātmya*. In the *Bhāgavata Purāṇa*, these observances are described in considerable detail, but basically they can be divided into four categories: hearing and telling the stories about Viṣṇu's *avatāras*; worship of images of these *avatāra*s located in temples dedicated to them; association with pious devotees (*satsaṅga*); and hearing and chanting the names of Viṣṇu. All these practices must necessarily be done with a heart and mind filled with devotion. The *Bhāgavata Purāṇa* gives this attractive summary of this devotion cast in an ironic mode:

> Human ears that do not listen to the exploits of Viṣṇu are mere holes. A tongue that does not sing the songs of Viṣṇu is as bad as the tongue of a frog. A head, even one wearing a silk turban, that does not bow to Viṣṇu is a mere burden. Hands, even those with flashy gold bracelets, that do not worship Viṣṇu are the hands of a corpse. Human eyes that do not see the emblems of Viṣṇu are of no more use than the eyes of a peacock's tail. Human feet that do not walk in Viṣṇu's fields are mere roots of trees. A person who never has contact with the dust from the feet of Viṣṇu's devotees is a living corpse. A person who does not know the smell of *tulasī* leaves offered to the feet of Viṣṇu is a breathing corpse. A heart that is not moved by hearing Viṣṇu's names is a heart of stone. When one's heart is moved, tears come to one's eyes and the hairs on one's body stand erect.
>
> (2.3.20–24)

Here each of the sense organs and the heart of the devotees are enlisted in the service of Viṣṇu. The only missing sense is that of touch, which was apparently reserved for the *gopī*s. In temple worship, it is only the guardian priests who normally have the opportunity to actually touch, dress, and care for the sacred images. In household shrines, of course, a family member may do this, most often a female. In any case, the senses that are most important are those of hearing and seeing. In all manifestations of *bhakti* religion, hearing and telling stories and songs about the deity or early *gurus* and saints of the movement are essential means of transmitting the messages and emotions of *bhakti*. In this, *bhakti* uses the immense power of narrative to activate and preserve human memory and emotion (Bruner 1996: 115–59).

Similarly, the visual sense plays a key role in *bhakti*, principally through the dramatic display of images of the deities and meetings with saintly persons. The word for such mutual encounters between the god or the *guru* and the devotee has even been accepted into English. It is "*darśana*" or "visual contemplation." One "makes" (*karanā*) a *darśana* of saint or divine image, and the saint or god "gives" (*denā*) his *darśana* (Eck 1981b). Such *darśanas* are normally most impressive in temple settings where the images are bigger and better adorned and located in a special sacred space filled with sacred sounds and smells. The historical growth of *bhakti* religion closely coincides with its institutionalization as ritual worship in public temples that the devotees periodically visit. When the temples are located far from the devotees' homes, the visits become pilgrimages.

Several academic scholars, most notably Friedhelm Hardy (1983: 7–48), have argued that *bhakti* in the *Bhāgavata Purāṇa*, particularly the *bhakti* of the *gopīs*, represents an "emotional *bhakti*" that stands in sharp contrast to the "intellectual *bhakti*" of earlier works, such as the *Bhagavad Gītā* and the *Viṣṇu Purāṇa*, and to that of the Sanskrit commentaries of the famous theologian Rāmānuja. Other scholars such as J. A. B. van Buitenen (1968: 1–41) have argued that the *bhakti* found in all these Sanskrit texts is essentially emotional and nonintellectual. On the other hand, Krishna Sharma (1987: 109–29) has claimed all these texts propound an intellectually oriented *nirguṇa bhakti* as the highest ideal, even the *Bhāgavata Purāṇa* where an emotional *saguṇa bhakti* seems to hold center stage. All these views can be defended by selected quotations, but it seems more reasonable to argue that all these texts contain elements of both intellectual and emotional *bhakti*, each text with a different emphasis on one or the other.

THE ĀḺVĀRS

At no time during the last two millennia has Sanskrit been understood or spoken by more than a small percentage of the population of the Indian subcontinent. Throughout this long period, vernacular languages must have been the main medium through which the religious sentiments of the vast majority of persons have been expressed. Unfortunately, no vernacular religious texts composed before the fifth or sixth centuries of the Common Era survive. Vernacular religious literature has always had a predominately oral character. The biggest part of this literature has been the songs and verses of poets, many of whom were illiterate and belonged to non-Brāhmaṇ castes. Starting in the Tamilnadu region in about the sixth century, however, some of these vernacular religious songs began to acquire a canonical status and were eventually written down. Three groups of Tamil poets and saints emerged, the twelve Vaiṣṇava Āḻvārs, the sixty-three Śaivite Nāyaṉārs, and the *yoga*-centered Siddhas. Here the discussion will focus primarily on the Āḻvārs.[2]

The songs and verses of all three groups display many common characteristics (Champakalakshmi 1996). All preach some form of *bhakti* religion. In the case of the Āḻvārs and the Nāyaṉārs, this *bhakti* was centered in temple worship to forms of Viṣṇu and Śiva represented primarily through anthropomorphic stone and metal images, or stone *liṅgas* in the case of Śiva, and through Purāṇic myths. All three groups are to some degree critical of the religious privileges of orthodox Brāhmaṇs. In the case of the Siddhas, this sometimes extends to a more radical criticism leveled against the traditional social ideology of *varṇadharma* and most ritual practices (Meenakshi 1996). On the whole, however, it seems best to count the Āḻvārs and Nāyaṇārs among the *varṇadharmī*s and the Siddhas among the *avarṇadharmī*s.

The Āḻvārs and Nāyaṇārs often express considerable hostility to the rival religious traditions of the Jainas and Buddhists. The historian R. Champakalakshmi (1996: 155–63) argues that all these common concerns of *bhakti* "seem to have emanated and spread in a context of rivalry for social dominance and royal patronage" (157) in which first the orthodox Vedic Brāhmaṇs, Jainas, and Buddhists gradually lost out to the Vaiṣṇavas and Śaivites during the seventh to ninth centuries. Then the Śaivites gained the upper hand over the Vaiṣṇavas during the ninth to thirteenth centuries, mostly as a result of the patronage given to them by Cōḻa kings. Finally, the Vaiṣṇavas gained back much of their influence through the reforms introduced by the great theologian Rāmānuja in the twelfth century.

The fact that vernacular religious compositions in India were first written down in Tamilnadu reflects the early strength of the Tamil language and culture. Tamil literature begins with the compositions of the three so-called "academies" thought to date from the early centuries of the Common Era. The poetic conventions first developed in this literature—for example, the division between "internal" and "external" themes and the use of initial rhyme—also shape the poetry of the Āḻvārs and Nāyaṇārs (Carman and Narayanan 1989: 14–17).

Since the earliest examples of vernacular *bhakti* literature are in Tamil and since there seems to be a gradual historical movement in such literature from south to north—from Tamilnadu to Karnataka to Maharashtra to the Gangetic plain and beyond—it is sometimes said, even in premodern sources, that *bhakti* was somehow passed from one region to the next in a regular progression (e.g. Ramanujan 1973: 39–40). This view ignores the fact that a clearly identifiable form of *bhakti* first appears in presumably northern Sanskrit texts, such as the *Śvetāsvatara Upaniṣad* and the *Bhagavad Gītā.* More importantly, it ignores the fact that the vernacular *bhakti* of each region has decidedly individual characteristics. Most likely, the apparent progression from one region to the next is an artifact caused by historical accident. In reality, vernacular *bhakti* in each region must have roots going back to at least the early centuries of the Common Era. The appearance of powerful sociocultural movements based on *bhakti* in different regions in different centuries must be explained treating each case in its own historical context.

The poems of the Āḻvārs are collected in the *Divyaprabandham*, an anthology of four thousand verses. These Tamil poems became a key part of the Śrīvaiṣṇava canon together with Rāmānuja's Sanskrit commentaries and works by other authors composed in both Tamil and Sanskrit. The Śrīvaiṣṇavas call this dual intellectual heritage "dual Vedānta" (Narayanan 1987: 2–14).

Among the Āḻvārs, one poet stands out above all others, a man of a Vēḷāḷar peasant caste who lived in about the ninth century. He was called Caṭakōpaṉ or Māṟaṉ but became best known as Nammāḻvār. Nammāḻvār's most revered composition is the *Tiruvāymoḻi,* itself a collection of 1,102 independent stanzas. Although adequate translations into English of most of Nammāḻvār's compositions still do not exist, three good short selections are available: one by the poet-scholar A. K. Ramanujan (1993a), another by John Carman and Vasudha Narayanan (1989), and a third by Narayanan alone (1987).

The Śrīvaiṣṇava thinkers who succeeded Rāmānuja developed a theology in which the more difficult discipline of *bhakti* was largely superseded by the easier path of self-surrender to Viṣṇu (*prapatti*). Although this idea is not fully developed in the poems of the Āḻvārs, they do emphasize the closely related idea of Viṣṇu's saving grace. Since salvation depends on this grace, bestowed on men because of Viṣṇu's infinite compassion, human efforts to attain salvation have only a secondary role to play. Here is one of Nammāḻvār's stanzas on Viṣṇu's grace (*Tiruvāymoḻi* 6.10.2; Vasudha Narayanan's translation):

O divine king!
Triumphant lord, whose fiery wheel
chops, razes, and reduces to the ground
entire clans of wicked demons!

O lord of holy Vēṅkaṭa
where lotus flowers, red as fire,
blossom in the muddy banks and pools.
Show your grace
so that I, your servant,
filled with unending love,
may reach your feet.

THE VĪRAŚAIVAS

In about the eleventh and twelfth centuries, a new *bhakti* movement appeared in what is now the southern state of Karnataka. Its followers, both men and women, are now known as Vīraśaivas or Liṅgāyatas. A Brāhmaṇ named Basava or Basavaṇṇa (1106–68) was the chief organizer of this movement into a well-defined sectarian tradition. Its followers worship the god Śiva in his manifestation as a *liṅga*, and the men are visually identifiable by their practice of wearing a small *liṅga* in a silver case on a loop of string hung over their left shoulder like a sacred thread. The most important texts of this tradition are the devotional songs composed in Kannada, the vernacular language of the region, by Basava and his associates. Almost all of these poets are non-Brāhmaṇs and several are women. Today the followers of this movement number about eight million. Useful general studies of the movement have been written by K. Ishwaran (1992), S. C. Nandimath (1979), and R. Blake Michael (1992).

Although there is little evidence of any direct historical connection, the Vīraśaiva movement has several similarities with the later northern *bhakti* movements led by men, such as Kabīr and Raidāsa, who worshiped a formless (*nirguṇa*) god and preached a radical social and religious ideology. Since the god of the Vīraśaivas is Śiva, embodied in material form as a *liṅga*, they cannot easily be counted among the *nirguṇī*s. Their social radicalism, however, does place the Vīraśaivas among the *avarṇadharmī*s. The songs of the early Vīraśaiva saints reject many of the beliefs and practices of both orthodox Brāhmaṇical religion and traditional local cults. The ideology of the movement rejects the hierarchical caste system, or at least greatly softens adherence to it, accords a more positive social and religious status to women, and attributes an unusually positive value to manual labor.

The Vīraśaivas' positive attitude to manual labor is found in only a few songs but is a notable feature of the story of the early saint and poet, Nuliya Candayya, who was a rope-maker by trade and dedicated all his earnings to the Vīraśaiva community. Here is one of his songs in which he stresses the *Bhagavad Gītā*-style message that one's work should be dedicated selflessly to god. The Jaṅgama mentioned in this song is a Vīraśaiva priest, regarded as a "moving" (*jaṅgama*) *liṅga*, while Madivalayya is the fellow saint whom Candayya is addressing (Bhoosnurmath and Menezes 1970: 218):

From whatsoever kind of work it comes,
To offer it with purity of heart
To Guru, Liṅga and Jaṅgama, that is
Worship of Śiva; will it not
Be welcome to Caṇḍeśvaraliṅga,
O Madivalayya?

THE VĀRKARĪS

Somewhat later than the early Vīraśaivas are the early poets of a Vaiṣṇava *bhakti* movement in the west-central region of India where the dominant vernacular language is Marathi. The followers of this movement are called Vārkarīs. The poet and theologian who is regarded as the founder of the movement is the Brāhmaṇ Jñāneśvara or Jñānadeva. His most famous work is a commentary and paraphrase of the *Bhagavad Gītā* in the Marathi language, said to have been completed in 1290 CE. This text, commonly called the *Jñāneśvarī*, is one of the oldest and probably the most influential of all compositions written in this language.

The Vārkarī movement has produced a large number of poets and intellectuals from a variety of castes: men like the Brāhmaṇs Jñāneśvara, Ekanātha, and Mahīpati, the merchant Tukārāma, the untouchable Cokāmeḷā, the tailor Nāmadeva, and the potter Gora and women like the Brāhmaṇs Muktābāī and Bahiṇābāī and the servant Janābāī. In their compositions we find a wide range of different religious and social points of view: both *saguṇa* and *nirguṇa* visions of god and both defenses of and attacks against caste ideology (*varṇadharma*). What holds the movement together is, first, worship of Viṣṇu as Viṭhobā whose image is located in a temple in the town of Pandharpur near the border of Karnataka, second, the annual pilgrimages to this temple by large groups of Vārkarī devotees from different parts of Maharashtra, and, third, the many songs of the Vārkarī poets that their followers sing on these pilgrimages or whenever they are in the mood. Useful scholarly studies of the movement include those by G. A. Deleury (1960), Eleanor Zelliot (1981), and Zelliot and Maxine Berntsen (1988). Of special interest is D. B. Mokashi's (1987) modern Marathi novel *Pālkhī* about the annual pilgrimage to Pandharpur.

A fair sample of the Marathi texts by poets and theologians of the Vārkarī movement has been translated into English. The translations include Jñānadeva's *Jñāneśvarī* (Kripananda 1989), Mahīpati's collection of stories about Vārkarī saints (Abbott and Godbole 1982), and some of the songs by Tukārāma (Chitre 1991). A few songs by Cokāmeḷā are translated in articles by Zelliot (1981, 1995). Winand Callewaert and Mukund Lath (1989) have produced a complete collection of texts and translations of Nāmadeva's Hindi songs.

The Vārkarī poet Nāmadeva played a key role in the transition to the *nirguṇī* poets of North India, like Kabīr, Raidāsa, and Nānak, who exalted the worship of a formless god and who refused to accept the validity of distinctions of social class (*varṇa*) and caste (*jāti*) or, somewhat less consistently, of gender. Nāmadeva's dates are controversial, but he must have lived before poets like Kabīr, Raidāsa, Nānak, and Mīrābāī who composed songs in the early 1500s, since they all mention him. Many of the songs attributed to Nāmadeva, however, are likely to be somewhat later compositions "signed" in his name (a practice that has also occurred in the case of most of the major *bhakti* poets of North India with the possible exception of the Sikh *gurus*). Like many Vārkarīs poets, Nāmadeva sometimes shifts between *bhakti* directed at embodied forms of Viṣṇu and *bhakti* directed at his transcendent forms. When he directs his devotion to a transcendent form, he addresses his god by the name Rām. This Rām is not Rāma, the *avatāra* of Viṣṇu, but the same transcendent, formless Rām praised by *nirguṇī* poets, such as Kabīr, Raidāsa, and Nānak. This Rām enables Nāmadeva (Callewaert and Lath 1989: 258) to discard even reverence for the Vedas and the Purāṇas and to reject respect for the caste hierarchy. This fact places him among the *avarṇadharmī* poets, although some other poets of the Vārkarī movement with which he is associated belong more in the *varṇadharmī* camp. Like the *nirguṇī* poets Kabīr and Raidāsa, and also the Vīraśaiva Nuliya Candayya, Nāmadeva affirms the intrinsic worth of his own low-caste profession. In the following Hindi song, his work as a tailor becomes a symbol of his faith (Callewaert and Lath 1989: 263):

Why should I care about caste?
Why should I care about status?
King Rām I serve
day and night.
Mind is my yardstick, tongue my scissors,
happy with Rām I cut
the noose of Death.
I stitch the seams, sewing, and sewing.
How can I stay alive
without Rām?
Love is the thread, bliss the needle.
Nāmadeva's joins his mind
together with Hari.

NORTH INDIAN VARṆADHARMĪ BHAKTI

The *varṇadharmī bhakti* movements of North India have all been led almost exclusively by Brāhmaṇ *gurus*, poets, and theologians. This is generally less true of the *bhakti* movements of the south, such as Āḻvārs, Nāyaṉārs, and Siddhas of Tamilnadu or the Vārkarīs of Maharashtra, in which both low-caste and women poets won fame. The followers of *varṇadharmī* movements, as opposed to their leaders, have come from all classes and castes, including even untouchables, in both the north and the south.

Another trait virtually all *varṇadharmī* movements have in common is a preference for worship of *saguṇī* forms of god, in other words a god or gods imagined as anthropomorphic and theriomorphic beings. Often divine forms are embodied in explicit carved or painted images. Śiva however is a partial exception. He is usually imagined as a being with a human shape, but he is most often worshiped in the semi-iconic form of a *liṅga*. The chosen god of most *varṇadharmī* movements is Viṣṇu, most often in the form of his *avatāras* Rāma or Kṛṣṇa. Rāma's ally Hanumān has also become an important god in his own right. In Bengal, however, *bhakti* worship of Devī or goddess is also popular. Since the Devī is also called Śakti (power), her followers are often called Śāktas. The preference for an embodied *saguṇa* form of god does not mean that the worshipers do not also conceive of god as formless and transcendent (*nirguṇa*). Rather, it indicates that they believe that this transcendent god takes embodied form to make himself or herself known to his or her devotees.

The most popular *varṇadharmī* movements of North India are those of the followers of Vallabhācārya (1479–1531) and Rāmānanda (fifteenth century) in Hindi-speaking areas and that of the followers of Caitanya (1458–1533) in Bengal. The late sixteenth-century poet Tulasīdāsa—the author of the famous Hindi version of the story of Rāma—was perhaps the greatest proponent of *varṇadharmī bhakti*, but his many followers never organized themselves into a separate sectarian movement. Here the discussion will focus on Tulasīdāsa's retelling of Rāma's story and on the songs of Sūradāsa, a poet allied to Vallabhācārya tradition.

The famous Sanskrit epic, the *Rāmāyaṇa,* has been the primary, but not the only, source for the many later retellings of the story of the *avatāra* Rāma in various vernacular languages. By far the most popular and influential of these vernacular Rāmāyaṇas has been Tulasīdāsa's *Rāmcaritmanas*, written in the Avadhi dialect of medieval Hindi. Nowadays, this dialect has become difficult for most Hindi speakers to understand, but many popular editions give a modern Hindi translation together with Tulasīdāsa's medieval text. In addition, recitation-expositions of episodes of the text are often held at major temples of Rāma and Hanumān. These performances attract large crowds, and the best performers who recite and comment on the text become celebrities and command large fees. Tulasīdāsa's text also furnishes the basic script for the often week-long public festival-dramas known as Rāmalīlās that are held annually in many North Indian towns, most notably Varanasi (Lutgendorf 1991a). The text was also the principal source for the recent, immensely popular serial adaptation of the epic for television (Lutgendorf 1995).

The great popularity of the *Rāmcaritmanas* stems from the Tulasīdāsa's great skill as a storyteller, his poetic language, and his ability to evoke the human emotions and religious devotion of those who read and listen to the text. The story of King Rāma, his loyal wife Sītā, their monkey allies led by Hanumān, and their demon-enemy Rāvaṇa has been told elsewhere in this book. Here the discussion will be limited to a few comments about the rather ambiguous ideological messages found in the Tulasīdāsa's text.

At the time when the *Rāmcaritmanas* was written, there was much opposition among the orthodox to the innovation of retelling the story of Rāma in a vernacular language. Many orthodox Brāhmaṇs criticized Tulasīdāsa as a radical reformer and virtual heretic. Nonetheless, a close look at the text shows that Tulasīdāsa purveys a socioreligious ideology that is generally more conservative than, for instance, that of the authors of the *Bhāgavata Purāṇa*. Most notorious is Tulasīdāsa's claim that "Śūdras, fools, drums, cattle, and women are all eligible for a beating."

More interesting, however, is Tulasīdāsa's long description of the social, moral, and religious ills of the Kali Yuga and their cure through the medicine of *bhakti*. Toward the very end of the *Rāmcaritmanas*, the crow Bhuśuṇḍi tells Garuḍa, Viṣṇu's eagle, how he came to be a devotee of the *avatāra* Rāma. In the Kali Yuga of a former eon, Bhuśuṇḍi says, he was born in Rāma's capital as a Śūdra. Among the many ills of the time were the claims of Śūdras and untouchables to adopt the religious calling of the Brāhmaṇs:

> The ills of the Kali Yuga devoured all *dharma*. The holy texts were destroyed. Hypocrites invented their own doctrines and propounded many paths to salvation. Everyone was deluded. Greed gobbled up good deeds. Listen, Garuḍa, and I will tell you something about the *dharma* of the Kali Yuga. The *dharma* of the four classes (*varṇadharma*) and four stages of life does not exist. Men and women are opposed to the Vedas. Brāhmaṇs sell the Vedas and kings oppress their subjects. No one respects the sacred teachings. . . . All men are under the power of women and dance like beggars' monkeys. Śūdras teach knowledge to Brāhmaṇs. They put on sacred threads and accept improper alms. . . . Men and women who have no knowledge of *brahman* speak about nothing else. For the sake of a few coins they kill Brāhmaṇs and *gurus*. Śūdras debate with Brāhmaṇs and say: "Are we something less than you? Whoever knows *brahman* is a true Brāhmaṇ."
>
> (*Rāmcaritmānas* 7.97a–b, 98.1–2, 99.1–2, 99a–b; Poddar 1989: 983–85)

Bhuśuṇḍi's Kali Yuga of a past cosmic cycle is, of course, a double for Tulasīdāsa's own Kali Yuga. What is striking here is not only Tulasīdāsa's social conservatism but also the fact that he is implicitly attacking the low-caste devotees of *avarṇadharmī bhakti* like Kabīr and Raidāsa who had achieved great popularity in the decades before Tulasīdāsa composed his epic.

In his shorter poems and songs, Tulasīdāsa most often emphasizes his own role as god's servant, his extreme humility in the face of god's glory, and the power of god's name. Here is one such poem from Tulasīdāsa's *Vinaya Patrikā*:

> Poor fool, repeat Rām's name again and again,
> The name is your ship to cross the terrible ocean.
> By this alone you capture peace and perfection.
> The disease called Kālī murders our meditation,
> The world is a garden of flowers floating in air.
> Why look to castles of smoke? Do not be fooled.
> Tulasī says: If you leave Rām's name and trust
> in another, you leave a feast and ask for gruel.

Vallabhācārya (1479–1531) was born into a family of Brāhmaṇs whose ancestral home was in Andhra Pradesh. According to the traditional account, however, he spent his early life in Varanasi. Between 1493 and 1512, he made several tours throughout India. He became especially fond of the Vraja region around Mathurā where Kṛṣṇa spent his childhood and adolescence. In 1494 Vallabhācārya took over a small temple to Kṛṣṇa at the site where Kṛṣṇa lifted up the Govardhana Hill to protect the villagers of the region from the rain storms sent by Indra. Sometime in the first years of the sixteenth century,

Vallabhācārya married. He set up two houses, one near Illāhābhād and one near Varanasi, but he also traveled often to Mathurā. He had two sons, Gopīnātha and Viṭṭhalanātha. The latter played an essential role in developing his father's sectarian tradition or *sampradāya*. Vallabhācārya wrote exclusively in Sanskrit and composed important commentaries on the *Brahmasūtra* and on the tenth book of the *Bhāgavata Purāṇa*, the book that describes Kṛṣṇa's exploits (Barz 1976: 16–55).

Although Vallabhācārya's works are in Sanskrit, the best known works of his *sampradāya* are the Hindi songs of his disciples, particularly those of Sūradāsa (also called simply Sūra), who is said to have lived from 1479 to 1584. According to sectarian tradition, Sūra was born in a family of Sārasvata Brāhmaṇs in a village near modern Delhi. He was born without sight and left home at an early age and settled at a site a few miles away where he took up the office of a prophesier and religious mendicant. Since he had great talent as a musician and poet, he gradually acquired a large following. He grew dissatisfied with this life, however, and decided to travel to the Vraja region. Eventually he settled at a place called Goghāṭa on the Yamunā River between Mathurā and Āgrā. One day in the year 1511, Vallabhācārya came there, and Sūradāsa became his disciple. Vallabhācārya encouraged him to compose songs about Kṛṣṇa's childhood and youth (Barz 1976: 103–39).

This, at least, is how Sūradāsa's story is told in Vallabha tradition. Modern scholars have questioned the historical probability of several aspects of the story. It is possible that Sūra was a not a Brāhmaṇ, was not a disciple of Vallabhācārya, and was not even blind, at least until quite late in his life. More important, many of the songs attributed to Sūradāsa may, in fact, be later compositions by poets who followed in his tradition (Hawley 1984: 22–63).

However true all this may or may not be, many of the thousands of songs attributed to Sūradāsa have become essential parts of the popular religious culture of North India and are still remembered and sung by countless devotees of Viṣṇu. In addition, the blind singers of religious songs who today wander the streets and trains of North India are still called by the generic name Sūradāsa. Most famous of all Sūradāsa's songs are those that tell of Kṛṣṇa's adventures as a naughty child living among the cowherds of Vraja. Many tell how he stole the butter from his mother's kitchen. Here is one of the best loved of such songs, possibly a composition of the eighteenth century:

> Kṛṣṇa first steals some butter,
> Then runs about the lanes of Vraja,
>   exciting the milkmaids' desire.
> I'll go to every house in Vraja,
>   is what Kṛṣṇa decides.
> I took birth in Gokula to have some fun.
>   I'll eat everyone's butter.
> Yaśodā knows me as her child,
>   the milkmaids meet me for pleasure.
> Sūradāsa's lord with love declares:
>   These are my people of Vraja.

In many of his songs, particularly those of the earlier collections, Sūradāsa expresses a more sober sort of *bhakti*, where he turns away from petty human cares and petitions the lord's help and favor. John Hawley (1984: 121–60) has argued that these songs reveal a Sūradāsa whose thoughts come close to those of *avarṇadharmī* poets such as Kabīr. Here is one of Sūradāsa's petition or *vinaya* songs:

Let go of worldly things, my heart.
Why, parrot, do you wait in vain
  for the tricky semar fruit?
The heart grabs at gold and sex,
  but your hands will end up empty.
Let go of pride and call on Rām,
  or face the pain of fire.
The *guru* told you, and I repeat it:
  collect Rām as your wealth.
Remember Rām, Sūradāsa's lord,
  or dance like *yogī*s and *ṛṣi*s.

NORTH INDIAN AVARṆADHARMĪ BHAKTI

Several *avarṇadharmī bhakti* movements in North India actively opposed the traditional Hindu social and religious ideology of the caste system and patriarchal dominance. The leading poets and intellectuals of these movements were almost all non-Brāhmaṇs. Many of both the leaders and the followers belonged to low castes of Śūdras or untouchables. Several important poets were women, while several of the men were raised in Muslim families. Virtually all these movements have been associated with the worship of Viṣṇu rather than that of Śiva or Devī. With one important exception, these North Indian movements imagine Viṣṇu as a transcendent, impersonal, nonembodied being who is beyond all attributes (*nirguṇa*) rather than as any of the standard *avatāra*s or anthropomorphic images. For this reason, these movements are often called *nirguṇī* or followers of *nirguṇa bhakti*. The exception is the movement associated with the woman-poet named Mīrā or Mīrābāī, who preferred to worship Viṣṇu in his *saguṇa* form as the adolescent lover Kṛṣṇa. Here we will describe these movements as proponents of ideologically liberal *avarṇadharmī bhakti*.

In this chapter, the discussion will focus on three poets: Kabīr, Raidāsa, and Mīrābāī. Other important poets include Pīpā, Dādū, Rajjava, Sundaradāsa, Jana Gopāl, Haridāsa Nirañjanī, Dharmadāsa, and Palaṭū Sāhab. English language studies of these poets and the movements associated with them include books by P. D. Barthwal (1978), Daniel Gold (1987b), David Lorenzen (1991b, 1996), Parita Mukta (1994), W. G. Orr (1947), Karine Schomer and W. H. McLeod (1987), Monika Thiel-Horstmann (1983), and Charlotte Vaudeville (1974). Illustrative translations are found in many of these texts. Several more complete translations are available for the older collections of Kabīr's compositions. The best collection is that of Linda Hess's and Shukdeo Singh's (2002) selections from the *Kabīr Bījak*. The older songs attributed to Raidāsa have been edited and translated by Winand Callewaert and Peter Friedlander (1992). Many of Dādū's compositions are translated in the book by W. Orr. Some of Mīrā's songs have been translated by Usha S. Nilsson (1969). John Hawley's and Mark Juergensmeyer's attractive introductory text (1988) has translations of songs by Raidāsa, Kabīr, and Mīrābāī, as well as by Nānak, Sūradāsa, and Tulasīdāsa. Translations of songs by other *nirguṇī* poets are generally less available.

Two other important religious movements that are historically related to the *nirguṇī* current of *avarṇadharmī* Hinduism are those of the Nāthas and the Sikhs. The Nāthas, however, mostly abandoned *bhakti* for a meditative discipline, usually Haṭha Yoga, centered on a mystic anatomy (Eliade 1969). In premodern times this discipline was sometimes transmuted into a religious form of alchemy (White 1996). The Sikhs, for their part, based their movement on a form of *nirguṇa bhakti* but also established an independent, non-Hindu religious identity (McLeod 1997). The most revered book of the Sikhs, the *Guru Granth Sāhib*, contains many compositions by Kabīr and Raidāsa, as well those by other North Indian *avarṇadharmī* poets and of course those of the Sikh *gurus*. This complete text has been translated several times into English, but the literary quality of these translations leaves much to be desired.

More directly than Nāmadeva, Kabīr (*c.*1450–1520) was the founding father of *avarṇadharmī* poets. He lived most of his life in the city of Varanasi and was raised in a family of poor Muslim weavers. Legend claims that he lost faith in Islam and was attracted by the Hindu teachings of a Brāhmaṇ named Rāmānanda. He is said to have tricked Rāmānanda into giving him an initiation and then convinced his new *guru* of his spiritual worth despite his low-caste Muslim identity. Kabīr's talents as a religious singer and poet made him famous and soon aroused the jealousy of both Hindu and Muslim religious leaders. Their many attempts to discredit him all failed, however, and his fame continued to grow. Best known is the story of the many failed attempts of Sulṭān Sikandar Lodī to have him killed. When it came time for Kabīr to die, he moved to a place called Magahar, near Gorakhpur. It is said that after his death, his Muslim and Hindu followers fought over how to dispose of the corpse, to bury it Muslim style or burn it Hindu style. When they looked under Kabīr's shroud, however, all they found were flowers (Lorenzen 1991b, 1999a).

How much of these legends can be taken as true is difficult to say. The connection with Rāmānanda is particularly problematic. Rāmānanda is said to have been a teacher in a direct line of descent from the famous Tamil theologian Rāmānuja and also to have been the *guru* not only of Kabīr but also of the *camār*-poet Raidāsa (also called Ravidāsa), the royal Rājput poet Pīpā, the barber-saint Sen, and the Jāṭ peasant-saint Dhannā, as well as several Brāhmaṇ disciples (Caracchi 1999). The few songs attributed to Rāmānanda that survive show more affinities to Kabīr and his other non-Brāhmaṇ disciples than to Rāmānuja and the Śrīvaiṣṇavas. Nonetheless, Rāmānanda is considered to be the founder of an important North Indian *varṇadharmī* religious movement known as that of the Rāmānandīs. Although this movement has produced no poet of the stature of Kabīr, it has perhaps the largest and wealthiest monastic organizations in North India, its only rival being that of the Daśanāmīs (van der Veer 1988). The followers of Kabīr also established their own monastic organization. Currently it is divided in several branches with monasteries located throughout the Hindi-speaking area.

Three old collections of Kabīr's songs and verses have survived, each connected with a different sectarian tradition: the *Kabīr Bījak* of his followers in the Kabīr Panth, the *Kabīr Granthāvalī* associated with the Dādū Panth, and his many compositions found in the *Ādi Granth* or *Guru Granth Sāhib* of the Sikhs. In the centuries after Kabīr, a large number of apocryphal songs and verses have been attributed to Kabīr. Many of these later songs and verses have become essential elements of the popular culture of virtually all North Indian Hindus (Lorenzen 1996: 205–23). The main message of these songs and verses, both old and new, is a rather austere *bhakti* toward a formless *nirguṇa* deity combined with a religious and social iconoclasm that rejects ideology of the caste system as well as many of the beliefs and practices of both Hinduism and Islam.

Kabīr's iconoclasm is most evident in the songs collected in the *Kabīr Bījak.* Here is a song that attacks the opposing claims of the Muslims and Hindus (S. Singh 1972: 122):

Tell me, brother. How can there be
Not one lord of the world but two?
Who led you so astray?
God is called by many names:
Names like Allāh, Rām, Karīm,
Keśava, Hari, and Hazrat.
Gold may be shaped into rings and bangles.
Isn't it gold all the same?
Distinctions are only words we invent.
One does *namāz,* one does *pūjā.*
One has Śiva, one Muḥammad.
One has Adam, one Brahmā.
Who is a Hindu, who a Turk?
Both share a single world.
Both read their books, Qur'ān or Vedas.
One is a *paṇḍā,* one a *mullāh.*
Each bears a separate name,
But every pot is made from clay.
Kabīr says they are both mistaken.
Neither can find the only Rām.
One kills goats, the other cows.
They waste their lives in disputation.

Many of Kabīr's songs embody ironic commentaries on the vanity of human ambitions and the immanence of death. Here is a popular *bhajana* from a more modern collection (Lorenzen 1996: 210–11):

O mind, you merrily strut your stuff,
But who in this world can you find to trust?

The mother says: This is my son.
The sister says: He is my hero.
The brother says: He is my rock.
The woman says: He is my man.
His mother cries for the rest of her life.
His sister cries for less than a year.
His woman cries for a couple of weeks
Then goes to live with someone else.

The shroud they begged was four yards long.
The pyre was lit, just like at Holi.
The bones burned . . . like firewood.
The hair burned . . . like dried grass.
The body that once was gold is . . . [ashes]
And no one wants to come near to it now.

The women of the house begin to cry,
Wandering all over, searching in vain.
Says Kabīr: Listen, my brother sadhu[s].
Give up the hopes you hold for the world.

Rāmānanda's disciple Raidāsa also lived in Varanasi. His family belonged to an untouchable caste of leather workers known as *camārs*. Most of Raidāsa's followers still belong to this caste. Although they have not established a large monastic organization, Raidāsa temples are found in many North Indian town and villages. Nowadays, the Raidāsa movement has become highly politicized, and Raidāsa plays an important symbolic role in the *camārs*' fight for social respect, education, and economic well being.

Like the songs of Kabīr, those of Raidāsa combine criticism of the caste system with *bhakti* toward a formless, *nirguṇa* god. On the other hand, Raidāsa directs few attacks against Muslim and Hindu beliefs and practices and generally eschews the sharp social and religious satire found in Kabīr's compositions. The tone of Raidāsa's songs is less confrontational and more conciliatory. He laments the indignities he has to suffer as a *camār* and seeks consolation in god and the *guru*. In the following song, Raidāsa asks god to take away his distress (Callewaert and Friedlander 1992: 191):

I worry day and night,
  my vile contacts,
My twisted *karma*, my lowly birth.
O Rām, life of my soul,
  don't forget me.
I am yours, a devotee.
Take away my pain,
  make me your man.
I grab your feet, my body is dying.
I've come to your *darbār*.
  Don't delay.
Meet your man, says Raidāsa.

The *avarṇadharmī* poet Mīrābāī was a Rājput princess from Mevar in Rajasthan. Although her dates are uncertain, she is said to have been a contemporary of Kabīr and Raidāsa. According to legend, she was promised in marriage to a prince of the Sisodiā clan of Citor. Mīrā, however, had love in her heart only for Kṛṣṇa, the *avatāra* of Viṣṇu. She defied her princely husband and refused to accept her traditional role as wife and mother. His family was deeply offended by her challenge to patriarchal custom, and someone, either the prince or his father, tried to have her poisoned. Kṛṣṇa saved her, and she fled the palace to live as a wandering singer of songs dedicated to her divine lover. In some legends, she even takes the *camār* poet Raidāsa as her *guru*.

Today Mīrābāī is clearly the most popular of all the saint poets of North India. Her troubled life has become the subject of short stories, novels, and films. Recordings of her songs are available on cassette in almost any North Indian market, both in the popular film-song style and in the more austere semiclassical style. Only the songs of Sūradāsa and Kabīr can remotely approach this popularity in Hindi-speaking regions. Mīrābāī's songs appeal especially to women but men too enjoy them. Her most fervent followers, however, are the poor, low-caste women *bhajaniks* of Rajasthan and Gujarat who organize frequent all-night sessions to sing her songs (Mukta 1994).

Many of Mīrābāī's songs are autobiographical and tell how her husband and his family punish her for loving only Kṛṣṇa. Here is one such song (Chaturvedi 1966: 112–13):

O friend, I cannot stay alive without my Hari.
Mother-in-law fights against me, sister-in-law scolds,
  and the king is always angry.
A guard sits there waiting before my door,
  and a lock makes sure it's shut.
That long-enduring love from a former birth,
  how can I bear to leave him?
Mīrā's lord is the cunning Mountain Lifter,
  no one else can please me.

In other songs, Mīrābāī tells how Viṣṇu-Kṛṣṇa has accepted the devotion of non-Brāhmaṇ saints, such as Nāmadeva, Kabīr, Pīpā, and Sen. Several of these saints are women like Mīrābāī herself. Here is a song that praises the low-caste woman of the Bhīl tribe who offered plums to the royal *avatāra* Rāma after tasting them first to make sure they were sweet. Such food is considered highly polluted, but her devotion made the plums pure, and Rāma ate them (Chaturvedi 1966: 154):

A woman of the Bhīls brought him some plums
And tasted each to be sure it was sweet.
What sort of a way is this to behave?
What's more, this Bhīl was hardly a beauty.
Her family was low, her caste was worse,
Her clothes nothing but dirty rags.
But Rāma took the fruit she tasted
and knew it to be a sign of her love.
Rāma knows neither high nor low.
The Bhīl tasted the taste of love.
How could she read the Vedas?
That very instant she got into the car,
Tied to him with all her heart,
And went to swing in Viṣṇu's heaven.

Mīrā says: one who has such love
will float across to the other shore
My lord, it is you who saves the fallen,
and I am a humble milkmaid of Vraja.

CONCLUSION

This chapter has explored the historical development of different styles of *bhakti* from the *Śvetāsvatara Upaniṣad* to the medieval poet saints of North India. Particular attention has been paid to the combinations of religious and social ideologies embodied in *bhakti* literature. Virtually all styles of *bhakti* open the possibility of salvation to women and to persons from low-status castes. Nonetheless, in some *bhakti* movements the majority of poets and theologians argue in favor of one or another interpretation of the traditional social system of *varṇadharma*, and in other movements they flatly argue against the basic norms and principles of this system. The Vīraśaivas and the *nirguṇī* movements of the north also tend to downgrade the authority of the Vedas and the Purāṇas. Given the centrality of *varṇadharma* to the Hindu social order and the Vedas to Hindu identity, it is not surprising that the movements mostly opposed to this ideology have tended to be situated somewhat at the margins of the Hindu community. In one important case, that of the Sikhs, the movement has purposely established a separate, non-Hindu identity.

Another social dimension of almost all *bhakti* movements is their association with specific languages and cultural regions. For example, most of the *bhakti* movements discussed here are closely tied to regional cultural identities based on specific languages: the Āḻvārs and Nāyaṇārs are tied to the Tamil language and the Tamilnadu region, the Vīraśaivas to Kannada and Karnataka, and the Vārkarīs to Marathi and Maharashtra. The groups centered in the North Indian plains, such as the Vallabhas and Kabīr *panthī*s, tend to have a somewhat looser regional identity but are still mostly limited to populations that can understand Hindi dialects.

Most movements also developed their own unique theologies. Most obvious is the broad division between movements that worship Śiva, those that worship Viṣṇu, those that worship the Devī, and those that worship a formless *nirguṇa* god. Movements led by Brāhmaṇ theologians who could write in Sanskrit often developed their own schools of Vedānta. Among the movements devoted to Viṣṇu, the Śrīvaiṣṇavas led by Rāmānuja and his line of disciples followed a school that propounded Viśiṣṭādvaita Vedānta, the Vallabhas followed Sūddhādvaita Vedānta, and other movements followed schools of Vedānta called Dvaita and Dvaitādvaita. Śaivite movements and *nirguṇī* movements, on the other hand, have tended to associate themselves in looser fashion with variants of Śaṃkara's Advaita Vedānta.

Each movement has also tended to evolve its own distinctive theology of divine grace. For instance, the Śrīvaiṣṇava movement placed a strong emphasis on the self-surrender (*prapatti*) of the devotee to god as a prerequisite of a divine grace that was regarded as the only practical source of salvation. Most other *saguṇī* Vaiṣṇava movements (and also the *nirguṇī* Sikhs) similarly stress divine grace as the principal means to salvation. Most Advaita and *nirguṇī* movements, on the other hand, stress an interior mysticism in which the devotee seeks to discover the identity of the individual soul (*ātman*) with the universal ground of being (*brahman*) or to find god within himself. Since this interior mysticism implies that all human beings are equally grounded in divine reality, it is often associated with a more egalitarian social ideology and with a lesser emphasis on the traditional theodicy of *karma* and rebirth (Lorenzen 1987).

In recent years *bhakti*-based Hinduism has been changing in important ways under the double impact of Hindu cultural nationalism and the transmission of religious messages by mass media, such as music cassettes, films, and television (Babb and Wadley 1995; Thapar 1985). The immensely popular television serializations of the *Rāmāyaṇa* and the *Mahābhārata* are two noteworthy examples. All this has led to the development of a more militant, political, communal, and standardized sort of Hinduism, one that does not bode well for the social and religious harmony of civil society (van der Veer 1994). On the other hand, the mass media can also help create a new, socially progressive Hinduism, a Hinduism that can do much to ease communal tensions and sponsor a more positive social, moral, religious, and economic renewal of Indian society.

NOTES

1 All the translations from Sanskrit and Hindi are mine, while the translations from Tamil and Kannada are by the various scholars indicated in the text.
2 For the Nāyaṉārs, Peterson's (1989) excellent study and translations are recommended. For the Siddhas, one can consult the book by Zvelebil (1973).

PART IV

COSMIC ORDER AND HUMAN GOALS

CHAPTER TEN

DHARMA

Barbara A. Holdrege

Dharma is one of the most important and ubiquitous categories in the history of Indic religions and cultures. This pivotal category has assumed a central role not only in Hindu traditions but also in Buddhist and Jaina traditions. The term "*dharma*" conveys a complex array of meanings and has defied the attempts of both Western and Indian scholars to reduce it to a single English equivalent, such as religion, law, duty, norm, social usage, right conduct, morality, justice, or righteousness. Franklin Edgerton's definition of this multivalent term is representative: "*Dharma* is propriety, socially approved conduct, in relation to one's fellow men or to other living beings (animals, or superhuman powers). Law, social usage, morality, and most of what we ordinarily mean by religion, all fall under this head" (1942: 151). In Hindu traditions *dharma* is an encompassing category that incorporates and at the same time transcends the distinctions among religion, ritual, law, and ethics that are generally posited in Western traditions. Austin Creel cautions us against attempting to equate *dharma* with any one of the Western categories to which it has been compared: "One must avoid identification of *dharma* as directly equivalent to any of the various components of its meaning, such as law, duty, morality, justice, virtue or religion. All of these are involved, but we should cease looking for an equivalent for translation, inasmuch as premature identification with Western concepts tends to blind one to the particular multifaceted structure of meanings in the Hindu *dharma*" (1977: 2). Among more recent studies, Ariel Glucklich (1994) has suggested that the most fruitful approach to understanding *dharma* is to set aside the quest for conceptual frameworks and theoretical formulations and to adopt instead a phenomenology of *dharma* based on a "somatic hermeneutic" that explores embodied experiences of *dharma* in specific spatial and temporal contexts.

In the classical formulations of post-Vedic traditions, *dharma* functions as a paradigmatic category that includes both an ontological dimension and a normative dimension.[1] In its ontological dimension *dharma*—in accordance with its etymological derivation from the Sanskrit root *dhṛ*, "to uphold, support, maintain"—is the cosmic ordering principle that upholds and promotes the evolution of the universe as a whole and of each of its individual parts. *Dharma* structures the universe as a vast cosmic ecosystem, an intricate network of symbiotic relations among interdependent parts, in which each part has a specific function to perform that contributes to the whole system. *Dharma* establishes each part in its proper place and ensures that every aspect of the cosmic system is properly balanced and coordinated with every other aspect and thus contributes the maximum to its own evolution and to the evolution of the whole system. The principle of *dharma* can be found operating on multiple levels corresponding to the various planes of existence. At each level an organic unity is structured in which the separation of functions among the various classes of beings is clearly defined, specific functions or modes of activity being assigned to each class of beings in accordance with its inherent nature. For example, it is the *dharma* of the sun to shine, it is the *dharma* of the river to flow, it is the *dharma* of the bee to make honey, and it is the *dharma* of the cow to give milk.

In its normative dimension, *dharma*, the cosmic ordering principle, finds expression on the human plane in the ritual, social, and moral orders, particularly as represented in the Brāhmaṇical system of sociocultural norms. As Glucklich (1988: 47) has emphasized, *dharma*, as both an ontological and normative principle, includes both nature and law, or—in the language of McKim Marriott (1976)—"substance" and "code." On both the cosmic and human planes the principle of *dharma* ensures that nature and law—or innate constitution and external function—are properly correlated for every being. On the human plane the principle of *dharma*, operating in consonance with the cosmic law of *karma*, ensures that each individual's inherent nature corresponds to the code of conduct, or duty, allotted to that individual by virtue of the circumstances of his or her birth and social status. In the Brāhmaṇical tradition an individual's allotted duty, or *svadharma* (literally, "one's own *dharma*"), is virtually synonymous with *varṇāśramadharma*, the particular duties of his or her social class (*varṇa*) and stage of life (*āśrama*). The Brāhmaṇical system of *varṇāśramadharma* is presented in this context as the paradigmatic social order that is part of the natural order of things, instantiating the cosmic order on the social plane. This system assumes a pivotal role in defining the distinctive ethnocultural identity of the "Āryans," the people of the Indian subcontinent who refer to themselves as *ārya*s, "noble ones."

The principal sources of *dharma*, as will be discussed further later, are the two authoritative categories of sacred texts that constitute the Brāhmaṇical Sanskritic canon: *śruti* (that which was heard) and *smṛti* (that which was remembered). The term "*śruti*" was originally used to designate the four Vedic Saṃhitās—*Ṛg Veda*, *Yajur Veda*, *Sāma Veda*, and *Atharva Veda*—the versified portions of which are termed *mantra*s. The domain of *śruti* was subsequently extended to incorporate the entire corpus of Vedic literature, including not only the Saṃhitās but also the Brāhmaṇas, Āraṇyakas, and Upaniṣads. While the domain of *śruti* is in principle circumscribed, *smṛti* is a dynamic, open-ended category, which includes the Vedāṅgas, Dharmaśāstras, Itihāsas (epics), and Purāṇas, as well as a variety of other texts that have been incorporated within this ever-expanding category in accordance with the needs of different periods and groups. The primary criterion for distinguishing between *śruti* and *smṛti* texts is generally characterized by both Western and Indian scholars as an ontological distinction between "revelation" and "tradition." The *śruti*, or Vedic, texts are traditionally understood to have been directly cognized—"seen" and "heard"—by inspired "seers" (*ṛṣi*) at the beginning of each cycle of creation. Pūrva Mīmāṃsā and Vedānta, the formal schools of Vedic exegesis among the six orthodox systems of Hindu philosophy, maintain that the Vedic texts are eternal (*nitya*), infinite, and *apauruṣeya*, not derived from any personal—human or divine—agent, while the Nyāya, Vaiśeṣika, and Yoga schools of Hindu philosophy view the Vedic texts as the work of god. All other sacred texts are relegated to a secondary status as *smṛti*, for they are held to have been composed by personal authors and are therefore designated as "that which was remembered" rather than "that which was heard."

In this chapter we will examine the complex array of meanings that are interwoven in Hindu constructions of *dharma* in both *śruti* and *smṛti* texts. We will begin with an analysis of *śruti* texts, with particular emphasis on the Vedic antecedents of post-Vedic formulations of *dharma* found in the Saṃhitās and Brāhmaṇas, in which *dharma* functions primarily as a ritual category. We will then examine the hermeneutical strategies utilized in the Pūrva Mīmāṃsā philosophical school to legitimate the expansion of the domain of *dharma* beyond the ritual realm to encompass sociocultural practices. The major portion of the analysis will focus on the system of *varṇāśramadharma* that is elaborated in *smṛti* texts that are concerned with the science of *dharma*: the Dharmasūtras and Dharmaśāstras. We will then turn to a discussion of contending perspectives concerning the relationship between *dharma* and *mokṣa* (liberation), as represented in the Dharmaśāstras, renunciant traditions, and the *Bhagavad Gītā*. We will conclude our analysis with a brief discussion of the ways in which the category of *dharma* has been reformulated by modern Hindu thinkers.

VEDIC COSMOLOGY: ṚTA, DHARMA, AND YAJÑA

In Vedic cosmology, as represented in the Saṃhitās and the Brāhmaṇas, the cosmic order is a complex system that encompasses four distinct yet interconnected orders of reality: the natural order (*adhibhūta*), divine order (*adhidaiva*), human order (*adhyātma*), and sacrificial order (*adhiyajña*). In the early Vedic period the cosmic ordering principle that regulates and coordinates the various orders of reality is termed *ṛta*, with the term "*dharma*" or "*dharman*" used primarily in the plural to refer to the ordinances and sacrificial rituals that uphold the cosmic order. *Dharma* is thus closely connected in early Vedic texts with the *yajña*, the Vedic fire sacrifice. In order to understand the Vedic antecedents of post-Vedic constructions of *dharma*, we will briefly consider the roles and interrelations of these three categories: *ṛta*, *dharma*, and *yajña*.

Ṛta and dharma

In the *Ṛg Veda Saṃhitā* (*c.*1500–1200 BCE), the earliest and most authoritative of the Vedic texts, *ṛta* is the principle of cosmic order that ensures the integrated functioning of the natural order, divine order, human order, and sacrificial order. As the regulative principle of the natural order, *ṛta* governs the movements of the sun, moon, and stars, the rhythms of the seasons, and the cycles of day and night. *Ṛta* is the power of natural law that causes the rains to fall, the rivers to flow, and the sun to send forth its light. *Ṛta* also operates in the divine order as that power which the gods harness in order to perform their respective functions in administering and maintaining the cosmic order. *Ṛta* is also the governing principle of the human order—and more specifically the moral order—regulating the moral conduct of human beings. Finally, *ṛta* finds expression in the sacrificial order, determining the ordered course of the sacrificial rituals that is essential for the maintenance of the cosmos.[2] William Mahony remarks concerning the integrative power of this cosmic ordering principle:

> Vedic sages . . . understood Ṛta to be the inherent universal principle of balance and concord, a dynamic rule or order in which all things contribute in their own unique way to the smooth running of the cosmos as a whole. If they were aligned with Ṛta,

therefore, all things would be true to their own given nature and, in so doing, would properly express their particular function in that intricate and delicately aligned system of order. As the source of the inner integrity of all things and as the foundation of cosmic order, Ṛta was seen by Vedic poets to be inherent in or expressed by all things in the structured universe.

(1998: 48)

In the *Ṛg Veda*, *dharma* is explicitly connected with *ṛta* in a number of contexts (5.15.2, 5.51.2, 5.63.1, 5.63.7, 9.7.1, 9.110.4). While *ṛta* is used as the overarching term for the cosmic order, *dharma* is used to refer to the "upholding of *ṛta*" (*ṛtasya dharman*) (*Ṛg Veda* 9.7.1, 9.110.4) and in its plural form designates more specifically the ordinances and sacrificial rituals that maintain the cosmic order. *Dharma* is "the continuous *maintaining* of the social and cosmic order and norm which is achieved by the Aryan through the performance of his Vedic rites and traditional duties" (Halbfass 1988: 315–16; emphasis in original). In its role in upholding the cosmic order, *dharma* is closely associated in the *Ṛg Veda* with *satya*, truth, and the expression *satyadharman* is used as an epithet to praise a number of different gods "whose ordinances are true" (1.12.7, 5.51.2, 5.63.1, 10.34.8). *Dharma* is connected in particular with the special guardians of *ṛta*, the god Varuṇa and his divine counterpart Mitra, who govern the course of nature and oversee the moral order of human beings by means of *ṛta* (*Ṛg Veda* 5.63.1, 5.63.7, 6.70.1, 7.89.5, 10.65.5). In *Ṛg Veda* 5.63, Mitra and Varuṇa are celebrated as ruling over the entire cosmos by means of *ṛta* in conjunction with *dharma*: "O guardians of *ṛta*, you whose ordinances are true (*satyadharman*), you ascend your chariot in the highest heavens. . . . Wise Mitra and Varuṇa, by means of *dharman* and your divine power (*māyā*) you guard the ordinances (*vrata*). You govern the entire world by means of *ṛta*. You placed the sun in the heavens as an effulgent chariot" (vv. 1, 7).

In the Yajur Veda Saṃhitās (*c.*900 BCE) and the Brāhmaṇas (*c.*900–650 BCE), the sacrificial manuals attached to the Saṃhitās, the term "*dharma*" continues to be closely associated with Mitra and Varuṇa and is increasingly connected in this context with the king, who represents the human counterpart of the divine ruler Varuṇa.[3]

Dharma and yajña

In the early Vedic period the term "*dharma*" often occurs in connection with the *yajña*, the Vedic fire sacrifice, and the plural form *dharma*s is used in this context to designate the sacrificial ordinances and rituals. *Dharma* is thus associated not only with Mitra and Varuṇa but also with two gods who assume a central role in the *yajña*: Agni, who is embodied in the fire that conveys the sacrificial oblations to the gods, and Soma, who is embodied in the *soma* plant whose juice is extracted and used as the principal oblation in the Soma sacrifice. Agni is celebrated as *satyadharman*, "he whose ordinances are true," and as the guardian (*adhyakṣa*) of *dharma*s, who, when kindled, ensures the efficacy of the sacrificial rituals (*dharma*) (*Ṛg Veda* 1.12.7, 8.43.24, 5.26.6, 3.17.1, 5.15.2). Soma is associated in particular with *dharma*'s role in upholding the cosmic order, *ṛta* (*ṛtasya dharman*) (*Ṛg Veda* 9.7.1, 9.110.4).

In Vedic cosmology, the *yajña* is ascribed the status of a separate order of reality (*adhiyajña*), which is correlated with the other orders of reality—the natural order (*adhibhūta*), divine order (*adhidaiva*), and human order (*adhyātma*)—and is considered essential to the harmonious functioning of all levels of the cosmos. *Dharma*, as an aspect of *yajña*, assumes an important role in generating and maintaining the orders of reality.[4] In order to understand the complex network of significations in which the categories of *dharma* and *yajña* are embedded, we need to examine more closely the theurgic role ascribed to the sacrificial order within the taxonomic framework of Vedic cosmology.

One of the earliest formulations of the Vedic model of reality is found in *Ṛg Veda* 10.90, the *Puruṣasūkta*, which is the *locus classicus* that connects *dharma* to the cosmos-generating activities of *yajña*. The body of *puruṣa*, the cosmic man who is the unitary source and basis of all existence, is represented as the primordial totality that encompasses and interconnects the orders of reality. The hymn depicts the primordial sacrifice, or *yajña*, by means of which the wholeness of *puruṣa*'s body is differentiated, the different parts of the divine anthropos giving rise to the different parts of the universe. Verses 6 to 10 establish a reciprocal relationship between the sacrificial and natural orders. On the one hand, certain elements of the natural order—the seasons—are used as ritual materials in the primordial sacrifice. On the other hand, the sacrifice gives rise to various aspects of the natural order and more specifically certain animals—horses, cattle, goats, and sheep—which are the principal offerings used in animal sacrifices. This reciprocity is also reflected within the elements of the sacrifice itself. The Vedic *mantra*s and meters are described as emerging from the sacrifice of *puruṣa*, and they in turn provide the sound offerings that are essential to the sacrificial ritual. Verses 11 to 14 go on to establish a series of correlations between the different parts of the body of *puruṣa* and the different aspects of the natural, divine, and human orders:

> When they divided *puruṣa*, into how many parts did they apportion him? What was his mouth? What were his arms? What were his thighs and feet declared to be? His mouth became the Brāhmaṇ; [from] his arms the Kṣatriya was made; his thighs became the Vaiśya; from his feet the Śūdra was born. The moon was born from his mind; from his eye Sūrya, the sun, was born; from his mouth came Indra and Agni, fire; from his breath Vāyu, wind, was born. From his navel arose the midregions; from his head heaven originated; from his feet came the earth; from his ear, the cardinal directions. Thus they fashioned the worlds.

The sacrifice, as the means by which the primordial wholeness of the divine body is differentiated, is represented in the *Puruṣasūkta* as the cosmogonic instrument that distinguishes and at the same time interconnects the components of the natural, divine, and human orders. The three principal sections of *puruṣa*'s body—head, navel, and feet—are correlated with the three worlds that constitute the cosmos—heaven, midregions, and earth. Specific parts of *puruṣa*'s psychophysiology—mouth, breath, eye, ear, and mind—are correlated with specific components of the natural order—fire, wind, sun, cardinal directions, and moon—as well as with specific deities that form a part of the divine order—Indra, Agni, Vāyu, and Sūrya.

The body of *puruṣa* also encompasses the human order, including not only the human body—which is the microcosmic counterpart of the divine anthropos—but also the social order. The *Puruṣasūkta* establishes homologies between particular parts of *puruṣa*'s corporeal form—mouth, arms, thighs, and feet—and particular social classes (*varṇa*)—Brāhmaṇs (priests), Kṣatriyas (kings and warriors), Vaiśyas (merchants, agriculturists, and artisans), and Śūdras (servants). The social order is thus re-presented as a primordial manifestation of the divine body that is part of the natural order of things. In this organic model the social body, like the body of the divine anthropos, is organized according to a hierarchical division of functions in which each part has its own separate function to perform that is vital to the efficient operation of the whole, and yet some parts inevitably perform more "exalted" tasks than others. Although the duties of the four social classes are not explicitly mentioned in the hymn, the imagery of the *Puruṣasūkta*, which correlates each *varṇa* with a specific body part, is invoked in later Vedic and post-Vedic texts to provide cosmic legitimation for the separation of functions among the *varṇa*s. The Brāhmaṇs, as the "head" of the social body, take the lead, supplying the organizing principles of intelligence and speech that direct the activities of the other members of the body. The Brāhmaṇs are the priestly class of scholar-teachers whose duty is to recite and teach the Vedas and to perform sacrifices. The Kṣatriyas, as the "arms" of society, exercise their physical prowess and the force of arms in order to rule and protect the people and to guard the safety of the country from internal dissension and foreign invasion. The Vaiśyas are the "legs" that are the sustaining power of society, securing the economic well being of the community through their activities in commerce, agriculture, and cattle-breeding. The Śūdras are the "feet" of the social body whose duty is to serve the three higher *varṇa*s.

The *Puruṣasūkta* thus celebrates the sacrifice, *yajña*, as the cosmogonic instrument that generates and structures the cosmic order, establishing the distinctions among the orders of reality and interconnecting them as correlated parts of the cosmic whole. The final verse of the *Puruṣasūkta* identifies this cosmos-producing *yajña* with "the first *dharma*s," the first sacrificial rituals, which provide the prototype for all future rituals. "With the sacrifice (*yajña*) the gods sacrificed (root *yaj*) the sacrifice (*yajña*). These were the first *dharma*s" (*Ṛg Veda* 10.90.16, cf. 10.90.6–7). The connection of "the first *dharma*s" with the sacrifice is emphasized elsewhere in the *Ṛg Veda* (1.164.50, 1.164.43, 3.17.1). *Ṛg Veda* 1.164, for example, interweaves through its enigmatic riddles "the first *dharma*s," *yajña*, and *ṛta* (vv. 50, 43, 35, 8, 11, 37, 47). *Atharva Veda* 7.5.1 similarly identifies the primordial sacrifice with "the first *dharma*s," invoking the language of the *Puruṣasūkta*.

The sacrificial discourse of the Brāhmaṇas, building upon the speculations of the *Puruṣasūkta*, provides elaborate taxonomies to demonstrate the theurgic power of the sacrificial order—and the *dharma*s that constitute it—as the instrument that structures and maintains the cosmos through enlivening the inherent connections (*bandhu*) among the natural order, divine order, and human order. As Brian K. Smith has emphasized, this system of *bandhus* is founded on the Vedic principle of "hierarchical resemblance," which as a "central principle of Vedism" (1989: 78) encapsulates the "ancient Indian notion that the universe was composed of mutually resembling and interconnected, but also hierarchically distinguished and ranked, components" (1994: vii). The connections among the various components of the cosmic order operate on two axes: vertical and horizontal.

> Vedic connections are of two sorts: what we might call vertical and horizontal correspondences. The former connects an immanent form and its transcendent correlative. . . . This type of connection operates between the elements of the same species located on different and hierarchically ranked cosmological levels. Horizontal connections link resembling components of . . . different species located within the same cosmological plane which share a similar hierarchical position within their respective classes.
>
> (B. Smith 1989: 73)

This system of *bandhus* is elaborated in the Brāhmaṇas in complex, multileveled taxonomies that, building on the classificatory schemas of the Saṃhitās, establish homologies among the various categories of existence—gods, worlds, time and space, natural elements and forces, animals, plants, psychophysical components, social classes, ritual elements, and so on (see Holdrege 1996: 43–62; B. Smith 1994). The sacrifice is represented in the Brāhmaṇas not only as the means of mediating the connections among the orders of reality but also as the means of constituting these orders. The sacrificial order serves as the cosmogonic instrument by means of which the creator Prajāpati—who is identified with *puruṣa*—structures an ordered cosmos in which the natural world, the divine order of the gods, and the human realm function as interconnected planes of existence. On the divine plane, the sacrifice serves more specifically as the theogonic instrument through which Prajāpati himself, who is disintegrated and dissipated by his creative efforts, is reconstituted and restored to a state of wholeness. On the human plane, the sacrifice functions as the anthropogonic instrument through which the defective human being produced through biological reproduction is born anew out of the ritual womb and reconstituted through ritual labor. The sacrifice also serves as the sociogonic instrument that constructs and maintains the social order as a hierarchy differentiated according to social class (*varṇa*) and gender (see Holdrege 1998: 349–57; B. Smith 1989: 50–119).

In the taxonomic schemas of the Brāhmaṇas, the various aspects of the natural, divine, and human orders—the flora and fauna of the natural world, the hierarchy of gods, and the components of the human psychophysiology—are correlated with categories that are integral to the distinctive ethnocultural identity of the Āryan people—the *varṇa*s, the Vedic *mantra*s and meters, and the components of the Vedic sacrifice (see Holdrege 1996: 43–62; B. Smith 1994). The Āryan socioreligious system—including the *varṇa* system, the Vedic recitative tradition, and the Vedic sacrificial tradition—is thus presented as replicating the structure of the cosmic order in the social sphere. The Brāhmaṇ priests, in their preeminent position at the top of the social hierarchy, are represented in this context as the custodians of the cosmic order, who ensure the harmonious functioning of the cosmos through their periodic recitation of the Vedic *mantra*s and performance of the sacrificial rituals. They are portrayed as the earthly counterparts of the creator Prajāpati, who periodically reenact the primordial sacrifice and the cosmos-producing activities of "the first *dharma*s" as a means of regenerating and maintaining the cosmic order. "Prajāpati indeed is that sacrifice (*yajña*) which is being performed here and from which these beings were produced, and in the same manner are they produced thereafter even to the present day."[5]

PŪRVA MĪMĀṂSĀ HERMENEUTICS: FROM SACRIFICIAL RITUAL TO SOCIOCULTURAL PRACTICE

From the third century BCE onward, the category of *dharma* underwent several important transformations. First, the term "*dharma*" was invested with ontological significance and superseded *ṛta* as the encompassing term for the cosmic ordering principle. Second, as a normative principle comprising those specific modes of activity that uphold the cosmic order, the term "*dharma*" was extended beyond the ritual realm to include not only sacrificial rituals but also sociocultural practices. Third, the term was used more specifically to designate the totality of ritual and social duties that constitutes the Brāhmaṇical system of *varṇāśramadharma*, which is represented as the paradigmatic social order that instantiates the cosmic order on the social plane. This extension of the domain of *dharma* appears to have served as one of the mechanisms adopted by orthodox exponents of the Brāhmaṇical tradition to respond to the challenge posed by the expansion of Buddhist traditions under the emperor Aśoka in the third century BCE. Patrick Olivelle (2000) has suggested that Brāhmaṇical authorities sought to accommodate and domesticate Buddhist reformulations of *dharma* by generating a new genre of literature—the Dharmasūtras—that reflected an expanded understanding of the term.[6]

As part of the Brāhmaṇical response to the Buddhist critique, the Pūrva Mīmāṃsā philosophical school developed a number of discursive strategies to legitimate the extension of the domain of *dharma* from the ritual to the sociocultural realm. The central focus of Pūrva Mīmāṃsā, as a school of Vedic exegesis, is the investigation of *dharma* as enjoined in the Vedas. The foundations of the Mīmāṃsā philosophy of *dharma* are established in the *Pūrva Mīmāṃsāsūtra* (*c.*300–200 BCE), attributed to the sage Jaimini. Mīmāṃsaka perspectives on *dharma* are further explained and elaborated in the earliest known commentary on the *Pūrva Mīmāṃsāsūtra* by Śabara, the *Śābarabhāṣya* (*c.*200 CE). Śabara's *Bhāṣya* was in turn commented on by Kumārila Bhaṭṭa (seventh century CE) and Prabhākara (seventh century CE), from whom two divergent subschools of Mīmāṃsā philosophy developed.

Veda and dharma

In their investigations of *dharma*, the Mīmāṃsakas focus on the *karmakāṇḍa*, the section of the Vedas pertaining to action, and they are thus primarily concerned with the injunctive (*vidhāyaka*) statements regarding *dharma* contained in the Brāhmaṇas. In early Mīmāṃsā the term "*dharma*" is confined to the ritual sphere and refers more specifically to the sacrificial rituals that are enjoined in the Vedas. *Dharma* is defined in the *Pūrva Mīmāṃsāsūtra* as "that human good (*artha*) which is defined by Vedic injunction (*codanā*)" (1.1.2). In his commentary on this verse, Śabara remarks that those persons may be considered *dhārmika* who perform sacrificial rituals (*yāga*), and he invokes as a proof text the final verse of the *Puruṣasūkta*, *Ṛg Veda* 10.90.16, which identifies the primordial sacrifice with the "first *dharma*s" (*Śābarabhāṣya* 1.1.2, pp. 17.11–18.5). Elsewhere Śabara identifies *dharma* with Vedic rites such as the *agnihotra*, the daily fire sacrifice (*Śābarabhāṣya* 1.1.5, p.23.5).

One of the fundamental axioms of the Mīmāṃsā philosophical project is that *dharma* is transcendent in that the sacrificial rituals that are designated as *dharma* are not instrumental, utilitarian actions whose purpose is self-evident (*dṛṣṭārtha*), but rather they are actions whose purpose is not evident (*adṛṣṭārtha*) and that produce invisible effects. Because *dharma* is transcendent in nature, it can only be known through an authoritative source of knowledge (*pramāṇa*) that is itself transcendent. In their expositions of *dharma* the Mīmāṃsakas are thus concerned to demonstrate the intrinsic authority and infallibility of the Vedas as the only transcendent source of knowledge of *dharma*. In this context they developed three major doctrines concerning the nature and status of Veda: the Vedas are not derived from any personal agent, human or divine (*vedāpauruṣeyatva*); the Vedas are eternal and without beginning (*vedānādinityatva*); and the Vedas are a valid means of correct knowledge concerning *dharma* (*vedaprāmāṇya*). In order to prove that the Vedic statements are eternal, uncreated, and authoritative sources of *dharma*-knowledge, the Mīmāṃsakas developed an elaborate philosophy of language regarding the nature of *śabda*, word. They are concerned in particular to prove the eternality of *śabda* and to establish that in the case of Vedic words there is an inherent, eternal connection between the word (*śabda*) and its meaning (*artha*), between the name and the form that it signifies. *Pūrva Mīmāṃsāsūtra* 1.1.5 provides the cornerstone of the Mīmāṃsakas' arguments regarding the uncreated status, infallibility, and transcendent authority of the Vedas as a source of knowledge about *dharma*: "The connection (*sambandha*) of the word (*śabda*) with its meaning (*artha*) is inherent (*autpattika*). Instruction is the means of knowing it [*dharma*], and it is infallible with regard to imperceptible things. It is a valid means of knowledge (*pramāṇa*) . . . as it is independent."[7]

The Mīmāṃsakas, in their concern to ground the transcendent *dharma* in the transcendent authority of the eternal, uncreated Vedas, would appear to present a claim to universal knowledge. However, they use a variety of strategies to circumscribe *dharma* and bind it linguistically, ethnically, and culturally to a specific people: the Āryans, the inhabitants of Āryāvarta,[8] who are the custodians of the Vedas. In their speculations concerning the nature of language, the Mīmāṃsakas distinguish between Vedic language (*vedavacana*) and ordinary human language (*laukikavacana*). They are first and foremost concerned with Vedic Sanskrit, the language of the Vedas and the language of *dharma*. They are not concerned with languages and usages different from the Vedic language, for such languages are not considered to have the eternal, uncreated status of *vedavacana* and therefore cannot serve as valid sources of knowledge about *dharma*. The Āryans alone are designated as the authoritative exponents of *dharma*, for they alone are the custodians of the eternal Veda and of the eternal language, Sanskrit, in which the injunctions concerning *dharma* are recorded. Kumārila declares: "The knowledge of the inhabitants of Āryāvarta is considered authoritative with respect to words and their meanings concerning *dharma* and its branches, since they are grounded in the [Vedic] scriptures" (*Tantravārttika*, p. 220.3–4).

In the Mīmāṃsā philosophical project *dharma* is thus upheld as the emblem of Āryan ethnocultural identity that distinguishes the Āryans from the non-Āryans, who are deemed *mleccha*s, "barbarians." The transcendent *dharma* becomes embodied in the particularities of ethnocultural categories defined in relation to a particular people (Āryans), a particular land (Āryāvarta), a particular language (Vedic Sanskrit), a particular corpus of sacred texts (Vedas), and a particular set of ritual practices (Vedic sacrificial rituals).[9]

Expansion of the domain of dharma

In early Mīmāṃsā the categories of Veda and *dharma* were both confined to the ritual sphere, and the *vaidika* ritual realm was clearly distinguished from the *laukika* nonritual realm. Sheldon Pollock (1990) has highlighted a number of interrelated hermeneutical strategies that the Mīmāṃsakas utilized in order to extend Vedic legitimation beyond the ritual realm into the sociocultural domain and thereby transform the ideological framework of Brāhmaṇical culture from a discourse of ritual to a discourse of social power.

First, Vedic legitimation, which originally applied only to ritual injunctions, was extended to sociocultural norms and traditions. In later Mīmāṃsā the boundaries between noninstrumental (*adṛṣṭārtha*) ritual rules and utilitarian (*dṛṣṭārtha*) sociocultural norms became permeable, allowing for the extension of Vedic legitimation to an ever-expanding corpus of śāstric injunctions in every sphere of Brāhmaṇical culture (Pollock 1990: 318–22).

Second, Vedic legitimation was extended to reformulations of *dharma* that expanded the term beyond the realm of ritual action to encompass sociocultural practices. This expansion of the term serves to resolve the "paradox of the *dharma*'s foundation in the Vedas" posed by J. C. Heesterman (1978: 92), who asserts that there is an insurmountable gap between Veda and *dharma*, between the transcendent order of *śruti* and the actualities of the mundane social world that are the domain of *dharma* (1985: 11, 82–83). Contrary to Heesterman's assertion, *dharma* does indeed have its foundation in the Vedas, but, as discussed earlier, the term was generally restricted to the ritual realm in the Vedic period. The gap was thus not between Veda and *dharma* but between *dharma* and the social world, and it was only by expanding the purview of *dharma* to include sociocultural practices that this gap was bridged.

Third, the domain of Veda was expanded to include not only *śruti* texts but also *smṛti* texts such as the Dharmaśāstras in which the regulations of the *varṇāśramadharma* system are elaborated. Pollock locates the mechanism through which this expansion occurred in the definitions of the terms "*śruti*" and "*smṛti*" themselves, which he argues have been incorrectly construed as representing a dichotomy between "revelation" and "tradition." He maintains rather that, according to the etymology derived from Mīmāṃsā that is still prevalent among certain traditional Brāhmaṇical teachers, *śruti* refers to the extant Vedic texts that can be "heard" in recitation, whereas *smṛti* is an open-ended category that encompasses any teachings or practices pertaining to *dharma* that have been "remembered" from Vedic texts that are lost, forgotten, or otherwise inaccessible. The meaning of the term "Veda" is thus extended beyond the circumscribed boundaries of the *śruti* texts—Saṃhitās, Brāhmaṇas, Āraṇyakas, and Upaniṣads—and through a process of "Vedacization" comes to include within its purview not only the Vedāṅgas, Dharmaśāstras, epics, and Purāṇas but potentially all śāstric teachings—enshrined in practices as well as texts—that are promulgated by Brāhmaṇical authorities (Pollock 1990: 322–28).

DHARMAŚĀSTRA: VARṆĀŚRAMADHARMA AND ĀRYAN ETHNOCULTURAL IDENTITY

While the Mīmāṃsakas developed hermeneutical strategies to legitimate the extension of the domains of *dharma* and Veda from the ritual to the sociocultural realm, it is the Brāhmaṇical exponents of Dharmaśāstra, the science of *dharma*, who were responsible for the articulation of a formalized system of ritual and sociocultural norms. The science of *dharma* is founded on two parallel systems: the system of *varṇa*s—Brāhmaṇs, Kṣatriyas, Vaiśyas, and Śūdras—and the system of *āśrama*s—student, householder, forest-dweller, and renunciant. These two systems are interwoven in *varṇāśramadharma*, which serves as the encompassing term for the ritual and social duties that are incumbent on male members of the social classes (*varṇa*) at different stages of their lives (*āśrama*).

The importance of *varṇāśramadharma* as a pivotal category of Hindu identity has been emphasized by both Western and Indian scholars. G. S. Ghurye remarks that "even now

Varṇāśramadharma, duties of castes and āśramas, is almost another name for Hinduism" (1964: 2). The pervasive and enduring power of the *varṇāśramadharma* system operates primarily at the level of discourse, and therefore the ideological representations of this sociocultural system in the Dharmaśāstra literature do not necessarily correspond to the historical actualities of the social institutions that the system purports to encompass. The idealized *varṇa* system of four social classes is not sufficient to account for the messy actualities of the innumerable castes (*jāti*), just as the idealized *āśrama* system is not coextensive with the social institutions that it seeks to classify and regulate (see Olivelle 1993: 24–30). Nevertheless, the discourse of *varṇāśramadharma* has functioned historically as a powerful tool of ideological persuasion that has served to legitimate and perpetuate asymmetrical relations of power in traditional Hindu society.

Dharmaśāstra literature

The discourse of *dharma* is elaborated in four principal genres of Dharmaśāstra literature: the Dharmasūtras, Dharmaśāstras, commentaries (*bhāṣya*, *vṛtti*, *vyākhyā*, *vivaraṇa*), and Nibandhas (digests).[10]

The Dharmasūtras (third to first centuries BCE) form the last section of the Kalpasūtras, one of the six Vedāṅgas, or subsidiary "limbs of the Vedas." The other two sections of the Kalpasūtras are concerned with ritual practices: the Śrautasūtras give detailed instructions for the performance of public Vedic (*śrauta*) sacrifices, while the Gṛhyasūtras are concerned with the domestic (*gṛhya*) rituals that regulate various aspects of householder life. In the Dharmasūtras the focus shifts from an exclusive focus on ritual matters to a broader concern with *dharma*, which is reformulated in this new genre of literature as an encompassing term for ritual, social, and moral norms. These short treatises, written in aphoristic prose or in prose interspersed with verse, are primarily concerned with the rules of conduct (*ācāra*) that regulate the *varṇa*s and *āśrama*s.[11] In addition, they lay out a system of penances (*prāyaścitta*) for infractions of *dharma*. The primary focus of the Dharmasūtras is on religious law, with less emphasis on matters of civil and criminal law. The four extant Dharmasūtras are the *Āpastamba*, *Gautama*, *Baudhāyana*, and *Vasiṣṭha*.[12]

In the early centuries of the Common Era the ritual and social obligations of *varṇāśramadharma* were further crystallized and expanded in the form of elaborate law codes, the Dharmaśāstras, which differ from the Dharmasūtras in origin, form, and content. While the Dharmasūtras originated as part of the Kalpasūtras belonging to the various Vedic schools (*śākhā*), the Dharmaśāstras derive from special schools of *dharma* that were not attached to particular Vedic schools but rather were concerned with expounding a science of *dharma* that was authoritative for all Āryans. With respect to form, in contrast to the elliptical prose of the Dharmasūtras, the Dharmaśāstras are much more extensive treatises written entirely in verse. With respect to content, the Dharmaśāstras cover the same topics as the Dharmasūtras, but they expand the scope of *dharma* to include more emphasis on civil and criminal law. In the Dharmaśāstras, the science of *dharma* is elaborated in three main branches: *ācāra*, the rules of conduct that constitute *varṇāśramadharma*; *prāyaścitta*, the system of penances prescribed for violations of *dharma*; and *vyavahāra*, regulations concerning the administration of justice that form part of *rājadharma*, the duties of the king. While *ācāra* and *prāyaścitta* are also treated in the Dharmasūtras, the Dharmaśāstras go beyond the *sūtra*s in their emphasis on regulations of a juridical nature, *vyavahāra*. By far the most celebrated of the Dharmaśāstras is the *Mānava Dharmaśāstra*, or *Manusmṛti* (first to second centuries CE). The *Yājñavalkyasmṛti* (third to fourth centuries CE) has also attained prominence for its systematic presentation of the discourse of *dharma*.

At the end of the period of the Dharmaśāstras, in the ninth century CE, two new types of Dharmaśāstra literature arose: commentaries and Nibandhas (digests). The commentaries are concerned with one particular Dharmaśāstra or Dharmasūtra, which they attempt to elucidate through explaining terms and construing difficult passages. There are at least seven extant commentaries on the *Manusmṛti*, among the most important of which are those of Medhātithi (ninth century CE) and Kullūka (thirteenth century CE). Of the five commentaries on the *Yājñavalkyasmṛti*, the most celebrated is the Mitākṣarā of Vijñāneśvara (eleventh century CE). Although commentaries continued to be written as late as the nineteenth century, digests became the preferred form from the twelfth century onward. These digests, or Nibandhas, gather together extracts from a vast number of *dharma* sources—including not only the Dharmasūtras and Dharmaśāstras but also the epics and Purāṇas—and classify them systematically according to topic. The authors of the Nibandhas also comment on their citations, clarifying obscure terms and passages and attempting to resolve apparent conflicts in order to establish definitive rules for proper conduct in every sphere of life. The *Kṛtyakalpataru* of Lakṣmīdhara (twelfth century CE) and the *Smṛticandrikā* of Devaṇṇabhaṭṭa (*c.*1200 CE) are among the most important of the Nibandhas. A number of the Nibandhas and commentaries assumed a legal status in British India and were frequently referred to in Anglo-Indian courts and subsequently by the jurists of independent India.

Epics and Purāṇas

Beyond the formal genres of Dharmaśāstra literature, the two great Sanskrit epics—the *Mahābhārata* and the *Rāmāyaṇa* of Vālmīki—and the Purāṇas are included among the *smṛti* texts that constitute sources of *dharma*. The epics and Purāṇas, which have been rightfully deemed the "encyclopedias of Hinduism" because of their all-encompassing character, contain a diverse array of didactic material, ranging from exemplary narratives to myths and legends to formal discourses on the topics of Dharmaśāstra.

The core narrative of the *Mahābhārata* (*c.*400 BCE–400 CE) recounts the great war between the Pāṇḍavas and the Kauravas on the battlefield of Kurukṣetra, "the field of *dharma*." The central narrative presents a series of moral dilemmas to which three responses are generally given: that of Yudhiṣṭhira, who embodies absolute adherence to *dharma*; that of Bhīma, who embodies brute force; and that of Arjuna, who assumes an intermediate position, embodying courage, strength, and discipline. The central narrative is embedded in a densely textured, multilayered textual repository that is rich in gnomic and didactic material, including ancient bardic poetry, myths and legends, fables and parables, and formal discourses on the ritual and social duties of *varṇāśramadharma*. The *Bhagavad Gītā*, which forms the third episode of the *Bhīṣmaparvan* in the *Mahābhārata*, presents the classic statement of the central importance of *dharma* on the path to salvation, as will be discussed in a later section.

The *Rāmāyaṇa* of Vālmīki (*c.*200 BCE–200 CE) recounts the story of Rāma, the paradigmatic divine-human king, who rescues his wife, Sītā, from the demon Rāvaṇa and establishes Rāmarājya, the "rule of Rāma," as the reign of *dharma*. Traditional Dharmaśāstra material, ranging from the duties of kings to the *dharma* of women, is interspersed throughout the central narrative. However, the significance of the *Rāmāyaṇa* as a source of *dharma* is primarily in its role as an exemplary narrative, in which the central protagonists are depicted as paragons of virtue who continually grapple with the conflicting demands of *dharma*. Rāma is represented as the perfect embodiment of *dharma*, who is willing to sacrifice everything in order to uphold the norms of correct sociopolitical behavior. Sītā is portrayed as the paradigm of the devoted wife, whose inviolable purity and unconditional devotion to her husband are celebrated as the quintessential expression of *strīdharma*.

The Purāṇas (*c.*300–1000 CE and after), according to the classical Hindu definition, are distinguished by five characteristics (*pañcalakṣana*): descriptions of creation (*sarga*) and re-creation (*pratisarga*) of the universe after its periodic dissolutions; genealogies of gods, sages, and kings (*vaṃśa*); accounts of the ages of Manu (*manvantara*); and histories of the royal dynasties (*vaṃśānucarita*). The Purāṇas are considered to be "ancient (*purāṇa*) histories" that assume the role of exemplary narratives, in which not only the protagonists—gods, kings, and sages—but also certain periods of history become paradigmatic. The Purāṇas are extolled among the sources of *dharma* and are frequently cited in the Nibandhas, containing large sections on *ācāra*, the rules of conduct that constitute *varṇāśramadharma*, and on *prāyaścitta*, penances for violations of *dharma*. Beyond this traditional Dharmaśāstra material, the Purāṇas emphasize certain popular devotional practices that are ascribed dharmic efficacy and that can be performed not only by male members of the three higher *varṇa*s but also by Śūdras and women,[13] such as *pūjā* ceremonies centered on ritual offerings to deities embodied in images, pilgrimages to sacred places (*tīrtha*), giving of gifts (*dāna*), and vows (*vrata*).

Sources of dharma

The exponents of Dharmaśāstra distinguish three principal sources (*mūla*) of *dharma*: *śruti*, the Vedas; *smṛti*; and *sadācāra* or *śiṣṭācāra*, the conduct of people who are virtuous (*sat*) and learned (*śiṣṭa*). While the Dharmasūtras uphold this threefold model (*Gautama* 1.1–2; *Baudhāyana* 1.1.1–6; *Vasiṣṭha* 1.4–6; cf. *Āpastamba* 1.1.1–3), the *Manusmṛti* and *Yājñavalkyasmṛti* add a fourth source: that which satisfies the self (*ātmatuṣṭi*, *priyam ātmanaḥ*). "The Veda, *smṛti*, the conduct of good people (*sadācāra*), and that which is pleasing to oneself (*svasya priyam ātmanaḥ*)—they declare this explicitly to be the fourfold means of defining *dharma*" (*Manusmṛti* 2.12, cf. 2.6; *Yājñavalkyasmṛti* 1.7).

In the Dharmasūtras and Dharmaśāstras the supreme source of *dharma* is *śruti*, the eternal Vedas, and acceptance of the transcendent authority of the Vedas is the primary criterion for distinguishing orthodox from heterodox traditions. The *Manusmṛti* (12.95–96, cf. 2.10–11) declares that any tradition or philosophy that is not based on the Vedas is worthless and untrue (*anṛta*) and produces no reward after death. While traditions that are not based on the Vedas arise and pass away, the Vedas are eternal (*sanātana*), beyond human power (*aśakya*) and beyond measure (*aprameya*) (*Manusmṛti* 12.94–96, 12.99, 1.23). According to the *Manusmṛti*, the eternal Vedas, unaffected by the ebb and flow of time, are drawn forth by the creator at the beginning of each new cycle of creation and serve as the archetypal blueprint that he employs in order to assign each class of beings its respective name, nature, and function. "In the beginning he [the creator] formed from the words of the Vedas alone the particular names, activities, and conditions of all [beings]" (*Manusmṛti* 1.21, cf. 1.28–30). The Vedas are thus represented as participating in the ontological function of *dharma* as the cosmic ordering principle that allots specific functions to the various class of beings in accordance with their respective natures. The Vedas are also represented as the source of the normative manifestation of *dharma* in the social order—the *varṇāśramadharma* system—which is described as emerging from the cosmic blueprint along with the three worlds and all beings. "The four social classes (*varṇa*), the three worlds, the four stages of life (*āśrama*), the past, the present, and the future are all severally brought about through the Veda. Sound, touch, form, taste, and, fifth, smell are produced from the Veda alone, together with their products, qualities, and activities. The eternal Vedaśāstra sustains all beings. Therefore, I regard it as the supreme means of fulfillment for these beings" (*Manusmṛti* 12.97–99).[14]

The Vedas are thus represented as the source of *dharma* both in its ontological function as the cosmic ordering principle and in its normative function as the social order. The Vedas are also considered the ultimate source of all the specific rules of *dharma* delineated in the Dharmasūtras and Dharmaśāstras. In this latter claim, however, the exponents of the Brāhmaṇical discourse of *dharma* were confronted with the problem of discontinuity between the content of the *śruti* texts, which are primarily concerned with sacrificial rituals, and the content of the *smṛti* texts, which are concerned with sociocultural practices. The *Āpastamba Dharmasūtra*, one of the earliest of the Dharmasūtras, proposes a hermeneutical principle that seeks to resolve this problem: since all rules of *dharma* have their source in the Vedas, if the basis for a particular practice cannot be located in an extant Vedic text, then it must be inferred that the practice derives from a lost Vedic text. A distinction is thus made between "explicit *śruti* texts" (*pratyakṣaśruti*), which are the extant Vedic texts preserved by the Brāhmaṇical recitative tradition, and "inferred Vedic texts" (*anumitaśruti*), which are Vedic texts that are inferred to have once existed but have subsequently been lost (see *Āpastamba* 1.4.8, 1.12.10–11; Olivelle 1999: xli).

This theory of the lost Vedas, which was promulgated by both the exponents of Dharmaśāstra and the Mīmāṃsakas, served as a pivotal hermeneutical strategy for bridging the gap between *śruti*, as the supreme source of *dharma* teachings, and *smṛti*, as a secondary source for ascertaining *dharma*. The term "*smṛti*" can be understood in three distinct senses in this context. First, as discussed earlier, *smṛti* is used as an encompassing term for those authoritative Brāhmaṇical texts that are held to have been composed by personal authors and are "that which was remembered" (*smṛti*) as distinct from "that which was heard" (*śruti*): the Vedāṅgas (including the Dharmasūtras), Dharmaśāstras, epics, and Purāṇas. Second, the term "*smṛti*" is used more specifically to refer to those texts that are concerned with the science of *dharma*: the Dharmasūtras and Dharmaśāstras. Third, in the Mīmāṃsaka rendering of the theory of the lost Vedas, as we have seen, *smṛti* functions as an open-ended category that includes any teachings or practices pertaining to *dharma* that have been "remembered" from Vedic texts that are lost or otherwise inaccessible. This third sense of the term provided an effective hermeneutical device through which commentators on the Dharmasūtras and the Dharmaśāstras sought to resolve conflicts between the rules of *dharma* found in *śruti* and *smṛti* texts. Certain commentators, following the Mīmāṃsaka interpretations of Kumārila, maintained that all *smṛti* teachings ultimately derive from the Vedas—whether from extant Vedic texts or from Vedic texts that are not accessible. Therefore, if there is a conflict between the injunctions of *śruti* and *smṛti* and no reconciliation is possible, it is permissible to choose between the injunctions, since both are ultimately Vedic in origin (see Kane 1968–77, 3: 833–35). All *smṛti* teachings are thus ascribed Vedic authority, and the gap between *śruti* and *smṛti* is overcome.

In addition to the theory of the lost Vedas, the Dharmaśāstras use various mechanisms to invest *smṛti* teachings concerning *dharma* with the transcendent authority of the Vedas. The *Manusmṛti* attempts to elevate its teachings to the status of *śruti* in three ways. First, the text claims that "whatever duty (*dharma*) has been proclaimed for anyone by Manu has been fully declared in the Veda," for the sage Manu was omniscient (*sarvajñānamaya*) and thus by implication had direct access to the eternal knowledge of the Vedas (*Manusmṛti* 2.7). Second, the text elevates Manu to the status of the supreme *ṛṣi*, or seer, who emerged from the self-existent (*svayambhū*) in the beginning of creation as the progenitor of the human race and himself brought forth the ten great *ṛṣi*s who served as the lords of created beings (*Manusmṛti* 1.102, 1.33–35). Third, the text grants Manu's teachings the status of divine revelation: just as the Vedic *ṛṣi*s obtained their cognitions of the Vedas through the practice of *tapas*,[15] so the creator brought forth the *smṛti* teachings through *tapas* and taught them directly to Manu, who in turn taught them to the *ṛṣi*s (*Manusmṛti* 11.244, 1.58, cf. 9.46).

According to the hierarchy of sources of *dharma* delineated in the Dharmasūtras and Dharmaśāstras, if a problem pertaining to *dharma* arises that is not explicitly addressed in either *śruti* or *smṛti* texts, then one may have recourse to the third source of *dharma* teachings: the conduct of people who are virtuous and learned (*sadācāra*, *śiṣṭācāra*). The Dharmasūtras specify four principal criteria that distinguish those people who are paradigmatic exemplars and authoritative exponents of *dharma*: such people are Āryans (*Āpastamba* 1.20.7–8, 2.29.14) who are inhabitants of Āryāvarta (*Baudhāyana* 1.2.9–12; *Vasiṣṭha* 1.8–15), who have a profound knowledge of the Vedas (*Gautama* 1.2, 6.21–22, 9.62, 28.48–51; *Baudhāyana* 1.1.6–8, 1.1.13; *Vasiṣṭha* 1.16, 6.43, cf. 3.20), and who are virtuous and free from vices such as desire, anger, pride, greed, and envy (*Gautama* 9.62; *Baudhāyana* 1.1.5; *Vasiṣṭha* 1.6). The *Āpastamba Dharmasūtra* declares: "That activity which the Āryans praise is *dharma*; that which they censure is *adharma*. One should model his conduct in accordance with that conduct which is unanimously approved in all regions by Āryans who are well-trained, elderly, self-possessed, and free of greed and deceit" (1.20.7–8, 2.29.14).

The *Manusmṛti* builds on the Dharmasūtras' characterizations of those virtuous (*sat*) and learned (*śiṣṭa*) people whose conduct and teachings may serve as exemplary sources of *dharma*. The text defines the conduct of the good (*sadācāra*) as that code of conduct which has been passed down by Āryan upholders of the *varṇa* system who dwell in Āryāvarta and more specifically in Brahmāvarta, an especially sacred region within Āryāvarta that is held to have been created by the gods (*Manusmṛti* 2.17–24).[16] The concluding section of the *Manusmṛti* indicates that in the case of issues of *dharma* that it has not explicitly addressed, such issues shall be determined by learned men, *śiṣṭas*. *Śiṣṭa*s are defined as Brāhmaṇ priests who, in accordance with *dharma*, have mastered the Vedas together with their supplements and who faithfully perform their allotted duties (*Manusmṛti* 12.108–14). "That which even a single Brāhmaṇ who knows the Veda (*vedavid*) declares to be *dharma* must be recognized as the highest *dharma*, but not that which is proclaimed by myriads of ignorant men" (*Manusmṛti* 12.113, cf. 2.20).

The authors of the Dharmasūtras and the Dharmaśāstras, like the Mīmāṃsakas, thus use a variety of strategies to circumscribe the universal applicability of *dharma* and tie it to the ethnic, geographic, linguistic, and religiocultural identity of the Āryans—and more specifically to the Brāhmaṇical custodians of *dharma* at the top of the Āryan social hierarchy. Wilhelm Halbfass remarks: "*Dharma* is the differentiated 'custom' and 'propriety' which constitutes the Aryan form of life, which upholds the identity of the *ārya* and distinguishes him from the *mleccha*, and which also legitimizes the privileged position of the Brahmins as the teachers and guardians of the *dharma*" (1988: 320). In the Brāhmaṇical discourse of *dharma*, the Āryans are distinguished from the non-Āryans, the *mleccha*s, as that special people who most perfectly embody the eternal truths of *dharma* in their blood lineages, their sacred land, their sacred language, and their sacred texts and practices. With respect to ethnic identity, the Āryans alone—as represented by the four *varṇa*s—are portrayed as emerging from the body of the creator at the beginning of creation, with all other peoples excluded from this claim to divine origins (*Manusmṛti* 1.31, 1.87, 10.44–45). Moreover, the Āryans alone claim to be the descendants of the *ṛṣi*s who cognized the Vedas, and thus it is the special prerogative of the Āryans—and more specifically of the Brāhmaṇical lineages—to preserve the *ṛṣi*s' cognitions in the form of the Vedic *mantra*s. With respect to linguistic identity, as the custodians of the Vedas, the cosmic blueprint that is the eternal source of *dharma*, the Āryans are also the custodians of the perfected (*saṃskṛta*) language, Sanskrit, the language of the gods and the language of *dharma* in which the *śruti* and *smṛti* texts are recorded. The sacred language of the Āryans is distinguished from the language of the *mleccha*s, and Āryans are forbidden from conversing with *mleccha*s and learning their language (*Gautama* 9.16; *Vasiṣṭha* 6.41; *Manusmṛti* 10.45). With respect to geographic identity, the sacred land of the Āryans, Āryāvarta, is distinguished from the land of the *mleccha*s as the land of the Vedas and the land of *dharma*, which alone is fit for the performance of the Vedic sacrifices (*Baudhāyana* 1.2.9–12; *Vasiṣṭha* 1.8–15; *Manusmṛti* 2.17–24).

The Āryans—born of the divine body, residents of the most sacred of lands, guardians of the sacred language of the gods, and preservers of the eternal Vedas and the cosmos-generating sacrificial rituals—are thus set apart from the non-Āryans as that special people whose destiny is to serve as arbiters of *dharma* and maintain the cosmic order through their religiocultural practices. The Brāhmaṇ priests in particular—in their privileged status as the direct descendants of the *ṛṣi*s who are responsible for preserving the Vedic recitative and sacrificial traditions—are celebrated as the quintessential embodiments of Veda and of *dharma* and are invested with the authority to define, redefine, and expand the domain of *dharma* beyond the circumscribed corpus of *śruti* and *smṛti* texts to include additional teachings and practices that they deem to be *dhārmika*.

Varṇadharma

According to the Brāhmaṇical discourse of *dharma*, as we have seen, in its ontological dimension, *dharma* is the cosmic ordering principle that is transhistorical, eternal, and universal, structuring the separation of functions among the various classes of beings on each plane of existence and interconnecting them in the complex network of symbiotic relations that constitutes the cosmic ecosystem. In its normative dimension, this cosmic ordering principle is represented as becoming embodied in a particular people and land, the Āryans of Āryāvarta, whose social order—the *varṇāśramadharma* system—constitutes the paradigmatic expression of the cosmic order on the human plane of existence. In this cosmic model of the social order, at the beginning of each cycle of creation the principle of *dharma*, in accordance with the cosmic blueprint of the eternal Vedas, establishes the separation of functions among the various classes of gods, plants, animals, and other beings in the divine and natural orders and also establishes the separation of functions among the various classes of human beings that constitute the social order (see *Manusmṛti* 1.21, 1.28–30, 12.97–99).

The Dharmasūtras and Dharmaśāstras elaborate on the cosmic origins of the *varṇa* system presented in the classificatory schemas of the Vedic Saṃhitās and Brāhmaṇas, explicitly invoking at times the imagery of the *Puruṣasūkta* in order to provide cosmic legitimation for the separation of functions among the four *varṇas* (*Vasiṣtha* 4.1–3; *Manusmṛti* 1.31, 1.87). The *Manusmṛti* establishes a cosmogonic foundation for the discourse of *dharma* by opening with an extensive creation narrative into which it interjects the imagery of the *Puruṣasūkta*: "For the sake of the welfare of the worlds, he [the creator] brought forth from his mouth, arms, thighs, and feet the Brāhmaṇ, the Kṣatriya, the Vaiśya, and the Śūdra" (1.31). The text invokes the same image again at the conclusion of its creation narrative in order to provide a transition to the discourse of *dharma* that is its primary concern. "In order to preserve this entire creation he, the effulgent one, assigned separate functions to those who sprang forth from his mouth, arms, thighs, and feet" (*Manusmṛti* 1.87). The text goes on to describe *varṇadharma*, the duties of the four *varṇa*s, and concludes with extended praise of the Brāhmaṇ class, which is born from the purest part of the divine body—the mouth—and hence is deemed to be preeminent among the social classes (*Manusmṛti* 1.88–101).

> Man is declared to be purer above the navel. Therefore, the purest [part] of him is stated by the self-existent (*svayambhū*) to be the mouth. As the Brāhmaṇ sprang from the highest part of the [divine] body, as he was the first-born, and as he preserves the Vedas, he is according to *dharma* the lord of this entire creation. For the self-existent, having performed *tapas*, brought him forth first from his own mouth in order to convey oblations to the gods and ancestors and to preserve this universe. . . . The very birth of a Brāhmaṇ is an eternal embodiment of *dharma*, for he is born for the sake of *dharma* and attains realization of *brahman*.
>
> (*Manusmṛti* 1.92–94, 1.98)

The image of the four *varṇa*s emerging from the divine body is also invoked elsewhere in the *Manusmṛti*, where it is used to define the non-Āryans as "all those peoples in the world who are outside [the community of] those born from the mouth, arms, thighs, and feet [of the divine body]" (10.44–45).

The imagery of the *Puruṣasūkta* is thus used in the *Manusmṛti* to legitimate the Āryan social order and establish a system of hierarchically ranked classes of human beings based on a series of successive dichotomies. First, the Āryans, as the four *varṇa*s born from the divine body, are distinguished from the non-Āryans, who are excluded from the claim to divine origins. Second, among Āryans, the "twice-born" (*dvija*)[17] Brāhmaṇs, Kṣatriyas, and Vaiśyas are distinguished from the "once-born" Śūdras, who are born from the most impure part of the divine body, the feet. Third, among the twice-born classes, the

Brāhmaṇs, as the first-born who emerge from the purest part of the divine body, the mouth, are distinguished from the Kṣatriyas and the Vaiśyas, who are born from less pure portions, the arms and thighs, respectively. The Brāhmaṇs, as the purest in the hierarchy of human beings, are celebrated as the "eternal embodiments of *dharma*" and the lords of creation (*Manusmṛti* 1.92–98, cited earlier).

Building on the taxonomies of the Brāhmaṇas, the Brāhmaṇical exponents of the discourse of *dharma* are concerned to establish not only that the *varṇa*s are inherent in the structure of the cosmos but also that the specific social function associated with each *varṇa* is the natural expression of its intrinsic nature. According to the *Baudhāyana Dharmasūtra*, the creator invests in each of the three twice-born *varṇa*s a special primordial force that constitutes its essential nature and that manifests in the propensity to perform duties that are consonant with that nature. The Brāhmaṇs are invested with the force of *brahman* and exercise religious power as priestly scholar-teachers whose duty is to uphold the cosmic order through preserving the eternal knowledge of the Vedas and performing the Vedic sacrificial rituals. The Kṣatriyas are invested with the force of *kṣatra* and exercise political and military power as kings and warriors whose duty is to protect the people and oversee the smooth functioning of the government. The Vaiśyas are invested with the force of *viś* and exercise economic power as merchants, agriculturists, and artisans whose duty is to promote economic productivity. The Śūdras, as the "feet" of the social body, are not associated with any special force or sphere of power but rather their duty is to serve the three higher *varṇa*s (*Baudhāyana* 1.18.2–5; cf. *Manusmṛti* 1.88–91, 11.236).

The Brāhmaṇical social system includes not only the four *varṇa*s but also the numerous *jāti*s, or castes, which the Dharmasūtras and Dharmaśāstras claim were generated through the intermixing of the *varṇa*s (*varṇasaṃkara*). The social hierarchy, in addition to ranking the four *varṇa*s according to their relative purity, is extended to include the mixed castes (*jāti*) that have been produced either through permissible *anuloma* (literally, "with the hair") unions between a man of a higher *varṇa* and a woman of a lower *varṇa* (hypergamy) or through unsanctioned *pratiloma* (literally, "against the hair") unions between a woman of a higher *varṇa* and a man of a lower *varṇa* (hypogamy). In this extended pyramidal hierarchy the Brāhmaṇs maintain their place at the apex as the paradigms of purity and the embodiments of *dharma*, while the large number of "debased" castes generated through adharmic *pratiloma* unions are deemed to be of impure origin and relegated to the bottom of the hierarchy. Moreover, the debased castes are generally assigned polluting occupations that involve constant association with impure substances—such as working with leather, handling corpses, or slaying animals—and that serve to reinforce their purported condition of congenital impurity.[18]

The status of a caste in the social hierarchy is not fixed but may be modified through interactions with other castes—more specifically through a complex network of transactions involving the exchange of women in marriage, food, and services. The norms of *varṇadharma* prescribed in the Dharmasūtras and Dharmaśāstras thus include laws of connubiality to regulate marriage transactions and laws of commensality to regulate food transactions among castes. The laws of connubiality delineate the effects of various types of marriage transactions—in particular, endogamous, *anuloma* (hypergamous), and *pratiloma* (hypogamous) unions—on a caste's status.[19] The laws of commensality circumscribe food transactions among castes, determining who may receive food and water from whom, and thereby serve to strengthen the hierarchical gradations of purity that both separate and connect castes.[20]

Āśramadharma

The Brāhmaṇical ideology of *varṇāśramadharma* interweaves *varṇadharma*, the duties of the four *varṇas*—Brāhmaṇs, Kṣatriyas, Vaiśyas, and Śūdras—with *āśramadharma*, the duties of the four *āśramas*—student (*brahmacārin*), householder (*gṛhastha*), forest-dweller (*vānaprastha*), and renunciant (variously termed *saṃnyāsin*, *pravrajita*, *parivrājaka*, *yati*, *bhikṣu*, and *muni*).[21] The earliest formulations of the *āśrama* system are found in the expositions of *dharma* in the Dharmasūtras. The *Baudhāyana Dharmasūtra*, for example, refers to the *āśramas* as "a fourfold division of *dharma*" (2.11.9, 2.11.12). However, the Dharmasūtras' representations of the *āśramas* differ in significant ways from the formulations of the classical *āśrama* system found in the Dharmaśāstras, in which the *āśramas* are depicted as four stages of life that are to be completed by male members of the three twice-born *varṇas*—Brāhmaṇs, Kṣatriyas, and Vaiśyas—in the course of the life cycle.[22]

As Olivelle (1993) has emphasized, the Dharmasūtras present the *āśramas* not as a sequence of four stages but rather as four alternative ways of life that may be undertaken by male members of the three higher *varṇas* who have undergone the *upanayana*, the Vedic rite of initiation, and have completed a period of Vedic study under the guidance of a teacher. The *Āpastamba Dharmasūtra* maintains that after completing the requisite period of Vedic study, a man may choose to undertake any of the *āśramas*, which constitute four equally legitimate paths, or lifelong vocations, that all lead to the supreme goal of peace.

> There are four *āśramas*: the order of a householder (*gārhasthya*), residing at the teacher's home (*ācāryakula*), the order of a renunciant (*mauna*), and the order of a forest-dweller (*vānaprasthya*). If one remains steadfast in any of these [*āśramas*], in accordance with the prescribed rules, he attains peace (*kṣema*). [A prerequisite] common to all [*āśramas*] is to live at the teacher's home following the *upanayana*. [A duty common] to all [*āśramas*] is not to abandon Vedic learning. Having learned the rites, he may undertake that [*āśrama*] which he prefers.[23]
>
> (*Āpastamba* 2.21.1–5; cf. *Vasiṣṭha* 7.1–3)

While the *Āpastamba* and *Vasiṣṭha Dharmasūtras* accept the validity of the four *āśramas* as alternative ways of life, the *Gautama* and *Baudhāyana Dharmasūtras* reject the fourfold system and assert instead that householder life is the only legitimate *āśrama* (*Gautama* 3.1–3, 3.36; *Baudhāyana* 2.11.9–12, 2.11.27).[24]

The earliest formulations of the classical *āśrama* system are found in the *Manusmṛti*, which, in contrast to the Dharmasūtras, presents the *āśramas* not as four distinct paths but as four stages of life that are to be completed in succession over the course of a man's lifetime. In the *Manusmṛti* the *āśramas* are represented as the ideal pattern of life to be followed in progression by male members of the three twice-born *varṇas*, the four stages corresponding to the four quarters (*bhāga*) of the life cycle: *brahmacarya*, the student stage, corresponds to the first quarter of a man's life (4.1); *gārhasthya*, the householder stage, to the second quarter (4.1, 5.169); *vānaprastha*, the forest-dweller stage, to the third quarter (6.33); and *saṃnyāsa*, the final stage of renunciation, to the fourth quarter (6.33). The *āśrama*s, as "the fourfold *dharma*," form an integral part of the social and cosmic orders and are described as emerging in the beginning of creation from the Vedas, the cosmic blueprint, along with the *varṇa*s, the three worlds, and all beings (*Manusmṛti* 6.97, 12.97–99, cited earlier).

The *Manusmṛti* provides an extensive treatment of the fourfold *dharma* of the *āśrama*s, devoting chapter 2 to the duties of the student, chapters 3 to 5 to the regulations of householder life, and chapter 6 to the conduct of the forest-dweller and the renunciant. The discussion of the student *āśrama* in chapter 2 (vv. 36–242) commences with the *upanayana*, the rite of initiation into Vedic study, in which the defective human being born from a woman's womb is born anew from the Veda in a "true" (*satya*) birth that is everlasting (*śāśvata*), free from old age and death (*Manusmṛti* 2.68, 2.146–48, 2.169–72). The twice-born student then goes to live in the home of his teacher, his second father, with whom he studies the Vedas and cultivates the proper habits of living. His regimen of duties combines ritual observances—daily recitation of the Vedas and ritual oblations to the gods, *ṛṣi*s, and ancestors—with ascetic practices—observance of celibacy, begging for alms, and performance of *tapas* and various vows (*vrata*).

In the second quarter of his life, the twice-born man undergoes the rite of marriage and enters into the householder *āśrama*. The *Manusmṛti* devotes three chapters (3.1–5.169) to the duties of householder life. In emphasizing the importance of householder *dharma*, the text invokes the Vedic notion of the three debts (*ṛṇa*)—to the *ṛṣi*s, ancestors, and gods—that are intrinsic to human existence. The central obligations of householder life are framed as means of paying these three primordial debts: the debt to the *ṛṣi*s is paid by studying the Vedas; the debt to the ancestors is paid by begetting sons who will perform the *śrāddha* rites to maintain the well being of the ancestors; and the debt to the gods is paid by performing *yajña*s, sacrifices (*Manusmṛti* 4.257, 6.35–37, 6.94, 9.106–7, 11.66). These three debts correspond to three of the five great sacrifices, or *mahāyajña*s, that are to be performed every day by the twice-born householder: recitation of the Vedas as a sacrifice to *brahman*, the ultimate reality; oblations of food and water (*tarpaṇa*) as a sacrifice to the ancestors; oblations in the sacrificial fire (*homa*) as a sacrifice to the gods; hospitality to guests as a sacrifice to human beings; and *bali* offerings of food as a sacrifice to semidivine beings, spirits, animals, and other beings (*bhūta*) (*Manusmṛti* 3.67–121, especially 3.67–74).[25] Through his daily performance of the *mahāyajña*s, which harness the theurgic power of the *yajña* within the domestic sphere, the householder upholds all of the orders of reality. "For he who is diligent in performing sacrifices maintains this [entire universe], animate and inanimate" (*Manusmṛti* 3.75). The *Manusmṛti* emphasizes the preeminent status of the householder *āśrama* as the foundation of both the social and cosmic orders, for it is the householder who supports the members of the three other *āśrama*s.

> Student (*brahmacārin*), householder (*gṛhastha*), forest-dweller (*vānaprastha*), and renunciant (*yati*): these four distinct *āśrama*s spring from the householder. Each and every one of these [*āśrama*s], undertaken in succession in accordance with the *śāstra*s, leads the Brāhmaṇ who acts as prescribed to the highest state (*paramā gati*). In accordance with the injunctions of Vedic cognition, the householder is declared to be the best of all these, for he supports the other three. As all rivers and streams converge in the ocean, so people of all *āśrama*s converge in the householder.
>
> (6.87–90, cf. 3.77–78; *Vasiṣṭha* 8.14–16)

The *Manusmṛti*'s privileging of the householder *āśrama* is evident in its cursory treatment of the two ascetic *āśrama*s that involve abandonment of householder life: the *āśrama*s of the forest-dweller (6.1–32) and the renunciant (6.33–85). Chapter 6 opens with a discussion of the proper time when a twice-born man may shift from the householder to the forest-dweller stage. When a man has fulfilled the obligations of the householder *āśrama* in accordance with *dharma* and when his skin has become wrinkled, his hair has turned gray, and his children have had children, then he may retire to the forest, either with or without his wife (*Manusmṛti* 6.1–3). The forest-dweller *āśrama* is represented as a transitional stage between the householder and the renunciant *āśrama*s, in which the twice-born man continues to uphold *dharma* through maintenance of the ritual fires and performance of the five *mahāyajña*s and other sacrifices, while at the same time he prepares himself for attainment of the ultimate goal of life—*mokṣa*, liberation from *saṃsāra*, the cycle of birth and death—through study of the Upaniṣads, meditation, and increasingly rigorous austerities.

In discussing the transition from the forest-dweller *āśrama* to the final *āśrama* of the renunciant, the *Manusmṛti* emphasizes that a man should not become a renunciant and devote himself to the pursuit of *mokṣa*, liberation, until after he has paid the three debts to the *ṛṣi*s, ancestors, and gods by fulfilling the obligations of householder life (6.35–37). Having discharged the three debts in the householder *āśrama* and retired to a hut in the forest for a period, the twice-born man may undertake the rite of renunciation (*Manusmṛti* 6.38) and enter into the final stage of life in which he abandons the last vestiges of worldly *dharma* that he had maintained in the forest—hut, spouse, food gathering, ritual fires, and sacrificial performances. A wandering mendicant, never settling in one place and living on alms, the renunciant devotes himself entirely to the pursuit of *mokṣa*, liberation from the bondage and suffering of *saṃsāra*. He adopts a regimen of yogic practices termed *dhyānayoga*, the *yoga* of meditation, which includes breathing exercises (*prāṇāyāma*), withdrawal of the senses (*pratyāhāra*), cultivation of one-pointed attention (*dhāraṇā*), meditation techniques (*dhyāna*), and various forms of *tapas* (*Manusmṛti* 6.49, 6.65, 6.69–82).[26] Through these practices, which are designed to discipline and purify the mind, senses, and bodily appetites, the renunciant overcomes the fetters of the mind-body complex and attains realization of the true nature of the Self, *ātman*, and its identity with *brahman*, the ultimate reality (*Manusmṛti* 6.49, 6.65, 6.79, 6.81–82, 6.85). "He should live in this world seated [in meditation], delighting in the experience of the Self (*ātman*), independent, free from sensual desires, with the Self (*ātman*) alone as his companion and bliss as his goal. . . . Having cast [the fruits of] his good deeds onto those he likes and [the fruits of] his bad deeds onto those he dislikes, he attains the eternal *brahman* through *dhyānayoga*" (*Manusmṛti* 6.49, 6.79).

Strīdharma

In the Brāhmaṇical discourse of *dharma*, an individual's *svadharma*, or allotted duty, is determined by three principal factors: gender, *varṇa*, and *āśrama* (in the case of men) or phase of life (in the case of women). In accordance with these three factors, the differential norms of *varṇāśramadharma* distinguish five separate groups with respect to their degree of participation in the *varṇa* and *āśrama* systems: male members of the twice-born *varṇas*—Brāhmaṇs, Kṣatriyas, and Vaiśyas—who are participants in both *varṇadharma* and *āśramadharma*; male Śūdras, who participate in *varṇadharma* but are excluded from the *āśramas*; women, who are similarly excluded from the *āśramas* but participate in certain aspects of *varṇadharma* and also have their own distinct set of duties; outcastes, who are beyond the pale of both the *varṇa* system and the *āśrama* system but whose status is nevertheless defined in relation to the broader social hierarchy; and non-Āryans, to whom the regulations of *dharma* do not apply.

Among these five groups, Śūdras and women are often linked in the Dharmaśāstras, with their connection framed in terms of a series of exclusions. Śūdras and women are excluded from undergoing the *upanayana* ritual that confers twice-born status, from study of the Vedas, and from offering sacrifices, and, as a consequence, they are excluded from the student *āśrama* as well as from the three subsequent stages of the classical *āśrama* system that presuppose completion of the first stage.[27] Moreover, Śūdras and women are in principle barred from becoming ascetics and are therefore excluded from initiation into the renunciant *āśrama*. Śūdras and women are, however, allowed to participate in the social institution of marriage, but their engagement in householder life is not ascribed the status of an *āśrama*.[28] While women, like Śūdras, are thus excluded from all aspects of the *āśrama* system, they nevertheless are ascribed an indispensable role within the householder domain. We will examine briefly the special sphere of *dharma* that is concerned with women—*strīdharma*—with particular attention to the *Manusmṛti*'s teachings pertaining to the status and role of women.[29]

While its principal concern is to delineate the obligations of *varṇadharma* and *āśramadharma* for male Brāhmaṇs, Kṣatriyas, and Vaiśyas, the *Manusmṛti* includes two sections that are devoted to the duties and rights of women: a short section on *strīdharma* (5.146–66) and a longer section on the *dharma* of husbands and wives (9.1–103). Both of these sections begin with a variant of the famous dictum that encapsulates the governing principle of *strīdharma* in Dharmaśāstra literature: women should never be independent. "Her father guards (root *rakṣ*) her in her childhood, her husband guards her in her youth, and her sons guard her in her old age. A woman is not fit for independence" (*Manusmṛti* 9.3, cf. 5.148; *Baudhāyana* 2.3.45; *Vasiṣṭha* 5.3; *Gautama* 18.1; *Yājñavalkyasmṛti* 1.85). Although a woman is excluded from participation in the *āśrama* system, her life is divided into stages corresponding to the life cycle—daughter, wife/daughter-in-law, mother/mother-in-law, and widow—and in each of these stages her *dharma* is defined in relation to men. As a daughter she is under the care and authority of her father; as a wife and mother, of her husband; and as a widow, of her sons. In every phase of a woman's life it is the duty of her male guardians to both "protect" and "guard" her, as the Sanskrit root *rakṣ* connotes: to protect her from external sources of harm and to guard against the expression of certain negative tendencies that are considered part of a woman's inherent nature.

The *Manusmṛti* expresses an ambivalent attitude towards women that is characteristic of Brāhmaṇical sources. The text at times praises women, celebrating them as gifts from the gods and embodiments of Śrī, or Lakṣmī, the goddess of good fortune, who are sources of blessings and auspiciousness for their families (*Manusmṛti* 9.95, 9.26). Fathers, brothers, husbands, and brothers-in-law are exhorted to revere women in order to please the gods and ensure the well being and prosperity of their families (*Manusmṛti* 3.55–62, 9.26). A woman is particularly celebrated for her roles in procreation and religious rites, for it is through these means that she helps her husband to discharge two of the three debts: the debt to the ancestors by bearing sons, and the debt to the gods by accompanying her husband in the performance of sacrifices and other rituals. "There is no difference whatsoever between wives (*striyaḥ*)—whose purpose is procreation, who embody good fortune, and who are worthy of worship and the splendor of their houses—and the goddesses of good fortune (*śriyaḥ*) who are [worshiped] in houses. . . . Offspring, religious rites, service, the highest conjugal happiness, and heaven for oneself and one's ancestors depend on one's wife" (*Manusmṛti* 9.26, 9.28, cf. 9.96). In discussing the relative importance of teachers, fathers, and mothers, the *Manusmṛti* maintains that the father is a hundred times more venerable than the teacher and the mother is a thousand times more venerable than the father (2.145; cf. *Vasiṣṭha* 13.48).

While the *Manusmṛti* thus glorifies women as embodiments of the fertile, life-sustaining, and auspicious powers of the goddess, it at the same time emphasizes the importance of safeguarding a woman's inherent power from possible misuse or abuse. The dictum regarding the need for women to be guarded by men is linked in particular to the concern to control female sexuality. The text maintains that if a married woman remains chaste and faithful to her husband, she will be a source of procreative power and blessings for her husband and family. However, if she violates her wifely *dharma* by being unfaithful to her husband, she will endanger the purity of her offspring and of the entire family (*Manusmṛti* 9.2–9). "By diligently guarding (root *rakṣ*) his wife, he guards his own offspring, conduct, family, and himself as well as his own *dharma*. . . . A woman brings forth a son who is just like the man with whom she has sexual union. Therefore, in order to preserve the purity of his offspring, a man should diligently guard his wife" (*Manusmṛti* 9.7, 9.9). In the *Manusmṛti*'s theory of reproduction, the male "seed" is more important than the female "field" into which it is sown, for it is the seed that determines the status and characteristics of the offspring. Therefore, in order to ensure the purity of the offspring and maintain the family's status in the social hierarchy, it is vital to safeguard the female field from being polluted by the seed of men other than her husband (*Manusmṛti* 9.31–55).

The highest *dharma* of a woman, according to the *Manusmṛti*, is to serve her husband as a god and remain faithful to him throughout his lifetime and even after his death (5.151–66). A woman's selfless devotion to her husband is represented as a path to salvation in its own right. The marriage ceremony is upheld as the only Vedic sacrament (*saṃskāra*) for women and is ascribed the transformative power of an initiation ritual in the female life cycle that is equivalent to the *upanayana* ritual that inaugurates the student *āśrama* in the male life cycle. A woman's devoted service to her husband is equivalent to the student's service to his teacher, while a woman's performance of her domestic duties is equivalent to the student's daily offerings into the ritual fire (*Manusmṛti* 2.67). A woman's path to salvation is not through performing sacrifices or undertaking vows but rather through faithful devotion to her husband she secures a place for herself in heaven alongside her husband. "There is no separate sacrifice (*yajña*) nor vow (*vrata*) nor fast for women [apart from their husbands]. If a wife serves her husband, by that means [alone] she will be exalted in heaven. . . . She who, self-controlled in mind, speech, and body, is not unfaithful to her husband attains the [heavenly] world with her husband and is called by virtuous people a *sādhvī* (virtuous woman)" (*Manusmṛti* 5.155, 5.165, cf. 9.29).

Karma and dharma

The Brāhmaṇical exponents of the discourse of *dharma* use two mechanisms to link the ontological and normative dimensions of *dharma* and provide a cosmic rationale for the *varṇāśramadharma* system. First, as we have seen, they claim that the *varṇa*s are not social constructions but rather are ontological realities that are integral to the cosmic order. Second, they maintain that an individual's *svadharma*—or allotted duty according to his or her gender, *varṇa*, and *āśrama* or phase of life—is ultimately determined by the cosmic law of *karma*, which ensures that the external circumstances of an individual's birth and social status are properly correlated with his or her inherent nature.

The Dharmasūtras and Dharmaśāstras, in discussing the consequences of *dharma* and *adharma*—and more specifically of observing or neglecting one's *svadharma*—often invoke the law of *karma*, the cosmic law of cause and effect that governs *saṃsāra*, the cycle of birth and death, and that dispenses justice to living beings in accordance with their deeds. This inexorable law extends the principle of natural causality to the realm of human morality. The *Manusmṛti*, which draws on a number of earlier theories of *karma*, provides a basic definition of this cosmic law: "Action (*karma*), which arises from the mind, speech, or body, produces good or bad fruits. The highest, intermediate, and lowest conditions of human beings are born of action (*karma*)" (12.3). The text cautions that a person should consider the fruits that his or her actions will generate in future births and should engage accordingly in meritorious actions with mind, speech, and body (*Manusmṛti* 11.232, cf. 12.81).[30]

The law of *karma* is understood as functioning simultaneously on the subjective and objective levels, establishing a link between the ontological and normative dimensions of *dharma*. On the subjective level, the karmic residues that an individual soul, or *jīva*, accumulates through actions in successive births shapes the soul's essential character, influencing inclinations, propensities, and aptitudes. On the objective level, the law of *karma* determines the external circumstances of an individual's birth in each lifetime, including the species, gender, family, social class or caste, and community in which the *jīva* is born and—in the case of human beings born in Āryāvarta—the corresponding social function that the individual will assume in accordance with his or her birth into a particular *varṇa* or *jāti*. In this perspective it is the law of *karma* that ensures that the subjective and objective dimensions of individual existence—inherent nature and external function—do not contradict one another but, on the contrary, are properly correlated in order to enable the individual to fulfill most efficiently his or her allotted destiny in each lifetime.

The Dharmasūtras and Dharmaśāstras invoke the law of *karma* as a cosmic incentive to inspire adherence to one's *svadharma*, especially with reference to the duties of one's *varṇa*. According to this law, an individual's birth in a particular *varṇa*, such as the Śūdra class, is not arbitrary but is a result of the soul's specific karmic heritage accumulated from previous births. Fulfillment of *varṇadharma* is held to be the most expedient path through which an individual can develop his or her natural faculties while simultaneously contributing the maximum to the social and cosmic orders. Although an individual is free—at least hypothetically, notwithstanding social pressures and sanctions—to choose another path and attempt to undertake the *dharma* of another social class or caste, the exponents of Dharmaśāstra repeatedly emphasize that to do so would not be conducive to his or her personal welfare. Since the power of cosmic *dharma*, as expressed in the structure of the *varṇa* system and in the law of *karma*, has already determined each individual's station in life, it is not considered advantageous to contradict the cosmic order by attempting to follow another path. An individual's duty is allotted by the infallible authority of cosmic law, and this *svadharma* ought to be performed.

The Dharmasūtras and Dharmaśāstras vividly describe the fruits of adherence to *dharma* as well as the consequences of violating the injunctions of *dharma*. "*Dharma*, when violated, destroys; *dharma*, when preserved, preserves. Therefore, *dharma* must not be violated, lest violated *dharma* destroy us" (*Manusmṛti* 8.15). The fruits of *dharma* and *adharma* are described in terms of both mundane and transmundane consequences. With respect to those who abide by their respective *dharma*s, the karmic seeds of their meritorious actions will bear fruit in happiness, wisdom, virtue, prosperity, fame, and longevity. Moreover, the fruits of their actions will be enjoyed not only in the present lifetime but also after death and in the course of future births (*Āpastamba* 2.2.2–4; *Gautama* 11.29; *Manusmṛti* 2.5, 2.9, 4.156, 4.158). Through adherence to *dharma*, such people are promised steady progress on the path of evolution and enhanced status in the social and cosmic hierarchies through birth into progressively higher *varṇa*s in future lifetimes (*Āpastamba* 2.2–4, 2.11.10; *Gautama* 11.29; *Manusmṛti* 9.334–35). For example, a Śūdra who faithfully fulfills his or her *dharma* through serving the three higher *varṇa*s and who is also pure, gentle in speech, and free from egotism can look forward to a higher birth in the next lifetime (*Manusmṛti* 9.334–35). The *Gautama Dharmasūtra* proclaims: "[Members of] the *varṇa*s and *āśrama*s who are devoted to their allotted duties enjoy the fruits of their actions after death, and then with the residue [of those fruits] they are born again in an excellent region, caste (*jāti*), and family, with a beautiful body, longevity, profound Vedic learning, and virtuous conduct and with exceptional wealth, happiness, and wisdom" (11.29).

The discourse of *dharma* also emphasizes the negative consequences that ensue from transgression of the injunctions of *dharma*. Those who abandon their duties and follow the path of *adharma* will experience the karmic fruits of their sins in suffering, misfortune, disease, and shortened life spans and will be tormented after death in terrifying hells (*Āpastamba* 1.5.2–3, 2.2.5–7; *Gautama* 11.30; *Manusmṛti* 4.157, 6.61–64,12.74–80). As a consequence of their adharmic actions, such people will fall from their respective *varṇa*s and, depending on the seriousness of their transgressions, will descend in their subsequent births into the wombs of lower *varṇa*s, outcastes, animals, or malevolent beings (*Āpastamba* 2.2.5–7, 2.11.11; *Manusmṛti* 12.52–78). The *Manusmṛti* warns that "those *varṇa*s who have abandoned their allotted duties when they are not in distress become the servants of *dasyu*s (non-Āryans) after passing through wretched transmigratory states" (12.70).

CONTENDING PERSPECTIVES: THE DIALECTIC OF DHARMA AND MOKṢA

Dharma, as a paradigmatic category in Hindu traditions, can only be fully understood within the larger scheme of Hindu values, which recognizes four ends of human life, termed *puruṣārtha*s: *kāma*, *artha*, *dharma*, and *mokṣa*. *Kāma* is sensual pleasure, particularly as manifested in sexual and aesthetic experience; *artha* is economic and political well being, encompassing notions of wealth and power; *dharma* is the cosmic ordering principle that regulates every aspect of individual, social, and cosmic life, finding expression on the human plane in a comprehensive system of sociocultural norms and duties; and *mokṣa* is liberation from *saṃsāra*, the cycle of birth and death, which is the supreme goal of human existence.

Kāma, *artha*, and *dharma* together make up the *trivarga*, to which *mokṣa* is added as a fourth element. Edgerton (1942) has termed the *trivarga* "ordinary norms," in contrast to the "extraordinary norm," *mokṣa*. As Charles Malamoud (1981) has emphasized, the *trivarga* constitutes a "revolving hierarchy" in that, depending on the perspective adopted, each of these three values can be viewed in turn as the governing principle that encompasses the other values and provides a framework for understanding their interrelationship.[31] From the perspective of Dharmaśāstra literature, *dharma* is the governing principle that encompasses all temporal values and serves as a regulatory principle for the pursuit of *kāma* and *artha*. The fourfold structure of the *puruṣārtha*s has thus at times been characterized as a dichotomy between two spheres of value: *dharma*, the principle that regulates the temporal realm of *saṃsāra*, and *mokṣa*, the state of liberation from *saṃsāra*.

A number of eminent scholars of South Asia have sought to illumine the dialectic of *dharma* and *mokṣa* (van Buitenen 1957; Ingalls 1957; Larson 1972), along with the corresponding dialectic of householder and renunciant (Dumont 1960; Heesterman 1981; Thapar 1981), in a variety of Indic religious traditions. Building on the *Manusmṛti*'s notion that *dharma* regulates not only temporal values but also the sphere of *mokṣa*, Gerald Larson recasts the dialectic as a dichotomy between "ordinary *dharma*," which includes both the specific norms of *varṇāśramadharma* and the common norms of *sādhāraṇadharma*,[32] and "extraordinary *dharma*," which is *mokṣadharma*.

> Indian culture has produced various interpretations of the relationship between "ordinary *dharma*" and "extraordinary *dharma*"—some of which indeed are contradictory but others of which, in some important sense, are resolutions of the problem and all of which are necessary to consider if the issue of a "regulative principle" in Indian culture is to be seriously raised. In other words, the very tension or polarity between "ordinary *dharma*" and "extraordinary *dharma*" brings one to the very heart of the problem of *dharma* as a regulative principle in Indian culture and the Indian tradition's own ambiguity or uncertainty regarding the issue.
>
> (Larson 1972: 150)

The Brāhmaṇical system of "ordinary *dharma*"—more specifically, *varṇāśramadharma*—has been challenged by a variety of competing traditions—including renunciant traditions, devotional (*bhakti*) sects, and Tantric movements—which present a range of alternative perspectives concerning the dialectic of *dharma* and *mokṣa*. I will limit my analysis to three historically influential perspectives that present contending assessments of this dialectic: the Dharmaśāstras, as exemplified by the *Manusmṛti*, which relegates *mokṣa* to a subsidiary role within the framework of *dharma*; renunciant traditions, as exemplified by Śaṃkara's Advaita Vedānta, which advocates abandoning *dharma* for the sake of *mokṣa*; and the *Bhagavad Gītā*, the celebrated classic of Hindu *bhakti*, which emphasizes the indispensable role of *dharma* on the path to *mokṣa*.[33]

Dharmaśāstras

In the Dharmaśāstras *mokṣa* is subsumed within the framework of *dharma* as a special category: *mokṣadharma*. The dichotomy between *dharma* and *mokṣa* is reformulated in this context as a distinction between two spheres of *dharma*: *pravṛttidharma*, which involves engagement in worldly activity in order to maintain the ever-revolving wheel of *saṃsāra*, and *nivṛttidharma*, which involves withdrawal from worldly activity in order to attain liberation from *saṃsāra*. The *Manusmṛti* emphasizes that both of these spheres of *dharma* constitute valid forms of "Vedic activity":

> There are two kinds of Vedic activity (*karma vaidika*): that which causes the revolving [of the world] (*pravṛtta*) and leads to increased happiness, and that which causes the dissolution [of the world] (*nivṛtta*) and leads to supreme bliss. That action which is motivated by desire in this world or the next world is called *pravṛtta*, but that action which is free of desire and founded on knowledge is referred to as *nivṛtta*. He who is devoted to *pravṛtta* activity becomes equal to the gods, but he who is dedicated to *nivṛtta* passes beyond the five elements.
>
> (12.88–90)

In the classical *āśrama* system presented in the Dharmaśāstras, *pravṛttidharma* and *nivṛttidharma* are associated in particular with the householder and renunciant *āśrama*s, respectively. The twice-born male householder is the exemplar of *pravṛttidharma*, who engages in the ritual and social activities of *varṇāśramadharma* in order, on a personal level, to attain certain worldly ends and, on a cosmic level, to maintain the smooth functioning of all planes of relative existence. The renunciant is the exemplar of *nivṛttidharma*, who withdraws from the network of worldly desires and social obligations and focuses on gaining knowledge of ultimate reality as a means of achieving *mokṣa*, liberation from the relative world of *saṃsāra*. In the idealized scheme of the four stages of life, *pravṛttidharma* and *nivṛttidharma*—or *varṇāśramadharma* and *mokṣadharma*—are presented not as two competing ways of life but as two spheres of *dharma* to be undertaken in different stages of the life cycle. This scheme places *nivṛttidharma*, or *mokṣadharma*, at the end of life, to be undertaken only after a man has fulfilled the worldly obligations of *pravṛttidharma*, or *varṇāśramadharma*. Thus the *Manusmṛti* stipulates, as we have seen, that a man may enter into the renunciant *āśrama* and devote himself to the pursuit of *mokṣa* only after he has paid the three debts to the *ṛṣi*s, ancestors, and gods in the householder *āśrama*.

> After he has paid the three debts, he may set his mind on *mokṣa*. But if he devotes himself to *mokṣa* without having paid them, he will fall. After he has studied the Vedas in accordance with the rules, begotten sons in accordance with *dharma*, and offered sacrifices (*yajña*) according to his ability, he may set his mind on *mokṣa*. If a twice-born man seeks *mokṣa* without having studied the Vedas, begotten sons, and offered sacrifices, he will fall.
>
> (*Manusmṛti* 6.35–37)

The *Manusmṛti* is concerned not only to regulate at what period in life a man is entitled to renounce the world, it is also concerned to define the "*dharma* of self-restrained renunciants (*yati*)" (6.86) after they have renounced. In its discussion of the renunciant *āśrama*, the *Manusmṛti* prescribes rules of conduct to regulate the lifestyle and behavior of the renunciant, including his appearance, begging practices, sexual abstinence, meditation techniques, and other ascetic disciplines (6.38–85). Moreover, the *Manusmṛti* and other Dharmaśāstras also include regulations that seek to define the social status of the renunciant in relation to the broader society.[34]

While the exponents of the discourse of *dharma* thus seek to accommodate and domesticate the renunciant ideal of *mokṣa* by incorporating it within the system of *āśrama*s, the *nivṛttidharma* of the renunciant is ultimately relegated to the periphery of a system that centers first and foremost on the *pravṛttidharma* of the householder. As discussed earlier, the *Manusmṛti* (6.87–90, 3.77–78) celebrates the preeminent status of the householder *āśrama* as the foundation that supports the other three *āśrama*s. At the conclusion of its discussion of the renunciant *āśrama*, the text goes so far as to suggest an alternative path that will allow the householder to attain *mokṣa*, the supreme goal of human existence, without having to become a mendicant renunciant. As an alternative to the "*dharma* of self-restrained renunciants (*yati*)," the text proposes the "*karmayoga* of renouncers of Vedic ritual (*vedasaṃnyāsika*)" (*Manusmṛti* 6.86), in which the householder, having paid the three debts, abandons the performance of all rituals in his elder years and—rather than retiring to the forest or undertaking the life of a wandering renunciant—continues to live at home under the protection of his son. This retired householder, having cultivated the ten virtues contained in the "tenfold *dharma*" and studied the Vedas, attains the highest state (*paramā gati*) (*Manusmṛti* 6.86–96, cf. 4.257–58).[35]

Renunciant traditions

In contrast to the classical *āśrama* system delineated in the Dharmaśāstras, in which renunciation is the last of four stages to be undertaken at the end of life, exponents of the renunciant path, as initially formulated by the forest-dwelling Upanisaḍic sages and elaborated in later post-Vedic ascetic traditions, advocate undertaking renunciation as a lifelong vocation. In ascetic traditions associated with the mendicant renunciant—variously termed *saṃnyāsin*, *parivrājaka*, *pravrajita*, *bhikṣu*, *yati*, and *muni*[36]—*mokṣa* is not a subsidiary goal to be postponed until the final phase of life but is rather the central goal of human existence to be pursued one-pointedly throughout the course of one's life. The most expedient path to *mokṣa* is to renounce the world of *dharma* associated with the householder way of life and retire as a youth to a life of solitude, unhampered by the entanglements of social responsibilities.

Exponents of renunciant traditions, in attempting to establish the preeminence of the renunciant path over the householder path, tend to emphasize the discontinuity between *dharma* and *mokṣa* as two ontologically distinct categories. *Dharma* is the governing principle of *saṃsāra*, which is the manifest, active, ever-changing, bounded field of relative existence. *Mokṣa* is liberation from the bondage of *saṃsāra* in which the individual realizes the true nature of the Self as the absolute reality—variously designated in different traditions as *ātman*, *brahman*, or *puruṣa*—that in its essential nature is unmanifest, nonactive, nonchanging, and unbounded. The distinction between *dharma* and *mokṣa* is thus represented as a dichotomy between two spheres of reality: relative and absolute, manifest and unmanifest, active and nonactive, changing and nonchanging, bounded and unbounded. In this perspective *dharma* cannot lead to *mokṣa*, for *dharma* is associated with the bondage of *saṃsāra*. Every action, whether good or bad, produces karmic fruits that must be reaped in present or future lifetimes, and thus even dharmic actions generate a binding influence that serves to perpetuate the cycle of birth and death. If all actions bind the soul to *saṃsāra*, then the only effective means for an individual to escape rebirth is to minimize his or her involvement in the realm of action, abandon the dharmic obligations of worldly life, and become a lifelong renunciant dedicated to attaining knowledge (*jñāna*, *vidyā*)—in the sense of both intellectual understanding and direct experience—of ultimate reality.

The renunciant goal of *mokṣa* is defined more specifically in opposition to the Brāhmaṇical norms of *varṇāśramadharma*, which are viewed as inextricably linked to saṃsāric existence. The world-renouncing ideologies and practices of renunciant traditions are antithetical to the world-maintaining ideologies and practices promulgated by the Brāhmaṇical exponents of the Dharmasūtras and Dharmaśāstras. The renunciant path is predicated on the abandonment of the prescribed rituals, including Vedic sacrifices and domestic rituals, as well as the social duties of *varṇāśramadharma*. Brāhmaṇical householder practices and norms that are concerned with regulating marriage and sexual transactions are countered by ascetic practices that renounce householder life, marriage, and procreation altogether and seek instead to restrain the sexual impulse through the observance of celibacy. Brāhmaṇical food practices and norms that involve a complex system of food transactions and dietary laws are countered by ascetic disciplines that are aimed at minimizing food production and consumption through such practices as begging and fasting. Having abandoned the accoutrements of worldly *dharma*—home, family, caste affiliation, sexuality, food production, ritual practices, and social duties—the renunciant devotes himself to the lifelong pursuit of *mokṣa*.[37]

One of the most sustained philosophical justifications for the renunciant path is found in classical Advaita Vedānta as expounded by Śaṃkara (eighth century CE). Śaṃkara's philosophical system is based on a monistic ontology in which *brahman*, the universal wholeness of existence, is alone declared to be real. In its essential nature as *nirguṇa* (without attributes), *brahman* is pure being (*sat*), consciousness (*cit*), and bliss (*ānanda*) and is completely formless, distinctionless, nonchanging, and unbounded. As *saguṇa* (with attributes), *brahman* assumes the form of *īśvara*, the lord, who manifests the phenomenal world as an illusory appearance (*māyā*). Deluded by ignorance (*avidyā*), the individual self (*jīva*) becomes enchanted by the cosmic play and mistakenly identifies with the mind-body complex, becoming bound in *saṃsāra*. Through an analysis of the nature of bondage and liberation (*mokṣa*, *mukti*), Śaṃkara concludes that liberation from *saṃsāra* cannot be attained through any manner of activity or moral improvement. *Mokṣa* is attained through knowledge (*jñāna*, *vidyā*) alone, for when knowledge dawns the individual self awakens to its true nature as *ātman*, the universal Self, which is identical with *brahman*.

> He who, . . . before undertaking action, has realized his self as the nonactive inner Self (*ātman*) that abides in all and that is *brahman*, . . . such a renunciant (*yati*), engaging in action solely for the maintenance of the body, established in knowledge (*jñāna*), is liberated (root *muc*). . . . Because all of his *karma* is burnt up in the fire of knowledge (*jñānāgni*), he is liberated (root *muc*) without any obstacle.
>
> (*Śaṃkarabhāṣya* on *Bhagavad Gītā* 4.21)

Dharma, which involves activity in the illusory world of *saṃsāra*, the realm of bondage, can never lead to *mokṣa*. The only truly efficacious path to *mokṣa*, according to Śaṃkara, is to abandon the dharmic responsibilities of householder life, along with the desire for sons, wealth, and worldly pleasures, and become a lifelong *saṃnyāsin* whose sole focus is the attainment of knowledge of *brahman*. However, Śaṃkara, even though himself a renunciant, did not completely reject the value of worldly duties on the path to *mokṣa*. He championed Brāhmaṇical orthodoxy against the attacks of Buddhist traditions, recognizing the utility of sacrifices and other dharmic activities as preliminary means of purification in preparation for the attainment of that supreme knowledge which results in liberation.[38]

The Bhagavad Gītā

The *Bhagavad Gītā* (*c.*200 BCE), which has inspired commentaries by Śaṃkara and hundreds of other traditional and modern commentators,[39] presents the classic statement that seeks to reconcile *dharma* and *mokṣa* by establishing the importance of *dharma* on the path to liberation. The *Bhagavad Gītā* thus provides a mediating position between the perspective of the Dharmaśāstras, which give precedence to *dharma*, and the perspective of renunciant traditions, which give priority to *mokṣa*. The *Bhagavad Gītā*'s discussion of *dharma* and *mokṣa* takes place in the context of a practical dilemma posed by the warrior Arjuna to Lord Kṛṣṇa on the battlefield of Kurukṣetra, the "field of *dharma*" (*Bhagavad Gītā* 1.1). Should he fight and uphold his *svadharma* as a Kṣatriya, a member of the warrior class, or should he decline from fighting in order to avoid the great sin of slaying his own relatives and destroying the age-old *dharma*s of the family? Lord Kṛṣṇa teaches Arjuna that skill in action whereby he can fulfill his *dharma* as a warrior and at the same time rise to a state of liberation, *mokṣa*, in which he will not incur sin.

The *Bhagavad Gītā* uses a number of arguments to support its position. First, like the exponents of the discourse of *dharma*, it seeks to establish the indispensability of *dharma* in maintaining the social and cosmic orders. Second, like the exponents of renunciant traditions, it emphasizes the central importance of *mokṣa* as the supreme goal of human existence. Third, the *Bhagavad Gītā* maintains that the quest for *mokṣa* is not the exclusive prerogative of those who have renounced the world but is open to householders and renunciants alike. In this context the *Bhagavad Gītā* upholds the validity of two alternative paths to liberation: *jñānayoga*, the path of knowledge, for those who want to renounce the world and dedicate their lives to gaining knowledge of ultimate reality; and *karmayoga*, the path of action, for the majority of people who are householders dedicated to a life of worldly responsibilities. Instead of waiting until the end of life to seek liberation from *saṃsāra*, the householder—as represented by Arjuna—is encouraged to undertake the pursuit of *mokṣa* while continuing to uphold the social and cosmic orders through performing his or her *svadharma*. Finally, the *Bhagavad Gītā* emphasizes that the fulfillment of dharmic obligations is not a source of bondage but rather constitutes an integral part of the householder's quest for *mokṣa*. Contrary to the exponents of renunciant traditions, the *Bhagavad Gītā* maintains that it is not action itself that binds; it is the attachment of the doer to his or her actions and their fruits that binds. This is the crucial teaching that reconciles *dharma* and *mokṣa*: the path to *mokṣa* is not through abandonment of *dharma*, not through renunciation of the world of action, but through abandonment of the attachment to action and its fruits.

The *Bhagavad Gītā* provides an ontological foundation for this state of nonattachment by invoking the example of Lord Kṛṣṇa himself. Lord Kṛṣṇa is celebrated as Puruṣottama, the supreme *puruṣa*, who is identified with *brahman* and encompasses within himself the fullness of both the absolute and the relative, the nonchanging Self and the ever-changing field of *prakṛti*, material nature (*Bhagavad Gītā* 15.16–19). Kṛṣṇa, as the lord of creation, points to his own behavior as an example that is to be emulated by the wise. While remaining completely nonattached to action in his absolute status as the unmanifest, nonactive Self, he maintains the cosmic order through manifesting himself in the unceasing activity of relative existence by means of *prakṛti* (*Bhagavad Gītā* 3.22–24, 4.13–14, 9.8–10). "Resorting to my *prakṛti*, I send forth again and again this entire multitude of beings, which is powerless, by the power of *prakṛti*. And these actions do not bind me, O Arjuna, for I remain separate, not attached to these actions. With me as overseer, *prakṛti* brings forth animate and inanimate beings. For this reason, O Arjuna, the world revolves" (*Bhagavad Gītā* 9.8–10).

Lord Kṛṣṇa exhorts Arjuna to emulate the divine example and perform his *dharma* for the welfare of the world while remaining established in the nonactive Self, *ātman*, which exists in a perpetual state of nonattachment from the ever-active relative field (*Bhagavad Gītā* 4.14–15, 3.20). It is ignorance of the true nature of the Self as separate from the field of activity that gives rise to bondage. Although *prakṛti* is in reality responsible for all activity in the world, the mind becomes deluded by the sense of "I" and claims that "I am the doer" (*Bhagavad Gītā* 3.5, 3.27). The *Bhagavad Gītā* maintains that liberation from this state of bondage cannot be gained by simply renouncing the world and attempting to abandon all actions, for "not by abstaining from actions does a man attain nonaction, and not by mere renunciation (*saṃnyasana*) does he achieve perfection" (3.4). The key to *mokṣa* lies in developing a state of consciousness in which the sage realizes the true nature of the Self as separate from the field of activity and thus ceases to claim authorship for actions. The sage who becomes established in this inner state of nonattachment, in which the fruits of action are spontaneously relinquished, is the true renunciant (*saṃnyāsin*, *tyāgin*)—not the person who simply adopts the lifestyle of an ascetic and attempts to abandon the world of action (*Bhagavad Gītā* 6.1–2, 5.3, 9.28, 18.11, 18.49). "He who performs action that is his duty, without depending on the fruit of action, he is a *saṃnyāsin* and a *yogin*, not he who is without fire and who abstains from religious rites" (*Bhagavad Gītā* 6.1).

As a means of gaining direct experience of the Self, the *Bhagavad Gītā* (6.10–28) advocates the practice of meditation, *dhyānayoga*, and suggests that such meditation practices are not to be restricted to *jñānayogins* leading a renunciant way of life but are also to be undertaken by *karmayogins* actively involved in the world. Having become established in the Self, the silent witness of the realm of action, the *yogin* should engage in action and perform his or her *dharma* free from attachment, in a state of equanimity (*Bhagavad Gītā* 2.45, 2.48, 3.19). This state of nonattachment culminates in the surrender of all actions and their fruits to their supreme source: the lord of creation himself (*Bhagavad Gītā* 3.30, 9.27–28, 12.6–7, 18.57–58, 18.65–66). *Jñānayoga*, the *yoga* of knowledge; *karmayoga*, the *yoga* of action; and *dhyānayoga*, the *yoga* of meditation, find their fulfillment in the *Bhagavad Gītā* in *bhaktiyoga*, the *yoga* of devotion to the lord. "Whatever you do, whatever you eat, whatever you offer in sacrifice, whatever you give, whatever austerity you perform, O Arjuna, do that as an offering to me. Thus you shall be liberated (root *muc*) from the bonds of *karma* that produce good and evil fruits. Your Self established in the *yoga* of renunciation (*saṃnyāsayoga*), liberated, you shall come to me" (*Bhagavad Gītā* 9.27–28).

MODERN REFORMULATIONS OF DHARMA: SĀDHĀRAṆADHARMA AND SANĀTANADHARMA

In addition to the dichotomy between "ordinary *dharma*" and the "extraordinary *dharma*" of *mokṣa*, we can locate a second dichotomy within "ordinary *dharma*" itself: the distinction between *varṇāśramadharma* and *sādhāraṇadharma*. The differential norms of *varṇāśramadharma*, as we have seen, determine the *svadharma*s of specific groups according to their degree of participation in the *varṇa* and *āśrama* systems. The universal norms of *sādhāraṇa-dharma* or *sāmānyadharma*, in contrast, comprise "common" moral principles, such as noninjury (*ahiṃsā*), nonstealing (*asteya*), and truthfulness (*satya*), that are applicable to all human beings irrespective of their gender, social class or caste, and stage of life. The *Manusmṛti* (6.91–92), after providing a five-chapter exposition of the four *āśrama*s, concludes its discussion with an enumeration of the "tenfold *dharma*" that is to be upheld by members of all four *āśrama*s: steadfastness, forbearance, self-control, nonstealing, purity, mastery of the senses, wisdom, knowledge, truthfulness, and freedom from anger. Elsewhere the *Manusmṛti* (10.63) provides a list of five virtues as an encapsulation of the *dharma* that is common to all four *varṇa*s: nonviolence, truthfulness, nonstealing, purity, and mastery of the senses. Although occasional mention is thus made of norms common to all human beings, the primary focus of the Brāhmaṇical exponents of the discourse of *dharma* is on *varṇāśramadharma*. In cases of conflict between the differential norms of *varṇāśramadharma* and the universal norms of *sādhāraṇadharma*, the particular obligations of an individual's *varṇa* and *āśrama* are given precedence. For example, as illustrated in the teachings of the *Bhagavad Gītā*, in times of war a Kṣatriya may violate the principle of *ahiṃsā*, nonviolence, in order to fulfill his *svadharma* as a warrior.

In the modern period, from the beginning of the nineteenth century onward, the category of *dharma* underwent significant transformations as a result of the encounter between India and Europe that occurred with the establishment of the European presence in India and the corresponding development of Christian missionary activities in different areas of the Indian subcontinent. As a result of their encounter with Western categories and models, various modern exponents of "Neo-Hinduism"[40] in the nineteenth and twentieth centuries—such as Bankimchandra Chatterji (1838–94), Vivekānanda (1863–1902), M. K. Gandhi (1869–1948), Aurobindo Ghose (1872–1950), and Sarvepalli Radhakrishnan (1888–1975)—developed their own distinctive interpretations of *dharma* in which they abandoned the traditional emphasis on *varṇāśramadharma* and attempted instead to "ethicize and universalize *dharma*" (Halbfass 1988: 333) by invoking the universal principles of *sādhāraṇadharma* as well as the related notion of *sanātanadharma* as the "eternal religion" that is universal in scope.

Many Neo-Hindu thinkers have grappled with the relationship between European concepts of "religion" and Hindu notions of *dharma*, particularly in response to Christian missionaries' attempts to appropriate the category of *dharma* and use it to proclaim the superior status of the Christian religion as *satyadharma*, the "true *dharma*." As Halbfass has emphasized, both Neo-Hindu reformers and traditional Hindu *paṇḍita*s have invoked the notion of *sanātanadharma* in order to counter the Christian challenge and assert the preeminence of "Hinduism" as the eternal, universal, all-encompassing *dharma* within which all specific religions—including Christianity—are subsumed.

> At first, *sanātanadharma* was a concept of self-assertion against Christianity, a religion which had a temporal beginning and a historical founding figure; in this sense *sanātanadharma* was synonymous with *vaidikadharma* and had a restorative and apologetic function. Later, the expression *sanātanadharma* increasingly became associated with such Western concepts as the *philosophia perennis*, the "universal religion" or "eternal religion," appearing as a program of deistic openness and a search for common denominators of all religions. Yet even in this context, *sanātanadharma* still remained a concept of self-assertion, for Hinduism alone was supposed to provide the framework for the fulfillment of the universal potential inherent in the various religions. Accordingly, it was not considered merely as one religion among many but as a comprehensive and transcending context for these other religions.
>
> (Halbfass 1988: 345–46)

A second trend of analysis developed in response to European concepts of "ethics," in which a number of Neo-Hindu thinkers have attempted to construct a system of Hindu ethics founded on *dharma* as a constitutive category. In their explorations of the ethical dimensions of *dharma* from a variety of perspectives, these exponents of Neo-Hinduism tend to emphasize the importance of *dharma* not as a system of laws but rather as a system of values, with particular attention to the universal values of *sādhāraṇadharma*. In their reformulations of *dharma*, some Neo-Hindu exponents of Advaita Vedānta such as Vivekānanda emphasize the principles of universal love and compassion—born out of the realization that the Self is the same in all beings—as the basis for a practical program of ethics and social reform. Others, such as Bankimchandra and Gandhi, focus on *ahiṃsā* as the pivotal principle of *dharma* that provides the foundation for a Hindu system of ethics.[41]

Our investigation of Hindu constructions of *dharma* has involved excavating the complex layers of meaning in which the category is embedded in the core strata of Vedic and post-Vedic traditions. In the oldest strata—in the Vedic period, particularly as represented in the Saṃhitās and Brāhmaṇas—*dharma* is laden with ritual and cosmological significations and is ascribed theurgic efficacy as the designation for the sacrificial rituals that maintain the cosmic order. In the next strata—in the classical period of Brāhmaṇical synthesis, from the third century BCE onward—the term "*dharma*" is invested with new layers of meaning and is transformed from a ritual category into a sociocultural system. While the Mīmāṃsakas developed the hermeneutical strategies to legitimate this transformation, it is the Brāhmaṇical exponents of Dharmaśāstra—in particular, the authors of the Dharmasūtras and the Dharmaśāstras—who articulated the formalized system of sociocultural norms that came to be known as *varṇāśramadharma*. This Brāhmaṇical discourse of *dharma* has been challenged since its inception by a variety of competing traditions, including renunciant traditions and *bhakti* movements, which have developed their own contending assessments of the role of *dharma* within the larger scheme of Hindu values and more specifically in relationship to *mokṣa*, the supreme goal of human existence. In the latest strata unearthed by our excavations—in the modern period, from the beginning of the nineteenth century onward—the Brāhmaṇical discourse of *dharma* was presented with a new challenge. The exponents of

Neo-Hindu reform movements, in response to their encounter with European categories such as "religion" and "ethics," sought to universalize and ethicize *dharma* by displacing the differential norms of *varṇāśramadharma* with the universal norms of *sādhāraṇadharma* and *sanātanadharma*. Although the category of *dharma* has thus undergone significant transformations in the course of its history—from ritual category to sociocultural system to universal ideal—in each period *dharma* has retained its paradigmatic role as the defining emblem of Āryan ethnocultural and religious identity, distinguishing the Āryans from the non-Āryans and, in the modern period, "Hinduism" from all other religions.

NOTES

1 See Karve's (1968: 91–92) distinction between the "naturalistic" and "normative" dimensions of *dharma*.

2 For an extended discussion of *ṛta*, see Lüders (1959). See also Bloomfield (1908: 122–29); Kane (1968–77, 4: 2–5); Mahony (1998: 46–58, 104–10).

3 In an unpublished paper, Olivelle (2000) has argued that in the middle Vedic period the semantic range of the term "*dharma*" was increasingly restricted to issues pertaining to the king, his governance, and his consecration.

4 For an analysis of the relationship between the categories of *dharma*, *yajña*, and *ṛta* in the Vedic period, see Koller (1972: 134–40).

5 This formula is frequently repeated in the *Śatapatha Brāhmaṇa* (see e.g. 4.2.4.16, 4.5.5.1, 4.5.6.1, 4.5.7.1).

6 For an illuminating analysis of early Buddhist reformulations of *dharma*, see Tambiah (1976: 9–72).

7 For analyses of the Mīmāṃsā philosophy of language and of *vedaprāmāṇya* as expounded by Śabara, Prabhākara, and Kumārila, see D'Sa (1980); Holdrege (1996: 115–23); G. Jha (1964: 97–135, 147–86).

8 Within India, or Bhārata, which is the homeland of the Āryan people, the area north of the Vindhya Mountains is ascribed a special role as Āryāvarta, the sacred land of the Āryans. The *Manusmṛti* (2.22) defines Āryāvarta as the region of northern India between the Himālayas and the Vindhya Mountains that extends from the eastern sea to the western sea.

9 For a discussion of the xenological implications of Brāhmaṇical notions of *dharma*, see Halbfass (1988: 172–96, 319–33). For an analysis of the distinctive nature of the Brāhmaṇical tradition as an "embodied community," see Holdrege (1999).

10 For discussions of the various genres of Dharmaśāstra literature, see Derrett (1973); Lingat (1973: 3–132).

11 As will be discussed later, the Dharmasūtras' representations of the *āśrama* system differ in significant ways from the formulations found in the Dharmaśāstras.

12 For a discussion of the dates of the Dharmasūtras, see Olivelle (1999: xxv–xxxiv).

13 The status of Śūdras and women will be discussed in a later section of this chapter.

14 The verb *prasidhyati* in verse 97 means "to result from" when used with the ablative. The verb in verse 98 is *prasūyante*, "to be born, produced," although the commentators construe the verb as *prasidhyanti*. The last part of verse 98, *prasūtir guṇakarmataḥ*, has a number of variant readings, and its meaning has been variously construed.

15 The term "*tapas*" literally means "heat" and is often used in Vedic texts to refer to meditation and ascetic practices by means of which the practitioner experiences the illuminating fire of pure consciousness and accumulates spiritual and creative power. For an analysis of the category of *tapas* in Vedic texts, see Kaelber (1989).

16 As mentioned earlier in note 8, *Manusmṛti* 2.22 defines Āryāvarta as the area of northern India between the Himālayas and the Vindhya Mountains that extends from the eastern sea to the western sea.

17 Male members of the three higher *varṇas*, Brāhmaṇs, Kṣatriyas, and Vaiśyas, are referred to as "twice-born" (*dvija*), for they have undergone the "second birth" of the *upanayana*, the Vedic rite of initiation. Śūdras and women are "once-born" in that they are excluded from the *upanayana* and are therefore permanently subject to the condition of natural deficiency associated with biological reproduction.

18 The *Manusmṛti*, building on the earlier discussions of the Dharmasūtras, delineates a complex system of mixed castes that derive from *anuloma* and *pratiloma* marriages (see 10.5–72, 3.12–19). See also Tambiah's (1973) incisive analysis of the generative rules that govern the production and ranking of mixed castes in the *Manusmṛti*'s account. The importance of the categories of purity and impurity in the Indian caste system has been emphasized by Tambiah as well as by other eminent anthropologists and sociologists, such as Dumont (1970, 1980), Orenstein (1965, 1968, 1970), M. Srinivas (1965), and Stevenson (1954). Dumont, in his classic study of the caste system, *Homo Hierarchicus* (1970, 1980), maintains that the opposition between the pure and the impure constitutes the fundamental ideological principle that undergirds the Indian social hierarchy. Although, as Dumont's critics have argued, the pure/impure opposition alone is not sufficient to account for the historical actualities of the caste system, issues of purity and pollution are nevertheless a central preoccupation in the Dharmasūtras' and Dharmaśāstras' ideological representations of the social hierarchy. For an analysis of the Dharmaśāstras' representations of the "purity body," see Holdrege (1998: 363–69).

19 See *Manusmṛti* 10.5–72, 3.12–19 and Tambiah's (1973) analysis of the *Manusmṛti*'s discussion of marriage transactions.

20 See, for example, *Manusmṛti* 4.205–23, 11.176, 10.181. My analysis here concurs with Tambiah's "transactional theory of purity and pollution" (1973: 217), which emphasizes not only the boundaries that separate (Douglas 1966) but also the interactions that connect castes. Such an approach provides a mediating position between Dumont's (1970, 1980) structural model of a fixed caste hierarchy based on the pure/impure opposition and Marriott's (1968, 1976) transactional model of a dynamic system of caste interactions involving the exchange of food, women, and services.

21 For a discussion of the use of the term "*saṃnyāsin*" and other terms for a renunciant in the Dharmasūtras and Dharmaśāstras, see Olivelle (1984: 81–82, 129–36, 1981: 268–71).

22 For an extensive study of the origins and history of the *āśrama* system, see Olivelle (1993).

23 My translation of *Āpastamba* 2.21.1–5 is indebted to Olivelle's insightful translation (1999) and analysis (1993: 73–81).

24 For an analysis of the Dharmasūtras' perspectives on the *āśramas*, see Olivelle (1993: 73–103).

25 For analyses of Brāhmaṇical constructions of the three debts and the five *mahāyajñas*, see Biardeau (1976: 40–47); Malamoud (1983); Olivelle (1993: 46–55); B. Smith (1989: 196–99).

26 *Prāṇāyāma*, *pratyāhāra*, *dhāraṇā*, and *dhyāna* are four limbs of the eight-limbed path of classical Yoga (*aṣṭāṅgayoga*) delineated in the *Yogasūtra* of Patañjali.

27 For the prohibitions against Śūdras learning, reciting, or even hearing the Vedas, see *Āpastamba* 1.9.9; *Gautama* 12.4, 16.19; *Vasiṣṭha* 18.11–15; *Manusmṛti* 3.156, 10.127, 4.99; *Yājñavalkyasmṛti* 1.148. For the restrictions against women studying the Vedas or offering sacrifices, see *Manusmṛti* 9.18, 4.205–6, 11.36–37. Although women are not allowed to serve as the sacrificial patron, or *yajamāna*, they are allotted an essential role in Vedic *yajñas* as the *yajamāna*'s wife, whose presence is required at *śrauta* sacrifices. For discussions of the ritual roles of women in the Vedic period, see Jamison (1996); Schmidt (1987). There is substantial evidence that women were initiated into Vedic study in the Vedic period, even though women were excluded from Vedic education from the period of the Dharmaśāstras onward. See Kane 1968–77, 2.1: 293–96, 365–68.

28 For a discussion of the status of Śūdras and women in relation to the *āśrama* system, see Olivelle (1993: 183–95). As Olivelle points out, even though Brāhmaṇical ideology generally prohibits Śūdras and women from becoming ascetics, there is literary evidence that indicates that both women and Śūdras did at times become ascetics, even during the period of the Dharmaśāstras.

29 While many Dharmaśāstra texts include sections on the duties of women, the eighteenth-century *Strīdharmapaddhati* of Trayambakayajvan constitutes the only extant Brāhmaṇical Sanskritic work that focuses exclusively on *strīdharma*. Among the numerous studies of the status, duties, and rights of women in various Vedic and post-Vedic traditions, see Jamison (1996); Kane (1968–77, 2.1: 556–82); Leslie (1991); Schmidt (1987).

30 For an analysis of the various theories of *karma* that are interwoven in the *Manusmṛti*'s discourse of *dharma*, see Glucklich (1988: 39–63). For a discussion of theories of *karma* and rebirth in a range of classical and modern South Asian traditions, see Neufeldt (1986); O'Flaherty (1980d). See also O'Flaherty's (1976) analysis of Hindu mythological representations of the problem of evil, which frequently invoke the categories of *karma*, *dharma*, and *adharma*.

31 In addition to Malamoud's (1981) illuminating analysis of the *puruṣārtha*s, see also Holdrege (1991: 16–19); A. Sharma (1982).

32 *Sādhāraṇadharma* will be discussed in the final section of this chapter.

33 For an alternative treatment of various Indian perspectives concerning the relationship between *dharma* and *mokṣa*, see Larson's fivefold typology (1972: 150–53).

34 For an analysis of the status and role of the renunciant in the Dharmasūtras and Dharmaśāstras, including a discussion of the rules of renunciation, see Olivelle (1984).

35 For an analysis of the *Manusmṛti*'s portrayal of the *vedasaṃnyāsika*, see Olivelle (1984: 132–36, 1993: 140–42).

36 For a discussion of the history of the terms "*saṃnyāsa*" (renunciation) and "*saṃnyāsin*" (renunciant) and their relation to other terms used to designate a renunciant, such as "*parivrājaka*" (wanderer) and "*bhikṣu*" (mendicant), see Olivelle (1981).

37 Among studies of Hindu renunciant traditions, see Olivelle (1986–87, 1992, 1995); Sprockhoff (1976).

38 For analyses of Śaṃkara's perspectives on liberation and renunciation, see Fort (1998: 31–46); Nelson (1993, 1996); Sawai (1986).

39 For a survey of the interpretive perspectives exemplified by representative English translations of the *Bhagavad Gītā*, see Larson (1981). Among modern Indian interpretations of the *Bhagavad Gītā*, see Gandhi (1946); Ghose (1959); Maharishi Mahesh Yogi (1969); Tilak (1935–36).

40 Hacker (1978b) uses the expressions "Neo-Hinduism" and "surviving traditional Hinduism" to characterize the two principal modes of responding to the West in modern Hindu thought. See also Halbfass 1988: 219–21.

41 For an analysis of modern Hindu reinterpretations of *dharma*, see Halbfass (1988: 334–48). For discussions of modern Hindu reformulations of *dharma* as a central category of Hindu ethics, see Creel (1977); Holdrege (1991: 50–56).

CHAPTER ELEVEN

ARTHA

Hartmut Scharfe

ARTHA AS A GOAL OF LIFE

Artha, its meaning ranging from "goal" to "worldly objective" and "wealth," has been considered in India one of the driving forces in human life for more than two thousand years. It did not always play such a role, though. The oldest text in the Hindu tradition is the *Ṛg Veda*, a collection of more than a thousand hymns, which may roughly be dated between 1500 and 1000 BCE. In these hymns *artha* denotes a goal, especially the goal of a journey ("going to the same *artha*") but also of an enterprise ("the matter at hand"). It is an old inherited word; for in the closely related language of Eastern Iran we find a corresponding term "*arəþam*" surviving with the meaning "matter, object of a lawsuit." Grammatically speaking, the word "*artha*" originally was a neuter, but in the latter parts of the *Ṛg Veda*, as in all later Hindu texts, it has masculine gender. There were fleeting hints in the *Ṛg Veda* of the things to come: *artha* was linked, or rather contrasted, with *kāma* (desire). The priests once are asked to deal with the matter at hand (*artha*) so as to get a honorarium, and it is hoped that they will escape the desire (*kāma*) of greedy men (*Ṛg Veda* 8.79.5), and in *Ṛg Veda* 10.29.5 the god Indra is implored to steer those to the other shore who agreed to his desire (*kāma*), as the sun goes to its goal (*artha*).

Only toward the end of the Vedic period, *artha* expanded its meaning and assumed a major role in the ethics and religion of the Hindu people—roughly speaking, contemporaneous with Buddha and other religious reformers who marked the turning point towards a new religious age. As "object" or "objective" of various actions, *artha* acquired meanings of substantial and material content. Verbal expressions refer to an object or denote a meaning (*artha*) in everyday language as in the important injunctions of the Vedic ritual: "A Brāhmaṇ shall light the sacred fires." For the ritualists, the connection of word and meaning was eternal and unchanging (just as the Veda itself was held by them to be eternally existing), whereas others considered it as a divine creation; only the definitions found in scholarly works of grammar or metrics are based on human conventions. As an object of commerce or agriculture, *artha* came to denote wealth and worldly possessions, and as the object of statecraft, it denoted a wide range of political duties and objectives: "The livelihood of men is the goal (*artha*); the earth is inhabited by men—thus [the earth] is the goal. The science [or manual] which is the means of attaining and protecting that earth is hence the science/manual of [secular] goals (Arthaśāstra)." This is the definition offered by the most famous of such manuals of political science, the *Arthaśāstra*, attributed to the legendary Kauṭilya (15.1.1–2); it marks a new meaning for *artha*. The notion of material well being in the Vedic texts was usually expressed by *yogakṣema* (literally, the "yoking [of the draft-animals] and settling down") (*Ṛg Veda* 10.166.5), which comprised the action of man in the world according to *Yajur Veda* 5.2.1.7: "The mind of some people is directed at yoking, that of others on settling down; therefore, he who moves about rules over him who rests." Taken together, "yoking" and "settling down" characterized the normal lifestyle of the times and what passed for well being. The expression *yogakṣema* (well being) survived as a venerable fossil in the language of later times. But towards the end of the Vedic period, the seminomadic society of the early Veda had become a society of sedentary peasants, and the many tribes had been joined in a number of larger states. A new expression for material well being was required: this expression was *artha*.

From about the third century BCE onward, we find another new concept under the heading of the "goals of man" (*puruṣārtha*), in which three terms are linked together that were to play an important role in Hinduism: *dharma*, *artha*, and *kāma*. The earliest reference to this triad (*trivarga*) that can be dated with some confidence is found in the annotations of the grammarian Kātyāyana (*c.*250 BCE) to Pāṇini's Sanskrit grammar (rule 2.2.34). Kātyāyana allows the formation of compounds with "*dharma*, et cetera" in either sequence; an old commentary explains what is meant: both *dharmārthau* and *artha-dharmau* and both *kāmārthau* and *artha-kāmau* are permitted. *Dharma*, *artha*, and *kāma* stand next to each other in the first-known instance in a long list found in one of the concise manuals that ruled domestic life and ritual, the *Hiraṇyakeśi Gṛhyasūtra* (2.19.6). The exact date of this text is not known, but the third or second century BCE may be not far off the mark. By the epic period, the poet poses the questions: "Do you not hurt righteousness for profit, or profit for righteousness, or both for desire of which joy is the essence? Do you always pursue, greatest of conquerors, profit, righteousness, and desire (*artha*, *dharma*, *kāma*), distributing them over time, knowing their time, granter of boons?" (*Mahābhārata* 2.5.9–10). In the *Bhagavad Gītā*, Lord Kṛṣṇa distinguishes three kinds of steadfastness, based on the three strands (*guṇa*) that make up the physical world. The one based on *rajas* (passion, agitation) is of middling quality: "The steadiness of the nature of *rajas* is the steadfastness by which one holds fast to *dharma*, *kāma*, and *artha* in a desire to reap the fruits that derive from them" (18.34). Here one may render these three terms with "duty," "pleasure," and "wealth"—useful and meritorious goals with a prospect of pleasant results but not quite leading the self to god.

This triad of goals or values of man is often expanded into a group of four (*caturvarga*) by the addition of *mokṣa* (liberation), attested first in the more recent passages of the epic: "All this is clearly spelled out in the instruction of the 'grandfather,' as also *dharma*, *kāma*, *artha*, and *mokṣa* with all detail" (*Mahābhārata* 12.59.85). We had seen above, how Kṛṣṇa had devalued the triad of goals somewhat by linking them to the middling strand of the universe, still striving for "success" and concerned for the benefits that derive from their actions. Seen properly, in Kṛṣṇa's mind, the first three are, as it were, but a preparatory stage for the fourth; the first three face the duties and challenges of this world but lead ultimately up to the fourth which looks to the hereafter, the liberation of the self from the world and from the slavery of being reborn again and again. The first three are hence said to lead to prosperity (*abhyudaya*), while the last leads to transcendental bliss (*niḥśreyas*). Many Hindus believe, therefore, that *dharma*, *artha*, and *kāma* should occupy the first half of one's life, *mokṣa* the second (B. Das 1956: 14). This "group of four" may be considered the dominant vision in modern India of the proper goals of man. The great Sanskrit poet Kālidāsa (fifth century CE?) pointed to the elegant homology of the four goals of man, the four aeons of the world, and the four social orders (*Raghuvaṃśa* 10.22). But we find abundant references both to the *trivarga* (group of three) and *caturvarga* (group of four) in Hindu literature throughout the ages.

Historically, they reflect different phases in the religious development in India. Originally the triad of *dharma*, *artha*, and *kāma* was, no doubt, designed to meet both the secular and transcendental needs of man: *dharma* led to heaven, while *artha* and *kāma*—sustaining life in this world—allowed *dharma* to flourish. The concept of the four goals puts heavier emphasis on the salvation and on the newer methods and ideals: devotion replacing or complementing ritualism, the union with the absolute or a personal god emerging as the ultimate goal. An Upaniṣadic author had contrasted the blissful (*śreyas*) and the pleasant (*preyas*), praising the former over the latter (*Kaṭha Upaniṣad* 2.1); later Vedānta authors applied this distinction to the goals of man: *artha* and *kāma* were merely pleasant, whereas *dharma* and *mokṣa* were blissful. "For one who desires *mokṣa*, however, even *dharma* is a fault, in as much as it causes bondage," as Śaṃkara states in his commentary on *Bhagavad Gītā* 4.21. Authors of the Nyāya school of logic create a similar dichotomy from the application of another concept borrowed from the ritualists: *artha* and *kāma* have visible aims and results in this world, *dharma* and *mokṣa* have invisible aims and results in the afterlife. In the view of the ritualists and philosophers, the transcendental has the higher value (Halbfass 1994: 133), just as a Vedic injunction for which no earthly benefit can be seen is presumed to be of a higher truth and beyond all challenge (Heesterman 1994: 144).

The mutual relation of *dharma*, *artha*, *kāma*, and *mokṣa* and their ranking is extremely complex, in part due to the use of these words on different levels; the distinction between these levels are often blurred. The first three or the four together are called *puruṣārtha* (goals of man), making *artha* one of the group and its umbrella as well. One may act *dharmārtham* (for the sake of *dharma*), where *artha* has a nontechnical meaning "for the sake of, for the purpose of," or one may act *dharmakāmāt* (out of a desire of *dharma*), where *kāma* is the motive for *dharma*. Moreover, when everyone is expected to live up to his *svadharma* (his functional identity, duty), it turns out that the most prominent duty of a king is the pursuit of *artha*, making *artha* a subclass of *dharma*. But besides these semantic conundrums, there are questions of the relative value of these goals. Since the majority of our textual sources, at least down to the middle of the first millennium CE, are religious texts—some explicitly dedicated to the questions of *dharma*—it is not surprising that they put *dharma* on top. But when the topic is discussed in the *Mahābhārata*, Arjuna, the most soldierly and worldly of the five Pāṇḍava brothers, proclaimed *artha* the foremost of the three, and his impetuous brother Bhīma proclaimed *kāma* (12.161.11, 12.161.28, also 12.161.8), while the mild-mannered twins Nakula and Sahadeva extolled *dharma* above the others. The mutual relation of these three goals must be viewed at various semantic levels.

All three terms of the *trivarga* are used on different levels that are not always kept rigidly apart, and on each level we can observe a revolving hierarchy. On the highest level of abstraction, *dharma* is "functional identity," that which a person (or even a thing) is or does or should do: hence the Buddhist concept of the *dharma*s as the ultimate monads of the universe. In this sense, it surely would be all-encompassing. But so would *artha* be taken as "goal, aim," since nobody would do anything without having a goal. Indeed, the *Kāmasūtra* (6.6.5) speaks of an *artha* of wealth, of righteousness, and of pleasure (i.e. an *artha* of *artha*, of *dharma*, and of *kāma*). The Vedic ritualists of the Mīmāṃsā school stress the importance of *artha* as the motivating force behind the Vedic injunctions to offer sacrifices to the gods: "*dharma* is an *artha* characterized by [Vedic] injunctions." Here *artha* clearly is the encompassing entity, with *dharma* (ritual duty) a derived function. And then again without *kāma* in its widest sense as "desire, drive" nothing, not even the pursuit of spiritual liberation (*mokṣa*), would get underway. Indeed, *Manusmṛti* condemns being ruled by desire but admits that desire is an integral part of life: "For the study of the Veda and the performance of ritual that are prescribed by the Veda are based on desire (*kāma*). Not a single act in this world is found ever to be done by a man free from desire; for whatever one does that is the action of desire" (2.2–4).

A surprising aspect of the *trivarga* is that its components are now all masculine nouns. Only *kāma* (desire) was masculine to begin with; *artha* (the goal, end point of a journey) was a neuter that later became masculine and gained the added meaning "object, wealth, purpose," and the Ṛg Vedic neuter n-stem *dharman* (support, established order) survived only under a few grammatical conditions and was otherwise replaced by a masculine a-stem *dharma* (functional identity, duty, virtue). It is common to say that the neuter word became masculine; but it would be more correct to say that instead of the neuter *dharman* we have another, masculine stem *dharma*—which corresponds directly to Latin *firmus* (steady, firm). This trend extended even to the fourth goal: the word for "liberation" in the *Śatapatha Brāhmaṇa* was the feminine term "*mukti*," which was later replaced by the masculine *mokṣa* in the *Mahābhārata*—which itself is a replacement for an older feminine *mumukṣā* (desire for release)! It is problematic to read a deeper meaning into such formal changes. But the parallel developments are quite striking and may indicate a subtle shift: from an impersonal process to a static and personal concept.

On a more practical second level, *dharma* as "duty, law, righteousness," *artha* as "material goal" (mainly in politics), and *kāma* as "desire, love" are the topics of a large number of works and constitute specialized branches of learning. In a well-run society, everybody's role and duties are circumscribed by custom and by a moral code based on considerations of religious merit: going to heaven, escaping the unpleasant cycle of rebirth, or reaching a union with the absolute. This quest is ruled by *dharma*, often translated as "duty, law, righteousness," and it is the central concern of a large body of texts, especially the Dharmasūtras and Dharmaśāstras. We should include in this corpus also the Gṛhyaśāstras, Vedic guides to domestic duties and the life-cycle rituals, the *rites de passage*: naming, initiation, graduation, marriage, funeral. But in this context, *dharma* cannot function without a material base and without considerations of secular concerns and procedures comprised by the term "*artha*," "material goals, worldly objectives."

Arthaśāstra (Science/Manual of Worldly Objectives) is sometimes considered an offshoot of Dharmaśāstra, but the texts on Artha proclaim a separate spiritual ancestry; their alleged founders were Śukra and Bṛhaspati, the former the chaplain and preceptor of the counter-gods (*asura*, often translated as "demons"), the latter of the gods of heaven. Vedic texts have a few theoretical statements that point to an early political and military science independent from the large literature on *dharma* and its saintly authorities. In the *Aitareya Brāhmaṇa* a king gives political advice: "One shall not sit down before the enemy does but shall stand if one thinks he is standing; one shall not lie down before the enemy does but sit if one thinks he is sitting; one shall not fall asleep before the enemy does but stay awake if one thinks he keeps awake; and even if his enemy has a head of stone, quickly will he strike him down" (8.28). Both branches, though, overlap a great deal. Dharmaśāstras like the *Mānava Dharmaśāstra* deal extensively with matters of state and politics, while the *Arthaśāstra* attributed to Kauṭilya has a long section on the judges' handling of legal disputes, duplicating the statements of the Dharmaśāstras. Many of these worldly objectives are commonsensical and hence not encoded in systematic works; they are more likely to be summed up as "wise sayings" in popular poetry, such as Bhartṛhari's *Nītiśatakam* or Tiruvaḷḷuvar's *Tirukkuṟaḷ*. Many are skills taught by example and praxis as the know-how of the peasant or a merchant; such skills are passed on from father to son without the help of formal manuals.

Only a portion of the wider meanings of *artha* is the topic of the Artha texts. The most prominent of them by far is the *Kauṭilīya Arthaśāstra*, the "*Arthaśāstra* ascribed to Kauṭilya"; we must be mindful of the usual double meaning of the word "*śāstra*," denoting both a branch of learning and a text devoted to it. The date of this text has been the subject of much controversy. It may not be what it claims to be, a work from the time of the Maurya dynasty and Alexander—it is now presumed to be considerably younger. We must consider, though, that changes came slowly in ancient India, and the content of the text could be representative of Hindu political life of the whole era, even if it turns out to be a compilation dating from the first or second century CE. Addressed to the prince and his courtiers, this *Arthaśāstra* deals primarily with the problems of state administration and the rough and tumble of politics both within the kingdom and the world outside it. With a term borrowed from the weavers' art, internal policy was called the basic "warp," foreign policy the "weft" that was inserted as the highlight in this tapestry of public life. The prince and his courtiers needed basic information on many topics concerning the life of their subjects, and therefore a text like the *Kauṭilīya Arthaśāstra* has chapters on the evaluation of warehoused goods, the training of elephants, and the investigation of suspicious deaths—not as training manuals for warehousemen, mahouts, or detectives but to enable the top administrators to evaluate the performance of their subordinates.

Later texts of this genre concentrated on the treatment of foreign affairs and political ethics rather than on state administration. The king was the protector and upholder of *dharma* who made it possible for the Brāhmaṇs to observe their ritual duties and for all his subjects to strive unimpeded for their spiritual betterment. His way to this goal was *artha*, his theoretical and practical guidance, the Arthaśāstra; Dharmaśāstra for the king offered secondary guidance in general matters and in dealing with community affairs. For the Brāhmaṇs, the Dharmaśāstra as an adjunct to the Veda had higher authority than the Arthaśāstra which could not claim to be based on revelation. Thus *Yājñavalkyasmṛti* 2.21 claims higher authority for Dharmaśāstra, and its commentary *Mitākṣarā* interprets this statement as a suggestion that Arthaśāstra is embedded in Dharmaśāstra. The famous *Kāmasūtra* conceded to *dharma* the top position—except in the case of kings for whom *artha* is paramount. This may be due to its limitation to erotics, leaving out a large part of the psychology of human emotions.

On a third level, *dharma* refers merely to the religious duties and good deeds that are expected from a member of one's community who wants to be in good standing; *artha* to material wealth; and *kāma* to erotic pleasures. A stanza quoted by Nīlakaṇṭha in his commentary on the *Mahābhārata* adheres to such a narrow definition of the three basic goals: "Forenoon is for religious duties (*dharma*), midday for acquisition of wealth (*artha*), and evening for diversion (*kāma*), such is the Vedic saying" (2.55.10). No such statement is found in our Vedic texts, which only in the latest compositions make even fleeting reference to the three goals of man. It would appear that many Hindus in India did indeed adhere to the "command" that the three goals of man should be practiced in due time. Bankimchandra Chatterji, the great Bengali novelist (and magistrate!), wrote in 1884 about a Brāhmaṇ landowner of his acquaintance:

> In winter as in summer he gets up very early in the morning and takes his bath. After that he performs his daily worship for many hours with the utmost scrupulousness. He feels as if stunned by a blow on the head if there is even a slight interruption of it. He takes only one vegetarian meal during the day and that in the afternoon. He then attends to the business of his properties. At that time his mind becomes wholly intent on the problems of ruining one or other of his tenants, depriving an unprotected widow of all her possessions, cheating his creditors, securing false witnesses to send some innocent person to jail, or concocting evidence to win his cases, and his efforts in all these directions are successful.
>
> (1986: 776)

We may assume that in the evening he labored to secure the line of succession by begetting sons. He was totally sincere in his devotion and considered himself a true Hindu. Chatterji (many would say, to his credit) disagreed (Chaudhuri 1979: 16). For this landowner, *dharma* was no longer a righteous life but an empty course of ritual observances and restrictions, and *artha* was not the pursuit of worldly success and a decent living but a naked grab for wealth and power, unrestrained by the rules of righteous behavior or even legal propriety. His actions also lacked compassion. The rule that each of the goals is appropriate for its time and occasion has been distorted by some into a rigid daily timetable.

The *dharma* which the character observed so meticulously was only on the level of the prescribed rituals, not of righteousness and even less of functional identity in a divine cosmos. We must acknowledge, though, that the landowner for all his superficial and mechanical observation of his ritual duties followed a traditional path. The late Vedic texts indeed contain elements of such regulations of *dharma* in the Gṛhyasūtras and Dharmasūtras, meant to be carefully observed by every man, and the *Arthaśāstra* suggests a good number of ruthless practices—but these are only available for the king in his official role as protector of the state and public well being. The citizens are held to strict standards of law and custom. In fact, Hindu merchants enjoyed an enviable reputation for honesty, according to such world travelers as Hsüan-tsang and Marco Polo. Large merchant guilds such as the medieval Maṇigrāmam or the modern Ceṭṭis held their members to a strict code of conduct and enforced compliance; temples and educational institutions were the recipients of their generosity.

The *Kāmasūtra* does not concern itself with all aspects of human will or desire but only with the relationship of men and woman towards each other inside and outside of marriage, and, especially in the later texts, the concern is primarily or even exclusively with sexual practices, that is, *kāma* on this third semantic level; it does not claim dominant position for *kāma* over *dharma* and *artha*. But such a claim was allegedly made by the much maligned materialists, the Cārvākas. According to Medhātithi (on *Manusmṛti* 2.224), they asserted that *kāma* is the ultimate goal of man and that *artha* is instrumental in achieving it: the lack of material goods and power puts a damper on sexual exploits. *Dharma* is dismissed altogether. Medhātithi's account is consistent with other information we have of the ancient materialists of India, but we must keep in mind that all references to the materialists' doctrines are culled from works of their opponents, opponents who loathed them with a vengeance.

There was a broad consensus, though, that only harmonious devotion to all three of these goals, *dharma*, *artha*, and *kāma*, yields the desired result, even if the emphasis may change due to circumstances. Says *Manusmṛti* 2.224: "The chief good is said to be [the combination of] righteousness and purpose (*artha*), [or] desire and purpose, or righteousness alone, or purpose alone is the chief good. But the correct decision is that it consists of the aggregate of the three." The same can be said on the level of practical life in the words of the *Arthaśāstra* 1.7.3–5: "[The king] should enjoy sensual pleasures without contravening his spiritual good and material well being; he should not deprive himself of pleasures. Or [he should devote himself] equally to the three goals of life which are bound up with one another. For any one of these [three, that is,] spiritual good, material well being, [and] sensual pleasures, [if] excessively indulged in, does harm to itself as to the other two." Still, the religious emphasis, so widely evident in Hindu texts, makes itself felt even in Kālidāsa's poetry, where for the good king Dilīpa *artha* and *kāma* have become one with *dharma* (*Raghuvaṃśa* 1.25): the triad has been reduced to one.

PREVIOUS SCHOLARSHIP

If one considers the role of *artha* among the goals of man (*puruṣārtha*), it is surprising how little comment *artha* has evoked from traditional or modern scholarship. The abundant literature on *dharma* and *mokṣa* is not at all matched with writings on *artha* and *kāma*—and even the few that we have fall far short: the works on *artha* are mostly confined to the topics of statecraft, those on *kāma* to questions of sex. That goes also for much of the Sanskrit literature in general of the last two millennia as for writings in the regional languages. Their authors, whether they were Brāhmaṇs or other Hindus, Buddhists, or Jainas, seem to have had as much distrust or disinterest in the pursuit of worldly goods as in the yearning for pleasure. Their predominant orientation was toward the "higher" goals of virtue and liberation from this world. Buddhist authors especially regarded the teachings of Kauṭilya's *Arthaśāstra* as outright immoral, worthy of every condemnation. As a consequence, modern scholars found little to comment upon when it came to the topics of *artha* and *kāma*. The sections in most modern handbooks dealing with *artha* as one of the goals of man are insignificant indeed.

The inattention to the pursuit of material and political goals suited not only pious traditional Hindus but also those who liked to find in India their religious utopia. When manuscripts of the *Arthaśāstra* were discovered at the beginning of the twentieth century, it aroused great interest for the wealth of details on Hindu life, but it found a mixed reception as far as its ethics were concerned. While the German scholar Hermann Jacobi praised its reputed author as "the Indian Bismarck" for his efficient *Realpolitik*, others compared him to the Italian Renaissance politician and author Niccolò Machiavelli, not always in a flattering manner. Moritz Winternitz (1963–83, 3.2: 632) remarked that Kauṭilya grossly abused the religious beliefs and prejudices of the people when the survival of the dynasty was at stake in spite of an abiding devotion to Brāhmaṇical religion, just as strong faith and devotion to the Church did not stop Machiavelli from using any means necessary to achieve his goal. It is worth noting that the *Arthaśāstra* made a distinction between the popular religion and its temple cults and the sacred Vedic traditions. The author condoned, on the one hand, the deployment of secret agents and assassins under the guise of "holy men," the surreptitious smearing of temple idols with blood in a rival's country as an ominous sign against that king (*Arthaśāstra* 13.2.27–28), and the theft of temple property in his own state during a fiscal emergency; on the other hand, Vedic scholars may not be used as cover of secret operations, their property was to be beyond reach, and they ranked high among the state dignitaries. The author had no hesitation to use (and abuse) the popular religion for political ends but guarded the sanctity of the Vedic tradition. A reversal of sorts is found in the *Mahābhārata* (2.18.22) where Arjuna, Bhīma, and Kṛṣṇa disguised themselves as *snātaka*s to gain access to King Jarāsandha—to present him with an ultimatum and eventually kill him: the *snātaka* was a young man in that pure and sanctified state between the completion of his Vedic studies and his reentry into the world as husband and householder. The action of these three was a terrible violation of Vedic conventions.

The Indian historian U. N. Ghoshal spoke for many:

> Kauṭilya in some ways upheld . . . the application of ethical principles to statecraft. . . . The policy towards the highly disaffected and dangerous elements of the kingdom as well as the enemy outside, involves on the contrary the flagrant violation of morality for political ends. . . . Not without reason did the judgement of posterity fix upon Kauṭilya the stigma of being the symbol of a thoroughly unscrupulous, if highly successful, statecraft.
>
> (1966: 153)

The Indologist and avowed Marxist Walter Ruben (1968: 117, 229), though, declared him a "great statesman" even though an "ideologue of patriarchal despotism." The name for the diplomatic quarter in New Delhi is now Chanakyapuri (Sanskrit Cāṇakyapurī; Cāṇakya is considered another name of Kauṭilya). After India gained independence in 1947, the number of publications that delve into the deeper aspects of *artha* and Arthaśāstra (and the *Kauṭiliya Arthaśāstra*) has grown and may signal a more positive attitude to the Hindu tradition of statecraft. But the wider aspects of *artha* are addressed as little as those of *kāma*.

The French anthropologist Louis Dumont (1967: 331–32) saw a hierarchy of the three goals of man: "duty," "gain," and "pleasure," in which each preceding holds sway over the one that follows. He compared the hierarchy of the social orders (*varṇa*); in his view "duty" (*dharma*) corresponds to the Brāhmaṇ, "gain" (*artha*) to the Kṣatriya, and "pleasure" (*kāma*) to all others. In some oppositions inspired by the thought of Talcott Parsons, Dumont saw in *kāma* immediate satisfaction, in *artha* deferred satisfaction, and in *dharma* the ultimate goal—or seen in another way, *kāma* is expressive action, *artha* instrumental action, and *dharma* moral action. These two oppositions reveal meaningful distinctions, but they do not take into account the several semantic levels in which these terms are used. Dumont followed the viewpoint of our Brāhmaṇ authors throughout, giving some credence to the criticism that he "has been taken in" unduly by the persuasive advocates of the priestly class.

The American philosopher Karl H. Potter (1963: 5–10) defined the *puruṣārtha*s as "attitudes," *artha* dealing with material prosperity, *kāma* with sexual relations, and *dharma* with one's duty to family, caste, or class. He called *artha* "the attitude of minimal concern" (6), *kāma* the attitude of "passionate concern" and possessiveness (7), and *dharma* "an attitude of concern greater than that involved in *artha* or *kāma*," in which "one treats things commonly thought of as other than oneself as oneself . . . in a spirit of respect" (8). Potter's view of *artha* as an attitude of minimal concern for the trivia in one's life may share the deemphasis of *artha* found in many religious texts but does not do justice to its role in life and the emphasis it receives in nonreligious texts. The gradation from greatest to passionate and minimal concern (i.e. from *dharma* to *kāma* to *artha*) is not found in Hindu texts; where there is a ranking at all, *kāma* usually comes out at the bottom.

The French musicologist Alain Daniélou (1976: 8–9) presented essentially the concept of *artha* and the other goals of man as it is current now among many educated modern Hindus who impose a homology on the four goals of man, the four social orders (*varṇa*), the four stages of life (*āśrama*), and even the four aeons of the world (*yuga*). The four social orders are Brāhmaṇs, Kṣatriyas (ruling class), Vaiśyas (farmers and traders), and Śūdras (servants and artisans). The four stages of life are life as a student, a householder, a recluse, and a wandering ascetic, and they are now usually seen as successive stages in one's life. The four aeons (Kṛta, Tretā, Dvāpara, and Kali) represent the continuing deterioration of the world, comparable to the Western notion of a golden age in the past and the iron age at present. Such a homology is, however, not expressed in the classical texts, and any attempt to be specific meets with great difficulties. Saying that intellectuals (essentially Brāhmaṇs) are dedicated to *mokṣa*, warriors and kings to *dharma*, farmers and traders to *artha*, and craftsmen (essentially Śūdras) to *kāma* goes against common statements that Brāhmaṇs are the propounders of *dharma* and that *artha* is the primary concern of kings, but it reflects the modern view that the "higher" goals should be linked with the higher social orders with the Brāhmaṇs at the apex. Daniélou sees a link between *kāma* and *mokṣa*, on the one hand, being antisocial, liberating, and beyond reason, and *dharma* and *artha*, on the other, being attached to the world and the society of men. Classical Hindu authors usually have seen *artha* and *kāma* as worldly with immediately visible consequences and *dharma* and *mokṣa* as transcendental with consequences that are visible only to the perception of a *yogī*.

Arvind Sharma (1982: 16–17), a historian of religion, saw a rather strict correlation of the four goals of man, the four social orders, and the four stages of life. The student is presumed to pursue *dharma*, the householder *artha* and *kāma* as regulated by *dharma*; but then Sharma proposed also a compounded correlation in which *dharma* corresponds to Brāhmaṇs and Kṣatriyas, to students and hermits, *artha* to Kṣatriyas and Vaiśyas, to hermits and householders, and so on. His scheme is not only self-contradictory but also totally unsupported by authoritative texts, as Patrick Olivelle (1993: 216–19) has pointed out. The one source that does give a relation between age and goals has a totally different scheme in mind: the *Kāmasūtra* which divides the ideal life span of man threefold says that in one's youth man "should attend to profitable aims (*artha*) such as learning, in his prime to pleasure (*kāma*), and in his old age to righteousness (*dharma*) and liberation (*mokṣa*)" (1.2.1–4). It is remarkable that here "study" (presumably of the Veda) is considered as *artha* and that the life of the householder, that is, the working, earning, and tax paying man in his prime, is presumably dominated by *kāma*!

More restrained is the attempt of Charles Malamoud (1981: 49–52) to establish correspondences. He flirted with Georges Dumézil's flawed theory of the tripartite ideology of the Indo-Europeans but concedes that no clear correspondences between the three basic goals of men and the three Āryan social orders can be demonstrated (of the four social orders, only Brāhmaṇs, Kṣatriyas, and Vaiśyas are usually considered Āryan; the Śūdras stand apart and below). As far as the stages of life are concerned, he made arbitrary attributions and created specific blends of the goals of life for each of the four stages of life (*āśrama*): *dharma* is valid for the first three stages, that is, as student, householder, and hermit, and *mokṣa* for the renouncer, while *artha* and *kāma* are practically forbidden for the student and the hermit. The householder, the man in the midst of life as husband, father, and breadwinner, is to practice and balance the basic triad of *dharma*, *artha*, and *kāma*. This may be called a common sense attribution based on our concept of these goals, but it has no support in traditional texts. The *Kāmasūtra*, in fact, considers the student's pursuit of knowledge an *artha* (as was pointed out earlier), and an ardent desire (*kāma*) to study could be essential for a student's success. One correspondence that is found in authoritative texts relates the three goals of man to the three strands that make up the material world in Sāṃkhya philosophy. We saw this earlier in the *Bhagavad Gītā*, and it is also found in the *Manusmṛti*: "The craving after sensual pleasures is declared to be the mark of darkness (*tamas*), [the pursuit of] wealth the mark of activity (*rajas*), [the desire to gain] spiritual merit the mark of goodness (*sattva*); each later [named quality] is better than the preceding one" (12.38).

The correspondence proposed by Manu is not a happy one as it is not found in the Sāṃkhya texts; it is purely motivated by the fact that there are two triads whose members are often ranked hierarchically. The principal merit of Malamoud's contribution is that he has perceptively differentiated the various levels in which terms like "*artha*" are used and elucidated the revolving viewpoints that attribute priorities to one or the other of the goals and how they combine in the activities of man.

Lately, the philosopher Wilhelm Halbfass (1994: 130–32) has recognized in the concept of *puruṣārtha* the rudiments of a Hindu anthropology; for these goals, values, and orientations define one's being and constitute man's humanity. One could go even further—man is defined by being oriented towards goals and needs: he is *arthin* (goal oriented). It is his direction towards an object or goal (*artha*) that translates into a purpose (*prayojana*), leading to action. Only man can plan far ahead, even beyond his demise, raising him above all other creatures. This definition of man as goal oriented created a potential problem for certain Hindu philosophers. If their philosophical systems were not targeted on one of the "goals of life," they were irrelevant and not worth the effort; the ancient school of atomism and ontological categories (Vaiśeṣika) was especially vulnerable to such criticism. The Austrian Indologist Erich Frauwallner (1956: 28, 1984: 35–41) has, in fact, asserted that this philosophical system was originally a pure nature philosophy with no soteriological ambitions; but this claim has been rejected by Halbfass (1986: 857) and Jan E. M. Houben (1994: 711–48): it cannot be proven, and is indeed improbable, that the interest in spiritual liberation has been added secondarily to a basic text of this school of philosophy. The ancient Hindus did not believe in science for its own sake which was considered merely the vain activity of men plagued by curiosity. "All sciences deal ultimately with the goals of man, not with the objects in themselves," as the philosopher Jayanta (ninth century CE) said in the introduction to his *Nyāyamañjarī*. Hence philosophers defended themselves with the assertion that their doctrines, even the nature philosophy of the Vaiśeṣika school with its classifying analysis of the world, were directed at the goals of man, especially "liberation" (*mokṣa*).

ARTHA IN HISTORY AND INSTITUTIONS

Kauṭilya's *Arthaśāstra* (as we saw in the previous section) defines its own role and what *artha* means for a king: "The livelihood of men is the goal (*artha*); the earth is inhabited by men—thus [the earth] is the goal. The science/manual which is the means of attaining and protecting that earth is hence the science/manual of [secular] goals (Arthaśāstra)" (15.1.1–2). This text was obviously not intended for wide dispersion among the public whose awe and veneration for the "good king" should not be threatened by a detailed knowledge of how unsavory the business of politics could be. It was instead composed for the guidance of the ruler and his high officials. In the *Rāmāyaṇa*, Lakṣmaṇa warns his brother Rāma: "Righteousness (*dharma*) without means (*artha*) cannot protect you from evils, when you stand on a pure road with your senses controlled" (6.70.14). The king to survive needs to supplement his high moral standing with resolute even ruthless efficiency, substantial force, as well as intrigue and subterfuge. Kauṭilya's *Arthaśāstra* deals with the situation in which the king might face powerful dignitaries who threaten his rule and cannot be brought to heel directly. So he is told to send a female secret agent posing as a nun to the man's wife, winning her confidence by providing her with love potions, then double-crossing her by giving her poison instead—the wife naively administers the drug and kills her husband. Or rebellious dignitaries may be invited to the king's palace. Secret agents infiltrate their entourage and pretend to make an assassination attempt on the king; the dignitaries are killed by the king's bodyguards, and convicted criminals are quickly substituted for the secret agents and killed as "the dignitaries' hitmen." Such action, however, should not be taken frivolously: "But against those hostile principal officers, who cause harm to the kingdom, who cannot be suppressed openly, he shall employ silent punishment, taking his pleasure from duty (*dharma*)" (*Arthaśāstra* 5.1.1–57; Scharfe 1979). If the state is in dire straits financially, he may confiscate temple property (the property of Vedic scholars is exempt) or set up a secret agent as a trader who collects deposits and loans from other merchants—only to have everything stolen at night by other agents posing as common robbers (*Arthaśāstra* 5.2.1–70). A rival king that cannot be won over by friendly overtures or by bribes may be neutralized by assassins who lure him from the safety of his palace to a horse traders' *bāzār* or to meet a "holy man" in a mountain cave with the prospect of the secret of eternal life (*Arthaśāstra* 13.2.1–20).

The *Mahābhārata* (12.129–67) refers to the above practices as "rules allowed in times of distress" (*āpad-dharma*). "For some righteousness has the appearance of unrighteousness, O lord of men, and what has the appearance of unrighteousness is [in fact] righteous: that should be understood by the wise" (*Mahābhārata* 12.34.20). The king has to fill his treasury, the basis of all power that finances the army and state operations. "Because the gain of wealth is not found unambiguously, in distress—so it is heard—even unrighteousness has the characteristics of righteousness" (*Mahābhārata* 12.128.15). The most outrageous acts can be condoned with the *raison d'état*, the preservation and welfare of the state, which ultimately benefits everybody: *artha* in effect decides what is *dharma*. But the king is strongly warned off any obnoxious acts caused by greed, lust, or bad temper that may cost him his life and destroy the kingdom (*Arthaśāstra* 1.6.4–12).

Different rules apply to the common citizen who cannot generally appeal to these "rules allowed in times of distress"; he has to obey the law at all times, but allowances for hardship are made in the case of customs and taboos. If no Brāhmaṇ teacher can be found, even a Brāhmaṇ may learn the Veda from a Kṣatriya or Vaiśya, and a Brāhmaṇ in dire straits can take up professions like soldiering. In an extreme example, the great Vedic poet Viśvāmitra, starved for food, stole dog meat from the hut of an untouchable—committing what would normally be considered heinous offenses: stealing, taking food from an untouchable, and eating dog meat. Viśvāmitra did not consider this act, necessary to save his life, as a criminal act of theft (*Mahābhārata* 12.139.37–39). Unlike the king who is urged to gather an immense treasury as a bulwark against difficult times (to the perverse consequence that these treasures attracted foreign raiders into India!), the citizen is expected to circulate the currency and share his wealth. "There are three ways of wealth: charitable giving, enjoyment, [and] ruin. If one does not give or enjoy [it], he follows the third way," said the poet Bhartṛhari (*Nītiśataka* 35); stagnant wealth of the miserly is doomed to come to naught. Generosity is clearly seen as the most virtuous use of one's wealth.

The *Bhāgavata Purāṇa* warns against avarice and complacency:

> In most cases, the riches of the miserly do not bring happiness at any time: in this world they lead to suffering of oneself and for the deceased to hell. The pure fame of the famous, the praiseworthy virtues of the virtuous—even a little greed destroys them like vitiligo the desired beauty. When wealth has been acquired, men have to make an effort, be anxious, thoughtful, and avoid errors in order to augment it, guard it, and expend it in loss and enjoyment.
>
> (11.23.15–17)

Somadevasūri, a Jaina author from tenth-century Kashmir, in his *Nītivākyāmṛta* (a compendium of political and moral advice) (2.6–11) chastises those who expend earned money without careful thought, those who run through their inheritance, and those who greedily gather wealth while hurting their servants and themselves: no good future awaits the first two, and the accumulated wealth of the third eventually falls to the king, the heirs, or the thieves. But properly applied, *artha* is of crucial importance: "That from which comes success in all tasks, that is *artha*" (*Nītivākyāmṛta* 2.1) and "*Artha* is the root of *dharma* and *kāma*" (3.17). The last two statements are echoes of more elaborate assertions made in the *Arthaśāstra* of Kauṭilya.

The state of a householder (*gṛhastha*) is the common way of life for a man of the upper social orders, contrasting with the life of a student, the man who in his old age retires to the forest, and the homeless renouncer. The late Vedic literature describes these four ways of life (*āśrama*) as options (exercised once and for all time), available to the young man at the end of his basic instruction in the house of his teacher; later they were seen as stages to pass through one by one. But only the life of a householder is demanded by Vedic injunctions, as only he can beget offspring needed to perpetuate the Vedic tradition and only he has the wherewithal to support the expensive Vedic rituals and the people in the other modes of life who are not themselves productive. The householder is not only entitled but even expected to follow righteousness (*dharma*) in his life, to pursue the gain of material wealth (*artha*)—not only for himself but also to meet his obligations concerning his family, to make charitable donations, and to sponsor Vedic rituals—and is allowed sensual desires (*kāma*), in fact he is obliged to observe his marital duties and produce a number of sons. Some authors therefore considered his status as the only way of life sanctioned by the Veda, others at least regarded his status as superior to the others (Hara 1997: 221–35). Thus *Manusmṛti* declared: "As all living beings depend on air for their survival, so all the ways of life (*āśrama*) depend on the householder for their survival. The householder constitutes the most excellent *āśrama* because it is the householder who daily supports everyone belonging to the other three *āśrama*s with knowledge and food" (3.77–78). The Brāhmaṇical establishment, including the orthodox school of Veda exegesis, Mīmāṃsā, therefore voiced strong support for the married life which maintained them and obeyed the Vedic injunctions at the same time.

There was also strong interest in the married life on the part of the state: only men active in the world as householders grew food, paid taxes, and participated in various other ways in the affairs of the country, supporting thus the state. It is therefore not surprising that Kauṭilya's *Arthaśāstra* (2.1.29–34) contains a recommendation not to allow such unproductive people as wandering ascetics to settle in a newly acquired province, that is, a province acquired either by conquest or by jungle clearing. The recommendation, though, would allow men settled in the province to renounce worldly life if they made provision for the maintenance of their dependents and for old people to retire to the forest. There was clearly no sympathy for the ascetics and monks of the various traditions like Buddhists or Jainas.

The *Arthaśāstra* attributed to Kauṭilya reverts several times to the problematic relation of the three goals of man; the fourth goal, liberation (*mokṣa*), either was not a concern of the politicians or did not in any way form part of the problem: it was transcendental. *Arthaśāstra* 1.7.3–7 says:

> He should enjoy sensual pleasures without contravening his spiritual good and material well being; he should not deprive himself of pleasures. Or [he should devote himself] equally to the three goals of life which are bound up with one another. For any one of the [three, that is,] spiritual good, material well being, [and] sensual pleasures, [if] excessively indulged in, does harm to itself as well as to the other two. "Material well being (*artha*) alone is supreme," says Kauṭilya. For spiritual good (*dharma*) and sensual pleasures (*kāma*) are rooted in material well being.

Arthaśāstra 3.1.44 gives the appearance of raising *dharma* over *artha*; but this is an illusion: "In a matter (*artha*) where settled custom or a procedural command conflict with the rules of righteous conduct (Dharmaśāstra), [the king] shall decide the matter (*artha*) according to the principles of righteousness (*dharma*)." The illusion is caused by the crossing of two semantic levels: *dharma* refers here to the rules of conduct and specifically to the body of such rules contained in several well-known texts, whereas *artha* is used here in its nontechnical common meaning "matter, point of dispute" (remember the related Avestan word "*arəþam*" (matter, object of a lawsuit).

Arthaśāstra 9.7 weighs the relative importance of the members of the triad.

> Material gain (*artha*), spiritual good (*dharma*), pleasure (*kāma*): that is, the triad of gain. Of that, it is better to attain each earlier one in preference to each later one. Material loss, spiritual evil, misery: that is, the triad of disaster. Of that, it is better to remedy each earlier one in preference to each later one. "Is it material gain or loss?" "Is it spiritual good or evil?" "Is it pleasure or misery?" This is the triad of uncertainty. Of that, it is better to secure the first alternative after overcoming the second [in each case]. . . . And since material wealth is the root of spiritual good and has pleasure for its fruit, that attainment of material gain which continuously results in spiritual good, material gain, and pleasures is attainment of all gains.
>
> (60–65, 81)

MANIFESTATIONS OF THE PURSUIT OF ARTHA

The pursuit of *artha* (worldly objectives) manifested itself most clearly in the king's activities in three areas: conquest, the justice system, and his societal relations.

The Hindu ruler had always the ideal before his eyes to become a ruler of the world, that is, the Indian subcontinent. At the same time, however, he had to avoid being conquered by his neighbors. It was the traditional attitude of the conqueror to be satisfied with the acknowledgment of his overlordship (and the right to receive some tribute) and to leave his vassals otherwise undisturbed. A blissful state of peace was supposed to descend upon the world once this goal of world dominion was attained. Some of the major Hindu empires, such as those of the Mauryas and Guptas, went beyond this ancient code and eliminated local dynasties, especially at the core of their empire. An early critique of this practice is found in an episode of the *Mahābhārata* (2.13.63, 2.22.10), in which Jarāsandha, king of Magadha, jailed the defeated princes with the intent of killing them—and then is himself killed by Bhīma for this unethical behavior.

Shifting alliances and conflicts had to be managed with tact and flexible methods. One scheme involved what was described as the four means (*upāya*): conciliation, gifts and bribes, the causing of dissension among the rivals, and the use of force; each following is less desirable than the foregoing. Some authorities added indifference and deceitful tricks as useful means. All authorities agreed that military force is the least desirable option because the fortunes of war are uncertain. If force must be used, then the king was advised not to stake everything on a single battle. Another scheme proposed for the ruler to follow was that of the six strands (*ṣāḍguṇya*): one had the option to march against the enemy, form an alliance with him that ended the hostility, or follow various strategies in several degrees of "cold war" or limited confrontation. If war broke out, then one would try to make friends with the king at the enemy's back and be wary of the enemy's efforts to use the same stratagem; the hostile king in one's back, allied with the enemy, is called by the colorful name of "heel catcher" because he would try to attack from the back, catching one by the heels, as it were. Political tactics are the topic of several popular literary works, of which one, the *Pañcatantra*, treated political tactics in the form of animal fables; it made its way to the West and inspired several recasts in European languages. A board game called *caturanga* (based on the moves of two opposing armies) traveled through Iran and North Africa and took hold in Europe in the late Middle Ages as *chess*. Simple theoretical manuals of politics reached Indonesia and Tibet with the expansion of Hindu cultural influence.

With the transition from a society of tribes to fixed political structures more deserving to be called states, came the king's claim to the exclusive use of force against serious offenders. The king and his appointees used the power of the "rod" (*daṇḍa*) to enforce the rules accepted by society and to suppress, with great brutality if necessary, any attempt to usurp the authority of the ruler. Even draconian measures were defended as ultimately beneficial to the people: they guaranteed social stability—and the individual and society as a whole could attain their spiritual goals only in a state where the traditional values were upheld and people felt assured of their personal safety. The "rod" was pictured as a dark being with red eyes, and where it roams the people do not go astray. Pure people are rare, and without the constant fear of the "rod" the world would sink into brutality, ruled by the "principle derived from fish" (*mātsya-nyāya*), that is, a state where the bigger would devour the smaller (Scharfe 1980). The king's rule also maintained the distinctions of the four social orders (Brāhmaṇs, Kṣatriyas, Vaiśyas, and Śūdras) and prevented the dreaded "confusion of the social orders" (*varṇasaṃkara*). There are several instances in Hindu recorded history where kings used their authority to enforce the rules laid down by religious communities for their own members and the conduct of their own affairs, but only rarely was his power used against a religious community. The few exceptions are often noted with disapproval.

Kings occasionally benefited their subjects actively by the construction of large dams for irrigation of the fields and by organizing relief in the case of disasters, but more often the king gained the affection of his subjects simply by staying out of their lives. "Villagers whose lord is not oppressive will say: 'We are happy, thanks to our lord' " (*Abhidharmakośa* 2.50a)—reminding us of Machiavelli's observation: "[The people] want only not to be oppressed" (*The Prince* chapter 9).

CHAPTER TWELVE

KĀMA

Dermot Killingley

THE VARIETIES OF KĀMA

Kāma is a Sanskrit noun which we will usually translate as "desire." Desire is familiar to all human beings, whether we think of it as something to be followed or as something to be resisted. We may say, therefore, that *kāma* is a constant, given in nature. On the other hand, like any of the apparent constants of human experience, it varies from culture to culture. This chapter will examine some aspects of the concept of *kāma* and its various cultural contexts.

Kāma is by no means the only word with the meaning "desire"; like many words in Sanskrit, it has many synonyms or near-synonyms. However, *kāma* is preferred as a technical term in religious and philosophical contexts as well as in the literature of *kāma* itself. "Desire" is not the only possible translation, and sometimes we will have to use others because the word "*kāma*" has various shades of meaning. However, to keep the identity of the word clear, we shall often leave it untranslated.

In some contexts it refers to what is usually meant by "desire" in English: a particular mental attitude towards certain objects, which can be satisfied only by the possession or enjoyment of those objects. For instance, the *Bhagavad Gītā* describes the state of the ordinary person, who has not learnt to withdraw himself from objects of desire: "When a man contemplates objects, there arises attachment to them. From attachment arises desire, and from desire arises anger" (2.62).

Like "desire" in English, *kāma* can also mean "object of desire, desired object." For instance, when Yama, the lord of the dead, has offered the young Naciketas a boon, and Naciketas has asked for the secret of what happens after death, the god tries to buy him off by offering him various worldly desires. He tells him: "Whatever *kāma*s are hard to get in the world of mortals—ask for all those *kāma*s just as you like" (*Kaṭha Upaniṣad* 1.25). Both meanings, "desire for an object" and "object of desire," appear in the compound *kāma-kāmāḥ* (*Bhagavad Gītā* 9.21), meaning, literally, "those who have desire for desires." From the meaning "desired object" we come to the meaning "pleasure"; in many contexts, either of these can be used to translate *kāma*.

Occasionally, the word "*kāma*" can refer to an altruistic wish. For instance, a text on Sanskrit grammar, Pāṇini's *Aṣṭādhyāyī*, tells us that it is possible to say "I have a desire that you should eat" (*kāmo me bhuñjīta bhavān*) (3.3.153).[1] But *kāma* is typically directed towards the subject's own gratification, not someone else's. Closely related to the noun *kāma* is the verb *kāmayate*, which usually means "loves [sexually]," though it can also refer to an altruistic wish such as "I desire that you should eat" (*kāmaye bhuñjīta bhavān*) (*Aṣṭādhyāyī* 3.3.157). But this, like the previous example from the same source, is an unusual use of the word.

As an aspect of the general meaning "desire, pleasure," the word "*kāma*" often refers specifically to sexual desire or pleasure. This sense is the one that nonspecialist readers are most likely to know, through the compound *Kāmasūtra*, the title of a book of instruction on sexual pleasure in the form of a set of rules (*sūtra*). This more specialized sense of *kāma* is so closely interwoven with the general sense that it will be discussed before the other aspects of *kāma*.

The Hindu tradition has also developed a body of theory about desire (*kāma*) in the general sense and its part in human behavior. It is located in the heart, which is the seat of the mind (*manas*). Desire is a product of the mind; it is not, as often in Western psychology, fed into the mind by the body.

Kāma is listed as one of the four human aims, the others being wealth or power, righteousness, and salvation. It is also spoken of in the Veda, and later, as a cosmic creative force. In ritual theory, *kāma* is the motive behind every ritual act. But it also binds a person to this world through continued rebirth; freedom from rebirth can only be reached when desire is overcome. On the other hand, desire for freedom from rebirth is itself a kind of *kāma*; so too is the longing for god which is characteristic of *bhakti*. This longing is often expressed in sexual terms, so that the language of *kāma* is used in the service of religion. This is carried furthest in the Tantric tradition. *Kāma*, particularly sexual *kāma*, is personified as a god, Kāma or Kāmadeva, with his own iconography and a mythology which interacts with that of other deities. After discussing these aspects of *kāma*, we shall consider what is distinctive about this Hindu concept.

SEXUAL KĀMA

The sexual sense of *kāma* has existed alongside the more general sense throughout Sanskrit literature and in modern Indian languages. In the Vedic *vaiśvadeva* ritual, where offerings are made to various entities at appropriate parts of the house—to water at the water jar, for instance—the offering to Kāma is made by the bed (*Āpastamba Dharmasūtra* 2.2.4.1; *Hiraṇyakeśi Dharmasūtra* 2.1.54, cited in Einoo 1993: 218). Similarly, in a list of what are called "men" (*puruṣa*), which are aspects of the phenomenal universe, and their corresponding "deities" (*devatā*), the deity of the "man made of *kāma*" is said to be women (*Bṛhadāraṇyaka Upaniṣad* 3.9.11).

There is a rich literature of *kāma* in the sense of sexual love. While the *Kāmasūtra* of Vātsyāyana, composed perhaps in the fourth century CE, is the earliest extant treatise on the subject, it refers to previous authorities who are otherwise unknown, especially one named Bābhravya. Other technical works include the *Ratirahasya* or *Kokaśāstra*, composed by Kokkoka in the twelfth century, and the *Anaṅgaraṅga*, by Kalyāṇamalla in the sixteenth century. The central figure in this literature is the "man of the city" (*nāgarika*), meaning a wealthy and cultivated man who is able to appreciate not only the physical beauty of women but also their artistic accomplishments.

Sexual *kāma* is one of the staple topics of artistic literature (*kāvya*) in Sanskrit and other Indian languages, and a study of it is considered part of the training of both readers and writers. Recurrent motifs include not only aspects of female beauty, such as swelling breasts, slender waists, and elongated eyes, but also natural objects associated with love, such as flowers, the moon, cuckoos, spring which excites longing, and the rainy season which separates lovers. These motifs abound in the literature of other Indian languages, in painting, and in films. Many Sanskrit plays such as Kālidāsa's *Śakuntalā* move from love at first sight, through the vicissitudes which separate lovers, to their final union. The longing of separated lovers is the theme of many poems such as Kālidāsa's *Meghadūta*. Love is a major theme in Sanskrit novels: Daṇḍin's *Daśakumāracarita* and Bāṇabhaṭṭa's *Kādambarī*.

It is also a central theme of some of the stories which have been handed down in collections such as the *Pañcatantra*, and it is the main theme of one such collection, the *Śukasaptati*. This book, which exists in several versions in Sanskrit and other Indian languages and also in Persian and Turkish, tells of a wise parrot who repeatedly prevents an adulterous wife from going out to meet her lover by telling her stories. Most of these stories involve adultery, and many end with ingenious replies given by wives to prove their innocence when they are discovered in compromising situations by their husbands.

The fact that each of the erotic stories in the *Śukasaptati* is told to prevent an erotic adventure, which the parrot narrator pretends to encourage, illustrates a tension between the exaltation of sexual *kāma* in the world of the arts and the relatively low status given to it in the norms of society and in the ideals of religion. The same tension is a central theme of U. R. Anantha Murthy's Kannada novel *Samskara* (1976), whose hero is a sexually inactive *paṇḍita* with a vast knowledge of erotic literature. It is also expressed in a story included in the hagiography of the theologian Śaṃkarācārya. In order to study the science of *kāma*, Śaṃkarācārya is said to have left his body and entered that of a recently deceased king, Amaru. In this form he not only experienced the pleasures of love which are commonly enjoyed by kings but also wrote a series of poems on the subject, the *Amaruśataka*, which is still extant in several versions. In this way, Śaṃkarācārya was able to complete his mastery of all sciences, without violating his status as a *saṃnyāsin* by experiencing sex in his own body. This story has been used by Lee Siegel (1983) as the basis of an imaginative exploration of the relation between asceticism and *kāma*.

Those who first learnt the word in a sexual context should note that *kāma* does not necessarily have such connotations. Indeed, the *Bhagavad Gītā*, in which *kāma* is an important topic, avoids mentioning sexual desire, even in contexts where it is expected (Killingley 1997b: 68–69). On the other hand, sex is often taken as the typical example of desire and pleasure, especially in texts on renunciation.

A particularly instructive example occurs in the *Buddhacarita*, the poetical life of the Buddha by Aśvaghoṣa, a Buddhist with a background of Brāhmaṇ learning. In chapter 4 of the *Buddhacarita*, the future Buddha, deeply disturbed by his first sight of old age, sickness, and death, is in the process of turning from the life of pleasure in which he has been brought up to one of renunciation. To dissuade him from this course, he is taken to a garden, the preferred setting for all pleasures including sex, where he is confronted by a bevy of beautiful, accomplished, and libidinous young women. This gives the poet the opportunity to display his familiarity with the kind of knowledge that is taught in the *Kāmasūtra*, while making it clear that his real theme is the renunciation of all pleasures, and the impossibility of indulgence in them for anyone who is truly aware of the human condition. To the courtier who adds his arguments to the blandishments of the women, the future Buddha replies with mock admiration: "Ah, your mind must be very resolute and strong, if you see substance in unstable pleasures. In most acute danger you cling to objects of sense, as you observe creatures on the road to death" (*Buddhacarita* 4.97).

The chapter ends with the triumph of the future Buddha's resolve over the attractions of sense-objects; the women, as representatives of those sense-objects, retire frustrated and humiliated. Their frustration is the greater because he is presented as sexually attractive. This arises from the very fact that he resists them; for in the Hindu view, those who abstain from sex accumulate a power which can take the form of great sexual potency and attractiveness, as we shall see in the case of Śiva.

A similar but briefer use of the libidinous woman to represent sensual pleasures in general occurs in the *Maitrī Upaniṣad*: "Now, like the man in an empty room who does not touch the sexy women when they come in, someone who does not touch sense-objects when they come in is a renouncer, a *yogin*, a sacrificer to the self" (6.10).

The noun *kāmin*, formed by adding the possessive suffix *-in* to the noun *kāma-*, regularly has the sexual meaning "lover." As in English, this is often a term of relationship: a particular man can be referred to as a particular woman's *kāmin*, and similarly a woman can be a man's *kāminī* (the same word with a feminine suffix). As far as the vast majority of Sanskrit literature is concerned, such relationships are invariably heterosexual. They are also usually extramarital and clandestine, except where kings confer on their lovers the status of secondary wives. The feminine form *kāminī* can also refer to a woman who is desirous of male contact in general, rather than one who is in love with or has a relationship with a particular man; in the above quotation from the *Maitrī Upaniṣad*, I have translated it "sexy women." Since Sanskrit literature is written almost exclusively from the male point of view, it treats woman as an object of desire and also credits her with inordinate sexual desire of her own (Leslie 1989). The word "*kāminī*" is therefore used as one of the many words for "woman."

KĀMA AS ONE OF THE HUMAN AIMS

Kāma, in the general sense of "pleasure," appears third in the well-known list of *puruṣārtha*s (aims of man): *dharma* (righteousness), *artha* ("worldly power," especially wealth), *kāma*, which in this context is usually translated "pleasure." The three aims are often referred to simply as the set of three (*trivarga*). However, to this set of three worldly aims is sometimes added a fourth, transcendent aim: *mokṣa* (salvation, release from rebirth). The list of three aims appears in the oldest text on *dharma*, the *Gautama Dharmasūtra*. They form a common topic in the literature of *dharma* and in other literature dealing with human conduct, including the two great epics, the *Rāmāyaṇa* and the *Mahābhārata*.

Several of the passages in the epics and the Dharma literature on the set of three discuss the question of priority among them (Kane 1930–62, 2.1: 8, cf. 1968–77, 1.1: 22). The context, and often the content, of many such discussions shows that they are concerned with the proper conduct of a king and the way in which the opportunities for pleasure (*kāma*) which his position gives him are related to his need to maintain that position through political, economic, and military means (*artha*) and to the demands of morality (*dharma*). A typical example is the following passage in the *Mahābhārata* (Wilhelm 1978: 67–68), in which Kṛṣṇa admonishes Duryodhana: "The wise involve the set of three in whatever they undertake, O bull among the Bharatas. When all three are not possible, men keep to *dharma* and *artha*. But when the three are taken separately, the wise man keeps to *dharma*, the second-rate man keeps to *artha*, and the fool keeps to *kāma*, which is the worst" (5.122.32–33). This passage gives the usual answer to the question of priority: *dharma* comes first, then *artha*, and *kāma* last. Some ancient authorities, however, give importance to the group of three together, rejecting all attempts at ranking them: "Some say *dharma* and *artha* are the highest good, some say *kāma* and *artha*, some *dharma* alone, and some say *artha* alone is the highest good in this world. But the answer is that the group of three is the highest good" (*Manusmṛti* 2.224).

An extensive discussion of the matter is contained in the *Mahābhārata*. After the great battle which is the climax of the epic, the victor, Yudhiṣṭhira, spends a month in mourning and reflection on the banks of the Gaṅgā, with his four brothers and their uncle Vidura. During that time, Yudhiṣṭhira asks what is the order of priority of the three aims of man. Vidura extols *dharma* and gives the usual order: *dharma*, *artha*, *kāma*. Arjuna extols *artha*, since it is the motive of all activity, making *dharma* and *kāma* possible. Nakula and Sahadeva also extol *artha* but conclude by giving the usual order: "One should first practice *dharma* and next *artha* in conformity with *dharma*. Then finally one should practice *kāma*, for it is the reward of someone who has achieved *artha*" (*Mahābhārata* 12.161.8).

But the longest speech is given by the boisterous and voracious Bhīma, who argues for *kāma*. "Someone with no *kāma* does not desire *artha*; someone with no *kāma* does not want *dharma*. Someone with no *kāma* does not desire pleasure. Therefore, *kāma* is the most important" (*Mahābhārata* 12.161.28). So far Bhīma's argument could be just a play on words: to pursue any of the three aims is, in a sense, to have a desire for it, and indeed the notion of an aim implies a desire. But he goes on to make *kāma* the motive for all activity. Even ascetics, reciters of the Veda, those who make ancestral offerings or sacrifices and those who give and receive ritual gifts, are motivated by *kāma*. Traders, farmers, herdsmen, artisans, craftsmen, priests, and seafarers are all driven by various kinds of *kāma* (*Mahābhārata* 12.161.29–32). In short, "There is not, never has been, and never will be a creature that is above *kāma*. *Kāma* is the essential thing, O king; *dharma* and *artha* depend on it" (*Mahābhārata* 12.161.33). Bhīma, therefore, urges Yudhiṣṭhira to enjoy *kāma* and particularly women (*Mahābhārata* 12.161.36).

Bhīma's view that *kāma* underlies all activity is echoed elsewhere in Sanskrit literature, as we shall see; but his judgment that *kāma* is the highest of the three aims remains an eccentric one. Yudhiṣṭhira concludes the discussion by rejecting the pursuit of the three aims, on the grounds that all human efforts are overridden by fate; instead he extols *mokṣa* (*Mahābhārata* 12.161.43). It is only in later literature, however, that *mokṣa* is regularly added to the three to make a group of four aims (Flood 1997: 20).

The *Arthaśāstra*, the treatise on the conduct of kings attributed to Kauṭilya, discusses the order of the three aims briefly and ends with the unusual view that *artha* comes first: "Some say: 'He should pursue *kāma* so long as it does not conflict with *dharma* and *artha*; he should not be without pleasure.' Others say: 'The whole group of three is interconnected; for if one of them, *dharma*, *artha*, or *kāma*, is pursued to excess, it impairs itself and the other two.' Kauṭilya's own view is that *artha* is the most important because *dharma* and *kāma* are rooted in *artha*" (1.7.3–7). The passages which are translated in single quotation marks represent the views of other authorities. This is a common practice in the *Arthaśāstra* and other technical literature; often, but not invariably, each view is ascribed to a particular authority, and the summary of views is followed, as here, by the writer's own view. It is remarkable that although he quotes one view placing *kāma* first and one placing all three equally, Kauṭilya does not mention the well-known view that *dharma* comes first. His own view is similar to Arjuna's described earlier; both imply that a king who lacks wealth or other forms of worldly power is unable either to enjoy pleasure or to fulfill his moral duties. Pragmatically, therefore, if not axiologically, *artha* comes first.

While the *Arthaśāstra* gives priority among the three to its own topic of *artha*, the *Kāmasūtra*, despite being modeled in some ways on the *Arthaśāstra* (Winternitz 1963–83, 3.1: 620), does not privilege *kāma* in this way (Wilhelm 1978: 72). Whereas Kauṭilya can reasonably claim that *artha* is the root of *dharma* and *kāma* because it is the means for achieving them, Vātsyāyana cannot extol *kāma* as the means to anything else, since by definition it is desirable in itself. Instead, he ranks *dharma* first, *artha* second, and *kāma* last, following the usual ranking, but adds that there are two classes of people for whom *artha* comes first: kings and prostitutes (*Kāmasūtra* 2.14–15).

However, he also relates the four aims to different natural stages in human life, assigning *artha*, including the acquisition of knowledge, to childhood (*bāle vidyāgrahaṇādīn arthān*), *kāma* to youth (*yauvana*, the stage of life which begins with puberty), and *dharma* and *mokṣa* to old age (*Kāmasūtra* 2.2–4). (Here, the word "*artha*" can hardly mean "wealth"; it seems to be understood in its more general meaning "matter, purpose, aim.") The effect of this passage is to place *kāma* in the central position which in Dharma literature is occupied by the householder. The householder is central because he is the man in the economically and sexually active stage who acquires wealth and raises a family. This stage is preceded by *brahmacarya*, the stage of the celibate student, who acquires learning while abstaining from material goods and from sex; it is followed by the stages of the forest hermit (*vānaprastha*) and the renouncer (*saṃnyāsin*). But since the householder provides the other three with the necessities of life, the householder stage is said to be the support, the source, and the chief of the stages (*Manusmṛti* 3.77–78, 6.87, 6.89–90). When read with this doctrine in mind, the *Kāmasūtra*'s assignment of *kāma* to the second stage of life implies that *kāma* is the chief concern of the householder.

So far, we have looked at *kāma* as a factor in the behavior of human individuals. As such, it tends to conflict with *dharma* and *mokṣa* (as well as with *artha*) and appears to belong to the secular rather than the religious sphere. However, to appreciate the place of *kāma* in Hindu culture, we should look in the next section at its role as a cosmic force.

KĀMA AS A COSMIC FORCE

Kāma appears as a creative force in many of the accounts of the origin of the universe which appear in the Veda. Though these accounts vary, there is a common pattern: in the beginning, an original single divine being caused many beings to appear, thus making possible the varied world which we see around us. In some versions the event is seen as a combat, in which the many beings are rescued by the one from an enemy; in many hymns of the *Ṛg Veda*, for instance, the god Indra releases cattle by defeating the demon Vala or releases the waters by defeating the demon Vṛtra. In other hymns, a god measures out the world or places it in order or constructs it out of timber (*Ṛg Veda* 10.81.4); all these imply the preexistence of the world, albeit in a chaotic form (cf. Varenne 1982: 64). But the version of the pattern which prevails from the Upaniṣads onwards, and is found also in the Brāhmaṇas, does not involve any preexisting material: the one being which is the cause of the universe produces the many from itself or himself.

One early cosmogony of this kind, *Ṛg Veda* 10.129, gives an important place to *kāma*. This text might be claimed as the earliest clear appearance of the production of the many from the one, except that the dating of Vedic texts is so uncertain that such a claim would be merely speculative. A more substantial claim is that while many Vedic hymns speak in mythological terms about the origin of the universe, this hymn is the only one in the entire Veda which deals exclusively with cosmogony (Varenne 1982: 224). Since it is also one of the most influential hymns of the *Ṛg Veda* in the subsequent history of ideas, it is worth spending some time examining what it says about desire. While it resembles many other hymns of the *Ṛg Veda* in attributing the entire universe to one power, it is unique among those hymns in its refusal to describe that power or identify it by name. It is thus the first presentation of the idea that ultimate reality is without name and form. This idea is developed more fully in the Upaniṣads and in Advaita Vedānta.

The few positive statements in the hymn are outnumbered by negative statements and questions; it draws on a tradition of riddling which is apparent throughout the Veda. It begins by describing, or rather refusing to describe, the situation before the beginning of the world: "Not-being was not, and being was not at that time; space was not, nor the sky that is above. What moved? Where? In whose protection? Was there water, profound, deep?" (*Ṛg Veda* 10.129.1).

The second verse introduces a being, referred to simply as "the one," with neuter gender, which "breathed without wind, by its own power" (*ānīd avātaṃ svadhayā tad ekam*). This suggests a living being, animated by the power which later texts call *prāṇa*, "breath," yet not dependent on any surrounding air: it is thus self-existent and self-sufficient.

The third verse describes the one as being born by the power of heat (*tapas*). This heat is no doubt suggested by the fact that heat, like breath, is present in living beings; but the word "*tapas*" is more complex than that. The contexts in which it is used indicate variously the warmth which hatches eggs, the heat of sexual desire or activity, the heat of the sacrificial fire, ascetic practice and the power which it generates, and many more (Kaelber 1989: 2–4). As we shall see, it is frequently mentioned in cosmogonic myths as the means by which the one original being created the many; indeed, a brief hymn (*Ṛg Veda* 10.190) suggests that *tapas* itself is the original being.

The fourth verse of our hymn introduces *kāma*, giving it a crucial role in the creative process: "Desire came upon it in the beginning, which was the first emission of mind. Searching in their hearts, the poets found through thought the bond of being in not-being" (*Ṛg Veda* 10.129.4).

The word "emission" is used here to translate *retas*, which can have the general meaning "flow" in Vedic Sanskrit but can also have the particular meaning "semen"; this is what it regularly means in later Sanskrit. This word appears again in the next verse: "Their cord was stretched across. Was there below, was there above? There were emitters, there were powers; autonomy below, gift above" (*Ṛg Veda* 10.129.5). The recurrence of *retas* in these two verses suggests, in the deliberately indefinite manner which characterizes the whole hymn, that the *kāma* mentioned in verse 4 is sexual desire. It further suggests that the primal one, though grammatically neuter in the language of the hymn, is biologically male. However, the second half of verse 4 and the first half of verse 5 are more obscure and resist the efforts of modern interpreters to give them an explicitly sexual meaning.

The first half of verse 4 appears again (with a slight adjustment to fit a different meter) at the beginning of a hymn to Kāma in the *Atharva Veda* (19.52). Here, Kāma is invoked as a deity and called on to bring power and wealth to the sacrificer. In another hymn of the *Atharva Veda*, where Kāma is asked to subdue and kill the speaker's rivals, it appears as a cosmic or even cosmogonic power. It is called a bull that kills rivals (*Atharva Veda* 9.2.1), perhaps alluding to the way bulls in the wild fight for the position of sole mate of all the cows in the herd. In this hymn, the cow which is speech is Kāma's daughter. To call *kāma* the father of speech, in a Vedic context, means not merely that everyday speech acts are prompted by desire but also that Vedic ritual itself, in which speech plays a central role, is founded on *kāma* (see pp. 273–76). The hymn also calls Kāma the first-born, superior to gods, ancestors, and mortals (*Atharva Veda* 9.2.19) and also to heaven and earth, water, fire, and much besides (9.2.20–24). Evidently *kāma* is more than desire; it not only wants things but also brings them about.

The noun *kāma* and the verb *kāmayate* (he or she desires) appear in many other Vedic cosmogonic narratives, usually without an explicitly sexual meaning. The name given to the original being varies, but the creative process is still initiated by desire. For instance, the waters desired to procreate (*Śatapatha Brāhmaṇa* 11.1.6.1). To do so, they used the power of heat (*tapas*); the result was a golden egg, which floated for a year and was then born as a man, named Prajāpati (*Śatapatha Brāhmaṇa* 11.1.6.2). Like many narratives in the Brāhmaṇas and later literature, this passage expands material found in the hymns. The source is *Ṛg Veda* 10.129; this is shown not only in the motifs of desire, heat, and water but also in the use of the unusual word "*salila*" (water) (*Śatapatha Brāhmaṇa* 11.1.6.1; *Ṛg Veda* 10.129.3). It uses, more explicitly than that hymn, the image of childbirth: the egg floating on the waters suggests the embryo in the amniotic fluid, and the passage explicitly presents the (approximate) period of Prajāpati's gestation, his first words, and his first standing upright as prototypes for the human infant.[2] Extrapolating from these points, we may suppose that the heat which started the primordial process of reproduction represents sexual desire, although the process itself is asexual.

The narrative continues with Prajāpati's desire for offspring. This desire is not directly sexual; it arises from his awareness of his own life span, which is a thousand years. That is, the prospect of his own mortality prompts him to wish for sons to perpetuate his lineage. His response is to perform ritual: "He went on chanting and laboring, desiring offspring" (*Śatapatha Brāhmaṇa* 11.1.6.7). Here again, though it is not stated in the passage, the action is prototypical; for Prajāpati in the Brāhmaṇas is the prototype both of the sacrificer (*yajamāna*) and of the father. As sacrificer, he performs the primordial sacrifices on which all subsequent sacrifices are based; and as father, he begets the gods and the demons. The act of begetting is usually asexual; in this narrative he produces the gods and the demons, and also day and night, from his breath.

The theme of primordial desire occurs once more when the narrative turns to the institution of a particular form of sacrifice, the offerings at the new and full moon (*darśapūrṇamāsa*). The first to perform them is Parameṣṭhin, one of the four gods begotten by Prajāpati. "After performing the two sacrifices, he desired: 'May I be this whole world!' " (*Śatapatha Brāhmaṇa* 11.1.6.16). The wish to be the whole world is a wish to transcend the limitations of worldly existence; we find it in many places in the Brāhmaṇas and Upaniṣads (e.g. *Bṛhadāraṇyaka Upaniṣad* 1.4.10). Parameṣṭhin achieves this wish by becoming the waters (from which, according to this cosmogony, the world originated). He then performs the same sacrifice for his father Prajāpati, who then performs it for another of his sons, Indra, who in turn performs it for the other two sons, Agni and Soma. Each of them, Prajāpati and his four sons, has the same desire to become the whole world, and each achieves it through the sacrifice. The narrative thus places desire not only at the beginning of the cosmos but also at the beginning of the sacrificial order which links the time-bound cosmos to eternity and which provides an escape from the limitations of human existence. We shall return to this point later (pp. 273–76).

The motif of Prajāpati's desire to procreate himself recurs, with variations, in many cosmogonies throughout the Brāhmaṇas and similar texts (e.g. *Śatapatha Brāhmaṇa* 6.1.1.8; *Taittirīya Saṃhitā* 7.1.1.4; *Aitareya Brāhmaṇa* 5.32). By procreating himself he fulfills his name, which means "lord of offspring." In doing so, he also initiates the patrilinear succession which is essential to the Brāhmaṇical ideology; and in many versions of the motif he does so without the participation of a female. Sometimes he himself becomes pregnant (*Śatapatha Brāhmaṇa* 6.1.2.11) or lactates (2.5.1.1; Varenne 1982: 243–44; O'Flaherty 1980a: 26, 28); yet he remains male, the father of all beings. Running through these variants is the theme of *kāma*, which takes the form of desire for progeny, for a wife, for wealth, and for the rewards to be obtained by ritual.

Prajāpati is not the only figure to be prompted to create by the primordial desire; or, to put it another way, the figure who is so prompted is known by other names besides Prajāpati. In one of the most sophisticated Upaniṣadic cosmogonies, the creator is called Sat: literally, "being." It existed alone, without a second, until it thought: "May I be many; may I procreate" (*Chāndogya Upaniṣad* 6.2.3), echoing the desire of Prajāpati. It produced heat—a motif we have met with already, though the word used here is not *tapas* but *tejas*. Then heat had the same thought and produced water, just as people sweat in the heat. Then water had the same thought and produced food, just as crops grow when it rains. The passage goes on to show how all living beings, all phenomena of the universe, and all parts of a human being are formed from combinations of these three: heat, water, and food (*Chāndogya Upaniṣad* 6.3–7).

In the *Bṛhadāraṇyaka Upaniṣad* 1.4.1, it is a "self, alone in the form of a man" who desires a companion, divides himself into male and female, and begets various species, from human beings to ants, by a series of incestuous, and perhaps violent, copulations. This is followed by three similar cosmogonies. In two of these, the original being is called *brahman* (*Bṛhadāraṇyaka Upaniṣad* 1.4.10–11). In the last, it is again called a "self" (*ātman*). This last cosmogony is particularly instructive on the subject of desire.

"In the beginning the world was only a self. He desired: 'May I have a wife; then I would procreate. Then may I have wealth; then I would perform rituals.' Indeed, desire is just this much. Whatever one wants, one will not get more than this. That is why even now, one who is single desires: 'May I have a wife; then I would procreate. Then may I have wealth; then I would perform rituals' " (*Bṛhadāraṇyaka Upaniṣad* 1.4.17; discussed by Biardeau 1989: 38). This passage tells us that the whole extent of desire is encompassed by these two desires, for a wife and for wealth. If this seems too limited to account for all human desires, we should remember that both wealth and a wife are required for the performance of Vedic ritual, and ritual is regarded as capable of satisfying all desires; it is compared to Kāmadhenu, the mythical cow from which all wishes can be milked (*Bhagavad Gītā* 3.10). The need for wealth is clear when we consider how much time, material, and personnel are required to perform the rituals described in the Brāhmaṇas. A wife is needed because she has a role in the rituals, and a man without a wife cannot perform them (Olivelle 1992: 25–26). She is also needed for offspring; and male offspring are needed to continue the patriline, which is essential for the continuance of rituals, particularly those for the maintenance of the deceased in the world of the ancestors. The passage also tells us that the desire for a wife and the desire for wealth are built into the structure of the universe, since they have their prototype in the primordial desires of the original being. If we may use terms which became current later, the original being's first desires appear to be for *kāma* (in the narrower sense of sexual pleasure) and *artha*. However, these two are not treated as aims in themselves but as prerequisites for the performance of ritual. *Kāma* and *artha* are thus subordinated to *dharma*.

We have concentrated on some Vedic versions of cosmogony, but broadly similar accounts of the origin of the many from the one can be found in much later sources. A Tamil folk cosmogony tells of a creator god whose body exists in a state of equilibrium until it is disturbed by *kāma* (S. Daniel 1983: 53). In the Vedic cosmogonies, the primordial desire is satisfied through *tapas*, through ritual, or through some other means. But the satisfaction of this desire is not pure gain; it is always accompanied by a loss which has to be made good by further effort, which brings further loss. The primordial desire which precedes all activity initiates a descent from perfect and stable unity to imperfect and unstable multiplicity and an increasing involvement in the realm of *kāma*. When the Vedic cosmogonies are fitted into the cyclic view of time which prevails in the Dharma literature and the Purāṇas, the primordial desire becomes a link in an endless chain of desire and action (Varenne 1982: 158–59).

KĀMA AS THE MOTIVE OF RITUAL

Cosmogonies such as those we have looked at do not simply explain how and why our present world came into existence in the past: they are prototypes for all action and all desire in the world as it exists now. In many of them, the loss which accompanies the primordial action is remedied through ritual. For instance, after his creative act Prajāpati is exhausted or shattered and has to be restored through the *agnicayana*, a particularly demanding ritual in which a fire is built on an elaborate structure of bricks and stones (*Śatapatha Brāhmaṇa* 6.1.2.12–36). When the prototypical *agnicayana* is repeated in subsequent performances, its purpose is to restore the sacrificer in the same way as Prajāpati was restored (*Śatapatha Brāhmaṇa* 6.1.2.17, 6.1.2.36): that is, to raise him from this unstable world, which is a constant process of desire, effort, and loss and always subject to death, to a stable world, which is free from death. We have already seen how Prajāpati was prompted to perform rituals by his desire for offspring, which followed from his realization of his own mortality (*Śatapatha Brāhmaṇa* 11.1.6.6–7); and his sons in turn performed rituals because they wished to become the whole world and so transcend the limitations of their individual existence (*Śatapatha Brāhmaṇa* 11.1.6.17–20). In many Vedic narratives the primordial sacrifice is followed by further desire and therefore further descent into the world of differentiation, which leads to the need for further sacrifices (cf. Heesterman 1993: 28–29).

The idea that all ritual action is motivated by desire is built into the theory of Vedic ritual. Every ritual act has its fruit (*phala*) and is performed in order to obtain that fruit. According to Pūrva Mīmāṃsā, any ritual action is either performed for the benefit of a person (i.e. it is *puruṣārtha*)[3] or it has a purpose within the ritual itself (that is, it is *kratvartha*) (*Pūrva Mīmāṃsāsūtra* 4.1.1; discussed by Clooney 1990: 143–48). But since the purpose of a *kratvartha* act is to make possible the performance of a ritual which in turn is *puruṣārtha*, all ritual acts are ultimately performed for someone's benefit. Typical benefits to a person are wealth, cattle, sons, long life, and a blissful and secure existence after death; if no benefit is specified for a ritual, it is assumed to be performed for the attainment of heaven (*Pūrva Mīmāṃsāsūtra* 4.3.15; discussed by Clooney 1990: 141; G. Jha 1964: 262).

In the Veda and in texts supporting Vedic ritual, the person who initiates the ritual, and whose desires it is intended to fulfill, known as the *yajamāna*, is assumed to be a man. In many of these rituals his wife has an indispensable role, but it is a subordinate one; and it was progressively subordinated in the course of the history of Vedic ritual (F. Smith 1991). The desire which motivates the ritual is consequently a man's desire. However, outside the framework of Vedic ritual, both contemporary practice and textual sources show that women can initiate rituals for their own purposes. Such rituals include worship in temples and in home shrines and the annual, monthly, or weekly voluntary observances known as *vrata*s, marked by abstinence from certain foods, which are a ritual domain of women (Gopalan 1978; Jackson and Nesbitt 1993: 65–73). Women can also adapt rituals from the masculine repertory for their own ends (Kapadia 1994). Already in the *Atharva Veda*, there is ample evidence of women initiating rituals to fulfill their own desires, including desire for a man.

While all ritual is motivated by desire, certain rituals are prompted by desire alone, while others are prompted by desire to do what is appropriate on a particular occasion. Ritual theory divides rituals into three classes. First come those which are performed at certain recurrent times of the year, month, or day; these are called "constant" (*nitya*). Next, there are the "occasional" (*naimittika*) which are performed at other events which occur at irregular intervals: births or deaths, for instance. Finally, there are "desire-based" (*kāmya*) rituals, performed because the performer desires the fruit of the ritual, whether it be long life, birth of a son, cure of a disease, or any other desired object.

When any Vedic ritual is performed today, one of the necessary preliminaries is a declaration of intent, called a *saṃkalpa*, and this includes a statement of the purpose for which the ritual is to be performed. A well-known example is the marriage ritual, in which the father of the bride, or the priest on his behalf, pronounces a *saṃkalpa* stating that on such a time, on such a date, and in such a place he will make the gift of a daughter in order to fulfill *dharma*, *artha*, and *kāma*. A ritual outside the Vedic framework can also be marked by a *saṃkalpa*: for instance, a fast undertaken on Kṛṣṇa's birthday by women in Maharashtra for the birth of children (McGee 1991: 75) or a pilgrimage to a temple of Aiyaṉār by Tamil couples for the same purpose (Stork 1991: 94). It is thus widely recognized that any ritual act must have a purpose and that this purpose must be something that the performer, male or female, desires.

The term "*saṃkalpa*" is clearly relevant to the topic of *kāma*, but it is a term of complex meaning which needs a little discussion. Like *kāma*, it is one of the functions of the mind (*manas*); an Upaniṣadic passage lists it together with doubt, faith (*śraddhā*), lack of faith, steadfastness, lack of steadfastness, shame, insight, and fear (*Bṛhadāraṇyaka Upaniṣad* 1.5.3). In another list, which links the various faculties of sense and action with their objects and functions, *saṃkalpa*s are linked with the mind in the same way as flavors are linked with the tongue, sounds with the ear, actions with the hands, journeys with the feet, and so on (*Bṛhadāraṇyaka Upaniṣad* 2.4.11). This list is remarkable for the way it groups the five sense faculties and the five action faculties separately, in the manner of classical Sāṃkhya, and places the mind, linked with *saṃkalpa*s, and the heart, linked with knowledges, between the two groups. Thus the mind produces and perceives *saṃkalpa*s, in the way that the heart (regarded as the seat of consciousness and elsewhere regarded as the seat of the mind itself) produces and perceives knowledge, while the tongue and the ear perceive flavors and sounds, respectively, the hands produce actions, the feet produce locomotion, and so on.

In later philosophy, *saṃkalpa* is the process by which the mind organizes sense data in accordance with a preexistent conceptual frame by identifying each sense-object as a member of a class. In Vedic thought, however, the term implies an element of intention; it is a function of the mind which directs a person towards a goal and gives purpose to action (Gonda 1965a: 368). This is the sense which is implied in the current ritual use of the term as well as in texts which associate it with *kāma*. Manu, for instance, says in a discussion of the nature of *dharma*: "To be full of desire is not approved, and yet there is no such thing as desirelessness in this world; for study of the Veda results from desire and so does the practice of Vedic rituals. Desire is the root of intention, and sacrifices arise from intention; vows and rules of abstinence are all based on intention. An action without desire is never found in this world; for anything that is done is driven by desire" (*Manusmṛti* 2.2–4).[4] This view of the pervasiveness of *kāma* in human action recalls Bhīma's (see p. 268), though it does not lead to the same conclusion.

It is worth noting how easily the argument in these three verses slips from action in general to ritual action and back again; this is common in ancient Hindu discussions of ritual. In many contexts the words "*karman*" and "*kriyā*" mean "action, deed" in general, and this is the meaning to be expected from their etymology. However, in the Brāhmaṇas and the Upaniṣads and in later literature dealing with ritual, they regularly have the specialized meaning of ritual action. In many contexts—for instance, in parts of the *Bhagavad Gītā*—it is not clear whether the general or the particular meaning is intended. The general rule that desire for objects is the motive for action may have originated in discussions of ritual, but it is applied throughout ancient Hindu thought to all action and not just to ritual action. In the Nyāya system, knowledge of an object leads to desire, which leads to action. According to Pūrva Mīmāṃsā all action is painful, and therefore no one would engage in action if they did not think that the resulting pain would be compensated by happiness (Biardeau 1989: 70–73); this theory of action in general becomes the foundation of a theory in which all ritual action is based on desire.

Before leaving the topic of *saṃkalpa*, we should mention the ideal condition of *satyasaṃkalpa*: "whose intentions are true." This condition is described in *Chāndogya Upaniṣad* 8.2: "Whatever end he is desirous of, whatever desire he desires, it arises from his mere intention" (10). This condition is reached after death by those who know the true self (*Chāndogya Upaniṣad* 8.1.6); and the self is described as "having true desires and intentions" (*satyakāmaḥ satyasaṃkalpaḥ*)—that is, whatever it desires or intends becomes real, since the self is not subject to the limitations of our worldly condition. This is the condition of Prajāpati, who not only desires creation but also achieves it; it also helps us to understand why in the *Atharva Veda* hymns to Kāma (p. 271), *kāma* is not merely a mental state but also a power which can subdue rivals or even create the cosmos.

KĀMA AS THE CAUSE OF BONDAGE

As we saw (pp. 269–73), the existence of the universe is rooted in *kāma*. Individual existence, for which the primordial being provides the prototype, is similarly rooted in *kāma*. This idea appears in one of the earliest Upaniṣadic passages which introduce the idea of rebirth. The passage describes the process of death and then, rather cryptically, how the self acquires a new body. Then comes a statement relating the kind of body an individual self acquires to the previous deeds of that self: "As he acts, as he behaves, so he becomes. A doer of good becomes good; a doer of evil becomes evil. Good by good action, evil by evil" (*Bṛhadāraṇyaka Upaniṣad* 4.4.5).

The same idea, or similar ideas, of rebirth according to action are found in other passages of the Upaniṣads (see next paragraph). But the passage we are now considering adds, as if as an afterthought, a further factor which it seems to regard as more fundamental than action itself: desire. "Now they say: 'Man is made of desire.' As is his desire, so is his resolve. As is his resolve, so he performs action. As is the action he performs, so he becomes" (*Bṛhadāraṇyaka Upaniṣad* 4.4.6).[5] The passage continues with a verse summing up the idea of rebirth according to actions; but it then adds that this applies to the person who desires. The one who is free from desire has a different destiny: "Being nothing but *brahman*, he goes to *brahman*." This too is repeated in verse: "When all the desires that reside in his heart are got rid of, then a mortal becomes immortal; he reaches *brahman* in this world" (*Bṛhadāraṇyaka Upaniṣad* 4.4.7). Thus the ultimate determinant of rebirth is not action, as it appeared earlier in the passage, but desire.

Other passages in the Upaniṣads identify action, without mentioning desire, as the cause of rebirth and the determinant of the forms which an individual will take in future births. In *Bṛhadāraṇyaka Upaniṣad* 3.2.13, Yājñavalkya's answer to a question about what survives after death is not explicitly given, but it is summed up in the one word: *karman* (action). In *Chāndogya Upaniṣad* 5.10.7, good behavior is said to lead to birth as a Brāhmaṇ, a Kṣatriya, or a Vaiśya, while bad behavior leads to birth as an animal or a *caṇḍāla* (a member of a particularly low caste). In *Kaṭha Upaniṣad* 5.7, some are embodied in a womb, others in plants, "according to their deeds and according to their knowledge." The last passage refers to Vedic knowledge (*śruta*) as a factor affecting rebirth, which is not mentioned in the other passages.

However, although *kāma* is not mentioned in these passages as a cause of rebirth, freedom from desire is associated in the Upaniṣads with the quest for salvation. Desire, as we have seen, belongs to the world of multiplicity, which is time-bound and unstable. While Vedic cosmogony begins with a primordial unity, which is prompted by *kāma* to become many, the way to salvation lies in the opposite direction: from multiplicity to unity through the abandonment of *kāma*. The search often starts with a realization that desires are by nature many, which implies that they are unstable and unsatisfactory: "Many are the desires within a man, and multifarious" (*Chāndogya Upaniṣad* 4.10.3). In the elaborate narrative which frames the *Kaṭha Upaniṣad*, the persistent inquirer Naciketas refuses the many *kāmas* (objects of desire) which are offered to him by Yama, the lord of the dead, and insists on the one thing he has asked for, knowledge of what happens after death. Yama thereupon congratulates him on choosing knowledge rather than objects of desire, again mentioning their multiplicity: "I consider Naciketas to be a seeker of knowledge; the many desires did not confound you" (*Kaṭha Upaniṣad* 2.4). The contrast between worldly desires and the search for salvation is made clear later in the same Upaniṣad: "Fools go after outward desires; they enter the snares of widespread death. But the wise, who know immortality, do not seek the stable among the unstable things of this world" (*Kaṭha Upaniṣad* 4.2). Freedom from desire is therefore the key to salvation. The contrast between the bondage of desire and the freedom of desirelessness is clearly put in another Upaniṣad: "Desirelessness is like the best selection from the best treasury. For the man who is made of all desires, who is marked by resolve, intention, and self-conceit, is bound. One who is the opposite of that is released" (*Maitrī Upaniṣad* 6.30).

Thus salvation in the Upaniṣads requires either freedom from action or freedom from desire; but the possibility of action without desire is not considered, perhaps because desire and action are assumed to be inseparable. Because action is often thought of in terms of ritual action, those who seek salvation may abandon all ritual activity and with it all marks of status and kinship. For instance, it is said that those who know the true self do not desire offspring—a desire which, as we have seen, is typical of the Veda. "Knowing this, the ancients did not desire offspring. 'What shall we do with offspring, we who have this self, this world?,' they said. So they rose above the desire for sons, the desire for wealth, and the desire for worlds and lived the life of beggars. For the desire for sons is the same as the desire for wealth and the desire for wealth is the same as the desire for worlds; for both of them are just desires" (*Bṛhadāraṇyaka Upaniṣad* 4.4.22).[6]

Such ideas provide a rationale for the figure of the *saṃnyāsin*, who lives without ritual or social ties because he seeks, or has already reached, salvation (Olivelle 1993). Although he cannot be totally inactive, the *saṃnyāsin*'s actions are totally unlike those of the householder. He avoids all action which has ritual, social, or economic significance, since such action creates bonds which are incompatible with salvation. Thus he has no sacrificial fire and no family and lives by begging or from the wild, getting his food neither by trade nor by agriculture. Besides the Upaniṣads, other texts similarly oppose action, rather than desire, to salvation. Since salvation is reached by supreme knowledge, this opposition becomes an opposition between knowledge and action, which was developed in an extreme form by Śaṃkara. A verse in the section of the *Mahābhārata* called the *Mokṣadharma* expresses the opposition very clearly: "By action a person is bound; by knowledge a person is freed. Therefore sages who have seen the beyond do not perform actions" (12.233.7).

In the *Bhagavad Gītā*, however, the possibility of action without desire becomes the key to a radically new way to salvation, in which the opposition between action and salvation is resolved (Killingley 1997b). Existence without action, the *Bhagavad Gītā* argues, is impossible, since everyone is made to act by the three *guṇas* which make up their personality and which are also part of nature: "For no one remains even for a moment without performing action; for everyone is made to do action, willy-nilly, by the *guṇas* which are born of nature" (3.5). On the other hand, action without desire is possible, despite the statements of Manu and others to the contrary. "The disciplined man who has abandoned the fruit of actions reaches constant peace; the undisciplined, who is attached to fruit, is bound by his desire-driven action" (*Bhagavad Gītā* 5.12). This way of acting without desire is referred to in the *Bhagavad Gītā* as *karmayoga* (discipline of action).

It is also said in the *Bhagavad Gītā* (3.9) that sacrifice (*yajña*) is the only kind of action that is not binding. But this does not conflict with the idea of *karmayoga*; rather it is another way of stating it. Sacrifice is not necessarily Vedic ritual. In fact, the *Bhagavad Gītā* disparages such ritual, since it is driven by *kāma* (2.43); the true *yogin* is the one who abandons intention (*saṃkalpa*) (6.2), which, as we have seen, is an essential element in ritual. If sacrifice were understood as necessarily motivated by desire, as it is in Pūrva Mīmāṃsā, there would be no escape from desire. It is not denied that sacrifice can be motivated by desire; indeed, it is likened to Kāmaduh (the desire-milker), the mythical cow of the gods that will grant any object of desire (*Bhagavad Gītā* 3.10). But, for the ideal *yogin* of the *Bhagavad Gītā*, who is free from desire, sacrifice is an unmotivated offering to god. Moreover, the *Bhagavad Gītā* (9.27) redefines sacrifice by saying that any action can be made into an offering to god. Thus action is not abandoned but performed in a new way, in which it is motivated not by the desires of the individual but by devotion to god (De Smet 1977; Olivelle 1978). This new way of acting has been referred to by the modern commentator Aurobindo as "acting Godwards" (Ghose 1959: 151).

This resolution of the problem of desire is made possible by the devotional theology of the *Bhagavad Gītā*, in which the devotee has a personal relationship with god which provides him with a motivation for action which does not depend on his own desires. The same theology solves the problem of god's motivation: he acts for the maintenance of the world (*Bhagavad Gītā* 3.20, 3.25) to restore *dharma* (4.8) or to return the love of his devotees (12.14–20, cf. 10.1, 11.54) but not out of desire, since he has no needs of his own (3.22).

The idea of action without desire for personal reward was used by Bankimchandra Chatterji (1838–94) as a key to the interpretation of the *Bhagavad Gītā*. He summarized this idea in the phrase *niṣkāma karma* (desireless action). Though it does not occur in the *Gītā* itself, this phrase became associated with its teaching, particularly when the *Gītā* was taken up by the Bengali nationalist movement in the early twentieth century.

The idea of salvation through freedom from desire contains a paradox. In the Vedic narratives which we looked at above, cosmogony is a descent into the world of desire and leads to a wish to escape from that world. Thus salvation, which is to be reached by abandoning desire, is itself an object of desire. A person seeking salvation is referred to as *mumukṣu*, "wanting to be released" or "one who wants to be released" (e.g. *Śvetāśvatara Upaniṣad* 6.18; *Bhagavad Gītā* 16.20), a desiderative adjective or noun related to the root *muc* (release). Moreover, such desire for release can be referred to as *kāma*. In the passage on rebirth quoted earlier, the person who is not destined to be reborn is described as "not desiring, without desire, desireless, whose desire is achieved, whose desire is the self" (*Bṛhadāraṇyaka Upaniṣad* 4.4.6). These seem to be alternative descriptions of the same person, implying that the ultimate desire is paradoxically no desire or else is a desire of a higher order in which lower desires are eclipsed.

The same paradox occurs in a passage in the *Bhāgavata Purāṇa*. It begins by listing the various deities which are to be worshiped by people desiring particular things: "One who desires the splendor of *brahman* should worship Brahmaṇaspati; one who desires powers should worship Indra, and one who desires offspring should worship the

Prajāpatis" (*Bhāgavata Purāṇa* 2.3.2). Other desires are similarly assigned to appropriate deities. Finally, to the ultimate deity is assigned the ultimate desire which is no desire: "One who is without desire, or who desires everything, who desires salvation with exalted thought, should worship god with intense discipline of devotion" (*Bhāgavata Purāṇa* 2.3.10). Here, again, we may regard these descriptions as three alternative attempts to describe the same kind of person rather than as descriptions of three kinds of persons who are qualified for the highest form of worship. Thus desire for salvation is no desire; otherwise, the desireless state on which salvation depends would be unattainable.

KĀMA, BHAKTI, AND PREMAN

We saw just now that desire for salvation could be referred to as *kāma*, though we also saw that this was desire of a particular kind, that could paradoxically also be called desirelessness. In the theistic traditions of Hinduism, desire for salvation is desire for god, and this can be expressed in sexual terms. There is a hint of this in the *Bhagavad Gītā*, where Arjuna, terrified when Kṛṣṇa reveals himself as god, begs his forgiveness for having treated him in the past as a familiar equal. He asks him to bear with him as a father with a son, as a (male) friend with a (male) friend, or as a (male) lover with a (female) beloved (*Bhagavad Gītā* 11.44). Here, Arjuna sees the devotee's relationship with god as analogous with three human relationships, and in the third of them the devotee is necessarily female, since god, at any rate in the *Bhagavad Gītā*, is male. However this hint is not taken further.

It was the group of twelve Tamil poets known as Āḻvārs who developed a form of religious expression drawing on the experience of sexual love. Among other motifs, they made use of the stories in the *Harivaṃśa*, the *Brahma Purāṇa*, and the *Viṣṇu Purāṇa* of Kṛṣṇa's life in the cowherds' village to which he had been taken as a baby. Many of these stories tell of the cowherd women (*gopī*), who were attracted and distracted by his beauty and the music of his flute. The Āḻvārs used the figure of Māyōn, who appears in earlier Tamil poetry and whose name, literally "dark-complexioned," is a Tamil translation of Kṛṣṇa (Hardy 1983: 218). They also used the conventions surrounding one of the stock figures of Tamil poetry, the lovesick girl separated from her lover, and identified her as a *gopī*. Thus one of these poets, Nammāḻvār, says: "Māyōn embraced me, clasped my breasts and shoulders, and then abandoned me" (*Tiruvāymoḻi* 9.9; Hardy 1983: 356). The fact that Nammāḻvār was a man did not prevent him from adopting the persona of a woman. Indeed, it is said (in the *Īṭu*, a commentary on the Tamil anthology *Akanāṉūru*) that god is so extremely male that when faced with him the male devotee loses his maleness (Hardy 1983: 563)—an explanation which implies a close relation between maleness and dominance. Āṇṭāḷ, the only woman among the Āḻvārs, makes one of her poems a prayer to Kāma to gain the love of Kṛṣṇa (Hardy 1983: 418).

The theme of the *gopī* as devotee, which had been developed in this way in Tamil, was later presented in Sanskrit in the *Bhāgavata Purāṇa*. This text, southern in origin, became part of the heritage of Vaiṣṇava *bhakti* movements throughout India. The theme was taken up in Sanskrit poetry, notably by Jayadeva in Bengal in the twelfth century and by Vidyāpati in Mithilā in the fourteenth century, who use vivid sexual imagery in their devotional poems. These poets dwell particularly on Rādhā, the most beautiful of the *gopīs*, a figure mentioned but not named in the *Bhāgavata Purāṇa*. Poems in modern Indian languages, dwelling on her longing for Kṛṣṇa, her joy at being with him, her anguish at separation from him, their quarrelling and reconciliation, are sung in many parts of India, particularly Bengal (Dimock and Levertov 1967). Such poems use all the resources of the literature of sexual *kāma* to describe devotion to god.

While the figure of the *gopī*s makes the story of Kṛṣṇa particularly appropriate for the use of sexual longing as a model for devotion to god, this model was also used by devotees of Śiva. Akkā Mahādevī or Mahādēviyakkā, a twelfth-century member of the Vīraśaiva sect, uses it in some of her poems, composed in the Kannada language (Ramanujan 1973: 111–42). She speaks of Śiva as the lover for whom she will abandon her husband or whose coming she awaits as she pines and grows thin (Ramanujan 1973: 141, 140). Male Śaiva devotees, like male devotees of Kṛṣṇa, also can express themselves in feminine terms. Basavaṇṇa, the founder of the Vīraśaiva movement, says that he becomes female in order to be the bride of the devotees of Śiva (Ramanujan 1973: 87).

A particularly elaborate theory of *bhakti* was developed in the sixteenth century, in the *Bhaktirasāmṛtasindhu* by Rūpa Gosvāmī, a disciple of Caitanya, the founder of the Bengali Vaiṣṇava tradition. *Sādhanabhakti* or devotion achieved through a program of striving is divided into *vaidhībhakti*, achieved by following rules, and *rāgānugābhakti*, reached by following a natural trend (De 1961: 173, 176). The latter is divided into *sambandhānugā*, which is based on relations of kinship and friendship, and *kāmānugā*, which is based on *kāma*. Since the *gopī*s provide the model for this form of *bhakti*, it is more natural to women, while men have to bridge the gender gap. Rūpa quotes a statement in the *Padma Purāṇa* that the sages of the Pine Forest, better known for their place in the mythology of Śiva (O'Flaherty 1973), longed to take part in Kṛṣṇa's pastimes and were accordingly reborn as *gopī*s (De 1961: 179; Hardy 1983: 564).

Although a devotee's love for Kṛṣṇa is modeled on the love of a woman for a man, it is clearly not the same thing. Some Vaiṣṇava theologians in the Caitanya tradition apply the aesthetic theory of *rasa* (flavor) to account for this difference. According to this theory, what is enjoyed in aesthetic experience, for instance, by the audience at a play, is triggered by the experiences (*bhāva*) which are being represented by the performers but is quite different from them. This aesthetic experience is called *rasa* (juice; flavor). It is through contemplation of the activity of the *gopī*s, not by participation or imitation, that the devotee experiences love for god. On the other hand, some forms of Vaiṣṇavism encourage the devotee to imitate or participate in the actions of the *gopī*s; in the case of male devotees, this requires a change of gender. Caitanya himself is said to have felt and behaved like Rādhā, the foremost among the *gopī*s, when she experienced the pangs of separation from Kṛṣṇa. The nineteenth-century Bengali mystic Rāmakṛṣṇa similarly feminized himself as a way of experiencing divine love.

Jīva Gosvāmī, Rūpa's nephew, distinguishes two terms, "*kāma*" and "*preman*" (love, affection). *Kāma* seeks one's own pleasure; *preman* seeks only to please the beloved (De 1961: 378–79). In the Caitanya tradition this distinction is applied to the story of the *gopī*s, whose feeling for Kṛṣṇa is not *kāma* but *preman*. A different view was taken by the Sahajiyā form of Vaiṣṇavism in the seventeenth and eighteenth centuries. There, *kāma* is the necessary origin of *preman*, which is a purified form of it (Dasgupta 1962: 135; Dimock 1966: 15–16). *Kāma* and *preman* are not necessarily so clearly distinguished as Jīva claims, and even he allows that the former may be used in the sense of the latter.

KĀMA AS A WAY TO SALVATION

Already in the early Upaniṣads, we sometimes find ultimate bliss described in terms of sexual pleasure. The conscious self in union with the absolute *ātman* is compared to a man in the embrace of the woman he loves, knowing nothing within or outside (*Bṛhadāraṇyaka Upaniṣad* 4.3.21). The person who has found perfect freedom is described as having pleasure (*rati*) in the self, playing with the self, coupling (*mithuna*) with the self, delighting in the self (*Chāndogya Upaniṣad* 7.25.2). In such passages, however, sexual terms are used as a metaphor. There is no suggestion that worldly pleasure can be a route to ultimate bliss; on the contrary, such bliss is for the person who has no interest in material possessions (*Chāndogya Upaniṣad* 7.24).

Kāma is more positively valued in the Tantric tradition, where the world and human personality are seen as manifestations of the ultimate being rather than as falling away from it. The divine is represented not as an asexual being or even a sexually inactive being but as a couple. In Śaiva Tantrism, Śiva and the goddess are lord and lady of desire or pleasure (*kāmeśvara*, *kāmeśvarī*) (White 1998: 177). Similarly in the Vaiṣṇava Sahajiyā tradition, a Tantric form of Kṛṣṇa worship, the most important aspect of Kṛṣṇa's essence is bliss (*ānanda*), and his consort Rādhā is his power to delight (*hlādinīśakti*) (Dimock 1966: 133–34). This means that not only sexual desires and relationships but also desires and relationships of all kinds have a place in the divine essence.

Tantrism shares with Vedic ritual theory the view that ritual is based on desire (see pp. 273–75). However desire is here valued positively, so that ritual is not regarded as something to be left behind by the seeker of ultimate bliss but as an embodiment of the divine itself. The value set on ritual, as an activity of advanced initiates as well as ordinary worshipers, is one of the features that distinguish Tantrism from other forms of Hinduism. Moreover, Tantric ritual seeks power and pleasure as well as the ultimate goal of assimilation to the divine.

In Tantric ritual the worshiper is transformed into the deity to be worshiped, and each part of the worshiper's body and personality is transformed into the corresponding part of the cosmos. This transformation includes *kāma*, both in general and in the sexual sense: the worshiper's *kāma* becomes cosmic *kāma*. An important element in Tantric practice is the *kāmakalā*, a term which may be understood as "a portion [or specifically 'one sixteenth'] of *kāma*" or as "the art of *kāma*." Whatever the intended meaning of the term—and it is typical of Tantrism to intend several meanings at different times or simultaneously—the *kāmakalā* is a diagram which represents, among other things, the face or mouth, breasts, and vulva of a woman. This woman may be the goddess herself, an actual woman present in a ritual, or an ideal woman in the male meditator's mind. In any case, the purpose of the *kāmakalā* is ritual or meditation based on the sexual act which is the origin and driving force of the cosmos, whether or not the act itself is ritually performed (White 1998).

KĀMADEVA, BODILESS AND EMBODIED

As we saw (p. 271), Kāma is regarded as a god in the *Atharva Veda*. The arrow of Kāma appears in a hymn recited as part of a spell to secure a woman's love; it is described as terrible, piercing the heart, and drying up the spleen (*Atharva Veda* 3.25.1–3). In post-Vedic literature, people who are madly in love are described as afflicted by the arrow or arrows of Kāma—for instance, the princess Ambā, when Śālva refuses to marry her (*Mahābhārata* 5.172.8). The god of love, whose arrows cause torment in both male and female hearts, acquires a distinct mythology and iconography. Sometimes these point to desire in general, but more often they point specifically to sexual desire.

One of Kāmadeva's epithets is Saṃkalpaja, "born from Saṃkalpa ('intention')." Here Kāma represents desire in general. He is also described as one of the three sons of Dharma, the others being Calm (*śama*) and Joy (*harṣa*) (*Mahābhārata* 1.60.31). A more elaborate genealogy makes him the son of Saṃkalpa who is the son of Dharma by one of his six wives, Saṃkalpā (*Bhāgavata Purāṇa* 6.6.10). This is a mythological way of saying that desires are preceded by intentions and can only be achieved by following *dharma* (since one's actions affect one's destiny); it can be more easily understood if we take *kāma* to refer to desired objects rather than the desire for them.

Kāma's parentage is evidently not fixed. The *Brahmavaivarta Purāṇa* makes him a son of Brahmā, who created him on finding that the sons he had previously created, born from his mind without the aid of any female, had no desire to procreate. Brahmā equipped him with arrows and told him to delude the hearts of all creatures. Kāma, however, began by trying his weapons on his father Brahmā, causing him to lust after his own daughter (O'Flaherty 1973: 71). This is a variant of the story of primal incest (*Bṛhadāraṇyaka Upaniṣad* 1.4.3–4), which we noted earlier (p. 272). It illustrates the point made earlier (p. 273) that creation is a descent into the realm of desire and imperfection.

Kāmadeva's wife is Rati ("delight, pleasure," especially sexual pleasure), another word which is both an abstract noun and the name of a mythological figure. Prīti (affection) is sometimes named as his second wife, and Vasanta ("spring," the season most appropriate to love) as his friend. In the eleventh-century allegorical play *Prabodhacandrodaya*, Kāma appears, accompanied by his wife Rati, as the minister of King Moha (folly, delusion); they are eventually defeated by King Viveka (discernment, discrimination) and his daughter Vidyā (knowledge) (Winternitz 1963–83, 2.2: 283).

Like other gods, Kāma is known by several names. As well as Kāma, or Kāmadeva (love-god), he is called Kandarpa. He is also known by various epithets or descriptions; he is called Smara (memory, recollection; love), Madana (the one who intoxicates), Manmatha (the one who stirs or churns the mind), Manobhava (the one who is born or exists in the mind), or Hṛcchaya (the one who lies in the heart).

Since Kāma resides in the hearts of lovers instead of having a body of his own, he is often referred to by the epithet Anaṅga (bodiless). The story of how Kāma became bodiless is a part of a complex myth which occurs in many forms. In the *Mahābhārata* the story is mentioned very briefly, in a series of examples of gods and men who have foregone the happiness that their good deeds have earned them: "Also the universal lord, the husband of Umā, when Kāma was getting the better of him, subdued him by making him bodiless" (*Mahābhārata* 12.183.10.5; discussed by O'Flaherty 1973: 144). This suggests that Śiva destroyed Kāma's body in the course of a struggle between the two, to ensure that Śiva would not succumb to desire; but the passage gives no details.

The *Matsya Purāṇa* links this story with the theme of Brahmā's incest, mentioned above. To punish Kāma for inciting him to lust with his arrows, Brahmā condemns him to be reduced to ashes by Śiva (O'Flaherty 1973: 117). In many other versions, as in the story first quoted, it is Śiva himself whom Kāma attacks. The heat of desire which he tries to arouse in Śiva becomes instead the heat of anger, flashing from Śiva's third eye and incinerating Kāma.

Kāma is also mentioned in an early version of the myth of Tāraka, one of the powerful demons who threaten the gods. None of the gods is capable of killing Tāraka; he can only be killed by a son, yet to be born, sprung from the semen of Śiva. This son is eventually born as Skanda. In this early version, found in the *Mahābhārata*, he is to be born from a drop of Śiva's semen which has fallen into fire (O'Flaherty 1973: 104). Brahmā, when predicting that this drop will be the origin of the savior of the gods, identifies it with Kāma: "For everlasting intention is called desire; it is Rudra's [that is, Śiva's] vigor which leapt out and fell in the fire" (*Mahābhārata* 13.84.11). In the same passage Brahmā identifies Kāma with fire, as an irresistible creative and destructive force: "Desire, which is intention and liking, is the most everlasting fire; it would kill even the unkillable, givers of boons, and ascetics" (*Mahābhārata* 13.8.16).

Later sources weave the bodilessness of Kāma and the origin of Skanda into one story, of which there are so many versions that any attempt to reduce them to a standard form would be a distortion. Both Kāma and Śiva play important roles in all of them, and a recurrent theme is the power which can be accumulated through sexual abstinence, which can take the form of heat, fire, destructive power, creative power, anger, or even sexual desire. The following summary gives some features of the various versions.

When the gods are threatened by the demon Tāraka, who can only be destroyed by a son of Śiva, Śiva is engaged in asceticism. To save the gods, Śiva must give up his asceticism and marry Pārvatī, the daughter of Himālaya, and beget a son. The outcome is not so simple; for, although Śiva and Pārvatī do marry, when the son Skanda is eventually born (and there are many versions of how this comes about), he is born from Śiva's semen but not from Pārvatī's womb. However, the marriage of Śiva and Pārvatī necessitates the resuscitation of Kāma, who has been destroyed by the fire of Śiva's third eye, and the reinstatement of the widowed Rati as his wife.

Pārvatī pleads for Kāma's resuscitation, since without him her marriage will not take place or will be unconsummated. In most versions, Śiva allows Kāma to live, but without a body of his own. Instead of depriving Kāma of power, Śiva's fire becomes Kāma's fire, while Kāma's disembodiment increases his power by allowing him to take many forms. He is embodied in the beauty of women and in all things that inspire love; a typical list is the mango, Spring, the moon, flowers, bees, and cuckoos (*Matsya Purāṇa* 154.251–52, cited in O'Flaherty 1973: 158).

Another aspect of Kāma's bodilessness is that particularly handsome men are often described as embodying him. The chapter of the *Buddhacarita* which we quoted (p. 267) gives an example: "For those women thought he was Kāma embodied, adorned by the marks of his greatness that blazed as if they were jewels he was born with" (4.4). Nala, the hero of an ancient love story, is described similarly: "In appearance he was like Kandarpa [Kāma] himself, embodied" (*Mahābhārata* 3.50.14). In each of these examples, a man is called an embodiment of the bodiless god as a deliberate paradox, indicating that his beauty is miraculous. This use of the motif of Kāma's bodilessness is older than the attested forms of the myth of his destruction; the myth probably arose to explain the motif.

Although bodiless, Kāma is represented in iconography. He has arrows made of flowers and a bow of sugar cane with a string of bees, and he rides on a parrot. The emblem on his banner is a crocodile (*makara*) (Gopinatha Rao 1968, 1: 276–79). These attributes not only appear in sculpture but also are frequently mentioned or alluded to in Sanskrit literature.

Kāma occurs among the thousand names of Śiva (*Mahābhārata* 12, Appendix 1, 28.246) and also among those of Viṣṇu (*Mahābhārata* 13.17.41 [variant for *kāmya*], 13.17.68 [variant]). These occurrences indicate the all-embracing nature of each of these two gods. In the *Bhagavad Gītā*, Kṛṣṇa identifies himself with Kandarpa (10.82) and with *kāma* that does not conflict with *dharma* (7.11). Śiva, because of his sexual power and attractiveness, is closely linked with *kāma* or even called an embodiment of him (O'Flaherty 1973: 169–71).

More remarkably, Kāma is sometimes identified with Pradyumna, the son of Kṛṣṇa and Rukminī (Hardy 1994: 204). This is hinted at in the *Mahābhārata*, where Pradyumna, like Kāma, has the emblem of the crocodile (*makara*) on his banner. The identification is made explicit by a myth found in the *Viṣṇu Purāṇa* (5.26–27) and in the *Bhāgavata Purāṇa* (10.55). This myth builds on the incident in which Kāma is made bodiless by Śiva's ascetic fire. After this incident, Kāma (or a portion of him, according to the *Viṣṇu Purāṇa*) was born as the son of Kṛṣṇa and Rukminī. The baby was stolen by a demon, Śambara, and thrown into the ocean, where he was swallowed by a fish. The fish was caught and delivered to Śambara's kitchen, where a cook found the baby inside it. He was brought up by Śambara's wife (in the *Viṣṇu Purāṇa*) or his cook (in the *Bhāgavata Purāṇa*), Māyāvatī. She was a reincarnation of Kāmadeva's wife Rati, who had been waiting for her husband ever since he had been reduced to ashes. Recognizing him, she accepted him again as her husband and taught him magical arts (*māyā*) which helped him to defeat Śambara. The pair then went to Kṛṣṇa's city, Dvārakā, and presented themselves to Kṛṣṇa and Rukminī as their long-lost son and new daughter-in-law.

THE HINDU CONCEPT OF KĀMA

What is distinctive about the Hindu understanding of desire? First, *kāma* is not only part of human experience but also a constituent of the cosmos. It is a product of the mind, but mind itself is a cosmic concept, existing prior to the individual. In the Vedic cosmogonies, the question of what caused the primordial desire does not arise; like the Big Bang of modern cosmology, the primal impulse is beyond time and causation, so it makes no sense to ask what preceded it or what caused it. However, in the Hindu cosmology which we find in the Purāṇas and other non-Vedic Sanskrit texts, time has no absolute beginning; it is infinite and cyclic, and so is *kāma*. The *kāma* that triggers the beginning of each cosmic day has lain dormant throughout the preceding cosmic night.

Sexual desire is the paradigmatic form of *kāma*, so much so that the word "*kāma*" alone is sufficient to imply it, whether on the level of the individual or on that of the cosmos. This particular form of *kāma* is celebrated in literature, dance, painting, sculpture, and song in every period to which we have access; and this celebration can be found in religious and secular contexts. Although women are often presented as the objects of desire and men as the desiring subjects, in *kāvya* and especially in *bhakti* literature we find an intense interest in a woman's love for a man.

In approaching Hindu culture, modern views of sex can be misleading. Sexual *kāma* is not just a matter of body chemistry. It arises in the mind and reaches its highest form in a cultivated mind which can appreciate cultivation in a member of the opposite sex. The body itself, in the Hindu view, is a part or a counterpart of the cosmos.

Kāma is a morally neutral concept. Although it is incompatible with salvation, *kāma* is not necessarily regarded as evil. It is true that in the *Skanda Purāṇa*, for instance, Śiva as lord of ascetics calls Kāma evil when he burns him with his third eye (O'Flaherty 1973: 144–45). But this view is only one side of a dialectic in which Śiva, Kāma, and the other gods are engaged, between activity (*pravṛtti*) and withdrawal (*nivṛtti*); if everyone took the same side, there would be no dialectic and no world. Sexual desire typifies *pravṛtti* not only because it is a particularly powerful desire but also because sex is the foundation of the family which is the center of a person's network of relationships, and these relationships in turn involve him or her in various activities, including ritual. But *pravṛtti* as a whole is driven by desires of many kinds: for wealth, for pleasure, for the approval of others, or even to please god.

While *kāma* is a product of the mind, this does not mean that it results from a conscious act of will. The mythology of Kāmadeva represents *kāma* as a force which attacks the individual from the outside, both when his flower arrows cause love at first sight in ordinary mortals and when he attacks Śiva.

What makes *kāma* a bar to salvation is that it is concerned with the world of multiplicity. While *kāma* in the general sense of "desire" is normally used in the singular, when it has the sense of "desire for a particular object," "object of desire," or "pleasure" it is often plural because desire is typically directed towards a plurality of objects, and the number of possible objects of desire is limitless. Salvation, on the other hand, requires the mind to be directed towards a single goal, whether through devotion to a deity or through awareness of the oneness of *brahman*. To achieve salvation, therefore, one must be free from desire: "When he abandons all desires that are in the mind, son of Pṛthā, and is content by himself in the self alone, he is said to have a stable intellect" (*Bhagavad Gītā* 2.55).

For the same reason, *kāma* is the necessary impulse for the creation of the world. It is *kāma*, in other words, which initiates the transition from a unitary absolute being to the world of multiplicity. The way to salvation is the reverse of the cosmogonic process and thus requires the abandonment of *kāma*.

We have seen that desire is given a higher value in the Tantric tradition, where it is an intrinsic part of the nature of the original being or the original couple. Creation here is not a descent but an outpouring of the divine essence. The ultimate human goal is not to regain a primordial tranquillity but to participate in the cosmic, desire-driven activity. However, what we have said about unity and plurality may still be relevant: the cosmic desire which the Tantric initiate replicates in himself is not directed at a multitude of objects but at desire itself, transcending the distinction we have drawn between *kāma* as "desire for an object" and *kāma* as "object of desire."

In the Vedic texts, the primordial act itself results from *kāma*, whether this is pure desire with no specified object (*Ṛg Veda* 10.129.4) or desire for multiplicity and progeny (*Śatapatha Brāhmaṇa* 11.1.6.1, above; *Chāndogya Upaniṣad* 6.2.3) or for a wife or wealth (*Bṛhadāraṇyaka Upaniṣad* 1.4.17). Since it is in the nature of any action that it should result from *kāma*, the primordial action must also result from *kāma*. In the case of Prajāpati, we may say that it results from a desire to fulfill his own nature, as expressed in his name, "lord of progeny." This is sometimes implied by the words used: "Prajāpati desired: 'May I be many, may I procreate (*prajāyeya*) myself' "

(*Taittirīya Saṃhitā* 7.1.1.4). There is no teleology in this view of the universe: Prajāpati is merely, so to speak, doing his own thing. The universe, therefore, appears in these cosmogonies as an unpredicted and unintended consequence of the primordial desire (cf. Varenne 1982: 158). Here too the primordial act is prototypical: in the Hindu view, as shown by many myths of the gods and stories of the rebirths of human and other beings, acts have consequences beyond the desire which prompted them, whether or not they also fulfill that desire. We have seen some examples of this before.

While the universe may be the unplanned result of an act which was prompted by *kāma*, there is no suggestion that this *kāma* or the act which fulfilled it is reprehensible. The desire for progeny, a wife, or wealth is thoroughly in accordance with the desires which are expected of the Vedic sacrificer. The Vedic account is thus unlike the Manichaean one, in which the universe results from a primordial desire which is both sexual and evil (Widengren 1965: 56–59). It is true that incest, and perhaps also rape, is involved in the account of the origin of human and animal species in *Bṛhadāraṇyaka Upaniṣad* 1.4.3–4 (p. 272); but this comes at a later stage than the original cosmogonic desire.

In *bhakti* as well as in the Tantric tradition, *kāma* plays a part in the devotee's relationship with god, and the language of *kāma* can be used in religious contexts: so much so that it is sometimes hard to tell whether a given poem is primarily devotional or erotic. Indeed, Jayadeva explicitly presents his *Gītā Govinda* as having either purpose: he invites one to listen to his poem "whether one's mind has a taste for remembering Kṛṣṇa or whether one is keen on the arts of pleasure" (1.3). The biblical *Song of Songs* is a well-known parallel: it may have originated as a collection of love poems, but it has been used as a religious text in the Jewish and Christian traditions for centuries. In parts at least of the Hindu tradition, sexual love and devotion to god are parts of one continuum; the former is not opposed to the latter, nor is it discarded in order to enter on the latter (Hardy 1994: 205–11; cf. Dasgupta 1962: 134–35).

NOTES

1 Given as an example of the use of the optative mode.

2 This passage states that a woman, a cow, or a mare gives birth within a year (*Śatapatha Brāhmaṇa* 11.1.6.2). This is inaccurate, but it is motivated by a wish to present Prajāpati not only as a prototype but also as encompassing the whole of space and time, as understood in the Vedic worldview. The year is identified with Prajāpati (*Śatapatha Brāhmaṇa* 11.1.6.13); it is the largest unit of time and therefore stands for time itself. Prajāpati's first words are the sacred utterances *bhūḥ bhuvaḥ svaḥ* (*Śatapatha Brāhmaṇa* 11.1.6.3), which correspond to earth, air, and heaven and so encompass the whole world.

3 The term "*puruṣārtha*" used in Pūrva Mīmāṃsā is identical in form with the term used for the three or four aims of man, but it has a different grammatical structure. The former is a *bahuvrīhi* compound (an exocentric adjectival phrase) meaning "whose aim is related to a man," while the latter is a *tatpuruṣa* compound (an endocentric noun phrase) meaning "aim of man."

4 "*kāmātmatā na praśastā na caivehāsty akāmatā. kāmyo hi vedādhigamaḥ karmayogaś ca vaidikaḥ. saṃkalpa-mūlaḥ kāmo vai yajñāḥ saṃkalpa-saṃbhavāḥ. vratāni yama-dharmāś ca sarve saṃkalpajāḥ smṛtāḥ. akāmasya kriyā kā cid dṛśyate neha karhi cit. yad yad dhi kurute kiṃ cit tat tat kāmasya ceṣṭitam.*" The compound *saṃkalpa-mūla* in verse 3 is ambiguous: it could mean that desire is "rooted in intention." This is how Kullūka and other commentators understand it, followed by Bühler (1886: 29). However, the little-known South Indian commentator Nandana (Bühler 1886: 29, cxxxiii–cxxxv) understands it in the way translated here, and this

interpretation gives a causal chain *kāma-saṃkalpa-yajña* which supports the argument of verse 2. *Bhagavad Gītā* 6.24 uses the similarly ambiguous phrase *saṃkalpa-prabhavān kāmān*, meaning either "desires which arise from *saṃkalpa*" or "desires which give rise to *saṃkalpa*." Both Śaṃkara and Rāmānuja understand it in the first sense, but the second would be in line with the interpretation of Manu suggested here. It also fits the translation of *saṃkalpa* as "will" (Radhakrishnan 1953: 472), "decision" (Olivelle 1996: 19), or "intention" (1996: 167, 168), terms which seem to refer to effects of desire rather than its cause. On the other hand, the mythological statement that Kāmadeva is the son of Saṃkalpa (p. 282) supports the other interpretation.

5 The statement "Man is made of desire," together with the word "*kratu*" (resolve) in the next sentence, recalls *Śatapatha Brāhmaṇa* 10.6.3.1: "Man is made of resolve" (*atha khalu kratu-mayo 'yaṃ puruṣaḥ*). A near-repetition of the same text, again associated with destiny after death, occurs in *Chāndogya Upaniṣad* 3.14.1: "Now a man is made of resolve. As is his resolve in this world, so he becomes when he leaves this world" (*atha khalu kratu-mayaḥ puruṣo yathā-kratur asmilṃ loke puruṣo bhavati tathetaḥ pretya bhavati*). The word "*kratu*" has a similar meaning to *saṃkalpa*: the resolve to perform a ritual act.

6 The noun translated "desire" in "desire for sons" is not *kāma* but a rarer word *eṣaṇa*. However, the verb translated "desire" in the first sentence is *kāmayate*.

CHAPTER THIRTEEN

MOKṢA

Klaus K. Klostermaier

Among the *puruṣārtha*s, the recognized Hindu life values, the highest position was always accorded to *mokṣa*, variously translated as liberation, emancipation, or salvation from rebirth. (The noun *mokṣa*, as also its synonym *mukti*, is derived from the Sanskrit verbal root *muc*, to liberate, to make free. Someone who has found *mokṣa*/*mukti* is called a *mukta* [m]/*muktā* [f].) Hindus were convinced that humans needed most of all an orientation towards the absolute, that one had to be guided by a great idea that transcended the petty concerns of everyday life, a goal that made life as a whole meaningful and worthwhile. Thus it is not surprising that much of Hindu literature is concerned with *mokṣa* and the ways to find it.

Mokṣa, although the subject of intense preoccupation by the greatest of Hindu philosophers, has always remained a concern of the people at large as well. Thus it also forms a major topic in popular Hindu writings and is discussed at length in the epics and the Purāṇas as well as articulated in poetic compositions. Liberation philosophy in India is intimately connected with mythology. In the following we will refer both to philosophies and mythologies to capture the full meaning of this term, so central to the life and thought of the Hindus.

To structure the virtually limitless material, a thematic approach has been chosen. While it may be of interest to Indologists to follow through the notion of *mukti*/*mokṣa* in the Upaniṣads, the *Bhagavad Gītā*, the epics, and the Purāṇas, the Darśanas, as well as the sectarian Āgamas, Saṃhitās, and Tantras, the readers for whom this book had been intended would feel bewildered, unable to see the forest for the trees. In order to communicate something of the meaning of *mokṣa* in Hindu life, it will be presented as a human journey from the condition of bondage and darkness to the freedom and light of the final state of being. Consequently, the chapter will be divided into three parts: the unliberated, "natural" human condition (*bandha*); the various ways designed by Hindu teachers to overcome this state of bondage and darkness (*mārga*); and the final state of freedom and enlightenment (*mokṣa*).

THE HUMAN SITUATION

Hindu myths as well as philosophies describe humans as being in a condition that is not yet the ultimate one, as estranged from their true self.

The powerful Vedic Indra-Vṛtra myth, which is first narrated in *Ṛg Veda* 1.32 and alluded to in innumerable later texts, depicts the distress of humankind under demon rule. The same motif recurs in many later myths, connected with Viṣṇu, Śiva, and Devī: the world has been overpowered by evil forces; the *asura*s (demons) expel the *deva*s (gods) from their realm; and humankind suffers under their reign of terror.

The Pūrva Mīmāṃsā school analyzes the human situation as yet in a rather pragmatic way: humans are in want of riches, children, and ultimately heaven. All those wants can be supplied by the *yajña* (Vedic sacrifices) (*Mīmāṃsāsūtra* 1.2.1ff.). The Upaniṣads show much deeper insight by depicting human life as threatened by fear and hunger, by old age and disease, by time and matter, by death and rebirth. The satisfaction given by wealth, long life, family, and heaven does not suffice (*Bṛhadāraṇyaka Upaniṣad* 3.1.3ff.). Life on the physical plane is no longer considered the highest value. It is rather viewed as a burden, a meaningless existence that repeats itself time and again. Analyzing the root of this *saṃsāra*, this constant cycle of death and birth, the Upaniṣads decide that the human situation is determined by *avidyā*, ignorance concerning the true nature of reality, and that the real evil which besets us (and prevents us from being truly human) is not our physical deficiency but our spiritual darkness (*Muṇḍaka Upaniṣad* 2.2.10). Going further, the Upaniṣads find that the root of all unhappiness inherent in the given human situation is the psychological split between the ego derived from changing sense experiences and the self, unchanging consciousness. Estrangement from our real self is the real human tragedy (*Chāndogya Upaniṣad* 7.1.3).

Vedāntic philosophy in its various branches takes up this idea and further develops it to show how at the root of all human misery is this "forgetfulness" of the true nature of the self, this falling out from the center of reality, the ignorance regarding our inherent divinity, the entanglement in the finite. Existence in the visible universe is, according to Vedānta, inauthentic, unreal, painful. The senses, material existence, and the body are fetters that keep the spirit, the true self, tied down and imprisoned.

Sāṃkhya-Yoga, the basic philosophy of many religious schools, describes the human situation as characterized by "threefold misery," caused by extra- and intra-human elements, mistakenly identifying spirit with matter (*Sāṃkhyakārikā* 1). Individuality itself is seen by some Śaiva schools as intrinsically sorrowful and unhappy. The limited *jīvātman* (individual living being) lacks the essential fulfillment of being. All are fettered by *karma* (effects of past deeds), *māyā* (illusion), and *āṇava* (egotism, the root evil), say the Śaiva Siddhāntins: our true nature is hidden. This separate individuality is even called a state of "sinfulness" (Devasenapathi 1960: 186). A seemingly paradoxical formulation of the human situation is given by the Śākta schools: it is Śakti, the divine power itself which binds us and makes us unhappy, and it is Śakti again which frees us and makes us blissful; our fate is determined by the supreme power.

Very few texts give an answer to the question: What is the origin of evil, the beginning of human unhappiness? The myths simply accept the existing order of the universe in which the presence of evil forces, side by side with good forces, is taken for granted. They presuppose that from time to time the evil forces prevail, only to be defeated by god.

There are, however, a few quite significant myths explaining the origin of demons: we are told that both *sura*s (gods) and *asura*s (demons) have sprung from the same father Prajāpati. In another context we hear that evil is the shadow of Brahmā or even his creature, that salvation and well being spring from his face, evil and bondage from his backside (*Bhāgavata Purāṇa* 7.1.12). The coexistence and co-origin of good and evil are two of the most striking features of mythology: the churning of the milk-ocean produces both *halāhala*, the deadly poison, and *amṛta*, the nectar of immortality. Śiva has a *saumya* (peaceful) and an *ugra* (wrathful) aspect, he is both life-giving and life-destroying. Śakti appears in many forms, as the mother of the universe and as Kālī, the fierce power of death and destruction.

Vedānta declares that bondage is beginningless: it has no origin. Sāṃkhya makes *puruṣa*'s infatuation for *prakṛti* responsible for the beginning of evolution and involvement in the process of becoming. Various Vaiṣṇava schools trace the beginning of the *jīva*'s limitation of bondage back to Viṣṇu's *krīḍā* or *līlā*: a playful act of god has set the wheel of *saṃsāra* into motion. Others make a special power of god, *māyāśakti*, responsible for bondage. Pañcarātra assumes that from the very beginning there were different kinds of *jīva*s, some eternally bound and some eternally free. It is again the will of god that is responsible for human bondage. Pāśupatas consider bondage as beginningless caused by the superimposition of the five *mala*s (restrictions). Śaiva Siddhānta similarly accepts the fact of *āṇava*, the limitation of Śiva-hood of the *jīva*, as beginningless, though ultimately caused by Śiva. In *pratyabhijñā* bondage is the work of Śiva's Śakti. Śākta doctrines too consider *avidyā* beginningless: it is the sleep of *śakti*, the split between reality and consciousness that accounts for our unhappiness.

Against the teaching that holds that evil is different from good, both mythology and the philosophies teach that reality is one, and it is only due to a wrong viewpoint that one differentiates: it is exactly this differentiation which is responsible for our unhappiness.

Evil as a constant of human existence seems to be accepted both by myths and philosophies of salvation. Hindu myths describe repeated encounters of gods with demons. Thus Indra battles against Vṛtra, against Vala, against *dasyu*s, and against a host of other demons and foes; all are "Vṛtras."

Viṣṇu in the form of Varāha-*avatāra* liberates the world from Madhu and Kaiṭabha. But evil incarnates again in Hiraṇyakaśipu, in Kaṃsa, in Bali, in Kālī, and in innumerable other demons (*Viṣṇu Purāṇa* 1.4.45ff.). God has to descend again and again to cope with evil. Evil and suffering cannot be vanquished once and forever. Nor can evil prevail for ever. An individual demon, representing a particular evil for a certain time, can be overthrown and defeated, but evil as such will reincarnate, rise again to challenge the forces of good. After one liberation, an other oppression will occur; the most treasured promise given by Viṣṇu after his interventions is the assurance that also in future he will save his devotees in distress.

Śiva too has to battle against a host of demons, and the divine dance in which he crushes *apasmāra*, the embodiment of evil, beneath his foot goes on as long as his creation lasts. Though Śiva always triumphs over evil, the world is never completely free from it.

Likewise, Devī does not intervene only once to put down evil. Knowing well that evil will beset humankind again and again, she promises, after the final victory over Mahiṣāsura, the buffalo demon, to return and defeat the powers of evil again in whatever form they appear.

The philosophical analysis of the human situation leads Jayanta Bhaṭṭa, a Naiyāyika, to the insight that ordinary activity can be traced to three roots: *moha* (delusion), *rāga* (attraction), and *dveṣa* (aversion). This view is shared by most Hindus, to whatever school they belong, though not all may go as far as Jayanta in the further description of these three basic instincts in man. He defines *moha* as "the erroneous judgement implying an assent of the will which arises from the failure to discriminate the ultimate transcendental nature of things," the "crowning folly," and the parent of *rāga* and *dveṣa*. Expressions of it are false cognition, perplexity and skepticism, and vanity and carelessness in one's duties. Signs of attraction are sexual craving (*kāma*), selfishness, worldliness, thirst for enjoyment of life, and greed. Expressions of aversion are anger, envy, jealousy, malevolence, and malice (Jayanta Bhaṭṭa's commentary to *Nyāyasūtra* 1.1.17 in *Nyāyamañjarī*).

The more popular enumeration of the three "root-instincts" is that found in the *Yogasūtra*: *lobha* (greed), *krodha* (anger), and *moha* (delusion) are the roots of all the other vices, varying in intensity in a particular individual.

The *Bhagavad Gītā* (16) works with an implicit idea of predestination in its analysis of the human situation by distinguishing between people "born with a divine nature" (*daivīsampad*) and those "born with a demoniac nature" (*āsurīsampad*), the former destined for deliverance, the latter forever bound. The characteristics of one with a "divine nature" are fearlessness, purity of mind, firmness in knowledge and concentration, charity, self-control, sacrifice, scripture study, austerity, uprightness, nonviolence, truth, freedom from anger, renunciation, tranquillity, aversion to faultfinding, compassion towards living beings, freedom from covetousness, gentleness, modesty, steadiness, vigor, forgiveness, fortitude, purity, and freedom from malice and excessive pride. Those with a "demoniac nature" are guided by ostentation, arrogance, excessive pride, anger, harshness, and ignorance; neither purity, good conduct, nor truth is found in them; they do not believe in a creator god; they are "bound by hundreds of ties of desire, given over to lust and anger they strive to amass hoards of wealth, by unjust means, for the gratification of their desires."

Vidyāraṇya traces anger and the other propensities back to *vāsana*s, latent tendencies in the mind that may be either *śubha* (good, auspicious) or *aśubha* (evil, inauspicious). They are specified as *lokavāsana* (desire for popularity), *śāstravāsana* (desire for learning and reputation for piety), and *dehavāsana* (desire for carnal pleasure).

The good tendencies are working towards liberation from *saṃsāra*. They are not unreflective and spontaneous like the evil urges, but they involve judgment. They are specified as *maitrī* (friendliness), *karuṇā* (compassion), *muditā* (rejoicing at the well being of others), *upekṣā* (indifference), *śama* (tranquillity of mind), *dama* (repression of sense-desire), *titikṣā* (endurance of pain), and *saṃnyāsa* (renunciation) (*Jīvanmuktiviveka* chapter 2).

For Śaṃkara evil is coextensive with individual existence and material creation; it is radically and necessarily connected with the world and its multiplicity, so much so that *saṃsāra*, the world, becomes the very expression for painful existence and evil (*Śārīrakabhāṣya* 1.1.1).

Not content with the evils of worldly existence, mythology knows of an eschatological evil too, namely, hell. The numerous colorful descriptions of various hells, as offered by the *Pretakalpa* of the *Garuḍa Purāṇa*, vividly demonstrate the possibility of an intensification of suffering and pain in afterlife.

Whatever the differences as regards the way and aim of salvation, all are agreed that humans can be redeemed, that the *jīva* can be liberated from unhappiness. The myths show it in a rather direct way: given a certain occasion, a devotee in distress, or a petition from those who are in need of salvation, the supreme intervenes, and the myths never leave the slightest doubt that the god of their choice can do anything and save any being from any calamity and give it supreme bliss. The various philosophical systems owe their very existence to this conviction of the possibility, nay, the necessity, of salvation. The human situation is not hopeless, despite suffering, evil, and ignorance. Ultimately, we will be free, blissful, good, and knowing. Though there are extreme statements in Advaita Vedānta to the effect that nobody can be liberated, these affirm rather than deny our contention: they hold that we are already free, though perhaps not phenomenologically and psychologically.

A deeper analysis reveals not only our bondage and our limitation but also our potential infinity and divinity, an immanent principle working in us towards liberation and fulfillment. In this regard there is hardly any substantial difference in practice between the different schools: Sāṃkhya explicitly states that *prakṛti* is not only the reason for *puruṣa*'s bondage but also the cause for his liberation (*Sāṃkhyakārikā* 56–57). The various Vedānta systems also assume that the same power which had been responsible for individuation and existence in the world is working towards reunification and liberation. For Śaṃkara the world is the play of *brahman*, its *vilāsa*, its *māyā* (the expression of the urge in *brahman* to become many) (*Śārīrakabhāṣya* 1.1.2). The unsatisfactory existence in time and multiplicity is the inner motive for the individual to return to the state before multiplicity and individuality to become once more one with *brahman* (*Śārīrakabhāṣya* 4.4.4). For Bhāskara the visible world is the *kāryarūpa* (effected form) of *brahman*; it is the presence of *brahman* beneath the *upādhi*s (the attributes of phenomenal existence) which leads the *jīva* back to *kāraṇarūpa brahman*, the source and plenitude of being. Yādava Prakāśa considers the *jīva* an *aṃśa* (part) of *brahman*; the part is striving to reintegrate itself into the whole; that is essentially the way of liberation.

Rāmānuja emphasizes the dependence of the *jīva* on Viṣṇu, a dependence that is ontological and essential: there is an innate tendency in the *jīva* towards Viṣṇu, a consciousness of the *jīva*'s need for god's grace in order to reach true selfhood (*Śrībhāṣya* 2.3.19). Madhva holds that not all *jīva*s are meant for liberation and that there is no natural principle connected with *jīva*-hood which works towards divinization. But he also accepts the immanent working of divine grace in those who are chosen (*Brahmasūtrabhāṣya* 2.3.41). Śrīkaṇṭha—with Pāśupatas, Śaiva Siddhāntins, and Vīraśaivas—accepts a basic Śiva-hood of the individual soul, which is connected with its very being. Due to this innate *śivatva*, the *jīva* is able to overcome all limitations, veils, and bonds and gain freedom (*Śrīkaṇṭhabhāṣya* 4.4.9).

For Nimbārka the ultimate reason for the possibility of release lies in the fact that *brahman* is the very self of the *jīva* (*Vedānta Parijāta Saurabha* 2.3.5). Vallabha maintains that the *jīva*s come out from *akṣara brahman* like sparks from fire and that all activities of the *jīva* are controlled by *brahman*: thus *brahman* itself is the principle urging the *jīva* towards salvation. Vijñānabhikṣu, reconciling Vedānta and Sāṃkhya, holds that every *jīva* is in essence one with *brahman*, and this potential *brahmarūpa* is the inner principle responsible for liberation.

THE WAY TO FREEDOM

At the core of the salvation myths is a description of the drama of liberation. This drama has inspired religious artists in India throughout the centuries. The Darśanas interiorized it in their *sādhana*s (spiritual practices): the battle between good and evil is no longer fought upon a cosmic battlefield but in the human soul.

In the Indra-Vṛtra fight the very position of the high god is at stake. It is Vṛtra, the demon, who challenges Indra. Indra, after killing Vṛtra, is not yet sure of his lordship over the universe, and he hides. But through this very act of demon-killing, Indra has established himself as the supreme, "He raises the sun for all to see; he bestows food and wealth" (*Ṛg Veda* 1.51).

Viṣṇu's intervention is the climax of the numerous Vaiṣṇava salvation myths. In Vaiṣṇavism good and evil assume many forms, and in the numerous divine interventions there is purpose and progress: the successive *avatāra*s (divine descents) form a "salvation history" which is to culminate in the final and last intervention of Viṣṇu as Kalkin, who will initiate the final defeat of evil and universal salvation.

Viṣṇu's intervention is always salvific, redemptive, and for the good of humankind. Śiva's is ambivalent. His coming can mean destruction and death—as in the case of Dakṣa—or liberation and bliss. We see ambivalence also in the manifestation of Devī. She is both Ambikā and Kālī, giver and taker of life.

One of the most frequent features of salvation myths is the creation of particular *hypostases* of the supreme god for the purpose of defeating evil. The stories themselves describe these sometimes as "parts" of the supreme god, as "creations" of god, as identical with the supreme, and as different from it. By its very nature the supreme being is uninvolved, calm and blissful, transcendent, beyond the duality of good and evil, unaffected by anything in the material universe: it cannot take part in a battle against a demon; it cannot become angry; it cannot take sides. It has to act through a proxy in which the might and power of the supreme is present.

There is, however, a rather remarkable instance of direct self-involvement of the supreme in the image of Śiva Nīlakaṇṭha: Śiva in his own person swallows the deadly poison which leaves its traces permanently upon him.

Often the intervention of the supreme is made dependent upon certain outward rituals or *mantra*s, so much so that a personal savior god has to give salvation to anyone who fulfills the conditions, irrespective of moral qualities or inner disposition. The often told story of Ajāmila is a case in point: Ajāmila, a Brāhmaṇ, abandoning his lawful Brāhmaṇ wife, lived for many years a sinful life with a low-caste woman from whom he had many children. He neglected his ritual duties and committed every conceivable act of impiety. When he felt death approaching, he wanted to see his youngest son, of whom he was very fond. Calling out "Nārāyaṇa" he not only summoned his child but also gained salvation from Viṣṇu, one of whose names is Nārāyaṇa. The *Bhāgavata Purāṇa* (6.2) adds to the narrative the explanation that any invocation of god's name, even involuntary or spiteful, brings about god's grace and salvation.

We find numerous artistic representations of important salvation myths connected with Viṣṇu, Śiva, and Devī. The icons not only figuratively represent a salvific deed of the supreme but also become in their turn the salvific presence of god. Similarly the temple was not only the home but also the body of god who made himself available for worship to humans. This is underlined by depicting the breaking forth of the supreme from an icon, a *liṅga* or another *mūrti*—a motif found both in myths and works of art. In some of the iconic representations we find already a blend of mythology and philosophy. Thus the South Indian Naṭarāja image embodies both the mythological *tāṇḍava* dance of Śiva and the philosophy of Śaiva Siddhānta. Though it is not possible to draw parallels in all details, we can consider the *sādhana*s of the different philosophical schools as the interiorized counterpart of the mythological drama of salvation. In Śiva's dance it is easy to see the parallelism: Śaiva mystics assert that Cidambaram, the place of Śiva's mythical dance, is everywhere: the human heart is the place of Śiva's redeeming dance.

Almost all schools define the *adhikāra*, the presuppositions, for entering the way of salvation. Some Upaniṣads require birth as a Brāhmaṇ and performance of the prescribed *saṃskāra*s, but above everything else a desire to acquire *brahmavidyā* is necessary. Some speak also of certain physical qualities, "auspicious marks on hand and feet," a pleasing appearance, unimpeded speech, absence of physical defects. The presence of a *guru*, someone who has already reached the goal, is also among the requirements (*Muṇḍaka Upaniṣad* 1.2.12ff.).

Śaṃkara describes in the introduction to his *Śārīrakabhāṣya* (1.1.1) the *adhikāra* in terms of *nitya-anitya-viveka* (discrimination between eternal and noneternal), *vairāgya* (renunciation), virtues, and *mumukṣutva* (intense desire for liberation). Sadānanda, author of a popular Advaita Vedānta text, specifies this in the following way in *Vedāntasāra* (chapter 1):

> The competent student is an aspirant who, by studying in accordance with the prescribed method the Vedas and the Vedāṅgas, has obtained a general comprehension of the entire Vedas, who, being absolved from all sins in this or a previous life by the actions known as *kāmya* [rites performed with a view to attaining a desired object] and *niṣiddha* [those forbidden in the scriptures] and by the performance of actions called *nitya* [daily obligatory rites] and *naimittika* [obligatory on special occasions] as well as by penance and devotion, has become entirely pure in mind, and who has adopted the four *sādhana*s or means to the attainment of spiritual knowledge.

The latter are more precisely defined as follows: *Viveka* is the insight that "*brahman* alone is permanent and that all other things are transient." *Vairāgya*, renunciation of the fruits of action in this world and hereafter, consists in "utter disregard for immortality because it is as transitory as the enjoyment of earthly pleasures." Under virtues Sadānanda enumerates *śama* (restraining of the outgoing mental propensities), *dama* (restraining of the external sense organs), *uparati* (withdrawing of the self), *titikṣā* (forbearance), *samādhāna* (contentment), and *śraddhā* (faith). *Mumukṣutva* is the yearning for freedom.

Rāmānuja emphasizes above all the aspect of grace and election from the side of god (*Vedārthasaṃgraha* 251). The *guru* gains an increasingly important role in some Vaiṣṇava schools: Sundarabhaṭṭa says that the *guru* has the task of leading the erring and straying soul back to its proper home, the lord (*Mantrārtharahasya* 21).

Various Śaiva schools see in Śiva himself the true *guru*. The Pāśupatas hold that Śiva himself taught the five topics of knowledge which bring about liberation. Śaiva Siddhānta asserts that Śiva appears in bodily form as the *guru* to show his great love and to free the *paśu*s (Paranjoti 1954).

Śāktas attach great importance to the right *dīkṣā* (initiation) as presupposition for entering Śākta *sādhana*. Only this *dīkṣā* opens the eyes of the *sādhaka* (aspirant to perfection) to view the world under the aspect of *śakti*, it purifies and is the means of salvation. "All things are purified by the look, touch, and grasp of the initiated." Initiation may also mean to arouse the dormant Kuṇḍalinī *śakti* and so to start the process of salvation. It is *śakti* that binds and *śakti* that frees (Woodroffe 1963: 135).

In this respect Śākta systems show the closest affinity to Sāṃkhya. At a given moment in the process of *nivṛtti* (withdrawal), *prakṛti* (primal matter), which had been instrumental in the process of evolution and bondage of *puruṣa* (the spirit), becomes an aid in the process of liberation.

In all these systems the dramatic battle of good against evil, of *vidyā* against *avidyā*, knowledge against ignorance, *sattva* against *tamas*, and light against darkness is being fought in the human soul. Though we find statements in the Upaniṣads that the one who has attained *brahman* dwells beyond good and evil and though we read often in the Purāṇas how the supreme god takes away the bad *karma* of sinners who have taken refuge to him without punishing them for their wicked deeds, throughout the Hindu tradition a strong ethical consciousness prevailed and righteousness in a moral sense was always regarded as a precondition for entering the way to salvation and freedom.

The Nyāya school has the most systematic accounts and classifications of vices which exclude from the "way" and virtues to be cultivated in order to achieve spiritual freedom. Vātsyāyana offers the following analysis of the elements of *adharma* (unrighteousness) and *dharma* (righteousness): *adharma* as well as *dharma* depend either on body or speech or mind. Unrighteousness relating to the body is threefold: violence, theft, and unlawful sexual indulgence. Righteousness connected with bodily activity is charity, succor, and social service. The vices originating from speech are mendacity, causticity, asperity, tartness of expression, calumny, insinuation, and gossip. The virtues of speech are veracity, speaking with a view to doing good, speaking gently and agreeably, and recitation of scriptures. *Adharma* connected with the mind is threefold: malevolence and ill will, covetousness of another's property, impiety, lack of faith. *Dharma* originating in the mind is kindness, indifference to worldly advantages, and faith or piety (*Nyāyasūtrabhāṣya* on *Nyāyasūtra* 1.1.17).

Patañjali offers a less systematic, but more popular, series of virtues necessary for the attainment of peace of mind and spiritual freedom under the two categories of *yama* and *niyama*, restraints and observances. The former comprises nonviolence, veracity, abstinence from theft, continence, and abstinence from avariciousness. "These are the great vows, universal and not limited by life-state, space, time, and circumstance." The *niyama*s are cleanliness, contentment, purificatory action, study, and the making of the lord the motive of all action (*Yogasūtra* 2.30–32). Almost all schools have similar, if not identical, lists of virtues considered indispensable as part of the way to complete inner emancipation and to being human. Most important is *vairāgya*, detachment from possessions, from enjoyment, from desires. *Vairāgya* means in many cases *brahmacarya* (celibacy). Various kinds of *tapas* (self-mortification) are also quite commonly accepted as part of the way to liberation: fasting, night vigils, and *prāṇāyāma* (breath control) contribute to a gradual liberation of the seeker.

Patañjali in his *Yogasūtra* enumerates among the eight *yogāṅga*s, limbs or accessories to *yoga*, *āsana* (postures), *pratyāhāra* (withdrawal of the senses), *dhāraṇa* (concentration), *dhyāna* (meditation), and *samādhi* (trance). The sustained practice of these, he tells us, destroys all impurities, and as a consequence, the "light of wisdom reaches up to *vivekakhyāti*" (discriminative knowledge, perception of truth, intuition). Very common spiritual practices are *nāmajapa* (repetition of the name of god), *satsaṅga* (religious gatherings), *bhikṣā* (begging), and *yātrā* (pilgrimage). The application of external marks is also considered by many sects to be essential of the attainment of *mokṣa* (liberation).

The principal ways of salvation have been classified into *karmamārga* (way of works), *bhaktimārga* (way of devotion), and *jñānamārga* (way of knowledge). The division does not imply exclusiveness but emphasis: often we find the three *mārgas* or some of their elements combined in a particular *sādhana*.

A pure *karmamārga* is defended only by Pūrva Mīmāṃsā: *yajña* (Vedic sacrifice) had as its direct and supreme end heaven; *apūrva*, the hypostatized merit of *yajña*, is instrumental in acquiring it (*Mīmāṃsāsūtra* 2.1.5). Kumārila Bhaṭṭa and Prabhākara suggest that *mokṣa* beyond *svarga* can also be attained through the performance of *nityakarma* and *naimittikakarma*, regular (i.e. prescribed) and occasional (optional) religious rites alone. Rāmānuja and Madhva mention the necessity of performing *nityakarma* and *naimittikakarma* along with *bhakti* as the principal means. Bhāskara maintains that *karma* is a direct means to salvation, as important as *jñāna*. His *sādhana* is called *jñāna-karma-samuccaya* (combination of knowledge and works). Śrīkaṇṭha also maintains that *karma* is a coprinciple of liberation together with the grace of Śiva. Though Śiva is all-merciful, he is not in a position to remove the sorrows of all, unless by their deeds the veil of ignorance and impurity is removed. *Karma* is one of the manifestations of divine law and grace.

The most popular *sādhana* is certainly *bhaktimārga*: it is found in Vaiṣṇavism, Śaivism, and Śaktism in some form or other. But it is not possible to give any one common meaning to *bhakti* in different schools.

Rāmānuja virtually identifies *bhakti* with *jñāna*. *Parabhakti*, the highest degree of *bhakti* is identical with *prapatti*, surrender to the lord (*Vedārthasaṃgraha* 238ff.). In his thought *jñāna* must assume the form of *bhakti*, and both together must result in consecrated *karma*. *Prapatti* is the final stage. It is also called *śaraṇāgati*, complete surrender to the lord seated in the heart who accepts the *bhakta* as his eternal servant and allows the devotee to stay with him forever. *Bhakti* has, according to Rāmānuja, six prerequisites: discrimination of food, complete disregard for worldly objects, continued practice, performance of worship, virtuous conduct, and freedom from dejection (*Bhagavadgītābhāṣya* 11.55ff.).

Madhva in the *Mahābhārata Tātparya Nirṇaya* provides the following definition of *bhakti*: "That firm and unshakeable love of god, which rises above all other ties of love and affection and is based upon an adequate knowledge and conviction of his great majesty, is called *bhakti*. That alone is the means to *mokṣa*" (1.86). Vallabha derives *bhakti* from the root *bhaj* (to serve) and the suffix *kti* (love). *Bhakti* means loving service (*sevā*). Complete *sevā* implies love; without love service would be troublesome and not desirable. Vice versa, love, in order to be complete, requires service. The Nimbārka school defines *bhakti* as "a special kind of love for the lord." *Bhakti* is essentially given through the lord's grace. Through god's grace the *sādhaka* recognizes his nothingness and becomes humble.

In several *bhakti* schools, *gurūpasatti*, "renouncing one's self together with what belongs to oneself to the lord through the *guru*," is one of the means to achieve liberation. According to Sundarabhaṭṭa, it is the best of all *sādhanas*, uniting *karma*, *jñāna*, and *bhakti*. Obeying the *guru*'s precept is *karmayoga*; knowing that the essence of one's self is the *guru* is *jñānayoga*; being devoted to the *guru* is *bhaktiyoga*. In this school the *guru* is the only savior. The *sādhaka* has formally to ask the *guru* to be allowed to be his servant, son, wife, and friend.

For Baladeva, a follower of Caitanya, the highest form of *bhakti* is *premabhakti*, which is the sole and direct cause of salvation. It has two complementary aspects: *vairāgya*, disgust for whatever is not *brahman*, and *prema*, yearning for *brahman*. The choice by the lord is decisive. *Bhakti*, finally, is the feeling of the *hlādinīśakti* (the power of delight) of the lord. Through it the devotee becomes united with the lord. All the activities of the devotee become then the source of immense joy, being a constant god realization.

Nārada describes in his *Bhaktisūtra* (32) eleven grades of *bhakti*: glorification of the lord's qualities, love of his beauty, formal worship, constant remembrance, service as the lord's slave, friendship, childlike love, love as of a wife for her husband, self-surrender, complete absorption, and pain of separation from the lord. According to Nārada, the highest possible love is that which the *gopī*s of Vṛndāvana felt when Kṛṣṇa was absent, and they were ardently longing for him.

Pāśupatas follow a combination of *yoga* (discipline) and *vidhi*s (observances), which comes close to *bhakti*. It comprises *japa* (repetition of certain words or syllables), *dhyāna* (meditation), bathing in ashes, behaving like a madman, singing, laughing, trembling, and so forth. Vīraśaivas consider *bhakti* as a means to liberation because *bhakti* reunites *liṅga* and *aṅga* (Śiva and his devotee).

Jñānamārga plays a role in almost all schools but with different emphases. It usually proceeds by steps: the Upaniṣads generally speak of four steps, while Śaiva Siddhānta has seven. The *sādhaka* has to transcend the various levels of body-bound consciousness before arriving at self-knowledge.

Śaiva Siddhānta, which distinguishes four *mārga*s, recognizes *sanmārga* (the true way) as the highest. *Sanmārga* consists of the practice of *jñāna*: of the three kinds of *jñāna* only *patijñāna* (knowledge of Śiva, the lord) leads to *mukti* (Devasenapathi 1960: 243).

In the schools and systems that are closely linked up with a particular religion and which accept Purāṇas and Āgamas as doctrinal authorities, the intervention of god in the *sādhana* plays an equally decisive role as "grace of god." This grace in some form or other becomes an integral principle of spiritual reality, the immanent seed of the divine essence working towards liberation.

The *Bhāgavata Purāṇa* (3.26) explains the presence of god as *antaryāmi* as the ontological principle of salvation. Pañcarātra theology considers the presence of the *vyūha*s (divine emanations) as the motive force. Over the exact role of the grace of god in the process of salvation the Śrīvaiṣṇava school split: in the "cat school" active cooperation is not required; the "monkey school" demands active effort, without which god would not save a person (Mumme 1988: 1). The element of grace comes out extremely strongly in the Madhva school. Every detail in the process of salvation depends on god's will alone.

THE GOAL

The great Vedic salvation myth describes a cosmic battle between Indra and Vṛtra: demon rule is a disturbance of the three worlds, and Indra's salvific deed restores peace and order and divine rule in *triloka*. The result of Indra's victory is the liberation of the waters and the cows, the appearance of the sun, the moon, and the dawn, and the supremacy of the *deva*s. Indra's victory gives "room and freedom" to his worshipers (*Ṛg Veda* 2.15).

Viṣṇu as Varāha-*avatāra* saves the earth from the depth of the waters; in other *avatāra*s he saves *dharma*, the cosmic law which is responsible for the well being of the universe. Significantly, the *Bhāgavata Purāṇa* in its description of the birth of Kṛṣṇa enumerates cosmic signs that accompany it, indicating also cosmic salvation brought through Kṛṣṇa.

Similarly, we see that Śiva's salvation is cosmic in its extent: by swallowing the poison *halāhala* he saves the entire world from ruin; through the destruction of the demon-fortress, he returns peace and prosperity to the demon-ravaged worlds. Śiva Naṭarāja effects a cosmic salvation. Devī's victory over the buffalo demon brings bliss and happiness to the whole world.

In this unbroken archaic view of reality, creation is good and enjoyable. Heaven is not necessarily an absolutely superior state, and people have no "desire for heaven" before their appointed time of death. Heaven is the place where the *deva*s live and where the fathers go to when life is over.

The Purāṇas introduce a more individualistic view of salvation, promising eternal existence in heaven as reward for certain acts of piety and faith. They abound in colorful descriptions of the joys of heaven, which are superior to those of earth. Vaiṣṇavas and Śaivas alike assume that those who reach heaven receive an incorruptible body and share most of the qualities of the supreme being, including the freedom to enter a body at will and to roam about on earth (*Bhāgavata Purāṇa* 3.15.12; *Śiva Purāṇa*, *Umā Saṃhitā* 1–6).

Vedānta regards *svarga* (heaven) as a temporary condition of finite bliss and strives for transcendence even of *svarga*, that is, complete freedom in *mokṣa*. In the interpretation of Śaṃkara, *mokṣa* is not an acquisition but the realization of the true essence of being. The final state is ultimate identity of self and being, of *ātman* and *brahman*, of subject and universe. This state alone, independent of space and time, is worth being pursued. It is the return of the particular to the universal, of the *jīvātman* to the *brahmātman*, of the multiple into the one.

In Sāṃkhya *mokṣa* means isolation of *puruṣa* from *prakṛti*—a cessation of all change, a *kaivalya* (aloneness), and a return to the pristine detached existence.

Nyāya and Vaiśeṣika have only a negative definition of *mokṣa*—absolute freedom from pain or even absolute freedom from all experience, freedom from distress, and freedom from activity.

Vaiṣṇava schools make use of both the Sāṃkhya and the Vedānta patterns when describing the ultimate state, but they always insist on the perpetuation of the individual *jīva*: the ultimate state is a personal relationship between the *jīva* and the supreme.

Rāmānuja rejects the idea of the *jīvātman* merging into *brahman*: *mokṣa* is not loss of individuality but restoration of the initial and blissful relationship with the absolute. *Mukti* is cessation of egotism but not of individuality; it rules out the possibility of rebirth, but the *mukta*s (liberated ones) can assume bodies at will.

Madhva sees in *mokṣa* the reunion of the *jīva* with its lord through the acquisition of a nonmaterial body whose essence is pure and unmixed bliss. The *jīva* remains eternally different from the lord: it always remains *paratantra*, dependent on Viṣṇu, and its bliss consists in this. The *jīva* "sees, as it were, with the eyes of Hari, walks with the feet of Hari, takes everything with the hands of Hari" (*Brahmasūtrabhāṣya* 4.4.5).

Nimbārka sees *mokṣa* as *ātmasvarūpalabha*, attainment of the self's proper form and nature; the difference between *jīva* and *brahman* remains forever. Vallabha knows different ultimate states according to the way followed by the individual.

The Caitanya school has also some original contribution to the understanding of final freedom. Caitanya himself avoids the term "*mokṣa*" and uses *bhakti* for the ultimate goal. In his *Śikṣāṣṭaka* (verse 4) he prays to be given "birth after birth uncaused devotion (*ahaitukibhakti*) towards the lord's lotus feet." Bhaktisiddhānta Sarasvatī's *Vivṛti* on this verse amplifies this into the explicit rejection of *mokṣa*: "I reject not only *bhukti*, material enjoyment, in the form of *dharma*, *artha*, and *kāma*, but *mukti* as well. I do not desire liberation from the cycle of repeated birth and death" (1994: 76). But some of his followers use the word "*mukti*" without hesitation, and they even speak of *jīvanmukti*, liberation while still living in a body on earth, besides five forms of *mukti* after death. The *jīva* never loses its identity; but in *sāyujyamukti*, the highest form of perfection, it is completely immersed in divine bliss and experiences the *hlādinīśakti* of Kṛṣṇa as its own.

The Vaiṣṇava mystics emphasize their experience of god as *vastu*, reality. It is accompanied by supersensual phenomena, especially the *anāhata śabda*, a mysterious sound which breaks forth from within. They know the sweetness of god, they speak of the sharing of *rāmarasa*, the "sweet god-essence," by the *mukta*.

Śaivas have a tendency to see *mokṣa* more in terms of Advaita Vedānta. *Śaiva Purāṇa*s contain sections in which the state of *mokṣa* is described in terms of Advaita. The Pāśupatas call the final state *duḥkhānta*, "end of suffering," which is of a twofold nature. The lower form is *anātmaka*, impersonal; the higher form is *sātmaka*, personal—it means to be like *īśvara* with regard to knowledge and active power. Almost all Śaiva systems know a plurality of forms of *mukti*. The ultimate aim is "to be similar to Śiva," not to be identical with him. In Śaiva Siddhānta "Śiva includes all beings who have attained the state of Śiva." *Śivatva*, Śiva-hood, is the highest stage in our development, the realization of our true self. The difference between Śiva and the liberated *jīva*s consists in the fact that the *jīva*s have been liberated through Śiva's grace whereas Śiva himself is eternally free.

According to Śrīkaṇṭha, the *mukta*s realize the *saviśeṣa* body of Śiva, and though they cannot be distinguished from *brahman*, they are not identical with it. Attaining the final stage means realizing *śivatva* and sharing the qualities of Śiva. The *mukta* is not only omniscient like Śiva but also independent and can assume and discard bodies at will. The *mukta*s are also all-pervasive, but they do not share the power of Śiva to create and to destroy the world. Though they enjoy the same bliss as Śiva, there is only one lord. Śrīkaṇṭha describes the abode of Śiva as a place blazing "like millions of suns" (*Śrīkaṇṭhabhāṣya* 4.4.22).

Pratyabhijñā claims that the state of perfection achieved by its *sādhana* is beyond and above the *turīya*, the "fourth state" of the Upaniṣads: it is *turīyātīta*, Śiva-consciousness, in which the individual experiences the self as identical with the entire universe and with Śiva.

Vīraśaivism, as interpreted by Śrīpati, asserts that the final goal of the soul is *aikya* or unity with Paraśiva. The soul in union with Śiva enjoys unexcelled bliss. The *mukta* increasingly participates in the functions and powers of Śiva until completely absorbed in Śiva and attaining the condition of Paramaśiva. Śāktas see the attainment of supreme bliss in the union of Śiva and Śakti in the body of the devotee. *Mukta*s assume all the forms of Śakti in their own subtle body and become one with the force that creates the universe and gives liberation.

One of the major controversies in Hindu religious history concerned the possibility of *jīvanmukti* or final liberation while still living in the body. Śaṃkara, on account of his teaching that reality is identical with consciousness, comes to the conclusion that *jīvanmukti* is definitely possible. Thus he describes in his *Vivekacūḍāmaṇi* the state of the one who is completely free while still living in his body:

> Satisfied with undiluted, constant bliss, the *jīvanmukta* is neither grieved nor elated by sense-objects, is neither attached nor averse to them, but always disports with the

> self and takes pleasure therein. A child playing with its toys forgets hunger and pain; exactly so does the person of realization take pleasure in reality, without ideas of "I" and "mine," and is happy. . . . Though without riches, yet ever content; though helpless, yet very powerful, though not enjoying the sense-objects, yet eternally satisfied; though without an exemplar, yet looking upon all with an eye of quality. Though working, yet inactive; though experiencing fruits of past actions, yet untouched by them; though possessed of a body, yet without identification with it; though limited, yet omnipresent. Neither pleasure nor pain, nor good nor evil, ever touches this knower of *brahman*, who always lives without a body-idea.
>
> (536–37, 543–45)

Rāmānuja, with equal logical consistency, denies the possibility of *jīvanmukti*: in order to attain ultimate bliss, the *mukta* requires a supernatural body, which replaces the physical and the subtle body (*Vedārthasaṃgraha* 123). Most Vaiṣṇava schools agree with Rāmānuja, whereas many Śaiva schools accept the possibility of *jīvanmukti*. Śaiva Siddhānta knows of *jīvanmukta*s who are "beyond good and evil" and who behave in ways that would be sinful for normal people (Devasenapathi 1960: 258). Śāktas also recognize the possibility of *jīvanmukti* in very much the same way as Advaitins do. The *Tripurārahasya* describes the *jīvanmukta* as "neither happy when enjoying nor unhappy when deprived of enjoyment, looking upon the whole world as if it were a play on a stage, always appearing somewhere far away and yet ever doing what is to be done at the moment" (chapter 10).

Krishnachandra Bhattacharyya, a modern Hindu thinker, thus describes the role of the *jīvanmukta*s: They

> elect to continue the divine system of justice and grace by remaining in the body, by freely continuing in the illusory form in relation to other souls. So the jīvan-mukta souls assist as the high priests at the cosmic yajña . . . . They move about like the impersonations of the Divine grace that is dimly stirring in the bosom of the age, the beacon lights of the universe, the realised hopes of the army of the good—never self-assertive, sometimes even despondent—fighting out the great battle with the army of evil.
>
> (1956: 59)

THE RELEVANCE OF MOKṢA IN OUR TIME

The texts referred to here, articulating the notion of *mokṣa* by the various Hindu traditions, are, without exception, "premodern." The question arises about their relevance for today.

Modernity in the West began with an emancipation of society from the domination of religion and thus came to be equated with secularism. The modern Western mind is, almost by definition, a secular mind, dedicated to pursuing aims in this world rather than looking towards a world to come, loath to spend energies and money on anything but the betterment of life on earth. Modernity reached India towards the end of the eighteenth century, when the British East India Company began to settle in India with the goal not only to do business but also to modernize a country which was still largely living in the middle ages, controlled by religion and oriented towards transcendent goals.

With the gradual spread of the British administration over large parts of India and the expansion of the British educational system there, it was unavoidable that modern Western secular ideas of life would influence the Indian educated classes. Seeing themselves in the mirror of an alien civilization, pricked by unsympathetic observations of apparently successful people, but also made aware by these self-same foreigners of the great heritage which they possessed, some enlightened Hindus set out to modernize without losing their souls. It was a comparatively small minority which saw in European-style secularization the ideal to be achieved; most attempted to blend and integrate traditional Hindu values and attitudes with Western science and technology.

In spite of the unquestionable change which India has undergone during the past two hundred years—industrialization, modernization of administration, urbanization, and a tremendous increase in population—traditional religion still plays a great role in India, and the recent past has seen significant efforts to reassert the place of religion in the political life of the country.

Modernity in India also meant analysis and criticism: no longer were the absolute and total claims of religion accepted uncritically, but tradition and religion itself became the focus of scrutiny and critique. Thus Rammohan Roy (1772–1833) successfully fought against *satī*, the burning of wives at the death of their husbands, a custom which had received the sanction of the religious authorities and was defended by the traditionalists as part and parcel of Hinduism. Dayānanda Sarasvatī (1824–83) attacked the popular Hinduism of his time as corrupt and alienated from his Vedic roots. He condemned many traditional practices such as child marriage and insisted that religion should also aim at improving the social and material conditions of people.

Bal Gangadhar Tilak (1856–1920) in his *Gītā Rahasya* propounded a new "gospel of action." His *karmayoga* was not otherworldly. He rejected the ancient ideal of renunciation and saw fulfillment in terms of work for society and nation. Although he was a staunch defender of the faith of his fathers, he gave it a new direction towards social and political liberation instead of inward spiritual individual *mokṣa*.

Gopal Krishna Gokhale (1866–1915), founder of the Servants of India Society, considered "the basic task" to be "the liberation of man by the development and enhancement of his moral, intellectual and physical abilities and talents" (1916: 1231). For him service of the nation was a *sādhana*. Many other less-known men and women took this suggestion up and devoted themselves to social work in a religious spirit in the conviction that this was the *sādhana* for our time, not based on myths and speculation, but on economic progress and social welfare.

The contact with modern ideas resulted not so much in a rejection of tradition but in attempts to reinterpret and further develop traditional teachings. The greatest personalities of the Indian Renaissance consciously took up the essential concepts offered to them by the philosophical, religious, and spiritual traditions of India and tried to integrate into them modern ideas according to the necessities of time and circumstances.

Rabindranath Tagore accepts the modern idea of the human person as "creator" and enthusiastically endorses the idea of a "paradise on earth" created through common human efforts. He declares in his *The Religion of Man*: "The idea of the humanity of our God, or the divinity of Man the Eternal, is the main subject of this book . . . . On the surface of our being we have the ever-changing phases of the individual self, but in the depth there dwells the Eternal Spirit of human unity beyond our direct knowledge" (1931: 15). He also has his own individual "religion of an artist" in which the concept of beauty is central: the realization of truth is identical with harmony and beauty. He emphasizes modern social concerns and sees a person not so much as a monadic individual but as an integral part of humanity; human life is meant to be lived in and for society. But he very clearly professes his faith in the tradition of his forefathers when explaining his *Sādhana*, "the realisation of life." We have to realize the inherent divinity in humanity; the means of this realization is spontaneous, selfless action in the sense of the *niṣkāma karma* of the *Bhagavad Gītā* or "realization of love." The way to realization is love, "for love is the perfection of consciousness" (Tagore 1913: 106). "Love is the ultimate meaning of everything around us. It is not a mere sentiment; it is truth; it is the joy that is at the root of all creation. It is the white light of pure consciousness that emanates from Brahma. . . . It is through the heightening of our consciousness into love, and extending it all over the world, that we can attain *Brahma-vihāra*, communion with this infinite joy" (Tagore 1913: 107).

At the same time Tagore emphasizes the need of action in the process of self-realization: an emphasis not against tradition but in accordance with it, though with a new connotation.

> The true striving in the quest of truth, of *dharma*, consists not in the neglect of action but in the effort to attune it closer and closer to the eternal harmony. The text of this striving should be: *Whatever works thou doest, consecrate them to Brahma.* That is to say, the soul is to dedicate itself to Brahma through all its activities. This dedication is the song of the soul, in this is its freedom. Joy reigns when all work becomes the path to the union with Brahma; when the soul ceases to return constantly to its own desires; when in it our self-offering grows more and more intense. Then there is completion, then there is freedom, then, in this world, comes the kingdom of God.
> (Tagore 1913: 128–29; emphasis in original)

Aurobindo Ghose (1888–1950) was brought up with modern Western thought; ideas of evolution, of development, of progress deeply influenced him. He remained, nevertheless, in the tradition of the *ṛṣi*s and the *ācārya*s. He revitalized ancient myths and philosophies in his great panoramic view of *The Life Divine*. He analyzes the evils of our age and comes to the conclusion that the West has created in its technical civilization a means for self-destruction and the East in its spiritual search has stagnated and become corrupt. The combination of the positive elements of both East and West—progress and spiritualization—can bring about liberation from the deadly cycle of periodic destruction or inertia. Aurobindo sees liberation not only in terms of the individual but also of society, of whole nations, of humankind, and, ultimately, of the cosmos. He distinguishes—as the whole Hindu tradition does—between the "ego" and the "self," between "mental" and "gnostic" beings. The way to the freedom of the self and the ultimate unity of being is what Aurobindo calls the Integral Yoga: it not only aims at the development of a part of the human personality but also at transforming the entire person into something higher, something spiritual and not only to lead an elite to this goal but all of humanity.

Guidance for this *sādhana* is not provided by any particular religion or philosophy but by the "eternal Veda secret in the heart of every" thinking and living being (Ghose 1971: 55). The true *guru* is in us: "It is . . . [the *jagadguru*] who [enlightens us, who] progressively [reveals] in us his own nature of freedom, bliss, love, power, immortal[ity]" (Ghose 1971: 55). This Integral Yoga is the "rebirth" into a higher sphere. Aurobindo stresses the need for "work" in the sense of the *Bhagavad Gītā* as liberating power and as way to truly integral knowledge. The perfect person is a *jīvanmukta*, one who has realized the ultimate in this life and while fully participating in life, exercises a divine activity. The same principle that is working towards the liberation and realization of the individual applies to the social forms of life: they also have to be reborn, transcend themselves, take part in the all-embracing process of spiritualization, which is ultimately a process of salvation through the immanent *jagadguru*. Humanity, as a whole, is the supreme manifestation of the universal self. Therefore, the *sādhana*, the means to the spiritual end, would not be a purely personal spirituality, *vairāgya* and *saṃnyāsa*, but it would encompass the totality of life, both individual and social.

> [A] society which was even initially spiritualised, would make the revealing and finding of the divine Self in man the whole first aim of all its activities, its education, its knowledge, its science, its ethics, its art, its economical and political structure. As it was to some extent in the ancient Vedic times with the cultural education of the higher classes, so it would be then with all education. It would embrace all knowledge in its scope, but would make the whole trend and aim and the permeating spirit not mere worldly efficiency, but this self-developing and self-finding.
>
> (Ghose 1962: 343)

Aurobindo is aiming at the "coming spiritual age" in which the ideal of spiritual person and spiritual society would be fulfilled—a liberated humanity, humanity that has realized the self.

If we can see in Tagore a modern *bhakta* and in Aurobindo a modern *jñāni*, we may call Mohandas Karamchand Gandhi a modern *karmayogī*. More explicitly than anyone else, Mahātmā Gandhi affirmed both his indebtedness to his traditional religion and his commitment to his own time. His "book of books" was the *Bhagavad Gītā*, which gave him solace, strength, and a philosophical basis for his action. Two tradition-laden concepts—*satya* and *ahiṃsā*—circumscribe his whole work and thought.

Gandhi's life was devoted to win freedom for his people. He himself understood *svarāj* (self-rule) always as transcending mere political independence. In and through *svarāj* he wanted to realize truth and love; that was the real freedom he was aiming at. He often said that he would not bother with "freedom" if it did not mean an increase in truth and love, if it did not make those, for whom he wanted freedom, better people. He preferred Truth to *svarāj*. He confessed that he considered his national service part of his *sādhana*, the process that frees the spirit from the bondage of flesh. He did not desire any earthly kingdom but only the heavenly kingdom, which is *mokṣa*. But he did not consider it necessary to seek refuge in a cave of the Himālayas in order to attain *mokṣa*. He felt that his *sādhana* was in and through his social service. We need not doubt that "freedom" for Gandhi meant "liberation" and "self-realization" in a religious sense. The *sādhana* he developed, and into which he initiated his closest fellow workers, is contained in the *Ashram Observances in Action*. Not by accident he insisted on the vows of truth, *ahiṃsā*, *brahmacarya*, poverty, body-labor, fearlessness and tolerance, *svadeśī*, and abolition of untouchability. They are meant to purify the soul, to make humanity unselfish, to "humanize" the individual and society. His is not a *saṃnyāsī*'s *sādhana* but nevertheless a true *sādhana*, a true way to self-realization. The ultimate he was aiming at was truth, a truth which had to find its expression in daily life as selflessness, sharing the lot of the poor, social justice. But this truth was also transcendent, was identical with god and the kingdom of god. "What I want to achieve, —what I have been striving and pining to achieve . . ., —is self-realization, to see god face to face, to attain *Moksha*. I live and move and have my being in pursuit of this goal. All that I do by way of speaking and writing, and all my ventures in the political field, are directed to this same end" (Gandhi 1993: xxvi).

There are unbroken traditions of Vaiṣṇavism, Śaivism, and Śaktism (as well as of Advaita Vedānta), and the ancient myths and the philosophies developed many centuries ago still give inspiration and solace to millions of Hindus who see in them the expression of eternal and timeless truths and a way to salvation. The centers of these religions continue to draw large crowds, and the heads of the various *sampradāya*s still command the respect of a vast following. The classical texts are reprinted time and again and read and reread by a large section of the population. Modern *guru*s and heroes, like Rāmakṛṣṇa, Vivekānanda, Ramaṇa Maharṣi, Rāmatīrtha, Rāmadāsa, Śivānanda, to mention only a few, never claimed to have found a "new salvation" but were faithful representatives of ancient ways and thoughts.

Also among twentieth-century professional academic philosophers we find a large number who affirm their acceptance of the traditional insights into the human situation, the way to liberation, and the aim of self-realization. They incorporate modern ideas, but basically they remain within traditional doctrines.

For K. Bhattacharyya, "Vedānta is primarily a religion, and it is a philosophy only as the formulation of this religion" (1956: 118). He accepts its basic tenets of the illusoriness of the individual self. "All religion makes for the realization of the self as sacred, but the religion of Advaita is the specific cult of such realization understood explicitly as self-knowledge" (K. Bhattacharyya 1956: 118). T. R. V. Murti describes his conviction as follows:

> As a Hindu, I had always believed in the Law of Karma. Reflection on it has induced in me a kind of conviction that it is quite a plausible explanation of the governance of the universe. The conception of the hierarchy of Values (puruṣārtha) with Freedom as the highest value has been no less a conviction. That Philosophy is not an affair of intellectual curiosity or theoretic analysis but a serious spiritual discipline (sādhanā) directed towards the attainment of Freedom is basic to Indian Philosophy, and I subscribe to it without reservation.
>
> (1952: 457)

For Murti philosophy is *adhyātmavidyā*—as for the ancients, the aim of both religion and philosophy. "Realisation of Spirit is the realisation of all Values, as it is Truth, Freedom and Bliss. It is not only a vision of reality, but a consummation of life as well" (Murti 1952: 470).

Sarvepalli Radhakrishnan, the best known among modern Hindu philosophers, deals in his numerous publications mainly with one theme: the crisis of modern humanity and the way out of it. He is sensitive enough to hear the "sound of things crumbling" in every field of human endeavor, in political and economic structures, in beliefs and systems of thought (Radhakrishnan 1947: 10). He is aware of the "crisis that touches the very roots of our civilization." The great challenge of our time lies in the fact that we possess almost unlimited energies derived from nature by science, while our moral stature has not grown proportionately. Thus these enormous powers are being used and misused against humanity.

Radhakrishnan sees the root of all evil in our estrangement from our real self, in our "split spirit." Our crisis is in the last analysis a spiritual crisis: we are "secularized," unintegrated, fragmented, divorced from spirit, cutoff from our spiritual source. Dictatorship, mechanization of life, rootlessness, shallowness, and lack of inner orientation, all are due to this deep-seated egoism which is born of humanity's misunderstanding of true self. What applies to the individual also applies to society: the structures of capitalism, militarism, and nationalism are intrinsically evil, inhuman, against the spirit. Radhakrishnan points out that those who were called to show the way—philosophers, thinkers, and writers, statesmen, and religious leaders—have failed to do so. At best they are able to point out the ills of our time, but they cannot provide any remedy. The remedy that Radhakrishnan offers is the remedy of Hindu tradition: self-finding, spirituality, a return to the origin. Spirituality is the spirit of unity, of universality, of transcendence. This spiritualization is meant to transform not only individuals but also society and humankind as a whole. The religion of the spirit is the path by which Radhakrishnan wants to lead humanity back to salvation. It is only by the reintegration and spiritual rebirth of the individual that society and nations can be saved. Only the individual has the spark of the spirit, which cannot be extinguished by any power on earth. "We are all fragments of the divine, sons of immortality, *amṛtasya putrāḥ*." In the details of this reintegration and respiritualization of the individual and humanity, Radhakrishnan also follows ancient tradition; individually, meditation and concentration are recommended; for society as a whole, the *caturvarṇāśrama* system is supposed to make for liberation and restoration of harmony.

The result of the "rebirth" would be a "perfect individual," a being that comes very close to the ancient *jīvanmukta*. Those "free beings" are able to act as instruments of the spirit, to realize the purpose of the spirit in society and humankind. Salvation does not mean to be taken out from the world but to live in the world with a transformed spirit. All are called to attain this status, and it is the role of society to create the necessary structures for an education towards freedom of the spirit. The reborn live not for themselves but for their fellow humans. The process of *mokṣa* comes to an end only then, when all individuals have reached perfection and freedom. Nobody is fully liberated unless all injustice and all evil in the world has been overcome (Radhakrishnan 1932: 306).

The realization of perfect freedom for all individuals means the rise of the perfect society. When perfect "spirituality" and perfect "unity" are reached, all individuals will merge into the oneness of spirit, the cosmic creator god too will become one with the spirit:

> The God who is responsible for this world, who is the consciousness of the universe, is working through brute matter from which He has to liberate Himself and liberate us. He Himself is suffering in each and all of us. This suffering will be at the end when the spirit which is imprisoned in transitory matter is released, when the potential world-spirit or spirit of the whole becomes the actual consciousness of each part, when God becomes (in the Apostle's word) "all in all," when the solitary limited God becomes the pantheistic Absolute.
>
> (Radhakrishnan 1958: 124–25)

PART V

SOCIAL ACTION AND SOCIAL STRUCTURE

CHAPTER FOURTEEN

KARMA

Herman W. Tull

India is renowned for its diversity. Dissimilitude abounds in every sphere—from the physical elements of its land and people to the intangible workings of its beliefs and practices. Indeed, given this variety, India itself appears to be not a single entity but an amalgamation, a "construct," arising from the conjoining of innumerable, discrete parts. Modern scholarship has, quite properly, tended to explore these elements in isolation. (In part, this trend represents the conscious reversal of the stance taken by an earlier generation of scholars whose work reified India into a monolithic entity—a critical element in the much maligned "Orientalist" enterprise.) Nonetheless, the representation of India as a singular "whole" is not an entirely capricious enterprise; for India is an identifiable entity, united by—if not born out of—certain deep and pervasive structures. Thus, for example, the Hindu tradition has long maintained a body of mythology that weaves the disparate temples, gods, even geographic landscapes that exist throughout the subcontinent into a unified, albeit syncretic, whole.

In the realm of thought, there is no more pervasive, unifying structure than *karma*. It is the "doctrine" or "law" that ties actions to results and creates a determinant link between an individual's status in this life and his or her fate in future lives. Following what is considered to be its earliest appearances in the Upaniṣads, the doctrine reaches into nearly every corner of Hindu thought. Indeed, its dominance is such in the Hindu worldview that *karma* encompasses, at the same time, life-affirming and life-negating functions; for just as it defines the world in terms of the "positive" function of delineating a doctrine of rewards and punishments, so too it defines the world through its "negative" representation of action as an all but inescapable trap, an unremitting cycle of death and rebirth.

Despite—or perhaps because of—*karma*'s ubiquity, the doctrine is not easily defined. Wendy Doniger O'Flaherty reports of a scholarly conference devoted to the study of *karma* that although the participants admitted to a general sense of the doctrine's parameters, considerable time was consumed in a "lively but ultimately vain attempt to define . . . karma and rebirth" (1980b: xi). The base meaning of the term "*karma*" (or, more precisely, in its Sanskrit stem form, *karman*, a neuter substantive) is "action." As a doctrine, *karma* encompasses a number of quasi-independent concepts: rebirth (*punarjanman*); consequence (*phala*, literally "fruit," a term that suggests the "ripening" of actions into consequences); and the valuation or "ethicization" of acts, qualifying them as either "good" (*puṇya* or *sukarman*) or "bad" (*pāpman* or *duṣkarman*) (O'Flaherty 1980b: xi). In a general way, however, for at least the past two thousand years, the following (from the well-known text, the *Bhāgavata Purāṇa*) has held true as representing the principal elements of the *karma* doctrine: "The same person enjoys the fruit of the same sinful or a meritorious act in the next world in the same manner and to the same extent according to the manner and extent to which that (sinful or meritorious) act has been done by him in this world" (6.1.45; Tagare 1993: 779). Nevertheless, depending on the doctrine's context, which itself ranges from its appearance in a vast number of literary sources to its usage on the popular level, not all these elements may be present (though in a general way they may be implicit).

How the elements underlying the *karma* doctrine coalesce, or, alternately, how they diverge in context is treated in detail in a collection of essays—the fruit of two "*karma* conferences"—published in 1980 (O'Flaherty 1980d). This collection advances considerably the study of the *karma* doctrine; yet, because the published findings tend to be highly specialized, it is neither possible nor desirable to restate them here. Rather, in the following pages the *karma* doctrine will be sought out on general grounds, from its ancient Hindu origins, to its development as a central element in Hindu thought, and, finally, to its continuing existence as a defining element of the Hindu world.

THE HISTORY OF KARMA: THE PROBLEM OF THE SOURCES

Despite *karma*'s dominance in Hindu thought, a detailed knowledge of its history long eluded scholars. As W. D. Whitney, the eminent American Indologist, noted more than a century ago: "one of the most difficult questions in the religious history of India, [is] how that doctrine arose, out of what it developed, to what feature of the ancient faith it attached itself" (1873: 61). The difficulty scholars encountered in seeking out *karma*'s roots may be attributed to some degree to the arcane nature of India's ancient textual tradition, the vast corpus known collectively as the Veda. This body of texts is divided into several layers: Saṃhitās, consisting chiefly of paeans to the god, invoking them to share in the sacrifice; Brāhmaṇas, in which the sacrificial rites are described and discussed in detailed, though highly idiosyncratic fashion; and Āraṇyakas and Upaniṣads, texts which purport to expound a "secret" knowledge (presaged in the Brāhmaṇas) that frequently begins with the metaphysics of the sacrifice and extends into sophisticated inquiries into the nature of reality and the possibility of its direct perception through some form of transformative knowledge (gnosis).[1]

The Vedic texts were composed over an enormous period of time, a period generally agreed to have begun—albeit on somewhat speculative grounds—roughly 1500 BCE and ending about 500 BCE. At the outset of this period, Vedic culture was situated in the northwest corner of the Indian subcontinent and had already shed its overt connections to its Indo-Āryan past. Over the next thousand years of its development, Vedic culture penetrated deeply into the eastern portion of the subcontinent, to modern Bengal, and at least as far south as the Narmadā River (Majumdar 1951: 222, 246, 266). This movement into the subcontinent undoubtedly influenced the Vedic tradition's development, as the Vedic people encountered and commingled with other settled ancient Indic populations. However, it is impossible to judge with any precision how this commingling may have affected the course of the Vedic religion's development. On the one hand, the Vedic texts do not disclose clear lines revealing the origins of specific beliefs; on the other hand, there is no extant textual record from the ancient non-Vedic cultures. (Substantial archaeological remains have been recovered from the Indus Valley civilization, which clearly predates the rise of Vedic culture; yet this civilization's writing remains indecipherable.)

Because the *karma* doctrine has no obvious, clear antecedents in the earliest layers of the Vedic literature, some scholars have suggested that *karma*'s origins lie outside the sphere of ancient Vedic culture. The prominence of agricultural themes in the doctrine's early presentations—in particular those relating to rice cultivation—has been cited as evidence of the doctrine's non-Vedic, "tribal" origin (O'Flaherty 1980b: xvi–xvii). The anthropologist Gananath Obeyesekere (1980) has investigated the possibility of *karma*'s non-Vedic origin by looking to the beliefs of modern Indian (and non-Indian) tribal populations and then extrapolating from them a model of belief that may have existed among the ancient Indian populations. According to Obeyesekere, nearly all primitive and preliterate societies possess simple theories of rebirth, theories that through a simple transformation can evolve into a karmic eschatology. This transformation occurs with the introduction of a link between the nature of actions in one life to either a state of retribution or reward in the next life, a transformation that Obeyesekere refers to as the "ethicization" of the simple rebirth eschatology.

Obeyesekere's supposition that the non-Vedic stream made a significant contribution to the *karma* doctrine is likely correct. Moreover, his developmental paradigm opens up what may be the most significant question in understanding the history of *karma*; that is, where (and how) does the systematic ethicization of actions occur? Obeyesekere and others have argued that the ethicization of actions cannot be seen in the Brāhmaṇic-Upaniṣadic milieu (Keith 1925, 2: 468, 584; Obeyesekere 1980: 161). However, within the context of the ritual performance, the Brāhmaṇic authors do distinguish between good and bad (ritual) acts, and, as in other ethical systems, this valuation is based on the consequences of actions (Mackie 1977: 59). Thus a typical Brāhmaṇic passage declares: "When the *agnihotra* is being offered, what he does mistakenly, either by word or deed, that cuts off his vigor, his own self, or his children" (*Śatapatha Brāhmaṇa* 2.3.4.18, see also 1.5.2.15). In other words, within the narrow confines of the Vedic ritual system a rudimentary ethical system does indeed exist.

The supposition that such an ethical system is part of Vedic culture is an important one. The Hindu tradition, for at least the last two thousand years of its development, has looked to the Veda as a model of cultural prestige and the legitimizing force for all sorts of religious behavior. Vedic culture however is not a monolithic entity; the texts, as well as the beliefs and ritual practices contained in them, admit to significant variations. Moreover, because these texts were created not by individual authors but represent the thoughts, directives, and observations of communities of inspired sages as they were recorded over successive decades or perhaps even centuries, they are not highly systematized. As a result, as they now stand and as they have stood for perhaps the past 2,500 years, the Vedic texts contain multiple, and sometimes contradictory, teachings on the same subject (a situation that does not differ markedly from the textual traditions of other great religions).

This fluidity however is not without limits; for at the core of the Vedic tradition certain key values exist. Foremost are those relating to the act of sacrifice. Despite the changes in thought and practice that may have occurred over the millennium or so of the Vedic texts' composition and compilation, this core remains clearly discernible; the act of sacrifice—though variously enacted and variously interpreted by the Vedic religionists—stands *always* at the center of the Vedic tradition.

Karma is a critical component of this core. In the early Vedic texts, the term "*karman*" typically denotes the action or performance of the sacrificial ritual; a usage that is so common that the term "*karman*" is there synonymous with the Vedic rites (this meaning is retained in later Hinduism, where it stands along with *karma*'s other connotations). By the end of this period, as reflected in the Upaniṣads, *karma* emerges as a *doctrine*; that is, in a formulation that has a definite and extensive meaning and is reified above and beyond its ordinary connotations. To understand *karma*'s history, it is first necessary to examine these early doctrinal formulations, a point that leads back to the action of the Vedic sacrifice.

THE FORMULATION OF KARMA IN THE UPANIṢADS

The term "*karman*" occurs frequently in the Vedic texts. As such, *karma* is not understood here as a doctrine but simply as a term denoting action, in particular, the action of the sacrificial ritual. However, by the end of the Brāhmaṇa period, which is synchronous with the composition of the early Upaniṣads, *karma is* presented as a doctrine, one in particular that expresses the notion that actions in one life directly affect the conditions of a future life.

In its first formulation in the *Bṛhadāraṇyaka Upaniṣad*, the doctrine appears as part of a discussion between two well-known sages, Ārtabhāga and Yājñavalkya, regarding the fate of the individual after death. Ārtabhāga first describes the dissolution of the dead person on the funeral pyre, drawing on an image deeply embedded in Vedic thought: upon cremation the deceased's speech enters into the air, his eye into the sun, his mind into the moon, his hearing into the quarters (*Ṛg Veda* 10.16.3, see also 10.90.13–14; *Atharva Veda* 18.2.7). He then asks his companion Yājñavalkya, "What becomes next of this person?" Yājñavalkya, however, prefers not to discuss this in public, as he states: "My dear Ārtabhāga, take my hand. We two alone shall know of this, this is not for us two to speak of among [other] people." The text then continues in the third person: "Having gone aside, they entered into a discussion. That which they spoke about was action (*karman*) and that which they praised was action: one indeed becomes good by good action, bad by bad [action]" (*Bṛhadāraṇyaka Upaniṣad* 3.2.13).

To many scholars this passage appears to present the fundamental premise of the *karma* doctrine as it dominates later Hindu thought; that is, that an individual attains a state after death that is a direct result of the ethical quality ("good" or "bad") of his activities before death (Deussen 1906: 329–30; Farquhar 1920: 34; Keith 1925, 2: 573; Oldenberg 1915: 109; Rao 1987: 28). Although the central idea presented here "that one becomes good by good action, bad by bad" does evoke later formulations of the *karma* doctrine, the passage fails to explicate several key elements that would tie it with certainty to the later *karma* doctrine. In particular, the questions of what constitutes "good" and "bad" action (is it action in general or a special form of activity such as that of the sacrificial ritual?) and what is the precise nature of the individual's postdeath existence (is it a new birth in a human or animal form in this world or a movement into an otherworldly existence?) stand unanswered here.

Karma, as a doctrine, appears again in another *Bṛhadāraṇyaka Upaniṣad* passage (4.4.1–7). This passage also begins with a discussion of the fate of the individual upon the event of his death. Unlike the previous passage, however, which relates an individual's component parts (hearing, breath, and so forth) to the numerous spheres of the cosmos, this second passage notes that the individual approaching death "becomes one," as the vital energies together enter the individual's heart. Gathered in the heart, these elements then depart through one of the body's orifices, an event signifying the end of the individual's current existence. At this moment, at what appears to be the brink of dissolution, the "deeds (*karman*) and knowledge and memory take hold of him [the deceased]." This "taking hold of" apparently leads to the acquisition of a new body, as the passage continues: "Just as a goldsmith takes a piece of gold and turns it into another . . . so the self [of the individual] makes another new and more beautiful shape, like that of the ancestors, *gandharvas*, gods, Prajāpati, Brahmā, or other beings." (Another recension of this text adds "men" to the list.) The passage ends recapitulating the notion that: "How one acts and how one behaves so that one becomes: the doer of good becomes good, the doer of bad becomes bad" (*Bṛhadāraṇyaka Upaniṣad* 4.4.5).

Although this passage does refer to the acquisition of a new body after death, it does not refer specifically to rebirth in this world—a critical component of the later *karma* doctrine—but to some sort of otherworldly afterlife existence (the beings listed here are all denizens of the various Vedic heavens). Immediately following this description of the acquisition of a new body, however, the authors or compilers of the text include a verse that describes the possibility of returning to this world: "That one together with his action, he goes where his inner mind is attached. When he reaches the end of that action (*karman*) which he did in this world here, then he comes back to this world, back to action." Not everyone returns to this world: "the man who does not desire . . . his breaths do not depart; Brahmā he is, to Brahmā he goes" (*Bṛhadāraṇyaka Upaniṣad* 4.4.6). Although these final passages are quite possibly an interpolation—evidenced by their verse form and the fact that they follow a passage that itself expresses a terminal thought—it is the sort of accretion typically found in the early Upaniṣads, texts in which contiguous passages, though perhaps unrelated in origin, reiterate specific concepts. Thus, although the teachings presented in these two passages—the one that proposes actions lead to a rebirth only in the next world, the other that actions lead to a new birth in this world—are nominally distinct, in juxtaposition they emphasize a common message; namely, that actions affect the conditions of the afterlife.

The intimation here that the individual, on the basis of the deeds performed in life, may be reborn in this world, or alternatively attain the world of Brahmā, appears again in an extensive discussion found in another *Bṛhadāraṇyaka Upaniṣad* passage (6.2), a passage that is repeated with variations in detail in another early Upaniṣad text, the *Chāndogya Upaniṣad* (5.3–10). The passage begins with an intriguing set of questions posed by an ancient king, Jaivali Pravāhaṇa, to the young sage Śvetaketu: "Do you know how people, when they die, go by different paths? Do you know how they return to this world? Do you know how the world beyond is not filled up, even as more and more people continuously go there?" (*Bṛhadāraṇyaka Upaniṣad* 6.2.2). Śvetaketu professes ignorance to each successive question (as well as to a number of other related questions) and returns home to report his encounter with the king to his father, the sage Gautama. Gautama, intrigued by his son's encounter, approaches the king and asks him to take him on as his pupil. King Jaivali Pravāhaṇa accedes to this request and then states enigmatically that the answers to these questions have never before been in the possession of Brāhmaṇs. Although considerable scholarly ink has been spilled over the representation of a sage entreating a king for knowledge, where one would expect the reverse (see, e.g. Keith 1925, 2: 492–97), scholars tend now to view this situation as part of the broadening intellectualization of the warrior class that occurred at this time in several contemporary Indian movements (Buddhism, Jainism) (Olivelle 1996: xxxiv–xxxv). The more significant point here is that knowledge of this doctrine is represented as a secret—a point that echoes Yājñavalkya's declaration (cited above) that *karma* should not be spoken of in public; for the representation of a teaching as secret strikes to the center of the Upaniṣadic mission of explicating the mysteries of existence and so underscores the significance of *karma* as a key element of Upaniṣadic thought.

In the ensuing narrative, the king describes creation—in each of several planes of existence: the world above, the clouds, this world, and man himself—as being based on and homologous to the elements of the Vedic sacrificial fire, its flames, its fuel, and its smoke: "That other world is a fire, O Gautama. The sun is its fuel; the rays its smoke; the day its flame. . . ." The last of these creations occurs in the fire of the cremation. Here the homology ends, for this fire symbolizes nothing more than itself: "the fire is the fire, the fuel is the fuel; the smoke is the smoke. . . ." The material of the offering of this last creation is the body of the deceased, from which, placed in the sacrificial fires, a "shining" or "radiant" man emerges. The radiant man follows one of two paths: the path of the gods (*devayāna*), which leads to a final existence in the world of Brahmā (those who attain it are said not to return), or the path of the fathers (*pitṛyana*), which leads to the moon and eventually to another birth in this world. The attainment of one or the other of these paths is based on the *type* (though, significantly, not the *quality*—for example, "good" or "bad") of activity performed before death. Whereas the one who meditates in the forest and possesses an understanding of the homology of the elements of the cosmos and the elements of the Vedic sacrificial fire (as described previously in this passage) attains the path of the gods, the one who sacrifices and gives gifts to the priests attains the path of the fathers (*Bṛhadāraṇyaka Upaniṣad* 6.2.9–16).

The description of rebirth for the one who follows the path of the fathers is distinctive for its representation of the physical aspects of this process (*Bṛhadāraṇyaka Upaniṣad* 6.2.16). Through the flames of the cremation fires, the deceased individual is first transformed into smoke and then successively joins with the various worlds and elements that make up the Vedic cosmos. Reaching finally the moon, the deceased individual becomes the food of the gods; when this comes to an end (suggesting the depletion of his store of merit, built through a lifetime of sacrificial performances), the deceased individual passes into the sky, then into the wind, then into the rain, then to the earth and rebirth in this world. The progression has obvious agricultural connotations: for once the rain falls on the earth it generates plants, which are in turn eaten by living beings and thus contribute to the formation of semen, impregnation, gestation, and birth. The *Chāndogya Upaniṣad* version of this description alone adds that "people whose conduct is pleasant can expect to enter a pleasant womb, like that of a priest, warrior, or common woman; but they who are of stinking conduct can expect to enter a stinking womb, that of a dog, pig, or an outcaste" (*Chāndogya Upaniṣad* 5.10.7). (It is interesting to note that the term used here is "conduct," *caraṇa*, and not "action," *karman*.) Both passages refer to a third path, that of the worms, insects, and other small creatures that revolve ceaselessly through birth and death. Neither a type of action nor a quality of action is specified for the creatures that follow this third path.

The *Kauṣītaki Brāhmaṇa Upaniṣad*, also considered an early Upaniṣad, contains a description of the fate of individuals after death that reiterates the themes found in the *Bṛhadāraṇyaka Upaniṣad* and the *Chāndogya Upaniṣad*. According to the *Kauṣītaki Brāhmaṇa Upaniṣad*, when people depart from this world they go to the moon. The moon is the door to the heavenly worlds; to pass beyond the moon to the other worlds, the deceased must answer the moon's question: "Who are you?" The one who fails to correctly answer this question (the answer is, "I am you," a statement that typifies the Upaniṣadic notion that man and the cosmos are in essence homologous) becomes rain, thus leading to rebirth in this world "as a worm, an insect, a fish, a bird, a lion, . . . a man, or some other creature, in accordance with his actions (*karman*) and his knowledge." The one who correctly answers the moon's question continues his journey through the heavenly worlds, eventually reaching the world of Brahmā. At this point, the deceased shakes off his good and bad deeds (literally, "that which he has done well" and "that which he has done badly," *sukṛta* and *duṣkṛta*), passing them on respectively to the relatives he holds dear and to the ones he despises. The deceased passes no further but sojourns eternally in the world of Brahmā (*Kauṣītaki Brāhmaṇa Upaniṣad* 1.2).

If a single, clear representation of the *karma* doctrine does not emerge from these Upaniṣad texts, it is important to consider that the early Upaniṣads were composed as anthologies, with portions of their texts built out of stock narratives (Olivelle 1996: xxxiv). In the case of the *karma* doctrine, the fundamental elements of these stock narratives—the recurring themes of the journey to the other world (frequently bifurcated into two paths, the path of the gods and the path of the fathers) and the physical nature of the rebirth process (from smoke to clouds, to rain, to plants, to semen, and to rebirth in this world)—have clear antecedents in other Vedic texts. Thus, for example, the homology of the cosmos and the sacrificial fire is found in the *Jaiminīya Brāhmaṇa* (45–46); the journey of the deceased to the moon and sun occurs in the *Jaiminīya Upaniṣad Brāhmaṇa* (3.20–28); the representation of the process of rebirth as a cycle of generation (smoke, rain, the generation of plants, semen, birth) is found in the *Śatapatha Brāhmaṇa* (7.4.2.22); and the two paths to the other world are intimated in the funeral hymns found in the *Ṛg Veda* (10.14, 10.16). The question that now arises is why is the *karma* doctrine—that is, as it is presented in these several Upaniṣadic passages, a specific rule relating action or conduct to the conditions of the afterlife—grafted onto these stock teachings? This question, however, cannot be broached without a clear understanding of the import of these teachings within their "original" context; that is, the Brāhmaṇic milieu, a milieu dominated by the ideology and performance of the Vedic sacrificial ritual (the "original" *karma*).

KARMA AND THE VEDIC SACRIFICE

In its basic form, the Vedic sacrifice may be characterized simply as "the offering of a cow to win more cows" (see *Śatapatha Brāhmaṇa* 11.7.1.1; Heesterman 1978: 87). Even at this fundamental level, the sacrifice is an event fraught with extraordinary danger, dominated by death and destruction, as the sacrificer gives up a life in the attempt to win renewed life, if only in the form of increased cattle, crops, and so forth. Adding to the dire nature of the sacrificial event, as the Vedic religionists implicitly recognized, is that the animal victims do not necessarily die willingly (see *Śatapatha Brāhmaṇa* 3.7.3.3) but that in effect are innocent victims, their fate a thinly veiled murder. At a deeper level, the logic of the Vedic sacrifice, which demands an offering of a life for renewed life, implies that the death that occurs in the sacrifice should be that of the sacrificer, for it is he and not the victim that is the beneficiary of the sacrificial largesse. The Vedic religionists acknowledged this point, as the authors of the Brāhmaṇas observed: "Now the sacrificial fires become determined for the flesh of the sacrificer when he sacrifices; they think about the sacrificer; they desire the sacrificer" (*Śatapatha Brāhmaṇa* 11.7.1.2). Self-sacrifice however is self-defeating; though its ideology is pervasive, in practice its occurrence is limited to the exceptional circumstances of the "final sacrifice" (*antyeṣṭi*), the cremation rite, in which the body of the sacrificer forms the material of the oblation.[2]

The Vedic sacrifice is not a spontaneous event but a replication of the primeval acts that created the cosmos; as the Brāhmaṇic authors frequently declare: "This [sacrifice] done now is that which the gods did then [in the beginning]" (*Śatapatha Brāhmaṇa* 7.2.1.4, 9.2.3.4; *Taittirīya Saṃhitā* 1.5.9.4). What the gods did then was to dismember a primordial being (*puruṣa*/Prajāpati), whose body parts, mind, and senses gave rise to specific elements of the cosmos: "The moon was born from his mind; from his eye the sun was born. . . . From his navel the atmosphere arose; from his head the heavens; from his two feet the earth; from his ear the quarters" (*Ṛg Veda* 10.90.13–14; see also *Śatapatha Brāhmaṇa* 6.1.1.1–3.20). As a replication of this primordial event, the Vedic sacrifice holds enormous creative potential; each ritual performance holding out the promise of creating new worlds that the sacrificer might inhabit (Gonda 1966: 49).

That the sacrifice is a replication also means that to be effective, its performance must not deviate from its underlying model. One widespread Brāhmaṇic myth thus presents a cautionary tale about a sacrifice enacted by Aditi, a divine antediluvian being, for the sake of obtaining progeny. Following the proper form of first offering an oblation to the gods and then eating the remainder, Aditi is rewarded with healthy offspring. With the same goal in mind, Aditi sacrifices again but decides this time to partake directly of the gods' portion, reasoning that: "If I eat first, then stronger ones will be born from me." This act results not in a healthy issue but in a miscarriage; that is, the wrongly enacted sacrifice leads to wrongly formed offspring (*Taittirīya Saṃhitā* 6.5.6). The message here is simple: the power of the sacrifice lies not in any quality inherent in the oblation but in the *process* of its performance; properly enacted the sacrifice yields the desired result.[3]

The ideology of the Vedic ritual complex did not stop with the notion that the sacrificial performance wins from the gods only the "goods of life" for the sacrificer (the "do ut des" principle) but further attributes to the Vedic ritual the power to grant renewed life to the sacrificer. To indicate the element of rebirth, the sacrificial performance is replete with symbols of birth and death—a necessary prerequisite and concomitant to new birth. Thus, in entering the sacrificial arena, the sacrificer prepares himself for the new birth; here, he assumes several attributes of an embryo, restricting his movement, remaining in a womb-like enclosure, and keeping his hands closed, "since embryos have their hands in a closed manner" (*Śatapatha Brāhmaṇa* 2.3.1.3, 3.1.3.28, 3.2.1.6; *Aitareya Brāhmaṇa* 1.3). That the sacrificer dies, at least symbolically, in the ritual performance is indicated through his intimate association with the victim. The Vedic religionists described this ritual death and birth as part of a continuum, a middle point standing between the sacrificer's natural birth and natural death (*Śatapatha Brāhmaṇa* 11.2.1.1; *Jaiminīya Upaniṣad Brāhmaṇa* 3.11.2–4).

The mechanism of the sacrificer's rebirth in the ritual is a journey to the world of the gods. Here, the intimate identification between sacrificer and oblation is critical; for the sending forth of the oblation to the world of the gods—through the vehicle of the sacrificial fire's smoke—effectively carries the sacrificer to the other world: "Now it is to the world of the gods that the sacrifice went, and thereby it leads the sacrificer" (*Śatapatha Brāhmaṇa* 1.8.3.11, see also 4.3.4.6, 1.9.3.1).

Though the sacrifice entails a journey to the other world, it is incumbent upon the sacrificer to return to this world. Vedic mythology makes it clear that the gods do not want men in their world and long ago sought to make it inaccessible to them (*Śatapatha Brāhmaṇa* 3.1.4.3, 1.6.2.1). Moreover, there is the simple fact that if the sacrificer were to remain in the other world, his real death would ensue; accordingly, the authors of the Brāhmaṇas point out that the sacrificer's journey to the other world is one fraught with danger (*Śatapatha Brāhmaṇa* 2.3.4.7; *Taittirīya Saṃhitā* 2.5.6). The Vedic religionists clearly sought to avoid this possibility; indeed, the ritual system itself seems to have been designed to entice the sacrificer to return to this world, to live, and to sacrifice again another day.[4]

The sacrificer's death and rebirth in the sacrifice, effected through the journey to and return from the other world, is a necessary element in the sacrificer's acquisition of the rewards of the sacrificial performance. Journeying to the other worlds, the sacrificer is said to become one with the world of the god to whom the sacrifice is directed (*Śatapatha Brāhmaṇa* 2.6.4.8). The unification of deity and man is further expressed in the notion that in the other world the sacrificer becomes the "food" of the gods (*Śatapatha Brāhmaṇa* 3.6.3.19), which suggests an element of transubstantiation but also underlines the precarious nature of the journey to the other world. The sacrificer returns to this world utterly transformed by this experience; "reborn" in the sacrifice, he is now in a condition to acquire the sacrificial largesse, the results of his sacrificial work (*karman*).

The lifelong process of sacrificing—of journeying to and returning from the other world and of acquiring the sacrificial largesse—ends with the sacrificer's death and the "final sacrifice" (*antyeṣṭi*), as the cremation rite is known. Here, the sacrificer's body forms the material of the offering (which incidentally effectively allows the sacrificer to attain the core ritual ideology of self-sacrifice). The journey to the other world and the subsequent rebirth that was realized in symbolic terms within the ritual arena is, in the event of the cremation, actualized in real terms. And here, the sacrificer's experience in performing the great Vedic rites may be said to represent the "empirical" evidence for the attainments which he will then experience again at the end of his lifetime; for just as the type of sacrifices that the sacrificer performed in life led to the attainment of specific other worldly realms, so too these performances clearly affect the conditions attained in the sacrificer's final journey.

The early formulations of the Upaniṣadic *karma* doctrine draw heavily on the Vedic ritual substratum. First and foremost, the mechanism of the sacrifice—that the action of the ritual performance necessarily yields a corresponding result, that the sacrifice entails a journey to the other world and a return to this one, and that through the sacrifice the sacrificer acquires a new birth (and so too implicitly must die)—is a fundamental premise to the Upaniṣadic presentations of the *karma* doctrine. Yet, whereas in the Brāhmaṇas this mechanism is applied to the sacrifices performed through the course of a lifetime, in the Upaniṣads, in discussions of the *karma* doctrine, it is applied directly to the individual's fate after death. That the Brāhmaṇic thinkers do not directly confront the problem of the sacrificer's fate after death is not surprising, for such thoughts rarely intrude into the Brāhmaṇic discussions. Although death and destruction—of the victim and implicitly of the sacrificer—stand at the center of the Vedic sacrifice, the Brāhmaṇic ritual itself was constituted to circumvent the reality of the sacrificer's death. The Brāhmaṇic ritualists achieved this through ceaselessly employing complex sets of symbolic identifications that effectively conceal the brutal facts of the sacrificial performance, creating, as more than one scholar has observed, a "dream" world in which the ritualists appear to have "left realities far behind them" (see, e.g. Farquhar 1920: 27). However, as J. C. Heesterman has noted, as a result of this, "the ritualists found themselves confronted with the problem of meaning; that is, they had to construct a way back to the lived in world of mundane reality" (1983: 6).

The Upaniṣadic confrontation with the sacrificer's real death—expressed clearly in the simple questions asked of the fate of the individual that frame the early presentations of the *karma* doctrine—suggests just such a return to the "lived in world." Yet, the mechanism of the sacrifice—the nearly automatic acquisition of the results of the sacrificial acts and the journey to and return from the other world through which the sacrificer is reborn and thus prepared to acquire these goods—cannot be left behind. These elements re-emerge in the Upaniṣadic formulation of the *karma* doctrine, the principles of which are no longer limited to the actions performed in the ritual world but are now extended outward to the lived-in world and so encompasses *all* acts.

KARMA AS A MODEL OF ACTION

The post-Upaniṣadic history of the *karma* doctrine is that of near universal pervasiveness; for, at least implicitly, *karma* penetrates even the furthest corners of Hindu thought. Here, it stands along with a handful of other doctrines that, following the Upaniṣad period, are consistently presented as "presuppositions" of Hindu thought, such as the doctrines of an underlying ego element (*ātman/puruṣa*) and its relationship to a cosmic ground of being (*brahman*), of illusion (*māyā*), and of liberation (*mokṣa*) (Eliade 1969: 3). Even the so-called Indian materialists, the Cārvākas, who deny references to all immaterial categories, and therefore repudiate the existence of *karma*, call attention to its dominance by placing the doctrine prominently among their disavowals (Radhakrishnan and Moore 1957: 235; Stcherbatsky 1978: 32).

Given its ubiquity, the doctrine is frequently defined by default; in the post-Upaniṣadic period, *karma* means, quite simply, that actions lead inevitably to certain results and that these results are realized after death (O'Flaherty 1980b: xi; Rao 1987: 23). These two components—the effectiveness of action and its realization in a future birth—emerge from the pattern of ritual action deeply embedded in the doctrine's Vedic past; that is, that an action performed in the work of the sacrifice necessarily generates a result and that death and rebirth—even if realized only symbolically—are necessary prerequisites to the realization or acquisition of that result. In the post-Upaniṣadic period, this relationship between act, death, rebirth, and consequence leads to the notion that the nature of the existence into which the individual is reborn—whether measured by form (human or nonhuman), or by class ("caste," a nonindigenous and somewhat misleading substitute for the general Indic term "*jāti*," literally "birth"), or by circumstance (wealthy, poor, and so on), or alternatively by no rebirth whatsoever—results directly from the deeds performed in a former life.

Although these principles stand as the *karma* doctrine's recognizable core and can be deduced from discussions of *karma* that appear in a wide range of Hindu texts, the doctrine is in application an entity of considerable complexity. In particular, lurking beneath the general depiction of *karma* is the question of what precisely is the nature of action; how is it constituted and how is it qualified. In the Brāhmaṇic-Upaniṣadic milieu actions are qualified on two bases, neither of which excludes the other: by the nature of the action, in and of itself; and by the way in which the action is actually performed. In the first instance, actions are valued on the basis of a general morality; for example, murder may be considered in a general way to represent a "bad" act and hence generates a bad result: "A man who steals gold, drinks liquor, takes to the bed of his teacher, or kills a priest; these four fall, and also the fifth who follows them" (*Chāndogya Upaniṣad* 5.10.9). On the other hand, actions that are "good" in a general way, such as feeding a guest or rewarding a priest for his work in undertaking the sacrificial rituals, clearly leads to a good result (*Chāndogya Upaniṣad* 2.23.1). The values associated with these sort of acts—murder, feeding the poor—reflect general mores or values that cross cultural and chronological boundaries; for nearly all cultures at all times have spurned such actions as murder, adultery, and thievery, while they laud acts of charity and munificence.

Along with this notion that certain acts may in and of themselves be qualified as either "good" or "bad" exists the notion of placing a value on actions on the basis of *how* they are performed; that is, whether an action is performed correctly (represented as "good") or incorrectly ("bad"). The principle underlying this valuation is that of a correspondence to an established model of action. In the case of the sacrifice, the model is presented as one of divine provenance: "This [sacrifice] done now is that which the gods did then [in the beginning]" (*Śatapatha Brāhmaṇa* 7.2.1.4, 9.2.3.4; *Taittirīya Saṃhitā* 1.5.9.4). Whereas precise imitation—in symbolic if not in actual terms—leads to rich rewards, imprecision leads invariably to disaster (*Śatapatha Brāhmaṇa* 2.3.4.18; see also Keith 1925, 2: 463).

In the Brāhmaṇas, this second model of action is clearly the primary one. Herein, where the action of the sacrifice is the only action contemplated and the actors themselves are defined by their roles (either as priest or as patron) in the ritual performance, the question of the value of actions in and of themselves is not raised. Indeed, within the narrowly defined ethic of the ritual system any act insofar as it fulfills the demands of the ritual, is morally "good"; as the French Indologist Sylvain Lévi observed, "le bien est l'exactitude rituelle" (1966: 10). In the Upaniṣads, however, the limitations of the Brāhmaṇic world begin to yield to a broader set of concerns. Among the signature developments seen in these texts is the movement away from traditional sacrificial forms and toward a pattern of activity in which the sacrifice is "interiorized," as meditative states and the quest for a transformative gnosis replace the physical performance of the sacrifice. One of the early Upaniṣadic presentations of the *karma* doctrine thus draws a distinction between individuals who meditate in the forest and those who sacrifice and give gifts to the priests. Each sort of activity garners its own result; whereas meditation in the forest leads to the acquisition of a certain esoteric knowledge and thus eventually to the path of the gods and freedom from rebirth and sacrifice, giving gifts to the priests leads to the attainment of the path of the fathers and rebirth in this world (*Bṛhadāraṇyaka Upaniṣad* 6.2.9–15).

The distinction between these two paths, and the distinct types of activities that lead to them, becomes a leitmotif in the Upaniṣads (*Bṛhadāraṇyaka Upaniṣad* 6.2.9–15; *Chāndogya Upaniṣad* 5.10.1–6; *Kaṭha Upaniṣad* 2.1–12; *Muṇḍaka Upaniṣad* 1.2.7–11; *Praśna Upaniṣad* 1.9–10, 5.3–4). In the *Bṛhadāraṇyaka* and the *Chāndogya Upaniṣads*, texts with evident connections to the Brāhmaṇas and thus counted among the earliest Upaniṣads, the two paths are described as simple alternatives: meditation in the forest leads the individual after death to a heavenly path that carries him through the sun and eventually to a permanent sojourn in the worlds of Brahmā (the path of the gods); sacrifices, on the other hand, lead the deceased on a path that carries him to the moon and eventually back to rebirth in this world (the path of the fathers). As described here, one path is not elevated above the other, and there is no explicit suggestion that one path is more desirable than the other.

In other Upaniṣadic presentations of these two paths, however, the activity of the sacrifice and the subsequent attainment of the path of the fathers is harshly depreciated: "The fools that consider sacrifices and gifts to be the best, they who know nothing better; having lived in joy in the heavens [after death], enter again this inferior world" (*Muṇḍaka Upaniṣad* 1.2.10; see also *Kaṭha Upaniṣad* 2.5–6). This denigration of the sacrifice signals a profound change in the ancient Indian worldview, leading eventually to the expression of a deep antipathy to the Vedic ritual tradition (seen in particular in the rise of the heterodox schools of Buddhism and Jainism). To a great degree, this antipathy develops from the *karma* doctrine's success; that actions inevitably generate results, and that these results are an organic element in an unremitting process of rebirth, weighed heavily as a vast burden, if not sorrow (the Buddhist *dukkha*), on the Indian psyche. Taken to its logical conclusion, this position leads to a paralysis in all actions. And, indeed, numerous ancient Indian traditions seem to have adopted this notion of seeking the cessation of all activity, a position that in practice leads to the dissolution of society if not culture. These traditions are widely represented: Hindu texts describe *yogin*s who practice "inactivity" (Eliade 1969: 140–42); the Buddhist texts refer to seemingly well-known teachers who decry the utility of all activity (E. Thomas 1927: 129); and the Buddha himself, before finding the path to enlightenment, attempts to abandon the world of action (*Buddhacarita* 12.92).

Neither Hinduism nor Buddhism, in the mainstream, adopted the extreme position of abandoning activity for inactivity. Both Hindu and Buddhist texts invariably describe the path of inactivity to exemplify a "wrong" path (Eliade 1969: 140–42; E. Thomas 1927: 129–30). Even the Upaniṣadic depreciation of the sacrifice is not a call to turn to a life of complete stasis; for meditation in the forest is still a form of activity. Moreover, it is an activity built on the framework of the ancient Vedic sacrifices, albeit in a "contemplative, cognitive, and interiorized" fashion; for the Upaniṣadic path of meditation takes the activity of the Vedic sacrifice and internalizes it (Kaelber 1989: 96). Here, the Vedic offerings to the gods are absorbed in the activity of "an 'inner sacrifice,' in which physiological functions take the place of libations and ritual objects" (Eliade 1969: 111). Given this assimilation, it appears that the Upaniṣadic sages direct their disparagement not at the ideology of the sacrifice but at the nature of its performance; in particular, taking an unfavorable view of the corporate and cooperative nature of the traditional Vedic sacrifice.

The traditional sacrificial format is an act of social cooperation with assorted priests working in consort: one priest chants the prayers, another performs certain ritual actions, yet another watches for errors, all at the behest of another actor, the patron who stands at the edge of the ritual arena but is also intimately identified with the victim, the focal point of the sacrifice. In expressing the intimate association of this group of actors, the Brāhmaṇic authors liken them to a single being, "the patron is the body of the sacrifice and the officiants the limbs" (*Śatapatha Brāhmaṇa* 9.5.2.16).

The communal performance of the sacrifice engendered its own peculiar set of problems regarding the benefits of the sacrifice; for the deep involvement of the priests, who actually perform the sacrifice and take its inherent danger upon themselves, suggests it is they and not the sacificer who should be the recipients of the sacrificial largesse (Lévi 1966: 113; Tull 1989: 77). To some degree, a resolution to this problem was found in the giving of gifts (*dakṣiṇā*) that closely approximate the offerings to the officiants, thereby allowing the sacrificer to "ransom" the benefits of the sacrifice for his own use (*Śatapatha Brāhmaṇa* 4.3.4.5–6). Nevertheless, the problematic nature of the "karmic web" created by the traditional sacrificial format remains a troubling factor, as reflected in a number of Brāhmaṇic-Upaniṣadic notions regarding the dispensation of an individual's merit (and demerit) after death; that is, that it is "eaten" or given to the gods and ancestors; or it is passed on to the relatives he holds dear and to the ones he despises; or it is given directly to his offspring (*Bṛhadāraṇyaka Upaniṣad* 6.2.16; *Jaiminīya Brāhmaṇa* 1.46, 1.50; *Kauṣītaki Brāhmaṇa Upaniṣad* 1.2, 2.15).

Against this background, the Upaniṣadic representation of "meditation in the forest" as an acceptable, if not superior, alternative to the traditional sacrificial performances indicates a significant sociological and soteriological shift in the ancient Hindu way of life. For, unlike the traditional sacrificial format with its complex web of actors, meditation in the forest is clearly a path of individual attainment, a point underscored by the fact that it is undertaken beyond the pale of the ordinary social life of village and town. Although the model of action underlying meditation in the forest is still the sacrifice—albeit in an internalized form—the rigid social web necessary for the traditional sacrificial performances is collapsed, and these circumstances are mirrored in the conditions of the afterlife. On one level, this collapse eliminates the need to disperse the sacrifice's consequences (in this world and after death); for just as the path of meditation is an individual path, so too the acquisition of its consequences belongs wholly to the individual. On another level, by removing themselves from normal social intercourse, those who follow this path remain even after death outside the ordinary world; accordingly, after death there is "no return" for them (*Bṛhadāraṇyaka Upaniṣad* 6.2.15).

In the post-Upaniṣadic period, the practice of *yoga* is the direct successor to "meditation in the forest." The fundamental purpose of *yoga* is the suppression of the body's and mind's involvement in the ordinary, everyday world of existence. To achieve this goal, the *yogin* disciplines his mind and body using highly developed techniques of breath control, concentration, and body postures. Through this discipline, the *yogin* no longer confuses the "noneternal with the eternal" (*Yogasūtra* 2.5) and eventually gains a state of "ultimate freedom," in which his inner being (*ātman*/*jīva*/*puruṣa*) is liberated from all material existence (Radhakrishnan 1931: 351, 363).

Among the explicit concerns of those who follow this discipline is the breaking of the karmic process. This process begins with desire and continues to build up through attachment to the things of this world. Acting on these desires creates good and bad results, the realization of which then carries the individual through an unremitting cycle of birth and rebirth (*Yogasūtra* 2.12–14). These notions clearly represent *karma* in a pejorative light; for it is the link between act and results that keeps the actor in a state of nescience. Awareness, and with it freedom from rebirth, is won only when this cycle is broken. Nevertheless, the discipline of *yoga* is not built on a model of inaction but on one of "right action," a path that leads ultimately to the cessation of action. Thus, initially, the *yogin* adopts a set of precepts or "restraints" (*yama*) that have broad moral implications: nonviolence, truthfulness, not-stealing, chastity, and the renunciation of material objects. The ethical tenor of these restraints is a universal one, focusing on the nature of action in and of itself. At first, the purpose of these restraints is to push the individual toward the "good" and thus to generate "good *karma*." However, as the discipline proceeds, the *yogin* seeks to generate no *karma* whatsoever (*Yogasūtra* 4.7). However, since this is accomplished in the ordinary world of existence, the *yogin*'s "awakening" occurs while there is still a karmic residue, a state known as "liberated-in-this-life" (*jīvanmukti*). When this residue is consumed, freedom from ordinary existence is won and no further rebirths occur (Eliade 1969: 30).

Like the Upaniṣadic meditator, the *yogin* eventually must remove himself from the ordinary world of everyday existence, engaging in a discipline that necessarily leaves aside all familial and societal relationships. Although by the first century CE, the practice of *yoga* attained considerable cultural prestige in India (Eliade 1969: 143), the demands of this discipline put it out of reach for all but a few religious specialists. Nevertheless, its existence as an ideal serves as a constant reminder that a significant segment of the Hindu population viewed the *karma* doctrine as an oppressive structure. The path leading to its escape, however, is one that necessarily leads away from society and ordinary existence; for fundamental to the *karma* doctrine is the proposition that the conditions of an individual's existence are invariably mirrored in the conditions of future lives. In other worlds, involvement in the ordinary world of everyday existence necessarily means a return after death to that same world of existence. Its negation, though it leads to personal freedom, necessarily requires individuals to remove themselves from the world of mundane affairs, participation in which is a natural element of human existence. In the end, it also leads to the dissolution of the social fabric.

KARMA AND SOCIETY

The Hindu texts reflect a clear awareness that the elevation of "meditation in the forest" and the path of *yoga* which succeed it as a viable means of life lead to the demise of society; for they promote a way of life that nullifies an individual's need as well as ability to meet his or her social responsibilities, from raising a family to undertaking the sort of labor—farming, trade, soldiering—that allows for society's continued existence. The *Bhagavad Gītā*, perhaps the most widely disseminated and certainly the single most influential Hindu text in India, contains among its deeply layered teachings what is clearly a direct response to this problem. Here, in a position that became the dominant one in the orthodox tradition, action is enjoined with the significant caveat that an individual should do the work ordained by his or her nature (*Bhagavad Gītā* 3.8). This last notion refers to the underlying Hindu ideology of "caste" or class (*jāti*); that is, that individuals possess inherent qualities that constitute them into specific sorts of social beings. These are defined as four types that, in accord with their inherent qualities, are possessed of a signature set of duties: priest (Brāhmaṇ), warrior (Kṣatriya), commoner (Vaiśya), and servant (Śūdra).

The discussion of Hindu society as composed of four component classes and the duties and activities assigned to each class is the chief topic of a class of texts collectively known as the Hindu law books or Dharmaśāstras. These texts became authoritative sometime in the early centuries CE but encompass directives that reach back to the Vedic period. (The ideology of caste is extant in the Vedic period [see *Ṛg Veda* 10.90], though given the limited concerns of the Brāhmaṇic-Upaniṣadic milieu, it is rarely discussed.) The *Manusmṛti*, which stands out among the texts in this class as a work of singular authority (Doniger 1991: xviii), expresses from its outset that its purpose is to explicate the duties associated with each of the classes (*Manusmṛti* 1.2). These duties are:

> For priests, he [the lord] ordained teaching and learning, sacrificing for themselves and sacrificing for others, giving and receiving. Protecting his subjects, giving, having sacrifices performed, studying and remaining unaddicted to the sensory objects are, in summary, for a ruler. Protecting his livestock, giving, having sacrifices performed, studying, trading, lending money, and farming the land are for a commoner. The lord assigned only one activity to a servant: serving these [other] classes without resentment.
>
> (*Manusmṛti* 1.88–91)

Following closely on this idea that each class possesses a unique and definitive set of duties is the notion that certain *actions* are either incumbent upon or prohibited to the members of each social class. On one level, these notions redefine the *karma* doctrine; for they place a value on actions in accord with the parameters set forth by the duties of each social class. In concrete terms, this means that, for example, killing an enemy is for a warrior a "good" act, whereas for a priest it is a "bad" act. On another level, however, these notions may be seen as a return to the dominant Brāhmaṇic-Upaniṣadic pattern of valuing actions on the basis of their conformity to an established model (which, as the *Manusmṛti* expresses, is a divine one); for, insofar as individuals perform actions that replicate those ordained for the class to which they belong, those actions are "good" and so generate a good result: "Tirelessly he should engage in the good conduct appropriate for his own activities" (*Manusmṛti* 5.155).

An individual does not choose to become a member of a particular class but is by birth constituted as a member of a class. This is not a random process but occurs as a result of the deeds (*karman*) of a previous lifetime. As described in the *Manusmṛti*, the process that carries these deeds through successive rebirth begins at death, as the individual's material body returns to the five elements of earth, water, fire, air, and ether. Following this, another material body, to be used in a temporary otherworldly existence, is formed from the five elements. Those whose deeds were "lawful" (*dharma*) or "good" now enjoy a temporary sojourn in heaven, whereas those whose deeds were "unlawful" (*adharma*) or "bad" go forth to suffer the tortures of hell (*Manusmṛti* 12.16–21). It is important to point out that the terms used here, "*dharma*" and "*adharma*," suggest a valuation of deeds based on their conformity to or violation of specific class rules of behavior, such as performing a sacrifice for a priest, fighting in war for a warrior, and engaging in trade for a merchant.

Following this temporary period of reward or punishment, the body again returns to the five elements. The three qualities of lucidity, energy, and darkness now play a determinant role leading up to the individual's next birth. The authors of the *Manusmṛti* first describe this process in brief: "people of lucidity become gods, people of energy become humans, and people of darkness always become animals" (*Manusmṛti* 12.40). To accommodate the full breadth of individual behaviors, which variously mixes good with bad actions, each of these three types admits to three orders, low, medium, and high; thus, rebirth as a god (for those in whom lucidity prevails) ranges from priests and gods who fly on chariots all the way to the supreme godhead, Brahmā; rebirth as a human (for those in whom energy prevails) ranges from wrestlers and kings to the celestial nymphs; and rebirth as an animal (for those in whom darkness prevails) ranges from worms and horses to ogres.

Having set out this general theory of how actions in one life lead to the conditions of a future life, the authors of the *Manusmṛti* present a detailed list of specific acts and their specific results. The list begins with the fruits of bad actions: "A priest killer gets the womb of a dog, a pig, a donkey, a camel, a goat. . . . A priest who drinks liquor enters the womb of a worm. . . . For stealing grain, a man becomes a rat. . . . For meat, a vulture. . . . Whenever a man has forcibly taken away another man's property . . . he inevitably becomes an animal" (*Manusmṛti* 12.55–68). Here, the underlying mechanism of the *karma* doctrine appears to be a concrete relationship between cause and effect; in essence the punishment fits the crime. The authors of the text thus declare: "a man reaps the appropriate fruit in a body that has the qualities of mind in which he committed that act" (*Manusmṛti* 12.81). Once again, the acts described here—adultery, being disrespectful to elders and teachers—and the negative consequences they engender, perhaps indicate a valuation of actions based on the type of action performed. However, the authors of the text note specifically that the nature of the actor—as defined by class (priest, warrior, and so forth)—is a critical factor in determining the valuation of these acts, as they declare that priests, rulers, commoners, or servants who "slip from their own duty" suffer as ghosts after death (*Manusmṛti* 12.71–72).

The notion that the value of actions lies in the performance of class-specific duties is deeply embedded in the teachings of the *Bhagavad Gītā*. This text, composed around the second century BCE, integrates and offers fresh interpretations of a number of significant trends from Hinduism's formative period, among them sacrifice, meditation and *yoga*, the relationship of the individual to the cosmos, the nature of the godhead, and, of course, the nature of action (*karman*) and duty (*dharma*), the subject presented as the ostensible concern of the text's opening scenes.

The *Bhagavad Gītā* begins with a description of the warrior Arjuna standing amidst the great warriors of his day, nearly all of whom are either kinsmen or friends, arrayed into battle formations. As a fighter without peer, Arjuna foresees the immense carnage and destruction that will ensue from his involvement in the battle and suddenly realizes the purposelessness of "winning" on these grounds. In what stands among the most poignant scenes in all Hindu literature, Arjuna's eyes fill with tears, his bow and arrows slip from his hands. He turns to his charioteer, Kṛṣṇa (the supreme divinity, though as yet unknown to Arjuna in this form), and declares that the forthcoming war is nothing more than a monstrous evil, even suggesting that a life of mendicancy is preferable to engaging in all out warfare. Kṛṣṇa, however, responds to Arjuna's despondency with contempt, observing that Arjuna's reasoning is that of a coward, unmanly, and inappropriate for a warrior. Kṛṣṇa then declares (after first delivering a lengthy discourse on the nature of the underlying ego element and its relationship to the phenomenal world) that: "It is better to do one's own duty, though ineffectively, than to perform another's duty as it should be done; it is better to die in following one's own duty; dangerous is the duty of other men" (*Bhagavad Gītā* 3.35). At the end of the *Bhagavad Gītā*, this statement is again repeated, albeit with the added caveat that an individual, by doing the work (*karman*) appropriate to his or her class, can never be defiled.

Arjuna's dilemma arises from the coexistence of the two models of action within the *karma* doctrine. The first model, that of valuing actions in and of themselves, suggests Arjuna's actions are "bad"; for, in a general way, killing represents a "bad" action and thus can only have a bad outcome. The second model, that of valuing action based on the degree to which it replicates a preordained pattern of activity, suggests Arjuna's actions are "good" insofar as killing is the model behavior for a warrior on the battlefield; as Kṛṣṇa tells him, not to perform these prescribed actions is "dangerous."

Here again, this second model of action hearkens back to the doctrine's origins in the Vedic sacrificial performance. Just as the Vedic sacrificers won the goods of life through following a particular model of action, so too the *karma* doctrine demands that to achieve the good, actors must follow the model of action inherent to their class. Yet, there is an obvious conflict between this model of action and the general ethical precept regarding killing. This conflict was a troubling fact for the Vedic religionists who sought, through the artifice of ritualization, to avoid the killing demanded by the act of sacrifice. In Upaniṣadic thought and its successor the discipline of *yoga*, this conflict is subsumed through the internalization of action, effectively removing the individual from the world of physical performance. That this conflict appears again as an underlying theme in the *Bhagavad Gītā* clearly indicates that over the centuries it persisted unresolved in Hindu thought.[5]

The authors of the *Bhagavad Gītā* propose a unique solution to this problem of what might be termed "necessary evil" actions by uniting the two streams of yogic practice and sacrificial action. Yogic practice, on the one hand, seeks the renunciation of desire as a means of breaking away from attachment to things of this world, thereby breaking the cycle of rebirth. The path of the sacrifice, on the other hand, enjoins individuals to perform the ritual acts and to enjoy their fruits, thereby keeping them in the cycle of rebirth. Kṛṣṇa, whose teachings constitute the bulk of the narrative of the *Bhagavad Gītā*, recognizes both positions, declaring, on the one hand, that sacrifice leads to "highest good" (*Bhagavad Gītā* 3.11) while, on the other hand, noting that the "man who, having abandoned desires, goes about free from desires . . . attains a state of peace" (*Bhagavad Gītā* 2.71). Kṛṣṇa then brings the two paths together, proclaiming that a man should act in the world—for this is mandated by human nature (which in India is further defined by an individual's class: priest, warrior, and so forth)—but that he should take no interest in the results of his actions: "Thus detached, carry out the actions that must be done; for the man who carries out actions unattached, gains the highest goal" (*Bhagavad Gītā* 3.19).

The path recommended here is inherently contradictory. For, in essence, it recommends that an individual remain in society, perform the duties incumbent upon him, while at the same time it demands that he act like the *yogin* who has removed himself from the attachments of ordinary existence. To overcome this contradiction, the authors of the *Bhagavad Gītā* introduce a novel understanding of the *karma* doctrine, separating actions from the results that, according to the doctrine, they necessarily generate: "Action (*karman*) alone is your primary concern, not the consequences (*phala*)" (*Bhagavad Gītā* 2.47). Taking this one step further, the fruits are to be offered up—in effect, renounced—and given over to the deity (*Bhagavad Gītā* 9.26), who accepts them as a concrete manifestation of man's love and devotion (*bhakti*) to him (4.11).

These teachings do not negate the *karma* doctrine's fundamental premise that certain actions generate certain results. Rather, they promote the notion that these results need not bind the individual actor to a karmic chain in which "bad" actions such as killing necessarily lead to a "bad" result. Through offering up the results to the deity (in effect, a sacrifice, itself a defining element in the constitution of the *karma* doctrine), actors win the same type of freedom as that won by those who follow the path of renunciation. In this way, the conflict of action is resolved; and the authors of the *Bhagavad Gītā* can unaffectedly recommend that individuals "perform the actions [they] are bound to do [by their inherent nature]" (3.8).

KARMA AND THE HINDU WORLD

In separate studies, Ursula Sharma (1973) and C. J. Fuller (1992) have noted that although the classical formulation of the *karma* doctrine is well known in popular Hinduism, ideas about *karma* on this level sometimes exhibit significant variations. This is not surprising given that in practice, as Sharma notes, "the individual receives the concept of *karma* as part of a living folk tradition" (1973: 359). This living tradition is built up out of both textual and nontextual sources; the textual generally represented by the epics, the *Mahābhārata* and the *Rāmāyaṇa* (*c.*200 BCE to 200 CE), and a class of texts known as Purāṇas (*c.*400–1000 CE), which are amalgamations of devotional, social, and quasihistorical material, and the nontextual by innumerable parochial traditions localized throughout the Indian subcontinent. On this level, *karma* is not an isolated concept but is frequently joined with other concepts that suggest different types of causes for an individual's circumstances. These include fate, the will of the deity, and sorcery (Sharma 1973: 355).

Perhaps the most significant divergence between the popular and textual renditions of the *karma* doctrine is that in practice Hindus tend to see events—in particular those that contain elements of misfortune or are in some sense tragic—as being the karmic results of deeds performed in *this* lifetime. Though on this level Hindus do not deny the connection between *karma* and rebirth, they seemingly pay scant attention to it (Fuller 1992: 246–48; U. Sharma 1973: 351, 353, 356; see also M. Srinivas 1976: 317–18). At the very least, as U. Sharma notes, in village Hinduism, Hindus "seem to feel immediate responsibility only for offenses committed in the present incarnation"; offenses from past incarnations belong to "a rather remote kind of self" (1973: 356). Although in its classical formulations the doctrine is nearly always presented as linking actions performed in one life with consequences to be realized in future births, there are textual references to the notion that actions might generate immediately realized consequences. Thus, in the *Manusmṛti* (4.156–57) it is said that good conduct (*caraṇa*), such as maintaining habits of cleanliness and showing respect to teachers and guests, leads to longevity, progeny, and wealth, whereas bad conduct results in illness and a short life. Although the term used here is "conduct" (*caraṇa*) rather than "action" (*karman*), the determinative relationship between act and consequence is in essence that of the *karma* doctrine.

The notion of the "transfer" or sharing of *karma* is another peculiar aspect of the *karma* doctrine that appears with some frequency on the popular level. In evidence of this, Fuller cites a village's general response to a devastating fire. Overall, the villagers perceived the fire to be a result of the recent sins of the village leaders. However, they also saw the fire as retribution for the villagers' accumulated sins, a proposition suggestive of a group enactment of *karma*; "the fruits of the sins of some especially evil people had been visited on others, just as a boatload of passengers can all drown if one awful sinner is on board" (Fuller 1992: 247). In a similar vein, U. Sharma cites an example in which a villager claims he was unhurt in a truck accident because "someone among the company must have had a very good *karma* to counteract the danger of the situation" (1973: 353). Both Fuller (1992: 248) and U. Sharma (1973: 352) observe that this idea of transference is especially effective among kin groups; in particular between a husband and wife—though a man's good and bad *karma* accrues to his wife, while none of the wife's *karma* accrues to the husband.

The transference of merit between family members recalls the Upaniṣadic notion that the deceased disperses his good and bad deeds to his kin (those he likes and those he dislikes, respectively). In the Purāṇas, the transfer of merit and demerit is represented with some regularity; the mistreatment of a guest, for example, is said to result in the guest taking the good *karma* of the host and giving his bad *karma* in return (O'Flaherty1980c: 29; cf. *Manusmṛti* 3.100). In a similar vein, the authors of the *Manusmṛti* (8.308) declare that a king who unjustly taxes his subjects acquires as a result their collective demerit. These representations stand as an emphatic reminder of the doctrine's origins in the Vedic sacrifice, which is enacted as a corporate event and so garners results for all the participants (the patron and the officiants). Indeed, on a larger scale, the good results of the correctly performed Vedic rites—that is, "the offering of a cow to win more cows"—benefits not just those who perform the sacrifice but is also shared among the larger community of family and settlement.

On its surface, however, this idea of a sharing or transfer of *karma* appears to contradict the doctrine's fundamental premises; as E. Hopkins observed: "Obviously such a view as this is inconsistent with the doctrine of Karma. If a man's sin is inherited it cannot be the fruit of his own actions" (1906: 589). That the idea of transferring *karma* was problematic, as E. Hopkins suggests, can be seen in the negative references to it in the epics. In the *Rāmāyaṇa* (2.27.4–5), a husband and wife alone are said to share *karma* and all other kinsmen are specifically excluded; in the *Mahābhārata* (12.291.22), it is said that it is impossible for anyone to enjoy the good and bad acts of another. (However, the *Mahābhārata* [1(7)87] also contains a reference to a sage who offers to transfer to a king all the worlds he has won through his own meritorious acts.) The negative view of *karma* transference in these texts may reflect the influence of the general yogic philosophy that isolates the individual as he strives to perfect and eventually conquer his *karma*. In both the *Mahābhārata* and the *Rāmāyaṇa*, yogic activity is frequently portrayed as an ideal behavior, providing a sharp counterpoint to the worldly concerns of the warrior kings whose stories form the backbone of the epics.

In a general way, the reliance on *karma* allows Hindus to account for their existential circumstances. The relationship between act and result, however, ranges from the obvious to instances of sheer opacity. An example of the latter case can be seen in a tale recounted in the *Mahābhārata* of the grisly punishment meted out to a certain sage. The narrative begins by describing a sage who unknowingly has his hermitage occupied by a group of thieves. The king's guards, having followed the thieves to the hermitage, seize both thieves and sage. Failing to receive any answers from the sage, who has taken a vow of silence, the guards take the entire group before the king who sentences them to be impaled on stakes. Though impaled, the sage remains alive for a long period of time. Eventually, the king realizes his error and begs forgiveness from the sage. The stake however is irremovable, and the sage is forced to spend the rest of his days wandering about with it still inside him. After many years of suffering in this condition, the sage approaches the lord Dharma and asks him why he had been punished so harshly. Dharma responds by informing him that in a former life "You had stuck blades of grass in the tails of little flies, and this was the punishment you received for that deed" (*Mahābhārata* 1[7]101; van Buitenen 1973–78, 1: 238). Though eventually the god Dharma is punished for meting out this penalty that it is so far in excess of the sin ("hurting a fly") that led to it, the tale indicates that no simple equations exist to determine an individual's karmic fate. Here, the apparent severity of the punishment may hearken back to the notion expressed in the Dharma texts and in the *Bhagavad Gītā* regarding the importance of each individual performing the actions appropriate to his class. The sage, who is undoubtedly a member of the Brāhmaṇ class, receives this severe punishment for hurting flies because it so deeply violates the general prohibition against violence for Brāhmaṇs. A member of the warrior class would perhaps not receive the same punishment, for this act would not violate his class duties as it does a priest's.

On the other hand, in the Purāṇas, texts that generally exhibit a nearly manic concern with *karma* and its effects on future lives, the relationship between deed and effect is quite direct; a typical passage from one text thus depicts the servants of the king of the underworld as meting out punishments that are correlated precisely to the nature of the deed: "Pierce the ears of him who has given false evidence. . . . Cut off the tongue of the man who has offended anyone by his words. . . . Cut off the . . . [genitals] of the man who has committed adultery" (*Vāraha Purāṇa* 202.10–13; Iyer 1993: 619). Passages such as this seem to occur ad infinitum in these texts, for there are "hundreds and hundreds" of hells (*Bhāgavata Purāṇa* 5.26.37), each one with its punishments correlated to specific wrong acts. This pattern continues as the individual attains another birth; thus, for example, dealers in flesh, after suffering the torments of the underworld, "take birth as human beings again, but with mutilated limbs and immersed in injury. Because of their actions, they meet with injuries in the ear, nose, hands and feet" (*Vāraha Purāṇa* 203.13–15; Iyer 1993: 623–24).

Despite the dire conditions depicted here, the *karma* doctrine is not seen in the Purāṇas as an overwhelmingly oppressive structure. On one level, the Purāṇic authors recognize that good deeds lead to good and just rewards and that those who follow this path attain "happiness in heaven and other pleasures" and that these can be enjoyed through numerous lifetimes (*Bhāgavata Purāṇa* 6.1.2). On another level, the authors of these texts look to the gods for the alleviation of human suffering, even though that suffering is generated by unworthy deeds. In the *Bhāgavata Purāṇa*, a story is told of a certain Brāhmaṇ, said to be well versed in the Vedic lore, who becomes infatuated with a low-class prostitute. The Brāhmaṇ eventually abandons his wife and family, sells his ancestral property, and leads "a licentious life censured by noble persons . . . in an impure condition and eating dirty (polluted by a harlot's touch) food" (*Bhāgavata Purāṇa* 6.1.67–68; Tagare 1993: 782). After many years of living in this state, the fallen Brāhmaṇ approaches his death, while the servants of Yama (the god of death) wait anxiously for their chance to drag him to hell. However, with his last breath the fallen Brāhmaṇ utters, in evidence of his deep devotion, the name of the god Viṣṇu. Viṣṇu, in turn, rescues him from Yama's servants, granting him not only expiation for his sins but also declaring that he has atoned for his sins from thousands of past lifetimes (*Bhāgavata Purāṇa* 6.2.7). According to the *Bhāgavata Purāṇa* (6.2.5), the god's intervention here is not only a reward for his devotion but also reflects the god's assurance that the common man who "does not understand, of his own accord, what is righteousness and unrighteousness" is not punished undeservedly.

On the popular level, too, the interweaving of *karma* with notions of fate and divine intervention temper for ordinary Hindus the oppressiveness suggested by the doctrine's supposition of the inevitable and inescapable retributive effects of actions (Fuller 1992: 249; U. Sharma 1973: 357). Although, as Fuller notes, on this level, *karma* is rarely denied, its acceptance as the one and only cause of an individual's circumstances tends to reflect certain societal factors as much as it does deeply embedded structures of belief. Thus, women, members of low castes, the poor, and the uneducated tend not to explain misfortune in terms of *karma*; rather, belief in the absolute efficacy of *karma* dominates that segment of society, the "socioreligious elite," who have at least some understanding of its textual validity (Fuller 1992: 250). Fuller suggests that given the complex of causal agents ordinary Hindus rely on to explain their circumstances, "in popular Hinduism, *karma* does not enjoy the currency that its fame might suggest" (1992: 250). However, it may also be the case that the doctrine's fame may have caused it, over the centuries, to become embedded—though certainly not lost—within this larger complex of causality. Given its extraordinarily deep roots in the Hindu world, the doctrine may have been, and almost certainly still remains, the defining factor for a worldview that sees causal links—karmic or otherwise—as a central tenet of existence.

CONCLUSION

A well-known Vedic myth recounts how the ancient sacrificer Bhṛgu journeyed to the other worlds, where he observes the horrifying sight of men eating men. Returning to this world, he seeks out his father for an explanation. Bhṛgu learns from his father that the men who eat other men in these worlds are the trees, animals, and plants that are eaten in this world; and the men who are eaten there are the men that ate and used these things in this world (*Śatapatha Brāhmaṇa* 11.6.1.1–13; *Jaiminīya Brāhmaṇa* 1.42–44; O'Flaherty 1985: 32–37). This tale, which almost certainly predates the articulation of the *karma* doctrine, is reminiscent of Western depictions of the punishments of hell, where blasphemers hang by their tongues or eat fiery coals; adulterers hang by their genitals; and those who defiled their bodies in life are maimed even in death as they are repeatedly cast from a precipice (*Apocalypse* of Peter 22–32; Gaster 1893: 602–3). In both cases, the Hindu and the non-Hindu, these images appear to be simple effects that reverse and punish actions performed in this world. Yet, there is a critical difference between these depictions, in particular, in the understanding of action and its valuation. On the one hand, the non-Hindu representation of sinners being punished for defiling the body, blasphemy, and adultery suggests a clear-cut valuation of certain actions based on specific ethical mores; thus, not all sexual relations but a certain type of sexual relationship, adultery; not all types of speech but a particular type of speech, blasphemy, are reviled here. On the other hand, the

Hindu representation of punishments being meted out for eating meat and for the use of plants and wood suggests a broad characterization that values actions without regard to their context; that these acts are necessary for survival does not mitigate for the Hindu thinkers the violence and killing they entail and the potential consequences they engender. Herein lies the potential to indict all acts and, along with it, the establishment of an unbearable psychic burden. Taken to its extremes, this burden cannot be relieved until the cessation of all activity is achieved, a goal that is as unattainable in practical terms as it is undesirable.

The Hindu *karma* doctrine removes at least to some degree the onus of action by valuing acts not in and of themselves but in relationship to the actor who performs them. Accordingly, despite the burdens it places on the individual, the Hindu thinkers enjoined action; as the authors of the *Bhagavad Gītā* long ago declared: "even though it is tainted, a man should never abandon the work (*karman*) to which he is born" (*Bhagavad Gītā* 18.48). This relationship between act and actor—carried through an unremitting process of rebirth—lies at the heart of the Hindu *karma* doctrine: "That which they spoke about was action (*karman*) and that which they praised was action: one indeed becomes good by good action, bad by bad [action]" (*Bṛhadāraṇyaka Upaniṣad* 3.2.13).

NOTES

1 Although the Brāhmaṇas stand as the conceptual as well as the chronological center of the Vedic texts, the first generation of Western scholars to examine them had an unfortunate tendency to view their richly symbolic (and often abstruse) language as evidence of intellectual degeneracy, if not debility (E. Hopkins 1895: 199; Müller 1926: 228; Whitney 1873: 69); a situation that spelled certain doom for the fruitful investigation of these texts as the source of the Hindu doctrine of *karma* (Tull 1989: 14–19). Thus, Müller famously characterized the Brāhmaṇas as "simply twaddle, and what is worse, theological twaddle" (1867: 116); a characterization repeated ad infinitum by a number of great Indologists: "puerile, arid, [and] inane" (Lanman 1884: 357); "monuments of tediousness and intrinsic stupidity" (Bloomfield 1908: 44); "[unequaled] for wearisome prolixity of expression . . . rather than by serious reasoning" (Eggeling 1882: ix).

2 To circumvent the death of the sacrificer in the sacrifice, the Vedic religionists employed a substitute, frequently an animal, with whom the sacrificer was identified through various ritual subterfuges. One means of achieving this was through correlating the implements used in the sacrifice to the sacrificer's physical proportions; the Brāhmaṇic authors thus asserted that: "the man arranges the sacrifice to the same extent as a man; therefore the sacrifice is a man" (*Śatapatha Brāhmaṇa* 1.3.2.1, 3.5.3.1). This process of identification is problematic, however. In one instance it leads the Brāhmaṇic authors to forbid the sacrificer from eating the offering; for, through the symbolic connection of sacrificer and victim, such a meal implicitly suggests autophagy (*Aitareya Brāhmaṇa* 2.3; *Kauṣītaki Brāhmaṇa* 10.3; *Taittirīya Saṃhitā* 6.1.11.6). In another instance, the Brāhmaṇic authors express uncertainty over whether or not the sacrificer should touch the victim who stands in his place. Whereas distance may indemnify the sacrificer from the killing of the victim, proximity is needed to ensure the establishment of a firm identification between sacrificer and victim: "Now they say: 'There [should] be no touching [of the victim] by the sacrificer; for they lead it to death. Thus he should not touch it!' But he should touch it; for what they lead by the sacrifice they do not lead to death. Thus he should touch it. For indeed when it is not touched he excludes his own self from the sacrifice; therefore he should touch it" (*Śatapatha Brāhmaṇa* 3.8.1.10).

3 This emphasis on process underlies the development of the Vedic sacrifice into a complex system of strict ritual forms—into what Staal has called, "the richest, most elaborate and most complete

among the rituals of mankind" (1980: 122)—a development that stands as the driving force of the Brāhmaṇa period. On one level, ritualization ameliorates the danger of the sacrifice; for the ritual sphere represents a world unto itself (indeed, the Vedic sacrifice takes place within a specific arena, a physically established ritual space), thereby granting the ritualists freedom to attribute new meanings to their actions. For example, the killing that occurs as the central element in the sacrifice becomes in the ritual world not a killing at all, as the Brāhmaṇic authors assert: "That which they lead to the sacrifice they do not lead to death" (*Śatapatha Brāhmaṇa* 3.8.1.10; see also *Ṛg Veda* 1.162.21) or that "One does not say: 'He strikes [the victim], he kills it' . . . but that [the victim] 'went away' " (*Śatapatha Brāhmaṇa* 3.8.1.15). On another level, ritualization—insofar as the ritual events are correctly enacted—ensures that the sacrifice will yield its desired goal; just as the primordial model yielded a certain result, so too every sacrifice that follows it yields its reward. As evidence of the workings of the ritual, the Brāhmaṇic authors frequently refer to ancient sacrificers who benefited from the sacrifice and present lists of the goods of life that can be acquired "automatically" through its performance (see *Śatapatha Brāhmaṇa* 1.6.2.7; Keith 1925, 2: 463). However, that the sacrifice—once ritualized—guarantees a result is, as already noted, a double-edged sword; for the failure to properly enact it leads potentially to disaster.

4 In the Vedic ritual system, the sacrifices are ordered according to the complexity of their performance, each succeeding ritual presupposes elements from—and the performance of—its antecedents (see Staal 1980: 125). Those who lived to the greatest age thus performed sacrifices of the greatest complexity and thereby won the greatest rewards (see *Śatapatha Brāhmaṇa* 10.2.6.8, 10.1.5.4).

5 The general confusion and lack of resolution that long dogged this conflict in Hindu India can be seen in a discussion of meat eating and sacrifice that occurs in the *Manusmṛti*. The authors of this text note first that: "A twice-born person who knows the true meaning of the Vedas and injures sacrificial animals for these [correct] purposes causes both himself and the animal to go to the highest level of existence"; and then, a few stanzas later, appear to reverse this position as they observe that the "killing of creatures with the breath of life does not get you to heaven" (*Manusmṛti* 5.42, 5.45). Finally, rather than take a hard stance indicating a preference for one model of action over the other, the authors of the text state that the rewards gained by the man who performs a horse sacrifice every year for a hundred years are the same as that gained by the man who abstains from meat eating (*Manusmṛti* 5.53).

CHAPTER FIFTEEN

SAṂSKĀRA

Mary McGee

Alliance for Bombay settled Keralite (N. Malabar) Dhivara (Mukkuvan) graduate employed girl 28/158 Revathi Shudha Jathakam invites from suitable boys of same caste, well settled. Reply with full details to Box No. C-8201, Indian Express, Nariman Point, Bombay–21.

This advertisement, from the "Match Makers" section of the Sunday edition of the *Indian Express*, a Bombay-based national newspaper, is one among thousands found weekly in newspapers throughout India and abroad. The marketing division of the *Indian Express* solicits such ads with this pitch: "There could be no better matchmaker than Indian Express. With its wide and varied readership. Ensuring the right response. For just the mate you want. Make your first choice the right choice!" Behind the facade of this modern and commercial solicitation for a marriage partner via local, national, and even international news publications is an age-old tradition of families actively engaged in the process of perpetuating their lineage while at the same time protecting it. Qualities valued in a marriage alliance, as recorded in the ancient *Manusmṛti*, emphasized the integrity and orthodoxy of the extended family, not just of the intended partner, whereas among those qualities prized today are the education and financial stability of the potential partner. In the search for the perfect wife or husband, second century as well as twenty-first century Hindu communities share a concern for physical traits as well as for common social values and experiences, evidenced in a preference for attractive mates from similar caste groups or geographical regions. In this respect, Hindu families are no different than many other social groups throughout the world. The Hindu marriage ritual that consecrates the union of the bride and groom—be they brought before the sacred fire by a matrimonial advertisement, a family matchmaker, a childhood friendship, a synchrony of horoscopes, or a deep love for each other—consists of rites and *mantra*s that, through symbol and metaphor, provide reference to the responsibilities and qualities of men and women especially in their roles as domestic partners. This ritual, in both its ancient and contemporary forms, sanctifies this domestic partnership and marks a social as well as moral transition for the bride and groom. The marriage ritual effects the transformation of these two individuals into one body, one dharmic unit, with new responsibilities; they are incorporated into each other's lives as well as into a larger community of householders.

The ritual of marriage, known as *vivāha* in Sanskrit, is the most preeminent of *saṃskāras*, rituals of sanctification and incorporation marking the life cycle of a Hindu. While a close analysis of each of these *saṃskāras* is not possible in such a short chapter, this overview of Hindu *saṃskāras*, with reference both to ancient textual prescriptions and to changes in contemporary practice, provides examples of how religious and social values are embedded within the ritual performance of *saṃskāras*, thereby shaping, educating, and transforming individuals and communities. Ritual change often suggests changes in social values, and as we explore the world of *saṃskāras*, we will see that the practice of several of these life-cycle rituals has waned in modern times, others have been modified to reflect changing priorities and social practices (e.g. marriage), while yet others (such as initiation) have become a political tool meant to emphasize the inclusion of women and low castes as full and vital members of Hindu society.

Before we look at some of these individual *saṃskāras*, including a much fuller analysis of the marriage ritual, it is important for us to situate these rituals in their religious milieu and cultural context. One way we can do this, being situated as we are in the twenty-first century, many of us sitting in classrooms or libraries, is to look at the textual prescriptions for these rituals and the kind of texts such rituals are found in. This textual approach will provide us with a sense of the continual legacy of *saṃskāras* over some two millennia and help us to better understand the idea of *saṃskāra*, for *saṃskāras* are more than just rites and ceremonies; they constitute an idea, a belief about human beings and their development in the world. While we want to understand the significance of individual *saṃskāras*, how and why they have died out or have changed, we also want to better comprehend the traditional classification of certain rituals as *saṃskāras* and how Hindu scholars and practitioners have interpreted the presence and purpose of these rituals as part of Hindu culture or a Hindu worldview.

SAṂSKĀRAS: AN OVERVIEW OF TEXTUAL SOURCES

The Sanskrit term "*saṃskāra*," often translated as "rite of passage" or "sacrament" in reference to those Hindu ceremonials that punctuate the life cycle, also means to perfect, refine, polish, prepare, educate, cultivate, and train. The rituals classified as *saṃskāras* in Hindu texts—variously enumerated from sixteen to forty-eight—such as initiation, marriage, and even the first haircut, formally mark different stages in the physical, psychological, and moral development of a Hindu while also preparing the person spiritually, socially, and culturally to assume the dharmic duties and responsibilities of adulthood. Ideally *saṃskāras* educate and shape an individual's moral values in their aim to perfect and sanctify the whole human being. Situated at key developmental stages in the human life cycle ranging from conception to death, *saṃskāras* enable and mark transitions from one stage of life to another, serving to incorporate the individual into the new stage be that in this world or the next. Each *saṃskāra* encodes within the rites, gestures, and speech acts of its ritual process the expectations of each new stage. For example, the wedding *saṃskāra* is filled with symbols and *mantras* with specific reference to fertility because the main purpose of marriage is procreation. The religious contexts within which these rituals are performed further sanctify these stages of life, linking them to the sanctity of the social and cosmic orders recognized by Hindu tradition.

These Hindu life-cycle rituals are described in ancient Hindu texts on domestic ritual, called Gṛhyasūtras, as well as in contemporary ritual handbooks, such as *Svayaṃ Purohita*, designed for household use. Very little has changed in the textual prescriptions for these rituals, although notably fewer of these *saṃskāra*s are observed today. The *saṃskāra*s accompanying marriage (*vivāha*) and death (*antyeṣṭi*) are the most widely observed and publicly visible *saṃskāra*s still in practice today among Hindus. Most of the other *saṃskāra*s have lost their popularity and prestige, and although some of them are still performed by orthodox Hindu families, economic factors as well as certain Hindu reform movements have caused them to be streamlined, and family traditions have introduced variations.

The ancient Vedas provide us with our earliest evidence of life-cycle rituals, especially those associated with childbirth, marriage, and death. The *mantra*s recited during the performance of most *saṃskāra*s are drawn from the Vedic corpus of hymns, prayers, and blessings. The earliest codification we have of these rituals is found in the Gṛhyasūtras (*c.*800–300 BCE), Sanskrit texts which describe the domestic rituals and responsibilities of householders. The Gṛhyasūtras represent particular ritual schools associated with different branches of the Vedas, and therefore we would expect some variations in their prescriptions for life-cycle rituals. One particular point on which there is a divergence concerns an individual's birthdate: some schools count from the date of conception, others from the date the child came into the world. This seemingly small difference helps to account for why there are discrepancies among the texts concerning the age at which one should undergo a particular life-cycle ritual. The corpus of Vedic texts, including the Gṛhyasūtras, form the basis for the development and prominence of what later came to be referred to by scholars as Hindu Brāhmaṇical culture, with its emphasis on hierarchy, purity, and class-based social duties (*dharma*). As *saṃskāra*s are an example of orthopraxy, rites that initiate and incorporate an individual into Brāhmaṇical culture, authoritative texts also address the applicability of these rites to men and women of the four different Brāhmaṇical classes (*varṇa*), namely, the priestly class (Brāhmaṇ), the warrior or ruling class (Kṣatriya), the merchant class (Vaiśya), and the servant class (Śūdra).

The Gṛhyasūtras discuss *saṃskāra*s in the same category with daily domestic sacrifices (*yajña*). As explained by Hindu scholastics, both are types of rituals (*karma*) meant to generate merit while purifying the mind and soul. Later texts distinguish life-cycle rituals from other types of daily and occasional sacrificial rituals, and in the influential Hindu law books (Dharmaśāstras), rites of passage rituals are specifically classed as *śarīra saṃskāra*s, that is, sanctifications of the body. Whereas the earlier domestic ritual manuals provide detailed descriptions on how these rituals are to be performed, the Dharmaśāstras, which codify standards of living for different classes (*varṇa*) and stages of life (*āśrama*), list *saṃskāra*s among the duties of a Hindu without attention to the actual performance of the ritual. The Purāṇas (traditional scriptural sources for Hindu myth and ritual) and Dharmanibandhas (medieval compendia of Hindu law) drew on popular custom as well as on the legal and ritual authority of the Gṛhyasūtras and Dharmaśāstras for their detailed discussion and prescription of life-cycle rituals. The same sources, Purāṇas and Nibandhas, are still consulted today by Hindu priests as well as scholars of Hindu traditions, who seek clarity on the proper procedure for Hindu *saṃskāra*s as well as other types of rituals. Within all these sources, the list of *saṃskāra*s varies not only in number but also in the specific rituals included in the list, and the order in which the rituals are to be performed within a given life cycle. In the more comprehensive lists, which include daily sacrifices, we find forty-eight *saṃskāra*s enumerated, whereas some sources treat only twelve *saṃskāras*. By the medieval period, many authorities settled on a common treatment of sixteen principal *saṃskāra*s of the body. Most contemporary ritual manuals follow this practice; however, there are still some discrepancies concerning which *saṃskāra*s are included among the sixteen. The sixteen *saṃskāra*s I discuss in this chapter, along with their respective purposes and principal constituent rites, are examined in the following order:

garbhādhāna	rite of insemination
puṃsavana	bringing about a male child
sīmantonnayana	ritual parting of the hair
jātakarma	birth ceremonies
nāmakaraṇa	naming ceremony
niṣkramaṇa	first outing
gannaprāśana	first feeding with solid foods
cūḍākaraṇa	first haircut
karṇavedha	piercing of the ears
vidyārambha	beginning one's studies
upanayana	initiation into sacred knowledge
vedārambha	introduction to the Vedas
keśānta	shaving of the beard
samāvartana	taking leave of one's teacher
vivāha	marriage
antyeṣṭi	last rites

Like life-cycle rituals in many other cultures, *saṃskāra*s provide a sense of identity marked by certain religious, social, and cultural values. *Saṃskāra*s, in particular, reflect a Brāhmaṇical system of values in which much emphasis is placed on hierarchical purity. Therefore, it is not surprising that in practice the actual performance of *saṃskāra*s has been restricted by the orthodox tradition largely to those of higher classes and the male gender, groups viewed as having relatively greater purity. This bias in practice differs somewhat from prescriptions found in authoritative texts concerning the observance of *saṃskāra*s. While these ritual sanctifications are prescribed for all within Brāhmaṇical society, certain restrictions and limitations attend the performance of *saṃskāra*s upon females and members of the lower classes, reflective of traditional Brāhmaṇical values and ideologies. For example, most authorities deny the rite of Vedic initiation (*upanayana saṃskāra*) to Śūdras (*Manusmṛti* 10.4), deemed the lowest of the four classes (*varṇa*). By virtue of undergoing the *upanayana*, a Hindu traditionally gained the right to study and recite the Vedas as well as the privilege of cultivating and maintaining the sacred fire, both signs of orthodoxy, purity, knowledge, and authority. Śūdras, whose duty it was to serve the upper three classes, were denied access to the Vedas as well as the privilege of maintaining the sacred fires and thus were considered ineligible for Vedic initiation. Some texts deny the privilege of *upanayana* to females, but *Manusmṛti* (2.67) identifies the marriage ceremony (*vivāha*) as the rite of initiation (*upanayana*) for women, by which they became full members of Hindu society, taking part in the ritual and social responsibilities of householder life alongside their husbands.

The religious law texts of Manu (200 BCE–200 CE) and Yājñavalkya (*c.*200 CE) address *saṃskāras* as the first topic under the duties of the four classes. They observe that these rituals, beginning with insemination and concluding at the cremation grounds, are to be accompanied by *mantras*. Manu and Yājñavalkya both mention twelve *saṃskāras*. *Yājñavalkyasmṛti* 1.13 specifically mentions that these rites are performed for females, although he adds the qualification that the rites for females are to be done silently or, as commentators on his text explain, without Vedic *mantras*. This use of *mantras* is one of the important distinctions in how these rites are distinctively performed according to class and gender. While most authorities agree that *saṃskāras* are necessary for all members of the upper three classes, there is a variety of opinions about whether Śūdras, the lowest of the four classes, are meant to undergo *saṃskāras*. Manu presents both sides of the argument, noting that since Śūdras do not have access to the Vedas and indeed are unfit to study or even to hear the Vedas, there is no need for them to participate in the process of *saṃskāras* which ultimately prepare one for Vedic study and the performance of sacrifices (*Manusmṛti* 3.156, 4.99, 10.126). Yet Manu also says (*Manusmṛti* 10.127) that Śūdras can perform those religious acts undertaken by the twice-born classes, although they must perform them without Vedic *mantras*. There is a general consensus among the authorities who address this question about Śūdras' right to undergo *saṃskāras* that Śūdras can and do perform the prenatal and postnatal *saṃskāras* from insemination (*garbhādhāna*) to ear-piercing (*karṇavedha*), as well as marriage (*vivāha*), but that they must not employ Vedic *mantras* in these rituals. Males of the upper three classes were expected to undergo *saṃskāras* from the rite of insemination (*garbhādhāna*) to Vedic initiation (*upanayana*). Some authorities held that the *saṃskāra* marking one's graduation from Vedic studies as well as the *saṃskāra* of marriage were not necessary for those men who chose to continue with a life of study and celibacy. Women in contrast were expected to marry, and key authorities allow most if not all the *saṃskāras* to them, although without the use of the sacred Vedic *mantras*.

Most authorities assert that when these life-cycle rituals are performed for women or Śūdras, Purāṇic *mantras* should be used instead of Vedic *mantras*. Purāṇas are part of the corpus of traditional, remembered sacred lore (*smṛti*) derivative of the more sacred and authoritative Vedic revelation (*śruti*). Purāṇic *mantras* constitute a more popular, accessible form of ritual prayer than the Vedic *mantras* and apparently were as efficacious for Śūdras and women as were the Vedic *mantras* for the men of the upper three classes. By substituting Purāṇic *mantras* in the *saṃskāra* rituals of women and Śūdras, the Vedic *mantras* remained pure, untainted by association with those classes of people who were potential sources of pollution, such as Śūdras and women. The exception to this rule is found in the *saṃskāra* of marriage where Vedic *mantras* are used in marriages between men and women of the upper three classes. Even when Vedic *mantras* are used, the most sacred and powerful of these, the Gāyatrī-*mantra*, has traditionally been reserved for the highest and most pure of the three classes, namely, the Brāhmaṇs (*Manusmṛti* 2.77–79). Similar modifications in the performance of rites within the various *saṃskāras* accommodate different classes. According to ancient textual prescriptions concerning the ritual of initiation (*upanayana*), certain accoutrements distinguish the class of the initiate. For example, the upper and lower garments of the initiates differ in material and color, and the wood and height of their staff varies according to their classes. In marriage, class distinctions were evident in the rite of *pāṇigrahaṇa*, during which the couple grasped hands. According to textual evidence, if the bridal couple were of the same class they were to hold hands; otherwise, according to Manu and Yājñavalkya, if a young woman was marrying a man of a different class, they held between them a symbol of the woman's class: a Kṣatriya bride grasped an arrow, a Vaiśya bride an animal prod, and a Śūdra the hem of the groom's garment. While marriage (*vivāha*) and to a lesser extent initiation (*upanayana*) are two of the most visible *saṃskāra*s still in practice today, the class distinctions within the rites are not as evident. However, whereas contemporary marriage rituals may not embed symbols of class difference in their actual performance, as did ancient practitioners, evidence from contemporary matrimonial advertisements suggests that class, caste, and even subcaste are still of significance when selecting a life partner.

THE RITUAL PROCESS OF PURIFICATION AND ORIENTATION

*Saṃskāra*s in general focus on two key processes: purification and orientation. The *saṃskāra* process orients individuals towards that which is considered right, good, pure, true, auspicious, moral, and responsible within Hindu culture, and each subsequent *saṃskāra* reinforces these cultural values, since they orient and prepare the individual for the next stage of his or her development and the expectations incumbent on one during this stage. Purity is a quality greatly valued in Hindu culture as it is believed to make one more receptive to truth and the knowledge or experience of god. Purity itself must be pursued on several levels: physical, mental, verbal, moral, and spiritual. Various preliminary rites help one to maintain purity or dispel impurities that may impede the efficaciousness of the *saṃskāra*. For example, ablutions, sipping water (*ācamana*), and ritual baths (*snāna*) are preliminary rites meant to purify the body of those about to undergo a *saṃskāra*, whereas breathing exercises (*prāṇāyāma*), fasting (*upavāsa*), and sexual continence (*brahmacarya*) are variously practiced to purify the senses and the internal body. Aspersion with water is used to purify the place for the ritual as well as the objects to be used in the ritual. The emphasis on purity within the context of these *saṃskāra*s also includes practices and prohibitions meant to keep out the impure, since impurity is highly contagious and an impure substance, person, or object could easily contaminate and jeopardize the proceedings.

The purification process itself is one way that *saṃskāra*s orient one towards particular cultural values and goals. In addition to the value placed on purity, auspiciousness is another value greatly sought after when performing *saṃskāra*s. Associated with prosperity and good fortune, auspiciousness increases the effectiveness of these life-cycle rites. To that end, a person undergoing a *saṃskāra* is usually oriented in an auspicious direction (east or north), and the date and time chosen for the ritual performance conform to astronomical configurations deemed auspicious, such as morning time, the waxing phase of the moon, and the northern progression of the sun, thus augmenting if not ensuring the efficaciousness of the ritual.

Commentators and authorities agree that *saṃskāra*s are primarily observed either to remove impurities or to make one fit for a particular responsibility (*dharma*); in many cases, *saṃskāra*s entail rites that fulfill both purposes. The prenatal and postnatal *saṃskāra*s in particular are concerned with the removal of impurities that are derived from blood, semen, and womb, the impure substances that comingle to give birth to a child. *Upanayana*, the *saṃskāra* that marks the transition from childhood to adulthood, prepares one to undertake Vedic studies, and the marriage *saṃskāra* anticipates the joint responsibility of sacrificing, parenthood, and householdership during which a Hindu will pay off two of the three debts that hold him or her back from reaching the ultimate goal of *mokṣa*. The three debts (*ṛṇa*) are those owed to the sages (*ṛṣi*), the ancestors (*pitṛ*), and the gods (*deva*), and they are paid off, respectively, by study, progeny, and sacrifice. Marriage is a necessary preliminary for two of these debts, namely, procreation and the eligibility to sacrifice.

The preeminent *saṃskāras* of initiation (*upanayana*) and marriage (*vivāha*) also mark transitions from one stage of life (*āśrama*) to another. Classical Hindu texts speak of four stages of life represented by the student (*brahmacārin*), the householder (*gṛhastha*), the forest-dweller (*vānaprastha*), and the renunciate (*saṃnyāsin*). To each stage are assigned particular duties and goals (*āśramadharma*). The duties and goals of the student and the householder, which I discuss later, are made evident during *upanayana* and *vivāha*, the respective life-cycle rituals that initiate Hindus into these two stages of life. No particular *saṃskāra* is designated to signify the transition from householder to retiree, although in modern times the sixty-first-birthday *yajña* has significantly gained in popularity and practice among middle-class Hindus and includes all the constituent rites of a *saṃskāra*. The formal transition to a life of renunciation as a *saṃnyāsī* is dramatically marked by the renunciant performing his own funeral rites (*antyeṣṭi*), burning an effigy of himself on a small funeral pyre. It is because the *saṃnyāsī* has already died to his life as a contributing member of society that on the actual physical death of their bodies the corpses of *saṃnyāsī*s are usually buried or released into a river rather than being cremated.

Many of the Sanskrit texts that detail the cycle of *saṃskāra*s as significant and (trans)formative moments in the dharmic life of a Hindu begin their treatment with either marriage or initiation: marriage because new life and the process of *saṃskāra*s begin as a result of marriage, and initiation because it not only signifies a second birth but, with the exception of Śūdras, also qualifies the twice-born classes for marriage and sacrificing. This choice of beginnings is not insignificant. For many of us who think of the life cycle as beginning with birth, the idea that life as a social being begins in early adulthood or with the act of procreation can provide us with a fresh perspective and help us to think more deeply about how cultural values shape the way we think. *Saṃskāra*s are part of a ritual process that gradually incorporates the individual into a social, moral, and cultural community. *Saṃskāra*s also participate in a belief system that recognizes that an individual may cycle through multiple births while striving for perfection. The social life of humans on this terrestrial world is but a small part of a much larger and vital cosmos comprehended by the Hindu tradition. *Saṃskāra*s help to situate human life within the larger cycle of the cosmos. Indeed, that all *saṃskāra* rituals are specifically tuned into larger cycles of time is apparent from the *saṃkalpa*, the ritual statement of intention, with which each *saṃskāra* begins. The *saṃkalpa* notes the coordinates of the sun and the moon and their conjunctive asterisms at the time of the ritual; the current eon, era, year, solar cycle, season, month, fortnight, lunar day, solar day, and division of the day during which the ritual is to be performed; the continent, region, town, longitude, and latitude where the ritual is to be performed; and the place in the family lineage of the individual undergoing the *saṃskāra*.

With the exception of *jātakarma* and *antyeṣṭi*, *saṃskāra*s that immediately follow birth and death, respectively, auspicious dates and times are deliberately chosen for the performance of *saṃskāra*s in order to ensure the well being and protection of the individual undergoing the sanctification. The ritual formula of the *saṃkalpa* situates one in time (*kāla*) and place (*deśa*), requiring acute awareness of one's coordinates within the immensity of time and territory, as well as within the history of one's family lineage. Each *saṃkalpa* also briefly states the purpose of the *saṃskāra* about to be performed. Thus we learn from these statements of intention that the rites of insemination (*garbhādhāna*) and parting of the hair (*sīmantonnayana*) are performed in order to purify the womb, the *puṃsavana saṃskāra* to make the fetus male, and the naming ceremony (*nāmakaraṇa*) and first haircut (*cūḍākaraṇa*) to ensure the long life of the child.

Most of the life-cycle rituals include preliminary and concluding rites found in other forms of Hindu ritual, many of them derived from Purāṇic rather than Vedic traditions. For example, all *saṃskāra*s begin with the purifactory rites of sipping of water (*ācamana*) and yogic breathing exercises (*prāṇāyāma*), followed by the utterance of the *saṃkalpa*. These preliminaries are usually followed by the worship of Gaṇapati (Gaṇapati-*pūjā*) and various other deities, such as the family deities, guardian deities, mother goddesses, as well as planetary and directional deities. The rite of *puṇyahavācana*, a declaration of the auspiciousness of the occasion by the assembled Brāhmaṇs, along with *nandiśrāddha*, auspicious memorial rites bringing joy to the deceased family ancestors, are pro forma in many *saṃskāra* ceremonies as well. Ritual feasts and gifts to Brāhmaṇs or relatives conclude the ritual process of most *saṃskāra*s. Water and fire, symbols of purification and protection, play a significant part in *saṃskāra* rituals, although the observance of fire-sacrifices (*homa*) are no longer part of most prenatal and postnatal *saṃskāra*s.

The life-cycle ceremonies discussed here are largely described according to their textual prescriptions in authoritative ritual texts, although we find some variation among the texts and in practice, reflective of the expected as well as accepted adaptability of these rites to family and regional traditions. These rituals continued to develop and change over time, some dropping out of usage, some becoming conflated with other *saṃskāra*s, others being revived yet simplified by modern Hindu reform movements, such as Sanātana Dharma and the Ārya Samāj. One should not assume that all Hindus observe the classical *saṃskāra*s, nor that those who do necessarily follow the order or procedures profiled in the composite portraits given here. Family tradition, influenced by such things as region, sectarian affiliation, degree of orthodoxy, class, caste, gender, health, and wealth, all greatly affect the performance of *saṃskāra*s both historically and in current practice. This chapter focuses on those rituals classified as *saṃskāra*s within authoritative, largely Brāhmaṇical, Hindu texts and does not include attention to other types of rites of passage observed among some Hindus communities, such as marking a girl's first menstruation or initiation (*dīkṣā*) into a particular sectarian community.

PRENATAL AND POSTNATAL SAṂSKĀRAS: TRANSITION AND INCORPORATION INTO THE HUMAN WORLD

*Saṃskāra*s begin even before birth with the sanctification of the womb and seed in the prenatal *saṃskāra* of *garbhādhāna*, less commonly known as *niṣeka*. This *saṃskāra* is to be performed immediately after the wedding because the prescribed purpose of marriage is to secure progeny. Most texts advise that *garbhādhāna* be conducted on the fourth day after monthly menses begin, when a woman's womb is considered ripe for the planting of the male seed. If a male child is preferred, even-numbered lunar days are advised for this insemination ritual, whereas the full moon, new moon, and asterisms (*nakṣatra*) of Mūla and Maghā are times deemed inauspicious for this ritual. Among the *mantras* employed during this ceremony is the following one from the *Ṛg Veda* 10.85, also found in the *Bṛhadāraṇyaka Upaniṣad* (6.4.20). The *sa* and *ama* mentioned in this hymn are understood as the two component parts of the word "*sāman*," referring to the *sāman* chant that overlies the Ṛg Vedic verse when it is sung; the components are gendered as feminine and masculine, respectively, and their coming together creates *sāman*. *Chāndogya Upaniṣad* 1.6 also describes the union of *sa* and *ama*, in which *sa* is equated with the earth, the intermediate region, the sky, the stars, and the luster of the sun, whereas *ama* is compared to the fire, the wind, the sun, the moon, and the dark. In comparing the married couple to the union of *sa* and *ama* and earth and sky, the Brāhmaṇical tradition recognizes not only the inherent nature, if not necessity, of this union in accordance with natural and cosmic law (*dharma*) but also sanctifies the procreative benefits of such natural unions:

> I am *ama*, you are *sa*.
> You are *ama*, I am *sa*.
> I am the *sāman* chant, you are the *Ṛg* verse.
> I am the sky, you are the earth.
> Come, let us unite,
> Deposit the seed,
> To get a son,
> A male child.

Traditionally male progeny have been preferred, as the continuity of the family was maintained through the male lineage, and sons were required to perform the necessary rituals that would guarantee the passage of the father's and mother's souls to heaven after death. However, that daughters were also welcomed and desired, in addition to sons, is evident in various authoritative texts such as a passage from the *Bṛhadāraṇyaka Upaniṣad* (6.4.17) which advises that a man who wishes "a learned daughter who will live out her full life span" should instruct his wife "to cook that rice with sesame seeds and the two of them should eat it mixed with *ghī*. The couple thus becomes capable of begetting such a daughter."

Ancient Hindu medical texts assumed that the gender of the fetus was not determined until the fourth or fifth month. Therefore, an additional *saṃskāra* to ensure a male fetus was prescribed for the third or fourth month of pregnancy before the quickening of the fetus. Performed when the moon is in a male constellation, this ritual, known as *puṃsavana*, is meant to stimulate, consecrate, and influence the fetus bringing about a male child. The woman who undergoes this *saṃskāra* fasts and bathes in preparation for it. During the ritual process she ingests a concoction of yogurt mixed with grains or beans; the texts also prescribe that a whitish fluid resulting from the pounding of a banyan branch (*nyagrodha*) be poured down her right nostril. The resemblance of these substances to semen is unmistakable and the fertility symbolism of the rite is unambiguous. This *mantra* from the *Atharva Veda* (3.23.2, 3.23.4), or a variant found in one of the Gṛhyasūtras, is recited during the rite: "May a male embryo enter your womb as an arrow into a quiver.

May a man be born here, a son after ten months. By the effective seed which bulls put forth may you obtain a son. Be a fruitful milch cow." This ritual is followed some months later by the *saṃskāra* of *sīmantonnayana*, which entails a ritual parting of the pregnant woman's hair and is meant to ensure the safe development and delivery of the child during the last trimester. According to some authorities, this *saṃskāra* begins a process by which the pollution of the fetus derived from the parents begins to be removed. Popular tradition understands this as a rite focused on the mother, educating her while entertaining her, encouraging her to concentrate on her own well being so as to ensure the full and healthy development of the child. The texts discuss feeding the woman auspicious foods as well as those that satisfy her special cravings (*dohada*), entertaining her with songs, anointing and massaging her, and garlanding her with a string of unripe fruits. During the last trimester of her pregnancy following this ritual, relatives pamper and protect the mother-to-be, catering to her various whims. *Yājñavalkyasmṛti* 3.79 warns: "By not meeting the wishes of the pregnant woman, the fetus becomes unhealthy; it becomes deformed or falls down. Therefore one should do what is desired by her." Every precaution is taken to protect the well being of the fetus. To that end, a pregnant woman is advised to avoid inauspicious activities as well as overexertion; similarly, her husband is to avoid impure and inauspicious activities, as well as travelling, after the sixth month of pregnancy. These particular prenatal rituals, especially that of *puṃsavana*, are rarely observed among Hindus today. The *garbhādhāna*, for the most part, has been incorporated into the wedding ritual. Modern vestiges of the *sīmantonnayana saṃskāra* have been transformed into occasions for celebration, for showering the mother-to-be with attention and gifts.

The purpose of the prenatal rites, as explained by the ritual utterances, is to sanctify the mother, the womb, and the fetus to ensure the long life of the child. Ancient ritual theorists debated whether these prenatal *saṃskāra*s were performed upon the mother or the fetus. The ramifications of these discussions concerned whether the rites had to be performed more than once during the lifetime of a childbearing mother. Although opinions varied on this matter, the general consensus was that all the prenatal *saṃskāra*s, with the exception of *sīmantonnayana*, were sanctifications of the embryo (*garbha saṃskāra*) and should therefore be repeated during each pregnancy. The ritual parting of the hair, many agreed, was a *kṣetra saṃskāra*, that is, a *saṃskāra* of the field or mother, not the fetus, and need not be repeated for subsequent pregnancies. As advised by Mitramiśra in his seventeenth-century commentary on the *Yājñavalkyasmṛti*: "Once a woman is purified by the *sīmantonnayana*, every child produced by her becomes consecrated" (*Vīramitrodaya* 1.176).

Jātakarma is the first *saṃskāra* to be performed after the birth of the child, typically taking place immediately after the delivery even before the umbilical cord is cut. According to tradition, *jātakarma* includes several minor rites, among them *medhājanana* in which drops of *ghī* and honey, in unequal proportions, are trickled onto the newborn's lips to ensure strength and intelligence. *Āyuṣya*, also part of the birth ceremonies, entails uttering the names of those who have lived long lives so as to ensure the longevity of the child. *Bṛhadāraṇyaka Upaniṣad* 6.4.24–28 provides us with a very early description of this ritual, in which the newborn is placed on the lap of the father who whispers into the child's ear various sacred syllables, a secret name, and the word "*vac*" (speech) three times. The father prays: "In this boy may I prosper a thousandfold and thrive in my own house. Rich in offspring and livestock, may disaster never strike his line. Svāhā!" The rite of *stanapratidhana* follows, in which the father gives the child to the mother to begin suckling while reciting: "The breast with which you nourish all you choose, give it here for him to suck." The rites of *jātakarma* instill in the child breath, speech, and nourishment, meant to provide the child with the intelligence and strength to live a long and full life. Touching his newborn child, the father prays: "Be a stone, be an axe, be like imperishable gold . . . live a hundred autumns" (*Pāraskara Gṛhyasūtra* 1.16.18; *Āśvalāyana Gṛhyasūtra* 1.15.3).

While birth is largely an auspicious occasion, the physical process of birthing creates a context in which impurity is rampant, making all those associated with the process vulnerable, including *sapiṇḍa* relations of the birthing parents. *Sapiṇḍa* relationships in general refer to blood relatives. Marriage and death rites require specific knowledge of deceased *sapiṇḍa* relatives going back as far as seven generations. Depending on their degree of relation, *sapiṇḍa*s can experience the ritual pollution that attends birth as well as death; during this period of pollution, *sapiṇḍa* relatives should eat only with each other. The ritual period of impurity usually extends from three to ten days, during which normal religious activities are suspended. Purification rites for the mother and the newborn take place on the eleventh day with prayers and ritual bathing. *Nāmakaraṇa*, the naming ceremony of the child, is prescribed for the eleventh or twelfth day after birth, allowing for the period of impurity to pass. The natal horoscope, cast on the basis of the configuration of stars and planets at the time of the child's birth, often provides clues for an appropriate name, which is different from the secret name given to the child by the father during the birthing ceremonies. On the day of this *saṃskāra*, after the infant is bathed and dressed in new garments, it receives its new name, marking the child as an individual and beginning the process by which a child is gradually incorporated and socialized into the world around him or her. Naming the child frees the child from sin, according to the *Śatapatha Brāhamaṇa* (6.1.3.9). Gifts are presented, and a feast of auspicious foods follows. So begins the sequence of early childhood *saṃskāra*s.

The Gṛhyasūtras and Dharmaśāstras provide guidelines for choosing names, which differ depending on one's class (*varṇa*) and gender (*Manusmṛti* 2.31–33). They recommend that boys' names be of two or four syllables, have an initial sonant, a semivowel in the middle, and end in a *visarga* (an unvoiced aspiration) or long vowel; girls' names, on the other hand, ideally should consist of an uneven number of syllables, end in a long "a" or "i," and be easy to pronounce. In the case of both boys and girls, inauspicious names and those with unpleasant associations are to be avoided. Auspicious names are recommended, such as those affiliated with a deity, a lucky constellation, or a desirable quality. An exception to this tradition are names given to children born into families with recurring tragedies, such as infant death or hereditary illness. Such families are popularly advised to give their newborns repulsive names in order to avert the bearers of the evil eye which may hasten a child's death. Other common names include those derived from an auspicious asterism (*nakṣatra*) or its presiding deity, derivatives of the name of the father, mother, or clan (*gotra*) or ones associated with the family deity, the locality, or nature's beauty (trees, flowers, birds).

A child's first outing is also occasion for a *saṃskāra*. The *niṣkramaṇa saṃskāra* is recommended for an auspicious day during the fourth month after birth. Some texts specify that it should be observed on the third lunar day during the waxing fortnight of the third month after the child's birth; others suggest that it be performed on the same lunar day (*tithi*) as the birth *tithi* during the fourth month. On this ritual occasion the newborn is taken out of the house for the first time and shown the sun (*sūryadarśana*) and sometimes the moon (*candradarśana*). Looking at the sun is a rite that will be repeated again in the Vedic initiation and marriage *saṃskāra*s. This ritual outing briefly initiates infants to their expanding universe, exposing them to the physical environment to which they must soon begin to adapt. A ritual bath and new clothes are also called for on this occasion. Some families use this opportunity to take the child to the temple for the first time. Continuing this process of socialization and physical adaptation, in the sixth month the *saṃskāra* of *gannaprāśana* takes place. This ritual first feeding of solid foods is sometimes accompanied by weaning, but some children are nursed well into their second year. The ritual food fed to an infant on this occasion varies according to family tradition, although sacrificial food (*haviṣyanna* or *sthālīpāka*) is the most highly recommended according to textual authorities. Food of any kind is to be treated with reverence and thanks, a lesson underscored by this ritual and echoed in the daily prayers of a Hindu that precede meals. The ritual feeding of the child is followed by a feasting of Brāhmaṇs or relatives. Some texts advise that the mother should eat the leftovers of the ritual foods prepared for the child. The first feeding *saṃskāra*, while beginning a process of weaning the child from dependency on its mother, also subtly furthers the child's developmental awareness of its dependency on the larger world's resources for its survival.

The first haircut, *cūḍākaraṇa* or *caula*, is next in the sequence of early childhood *saṃskāra*s. Intended to ensure the long life, stamina, and beauty of the child, this *saṃskāra* is meant to remove impurities. A full *cūḍākaraṇa* includes not just a haircut but also a trimming of the nails. Concern with beauty as well as with the threat of impurities signifies a transition in a child's life. Lessons of good hygiene and the importance of ritual purity are instilled early on in childhood and reinforced in subsequent *saṃskāra*s. As toddlers, children increase their movement and thus their interactions with their environment, bringing them into more frequent contact with receptacles of impurity. The texts vary in their prescriptions as to when this *saṃskāra* is to be undergone: some advise its performance for the end of the child's first year, others say that it should be done by the third or seventh year. Today this *saṃskāra* is usually incorporated into *upanayana*, Vedic initiation. The actual ritual cutting may involve a mere trim or a full tonsure, in which case a tuft of hair is left to cover the soft spot near the top. This critical juncture in the body or *sandhi* is known as the *adhipati*, and injury to this part of the head can be fatal (notably, this is the section of the skull cracked open during obsequies to release the soul of the deceased). The *mantra*s that accompany this *saṃskāra* pray for the long life, fame, and happiness of the child.

Before the age of four a child undergoes the *saṃskāra* of *karṇavedha*; in practice this ear-piercing usually takes place within the first month after birth. This is a minor *saṃskāra* not singled out in many of the early authorities on *saṃskāra* but found in later lists of *saṃskāra*s where it is noted that its purpose is primarily an ornamentation of the body. As yet another rite in the socialization process of the child, the *karṇavedha*, with its emphasis on ornamentation of the body, provides cultural lessons on Hindu notions of beauty. However, Suśruta, an Āyurvedic authority, explains that ear-piercing is done for both decoration and protection, prescribing a needle of gold for piercing the ear of a Kṣatriya and a silver needle for Brāhmaṇs and Vaiśyas. The right earlobe of a boy is pierced first; of a girl child, the left lobe. Piercing the left nostril of a girl may take place at the same time. The piercing of the earlobes symbolizes attentiveness, the importance of hearing and speech, and opening the mind and ears to the wisdom of the Vedas: "O gods, may we hear bliss with our ears" (*Ṛg Veda* 1.89.8).

A more important *saṃskāra* introducing a child to its culture is that of *vidyārambha*, the beginning of one's studies. However, like the piercing of the ear (*karṇavedha*), this *saṃskāra* is not singled out in the Gṛhyasūtras and is a late addition to the list of *saṃskāra*s. This *saṃskāra* is also known as *akṣarārambha* or *akṣaralekhana*, that is, learning to recite, recognize, and write syllables, the equivalent of learning one's ABCs. The rite that initiates this process signifies a child's readiness to learn and, depending on the authority consulted, is performed sometime between the fifth and the seventh year. Because of the value placed on learning and knowledge in Brāhmaṇical culture, great care was taken that this *saṃskāra* be carried out at an auspicious time. The learning process was not to be initiated during the rainy season or during the southern progression of the sun, both periods of inauspiciousness. Although most texts advise that this *saṃskāra* should not be observed during *caturmāsa* (a four-month "lenten" period), a popular exception to this rule is the celebration of this ritual on the tenth lunar day in the month of Āśvina (September-October) immediately following the festival of Sarasvatī, the goddess of wisdom. However, today this minor *saṃskāra* is not widely performed. Instead, many mark the beginning of a child's schooling or the first day of school with special blessings and sweets.

EDUCATIONAL SAṂSKĀRAS: TRANSITION AND INCORPORATION INTO ADULTHOOD

The process of learning begun with the *vidyārambha saṃskāra* is further refined and solemnized during the period of studentship (*brahmacarya*), inaugurated by the *saṃskāra* of *upanayana* (also known as *vratabandha* and *mauñjībandhana*). This *saṃskāra*, which emphasizes the value of education and knowledge, was traditionally recommended for Brāhmaṇs in their eighth year, Kṣatriyas in their eleventh, and Vaiśyas in their twelfth. This period of studentship prepares one for a significant life transition from childhood to adulthood. Like initiations in other religious traditions, such as confirmation within Roman Catholicism or bar mitzvah within Judaism, the *upanayana* is a ritualized process by which a child is introduced to the privileges, responsibilities, and sacred knowledge held in trust by adult members of the religious community. *Upanayana* confers special rights and privileges, and with that comes enhanced responsibilities and status.

In order to impart mastery of the Vedas as well as to instill in students the values and discipline required to maintain and adhere to the sanctity of religious knowledge, Brāhmaṇical tradition prescribed a prolonged period of studentship for the initiate, ranging from twelve to forty-eight years. This concentrated period of study required discipline and restraint of the senses. Students developed these virtuous habits through the practice of celibacy, various austerities, and simple living. Other important values for the student to learn included humility, duty, and respect for authority, which were reinforced daily through service and obedience to the preceptor. Students were also taught the mechanics of ritual performance, were trained to memorize and recite sacred verses and *mantra*s, and were schooled in various methods of purification in order to keep mind, body, and speech pure. Brāhmaṇs, traditionally entrusted with the study, preservation, and teaching of the sacred knowledge contained in the Vedas, required a longer period of studentship in order to master all the Vedas. While Kṣatriyas and Vaiśyas also were expected to acquire some Vedic knowledge so that they could maintain the ritual purity expected of those who maintained sacred fires and performed sacrifices, their primary duties (*dharma*) lay elsewhere and thus their Vedic education was not as prolonged. Today such Vedic education is greatly foreshortened and often merely entails some after-school or weekend lessons in Sanskrit, Vedic texts, or ritual performance in the months or weeks leading up to the initiation ceremony.

One who has undergone *upanayana* is referred to as twice-born or *dvija* because the student is given a cultural and spiritual rebirth by way of the *guru* or teacher who initiates him into his new life, its expectations and responsibilities. As explained in the *Śatapatha Brāhmaṇa*: "By laying his right hand on the pupil, the teacher becomes pregnant with him. In the third night he is born a Brāhmaṇ with the Sāvitrī" (11.5.4.12). Twice-borns not only have special access to the Vedas, which is denied to those who have not received or are not eligible for *upanayana*, but the sacramental initiation also confers upon them the *adhikāra* or right to perform sacrifices.

The actual ritual performance of the Vedic initiation, still in practice today within Hindu communities around the world, contains many rites and symbols indicative of the values and lessons meant to be instilled in a child as he makes his transition to adulthood. Several of the ceremonials within the ritual mirror those performed by the bride and groom during the wedding ceremony. For example, the rite of *hṛdayaspṛś*, involving a touching of the heart, symbolizes the intimacy between teacher and student and between husband and wife. *Āśmārohaṇa*, a rite in which the student and the wife mount a stone, symbolizes the student's steadfastness in devotion to his teacher and studies and a wife's devotion to her husband and household duties. Holding hands (*hastagrahaṇa*), looking at the sun (*sūryavilokana*), and gazing at the pole star (*dhruvadarśana*) are all rites found in both the Vedic initiation and marriage *saṃskāras*. A sacred thread is draped around both the student initiate and the bride during these ceremonies. A student receives a sacred thread (*yajñopavīta*) during the *upanayana* which he is to wear daily as a reminder of his responsibilities to a life of purity and righteousness. Similarly, a bride is presented with a thread of auspiciousness (*maṅgalasūtra* or *tali*), which she wears as a symbol of her auspicious married state and as a reminder of her duties to maintain the well being and auspiciousness of the household. The investiture with sacred thread is not a prominent feature in ancient textual prescriptions for *upanayana*. However, in modern times it has become one of the most central and prominent rites of this *saṃskāra* so that the Vedic initiation ceremony itself is commonly referred to as "the sacred-thread ceremony" in English-language publications.

The *yajñopavīta* donned on the occasion of the *upanayana*, although traditionally permitted to Vaiśyas and Kṣatriyas who also were eligible to undergo *upanayana*, has largely become a hallmark of Brāhmaṇ-hood. The sacred thread thus has become more of a mark of social status rather than of religious knowledge, although the wearers of sacred threads are expected to adhere to stricter codes of purity and behavior than those who have not undergone initiation. The sacred thread is usually made up of three strands, each strand made of three threads and tied with a special knot. The significance of the number three for the sacred thread is variously explained; some identify it with the three Vedas, others with the three qualities or *guṇas*—goodness (*sattva*), passion (*rajas*), and lassitude (*tamas*)—some with the three debts or three *pravaras* (*ṛṣi* clans), others with the three gods (Viṣṇu, Brahmā, Śiva) or three families of gods (Vaiṣṇava, Śaiva, Śākta). Hindu women do not customarily undergo *upanayana* or wear a *yajñopavīta*, although some scholars have found ancient textual references that include a sacred thread listed among the vestments worn by a bride during her marriage ceremony. Originally the *upavīta* referred to a particular configuration of the upper garment that was worn during the performance of Vedic sacrifices; later it became stylized into a thread. The thread is worn differently for different occasions. For everyday rituals and auspicious occasions, the sacred thread is worn suspended from the left shoulder encircling and crossing the chest to the right, falling above the navel. The thread is reversed, that is, hung from the right shoulder crossing to the left side, when performing funerary and memorial rites for the deceased. When engaging in activities deemed impure, such as carrying a corpse, defecating or urinating, or having sexual intercourse, the thread is hung around the neck from both shoulders, reaching below the heart but above the navel. Today many Brāhmaṇ men wear the sacred thread daily, ritually changing it on the full moon day in the month of Śrāvaṇa (July-August).

Additional rites within the *upanayana saṃskāra* emphasize the importance of purity and the sanctity of knowledge. A boy is ritually tonsured, and his nails are pared by a barber. This process is followed by a ritual bath, and then the initiate is dressed in a simple garment appropriate to the austere period of his studentship soon to follow. After his external body is purified, the boy is taught special breathing techniques (*prāṇāyāma*) meant to purify him internally. This process of purification prepares him to receive the most sacred of Vedic *mantra*s, the Gāyatrī, which is whispered into his ear by his teacher or his father. According to the *Yājñavalkyasmṛti* (1.22), every day a twice-born Hindu should ritually bathe, practice controlled breathing, venerate the sun, and recite the Gāyatrī. The Gāyatrī is considered so sacred that precautions are taken to prevent this sacred utterance from inadvertently reaching the ears of the uninitiated. In some *upanayana* ceremonies, this secrecy is guarded by draping the father (or teacher) and initiate with a white cloth. Underneath the cloth the father whispers the *mantra* into his son's ear, asking him to repeat it syllable by syllable. The Gāyatrī-*mantra*, addressed to Savitṛ, the sun, is found in the *Ṛg Veda*: "We meditate on the brilliance of the god Savitṛ. May it inspire our intellect" (3.62.10). Hereby the student is initiated into the sacred utterances of the Vedas, which his studentship will lead him to further appreciate, respect, and understand. The teaching of the very powerful Gāyatrī-*mantra* is one of the most important rites of the *upanayana saṃskāra*.

In former times, the rite of girdling the boy with a belt of *muñja* grass was one of the preeminent rites of the *upanayana*. The boy was expected to wear this "chastity belt" for the duration of his studentship as a reminder of his vow of celibacy. While the girdling is still part of the *upanayana* ritual performed today, the investiture of the sacred thread seems to have eclipsed the significance of the girdle. After the girdling, the teacher instructs the initiate in the rules governing his duties and behavior as a student: "You are a student. Do service, do not sleep in the day time, depend on your teachers, learn the Vedas . . ." (*Śatapatha Brāhmaṇa* 11.5.4.6ff.; *Pāraskara Gṛhyasūtra* 2.3.2; cf. *Manusmṛti* 2.69–73). The initiate is now ready to join his preceptor in kindling the sacred fires and making sacrificial offerings into the fire. This ritual art, to which the student is initiated during the *upanayana* ceremonies, will be refined during his apprenticeship with his teacher.

Traditionally the *upanayana* required a boy to take leave of his family to go live with his preceptor where he underwent his studentship. This transition also meant a move from a female-dominant world to a male-dominated environment, symbolized by the boy's taking his last meal with his mother. The last meal with the mother, ritually incorporated into the *upanayana* and still part of the ritual process today, signifies the end of childhood for the boy. During his period of studentship a young man was dependent on alms which he begged for on behalf of his teacher so that they both might subsist. One of the last ceremonies in the *upanayana saṃskāra*, still observed today, entails a symbolic begging procession. The first person the boy approaches for alms is his mother, who, until this moment, has been his primary nurturer and caregiver. As the first in line to fill his bowl, which she does generously, she conveys a blessing that his bowl will always be full, guaranteeing that his future alms-rounds will be fruitful, the patrons compassionate.

According to śāstric teaching, those among the classes of Brāhmaṇs, Kṣatriyas, and Vaiśyas who remained uninitiated, and thus uneducated in Vedic lore, suffered a kind of excommunication. These men, known as *vrātya*s, were denied access to privileges merited by those of their class who underwent *upanayana* and a period of studentship. Śūdras had no choice in the matter and have traditionally been denied *upanayana*, which would gain them access to the sacred wisdom of the Vedas (cf. *Manusmṛti* 10.4). A modern Hindu reform movement founded in the late 1800s by Dayānanda Sarasvatī, the Ārya Samāj, opposed untouchability and the exclusion of Śūdras from Vedic wisdom, which Ārya Samājists believed should be accessible to all members of society, regardless of class and gender. The Ārya Samāj developed a ritual known as *śuddhi*, meant to purify those converting to the ways and beliefs of the Ārya Samāj. This rite contains an investiture with a *yajñopavīta*, a modified version of *upanayana*, signaling the purity and twice-born status of the new convert, many of whom come from the lowest classes. The *śuddhi* rite includes a fire sacrifice (*homa* or *havana*) and recitation of the sacred Gāyatrī-*mantra* along with readings from the Vedas, all conventional marks of Brāhmaṇical ritual and status long denied to Śūdras. While the Ārya Samāj recognizes sixteen *saṃskāra*s as described in Dayānanda's *Saṃskāravidhi*, its performance of all rituals is greatly simplified in keeping with Dayānanda's rational philosophy.

While there is ample textual evidence that girls underwent *upanayana* in earlier times, it is likely that by the time of Manu the practice had gone out of fashion, since Manu states that the marriage ceremony takes the place of *upanayana* for women. In more recent times, *upanayana* ceremonies for girls have been revived in a few Hindu communities, but the *upanayana* is now observed mostly by Brāhmaṇ families who use the opportunity to initiate pubescent boys (usually between the ages of eight and twelve) into the rituals, traditional knowledge, and responsibilities of the Hindu religion.

*Saṃskāra*s that usually fell during a boy's studentship included *vedārambha*, a ritual initiating a student into Vedic studies (not included in the list of *saṃskāra*s found in the Gṛhyasūtras or Dharmaśāstras but included within later lists), and *keśānta*, a ritual shaving of the beard performed in a boy's sixteenth year. In modern times these *saṃskāra*s are incorporated into the *upanayana* ritual. The introduction to Vedic studies is initiated with instruction on the proper pronunciation of the Gāyatrī-*mantra*. *Keśānta*, very similar in form and purpose to the early childhood *saṃskāra* of first haircut (*caula*), is increasingly performed as a preliminary rite to the marriage rituals. It entails shaving or trimming of a man's head, facial hair (beard, nose, and ears), and armpits, as well as paring of the nails. This rite acknowledges the boy's transition to puberty and manhood and symbolizes the need to curb one's physical appetites. Celibacy (*brahmacarya*) was a highly esteemed value as well as a serious vow undertaken by a *brahmacārin* during his studentship, and shaving was a regular reminder of this commitment and restraint. This *saṃskāra* anticipates the conclusion of a stage in the Hindu life cycle, and soon after this acknowledgement of manhood, a twice-born male is ready to move on to the next stage of life, that of a householder.

The period of studentship ends with a ritual bath. The *saṃskāra* that marks the completion of this stage of life is often simply called "bath" or *snāna*. This *saṃskāra* is also referred to as *samāvartana*, taking leave of the teacher and returning home. As part of this ritual, the student presents his teacher with a gift or honorarium (*dakṣiṇā*) signifying his thanks and respect and asks the teacher's permission to take leave. The student leaves behind the staff and girdle that were marks of his studentship, bathes, puts on new clothes, and is welcomed home with sweets and offerings of water to cool and cleanse him after his journey. This *saṃskāra* constitutes the student's graduation ceremony, so that one who has completed his studies is called a *snātaka*, literally "one who has bathed," signifying the new status and purity of this twice-born young man. In more recent times, this *saṃskāra* has been minimized and incorporated into either the conclusion of the *upanayana* process or the marriage preliminaries. Through this ritual process the young man, who in ancient times spent his lengthy studentship in the hermitage of his teacher away from the hustle and bustle of everyday life, is reincorporated into society and the values instilled in him during that liminal period are put to the test. It is expected that during his studentship he will have acquired Vedic learning and discipline that will serve him well as he moves into the world of householdership, politics, and commerce. (Today a young Hindu does not have the benefit of this prolonged religious education, and with the folding of the educational *saṃskāra*s into the initiation and marriage *saṃskāra*s, which themselves have become abbreviated, these rites become mere symbols of important values rather than celebrations of the actual inculcation of such values.) Having completed his studies and undergone the appropriate *saṃskāra*s, a young man is considered qualified to establish an orthodox household in which he will set up and maintain his own sacred fire for the first time. But first he must marry, a prerequisite to establishing his own ritual household fires.

The *saṃskāra* of marriage, known as *vivāha*, is the most central of all the *saṃskāra*s, initiating men and women into householdership and its respective duties and responsibilities (*dharma*). Manu praises marriage as the highest *dharma* of men and women. According to the *Yājñavalkyasmṛti* (1.51), marital life helps one to fulfill prescribed duties (*dharma*) and pay off debts (*ṛṇa*) and, moreover, can be a source of prosperity (*artha*) and pleasure (*kāma*). Many Gṛhyasūtras and Dharmaśāstras begin their exposition of *saṃskāra*s with marriage, since all other ceremonials and rituals are dependent on the fruitfulness of marriage. More importantly, all other *āśrama*s depend on the hospitality of householders. "Just as all living creatures depend on air in order to live, so do members of the other stages of life subsist by depending on householders. Since people in the other three stages of life are supported every day by the knowledge and the food of the householder, therefore the householder stage of life is the best" (*Manusmṛti* 3.77–79).

Most authoritative Sanskrit texts list eight types of marriage. While few of these forms of marriage are still in practice, we find examples of them described in the Sanskrit epics, the *Rāmāyaṇa* and the *Mahābhārata*, as well as in other classical Hindu literature. Of the eight forms of marriage recognized in the Sanskrit legal texts, the highest and most honorable is the *brāhma* form, in which a daughter is given freely by her father to a man of good character who is her equal. The worst form is *paiśāca*, marriage by rape. Only four of the eight types of marriage receive approval by traditional authorities. Families with daughters have traditionally borne a great responsibility for arranging their marriages. Many authorities warn of the sin that incurs to families who do not arrange the marriage of their daughters, and some even advise women to choose their own husbands if their families have failed them. According to classical Hindu authorities, an unmarried woman—or a woman who does not have sexual intercourse during her fertile cycle—is like a fertile field whose potential prosperity is wasted. Such a waste, particularly of an embryo, is deemed sinful, classified by some authorities alongside abortion.

The fertility and prosperity of the marriage union has always been of great importance in Hindu culture. Therefore families take great care in their selection of marriage partners for their sons and daughters. Family priests and astrologers are consulted, family lineages examined, natal horoscopes of potential partners compared, and the physical characteristics of the prospective bride and groom are scrutinized by potential in-laws. Families traditionally based their assessment of the compatibility of the bride and groom on their examination of class, caste, horoscope, and family. The main guideline in selecting a marriage partner, according to Hindu law, is to marry someone of the same class (*varṇa*). While authorities such as Manu and Yājñavalkya, permit marriage of a lower-class woman to a higher-class man (known as an *anuloma* alliance), this is not the ideal. On the other hand, *pratiloma* unions, in which a lower-class man marries a woman of a higher class, are greatly discouraged by tradition and in some cases banned by Hindu law. Marriage within the same clan lineage (*sagotra*) or bloodline (*sapiṇḍa*) amounts to a kind of incest and is legally forbidden by most Hindu schools of law. The Hindu Marriage Act of 1955 revoked some of these impediments to marriage unions. However, modern matrimonial advertisements, ubiquitous in Indian newspapers, are evidence that many Hindu families still value unions between partners of the same class and caste, while education and occupation are increasingly important factors in evaluating potential brides and grooms. Once family issues have been scrutinized, such as class and consanguinity, the merits and characteristics of the individual are considered. Ideally a prospective bride bears auspicious markings, is pleasing to look at, has brothers, is free from disease and ill-health, and has not previously married. Handsome, virile, well educated in the Vedas, virtuous, and wise were among the traditional characteristics sought in a groom. Once the marriage has been arranged between two well-suited partners, the *saṃskāra* of marriage is performed to bless and consecrate this union and to ensure its fertility. Many of the rites and ceremonials that are encompassed within the marriage *saṃskāra* are directly related to the fertility of the couple and their joint duty (*dharma*) to bear offspring. Progeny ensures the continuity of the family and aids the family ancestors' access to heaven through the performance of sacrifices and memorial rites (*śrāddha*).

The wedding *saṃskāra* begins with the premarriage ceremonials of betrothal (*vāgdāna*) and acceptance of the bridegroom (*varavaraṇa*). Traditionally these rites could take place years before the ritual completion and consummation of the marriage, especially if the betrothed were a young boy and girl promised in marriage. Today the betrothal ceremony is performed anywhere from a few years in advance to the eve of the wedding ceremony. The order of the marriage *saṃskāra*, following upon the premarriage rites, falls into three parts: the marriage sacrifice (*vivāhahoma*), the entry into the home (*gṛhapraveśa*), and the consummation (*garbhādhāna*). The marriage ceremony proper begins with the rite of *kanyādāna*, the giving away of the bride by her parents to the groom. This is followed by the rite of *pāṇigrahaṇa* by which responsibility for the bride is transferred from the father to the groom. The groom, grasping the hand of the bride declares: "I take your hand for the sake of marital felicity (*saubhāgya*) so that with me, your husband, you may attain ripe old age. . . . Come, let us marry." The intimacy of this marriage is then indicated by the performance of the *hṛdayaspṛś* ceremony: touching the heart of the bride, the groom mutters a prayer celebrating their union of mind and heart. Resolute in their commitment to this marriage, the couple circle the sacred fire three times (*agnipariṇayana* or *agnipradakṣiṇā*) while the groom recites a prayer (*Āśvalāyana Gṛhyasūtra* 1.7.6; *Pāraskara Gṛhyasūtra* 1.6.3), a variation on the *mantra* used during the rite of insemination:

> I am this, you are that.
> That are you, this am I.
> I the heaven, you the earth.
> I the *sāman*, you the *Ṛg*.
> Come, let us both marry here. Let us unite our sperm.
> Let us beget offspring. Let us have many long-lived sons.
> Dear to each other, bright, having well-disposed minds,
> May we live a hundred years.

With the sacred fire before the wedding couple as witness to their vows and joint *dharma*, the bride makes sacrificial offerings (*lājāhoma*) into the fire of grain and *ghī*, symbols of the prosperity and fertility of this union. As she offers the grain into the fire she prays, "May my husband live long and my relations prosper. May these grains bring prosperity to us and unite us." The fire sacrifice is followed by *saptapadī*, the rite of seven steps, which many consider to be the rite by which the marriage becomes legally binding. Accompanied by the groom, the bride takes seven steps, each time placing her right foot on a separate pile of rice grains. This prayer, or some form of it, is recited during this rite and encapsulates the significance of marriage within the Hindu tradition (*Āśvalāyana Gṛhyasūtra* 1.7.19; *Pāraskara Gṛhyasūtra* 1.8.1):

> One step for vigor; two steps for vitality;
> three steps for prosperity; four steps for happiness.
> Five steps for cattle (or progeny); six steps for seasons.
> Seven steps for friendship.
> With this seventh step may we become friends,
> devoted to each other.

During the rite, known as *āśmārohaṇa*, the bride, standing alongside the groom, places her right foot on a millstone, symbolizing her inner strength as well as her firm commitment to this marriage and her duties as a wife. This rite is followed by the *sūryavilokana* rite, looking into the sun, and the *dhruva-(arundhatī)-darśana*, gazing at the pole star and, some authorities add, at the star of Arundhatī. During these rites, the bride murmurs various prayers: "May I be constant (*dhruva*) in my husband's family"; "I shall be near you like Arundhatī"; "May my husband live long and I bear offspring." These three rites, all performed by the bride, have counterparts in the *upanayana* in which they are performed by the boy initiate. The boy and the bride both affirm their purity (looking at the sun), their commitment and fidelity to their vows (mounting the stone), and their steadfastness (gazing at the Pole Star, a symbol of constancy, as is the star Arundhatī, which shares its name with the faithful and respected wife of the sage Vasiṣṭha). In performing these rites, the bride and the student both publicly affirm their respective duties; they take on the ritual and social responsibilities of an initiated and mature Hindu, as expected of them by society and as recognized within the community by this sequence of rites. There is, of course, variation in the order, procedure, *mantra*s, and rites that make up the marriage sacrifice. Indeed the texts advise that when it comes to marriage rituals, the best authorities on regional and family customs are women, and they should be consulted concerning such procedures.

Today the rite of *maṅgalasūtra-dāna* or *tali-bandhana*, tying the thread of auspiciousness, is one of the more significant rites during the marriage *saṃskāra*. Styles of *maṅgalasūtra*s vary among class, kin, regional, economic, and religious groups: the *sūtra* may be as simple as a cotton thread soaked in turmeric until it attains a golden hue, as ornate as a solid gold necklace, or as intricate as a black string threaded with heirloom gold ornaments and black beads. As one of the final rites of the marriage ceremony, the groom places the *maṅgalasūtra* around his wife's neck, symbolizing her good fortune (*saubhāgya*) and her auspicious status and prestige as a wife. *Maṅgalasūtra*s have become one of the predominant symbols of marriage worn by Hindu women, similar in function to wedding rings worn by women in some other cultures. When the husband dies, a woman usually removes her *maṅgalasūtra*, along with other ornaments marking the auspiciousness of marriage. This particular rite is not found within the ritual rubrics for marriage in ancient Sanskrit texts, and because of this, despite its incorporation into even the most orthodox of Hindu marriage ceremonies, Sanskrit *mantra*s do not usually accompany the presentation of the marriage thread.

The marriage sacrifice concluded, a grand feast usually follows during which the newlyweds practice hospitality, one of several virtuous duties incumbent upon householders. Often the bride and groom serve their guests going from seat to seat, pouring a stream of thick, rich *ghī* upon the rice dish of each guest. The next segment in the marriage *saṃskāra* process entails the ritual journey to the home where the couple will set up household and sacrifice together. As the bride enters the home, auspicious right foot first, she knocks over a container of rice or wheat perched on the threshold, symbolizing the prosperity and fertility this marriage and this bride bring into the family. The bride is welcomed into her new home (often the joint family home of her husband) and blessed by the women of the family. A series of women's rites (*strī-ācāra*) may then be performed according to the customs of the family or region. In earlier times, the ritual of entry into the home (*gṛhapraveśa*) included an entry sacrifice (*praveśahoma*), focused on oblations to ensure the fecundity of the new wife. With each offering the groom prayed "May Prajāpati create offspring for us" (*Ṛg Veda* 10.85.43–46). Today very few families maintain the special domestic fires needed for such sacrificial rituals.

The ancient texts prescribe for newlyweds a three-day period of fasting, austerities, and celibacy (*trirātravrata*), followed by a formal coming together on the fourth day during which the couple undertook together their new responsibilities of sacrifice and procreation. Touching the heart of the bride in the rite of *hṛdayāvamarśana*, the groom prays, "May all the gods unite our hearts" (*Ṛg Veda* 10.85.47). With this union of hearts, the couple established the sacred household fire, shared a meal, and then consummated their union. This ritual consummation later became equated with the *saṃskāra* for fertilization of the womb, the *garbhādhāna* ritual with which we began this explication of the Hindu sanctification of the life cycle. This *mantra*, taken from one of several such *mantras* to be recited as part of the consummation ritual on the fourth day of marriage, leaves us with little doubt that procreation is the central duty of householders (*Hiraṇyakeśi Gṛhyasūtra* 1.7.25.1):

> May Viṣṇu make your womb ready. May Tvaṣṭṛ frame the shape.
> May Prajāpati pour forth; May Dhātṛ give you conception!
> Give conception, Sinīvālī. Give conception Sarasvatī.
> May the two Aśvins, wreathed with lotus, give conception to you!
> The embryo which the two Aśvins produce with their golden kindling,
> that embryo we call into your womb,
> that you may give birth to it after ten months.
> As the earth is pregnant with Agni [fire],
> as the heaven is pregnant with Indra [rain],
> as Vāyu [wind] is in the womb of the region directions, so I place an embryo into your womb.

OBSEQUIES AND MEMORIAL RITES: TRANSITION AND INCORPORATION INTO LIFE AFTER DEATH

The *saṃskāras* performed upon a Hindu during the various stages of his or her life, from the rite of insemination up to marriage, are known as *jāta saṃskāras*, sanctifications of the living, which prepare one to live a full and fruitful life in this world. *Mṛta saṃskāra* refers to *saṃskāras* of the dead which prepare one to negotiate life and the worlds after death. The death *saṃskāra* of *antyeṣṭi* and relevant memorial rites (*śrāddha*) are not usually treated in the same sections of ritual texts as *saṃskāras* for the living. Most often death and its related rites are expounded in sections dealing with purity (*śauca*) and impurity (*aśauca*) and rites of expiation (*prāyaścitta*).

For Hindus death rites constitute the "last sacrifice," *antyeṣṭi*. This final *saṃskāra* marking death is also known *antyakarma*, the final ritual or last rite. Hindu death rites involve the consignment of the deceased's body to the fire, from which the *saṃskāra* gets its other name, *śmaśāna* or cremation. Once again the fire acts as a witness and purifying agent, consecrating yet another transition in the life of a Hindu. Like Vedic initiation and marriage, the *antyeṣṭi saṃskāra* is a process involving a series of rites over several days. In preparation for the cremation, the body of the corpse is ritually washed (*abhiṣeka* or *abhiṣincana*) by members of the same sex, anointed, and wrapped in a new white shroud; the corpse of a male is shaved. The deceased is to be cremated as soon as possible after death. The chief mourner by tradition is the nearest male relative, preferably the eldest son, who leads the funeral procession from the home of the deceased to the cremation ground. The corpse is carried through the streets on a bier followed by friends and family. Sometimes the bier is accompanied by a cow, which in ancient times was sacrificed in order to accompany the deceased on his or her journey to the next world but which later came to be offered as a gift. Depending on local or family custom, women follow at the rear of the procession but very few of them accompany the corpse to the cremation grounds, a place typically associated with inauspiciousness and impurity.

The funeral pyre is built up and the grounds are sprinkled with sacred waters to drive away any evil or unsettled spirits (*bhūta* and *preta*) that may linger in the area. The body is placed on the funeral pyre, on a north/south axis, lined up toward the southern world of Yama, god of death. According to some authorities, all clothing and ornamentation are removed—shroud, sacred thread, jewelry—with the idea that a body should depart this world just as it came into this world. But there are many exceptions to this practice; for example, some families customarily place a coin in each of the seven openings in the head, while others place coins or jewels in the mouth of the deceased to help pay the way across the river of death. The chief mourner circles the fire three times before lighting the pyre with this prayer: "Agni, consume not this body to cinders, nor give it pain nor scatter about its skin or limbs, O Jātavedas, when the body is fairly burnt, convey the spirit to its ancestors" (*Ṛg Veda* 10.16.1). Oblations are offered to the fire, and the chief mourner cracks the skull of the deceased (or pours water over the skull after it has burst) to allow the soul to escape before the body is consumed. As the body is consecrated to the fire, a prayer is offered, such as this one derived from the *Atharva Veda* (18.2.7):

> May the organ of vision proceed to the sun.
> May the vital air merge in the atmosphere.
> May you proceed according to your virtuous deeds
> to either heaven or earth or the regions of the waters,
> whichever place is beneficial to you.

After the cremation, the chief mourner is shaved (head, beard, nails pared), dons new clothes, and observes a period of mourning during which he practices celibacy and other austerities for the next ten days, depending on the family's tradition. Close relatives of the deceased are affected by a period of ritual impurity following the death, which entails a period of social segregation as well as various restrictions in dress, diet, and interaction. Periods of ritual impurity may last from one to ten days, depending on the degree of one's relationship to the deceased. Age, class, gender, and marital status may influence not only the prescribed periods of mourning (or ritual pollution) but also the treatment of the corpse. For example, the *Manusmṛti* (5.67–70, see also 5.58–62) prescribes different obsequies for a deceased child depending on which postnatal *saṃskāra*s the child has undergone. Manu (*Manusmṛti* 5.72) also advises that the relatives of an unmarried girl endure ritual pollution for only three days rather than the usual ten.

Offerings of water to cool the dead after the cremation process are accompanied by *mantra*s. Water is also used to purify family relatives of the deceased who have become temporarily polluted by the death. Within three days of the cremation, the remaining bones and ashes are collected by the chief mourner and are either buried in an urn and commended to Mother Earth or are cast into the flowing waters of a river. Following this rite, the chief mourners undergo yet another purification rite with ablutions. Although cremation is the most widespread method of processing the body of the deceased, there is also a tradition of burial in Hindu communities. Burial is variously advised for infants, unmarried girls, and uninitiated boys, those who die of smallpox or other epidemics, and *saṃnyāsī*s (renunciants who have already renounced normal life and performed a ritual cremation as part of their transition to a life of renunciation). An alternative to burial is the ritual immersion of a corpse into a sacred river. Some sectarian groups such as the Liṅgāyatas choose to bury rather than cremate their dead. Many of the ceremonials surrounding death, such as preparation of the corpse and the memorial rites, remain the same whether the corpse is cremated or buried.

Śrāddha ceremonies, memorial rites performed in many different Hindu ritual contexts, honor and propitiate deceased ancestors. A special *śrāddha* rite, known as *sapiṇḍīkaraṇa*, is performed on the twelfth day after death, once the period of impurity has subsided. Another special *śrāddha* is performed a year later on the anniversary of the death. In preparation for the special *śrāddha*s, relatives take a ritual bath and dress in new clothes. The *śrāddha* rites are critical to the deceased soul's journey from bodiless spirit (*preta*) to ancestor (*pitṛ*). The offerings of rice balls (*piṇḍa*) and libations of water (*tarpaṇa*), offered both during the funerary *antyeṣṭi* rites and the memorial *śrāddha* ceremonies, help the soul of the dead to form an intermediate body (*bhogadeha*) so that it may cross over the river of death and join the ancestors. The *sapiṇḍīkaraṇa śrāddha* ceremony performed on the twelfth day completes the union of the newly deceased with his or her ancestors, and Brāhmaṇs are invited to be the vicarious recipients of the feasts of *śrāddha* foods offered to the deceased. Memorial rites are performed annually, but the *śrāddha* ceremony immediately following a death has special significance and purpose as it helps transform the newly deceased into a revered ancestor (*pitṛ*). Without these rites, a soul would wander aimlessly in the intermediate world, threatening the order and well being of the family. Here again we see how the ritual process of *saṃskāra*s not only signifies but actually accomplishes the transformation from one status to another.

In the funerary process, death and cremation separate the deceased from his or her relatives. The period of ritual impurity experienced by relatives is a liminal period that parallels the liminality of the deceased's soul, which is in the process of forming a new body as it moves through the spirit world. The *sapiṇḍīkaraṇa* memorial rites literally make (*karaṇa*) into an ancestor (*sapiṇḍa*) the spirit (*preta*) of the deceased, incorporating the soul of the deceased into its new realm in the world of the ancestors (*pitṛ*). Just as prenatal *saṃskāra*s abet the formation of a body in the womb of the mother and the later postnatal *saṃskāra*s work at incorporating this body into its new environment and community, so mortuary *saṃskāra*s contribute to the formation of an ethereal body and its subsequent incorporation into a new life after death. Both in life and in death, *saṃskāra*s sanctify the human body; they acknowledge the transformation of the body, taking account of its physical developments and natural bodily functions. Ideally a twice-born Hindu was expected to undergo all sixteen *saṃskāra*s, a process believed to make the body whole, perfect, and pure, and thus a fit offering for the final sacrifice.

SAṂSKĀRAS IN TRANSITION: THE PERFORMANCE OF SAṂSKĀRAS YESTERDAY AND TODAY

Hindu *saṃskāra*s are conventionally described in English reference works as "sacraments" or "rites of passage." "Rites of incorporation" may be a more appropriate and evocative label for *saṃskāra*s, if we consider both the Latin root and contemporary meanings of incorporation. The Latin verb *incorporare* means "to form into a body," and indeed these *saṃskāra*s, notably singled out as bodily *saṃskāra*s (*śarīra saṃskāra*), quite literally aid in the formation of the body, from the prenatal rite of *garbhādhāna*, which gives rise to an embryo, to the postmortem rite of *sapiṇḍīkaraṇa*, which aids in the transformation of the deceased from a food-body (*bhogadeha*) to an ancestor (*pitṛ*). In contemporary usage, incorporation signifies a process by which one thing becomes *united* with something already existing or by which someone is *admitted* to an organization. *Saṃskāra*s indeed serve to admit and unite individuals into an idealized corporate body, best represented by the cosmic human body in the *Puruṣasūkta*, a famous *Ṛg Veda* hymn (10.90) which describes the creation process, the evolution of society, and the natural duties of the different classes. *Saṃskāra*s incorporate individuals into an ideal culture of duties and responsibilities (*varṇāśramadharma*), traditionally governed by an organic ethos of interdependence. From a religious perspective, *saṃskāra*s constitute and sanctify the individual and corporate body simultaneously.

The early Brāhmaṇical Hindu tradition conceived of these rituals as compulsory, necessary for the development of the total person. Penalties for laxity in performance were prescribed for those who failed to undergo the full course of *saṃskāra*s. The decline in the number of *saṃskāra*s observed as well as changing attitudes toward their performance suggest that most Hindus in modern times do not feel obligated to undergo these *saṃskāra*s in order to fulfill religious or social goals, although many choose to do so.

The *saṃskāra* rites as prescribed in the ritual and classical texts of the Hindu tradition not only require a great technical expertise in their performance but also involve a significant outlay of goods and funds by the head of the household. Most *saṃskāra* rituals detailed in the texts entail knowledge of special *mantra*s and their correct pronunciation, oblations into the sacred fire, feasting of Brāhmaṇs and relatives, new clothes, and gift-giving. Nowadays few families maintain the traditional household fire around which these *saṃskāra* ceremonies were to be performed, and over time popular (*laukika*) family traditions and customs have come to replace many of the orthodox (*śāstrika*) Sanskritic rites, decreasing the need for and expense of priests with specialized ritual knowledge. As traditional education declines among Brāhmaṇ priests, so does the number of young men choosing to enter this hereditary profession. As a result of this trend, families increasingly rely on ritual expertise within the family, often in the hands of the women, or on popular ritual handbooks for the maintenance of life-cycle rituals. Ritual handbooks are readily available in the marketplace, providing procedural guidelines in vernacular languages for streamlined ritual formats as well as appropriate Sanskrit prayers, blessings, and *mantra*s for use in *saṃskāra*s. While many families still observe some form of temporary segregation due to the ritual pollution attending birth and death, this practice has also been greatly modified by many families to fit the economic and social realities of the contemporary work world. The traditional Hindu calendar (*pañcāṅga*) found in most Hindu homes usually contains an appendix that succinctly summarizes rules on ritual pollution due to births and deaths within a family.

Today few of the classical *saṃskāra*s are observed, and those that are still performed have been significantly modified. Of the few prenatal and postnatal *saṃskāra*s still celebrated today, most are performed in the context of the home without the formality of priests or *mantra*s, the fanfare limited to the immediate family. The more orthodox the family, the more orthodox the observance. The long period of traditional studentship initiated by *upanayana* is no longer observed, and *upanayana* now serves a symbolic function celebrating a child's coming of age and his increased social and religious responsibilities. However, for those increasingly few young men from Brāhmaṇ families who choose to carry on hereditary roles as *pujārīs* (priests) and *paṇḍitas*, a significant amount of traditional learning and training in ritual as well as the oral transmission of the Vedas is still required. For those who do not pursue the priestly occupation, minor *saṃskāras*, such as tonsure (*caula*) and introduction to the Vedas (*vedārambha*), are usually incorporated into the initiation of adolescents to their Vedic heritage, and increasingly *upanayana* itself is becoming a perfunctory rite within some communities, tacked on to the preliminaries of the marriage ceremonies. While most families spare no expense when it comes to marriage, the wedding *saṃskāra* itself has been economized into a more concise ritual format of a half-day, although some weddings with their related preliminaries and receptions span three days. *Maṅgala kāryālayas*, "halls of good fortune," have sprung up throughout urban centers in India and are rented out for auspicious functions, such as initiations, marriages, and sixty-first birthday celebrations. In the United States and Great Britain, *saṃskāras* are one of the many services provided by priests affiliated with the Hindu temples that serve growing communities of immigrant and second-generation South Asian families. Temple brochures list special occasion rituals, which largely include *pūjās* and *saṃskāras* and their respective tariffs, to be performed by priests either at the temple or in homes, depending on the wishes of the patron. Both in India and abroad, family tradition largely dictates which *saṃskāras* are celebrated and how, whereas family finances influence the degree and pomp of the celebration.

Significant stages in the life cycle continue to be marked in Hindu communities by social and ritual occasions, although the religious elements of these celebrations may be less obvious in some observances today. The religious acknowledgment of these stages incorporates the human cycle into the cosmic cycle, providing human life with a sense of purpose and destiny. Such occasions and ritual performances like *saṃskāras* express the Hindu tradition's acknowledgment of the natural and social development that is part of the human life cycle. There is still a strong sense that *saṃskāras*, like sacraments in the Roman Catholic tradition, prepare one to lead a moral and socially responsible life, as a Hindu fulfills his or her religious and social duties. This moral life, sanctified by *saṃskāras*, also leads one towards *mokṣa*, liberation, the ultimate goal articulated by many great Hindu teachers and philosophers. *Saṃskāras* serve to bring out one's fullest potential, as they refine, polish, transform, and perfect different dimensions of a human being. Like a photograph developing before one's eye, blurred splotches of color intensifying and transforming to define precise lines and features, so the development of human character unfolds during a lifetime, aided by *saṃskāras* which refine and purify individual traits and qualities, bringing out the best in an individual. As the *Parāśarasmṛti* so elegantly explains: "Just as a picture of myriad parts gradually becomes perceivable, in that manner, the state of Brāhmaṇ-ness [individual perfection] is brought out by *saṃskāras* when properly performed" (8.19).

CHAPTER SIXTEEN

VARṆA AND JĀTI

McKim Marriott

DEFINITIONS AND ASSUMPTIONS

The word "*varṇa*," which means "light" or "color" in the language of the *Ṛg Veda*, is used in later Vedic and subsequent discourse for each of four cosmogonic human types whose properties are attributed also to gods, animals, plants, and other things. *Jāti*, an equally early word meaning "birth" or "genus," is used for any set of beings supposed to cohere as a biological and/or social "community" (*samāja*)—a race, clan, region, occupation, religion, language, nation, gender, or *varṇa* (Kane 1930–62, 5.2: 1632–33); most often it designates one of the many, now thousands of marriage and kinship networks existing among South Asian families. The varied ways such networks have related to each other and to *varṇa* types over three millennia are summarized here from texts, histories, and twentieth-century observations, with special attention to indigenous categories and logics.[1]

Varṇa and *jāti* names evoke "particular coherences" (*svadharma*) or styles of life and thus suggest an English gloss of "class." But unlike social classes, which are attributed to human action, the style of a *jāti* is conventionally attributed to its original "natural substance" (*prakṛti*) as well as to the kinds of "action" (*karman*), more or less coherent with that origin, by which its members have since lived. A *jāti*'s, like a person's, substance is malleable and carries whatever "markings" (*saṃskāra*, *vāsanā*, *doṣa*, and the like) are inscribed in it through nutritive and other actions—personal, interpersonal, ancestral, and cosmic—starting before conception and continuing after death (M. Davis 1983: 81–107; Inden and Nicholas 1977: 36–66; Pandey 1996). Earlier markings are thought alterable by later actions, and alterations too are thought transmissible to associates and descendants (E. Daniel 1984: 9, 102; S. Daniel 1983; Lamb 2000: 30–37; Wadley and Derr 1989). The idea that acquired characteristics are heritable aligns Hindu thought with Chevalier de Lamarck rather than Charles Darwin and distinguishes it from purely genetic racism. The assumed vulnerability to change of most Hindu entities (M. Davis 1983: 45–80) and their capacity for mutual influence encourages diverse strategies—greater openness by those who would give their own or take some other's markings, attempted closure by those who would not, and alienation by those who are denied wanted markings from others or are rejected because of their own.

Since the nineteenth century, *jāti*s have been widely but mistakenly equated with theoretical "castes"—entities imagined from fragmentary, mostly priestly information to be uniform, strictly hereditary isolates assigned by divine fiat to certain fixed *varṇa* ranks. Such entities have been imagined as determining the occupations, political behavior, and religious beliefs of their members and as forbidding the exchange of food or making of marriages with others. The "rigid caste system" made up of a collection of such entities is not likely ever to have existed, although, as Ronald Inden (1990) and Nicholas Dirks (2001) point out, its prevalence has been asserted rhetorically by most of India's published critics—Christian missionaries (Forrester 1980), colonial officials like James Mill (1817), and Indian reformers such as Jawaharlal Nehru (1946)—and elaborated in armchair theorizing by Max Weber (1958), Louis Dumont (1970), and others. The supposition of such a caste system guided the gathering of official information and influenced social policy debates throughout the final century of colonial rule. It continues to preoccupy many recent descriptions of Hindu society.

As observed in the late twentieth century, however, most *jāti*s consist of dispersed, named networks of families, also larger, internally stratified clusters of such networks, that attempt to preserve or raise their collective natures by the ways they intermarry, interdine, and subsist. *Jāti*s may mark themselves with distinctive titles, genealogies, and *varṇa* styles and may maintain some specialized occupational skills, but unless concentrated in cities, may lack political organization. Members may collectively worship one deity, yet personally worship many others. They may be ready to give food to people of other *jāti*s who are willing to receive it but prefer to take food from and exchange wives only with others with whom they are either previously related or whom they consider to be similar to or better than themselves. *Jāti*s' so-called "rules of endogamy" (marriage within a network) vary if members differ about their *jāti*s' exact extent and may be qualified by preferences for females to marry hypergamously (into better networks). Such interactions, like the work members do for and have done for them by others, affect *jāti*, family, and personal substances and reputations, as exemplified by studies in Gujarat (Pocock 1972; Shah and Desai 1988), Bihar (C. H. Brown 1983), Tamilnadu (Dumont 1986: 145–69), and elsewhere (Karve 1968: 16–49; Silverberg 1968).

People of Hindu culture commonly evaluate the natures and actions of *jāti*s, persons, and other entities for their appropriateness or "*dharma*," a term that is conceivable as a comprehensive moral and cosmic order and is thus often glossed as "law" or "religion." However, since *dharma* judgments are made from diverse perspectives rather than one, concern complementarities rather than uniformity, and attend to practice and substance rather than faith, "*dharma*" is glossed herein as moral "coherence"—a contextually variable value (Ramanujan 1989).

VEDIC LOGICS

Differences are emphasized from the beginning. Before the first millennium BCE, Vedic recitations of knowledge "heard (from the gods)" (*śruti*) by priestly "seers" (*ṛṣi*) attribute inherent "brightness" (*tejas*) to their own "noble" (*ārya*) people and "darkness" (*tamas*) to their non-Āryan "enemies" or "slaves" (*dāsa, dasyu*). Within Āryan society the earliest recitations name two elite types—those of the "priest" (Brāhmaṇ) and the "ruler" (Rājanya)—plus a nonelite comprising the Āryan commoners or "householders" (Vaiśya). Later these three types are called "*varṇa*s" and the ruling type "protector" (Kṣatriya). If instructed and vested with their distinctive *varṇa* threads by priests, the young males of all three are declared "twice-born" (*dvija*) and are charged with the powers and duties respectively called "knowledge" (*brahman*), "protection" (*kṣatra*), and "productivity" (*viś*) (derived from a word for "house"). Named in the Vedas but not explicitly classified in any of the three types are numerous other occupational *jāti*s—bards, chariot-makers, ironsmiths, potters, barbers, medicine men, tanners, and so on.

Twice-born Āryans may participate in the Vedic sacrifice and enjoy its fruits, which include dominance over enemies and immortality for their souls. Their hymns represent them as subsisting on herding, hunting, and predatory warfare in which each Āryan *varṇa* "feeds" itself upon the next or all three feed upon the non-Āryan peoples whom they conquer (B. Smith 1994: 46–48). Added to Āryan society as it expands is a fourth, initially peripheral "servant" (Śūdra) *varṇa*, consisting of people who work for the twice-born but are excluded from Vedic learning and the sacrifice (Kane 1930–62, 2.1: 25–54).

In "priestly manuals" (Brāhmaṇas) and "teaching texts" (Upaniṣads) from the early first millennium BCE, priests represent themselves as able to control the universe and manipulate people of the other *varṇa*s through the sacrifice by metonymic gestures, some of them violent. Ordered lists in the sacrificial texts link the *varṇa*s with growing numbers of cosmic concepts: Agni, god of the heaven-reaching sacrificial fire, is allied with the priestly *varṇa* in its functions; Indra, the divine king, is allied with the *varṇa* of rulers; and Prajāpati, the god of reproduction, among others, is allied with the commoner *varṇa*. Other lists link the *varṇa*s with celestial bodies, layers of the cosmos, cardinal directions, elements, seasons, times of day, sacrificial personnel and equipment, kinds of texts, utterances, hymns, meters, gestures, the species and ages of animals, and degrees of virility (B. Smith 1994: 27–82). Although the contents of these lists vary in later centuries, thinking in triads and the making of such metonymic "homologies" (*bandhu*) are logics that continue strongly in later Hindu discourse (B. Smith 1994: 314–22).

Extensive cosmic analogies develop similarly in classical Chinese civilization, as represented by speculation based on the I Ching (Ronan 1978: 127–90). Linkages like the Vedic ones between human and environmental features have been called "humoral" in classical Greece and the medieval West, while alliances between kinship categories and natural species in many nonliterate societies have been called "totemic" (Lévi-Strauss 1963). In the terms of C. S. Peirce (1934: 73), Vedic and later homologies are "indexical" to the extent that they are understood as sharings of substantial properties or components rather than as mere poetic fancies.

Cohesive, competing, and ranked relationships are described as occurring among persons of different *varṇa* style through their transactions around the sacrifice. Libations of the legendary *soma* juice are described as being drunk communally, or first by priests, then by other sacrificers (Wasson 1968), or by both, possibly in ludic combat. The remains of oblations to the gods are bestowed on loved ones as favors or are forced upon guests as defeated rivals of the sacrificing host. Each transaction is construed as transforming the participants' natures and relationships—uniting givers and takers, or reconstituting the givers as winners or auspicious, the takers as losers and burdened with evil, or vice versa (Heesterman 1985). Constructing moral order through prestations is a continuing social process, explicit in the texts and rituals of all South Asians.

In late Vedic and classical texts, priests claim that they can destroy evils in sacrificial fires developed within themselves; they end, thereby, the agonistic transfers among the twice-born that had previously been at issue in many *soma* sacrifices, J. C. Heesterman notes. Yet transfers not only to priests but also to gods, spirits, wife-taking affines, and persons of other *jāti*s specialized in the disposal of evils are reported as continuing at births, marriages, funerals, harvests, elections, and otherwise in twentieth-century India (Mines 1997: 179–82; Parry 1994: 75–81; Raheja 1988: 68–92).

In late Vedic texts, the *varṇa*s are further related and ranked by their greater or lesser scope. The priestly authors declare their own *varṇa* to embrace the universe as defined either by the earth and all that it generates or by all that the sky surrounds. They assign to the ruling *varṇa* control of the stormy air or the earthly human domains and populations for which the rulers offer sacrifice. To commoners they ascribe the myriad denizens of the sky or the numerous animals, crops, and other goods produced in their domestic sphere, but to servants they ascribe just their houses and persons (B. Smith 1994: 133–36). Such rankings by inclusion occur in taxonomies and bureaucracies throughout the world, although the domains ascribed to the *varṇa*s are peculiar to the late Vedic social cosmology.

Debated are speculations as to whether the early "color" meaning of *varṇa* is pejorative, descriptive of biological differences, and/or arbitrary; how the *varṇa* styles became attached to *jāti* collectivities from what seem initially to have been personal roles (Kane 1930–62, 2.1: 25–49); whether thinking in threes, a general Indo-European trait, preceded (Dumézil 1958) or followed (Durkheim and Mauss 1963; Gonda 1976) the Vedic institution of *varṇa*s; and whether the Vedic *varṇa*s' cosmic homologies are chaotic or systematic (B. Smith 1994: 13–19).

In the much-cited "sacrifice of the cosmic man" (*Puruṣasūkta*) hymn near the end of the *Ṛg Veda* (at 10.90), the four types later called *varṇa*s are depicted as metonymic products of a primordial action by the gods: they emerge, along with gods, animals, planets, elements, and the seasons, from the severed higher and lower parts of the victim, a body of universal scope. The Brāhmaṇ emerges from the body's mouth, the Rājanya from its arms, the Vaiśya from its thighs, and the Śūdra from its feet. Elsewhere in priestly literature all the *varṇa*s are said to have been emitted by the original divinity or to have been successively generated by the first-emitted of them—the Brāhmaṇ—which is itself reckoned as divine (B. Smith 1994: 89). In each of these scenarios, as in the predatory feedings favored earlier, the four *varṇa*s and sometimes other entities are depicted as connected with divinity by asymmetric movements of bodily or body-nourishing "matter" (*dravya*). All *varṇa*s are thus said to participate, if only sequentially, passively, or indirectly, in divinity and in a single ranked, organic order.

In the sixth century BCE, a time of heterodoxies, Gautama Buddha and Vardhamāna Mahāvīra, both born rulers and thus potential sponsors of collective "coherence-making" (*dharmakārya*) or "ritual" for their domains, refuse to participate in the Vedic sacrifices. Mahāvīra and his Jainist followers recoil from the sacrifices' extravagant violence against animals, while the Buddha declares all Vedic ritual irrelevant to the root cause of human suffering, which he sees as worldly attachment. Jainism and Buddhism are two among the several movements led by "ascetics" (*śrāvaka* or *śramaṇa*) who abandon attachments to their elite households in favor of wandering, meditating, and (in later centuries) monastic living. Both Buddhists and Jainists develop alternative forms of coherence: they devise rituals without animal sacrifice and openly recruit celibate males to perform learning, teaching, and gift-taking functions like those provided by noncelibate Vedic priests. For myths of the *varṇas*' emergence from divinity the Buddhists substitute myths of social contract between rulers and others, but while they and the Jainists ignore Vedic gods and cosmogonies, the texts of both continue to describe people by their *varṇa* styles. The Jainists revalue people by their avoidance of violence and by their souls' separation from bondage to substance, while Buddhists often list rulers ahead of priests and in their judicial doctrines evaluate personal conduct without regard to *varṇa* claims (Basham 1954: 82, 141, 246; Jaini 1979: 134–85, 241–73).

Two or three centuries later a partial overriding of *varṇa* distinctions is offered to Hindus of Vedic tradition, too, in the *Bhagavad Gītā*, where at 9.32 Lord Kṛṣṇa, a supreme deity, invites direct access to himself by both females and males of all *varṇas* without mediation by the Vedic sacrifice or Brāhmaṇ priests. His offer may have been stimulated by Buddhist, Jainist, and other non-Vedic competition and encourages the "devotional" (*bhakti*) movements, especially those of the theistic, northern variety that grow and flourish thereafter, gradually capturing adherents from the non-Vedic systems.

CLASSICAL CODIFICATIONS

Transitional for peoples of Vedic culture to the agrarian, classical phases of their civilization early in the first millennium CE are attempts, reflected in debates within the princely *Mahābhārata* epic and elsewhere, to collect and reconcile various ideas on social order. While the texts of Jainists, Buddhists, and other non-Vedic systems stress personal action and intention, the conservative priestly "Manu Memorandum" (*Manusmṛti*), also called the "Manu Group's Coherence Book" (*Mānavadharmaśāstra*), foregrounds substantial distinctions among the *varṇas*. Assembled between about 200 BCE and 200 CE from a range of views held by priests of the Vedic tradition, it is the largest and most authoritative of such social "compilations" (*saṃhitā*) (Doniger 1991). Its opening statement regarding the *varṇas* may be rendered as follows:

> For Brāhmaṇs (the lord) ordained teaching and learning (the Veda), sacrificing for themselves and sacrificing for others, giving gifts and receiving gifts. For a Kṣatriya, protecting his subjects, giving gifts, having sacrifices performed, learning, and remaining unattached to sensory objects. For a Vaiśya, protecting his animals, giving gifts, having sacrifices performed, learning, trading, lending money, and farming the land. For a Śūdra he ordained only one activity—serving the other *varṇas* without resentment.
>
> (*Manusmṛti* 1.88–91)

Presuming familiarity with *Ṛg Veda* 10.90, Manu (*Manusmṛti* 1.31) further urges acting in consonance with the unilinear order of the *varṇas*' first emergence as described there. It treats the priority of the priestly and ruling *varṇas* as proving their superiority and the posteriority of the others as proving their relative inferiority. In contrast with the predatory attitudes voiced in the earlier Vedas, however, it has the *varṇas* relating usefully to each other.

Although Manu (*Manusmṛti* 6.91–92, 10.63) lists virtues, such as self-control and truthfulness, as incumbent on all people, it discriminates strongly when estimating their incidence in the different *varṇas*. Truths affirmed by Brāhmaṇ priests are to be credited more than those affirmed by others (*Manusmṛti* 8.73, 12.108–15), and "punishment" (*daṇḍa*) for delicts, often physical, is to be graded from lightest for priests to heaviest for servants (4.169, 8.124, 8.267–69, 8.276, 8.279–81, 8.337–38, 8.374–85). The afterlife envisioned by Manu (2.201, 12.39–50) is even more stratified: following divine punishment or reward, souls must await rebirth in wombs of nine suitable ranks, each subdivided into three further grades that mingle gods, animals, and human *varṇa*s.

The appropriateness of earthly conduct is to be judged by Veda-knowing elites (*Manusmṛti* 2.6–12) whose decisions seem likely to reinforce the privileges that they claim for themselves. It is so for example with wealth: a priest may seize any property he wishes from a servant (*Manusmṛti* 8.417). However, priests' concerns with their relative standings in wealth or influence ("advantage-disadvantage" [*artha-anartha*]) are treated as secondary to their special concern with "coherence-incoherence" (*dharma-adharma*) (*Manusmṛti* 4.3, 4.33, 12.38)—a conceptually distinct scale in knowledge of which members of their own *varṇa* potentially excel.

While Brāhmaṇs may not generally expect to excel on the scale of advantage, they do claim to stand first on two other scales—those of cosmic precedence and moral coherence, which they see as parallel. However, since they control divine knowledge that is indispensable to rulers and since rulers control most advantages, these two *varṇa*s are expected by Manu to agree and to make social reality out of a partial correlation also between advantage and coherence. The text accordingly advises nonelites to accept relatively marginal and less advantageous placements that match the less coherent natures imputed to them by the elites. Popular uses of cover terms like "high" and "low" in the twentieth century continue to conflate these several scales.

Persons of the putatively more coherent ruling and priestly *varṇa*s are assumed to need less time to heal the social ruptures of birth and death (*Manusmṛti* 5.83; Mines 1989) as well as other disasters. As innate embodiments of cosmic coherence, persons of the priestly *varṇa* are allowed the most flexibility in ways to survive incoherent "emergency" (*āpad*) conditions such as famine: unlike people of other *varṇa*s, they may eat anything or earn by any means without corrupting their natures (*Manusmṛti* 10.101–17). Made into centers of coherence for their kingdoms by extensive priestly affusions (Inden 1978), kings need observe no breaks for mourning in their capacities to reign (*Manusmṛti* 5.93–94).

Manu also prescribes differences in "attachment-nonattachment" (*kāma-niṣkāma*), a concern that rearranges the *varṇa*s (also the life "stages" [*āśrama*]) along a scale that is orthogonal to both of the other scales. It urges priests, students, and servants to minimize their outer attachments by practicing a meatless diet, fasting, and reciting—techniques employed to "(internalize) heat" (*tapasyā*). For servants this urging is consistent with the advice that they content themselves with whatever they receive from their masters. For rulers, commoners, and married householders (who are the principal patrons of priests), however, Manu urges disciplined attachment to their productive, often externally heating tasks.

Manu lists the above "trio" (*trivarga*) of "principal human concerns" (*puruṣārtha*) in an order of priestly preference, with coherence first, advantage next, and attachment last. (It also mentions a fourth and ultimate concern not discussed further here—obtaining total "freedom" or "release" [*mokṣa*] from engagement with this world—a goal available only to twice-born ascetics [*Manusmṛti* 2.244, 6.34–37] and ideally sought by all Buddhists and Jainists [see Babb 1996].) Rather than assigning each concern to a different *varṇa*, however, Manu (*Manusmṛti* 2.2–5, 2.224) treats all concerns as incumbent on all persons, but variously according to their circumstances. A king for example should consider all three concerns, even though they may seem mutually conflicting (*Manusmṛti* 7.151–52), and a priest may properly overrule even coherence when the other two concerns are especially pressing (4.176). Often stated as three pairs of contraries (as "coherence–incoherence" and so on), the three moral concerns constitute an indivisible set of nonparallel scales to be artfully combined (Malamoud 1981).

Typically, however, the *varṇa*s are assumed to differ innately in their default combinations of concerns, and these should guide them, for example, to appropriately different ways for a man to get a wife—as a prize, payment, or gift, with dowry, or by purchase, mutual choice, capture, or stealth (*Manusmṛti* 3.20–44). The first four ways (all nonattached, advantageous, and coherent) are advised for the Brāhmaṇ *varṇa*, while stealth, a cold, low, messy (i.e. a nonattached, disadvantageous, incoherent) way is recommended only for the one *varṇa* presumed to embody those traits—the Śūdra. Mutual choice (an attached and coherent way) is approved for others, while capture, dowry, or purchase (which allow display of power and wealth) are declared suitable for rulers, who are typically attached as well as advantaged and coherent. By calculations especially involving two concerns—disadvantage and incoherence—the offspring of matings between persons of different *varṇa* are assigned by Manu to diverse *jāti*s (see pp. 378–79).

Recent scholars model classical India by variously applying European concepts and comparisons, and few go beyond priestly texts. Thus Dumont (1970: 33–91) following Marcel Mauss (1947: 9–10) sees Hindus as wholists, but following Émile Durkheim (1947) also as split between sacred and profane, and following Claude Lévi-Strauss (1963) as also splitting cultural and natural domains; he posits further a church-like "hierarchy" linking priests with untouchables by an "ideology" (Marx 1948) or "value system" (Parsons 1949) whose ideal of "purity" (translated as "freedom from the organic") "encompasses" (surrounds but does not penetrate) a "middle" domain where other *jāti*s compete "shame-facedly" for secular "power" (Weber 1946). Faulting Dumont for reifying religion and for crediting archaic priestly claims of hegemony that gained plausibility only after British administration had deprived the native rulers of their powers to decide on *jāti* ranks, Dirks (2001) holds all structures to be "political" in origin.

Seeking indigenous formulations and observing that "organic," "political," and other concerns are aspects of all Hindu interactions, McKim Marriott (1968, 1976, 1989), Gloria Raheja (1988), and others reject the unilinear postulations and dualities of all the above-mentioned models. Recognizing the several Hindu scales that invite social diversity, they also obviate Dumont's effort to combine dualities with holism by means of the ambiguous term "encompassment." Other scholars offering two- or three-dimensional models are Richard Burghart (1978), Veena Das (1977), and J. P. S. Uberoi (1996), who relate *varṇa*s and *jāti*s through the contrasting roles of priest, king, ascetic, and householder.

INDIGENOUS ANALYTICS: SĀṂKHYA

By systematizing ancient categories and logics that are still in everyday use, the early classical, nonpriestly Hindu philosophic tradition called "Enumeration" (Sāṃkhya) (Larson 1987) affords fuller, more analytic understandings of *varṇa*s and *jāti*s than are available in either priestly writings alone or in the European social sciences. Some of

Sāṃkhya's components resemble the humors and elements of early Greek and Chinese sciences but are configured differently. Its terms often appear in the *Manusmṛti*, in the *Mahābhārata*, in many "ancient (tales)" (Purāṇas), in classical Hindu "biology" (Āyurveda), in Jainist cosmology, and in the common food, health, and social practices of both Hindus and Buddhists (Kane 1930–62, 5.2: 1352–84). Although they or their equivalents still permeate popular discourse in South Asia (as exemplified by M. Davis 1983; Khare 1976b; Kurin 1981), they have yet to be used by scholars to analyze the topics addressed here.

Adding to Manu's trio of moral concerns, Sāṃkhya thinking elaborates on four sets of components that are fundamental to Hindu ideas of physics, biology, and human social and pscyhological life—the five "gross elements" (*mahābhūta*), the five "impulses" (*indriya*), the three "humors" (*doṣa*), and the three "strands" (*guṇa*). Apart from Sāṃkhya's "pure consciousness" (*puruṣa*), which like *ātman* and *mokṣa* has no substantial properties, everything else in its dual universe, including the subtle substance of human minds, is linked indexically with the elements ether (sky), air, fire, water, and earth combined in various proportions. Such a "reductive materialism" (Larson 1987: 76–77) approximates the common sense of South Asia's peasants, who know those elements firsthand.

Sāṃkhya does not merely list its components but also correlates and always combines them. It correlates the five elements with the five sensory-motor impulses—ether with sound, hearing, and speaking; air with touch, feeling, and grasping; fire with light, heat, seeing, and walking; water with flavor, tasting, and excreting; and earth with place, smelling, and coupling (Larson 1987). From the inner trio of the elements (air, fire, and water), it derives the "three humors" (*tridoṣa*) called "wind" (*vāta*), "bile" (*pitta*), and "phlegm" (*kapha*)—principal terms of popular dietary, medical, seasonal, and political discourse. Not explicitly derived from the elements, humors, or moral concerns, but popularly treated as homologous with them is the subtle set of Āyurvedic mental components called the "three strands" (*triguṇa*)—"goodness" (*sattva*), "passion" (*rajas*), and "darkness" (*tamas*)—prime constituents and causes of human behavior as revealed by Lord Kṛṣṇa in the *Bhagavad Gītā* (14, 17–18) and employed widely elsewhere.

Using any of these triadic sets assumes that each of its components varies independently between "more" and "less" (*pāra-apāra*) (*Caraka Saṃhitā*, *Sūtrasthānam* 1.49; *Bhagavad Gītā* 14.10). Each set can thus be visualized as an inseparable group of variables or scales intersecting orthogonally in a three-dimensional space (as in Figure 16.1). At each point in such a space the three components combine in different proportions, necessarily creating diversity.

Since the several sets of components are conceived as homologous—mutually constitutive and formally congruent (thus overlapped in Figure 16.1)—inferences can be made from one set to another. For example, a human entity showing itself to be morally "pure" or *śuddha* (nonattached, advantaged, and coherent in Manu's terms) can be presumed also to be pure biologically (cool, refined, and stable) and mentally (dispassionate, truthful, and enlightened) (*Caraka Saṃhitā*, *Sūtrasthānam* 7.39–40, *Śarīrasthānam* 4.34–37). Furthermore, this entity should find gold, honey, and *ghī* congenial, since such things are understood to be pure physically. Should any such presumption prove incorrect, explanation must be sought in the componential analysis.

Orthogonal to the scale of "pure–impure" (*śuddha-aśuddha*), different combinations of the same components generate other common Hindu social variables, such as "great-small" (*mahā-hīna*), "subtle-gross" (*sūkṣma-sthūla*), and "violent–nonviolent" (*hiṃsrā-ahiṃsrā*), contrary qualities shown at the eight corners of Figure 16.1. The humors and elements combine variously to generate in six of those corners the "flavors" (*rasa*) of both foods and the seasons—sweet, salty, bitter, sour, astringent, and pungent (*Caraka Saṃhitā, Sūtrasthānam* 1.64–66, 6.5–48). A similar set of eight personal "emotions" (*bhāva*) paired with a set of sentimental "essences" (*rasa*)—pleasure, pity, pride, wonder, mirth, anger, fear, and disgust, later also tranquility—can be seen as differently combining the major moral concerns (*Nāṭyaśāstra* 6–7). These flavors and emotions correlate with each other and with the above-mentioned social variables—for example, sourness with anger and violence and sweetness with purity. Further combinations of the same components, including mixtures of the contraries, are theoretically countenanced and perceived in everyday practice as well as in literary discourse.

COMPONENTS OF THE VARṆAS

The mutually corresponding elements, humors, strands, and moral concerns are collated here under five headings and are written together on those sides of the cube in Figure 16.1 where they are most strongly present. A component's contrary, if textually named, is written on the cube's opposite side, where written or not, the same component should be understood to be weakly present. The eight major social qualities shown at the cube's corners are commonly attributed to the *varṇa*s, *jāti*s, and persons whose components and social relations are estimated to put them at those loci.

Sky, ether, heaven, space

"Sky" (*ākāśa*), an invisible element distinct from but often conflated with air, may be understood also as "empty space," "ether" (the medium of sound), and "heaven." It has no homologue among the strands, humors, or moral concerns but fills the background, also the channels among, pores through, and cavities within all entities. Being pervasive and extensive, it allows all the other elements to operate, particularly permitting movements everywhere of human and divine spirits and other "(ethereal) energies" (*śakti*). Whoever speaks or hears deals with this element, but adepts in the gods' own Sanskrit language claim greater skill in transacting with heaven. Pronouncements by ether's adepts—blessings for coherence, curses for the contrary—are thought to be particularly potent. Conceived in the twentieth century as the medium for electronics, ether began to attract many new masters, many of them from Brāhmaṇ *jāti*s, following their priestly antecedents.

Air, wind, darkness, and (in)coherence

These are the components that cause such transformative changes (flux, inertia, or entropy) as celestial movements bring to the seasons, breathing brings to the body, birth and death bring to life, night brings to day, and peripheral beings—gods, spirits, or other alien, subtle, violent, or impure persons—may bring to social situations. Their intransitive actions tend to reverse, negate, divide, or distance whatever they encounter. The positive contraries of these components—calm, illumination, and coherence—are cultivated by gross and nonviolent nonelites as well as by elite priests and rulers in the orderly centers where their interests reside. A similar opposition between the order established by cultivators and the disorder of the jungle has long been a prime axis of distinctions among *jāti*s, especially in Tamil and other southern areas (Pfaffenberger 1982).

The central elites typically express anaerobic, windless, bright, and coherent attitudes—satisfaction with their purity, pride in their greatness, continuity with their ancestry, and pity for the weaker, less pure people among whom they attempt to enforce tranquility, deference, and humility. Controlling their own food, regularizing their actions, and keeping in touch with each other help elites to limit disruptive change, as does their gifting of troubles to priests and others (Raheja 1988). Priests receiving such troubles counteract them by fasting, repeating *mantra*s, and "(controlled) breathing" (*prāṇāyāma*)—practices intended to replace air's incoherences with the emptiness of ether—while nonpriests may hand troubles along to affines.

The subtitled components are likely to figure largely in the lives of servant *jāti*s that deal with loose, messy materials. Scavengers are "the worst of men" according to Manu (*Manusmṛti* 10.12) because, like twentieth-century untouchables, they not only live on trash but also are reputed to descend from mismatched parents. Other experts in incoherence include Vedic "hunters" (*niṣāda*) and twentieth-century peripatetic "tribals" who deal in wild, distant things and possibly in witchcraft (Selwyn 1981), also barber and washerman *jāti*s who are charged with removing loose human substance domestically.

Alcohol, being produced by fermentation and producing incoherent human action, is reputed to be Śūdras' drug of choice, as darkness is their favored time, sleep their refuge. At a superior altitude, the influential "subtle" professions (discussed next as a Brāhmaṇ variant) exemplify a positive mastery of incoherence.

Fire, bile, attachment, and passion

These components with their contraries constitute a thermal variable running laterally throughout Hindu life, indexing any entity's relative openness (heat) or closure (coolness) and thus its greater or lesser readiness to exchange properties (Kurin 1981; McGilvray 1998; Marriott 1976; Moreno and Marriott 1989). Temperature thus differentiates the *jāti*s (or persons) of rulers and ascetics, locals and immigrants, carnivores and vegetarians (Hiebert 1971: 54–62; Mayer 1960: 33–60; Srinivas 1955: 19–26). It also distinguishes between entities of the "impure" and "small" and "violent" and "subtle" types shown at the corners of Figure 16.2 (and discussed as "Varṇa Variants" later). The same components also index larger and smaller group size.

Relatively strong in expansive, hot components are *jāti*s of the ruling style, which tend to develop large populations. These *jāti*s' more open, nonreflexive natures, and their efforts to control, protect, and punish others, move them toward intense interactions with allies and rivals. As warriors, commanders, employers of many servants, enjoyers, and providers of salty food, and often eaters of wild or domestic meat, they are dealers in human and animal flesh as well as creators of social friction. They thrive not by reflecting on principles, as suits priests, but on vigorous, impulsive action (*Bhagavad Gītā* 18.20–21, 18.41–42). Their openness and heat favor friendship and generosity but also stimulate greed, lust, and anger (*Manusmṛti* 4.185)—external attachments and deployments of energy that Manu (1.89, 7.221) seems to recognize as inevitable for warm-blooded rulers but would restrain.

Brāhmaṇs' classically ordained tasks of learning and teaching require them to minimize their fire component, to restrict inputs and outputs, to seek auricular and visual rather than actional experience, and to store up energy rather than expending it kinetically. To cool attachments and to incinerate both sins they have committed and faults received from others, Manu (*Manusmṛti* 6.69–72, 11.234–47) advises everyone, but especially priests, to practice heat-internalizing austerities. Although priests also continue performing fire sacrifices in the twentieth century, their aggressive alliance with the Vedic fire-god Agni fades from its former textual prominence (Heesterman 1985).

The sweet, vegetable diets classically urged for priests and ascetics, which contrast with the regimes of extravert rulers, reinforce the thermal differences appropriate to these two *varṇas*. In maintaining their outer cool, priests tend to keep their *jāti*s small and make less expansive alliances, both prandial and marital. Their characteristic attitude of "pity" (*karuṇā*) for others is paralleled by their preference for colorless, delicately flavored, gently ripened foods and for white clothing (*Manusmṛti* 4.35)—features that contrast with the fiery, engaged, hyper-"male" (*vīra*) attitude represented by rulers' preferences for red and for elaborately cooked feasts.

Nonelite *jāti*s may differ on the same lateral dimension by moving in either thermal direction in complex ways: commoners may act with more passion but work alone in cooler places with closed substances like grain, metals, or money; servants may work less diligently in an outwardly cooler manner but do so in groups, in hot fields, interacting with animals and for more exposed rewards like cooked food or reciprocal labor. Cool Vaiśya *jāti*s, especially in urban areas, are famed for their small population sizes and close-knit structures; Śūdra *jāti*s, especially those in the hot work of rural labor, can on the other hand be large in numbers and diffusely organized (Shah and Desai 1988).

The vegetarianism of some Brāhmaṇ *jāti*s and the trend toward it in the sects favored by a wide range of aspiring commoner *jāti*s suggest a correlation between cool regimes and high rank (Srinivas 1955). But this correlation is probably low in the general population, for the warmer, carnivorous, ruling style remains common, especially among established agriculturists: the men of an estimated half of twentieth-century Hindu families (including those of several Brāhmaṇ *jāti*s) favor the eating of fish, chicken, or mutton (Marriott 1976; Shah and Desai 1988: 62), even if they cannot often afford it. Not fire and the other thermal components, nor the wind components as discussed here, but the set of components headed by water best distinguish differences of rank.

Water, phlegm, goodness, and advantage[2]

Gravitating as fluids or rising like vapors, these components readily index asymmetric movements between more and less valued entities. Movements between sky and earth, high and low, upstream and down, wet and dry, source and sink are essential to life and seen continually in speaking and hearing, giving and receiving, feeding and being fed, teaching and learning, marking and being marked. Upward movements of fluid from root to branch to flower may also be used to represent ancestry (Rossi 1998: 198–201) or sacrifice, although temporal sequences between before and after, past and future, and senior and junior are more often conceived as descending lines.

By assiduous bathings-away of lowness and by marking their progeny with divine learning, people of Brāhmaṇ *varṇa* support their claim to excel all others. Their *varṇa* also rises by teaching members of the other *varṇa*s and by sending the others' sacrifices to the gods that control the higher sources of water. As Brāhmaṇs rank high, so is "mind" (*sattva*) thought to reside high in the body, as are semen, the humor phlegm, and other "unctuous" (*snigdha*) substances (*Caraka Saṃhitā*, *Sūtrasthānam* 20.8). The influences of all these can be thought of as moving, much as do milk, food, oil, and love from parent to child, marking and ranking all those from and to whom the benefits descend (Inden and Nicholas 1977: 30–31, 87). Brāhmaṇs are said to thrive on mountains or deltas where water is sweet and plentiful (E. Daniel 1984: 85–86) and to prefer a relatively expensive sweet, white, and fluid diet. Manu's assignment of the duty of gift-receiving—preferably gifts of cows (*Manusmṛti* 2.246, 3.29, 3.53, 3.95)—exclusively to Brāhmaṇs (1.88) encourages a beneficent lifestyle close to, if not necessarily so affluent, as that of rulers.

Aided by their deep vertical lineages and numerous followers, rulers collect tribute and consequently have much to give. They are expected to bestow benefits upon their priests and servants and to provide water and food to their supporters and to the needy. If they distribute their gains generously, their goodness may be celebrated by their bards and subjects. They become experts in asymmetry through making such distributions as well as through commanding and punishing.

The commoner *varṇa* is enjoined in Manu to be the producer of food and livestock and the provisioner of other goods—superior gifts for priests, tribute to rulers, sustenance for servants, and a surplus to lend or exchange for profit. With assets thus usually in flux, however, a Vaiśya *jāti*'s net advantages are likely to be uncertain—a cause for both close calculation and flexibility in its strivings. Conventionally represented by the colors yellow or brown, it may be expected to feed variously on a wet and flavorful or on a dry diet, as its commercial fortunes vary.

Servants are subordinated to the twice-born *varṇa*s by receiving commands and benefits while being able to offer up only their labor—a lesser good—in exchange. Working on less advantageous lands, they are typically eating dry, pungent, or astringent foods, and represented by the color black, Śūdras are at the receiving end of social asymmetries. Vertical relations are generally less developed within each Śūdra *jāti*, while distances are more strongly kept between different Śūdra *jāti*s (Shah and Desai 1988), consistent with their supposedly greater wind or darkness components.

Earth, place

Earth is the locative, cumulative, and containing element that facilitates the other four components' combinations into viable entities. As in the common trope of the womb as the field needed by the male seed, earth provides places for reproduction and growth. In the figures the cubic outlines represent such places and the entities that develop in them.

People generally exchange qualities with the earth and houses where they reside (E. Daniel 1984: 61–104), but those absorbing more of the earth component should have narrower scope and outlook, becoming less pure, more odorous, and less sensitive to odors and more capable of stable, engrossing, womb-like reproductive functions. Agricultural workers—usually commoners and servants by classical theory—are thus more subject to control by local elites. They may also be seen as inherently fertile, participating as they do in the often low and dirty but "auspicious" (*śubha*) places where they raise crops and animals.

Less earth in an entity's nature favors a broader outlook, greater purity, more sensitivity to odors, distaste for root crops, and a subtler (that is, male) role in sexual reproduction. People of the Brāhmaṇ *varṇa* evince all these effects, as they are the most widely distributed, the principal users of perfume and incense, the inseminators in ritual (E. Daniel 1984: 117–26; Marglin 1981).

The wanderings of renouncers and the journeys of pilgrims to remote shrines are ways to loosen bonds to particular loci (A. Gold 1988: 262–98); processions to the farthest lands or anointment with tokens of all the world's soils may similarly raise kings to a transcendent, Brāhmaṇ-like status—that of earth's god-like husband (Inden 1978: 43–44).

VARṆA VARIANTS

Since the sets of components outlined here have been in continual use over the past two millennia, various past ratings of the *varṇa*s can be compared with each other and with twentieth-century ratings, as in Figure 16.2. Used for comparisons here is the set of three strands—goodness, passion, and darkness—and the strands' popular, regional homologues.

Not shown in Figure 16.2 but adding to its set of *varṇa*s are four other, *varṇa*-like types whose qualities are logical extensions of the same variables into the unfilled corners of the Sāṃkhya paradigm (Figure 16.1). Although lacking standard names, these additional types are populated with kinds of people who are already well known from learned and popular texts—people who seem mostly to have been either elites moving competitively toward less coherence (priests toward greater subtlety and rulers toward violence) or nonelites moving toward more coherence (Vaiśyas toward nonviolence and Śūdras toward the gross style). Along with the other moves with and among the *varṇa*s (as sketched below), the moves of people toward these spaces are likely to have generated many new *jāti*s.

Brāhmaṇs: pure and subtle

Rated by the three *guṇa* strands, the Brāhmaṇ *varṇa* (B) is unique: according to all the six sources cited in Figure 16.2, it is the sole *varṇa* that is high in goodness, minimally passionate, and (being enlightened by knowledge) minimally afflicted by darkness. Manu parallels these evaluations by portraying the Brāhmaṇ type as properly nonattached, moderately advantaged, and highly coherent. In all these ways the Brāhmaṇ *varṇa* exemplifies the quality called "purity" (*śuddhatva*).

So much agreement on *guṇa* ratings is not found regarding any other *varṇa*. This does not mean that different appraisals of Brāhmaṇs cannot be found using other criteria. For example, Brāhmaṇ priests' demands for small ritual fees may be seen as gross or servile. Brāhmaṇs who have become rulers, soldiers, farmers, or artisans, as some have done throughout the centuries, might also, of course, evoke quite different evaluations.

Resembling the Brāhmaṇ *varṇa* in most respects (located just behind it in a high and cool but dark corner of Figure 16.2) and often recruiting priestly as well as Śūdra personnel is the alien and less coherent but influential social type that is here called "subtle" (*sūkṣma*) and that is sometimes popularly designated simply as "other" (*anya*). The subtle locus is crowded with playful and elusive gods, spirits (auspicious and otherwise), renouncers (both genuine and phony), fortunetellers, sorcerers (Raheja 1988: 37–67),

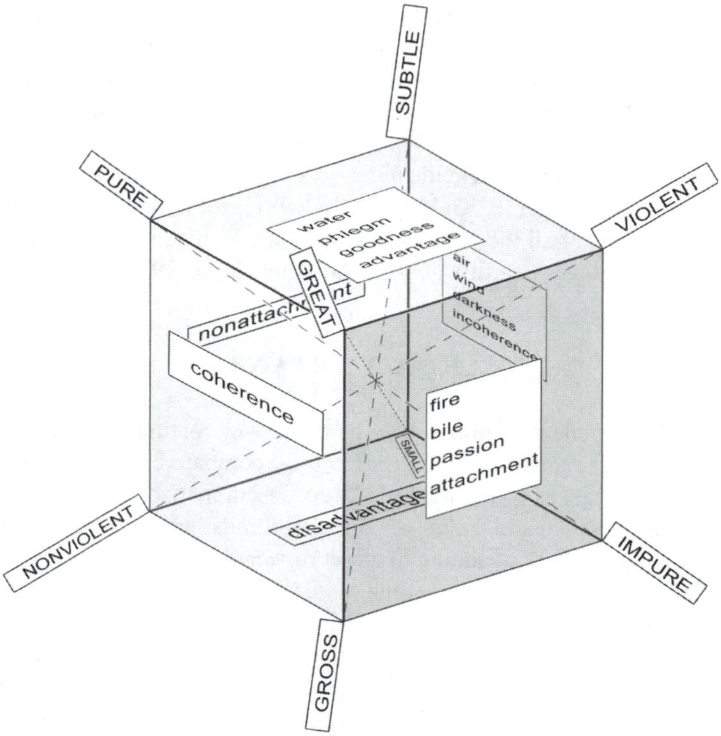

Figure 16.1 Classical paradigm.

courtesans, musicians, dramatists, and clowns (Shulman 1985). They may perform visual and sonic transformations that astonish or transport audiences, especially devotees and admirers of the ordinary or gross type located diametrically opposite to them. Hallucinogens are favored among them, ecstasy and trance are not uncommon responses to them. Some subtle people use their more ethereal components to create lyric, narrative, or philosophic works on aesthetics, erotics, devotion, or "release" (*mokṣa*).

The large gifts that certain Brāhmaṇ priests receive for representing the spirits of the deceased or for absorbing evils make them objects of both honor and fear. Jonathan Parry (1994: 75–81) calls the latter variety "degraded," although their combination of cool strangeness and superiority likens them more to other subtle specialists than to untouchables. Other high but arcane specialties, such as astrology, accounting, banking, and medicine, may inspire similar combinations of admiration and distrust, whether the practitioners claim affiliation with the Brāhmaṇ *varṇa* (*Manusmṛti* 4.220).

Kṣatriyas: gross, great, and violent

Notably diverse opinions are found regarding the relative rank of the Kṣatriya *varṇa* (K in Figure 16.2). While this *varṇa* is always rated both passionate and coherent, literary sources of two earlier millennia rate it low in goodness, hence as "gross." In Śaṃkarācārya's more inclusive and refined 3 × 3 × 3 ratings, however, Kṣatriyas rise to

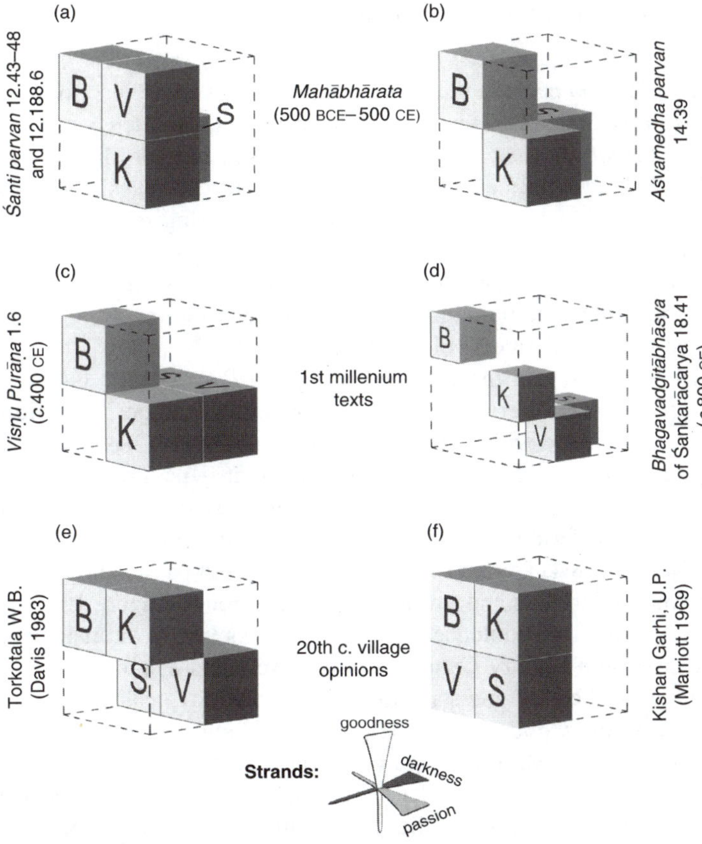

Figure 16.2 *Varṇas* rated by strands (*guṇas*).

intermediate goodness, and in the two rural assessments sampled from the twentieth century (Figures 16.2[e] and [f]), they join Brāhmaṇs on the upper level, occupying the "great" corner. In these villages no local group actually claims the Kṣatriya label or wears its thread, but in both, as often elsewhere in rural India, the resident landholders operate as local rulers. Increased security in their landholdings seems a probable cause of these lordlings' rise and of the *varṇa*'s higher rating.

Not represented among the evaluators of Figure 16.2 are those who may resent their rulers' punitive controls (Gold and Gujar 2002) and relegate the Kṣatriya *varṇa* to the "violent" corner of Figure 16.1 (Bharati 1983). Those competing for rule necessarily employ or threaten destructive tactics like those suggested in the classical "treatise on advantage" (*Arthaśāstra*) of Kauṭilya. In the same remote corner of the paradigm may be found angry gods, "giants" (*daitya*), sour-faced "demons" (*rākṣasa*), "barbarians" (*mleccha*), bandits, and ruffians—any energetic antagonists of an existing order. Colonialists, communists, capitalists, strong ethnic minorities, and enemy nations have all been cast in this well-known role in recent centuries.

Vaiśyas: great, impure, and nonviolent

This large *varṇa* (V in Figure 16.2) is even more variously rated than the Kṣatriya in the present sources, probably because it comprises a miscellany of ordinary occupations, some rural, others urban—classically farming, livestockbreeding, commerce, and moneylending. Perhaps because the word "*vaiśya*" implies no one salient style of life, it is ignored by the elite-focused *Mahābhārata* in one of its few comparisons of *varṇas* at *Aśvamedhaparvan* 39 (Figure 16.2[b]). Elsewhere, however, possibly comparing rich and generous traders with landless warriors claiming Kṣatriya status, another book of *Mahābhārata* (*Śāntiparvan* at 188.6) treats the Vaiśya *varṇa* as superior to the Kṣatriya and equally central—as manifesting a combination of goodness, passion, and enlightenment that is usually reserved for "great" rulers (Figure 16.2[a]).

On the other hand, both in the fifth-century *Viṣṇu Purāṇa* (at 1.6; shown in Figure 16.2[c]) and among some very rural twentieth-century villagers of Midnapur, West Bengal, who are acquainted with no actual group called "Vaiśya," people of that designation are reckoned to be just another *jāti* of poor peasants—passionate, low in goodness, and dwelling in unenlightened darkness (M. Davis 1983: 51–52; shown in Figure 16.2[e]). Śaṃkarācārya, again offering more refined and moderate opinions in his tenth-century *Bhagavadgītābhāṣya* (18.41), concurs on Vaiśyas' low and passionate natures but brings them half-way out of darkness and toward "gross" coherence (Figure 16.2[d]).

Vaiśya-style heroes of nonviolence are Jainist ascetics whose ultimate exercise is self-starvation and twentieth-century Gandhian passive resisters against colonial oppression. Peaceful commoners, such as traders and moneylenders, are typical victims of their violent contraries—bandits, angry gods, and predatory rulers. Such are the reputedly nonpassionate "Vaiśyas" observed by Marriott (Figure 16.2[f]) in a village of western Uttar Pradesh where that label is preferred by a landed, vegetarian, thread-wearing *jāti* of farmers and traders otherwise known as Bārahseni Baniyās. Skilled in marketing, this group is locally considered to be at least as central and coherent, if not so advantaged in land or influence as the dominant Sanādhya Brāhmaṇ and Jāṭ farmers with whom its members exchange feasts.

Śūdras: small, impure, and gross

Ordained in Manu to work as directed by people of the three other *varṇas*, persons of this servant category (S in Figure 16.2) often have to shift among different low tasks and food sources that they do not themselves control. Śūdras' natures are accordingly rated by all the classical sources as low and dark. While decreasing numbers of *jātis* label themselves as "Śūdra" in the twentieth century, any who work under the commands of others are likely to be classed as "servants," using equivalent words of the regional languages.

The Bengali villagers of Figure 16.2(e) describe Śūdras as embodying the combination of classical components called "small" in Figure 16.1, which amounts to calling them weak, lazy, and fearful, although their local populations may be among the largest. On the energy levels of Śūdras, however, these sources vary. Śaṃkarācārya (Figure 16.2[d]) credits them with an intermediate degree of passion, which brings them closer to the quality "impure." Likewise in twentieth-century Kishan Garhi, an old village of western

Uttar Pradesh (Figure 16.2[f]), the category "*kamīn*" (a Hindi equivalent of Śūdra) implies a notable output of energy and a corresponding demand for a heavy, bland diet. As the dozen *kamīn jāti*s in that village include artisans, specialized agriculturists, and service providers who contribute both new skills and outside earnings to the local economy, public opinion is also moving them closer to the central establishment—into the more coherent corner labeled "gross" in Figure 16.1. What endures, it seems, is less the natures of the *jāti*s than the paradigm in whose terms they are compared.

JĀTIS FROM VARṆAS

Twentieth-century scholars hold from good evidence that for at least three millennia South Asian *jātis* have been many and that their present large number has developed mostly from the internal processes noted above but also from the absorption of alien groups, both autochthonous and invasive (S. Bayly 1999: 25–63; Karve 1968: 58–65). Colonial policy emphasized the latter interpretations to portray India as needing foreign administration to organize its heterogeneity: in provincial compendia hundreds of *jātis* were described as culturally distinct entities—specimens of arrested progress toward an assumed goal of national homogeneity (Risley 1915: 154–301).

Manu, as noted, holds the reverse of this view, insisting on humanity's single origin and its subsequent devolution toward heterogeneity and chaos. As outlined below, that text shows how degeneration may continually produce separations from the Brāhmaṇ *varṇa* and how miscegenation among the primordial four *varṇa*s has produced many more. But it fails to note the contrary tendency for rulers to agglomerate *jāti*s and for commoners to move flexibly about the middle of society. *Jāti*s of each *varṇa* have actually displayed several distinctive styles for forming additional *jāti*s.

Brāhmaṇs divide

Medieval texts describe the Brāhmaṇ *varṇa* as having anciently comprised just five regional divisions in the north and five linguistic divisions in the south, but nineteenth-century surveys name hundreds of Brāhmaṇ *jāti*s. More detailed twentieth century inquiries show many of those to be further divided by region, dialect, Vedic branch, sect, occupation, class, diet, or other traditions into smaller marriage networks of unknown number (Saraswati 1977: 39–81). The prominence of this small but most divisive *varṇa* may explain the prevalence of the notion that all *jāti*s are segments of *varṇa*s, while in fact only a minority of non-Brāhmaṇ *jāti*s make any *varṇa* claim and no other *varṇa* presents so elaborate an internal taxonomy as the Brāhmaṇ.

The plethora of Brāhmaṇ *jāti*s is easily explained in classical terms, as their *varṇa* is conceived as initially most pure—heavenly in speech, minimally attached, superior in intellect, expert in moral coherence, universal in domain, and transcendent in consciousness. Such purities permitted Brāhmaṇs the widest liberty but also the widest opportunities for impurity and schism. Departure from the *varṇa*'s reputed original residence in the "noble land" (*āryāvarta*) where the gods' own language was spoken was one early cause for splits that have since continued on a vast scale. Concurrently deplored were some errant Brāhmaṇs' failures to provide full initiations—necessary rituals of marking—to their members (Kane 1930–62, 2.1: 188–201), a game in which twice-born *jāti*s of twentieth-century Bengal continue to compete (M. Davis 1983: 91–98; Nicholas 1995).

Males subsisting solely by priestly activities seem from Manu (*Manusmṛti* 4.4–6) never to have constituted more than a small minority of the Brāhmaṇ *varṇa* but had become rarities by the end of the twentieth century. By then, few received their *varṇa*'s full classical set of sixteen major marking ceremonies or spent more than a fraction of the recommended twelve or more years in Vedic study. Of the learned, fewer still were wanted for Vedic teaching or found sufficient employment to live by reciting or performing sacrifices for others. Lacking the knowledge to conduct even their own domestic rites in Vedic style, most others subsisted by agricultural or other nonpriestly work. Although Brāhmaṇs should be feasted at funerals and other occasions, says Manu, and although feeding any starving priest earns merit for the feeder, those Brāhmaṇs who are unlearned or corrupt in the above-mentioned ways should not be fed and should be excluded from other transactions with the networks of learned and orthoprax families (*Manusmṛti* 3.150–82).

Brāhmaṇs' unique duty of receiving "gifts" (*dāna*) threatens them with incoherence, for what is given may contain the donors' unwanted problems. If the receivers are unprepared—if they have not undertaken the austerities needed to digest evil—they are advised not to risk trying to live on such prestations (*Manusmṛti* 3.179, 4.84–91, 4.186–91). Nor would donors benefit because undigested evils would remain attached to the donor. Priests who subsist by accepting the larger gifts made at funerals especially endanger themselves and their chances for continuing food and marital exchanges with others of their respective *jāti*s (Fuller 1984: 65–68).

The greater or lesser advantages enjoyed and attachments avoided by Brāhmaṇ *jāti*s also help to explain their *varṇa*'s continual diversification. The most learned, wealthy, and independent Brāhmaṇs contend for the highest degree of goodness and purity: they prefer not to accept either gifts or employment (*Manusmṛti* 4.159–60, 4.186, 4.218), especially not from kings of doubtful reputation (4.85–91). Beneath them are domestic priests, the higher serving only selectively, the lower accepting jobs from anyone of any *jāti* willing to pay (*Manusmṛti* 3.151, 4.205). Temple priests, who must deal with masses of worshipers for petty fees, are generally ranked still lower (*Manusmṛti* 3.152). Even less advantageously employed are those many who work at astrology or medicine (*Manusmṛti* 3.152, 3.162), or at cooking, for which their supposed purity qualifies them, or at other menial tasks (4.6).

Advantaged by their relative independence, yet more attached to worldly matters are the many Brāhmaṇs who subsist by farming, although if they plow themselves, violating Mother Earth and killing her small creatures, they lose moral purity (*Manusmṛti* 10.84). If they take up professions that may be more remunerative, such as stockbreeding, trade, crafts, or a ruler's civil or military service, they may be scorned as subordinate and morally dubious by the priestly types whose opinions Manu (*Manusmṛti* 3.64, 4.218) continues to represent. Thus prominent Brāhmaṇ *jāti*s, such as Nāgar administrators of Gujarat, Citrapur Sārasvat professionals of the Konkan, Niyogī soldiers of Tamilnadu, and Bhūmihār landlords of the middle Gaṅgā, are admired for their nonpriestly achievements but have generated sections that dine and marry separately. The movements of Brāhmaṇs into occupations of the subtler type as noted earlier—astrology, medicine, moneylending, gambling, and so forth—involve kinds of incoherence also meriting division (*Manusmṛti* 3.159). While some Brāhmaṇ *jāti*s continue to fracture along these dimensions of impurity, others seeking to regain lost coherence reconnect (scandalously, according to conservatives) across previous lines of fission.

Some features of the Brāhmaṇic priestly style—mastery of Sanskrit texts, command of ritual, knowledge of the gods, abstention from corruptions such as liquor, heat-producing foods such as meat, and widow remarriage—are emulated by non-Brāhmaṇ *jāti*s hoping thereby to gain respect. Such emulations, which have flowered at intervals in the past and in the later nineteenth and early twentieth century, have been called "Sanskritization" by M. N. Srinivas (1962). Epitomizing such emulation and its frequent futility is a common version of a famous ancient story in which the ruler Viśvāmitra is continually frustrated in his attempts to gain powers like those of the priest Vasiṣṭha. Especially to be shunned, says Manu (*Manusmṛti* 3.169, 4.200), are those non-Brāhmaṇs who counterfeit Brāhmaṇs' priestly roles. Non-Brāhmaṇ ascetics, fortunetellers, preachers, singers, temple custodians, and the like do nevertheless successfully purvey their services to low and peripheral *jāti*s as substitutes for those offered or denied to them by Brāhmaṇ priests.

Like competing Jainist, Buddhist, and other movements that had begun during preclassical times, alternatives to the Vedic tradition with its Brāhmaṇ priesthood have been continually presented by immigrant missionaries—Christians from the first century CE, Muslims from the eighth, Neo-Buddhists in the twentieth. In medieval times popular indigenous devotional movements such as that of the Śrīvaiṣṇavas of South India seized the imaginations even of Brāhmaṇs. The Gauḍīya Vaiṣṇavas of Bengal and the Vīraśaivas of Karnataka from the twelfth, the Vārakarīs of Maharashtra from the thirteenth, and the Sikhs of Punjab from the sixteenth—all preferred regional vernaculars to Sanskrit, a move that parallels the abandonment of Latin by reformist Christian sects; these also developed their own non-Brāhmaṇ, nonhereditary equivalents of Brāhmaṇ priesthoods. During the nineteenth and twentieth century, some literacy movements in Bengal, Maharashtra, Punjab, and Tamilnadu more sweepingly urged every Hindu to be his own priest. Many such devotional movements together with that of Kabīr and the other greatly simplified, noniconic "strandless" (*nirguṇa*) cults beginning in the fifteenth century have taken with them one-sixth or more of the non-Brāhmaṇ population and some Brāhmaṇs, too.

In the twentieth century, more people nevertheless still claimed membership in the Brāhmaṇ *varṇa* than in any other—about 5 percent of independent India's total population. The Brāhmaṇ *varṇa* is the only one that is well represented in all regions of the country, its proportion varying from 2 percent in parts of peninsular India to nearly 10 percent in Hariyana and Uttar Pradesh.

Accretions to the Brāhmaṇ *varṇa* from outside have probably been few, as even nonpriestly and less learned Brāhmaṇ populations have defended their purity by refusing any attachments that seem doubtful. Learned Brāhmaṇs are organized according to branches of Vedic study that require proof of ancestral enrollment. The preceptorial lineages of most Brāhmaṇ *jāti*s, named for semidivine Vedic seers, are enshrined in well-known texts and refreshed through frequent repetitions (Saraswati 1977: 41–43), while their clan genealogies are guarded by officers within the *jāti*. Where disputes have arisen within the elite Brāhmaṇ or non-Brāhmaṇ *jāti*s of their kingdoms, local rulers have often had to decide on clan ranking, such formality further suggesting fixity; but since clan ranking decisions depend on the flux of actual marriages, change is always threatened and has often produced further divisions among *jāti*s (C. H. Brown 1983; Inden 1976: 45–76; Khare 1970: 96–98; Parry 1979: 195–317). Nevertheless, by competing for more perfect "purity" (or honor) in these divisive ways, Brāhmaṇ *jāti*s have in the aggregate kept their *varṇa* closed to others.

Kṣatriyas multiply

No Kṣatriya genealogy is continuous from the Vedas; indeed, according to legends widespread in India's southwest, the original ruling *varṇa* was exterminated early by Paraśurāma, a vengeful figure of partly Brāhmaṇ descent (Shulman 1985: 110–29). To fill the gap legends have it that the great Kṣatriya clans emerged either from the primordial Brāhmaṇ or directly from the sun, moon, fire, or serpents (Karve 1965: 165–70).

Greek, Śāka, Pahlava, Yüeh-chih, Kuṣāṇa, and other invaders from Central Asia are likely to have replaced some Vedic lineages during the early centuries of the Common Era, adding to the class of ruling *jāti*s (Basham 1954: 58–62). Jainist legends tell of certain Kṣatriyas who abandoned their kingdoms when converted to Jainism (Babb 1996: 139–70). Traditions of the northern Himālayan slopes tell that the Hindu rulers surviving there had been driven out of their domains in the plains by Muslim invaders beginning from the eleventh century, but interactions between Hindus and their Mughal overlords during the sixteenth to nineteenth centuries also helped to replace them with the hybrid, ostensibly indigenous Kṣatriya warrior *jāti*s of northern India called "ruler's sons" (Hindi Rājpūts) (S. Bayly 1999; Kolff 1990).

Weaknesses in existing kingdoms, if not filled by non-Vedic invaders, have generally been filled by lesser chiefs from nearby ruling or landed lineages, not all of them of Kṣatriya pedigree. New aspirants to rulership have generally demonstrated their "greatness" (*mahattva*) first by mobilizing a superior fighting force, a task understood to require divine support. The benisons of Viṣṇu, Śiva, or Allāh may help, but particularly vital is the "energy" (*śakti*) that can be provided by autochthonous goddesses, as exemplified from Kathiawar by Harald Tambs-Lyche (1997).

Once in control, aspirants claim connection by descent and/or by marrying with established ruling groups. The providers of suitable genealogies to Rājpūts are neutral professionals of Brāhmaṇ or bardic *jāti*s (such as Bhaṭs or Cāraṇs), who keep secret books to please their most generous patrons (Shah and Shroff 1959). Ceremonial inauguration into rulership then requires several other sorts of priests. The seventeenth century, Brāhmaṇ-assisted rise to quasi-Kṣatriya status by the Maharashtrian Kuṇbī king Śivājī is the most prominent and best-documented case, although many lesser chieftains of peripheral peoples in other and marginal regions have traveled similar paths, bringing their *jāti*s with them (S. Bayly 1999: 39–63).

The advantage that a large fighting force and many allies gives to rulers encourages them to disdain the exclusivity and divisiveness by which Brāhmaṇs have cultivated their vaunted purity. To expand their territories, rulers have made wide alliances both marital and prandial, opening their groups to still others' claims of belonging and continually increasing the Kṣatriya *varṇa*'s internal heterogeneity. Passionate competition for honor among lineages within and among ranked clans has raised some to kingship while lowering others to servitude, but marriages among higher and lower, central and peripheral families continually spread the ruling style and blur what might otherwise have been *jāti* distinctions (Karve 1968: 19–22, 41).

Probably less than 1 percent of males wore the thread of twice-born Kṣatriyas before India's twentieth-century independence, after which hundreds of kingdoms disappeared.

But some 15 to 20 percent of the population retained personal or group names or myths that suggest their descent from former rulers. At least 5 percent of people in northern and central India belong to lineages that since later medieval times have been calling themselves Rājpūts, while larger proportions in peninsular India use *jāti* names, such as Marāṭhā, Khaṇḍāit, Kamma, Reḍḍi, Okkaliga, Vēḷāḷar, Kavuṇṭar, or Nāyar, that imply their present or one-time regional dominance as landholders or warriors. The widespread use of courtly and military titles as personal names or affixes—words translatable as "king," "lord," "prince," "chief," or "lion," for example—also keep the ruling style alive for many groups that actually have little landed power. Counterfeiting may be punished where there are locally dominant Rājpūts (Cohn 1955; Rowe 1968), but elsewhere the Kṣatriya style is readily accessible: thus in Tamilnadu some Śāṇārs whose toddy-tapping labors had kept them low and peripheral gained wealth through trade, invested in land and politics, and renamed their *jāti* "lords of the land" (Nādār) (Hardgrave 1969).

Vaiśyas flex and burgeon

The commoner or Vaiśya *varṇa* is known for its occupational breadth, mobility, and flexibility, its most conspicuous trend being toward society's middle, into tranquil but energetic commerce. By the twentieth century the term "*vaiśya*" usually signified only "trader," any former *varṇa* and *jāti* names for persons of commercial occupation being replaced with regional mercantile titles, such as Śeṭh, Ceṭṭi, or Mahājan.

Commoner *jāti*s specialized in cultivating and herding are usually large and widely dispersed over the rural landscape; when able to rise above subsistence, they have tended to move into Rājpūt-like roles, as did the Kanbīs of Gujarat in medieval times. But in twentieth-century central Gujarat when (as perhaps in Figure 16.2[a]) traders became wealthier than village rulers, "Pāṭidār" farmers dropped first their Rājpūt, then also their Vaiśya claims, and settled in cities, thereafter calling themselves simply "village headmen" (Paṭels) (Pocock 1972; Shah and Desai 1988; Shah and Shroff 1959).

When peaceful conditions prevail, some people of all social categories and faiths (about 4 percent in the twentieth-century population) turn to commerce in the cash markets. In Tezibazar, a crossroads town of eastern Uttar Pradesh, alongside shops run by longstanding Vaiśya *jāti*s, members of the rural oil presser, brass worker, and distiller *jāti*s all became "merchants" to their customers (Fox 1969: 83) and formed cross-*jāti*, guild-like relations that must have developed often in the pasts of India's urban places. So also networks of the Māhisya (formerly Kaivarta) *jāti*, formerly lowly cultivators of West Bengal, shifted to Howrah City and gained a predominant place in the manufacturing and selling of machine parts, importantly aided by their hands-on approach to factory careers and their frank reliance on *jāti*-fellows (Owens and Nandy 1977: 98, 131). The authors call the Māhisyas "the new Vaiśyas."

More advantaged near-elites such as the small but privileged and ubiquitous "scribe" (Kāyastha and other) *jāti*s are reputed to have grown by defections to state service from *jāti*s of priestly, ruling, or other *varṇa*s. In Punjab, the several *jāti*s of Khatrīs represent similar blends of landholding, trading, and other literate service professions. The Jainists of western India, now generally known as "Vaiśyas," declare their ancestors to have converted from ruling to trading (Babb 1996: 137–73).

Many such traders such as the Jainist Mārvāṛīs are wealthy and influential in political life, yet exhibit styles of life that attempt no such extremes of purity or greatness as typify the old elites (D. Gupta 2000: 124–27). In general, they appear to mix moderate doses of all the classical components, retaining the flexibility needed to exploit new opportunities as they appear. The Sikh faith honored by many *jāti*s of Punjabi farmers, soldiers, traders, and artisans seems to celebrate its centrality by the balanced set of five signs it requires its adherents to wear—hair that is long (dedicated) but combed (controlled), dagger (masculinity), iron bracelet (femininity), and short pants (sexual discipline) (Uberoi 1996: 10–13).

However heterogeneous the *jāti*s from which they are recruited, people who earn their livelihoods in cash markets, particularly those mainly residing in cities, tend toward a style of life that minimizes dependence on priests or rulers, on other *jāti*s, or on extrafamilial attachments generally. Their households and *jāti*s tend to be self-sufficient, contrasting with the maximally interdependent style of rulers. The family firm is its own center (C. Bayly 1983: 369–93), and since traders can often operate efficiently using only close relatives, they tend to minimize both lineal and marital ties. Specializing in commodities like grain, cloth, and metals helps them further to minimize outside labor costs. Reputed as cold and closefisted, the merchants of Tezibazar limit intimate feedings to their own *jāti*s and generally elide ranking issues (Fox 1969: 82–107)—tactics that gain traders wealth but may earn them goodness estimates well below the top (Carstairs 1957: 119–24).

If they reside in agricultural villages but deal in the subtle media of money or metals and do not hold land or participate in local cults, artisans, merchants, and moneylenders may be regarded as permanent strangers, assigned to the "left-hand" faction in some Dravidian regions or to a separate set of ranks as regards food (Srinivas 1955: 22–24). They may favor Jainist, Vīraśaiva, Vaiṣṇava, or other faiths unconnected with the land or develop forms of worship ministered by priests of their own *jāti*s.

Śūdras permutate

Characterized by the classical priestly authors as low, morally "incoherent" (*adhārmik*), and therefore of Śūdra *varṇa* are all people in the world who do not perform Vedic sacrifices. If nonsacrificers' ancestors did not originally emerge as Śūdras, they must be supposed to have sinfully given up sacrificing, thus degenerating into that *varṇa*—so reason the classic texts (*Manusmṛti* 10.43–44). Like such explanations in their theme of loss and decline, many origin myths told in the twentieth century by people of nonelite *jāti*s assert their origin from a deity or person of elite *varṇa*, followed either by rejection for some sinful act, such as killing a cow or eating impure food, or by being forced into servitude (Deliège 1999: 71–88). B. R. Ambedkar (1948), political champion of untouchable *jāti*s and constitutional lawyer, endorses the latter explanation as part of his general theory of Śūdra origins.

Sexual "mixing of the *varṇa*s" (*varṇasaṃkara*), another common kind of incoherence, is attested in Manu as another way of continually producing lower and more peripheral *jāti*s. Only matings within one *varṇa* are seen as fully reproducing the parents *varṇa* qualities. For the *varṇa* of an offspring to approximate that of its father, texts hold that its mother's *varṇa* must be, if not the same as the father's, then no more than one step lower in the *varṇa*s' primordial order. If she is of a *varṇa* two or more steps lower, her offspring will belong either to an inferior grade of her *jāti* or to a new, still lower *jāti*—one that may bear an insulting name (Kane 1930–62, 2.1: 51–104).

When evaluating the offspring of inter-*varṇa* marriages, Manu considers not just the parents' *varṇa*s and their relative ranks but also the correlation (the degree of coherence) between the ranks of their *varṇa*s and their ranks as spouses, the husband being presumed sexually superior to the wife. The pairing of a higher-*varṇa* man and lower-*varṇa* woman agrees "with (the natural slope of) the hair" (*anuloma*), that is, it correlates their sexual and *varṇa* rankings positively and makes the natural fault in the offspring less. Although unlikely to be achieved or proven, repetitions of positive marriages for seven generations should in theory restore the faulty descendants to their male ancestor's *varṇa* (*Manusmṛti* 10.64–65; Kane 1930–62, 2.1: 61–66).

But a lower-*varṇa* man's impregnating a woman from a higher *varṇa* goes "against (the slope of) the hair" (*pratiloma*), that is, it correlates the two rankings negatively and produces a very faulty offspring suited only to a different *jāti* that is both lower and less coherent than either of the parents'. Implicitly concurring with Manu are many twentieth-century Hindus: people of the woman's *jāti* generally feel themselves dishonored and, if they do not disown the errant couple, may find themselves equally degraded and peripheralized.

Manu (*Manusmṛti* 10.5–39) names twelve separate *jāti*s that have been generated by marriages mixing the four original *varṇa*s and further names at least thirty of the one hundred ninety-two lower and less coherent *jāti*s that are or can be generated by a second round of mismatchings among those twelve and the original four. The most negatively correlated marriages are those that yielded the Cāṇḍāla and the Niṣāda *jāti*s, foreshadowers if not actual forbears of recent history's most incoherent and disadvantaged "untouchable" (Hindi *achūt*) or "oppressed" (Hindi *dalit*) *jāti*s. During the present "degenerate era" (Kali Yuga), classical texts anticipate a continuing increase of inappropriate matings and the production of even more disadvantaged and incoherent *jāti*s.

Most recent scholars dismiss such mismatchings as incapable by themselves of providing plausible origins for the innumerable *jāti*s that exist. The names of the new *jāti*s claimed by Manu as products of miscegenation—a miscellany of occupational, regional, linguistic, and tribal designations—suggest a society that is differentiating internally and simply outgrowing the classical prescriptions as it absorbs other populations. Yet inter-*varṇa* matings by marriage, concubinage, and informal liaisons are also attested throughout Hindu literature, history, and ethnography (Karve 1968: 16–17; Nicholas 1995). Even if such matings in the past never constituted more than the tiny fraction reported in recent surveys, continuation of those rates for two millennia could have large cumulative effects. Since dozens of *jāti*s are today understood to have been generated not only through incoherent matings but also by inversions of relationships in feeding, fighting, and work, Manu's permutative formula might better be extended than rejected as a historical hypothesis.

Untouchables separate

Any *jāti*, person, or thing whose impurities—attachments, disadvantages, and/or incoherences—are relatively greater may be regarded as "untouchable" by others who would avoid acquiring such qualities. In the twentieth century, the label was applied most widely to *jāti*s dealing professionally with incoherent materials, such as dirt, garbage, human exuvia or excreta, and dead animal bodies or their parts.

Kept at a distance by other *jāti*s, often required to reside in separate settlements, some impure *jāti*s specialize in worshiping deities that exhibit incoherent properties like those imputed to themselves, such as Kālī with her necklace of skulls or Māriamma<u>n</u> who may bring polluting diseases. In the same way that priests of Brāhmaṇ *varṇa* may mediate with elite gods to convey spirits from impure *jāti*s to heaven, so priests of Śūdra and untouchable *jāti*s may be employed by purer people to propitiate deities whom they fear to approach themselves. As in incoherence-removal and in much other work, more-and-less pure *jāti*s need each other to be distinct and different in just these ways and may be reluctant to see their mutually exploitative relations redefined (S. Bayly 1999: 306–41). Thus a century of colonial-period agitations to abolish discrimination against impure *jāti*s in temples, military service, and education succeeded only partially and then against much resistance.

Members of disadvantaged and peripheralized *jāti*s themselves often seek spiritual and social advancement in devotional cults, for while servitude is despised in classical priestly doctrine, it is celebrated in devotional discourse as a means of approaching deities more intimately. Without abandoning *varṇa* distinctions, in the early twentieth century M. K. Gandhi tried by devotional service to ameliorate the lives of untouchables (whom he renamed "children of god" [*harijan*] with moral but slight practical effect). Untouchables who are less hopeful both use and reject parts of the classical paradigm in diverse, often confusing ways (Deliège 1999)—some imitating more advantaged *jāti*s, some joining one of the many "strandless" cults that attend only to souls (Khare 1984), some insisting on personal autonomy from all categorization (Vincentnathan 1993). Still others have converted, usually in clusters of families, to non-Vedic faiths, mainly to Christianity and Islam in previous centuries, and since 1957 to Buddhism, led by the militant Ambedkar, himself of untouchable origin.

RECENT RECLASSIFICATIONS

Governmental reforms of the twentieth century had encouraged victims of *jāti* discrimination to seek more tangible remedies through political agitations, and these were led in divergent ways by Ambedkar and Gandhi. Although still limiting voting rights to a literate minority, the Government of India Act of 1935 guaranteed proportional legislative representation to candidates from the previously most disadvantaged and peripheralized *jāti*s (14 to 17 percent of India's Hindu population). These hundreds of "scheduled castes" included dozens of small, scavenging *jāti*s along with the large leatherworking and laboring *jāti*s. Legislative seats were later reserved also for three hundred more *jāti*s (6 to 8 percent of the population) living mainly in economically marginal areas and called "scheduled tribes." Seats were reserved, too, for other minorities—Muslims, Christians, Anglo-Indians and European minorities, women, and certain occupational categories.

Independent India's 1950 Constitution confirmed the 1935 provisions and went further. It avoids the words "*varṇa*" and "*jāti*" but opposes discrimination by birth and declares that "untouchability is abolished and its practice in any form is forbidden." Consequent legislation against discrimination proved difficult to enforce, however. Aiming for greater future equality, the Constitution also directs that "special care" be given to the nation's "backward classes" and "weaker sections"—terms later construed as referring to categories whose past exclusion from public facilities had kept them relatively ignorant and disadvantaged. Legislation accordingly prescribed compensatory discrimination in public education and governmental employment as the remedy (Galanter 1984). Successive commissions interpreted the excluded categories to have been *jāti*s, rather than individuals or families, so millions organized formally through their *jāti* networks to document their collective disabilities and to demand future preference for all their members.

By the end of the twentieth century, *jāti*s containing nearly half the nation's Hindus had been listed for help and classified in four large categories. To the colonial scheduled caste and scheduled tribe categories were added a large (20 percent of the population and still growing) category of "other backward classes," initially comprising over four thousand *jāti*s (S. Bayly 1999: 266–305). While the more assertive scheduled caste and scheduled tribe *jāti*s were and are often called "impure," the other backward class *jāti*s were once called "small" in popular discourse—a now obsolete power distinction along the familiar hot-cool scale. The dwindling other half of India's Hindus, economically diverse but including all Brāhmaṇs and most other *jāti*s that once claimed twice-born status, remained without preferment—an elite by omission. A categorization of *jāti*s whose distinctions resemble those classically made among the *varṇa*s has thus been legally reinstituted in inverted form. While in the name of equality *varṇa* labels are used less and less, most *jāti*s have been politically activated. The legal duration of these categories and logics remains indefinite, and so their long-term effects remain to be assessed.

CONCLUSION

Cosmogonic types in Vedic thought and ritual, the four "color" (*varṇa*) classes of "priest," "ruler," "commoner," and "servant" became major categories of classical social discourse. Their ranked, contrasting, and interdependent styles came to be understood in both popular and learned terms as differing combinations of the universe's natural components—its elements, humors, moral concerns, and strands. *Varṇa* styles were pursued and varied by hundreds of kinship and marital-"birth" (*jāti*) networks competing for advantage by managing their attachments and coherence through relations in food and work. Over the centuries, *jāti*s divided, multiplied, shifted, and intermingled, producing today's thousands of networks of still more diverse natures and unequal resources. Without using *varṇa* labels but aiming to correct inequities, Indian governments of the twentieth century recognized thousands of *jāti*s as units for compensatory discrimination and classified them in four categories that roughly invert the *varṇa*s' primordial ordering.

NOTES

1 Indigenous concepts are identified herein by Sanskrit or Hindi words that have near-equivalents in most of the regional languages of South Asia. Of the thousands of published twentieth-century ethnographic observations, it has been practicable here to cite only representative examples.

2 Consistent with the homologies noted earlier among the other moral concerns and strands, namely, attachment with passion (as at *Bhagavad Gītā* 3.37) and incoherence with darkness, a logical and popular but noncanonical homology is recognized here between the concern for "advantage" (*artha*) and the strand of "goodness" (*sattva*). Both terms state axioms of the Hindu

world, advantage and goodness agreeing that nonsymmetry—a relation of superiority and inferiority—generally exists between any two entities. This homology differs from *Manusmṛti* 12.38, which links goodness with coherence (the prime concern of priestly instruction) rather than with advantage, and goes on to link advantage with passion and attachment with darkness—linkages that may suit priestly homiletics but do not agree with the Sāṃkhya logics employed here.

CHAPTER SEVENTEEN

ĀŚRAMA

Walter O. Kaelber

THE "ĀŚRAMA SYSTEM" AS IDEAL-TYPICAL CONSTRUCT

The term "*āśrama*" in mainstream Brāhmaṇic thought generally refers to four distinct social locations within which the Hindu male may pursue cultural as well as specifically religious goals. These social locations—often correlated with particular spatial locations as well—are quite clearly "places of toil or exertion." Such "exertion" (*śram*) was ultimately perceived to serve a moral and/or spiritual purpose. The correlation of *āśrama* with ascetic activity is evidenced by the repeated pairing of the roots *śram* and *tap* in Brāhmaṇic literature (Kaelber 1989: 30; Olivelle 1993: 9–11). The term "*āśrama*" takes on its best-known meaning in the context of a preeminent construct of Hindu theology or self-interpretation: the "*āśrama* system," a system of four "orders of life."

Although the *āśrama* system was reinvented and reinterpreted over time, the best-known or "classical" (Olivelle 1993: 129–30) formulation of the system can be found, with varying degrees of consistency, in the Dharmaśāstra literature composed during the early centuries of the Common Era. The *śāstra* literature prescribed normative or ideal-typical stages in the life of the "twice-born" (*dvija*) Hindu male. In time, this system of stages became an integral element of Hindu *dharma*, the moral order. The *āśrama* system coupled with the system of four social classes (*varṇa*) constituted *varṇāśramadharma*. This term, referring to the duties appropriate to one's social class and stage of life, is often regarded as synonymous with Hinduism itself. The progression or succession of four stages culminates, according to many Hindu sources, in *mokṣa* or release from transmigration, ignorance, and suffering, a soteriological goal embodied in the term "*mokṣa-dharma*." Thus, appropriate place and opportunity are given—at least in theory—to both participation in the socioritual world *and* renunciation of that world.

The classical *āśrama* system delineates four successive stages. According to *Manusmṛti*, for example, the first *āśrama* was that of a celibate student (*brahmacārin*). Following a period of prolonged study, lasting possibly twelve years, the twice-born male married, thereby entering the second *āśrama*, that of householder (*gṛhastha*). When his hairs turned gray, however, and when his skin became wrinkled and he saw his children's children, it was time for him to enter the third *āśrama*, leaving society behind and becoming a forest hermit (*vānaprastha*). Here, dedicated to austerity, his intentions turned progressively toward release from worldly and social entanglements. Finally, renouncing the material world and its attendant desires, the twice-born Hindu male was initiated into the fourth and final *āśrama*. Throughout these four, successive life stages of the classical system, the *dvija* thus traverses a path characterized by distinctive goals and corresponding forms of ascetic activity. The Brāhmaṇic path of moral and religious exertion articulated in the *āśrama* system is therefore a path of asceticism or *tapas* as well.

This system of *āśramas*, however, was never equivalent to—or identical with—social institutions as they actually existed in space and time. The system—with its description of stages and respective duties, goals, and activities—was presented by the Hindu authors as a normative, ideal-typical system. Engaged in a grand process of inclusion, the *sūtra* and *śāstra* literature sought to bring at least theoretical order to the multiplicity of ascetic lifestyles present in ancient India as well as to the often conflicting aims and inclinations expressed through those lifestyles.

THE HINDU TRADITION: CHALLENGE, TENSION, AND RESOLUTION

Simply stated, the fundamental tension which the *āśrama* system sought to resolve was centered in the conflicting, even mutually exclusive, aims of the ritual world of marriage, on the one hand, and the aims of "liberation," which sought to leave that world behind, on the other. That socioritual worldview, challenged by the ideologies of "liberation," was in fact the very heart and essential legacy of the ancient, Vedic tradition as articulated in the Saṃhitās, the Brāhmaṇas, and the Śrauta literature.

Āśrama: misconceptions and modern scholarship

Misconceptions regarding the origins and development of the *āśramas* are clearly visible not only in the Hindu tradition itself but also in modern, critical scholarship. Modern scholars, many of them Western, have opined with Albert Schweitzer that the *āśramas* were "born as it were in a cloudless sky." That is, they—along with the ideal and practice of renunciation—were "self-originated" or present in Hinduism "from the very beginning" (Olivelle 1992: 19). Even more critical scholars, such as Robert Ernest Hume, Paul Deussen, and Nikhilānanda, saw the system already present in some embryonic or latent form as far back as the earliest of the principal Upaniṣads. Consider, for example, Hume's ill-founded observation regarding the celebrated passage in the *Bṛhadāraṇyaka Upaniṣad* wherein the renowned sage Yājñavalkya "goes forth," leaving his domestic world behind. Hume states that Yājñavalkya is here going forth to become a *vānaprastha*, thereby entering stage three of the fourfold *āśrama* system (Hume 1921: 98). Sarvepalli Radhakrishnan's (1953: 195) comment on the passage is virtually identical. These observations are indefensibly speculative. Neither the terms "*vānaprastha*" nor "*āśrama*" appear in the text. In point of fact, Hindu *paṇḍitas* such as Śaṃkara himself granted the *āśramas* an ancient legacy, in order to hallow the ideal of renunciation and a quest for liberation or *mokṣa*.

More recent scholarship, however, particularly the work of Patrick Olivelle, J. F. Sprockhoff, J. C. Heesterman, and Walter Kaelber, has shed new light on the complex issue of the emergence and formation of the *āśrama* system. Despite remaining uncertainties and ongoing discussion, it is evident that the classical system of four successive life stages, as presented in *Manusmṛti* and other Dharmaśāstra literature, came as a response to—and as a hoped for resolution of—a fundamental tension or even conflict within the Hindu tradition. Any attempt to understand *āśrama*, the classical *āśrama* system, as well as the ongoing Brāhmaṇic debate must do so with an eye to that fundamental tension.

Building blocks: the Vedic heritage

The central social institution of Vedic India was the family. Marriage, domestic life, procreation, and ritual performance were the initially unquestioned foundations of cultural stability. A confident affirmation of Vedic tradition and its complex ritual structure held sway in an essentially tribal world still centered in village life.

The Vedic Student: Members of the upper three classes were initiated into adulthood through a ritual of purification and transition known as the *upanayana*. Through this most significant of all adolescent *saṃskāra*s (consecrations), the individual enjoyed a spiritual rebirth, therewith receiving the title of "*dvija*" (twice-born). The "Vedic student" (*brahmacārin*) is already described in the *Atharva Veda*. Although the first extended reference to the *upanayana* is found in the *Śatapatha Brāhmaṇa*, there is no question that this initiation—as well as other activities of the *brahmacārin*—are of archaic origin (Gonda 1965b: 233; Kaelber 1989: 111). For as many as twelve years or more following the *upanayana*, the student prepared himself for full participation in the cultural world of his day.

The ancient term "*brahmacarya*" refers to the sexual abstinence enjoined upon the initiate until marriage. In fact, sexual abstinence was only one of many ascetic restraints that the student observed in order to fully immerse himself in the power-generating world of Vedic study. The ancient *brahmacārin* was in fact a *tapasvin*, one dedicated to the practice of *tapas*, one absorbed in *tapas*, one saturated with the power-laden heat of *tapas*. *Atharva Veda* 11.5 glorifies the "Vedic student" in exaggerated fashion. Here the *brahmacārin* protects the Brāhmaṇic life with *tapas*, filling the world with his asceticism (*śram*; *tap*). Jan Gonda (1965b: 295) has, in fact, observed that the entire learning endeavor of the *brahmacārin* rested upon a foundation of *tapas*. The observance of several *vrata*s (vows of austerity) by the Vedic student clearly indicates his dedication to *tapas*. As part of his learning endeavor, the *brahmacārin* is obligated to engage in such ascetic practices as fasting, prolonged silence, begging, isolation in the forest, remaining awake at night, sleeping on the ground, standing for prolonged periods of time, and, of course, the observance of chastity (Kaelber 1989: 110–24).

Clearly, the institution of "studenthood" was part of the Vedic heritage. It existed before the *āśrama* system came into being and, in a very real sense, continued to exist independently of that system once the latter came into being. The institution of *brahmacārin* must, therefore, be seen as a component or building block later integrated theoretically into the various configurations of the "*āśrama* system."

The Householder: In a similar fashion, the institution of marriage—as well as the complex rituals of sacrifice which characterized the householder's life—preceded the construction of even the earliest *āśrama* system. Marriage and sacrifice must, therefore, be seen as components later integrated into the various "systems." The norms of Brāhmaṇic tradition stipulated that only married men could perform sacrifice. In fact, for sacrificial purposes the man of the house together with his wife constituted a single ritual persona (Olivelle 1993: 40–41). From the Vedic perspective, a man becomes complete only after marriage and the birth of a son.

Sacrifice was, in fact, the central religious activity of Vedic life. The intricacies of the sacrificial procedure—if properly executed—produced a cornucopia of benefits for the householder. In addition to rainfall, fertility, and abundant crops (Kaelber 1989: 15–28), the sacrifice generated progeny, therewith ensuring immortality for the sacrificer through offspring (29–33). Unlike the far more elaborate Śrauta sacrifices performed by specialized priests and requiring three fires, the domestic rituals could be performed by the householder (i.e. *gṛhastha*) himself. The daily sacrifices of the householder were relatively simple procedures. *Homa* sacrifices, in which cooked food was offered to various gods, were essential. So also were the *pañca-mahāyajña*s, the "five great sacrifices," articulated in the Dharmaśāstras. These, in fact, are still observed in many Hindu homes today. They are *devayajña*: the obligation to burn an offering to the gods, or to make a sacrifice of milk, curds, or butter, or to place a bit of wood sprinkled with *ghī* in the fire; *brahmāyajña*: the daily expression of debt to the sages by studying, repeating, or meditating upon some portion of the Vedic scriptures; *pitṛyajña*: libations of water or the setting aside of rice balls as a daily remembering of ancestors; *bhūtayajña*: the recognition of spirits or an offering to animals, birds, and insects; and *narayajña*: the daily obligation to honor ties of fellowship with humans by showing hospitality to guests, friends, or even a beggar (Organ 1974: 206).

A large number of *saṃskāra*s or ceremonial sacraments also punctuated the life of the householder and his family, celebrating significant events in domestic life. Although the precise number of *saṃskāra*s varied from source to source, the Gṛhyasūtras, in the first systematic description of the rites, detailed sixteen specific performances. Among the most important of the *saṃskāra*s were the *upanayana*, initiating the son into adulthood, and *vivāha*, the marriage rite, through which he himself became a householder.

It was also the sacrifice that enabled the householder to be reborn spiritually, thereby ensuring his ultimate immortality after death. Just as the gods had attained their own immortality through the ritual sacrifice, so now does the householder. During the ritual scenario, the sacrificer became an embryo, soon to be reborn out of the sacrifice itself. So had it been for the paradigmatic god, Prajāpati. So too was it now for the householder.

The final *saṃskāra* of an individual's life was the funeral rite. This too however was understood as a sacrifice. The cremated body of the deceased was now offered up in the sacrificial fire, this rite generating the third and final rebirth of the *dvija*. After a liminal period, usually lasting twelve days, the *yajamāna* was fully reborn in heaven, now joining the "fathers," the ancestors, for his immortal reward.

The changing cultural world of the sixth century BCE

During the sixth century preceding the Common Era, gradual but dramatic changes took place in the social, economic, and religious life of northern India. Starting in the west, these changes gradually spread eastward, dramatically affecting life in the Gaṅgā River Valley. Concurrent with agricultural abundance and food surplus was the rise of an urban culture. Relatedly, older, traditional political units were slowly challenged, even eclipsed, by the rise of monarchies and the rule of kings. With the increased possibility of safe travel and the lure of economic gain, an enterprising merchant class began to emerge. Commerce and a related communication of ideas over ever-wider areas became more commonplace.

The provincialism of village life, with its emphasis on kinship ties, was challenged by a new worldview. Old allegiances and values were questioned under the impact of a new freedom—indeed, a new individualism—and an urban perspective. This new world gave rise to social organizations different from the traditional allegiances of "tribe" and family. Merchants, for example, began to organize themselves with an innovative eye toward common goals and shared concerns. This new world with its growing sense of individualism (Olivelle 1992: 32–34) nourished a new and growing phenomenon: the possibility of choice. With a widening range of cultural options came the wish among many urban individuals to choose from this growing array of values and visions.

But with the possibility of choice came also the possibility—even the anxiety—of making incorrect choices. A new uncertainty hovered in the Indian air. The challenge, even the threat to village-centered life—as well as to the tradition kinship ties and values upheld by that life—troubled the Hindu psyche. Not only were the old social structures thrown into question, but so too was the soteriological value of ritual itself. The efficacy of the sacrifice, the very heart of Vedic stability, was now in doubt. Innovative members of society, particularly Brāhmaṇs influenced by the new currents, sought alternative avenues toward salvation. Rather than affirming the old values and the social world out of which they emerged, these new soteriological visions often challenged—even threatened—traditional views and practices.

This new worldview, emerging in northern India, would eventually become a fundamental feature of Hindu thought. Although never eclipsing the traditional worldview, the new vision and the religious practices it fostered altered Hindu culture as it continued to develop through the centuries. The salient features of that new worldview are well known. They include the doctrines of *karma*, transmigration, and liberation from an endless cycle of rebirth.

The word "*karma*," long applied to ritual activity, began to assume an additional meaning. No doubt influenced by the growing individualism of the day, *karma* now referred to the deeds, both positive and negative, performed by the individual as well as to the consequences of those deeds. Immortality in heaven, long seen as attainable through traditional ritual, was no longer assured. The notion of a "re-death" (*punarmṛtyu*) in the heavenly realm eventuated in a firm conviction that the individual would be reborn in another earthly form. The characteristics, the circumstances of that rebirth would be determined by the *karma* of one's preceding life. Good *karma* led to a good life; bad *karma* to the contrary. In many ways the doctrines of individual *karma* and transmigration (*saṃsāra*) embodied the pessimism of the age.

Accompanying the doctrines of *karma* and *saṃsāra*, there emerged a new soteriological vision. Ultimate salvation was now possible only through "release," deliverance, or freedom from the cycle of rebirth. A new religious ideal began to sweep over the landscape of northern India. In many circles, *mokṣa* or liberation began to challenge the traditional values, long associated with village life: marriage, kinship ties, and sacrifice.

It is during this period as well that the two most evident rivals of the Vedic tradition unfolded themselves on the Gaṅgā plain: Buddhism and Jainism. Rejecting a worldview centered in Vedic ritual, these ascetic communities were nourished by a growing individualism, cosmopolitanism, and freedom of motion. Just as the emerging merchant guilds constituted a voluntary order with values appropriate to their distinctive secular goals, so the early Buddhist and Jaina monks constituted a voluntary order with values and practices appropriate to their distinctive soteriological goals.

Building blocks: renunciation

It is difficult to accurately assess the impact that these radical soteriological systems had upon the evident changes that would take place in Brāhmaṇic thought and practice. Scholars remain divided on the issue. Clearly, however, Brāhmaṇic orthodoxy with its Vedic heritage did not turn a blind eye to these movements. Coupled with the other social and economic changes of the century, mainstream Brāhmaṇic thought was compelled to respond to the challenges of a new age, challenges coming not only from without but also from liberal-minded Brāhmaṇs within.

As the temporal efficacy and soteriological guarantees of the traditional Vedic ritual were thrown into question and as new visions of salvation eased the anxiety of a changing world, rejection—indeed, renunciation—of that ritual-centered world became more and more prevalent. The culturally sensitive, even skeptical, liberal-minded members of the Brāhmaṇic world saw renunciation of that world as a growing option. Renunciation of that traditional world entailed, then, a rejection of traditional institutions, among them: marriage, procreation, and extended kinship ties. But perhaps most evidently, renunciation of the traditional worldview meant renunciation of its ritual and sacrificial procedures.

From an ideal-typical point of view, the village householder with his traditional values now stood in contrast or opposition to that new "individual" who chose to renounce the traditional world and its sacrificial structure. Within the context of Brāhmaṇic self-understanding, the renouncer is first and foremost one who abandons the implements and procedures of the sacrifice. On the theoretical level, the renouncer stood over against the conservative, tradition-minded "man-in-the-world" and his defense of Vedic ritual.

This "debate" is well evidenced in the early Upaniṣads. Proponents of the new soteriology are clear in devaluing the efficacy of sacrificial procedure. Ritual activity, at best, can lead one to the "realm of the fathers," a postmortem state which—from the perspective of this new worldview—is less than optimal. Only by leaving behind the entanglements of domestic life, only by renouncing the concerns of society and sacrifice, could one travel a higher path to a more desirable state. More and more, it was a particular form of gnosis, a mystical knowledge, which came to be seen as the preeminent means of attaining such release from the woes of *karma* and transmigration. From the perspective of this new worldview, it was not through *doing* but through *knowing* that one could attain release and freedom.

A clear watershed emerged in Hindu thought and self-understanding, a watershed theoretically separating "action" (*karma*) from "knowledge" (*jñāna*). From a certain point of view this watershed is historical. The soteriological significance of a mystical knowing is new, at least in terms of emphasis. But the watershed is also and more significantly structural. The values of both *karma*—with its traditional activity in a world of kinship ties and ritual—and *jñāna*—with its renunciation of that traditional world—sought inclusion within a robust new theology. These two soteriological visions eventuated in the *karmakāṇḍa* and the *jñānakāṇḍa*, respectively. It is this opposition, this conflict, this tension between two soteriological visions and the effort to somehow resolve that opposition which gave birth to the *āśrama* systems. In fact, the early and ongoing debates in Hindu theology over the respective importance and place of the various *āśrama*s can be fully understood only from the perspective of this tension (Kaelber 1989: 73–81).

The opposition between renouncer and householder was, however, often more theoretical than real. This can be seen clearly in the paradoxical position taken by Brāhmaṇic thought regarding one's postmortem condition. From the perspective of the *karmakāṇḍa*, the properly performed funeral rite still delivered one to immortality with the ancestors for whom ritual gifts were still offered. From the perspective of the new soteriology and the *jñānakāṇḍa*, however, the individual's postmortem fate was the consequence of his or her very own past deeds. From this perspective, one was reborn biologically from an earthly womb rather than spiritually with a new immortal body in the beyond. These two views, dramatically opposed to each other at a theoretical level, coexisted at the more pedestrian level of day-to-day life.

There was, in fact, actual dialogue and social interchange between members of both "worlds." This is well reflected, for example, in the life of Yājñavalkya as presented at *Bṛhadāraṇyaka Upaniṣad* 3.5.1. Having attained a mystical knowledge of ultimate reality, Yājñavalkya does not retire to perpetual solitude in the forest, imparting his wisdom secretly and serenely to only select disciples. He rather appears at the glorious court of King Videha. This ruler had, in fact, called together priests and self-proclaimed wise men from the entire kingdom in order to see who among them had the supreme knowledge. Although challenged by other participants, Yājñavalkya emerges victorious, claiming the very worldly prize of cows and gold.

At the ideal-typical level, however, the conflict between the older and the newer worldviews was often stark, over simplified, and sharply drawn. Traditional ritual and its rewards were challenged by a soteriologically empowered knowledge. The prestige of priest and sacrificer was challenged by ascetics of the forest. Asceticism in service to sacrifice was challenged by asceticism in service to meditation. Asceticism of limited duration was challenged by asceticism as a lifestyle. The value of worldly goals was challenged by a pessimism regarding rebirth. The value of *karma* was challenged by a salvation beyond conventional morality. The efficacy of funeral rites was challenged by the doctrine of transmigration.

In time, Brāhmaṇic theology forged a synthesis of these theoretically conflicting worlds. Room was made for innovation, yet tradition was maintained. Throughout this process of Hindu reinterpretation and self-understanding, however, Brāhmaṇic literature bears witness to an ongoing tension, even conflict of opinion.

EMERGENCE OF THE ĀŚRAMA SYSTEM AND THE POLITICS OF INCLUSION

Heuristic models

The emergence and development of ascetic lifestyles, renunciation, and the later *āśrama* system is a complex issue and therefore best illuminated from various perspectives. Any investigation of Brāhmaṇic asceticism and renunciation is thus greatly aided by considering a number of heuristic models, each throwing light on the issue from a particular perspective.

Although such models often conflict with each other in theory, their consideration and application can help us to apprehend the "robustness" of the phenomena in question.

A particular model for understanding the relationship between ritual and renunciation emerges implicitly but clearly in the work of Madeleine Biardeau (1976). Biardeau singles out sacrifice as being the most significant aspect of Vedic culture, the unifying and organizing principle of its religious life. She then moves beyond the Vedic tradition into Hinduism, using sacrifice as the "unifying theme to organize the confusing richness of Hindu religious thought and practice" (Heesterman 1985: 81). The model that emerges from Biardeau's investigation is, therefore, one of sacrifice as a protean and ever-expanding concept, capable of engendering and embracing diverse and variegated aspects of Vedic and post-Vedic tradition. Given its protean and embracing quality, sacrifice itself is able to establish continuity between diverse and sometimes opposing elements within the socioreligious complex. Working from her particular perspective, Biardeau is able to demonstrate continuity in areas where it has frequently been overlooked.

A number of her observations are relevant in the present context, bearing as they do upon the relationship between the theoretical institutions of sacrifice and renunciation. In her discussion of the *prāṇāgnihotra* (the inner sacrifice performed in the fires of breath), Biardeau (1976: 64) emphasizes the continuity between the traditional external sacrifice of the *yajamāna* and the ongoing but revalorized sacrificial concerns of the *vānaprastha* and the *saṃnyāsin* or renouncer. The practices of the renouncer are seen, therefore, not in opposition to the traditional institution but as an extension or modification of it. In a related fashion, she is able to demonstrate continuity between the second and the third *āśrama*s by observing that the "five great sacrifices" were essential in both life stages. In fact, Biardeau's observations regarding the *vānaprastha* show how the hermit could serve as a transitional figure, bridging the institution of sacrifice as upheld by the *gṛhastha* with the renunciatory "sacrifice" of the *saṃnyāsin*. Relatedly, Biardeau points to the practice of purification that links the *yajamāna* to the renouncer. The *saṃnyāsin*, because he unintentionally kills minuscule creatures, requires purification as does the *yajamāna*, who takes the life of the sacrificial victim (Biardeau 1976: 64–68).

Biardeau's model, despite its evident heuristic value, is not without its limitations. But this is virtually inevitable. Illuminating a tradition from a particular perspective invariably leaves certain phenomena in the shadows. Heesterman (1985: 82) therefore suggests that sacrifice may indeed be too limited a rubric under which to subsume the variegated aspects of Hinduism. One might also observe that the growing significance of knowledge, particularly in the early Upaniṣads, is not always well served when comprehended solely from the perspective of the sacrifice. Biardeau's model, with its focus on continuity, is less able to apprehend the tension and conflict so often conspicuous in the tradition. Biardeau's model appears unconcerned with what Wendy Doniger O'Flaherty (1971: 279) has called the "deep-seated anti-asceticism" in orthodox Hinduism. With her insistence on continuity, Biardeau highlights how the tradition of renunciation grew rather naturally out of the householder's life. The model is thereby less concerned with the effort required by the mainstream Brāhmaṇic tradition to assimilate innovative and often challenging beliefs and practices. The Brāhmaṇic tradition most certainly demonstrates continuity. The issue, however, is often whether that continuity emerged rather smoothly and naturally from within or whether it was diligently put in place despite reluctance, resistance, and ambiguity. Although Biardeau (1976: 65) characterizes renunciation and sacrifice as the poles of Hinduism, she clearly stresses the continuity rather than the tension between them.

Heesterman, in an effort to explain the emergence of renunciation and Brāhmaṇic asceticism, has generated a heuristic model of his own. His model, in many ways, aligns itself with that of Biardeau, in that both models affirm the continuity between sacrificial endeavor and renunciation. In fact, Heesterman, even more emphatically than Biardeau, maintains that renunciation as a lifestyle is the logical, indeed, inevitable outgrowth of ritual concerns.

The Śrauta sacrifice, for Heesterman, is a self-contained, transcendent realm of perfect order, guaranteed success, absolute purity, and unchanging grandeur. It is also, according to Heesterman (1985: 3, 26, 82, 188), a realm of no utilitarian benefit and no connection with the world of change, turmoil, and uncertainty surrounding it on all sides. But it was not always so. The Vedic myths still bear witness to an earlier time in which the sacrifice was clearly a part of the worldly realm including its struggles and violence. Heesterman (1985: 26–35, 50, 68, 86–87) observes that the enemies of the ritual, so evident in myth, were once the flesh and blood adversarial partners in an "agonistic," indeed life-threatening, ritual combat. This agonistic and precarious sacrificial endeavor was, however, changed in what Heesterman (1985: 91) regards as a dramatic ritual reform. The sacrifice was removed from the realm of turmoil and enshrined unchangingly in its own sacred enclosure. This reformation produced a sacrifice that was both "individualized" and "desocialized" (Heesterman 1987: 234). It no longer performed a public function, serving now only the individual, the *yajamāna*, for whom the rite was performed. Making reference to the mythical scenarios in which Prajāpati overcame death, Heesterman sees the paradigm of the *yajamāna*'s own autonomy. The *yajamāna*, like the sacrifice itself, unifies all opposites through mythical and ritual connections. Leaving behind the conflict-ridden and mundane world, the sacrificer could enter, for a time, the sacrificial enclosure and enjoy the transcendence afforded him by the ritual. As an individual, the *yajamāna* fashioned his own transcendence. With its attained perfection the ritual lost all connection with the mundane order; and the *yajamāna*—or more correctly, Heesterman's "ideal Brāhmaṇ"—achieved his autonomy and transcendence only by turning his back upon the world of change and turmoil (Heesterman 1985: 4, 32–34, 45, 50, 91, 101). There is then an unbridgeable gap and tension between ritual and reality. But, suggests Heesterman, that gap is bridgeable by the ideal Brāhmaṇ who, as an individual, voluntarily chooses to move from one realm to the other. "Janus-faced," the ideal Brāhmaṇ renounces the world during the ritual and returns to it at the conclusion of the rite (Heesterman 1985: 3, 5, 9).

The autonomy of the *yajamāna* was, however, not yet complete. Although he had been delivered from his dependence upon a rival, he found himself still dependent upon the officiating priests. It is for this reason that Heesterman regards the *prāṇāgnihotra*, the internal sacrifice of the *vānaprastha* and the *saṃnyāsin*, as the inevitable outcome of the ritual search for individuality as well as autonomy. From this perspective, the permanent renunciation of the *saṃnyāsin* is the inevitable endpoint of the ideal Brāhmaṇ's quest for transcendence. Turning his back on the world, not only temporarily but also permanently, the *saṃnyāsin* disengaged himself from the opposites of the worldly order (Heesterman 1985: 38–44). In his quest for purity, the ideal Brāhmaṇ had to break all relations with the impure social realm. "Ideally, the brahman should stand outside of society, the highest brahman being the one who has no power or wealth or even provisions for the next day, and who performs the ritual in and for himself alone" (Heesterman 1987: 238). But herein lies one of the many paradoxes that Heesterman throws into relief. By turning his back upon the world, the *saṃnyāsin* may speak to it. Because he is disengaged from the world, he may engage himself with it. So again, the ideal Brāhmaṇ bridges the unbridgeable gap between the transcendent realm of renunciation and the mundane order. "Having emancipated himself from the world, the renouncer can from his sphere of independence reenter into relation with the world, where he now enjoys unequalled prestige" (Heesterman 1985: 43).

Heesterman's model is bold and enriching. It is unafraid of embracing the paradoxical aspects of Vedic and post-Vedic culture. For Heesterman, even more than for Biardeau, the *saṃnyāsin*'s renunciation seems to grow naturally, in fact inevitably, out of the Śrauta rite of the householder.

> It is often thought that the institution of renunciation emerged as a protest against brahminical orthodoxy or that it originated in non-brahminical or even non-Aryan circles. The theory of the four āśramas, or stages of life, would then have been an attempt at legitimizing the renunciatory modes of life and drawing them within the orbit of brahminical orthodoxy. There is of course full scope for recognizing the influence of extraneous beliefs and practices, for instance, in the matter of various forms of ascetism. But the important point is that these influences do not seem to have made a decisive irruption in the development of religious thought. They seem rather to have fitted themselves into the orthogenetic, internal development of Vedic thought.
>
> (Heesterman 1985: 39–40)

Heesterman's use of the term "orthogenetic" is significant here. His model clearly perceives the full-blown institution of renunciation as emerging naturally and in a "straight line" from within the orthodox tradition itself (Heesterman 1987: 236).

An alternative to this "orthogenic" model may be termed the model of "challenge and assimilation." It is now quite clear that the institution of renunciation, once alien to mainstream Brāhmaṇic *dharma*, became an integral element of Dharma literature only gradually and in the face of clear resistance. Emphasis on continuity should, therefore, not blind us to the challenges faced by Brāhmaṇic theology and the long struggle for resolution.

An influential example of the "challenge and assimilation" model is already found in the classic essay by Louis Dumont, "World Renunciation in Indian Religions" (1960). The author observes how Indian society and religion have "tended to absorb formerly heretical inventions" (Dumont 1960: 36). Dumont's specific concern here is the *saṃnyāsin* and the way in which his initially challenging conceptions ultimately enriched the orthodox tradition. Influenced by the typology of Max Weber, Dumont highlights two distinct and "ideal-typical" individuals: the "man-in-the-world" and the "renouncer." Relatedly, Dumont poses a clear dichotomy or bifurcation between two disparate realms. One may remain in "the world" and thereby be denied any real individuality, or one may turn his back upon that (sociocultural) realm, becoming a renouncer and simultaneously an "individual." Only the renouncer "thinks as an individual and this is the distinctive trait which opposes him to the man-in-the-world" (Dumont 1960: 46). Dumont perceives the ideal Brāhmaṇ as very much the man-in-the-world and not the renouncer at all. "We must in fact make a distinction. The Brahmans, as priests superior to all other men, are comfortably enough settled in the world. On the other hand, it is well known that classically whoever seeks liberation must leave the world and adopt an entirely different mode of life" (Dumont 1960: 44). For Dumont, only the *saṃnyāsin*, not the *yajamāna*, may be described as the "extramundane individual" (1960: 52). In generating a "system of oppositions" (Dumont 1960: 41), the author also juxtaposes the "worldly" values of *kāma*, *artha*, and *dharma* against the *saṃnyāsin*'s "value," namely, *mokṣa*.

Initially, according to Dumont, there was "hostility" to renunciation as a lifestyle. Relatedly, *mokṣa* was perceived as "fatal" to the other three values (Dumont 1960: 45). But the poles of worldly life and renunciation may be seen as "complimentary" (Dumont 1960: 41). In time, a dialectical relationship emerged between them. The man-in-the-world supports the *saṃnyāsin*, and the *saṃnyāsin* in turn provides the man-in-the-world with alternative perspectives, new religious possibilities, the hope for individuality, and the promise of liberation. What is crucial for Dumont is the growing "dialogue between the renouncer and the man-in-the-world" (1960: 37–38). That "extraordinary post-Vedic and pre-Hindu" period beginning with the first Upaniṣads and ending with the *Bhagavad Gītā* is seen by Dumont as a "golden age of speculation in which emerge . . . the dominant tendencies of Hindu thought" (1960: 49). The creative and fructifying force behind this process is the *saṃnyāsin*. "Rich and diverse as this movement appears," continues Dumont, "it is the work of renouncers" (1960: 49). The emergence of Hinduism is therefore a "process of aggregation to orthodoxy of sanyasic values" (Dumont 1960: 51). To simplify: for Heesterman, the *yajamāna*, the ideal Brāhmaṇ, "informs" the *saṃnyāsin*; for Dumont, the *saṃnyāsin* "informs" the *gṛhastha*, the "man-in-the-world" (1960: 46). Quoting Dumont: "The man-in-the-world, and particularly the Brahman, is given the credit for ideas which he may have adopted but not invented" (1960: 47). Relatedly, "the true historical development of Hinduism is in the sanyasic developments on the one hand and in their aggregation [that is, assimilation] to worldly religion on the other" (Dumont 1960: 47n21).

Recent and more sophisticated attempts to understand the emergence of renunciation, ascetic lifestyles, and the *āśrama* system have interwoven insights from both the "orthogenic" and the "challenge and assimilation" models. The insights and scholarship of Olivelle, in particular, demonstrate the rewards of critically integrating previous models, rejecting or accepting their perspectives under the impact of careful textual consideration. Further, by drawing critically on the sociological theories of Peter Berger and Thomas Luckmann (1966), Olivelle (1992: 46, 51) raises the traditional investigation to a new level of understanding.

Not only were the traditions and values of the Vedic world challenged from without by new goals and lifestyles, they were also challenged from within by what Olivelle regards as more liberal-minded Brāhmaṇs, cosmopolitan Brāhmaṇs receptive to the emerging urban culture of the day with its ability to foster more "individualistic" points of view. It was this cultural milieu—and not that of the village—which nurtured the possibility of individual choice (Olivelle 1992: 36–37). Lifestyles were no longer simply given by tradition; they were now presented as possibilities.

The process of assimilating these new worldviews and lifestyles was, according to Olivelle, a "two-way street" (1992: 52). Going beyond Berger and Luckmann, who argue that the process of assimilation is initiated solely by the "custodians of the established order," Olivelle (1992: 52) suggests that it was also the "champions of the new world" that sought acceptability and power at the institutional as well as at the ideological level. Therefore, rather than seeing the new worldview as simply a threat from without that had to be neutralized through compromise and inclusion, Olivelle sees the proponents of this new worldview as willing participants in the process of inclusion or assimilation.

Significantly, it was the original or "preclassical" *āśrama* system that emerged as the most significant product of that drive toward inclusion. "The purpose of creating the system was clearly to legitimize celibate modes of life by providing a place for them within the sphere of *dharma*. In so doing they expanded the meaning of *dharma*; it is made to include institutions and ideals of the old as well as the new world" (Olivelle 1992: 53). The *dharma* of society is now supplemented with a *dharma* of renunciation and liberation. The traditional values of *dharma* (moral behavior), *artha* (worldly success), and *kāma* (sensual pleasure) are supplemented with a fourth value or goal, namely, liberation or *mokṣa*.

The *āśrama* system, with its drive toward inclusion, is in many ways similar to the older system of class (*varṇa*). Both systems "aim at managing diversity not by eliminating it but by recognizing and including the diversities within an overarching system. The creators of the *āśrama* system intended to do to the diversity of religious life styles what the creators of the *varṇa* system did to the diversity of social and ethnic groups. In this sense it was a forward-looking and reformist scheme rather than a defensive wall put up by beleaguered conservatives" (Olivelle 1993: 101).

The original system and the issue of choice

The original *āśrama* system differed significantly from the better-known, classical system that evolved from it. In the original system the four *āśrama*s of Vedic student, householder, forest hermit, and renouncer were understood to be permanent careers or vocations. The four orders were not sequential, as they would be in the later system. According to the original system, the twice-born Hindu male would choose one of these four orders as a lifelong vocation. This choice was made after the *dvija* had completed a period of Vedic study. This preliminary period of study was not regarded as an *āśrama* in the original system. It was rather a precondition for any of the four careers, including that of perpetual student.

It is important to realize in this context that the *āśrama* system did not create the institutions that it sought to organize. As indicated before, the *brahmacārin*'s career—the career of perpetual Vedic student—was part of the Vedic heritage. As such, it was a component or building block used by Brāhmaṇic theologians in constructing their system. So too, quite obviously, the institution of marriage preceded its incorporation into the system. The same is true also of the many and varied ascetic lifestyles of renunciation. The system—either in its original or in its classical forms—should never be confounded or confused with the actual social institutions it sought to stylize, organize, and even prioritize. Relatedly, the fact that women, for example, are not given an autonomous place within either the original or the classical system in no way implies that women did not engage in renunciation or lead ascetic lifestyles. It means only that the *āśrama* systems did not legitimize these activities. The same may be said of Śūdras.

Acceptance of the original system by Brāhmaṇic theology was hardly immediate. Initial opposition in the fourth and fifth centuries BCE is rooted largely in the challenge carried by the new system to married life and the generation of offspring. Because the *āśrama*s were perpetual and because three of the four career options were institutions of celibacy, only individuals choosing the householder *āśrama* would produce (legitimate) offspring. Although one was free to choose one's *āśrama*, one was not free to change *āśrama*s or to pursue another *āśrama* at some later point. The *āśrama*s, as originally conceived, were permanent.

By the second century BCE, however, this original system became somewhat more acceptable to Brāhmaṇic theology and found its way uneasily into Brāhmaṇic tradition. The Dharmasūtras of Āpastamba and Vasiṣṭha accept the system (Olivelle 1992: 93). They do, however, argue against a privileged status for renunciation, praising instead the householder. Although the virtues and legitimacy of renunciation have here made their way into the Brāhmaṇic fold, the ongoing tension remains evident.

The possibility of avoiding married life was, however, not the only aspect of the original system that troubled mainstream Brāhmaṇic thought. The element of choice inherent in the system was just as problematic. Cultural life in the Gaṅgā Valley was now offering a greater range of personal choice than did the preceding period. This is evidenced by the emergence of non-Brāhmaṇic ascetic communities as well as secular organizations and institutions. But Brāhmaṇic thought, always characterized by its priestly need for regulation and conformity, found the element of individual choice unsettling.

The question was then simply this: How could the Brāhmaṇic tradition make a place for renunciation and "careers" of asceticism while simultaneously reducing the range of individual choice and virtually mandating marriage and offspring? The solution to this double-edged problem came in the form of a new, more acceptable configuration of the existing *āśrama*s.

The classical system: challenge, tension, and assimilation

Unlike the original system, the new or classical configuration presented the *āśrama*s not as permanent vocations but as a sequence of temporary "careers." Rather than choosing one *āśrama* for life, the adult Hindu male was now required—or strongly encouraged—to pursue all four *āśrama*s in a logically crafted sequence, leading him from youth to old age. The preliminary and temporary student period, not regarded as an *āśrama* in the original system, was now merged with the *brahmacarya āśrama* to form the mandatory first "stage." Not only did the new configuration seek to eliminate choice, it sought also to guarantee or secure the institution of marriage and therewith procreation. Renunciation, according to the classical scenario, was clearly an acceptable aspect of Brāhmaṇic life, but only if pursued at the right time in one's career. Having paid one's "debt" to the sages in stage one by being a student and having paid ones "debt" to the gods and to the ancestors through sacrifice and offspring in stage two, the mature, even aging Hindu male was now able to pursue liberation in the waning years of his life.

As Olivelle (1993: 127, 131) has suggested, an effort was now made to correlate passage through the four sequential *āśrama*s with a number of *saṃskāra*s or initiatory consecrations. These well-established rites had long punctuated the *dvija*'s life. According to the theoretical formulation, one entered each *āśrama* by means of an appropriate initiation. The age-old *upanayana* now constituted one's entry into the first stage or *brahmacarya āśrama*. Having completed his Vedic studies, having performed a ritual bath, and having returned home, the *dvija* was now ready for marriage and therewith initiation into the second *āśrama*, that of *gṛhastha* or householder. When old age approached, his domestic and ritual obligations fulfilled, the twice-born Hindu male—either alone or accompanied by his wife—was initiated into the third *āśrama*, that of forest hermit. Even one who entered the fourth *āśrama*—thereby embarking upon renunciation and leaving the ritual complex behind—was required to do so through a clearly defined *dīkṣa* or rite of passage. The new or classical formulation did not permit return to a previous *āśrama*. Each *āśrama* or stage led logically to the next. The fourth *āśrama* alone could be seen as a permanent state, in that it ended only with biological death.

It is important to realize that the classical system, like its predecessor, was a diligently crafted and evidently theoretical formulation. The system embodied normative prescription rather than social fact. It struggled to present in a neat, comprehensible, and acceptable sequence a montage of goals, lifestyles, and practices that often defied the efforts of system-seeking priests. But even more importantly—and more surprisingly—even in Brāhmaṇic literature itself, the system is rarely, if ever, "encountered in its pure form" (Olivelle 1993: 173). Even *Manusmṛti*, so frequently cited as the *locus classicus* of the system, deviates conspicuously from the ideal-typical formulation. Not only in *Manusmṛti* but also in the entire body of Brāhmaṇic literature deviations from the ideal-typical norm are evident, particularly in prescriptions and descriptions regarding "renunciation." The *āśrama* system must be seen as an exercise in Brāhmaṇic self-understanding and theology. As such, it is fraught with ambiguities, even contradiction. Not surprisingly, the fundamental debate over renunciation surfaced again and again, taking the form of specific issues.

One such issue centered on the appropriate time when one might renounce. According to the original system, the twice-born male might choose to do so directly after a period of study. The situation was, however, quite different with the *saṃnyāsin* of the classical system. The classical *saṃnyāsin* was quite literally one who "abandoned" or "threw down" the implements of sacrificial procedure. The term, which first appears in the Brāhmaṇic thought around the second century BCE, is found in neither Buddhism nor Jainism. It is a Brāhmaṇic term, fully comprehended only against a background of the sacrificial rite. Only the *dvija* who had fully engaged himself in the sacrificial complex was able to "abandon" that complex of activities. The *saṃnyāsin* was, quite strictly, one who abandoned the sacrificial fire, the sacrificial string, and various sacrificial implements.

There were, however, logically argued "exceptions" to this norm. Quite clearly, individuals—Hindu, Buddhist, and Jaina alike—were leaving society in pursuit of a transcendent liberation. Somehow the new *āśrama* system—normative or ideal-typical as it might be—had to make logical provision for observable fact. As a consequence, it was argued in a number of the *Saṃnyāsa Upaniṣad*s that an individual might in fact renounce at any time, assuming that he felt sufficient "detachment" (*vairāgya*) from worldly concerns. According to *Jābāla Upaniṣad* 64, for example, one might renounce directly from studentship, domestic life, or the forest.

In apparent paradox, many Brāhmaṇic texts describe in some detail the ritual procedure by means of which one correctly abandons the ritual, thereby becoming a renouncer. Simply stated: for the ritually minded Brāhmaṇic tradition, it was only through ritual that one could properly abandon ritual. The rite of initiation, lasting two days, required the *dvija* to formally declare that he "belonged to no one and that no one belonged to him" (T. Hopkins 1971: 83). Vowing to injure no living thing, he made the transition to homeless wanderer. Central to the two-day rite was the performance of the *dvija*'s final external sacrifice. That sacrifice completed, he now placed the ritual fires within himself. From this point on he would be without fire, performing the fire-sacrifice through breath (and mind) alone. Significantly, this inner sacrifice, the *prāṇāgnihotra*, was interpreted to be the very *perfection* of ritual procedure (Olivelle 1992: 68). Herein lies perhaps the quintessence of Brāhmaṇic logic. The renunciation or abandonment of ritual was synonymous with the interiorization of ritual that, in turn, was synonymous with the perfection of ritual. Further, although the *saṃnyāsin* gave up his (external) sacrificial string, he now wears a more perfect string, the "internal" string of knowledge. These subtle exercises in paradoxical logic did not, however, fully resolve the issue of whether the *saṃnyāsin* was without ritual or not. Although it was a general rule that the wandering, begging *saṃnyāsin* would now be without external string, external fire, and external rite, logical exceptions to this rule were plentiful. Quite clearly, the fundamental tension of Brāhmaṇic theology remained alive. The *saṃnyāsin*, with a life beyond society, remained a challenge to tradition. By abandoning the external ritual, he appeared to abandon not only society but also social classification and, thereby, social regulation as well (Kaelber 1989: 119).

Whereas the *Saṃnyāsa Upaniṣad*s regularly declare that the sacrificial cord, and therewith external sacrifice, should be given up, a more orthodox position states that the sacrificial cord "is the means for acquiring mokṣa for all the twice-born. Those who renounce it . . . go to hell" (H. Sharma 1939: 35). It is not surprising but certainly interesting that in many texts the *saṃnyāsin* again performs external sacrifices (H. Sharma 1939: 49). Many Upaniṣads also stipulate that the *saṃnyāsin* give up his animal skin and go naked. A more orthodox position, however, often requires the wearing of a black antelope skin, a time-honored symbol of Brāhmaṇic sacrifice. The same conflict may be seen in the issue of whether the *saṃnyāsin* should have a girdle and a staff.

Although a simplification, it is in many ways accurate to say that those Upaniṣads reflecting the spirit of the *jñānakāṇḍa* are more faithful to the ideal of liberation and its concrete consequences—including liberation from *dharma*—in their description of the renouncer than is the legal literature of the *karmakāṇḍa*, which is far more concerned with bringing the *saṃnyāsin* back under the umbrella of regulation, obligation, and classification. A striking example of this conflict in the legal literature is the evident glorification of the fourth *āśrama* in the Upaniṣads and the almost persistent glorification of the second *āśrama* in the legal literature. Despite perpetual lip service to "release" as the ultimate goal in the *karmakāṇḍa*, the second *āśrama* is invariably regarded as being superior. This position is evident for example in *Manusmṛti* (T. Hopkins 1971: 75; Kaelber 1989: 119–20). His glorification of the householder *āśrama* of necessity obligates *Manusmṛti* to conclude that the "highest goal" is attainable not only by the *saṃnyāsin* but also by the householder.

Manusmṛti's position on social location and the "highest goal" did not, however, resolve the issue. Many authors within the *jñānakāṇḍa* tradition argued that only the *saṃnyāsin* could attain that goal. But the issue was even more complicated. Simply put: Was the fourth *āśrama* a social location in which one *sought* liberation, or was it rather a social location for those who had *already attained* liberation? This issue cut to the very core of Brāhmaṇic self-understanding. Not surprisingly it was never fully resolved. Was liberation possible while still alive? Could one in fact be a *jīvanmukti*, a person "liberated-in-life?" Further, was it in fact possible to regard the fourth *āśrama* as a preparation for the highest goal and also hold that in fact one could be liberated in life? Such questions led some authors to postulate a fifth *āśrama*, a social location that transcended the traditional four (Olivelle 1993: 223, 232).

These many issues cut to the very heart of Brāhmaṇic theology simply because they were all, in one way or another, variations on one central issue: *dharma*. Was it possible for one to achieve a state of liberation in which one was actually freed from the obligations of social life? Did the somewhat theoretical state of a liberating gnosis actually liberate one from the constraints of moral behavior? Although the *saṃnyāsin* was, according to many authors, legally, socially, and ritually "dead," did that free him from legal and moral constraint? Even Śaṃkara, despite his theoretical consistency in spelling out the consequences of liberation, pulled back repeatedly from the antinomian ramifications of his position (Olivelle 1993: 225–30). One solution to this quandary was to suggest that not all *saṃnyāsin*s were alike. It could then be argued that only the highest form of *saṃnyāsin*, the *paramahaṃsa*, both sought and achieved the highest goal.

What began then, particularly in the early Upaniṣads, as a simple description of ascetics renouncing the world, became over time a complicated system of rules and regulations covering virtually every aspect of life. Renunciation was no longer peripheral or even external to *dharma* in most texts. In fact, it had become one of its most important areas. The increasingly prevalent term "*mokṣa-dharma*" beautifully represents the boldness of Brāhmaṇic theology. Interestingly enough, the practice of *tapas* or asceticism—theoretically no longer necessary for one who has attained the highest goal—is now frequently prescribed as a crucial aspect of the renouncer's life. I suggest that had the orthodox tradition permitted the *saṃnyāsin* his asceticism, its victory would have been less impressive. By making that asceticism *obligatory* it won a victory of far greater proportion (Kaelber 1989: 121). This is dramatically accentuated by the fact that the conservative tradition often regarded the asceticism of the third and fourth *āśrama*s as a means of penance and purification for past misdeeds. From the perspective of *this* tradition at least, the objective of asceticism and renunciation remained to a large degree atonement for previous transgressions and therewith preparation for death.

In the ongoing efforts of Brāhmaṇic self-interpretation to assimilate the *saṃnyāsin* into the orthodox fold, the age-old institution of *brahmacārin* or Vedic student appears to have played a significant role. Despite their very different objectives, the more recent practices of the *saṃnyāsin* were impressively similar to the well-established and clearly acceptable practices of the *brahmacārin*. It was this similarity in praxis between the well-established career of the *brahmacārin* and the challenging career of the *saṃnyāsin* that helped facilitate the theological acceptance of the latter. The *brahmacārin* did, in fact, serve in many ways as a forerunner and legitimizing model through which both the *vānaprastha* and the *saṃnyāsin* could be assimilated into mainstream thought (Kaelber 1989: 116). The activities of the *brahmacārin*, the *vānaprastha*, and the *saṃnyāsin* are often striking in their similarities (Kaelber 1989: 151): the practice of *tapas* or asceticism, the practice of *prāṇāyāma* or control of breath, the observance of *brahmacarya* or celibacy, begging, fasting, total abstinence from certain foods, recitation of the Veda (Kaelber 1989: 118).

Because he was an integral member of the orthodox fold, the *brahmacārin* could serve as a legitimizing model for the asceticism of the fourth *āśrama* in many ways. This is perhaps nowhere more evident than at the initiation of the ascetic into the fourth life stage. This initiation is quite evidently modeled on that of the *brahmacārin*—an ascetic, to be sure, but one who is very much a part of society and its classifications. Whereas the *Saṃnyāsa Upaniṣad*s often state that the *saṃnyāsin* gives up his sacrificial cord (H. Sharma 1939: 34), girdle, antelope skin, and upper garment, *Vaikhānasasmārtasūtra* 2.5

makes it explicitly clear that the *saṃnyāsin* receives these things anew at his initiation in exactly the way prescribed at the *upanayana*. The instructions given for the reception of the ascetic by his new teacher are virtually identical in each case (H. Sharma 1939: 50). As part of the initiation, the *saṃnyāsin* has his hair, beard, and nails cut, receives a new name, swears obedience to his teacher, and takes a vow of truthfulness and noninjury just as the *brahmacārin* had done before him. It is accurate to say that the more the *saṃnyāsin* resembles the *brahmacārin* the more he has been assimilated into the orthodox fold (Kaelber 1989: 121).

Most of the above-mentioned practices of the *vānaprastha* and world renouncer are clearly set forth in *Manusmṛti*, which characterizes both *āśramas* by severe austerities. Significantly, however, for *Manusmṛti* the *brahmacārin*'s activities are hardly characterized by austerity at all, certainly not to the extent set forth in the *Atharva Veda* and the Gṛhyasūtras for the "old" *brahmacārin*. It is not the *brahmacārin* of *Manusmṛti* who inherits the characteristics and activities of the old *brahmacārin* but *Manusmṛti*'s *vānaprastha* and world renouncer. The *brahmacārin* of *Manusmṛti* has become something quite different. Thus, *Manusmṛti* 2.229 states that for the *brahmacārin* obedience to father, mother, and teacher is the best form of austerity. The student who pleases these three obtains all the rewards that the performance of *tapas* can yield (*Manusmṛti* 2.228). In fact, according to *Manusmṛti* 2.234: "All the duties of [the *brahmacārin*] have been fulfilled by him who honors parents and teacher." For the *brahmacārin* of the *Atharva Veda* and the Gṛhyasūtras, study of the Veda was always related to the practice of austerity, but for *Manusmṛti* (2.166) austerity may be almost eliminated for "the study of the Veda is . . . the highest austerity." The student must still remain chaste and beg alms, but fasting is no longer necessary, for, as *Manusmṛti* 2.188 observes, "The subsistence of a student on begged food is declared to be equal to fasting." *Manusmṛti*'s *brahmacārin* is concerned not with fasting but with avoiding "excessive eating," which is "prejudicial to health" (2.57). In general, *Manusmṛti*'s *brahmacārin* is concerned primarily with obedience to and respect for elders, social graces, purity of heart, doing his duty, and a disciplined life in a more conventional sense, but not with the creation of an ascetically powerful *tapas*. It is also significant that *Manusmṛti* no longer requires the *brahmacārin* to leave his hair, beard, and nails uncut. The old *brahmacārin*, essentially concerned with *tapas*, largely passes from the scene; the *vānaprastha* and *saṃnyāsin*—and eventually the *saṃnyāsin* alone—become his true successors.

The Āśrama system today

Any attempt to generalize about the modern-day householder's life, the modern-day renouncer's life, and their relative value invites evident frustration. As T. N. Madan has said in this context: "It is . . . well known that cultural diversity within Hindu society, in terms of inter-regional and inter-caste differences . . . is so great that every general statement . . . is suspect. . . . And . . . the more trained we are the more likely it is that we will doubt what we write or say" (1987: 4). The profusion of options in India today—particularly ascetic and renunciatory options—is often bewildering. It is, in fact, sometimes difficult to disentangle the Brāhmaṇic or more orthodox practices from the non-Brāhmaṇic and often baroque endeavors of unorthodox *sādhus*. Three things however appear certain. The "*āśrama* system"—always more theoretic than real—is less a reflection of reality today than ever before. Nonetheless, the influence of these theoretical norms continues to inform Hindu sensibilities and value. Lastly, the two primary "building blocks" that predated the classical scenario, namely, domestic life and renunciation, both clearly thrive despite the fading reality of a theoretical system.

Many of the domestic sacrifices, ancient enough to predate the *āśrama* system, are in full vigor today. Rural life in particular remains centered on the immediate family, extended kinship ties, and rituals that bind the cosmos and its inhabitants—both human and otherwise—together. For many Hindus, the *saṃskāra*s that became interwoven with the *gṛhastha āśrama* in the classical system remain an avenue of social cohesion and shared value. The centrality of domestic life in rural India is well articulated by Madan in his study of Brāhmaṇs in the Kashmir Valley: "The best place to die . . . is one's own home, the house in which one has lived. For most men this would also be the house where one was born, but in the case of women it would be the house where one has lived after marriage and borne children. The house is not a mere dwelling but the microcosm of the universe" (Madan 1987: 122).

For most Hindus family and "household" remain central. Particularly in village India, however, it is common to find an increased interest in spiritual issues as one grows older as well as greater detachment from "worldly" concerns. As S. C. Dube observes: "Though it is rare for people to renounce their home and property in old age, old men and women excessively attached to material goods come in for a good deal of criticism. . . . It is at this time that their thoughts turn more to religion and to the destiny of their souls in the future life" (1967: 132). This change of attitude, then, rarely entails an actual renunciation of domestic life. The key seems to be not "renunciation" of social and domestic concerns but a growing emotional "detachment" therefrom. The values of the *saṃnyāsin* thus prompt the householder to alter his attitude and perspective if not his spatial and social location.

The role of the third *āśrama*, that of the *vānaprastha*, is perhaps the most elusive. So it has always been. Even scholars cannot agree regarding the vitality or even the existence of the *āśrama*. As early as the classical period itself, Hindu law givers argued that the third *āśrama* was no longer an option in the present Kali Yuga, the dark age (Olivelle 1993: 236). More recently, scholars have suggested that the *āśrama* was always too theoretical to sustain an actual existence. It appears clear, however, that if indeed the *āśrama* has melted away in the modern world, it has "melted into" the householder *āśrama* rather than into that of the *saṃnyāsin*. I suggest this for a number of reasons. The *vānaprastha* rarely picks up and retires into a forest, as the name would suggest. He continues, rather, to function in the social and even in the political world. Although possibly "retired" from his previous occupation, he devotes his energies to serving others through charitable endeavors, counseling, and mediating social issues. He may continue in a married state, although celibate coexistence becomes an option as he turns his attention to more spiritual concerns (Housden 1996: 160). Although progressively "detached" from the sociopolitical world, he continues to function in it (Organ 1970: 232).

The age-old issues and controversies surrounding the *saṃnyāsin* persist into the modern world. Śaṃkara's distinction between renouncer's who were part of the *āśrama* system and renouncers who were beyond that system (Olivelle 1993: 225) remains alive—in varying guises—today. As stated above, *Jābāla Upaniṣad* 64 asserted that the individual who felt sufficiently "detached" could renounce at any time, even bypassing the duties of a householder. So also today, the individual may bypass both the second and the third *āśramas* in pursuit of perfection (Organ 1970: 231). The modern-day *sādhu* may, therefore, be understood in the light of a long tradition. Viewed from a different perspective, however, many modern-day *sādhus* or "holy men" fall outside of the Brāhmaṇic tradition, neglecting the traditional rites of transition and adopting values and practices that place them beyond any recognizable Brāhmaṇic framework.

According to one source, there are "between four and five million ascetics, or sadhus, in India today, perhaps ten percent of whom are women" (Housden 1996: 139). Many of these renouncers—covered in ashes, with their long matted hair, and only a rag or animal skin for clothing—differ little from early ascetics described in the Vedas. Many modern-day ascetics are baroque even by Indian standards and fall well beyond the pail of Brāhmaṇic orthodoxy. Indeed, the honor afforded wandering holy men has waned appreciably, particularly over the last thirty years. The influx of Western values has also eroded the honor and respect paid to *sādhus*. Begging is no longer as acceptable as it once was and free passage on trains and buses is being curtailed (Housden 1996: 142). In fact, one often sees an increasing mistrust of renouncers, *sādhus*, and even the values they uphold. After careful study of Brāhmaṇs in the Kashmir Valley, Madan (1981: 243) observes that renouncers and their values are often felt to challenge domestic life. Renouncers are even denigrated as charlatans or as undesirables. Nonetheless, viewing India as a whole, the ideal of the *saṃnyāsin* continues to stir the Hindu psyche. The alluring tones of renunciation serve still as counterpoint to the complex symphony of "worldly" life.

"WORLD REJECTION" AS A CROSS-CULTURAL ISSUE

Robert Bellah, in a seminal essay entitled "Religious Evolution" (1964), has succinctly delineated what he believes to be some of the critical shifts characterizing religious worldviews in the first millennium BCE. Like Karl Jaspers and others, Bellah sees this period as being pivotal in the development of religious thought and human self-interpretation. Central to religious change during this period was the virtually universal emergence in literate cultures of what Bellah, like others before him, terms an attitude of "world rejection" or "world denial." Significantly, the particular issues with which Hinduism grappled, issues that gave birth to the *āśrama* system, can be clearly seen as a quintessential illustration of the shift in worldview which Bellah articulates.

For Bellah, the periods preceding this "Axial Age" may be termed "primitive" and "archaic," respectively. Viewed universally and cross-culturally, the first of these periods is one in which no religious organization or intent exists independently of—or in opposition to—society at large and its values (Bellah 1964: 363). Religious ritual here reinforces social solidarity and tribal values. Kinship ties, including those to ancestors, are of paramount importance. Citing the eminent student of Australian religion, W. E. H. Stanner (1963), Bellah characterizes life in such a culture as a "one possibility thing" (1964: 365). Religion here provides "little leverage . . . to change the world" (Bellah 1964: 364) or to speak to it from a "world-transcending" perspective.

In essential ways—and certainly for our purposes here—the archaic period is little different. Viewing the issue from a cross-cultural perspective, Bellah observes that social and religious structures are now more complex. Intricate sacrificial rituals emerge, priestly structure and function become more complicated, mythologies are self-consciously elaborated. Nonetheless, the religious world remains a "one possibility" exercise. "There is little tension between religious demand and social conformity. Indeed, social conformity is at every point reinforced with religious sanction" (Bellah 1964: 365). But with developing complexity "an increased burden of anxiety enters the relations between man and the ultimate conditions of his existence" (Bellah 1964: 365). In fact, traditional mythologies, supporting the status quo, are now gently thrown into question.

Significant changes gradually occur, however, not only in India but also in literate societies throughout the world. During the next period, the "historical" period, religions the world over give birth to a new "transcendent" perspective. "Under these circumstances the religious goal of salvation (or enlightenment . . . [or] release . . .) is for the first time the central religious preoccupation" (Bellah 1964: 366). The given empirical cosmos is now devalued. Traditional social and religious values are questioned, challenged, even rejected. The value of the traditional "world" is for the first time "denied" by significant constituencies of society. Bellah and others have observed on a universal plane the growing tension between traditional tribal, ritual, and mythological values and the new, transcendent worldviews that now emerge. So, too, Bellah has made reference to the evident "individualism" which accompanies—even spurs—these religious developments (1964: 366–67). Not only are traditional social values challenged and left behind by innovative individuals, but so too is society itself, in what may be termed a "religious withdrawal from the world" (Bellah 1964: 367).

With the appearance of these "world-transcending" or "world-denying" perspectives, an inevitable tension emerges between traditional values and social structures, on the one hand, and the new values and religious institutions, on the other. It is precisely because this emerging tension appears throughout the literate world that an understanding of the Hindu situation is of particular importance. It is hardly an exaggeration to suggest that no culture has made the recognition and resolution of this fundamental tension more central to its religious self-interpretation than has Hinduism. The need to incorporate both "worldly" and "otherworldly" concerns into a unified and mutually reinforcing system is nowhere more evident than in Brāhmaṇic thought. The hoped-for resolution of this fundamental tension in Brāhmaṇic self-understanding is, in fact, the core of *varṇāśramadharma* and therewith Hinduism itself. Issues, tensions, and conflicts, often implicit in other cultural traditions, are explicitly articulated, debated, and continuously reexamined in Hinduism. Simply stated, an understanding of the *āśrama* system, its inherent dilemmas, and its hoped-for resolutions sheds invaluable light on a crucial cross-cultural issue in humankind's religious and spiritual self-interpretation.

Despite recognizing the contributions of Bellah and earlier scholars, such as Max Weber, Ernst Troeltsch, and Louis Dumont, more recent scholarship has become increasingly critical of the terms "world denying" and "world rejecting." Nowhere is this more evident than in the work of Steven Collins. Although recognizing his debt to Dumont, Collins rightly observes that Dumont "nowhere defines the term ['world'] in his writings" (1988: 103). Referring to the manner in which Weber and Troeltsch used the term "world," Collins observes that their definitions, although "conversationally . . . applicable to Indian materials," are too much a "blend of Christian theology and sociological description." As a consequence, according to Collins, the term "world" does not "function precisely [enough] when dealing with non-Christian materials" (1988: 103).

Despite his objections to an uncritical use of the term "world," however, Collins does believe that there is a "genuine sociological constant which can give a precise fulcrum on which to balance cross-cultural reflections about 'world-renunciation' " (1988: 105). For Collins, this "sociological constant," this analytically acceptable equivalent or substitute for the term "world" is the more precise: " 'world' of inter-connected reproductive-kinship relations" (1988: 109). And for Collins, the most significant characteristic of the individual who has liberated himself from the " 'world' of . . . reproductive-kinship ties" is his celibate lifestyle. Moreover, for Collins, the celibacy of the "renouncer," his "singleness," is directly related to his self-sufficiency and his individuality (1988: 109).

This has brought us full circle. Given the evident significance of sexual and reproductive activity in human life, the practice of celibacy—the deliberate abstinence from sexual and reproductive activity—makes a dramatic value statement about human existence as normally lived. As Daniel Gold has observed in his cross-cultural discussion of celibacy:

> The most highly structured relationships between abstinence and procreation are found in traditional India. . . . The classical Hindu life cycle . . . begins and ends in celibacy, but prescribes a sexually fruitful period of life as a householder in between.
>
> Giving celibacy an explicit place in the individual life cycle, Hindu tradition also gives the celibate individuals an explicit place in society. . . . Hindus recognize that exceptional individuals will want to live all their lives as celibate ascetics, either prolonging their studies . . . as *brahmacārin*s or bypassing the householder stage by making early formal renunciation. . . . In most Indian cosmologies, the participation of householders as well as celibates is required in the proper economy of salvation in the cosmos.
>
> (1987a: 146)

PART VI

VITALITY IN PERSONS AND IN PLACES

CHAPTER EIGHTEEN

ANNA

R. S. Khare

SCOPE, FOCUS, AND MEANINGS

Anna or Hindu food has wide-ranging meanings, and its religious, ritual, and social conceptions relate distinctly to Hindu philosophy and cosmology. This interdependent, "holistic" view perhaps best encapsulates the distinctness of Hindu approach to food. Although customary Hindu ideas, norms, and practices may distinctly differ from what modern, scientific accounts of food now assume or stress, any simplistic traditional/modern contrasts and dichotomies are often inadequate in accounting for the enormously significant uses, representations, and meanings foods acquire in Hindus' (and Indians') life. To get to such a complete picture, however, we not only need to explicate several major cultural assumptions, values, and ideals constituting the Hindu conception of *anna* but we must also see how pervasively this conception weaves itself through changing historical, economic, and political conditions.

Correspondingly, we encounter rather difficult questions of the definition and scope of "Hindu food." Historically and culturally, how do we identify what is (or is not) truly, exclusively, or completely "Hindu" in people's daily selection, classification, cuisine, sharing, and eating of foods and food practices? Conversely, how does one know in India what (and how much) is exclusively "non-Hindu" in these domains? These questions are doubly difficult because there are no authoritative and consistent markers and pointers for Hindus across India. Beyond regional customs, local orthodox and major religious leaders differ among themselves about the "proper" and "improper" in Hindu food ways. Since even the issue what is (or is not) "Hindu food" regionally so varied, it is best to stipulate as follows. Given no single, consistent, and uniformly applicable religious and social model for an all-Hindu (much less all-Indian) approach to *anna* and given no composite all-Indian empirical food survey on the "Hindu"/"non-Hindu" cultural zones, we will approach *anna* mostly by explicating major prevalent constellations of religious, cultural, and social knowledge. This stance will allow us to address religious distinctness as well as social sharing that Hindu foods display in ideas as well as life. Major historical changes in India further demand that our discussion must also address some competing economic and political changes in food availability and their impact on the Hindu world.

Yet, our exercise cannot but be limited in scope and distinct in focus. Our discussion will stress interrelated sets of major cultural and religious characteristics of *anna* in different conceptual, ritual, social, and pragmatic settings, showing how over time Hindu food continues to reflect continuities as well as changes within Hindu society, its worldview, and in India. The account will explicate how *anna* weaves together crucial philosophical ideas, religious values, and ritual traditions with, first, a distinct moral order, moral economy, caste customs, and ritual schemes; second, major regional and local socioritual ways; and third, "food problems" as related to religious and political changes.

After a brief introductory overview of the conception of *anna* in the opening section, we will discuss in the second section distinct classical religious and philosophical conceptions of *anna*. The two subsequent sections present selected major contemporary caste and ritual food usages, including some of those that directly illustrate interdependence across Hindu spiritual, sacred, therapeutic, and everyday practical issues. Simultaneously, as the next section shows, British colonial and Indian postcolonial changes also show their distinct yet pervasive impact on the Hindu food system. This, as the concluding segment illustrates, led virtually to a historical and political *reframing* of Hindu food and food problems during the twentieth century, displaying religious continuities as well as changes.

To start with, the classical literature firmly guides us while reviewing the conception, definition, and uses of *anna*. Overall, the ancient classical texts provide us with a civilizationally distinct philosophical treatise on food, accompanied by corresponding religious, ritual, mythological, and social provisions. In contrast, the subsequent accounts of *anna* have been often distinctly regional, caste oriented, and locally customary. Comprehensive disquisitions are very scarce. The studies written in English were not any different. We get fragmented "administrative accounts" during the nineteenth century when British colonial administration began to map, survey, record, and count things, people, and land in India. The local family, caste, and religious food ways attracted, as we will see later, only incidental interest, for these remained peripheral to the colonial control of issues of land, agriculture, and taxation and even to food production, marketing, and distribution.

Correspondingly, there was little attention given to shared food ideas along (or across) the learned and folk traditions of the Hindus, Buddhists, and Jainas. The entire subject became either "esoteric" or simply a matter of "tribal," "caste," or "religious" customs and practices. These colonial constraints notwithstanding, *anna* for Hindus (and Jainas and Buddhists) continued to be the most intimate yet ubiquitously transacted bodily, interpersonal, social, and spiritual substance. More recent studies notwithstanding (see below), there is still a distinct dearth of systematic social and historical studies of all that comprises and constructs the Hindu—and Indian—food and food ways. At present, even reliable bibliographies are rare (for two bibliographies, one on ancient India and the other a highly eclectic one, see, respectively, Prakash 1961; Achaya 1994, 1998).

Distinct meanings: philosophical, religious, and cultural

Anna means food in a very intimate yet comprehensive and cosmic way. In classical philosophy, if it represents the lowest form in which the supreme soul (*brahman*) manifests itself; it is also the coarsest or the last vesture (*annamayakośa*) of the soul, creating the visible body (*sthūlamayaśārīra*). In mythology, food represents major cosmic deities; thus, for example, if *anna* is a name of Viṣṇu, it also represents the sun and the earth. In popular religious and social usage, *anna* by itself becomes a deity (*annadevatā*), and

Śiva and Goddess Durgā, like Viṣṇu, are called food-givers (*annadātā*). Durgā is known as Annapūrṇā, comprising food's chief presiding deity. In everyday life, regionally varying terms (e.g. in Hindi *bhojana* and *āhāra*; in Urdu *khānā* and *gizā*) amplify on different forms of *anna*, including those uncooked or cooked edible foods and a meal or diet. Popularly, *anna* stands for a wide variety of raw, ripe, uncooked, edible, and staple foods, while also conveying a full range of distinctly religious, ritual, and cosmological meanings (Apte 1965: 89; for more discussion of textual conceptions, see below).

Thus, any composite review of food in India is impossible without addressing religious conceptions of *anna*, and any review of writings on *anna* begins with a core of Vedic and Vedāntic contributions. The subject is repeatedly raised and discussed in several core and major classical texts (i.e. the vast *śruti* and *smṛti* literature), treating food in a philosophically comprehensive, mythically transforming, ritually elaborate, and socially ordered and ranked contexts. Surviving scores of centuries, these contributions constitute the most basic—and enduring—paradigms of Hindu thought and action on food (for distinctly abstract discussions of food in the Upaniṣads, see Nikhilananda 1963; see also Hume 1921; for a related study of foods in ancient India, see Prakash 1961).

Often aphoristic, these formulations, in turn, became the basis for succeeding discussions in that large and diverse corpus of the Epic-Purāṇa literature, setting ideals and norms for regionally diverse yet shared "pure" Hindu moral, religious, and spiritual life. All textual injunctions on *anna* thus remain remote and incomplete until they filter through regionally different sectarian ideologies, holy men, and regional/local caste customs and folk practices. These different layers (and lenses) of knowledge and practice not only order Hindu's notions and distinctions of ritual purity and impurity (with implied notions of clean and unclean), but they also factor in what is considered auspicious and inauspicious under different sectarian values. Thus, for example, the "right-handed" sects and rituals (as of Vaiṣṇavism) clearly distinguish themselves by identifying their "proper foods and food ways" from those "left handed" (Tantrism). Similarly, upper castes elaborately distinguish their food ways from those of lower castes, and lower castes in turn separate themselves from *dalit*s and tribes.

For majority of Hindus, thus, "proper food handling" remains a serious lifelong caste, ritual, and religious concern. A crucial goal is to eat everyday only ritually appropriate foods, cooked and served by properly ranked persons, so as to meet one's worldly obligations as well as otherworldly spiritual goals. In such matters, a whole class of authoritative traditional texts, commonly called Dharmaśāstras, continue to guide the Hindus (for a judicious rendition and commentary on food in these texts, see Kane 1968–77, 2.2, especially on *bhojana*; for further details, see below). Within such a corpus of literature, *Manusmṛti* particularly stands out (Bühler 1886). Elaborating systematically on the distinct social and ritual roles of food throughout one's life, this text has continued to date an authoritative guide for Hindu life. On the other hand, it has also attracted severe social criticisms and political debates for over last two hundred years. If Hindu revivalists today seek to emphasize its primacy, then low castes and *dalit*s condemn it for justifying social inequality and exploitation.

But the long journey of Hindu food between those early classical writings on *anna* and the modern British and independent India's food handling is hardly well studied. Even the twentieth-century governmental, historical, and scholarly studies of food face yawning gaps, especially on people's changing family and community food ways. For the Hindu, the classical period still stands unmatched in religious authority. In recent scholarship on ancient India, however, we encounter only a limited number of thoughtful attempts. Most treated the subject by way of ancient sacrificial, "cooking," and gifting rituals (e.g. see Heesterman 1993; Malamoud 1996). A discerning history-of-religions approach to the subject is also rare (for a mythological study of food under life-death, ritual-spiritual quandaries, see White 1992). Similarly, since medieval accounts of food remained mostly anecdotal, indirect, or limited to the royalty, we rarely encounter a carefully documented social and regional historical study of food for elaborate distribution and consumption (for food transactions found within and around a major South Indian temple complex, see Breckenridge 1986).

Still rarer are those comprehensive overviews of Hindu food that attempt to weave together, in one stroke, the classical with the literary, religious, social, hagiographic, aesthetic, folkloric, and the commonsensical (Ramanujan 1992). Such an attempt captures that distinct cultural sense and sensibility that shows how *anna* still commands an interwoven and comprehensive moral, religious, spiritual, social, and practical presence within the Hindu world. This Hindu view also links up with rich regional narrative and folk literature that delves, with wit and verve, into "living" social uses and meanings of food. These are pursued as much for ritual feasting, fasting, celebrations, and religious devotion as under friendship, hospitality, competition, and social discord. Foods faithfully stand as much for human intimacy as domination, deceit, enmity, famine and torture (for illustrative examples from some major sources in Hindu narrative literature, see Abbott and Godbole 1982 on *Bhaktavijaya*; Balasubrahmanyam 1989 on *Hitopadeśa*; Beck, Claus, Goswami, and Handoo 1987 on folk tales and stories; Rajan 1993 on *Pañcatantra*; and Tawney 1968 on *Kathāsaritsāgara*).

Contributions of modern studies

Modern systematic studies of Hindu food (and of Indian food systems, more generally) start with the end of the Second World War. Whether textual, documentary, or "field" based, such accounts distinctly narrowed, intensified, and systematized the focus on the subject. Food was often studied as integral to lives of diverse Hindu religious communities, numerous castes and tribes, and remote towns and villages, allowing for an empirical picture of food in Hindu society. Unfortunately, food still remained a secondary—dependent—subject of study. Sometimes the attention was just incidental. Thus, as philosophy, Indology, history of religions, social history, sociology, and anthropology pursued their distinct disciplinary quests, they pursued "real" subjects in history like philology, theology, mythology, rituals, caste system, economics, and politics. Even during the fifties and the sixties, social sciences treated food as a foil for sociological and anthropological analyses of the Hindu caste system (Dumont 1980; Marriott 1968).

However, as the late sixties stressed global problems of food scarcity, hunger, and malnutrition, often as a corollary of the "population problem," food-focused studies attracted greater attention. In India, this meant that the government had to increase food production and distribution to feed the multiplying millions. Yet, as people protested inequity in food availability and hunger, attention slowly but surely also moved to what Indians (and Hindus) did in life with their food. And what they did with food related closely to what food meant to them. In anthropology, this led to a structural-symbolic study of food within the Indian—and primarily Hindu—religious and social worlds (for an ethnographic study and analysis of Hindu castes in a North Indian city, see Khare 1976a, b; for other related studies and their review, see below).

However, such studies still faced major handicaps, as long as such basic research tools as a reliable encyclopedia, a historical gastronomic atlas, and a basic dictionary on the subject were absent. We still lack these, although recently an Indian food scientist, as his hobby (see Achaya 1994, 1998), published a "historical companion" and a "dictionary" on Indian foods and food ways. Though without a systematic plan of professional historical and social scholarship, these works regionally classify and describe, historically showcase, and culturally index an array of Indian foods and culinary practices. As a gastronomic tour guide, these works, although reflecting the author's uneven cultural knowledge, interests, and biases, give the reader an idea of diverse and striking Indian food ways.

THE SELF-EVIDENT ANNA: PHILOSOPHICAL MODELS AND A CULTURAL GRAMMAR

The essence of *anna* (the edible substance, also called "the *virāj*" or the material aggregate of *ātman*) is found in its circulation. This food, so conceptualized, distinctly expresses ways that *conjoin* rather than separate and isolate the creation from creatures, nature from culture, transaction from value, and the "outer" material world from the "inner" spiritual one. Some of the clearest statements of this inspiration, including the root meaning of *anna*, are found in the aphoristic formulations of the Upaniṣads. For instance, "They who worship food as *brahman* obtain all food. Food alone is the eldest of all beings, and therefore it is called the panacea for all." And here is the definition: "Because it is eaten (*adyate*) by beings and because it eats (*atti*) beings, therefore it is called food (*anna*)" (*Taittirīya Upaniṣad* 2.1.1–2).

Culturally, these distinctly interdependent classical conceptions and cosmological relationships are indispensable for explicating how even illiterate Hindus conjoin food with matters of bodily and ritual states, health, caste status, social honor, cosmic moral order, and spiritual goals. Many orthodox Hindus recall these verities as they daily recite their "meal prayers." Calling food *annadevatā* (food god), they revere "the sustainer of life" at the beginning and end of a meal. They fold hands and bow before their food plate, praying for health, wellness, longevity, and spiritual calm. These customary practices resonate with that ancient Upaniṣadic inspiration that conceives food as *annambrahman*, a self-evident essence of the absolute. Simultaneously, in practice, everybody, whether high or low, rich or poor, dominant or dependent, friend or foe, or saint or scoundrel, seeks out *anna* to sustain life.

Those knowledgeable, therefore, see *anna* as having both gross (*sthūla*) and subtle (*sūkṣma*) properties, binding beings with their bodies and binding both of these to inescapable cosmic laws of *dharma* and *karma*. At the core are the principles of unchanging and "timeless" *dharma* and *karma* that create and regulate food for all the creatures. Only with food, as major religious texts repeatedly declare, humans uphold their *dharma* and *karma*. This basic awareness constructs the core of Hindu food, binding the innermost of all creatures to the outermost—the entire cosmos.

Within human society, *anna* is marked by distinct moral and religious "debts" and social obligations, requiring everybody to discharge these as a part of their lives. Foods mark—and are marked by—people's social life, quickly absorbing and reflecting different ranks, actions, emotional states, conditions, and goals. The Hindus routinely organize these around their criteria of ritual purity and pollution (*pavitra* and *apavitra*), moral sin and merit (*pāpa* and *puṇya*), and auspiciousness and inauspiciousness (*maṅgala* and *amaṅgala*). So pursued, food becomes one of the most crucial material-moral thresholds that bridge this-worldly (*laukika*) pursuits with those otherworldly (*ādhyātmika*). Once "inside" (*antarīya*) a person, foods reflect—and influence—that person's innate properties (*guṇa*), morality, hidden intentions, emotions, and social dispositions. On the "outside," same foods reflect—and get modified by—the natural environment, ecology (*paryā-varaṇa*), seasonal changes, and people's tastes and food habits.

Cosmic models and perspectives

To make sense of such diverse properties, Hindus view *anna* as a paramount "uniter" of material, moral, and spiritual domains of the cosmos. Focusing on the body and soul, the Upaniṣads recognize transforming relationships between the "breath of life" (*prāṇa*) and food, body and food, and body and breath. Another general formulation seeks to establish interdependence between water, food, and fire (eater), enabling the *Taittirīya Upaniṣad* (3.7.1, 8.1, 9.1, and so on) to declare, "Thus food rests on food."

Such interdependent—and transmuting—reasoning patterns are at the heart of the Vedāntic philosophy of *anna*. Here food, eater, and eater's body and life breath (*prāṇa*) are not only found transforming into one another, but these also reduce, at death, into such primary (or cosmic) elements as the earth, water, fire, rain, and sky. Within a person, *anna*, by generating bodily strength, makes possible such crucial functions as cognition, knowledge, speech, pleasure, procreation, bliss, and liberation. Thus, whether inside a person or outside, food is called the "uniter." The Upaniṣads pursue this idea further by treating food as a basis for—and a cosmic "thread" of—all "life" (i.e. of *prāṇa*, in its five constituent—breathing, animating, feeding, evacuating, and soul-ejecting—functions).

Next, the Upaniṣadic texts refer to a list of fourteen life-identifying and life-sustaining components that help conceptualize food-body-soul-cosmos relationships in two distinct models. One is a hierarchical or "scale" model, while a "wheel" represents the other. In the hierarchical model, the recognized fourteen components, each successively less inclusive (or more dependent), are identified as follows: *prāṇa* > memory > space > fire > water > food > strength > understanding > meditation > consideration > will > mind > speech > name. *Anna*, let us note, appears sixth in (or in just about the middle of) the sequence, controlling eight crucial bodily and mental functions of humans. The second model arranges the same chain into "a wheel of fourteen spokes" (for a detailed discussion, see Khare 1992c: 205–9, 218n4). Commenting on such a "cosmic" view, food in the Upaniṣad proclaims: "I [food] am the first-born of the true, prior to the gods, and the navel of immortality. He who gives me away, he alone preserves me. He who eats food—I, as food, eat him" (*Taittirīya Upaniṣad* 3.10.6).

Sustaining one's subtle life breath (*prāṇa*), food is also called the "body" or the outermost "sheath" (*annamayakośa*). In life, since food sustains both life and body, prolonged periods of voluntary fasting are recognized as abnormal and even undesirable. Since hunger disorients, the *Chāndogya Upaniṣad* remarks, "Food is, verily, greater than strength. Therefore if a man abstains from food for ten days, even though he might live, yet he would not be able to see, hear, reflect, become convinced, act, and enjoy the result" (7.9.1). Correspondingly, if voluntary fasting requires moderation for normal bodily and mental functions, severe droughts and famines invoke special moral provisions, relaxing normal codes of *dharma* and *karma*.

In ancient India, as some studies show, the preceding conceptions, relationships, and meanings of *anna* developed slowly and over time, starting often with Vedic sacrifices. For instance, J. C. Heesterman recently noted, "Thus, sacrifice can be seen as the solemnization of food and its distribution at a communal meal" (1993: 10). Similarly, Charles Malamoud, explicating "cooking," remarked, the "theme of cooking, of actual and metaphorical cooking, displays itself in its fullness and coherence in the brahmanical doctrine of sacrifice" (1996: 27). Here, as in daily cooking, residual food (*ucchiṣṭa*) acquires special significance; it easily taints a sacrifice, and it demands careful separation and disposal (Malamoud 1996: 7). And both food and sacrifice successively transform each other until the sacrificer/eater internalizes cosmic moral, material, and supernatural qualities. Thus, the act of eating became a form of sacrifice to self (e.g. *Bhagavad Gītā* 3.14).

The continuing impact of these classical ideas is amply evident in contemporary Hindu life and the related worldview. With the *Bhagavad Gītā* (or the other sectarian texts inspired by it) as perhaps the most influential religious-spiritual anchor for contemporary Hindus, food is viewed through the threefold lens of *guṇa*s (inherent qualities)—"good" (*sāttvika*), "passionate" (*rājas*), and "dull" (*tāmas*), closely interrelating a person's this-worldly goals to those otherworldly. Here a person's actions, sacrifices, knowledge systems, and devotion also undergo a similar three-*guṇa* classification (*Bhagavad Gītā* 17.7–10, for an interpretation, see 17.11–22).

In brief, the preceding classical schemes emphasize how *anna* constitutes an irreducible ground for the continuation of life. Anthropologically viewed, the classical conception of *anna* overarches, transforms, and negotiates across such modern dichotomies as nature/culture, body/soul, practice/value, history/myth, and self-interest/altruism. The same cultural logic is extended to issues of food production, distribution, and consumption, drawing on the divine-ordained forces of nature, environment, rulers, human efforts, and the cosmic moral order (*dharma-karma*). Similarly, issues of food abundance, availability, and scarcity are also tackled, with equally distinct moral and social commentaries. For instance, just and unjust kings are known to cause as well as control food abundance, drought, and hunger. If virtuous rulers enjoy gods' benevolence, including people's support, ushering in prosperity and abundance, injustice, tyranny, and immorality are known as surely to cause drought, famine, disease, unrest, and migration in the society.

Together, as we will see next, the preceding considerations yield a distinct Hindu ethics, produced by interrelating status-and-ritual appropriate foods and food transactions with concerns for bodily health, mental peace, ritual debts, social order, and ultimate spiritual goals.

Hindu food ethics

Hindus routinely learn within their families about how to give and receive foods according to their caste rank, gender, age, kinship position, health condition, and personal circumstance. The knowledgeable debate the intricacies of associated *dharma*, especially while transacting foods by recognizing the crucial roles of (and a triadic interplay between) the situation (*sthiti*), time (*kāla*), and the givers/receivers (*pātra*) involved. The goal of a Hindu is to enter into status-appropriate, ritually "proper," and morally balanced giving, gifting, and receiving of foods. While most food transactions are reciprocal, although often with an emphasis on giving more than receiving, there are also one-way (or lopsided) transactions among those highly unequal and deeply indebted. Most social relations demand commensurate reciprocation in cash or kind, including a specific service performed in return. Concurrently, as already indicated, a person inclines or disinclines toward food according to his or her *guṇa*s or innate tendencies. Thus, those of "good" or *sāttvika* disposition are known to incline only toward "good" (i.e. savory, smooth, firm, and appealing) foods, while those of "passionate" or *rājas* disposition like foods that are sour, salty, pungent, stinging hot, and burning. In contrast, those "dark" or *tāmas* in disposition like stale, tasteless, rotten, and decayed foods. These formulations, put another way, ascribe to the axiom: "You eat what you are."

Simultaneously, Hindu food, being an all-encompassing "connector," also upholds the opposite formulation: "You are what you eat." This axiom, found routinely within families as well as in the Āyurvedic medical system, classifies foods according to their innate (i.e. "hot" and "cold"), "natural" (i.e. weather/season-dependent), and cooking-induced properties. Such differences in innate qualities of foods, including the intricate alchemy of "hot" and "cold" foods, help Hindus interrelate innate properties of persons with innate qualities of foods. When handled harmoniously in life, these distinctions promote physical health, create mental peace, prevent illness, encourage social cohesion, and enhance spiritual quest.

These innate properties of food are also seldom unrelated to issues of personal morality, especially while identifying and acquiring one's food. Thus, immorally (and violently) acquired foods are widely known to cause spiritual harm, physical diseases sooner or later, and social enmity. These consequences occur irrespective of the ritual care taken in cooking and eating such foods, showing that these subtle influences are ultimately not any less crucial, and these comprise the moral economy of Hindu food (for more details, see below). Similarly, availability of food in life depends on one's own good *karma*s and on the will of the divine (*daivī icchā*). Thus, in popular Hindu worldview, god's will and human efforts, only both together, ensure food crops and food availability. This is indisputable for Hindus, since, at the cosmic level, only god feeds (and ensures the well being of) all creatures, including humans. Thus, a popular expression often heard in the Avadh (a North Indian) region is: "God provides food before creating a mouth." In the same train of thought, another expression is: "every grain comes stamped with its eater" (*dāne dāne pe likhā hai khānevāle kā nāma*; actually, a line from a popular Hindi film song). Thus, the causes as well as cures of food scarcity, drought, and famine are located in the divine will as well as human endeavor. This approach, some Hindus argue, not only encourages people to be frugal, practical, and hard working under crisis but that they also read divine, religious moral-ethical messages for survival under food scarcity and social distress.

CASTE RULES, RITUAL NORMS, AND THE CUSTOMARY FOOD CYCLE

The preceding philosophical, religious, and ethical discussion prepares the necessary ground for approaching interwoven customary Hindu caste, kinship, and ritual practices. Food to Hindus is a matter of lifelong religious and social concern. In life, it stands at the core of society and religion, shaping powerfully people's actual family life, caste-and-marriage rules, and religious and spiritual values. Though this core varies in practice with caste, locality, and region, its underlying values are nevertheless crucially shared, organizing comparable ritual and social scales of hierarchical status, honor, and ultimate goals of life. Numerous taboos, ritual exclusions, religious preferences, and prescriptions of foods also appear here, including complicated Hindu conceptions of "vegetarianism" and "nonvegetarianism." And an equally complex (and changing) set of moral, religious, and sectarian considerations guide diverse castes', subcastes', and families' conceptions of vegetarianism and nonvegetarianism. In life, few totally—that is, uniformly and consistently—"vegetarian" and "nonvegetarian" Hindu castes are found. Given the regional, historical, and political issues long involved in this crucial distinction, this issue flags the crucial importance of regional gastronomic diversity in India and its different religious and social evaluations.

Broadly, we have, at least, the following identifiable food-cuisine-culinary-ritual zones or regions: the "northern" (i.e. extending from Kashmir and Punjab to Delhi, Uttar Pradesh, and Madhya Pradesh), the "western" (as in Rajasthan, Gujarat, and Maharashtra), the "eastern" (as in Bihar, Bengal, Assam, other Northeastern states, and Orissa), and the "southern" (as in Kannada, Tamilnadu, Kerala, and Andhra Pradesh). But, since seldom a geographically clear and consistent boundary exists across these regions in religious, ritual, culinary, and cultural matters, a gastronomic map of India always shows zigzag boundaries, with overlaps and sharing. Hindu food, over time and space, has traded significant influences with all other major Indian culinary traditions, including tribal, Islamic, and Christian. Simultaneously, every major cultural region does have its own distinct but heterogeneous internal profile, alongside locally different caste-family-ritual maps of staple foods, culinary-cooking-spice use patterns, and dietary patterns (for a rough-and-ready overview of such regional diversity, including references to some distinct non-Hindu influences and tribal food ways, see Achaya 1994: 118–53).

Given these diverse but socially very real regional dietary patterns, Hindu gastronomy is best described as socially highly adaptable. If it has a deeply entrenched and restrictive caste-kinship-ritual core, then its culinary and gastronomic contours openly adjust, assimilate, and modify by regions and by changing social situations. Like any other human food system, this system also diversifies its cooking techniques, culinary recipes, food sharing, hospitality, and commercial food vending. This "opening up" has particularly increased in independent India, especially as modern transportation and communication took hold and as Indian cuisine has traveled abroad as a major ethnic Asian food. But, for most Indians living in India, the nature of this social expansion often complements rather than drastically replaces Hindus' food taboos, sectarian religious injunctions, and meat-eating preferences.

Food taboos, meat eating, and sectarianism

Thus, whether rigid, flexible, or eroding, many intercaste and intracaste rules and customs, combined with prevailing local food taboos and prohibitions, still regulate the family food system of vast rural and urban Hindu masses. These customary ways, passed on for many generations, identify what is tabooed, disapproved, conditionally accepted, or newly rejected. Food taboos are a historically complicated subject for Hindus. For instance, in beef taboo, ecology, competing religious ideologies, historical changes, and political conflicts are known to have played significant roles for millennia. In creating and sustaining the beef taboo, for example, Brāhmaṇical deification of cow played a crucial long-term role vis-a-vis Buddhism, producing a prolonged religious, historical, and regional tussle, yielding, in the process, changing definitions of both nonviolence and vegetarianism.

For major upper castes and many middle-caste clusters, this tussle reinforced beef taboo and downgraded meat eating in general. For others, selective meat eating continued for social, religious, or health reasons. Studies of ancient India see such developments as a complex response to competing regional ruling ideologies, sectarian rivalries, ecological conditions, and natural calamities (Basham 1954: 195ff.). However, in the absence of adequate information for succeeding periods, such explanations still remain either tentative or controversial for Hindu India as a whole.

Similarly, "abnormal" and "unusual" foods, especially meats of unfamiliar or strange animals and unusually intoxicating drinks, herbs, and plants, also attract special religious and social attention. Meat eating, in particular, draws on a complicated social, religious, and sectarian history. Today, for example, if Vaiṣṇavite Hindus, the followers of "right-handed rituals," are most often vegetarians and teetotalers, then worshipers of the goddess (the Śākta) justify meat eating and drinking, especially under the left-handed, Tantric rituals. Grounded in distinct sectarian philosophy, religious observances, and rituals, these practices create continuing historical and cultural tensions, anomalies, as well as social compromises. For instance, in a high (and predominantly vegetarian) caste, some could remain meat eaters because they worshiped the goddess. But such "anomalous" features have long been integral to living Hinduism, and these cannot—and should not—be either somehow easily dismissed or explained away as "exceptional" (see Khare 1976a).

As some recent studies show, staunch followers of major sects of Vaiṣṇavism, Śaivism, and Śaktism today foster their own distinct food ways, devotional attitudes, and domestic food rituals. Offerings (*prasāda*) appropriate to sectarian deities correspondingly differ, along with duties of feeding different sectarian gods, saints, *guru*s, and followers. Popular deities, like Viṣṇu, Rāma, Kṛṣṇa, Gaṇeśa, and Hanumān, routinely receive vegetarian food offerings throughout the year, and they in turn yield the "blessed food" or *prasāda*. Major temples, sacred pilgrimage centers, and even domestic shrines widely distribute, either free or for a charge, such food offerings to pilgrims. Some of these are extremely elaborate. For example, a major Kṛṣṇa temple of the Vallabhite or Caitanya sect in Vrndavan follows its own highly socially restrictive-yet-elaborate gastronomic and ritual traditions in feeding its regal deity, daily as well as on special occasions (for two elaborate and distinctly contrasting sectarian food styles in the worship of Kṛṣṇa, see Toomey 1986; for a historically documented detailed food use in a major South Indian temple complex, see Breckenridge 1986; for Vaiṣṇavite food offerings in domestic shrines in Avadh, see Khare 1976b: 81–115, see also 1992b). On the other hand, not all deities (e.g. Śiva—impure but auspicious) leave behind human-edible leftovers (at least for North Indians). Nor is it unusual for the goddess (in Tantric worship) to yield both vegetarian and nonvegetarian blessed foods. In many major temples of the goddess, spectacular animal sacrifice is performed during the most important annual occasion (often during the goddess worship in October-November), while routinely the deity accepts either smaller animals or only a vegetarian substitute.

However, assessing the religious basis of these sectarian meat-eating practices is still difficult. For, once special ritual observances are over, the dominant customary familial and local food ways, often mostly vegetarian, return. Thus, all goddess worshipers are not uniformly meat eaters, nor are all Hindus goddesses meat eaters. Actually, many Hindus today eat (or do not eat) meat for diverse social—often modern—reasons. But modernity is today an internally heterogeneous, even divergent value system. If some today try to justify their meat eating for either becoming "progressive," physically strong, or regaining health, others cut back on meat "to be smart moderns" (by reducing chances of getting coronary disease or cancer). Overall, entrenched caste and family food ways usually play a sustained role in such matters in India.

Customary food cycles

It is in daily family life and during the major rites of passage that caste and kinship rank-related food restrictions show their maximum strength. Yet, since significant social changes have occurred in these areas, particularly during the last fifty years, the following mid-century account of orthodox Hindus must be read with sufficient room for ongoing changes.

All major Hindu rites of passage usually amplify on what people of different castes are supposed to do in their daily family life as they cook, store, serve, eat, dispose off foods. In daily practice, as households prepare their daily meals at the domestic hearth, they engage in repetitive daily "cycles" of food cooking, eating, and cleaning activities. Situated at the heart of Hindu family life, these food cycles help interrelate, pace, and bind family members to one another, with distinct roles carved out for family women as cooks and managers of the family kitchen. The supervisory roles come to them by marriage, age, motherhood, and kinship position. While women's duty is to manage kitchen within the family to feed equitably all family members, beginning with male elders, men are expected to secure adequate food for all. Caste ranks and social customs regulate the cooked food, once it steps out of the domestic hearth.

As anthropological studies have amply shown, a majority of Hindus still elaborately rank order and measure intercaste distance by carefully monitoring and calibrating who can give to and/or receive different foods from different castes. Food transactions thus help them establish and "measure" degrees of social distance, ranging from those most intimate to those of lowest castes and non-Hindus. While doing so, Hindus follow a distinct and elaborate transactional logic in the way they admit, rank, and exclude different persons, families, caste groups, and strangers for food sharing. To transact food in customary "appropriate" ways is most often to follow the locally prevailing social norms and to reinforce the related comprehensive Hindu worldview (see Marriott 1968, 1976).

For those ritually high and orthodox, caste status and its associated rules of ritual purity and impurity closely regulate daily domestic food cooking, sharing, feeding, eating, and disposing off of leftover foods (see Khare 1976a, b). As these rules address questions of who can (or cannot) give/receive and eat/not eat what and with whom, they also specify by caste status and kinship position women relatives who can (or cannot) cook at the family hearth. These cooks, usually mothers, sisters, wives, or women cooks of equal or higher castes status, know the prevailing family customs, and they ensure observance of all appropriate ritual and social rules during every domestic cooking cycle. They are expected to observe, out of family affection, preferences of every family member, young or old, and intimate, near or distant. Before eating, they know, for example, how to accommodate orthodox elders who purify themselves by bathing or by washing hands and feet and know who consecrate cooked food to appropriate gods, including, as already indicated, to "food god" (*annadevatā*) itself. The family head, an aged male relative or one's spiritual *guru*, thus, receives the first food plate from the new kitchen, followed by all other males, women, and servants. Children are fed any time. Since kitchen is located in the innermost part of the house, the access to lower castes and strangers is automatically excluded. Until recently, even the sight of an untouchable or *dalit* was sufficient to pollute an orthodox person's kitchen (and all cooked food in it).

A North Indian distinction

This strong emphasis on regulating intercaste contacts in food sharing developed some regionally distinct ways of separating ritually better protected foods from those less so. In a distinct development, for example, a segment of northern upper-caste Hindus (particularly those living in Uttar Pradesh and in parts of Bihar and Madhya Pradesh) developed the "boiled"/"fried" (or the *kaccā/pakkā*) ritual distinction in cooked foods. Within this scheme, everyday family foods (i.e. the staple lentil-rice-bread or the *dāl-bhāt-roṭī* meals cooked at the family hearth) were called *kaccā* because they were "boiled/cooked in water" and were easily polluted. Accordingly, these are prepared with great ritual care and usually *within one's household* by family women (or by hired male/female cooks of equal or higher caste rank). The foods so prepared are shared only among immediate family members, kin groups, or the prospective marriageable *jāti* members. In contrast, the *pakkā* (or the *ghī*-fried) foods can be socially widely shared, even across divergent castes, because, once cooked in clarified butter (*ghī*), they resist ritual impurity much better during diverse social transactions.

In determining whether a cooked food is *kaccā* or *pakkā*, knowing the *primary cooking medium and its actual sequence* in cooking is crucial (cf. Khare 1976b). The orthodox carefully watch the basic cooking medium (i.e. whether it is water, some sort of cooking oil, or the clarified butter) employed in every food cooking sequence. Thus, for instance, rice cooked simply in water is considered *kaccā* (and hence can be served only to one's family, kin, and *jāti* members), while *ghī*-basted rice, even when boiled next in water, becomes *pakkā*. Equally important, once the fried food comes in contact with the boiled food, *pakkā* foods become *kaccā*, and they are so treated in all later transactions. Thus, while serving or eating a *kaccā* meal (or gifting a *kaccā* cooked food item), traditional Hindus purify themselves (by bathing or washing hands and feet) both before and after such eating. Similarly, the cooks and servers of *kaccā* food not only should be of appropriate caste rank, but they must also scrupulously maintain the state of required bodily and ritual purity (for details, see Khare 1976a, particularly 1976b). In brief, everybody participating must carefully follow all the intricate provisions of ritual purity/pollution until the *kaccā* meals are over.

The orthodox extend this ritual regimen to the cooking fuel (e.g. the ritually pure wood vis-a-vis the increasingly impure charcoal, kerosene oil, and cooking gas), cooking-serving utensils, food containers, and food storage areas (for uncooked, cooked, and leftover foods) within the house (see Khare 1976b). For example, containers made of leaf and clay very easily pollute (and hence are disposed after one use), while those made of steel, brass, bronze, silver, or gold (the purest) last successively longer. The silver and gold are considered purest and require least cleaning and scrubbing. Different cooking techniques (e.g. from roasting, boiling, grilling, basting to frying) are also similarly ritually ranked on the scale of ascending purity (along with ever greater resistance to impurity).

A crucial public test of most of these intricate food-ranking ritual schemes occurs during a traditional North Indian Hindu marriage. Elaborate feasts on this occasion serve both *kaccā* and *pakkā* foods, and both are closely scrutinized by the orthodox for observing crucial norms of caste rank, age, and kinship seniority, ritual status, and social honor. Despite the relaxation of many ritual requirements, the bride's side, as the host, still bears full responsibility for observing all the applicable ritual and social standards. Its precautions in food preparation and hospitality must pass all the tests the bridegroom's party expects. The groom's party, recipients of special social deference and ungrudging open hospitality, expect "all due ritual observances, social recognition, and individual honor" during the entire marriage ceremony. This is now often an explicit social demand rather than a ritual expectation, and any neglect results in loud complaints. For some, this is as serious as the dowry settlement. Traditionally, feasts at marriage become witness to that crucial (and fragile) "*roṭī-beṭī*" (i.e. the *kaccā* food and "virgin") exchange relationship. Every participant well knows that a serious ritual or social lapse at a marriage feast can initiate a lifelong grouse, resentment, and even a fierce social feud.

During a marriage, feasting involves much more than the issues of only social hierarchy and ritual purity and impurity. They also focus on Hindus' notions of the auspicious and inauspicious (*śubha/aśubha* or *maṅgala/amaṅgala*) and their cardinal roles and relevance in a prosperous and happy married life. However, the auspicious/inauspicious and pure/impure distinctions and their meanings do not always coincide, nor do they always mean the same thing. For instance, while foods marking birth ceremony are found auspicious and celebratory but ritually impure, foods at death become totally inauspicious and highly impure (until funeral rituals are over). Conceptually, Hindus find ritual pollution at birth qualitatively different from that at death (for a discussion of such notions and their meanings for food in orthodox families, see Khare 1976b: 46–80; for an overview of the subsequent discussion of the auspicious and the inauspicious, see Madan 1987: 48–71). In general, auspiciousness and inauspiciousness, whether located in foods, gods, events, or celestial bodies, allow Hindus to recognize many interweaving desirable/undesirable cosmic, celestial, spiritual, and aesthetic orders, forces, states, and relationships. Just as in ritual impurity, the effort invariably is to curtail, control, and confine the inauspicious, to let the auspiciousness prevail. A synthesizing overview of the highly diverse Hindu world gives us only more examples of different meanings that the auspicious and inauspicious attract (for a summarizing view of Hinduism, see Fuller 1992).

The preceding hierarchical ritual-social complex surrounding Hindu foods has a more general significance. As a system, it gives us clues about that "caste logic," even that "caste mind" that most Hindus still pervasively uphold in life. Food to Hindus is a serious lifelong concern, for it is to them the most crucial first material (external) need as well as the subtlest moral-spiritual (internal) essence that animates the body, mind, and soul. A scrupulous Hindu rigorously observes daily dietary rules to gain bodily, social, mental, and spiritual purity. And these, in turn, eventually lead one to that all-important "inner" (spiritual) purity that helps realize the ultimate goal, whether nearness to god or the spiritual liberation (*mokṣa*).

Once viewed against this expanded vision, Hindus' ideology of food is neither only about gross/subtle distinctions nor social barriers and ritual restrictions. Underneath these, Hindus insist, is that inclusive essence of *anna* that numerous rites of sacrifice, gifting, and charity express. The traditional Hindu calendar is filled with such numerous year-round religious fasts, festivals, and ceremonies, encouraging gifting of food by householders (see Khare 1976b). As a daily domestic duty, all guests must be fed, and food must be freely distributed to needy humans, alongside different creatures, like cows, crows, ants, and dogs. Even today's villagers know that "giving of food [is] the greatest [form of] gifting" (*anna dāna*, *mahādāna*). They also know that the needy, the hungry, the pious, and the stranger should be never turned away from the door. Even the poorest must do their best for these people.

Although these traditional injunctions still guide a vast number, there is also no denying the social fact that Hindus perpetuate social inequalities as well as face food scarcity. That hunger stalks many low-caste Hindu families in rural and urban India, the question therefore is also empirical: How much do the numerous age, gender, intercaste, and Hindu/non-Hindu social restrictions actually restrict food giving and sharing among Hindus? Further, if this question requires systematic empirical research before any quantitative estimates are made, some other practical aspects of Hindu food are already well known. This includes how food as a gross and subtle material plays highly significant therapeutic, psychological, and religious roles in Hindu society.

"GROSS/SUBTLE" PROPERTIES OF FOODS IN HINDU MEDICINE AND WITH SAINTS

The ground for wide-ranging transformations of food, both gross and subtle, is discovered in some of the earliest philosophical formulations on *anna*. For example, the *Chāndogya Upaniṣad* remarked: "Food when eaten becomes threefold. What is coarsest in it becomes feces, what is medium becomes flesh, and what is subtlest becomes mind. . . . The mind . . . consists of food, the *prāṇa* of water, speech of heat" (6.5.1, 6.5.4). Such classical formulations on the transformation of food set forth some basic Hindu ideas and relationships, illuminating gross and the subtle roles of food. If Indian systems of medicine and medical practices help illustrate one major domain of these, holy persons, saints, and sages exemplify another. Both, together, expand on the subtle qualities of *anna* for a healthy body, long life, tranquil mind, and spiritual attainment. The first field directly interrelates food selection and daily eating to issues of illness, health, and wellness, with interdependent relationships to ecology, climate, and seasonal changes. All these in turn fold, sooner or later, into that all-inclusive Hindu sacred and spiritual world of saints, who transform food into a curing, healing, and mystical—even miraculous—substance (Khare 1992b: 42).

The Hindus learn within their families about such special properties of foods. Transmitted routinely by older relatives, the knowledge of curative foods and diets is considered common and commonsensical rather than specialized. Family elders and neighbors routinely mention what to eat (or not eat) while suffering from an ailment. People know about medicinal uses of common foods for treating such common or minor ailments as indigestion, colds, low fevers, small cuts, and sprains. In India, dietary regimen is considered indispensable in all effective medical treatments, whether Āyurvedic, Homeopathic, or

Allopathic. For the first medical system, a patient's diet must conform not only to regional climate and seasonal variations, but it should also agree with that person's physical constitution, intrinsic individual (the *guṇa-doṣa*) configuration, and prevailing moral and social life situations. The other two medical systems survived in India only by giving therapeutic emphasis to the patient's diet.

The Āyurvedic medicine, for example, based on the humoral theory of disease causation, and cure, seeks to restore "equilibrium," as much within a patient's body as in the surroundings around him or her. To diagnose a disease in this medical system is thus to determine what is the nature and degree of imbalance between a patient's three cardinal humors—"wind," "bile," and "phlegm" (or *vāta*, *pitta*, and *kapha*). To be able to restore this basic equilibrium successfully is essentially to cure—and with suitable lifestyle to prevent—a disease in a patient. However, the ecological criteria of interdependence, balance, and "appropriateness" are crucial to such an Āyurvedic diagnosis of an ailment and its treatment (Zimmermann 1987). Translated in practice, it means as a rule to diagnose, among other things, the "offending foods" in a patient's diet and to indicate (and design) "a palliative diet" to start a patient's treatment. To maximize efficacy, a discerning Āyurvedic practitioner prescribes medicines and specifies dietary injunctions according to a patient's physique as well as the inner disposition and personal temperament (*śārīra*, *guṇa*, and *svabhāva* and *prakṛti* or *mizāj*).

In this scheme, if a carefully followed dietary regimen can keep a person healthy, then unsuitable foods can also equally surely predispose him or her to new ailments. Thus, disease-averting foods and food habits are in Indian family as surely identified as those that predispose one to get diseased. Āyurvedic practitioners, over time, therefore very carefully refine their expertise to calibrate the potency of a particular medicinal fruit, herb, plant, or tuber by knowing its distinct natural-ecological niche, including where and how (including purely or impurely or "justly" or "unjustly") these curative foods were raised and procured. Similarly, poor storage, crude preparation, and an undisciplined patient can quickly undo the cure underway (on close interdependence between ecology and pharmacy in the Āyurveda, see Zimmermann 1987).

In this morally sensitive medicinal world, acts of theft, dishonesty, and exploitation are therefore known to weaken distinctly the potency of even a rare, highly potent medicine. As observed elsewhere, "only morally just food . . . can be the truly healthy food for the Hindu" (Khare 1992c: 207). Accordingly, scrupulous householders, famous saints, renowned Āyurvedic healers, and accomplished ritualists (*karmakāṇḍin*) try to avoid eating all morally "tainted" (and just not only ritually impure) foods. For these tend to harm and dissipate their special curative powers. Known lapses therefore trigger among the scrupulous curers and healers a fast, a special worship, or some other suitable austerity.

On the other hand, a skilled therapeutic use of special foods or diets brings a distinct fame and renown to Indian medical practitioners. People distinctly remember physicians who cure difficult (and often chronic) diseases by putting their patients on distinct lifestyle altering dietary regimens. While treating, such physicians guide the patients and their families in specially designing, calibrating, and balancing different properties of ordinary as well as special foods—hot against cold, wet and dry, calming and stimulating, light and heavy, and diuretic against constipating. No less attention is given to the timing, doze, and duration of specific medicinal foods. Knowledgeable Indian medical practitioners this way constantly monitor that complex and comprehensive food-body-mind-medicine-ecology calculus, both within and around a patient.

Finally, for the medicines and prescribed dietary regimen (*parhez*) to have their full effect, both the doctor and patient evoke faith in god. A full and complete cure in India assumes, above all, that the doctor, medicine, and the prayers have converged and worked together (along the roles of *dākṭar*, *davā*, and *duā*, see Khare 1996). Taken one step further, most revered and effective Indian physicians are treated like saints. Not only that, some live like one, and for them spiritual purity (*ātmika pavitratā*), prayers (*duā*), and medicine (*davā*) work seamlessly.

In a complementary way, many major saints are known to cure and heal "difficult diseases," just as a result of their spiritual attainments. Viewed practically, many develop such expertise as they wander in far off jungles, mountains, and caves in spiritual search, meet healers, and discover (or are told about) rare *mantra*s, herbs, and potions effective against specific ailments. Many are known to make special use of common foods, with mysterious and dazzling therapeutic results.

Food with saints

In a related view, all foods acquire special sanctity, meaning, and potency once "genuine saints" handle them. Such saints renounce food accumulation, elaborate cooking, and eating just for taste. Pure in thought, speech, and action, they are known to live everyday "on only a few morsels of food." Eating just enough to survive, they do not look for quantity, variety, and flavor, and they discard morally tainted food. In most sects, saints and renouncers observe rigorous traditional rules of social and ritual purity. If they do not, ordinary Hindus reason, who will. To control undesirable food sources, scrupulous saints and renouncers subsist on foods prepared either in a monastery, a temple, or a designated disciple's home. Others cook their own simple meal, singly or in a small group, while rigorously observing rules of caste and ritual purity in cooking, food sharing, and eating. Still others (for example, *sādhu*s of devotional orders) eat "left-overs" (*prasāda*) of a temple's deity. Some undertake a vow to live only on single food—milk, a specified fruit, or just one grain—for several months, even years. These austere moral and spiritual acts help them control senses, gain spiritual power, and receive god's grace.

Major saints, thus, automatically leave miraculous food remnants or scraps for their devotees, who find them uniquely potent, pure, and auspicious. Some saints (e.g. Sāī Bābā) are internationally known for curing diseases of the faithful by magically creating curing edibles (or ash) out of thin air. Motivated to lessen human pain and suffering, other "genuine saints" cure either by touch or by giving a blessed fruit, a flower, their hairs, a piece of their own clothing, and even spittle (for examples of major sectarian saints and their efficacious ways, see Babb 1986; Kakar 1982; Khare 1992b).

On the other hand, saints running temples and monasteries supervise elaborate cooking to feed the regnant divine (Nārāyaṇa, Rāma, or Kṛṣṇa). To do so is also to feed the devotees, rich as well as the poor. To feed the poor (*daridra nārāyaṇa*) thus is to feed god. In such sacred institutions, food paradoxically acquires by context an austere as well as royal and regal face, interweaving a distinct web of spiritual, moral, devotional, and worldly meanings (for a discussion of the resulting "gastrosemantics," see Khare 1992a, b). Yet, all such miraculous curative powers of a saint must be ultimately, in the Hindu view, "a sideshow." These should not derail the ultimate spiritual quests.

This meaning-charged, spiritually dense *anna* is, however, also that life-sustaining social and economic commodity that bears imprints of complicated modern historical, social, and political changes. To Hindus, this is not surprising because their this-worldly needs must constantly interrelate with otherworldly goals, and vice versa. Given modern Indian history, it specially meant *anna* adapting to—and influencing—some major colonial and postcolonial forces and their values.

THE COLONIAL AND POSTCOLONIAL CHANGES

The Hindu food has faced distinctly different historical forces during the last two centuries, especially as India, first, experienced British colonialism and, next, as it launched its own freedom movement and gained independence in 1947. A central question for this account is: How did *anna* under religious differences, changing social forces, and political conflicts fare during these times? Specifically, for example, how did the "timeless" religious and moral conceptions of *anna* recognize, adapt, and respond to existing "food problems," including scarcity, hunger, and famine? More generally, how did Hindu food approach modern social values, economic realities, and political conflicts? Undoubtedly, this discussion can only briefly allude to these vital questions. Limited further to only a few observations, our purpose is, first, to indicate how the religious and moral constructs of *anna* relate to historically practical, economic, and political situations and, second, to underscore an undeniable religious and political "repositioning" of Hindu food.

Thus, for instance, recalling the nineteenth-century British colonial approach, foreign travelers accounted for Hindus' diverse food customs, rituals, and food ways (notably Jean Antoine Dubois' [1765–1848] *Hindu Manners, Customs, and Ceremonies* 1897). Several additional accounts appeared on different Indian regions, with their own distinct colonial emphases (for citations on other European travelers' contributions, see Achaya 1994: 142–52). Many such documents initially highlighted how "strange" and "backward" were Hindus' foods and food ways, compared to modern Europeans. But, by the same token, the British also realized the cultural distance they were somehow expected to "bridge" to colonize India.

Sociologically, real contacts started, first, as the British Rāj penetrated into districts, towns, and villages to control the land, the landlords, laborers, and agriculture and, second, as they mapped, counted, and documented all these to expand their rule and administer and tax Indians. The British thus created from the top a multilayered Rāj-serving chain of command that ran from all-India administrators to regional *rājā*s and state-district-local officials (including landlords or *tālluqedār*s). In this scheme, local landless and indentured laborers and *dalit*s stood last. Among other major changes, the Rāj increasingly rendered food a money-based scarce commodity, passing often through many capricious patrons (*mālik*) and grain dealers. Again, as this affected most, over time, landless peasants, indentured field laborers, and lowest castes, food insufficiency unless attended turned into a food problem of rising social concern. Yet, it was remarkable how most such Hindus (and Indians) successfully adapted their core family-based religious values and ceremonial customs, centered on sharing food.

They did so as their time-tested *jajmānī* system weakened, first in towns and then in villages. But, over time, the modern Rāj institutions did significantly erode, it would seem, the customary food-for-status, food-for-food, and food-for-work relationships among people. One might argue that traditionally effective channels of food distribution dried up in proportion to the Rāj's direct intervention in land revenue, agriculture, and major food markets at provincial and district levels. Further, with inequitable land ownership, food scarcity, and market manipulation, the traditional ways of, and religious morality in, regulating foods also declined. People encountered man-made food shortages, even famines. Such observations however remain tentative, requiring systematic studies of both positive and negative roles of the Rāj. Until then, we can only guess how their Christian ethical, modern rational economic, and divisive political interventions impacted Indian systems of food and agriculture.

On the positive side, the same Rāj had instituted systematic local and regional land surveys, created district records, and documented land ownership, transfers, and taxation. In turn, such documents and records helped track much better, among other things, food shortages, droughts, local famines, areas of endemic hunger, and epidemics. With accumulating records, surveys, censuses, and district gazetteers, the British virtually unveiled an all-India picture of social and religious diversity, including regional agriculture and people's food production and distribution patterns. Yet any systematic accounts of people's community food patterns and religious ideas were largely absent. The subject was as if beyond the colonial concerns. But whenever attended, accounts were incidental, reflecting the colonial cultural biases, blind spots, and aversions (see Crooke 1926, 1971). Later scholarly works on peoples' different religious ways and traditional cultures tried to be more "objective." In this category was, for instance, the *Encyclopedia of Religion and Ethics*, published at the beginning of the twentieth century (Hastings 1908–26). As this publication studied the world's major religious philosophical, historical, and philological forms, it also comparatively explicated different religious faiths, ideologies, ritual and ceremonial systems, including several—if separate and fragmented—religious conceptions of food.

Many early twentieth-century official and scholarly accounts also remained similarly fragmentary on the subject. Thus, one had to plod through mounds of major British district gazetteers on, and administrative studies of, cities, villages, castes, and tribes to find tits-bits on people's food taboos, community ways, and exchanges (Blunt 1931; Crooke 1926, 1971; Hastings 1908–27; Hutton 1946; Risley 1915). Exceptions were very rare. As a striking exception, food ways of a Hindu prince, for example, attracted the attention of E. M. Forster, a literary figure in the making at the time, and he documented Indian meals in exquisite detail in his personal correspondence (Forster 1983). Similarly, books on the Rāj nostalgia recounted some serious as well as humorous gastronomic encounters, events, and episodes, often comparing religiously scrupulous Hindu princes and the ruling British officials (Allen 1975, 1977; for more references, see Achaya 1994).

Amidst Gandhian religious and political reform

Next, we briefly turn to some distinct aspects of religious and national politics that kept Hindu food at the center, particularly during the modern twentieth century when Hinduism faced major political changes and challenges. Here M. K. Gandhi played a signal pre-independence role by debating, for instance, the orthodox Hindu caste system for its ritually restricted food sharing and by defending beef taboo and cow protection. All these also impacted Hindu-Muslim relations and communal violence (for crucial excerpts of his writings on these issues, see Gandhi 1947). Let us also remember that Gandhi, father of independent India, was "the paradigmatic Hindu" for the vast Hindu majority. He lived his convictions, showing how (and how far) to uphold, adapt, reform, or reject Hindu traditions for new India. Most importantly, he was pivotal as much for upholding the "timeless" Hindu *dharma*, with the essence of its caste order, as for accommodating modern humanistic values of social equality and justice.

A strict vegetarian with a simple, frugal, and well-regulated personal diet, he spotlighted how his closely watched diet and fasting led to moral and spiritual purity and national political mobilization. In his unique (if paradoxical) way, Gandhi sought to "reform" caste rigidities (a modernist goal) while also championing cow protection (a goal of the orthodox and Hindu right). If he arguably came closest in the twentieth century to living everyday on *anna* yielding "pure" thought and action, he also tried to accomplish two discordant goals, essentially by the magnetism of his saintly example and political charisma. Over time, cow protection, vegetarianism, abstemious eating, and celibacy virtually became Gandhi's political as well as spiritual signature (for statements on cow protection and vegetarianism, see Gandhi 1947: 127–30, 156, 158; for a contrasting ecology-based anthropological explanation of the "sacred cow complex" in India, see Harris 1985).

However, as is now well known, Gandhi's success was at best limited and fleeting. Soon, both orthodox Hindus (rallying against Gandhi's "dining and living with untouchables") and orthodox Muslims (against his Hindu-favoring politics of cow protection) criticized Gandhi's agenda, and it sank in Indian communal politics.

Simultaneously, a slow but distinctly revivalist *hindutva* politics also gathered momentum. Gandhi's appeals to Hindus for religious tolerance notwithstanding, major issues like beef taboo, temple entry (by *dalits*), and cow-protection congealed the rise of *hindutva* and Hindu nationalism (Jaffrelot 1996: 286–87, 113). Though these forces were in the making for some time (Jaffrelot 1996: 113, 204–11), *hindutva* agenda strengthened rather than weakened soon after Gandhi's assassination. And cow protection—powerfully symbolizing Hindu food—became the political centerpiece. Thus, as Jaffrelot (1996: 113) notes, a group of petitioners for cow protection in 1952, for instance, formed a five-kilometer-long line, with signature registers piled on bullock carts, for presentation to the governor of Madhya Pradesh. A cow-killing incident is still a surefire trigger for communal rioting in India.

Some post-independence changes

After independence, as modern food ways slowly—and selectively—began to influence the domestic Hindu food system, at first mostly in cities, popular Indian culture noticed the change first. However, emerging scientific and social science scholarship rarely looked beyond major problems in Indian agriculture and shortfalls in food supply. Anthropology and sociology studied food mainly as it helped explicate the proverbial Hindu caste system. Most studies showed how the close-knit family-kinship-caste order maintained the Hindu social order, especially as represented by upper-caste families and their food ways. Only few studies focused on food, however, remarked on how Hindus gingerly introduced measured social and ritual changes in urban (and some advanced rural) surroundings and how upper-caste food ways compared with those of lower castes (Khare 1986a, b). Yet, by the late seventies, cumulative social and ritual changes were evident in most people's food ways. Many orthodox villagers, for instance, while traveling in search of a job or on business to nearby cities, adapted to whatever was necessary or unavoidable. Most urban Hindus freely admitted that they were far less ritually punctilious in their food ways than were their parents and grandparents. Their modern office ethos challenged them, irrespective of their religious affiliations, to lunch, party, or dine together, at least whenever formally required. Once traveling abroad, ritual qualms further weakened, making many modern Hindus adopt the host country's dietary ways, including, for some, beef eating.

Correspondingly, villagers plying trade in cities also adjusted, exploiting to their advantage eating in roadside food stalls, "pure vegetarian hotels," and Western-style restaurants. At another level, enterprising villagers exploited cities for getting modern ideas on and support in new agricultural technologies and food marketing. A recent "postcolonial" study of a North Indian village, thus, showed how peasants unhesitatingly utilized modern agricultural technology to their advantage. Far from being passive or grudging participants, they, without compromising their core religious values and ritual ways, actively explored how to marry the new and the modern to their "indigenous" knowledge and practice. Akhil Gupta (1998) provided a detailed picture of how such convergence worked in a North Indian village around agronomy and ecology. While doing so, villagers repositioned and sharpened their indigenous knowledge systems and adapted domestic practices to link up to new regional and national political movements and their politics. However, follow-up is needed to see how (and how far) local and regional Hindu value dilemmas reconcile themselves with globalization, still struggling.

Though such postcolonial studies tend to emphasize conflicting economic and political interests, embedded in global forces over religious values, the deeply entrenched Hindu value questions are seldom far away. Basically, since Hindus know that their religious faith and traditional values define them as well as help create new political strategies of survival, their shrewd practical sense, especially in survival issues, closely nurtures both. The issue, however, requires careful further studies that will illuminate both the religious value and practical political issues together. Similarly, we need systematic empirical studies on roles of the government-initiated subsidized food distribution schemes. The fifties and the sixties saw the rise of "Indian population and food problems," and they created in response the government-subsidized "ration shops" to help low-income urban households procure basic foods and cooking fuel. Many low-income recipients, in response to the scarcity and hunger, simplified and shortened their customary rituals and ceremonies, preparing "rich foods" during only one or two annual festivals.

Though rarely recognized, such voluntary adjustments in the customary world played a distinctly supportive role in managing Indian food shortages. The people's daily ethics and morality in food also played a distinct role in tiding over droughts and famines. The diverse historical studies of Indian famines illustrate a similar intertwining of religious values and modern economic rationality (e.g. on the Bengal Famine of 1942, see Greenough 1982; on Indian famines in general, see Bhatia 1991; K. S. Singh 1975). Thus, if under food scarcity, distinct natural and human failures are as well recognized as an overarching role of the divine, then deeply held moral attitudes *initially* give the government not only time but also a much required social and political room to put its plans in action. But once the government, markets, and traders are found flagrantly mismanaging this opportunity and created artificial food shortages, the same people vociferously protest and rebel.

In a similarly pragmatic view, people's failures and shortcomings neither "disprove" those tenaciously held pictures of opulence and food abundance depicted in Hindu mythologies, nor do they mask the fact of actual food scarcity in life. Each, it seems, is dealt at its own place. Pursuing simultaneously these *paradoxical* moral-religious-pragmatic strategies, Hindus today, on the one hand, persevere as far as possible with the available food, and, on the other, some of them (in large cities) now loudly demonstrate to demand food as a human and civic right. Conceptually, Hindus have long pursued this "split strategy" to cope with food scarcity, hunger, and government failures (on the Hindu models of mythic plenty amidst actual scarcity, see Khare 1976b: 142–73; on traditionally diverse channels of food distribution in India, Khare 1986b; and on the question of "right to food" among Hindus, Khare 1998).

CONCLUSION

Overall, however, the impact of postcolonial forces on Hindu food is still far from settled, uniform, or internally cohesive. Nor are Hindu food's ties with the changing Indian moral and political economies always firm and clear. Yet, the classical philosophical and religious conceptions continue to endure, and they remain integral to Hindus' religious ideals, social practices, and spiritual goals. These continue to survive good times and bad, including major religious and political changes, as much as periods of food scarcity, hunger, drought, and famine. Simultaneously, however, in contemporary India, people more readily protest outright social inequality, injustice, and repression, especially if it concerns food. Given these changed social facts, twentieth-century Hindu food issues, as the previous sections showed, have been seldom free of politics of religion and nationalism.

In summary, although the preceding multistranded discussion of some major religious and social characteristics of *anna* is far from exhaustive, it is sufficient to convey some distinct cultural, religious, and historical properties of a major human food system. Anthropologically, our account of *anna* amply verifies what the structural-symbolic theories on human food explicate. People value, symbolize, and evaluate food by what traditionally matters—and socially means—most to them (Douglas 1966, 1974; Lévi-Strauss 1965). Today, Hindu food is indeed a multisided, elaborately structured, and multivocal cultural system, reflecting an underlying "cultural grammar" of comprehensive Hindu philosophical ideas, religious-spiritual values, social-ritual actions, therapeutic uses, and cultural meanings. The cultural logic of such Hindu food forges a wide range of *conjoining* relations rather than resolve into an array of such oppositions as ideals and practice, nature and culture, the raw and the cooked, and materiality and spirituality. The earliest formulations of food clearly set forth some distinct Indic paradigms, and these still prevail among the Hindus, Jainas, and Buddhists. Extending these insights, Hindus (and most Indians) approach food in highly pragmatic terms as long as it is in the market; but once it enters the household, caste, and community, it becomes highly ranked, ritualized, and socially constrained. Finally, once ingested, food expresses fine-grained affective, therapeutic, and spiritual properties.

Concurrently, Hindu food shows how it specifically encounters historical and political changes. A crucial and deep cultural assumption frames and guides such changes. Guided by it, that seamless and "timeless" *dharma* always frames and guides the significance and impact of all historical changes, however momentous. Thus, all Hindu accounting begins and finishes with this cosmic, all-encompassing *dharma*. The learned are not any more (or less) guided by it than those illiterate. Although the modern intellectual temper may find this stipulation problematic, it is nevertheless a massive social and cognitive fact for Hindus. Any critical religious and cultural study of *anna* can, therefore, neither ignore its distinct moral economy nor, as this section suggests, overlook its social weaknesses, historical difficulties, and political conflicts.

On the other hand, equally important, as long as the Hindu food system entertains open debates, adjusts, and responds constructively to protests and criticisms from within and without, there should be hope in its ability to cater to historically changing (including modern) religious goals, social needs, and political interests. The conception of *anna* in such a system, classical in religious conception but socially open to historical changes, continues to invite ever more changes in its production, distribution, and expanding-imbibing cuisine. Now caste restrictions are also slowly relaxing for many. Yet battles of equity, social equity, and justice are all still ahead. For only the *anna* that is equitable, sufficient, and satisfying to all (now over one billion people) can justify its defining time-honored Hindu inspirations.

CHAPTER NINETEEN

GRĀMA

Susan S. Wadley

Any analysis of Hinduism in India's villages requires that we consider it in the context of religion as practiced. Because of the cultural value placed on "the place to which one belongs," these practices differ in some critical ways from the prescriptions found in the myriad Hindu texts and also from those practices found in urban areas. Moreover, examining religion in the village requires attention to the ways in which the different groups of humans resident in any one village (families, lineages, castes) interact in the organization of religious activities that encompass specialists from categories far broader than the "priests" or Brāhmaṇ specialists who were the primary writers of the Sanskrit texts of classical Hinduism and who are the primary functionaries in most temple rituals. Further, urban Hindu practices are likely to be more heavily dominated by Brāhmaṇical practices than by the practices of the poor and lower caste. This chapter focuses on core practices of Hindu village religion while using more examples from northern India than from southern India in order to provide a more coherent capsule of village religious practices than we might get if we tried to capture the myriad variations that exist in religious practice across the hundreds of thousands of villages in India. Moreover, in the twenty-first century, the distinctions made between village (*grāma*), forest (*jaṅgal*), and city (*śahr*) are continually challenged by increasing migration to both urban areas and abroad as well as by a public culture and mass media that provide powerful linkages within and across regions and national boundaries.

CONCEPTUALIZING THE VILLAGE AND ITS INHABITANTS AS A RELIGIOUS COMMUNITY

Villages, as bounded, inhabited human communities, contain the vast majority of the Hindu population in India: even in the 1990s, more than 70 percent of India's population lived in village communities. These human village communities, moreover, are conceptualized by their inhabitants as different from both the forest, on the one hand, and the city, on the other. Villages differ from forests in being places of order and from cities in being places tied to the land of that specific place. Forests represent a site of demons and spirits that are out of control, while the village, *grāma*, is a place of order and control, with its various castes each allotted their own locations, with its women (at least those of higher caste) secluded in houses, and with its divinities sequestered in temples and shrines, all the while offering protection to the village inhabitants (Pfaffenberger 1982). While the older parts of cities may in fact replicate many of the features of villages, including the identification of spatial areas for different caste populations and the relationship of the "city" to a protecting deity (S. Srinivas 2001), it is in the religious practices of village communities where we can most clearly see how different categories of humans religiously relate to one another and to their deities. Looking at village Hinduism forces us to examine the ways in which different groups of humans interact with gods and goddesses and each other and enact, and thus refashion, and sometimes recreate, Hinduism.

Key to understanding village communities is the idea of *jāti* or caste, as distinct from the all-India categories of *varṇa*. Deriving from the same Indo-European root as the Latin word "*genus*," *jāti* implies a kind of being or origin (Marriott and Inden 1974). There are *jāti*s of humans as well as of snakes or even rocks. Each *jāti* represents beings with a similar moral and physical make up, that is, members of each *jāti* share physical characteristics such as level of innate purity and qualities represented by the idea of *guṇa*s, the qualities or substances of which beings are composed. In the textual view, adopted in large part by many practitioners of village Hinduism, Brāhmaṇs are thought to be mostly *sattva* (goodness or purity); those castes falling into the Kṣatriya *varṇa* are mostly composed of *rajas* (passion); and low castes are mostly *tamas* (ignorance, anger). The *dharma* (right actions and proper conduct) for each of the *jāti*s is distinct, based on views about the moral and physical qualities attributed to that *jāti*, so that it is "right" for a Rājpūt (a warrior caste) to drink liquor, but not for a Brāhmaṇ. Likewise, it is "right" for an untouchable of the Sweeper caste to eat meat, but not for a Brāhmaṇ.[1] And it is "right" for a Brāhmaṇ to avoid the polluting touch of the Sweeper. Because members of a given *jāti* are different physically and morally from other *jāti*, they should not intermarry: hence *jāti*s are endogamous. Moreover, most *jāti*s or castes are thought to represent a specific occupation, such as Barber (*nāī*), or Sweeper (*bhaṅgī*), or Goldsmith (*sunār*). In rural India, however, most castes also participate in farming, either as landlords, tenant farmers, or laborers. Finally, the *jāti*s that make up the rural populace differ from region to region, so that *jāti*s found in Bengal do not exist in Kerala or Gujarat; in this way, each region has unique constructions of the rural social order and hence of rural religious practice.

Each of the *jāti*s is thought to belong to one of the four *varṇa*s or to be outside of that system and untouchable. These *varṇa* identifications are often loose and a matter of ideology, with *jāti*s claiming a *varṇa* status that others in their community do not recognize. Related to these claims are *jāti* histories that often allege an original high status that the *jāti* was somehow cheated or tricked out of (for a detailed discussion of the origin myths of the Potters, see Caughran 1997; see also Wadley 1994: chapter 3). Further, the *jāti*s or castes in any given village are ranked; and while this ranking is connected to beliefs about the polluting aspects of their associated occupations, it is also heavily based on the economic standing of that *jāti* in that village. The major landholding caste, which tops the economic hierarchy, was termed the dominant caste by M. N. Srinivas (1959). This caste is usually accorded a high, if not the highest, status by the residents of that village, even though it is often not a Brāhmaṇ caste. Moreover, these caste statuses are malleable and change according to the changing material conditions of the castes in any specific village.

While not true for all of India (especially Bengal and Kerala), most Indian villages are nucleated: that is, the humans cluster together in houses packed into a small space, surrounded by their fields. Within the village nucleus, members of the village's various castes tend to live in caste neighborhoods; frequently the lowest castes are found at the edge of the village or in a nearby hamlet. These caste-based neighborhoods sometimes act as distinct religious communities, with their own temples and rituals not practiced in the nearby neighborhoods of other castes (see, e.g. Caldwell 1999).

The village's physical boundaries—off at the edge of the farmers' fields—are usually known, at least to the men. This physical locale, this village including its fields, is thought to be interconnected to its inhabitants via the soil that nurtures the crops and thus the humans. If the soil and its humans are compatible, then the humans will thrive and prosper; if not, the humans might sicken and perhaps die. Different kinds of soils are more or less compatible with varying kinds of humans, usually marked by their caste status. Thus Brāhmaṇs thrive in villages known for their "sweet" soils, while Śūdras thrive in villages with "sour" soils (E. Daniel 1984: 85).

In addition to being a physical location that nurtures humans and to which they are physically related through the eating of products of the soil, the village is also a moral community. The actions of members of the community intersect with those of others: sins and merit accumulate, for example, not just with an individual but also with his or her family, caste, and ultimately village. If the village as a whole is too sinful, a tragedy affecting it as a whole might occur, such as fire or flood or cyclone. One example of this mutuality of village residents comes from the village Karimpur in Uttar Pradesh in northern India. In 1984, a strong pre-monsoon dust storm led to a fire that destroyed many human and animal lives as well as thirty-five homes. In seeking an explanation of the fire, the village residents focused on the image of a pot of sins that had overflowed: they claimed that many residents had sinned, the pot overflowed and the village burned. No one person was singled out for sinning too much and causing the fire; rather, it was the collective accumulation throughout the village of sins that caused the fire. (Residents did state that the houses that were most badly burnt were thought to house people who had sinned more than those in houses that had not burned.) And while meritorious acts can counteract an individual's or the group's sins, clearly not enough merit had accumulated to outweigh the accumulated sin. Again, individual families may have had more merit and hence been spared. One family whose house was in the line of fire was said to have had a *satī*, a self-immolation of a widow on her husband's funeral pyre, a highly meritorious act, some generations before; and the result was the removal of sins for that family for the next seven generations. Since there was no sin in that house, it was spared. Here the merit accumulated by one individual is shared with her family, not just at the time, but over succeeding generations (see Wadley and Derr 1989).

Further, there are deities associated with a particular village, such as the goddess worshiped by every new bride in northern India or the protective goddess housed in a temple in southern India. The village Karimpur, mentioned before, has a guardian deity who is a Muslim saint, allegedly the conqueror who gave the village to its current Brāhmaṇ landlords several centuries ago. On Thursdays, the day thought sacred to him, women, mostly Hindu, climb the hill to his tomb/shrine and worship him with the help of a Muslim male whose family has responsibility for this service. The ritual itself incorporates elements of Islamic practice (e.g. "spreading a sheet," *cādar caṛhānā*, though a white one, not the green sheet used in major Muslim shrines), while they also make offerings of sweets and money, as in Hindu practice. (Note that no one in Karimpur thinks it peculiar that Hindu women worship a Muslim village protector or that they use Islamic styles of popular worship to do so. For a more detailed discussion of complex Hindu-Muslim interactions in rural communities, see Gottschalk 2000.) Only women who reside in the village Karimpur perform this ritual. Hence these village guardian deities are clearly seen as protective of the inhabitants of a specific physically defined village community, with the residents fully aware of what is inside of and outside of that border.

Some communities clearly mark the village community's border as in the ritual called *khappar*, also held in Karimpur (Wiser 1958). Once a year, a group of men collects offerings from all the houses of the village. In the evening, they worship the village goddess at her shrine under a tree, and possibly some individuals become possessed by her. Then, in the middle of the night with one man dressed as the goddess, they take a pot (*khappar*) around the village, entering every house to collect the inauspiciousness and sins found there. The pot is then carried to the village boundary out in the fields where it is tossed into a field belonging to a neighboring village, thus ridding their village of sins and delivering them to another village. In the North Indian state of Bihar, a similar ritual involves animal sacrifice either at the shrine of the presiding goddess of the village or at the boundary between villages (Gottschalk 2000: 50). (Brenda Beck [1981] notes a similar ritual for a community in South India where the collected evil spirits of a geographic area termed "*kirāmam*" are dumped into the territory of the next community.) Hence the village is a human and physically intertwined unit; and while much village religious practice is done by and for individuals, yet other practices recognize and enact the relationships with both humans and the place that exist within the village community.

Another set of relationships is related to the caste-specific occupational structures of the village community and their related ritual duties. Most Indian villages contain members from a variety of castes, ranging from those belonging to the Brāhmaṇ *varṇa* to those outside the *varṇa* scheme, the untouchables. Many rituals that take place in the village require the services of a number of these caste groups: these rituals could be life-cycle events, such as births or marriages or funerals; or annual cycle occasions such as the North Indian festival of Holī, when a bonfire is lit and the community celebrates the destruction of Holikā, who had prevented her nephew, Prahlāda, from worshiping god properly; or all-Indian festivals such as Dīvālī, the festival of lights that honors the goddess Lakṣmī and brings prosperity to the house for the coming year. Marriages, as the most elaborate of the life-cycle rituals, may require the most ritual services. For an upper-caste marriage in northern India, these might include a Brāhmaṇ, the village *paṇḍita* or *purohita*, who is able to read the Sanskrit texts and preside over the event; a Barber (*nāī*) and his wife who must help bathe and dress the bride and groom; a lower caste whose men act as musicians (nowadays playing brass band instruments in a tradition borrowed from the British); a Leatherworker (*camār*) whose family presents a model hearth of clay used in rituals that protect the house of the bride or groom from evil spirits; a Water carrier (*dhīmar*) who performs various functions for the family, such as bringing water or spreading sacred cowdung on the area where the actual marriage will take place; and a Potter (*kumhār*) who provides the pot that represents the goddess for the wedding ritual. Holī and Dīvālī require a similar set of services: the Potter must bring new pots for the household for the coming months and the small clay saucers used to light the house at Dīvālī; the Barber shaves the men before the ritual itself; the Tailor makes new clothes for the whole family; and so on.

These services have been tied to a system known as *jajmānī*, a system of hereditary patron-client relationships wherein the landowning castes guarantee a portion of their crops to a set of serving castes whose livelihood is thus guaranteed. Until the vast changes associated with the green revolution began in the 1960s, these services also included many which were only partially ritual or religious in the literal sense, such as a daily cleaning of the house's latrine by the Sweeper or the weekly washing of clothes by the Washerwoman (though the rules of purity and pollution prevented an upper-caste family from doing these tasks themselves). Nowadays in many villages, the more mundane tasks are no longer performed by the service castes because families have their own pumps and do not need water carried, would prefer to wash and iron their synthetic clothes themselves, have a septic tank and a modern toilet, and so on. In some cases, the only aspects of the *jajmānī* system that remain are those related to ritual duties: the Potter still brings the clay saucers for the Dīvālī lights (though these are now augmented by candles or even electric lights); the Barber and his wife still help dress the bride and groom; the Priest still conducts the marriage service itself; the Water carrier still purifies the floor with cowdung before the marriage arch is set up. What is clear is that a sense of ritual interdependence still exists: major rituals require the efforts of numerous kinds of people, and hence the members of the village community interact around rituals (Wadley 1994).[2]

In southern India where temple rituals are more elaborate and common for the village community as a whole, intercaste connections similar to *jajmānī* relationships are enacted in temple rituals. The temple priests are most commonly Brāhmaṇ (though many temples do not have Brāhmaṇ priests), while the musicians that play at major temple festivals are low caste. In her study of the marriage of the goddess Māriyammaṉ at the temple Kannapuram near Coimbatore, Tamilnadu, Brenda Beck (1981) briefly describes the roles of Brāhmaṇ priests, non-Brāhmaṇ priests, an untouchable "chief" officiant, untouchable musicians, and the leader of the main landowning caste of the region. Although presenting a different configuration of personae than found in northern India, a variety of ritual specialists are needed for this event, from a multitude of caste groups, including both a Brāhmaṇ and a non-Brāhmaṇ priest, as well as an untouchable.

There is yet another critical way in which humans are linked in rural communities, and no doubt in urban ones as well, and this concerns the removal of inauspiciousness. As noted earlier, the village Karimpur rids itself of inauspiciousness once a year by ritually dumping its accumulated sins in the neighboring village's territory. Critical to this action is the idea that inauspiciousness must be removed by transferring it to the physical space of another community. Inauspiciousness (*nāśubh* or *kuśubh*) is thought to be attached (*lagnā*) to the person, house, or village, thereby causing problems, such as illness, infertility, the decline of one's lineage, or poor crops. There are things one can do to prevent inauspiciousness from lodging in an individual, such as the lampblack (*kājal*) put on a baby's eyelid to prevent the evil eye or malicious thoughts from affecting that child or conducting rituals on astrologically auspicious days. But once inauspiciousness is attached, it can only be removed by passing it on to some other person or place (Raheja 1988).

This inauspiciousness is passed as a form of *dāna* or *dakṣiṇā*, ritual prestation, to those of higher-ritual rank (a Brāhmaṇ *purohita* or, in North India, an affinal kinsman) or, as in the village Karimpur, to a person of lower rank in the form of *nyochāvar*.[3] In northern India, when given to a higher person, sometimes with the mediation of deity, the ritual prestation is called *caṛhāvā* which signifies the inauspiciousness contained therein: the *caṛhāvā* must be given to a designated kinsperson or a person of a particular caste. Many of the rituals known as *vratas*, fasting rituals especially common to women, contain an offering called *udapān*, a form of *caṛhāvā*, which commonly contains grains and clothing. These offerings are made to the family *purohita* at the end of the woman's fasting ritual and effectively transfer the inauspiciousness attached to themselves or a member of their family to that receiving person (also called a vessel, *pātra*) (Raheja 1988). The Mahābrāhmaṇ funeral priests at Varanasi are also recipients of *dāna*, here representing the inauspiciousness of the deceased; and since they lack the heat (*tapas*) necessary to appropriately digest this inauspiciousness, they are thought to sicken instead, perhaps dying from diseases like leprosy as a clear manifestation of the inauspiciousness attached to their beings (Parry 1980).

In other instances, this inauspiciousness is passed to a lower person who has by the nature of their being (since lower-caste persons are generally thought to have more heat or *tapas* than high-caste persons) a greater capacity for digesting or eating that inauspiciousness. Thus at a marriage, coins or bowls of grain are circled over the head of bride and groom to remove any inauspiciousness attached to them at that time: these grains and coins are then piled up to be taken away by a lower-caste ritual servant (such as the Barber or Water carrier) or, if the ritual is in a lower-caste household, by a lower-ranked relative. A key point here is that the greater heat or digestive capacities of the lower person enable them to "digest" and hence control the inauspiciousness sent their way without sickening them as is the case with Brāhmaṇ or other high-caste recipients of *dāna*.

Hence, village religious action can be seen as intimately connected to a vision of the village as a defined physical location associated with a moral order and composed of individuals who are dependent upon one another, not only materially but also religiously. Without the high-caste *purohita*, the middle-ranked Barber, or the lowly untouchable, successful religious action would be impossible. It is not surprising, then, that there are religious stories that tell of how a village community is saved by the behavior of the lowest of the low, a Sweeper woman. What is also fundamental is that correct religious action is not just a matter of the behavior of the Brāhmaṇ priests but also is dependent upon the correct behavior of the various groups within the village and of the village as a whole. The Sweeper woman can destroy or save the village just as easily as the Brāhmaṇ priest can and neither can exist ritually nor materially without the other.

While the village is often thought of as a defined moral and physical unit, it is intimately connected nevertheless to other communities, through systems of temples connected to kingdoms, through pilgrimage, through marriage networks, and, increasingly, through popular media. So while the village may have a reality as a conceptual unit for some purposes, for yet others it is part of a much larger system.

Temples are intimately connected to kingship, and the ancient and medieval kingdoms of India were associated with particular temples, often built in order to substantiate the claim of that lineage to rule that territory through its identification of Viṣṇu or Śiva as the reigning monarch. For example, Śiva in the form of Sundareśvara ruled with his consort Mīṉākṣī the ancient Pāṇḍiyaṉ kingdom in Madurai (Fuller 1984). These royal temples such as Śrī Cannakeśara honoring Viṣṇu at Somnath, near Mysore, are often inscribed with the stories of mythological kings such as Rāma or Kṛṣṇa as a further claim to sovereignty, in this instance, of the Hoysala rulers (thirteenth century CE). It was the responsibility of this god in the temple (who was the true king) to protect the royal family, the kingdom, its people, and its territory. Annual festivals are then organized on a regional basis, drawing together participants from numerous village communities. Some temples are organized along lineage lines such as those belonging to the Tamil Pramali Kaḷḷar caste where Śiva is the principal god (Dumont 1986). These lineage temples also draw ritual participants from a variety of rural and urban communities, thus linking individuals of the same caste across village lines.

While many temples draw primarily from a local community or region, others are linked to pilgrimage routes that transverse India (and now the diaspora). Pilgrimage sites have become increasingly important as travel and communications become easier, but the idea of a *tīrthayātrā*, a trip to a "place of crossing," is ancient. Associated with rivers, most particularly the Gaṅgā, at Hardvar, Allahabad, Varanasi, or Gaya, these crossing places or fords are sites where divinity is particularly imminent and potent. Hence a visit to a pilgrimage site such as Varanasi is especially beneficial if a pilgrim wants her message heard by the resident deity. Varanasi is especially sacred to Śiva, as is Mount Kailāsa. Other pilgrims may be drawn to the region of Braj, around Vrndavan and Mathura on the border between Uttar Pradesh and Rajasthan, birthplace and playing ground of Kṛṣṇa. Many residents of the Braj region themselves take a pilgrimage to the Himālayas, to Nagarkot, to worship the goddess sometimes called Vrajeśvarī (the one of Braj). Pilgrims devoted to Rāma can make an all-India pilgrimage, visiting his alleged birthplace in Ayodhya, his wife Sītā's birthplace in Janakapur, the *āśrama* of Vālmīki (who was considered the composer of Rāma's story, the *Rāmāyaṇa*), an *āśrama* in Maharashtra where Rāma and Sītā are thought to have stayed in their forest journey, and so on, all the way to the tip of India at Kanyakumari, where the monkey army that purportedly aided Rāma rescue his captured queen built a causeway to Laṅkā, island home of the demon Rāvaṇa.

Whatever the god and goddess, whomever the pilgrim, and whatever spiritual goals they seek, pilgrimage links individuals across villages and regions and contributes enormously to the spread of an all-India Hinduism. Sometimes key identities cannot be transcended, as in the caste ties described by Irawati Karve (1988) about a pilgrimage to the temple of the god Viṭhobā in southern Maharashtra, while at other times links to a particular *guru* aid in transcending these ties. Pilgrimage is central to enacting a sacred geography of Hinduism and of linking individuals beyond their local communities, however influential those links may be.

India's rural communities are also intimately linked through marriage networks, through the movement of women from their natal homes to those of their husbands. Although there is a regional difference in the distances of these marriages (in southern India, the average marriage distance is less than five miles, while in the north it is more than ten miles; Sopher 1980), most women do leave their natal communities at marriage. In the north, this has traditionally been mandated by rules of village exogamy and marriage to persons not previously related as kin, while in the south, cross-cousin marriage has been prescribed, and although the groom may be a relative already, he most commonly still resides in a different community. This circulation of women, especially in the north, is a source of new rituals and everyday practices: one example is the bride who may want to perform an annual or weekly ritual unknown in her in-law's community. But there is a second aspect to the movement of women in marriage; and this involves the less permanent but nevertheless frequent movement of men. Fathers, brothers, and husbands visit their sisters, aunts, and cousins in their communities regularly and are still required to escort women between natal and affinal homes on many occasions. These all provide a frequent circulation of men across the region and also serve to link rural communities. The "isolated" rural community, as an economic and religious unity, is not the reality. Rather, regional temple rituals, pilgrimages, and the movements of men and women all reinforce the interconnectedness of humans across the rural landscapes of India and hence the circulation of religious ideas and practices across regions and the country and now to (and from) the diaspora in places like Birmingham, London, Queens, Pittsburgh, Fiji, or Trinidad.

UNDERSTANDING VILLAGE RELIGIOUS PRACTICES

While there are numerous volumes on everyday Hindu practices by missionaries, colonial administrators, and other travelers to India (e.g. Crooke 1926; Whitehead 1921), the work of M. N. Srinivas in the 1940s on the Coorgs, a caste group located in Karnataka in southern India, marks the real beginning of anthropological writings on Hinduism. Srinivas's work is especially important because of his ability to speak about nontextual traditions at a time when Indology remained focused on Sanskrit written works. Studies of village religious thought and practices also benefited from the shift in acceptable sites for anthropological fieldwork after the Second World War. Before the war, a few studies existed of so-called "peasant" communities such as Robert Redfield's work in Mexico, but the majority of anthropological work focused on "primitive" or "tribal" communities (and, indeed, there is a strand of writing on India concerned with its so-called tribal communities; e.g. see Furer-Haimendorf 1943–48). But the 1950s wrought a revolution in anthropological endeavors as the peasant communities of the world became acceptable sites for research.

In terms of conceptualizing village Hinduism, the students affected by Redfield's writings on Mexico are most influential. During the 1950s, scholars like McKim Marriott, Milton Singer, and M. N. Srinivas struggled with the task of understanding the relationships between village religious practices and textual Hinduism. Throughout his writing on the Coorg, M. Srinivas (1965: 89) makes the distinction between Sanskritic Hinduism or "all-India Hinduism" and regional or local Hinduisms, with their implied local gods, distinctive practices, and vernacular texts. While Sanskritic Hinduism implied pan-Indian deities and the salience of ideas such as *karma* and *dharma*, local Hinduisms might involve the worship of deities known only to that community and a lack of reference to concepts such as *dharma* and *karma* as guiding principles of people's lives.

Building on his work on the folk-urban continuum, where he develops the idea of the folk society as different from the civilization, Redfield collaborated with Singer on an article on the cultural role of cities that contained a vision of the relationship between rural and urban that was then followed up by Marriott. Essentially, Redfield and Singer (1954–55) propose that in the primary urbanization process that characterizes the first cities, the rural folk or little traditions are transformed by the growing urban literati into a coherent "great tradition" that becomes the standard for members of that civilization. Marriott (1955) takes the argument further, proposing that there is a continuous interchange between the textual "great" traditions and the folk "little" traditions and that this process is a two-way exchange. Ideas borrowed from the folk into the great tradition undergo the process of universalization, while those from the great that influence the folk traditions undergo a process of parochialization.

One example concerns the Hindu epic the *Rāmāyaṇa*, one of the most popular traditions in India; its best-known version is the Sanskrit rendition by the poet Vālmīki, who is considered by many to be the author of the *Rāmāyaṇa* as well as a key actor in it. But it also exists in numerous vernacular versions—in Bengali, Tamil, Avadhi, Marathi, and so on. In addition, it is enacted, usually in performances lasting ten to thirty days, in villages and cities throughout northern India every October (although the modern urban elite are more likely to perform in or see a professional one or two hour version, and similar short versions are found among Hindus in the diaspora). Each of these local enactments reframes the epic according to local traditions, building upon one or more written versions current in their community and possibly on the Vālmīki rendition as well.

In the late 1980s, the television producer Ramanand Sagar developed a multiepisode televised version of the *Rāmāyaṇa*. Sagar's *Ramayan* incorporates items from various regional and local *Rāmāyaṇa*s as well as from Vālmīki. For example, he takes the idea of a shadow Sītā from the *Rāmcaritmānas* of Tulasīdāsa, a Hindi (actually Avadhi) version of the *Rāmāyaṇa* (Hess 1999: 9–14). This allows him to have Rāma's wife Sītā captured by the demon Rāvaṇa without having her chastity truly tested. Unlike Vālmīki, he also has Sītā undergo a fire ordeal to prove her virtue. Using the ideas discussed here, we can say that the Sagar *Ramayan* represents an all-India version (for it was televised throughout India every Sunday morning and can now be rented in video stores in India and abroad, though in Hindi, not Sanskrit) and that it represents a process of universalization in taking elements from various regional *Rāmāyaṇa*s and incorporating them into a new all-India version. At the same time, in a process of parochialization, local communities are borrowing from both the Sagar *Ramayan* and their older regional versions and adapting these to their own local performance traditions in the village and community Rāmalīlās presented regularly throughout northern India. What this example demonstrates, in part, is that there is no one "great" tradition but a multiplicity of Sanskrit traditions as well as "classical" traditions in vernaculars. These interact in complex ways with the even greater multiplicity of local traditions even today. Further, universalization as a process has now been widened and reformulated as globalization, and parochialization becomes localization (see Wadley 2000).

By the 1970s, anthropologists and some historians of religion working in rural India had begun to devote their full attention to village religion rather than incorporating it into monographs in village life.[4] Attempts to understand local constellations of deities led to structural analyses that simultaneously focused on relationships among humans, among divinities, and among humans and divinities. To take one example, Beck (1981) examined the roles of Māriyammaṉ, "the vacillating goddess," in South India and speaks to the structure of the pantheon of Hindu gods and goddesses as understood when we look at village religious practice and belief, especially when tied to human structural differences such as Brāhmaṇ and low caste. Māriyammaṉ is understood as both the calm consort of Śiva (Pārvatī, Umā, Gaurī) but has a "violent underside as punisher and angry death dealer (Durgā-Kālī)" (Beck 1981: 86–87). Through annual ritual celebrations, Beck argues that the two sides of Māriyammaṉ are united. These celebrations bring into question animal sacrifice; the roles of males (as husbands or potential husbands); and the hierarchical extremes of Brāhmaṇ and untouchable. As she writes: "When the goddess comes home to earth things are also stirred up. . . . A fresh infusion of well-being flows from her presence and from a general lessening of categorical boundaries. . . . Most important of all, however, is . . . that these rites constitute a public restatement of mutual dependence on the goddess" (Beck 1981: 132–33).

Drawing on the work of Louis Dumont (1970), the encompassing nature of higher-ranked deities as well as an attempt to understand local pantheons reverberates through the work of Lawrence Babb (1975), Richard Brubaker (1978), Michael Moffat (1979), Susan Wadley (1975), and others. Supreme deities, such as Śiva and Viṣṇu, are seen as distant from humans, as unreachable because of their divinity. These deities encompass lower-ranked deities that take on aspects of the supreme deity's character, as do the incarnations of Viṣṇu—for example, Rāma as the warrior king or Kṛṣṇa as the child and lover. Kṛṣṇa in turn encompasses the snake deity, a more capricious deity whom he conquers by dancing on its seven heads until it relinquishes its control of the Yamunā River. Vāsuki, the king of snakes, in turn encompasses numerous named snake deities who are more malicious than Vāsuki himself. A second hierarchical arrangement has Śiva at the top: he gives power to and controls the Nāthayogīs who are his devotees. They in turn give power to the Rajasthani regional deity Gūgā, who cures snake bite. Gūgā in turn has control of Vāsuki and the snake deities. (Lapoint 1978 presents the legend of Gūgā where these roles are played out.)

Another approach to village religion is to see it as related to the seasonal cycles and agricultural seasons to which it is intimately connected. These seasons are best portrayed in a set of songs known as *bārah māsī* (twelve months), in which the characteristics of each month of the year are given within the frame of a narrative which is sometimes religious in character and sometimes more concerned with everyday woes such as the cheating landlord (see Vaudeville 1986; Wadley 1983). Normally the months are collapsed into three seasons, hot (March-June), rainy (July-October), and cold (November-February). The rainy and cold seasons, at least in North India, are followed by a major harvest: crops during the hot season are possible only with irrigation. Around the annual cycle and in sections within it, deities and rituals are organized in a more linear or narrative fashion. The two harvest seasons of northern India are celebrated with the cycle of rituals surrounding Dīvālī ("the festival of lights," a ritual honoring the goddess Lakṣmī and household prosperity) in the fall and Holī (a celebration of the new harvest of barley, fertility, and community) in the spring. Moreover, each of these major events is surrounded by other rituals that capture aspects of the core festival.

Looking again at an example from Karimpur, the festivals prior to and following Dīvālī are: Simāra Simāriya, a festival when young girls seek the goddess's support for an auspicious marriage; *karvācauth* (pitcher fourth), a day on which married women worship their husbands and seek their longevity; Dīvālī itself, with its celebration of Lakṣmī, the goddess of prosperity, and Gaṇeśa, the god who removes obstacles; *siyāūmātā*, a ritual early in the morning after Dīvālī in which women ask the gods for children, particularly sons; Govardhana, also the day following Dīvālī when household prosperity and survival are sought by honoring Kṛṣṇa, who held the mountain Govardhana (literally, "cowdung wealth") in his little finger as an umbrella over his village to protect it from a deluge; and *bhaiyā dūj* (brother's second), a ritual where women worship their brothers and seek their protection for the coming year.[5] If we list the goals of this set of festivals, as linked to the more general idea of household prosperity, the focus of the set is clear: hope for an auspicious marriage; a long-lived husband; sons; general household prosperity; protection by a woman's brother. All of these rituals are primarily enacted by women, and while the goals are broader than those of the women themselves, this set of fall rituals clearly focuses on those things that a woman would ideally need for happiness: husband, sons, prosperity, support of natal kin (Wadley 1980). That all occur within a five-to-six-week period makes the underlying message of prosperity generated by women even stronger.

Notably these rituals are organized and largely enacted by women, as indeed are the majority of annual cycle rituals in northern India. Not only do these rituals mark the powers of women in gaining household prosperity, they also provide a marked counterpoint to female devaluation and subordination as found in the dominant male-authored texts of Sanskritic Hinduism.

This emphasis on ritual enactments of female worth and power is captured in an analysis of another calendrical ritual cycle by Ann Gold (2000). In the Rajasthani village of Ghatiyali, the women practice a spring cycle of rituals that begins with Holī, the festival celebrating the destruction of the goddess Holikā and devotion to Rāma of her nephew Prahlāda, and ends sixteen days later with Gaṅgaur, a time when girls pray to be "auspiciously married to living husbands."[6] Between these two rituals fall two more: the first honors Sītalā (the cool mother or "smallpox goddess"), while the second celebrates the Dasa Mātā (the ten mothers). Gold sees these four linked festivals (and they are clearly linked in the minds of the women who enact them) as capturing "what female power is and does," and it is in large part because they are linked that they carry weight.

She summarizes the overall relationships and effects of these four rituals thus:

> 1) At Holi, conceptually, the female demonic [in the form of Holikā Mā] is humanized, her kinship acknowledged. Although complete identification is certainly avoided, complete horror is never posed. Ritually, it is men who vividly act out aggressive, demonic violence, while women take the part of rescuers and life-givers [as they symbolically save the child from the fire and return it to the house]. 2) On Sitala's day, conceptually, the goddess who . . . [afflicts children with] disease and fever is the very goddess who is pleased with female body grime and menstrual pollution, and who grants fertility to newlywed couples. Ritually, women transgress the taboo on ploughing and claim the right to bequeath property, recognizing the intimate connection between these two. Thus they assert an opposition to these doubled ritual and economic disempowerments. 3) On Dasa Mata's day, conceptually, women claim superior knowledge, superior intelligence. They teach men's folly in attempting to control wives and make them into passive objects. Ritually, women put on the "ugly" string that ensures that the Goddess's beneficent power will bless their households. 4) On Gangaur, conceptually, women enact self-determination in marriage arrangements, and a capacity for ascetic feats. Ritually, Gangaur celebrates couples. As high-caste pageantry, explicitly defined as important only for those groups who forbid widow remarriage or divorce, it is nearest among the four festivals to taking a view of females as subservient half-bodies. Yet, just as women plough like men on Sitala's Day, on Gangaur a girl acts the part of a groom, and women—officiating through their "interactive" wall art at the divine couple's union—act the parts of male Brahmin priests at weddings.
>
> (Gold 2000: 226)

Gold calls these "conceptualizations of gender evident in women's celebrations 'counterpoints' " and claims that they offer "both blunt and subtle denials of a dominant male-authored discourse of female devaluation and subordination" (Gold 2000: 226). In doing so, she joins other scholars in looking more carefully at the ritual practices of women and the ways in which Hindu women, through ritual, contest the dominance of male textual traditions.

These two examples illustrate a further concern of scholars working with religious practices in rural India (though it also permeates recent work on urban and textual religion)—the gendered nature of ritual practice. In addition to the major roles that women play in annual cycle rituals, they surround the more textual and Sanskritic practices of life-cycle rituals with their own rituals and texts, usually songs and stories sung and told in the local dialect. For the most part, a Brāhmaṇ priest conducts a birth ceremony, a marriage ceremony, or a funeral (priests are not always available to the lowest castes, who officiate at their own ceremonies). But these textual rituals (with the text often being read in Sanskrit from a pamphlet) are surrounded by the rituals of women, rituals that ultimately dominate in terms of time and energy. For example, a high-caste birth requires a tenth-day ceremony conducted by the priest who gives the child a ritual name and marks his or her coming out into the community. But on the birth day itself, women celebrate with songs (especially if a boy) and decorate a milk pot with cowdung and barley seeds in which to make foods for the new mother. Special "heating" foods must be prepared for the mother to replace the bodily heat that she has lost through childbirth, lest her body become too cool and illness befall her. Before the mother can nurse the child, her breasts must be ritually washed by her husband's sisters. In parts of India, the goddess of fate, Behmātā, is called to write the child's fate on its sixth day after birth. Various ceremonies lead to the ritual cleansing of the mother and child, until the "coming out" ceremony presided over by the priest on the tenth day after birth. This abbreviated synopsis of the rituals of childbirth clearly marks the critical role of women, even in one of the most important realms dealt with by textual traditions.

If women's roles in village religious practices loom large, in contrast to the roles of the practitioners of the Sanskrit textual traditions, so do those of non-Brāhmaṇ men. This is especially true of curing rituals, where expertise is not hereditary but often chosen or achieved through extraordinary circumstances. Typically, a diviner-priest or exorcist is a lower-caste male who has developed a special relationship with his own tutelary deity and who has chosen to learn the sacred ritual sayings that provide power for his curing. Thus by working with his more powerful spirit, the exorcist is able to confront the more malevolent lesser deity or spirit and induce him to abandon his victim, to move to another place, to return to his earthly body (as in snake possession),[7] or to accept the worship of others and be happy being thus worshiped. (The possession is usually identified because of illness or peculiar behavior on the part of the one possessed.) Sometimes the deity possessing a victim will become the tutelary deity of that person who is then recognized as an exorcist or diviner-priest. Hence roles as diviner-priests or exorcists provide a route to recognized religious specialization for lower-caste men, who are otherwise denied an authoritative role in religious practice (for several excellent examples from southern India, see Caldwell 1999; Hiltebeitel 1988–91; Kapadia 1998).

Possessions also provide an avenue for those oppressed—women, laborers, members of the lower castes—to speak out against their oppressors, often in violent terms. Thus a possessed young bride might speak about the unwelcome sexual advances of her husband, using aggressive language that is in marked contrast to proper female speech. Or the spirit possessing a laborer might speak in the most antagonistic ways about the abuse and poor pay, or lack of pay, he receives from his landed employer. Possession can also be used to explain other kinds of social problems, such as the son who quickly returns from the city where he has unsuccessfully sought employment in an alien environment and has a breakdown defined by his community as possession (Freed and Freed 1964).

It is also possible for a community to use ritual and possession for political purposes. One such ceremony is Holī, the North Indian ritual of reversal, where the lower castes and women are allowed to throw colors (or dung or urine) on their high-caste/male oppressors (see Marriott 1966). Holī provides an opportunity to mark anomalous behavior. For example, in North India a man should not live in his wife's village, although when a couple has no son, they frequently bring their son-in-law to their home, especially if land is available.[8] Holī frequently involves mocking the man living in his wife's house, as in the instance Marriott (1966) reports of the son-in-law led through the village lanes riding backwards on a donkey.

While possession rituals, especially, mark an opportunity for the oppressed to speak, F. G. Bailey (1994) provides an example where ritual is used to punish those who have become too uppity, transgressing the acceptable power structures of the rural community. He studies a collective community decision about witchcraft in a village in Orissa. In this case, the death of a young woman who may have had cerebral malaria is blamed, some months later, on a Potter who had unexpectedly become wealthier than his neighbors. After a series of rituals to divine the cause of the girl's death, it was claimed that his tutelary deity had gotten loose and caused the girl's death. Only with large monetary contributions from the accused Potter (thus taking away his "improper" wealth) could the community feel safe.

Thus we have come full circle: in village religion, men and women of various castes (and women of all castes) play a variety of specialty roles that support rituals such as Dīvālī or a marriage. But village religion also provides an outlet for those oppressed by the material and ritual hierarchy to speak out, as when a young wife is said to be possessed and the spirit is allowed to speak through her to the wider community, outlining her issues and concerns. Women gain power through rituals that they control, and so do lower-caste men. This in fact is one of the great sustaining values of village religious practices, as contrasted to the high-caste, male-dominant Sanskrit textual traditions. Many of these same practices are found in urban religious practice, so that we might often more profitably speak of nontextual traditions than of village traditions. (Exploring the nuances of these differences between village and urban practice is beyond the scope of the chapter.) Nevertheless, village religion and its urban counterparts allows a greater range of ideas, practices, and practitioners than does the religion of the Sanskrit tradition: one result is an enormous vitality as religious practice opens to everyone.

THE EFFECTS OF GLOBALIZATION ON VILLAGE RELIGION

As already noted, village religious practices are never stagnant but always responsive to new ideas brought through travel and pilgrimage and more recently through the media. The early effects of what we now term "globalization" reached a small range of people. One of the first sources of new ideas that reached a relatively wide audience was printed books, and for the rural audience these were often didactic manuals—how to perform the rites and festivals of the twelve months of the year or how to perform a weekly ritual such as that for Saturday. Even more popular were pamphlets of religious songs—either for particular seasons or life-cycle rites or around some given theme. Some of these pamphlets were written in a local dialect and hence were accessible only to audiences raised in that region; and as a result, they were particularly valuable in highlighting the traditions of local areas. Yet other pamphlets emphasized more all-India themes or rituals. But since the majority of India's villagers even today are illiterate, materials to be read reach a circumscribed audience.[9]

The modern printing press also contributed to the flow of visual ideas, especially with "god posters" or Hindu calendar art. Working with an ever-changing set of ideas of how to render the gods and goddesses visually, the proliferation of god posters has been enormous, with essentially every house, however poor, having at least one image hanging from an often dusty wall (see Inglis 1995; H. Smith 1995). Here again there is a contrast between local images and those with wider, perhaps all-India, circulation. Images of deities at local temples or temples reached on pilgrimage can be contrasted to such pervasive images as Lakṣmī, the goddess of prosperity.

The influence of motion pictures is also enormous. For example, in the mid-1970s, the "new" goddess Santoṣī Mā, who is thought especially to protect women whose husbands are absent (an increasingly common phenomenon as migration from rural to urban areas increased), had her cult vastly enlarged through a Bollywood film that purportedly told her story. It is important, however, to note that poverty denies many people, especially poor women, access to films. The rapid spread of television in the late 1980s and 1990s has further increased the reach of mythological films, which appear to be the primary focus of many women's television viewing.

More cheaply available are audio media—radios and tape players. Since electricity remains problematic in many rural areas (which either do not have electricity or are subject to frequent power cuts), both radios and cassette players are often run off of batteries, themselves expensive and hence a deterrent to their use. But cassette players have a particular niche not met by either films, television, or radio. Like printed pamphlets, audio cassettes are cheaply produced and easily marketed. They are thus responsive to the demands of audiences for songs, ballads, epics, and religious stories told in their local dialects, with local themes by artists renowned in that region. Frequently, then, the marketing range for audio cassettes is limited to a rather small geographic region (and possibly areas where migrants have moved). For example, the electronics market in Delhi has distributors that specialize in the audio cassettes from particular districts: they buy from a designated cultural region and then sell to shopkeepers with migrant audiences from those regions (not particularly difficult, as migration tends to follow kin and caste networks). Thus whereas the Bollywood (Hindi movies made in the enormous Bombay film industry) films shown on television and in cinema halls tend to have a homogenizing effect on local religious practices, widespread use of audio cassettes plays a crucial role in keeping local traditions flourishing (Manuel 1993).

India's rural communities are also caught up in the wider religious confrontations prevalent throughout India today. The crisis at Ayodhya in the early 1990s when Hindus tore down a centuries-old Muslim mosque that they claimed was built on the site of the birthplace of the god Rāma reverberates in the resurgence of performances of the story of Rāma (the Rāmalīlā) in local communities across northern India. Increases in education, both to more children and to higher levels, bring more and more ideas of Sanskritic Hinduism into village life: not only are students' textbooks filled with Sanskritic concepts, texts, and history, but their teachers usually advocate a strong all-India set of values based on their understanding of Sanskrit traditions.[10] At the same time, the increased education and general prosperity of a number of caste communities has meant that these once-silenced communities can now support a set of lectures by a religious leader of their own caste group or subsidize a Rāmalīlā performance in places where previously only higher-caste landlords could attempt such patronage. This is most evident in the Dalit movement in which hundreds of thousands of ex-untouchables have left Hinduism and converted to Buddhism in an attempt to rid themselves of old prejudices and hurtful behaviors. Their resistance is shown too in folk songs such as the one in the Anant Patwardhan film, *We Are Not Your Monkeys*, in which a prominent Maharashtrian folk singer claims that the low castes were enslaved by the Āryan high castes and turned in the monkey army that the god Rāma used in his battle with the demon Rāvaṇa in the *Rāmāyaṇa*.

The media also seem to affect some kinds of religious practices and symbols. Recently, I encountered a group of teenage girls (who were partially raised in an urban area) who refused to engage in the ritual cleansing of their courtyards with cowdung, as they had learned in school that dung was dirty and disease ridden. This denial of the ritual purity of the products of the cow strikes at the heart of Hindu belief and practice (Wadley 2000). Comparable is evidence from South India that women in rural Karnataka no longer are required to be segregated in a menstrual hut nor do they have to take a bath with cowdung at the end of their menstrual period (Helen Ullrich, personal communication, 2001).

In contrast to these signs of an opening up of Hindu symbols to new and vastly different interpretations is the behavior of some Brāhmaṇ village women who are more careful and conservative in their eating and ritual habits than their mothers-in-law were. In part, their conservative following of rules about what one can eat, and from whom, are a response to the Hindutva movement of the 1990s in which many "Western" practices have been condemned as "modern" and to be avoided by the devout Hindu.[11] These women refuse any food not cooked by a Brāhmaṇ, will drink tea only if made by a Brāhmaṇ and served in a metal (not china) cup,[12] and have the leisure time (given less involvement in the labor-intensive household chores such as grinding grain of their elders) to engage in daily and weekly rituals.

VILLAGE RELIGION AND THE DIASPORA

Slowly the village community is being transformed. Never itself an isolate, though envisioned by its residents as a particular place with a particular value and ethos, the village community is increasingly connected with urban India and with the rest of the world. Slowly India's rural population is decreasing in favor of residence in cities. Every year, more and more men, sometimes with their families, migrate from India's villages to seek their livelihoods in India's cities. Yet the movement between urban and rural sites is enormous, as members of families return to their "native place" for important rituals, such as Dīvālī or for weddings, births, or funerals. Recent migrants might retain their rural connections for a generation or more, never thinking to conduct a marriage in the city or of celebrating a major festival in the city. When return to the rural homesite is not possible, they seek to reconstruct, in the city and in altered form, the social and religious practices of their homeplace.

Some of these recreations are challenging, such as a North Indian ritual called *karvācauth* (pitcher fourth) held in a lower-middle class neighborhood in Delhi in 1998.[13] *Karvācauth* is a major festival for women in the Hindi-speaking regions of northern India and involves a full fast for the day, to be broken only when the moon rises. Held in honor of one's husband's long life, women consider it one of their most important rituals. In their home villages, they gather in family or lineage groups to celebrate, telling stories of the ritual, drawing the ritual design on their walls, and in the evening worshiping their husbands and breaking their fast together. In urban areas, often isolated from other family members, groups of women, often from different caste groups but living nearby in the same colony, gather to celebrate together. The ritual design is no longer drawn on a cow-dunged wall; rather, a paper version is bought in the market and hung on the cement wall. This cross-caste, nonfamily celebration is unknown in their home areas, but the need for community at time of religious festivity leads to the altering of old rules. Moreover, whereas in northern India a village (or a caste within a village) may have organized a Rāmalīlā enactment of the story of Rāma, now a colony in the urban area may do so.

The challenges are even greater in the Indian diaspora. But the resulting religious practices have a similar theme: the Hindu community of Syracuse, New York, for example, puts on a Rāmalīlā performance, ignoring original caste and regional differences. The women from northern India gather in someone's house for their *karvācauth* festival with paper designs bought in New York City or sent by kin in India.

Longitudinal studies that would allow us to understand the transformations of village religion as members move to other spaces are lacking. Autobiographies of Indian migrants to the West suggest that the shift to exceedingly rare visits to the home community, despite the importance of native place, takes place within one generation. Certainly, there are families from the community of Karimpur that have slowly, but finally, broken all their ties to their native place in the last thirty years. Owning houses in nearby urban areas and with children raised as city kids, they eventually sell whatever remaining property they have in the village and cut their ties. Now their village kin visit them in the city rather than their kin in the village.

With 70 percent of India's population still in rural communities, village religious practices are in no danger of dying out. Yet every such community is challenged by migration, by media, and by influences that are slowly eroding some practices in favor of new ones. Over time, many Hindus have cut and will cut their ties to their rural communities, yet periodically they too return to savor the connection to the "place to which one belongs."

NOTES

1 I am using caste and *jāti* interchangeably here: neither is the equivalent of *varṇa*. I have capitalized the names of caste groups as defined by their traditional occupations to distinguish them from individuals who might choose to follow that occupation, hence Tailor is a person whose caste occupation is sewing, while tailor refers to a person of any caste who has chosen to make clothes for a living.

2 Many of these caste-specific functions are also found in urban areas, in some sense replicating the social formations of rural communities (and, in many instances, are actually a rural community incorporated into a growing urban space). Hence ritual interdependence helps to characterize community, not just village communities.

3 The terminology changes from area to area: in Karimpur, there is a marked distinction between the *dakṣiṇā* given to the priest and the *nyochāvar* presented to those lower. Raheja (1988) finds a different set of terminology at work in a community several hundred miles north.

4 The unpublished dissertation by John Planalp (1956) is one early exception.

5 This event is particularly important for North Indian women who are married into previously unrelated families in villages at some distance from their natal homes. Moreover, the hypergamous marriage system is sometimes interpreted to mean that fathers cannot accept food or water in their daughter's affinal home, making it all but impossible for a father to visit his married daughter. The result is that brothers become the link between a woman's village of birth and her village of marriage and hence represent to women any protection against marital abuse that she may receive from her natal kin.

6 Taking place six months later than Simāra Simāriya, it seems that Gaṅgaur is nevertheless the Rajasthani equivalent of the Karimpur ritual.

7 The spirit of the snake who has bitten a victim is believed to reside in that victim's body and must be induced to return to its snake body. Hence, in North India at least, snakes that have bitten someone are not killed, for if they were, there would be no body for them to return to.

8 This practice is also related to ideas about a female's manifesting her sexuality before her parents: in some communities, a man cannot sleep with his wife when visiting her parents nor should the wife give birth in her parents' home. Clearly, the resident son-in-law breaks these taboos.

9 In the more rapidly modernizing cities, comic books became a key transmitter of religious ideas (see Babb and Wadley 1995).

10 Yes, this does make it difficult to be a Muslim student in many rural communities where Muslims are not in a majority. It also leads sometimes to anomalies, such as the best Sanskrit student in the Karimpur middle school in the late 1960s was a Muslim.

11 Two notable practices attacked by the movement are the birthday cake because it involves blowing out candles, when in fact a child's life should be celebrated with the lighting of a candle or lamp, and Valentine's Day, seen by the elements in the *hindutva* movement as decadent Westernism. Popular high-class restaurants in Mumbai were picketed on Valentine's Day by conservative Hindus in both 2001 and 2002.

12 Metal has centuries-old qualities of transmitting purity and pollution, while china is an unknown thing and hence is used by those who wish to break the rules, but not by those who intend to stick firmly to them.

13 I observed this ritual enactment in October 1998.

CHAPTER TWENTY

ĀLAYA

Vasudha Narayanan

Build a temple (*kōyil*)
in your heart.
Install the lord
called Mādhava [Kṛṣṇa] in it
Offer him the flower of love . . .
(*Periyāḻvār Tirumoḻi* 4.5.3)

So sang Periyāḻvār, a poet devotee, in the eighth century CE. Although most Hindus believe that the supreme being resides within them, they still go to the local temple or make long pilgrimages to visit a deity enshrined in a sacred place. Many Hindus, even in the diaspora, take their children to visit the temple in the Indian village from which their ancestors came or to a temple in which their families have worshiped. Such pilgrimages are undertaken to petition or express gratitude to the deity or to have different rites of passage performed in a place held sacred by their family for many generations.

Hindus of various *sampradāya*s or traditions have been worshiping in temples for more than fifteen hundred years. It is likely that there were many sites considered to be holy even before temples were built there. While the sacrality of many temples is inextricably connected with the sanctity of the land on which it is built, this chapter will deal more with the history, structure, theology, and functions of the place of worship and to a lesser extent with the place itself. The information is drawn from visits to hundreds of temples in India and a few dozen temples in the United States, Canada, and South Africa; dozens of Sanskrit and vernacular works extolling the glory of the place and the temple (Sthalapurāṇa); as well as pamphlets and brochures. The sources used—textual, historical, ethnographic, and participant observation—are integrated with personal reflection on pilgrimages made to these temples and participation in rituals conducted in the many shrines.

ACCOUNTS OF SACRED PLACES IN INDIA

Sacred epics and texts on deities known as Purāṇas mention specific places in India as holy and charged with power. Many Hindu texts say that if one lives or dies in the holy precincts of a sacred place, one is automatically granted supreme liberation. According to oral tradition, there are seven towns which are so holy that just by dying there one is assured of liberation (adapted from Eck 1982: 38):

> Ayodhyā, Mathurā, Māyā [Hardvar]
> Kāśī [Varanasi], Kāñcī, Avantikā [Ujjain]
> And the city of Dvārakā
> These seven bestow liberation.

There are other lists of such cities and villages. Many lists are regional, but some are pan-Indian and span the subcontinent, creating networks of sacred spaces and consolidating the various Hindu communities and traditions. South Indian Śrīvaiṣṇavas (a community that is about a thousand years old and whose members worship the deities Viṣṇu and Lakṣmī) count 108 temples as sacred. One hundred and six are in India, the other two are heaven (*vaikuṇṭha*) and the mythological sea of milk where Viṣṇu is said to lie on his serpent bed. Because the Śrīvaiṣṇava community is located in South India, most of the places are in the modern southern states of Tamilnadu, Andhra Pradesh, and Kerala. A few towns like Dvaraka and Ayodhya from northern India are deemed sacred because of their associations with the stories of Rāma and Kṛṣṇa (incarnations of Viṣṇu), but the most important temple for them is in the local island town of Srirangam in the Kāverī River in South India.

Worshipers of the deity Śiva who is said to be the husband of the powerful goddess Pārvatī/Śakti also have their lists of the most important pilgrimage places. In most of these temples, Śiva is represented in the form of a conical stone or upright shaft called *liṅga*. The word "*liṅga*" means "distinguishing symbol" and refers to the male procreative organ. It is placed in a receptacle called *yoni*, which represents the womb. The union between the *yoni* and *liṅga* reminds one that female and male forces are united in the spiritual and the material generation of the universe. Most Hindus, however, do not normally interpret the *liṅga* and *yoni* as physical objects. Rather than reminding them of sexual connotations, it serves as a reference point to the spiritual potential in all of creation and specifically to the positive energies of Śiva. In many narratives, the *liṅga* is seen as a column of light, a pillar with no beginning or end and depicts the infinite nature of Śiva.

In the Tamil-speaking lands of South India, there are five temples dedicated to five manifestations of the Śiva *liṅga*. These forms connote the five basic elements that, according to many schools of Hindu philosophies, come together in the creation of the universe. The five elements are water, fire, wind, earth, and air/ether. Muttusvāmī Dīkṣitar, a renowned musician (1776–1835), composed songs in honor of Śiva in these five temples.

Other narratives say that Śiva is said to appear as the flame of creative energies (*jyotirliṅga*) in twelve places in India, but the list of places is contested by many local devotees who would like to see their town on the pilgrimage route. Many of these places now advertise on the internet, narrate the history of the shrine, and describe the accommodations available to the pilgrim. The list of *jyotirliṅga* sites with home pages on the internet include Śrīśailam, Oṃkāreśvara, Girīśneśvara, Aundha-Nāganātha, Tryambakeśvara, and Bhīmaśaṃkara.

One may also count lists of the 108 places where there is *śakti* or the power of the goddess present. There are also lists of sixty-eight places where the Śiva *liṅga*s are said to have emerged "self-born" (*svayambhū*) (Eck 1982: 38), the eight places where Viṣṇu spontaneously manifested himself, and so on. When it is a small, local area that is being exalted, we see localized lists; thus there are supposed to be 108 shrines to the goddess Durgā in the state of Kerala alone. Pilgrimage programs sometimes include these thematic routes, and the map of India is filled with holy cities and places. Pilgrims through the centuries have gone from one place to another linking the many centers of the Hindu traditions.

GENERIC SACRALITY AND LOCAL SANCTITY

Indeed there are those who say that all the land of India is holy; it is here that actions bear fruit. The description of the sacrality of the land was confined to the northern part of India in the time of the Dharmaśāstras around the beginning of the Common Era. Manu says: "That land, *created by the gods*, which lies between the two divine rivers Sarasvatī and Dṛṣadvatī is . . . Brahmāvarta . . . . The tract between those two mountains which extends between the eastern and western oceans, the wise call Āryāvarta (the country of the noble ones). *The land where the black antelope naturally roams, one must know to be fit for the performance of sacrifices*; this land is different from the country of the barbarians" (*Manusmṛti* 2.17, 22–23, adapted from Bühler 1886: 32–33; emphasis added). In time, the concept of the sacred land extended beyond the land between the Himālaya and Vindhya mountains to cover the whole subcontinent.

In the late nineteenth and twentieth centuries, India as personified as the mother (Bhārata Mātā) has been important in political thinking. Mayuram Viswanatha Sastri (1893–1958), a musician who participated in the struggle to free India from colonial rule, composed a song popular among all South Indian classical singers called "Jayati Jayati Bhārata Mātā" (Victory, Victory to Mother India):

Victory, Victory to Mother India
  sung by the wise,
most exalted of all [lands]
filled with forests
comfort of the despondent,
Victory, Victory to Mother India

Holding all lives to be equal,
sustaining all honor and perfection
most esteemed of all lands
possessing supreme bliss,
Victory, Victory to Mother India.

Appearing with countless virtues
replete with compassion
manifest flower of joy
She who is the refuge of the fallen,
Victory, Victory to Mother India.

In this, and many such songs, India is personified and extolled as a compassionate mother goddess filled with sanctity. This image of Mother India has had political overtones as well; as we have seen in an earlier chapter during the freedom struggle against the British, Mother India was portrayed as being held captive by foreign forces. Bankimchandra Chatterji's song "Vande Mātaram" (We bow down to the Mother) is considered to be the national song of India. Every morning, all radio stations in India play the opening bars of this song when they begin transmission. In the late twentieth century, the notion of a personified Mother India is associated with political consciousness of Hindus, and there is even a temple built in her honor (McKean 1996a).

While India is personified as a mother and considered holy, most Hindus *localize* the sanctity and go regularly to the regional temple or a sacred place that has been important to their families for generations. A young married couple may go to such a holy city to pray for a child and will return there to conduct some sacrament for the child after its birth. A family whose ancestors may have hailed from a particular village may send money to that local temple for propitiatory rituals.

Although there are many standard itineraries—just Viṣṇu or Devī temples or a mixture of all the famous ones—almost every town is held sacred in some way. Practically every holy place has a Sthalapurāṇa, a text which lavishly describes the antiquity and the sacredness of a place. The whole town surrounding any temple is said to be sacred. Every tree, every stream near the precincts of the temple exudes this sense of sacredness. Bathing in the sea, river, stream, or pond near the temple is said to grant salvation. In South India, every village temple will have a story of how the lord or the goddess revealed himself or herself in that place to a particular devotee. Pilgrims believe that by remembering the stories of the devotees whose wishes were fulfilled in the past and in worshiping that local deity in a particular way, they will now receive divine grace. This grace will eventually give one liberation from the cycle of life and death.

The temple itself is like a port of transit, a place from where a human being can "cross over" (*tīrtha*) the ocean of life and death. Many of the temples and holy places are also located near bodies of water—one finds them near oceans, streams, rivers, or springs of water. When such a body of water was not readily available, temple architects dug a deep well or pool and used it for ritual purposes. In this context, one may recall that one of the main structures of Mohenjodāro in the Indus Valley civilization was called the great bath. This may well be one of the earliest sacred tanks, similar to the hundreds of temple-attached ponds that we find in South India.

Many temples and holy sites are also near mountains and caves, places where Hindu gods and goddesses resided in Purāṇic stories. Śiva lives in the mountain called Kailāsa, and for the devotee, every Śiva temple on earth is a Kailāsa. The innermost shrine in a temple usually has no window and is said to resemble a cave.

The sanctity of places is not frozen and immutable; while a few places like Srirangam and Varanasi have been continuously sacred for almost two thousand years, the popularity of a place in the past was dependent on the presence or visits of saints and singers, on the one hand, and political expansions and the caprice of emperors and royal patronage, on the other. Thus, the sanctity of a place has been constructed and reconstructed by poets and patrons, saints and singers, over the millennia and reimagined in every generation. Tirupati, for example, which was a relatively small temple in the hilly forests, became famous after the patronage extended to it by the Vijayanagara kings and the songs of Annamācārya in the fifteenth century (Narayanan 1995). When reimagining and reconstructing the sacrality of a place, new architecture and rituals are frequently introduced.

New rituals are also devised to go with the rising popularity of new temples. In Mel Maruvattur, a village about fifty miles from Madras, the temple of Ādiparāśakti has become celebrated since the mid-1970s. A new revelation to a young man who lived in this village proclaimed that land to be the place where the goddess abides. All pilgrims coming here now wear red clothes; it is said that the deity made her wishes known through a devotee and ordained it. The goddess, it is said, pronounced that although the skin of her devotees may be white, red, brown, or dark, the blood that runs in them is always red. To denote the equality between all devotees without consideration of gender, caste, or race, her followers should wear red when they worship her in the temple. For miles around the temple, one may see truckloads of red-clad worshipers or a solitary pilgrim walking sedately, all heading to the shrine of the goddess. Nor does the innovation stop there; in contra-distinction to most Brāhmaṇical temples, menstruating women worship here. In most Hindu temples, menstruating women are considered to be "polluted" and not allowed to enter. This rule is internalized by most women, and they traditionally do not go to a temple to pray during the time of their menstruation. In Mel Maruvattur, however, there is no discrimination against menstruating women.

Although it is the deity of the town who is said to grant favors and salvation, the pious devotee deemed every particle of dust in the town to be sacred. Just residing in a sacred place is said to grant one liberation from the cycle of life and death, and as we saw earlier, several towns figure in such lists. How do these grand statements and ardent worship fit into the Hindu traditions? What is the meaning of worship in the temple and visiting a holy place? How does the devotee view the deity in the temple? We will turn our attention to these issues and try to understand the importance of temple worship in this chapter.

HISTORY OF TEMPLES IN THE SUBCONTINENT

Most of the earliest surviving religious structures in India are either Buddhist or Jaina monuments, prayer halls, or caves dug into hillsides. Although there may have been places of worship even in Harappā and the great bath that was built in Mohenjodāro may have had ritual significance, we do not find any "Hindu" temple or religious structure until almost the beginning of the Common Era. This may simply be because the earlier structures were made of wood and bricks which perished easily or that royal patronage from Aśoka (third century BCE) and other emperors resulted in the sponsorship of many more Buddhist and Jaina monuments.

One of the earliest artifacts identifiable with Hinduism as we recognize it is from the second century BCE. An inscription on a pillar (*c.*120–100 BCE) found at Vidiśā (modern Besnagar in Madhya Pradesh) says that the original monument was a kind of flag post with Garuḍa, a bird which is a devotee of Viṣṇu. The inscription says that the pillar was built in honor of Vāsudeva (another name for Kṛṣṇa) by a Heliodorus. The inscription indicates that religious structures which were similar to later Vaiṣṇavaite ones were prevalent around the first century BCE (Huntington 1985: 57). Also from the second century CE, we find an image of Lakṣmī flanked by elephants in the entrance to Buddhist monasteries near Pitalkhora (Desai 1975: 21). Votive images of the sun-god Sūrya in northern India (Craven 1976: 116) and Śiva in southern Andhra Pradesh (Huntington 1985: 87–88) in the first century CE indicate that Hindu deities were being represented in forms that were worshiped.

Some of the earliest Hindu temples that have survived were built in what are now the states of Gujarat and Karnataka. About fifty temples were built around the fifth century CE in Saurashtra, Gujarat (Dhaky 1975: 121). In South India, several temples were built at Aihole (in the state of Karnataka) and some may date back to 520 CE (Venkataraman 1976: 4). Many of the temples built in Aihole around the sixth century CE are said to mark the first phase in the growth of the South Indian temple (Venkataraman 1976: 4). We do know that by the eighth century in South India, the poet devotees of Viṣṇu and Śiva went from temple to temple singing about the deity enshrined in it. Some temples like that of the famous Vaikuṇṭha Perumāḷ belonging to the eighth century are artistic presentations of elaborate theologies—in this case, of a sectarian tradition called Pāñcarātra. This temple has been called "the *Bhāgavata Purāṇa* in stone" (Hudson 1995: 137–82), and a case has been made for close links between theology and temple building. By the tenth century, the Cōḻa kings and queens built great temples in the south of India. Enormous towers built on elaborate temple structures replaced the smaller stone edifices, and various substyles of North and South Indian temple architecture were discernible by now.

Endowments to temples

Temple rituals and distribution of honors were financed by offerings and endowments of the devotees. Many women made such endowments in their own names, and it seems possible that many of these were either from royal families or from courtesans attached to temples. In the year 699 CE we hear that a great Śiva temple where Brahmā, Viṣṇu, and Śiva were all enshrined was dedicated by Queen Vinayavatī in Bādāmi, the capital of the Cāḷukya kingdom (Bolon 1988: 62). Samavai (966 CE), a Pallava queen, made the first monetary endowment to the temple at Tirumala-Tirupati (in modern Andhra Pradesh), which today is the richest temple in the country. Samavai's endowments made possible several innovative features in worship and, as the inscriptions show, funded the celebration of many festivals in that temple.

Samavai was not an isolated example; queens of the Cōḻa dynasty (*c.* ninth to thirteenth centuries CE) in South India were enthusiastic patrons of temples and religious causes for the Śaivaite community of South India around the tenth century (Dehejia 1990). People endowed cattle, money, lands, jewels, and so on, and the income was to be used for the cause specified by the donor. Sometimes people donated money for the performance of a ritual in the temple, sometimes to make a particular kind of food, offer it to the deity, and then distribute it to pilgrims or to other religious personnel like the Veda-reciters.

Queens like Sembiyan̲ Mahādevī (tenth century CE), deep in the south of India, built numerous temples and endowed liberally to the Śiva temples in their kingdom. She was widowed at a young age but obviously did not live a quiet secluded lifestyle that some Dharmaśāstras advocated for widows. Over a period of sixty years, she gave generous gifts to many temples in South India. We hear of Sembiyan̲ Mahādevī for the first time in an inscription dated 941; she is said to have made an endowment so that a lamp may be kept permanently lit in front of the deity. A village bearing her name was founded during her lifetime. The last inscription recording her activities is in 1001 (Venkataraman 1976: 12–13). She built new temples, renovated old ones, and gave generous donations to all of them (Venkataraman 1976: 16–64). Many other queens of the Cōḻa dynasty in the south also made liberal endowments to temples, and temple inscriptions record the details of their philanthropic gifts.

In addition to royalty, *devadāsī*s ("servants of the lord," a phrase referring to temple courtesans) also endowed money in their own names to the temples (Narayanan 1995: 100; Orr 1994, 2001). Looking at the inscriptions in a thousand-year period between 700 and 1700 in the state of Tamilnadu, Leslie Orr (2001) has distinguished various categories of women who regularly endowed to South Indian temples; these include queens, palace women, Brāhmaṇ women, temple women, slaves, and Jaina religious women/teachers. A study of these inscriptions also shows that many women seem to have had access to property, direct control over the land that they owned, and enjoyed a considerable degree of autonomy and independence from male-dominated family structures. It is also obvious that Dharmaśāstra rules and regulations insisting that women be dependent on men do not seem important in these inscriptions.

Some of the earliest recorded endowments by women can be seen in Cambodia. Queen Kulaprabhāvatī (*c.* fifth century CE) endowed the monies for the installation of Viṣṇu, the building of an *āśrama* (possibly a hermitage, in this context), with a tank and a dwelling house (Majumdar 1953: 1). There were many such endowments in Cambodia and Southeast Asia.

Many of these gifts were made in the hope that future generations would honor the commitment and perpetuate the charitable acts. Many inscriptions end with the exhortation hoping that the donation would be put to good use "until the sun and the moon shine." The donors also plead with future generations to preserve the endowment, saying that they are indebted to those who thus "protect and maintain" the charity (Venkataraman 1976: 22).

The endowments were made for various reasons. Some were built directly for building various parts of the temple, some for repair, some for offering food to the deity or for feeding the pilgrims who came to the temple. Some inscriptions specify what ingredients are to be bought for the cooking of a particular dish and even stipulate the amounts, so we are left with almost what looks like a recipe book in stone in some temples. Look at the following recipe for a dish that was supposed to be offered to Veṅkateśvara, a form of Viṣṇu and the deity at the temple in Tirupati. The endowments for the ingredients were made by various devotees between the fifteenth and sixteenth centuries (adapted from Viraraghavacharya 1997: 99):

> Dosai (a crepe-like dish)
>
> | | |
> |---|---|
> | Rice | 1 *marakkāl* (a unit of measurement) |
> | Urad lentils | 1 *marakkāl* |
> | Clarified butter | 1 and 3/4 *nāḻi* (a unit of measurement) |
> | Yogurt | 1/5 *nāḻi* |
>
> The ingredients were ground to a fine paste, fermented overnight, and made into thin pancakes over a griddle.

The temple authorities sometimes distributed the many food items they prepared free of cost to the pilgrims, but sometimes sold them at subsidized prices to pilgrims. Through the endowments, many temples became very wealthy and were centers of economic power and activity. In time, as we will note in the section on performing arts, these temples also became cultural centers where music and dance were performed regularly. These activities were also patronized by devotees.

Patronage of many religious traditions

Many patrons endowed not to one but to many religious traditions or sects. A magnificent temple known as Mārtāṇḍ to the sun-god Āditya was built by the king Lalitāditya (*r.*724) in Kashmir in the eighth century. The temple stood on a plateau with a dramatic sweeping view of the entire valley and had many images of Viṣṇu. He is said to have conquered territories all the way to the Deccan, and the poet Kalhaṇa, writing in the twelfth century CE, writes of him thus in his *Rājataraṅgiṇī*: "The king, eager for conquests, passed his life chiefly on expeditions, moving around the earth like the sun" (cited in Fisher 1988: 27). Lalitāditya patronized and endowed to both Hindu and Buddhist temple complexes, "making the eighth century Kashmir's greatest period of artistic achievement" (Fisher 1988: 27–28). He dedicated funds to Buddhist *stūpa*s and shrines in Uskur and Parihasapur (in Kashmir) as well as to (Hindu) Viṣṇu and Śiva temples; to quote Kalhaṇa again, "Who could determine accurately in number how many treasures, villages, and establishments he bestowed on these (shrines)?" (cited in Fisher 1988: 32). This patronage of shrines of many faiths is seen throughout India in many centuries alongside some clear cases of religious and sectarian intolerance. Further in the south, the Hōysaḷa queen Śantala Devī (*c.* eleventh to twelfth century CE) is said to have built both Jaina and Hindu (Viṣṇu) temples around Belur.

There was extensive temple building in parts of Maharashtra, Rajasthan, and Madhya Pradesh in the eleventh century (Deva 1975: 98–113). The Candella kings built the famous temple complexes at Khajuraho, renowned for their exquisite architecture as well as for their erotic sculpture.

Carvings: epic narratives and erotic sculptures

Most temples in India are characterized by the intricate carvings and sculptures on walls and towers. Many of them were decorative; some were put there to ward off the evil eye. Some temples like the lavishly carved ones at Halebid and Belur (Karnataka, eleventh to twelfth centuries CE) have extensive narratives from the *Rāmāyaṇa*, the *Mahābhārata*, and the Purāṇas carved on the walls. Many of the niches at Belur also have exquisite sculptures of dancers and musicians. Queen Shantala Devī, one of the principal patrons of the temple, was a dancer. The dance form and the beauty of the human body were celebrated through the sculptures.

Temples in India and Southeast Asia have hundreds of thousands of carvings from the two epics and the various Purāṇas. Some of the most spectacular carvings can be found in Halebid-Belur (Karnataka), India, and Angkor Wat (twelfth century), Cambodia. There are several depictions of the Churning of the Ocean of Milk, a story associated with the second of Viṣṇu's incarnations, in and around Angkor. Some of these are still found *in situ*, as the Churning of the Ocean of Milk, which flows along the long southeast corridor of Angkor, and museums such as the Musée Guimet all around the world. Stories from the *Rāmāyaṇa*, such as the killing of Vālin, and the epic battle of the *Mahābhārata* are to be found in Angkor.

Many medieval Hindu temples throughout India have sculptures displaying implicit or overt sexual acts. Many books on sculpture written after the Gupta period refer to the portrayal of sexual imagery in religious monuments, but none seem to have thought of these as incongruous in a temple setting. Many, though by no means all, temples have erotic imagery on walls and towers, both outside and inside. While the depictions of such imagery in artwork begins in the first millennium CE (Desai 1975: 1–21), it is after the sixth century that we begin to see pictures of copulating couples. We see this imagery in Hindu and Buddhist monuments and also in some Jaina temples.

While this seems entirely incompatible with our sense of religion in the early twenty-first century, it seems obvious from the lack of comment that this imagery was taken for granted rather than repudiated. The texts do not tell us the reasons as to why these carvings exist at all, and art historians try to understand the sculptures against the sociopolitical milieu of the various periods. Based on these pieces of information, a number of theories have come up to explain the prevalence of sexual motifs in temple architecture.

It is widely accepted that the sculptures are there for multiple reasons and have to be socially contextualized. Thus, we cannot say that they were all put there for any single reason like sex education. While it is sometimes assumed that these sculptures denote the value of *kāma* or sexual love and that this is an accepted goal (*puruṣārtha*) in human life, most art historians are dissatisfied with the simplicity of the explanation. Occasionally there are orgies depicted, and the *kāma* theory does not provide an explanation for such excesses (Desai 1975: 2). Many of the erotic sculptures depicting sex, it is assumed, are there for decorative purposes and carved for a sophisticated audience which approved of these motifs. They may have also served an auspicious function; that is, they depicted the happiness and well being of life and, in a magical way, caused further felicity to come to pass. Some of the sculptures are also there for promotion of fertility; it may well be that they were substitutes for and reminders of real fertility rituals. It is also held that "obscenity and indecency are believed to 'stimulate the generative powers of nature' " (Desai 1975: 105). In other words, these sculptures act as a charm to encourage nature—plants, birds, cows, crops—to multiply and add to the bounty of the land. They are also associated with life symbols of fertility and abundance. In some instances, where the sculptures are of aristocratic loving couples, it may well be portraits of the donors (Desai 1975: 34). Quoting anthropologists who had studied the importance of magic in many societies, Devangana Desai, an art historian, says that " 'The utilitarian effects of sexual activity extend, in early ritual, to practices intended to promote the general welfare of the community and to avert danger and misfortune' " (1975: 89, citing Briffault 1929: 45; see also Desai 1975: 98). Thus these sculptures, symbolically representing sexual acts, may be there to ward off the evil eye and be protective in nature.

The connections between these erotic sculptures and Tantric ritual is not clear. In some forms of Tantric practice, ritual copulation with one who is *not* one's spouse is seen under certain conditions to be part of a complex way to spiritual liberation. It may well be that in a few cases they do, in fact, depict ritual Tantric intercourse, but the associations between text and sculpture is not quite transparent. It is also possible that in cases where a celibate ascetic is seen in an erotic pose, a rival sectarian group is trying to poke fun at or denigrate the sect to which the ascetic visibly belongs. While it is difficult for us to ascertain the exact function of the erotic sculptures in the medieval temples, we may say that they were supposed to promote the quality of human life and fertility, enhance material abundance, and protect by warding off evil influences. The sexual metaphor is only one in the architectural syntax of a temple. The physical layout of the temple structure is also expressive of the many meanings and functions of the temple.

LAYOUT OF THE TEMPLES

According to texts and oral traditions, a temple may either represent the body of *puruṣa*, the cosmic person spoken of in some Vedic hymns and later texts, or be regarded as a physical extension of a deity. In other traditions, the temple is likened to a cosmic mountain like the gigantic Kailāsa described in the Purāṇas. Others consider the temple to be an abode of god like Vaikuṇṭha or heaven. In an extension of the body metaphor, the tower or the uppermost structure is called a *śikhara* (crest of a mountain or head), and the main shrine, which is in the innermost recesses of the temple, is the womb-house (*garbhagṛha*) (Michell 1977: 69; Ramanujan 1973: 20). The curved contours of a temple are said to be designed to reinforce the mountain metaphor. For some people, every temple may be the cosmic axis, the center of the world denoted by Mount Meru of the Purāṇas (Michell 1977: 69–70). The world then is filled with such centers, and depending on which temple one is in, *that* is the center.

Many of the small temples may be little more than a single shrine, sometimes jutting out into a crowded, urban street. There may be a single room with a deity installed inside, and, at appointed times, a *pujārī* or ritual priest will stay there and, if asked, will light a camphor flame in front of the deity. Some North Indian temples resemble houses and may be tucked away in residential and shopping complexes, indistinguishable from architecture around them (Asher 1997). Other temples, like the Liṅgarāja and the Raṅganātha temple complexes in Bhubanesvar and Srirangam, respectively, are elaborate structures, spanning several acres with several towers. In Srirangam the main shrine is encircled by seven concentric pathways. While the texts do not elaborate on the numerical significance of seven, there are many Purāṇas in which there are seven "upper worlds" or temporary paradises and seven netherworlds.

In the past, temples in South India were generally complexes built for a family of deities and had multiple shrines in one compound. Devotees did not visit all or even most of the shrines in large temples. The temple complex is like a buffet table; worshipers will walk in, pick and choose which deities they want to worship that day, and proceed there. Most of the Brāhmaṇical temples, that is, temples where there is some involvement by Brāhmaṇ priests in the performance of ritual worship, are dedicated to manifestations of Devī/Pārvatī, Viṣṇu, or Śiva and to their consorts, devotees, and/or families. Thus, a temple would be called Śiva or Viṣṇu or Amma<u>n</u> (mother goddess) temple. A Śiva or Amma<u>n</u> temple would have separate shrines for Śiva and Pārvatī, one for Gaṇeśa, one for Skanda/Muruka<u>n</u> (children of Śiva and Pārvatī), and others for various saints. Historically, most temples in India have been sectarian in character and have been dedicated to one of the major deities and his or her retinue.

Many temples also have shrines for the personification of the nine planets recognized by Hindu astrologers. In many temples in South India, and in the "South Indian" forms of the temple in the diaspora, this is one of the most popular shrines. Many of the worshipers consult the local astrologer regularly and may know that Śani (Saturn) and Guru (Jupiter) will not be in good positions in their horoscope for the next six months or six years. They then go regularly to the *navagraha* (nine planets) shrine in a local temple to propitiate a planet with prayers or offerings and petition them to do the least harm to them.

The orientation of the temple building is specified in many texts. The main deity in many of the temple complexes frequently faces east, though the large temple complexes have entrances from all directions. Many Viṣṇu temples in South India, including the famous eighth-century CE Vaikuṇṭha Perumāḷ temple at Kancipuram, face west. This is also an auspicious direction. Angkor Wat, built three centuries later, is very similar to this temple—west facing and three storied. Many scholars have assumed that the west-facing orientation of this temple is an indication of its inauspicious nature and that it is a funerary mound. This is emphatically not the case in similar temples in South India. When a temple faces an unusual direction, like south, there is usually a local story to explain how this came to be. For example, the image of Raṅganātha in Srirangam faces south; it is said that the lord is facing this direction, towards the country of Sri Lanka, to gaze on Vibhīṣaṇa, his devotee, who ruled over that kingdom.

In many North Indian temples, a pair of deities may be worshiped in the same shrine; thus, Viṣṇu and Lakṣmī would share the same room or Pārvatī and Śiva (both pairs being visualized as married couples) may be close together. In South India, however, frequently the male and female deities have their own space. Lakṣmī gets a room of her own in most Viṣṇu temples; many worshipers go there to get her blessings first. Art historians say that separate shrines to Lakṣmī were built around the twelfth and thirteenth centuries CE in many South Indian temples, including Srirangam and Kancipuram (Hari Rao 1967: 59; Raman 1975: 165). In most other temples, the shrines to the Devī or goddess came to be built during the Vijayanagara dynasty, that is, after the fourteenth century (Hari Rao 1967: 59). It is entirely possible that until the separate shrines were built, the female and male deities were worshiped in the same room. There is no conclusive evidence about the dates of the separate shrines because literary and architectural evidence is sometimes contradictory.

The paradigmatic temple at Srirangam: the temple of Raṅganātha

Let us now look at the plan of the large Raṅganātha (Viṣṇu) temple in Srirangam to see how an "ideal" temple was supposed to have been built. The problem with such an enterprise is that most of these temples were built and rebuilt over centuries and notions of the "ideal" changed regularly. Srirangam has about seventeen towers, thirty-nine pavilions, and several small bodies of water in it. There are a series of outer streets and pathways encircling the main shrine. The temple complex, the largest in India in terms of area, is about one-hundred-and-fifty-five acres, and there are almost fifty shrines inside.

Srirangam is supposed to be "heaven on earth," a description that is extended to every major temple by devotees in India. To physically extend this analogy, it is said that the river Kāverī encircles this island town, just as the river Virajā is said to encircle Vaikuṇṭha or heaven in Purāṇic mythology. The surrounding waters of the Kāverī form a natural boundary, marking off sacred space from the rest of the world.

The plan in a large South Indian temple like Srirangam is similar to many other temples. The entrance to the temple is generally marked by a *gōpura*, a structure that became popular after the twelfth century CE. Although this word originally meant "gateway," today it indicates the main tower over a vestibule that leads one into the temple complex. Many *gōpura*s are over a hundred feet tall, and some built in the sixteenth and seventeenth centuries have as many as eleven stages high. When many *gōpura*s are built on of the cardinal axes of the temple, they decrease in size and height as the center of the temple is approached (Harle 1963: 1). We see this progression and procession of towers in the large temple complexes of Cidambaram and Madurai. Frequently, it was a sign of prestige for a ruler to build a really tall tower or to gild the *vimāna*, the small tower on top of the main shrine, with gold. The small dome-like structure on top of the temples in Srirangam and Tirupati have been gilded with gold by munificent kings in the past.

In recent years, the outer tower for the Srirangam temple was completed in 1987 under the leadership of a religious teacher and the patronage of thousands of devotees. The replacement of royal patronage with a system where the public at large funds these projects has been a major change in the last few centuries. The completed tower stands over two-hundred-and-twenty feet tall and is billed as the tallest tower in all of Asia. These towers have sculptures depicting scenes from Hindu mythology. Frequently, these gateways are seen as liminal spaces marking the boundaries between the sacred space of the temple and the secular city. The importance of these towers is seen in everyday speech; in a hyperbolic saying that is current in many South Indian languages, it is held that "the vision of a temple tower is enough to destroy one's sins."

The outer streets of the Srirangam temple have houses, banks, and shops. While in earlier centuries these houses may have been occupied by priestly families, today anyone may occupy the houses. As one proceeds towards the main shrine, we notice that the inner pathways have several shrines located within them. In Srirangam there are shrines to various devotees of Viṣṇu and Lakṣmī. These include the poet saints called Āḻvārs who lived between the seventh and tenth centuries CE and theologians like Rāmānuja and Vedāntadeśika. There are also shrines to various incarnations of Viṣṇu like Rāma and Kṛṣṇa. The enclosure around the main shrine also has a large shrine for Lakṣmī. Many of the rituals celebrated for Viṣṇu in the main shrine are repeated and performed in front of Lakṣmī at a later time.

The innermost shrine is called the *garbhagṛha* (womb-house). Here is the womb, the place where the powers and energies that lead to the creation of the universe reside. Here the spiritual rebirth of the devotee is to take place. This is the room with the main deity, the room filled with potential for creation and spiritual transformation. Here the main deity is installed, consecrated, and worshiped. The room is usually quite dim, and the light from the oil lamps illumine the deities. Here the priest performs various rituals on behalf of the devotee. Devotees file past the main deity saying prayers, lingering, if possible, to see as much as they can of the manifestation of god within the shrine. While in smaller temples one can stand in the anteroom in front of the main shrine for as long as one wants, in most temples, because of the rush (especially on weekends), the pilgrims may simply have to stand in line and pass the main deity in a queue formation. To see and to be seen by the enshrined deity is the central act of worship in the temple.

INNER AND OUTER MANIFESTATIONS OF THE DEITY

The image and other forms of Viṣṇu

Some Hindus, like those who are members of the Śrīvaiṣṇava community and perform the rituals in Srirangam, believe that Viṣṇu and Lakṣmī are present on this earth in the "womb-house" in the same manner as they are in heaven. While Hindus generally emphasize the inner experience of god, most of them do not adopt the near iconoclasm of sects like the early Vīraśaiva community (Ramanujan 1973: 19–21, 30–31). Many Hindu traditions developed a theology that articulated an essential relationship between the external manifestation of the lord in the temple and the inner embodiment of god within the devotee's own heart.

While there are many interpretations of the "image," we can look at the Śrīvaiṣṇava tradition to see how some Hindu communities articulate their understanding of Viṣṇu's manifestation in the temple. They consider the image to be a permanent descent of the deity as an image (*arca avatāra*, literally, the "incarnation [of god] in a worshipable form") which makes possible the ascent of the human being to heaven, the celestial realm of Viṣṇu known as Vaikuṇṭha.

While the image of the deity may be made of earthly material, Hindus from many traditions believe that this is the real body of the deity. Far from regarding the image as a body made of stone or hewn out of rock or cast in metal, the image is considered to be made of a nonearthly transcendental substance which is unique to the deity and is made perceivable on earth only by virtue of god's desire to be accessible to his devotees. This image is an actual and real manifestation of the deity, neither lesser than nor a symbol of other forms. It is said to be wholly and completely god, though it does not exhaust his or her essence. This manifestation of Viṣṇu in the temple, however, does not exist in contradistinction to, nor is it lesser than, his manifestation in the heart of the devotee. The outer and inner experiences of the lord are both exalted in many Hindu traditions.

The human body as the temple for the deity

Just as Viṣṇu graciously descends from heaven and manifests himself in a temple, he appears in the worshiper's heart. Tirumaḻicai Āḻvār, a poet devotee who lived between the seventh and eighth century CE, expresses this idea clearly and says that the same deity whom he saw in the various sacred places resides in his heart (*Tiruccantaviruttam* 64):

> The days are gone when I saw
> at Ūrakam, the standing lord.
> At Pāṭakam I beheld my father sitting,
> and at Vēḥkā, he reclined.
> I was not "born" then; and when I was born
> I never did forget
> that he stands, abides, and reclines
> within my heart.

The poet clearly identifies the deity externally worshiped in the temples at Ūrakam, Pāṭakam, and Vēḥkā (all near the town of Kancipuram, about forty miles from Chennai) with the divinity that he realizes within himself. The external and internal images of the deity are not mutually exclusive; rather, it is the same divine being which manifests itself in the temple and in the human heart.

The god in the heart is the same as the god in the temple. For most Hindus, this god in a temple is the same who manifested himself in the incarnation form as Rāma and Kṛṣṇa. Thus, Viṣṇu who incarnated himself as Rāma, Kṛṣṇa, and others is the same deity who manifests himself in the local temple (Kulacēkara Āḻvār, *c.* eight century CE, *Perumāḷ*

Tirumoḻi 10.1):

> In the beautiful city of Ayodhyā, encircled by towers,
> a flame that lit up all the worlds
> appeared in the Solar race
> and gave life to all the heavens.
> This warrior, with dazzling eyes,
> Rāma, dark as a cloud, the First one, my only lord,
> is in Citrakūṭa, city of Tillai.
> When is the day,
> when my eyes will behold him
> and rejoice?

In this poem, Kulacēkara Āḻvār identifies Rāma, who was born in the royal "Solar race" according to the epics, as the same god in the local city called Tillai or Cidambaram. He longs to see him in this temple.

While many Hindu philosophical traditions have harmonized the concepts of the external deity and the divinity that exists within every human being, the Vīraśaiva tradition, which was organized around the twelfth century CE, rejected the notion of worship in a temple. The human being is the living, moving temple for the lord Śiva, they said, and repudiated the importance of building a temple with brick and mortar. Listen to the words of Basavaṇṇa (Ramanujan 1973: 88):

> The rich
> will make temples for Śiva.
> What shall I,
> a poor man,
> do?

In another part of this poem, Basavaṇṇa says that "things standing," like the temple, will eventually fall, but the moving body, the live temple for the deity, will always be there. From his devotional stance, he reverses the notion that the stone temple will stand and that the human body will perish; he assures us that this live human body is, in a sense, the true temple. The crafted, standing, immovable temple is static and stagnant; the worshiping human body is the loving, living temple for the god.

In the nineteenth century, the Brahmo Samāj, or the Society of Brahman founded by Rammohan Roy, also rejected the concept of "image" worship, saying that it was not present in the Upaniṣads. These traditions reject the outer manifestations of the deity in a temple and only accept that the divine person abides within the human being. Thus, although most Hindus go to temple to worship and understand that god is present there, some reject this idea.

The distinctive personalities of the regional manifestations and images

In many South Indian villages, there is a conflation of mythical and historical events to contribute to the sanctity of a place and the image. The movable and immovable images within each temple can thus have a distinct personality, as do each of the manifestations of the lord at the various places in which the images reside. While the primary image may loosely be classified as Viṣṇu, Śiva, Gaṇeśa, Pārvatī, and so on, in many temples in South India, Viṣṇu, Śiva, or Devī have a particular, distinct name. These are comparable to the differences ascribed to Viṣṇu's descents as Rāma or Kṛṣṇa. Thus, the goddess Pārvatī as enshrined in the temple at Cidambaram is called Śivakāmasundarī; in Kancipuram, where there is a major temple to Pārvatī, she is called Kāmākṣī, and in Madurai, Mīṉākṣī.

In each of these places, she has a unique history of how she manifested herself there. In Madurai, for instance, Mīṉākṣī is said to have been born in the Pāṇḍiyaṉ dynasty. She became the ruler, went on a *digvijaya* (a victorious military expedition in all directions), and encountered Śiva in a battle. She eventually marries him, and they both reside permanently in the temple at Madurai. Here she is called Mīṉākṣī, Śiva, Sundareśvara.

Similar stories and different names can be seen in many sacred places in South India. Viṣṇu in Tirupati is called Veṅkateśvara; in Srirangam he is known as Raṅganātha. Lakṣmī is called Padmāvatī in Tirucanur, near Tirupati. Viṣṇu, in his distinctive form as Veṅkateśvara, is one of the most popular deities in India and now has temples in Atlanta, Pittsburgh, Malibu, Chicago, and other places in the diaspora. The local nature of the gods and goddesses are stressed in the stories and names. It is generally only Viṣṇu, Lakṣmī, Śiva, and Pārvatī who have these local manifestations; all other deities usually go under their generic pan-Indian names of Gaṇeśa, Hanumān, Kārttikeya, and so on.

How are we to understand these multiple manifestations of one Viṣṇu, Śiva, Lakṣmī, or Pārvatī? Why is it so important for people to think not of one generic Viṣṇu but with a brand name, each with a distinctive story and history? Historians and scholars of religion sometimes see these stories as cases where a local mythic tradition becomes conflated with a pan-Indian Sanskritic tradition, and the local deity is identified with the Sanskrit epic or Purāṇic net. Most Hindus, however, would interpret the local nature of the deity as an example of its accessibility. The supreme being who is beyond human comprehension has, through its compassion, made itself manifest in human and worshipable image form just down the road in the local field or in the neighborhood temple. Most stories say that in answer to a holy person's prayers, Viṣṇu/Śiva/Lakṣmī or other deity was born in some local family or royal dynasty and remained in image form in the village for the welfare of human beings. In other words, most Hindus generally do not speak about an impersonal cosmic being who is removed from the day-to-day events of the world; the supreme being is supreme precisely because it is so eminently accessible and local. While there is some understanding that these local gods and goddesses are actually to be identified as a pan-Indian deity, frequently their distinctive, local nature is more renowned than their generic identity. Thus, residents of Srirangam would name their children as Ranga Nathan (lord of Śrīraṅgam) or Ranga Nayaki (lady of Śrīraṅgam) after the local names by which Viṣṇu and Lakṣmī are known in this sacred city. In Madurai the goddess is called Mīṉākṣī; and while people know she is one manifestation of Pārvatī, she is almost never referred to by the pan-Indian name.

These local deities are celebrated in poetry and songs all the way from the fifth century CE to the present. The particular story associated with a temple may be acted out in ritual regularly. Thus, the temple of Goddess Mīṉākṣī in Madurai has annual rituals to commemorate her conquest of all directions, meeting Śiva, and eventually marrying him (Harman 1989).

THE LAYERS OF NARRATIVES

The distinctive personalities of the local manifestations are revealed in the stories recorded in the history of each holy place (Sthalapurāṇa). Such histories create a sense of continuity; they fix events both in mythical and historical time. One may observe in them at least three different strands which are brought together to give an aura of legitimate sanctity to each holy place and to the image with which it is associated: (i) The origin of the image is recounted in a "Purāṇic" or epic history. This may involve the appearance of the deity on its own volition or its appearance before holy people. This strata of legend is usually located in mythic time. It is important because it lends an aura of scriptural approval from the Sanskrit tradition, and most Hindus consider this to be necessary for religious legitimation. (ii) The deity is associated with a poet saint or *guru*, that is, the image is usually praised by one or more poets in a devotional song. (iii) The temple is associated with a well-known philosopher/theologian.

Let us look at how this applies to Srirangam. According to local legend and Purāṇic stories, Viṣṇu is said to have manifested himself there about the time that Rāma was on earth. This is the mythic layer; it is said that Vibhīṣaṇa, Rāma's devotee, was returning to his kingdom of Laṅkā. According to the story, he asked Rāma to give him an image of himself. Rāma gave him a small image with the condition that Vibhīṣaṇa was not to set it on the ground on the way to Laṅkā. One day, Vibhīṣaṇa wanted to wash himself and looked around for someone to hold the image. Gaṇeśa the son of Pārvatī was on hand, disguised as a young boy. Gaṇeśa told Vibhīṣaṇa that he would only hold the image for a few minutes; after that he would put it down on the ground. Gaṇeśa did not wait long and placed the image on the ground; the image apparently grew in size and stretched along the island in the middle of the Kāverī River and became immovable.

Vibhīṣaṇa was upset but could not do anything. The story does not stop there; it is connected with a local narrative. It is said that Viṣṇu stretched himself in that spot in order to please another devotee, the local king of the Cōḻa kingdom, and also to honor the river Kāverī, which had wanted to be more esteemed than the river Gaṅgā.

In historic time, the Śrīraṅgam temple was honored in the songs of the poet saints, the Āḻvārs (seventh to tenth centuries CE); it was also the residence of several theologians like Rāmānuja. Thus, the historic sanctity is built on the Purāṇic stories of how it all came to be sacred in the first place.

The story also makes clear that god is simultaneously present in several places at the same time. Rāma was an incarnation of Viṣṇu, but he is also in the image that he gave Vibhīṣaṇa. This image is not a generic Viṣṇu but a southern Viṣṇu in the Tamil-speaking region and who is only known as Raṅganātha; here, he is one of hundreds of regional divine manifestations.

Thus, while the theological tradition may conceive of the one "full" lord who appears in several places and is "complete" in every sense, the oral devotional tradition of popular piety respects the individual personality of each image and treats each as a distinct person. Often several stories are interwoven, thus creating a cumulative significance for the image. Such stories attend both to "Purāṇic" origin and to associations with the historic teachers and poets. They establish connections between local deities and high gods and thereby establish a unique history and personality for each *arca* which provides both a mythological basis for its distinctive appeal and a rationale for particular rituals associated with a temple.

Sectarian Śākta, Vaiṣṇava, and Śaiva texts also insist that the deity is fully present in every temple. There are some variations on this theme; Śrīvaiṣṇavas may say that Viṣṇu and Lakṣmī are fully present everywhere, but South Indian Śaivas may feel that Śiva is in the whole universe, dwells in the heart of every human person, but is uniquely present only in *the temple*, that is, the temple at Cidambaram (D. Smith 1996: 2; Younger 1995). In theological terms, the same lord is said to reside in the many holy places with no difference in status among these local manifestations, just as the manifestation of Viṣṇu as image, as present in the heart (*hṛdaya*), and as incarnate in the world (*avatāra*) are ontologically equivalent. Although in popular belief and imagination each local manifestation is different from another form of Viṣṇu, theological texts may speak of one Viṣṇu with one eternal form. Thus, the prayer called the *Viṣṇusahasranāma* (thousand names of Viṣṇu) refers to him as the "one with an eternal form," who manifests himself in a manner that is fitting to particular occasions. The supreme being, therefore, is both one and many, and this is one of the paradoxes of the transcendent breaking into the temporal, material world.

THE MATERIAL IMAGE OF THE DEITY

The festival (*utsava*) or processional images of the deity in South India and all images in northern India are made of metal. In many temples we find bronze images; and in some, a very specific blending of metals is found. Bronze images seem to have become very popular at the time of the Cōḻa dynasty in South India after the tenth century CE (Dehejia 1990: 1–47) and was developed to perfection. The sculptors were trained in the science of metallurgy and the art of image-making. These cottage-industry foundries following traditional rules now flourish in many places: Swamimalai and Nacchiyar Koil, near the town of Kumbhakonam, and Mahabalipuram near Chennai are famous for casting these images for home and temple worship. The marble stone images from Jaipur (Rajasthan) are renowned for their exquisite features. These places now undertake orders for images not only for local shrines but also for temples in Tampa, Atlanta, Malibu, and Pittsburgh. A larger market is now found in the secular sphere—many of these images are now considered to be *objets d'art* and grace living rooms in India and around the world.

Metallic images are seen both in northern and southern India, but the features, clothes, ornamentation, and decorations differ according to the region. The stone images, however, have striking differences between the regions. If one walks into a temple in North India, one will generally see a white marble image; in the south, the primary, immovable image is usually in dark stone. While these images are ritually bathed and anointed in regular temple ritual every few years, they also undergo a thorough cleaning and maintenance. Before the work begins for such preservation, the "life" of the image is ritually transferred to the smaller festival image. Sculptors refinish the stone images, and during this period, they are not worshiped by devotees. Before regular worship begins, they are consecrated ritually and the spirit of the deity is requested to abide in them once more.

The stone images in South India may be between four to six feet in height, and the metallic, "festival" images used in processions and some rituals are usually between two and three feet in height. While the festival images are usually standing, the primary images of Viṣṇu and Pārvatī/Devī may be in one of many poses. Lakṣmī is usually seen as sitting, usually on a lotus flower. Śiva's main primary image in temples throughout India is usually in the abstract, aniconical form of a *liṅga* which emphasizes the creative forces of the universe. The festival form of Śiva may be in several poses; the most famous one in the twentieth century is one of him as Naṭarāja doing the cosmic dance of creation and destruction. Viṣṇu is represented as standing, sitting, or reclining. Every pose of the deities, every posture of the hand and legs are said to articulate a particular message that is meaningful to the devotee.

While the image is obviously made of stone, metal, or wood, devotees think of this as a living deity. The image is considered to be a material object until there is a ritual called *prāṇapratiṣṭhā* (establishment of life). Through these complex rituals, the image is transformed from a material article to one in which the supreme being resides. This image now is wholly, completely divine for some devotees.

The paradox of nonmatter

What exactly does a devotee see when he or she sees the image? Most Western missionaries in the eighteenth and nineteenth centuries were horrified at what they thought was blatant idolatry. We do know that the different traditions within Hinduism perceive the image in different ways. Some people may think of the image merely as a focussing point for their meditation, without any ultimate value. It is a translucent symbol of the supreme reality, they say, without any intrinsic value. Many other traditions like the Śrīvaiṣṇava and the Caitanya schools, however, think of the image as being fully, completely god. The paradox of the "worshipable image" at least in some Hindu communities is that while this manifestation of the deity is so obviously made of stone or metal, it is believed to be *aprakṛta* or nonmaterial. The deity's body in heaven, in the incarnate form (as Rāma and as Sītā) as well as in the image in the temple, is said to be formed of a transcendent, nonearthly substance called "pure purity" (*śuddha sattva*). This "purity" is not on par with the three qualities (*guṇa*) which constitute all living creatures and material things. *Śuddha sattva* is a "super" substance, transcending anything found on earth. It is a pure substance, unadulterated by any other quality, and is described as being "luminous." Only heaven (*vaikuṇṭha*), the deity's auspicious body, and the bodies of his attendants are made of this stuff. This is *one* form of Hindu perception, but one which is present in dilute ways in many traditions.

We are confronted with a paradox: What appears to many non-Hindu eyes as the most gross and material representation of the deity is understood by many Hindus to be a divine, auspicious form, composed of a nonmaterial substance that exists only in heaven and in the properly consecrated temple on earth. The image must not be regarded as a material object. It is a personal god, luminous, and complete with all auspicious qualities; it is transcendent and supreme, yet easily accessible—a bit of heaven on earth.

The image is often referred to as the ultimate means by which the lord makes himself accessible to humanity. Theologians often speak of the inaccessible supreme being who deigns to come down and manifests himself. Kūrattāḻvāṉ, an eleventh-century theologian, says that although the supreme being is inaccessible to the minds of *yogī*s and cannot be grasped by the philosophy of Vedānta, it manifests itself in temples (*Varadarāja Stava* 1, 3; *Sundarabāhu Stava* 119).

The image symbolizes the accessibility of the deity to the human devotee and reminds the devotee of their mutual relationship. The worshipable, image form of the deity simultaneously represents its supremacy and accessibility. The latter attribute is glorified by a thirteenth-century theologian, Piḷḷai Lokācārya, thus: "The lord, though omniscient seems ignorant, though omnipotent seems as if powerless, though self-sufficient seems otherwise. Although he is the protector, he seems to be the protected one, exchanging his lordship to be one who is extremely accessible. . . . He is thus graciously present in all temples and homes. This is the glory of the incarnation in the worshipable form" (*Śrīvacanabhūṣaṇa* 40–42). The temple and the form of the deity in the temple, therefore, are not comparable to heaven; they are, in the devotee's eyes, superior to it.

TEMPLE RITUALS

The camphor lamp and visualizing the deity

When a group of devotees pray, whether at home or in the temple, the ritual may end with an *ārati* or waving of lamps. The priest, or one of the worshipers, will light a piece of camphor in a plate and wave it clockwise in front of the deity. The lit camphor flame is then shown to the worshipers, who reverentially place their hands on top of the flame and touch their eyelids briefly as if to internalize the light of devotion or knowledge that showed them the supreme deity in the temple. The main act in this ritual is to see the deity (*darśana*) and to be seen by this god or goddess; this is as important as hearing the sacred words of Hindu scripture.

In many North Indian communities, a popular lyric that is sung during the *āratī*, both in India and in the diaspora, is one called "Jaya Jagadīśa Hare" (Victory to the Lord of the Universe). The song is sung slowly while the camphor flame is waved in front of the shrine, and worshipers have *darśana* or a vision of the deity.

Oṃ! Victory to the lord of the universe!
Hail to the lord!
Lord, victory to the lord of the universe,
you remove the difficulties
of your devotees in a second.
Oṃ! Victory to the lord of the universe!

You fulfill the wishes of those who meditate on you;
their mental anguish dissipates.
Wealth and happiness come to their homes
and the pains of their body fade.
Oṃ! Victory. . . .

You are the mother, the father,
who else will be my refuge. . . .
I place my hopes on you. . . .
Oṃ! Victory. . . .

You are the perfect, supreme soul,
you who reside in my soul,
supreme lord of all,
you are the supreme *brahman*,
you are the master of all.
Oṃ! Victory. . . .

You are an ocean of mercy,
you protect us, lord, you protect us;
I am a fool, caught in passion,
shower your grace on me. . . .
Oṃ! Victory. . . .

Friend of the poor, remover of sorrow,
you are my protector
Lord, extend your hand [in protection],
to me at your door. . . .
Oṃ! Victory. . . .

Destroy my lowly passions,
Lord, destroy my sins;
Lord, increase our faith and devotion,
so we may serve you and your servants. . . .
Oṃ! Victory. . . .

My body, mind, and wealth is all yours,
everything is yours.
Lord, I submit what is yours to you,
for what can I call my own?
Oṃ! Victory. . . .

This *ārati* is probably the most popular religious hymn in northern India. Many devotees from the northern part of India would think of seeing the deity and singing this song of adoration as an important part of the evening prayers. The deity is addressed in a personal manner—it is the mother, father, and the ocean of mercy. The worshiper asks the lord to fulfill the wishes of the devotees—to destroy one's lowly passions, to remove one's sorrow, to extend the divine hand of protection and for divine grace. One of the early verses asks for health and wealth for the worshipers. Most devotees who go to temples ask for some or all of these desires to be fulfilled.

While devotees ask for special rituals to be conducted at temples with petitionary or thanksgiving intentions, there are also regular ritual schedules. These temple schedules are very complex, with daily, seasonal, and annual festivals and celebrations. The rituals differ in the various regions of India, between folk and "high" tradition temples, between urban and rural areas, between various castes, and between large complexes and simple shrines.

INDIVIDUAL ACTS OF WORSHIP

Why do people go to the temple or on a pilgrimage? Most of the pilgrimage towns are called *tīrtha* or places where one crosses over the ocean of life and death. As we saw earlier, the sacrality of many places is considered to be so potent that just living or dying there is said to give one liberation from the cycle of life and death. And indeed, a few ascetics and pilgrims do go to holy cities with such a wish in mind. Most devotees and pilgrims who go to places of worship, however, go there for a variety of other purposes and usually pray for good health and prosperity. Others just go regularly to a local temple and undertake special pilgrimages whenever possible.

The temples in India are the nuclei for prayers, rituals, and festivals. Many are individual, devotional offerings, others are grand celebrations speaking of pomp, power, and prestige. In this section, we will discuss the activities that go on in a temple. We will talk about individual acts of piety, daily schedules in large temples, and annual celebrations of major rituals.

Worship in many Hindu temples is traditionally not congregational in the Judeo-Christian sense of the term with set services for the community and interactive participation. The temples have several shrines within them but no pews or seats either for temporary or permanent seating. In some temples in Northern India and certainly in houses throughout India, there are group songs (*bhajana*) accompanied by a percussion instrument and a keyboard, but that is not a formalized service. More of these group-worship rituals are also seen in the diaspora, where worshipers tend to congregate on the weekend.

One is supposed to go to a temple after bathing and cleansing oneself physically. In many large temple complexes or famous pilgrimage sites in India, there are nearby pools, rivers, or even showers for pilgrims visiting from a distance. City and neighborhood temples do not have such facilities, except outside India. Footwear is always left outside the temple precincts; and with it, one leaves the dust and grime of worldly thoughts and passions. Sometimes the worshiper may buy flowers, camphor, coconuts, or fruits from the dozens of shops and stalls outside the temple. The simplest act of worship in a temple is for the worshiper to go whenever the temple is open and make an offering of camphor, fruit, flower, or coconut to the deity. Many temples, except for the busy ones like Tirupati, are closed in the afternoons after lunch for rest. In a small temple the offering may be made directly; in most temples, the worshiper hands over the offering to a priest. In South Indian temples, the devotee may go up only to the threshold of the womb-house. Only the priests and ritual specialists who have been specially initiated are permitted to go beyond the threshold. In many of the North Indian temples, devotees may go all the way into the inner shrine. In all temples, however, it is having vision of the deity which is most meaningful to the devotee. Some communities call this viewing of the supreme being as *sevā* or service; to *see* the lord or the goddess is to be aware of one's finitude and to want to *serve* the deity and other devotees. Many women who come to the temple regularly and who may not be able to afford the fruit or flower offering may bring a piece of camphor or a small container of oil. This oil is added to the lamps that flicker in the shrines.

After first being offered to the deity, the flower or fruit that the devotee brought as an offering is returned as "blessed" and as holding the favor of the divine being. Such a piece of blessed food is usually called *prasāda* (literally, "clarity," used here in the sense of "favor" of the deity). This act of devotion, of seeing the deity, offering something and getting it back in a blessed state, is the simplest and most popular among votive rituals. Devotees frequently walk around the temple inside one of the enclosures, thus circumambulating the deity. This is an essential feature of the temple visit, as is bowing down before the deity.

Some worshipers may ask the temple priest to perform an *arcanā* (praise or adoration) to the deity. The priest then will recite 108 names of the local deity (most gods and goddesses have 108 names); some, like Viṣṇu, Lakṣmī, Śiva, and Pārvatī (in her manifestation as a goddess called Lalitā), have as many as 1,008 names. As the priest recites the 108 names, he offers flowers or *tulasī* (a form of fragrant basil) leaves to the feet of the god or a red powder called *kumkum* at the feet of the goddess. The *kumkum* offered in worship is then distributed among the worshipers. It is only on special events, which are frequently sponsored by a devotee, that a whole ritual with the 1,008 names is recited. After the recitation of names, the waving of the camphor flame, and the offering and distribution of *prasāda* (which could be a sweet dish, a piece of fruit, or a piece of homemade candy), the priest may give the devotee other marks of "favor" from the deity.

If it is a Viṣṇu shrine in the south, the worshiper may be given a spoonful of holy water to sip and some *tulasī* leaves sacred to Viṣṇu. The devotee then puts a pinch of the basil in his or her mouth to ingest. Occasionally, some fragrant sandalwood paste from the deity's body or flowers which adorned the form of the goddess may be given to the worshiper. The devotee receives this *prasāda* with his or her right hand (the left hand is considered polluting) and then puts some of it on his or her own hair or forehead as a form of ornamentation. It is an honor to wear what was once worn by the god. A priest in a Śiva shrine may give the devotee some temple-made ash. Ash is a symbol of Śiva, and the devotee respectfully puts a small amount on the forehead. One may get a red *kumkum* powder to put on one's forehead in the shrine of any goddess.

The entire worship ceremony may take less than five minutes in a single shrine in a temple that is not very busy. Most people would go to two or three shrines in a complex; if it is a Viṣṇu temple in South India, one would typically go to the separate shrines of Viṣṇu and Lakṣmī; if it is the north, one may visit possibly the shrines of Rādhā-Kṛṣṇa (kept in one shrine) and then perhaps Ambā/Durgā or Rāma. If one chooses to linger and go to many shrines or socialize, one may take up to an hour or so. But most regular worshipers, especially if they are dropping into a temple on the way to work or school on a busy week day, may simply go to one shrine and be in and out in a few minutes. From this perspective, one realizes how much the temple is part of one's everyday life.

After going around the shrines, a woman devotee may go to the official "temple tree" (*sthalavṛkṣa*), a tree that has been venerated by the community for centuries, and walk around it with reverence. The temples traditionally honored trees and groves; in medieval Tamil literature, the important Śiva and Viṣṇu temples seem to have had a resident, "official" tree which was venerated by the local women. The tree had implications of fertility, and women worshiped it daily; it is entirely possible that this has been so from the time of the Harappā civilization. Sacred trees are found both inside and outside temple precincts. In many villages and in many quiet places in the cities, there are sacred trees that have a simple platform built around them.

Under the trees may be many small stone images of intertwined snakes. These serpent images are venerated with red spots of *kumkum* powder that is used to adorn the forehead of women. Women come to these open-air shrines to worship at particular times of the year or when they need a wish to be fulfilled. The serpents, called *nāgas*, may well be one of the earliest features of the Hindu tradition; they may even predate the Indo-European culture. We have very little evidence that their worship was prevalent in the Harappā culture, since only one seal possibly depicting the serpent has been found there, but they were probably venerated in other parts of the subcontinent.

Monetary offerings to temples

In some temples, certain items of food are cooked, offered to the deity, and sold at subsidized prices as *prasāda*. Some temples give free food or *prasāda* from the monies received through the endowments made in the past by patrons. As we saw earlier, patrons frequently earmarked their donations for particular charitable deeds or functions in the temple, and their donations were inscribed on stone plaques on temple walls. The inscriptions on the walls of the old temples are a wonderful record of transactions within the temple and give us considerable information on who endowed the money. Through these we know of the many men and women who patronized temples and who generously donated money for pilgrims and festivals. The temples were and still are powerful economic institutions in which large amounts of money are endowed and where in return the devotee may receive some symbol of divine grace or tangible form of temple honor.

Most worshipers may drop some money into the large collection boxes known as *huṇḍī*. While many may contribute small change, if they can afford to do so at all, some pilgrims may donate large sums of money or gold jewelry. While some temples have minimal funds, others are endowed very well. An example is the Veṅkateśvara/Viṣṇu temple at Tirupati (Andhra Pradesh). It has enjoyed royal patronage during the last thousand years, but only in the last hundred years has it attracted large numbers of pilgrims and substantial revenues. The popularity of the temple is said to have increased phenomenally after a major reconsecration in 1958. The wealth of the temple is also frequently reported and commented upon by the media. In 1996 the reported cash income (not counting the investments and endowments) was upward of 36 million US dollar a year.

Cars and diamonds are collected, as are approximately 20 kilogram (640 troy ounces) of gold every month, from various pieces of jewelry deposited in the *huṇḍī*. The temple is located on 28 square kilometers (10.75 square miles) of the Tirumala Hills. Until 1965, when the government took them over, it owned more than 600 villages. The enormous funds of the temple are used for charitable purposes, universities, educational institutions, and hospitals. This temple has one of the busiest daily schedules, since it has to accommodate tens of thousands of pilgrims everyday.

DAILY ROUTINE IN LARGE TEMPLES

The suprabhātam

Lord Veṅkateśvara in Tirupati is "woken-up" every morning with the majestic recitation of the *suprabhātam* or a "good morning" prayer in the Sanskrit language, composed in the fifteenth century. The tradition of such wake-up panegyrics goes back to the Tamil poetic and royal customs, when the king was woken-up every morning with lilting music and words of praise. The Tamil poems were called *Tiruppaḷḷiyeḻucci* (Waking up from the Sacred Bed). A Tamil poem of this genre was used for Lord Viṣṇu in the eighth century CE in Srirangam, and later in the fifteenth century, a Sanskrit work was composed for the deity in Tirupati. The poet deems the deity to be a royal king and wakes him up with his song. This notion of the king as god and god as king permeates Hindu thinking in many levels and is particularly seen in a temple where the deity is treated as a ruler. The *suprabhātam* is the most famous in the genre, but now almost every major temple in South India has its own morning wake-up prayer addressed to the local manifestation of Viṣṇu, Śiva, or Devī.

Lord Veṅkateśvara is woken-up like a king, but he has a busy day ahead. The early morning rituals in most temples begin between five and six in the morning, but in Tirupati, because of the throngs of pilgrims, the wake-up call may be as early as 3 AM. By the time the last rituals are done and he is ceremoniously asked to retire for the night, it may well be midnight.

In many large temples, the deity is woken-up in a similar manner in the morning, frequently to the sounds of music and Sanskrit prayers. Large quantities of food are offered to the deity at regular intervals. In Tirupati, Veṅkateśvara is decorated with flower garlands (*mālāsevā*) in the morning and "receives" pilgrims like a king receives his subjects. The worshipers file past the deity in the dimly-lit main shrine, where they get glimpses of the manifest divinity, the lord, who has taken form to appear before them. Periodically, this procession of devotees is halted, and the deity is offered food or special prayers.

The recitation of prayers in temples may differ. At the devotee's request, the priest may say the 108 names of the deity. In many temples, sections of the Vedas known as *Puruṣasūkta* (hymn to the cosmic person) or *Śrīsūktam* (hymn to Lakṣmī) may be recited regularly. In some South Indian Viṣṇu temples, the Tamil poems of the Āḻvārs (eighth to tenth centuries CE) are considered to be the Tamil Veda or revelation and are recited at regular intervals.

The 1,008 names of the resident deity may be recited at the sponsorship of a devotee; the worshiper pays a stipulated amount to the temple office and the priest begins his recitation. While the priest recites the names, the worshiper and the accompanying family would sit on the ground in front of the deity and listen to the names. The worshiper usually has a passive role in these ceremonies. The prototype of such strings of names is found in the *Mahābhārata*, where Viṣṇu's 1,008 names are narrated. Śiva has several (about eight) sets of such 1,008 names. There is no definitive discussion in texts as to why these numbers are favored, though in general the number thousand seems to indicate a sense of largeness and suggestive of infinity. Thus in the Vedic *Puruṣasūkta*, the *puruṣa* or primordial person who is said to have a thousand heads, a thousand eyes, and a thousand feet extends through the universe and still goes beyond it by ten finger lengths. By reciting or hearing the thousand (or the abbreviated version of a hundred) names, the devotee is reminded of the infinite potential and manifestations of the supreme being. Some scholars also believe that the sanctity of the number 108 (and also 1,008) comes from the number 10,800, the number of time units (*muhūrta*) in a year. Vedic texts apparently explicitly acknowledge this number as 108 × 100 (Parpola 1997).

The deity may be adorned and decorated once or several times a day. In the famous Śrīnāthajī temple at Nathdvara, Rajasthan, the form of Kṛṣṇa is decorated and adorned several times a day in order to delight the throngs of devotees who flood into the audience chamber. In many of the larger temples, the deity goes through a ritual bathing and anointing (*abhīṣeka*) process once a week. In many South Indian temples in India and in the diaspora, this is a major ritual. The priests leave very few clothes on the deity and systematically bathe and anoint it with various substances—water, milk, honey, yogurt, and so on, symbolizing the various nourishing substances of the world. Finally, pitchers of water are poured over the image to the recitation of the *Puruṣasūkta*. A screen is drawn between the worshipers and the shrine; the deity is then offered incense and fragrances, clothed, and adorned in new splendor. After an afternoon rest, there are evening audiences with the worshipers and evening *āratī*.

In some temples there is a beautiful ritual of making the lord sleep at night to the strains of soft music and lullabies. In all these rituals, the deity is envisaged as a king-protector or, at times, an infant child in the form of Kṛṣṇa. The paradox of the ritual, of course, is that the lord or the goddess who is the supreme being indulges the whims of the devotee and takes on image form which is bathed, anointed, clothed, adored, and adorned by the human being.

These forms of worship in many South Indian temples follow one of two systems laid out in texts called Āgamas. There are Āgamas dedicated to Śiva, Śakti Devī (the goddess), and Viṣṇu. The Āgamas are texts parallel to the Vedas in some ways, but elements of their worldview are seen in parts of the *Mahābhārata*. Many Āgamic texts lay down specific rules for the time, manner, and details of the rituals and festivals. Male priests of the Brāhmaṇ caste are trained in these temples as apprentices, undergo special initiation ceremonies, and are empowered to attend to the deity in the main shrine.

While only male Brāhmaṇ priests do the rituals within the main shrine in the large, traditional temples, in many smaller, newer temples such as Mel Maruvathur, women are beginning to officiate in the main shrine. Traditionally, women were considered to be polluted during the time of menstruation and did not go to a temple. This is now being reversed in many newer shrines in India. The temple was supposed to be ritually pure, and menstruation and death polluted it. When there was a death in the family, those closely related to the dead person are considered ritually polluted for a few days and cannot visit the temple during this period. The number of days that one is ritually polluted depends on one's caste. It is interesting that although in devotional narratives a woman can pray to the lord or goddess anytime and surrender herself anytime, even if she was menstruating, the Brāhmaṇical structure of a temple ritual did not allow this in practice. For example, it is said in the *Mahābhārata*, Draupadī called upon Lord Kṛṣṇa and asked for protection when she was being abused. This surrender took place when she was (from the view point of the Dharmaśāstras) considered to be ritually polluted, that is, when she was menstruating. In the world of devotion, however, there is no physical pollution, no stigma to menstruation. It is in the ritual, male Brāhmaṇical world of the traditional temple, that a menstruating woman is excluded.

SPECIAL RITUALS IN TEMPLES: THE AUSPICIOUS WEDDING OF VIṢṆU AND LAKṢMĪ

There are periodic temple rituals which are sponsored by a devotee. A person may say that when a son gets married or if he or she gets a promotion, the family will celebrate the wedding of the god and the goddess in a temple. While this is done in many temples on a regular basis, it is celebrated almost everyday with eclat in Tirupati (in Andhra Pradesh).

By extension, this ritual is celebrated in all the temples where the manifestation of Viṣṇu is called Veṅkateśvara or "lord of Veṅkatam Hill," that is, in Pittsburgh, Malibu, Chicago, Atlanta, and Singapore, among other places. The ritual is *kalyāṇa utsava* or the celebration of the auspicious wedding between Viṣṇu and the goddesses Śrī (Lakṣmī) and Bhū (the earth goddess). This festival is different from other ritual wedding celebrations such as that of the deities Mīṉākṣī and Sundareśvarar in the city of Madurai. While the latter is an annual occurrence, the *kalyāṇa utsava* is celebrated almost everyday in Tirupati upon the request of devotees. In this ritual a priest acts out the part of the lord as a bridegroom, and all the ritual acts of an actual wedding are performed. In popular terms, devotees believe that the reenactment of the most auspicious event—the union of the male and the female powers of the universe, the wedding of the god and the goddess—there will be happiness and prosperity for all. The ritual also highlights Viṣṇu's accessibility. The devotee almost "plays" with the deity (as manifested in the image) and thus reenacts and participates in this most auspicious event, the marriage of Viṣṇu to Lakṣmī and Bhū. Such a reversal of the human-divine relationship is typical of devotion (Ramanujan 1993a). The human being is not an instrument of the lord's sport (*līlā*); rather, Viṣṇu, through his manifestation in the image form, participates in the sport of the devotee.

The images of Viṣṇu, Lakṣmī, and Bhū and the ritual of the wedding also represent the several relationships of the deity to the world. By assuming the form of the bridegroom of Lakṣmī, Viṣṇu reminds the human that he is the bridegroom for every soul; as the consort of Bhū, Viṣṇu can be seen as the support of the earth and as a friend to all humanity.

Annual rituals I: temporary shrines and local deities

In many suburbs of large cities and in rural areas, women from the so-called "lower" or "scheduled" castes (castes which Western academics call "untouchable") may set up an image in a small shrine under a thatched roof; with community contributions, it may eventually get brick walls around it. In the state of Tamilnadu, we find deities not found in the Purāṇic structure, local goddesses who are not known outside the immediate cultural area. Sometimes temporary shrines may be erected around an image only for one month when the goddess is celebrated. The goddess cannot be called a village deity; she is found in both rural and urban areas.

The goddess in this area manifests herself in seven forms, and a community will traditionally worship only one of these manifestations. In the suburbs of Chennai, for instance, in the month of Āṭi (mid-July to mid-August), Ammaṉ or the mother goddess is worshiped by women. The goddess may be called Cellattammaṉ, Nāgatammaṉ, or any one of seven names. On any given Sunday of the month, a small community builds a temporary shrine, surrounded by large canopies to hold the crowds. Visiting folk musicians and bards who know the relevant songs are hired for the day, as is a public address system, which blares to the world that the community is celebrating the goddess that day. From early in the morning, loudspeakers roar film songs dedicated to the goddess.

The expenses of the festival in this shrine may be picked up either by community contributions or through the major sponsorship of one family, with other families chipping in. For two days, the women cook large cauldrons of food which will be distributed to about a hundred visitors after the worship. Around mid-day, the film music stops and the hired (male) folk musicians sing ballads to the accompaniment of skilled percussion instrument players. As the drumming gains momentum, women may start swaying and become possessed with the spirit of the goddess. Anywhere between two to ten women may dance under possession for about an hour or so in front of the goddess, eventually slowing down as the drums decelerate. They eventually stop their rhythmic swaying, sip water, and relax as the next stage of the rituals begin. In some communities, the goddess enjoys meat; a goat is now sacrificed right there and offered to the deity. The large cauldrons of thick fermented cereal which is said to "cool" down the system are distributed to the visitors, and the film music glorifying the goddess begins to pick up speed again.

While the setting seems fairly informal, the events are planned months in advance. The Āṭi festival for the goddess will scarcely be over before planning for the next one begins.

Annual rituals II: the festival of recitation in Srirangam

The large Brāhmaṇical temples of India also have regular annual cycles of rituals celebrated with hundreds of thousands of devotees. The grandest festival in most temples is called *brahmotsava* or the festival of the supreme being. The most ostentatious celebration usually occurs on the last day or the day when the festival image of the deities is pulled slowly through the streets in an enormous chariot (*ratha*, *tēr*); a ritual anglicized locally as the "car festival." The temple best known for the car festival is Jagannātha in Puri, where the local form of Viṣṇu called Jagannātha, is pulled through the streets. In this temple, Jagannātha is understood to be Viṣṇu's incarnation, Kṛṣṇa. Kṛṣṇa's sister and brother, Subhadrā and Balarāma, are installed in the chariot and pulled slowly by human beings through the streets, with hundreds of thousands of people following them. (The English word "juggernaut," which refers to any massive force that crushes anything in it's path, is a mispronunciation of "Jagannātha." The chariot/cars are very tall and weigh several hundred tons.) In the last two centuries churches in South India have also celebrated chariot festivals in honor of the Virgin Mary or various Christian saints.

Let us look at one long festival called the *adhyayana utsava* or the festival of recitation in the temple city of Srirangam to see how complicated some of the annual celebrations are. The Viṣṇu/Raṅganātha temple here celebrates annual festivals for almost two-hundred-and-fifty days a year. "Śrīraṅgam" translates as "sacred stage" or "sacred arena." Unlike the dynamic Śiva, who is the dancer in the city of Cidambaram, here the manifestation of Viṣṇu, who is known as Raṅganātha (lord of stage), reposes in tranquility on his serpent couch. He is not the performer but the audience entertained by the recitation and the dance of human beings. Srirangam, during the *utsava*, becomes the cosmic stage, and here the devotion of a ninth-century poet, the Nammāḻvār, and his perceived ascent to heaven are enacted annually. During the festival, through song and dance, this place is affirmed to be *bhūloka vaikuṇṭha* or heaven on earth.

The mythical portrayal of heaven (*vaikuṇṭha*) seems similar to the physical description of Srirangam: an island garlanded by a river. Srirangam, which is near the large town of Tiruchirapalli, is circled by the Kāverī and Kolladam rivers, and it is said to resemble Vaikuṇṭha, circled by the Virajā River. The rivers form clear boundary markers; separating earth from heaven, the outside world from the realm of the sacred temple space. On the days of the *adhyayana utsava*, one is in a liminal state, for only during those ten days are the northern gates of the Srirangam temple, known as the "gates of heaven," opened and the distinction between the earth and the heaven is said to be removed; heaven and earth become contiguous with each other. Heaven is said to come to earth; the lord who cannot be grasped or perceived by the senses is said to be seen by all; the unheard sound resonates through the articulation of the Sanskrit and Tamil Vedas. Revelation is simultaneously visual and aural as the devotees see Viṣṇu/Raṅganātha enshrined in the Hall of the Thousand Pillars and hear the words of poet Nammāḻvār. At the conclusion of the ritual, Viṣṇu grants salvation to his ninth-century devotee Nammāḻvār; at the end of the sacred time, when heaven has descended to earth, Nammāḻvār, the human being, ascends to heaven.

The festival focuses on the recitation of the Sanskrit Vedas as well as the recitation and *performance* of the Tamil poems composed between the eighth and the tenth centuries in honor of Viṣṇu. In the eleventh century CE, Vaiṣṇava devotees introduced these poems into the temple and home liturgies and began to comment on it—initially orally and through the performing arts and then later in writing. A full recitation with verbal and performative commentaries is held during the annual *adhyayana utsava*. These ritual contexts comment upon the songs and inform us about the poems and the local devotional community—perhaps more so than even a verbal commentary. The whole festival is one of rejoicing and splendor, celebrating the quest of Nammāḻvār—and every devotee—for union with Viṣṇu.

The *adhyayana utsava* takes place in the month of Mārgaśīrṣa (December 15th to January 14th) in all temples where there is substantial representation from the Śrīvaiṣṇava community. Some rituals of the festival are celebrated in several temples in America. Over twenty-one days, Sanskrit Vedas and four thousand Tamil verses composed by poet devotees are recited. The highlight is the recitation of Nammāḻvār's *Tiruvāymoḻi*, a poem of 1,102 verses. The program for twenty-one days, starting with the new moon of the month Mārgaśīrṣa, involves carefully orchestrated rituals, including: the recitation of poems, processions of the festival image through the streets, the dressing up of the festival image in various costumes, enactment of particular episodes from the Tamil Āḻvār poetry or the Sanskrit epics by special cantors/actors (male Brāhmaṇs who belong to certain family which have the hereditary rights to perform) in some temples, and enactment of particular verses from the poetry. On each day, the movable, festival image of the Viṣṇu used for celebrations is dressed up in special costumes, and he is worshiped in his other manifestations.

The *adhyayana utsava* begins on the new moon day in the month of Mārgaśīrṣa. The recitation of the *Tiruvāymoḻi* begins on the eleventh day (*ekādaśī*) after the new moon; it is on this day that the "gates of heaven" will be open. On this eleventh day in the bright half of the moon in Mārgaśīrṣa, the heaviest crowds of the year are expected at the Srirangam and most other Viṣṇu temples in South India and in the diaspora. This day is one of the holiest days in the pan-Hindu calendar; fasting on this day and keeping a pious vigil through the night without sleeping is said to grant one the good merit to reach Vaikuṇṭha.

Beginning on this day, the tall, northern doors of the Srirangam temple, known as the "gates of heaven," are opened just prior to the recitation of the *Tiruvāymoḻi*. These doors are kept closed for the rest of the year and kept open *only on the ten days of this recitation and performance*; during these ten days, heaven is contiguous with earth. While the gates in Srirangam are very tall, most temples in India and in the diaspora have smaller doors which are considered to be a vestibule connecting heaven with earth. In the Viṣṇu temples of Atlanta, Pittsburgh, Chicago, and so on, these make-shift "gates to heaven" are formally opened during this day with throngs of devotees in attendance. In Srirangam, the festival image of Viṣṇu/Raṅganātha is brought from the main shrine and goes slowly around one of the enclosures of the temple and then passes through the "gates of heaven." In recent years, there has been extensive television coverage of the Srirangam temple when the lord passes through the "gates of heaven."

In Srirangam, for the ten nights of the festival, the processional image of Viṣṇu is brought through the "gates of heaven," taken to the temple tank, and then brought to the "Hall of a Thousand Pillars," a twelfth-century structure which is in one of the outer enclosures of the temple. This enormous hall is a grand form of a pavilion which may exist in many other temples—a pavilion in which music and dance were performed for the deities.

On the last day of the festival, the poet Nammāḻvār is said to be given salvation. The performance as enacted by priests and images in the temple depicts Nammāḻvār as reaching heaven and getting liberation from the cycle of life and death. At that point, a member from the crowds of devotees, who are witnessing this passion play of Nammāḻvār's devotion to god, goes up to the center stage and requests Viṣṇu to return Nammāḻvār to humanity. Viṣṇu agrees to let the poet come back to humanity, so that his words and his form in the temple will continue to inspire and save other devotees. Following this drama of the salvation of Nammāḻvār, the cantors are taken in a procession around the temple.

What is the meaning of this festival? On the simplest level, we can see a community—the Śrīvaiṣṇava tradition—asserting from the eleventh century that their vernacular language, Tamil, is equivalent to Sanskrit and that revelation is not frozen in the Sanskrit Vedas. Revelation is ongoing; it came through Nammāḻvār, and it happens every time the devotee *hears* the sacred words and *sees* the divine manifest form of the lord in the earthly place that is transformed to heaven.

Some other devotees give a symbolic meaning for the various parts of the rituals, saying that every small syntax of the ritual corresponds to a spiritual state in the path of the human soul to heaven. The journey of Viṣṇu from the main shrine to the Hall of a Thousand Pillars is said to express the pilgrimage of the human soul to heaven. Lord Viṣṇu/Raṅganātha is said to represent the human soul which wants salvation, and the details of his passage to the Hall (which is heaven) is considered to have allegorical meaning. Let us look at some details of this type of interpretation to get an idea of how devotees internalize temple rituals and see them as outer manifestations of inner, spiritual conditions:

Ritual	*Allegorical meaning*
doors closed when Viṣṇu leaves the main shrine	sense organs shut and controlled
bearers of palanquin	movement of *kuṇḍalinī* or glide-like serpent yogic energy within one's body
Viṣṇu goes through doorway	human life passes through head at death
Viṣṇu orders a gateway to be opened	various barriers broken and pathways to heaven opened
Viṣṇu reaches a well in one of the enclosures circles	soul reaches river Virajā which circles heaven
lord discards a shawl and wears new garland	soul assumes new spiritual body
lord wears clothes with gems	soul is radiant in glory at the time of liberation
images of saints brought near lord	soul renders continuous service with other devotees to the lord

Such allegorical interpretations for rituals are seen in many Hindu texts, but it must be noted that there is no common ground of acceptance for these meanings. Many rituals were initiated by patrons and devotees to commemorate various events which took place in known historical or mythical time and to enact moments in the tradition which they believed should be remembered and celebrated. The astrological exactness of these celebrations is critical, and these moments succeed in bringing together various segments of the Hindu communities in horizontal space as well as by tying in these devotees with their ancestors in vertical time.

Pilgrimages

Perhaps the times when we see the community coming together both vertically and horizontally is at times of major pilgrimages when there are movements of great numbers of people over the subcontinent. While there is no single pilgrimage which is incumbent on all Hindus and of the magnitude of the Hajj in Islam, almost every Hindu usually makes at least one or more pilgrimages in the course of his or her life. The popularity of pilgrimage centers and events may wax and wane according to political patronage and cultural relevance, but some towns like Varanasi and Ramesvaram have been important for centuries.

While some of these towns are important yearlong, many get a special significance and attract hundreds of thousands of pilgrims only on a few festival days of the year. Thus, the river waters in the cities of Haridvar, Ujjain, Nasik, and Prayāga (the modern Allahabad) attract millions of pilgrims during the *kumbha melā* or the festival of Aquarius/Pitcher. This festival commemorates a myth in the Purāṇas. Apparently the gods and the demons fought for the nectar of immortality, and when the gods eventually procured it, they used the four places as resting spots. Fertility and immortality are promised to pilgrims here; one may bathe for liberation from the cycle of life and death, but more probable, one may get drops of water to soak seeds and grains so that the harvest next year may be bountiful.

The festival occurs every three years and rotates between the four towns mentioned here. These towns are located on rivers which are generally considered holy; but during the astrologically correct days in January-February, the sanctity reaches a peak. Nasik is on the Godāvarī, Haridvar on Gaṅgā, Ujjain on Siprā, and Allahabad is on the confluence of the Gaṅgā, Yamunā, and the mythical Sarasvatī. Bathing in the waters at the astrologically correct moment is said to give one good *karma* and is said to cleanse one physically and spiritually. Millions of pilgrims congregate here, but it is the special place for *sādhu*s or holy (male) ascetics and *sadhvi*s or ascetic women. In 1995, more than twenty million pilgrims came to bathe in Allahabad. Accounts of the festival are found as far back as seventh-century literature, and in the eighth century, the philosopher Śaṃkara is said to have asked ascetics to assemble here during the astrologically beneficial moments. Prayers, religious songfests, sectarian debates, religious councils, and power brokerage all take place here during the days.

Most Hindus consider the rivers of India to be sacred. By bathing in the great rivers of India, one is said to be morally cleansed of sins *and* to acquire merit or auspiciousness. One not only gets physically cleansed by the rivers but one is morally purified and one's sins (*pāpa*) are destroyed as well. A story popular in oral tradition makes the point.

A king goes to sleep on the banks of the river Gaṅgā. When he wakes up in the middle of the night, he sees some women covered in filth taking a dip in the holy river. They emerge from the river cleansed and then disappear. The king returns on several nights and sees the same thing. Eventually he asks them who they are; they reply that they are the embodiments of the rivers of India. Everyday they tell him, human beings bathe in the rivers and their sins are absolved by that act. The rivers—embodied as women—absorb the moral dirt and then come to the Gaṅgā, the grand purifier, to purify themselves.

Variations on the story say where the Gaṅgā goes to get herself purified, although it is generally assumed that she needs no purification. In stories that extol the river Narmadā, Gaṅgā goes to bathe in that river. In a metastory ascribed to oral tradition, she goes to bathe in the holy city of Prayāga to absolve herself of the moral filth. This story obviously praises the sanctity of Prayāga but ends up being a circular narrative because the holy city itself gets it's importance because the rivers Gaṅgā and Yamunā meet there.

The generic version of the story distinguishes between two kinds of dirt: moral dirt and sin (*pāpa*), which is perceptible as physical dirt in the bodies of the river. In addition to moral and physical purities, one may also note that in other Hindu contexts there is a third kind of purity: ritual purity. When one bathes in them, rivers and other bodies of water may bestow the pilgrim and his or her clothes with ritual purity. Ritual purity encompasses physical purity, but all that is physically clean is not ritually pure (Alley 1998). Even if a person is physically and ritually clean, the mere association with people and garb which are deemed ritually unclean or impure may be contagious enough to "pollute" one.

Most of the rivers of India are considered to be female, and mountains are generically male. There are exceptions however: some rivers like Kṛṣṇa have male names and some mountains like Nandādevī bear women's names. Rivers are perceived to be nurturing (and sometimes judgmental) mothers, feeding, nourishing, quenching, and, when angered, flooding the Earth. The river Gaṅgā is hailed by millions of people as Mother Gaṅgā (*gaṅgāmaiyā*). Hindu girls in India are frequently named after rivers. Rivers are also personified as deities; Gaṅgā is sometimes portrayed as a consort of Lord Śiva. In the south, Kāverī Amma<u>n</u> (Mother Kāverī) is the name by which the river is fondly addressed. The river Kāverī rises in Coorg, Karnataka, and hundreds of girls born in the area are called Kāverī. In the plains of Tamilnadu, Kāverī is seen as a devotee and sometimes the consort of Lord Viṣṇu, and several temples (like Tēra<u>l</u>untūr, near Kumbhakonam) have a striking image of this personified river in the innermost shrine. By bathing in the rivers, by venerating and propitiating the divine personification of the rivers, the devotee prays for purity and prosperity.

The waters of these rivers are also used to extend sacrality wherever they are present. Little jars of water from the Gaṅgā are kept at homes and used for funeral rituals. Sometimes pilgrimage rituals involved carrying water from one sacred place to another, thus extending the mingling of the powers of these rivers. For instance, in popular practice, pilgrims worship Śiva at Ramesvaram, deep in the south of India. They then take sand from the beach of Ramesvaram to Allahabad. The rivers Gaṅgā and Yamunā meet at Allahabad, and, according to some Hindu texts, a third, mythical river called Sarasvatī joins them here under the ground. Pilgrims dissolve the sand they have brought from Ramesvaram at this confluence of rivers. They then take the holy water from this confluence in little bottles back to Ramesvaram and anoint the Śiva *liṅga* there. Many devotees consider the pilgrimage circle, from Ramesvaram to Allahabad and back to Ramesvaram, to be particularly meritorious. In other rituals, waters from the Gaṅgā and other rivers of India are taken to other countries, mingled with the waters of local rivers, and used to consecrate new temples. Thus, during special rituals at the Veṅkateśvara temples at Pittsburgh and Atlanta, waters of the Gaṅgā and Kāverī were mingled with the Mississippi, the Suwannee, and other American rivers, blessed with the recitation of Vedas, and used to consecrate the new or renovated temple structures. When the temples are consecrated in the new place, the daily and periodical cycles of rituals commence.

Millions of Hindus have thus connected old places of worship with new ones. Although there may not be formal, unifying links between the various traditions of the Hindu faith, pilgrimage rituals, like the one physically connecting Ramesvaram in the south with Allahabad in the north, served as strong connecting bonds. As Hindus settle in new countries, the land there is consecrated; the sacred waters of India are brought to mingle with the waters of the new host country, and sacrality is extended.

Building plans for Hindu temples in America are constantly in the works, and a project is finished only for another extension or renovation to begin. Building plans are constantly evolving—as are prayers, rituals, and functions. Sacred spaces and Hindu temples have overlapped in India and Southeast Asia for more than two millennia; now these sacred spaces are perceived in other parts of the world. Through temple rituals, some Hindus may establish connections between themselves and the deity, seek favors from and offer thanks to the presiding deity, aspire to eliminate old sins, acquire karmic and ritual purity, seek liberation from the cycle of life and death, establish connections with sacred places, both new and those going back to their ancestors, and extend their notions of holy land from India to the diaspora. The final blessings that ring out after most rituals in Hindu temples, both in India and in other countries, proclaim the aspirations of all devotees: *sarva jana sukhino bhavantu*: "May all people be happy!"

CHAPTER TWENTY-ONE

TĪRTHA

Surinder M. Bhardwaj and James G. Lochtefeld

Pilgrimage to sacred centers has occupied a venerable place in the long history of Hindu civilization and remains an important practice in modern Hindu life, both inside and outside of India. Although at the most literal level pilgrimage involves a place and people who travel to that place, both the places and the actions can have considerable symbolic content. When one investigates the meanings of these actions in light of their context—a particular time, place, and cultural milieu—the insights that one gains both reflect and reveal that context. As with any other realm of religious life, looking closely at pilgrimage can reveal a great deal about the fundamental assumptions in any religious tradition.

In Islam, for example, the centrality of Mecca is a symbol for the oneness of Allāh, and every adult Muslim is required to do the Hajj (assuming one is physically and financially able), as a sign of obedience to Allāh. Furthermore, the ritual patterns of the Hajj itself symbolize both the unity and the equality of the Muslim community and the lordship of Allāh. Yet many Muslims also pay visitations (*ziyārat*) to Ṣūfī tombs—sometimes to ask for favors, but sometimes simply to maintain a relationship with the saint buried there (Pinto 1989: 117). Here the emphasis is on compassion and grace and its accessibility to ordinary human beings. Unlike the Hajj, these journeys are not required as a religious obligation but are often prompted by compelling human concerns.

For Buddhists the notion of pilgrimage is very different, since the meanings of these actions are coded into a Buddhist context. No single place is deemed the most important sacred center; the emphasis is instead on the path, which reflects Buddhism's stress on self-transformation. When Buddhists visit the four sites associated with the historical Buddha—Lumbini, Bodhgaya, Sarnath, and Kusinagar—it is because these places serve as reminders of the Buddha's life and message and an exhortation to Buddhists to do the same. In a similar vein, Tibetan Buddhist pilgrimage around Mount Kailāsa can be interpreted as a symbol of transformation—the death of the old person and a new beginning. Although every action must take place somewhere, for Buddhists the critical factor is the path, as the vehicle to move one toward the ultimate religious goal.

Although it is commonplace to talk about sacred places possessing these qualities in themselves—and in many cases this reflects the understanding of the people who visit them—it is clear that different sorts of things are happening in each of these examples and that the meanings of these places are based on their context. Similarly, one can expect that Hindu pilgrimage will reveal the Hindu conceptual world (or worlds), and the most pervasive feature of Hindu tradition is its infinite variety. Hindu religion is diffuse and decentralized, and pilgrimage reflects this fundamental characteristic. Hindu sacred places are distributed throughout India—whether associated with particular deities, with events in Hindu mythology, or with particular rites in the life cycle—and millions of people visit them each year. These places are clearly important, but there is no single uncontested holiest place—the valuation of various places ultimately depends on who is speaking. Pilgrimage is clearly an important Hindu religious activity, and some of the largest gatherings of humanity take place at India's major sacred centers, particularly at the *kumbha melās* (Dubey 1987). Yet although the pilgrim's journey is important, no single model encompasses what people do on pilgrimage—again, one must look at the context. As a manifestation of Hindu cultural life, pilgrimage is also directly connected with many of the other cultural forces—social change, economics, and politics.

In connection with Hindu pilgrimage, this chapter will discuss these three notions: the pilgrim's journey (path), the pilgrim's goal (place), and the cultural forces that shape the ideas about these. Although all three are important in Hindu tradition, by far the greatest stress has been on the notion of place, a stress that reflects the deeply rooted conviction that certain places are powerful in their own right and that visiting them can promote or facilitate personal transformation. These are the *tīrthas*, the points of crossing, and they will receive first attention.

TĪRTHA IN THE HINDU WORLD: A PLACE AND A SYMBOL

The word "*tīrtha*" literally means a "ford" or a "crossing place"—a place where one can easily cross from one side of a river to the other. Metaphorically, *tīrthas* are places where the boundaries between the everyday world and the sacred become permeable and where one can more easily "cross over" or communicate between the two (Eck 1981a: 325). As mentioned earlier, such encounters cannot be ascribed under a single model, since pilgrims at the same place can often have differing motives. If the ultimate goal is conceived as freedom from the cyclical bondage of *karma* and the soul's ultimate merging with the infinite (*mokṣa*), then *tīrthas* are the place where this can happen. In other cases, *tīrthas* provide access to the divine presence, either for pragmatic reasons such as seeking favors, or to take part in the divine *līlā* and thus be in the divine presence. In other cases, *tīrthas* are believed to be places where ritual actions carry greater religious weight—whether bathing in a sacred pool, giving alms (*dāna*), or performing one of the life-cycle rites. In every case, however, such *tīrthas* are places where the religious goals are more easily attained. Generalizing from this concept of symbolic "crossing," all Hindu holy places are colloquially termed as *tīrthas*; this term is even applied to *gurus*, teachers, and other holy men and women, since their grace helps one to transcend this phenomenal world.

As one might expect from the word's literal meaning, in many cases *tīrthas* are associated with water, particularly with India's sacred rivers. The earliest mention of these, in *Ṛg Veda* 10.75.5–6, described an area in Punjab and Sind, but this area soon expanded. The most common classical list names seven sacred rivers—Gaṅgā, Yamunā, Godāvarī, Sarasvatī, Narmadā, Sindhu (Indus), and Kāverī—which between them span the subcontinent. Even among these the Gaṅgā occupies a special place and is often considered as a symbol of the sacred river itself—so much so that Godāvarī and Kāverī are often described as the "Gaṅgā" for their particular regions. Although all these rivers are considered holy throughout their length, their sanctity can be intensified during particularly auspicious times or augmented at certain unusual places: river sources (which could represent the origin of things or the purity of the just born), river junctions, and places where they empty into the sea (which could be seen as symbolizing an individual merging with the infinite). Another possible transition point is the place where a river disappears and becomes indistinguishable such as Vinaśana, where the Sarasvatī merges into the Rajasthan desert. Aside from rivers, any other body of water can also be a *tīrtha*; the term "*tīrtham*" is also used for *caraṇāmṛta* (water from washing a deity's feet). This is the holy water that the priest distributes to the temple devotees after worship, which the devotees sip as a mark of their visit to the temple deity.

Aside from rivers and bathing places, many topographic features or natural phenomena that evoke a sense of awe can be seen as what Mircea Eliade (1959b: 11) called "hierophanies" or manifestations of the sacred. These can include hot springs, natural gas emissions, waterfalls, conical hills, mountains, rock outcroppings, confluences, promontories, oceanic views, and beautiful lakes. Throughout the cultural history of India, the Himālayan mountain system has been considered to be a holy region because it is recognized as the abode of Śiva. More particularly, Mount Kailāsa is the paradigmatic symbol of Śiva himself. In the deserts of Rajasthan and in mountainous Himachal Pradesh, many Devī (goddess) temples are located on hilltops. Devī pilgrims often portray themselves as her little children who feel a natural attraction to her mountainous "palaces" and set out on her pilgrimage in response to her "call" to them (Erndl 1993: 61).

Such places are not only seen as holy sites but also may be identified often as manifestations of the divinities themselves. For example, Nandā Devī is a mountain and a goddess, Vaiṣṇo Devī is revealed as three lumps (*piṇḍa*) of rock in a cave in the Himālayan foothills, Jvālā Devī is present in a natural gas vent which has been lit for centuries, at Kedarnath a fold of stone is where Śiva showed himself, and, of course, the river Gaṅgā is considered to be the goddess Gaṅgā. Such places are not simply symbols but are also considered to be actual manifestations of the divinities themselves; at such sites one can thus directly encounter divinity. As examples of human religious behavior, such *tīrtha*s are a human social product. But many of the people who flock to these places, often at the cost of time, money, and trouble, see themselves responding not to a projection of social realities but to a genuine divine presence, and the significance of such places is repeatedly reaffirmed through activities such as pilgrimage and ritual.

The final way by which a place or region can come to be considered holy is by being identified with one or more of the divine activities (e.g. sport, hunt, play, love, battle, and miracle), and the circumstances sanctifying that place are invariably revealed by the site's Sthalapurāṇa (charter myth). For example, Triyuginarayan in the Himālayas is claimed to be the spot where Śiva and Pārvatī were married, and pilgrims can take ash from the smoldering fire (*dhuna*) which is claimed to have been burning since that time; the Cāmuṇḍā Devī temple in Himachal Pradesh is claimed to be on the spot which the *śakti* of the Devī killed the demon-generals Caṇḍa and Muṇḍa (Erndl 1993: 58).

Such divine activities may also sanctify an entire region, although such regions generally have a central core area. Such identification with whole regions is particularly characteristic of Kṛṣṇa and Rāma devotion, in which primary stress is not only in worshiping the deity but also in participation—taking part in the divine *līlā*. For example, Vrndavan is identified as Kṛṣṇa's "home town," but the surrounding Vraja region is filled with places identified with one or another of Kṛṣṇa's exploits (Entwistle 1987; Haberman 1994). The same is true for Rāma's devotees, who have special love for Ayodhya but also revere places associated with his years of exile. The area around Kuruksetra has many specific places especially identified for performing certain rituals, since this site is associated both with the Mahābhārata war, which was fought to uphold *dharma* (divine order), and for Kṛṣṇa's divine discourse, the *Bhagavad Gītā*.

TĪRTHA CLASSIFICATION

Since the Hindu tradition's hallmark is diversity and decentralization, it is no surprise that the Hindu *tīrtha* system contains multiple subsystems. These are not intertwined into a single formal hierarchy but stand as independent systems with their own nodal points—some more popular than others, but none universally recognized as the holiest. In many cases these sites and systems also show conceptual mirroring: "All-India" networks are often replicated on some smaller, regional scale, whereas local sites are identified with larger, more important ones (e.g. Morinis 1984: 30). It is also not uncommon to find that these networks intersect at pivotal places (e.g. Ujjain, Kancipuram) whose economic, political, or cultural significance made it imperative to have a presence there.

Greater and lesser pilgrimage networks have grown up around each of the major deities. The sacred places of the great goddess are described as *pīṭha*s (seats) rather than *tīrtha*s (crossing places), perhaps to connote an established divine presence. Each goddess in this network has a separate identity and a separate consort, but they are all seen as manifestations of a single female divine energy. Although there is no single consistent list of these sites—some sources list 51 and some 108—they are spread throughout the subcontinent. The charter myth tying all these sites together comes from the story of Dakṣa's sacrifice, which ended with the death of Goddess Satī (who was Dakṣa's daughter and Śiva's wife). While Śiva roamed India carrying Satī's body, grief-stricken, Viṣṇu used his discus to cut parts of the body away, and wherever a part of Satī's body fell to earth, it became established there as a particular goddess (Sircar 1973).

This story uses bodily imagery not only to link together a host of local Hindu goddesses, by identifying them as manifestations of this great goddess, but also to connect them and their places into a single unified whole. Yet even though this charter myth emphasizes their connections, some sites are more important than others, based on the body part believed to have fallen there. For example, Kāmākhyā in Assam and Jvālāmukhī in Himachal Pradesh are associated with Satī's pudenda and tongue, respectively. These are sexually charged parts of the female body, and both places are seen as being extremely powerful. Yet there is no unanimity in these claims, since one finds that differing spots claim the same body part. For example, local tradition at Kālīmaṭha (in the Garhwal Himālayas) claims that this was the place where Satī's pudenda fell, a claim that boosts its prestige as a sacred site.

This all-India goddess network is complemented by smaller regional ones. The best-known regional network is the "seven sisters" of the Śivalika Hills, which shares certain sites with the larger network. Of the seven, Jvālāmukhī and Vajreśvarī Devī are listed in Sircar's (1973: 40) enumeration of the *śaktipīṭhas*, and local sources claim this for Nainā Devī, Vaiṣṇo Devī, Cintpūrṇī, and Manasa Devī, but not for Cāmuṇḍā Devī (Erndl 1993: 37–59). Furthermore, this list of seven is not definitive, since Hindi sources list a set of nine goddesses. As with the larger network, the important feature here is that of place—tying together differing goddesses as members of one geographic group.

Similar interconnected patterns can be seen for Śaivite *tīrtha*s, for which the most important network is the twelve *jyotirliṅga*s (*liṅga*s of light). Śaiva myths describe Śiva's first manifestation as a gigantic pillar of light, and these twelve sites are deemed places where this *jyotirliṅga* came down to earth (Eck 1982: 290–91). Although each site has a particular Sthalapurāṇa (charter myth), in every case the charter describes how Śiva took up residence in that spot. The twelve sites are scattered unevenly over India: two are in Gujarat (Somanātha and Nāgeśvara), three in Maharashtra (Bhīmaśaṃkara, Ghṛṇeśvara, and Tryambakeśvara), two in Madhya Pradesh (Mahākāleśvara and Oṃkareśvara), two in South India (Rameśvara in Tamilnadu and Mallikārjuna in Andhra Pradesh), one in the Himālayas (Kedārnātha), and two in eastern India (Viśvanātha in Varanasi and Vaidyanātha in Bihar). Furthermore, some of these are important pilgrimage places—particularly, Visvanath, Vaidyanath, Ramesvaram, and Mahakalesvar.

Just as the *śaktipīṭha* network shows smaller regional variants, so does the Śaiva. In the Himālayas, the five different sites in the Pañcakedār—which is centered around Kedarnath, one of the *jyotirliṅga*s—are all described as part of Śiva's body. Another regional grouping, this one in South India, identifies each manifestation of Śiva with one of the five primordial elements, thus conveying the symbol of totality: Tiruvannamalai (fire), Kalahasti (air), Jambukesvar (water), Kancipuram (earth), and Cidambaram (space). Although none of these five are among the twelve *jyotirliṅga*s, the last three are important sites in very important places.

With Vaiṣṇavas, this all-India trend is not nearly so marked. One finds it with the devotees of Vallabhācārya, who have identified 84 *baiṭhak*s (seats) of Vallabha (S. Das 1985), which are spread through many of India's holy places. Unlike for Śiva and the goddess, one reason why Viṣṇu has no widespreading network may be that his two most widely worshiped *avatāra*s, Rāma and Kṛṣṇa, are strongly associated with particular places—eastern Uttar Pradesh and Vraja. These are areas in which Rāma and Kṛṣṇa are believed to have actually lived—and such specific identification may hamper the development of wider networks. Another possible reason is that Viṣṇu has tended to assimilate other deities, either through the doctrine of the *avatāra*s or by identifying him with autochthonous deities. At least three of these latter deities have taken on major importance: Veṅkateśvara in Tirupati, Viṭhobā in Pandharpur, and Jagannātha in Puri. One does see smaller Vaiṣṇava networks, such as the Pañcabadrī in the Garhwal Himālayas and the Vārkarī pilgrims at Pandharpur.

Other networks mark the boundaries of ethnic or religious identity. The largest such network is the *cār dhām*, four sites marking the "boundaries" of the sacred land of India: Badrinath in the north, Puri in the east, Ramesvaram in the south, and Dvaraka in the west. Each of these sites is associated with one of the *saṃnyāsī maṭha*s said to have been established by the philosopher Śaṃkarācārya—so these four places not only mark the boundaries of the sacred land but also carry associations with the greatest Hindu religious figure. On a smaller scale, other networks celebrate and solidify regional identities: there is another "*cār dhām*" in the Himālayas, composed of Yamunotri and Gangotri (the sources of two sacred rivers), Kedarnath (Śiva), and Badrinath (Viṣṇu). Tamilnadu's pilgrimage centers of Murukaṉ celebrate the Tamil landscape's diverse ecosystems and also provide a unifying factor for Tamil identity (Clothey 1972: 93). In the same way, Maharashtrian identity has been formed and reinforced by the eight shrines to Gaṇeśa, which make up the Aṣṭavināyaka network (Courtright 1985: 211–17), and the temples to Khaṇḍobā (Stanley 1977: 31–34).

Each Hindu cultural region of India has similar, though less universally well-known specialized *tīrtha*s. Many goddess shrines specialize in rites pertaining to male children, for example, their first hair offering, and many of these are places to which people come to request the birth of male children. Possibly originating as fertility rites, their association with mother goddess shrines is clear enough. A final *tīrtha* network depends not on the presiding deities but on their utility for performing certain rites and ceremonies, especially for the dead. These will be mentioned later.

Development of overseas Hindu sacred places

Although Hindu cultural influence has historically extended through Southeast Asia, until recently Hindu holy places have been limited to India itself. As larger numbers of Hindus have settled outside the subcontinent, one of the results has been the development of pilgrimage and pilgrimage sites in their new homes.

During British colonial rule, Hindus emigrated to virtually every part of the British empire. The greatest overseas diffusion was to East and South Africa and to certain tropical islands, such as Fiji, Mauritius, and the West Indies. Most of these emigrants served as laborers on plantations, as workers constructing railways and roads (especially the East African railway), and as small traders and artisans. These Hindu communities remained relatively isolated from India until quite recently and were unaware of the complexity of religious developments in India (Klass 1991: 23).

At this point, the best-developed Hindu pilgrimage activity outside of India is in Mauritius. In this festival Śaiva pilgrims draw water from Grand Bassin Lake—which is identified with the Gaṅgā—and carry the water as an offering to Śiva at their local temples, timing their journey to arrive on the evening of Śivarātri (Cascaro and Zimmerman 1987). This ritual is clearly modeled on the pilgrimage to Deogarh in Bihar, in which pilgrims draw Gaṅgā water at Sultanganj and then carry it seventy-three miles to the Vaidyanātha temple (Anand 1990: 123). Since the Hindus in Mauritius (and in the other sugar colonies) largely emigrated from Bihar and eastern Uttar Pradesh, this connection is quite reasonable.

Hindu migration to North America followed a very different pattern, especially after the major changes in the American immigration laws in the 1960s. Most Hindu migration to America occurred in the context of postindustrial society during the information age; many of these immigrants were very highly educated and came from relatively privileged backgrounds. Whereas the nineteenth-century emigrants to the sugar colonies became culturally isolated, these North American immigrants have been in constant touch with their Hindu heritage in India. One result of this has been the relatively rapid development of temples. Aside from being places of worship, these have often also served as community centers, a function one rarely finds in India (Narayanan 1992: 153).

Among the oldest of these temples is Pittsburgh's Śrī Veṅkateśvara temple, built in 1976, whose presiding deity is the same as that of the famous Tirupati temple of India. This is only one of a series of Veṅkateśvara temples in various places in the United States, including Orlando, Houston, Malibu, and Aurora in suburban Chicago; in many cases these have been built with help from the Tirupati temple trust (Narayanan 1992: 149). Although the Pittsburgh temple's festival calendar has been affected by United States cultural constraints—with greater activity on weekends and American secular holidays—the temple literature emphasizes the holiness of the site itself, which is compared to the hills around Tirupati. This emphasis on the site's holiness reflects Śrīvaiṣṇava theology, in which the consecrated image, known as *arca avatāra*, is a real form of the deity. Thus, in these ritually awakened images Veṅkateśvara is considered to be genuinely present at these temples. This contrasts with the pattern associated with Śaiva temples in the United States, which are described as being discovered rather than consecrated (Narayanan 1992: 157–61). Most Veṅkateśvara temple devotees are culturally connected with the Dravidian cultural region and consider this temple as the most important. On their trips back home to India, they also visit the Tirupati temple, turning it into an international pilgrimage center.

The people managing the earliest temples in the United States often seemed conscious of the need to serve the entire Hindu community. The presiding deity at the oldest Hindu temple in New York City is Gaṇeśa—a deity acceptable to most Hindus—and the temple has images of the other major deities. This same inclusive impulse can be seen in many of the Veṅkateśvara temples, which have images of non-Vaiṣṇava deities (Narayanan 1992: 170). Yet as the United States Hindu community has become better established, there has been the greater tendency to divide into smaller groups. This is most visible in places where Hindus are densely settled such as northern New Jersey, whose eight different temples serve well-defined regional and sectarian groups. Since such division reflects deep-seated sectarian and regional loyalties, one would suspect that this trend will continue.

SOURCES FOR THE STUDY OF TĪRTHAS: TEXTS AND HISTORY

Contemporary *tīrtha*s have resulted from the heritage and cumulative cultural processes of the Hindu people over several millennia. The earliest potential sources are the pre-Āryan traditions, which consist of the vast urban civilization of prehistoric northwestern India (the Indus Valley civilization), and numerous peoples and cultures of the forests, grasslands, and arid ecosystems. Any ideas about religious life in these cities are highly speculative since the only evidence is archaeological, and these sources are "silent" regarding abstract ideas such as religion.

The most important sources for pilgrimage and pilgrimage places come from Hindu sacred literature, beginning with the Vedas. Although it is difficult to fix an indisputable date for the Vedas, the ideas in them are fairly clear. An important feature of Vedic lore is the sanctity of rivers, which are eulogized in many verses (Kane 1968–77, 4: 556–57; Schwartzberg 1978: 13). The Sarasvatī is particularly prominent in Vedic literature, and although this river now flows only during the monsoon, and even then disappears in the Rajasthan desert, it was then a prominent river and joined the Sindhu (Indus). The Vedas detail ceremonies that pilgrims performed at the confluence of Sarasvatī and

Dṛṣadvatī and at the place where the Sarasvatī disappears. In addition to sacred rivers, these texts also mention several settlements as holy places, such as Hariyūpīyā (possibly modern Harappa) in the Saptasindhu region and Kāśī (Varanasi) in the east (Schwartzberg 1978: 13).

A more clearly developed picture appears in the epic literature, particularly in the *Mahābhārata*. The core events of this epic are probably of the eighth or seventh century BCE (Kulke and Rothermund 1998: 45). In its *Vānaparvan* (forest book), the *Mahābhārata* lists a large number of *tīrtha*s associated with water bodies, sages' hermitages, sacred mountains, forests, and other natural features. The grand pilgrimage described here begins at Puṣkar in Rajasthan, at the sacred lake of Brahmā, and moves clockwise through the entire subcontinent, finally ending in the Himālaya Mountains, the abode of Śiva (Bhardwaj 1973: 44; Schwartzberg 1978: 14). Aside from laying out the contours of the sacred landscape and extolling *tīrthaphala* (literally, the "fruit" or benefits of visiting a *tīrtha*), the *Mahābhārata* also emphasizes that such rewards are reaped by pilgrims who control their senses and are above hypocrisy and deceit—a theme which runs through Hindu pilgrimage to this day. Unlike the *Mahābhārata*, the *Rāmāyaṇa* gives few references to concrete sacred places despite its extended tale of Rāma's sojourn in the forest world.

In contrast, the Purāṇas name a large number of sacred places, and one of their most significant elements is the exaltation of sacred sites, particularly the glorification of *tīrthaphala*. The development of the present Purāṇas is generally accepted as taking place in the Gupta period (*c.*350–550 CE). These texts often describe pilgrimage as a ritual alternative to Vedic sacrifices—sacrifices whose performance was far beyond most people's means and ritual skills—and one sign of this is that the *tīrthaphala* is often equated with the merit from Vedic sacrifices such as the *aśvamedha* (horse sacrifice). *Tīrtha* toponyms in the Purāṇas reveal an intimate topographic knowledge of India but also clear sectarian biases. This is hardly surprising since many of the Purāṇas are unabashedly sectarian.

Although formerly one had to search through these texts to map their sacred sites, several helpful sources have been compiled. Surinder Bhardwaj (1973: 62, 66, 69) has mapped the identifiable *tīrtha*s in the *Garuḍa*, *Matsya*, and *Agni Purāṇa*s, and as a cultural geographer, he has also talked about the implications of these maps, such as pilgrim circulation and settlement patterns. A far more ambitious list can be found in P. V. Kane's *History of Dharmaśāstra* (1968–77, 4: 723–825), which provides a list of about 2,500 *tīrtha*s. In many cases Kane has matched these textual references with actual sites.

Some later religious digests utilized the lists in the *Mahābhārata* and the Purāṇas but kept their focus on some selected regions, possibly to favor a king or a patron. An interesting example is Bhaṭṭa Lakṣmīdhara's *Kṛtyakalpataru* (*Tīrthakalpataru*, according to Kane 1968–77, 4), a famous twelfth-century CE compendium. This work mentions a large number of *tīrtha*s, although the author's sources are relatively narrow—he draws only from the *Mahābhārata* and a few selected Purāṇas (Kane 1968–77, 4: 691). Mapping these *tīrtha*s (Bhardwaj 1973: 72) revealed a major bias toward northern India, although this may simply reflect his sources. Lakṣmīdhara's work was a model for later *tīrtha* digests, including Vācaspati Miśra's *Tīrthacintāmaṇi* (late fifteenth century), Nārāyaṇa Bhaṭṭa's *Tristhalīsetu* (*c.*1550), and Mitra Miśra's *Tīrthaprakāśa* (*c.*1625). These latter authors drew from a far greater textual corpus, including the Vedas themselves, and also wrote substantial commentary on the rites connected with pilgrimage and pilgrimage sites.

Although these texts extol many different places, considerable attention goes to sites in the Gaṅgā basin and particularly to Kāśī (Kane 1968–77, 4: 623–24).

All the sources based on Sanskrit texts have certain limitations. First, these texts cannot be read as factual descriptions—recall that some of the sites Kane lists cannot be found in real life. Many of these texts also show strong sectarian biases and exalt certain sites but completely ignore others. Even when the sites are certain, another vital consideration is that of the authors and their audience. These texts are the product of a small, educated elite and give a prescriptive picture of their views; one cannot assume that ordinary people followed these prescriptions—presuming that they even knew that such texts existed.

Within these limitations, several texts deserve serious consideration. As mentioned before, Kane's *History of Dharmaśāstra* (1968–77, 4) has an extensive list of individual pilgrimage places (723–825) as well as citations from these texts about the emphasis on the cultivation of moral qualities (562–63), through which alone pilgrims gained their goals. Similar sentiments can be found in K. V. R. Aiyangar's (1942) introduction to Bhaṭṭa Lakṣmīdhara's *Tīrthavivecanakāṇḍa*, which stresses the notion that pilgrimage's real affect is as a means to transform oneself. Consideration of the relative merits of various *tīrtha*s can be found in Richard Salomon's "*Tīrtha-pratyāmnāyāḥ*" (1979) and detailed prescriptions for pilgrimage practices in *The Bridge to the Three Holy Cities* (1985), Salomon's translation of the first section in the *Tristhalīsetu*.

Pilgrimage studies

Hindu pilgrimage studies run the gamut from (popular) descriptions of individual *tīrtha*s, to analytical studies focused on the meaning of holy places in Hindu life, to works that examine a pilgrim's journey in the larger context of that person's social and cultural life. The simplest pilgrimage studies are descriptive sources, many of which mirror the pattern in Sanskrit texts by naming collections of *tīrtha*s. One such source is the volume of the popular Hindi religious journal *Kalyāṇa* entitled "Tīrthāṅka" (1957), which contains descriptions of about 1,800 *tīrtha*s, though with a certain bias toward northern India. The 1961 Census of India took on the ambitious and unprecedented project to prepare detailed volumes on the fairs and festivals of each state and in some cases each district. These volumes give history and descriptions for sacred places from all religions, as well as estimated attendance at particular fairs and festivals. J. H. Dave's (1957–61) four-volume set describes a number of important Hindu pilgrimage sites but relies very heavily on Sanskrit texts and popular tradition. A general description of the importance of pilgrimage sites in Hindu civilization can also be found in two articles by Agehananda Bharati (1963, 1970).

An attempted quantitative typology is in S. M. Bhardwaj's *Hindu Places of Pilgrimage in India* (1973), written from a cultural geographer's perspective. Bhardwaj describes pilgrimage places as falling into various "levels," from "subregional" all the way to "pan-Hindu"; his primary criterion for determining these levels is based on the distance that pilgrims have traveled to get there. This work carefully locates the pilgrimage sites described in various Sanskrit texts and measures and monitors pilgrim flow in these places. He suggests that as pilgrims move to higher-level sites, their goals become more abstract—that is, less tied to immediate concrete needs. Some scholars considered this formulation appealing (Turner and Turner 1978: 237–39), but on the basis of their studies, others found it subject to many exceptions and unsupportable (Morinis 1984: 271; van der Veer 1988: 62).

Another genre is pilgrimage site studies, which have been done by scholars from a variety of disciplines. L. P. Vidyarthi's *The Sacred Complex of Hindu Gaya* (1961) provided a model for many other places, including Badrinath, Katmandu, Nathdvar, and Varanasi (Kāśī). Each of these works examines the site in question from the perspective of sacred centers, sacred performances, and sacred specialists. These are useful ethnographic studies but suffer from the underlying premise that pilgrimage to these places serves as a means of cultural integration between the "great" and "little" traditions—traditions that are often difficult to separate and discern (Morinis 1984: 241–43). This model also gives very little attention to pilgrims themselves, giving these accounts a strangely depopulated feeling—as if there were temples and buildings and specialists to service the trade but no customers!

Other site studies include Diana Eck's *Banaras* (1982), an account based primarily on the Sanskrit *māhātmya* literature and the geography of the city itself. It does an admirable job of drawing an idealized picture from these sources but gives little attention to grittier subjects, such as economics and social organization. G. A. Deleury's *The Cult of Viṭhobā* (1960) focuses on the temple at Pandharpur and the twice-annual Vārkarī pilgrimage there. The essays in *The Cult of Jagannath and the Regional Tradition of Orissa* (Eschmann, Kulke, and Tripathi 1978) carefully lay out not only the history and development of Puri's Jagannātha temple but also the larger cultural forces at work in Orissa, particularly notions of kingship. Given the depth of Kṛṣṇa devotion, it is not surprising that there have been several studies on the Vraja region. Alan Entwistle's *Braj* (1987) exhaustively surveys the sites in Vraja, the sources that describe them, and the history of both. Jack Hawley's introduction to *At Play with Kṛṣṇa* (1981) depicts the mood of participation so central in Kṛṣṇa-*bhakti* and sets the context for describing the liturgical dramas known as Rāsalīlā. A longer and more highly nuanced exploration of this is found in Margaret Case's *Seeing Krishna* (2000).

Several sources describe the experience of the pilgrims themselves. Irawati Karve's "On the Road" (1988) and D. B. Mokashi's *Palkhi* (1987) both describe the Vārkarī pilgrimage to Pandharpur; Karve in particular highlights the disjunction between Vārkarī egalitarian ideals and actual social practices. David Haberman's *Journey Through the Twelve Forests* (1994) not only describes his (often painful) experiences during a circular foot pilgrimage around Vrndavan but also gives a careful description of the history and development of the sites themselves.

The most valuable works either combine the study of a particular site with more theoretical understandings or examine pilgrimage in the larger context of social, cultural, economic, or religious life. Of the latter, Ann Gold's *Fruitful Journeys* (1988) is an example of village-based anthropology, in which she examines the villagers' differing sacred journeys—to local shrines for various purposes, to further shrines to fulfill life-cycle needs, and, finally, a tour of all-India pilgrimage sites. She richly describes all these journeys but admits that she had difficulty understanding pilgrims' motives for the final category (A. Gold 1988: 260). Kathleen Erndl's *Victory to the Mother* (1993) examines various manifestations of the goddess cult in northwest India and chapter three describes the pilgrimage to various hill temples, often in obedience to the goddess's "call." The most fascinating example is E. Valentine Daniels's *Fluid Signs* (1984). This text ends by describing the pilgrimage to Sabari Malai in Kerala but builds up to this by uncovering distinctively Tamil conceptions of person, environmental affinity, and sexuality.

Several sources combine extended site studies with more in-depth theoretical consideration, for which the best example is E. Alan Morinis's *Pilgrimage in the Hindu Tradition*

(1984). This text examines and compares three sites in West Bengal, then ends with a chapter entitled "Theoretical Perspectives on Pilgrimage." Morinis (1984: 233–75) divides these perspectives into typological schemes, functional analyses (such as promoting social integration, fostering group solidarity, or enacting elements of the social order), theories of individual motivation, and psychological theories. He compares each of these theories with his data from West Bengal and shows that every theory for explaining pilgrimage either suffers from internal inconsistencies or is so context-bound that it is of limited value elsewhere. Several scholars have disagreed with Victor Turner's view that pilgrimage is an analogue to tribal rites of passage (Morinis 1984: 257–58; Sax 1991b: 12; van der Veer 1988: 58–60). In his own work, Morinis (1984: 298–99) ends by propounding his own theory, which contrasts the pilgrim's "explicit" and "implicit" journeys—the former being the journey to a shrine, and the latter the journey of the soul to the "One."

In *Gods on Earth* (1988), Peter van der Veer exposes several problems with this last model: that it is a theological rather than an anthropological argument, that it draws its ideas from widely differing times and places, and that it largely ignores "the production and management of meaning by various interest groups involved in pilgrimage" (63). Van der Veer's study of Ayodhya takes up theoretical questions in his second chapter, and as his book's subtitle clearly shows, one of his major concerns is "the management of religious experience and identity." Since he was conducting fieldwork in Ayodhya while the Rāmajanmabhūmi movement was gathering strength and realized that his "scholarly" work had profound political implications, this emphasis on the way that interest groups manage religious meaning is not surprising. A final anthropological study is William Sax's *Mountain Goddess* (1991b). This looks at Nandā Devī's cult and pilgrimages in the context of Kumaoni society but begins with a chapter laying out the anthropologist's perspective.

A final category is shorter works and anthologies. In "The Lord of the Spirit World," Sudhir Kakar (1982) masterfully depicts how pilgrimage to the Bālājī (Hanumān) shrine at Mehndipur in Rajasthan effects healing in mentally troubled people. It not only considers the pilgrims' worldview, in which the deity's power is seen as driving off possessing spirits, but he also analyzes the therapeutic affect of these rites from his own psychoanalytic perspective. In "Creating the South Indian 'Hindu' Experience in the United States," Vasudha Narayanan (1992) looks at the Veṅkateśvara temple in Pittsburgh and examines how the social context in the United States is affecting both ideas and practice there. Finally, there are collections of sociological essays on pilgrimage edited by Makhan Jha (1985, 1991) and D. P. Dubey and Lallanji Gopal (1990); these essays tend more toward the descriptive than the analytic. Under the guidance of R. P. B. Singh, the *National Geographical Journal of India* has produced a large number of studies on various aspects of pilgrimage, especially Hindu *tīrtha*s (sacred places) and *tīrthayātrā* (pilgrimage) (R. Singh 1987).

YĀTRĀ TO TĪRTHAS: PILGRIM PATTERNS

Until now this chapter has focused on pilgrimage sites, but one cannot have these without pilgrims—that is, real men, women, and children who intentionally travel to these sites. As a religious activity, pilgrimage is a human behavior that takes place in the context of a time, place, and culture. In looking at this an outside observer may perceive things that are invisible to the participants or conceive of these things in different ways than the participants—such as describing notions of a *tīrtha*'s sacrality as tied to distances traveled, money spent, and the numbers of people going there. Yet this is an outsider's perspective, and to get the whole picture one must take into account what people themselves think they are doing—that is, one must recognize that they are conscious agents and take their perspectives seriously. It *is* true that many pilgrims visit these sites with the conviction that they are encountering a living, divine presence and not just a site validated by social projection. Yet even though there are enough "simple" believers to make this a genuine "insider's" perspective, many other people work on more abstract and symbolic levels. A good account of their behavior must recognize this, and the surest way to do so is to pay genuine attention to what real people say and do—not that one should uncritically accept everything that they say, but that one should hear their voices.

Just as examining the notion of *tīrtha*s reveals no single most sacred center but various networks reflecting strong differences of opinion, similarly there is no single overarching reason why pilgrims travel to these sites. The Hindu religious tradition is diffuse and decentralized, and pilgrimage sites and pilgrimage behavior reflect this fundamental reality. In many cases, pilgrims themselves may have no single clearly defined motive but several different ones, and these become evident only by examining each particular case. Yet even though each person's perceived reasons for traveling are his or her own, certain themes appear again and again: transformation, participation, obligation, purification and power, seeking "peace," and tourism.

Transformation and pilgrimage

There is a long history of understanding pilgrimage as a vehicle for spiritual development (*sādhana*) through voluntary austerities (*tapas*), and this notion has strong undertones in Sanskrit texts and pilgrimage manuals. It first appears in the *Aitareya Brāhmaṇa* (7.15.2) of the *Ṛg Veda*:

> Flower-like the heels of the wanderer,
> his body groweth and is fruitful:
> All his sins disappear,
> slain by the toil of his journeying.

This same theme is also echoed in the epics. Although the *Mahābhārata* extols the "fruit" of visiting *tīrtha*s, it also emphasizes that these rewards are reaped by pilgrims who control their senses and are above hypocrisy and deceit. As Kane (1968–77, 4: 553) reports from one of the Purāṇas, pilgrimage was seen as affirming and inculcating positive moral values, such as forbearance, truthfulness, restraint of senses, respect for elders, and compassion for others. Despite the exaggerated claims of rewards, the Hindu scriptures never considered pilgrimage as a substitute for moral and righteous action but as an act of piety in the context of a life lived according to one's *dharma*. According to the *Kūrma Purāṇa*: "That person who abandoning his proper duties resorts to *tīrtha*s does not reap the fruits of pilgrimage in this world as well as in the next" (2.44.20, cited in Kane 1968–77, 4: 570–71).

This transformative ideal can still be found. One contemporary *guru* described pilgrimage as a tool to break down the ego—that the difficulties of travel gradually transformed one, just as clothes are cleaned by beating them on rocks. Further benefits of pilgrimage came from having limited possessions, which helped people to simplify their lives, while their constant motion kept them from developing attachments. One also sees this notion of willingly accepting hardship in the Kāñvariyā pilgrims who carry Gaṅgā water on foot to the Vaidyanātha temple in Bihar or from Haridvar back to their homes and who undergo all sorts of hardships on the way. I (Lochtefeld) once accompanied this latter group for twenty miles and gave up with date-sized blisters on my soles, but they carried on, some limping with every step. Similarly, the ebullient pilgrims traveling to the Śivalika Mountain shrines of the great goddess (Devī) climb the steep slopes leading to her temples singing "Jai Mātā Dī" (Victory to the Mother), even while they are sweating at each step in the monsoon season (Erndl 1993: 61–83).

Yet many Hindus do not ascribe to this essentially romantic pilgrimage notion, as any investigation of pilgrim travel patterns clearly shows. Although some *sādhus* travel on foot as a religious discipline, ordinary pilgrims walk to pilgrimage spots only where there are no roads—primarily in the hills and the Himālayas. It is plainly evident that pilgrims will use conveyances when they are available and that they prefer to do so. Easier travel encouraged long-distance pilgrimage by reducing the time and effort needed to reach one's destination, but it also altered pilgrimage patterns. For example, before the railroad came to Haridvar in 1886, pilgrims came there mainly in early April, on their way to the Himālayas, whereas after the railroad pilgrims came throughout the year and also more often. Yet by 1898 train travel was so accepted that religious festivals could be shut down by simply suspending train reservations. In his well-documented study, Ian Kerr (2001: 304–27) has shown that the railways in India had a profound impact on the spatial origins, temporality, and the social patterns of pilgrimage. While the volume of pilgrims skyrocketed, their gender structure was profoundly altered—toward much greater female and family participation. A similar example can be seen on the roads to the Himālayan pilgrimage shrines, which as late as the 1930s had an elaborate network of pilgrim shelters (*caṭṭī*) every eight to ten miles. With the advent of roads this network simply withered away, and with it several traditional pilgrimage routes such as the path from Gangotri to Kedarnath. So even though the cultural tradition praises hardship and austerities, most people avoid them if possible.

Another mode of experiencing pilgrimage is participation, for which the best example is found in Kṛṣṇa devotionalism. For many pilgrims coming to Vrndavan or viewing a Rāsalīlā in some other setting, the real focus is not to get somewhere and do something but to savor the experience itself. As described by Case:

> Krishna's activity is called *līlā*—literally, play. He performed all his youthful feats in play, just for the fun of it. The pleasure that he felt in his actions was the pure pleasure of eternal bliss. . . . For the devotee, the līlās narrated in the *Bhāgavata Purāṇa* are taken as having happened historically, but they also happen eternally. Krishna participates in the recurring daily, monthly, and yearly patterns of the natural world, and his devotees can also participate in his activities in this eternal realm.
>
> (2000: 6)

The stress here is on becoming a participant in the divine *līlā* and in sharing the experience of Kṛṣṇa's presence. Groups emphasizing this tend to focus on visualization practices—on envisioning oneself as sharing god's activity in that sacred space. It is primarily centered on inner experience and the cultivation of that experience; the end goal is "the inducement and enhancement of bliss" (Case 2000: 92). Along with being (*sat*) and consciousness (*cit*), bliss (*ānanda*) is one of the qualities traditionally associated with the divine essence; and through these "sharing" practices, the devotee can enjoy this as well.

Obligation

Other travelers' journeys focus less on ascetic practice or participation in the divine *līlā* than on fulfilling immediate personal or familial obligations. In earlier times pilgrimages were sometimes undertaken as expiation (*prāyaścitta*) for an unbecoming or sinful act, and these pilgrimages were judged equal to various penances (Kane 1968–77, 4: 55–56). In contemporary times one major source of obligation is life-cycle rites, particularly rites connected with the dead. Pilgrims come to Haridvar bearing the "flowers" (bits of bone and ash) from cremation pyres to perform the final death rites by immersing them in the Gaṅgā. Formerly this rite may have been done years after a person's death; but with better transportation, it is now often done right away (see A. Gold 1988: 85). Whatever the timetable, this is still a religious obligation that someone must fulfill. The same holds true for Gaya in Bihar, which is one of the best-known places in North India for performing the *piṇḍadāna* rite for the ancestors, whereas in South India the preferred site is Ramesvaram. Kuruksetra (in Haryana) is the *tīrtha* of choice to perform funerary rites for those dying under unusual circumstances.

Perhaps the most unusual rite is religious suicide. The tradition extols this at certain *tīrtha*s either as a sure door to final liberation (*mokṣa*) or to gain the objects of one's desire. Kane (1968–77, 4: 701–2) cites the authority of the *Brahma Purāṇa*, which permits and even encourages suicide at Puruṣottama Kṣetra (Jagannātha Puri in Orissa). Accounts of suicide at Puri were part of standard British missionary polemic, although concrete cases are difficult to verify. Hindu religious literature prescribes suicide at *tīrtha*s such as Kāśī and Prayāga, and actual suicides at the latter site are attested by Hsüan-tsang (1969, 1: 232–34), al-Bīrūnī (1971: 170), and al-Badā'ūnī (1976: 179). Tradition reports that the Mughals took strong exception to this and took concrete steps to stop it (Sarkar: 1901: 27–28, 136).

A different sense of obligation comes when pilgrimage fulfills a vow. Vows in which one promises to carry out certain actions if one's requests are fulfilled are a common feature of religious life. Many of the Kāñvariyā pilgrims to whom I (Lochtefeld) spoke alluded to making vows to carry a *kāñvar* for a certain number of years, although few of them said anything about the content. What is generally accepted is that if one receives one's request, then one must fulfill what one has promised. Such a vow is essentially seen as a contract with god, and to renege on this is to risk terrible misfortunes. There is no required form or setting for making such vows—since god knows the content—but in many cases people make them at pilgrimage sites, since in many of these places the deities are seen as "awake" and more responsive to people's requests.

Seeking power and peace

The presuppositions behind such vows reveal one of the most important reasons why many people visit *tīrtha*s—the heartfelt conviction that doing so brings them in contact with divine power, through which they can gain blessings and grace. In many cases, this same notion lies behind much of people's religious practice in their everyday lives, and this is one reason why it seems mistaken to dismiss "local" sites as different from "pilgrimage" sites. The same sorts of things—connections with deities—happen in both places. For many pilgrims at Haridvar, the Gaṅgā is thus not merely water but a goddess with whom they can have direct contact. Temples in the hills, the Himālayas, and on the other side of town all house resident deities, whose *darśana* is both powerful and purifying. Some of these deities are renowned for granting people's wishes—Veṅkateśvara at Tirupati is said to fulfill any request made in his presence—but such requests usually require a return visit to give thanks in public. Such public displays affirm the shrine's power and thus encourage others that their requests will be fulfilled. As always, a site's Sthalapurāṇa reveals a great deal about what people might expect and what sorts of concerns might draw people there. Just as one chooses a medical specialist based on one's ailment, so many sites (and their presiding deities) often have "specializations."

This desire to gain access to divine power cuts across religious lines and sends Hindus to Ṣūfī *dargāh*s, such as Niẓāmuddīn Awliyā in Delhi and Muʿīnuddīn Chishtī in Ajmer, or to Christian shrines such as Saint John de Britto in Tamilnadu. Even pilgrims with no explicit request are believed to gain benefits, if only through charging their spiritual batteries through proximity to this power (Pinto 1989: 117). Not surprisingly, the places that most commonly draw pilgrims from different religious communities are those that are reputed to have healing powers (Bhardwaj 1987: 457–68). In the same way, many pilgrims travel to visit with religious *guru*s, who are not only seen as teachers and guides but also as giving access to divine power.

Although these places (and people) are considered both holy and powerful, it is also important to recognize that these qualities are not seen as static but that they can be enhanced by differences in place and time. It is clear that many pilgrims believe this, for festivals bring predictable spikes in pilgrim activity. For example, although the Gaṅgā is everywhere holy, certain places are considered more powerful, and this power is multiplied when combined with more ritually powerful times. People bathe everywhere in the Gaṅgā on the festival of Kārtika Pūrṇimā, but particularly at *tīrtha*s such as Haridvar and Garhmuktesvar. Similar bursts of activity can be seen on the festival days connected with particular deities.

The most dramatic enhancement can be seen in the *kumbha melā*s, which are held at Haridvar, Allahabad, Ujjain, and Tryambakesvar. The *kumbha melā*'s current charter (unattested before the twentieth century) connects these sites with the battle between the gods and the *asura*s for the nectar of immortality (*amṛta*). The charter relates that this nectar fell to earth at these four spots, during a twelve-day struggle between these groups. Since a divine day is believed to equal a human year, these festivals are celebrated in these spots every twelve years, and on that anniversary the waters are again said to be transformed into that primordial nectar. The *kumbha melā* at Allahabad is the best attended of all, in part because this site has far more usable space than the others, but mostly because of its excellent location in relation to the populous Gaṅgā plain.

For many pilgrims, this closeness to power is a powerful factor behind their journey. Yet as noted before, Hindu pilgrims come with a wide variety of attitudes, and many are not simple believers. Although religious texts describe the vast religious merit (*puṇya*) generated by visiting pilgrimage places, many pilgrims seem reluctant to claim this.

Perhaps this reticence comes from a reluctance to claim benefits for themselves or the notion that what they are doing is not difficult enough to "qualify" as pilgrimage—particularly since many wandering ascetics do uphold the traditional standard of foot travel, begging for food, and enduring privations. Yet for many people this reluctance is more strongly rooted in changing religious paradigms, particularly greater skepticism about the literal reality of religious merit. Sanskrit pilgrimage literature reflects the assumptions of an earlier time, and one cannot expect contemporary people to subscribe to these. Although some people retain simple, "traditional" faith, those who do not must either discard these symbols or reinterpret them in a modern context.

Several generations ago Kane recognized this reality and noted that

> The number of people visiting holy places in the belief of accumulating merit is sure to become less and less, as modern secular education spreads. But it would be a calamity for the moral and spiritual greatness of India if pilgrimage to holy mountains and rivers came to be stopped altogether. I would . . . recommend to all men, however highly educated, the undertaking of pilgrimages to certain hallowed spots.
>
> (1968–77, 4: 826)

He later exhorts that "Every Indian who is proud of the great religious and spiritual heritage of our country must make it a point to devote some part of his time to frequenting holy mountains, rivers and other places of pilgrimage" (Kane 1968–77, 4: 827).

Here Kane attempts to replace traditional religious sentiments with cultural pride, which is one sort of reinterpretation. Another type of response is to show how traditional practices have either "reasonable" or "scientific" explanations. Gaṅgā water, we have often been assured, has scientifically tested bacteriological properties. This explanation conflates ideas about religious and hygienic purity, and I (Lochtefeld) encountered many other examples of such reasoning. In interpreting the visitors guide to the Pittsburgh Veṅkateśvara temple, Narayanan observes the same phenomenon. She notes that a strong message in this literature is the notion that "All rituals have an inner meaning and significance which frequently have to do with promoting good health and a safe environment. . . . Such interpretations are seen in the 'antiseptic' properties of turmeric or cowdung, and I have even heard that the reason why we break a coconut in a temple is to let the 'ether' out of the coconut and thus replenish the ozone layer" (1992: 174). However far-fetched such explanations may seem, they are clear attempts to reconcile conflicting paradigms. Not everyone may agree with these explanations—Narayanan notes the pamphlets explicitly state that "the views expressed in the articles . . . do not necessarily reflect those of the S. V. Temple management" (1992: 168). Yet she also speculates that for many visitors, such pamphlets may provide the only explanation they receive.

In my (Lochtefeld) own experience, the most sophisticated responses somehow managed to combine the notion that pilgrimage places had some sort of transforming power, with which one needed to harmonize oneself. Although people may doubt the literal reality of *puṇya* and *pāpa* (religious merit and demerit), they may conceive of the benefits from pilgrimage in other ways. One man compared the effect of visiting the holy places to putting on fine perfume—even a small amount has a pronounced effect and continues to scent the body long after one has applied it. Another common image was the notion of seeking "peace," which I often heard during my work in Haridvar. People waxed on the calming effects of Haridvar's natural beauty, and one man explicitly stated that when one bathed in such a beautiful place, all of one's "mental tension" (he used this English phrase in a Hindi sentence) was relieved and gave one the feeling that one's sins had been washed away. This is another attempt to impart some special feeling to the place, phrased in a twentieth-century idiom of anxiety and relief rather than religious merit and demerit.

Tourism

The final important motive behind pilgrim behavior is tourism—whether recreational, cultural, or religious—which has greatly affected modern *tīrtha*s. The emphasis on tourism has undeniably increased since independence, partly because India's population has become more urban and thus tends to have more cash income to spend on traveling, but also because of tourism promotion by the national and state governments—which see tourism as a "clean," labor-intensive industry. Such promotion has not only included building and running the necessary infrastructure—on the premise that "tourists" demand more and better facilities than "pilgrims"—but also organizing cultural festivals and other attractions to stimulate visitor traffic. Although such promotion often makes it seem as though holiness is a commodity to be advertised, bought, and sold, such advertisements can be seen as a twentieth century equivalent of the Sthalamāhātmyas, which were also intended to attract people to pilgrimage sites by touting their merits.

Such development has had its costs—particularly in the Himālayas, where the fragile ecosystems have degraded more and more. More subtly, "tourists" tend to want comfort, ease, and entertainment, and as these sites have been marketed along those lines, many residents feel that this has transformed the atmosphere in these places. As one Haridvar *purohita* (hereditary pilgrimage priest) remarked, in earlier times people had stayed in *dharmaśālā*s, but now they stay in hotels, and this change signaled the loss of the *dharma* which had made Haridvar special.

A sharp distinction between "pilgrims" and "tourists" is often difficult to make at Hindu *tīrtha*s because many educated Hindus describe their visit to holy places simply as tourism. But whatever they prefer to be called, the number of visitors, tourists, or pilgrims has visibly increased, not declined. Their quest for merit is another matter. The phrase "pilgrim-tourism" (in German literature "pilgertourismus") perhaps more aptly encompasses the modern pilgrimage activity (Rinschede 1999: 197–221).

In any case, the "pure" pilgrimage reflected in this romantic view never really existed. Most Hindu families expect to have fun as part of *tīrthayātrā*. This does not deny that there have been real changes in pilgrimage over time. Better transportation has made it possible for people to travel more easily and often but has undoubtedly decreased the anticipation that would come in the long journey to a site to which one had never been and might never see again. Yet when one looks for evidence about fundamental attitudes, how much is really different?

At base, "pilgrim" and "tourist" are both idealized types, and almost all visitors to these sacred sites share both aspects. Any pilgrimage involves visiting places, often new ones, and this certainly brings the thrill of discovery. Most Hindus go on pilgrimage in a group—usually family but sometimes friends and neighbors—so the journey involves a great deal of social interaction, a break from routine, and fun. Furthermore, pilgrimage was one of the few travel opportunities for women from the most traditional Hindu families, which meant that this was an incredibly exciting time for them (A. Gold 1988: 217). As a laudable religious activity sanctioned by *dharma*, pilgrimage was also socially acceptable conspicuous consumption, whereas other sorts of status expenditure may have been seen as frivolous or wasteful. All these considerations indicate that "pilgrims" can and often do have multiple motives at the same time.

Another problem with this strict pilgrim/tourist dichotomy is that it assumes that the past was somehow different from the present. Is this true, and if so, how far back does one have to go to find this? As but one example of how little things have changed, for many years Haridvar's largest religious festival coincided with the biggest marketplace in North India. Many visitors then had no problem doing business and bathing in the Gaṅgā, although they presumably did these at different times! Furthermore, contemporary travelers' descriptions clearly show that this holy event was marked by thefts, confidence games, prostitution, gambling, and various "secular" entertainments.

Visitors with a variety of motives are encountered at the *tīrtha*s. In the same way, individual pilgrims' self-understandings of their journey can also be different. Some people may adhere to traditional understandings, seemingly unchanged for hundreds of years, while others are constructing new interpretations for existing practice. Yet there also remains a deep-seated conviction that these places have something to offer visitors—whether natural beauty, powerful *darśana*s, productive social interactions, or the guidance of a "saint"—if they will allow this to happen. Although this power is felt to be real, it is not automatic but depends on the individual's response and participation. In the end, a pilgrimage will mean something different to each person, and the major factor in generating such meaning will be the religious quality of their individual lives, since from a purely behavioral standpoint two people may perform the same action but understand it very differently. This emotional commitment and involvement may be the reason why the traditional texts claim that a person with faith gets the benefits of a *tīrtha*, while one without faith merely gets a bath.

This section has discussed some possible reasons why pilgrims travel and has focused on their individual choices and understandings, since the decision to travel is an individual choice. Yet people's religious lives take place in a larger cultural context, in which larger cultural forces shape the pilgrim choices. The following section will examine pilgrimage in the context of the forces that drive larger numbers of people, especially economic forces, politics, and religious conflict. If a complete analysis needs to take into account "the production and management of meaning by various interest groups involved in the pilgrimage" (1988: 63), as van der Veer insists, then such factors cannot be ignored.

ECONOMICS, POLITICS, AND SOCIETY: COOPERATION, CO-OPTATION, CONTESTATION

As the products of a particular religious and cultural process, *tīrtha*s carry great symbolic weight. Their importance is actively upheld and promoted by groups with interests in these places, particularly interests based on sectarian loyalties, on competition for patronage, on the struggle to control local resources, and for political gain. Such conflicting forces have meant that *tīrtha*s have high potential to be contested places, and this has often been true.

A pervasive but relatively innocuous contest involves claims about the primacy of sacred places, which can be seen in the Purāṇas and even more in the Sthalapurāṇas or local sacred texts. Such texts promise great rewards for visiting a particular *tīrtha* and compare this with the merit gained by visiting other sites, which is invariably less than the merit from the site the text is promoting. Most pilgrims recognize the nature of this genre and take such claims and promises in stride.

More serious competition arises when groups contest with each other for the same sacred place; this desire to control a site usually stems from competition for power, patronage, and prestige. Fierce competition is an everyday reality for businesses, such as pilgrim lodging houses and restaurants, but in many other cases, the contesting groups have worked out an amicable arrangement. For example, the *tīrtha purohita*s in most *tīrtha*s have worked out an arrangement based on a pilgrim's ancestral village, with each family drawing its *jajmān*s (pilgrim clients) from a different Indian region or regions. In the case of temples, families of local priests often take turns as the temple's resident custodians. During their tenure they are entitled to the offerings that are given, but they are also responsible for carrying out the necessary rites (Case 2000: 78).

Given this direct link with people's livelihood, competition is often particularly strong when large numbers of pilgrims are expected, and occasionally such contests break out into open violence or criminal activity, as one group tries to oust the other by force or guile. One excellent contemporary example is with the sometimes homicidal competition between Ayodhya pilgrimage priests (van der Veer 1988: 241–59), but there are many earlier examples. Both Abū al-Faẓl Allāmī (1972: 422–24) and al-Badā'ūnī (1976: 94–95) report a battle in April 1567 between two ascetic groups at Thanesar, which arose when one claimed that the other had usurped its right to claim the offerings there. Competition for prestige and patronage lie beneath many of the bloody conflicts that have marked the *kumbha melā*s, as various ascetic groups have sought primacy in the bathing order and the control over the site that this would imply. Such control had economic as well as ritual implications, and it is no accident that in three of the four *kumbha melā* sites—Haridvar, Allahabad, and Ujjain—the dominant ascetic groups were heavily vested in the local economy. In the eighteenth century, the primary rivalry was between the Śaiva and the Vaiṣṇava *akhāṛā*s, resulting in battles in Haridvar (1760) and in Tryambakesvar (1789). In the twentieth century, the primary tensions have been within the Śaiva *akhāṛā*s, and these erupted into violence in 1998. As the social circumstances have changed, so has the dynamic between competing groups.

The role of some regional empires

Given the *tīrtha*s' symbolic importance, they have often played a central role in Hindu life, but the social effects have often been far more positive than those just described. According to many historians, the economic and political strategy of medieval regional kingdoms emphasized patronage of the great temples, such as the Tirupati temple and the Jagannātha temple in Puri (Stein 1961; Kulke and Rothermund 1998: 137). These temples were important redistributors of the kingdom's economic resources. Large land grants to these temples meant a steady flow of grain. In turn the temples loaned money to the villages, thus maintaining economic control of the realm. The rulers considered these temples' presiding deities as their state deities (Mukherjee 1977: xii) and, in some cases, claimed to rule as the deity's deputy, thus upholding the sacred order. In other cases, kings patronized temples as a strategy to confer legitimacy. The Srirangam temple received considerable patronage from various South Indian dynasties, since this temple's primary image is Raṅganātha, Viṣṇu as the divine monarch. Such image-building even cut across religious lines. Even though Tipū Sulṭān Fath ʿAlī Khān was a Muslim, his capital at Srirangapatnam featured a Raṅganātha temple, and this powerful symbolism would have helped legitimate his rule in the eyes of his Hindu subjects.

Temple-building and patronage were significant element in many regional empires. The Cōḻa dynasty constructed many temples as symbols of their royal power and authority, such as at Thanjavur (Tanjore) and Gaṅgaikoṇḍacōḻapuram (Nilakanta Sastri 1963), and many of these temples ultimately became pilgrimage places. Following their example, many other South Indian regional Hindu kingdoms, including the Gurjāra-Praithāras, Pālas, Gajapatis, and later Vijayanagara, were energetic in building and endowing temples, which served as major links in pilgrimage networks.

With Marāṭhā ascendancy these same effects became evident in North Indian *tīrtha*s, which were reshaped by Marāṭhā patronage and piety. By 1680 Marāṭhās had replaced Rājpūts as the primary donors at Varanasi, Allahabad, Puri, and Gaya; such patronage was partly to underscore their claim to come from a lineage as illustrious as the Rājpūts. These claims were reinforced by lavish building projects. The houses of Holkar and Scindia both built huge stone bathing *ghāṭ*s in Varanasi, and Queen Abhalyābāī Holkar is largely responsible for constructing the present Viśvanātha temple (C. Bayly 1983: 137). As Marāṭhā influence widened, so did their largesse; Abhalyābāī is also said to have built the Kuṣāvarta Ghāṭ at Haridvar, a tradition attested by a plaque on the *ghāṭ*. Aside from their bequests, royal pilgrimages were a major economic stimulus to the regions through which they traveled, since they tended to travel in large companies (Deleury 1987: 195).

After the East India Company became the primary commercial and territorial power in India, the Company also assumed the role of the guardian formerly held by these regional empires. Protection of Indian religious customs and institutions was at the heart of the "Cornwallis Code" of 1793 (Cassels 1988: 1); this was reiterated in Queen Victoria's Proclamation of 1858, which explicitly pledged that the government would not interfere in her subjects' religious lives (R. Muir 1923: 382–83). Under the rubric of guardianship, the "East India Company played a prominent role in the administration of a Pilgrim Tax at three places—Gaya, Allahabad, and Puri" (Cassels 1988: 16). Under the Company, tax was levied on pilgrims to the Jagannātha temple in Puri, although there were some tax-exempt classes of pilgrims, such as *daṇḍī svāmī*s and *sādhu*s (Mukherjee 1977). In doing so, the Company was functioning appropriately as the local "ruler"—in upholding established custom—but this practice eventually ended because of opposition from English evangelical groups.

In addition to collecting pilgrim taxes at religious sites under its jurisdiction, the Company took on the responsibility for maintaining public order. After the Marāṭhās ceded much of Uttar Pradesh to the Company in 1803, the Company took responsibility for keeping order at the annual Haridvar fair, which combined a religious festival with the most important marketplace in North India. Haridvar's security needs were particularly pronounced during the *kumbha melā*s, given the history of sometimes sanguinary conflict between various ascetic groups. The Company not only stationed troops to maintain order at the fair, but it also enforced the "traditional" bathing order—an order which reflected the relative power of these groups when the Company arrived. The basic impulse behind all this was to safeguard life and property, which the British saw as integral to their colonial mandate.

This responsibility continued after Company rule gave way to empire, and in order to do this the colonial government was often forced into greater involvement with pilgrimage arrangements. One textbook case was the cholera epidemic of 1867, which began at the *kumbha melā* in Haridvar but was carried by pilgrims returning home by train to virtually every part of India. The government was reluctant to ban large religious festivals, since this would be considered undue interference in religious affairs, and so it responded by taking a greater public role in ensuring public health and safety at large pilgrim gatherings, especially the *kumbha melā*s.

These same patterns persist in independent India, even though it is a secular democracy. Religious gatherings such as the *kumbha melā* are still funded and regulated by the state governments, partly because of the government's responsibility for pilgrims' health and safety, and partly because local governments simply cannot fund and manage such enormous festivals. State governments have also used the appeal to popular welfare as a reason to take direct charge of religious institutions. Temple management at many important pilgrimage sites—among them Badrinath, Puri, and Tirupati—has been taken from the traditional owners and vested in a temple committee; such changes have often caused major changes in the distribution of the offerings at these places. The most recent case of this kind is the thirteen kilometer *yātrā* route to Vaiṣṇo Devī, which the government of Jammu and Kashmir took over in 1986. This action has resulted in much better facilities for pilgrims but was clearly detrimental to the traditional caretakers (Vasudev 2002).

Interreligious contestation

Contest for sacred places reveals another dimension when different religious groups are involved, especially when such conflicts have political implications. The most fruitful resolutions of such conflicts have come when such contests have resulted in multiple sites in a place, which magnifies their importance. Two examples where this happened are Ujjain and Kancipuram—both of which were royal capitals during their history, and both of which contain important Hindu sectarian sites.

Similar accommodation can be seen in Hindu interaction with Jaina and Buddhist pilgrimage traditions. Jainas, Buddhists, and Hindus share common cultural roots, and pilgrimage is an important activity for all three. The most important Jaina religious figures are the *tīrthaṅkara*s (ford-makers), the teachers who build the "fords" to make it possible for humans to cross the ocean of rebirths. The concept of a holy person as a *tīrtha*, which is well established in Hinduism (Bharati 1970: 89), is also applied to Jaina monks. During the four monsoon months when Jaina monks traditionally stay in one place, lay people undertake *tīrthayātrā* to seek the benefit of "crossing." During the rest of the year, Jaina monks themselves are like mobile *tīrtha*s (McCormick 1997: 240). These same patterns can also be seen for contemporary Buddhist monks and pilgrimage sites.

Many Buddhist and Jaina sacred places have been at least partly adopted by Hindus as well, although both groups are presently asserting a more separate identity, especially those Buddhists (like the Māhārs) who have converted to escape the disadvantages of the caste system. Nevertheless, there are several sacred places where Hindu, Jaina, and Buddhist sacred spots exist in close proximity (Schwartzberg 1978: 22). Among the most prominent are Varanasi and Gaya, in which major Hindu and Buddhist sacred spots are within a few miles of each other. There are also several places where two groups have temples in the same site, such as at Muktinath in Nepal (Hindu and Buddhist temples) and Junagadh and Girnar in Gujarat (Hindu and Jaina temples). Of course, in some cases these sacred sites have simply changed hands, such as Badrinath in the Himālayas. In earlier times this seems to have been a Buddhist site, but it has become one of the *cār dhām*s marking the boundaries of Hindu culture (Fonia 1998: 95–96).

Such intrareligious contests have not always been cooperatively resolved, especially when such competition reflects claims of identity. The early twentieth century saw the struggle between the Akālī Sikhs and the Udāsī *mahant*s (abbots) who controlled many important Sikh centers (K. Singh 1966: 193–216). Among these contested centers were Nankana Sahib, which is the birthplace of the first Sikh *guru*, Nānak; another central site was the Harimandir ("golden temple") in Amritsar, which has become the Sikh community's administrative headquarters. The Udāsīs are Hindu ascetics with close historical links to the Sikhs, since the order was founded by Sirī Cand, Nānak's eldest son. The twentieth-century Akālī struggle for control of these places was based on their claim that Sikhs were a separate religious community and should therefore control their religious sites. This conflict raised many thorny issues that further separated the two communities, such as removing images of Hindu deities at these sites, which Sikhs considered at odds with their monotheistic faith. In the end, the control was wrested from the *mahant*s and vested in an elected Sikh body, the Shiromani Gurdwara Prabandhak Committee.

Hindu-Sikh relationships have affected pilgrimage places in more recent times. As Sikh separatism in Punjab peaked during the 1980s, this sharply reduced the number of Sikh pilgrims going to the goddess shrines in Himachal Pradesh. Thus religious boundaries between Hindu and Sikh pilgrimage centers, at one time rather blurred, have now become clearer from the local to the national levels.

The most powerful and widespread intrareligious conflict has historically run along Hindu-Muslim lines, yet the influence of Islamic rule was not always pernicious. Some Hindu holy places received grants and remission of taxes from Muslim rulers, including Jalāluddīn Akbar and Salīm Jahāngīr, whereas several Hindu rulers imposed pilgrim taxes on Hindu pilgrims (Kane 1968–77, 4: 571–72). In addition, the advent of Islam in India brought the activity of the Ṣūfī saints, whose tombs often served as gathering places for people from many religious communities (Bhardwaj 1987: 457–68). It is easy to sketch a picture of a divided nation (Hindu against Muslim), but at the grass roots the picture is far more complex.

Nevertheless, certain Muslim rulers have had a profound impact on Hindu holy places, whether historians soft-pedal this impact (Ikram 1964: 24–26) or whether they acknowledge it (Rizvi 1987: 14–15, 138; Kulke and Rothermund 1998: 152–70). One clear example is Somnath, a major pilgrimage center in Gujarat, which was desecrated and destroyed by Maḥmūd of Ghazna in 1025 CE (Wolpert 1993: 106–7) and abandoned as a pilgrimage place until it was rebuilt in 1952. In the same way, numerous temples in Thanesar and Kanauj were reduced to the ground, and the latter never recovered from Maḥmūd's raid in 1017. During the Mughal empire, Aurangzēb ʿĀlamgīr became notorious for razing several important temples, including Mathura's Kṛṣṇajanmabhūmi and Varanasi's Viśvanātha—both destroyed in 1669.

It is easy to stereotype such destruction as Islamic religious fanaticism—and Maḥmūd called himself the "breaker of idols"—but other motives were always present. One of

Maḥmūd's important reasons for going to Somnath was to plunder its fabulous wealth, and his long series of annual raids (from 1001 to 1027) were clearly motivated by economic as well as religious goals. In Aurangzēb's case, there is speculation that these temples were destroyed not only to reflect religious zeal but also to assert his political authority over his Hindu subjects. One sign of this is that he built the ʿĀlamgīr mosque on the site of the razed Viśvanātha temple, and this would have powerfully underlined contemporary political realities.

In other cases, Hindu pilgrimage places were eclipsed for less direct reasons. Multan (now in Pakistan) declined partly because its hinterland had become predominantly Muslim but also because the Sun cult became less important to Hindus. Some *tīrtha*s stubbornly persisted in spite of repeated desecration, in particular Varanasi. Between 1194 and 1669 CE, numerous temples were razed by figures such as Quṭbuddīn Aibek, ʿAlā'uddīn Khaljī, and Aurangzēb (Kane 1968–77, 4: 631–32; Rizvi 1987: 138), yet despite this, Varanasi continued to occupy its status as one of the holiest Hindu *tīrtha*s. Perhaps one reason for this was Varanasi's traditional importance as a seat of learning, which fostered the conservation of traditional Hindu culture.

Tīrthas and contemporary politics

As mentioned before, during the past millennium many Hindu pilgrimage sites suffered at the hands of Muslim raiders and rulers—whether motivated by iconoclastic zeal, the desire for booty, or the desire to assert political control. In the past generation, a more assertive Hindu nationalism has been seeking to reverse this perceived pattern of injustice and oppression. The most obvious example has been the Vishva Hindu Parishad's struggle to build the Rāmajanmabhūmi temple in Ayodhya. This campaign reached a violent peak on December 6, 1992, when the Parishad and its allies razed the Babri Masjid and thus physically removed it as an obstacle to the temple's construction. The Rāmajanmabhūmi movement has always had clear political implications—not only was it the issue through which the Bharatiya Janata party rose to power but also many of the Parishad's mass action campaigns have coincided with state or national elections, thus using religious issues to maximize political gain. The Parishad eventually scheduled campaigns for *kār sevā* (volunteer construction labor) in Ayodhya during Ayodhya's annual *pañcakrośī yātrā*, the most important annual festival there; this then allowed them to claim that all the pilgrims were there to support their cause.

Another Hindu activist strategy has been to promote religious festivals as a way to create a higher Hindu profile and thus "awaken" Hindus to their political power. One such example is Haridvar's "Kāñvariyā" festival in the month of Śrāvaṇa, at which half a million pilgrims draw water from the Gaṅgā and then carry it on foot as an offering to Śiva. One of the favored spots to offer this water is the Augharnath temple in the eastern part of Meerut district, which means that hundreds of thousands of Hindu men travel through a district with a heavy Muslim population. Although individual pilgrims have their own reasons for doing this rite, their collective numbers make a powerful political statement. Similar political implications can be seen in the annual Amarnath pilgrimage. In the 1990s this became a vehicle to assert a Hindu presence in Muslim-dominated Kashmir, and participation jumped from 10,000 pilgrims in 1990 to 100,000 in 1993 (Joshi 1993).

Another festival with contemporary political significance is the *kumbha melā*, which has always reflected larger societal forces. For many years Haridvar's *kumbha melā* was the largest of all because it coincided with the annual Haridvar fair. When this trade dried up, so did the attendance at Haridvar's *kumbha melā*, only to rise when the *kumbha melā* became a voice and vehicle for nationalist and independence sentiments. Such sentiments have only increased in the recent past. Hindu nationalist sentiments have been a major factor in increasing the attendance at the Ujjain *kumbha melā* (held in the Hindi heartland of Ujjain), which for many years was a relatively minor event. During the 1990s the Vishva Hindu Parishad has used *kumbha* and *ardha kumbha melā*s, particularly those in Allahabad, as a platform to publicize its program. The media attention surrounding these events has only heightened their symbolic importance.

CONCLUSION

Hindu pilgrimage places are vital cultural symbols, and pilgrimage has had a central place throughout Hindu cultural history. Hindu *tīrtha*s are centers of power—either to cross from this world to the eternal liberty of *mokṣa*, or to gain blessings and grace to enrich one's present life. Yet as cultural practices, pilgrimage and pilgrimage places are in continual transformation as the societal forces shaping them are changed. As with any cultural practice, pilgrimage is both a window and mirror, revealing and reflecting the effects of these forces in people's lives. This continues in modern India and has become even more complex as Hinduism in the diaspora has extended Hindu sacred horizons. The diaspora also has political implications, since overseas Hindus who support the Bhartiya Janata party for its perceived support for Hindu values take pride in India as the source of Hindu civilization. Although Hindu *tīrtha*s and *tīrthayātrā* have roots in the sacred texts, their meaning in Hindu life is pervasive and not limited to a quest for holiness. *Tīrtha*s are powerful, culturally dynamic places, which serve as the reservoirs of Hindu beliefs. They are socially constructed and hence always in the process of becoming. *Tīrthayātrā* to these places is an expression of the richness and variety of life and culture within India and wherever else in the world Hindus are settled.

PART VII

LINGUISTIC AND PHILOSOPHIC ANALYSIS

CHAPTER TWENTY-TWO

BHĀṢĀ

Madhav M. Deshpande

The role of language in the Hindu tradition raises complex questions for a number of reasons. Chronologically, the languages used by the Hindus for religious expression have varied for reasons of pure linguistic change over time as well as through migrations and adoption of this religion by different communities in South Asia and elsewhere. While there tends to be a greater linguistic unity at the higher end of Hindu religious and philosophic expression, as one looks at the middle and the lower levels of the Hindu society, the languages vary considerably in different regions as well as in different social strata. Therefore, it is difficult to make broad generalizations about religious language as used by all Hindus. One must look at the specific social and regional contexts. The role of language in the religious tradition also needs to be looked at from various points of view, for example, the faculty of language, the role of specific languages, ritual performance of language, particular manifestations of language in various forms of texts, their reification into scriptural traditions, and the attitudes of the religious community towards all these phenomena.

The Hindu tradition goes back to the prehistoric mergers of various linguistic and cultural communities in the South Asian region. The two main prehistoric sources of this tradition lie in the Indus Valley civilization, on the one hand, and the migrations of the Indo-European speakers, on the other. As far as the Indus Valley civilization is concerned, its linguistic identity has not been conclusively determined, and the suggestions regarding its language range from Dravidian and Munda to some form of Indo-Āryan. In any case, since the linguistic identity of the Indus Valley civilization has not been fully established, we cannot say much about the role of language in that tradition at this point. The Indo-European tradition and its proposed invasion or migration into South Asia are also hotly debated, along with the suggestion coming from some that Sanskrit originated in India and was the mother of the Indo-European (and other) languages. We need not go into these debates here, except note that most of the languages of modern North India are members of the Indo-European language family, and Sanskrit, and particularly Vedic Sanskrit, is the oldest known language of this family in South Asia. As the language of the Vedas, the formal scriptures of the Hindu tradition, Sanskrit plays a very important role. Related to Sanskrit are a whole range of ancient vernaculars, generically called Prakrit, which were used as languages of religious expression by the Jainas and the Buddhists in ancient times, explicitly in opposition to the Sanskrit language used by the Brāhmaṇical tradition. The interactions among these various traditions and their conflicts and compromises over linguistic issues are an important part of the religious history of South Asia. In later times, vernacular languages throughout South Asia emerge as vehicles of devotional approaches to god, again in opposition to the Sanskrit language used by the Brāhmaṇ elites, and there are interesting conflicts and compromises between upholders of the prominence of various language varieties. These also form a significant part of the religious history of South Asia.

LANGUAGE IN THE VEDIC PERIOD

Early Vedic literature

The Vedic scriptural texts (1500–500 BCE) consist of four ancient collections, that is, the *Ṛg Veda*, the *Sāma Veda*, the *Yajur Veda*, and the *Atharva Veda*. These collections of hymns, ritual formulae, and recitations of many sorts have come down to us in various recensions. The next layer of Vedic texts consists of prose ritual commentaries that offer procedures, justifications, and explanations. These are called Brāhmaṇas. The last two categories of Vedic literature are the Āraṇyakas (forest texts) and the Upaniṣads (secret mystical doctrines). The Vedic texts are composed in different varieties of archaic Sanskrit, and the most ancient form of this archaic Sanskrit is found in the hymns of the *Ṛg Veda*. The Vedic texts are traditionally called *śruti* (heard texts) referring to their early oral transmission.

The word "*saṃskṛta*" is not known as a label of a language variety during the Vedic period. The general term used for language in the Vedic texts is *vāk*, a word historically related to "voice." The Vedic poet sages belonged to communities which are designated by the term "*ārya*," and they refer to non-Vedic outsiders by various terms, such as *dāsa* and *dasyu*. It is evident that they perceived significant differences between their own language and the languages of the outsiders. Similarly, they perceived important differences between their own use of language in mundane contexts and the use of language directed toward gods. The gods are generically referred to by the term "*deva*," and the language of the hymns is said to be *devī vāk* (divine language). This language is divine in the sense that it is believed to have been created by the gods themselves. The language thus created by the gods is then spoken by the animate world in various forms. The divine language in its ultimate form is so mysterious that three-quarters of it are said to be hidden from the humans who have access only to a quarter of it. The Vedic poet sages say that this divine language enters into their hearts and that they discover it through mystical introspection. The poet sages consider themselves to be craftsmen of language. They do not create it, but they shape the form of the religious expression by selecting the best expressions and leaving out the uncultured expressions. The process is explicitly compared to cleansing the grain with a sieve. This provides us with a distinction between the language in its common use and the language that is deliberately chosen and fashioned for its appeal to the gods. Just as the language used by the Vedic poet sages is the divine language, the language used by the non-Vedic people is said to be un-godly (*adevī*) or demonic (*asuryā*). The Vedic Āryans called their non-Vedic opponents *mṛdhravāk* (people with confused language).

The different uses of language are referred to by different verbs in the Vedas. For instance, we have verbs like "to praise," "to sing," "to invoke," each of which denotes a specific function of the scriptural language. The reification of various forms of language is also manifest in the Vedas in the use of various nouns, such as "praise," "song," "honeyed speech," "chant," "benediction," and "desires." The language is not only an act but also a reified object, it gradually appears in many more conceptual frames. Instead of simply saying "I praise God Indra," the Vedic poet says: "I direct my words of praise to Indra, like swift horses." Consider the following passages in the Vedic literature:

> With my words, I praise the wise Agni who is the essential means of our sacrifice.
> (*Ṛg Veda* 3.27.2)

> O God Agni, you, having been saluted, became the killer of the barbarian.
> (*Śaunakīya Atharva Veda* 1.7.1)

> We invoke Indra with our prayers so that he may have a drink of our *soma* juice.
> (*Ṛg Veda* 3.42.4)

> I make you sinless with my potent incantation.
> (*Śaunakīya Atharva Veda* 2.10.1)

> I crush the germs with potent incantations of Agastya.
> (*Śaunakīya Atharva Veda* 2.32.3)

The reified language objects like "prayer," "praise," and "chant" assume greater potency and durability. These linguistic objects are then looked at as instruments of achieving particular religious goals, as products of particular poet sages, and as objects that can be preserved and perpetuated as a scriptural tradition. For example, when a poet sage says "I crush these germs with the incantation of Agastya," we can see several dimensions of the religious language at work. There is a belief that Agastya produced a particular incantation at a particular time. Then there is the belief that this incantation was very effective in destroying the germs. Further, this widespread belief in the efficacy of Agastya's incantation led to its preservation by the priestly community and its repeated performance by them for the same effect. Here are the seeds for the creation of a scriptural text, which repeated on a massive scale led to the emergence of the voluminous Vedic corpus. The belief in the power of one's own incantations is expressed eloquently in the following passages of the *Śaunakīya Atharva Veda*:

> Whoso, O Maruts, thinks himself to be above us or whoso shall revile our incantation that is being performed for him, let his wrongdoing be burning; the sky shall concentrate its heat upon the hater of potent incantations.
> (2.12.6)

> Sharpened up is this incantation of mine; sharpened up is my heroism and strength; sharpened up and victorious be the warrior of whom I am the priest.
> (3.19.1)

> That incantation by virtue of which the gods do not go apart nor hate each other, we perform in your house; concord be for your men.
>
> (3.30.4)

> I am covered by the incantation-armor.
>
> (17.1.27)

The externalization and reification of language also led to the development of mystical and devotional approaches to it. Language was perceived as an essential tool for approaching the gods, invoking them, asking their favors, and thus for the successful completion of a ritual performance. While the gods were the powers that finally yielded the wishes of their human worshipers, one could legitimately look at the resulting reward as ensuing from the power of the religious language or the power of the performing priest. This way, the language came to be looked upon as having mysterious creative powers and as a divine power that needed to be propitiated before it could be successfully used to invoke other gods. This approach to language ultimately led to deification of language and the emergence of the goddess of speech (*vāk devī*), and a number of other gods who are called "lord of speech" (*brahmaṇaspati*, *bṛhaspati*, *vākpati*). Like offering oblations to gods like Indra and Varuṇa, we also see Vedic priests offering oblations to the goddess of speech and to the various lords of speech.

> When men, O Bṛhaspati, giving names to objects, sent out the first and the earliest utterances of speech, all that was excellent and spotless, treasured within them, was disclosed through their affection.
>
> (*Ṛg Veda* 10.71.1)

> By means of sacrifice they followed the path of speech and they found her entered into [the hearts of] the sages.
>
> (*Ṛg Veda* 10.71.3)

> Speech has been measured out in four divisions; the Brāhmaṇs with insight know them. Three, kept in a deep secret cave, cause no movement; of speech, men speak only the fourth part.
>
> (*Ṛg Veda* 1.164.45)

> Gods created the divine language. Creatures of many kinds speak it. May that pleasing speech, the cow that yields food and drink, being properly praised, come to us.
>
> (*Ṛg Veda* 8.100.11)

Here we notice the divinity of speech and its mysterious existence and powers. In contrast with the valorous deeds of the divine language, the language of the non-Vedic people neither yields fruit nor blossom (*Ṛg Veda*, 10.71.5). "Yielding fruit and blossom" is a phrase indicative of the creative power of speech that produces the rewards for the worshiper. From being a created but divine entity, the speech rises to the heights of being a divinity in her own right and eventually to becoming the substratum of the existence of the whole universe. The deification of speech is seen in hymn 10.125 of the *Ṛg Veda* where the goddess of speech sings her own glory:

> I roam with the Rudras and the Vasus, with the Ādityas too, and all the host of gods. I bear up both Mitra and Varuṇa. I sustain Indra and Agni, and the two Aśvins. I uphold the steaming Soma, and I sustain Tvaṣṭṛ, Pūṣan, and Bhaga. I endow with wealth him who brings an oblation and is a pious sacrificer-pressing Soma. I am the queen, who gathers together the riches. I am the wise one, first among those deserving a sacrifice. Therefore, the gods variously installed me in many places, residing in and entering many abodes. Whoever sees, breathes, or hears what is said eats food only through me. Without knowing, they reside with me. Listen, one and all. I am telling you the truth. I myself say these words that shall be welcome by gods and men. I empower the person I love. I make him a Brāhmaṇ, a seer, and a wise man. I bend the bow for Rudra so that his arrow may destroy the hater of potent words. I create battle for the people, and I pervade heaven and earth. I give birth to my father and set him up at the top. My origin is in the waters in the ocean. From there I pervade all the worlds. I touch the heaven with my head. I alone flow like a blowing wind, holding together all the worlds. Beyond the heaven and beyond the earth, I have become so immense through my power.

In this hymn, one no longer hears of the creation of the speech, but one begins to see the speech as a primordial divinity that creates and controls other gods, sages, and the human beings. Here the goddess of speech demands worship in her own right, before her powers may be used for other purposes.

Late Vedic literature

The "lord of speech" divinities typically emerge as creator divinities, for example, Brahmā, Bṛhaspati, and Brahmaṇaspati, and the word "*brahman*" which earlier refers, with differing accents, to the creative incantation and the priest, eventually in the Upaniṣads comes to assume the meaning of the creative force behind the entire universe. The creative power of the divine language is stressed in a number of Vedic passages. When a spiritually powerful being makes a certain pronouncement, it comes true. The powerful words produce the circumstances that show them to be true. The *Śatapatha Brāhmaṇa* says: "The Creator said to Agni, 'You are Rudra,' and because he gave him that name, Agni assumed that form" (6.1.3.10). This process is often generalized to creation at large. The *Kāṭhaka Saṃhitā* says: "Prajāpati, the Creator, created all creatures. . . . Whatever he spoke with his speech, that happened. Whatever one says with his speech, that happens. . . . He creates it" (7.10). On a more basic level, the Vedic sacrificer looked at the ritual language as a sure means of achieving the fulfillment of his desires:

> Speech indeed yields all desired objects, since one indeed expresses all his desires by means of speech. Speech yields all wishes of him who knows this.
>
> (*Aitareya Āraṇyaka* 1.3.2)

> I shall speak forth this speech, which will declare much, fare far, produce much, gain much, effect more than much, which goes to heaven, which will declare heaven, which will fare to heaven, produce heaven, gain heaven, carry this sacrifice to heaven, and carry the sacrificer—me—to heaven.
>
> (*Aitareya Āraṇyaka* 5.1.5)

While the Vedic hymns were looked upon as being crafted by particular poet sages in the earlier period, gradually their rising mysterious power and their preservation by the successive generations led to the emergence of a new conception of the scriptural texts. Already in the late parts of the *Ṛg Veda* (10.90.9), we hear that the verses (*ṛk*), the songs (*sāma*), and the ritual formulas (*yajus*) arose from the primordial sacrifice offered by the gods. They arose from the sacrificed body of the cosmic man, the ultimate ground of existence. This tendency of increasingly looking at the scriptural texts as not being produced by any human authors takes many forms in subsequent religious and philosophical materials, finally leading to a widespread notion that the Vedas are not only not authored by any human beings (*apauruṣeya*) but are in fact uncreated (*anādi*, without beginning) and eternal (*ananta*, without end), beyond the cycles of creation and destruction of the world. In late Vedic texts, we hear the notion that the Vedas are infinite (*ananta*) and that the Vedas known to human poet sages are a mere fraction of the real infinite Vedas. This shows an expanding conception of the Vedas, their delinking from the human authors and their elevation into transcendental spheres. The humans become mere vehicles for the manifestation of these eternal scriptures.

The Brāhmaṇas: Vedic ritual literature

In the late Vedic traditions of the Brāhmaṇas, the Āraṇyakas, and the Upaniṣads, we find further development of the conceptions regarding language. The Brāhmaṇas are concerned with the ritual use of language. Besides the general notion of efficacy of incantations, the Brāhmaṇas express concern about a number of specific issues. We are told that there is perfection of the ritual form when a recited incantation echoes the ritual action that is being performed. This shows a notion that ideally there should be a match between the contents of a ritual formula and the ritual action in which it is recited. This expectation leads to a heightened concern for maintaining the proper understanding of the preserved ancient incantations, because without a proper understanding of their meaning, one could not ensure their proper application. This led to a number of efforts to preserve the form as well as the understanding of the preserved scriptural texts. The Brāhmaṇas offer etymologies of words to explain their significance and offer justifications for particular applications of particular passages. There is also a greater emphasis on the maintenance of the correct pronunciation of the received texts. For instance, we are told a story of a demon mispronouncing a word during ritual. The demon wanted a son who would kill Indra. Thus, during a sacrifice, he asks for a son who would be Indra's killer. He should have used the word "*indraśatrú*" with the accent on the final syllable. However, the demon erroneously used the word "*índraśatru*" with the accent on the first syllable. With that pronunciation, the word came to mean "he, whose killer is Indra" rather than "Indra's killer" as the demon wanted. The story says that the mispronunciation was rewarded with the birth of a son who was killed by Indra. The texts also emphasize the daily recitation of one's inherited scriptural texts and promise glorious heavenly worlds as its reward.

The Āraṇyakas and the Upaniṣads: "secret Vedic doctrines"

In the Āraṇyakas and the Upaniṣads, one sees a rather different emphasis. Here we shall not make difference between the Āraṇyakas and the Upaniṣads, since many well-known Upaniṣads are themselves Āraṇyakas or parts of Āraṇyakas. Language acquires importance in several different ways in these traditions. Both in ritual and philosophical contexts, various persons attain a status of high eminence through their skill in priestly debate (*brahmodya*). In a slow shift from the tradition of the Brāhmaṇas, the Upaniṣads, without denying the rewards of rituals, generally suggest that the rewards of all rituals are limited and that the performance of rituals finally traps the performer in the cycles of births and deaths. The rewards of ritual, and the general good and bad rewards of one's actions (*karma*), define the nature of one's future births, such that one reaps the fruits of one's past actions during those subsequent births. The Upaniṣads, emphasizing the painful nature of these cycles of rebirths, point out that the ideal goal should be to put an end to these cycles of birth and rebirth and to find one's permanent identity with the original ground of the universal existence, that is, *brahman*. Putting an absolute end to the accumulation of *karma* through renunciation of possessions and withdrawal from binding ritual obligations is now the advised alternative. This shift in the goal leads to a gradual movement away from the rituals in the direction of a meditative life. As part of this meditative practice, one is asked to practice the meditation aided by the sacred syllable *oṃ*, which is the symbolic representation of *brahman*. Here the language, in the form of *oṃ*, becomes the tool for the attainment of one's mystical union with *brahman*, the ground of the universal existence. The syllable itself is explained as consisting of the elements *a*, *u*, and *m*, but finally ending with a portion of silence. These elements are said to represent different states of one's consciousness, the silence representing the final merger with *brahman*. Moving away from the knowledge of the Vedic chants (*mantra*), the Upaniṣads redirect a seeker toward the realization of the ultimate reality of *brahman*:

> Two kinds of knowledge must be known, this is what all who know *brahman* tell us, that is, the higher and the lower knowledge. The lower knowledge is the *Ṛg Veda*, *Yajur Veda*, *Sāma Veda*, *Atharva Veda*, and so on, but the higher knowledge is that by which the indestructible *brahman* is comprehended.
>
> (*Muṇḍaka Upaniṣad* 1.1.4–5)

> Respected Sir, thus I am only a knower of the ritual chants (*mantra*), but not a knower of the self. I have heard from people like your honor that a knower of the self crosses beyond grief. Sir, I am in grief. Please help me cross beyond grief.
>
> (*Chāndogya Upaniṣad* 7.1.3)

While the Upaniṣads shift the focus from the ritualistic understanding and application of the Vedas and treat the traditional Vedic collections as a lower form of knowledge, their spiritual quest is not completely delinked from linguistic concerns. The prominent tool for focusing upon *brahman* is now the syllable *oṃ*, the supreme syllable. The Sanskrit word "*akṣara*" refers to a syllable, but it also means "indestructible." Thus, the word "*akṣara*" allowed the meditational use of *oṃ* to ultimately reach one's experiential identity with the indestructible reality of *brahman*. The role of language and scripture in the Upaniṣadic mode of religious life is complicated. The traditional Vedas are perceived as advocating the wrong path of ritual action. The traditional gods of the Vedic religion are viewed as being almost an impediment to a seeker of *brahman*. Hence the use of language to invoke these gods becomes a lower goal. Can *brahman* be reached through language? Since *brahman* is beyond all characterizations and all modes of human perception, no linguistic expression can properly describe it. Hence all linguistic expressions and all knowledge framed in language are inadequate for the purpose of reaching *brahman*. In fact, it is silence that characterizes *brahman* and not words. Even so, the use of *oṃ*-focused meditation is emphasized at least in the nonfinal stages of *brahman*-realization. However, the Upaniṣadic practices and goals were practically beyond the reach of everyone. Therefore, the Upaniṣads represent an exclusive and elite tradition with rather limited participation. On the other hand, the religion of rituals, though requiring specialized priestly skills, offered relatively greater opportunity of participation, and its goals remained attractive to a larger proportion of people. Therefore, it continued unabated, and with it the ritual use of language.

POST-VEDIC DEBATES ON SCRIPTURAL TEXTS

Efforts to preserve the Vedas

As we gradually enter the post-Vedic period, the preservation of the ancient scriptural texts and their utility become subjects of very important debates. Some of the problems with the handling of the scriptures are created merely by the historical linguistic changes. The language of the ancient scriptures was increasingly becoming archaic, and a large percentage of the vocabulary and grammar of the ancient language did not survive in the newer forms of Sanskrit. Similarly, the time-gap, the migrations, and the cultural and ethnic contacts and mergers changed the pronunciation significantly, so that a number of features like the accents of the ancient language were lost in the later forms of Sanskrit. Under such conditions, the maintenance of the form and the understanding of the ancient texts became increasingly precarious. The beginning of such concerns is already manifest in the late Vedic texts. We have already seen such concerns regarding origins of words and the recitation with proper accents. By the end of the late Vedic period, we already see the beginning of some formal efforts to deal with this situation. It is manifested in the creation of multiple forms of recitation. There was the original undivided text of the scriptures that was handed down by the tradition orally. This text was called Saṃhitā, the joined unbroken form of recitation. A new form of word-by-word (*padapāṭha*) recitation was now created, and an understanding of word combinations was developed. This subsequently led to the development of the traditions of Sanskrit grammar, etymology, and phonetics.

Saṃhitā: (abcdefg . . .)
agnimīḷepurohitaṃyajñasyadevamṛtvijam . . . (*Ṛg Veda* 1.1.1)

Padapāṭha: (a / b / c / d / e / f / g / . . .)
agnim / īḷe / puraḥ-hitam / yajñasya / devam / ṛtvijam / . . .

Kramapāṭha: (ab / bc / cd / de / ef / fg / . . .)
agnimīḷe / īḷepurohitam / purohitaṃyajñasya / . . .

Jaṭāpāṭha: (abbaab / bccbbc / cddccd / deedde / effeef / fggffg / . . .)
agnimīḷaīḷegnimagnimīḷe / īḷepurohitampurohitamīḷaīḷepurohitam / . . .

Ghanapāṭha: (abbaabccbaabc / bccbbcddcbbcd / cddccdeedccde / . . .)
agnimīḷaīḷegnimagnimīḷepurohitampurohitamīḷegnimagnimīḷepurohitam / īḷepurohitampurohitamīḷaīḷepurohitaṃyajñasyayajñasyapurohitamīḷaīḷepurohitaṃyaj ñasya / . . .

The word-by-word (*padapāṭha*) version of the Vedic texts increasingly came to be viewed as the basic text from which the normal text of the Vedas, their continuous recitation, was deemed to be constructed by applying rules of morphophonemic combinations. By using various permutations and combinations of the words of the *padapāṭha*, numerous other versions of the Vedic texts were produced and have been kept alive in the recitational tradition till today. The recitational preservation of these various permutations and combinations was perceived to be a sure way of preserving the original Vedic text and protecting it from even the slightest change. Even the slightest change in the original would lead to hundreds of changes in the permutations and combinations, and hence if the permutations and combinations were fixed, the original could always be restored, in case of doubt. This way, the body of the Vedic texts came to be preserved with a great degree of accuracy, especially when the tradition was passed down entirely in oral transmission.

Emergence of phonetic analysis and description

A great deal of care was also given to ensuring the proper pronunciation of the Vedic texts. As the priestly communities migrated to different regions of South Asia, their mother tongues underwent great changes. With the increasing gap between the language of the original Vedic texts and the mother tongues of the reciters, there was a growing fear of mispronunciation of the scriptural texts. The Vedic accents were no longer observed in either the colloquial forms of Sanskrit or in the vernaculars. Many vowels and consonants of the Vedic Sanskrit did not occur in the vernaculars, the mother tongues of the reciters. It is clear from the modern recitation of the Vedic texts that the mother tongues of the reciters affect the recitation of these texts, and the same Vedic texts sound different if recited by a Bengali or a Tamil Brāhmaṇ priest. The fear of mispronunciation led to the development a full-scope tradition of phonetic analysis that is preserved in over a hundred different treatises called Śikṣās and Prātiśākhyas. These treatises analyze the articulatory features of each Sanskrit sound and point out specific mispronunciations to be avoided. On the whole, one must recognize that there was a great deal of success in preserving the phonetic shape of the Vedic texts.

Etymology and meaning

However, the efforts to preserve a comprehension of the ancient Vedic texts were not equally successful, though they mark some important developments in the scientific investigation into the nature of words and their origins. One of the early debates regarding the analytical understanding of words is found in Yāska's *Nirukta*, around 500 BCE. Yāska's *Nirukta* is a commentary on a list of Vedic words (*Nighaṇṭu*). Yāska says that the original sages (*ṛṣi*) had direct insight into the nature of things. These original sages received the Vedic texts in their mystical trances. They handed down these texts to later generations of sages who did not have such a direct insight into the nature of things. They transmitted these texts to later generations, who were worried about the survival of the transmission and produced the list of Vedic words as an aid. This perception of a gradual decline from an initial golden age is found in many post-Vedic traditions, and their efforts to preserve the texts and their comprehension need to be understood against the background of this perception of decline.

Yāska recognizes a problem in using the word-by-word (*padapāṭha*) text of the scriptures as it was available by his time. He says that we must first understand the meaning of a scriptural text before we can split it up into its component words. In trying to make sense of words, Yāska carries forward the tradition of (folk-)etymology that had made its appearance already in the late Vedic Brāhmaṇa texts. There is a greater emphasis in Yāska's work on the nouns rather than the verbs of the scriptural language. Yāska and a few grammarians proposed that all nouns are to be derived by adding affixes to verb-roots. On the other hand, he also refers to others who argued that not all nouns can be thus derived and that there must be some underived nouns. Some of the etymologies are regular and convincing, while others are irregular and some downright desperate. However, Yāska says that one cannot refuse to offer an etymology for a word because that refusal would amount to accepting that the word has no perceptible meaning. Recitation of scriptures without any comprehension of meaning is like carrying a burden. It does not produce any merit. For Yāska the science of etymology becomes an essential tool to understand the meaning of scriptural words. Yāska's efforts are clearly motivated by an old belief that goes back to the Brāhmaṇa texts, namely, that perfection of ritual form (*rūpasamṛddhi*) can only be achieved when the recited verse echoes the ritual action being performed. This requires that one is able to comprehend the meaning of the recited Vedic passages.

Kautsa: "Vedas are meaningless"

However, Yāska represents only one side of the debate. He also refers to an opposing view, that of Kautsa. Kautsa claimed that the science of etymology as a tool for comprehending the meaning of the scriptural texts was worthless because *the Vedas had no meaning at all.* Kautsa claims that the words of the scriptures, unlike those of contemporary Sanskrit, were fixed in order. If the words of the cited Vedic passages were meaningful, the Brāhmaṇas would not have offered their explanations. The Vedic passages, if understood as meaningful utterances, often seem to be contrary to facts of experience and contradictory to each other. Therefore, it is better to accept that they are completely meaningless, and there is a suggestion that their main utility lies in their value as magical sounds and not as meaningful linguistic utterances. Thus, in the opinion of Kautsa, the scriptural texts have been reduced to nonlinguistic magical sounds. This is indeed one direction in which some later traditions deal with sacred utterances. Yāska, on the other hand, insists on the etymological efforts to find out the meaning of scriptural words. The grammarian Patañjali and the Mīmāṃsā author Jaimini later support Yāska's stand. However, this debate makes certain points quite clear. The preserved ancient texts of the Vedas have become at least partially unintelligible due to language change. The texts are no longer considered as human-authored words but as a unitary body of words which are of some divine origin or completely uncreated and ideally should not contradict each other.

Vedas as magical sounds

The view represented by Kautsa that the words of the scriptures are not linguistically meaningful probably hints at the other alternative that they are significant in some magical mystical way. This interpretation of the scriptures finds support with the importance given to mystical utterances like *oṃ* in the Upaniṣads. Some of the ritual practices also hint in this direction. For instance, there is a prescription in an ancillary text of the *Atharva Veda* for the syllable-by-syllable reverse recitation of the popular Gāyatrī-*mantra*. The normal recitation of this chant and its reverse recitation are illustrated below:

Normal: *tat-savitur-vareṇyaṃ-bhargo-devasya-dhīmahi-dhiyo-yo-naḥ-pracodayāt* ।

Reverse: *yāt-da-co-pra-naḥ-yo-yo-dhi-hi-ma-dhī-sya-va-de-rgo-bha-yaṃ-ṇī-re-rva-tu-vi-tsa-tat* ।

It is evident that those who believed in the normal as well as the reverse recitation of the chants did not look at these stretches as meaningful normal linguistic utterances but as mystically empowered sounds. It is this dimension of magical sounds that is fully developed later in the traditions of Tantra, where the entire Sanskrit alphabet is invested with mystical powers, each sound being taken to represent some element in the Tantric cosmology, and the combinations of these sounds representing particular natural or divine forces. The strong belief in such mystical significance of Sanskrit sounds is very old, though it becomes more clearly manifest in later times. For example, the late Tantric text *Kāmakalāvilāsa* says: "The supreme Śakti is resplendent. She is both the seed and sprout as the manifested union of Śiva and Śakti. She is very subtle. Her form is manifested through the union of the first letter of the alphabet, 'a,' and the final letter, 'ha' " (3). In such texts, every single letter of the Sanskrit alphabet is looked upon as representing some phase of the manifestation of the creative power, Śakti. Several attempts have been made in modern times to interpret the ancient Vedic texts using the Tantric significance of the sounds of the Sanskrit language. While such efforts are philologically unacceptable to modern scholarship, their very existence reflects a continuity of particular lines of interpretive thinking found in ancient India.

VEDIC TRADITION VERSUS JAINISM AND BUDDHISM

It is clear that the Vedic tradition and the Brāhmaṇical religion as represented in that tradition placed the highest value on the role of Brāhmaṇs, the priests, as well as on the role of Sanskrit, the language of the scriptures preserved and guarded by the priests. Cosmological ideas about the origin of human beings placed the Brāhmaṇ priests above the warriors, who were above the trading castes and the lowly Śūdras. The perceived linguistic hierarchy paralleled the social hierarchy. The Brāhmaṇs placed the highest religious value on the Vedic scriptures and its language, Sanskrit, as the language of the gods. As the human speakers of the language of the gods, the Brāhmaṇs called themselves gods on earth (*bhūdeva*). While the Brāhmaṇical Sanskrit texts generally do not show us the voices of protest from other communities, who were accorded a lower place on the scale of socioreligious status, it is clear that others did not accept the claims of the Brāhmaṇs easily.

The protests against the Brāhmaṇical attitudes and practices are first seen most clearly in the religious traditions of Jainism and Buddhism, which emerge into prominence during the middle of the first millennium BCE. Mahāvīra and Buddha were contemporaries who promulgated two different religious traditions, subsequently known as Jainism and Buddhism, around the fourth century BCE. Both of them were born in princely warrior families in the region to the east of the north-central region of Āryāvarta, the religious center of the Brāhmaṇical tradition. In the dialogues of Mahāvīra and Buddha, we see the resentment of the warriors against the beliefs and practices of the Brāhmaṇs. In contrast with the restrictive strategies of the Brāhmaṇs, which denied access to the Vedic scriptures for large segments of the population, Mahāvīra and Buddha taught their doctrines to everyone and offered the possibility of salvation to everyone. In their zeal to reach the masses, both of these teachers preferred to teach their doctrines in the local Prakrit dialects which could be understood by the masses. This does not mean that they chose the lowly languages just to reach the masses because there is circumstantial evidence that they regarded the Prakrit languages to be languages of high status. The tradition of Theravāda Buddhism regards Pali, the Prakrit used for its canonical texts, to be the original language of all beings. The dialogues of Mahāvīra display an exalted place accorded to the language Ardhamagadhi, the Prakrit used by Mahāvīra. It is said to be the language of the gods, and this vernacular language used by Mahāvīra is said to have been automatically transformed into the languages of the listeners. In the lists of the four social classes, the Buddhists place the Kṣatriyas, the warriors, above the Brāhmaṇs. Thus there are good indications that the Buddhists and Jainas viewed the respective Prakrits used for their canonical texts to be languages of high status and of high religious value.

Both of these traditions questioned the status of Brāhmaṇs and argued for a caste-free access to spiritual life. The Buddhist dialogues show a great deal of criticism of the sacrificial practice of the Brāhmaṇs, their animal sacrifices, their ignorant claims to wisdom and truth, and their caste-centric beliefs of superiority. In doing so, the Buddhists depicted the authors of the Veda, the poet sages, as ignorant fools, and the contemporary Brāhmaṇs as blind followers of the blind. They reinterpreted many Brāhmaṇical terms of high value, such as the caste terms and the three Vedas, to suggest that these terms actually referred to Buddhist values. Buddha not only offered to teach his doctrine of salvation to the Brāhmaṇs, the Buddhists depicted Brāhmaṇical gods as being eager to become disciples of Buddha. We are told that there were Brāhmaṇ converts to Buddhism who wanted to translate the words of Buddha into the language of Chandas (Vedic language) and that this request was soundly rejected. Emperor Aśoka, who supported Buddhism and became himself a Buddhist, used Prakrits, rather than Sanskrit, for all his inscriptions (besides Greek and Aramaic for a few), indicating the high political prestige for the Prakrit languages. This set the stage for a very long and bitter debate about the social and religious status of Sanskrit and Prakrit languages.

Both the Jainas and the Buddhists also appropriated the high-prestige term "*ārya*" for themselves, producing another bitter conflict and debate. The Buddhists considered all those who accepted the path of Buddha to be *ārya*s. Thus, the term "*ārya*" no longer carried a sense of identity by Āryan birth, but it shifted the focus to moral and spiritual values as the determining factor. The Jainas also came up with a long list of various criteria for inclusion in the newly defined Āryan community. The Ardhamagadhi and the Pali Prakrits are now claimed to be the Āryan languages par excellence, and this poses a great challenge to the traditional conceptions of the Brāhmaṇical tradition. The Jaina and the Buddhist traditions openly admit that it is acceptable to use any language of convenience to communicate the religious doctrine to a willing listener. For the Buddhists and Jainas, the use of language is primarily a tool to communicate their religious message to anyone who is willing to listen, and hence the insistence on a particular language is not a characteristic feature of these traditions. Thus, in spite of the feeling of high prestige for Ardhamagadhi and Pali in these traditions, they were open to the notions of translations and vernacular explanations of their teachings.

This early preference for vernaculars in Buddhism and Jainism was eventually abandoned, and both the traditions gradually switch to the use of Sanskrit. The use of Sanskrit remained limited to expository and commentarial literature in Jainism, it never extended to scriptural texts. On the other hand, many later traditions of Indian Buddhism, including the Vaibhāṣikas, the Sautrāntikas, the Lokottaravādins, and the various Mahāyāna schools, began to exclusively use Sanskrit for their scriptural texts and philosophical and commentarial literature. This shift in favor of Sanskrit may have been motivated by the rising prestige of Sanskrit in post-Mauryan India. A similar shift is also noticed in the language of inscriptions from Prakrit to Sanskrit beginning around second century CE.

BRĀHMAṆICAL RESPONSE AND EMERGENCE OF POST-VEDIC HINDUISM

The rise of Jainism and Buddhism shaped the nature of Hinduism, both scholastic and popular, as it emerged in later times. It absorbed some of the ideals of both of these traditions, such as the more widespread practice of vegetarianism prompted by their emphasis on the doctrine of nonviolence (*ahiṃsā*). However, in other areas, the Brāhmaṇical tradition offered stiff resistance to the arguments offered by the Jainas and Buddhists. The response of the Brāhmaṇical tradition to the opposing traditions took many forms, but here we shall only focus on language-related issues. The main linguistic arguments came from the Sanskrit grammarians, the Mīmāṃsākas (ritualists) and the Naiyāyikas (logicians). The authors of the Hindu Dharmaśāstras also offered arguments.

Hindu lawbooks (smṛti)

Manu's Lawbook (*Manusmṛti*, 200–100 BCE) seems to reject outright the lax definitions of caste terms offered by the Buddhists and the Jainas and their redefinition of the notion of who was *ārya*. Manu's statements make it quite clear that the caste identity of a person is strictly defined by his or her birth, and moral qualities play only a secondary role. Manu, who says that one's identity as an *ārya* is strictly defined by one's birth, also discusses the question of language. In the world, there are non-*ārya*s who look like *ārya*s, and they may even speak like *ārya*s. However, unless they are born *ārya*s, they are not *ārya*s. The moral definitions of who is a true Brāhmaṇ, as offered by the Buddhists, Jainas, and others, were clearly unacceptable to Hindu legal writers. The Dharmaśāstra writers held steadfastly to their view that the Brāhmaṇs were the primary custodians of the Vedic scriptures. They were the only ones who could learn, teach, and use the Vedas. The communities of Kṣatriyas, the warriors, and the Vaiśyas, the trading castes, were deemed worthy of studying the Vedas, but they were not allowed to teach them. The Brāhmaṇs officiated as priests at the Vedic rituals performed by hosts from these communities. As for the Śūdras, they were completely beyond the reach of the Vedas. They were not only not supposed to study the Vedas, they were not supposed to even hear these texts being recited. The Brāhmaṇs were advised to stop reciting the Vedas, if they suspected that a Śūdra might listen to their recitation. Women were also treated the same way. In Brāhmaṇical rites, the women were mostly silent partners, with relatively little occasion to speak up. It is certain that over time the gap between the Brāhmaṇs and the Kṣatriyas and the Vaiśyas widened, and in medieval times, the Brāhmaṇs came to believe that there were no genuine Kṣatriyas and Vaiśyas left in the world and that the only two communities were Brāhmaṇs and Śūdras. Thus, the access to the Vedas became eventually restricted only to the Brāhmaṇs. There is a good deal of historical evidence that in the seventeenth, eighteenth, and nineteenth centuries even the ruling dynasties in regions like Maharashtra were not recognized as Kṣatriyas by the local Brāhmaṇs, and they refused to perform religious rites for these dynasties with Vedic chants. As we will see later, this dissociation of the non-Brāhmaṇ communities eventually led to the emergence of vernacular forms of devotional religion in all parts of India.

Another dimension of the scriptural status of the Veda in the context of the Hindu law may be mentioned here. The Dharma texts argue that all rules of conduct are ultimately based on the Vedas. The Vedas are the highest authority in any decision. The next authority is that of the remembered tradition codified in the *smṛti* texts. If there is a conflict between the Vedas and a *smṛti*, the Vedas override the *smṛti*. The third authority is the behavior of the elites in the society, who, by their exemplary conduct, set the norms for the behavior of others. Some Dharma texts admit that rules of conduct by people of specific regions, families, and communities were not specified in the Vedas, and hence Manu provided these rules. However, there is a more conservative approach in other texts. If a *smṛti* text is explicitly contradicted by a known Vedic text, then the Vedic text overrides the *smṛti* text. However, if a *smṛti* text is neither contradicted nor supported by a known Vedic text, one assumes that there must have been a supporting Vedic text which is now lost (*anumitaśruti*). Thus, in theory, all *smṛti* texts that are accepted as authoritative are supported by Vedic texts, whether attested or assumed. Such a notion of assumed Vedic texts, which are now presumed to be lost, is a legal fiction, which becomes possible because of the traditional conception of the infiniteness (*ananta*) of the original Vedas and the finiteness of the Vedas known to human beings. The finiteness of the known Vedas is due to the limits of human intellect and life span. Such a doctrine projects a perception of history where there is nothing new happening in the world. All events are essentially repetitions of the events in the past, and hence the ancient scriptural texts have anticipated them all.

Sanskrit grammarians

Pāṇini (400 BCE) composed his grammar of Sanskrit with a certain notion of an eternal language. For him, there were regional dialects of Sanskrit as well as its scriptural and contemporary domains of usage. All these domains are treated as subdomains of a unified language, which is not restricted by any temporality. The language of the Vedas is treated as a subdomain of this unified language and is not treated as a language of a bygone age, no longer alive. This gives us some idea of Pāṇini's conception of language, though he does not engage in an explicit discussion of philosophical issues.

The early commentators on Pāṇini's grammar, Kātyāyana and Patañjali (250–100 BCE), display a significant reorganization of Brāhmaṇical views in the face of opposition from Jainas and Buddhists. For Kātyāyana and Patañjali, the Sanskrit language at large is sacred like the Vedas. The intelligent use of Sanskrit, backed by the explicit understanding of its grammar, leads to prosperity here and in the next world, as do the Vedas. Kātyāyana and Patañjali admit that vernaculars as well as Sanskrit could do the function of communicating meaning. However, only the usage of Sanskrit produces religious merit. This is an indirect criticism of the Jainas and the Buddhists, who used vernacular languages for the propagation of their faiths. The grammarians did not accept the religious value of the vernaculars. The vernacular languages, along with the incorrect uses of Sanskrit, are all lumped together by the Sanskrit grammarians under the derogatory terms "*apaśabda*" and "*apabhraṃśa*," both of which suggest a view that the vernaculars are degenerate or "fallen" forms of the divine language, that is, Sanskrit. Kātyāyana says: "While the relationship between words and meanings is established on the basis of the usage of specific words to denote specific meanings in the community of speakers, the science of grammar only makes a regulation concerning the religious merit produced by the linguistic usage, as is commonly done in worldly matters and in Vedic rituals" (*Vārttika* 1 on Pāṇini's *Aṣṭādhyāyī*). Kātyāyana refers to these "degenerate" vernacular usages as being caused by the inability of the low-class speakers to speak proper Sanskrit. This implies that the speakers of Prakrit have a certain disability. This disability could be deadly in ritual terms. The grammarians tell the story of demons that used improper degenerate usages during their ritual, and hence they were defeated. On the other hand, the great sages named Yarvāṇastarvāṇaḥ used vernaculars to speak at home but used proper Sanskrit during their rituals. Thus the grammarians suggest that while the use of vernaculars may be acceptable in secular nonreligious contexts, their use in religious contexts was particularly objectionable. The relationship between Sanskrit words and their meanings is said to be established (*siddha*) before the grammarians begin their work. Patañjali understands this statement of Kātyāyana to mean that the relationship between Sanskrit words and their meanings is eternal (*nitya*), not created (*kārya*) by anyone. Since this eternal relationship exists only for Sanskrit words and their meanings, one cannot accord the same status to the fallen vernaculars, which are born of the disability on the part of their speakers. Thus, the use of the fallen vernaculars by the Jaina and Buddhist teachers only showed their low-class status. It was not worth imitating by Brāhmaṇs who had the superior option of using the divine Sanskrit language.

It is important to mention another philosopher of language in the grammatical tradition, Bhartṛhari (400 CE). Apart from his significant contribution toward an in-depth philosophical understanding of issues of the structure and function of language and issues of phonology, semantics, and syntax, Bhartṛhari is well known for his proposal that language constitutes the ultimate principle of reality (*śabdabrahman*). Both the signifier words and the signified entities in the world are perceived to be a transformation (*pariṇāma*) of the ultimate unified principle of language.

Mīmāṃsā: logic of ritualists

Beginning around 200 BCE, the ritualists (Mīmāṃsākas) and the logicians (Naiyāyikas and Vaiśeṣikas) were also eagerly defending their religious faith in the Vedas and in the Brāhmaṇical religion. The strategies of these traditions were, however, very different. The ritualists accepted the criticism of the Buddhists and the Jainas that one should not accept the notion of god if one accepts the doctrine of *karma*. The Buddhists had also argued that the authors of the Vedic texts were ignorant human beings and that their words could not be trusted, as they were bound to be colored by ignorance, passion, and deceit. In contrast, the figures of Mahāvīra and Buddha were perceived by their respective traditions as human, and yet omniscient persons (*sarvajña*), who were compassionate and free from ignorance and malice. The ritualists attempted to defend the Vedas under these criticisms. They contested the doctrine of omniscient person (*sarvajña*) and argued that no humans were omniscient and free from ignorance, passion, and deceit. Therefore, Buddha could not be free from these either, and hence his words cannot be trusted. On the other hand, the Vedas were eternal words, uncreated by any human being (*apauruṣeya*). Since they were not created by human beings, they were free from the limitations of human beings. Yet the Vedas were meaningful because the relationship between words and meanings was innate. The Vedas were ultimately seen as ordaining the performance of sacrifices, and the ritualists develop a theory of sentence-meaning which claims that the meaning of a sentence centers around some specific action denoted by a verb and an injunction expressed by the verbal terminations. Thus, language primarily orders us to engage in appropriate actions. The response to Buddhism from the ritualist Kumārila (650–700 CE) is even more specific. Kumārila faults Buddha for having forsaken his Kṣatriya duty and the duty of a householder and taken upon himself the role of a teacher, which was restricted only to Brāhmaṇs. Kumārila specifically says that the Buddhist texts are composed in degenerate fallen languages (*apaśabda*). How can texts composed in such degenerate fallen languages by deviant teachers who abdicated their own caste obligations be trustworthy?

In this connection, we may note that Mīmāṃsā and other systems of Hindu philosophy also develop a notion of linguistic expression as one of the sources of authoritative knowledge (*śabdapramāṇa*), when other more basic sources of knowledge like sense perception (*pratyakṣa*) and inference (*anumāna*) are not available. Particularly, in connection with religious duty (*dharma*) and heaven (*svarga*) as the promised reward, only Veda is available as the source of authoritative knowledge. For Mīmāṃsā, the Veda as a source of knowledge is not tainted by negative qualities like ignorance and malice, which could affect a normal speaker of a linguistic expression. According to Mīmāṃsā, the Vedas are the primordial self-existent words, not uttered by a human or a divine speaker, and hence they are untainted by the faults of a speaker and are intrinsically meaningful.

Naiyāyikas and Vaiśeṣikas: Hindu logicians and realists

The Naiyāyikas (logicians) and Vaiśeṣikas (realist ontologists) also offered their own arguments in defense of the Vedic traditions. They also believed that the Vedas were a source of authoritative knowledge (*śabdapramāṇa*). According to them, only the words of a trustworthy speaker (*āpta*) were a source of authoritative knowledge. They joined the ritualists in arguing that no humans, including Buddha and Mahāvīra, were free from ignorance, passion, and so on, and therefore the words of Buddha and Mahāvīra could not be accepted as infallible. However, they did not agree with the ritualists in their rejection of the notion of god. In the metaphysics of the logicians, the notion of god plays a central role. First, they had to defend this notion against objections from their Buddhist and Jaina opponents. Having established the notion of god, they claimed that god was the only being in the universe that was omniscient and free from the faults of ignorance and malice. He was a compassionate being. Therefore, only the words of god could be infallible and therefore be trusted. For the Naiyāyikas and Vaiśeṣikas, the Vedas were the words of god and not the words of some human sages about god. The human sages only received the words of god and transmitted them to later generations and had no authorship role. On a more specific level, this argument came to mean that god only spoke in Sanskrit, and hence Sanskrit was the language of god, and that it was the best means to approach god. God willfully established a connection between each Sanskrit word and its meaning, saying "let this word refer to this thing." Since such a connection was not established by god for vernacular languages, which were only fallen forms of Sanskrit, the vernaculars could not be vehicles for religious and spiritual communication. The Naiyāyikas argued that vernacular words did not even have meaning of their own. They claimed that the vernacular word reminded the listener the corresponding Sanskrit word that communicated the meaning.

Vedas and creation

In many classical Hindu traditions, the roles of the language, god, and creation are very closely related. The words of the Vedas assume an even more direct creative role. God not only authored the Vedas and created the relationship between words and meanings, he used the words of the Vedas as prototypes to create things of the world that these words refer to. Therefore, in a system like that of the Vaiśeṣikas, often the existence of a word is taken as a sufficient proof for the existence of the corresponding thing, even if that thing is beyond the reach of perceptive organs. The Vedas are believed to survive the cyclical destruction of the world and hence provide appropriate prototypes for the creator to create the world all over again. These notions are expressed both in explicit philosophical terms as well as in mythical images. In Vaiṣṇava mythology, we find that Viṣṇu, the ultimate god, is resting on the cosmic ocean. Out of his naval a lotus comes up, and seated on that lotus is the creator god, Brahmā, represented with four faces, each symbolizing one of the four Vedas. The idea of the creator god Brahmā having four faces, representing the four Vedas, is a powerful visual representation of the perceived role of the Vedas in the process of the creation of the world.

Vedas and infallibility

By the time we come to the classical philosophical systems, one more assumption is made by almost all Hindu systems, that is, that all the Vedas together form a coherent whole. The human authorship of the Vedic texts has long been rejected, and they are now perceived either as being entirely uncreated or created by god. Under the assumption that they are entirely uncreated, their innate ability to convey truthful meaning is unhampered by human limitations. Thus if all the Vedic texts convey truthful meaning, there cannot be any internal contradictions. If the Vedas are created by an omniscient god, who by his very nature is compassionate and beyond human limitations, one reaches the same conclusion, that is, there cannot be any internal contradictions. The traditional interpretation of the Vedas proceeds under these assumptions. If one observes seeming contradictions in Vedic passages, the burden to find ways of removing those seeming contradictions is upon the interpreter. We see contradictions because of our limitations and not because of any inherent problems with the texts themselves. Such a fundamental belief led to the emergence of many sophisticated ways of explaining away the seeming contradictions found in the Vedas.

Resolving seeming contradictions

If two passages seemed contradictory, one way was to argue that one of those passages was to be taken literally, while the other one was only metaphorical. Perhaps, the two seemingly contradictory passages refer to customs followed by people in different regions or time-spans. It is sometimes pointed out that one of such passages was meant to provide only a provisional, nonfinal answer, while the other passage was meant to provide a final conclusion. After trying all possible ways of removing a seeming conflict between two statements, if one cannot find any viable solution, then, and only then, the two seemingly contradictory passages are accepted as providing an option. Such rules of textual interpretation were perfected by the ritualists and were widely accepted by the legal tradition and by the philosophers belonging to different schools of Vedānta, which tried, each in its particular way, to reconcile (*samanvaya*) the various scriptural texts and to construct a systematic philosophical doctrine out of otherwise seemingly discordant Vedic texts.

Changing interpretation of the Vedas

While such was the explicit logic of the traditional interpretation of the Vedas, one should also recognize what happened in practice. While the Vedic texts were preserved as texts, preserving their original meaning was far more difficult. Hence, with a continuously changing cultural, religious, and linguistic environment, the meaning of the Vedic words became more and more negotiable. The belief that the Sanskrit language and the Vedas were eternal allowed the exegetes to apply latter-day meanings to ancient words. The interpretation of the Vedas at any given time brought their understanding close to the current religious practice in a given region and community. With the entry of vegetarianism, for example, older passages referring to the consumption of meat came to be reinterpreted. Similarly, with the rise of divinities like the elephant-faced Gaṇeśa, the ancient hymns that contained the word "*gaṇapati*" came to be interpreted as being in praise of Gaṇeśa. Coming close to modern times, both social reformers and conservatives found support for their views in the Vedic passages, and in modern India, many Western-educated Hindus fervently believe that all Western scientific ideas are already contained in the Vedas. One just needs to have a right interpreter. The more the texts became archaic, the interpretations proliferated because of the freedom provided by the ambiguities in the archaic texts.

Different versions of such theories widely circulated among the different schools of Hindu philosophy. They differed on the question of whether the Vedas were words of god or were eternal, but they all agreed on the high status of the Vedas and the Sanskrit language and the low status of the vernacular languages. This was the consolidated Brāhmaṇical response to the vernacularism of the Buddhists and the Jainas.

RISE OF DEVOTIONAL TRADITIONS AND THE NEW LANGUAGE DEBATES

Opening access to salvation

While responding negatively to the early promotion of vernaculars to the status of scriptural languages by the Buddhists and the Jainas, the Brāhmaṇical tradition itself was not fully immune to the same urges. This is seen in the emergence of the Sanskrit epics, the *Rāmāyaṇa* and the *Mahābhārata*, and the Purāṇas. This literature, though its oldest surviving manifestations appear in Sanskrit, is most certainly different in its intent as compared to the Vedic literature. The eligibility for the Vedic rituals was restricted to the higher three communities of priests, warriors, and trades people, but women and Śūdras were left out of this access. The *Bhagavad Gītā*, a new scripture, tries to spread its appeal to all communities. The doctrine of devotion to Kṛṣṇa/Viṣṇu is new in that it is aimed at providing access to salvation through devotion to all human beings. The *Bhagavad Gītā* makes a clear statement offering devotional access to everyone:

> I am equal to all beings, and no one is dear or hated for me. Those who serve me with devotion, reside in me and I reside in them. Even if one commits a great sin, if he devotes to me, and to none other, he should be considered to be a good person, because he has [now] chosen the proper path. . . . Having taken refuge in me, even those of low birth, women, Vaiśyas, and even the Śūdras attain to the highest spiritual goal. So what to speak of the holy Brāhmaṇs and devoted royal sages.
>
> (9.29–30, 32–33)

The *Bhagavad Gītā*, though composed in Sanskrit and representing a top-down approach, is extending the devotional path to Vaiśyas, Śūdras, and women without offering them access to the Vedas or even to the use of the Sanskrit language. Thus there is a suggestion that access to devotional religion for these non-high social groups, and women, must be achieved through their own languages and through means other than Vedic sacrifices. This is the first open indication of acceptance of non-Sanskrit languages and non-Vedic ritual forms of worship as possible alternative ways to approaching god. This acknowledgement of alternative linguistic and ritual paths to god, without diluting and abdicating the path of Vedic scriptures and sacrifices, points to the emergence of an essentially two-tier religious practice. Everyone had access to devotional religion, while the Brāhmaṇs continued to restrict access to the Vedas and the Sanskrit language. This is evident in the emergence of the so-called Purāṇic *mantras* in worshiping various divinities, by the side of the Vedic *mantras*. If the host was a Brāhmaṇ, the priest would perform the ceremony using both the Vedic and the Purāṇic *mantras*. On the other hand, if the host was a non-Brāhmaṇ, the priest would typically use only the Purāṇic *mantras* in the ceremony. For those who were too low to have access to a Brāhmaṇ priest, a devotional ceremony could still take place entirely in a vernacular language. In practice, even the Brāhmaṇ hosts had, generally speaking, little comprehension of the Vedic texts and the Sanskrit language, and while the Brāhmaṇ priest would recite the Vedic and Purāṇic *mantras*, these *mantras* were in most situations merely recited without offering an explanation of their meaning. The ritual instructions, in practice, were given by the priest to the host in the local vernacular. Thus, whatever understanding of the ceremony there was, it occurred ultimately through the vernacular of the hosts, even though recitation of Vedic and Purāṇic *mantras* would be considered an essential part of the creation of the holy atmosphere and the magic of the ritual. The devotional literature like the *Mahābhārata* and the Purāṇas, on the other hand, could be narrated in the vernacular languages. Such vernacular versions of these epics and Purāṇas were in all likelihood circulating from very old times, though recorded instances of vernacular versions become available at a later time.

Such a situation as gleaned from the Sanskrit epics and Purāṇas was indeed fraught with tensions. The *Bhagavad Gītā*, even while opening up access to women, Vaiśyas, and Śūdras, calls these groups "low birth" (*pāpayoni*). This gives us an indication of the upper-class view of the religious practices of the masses. While the masses were allowed to practice the devotional religion, the Brāhmaṇs looked down upon it as a reflection of the inferior nature of the practitioners. While the Sanskrit Dharmaśāstras generally include the Vaiśyas among the three higher groups, the *Bhagavad Gītā* seems to lump them with the lower groups. Just as the Buddhist and the Jaina traditions provide early evidence that the Kṣatriyas did not accept the lower status granted to them by the Brāhmaṇs, similarly one can suspect that other groups also did not happily accept the low status granted to them by the Brāhmaṇs and the imposed restrictions on access to the Vedas. The origin of the vernacular devotional movements lies in this sociolinguistic tension between the higher and the lower layers of the Hindu society. Judging from the evidence provided by Buddhism and Jainism, such tensions must have existed all along, though the vernacular devotional literature itself becomes available to us from a somewhat later period.

Emerging vernacular traditions

While the Vedic tradition seems to have moved from the northwestern parts of the subcontinent to eastern and then to the southern areas, the vernacular devotional literature, to the extent the available materials indicate, originated in the southern Tamil-speaking regions and then, in the form of a devotional movement, gradually moved northward, eventually covering all parts of South Asia. This vernacular devotional movement makes its appearance in the Tamil region in the second half of the first millennium CE, both in opposition to the dominant traditions of Buddhism and Jainism in this area as well as the dominant Brāhmaṇical religion expressed in the medium of Sanskrit. The majority of these Tamil-speaking "saints," the Vaiṣṇavite Āḻvārs and the Śaivite Nāyaṉārs, are fervent devotees of their respective gods. The Tamil poetic tradition itself, recorded in the Saṅgam literature, predates the emergence of these devotional poet saints by a few centuries and ensures the confidence of the Tamil poetic expression. The Jainas and the Buddhists also had been using Tamil for religious expression, and hence the use of Tamil for religious expression by the Āḻvārs and Nāyaṉārs is not entirely new. What is new is the orientation in the direction of fervent devotion to Śiva and Viṣṇu. While these gods were already worshiped in the Brāhmaṇical tradition, the Brāhmaṇical tradition provided little access and comfort to the lower classes of the Hindu society. They were kept out of the Brāhmaṇical rituals and temple establishments, and their mother tongue, Tamil, had no place in that Brāhmaṇical practice. The predominantly non-Brāhmaṇ Āḻvārs and Nāyaṉārs, who included a number of women saints among them, essentially claimed to have a direct relationship to their respective gods, which was ecstatic, personal, all-encompassing, and satisfying. Importantly, this relationship to god bypassed the Brāhmaṇical texts, practices, and establishments, and it engendered in the minds of the saint poets a new sense of freedom from that Brāhmaṇical tradition, almost verging on a feeling of superiority to it. The Tamil poet-saint Appar (seventh century CE), who was born in the Vēḷāḷar caste and was persecuted by the Jainas for his devotion to Śiva, expresses his devotion in these words.

Why bathe in the stream of Gaṅgā or Kāverī?
  Why go to Comorin in Kongu's land?
Why seek the waters of the sounding sea?
  Release is theirs, and theirs alone, who call
  In every place upon the Lord of all.

Why chant the Vedas, hear the Śāstras' lore?
  Why daily teach the books of righteousness?
Why the Vēdāngas six say o'er and o'er?
  Release is theirs, and theirs alone, who heart
  From thinking of its Lord shall ne'er depart.

Why roam the jungle, wander cities through?
  Why plague life with unstinting penance hard?
Why eat no flesh, and gaze into the blue?
  Release is theirs, and theirs alone, who cry
  Unceasing to the Lord of wisdom high.

Why fast and starve, why suffer pains austere?
  Why climb the mountains, doing penance harsh?
Why go to bathe in waters far and near?
  Release is theirs, and theirs alone, who call
  At every place upon the Lord of all.
(Kingsbury and Phillips 1921: 57)

While Appar, Campantar (seventh century CE), and Cuntarar (ninth century CE) opted for the vernacular and tried to open devotional access to Śiva for all castes, they also set out to establish or reestablish Āgamic temple worship for Śiva.

We can compare and contrast Appar's sentiments with those of the North Indian saint-poet Kabīr (1440–1518 CE), born in a different region and under different circumstances. Kabīr was born in a Muslim weaver family and developed a devotional approach to god which was critical of both the Hindu and the Muslim orthodox traditions. He says that Sanskrit is too narrow like the water of a well, while the vernacular language is like a flowing river. Kabīr rejects temple worship of the images of gods managed by the Sanskrit-chanting Brāhmaṇs and advocating a direct unmediated approach to god, says:

Pundit, how can you be so dumb?
You're going to drown, along with all your kin,
  unless you start speaking of Ram.

Vedas, Puranas—why read them?
It's like loading an ass with sandalwood!
Unless you catch on and learn how Ram's name goes,
how will you reach the end of the road?
(Hawley and Jurgensmeyer 1988: 51)

The works of the Tamil saint poets, the Āḻvārs and the Nāyaṉārs, became an alternative scriptural corpus for the followers of the vernacular devotional path. The works of the Vaiṣṇava Āḻvār saints, collected in an anthology called *Divyaprabandha* by the Brāhmaṇ Vaiṣṇava teacher Nāthamuni (ninth century CE), came to be looked upon as the Tamil Veda. This Tamil Veda was looked at as an authoritative source for devotional religion by the Vaiṣṇava Brāhmaṇs in the Tamil region, and the Sanskritic Vaiṣṇavism of Rāmānuja incorporated much of the devotional inspiration from the hymns of the Āḻvārs. This incorporation of the vernacular inspiration into the Brāhmaṇical traditions and the incorporation of the Brāhmaṇical tradition into the vernacular are to be seen as parallel processes in the history of Hinduism. In the region of Karnataka, the vernacular devotional tradition of the Vīraśaivas generally followed an independent course and stayed away from the Brāhmaṇical traditions. On the other hand, the Vaiṣṇava saints like Purandaradāsa and Kanakadāsa (sixteenth century CE) were not delinked from the Brāhmaṇical tradition. Vyāsatīrtha (1447–1539 CE), a scholar in the tradition of Madhva's dualist (*dvaita*) Vedānta school during the reign of the Vijayanagara king Kṛṣṇadēvarāya, simultaneously pursued Sanskritic and vernacular interests. While writing highly erudite Sanskrit philosophical works expounding his Dvaita Vedānta views, he simultaneously encouraged participation of non-Brāhmaṇ devotees of Viṣṇu into a devotional group called Dāsakūṭa. It was through Vyāsatīrtha's encouragement and inspiration that the saint-poets Purandaradāsa and Kanakadāsa produced their Kannada devotional poems.

Language and religion in Maharashtra

To illustrate this dual cultural and linguistic process, let us look at the region of Maharashtra in the second millennium CE. In the twelfth and the thirteenth century CE, we see several important figures at work. A Brāhmaṇ Sanskrit scholar Mukundarāja (twelfth century CE) wrote a Marathi work *Vivekasindhu* to provide a vernacular exposition of the Advaita Vedānta of Śaṃkara. This is clearly an attempt to provide access to classical philosophical ideas to those who did not understand Sanskrit. Mukundarāja clearly does not attempt to elevate the status of Marathi but explicitly argues for the use of Marathi for purposes of wider communication in spite of its low status. He compares Marathi to dust and Sanskrit to gold. The other group at work was Cakradhara (thirteenth century CE) and his followers, who constituted the Mahānubhāva tradition, a tradition of Kṛṣṇa-*bhakti* that generally moved away from Brāhmaṇical communities and used Marathi to spread its message. When some Brāhmaṇ converts to this tradition wanted to write in Sanskrit, their teachers asked them not to do so, as this would deprive the common man of the religious teachings. The most prominent religious figure of this period is Jñāneśvara (thirteenth century CE). Born to Brāhmaṇ parents, who were excommunicated by the local Brāhmaṇ community, Jñāneśvara was initiated into the Nātha tradition by his elder brother Nivṛtti.

Jñāneśvara, his two brothers, and a sister, after their parents' death, went to the Brāhmaṇs of Pratiṣṭhāna to be accepted back into the Brāhmaṇ community. However, after the Brāhmaṇs refused, Jñāneśvara performed many miracles, and this launched his career as a saint. Thus, as a rejected Brāhmaṇ, Jñāneśvara directed his attention to the religious needs of the people at large and produced the first vernacular commentary on the *Bhagavad Gītā*. This Marathi commentary, popularly called *Jñāneśvarī*, is not just an attempt to bring the philosophical contents of the *Bhagavad Gītā* into Marathi. It shows Jñāneśvara's full pride in Marathi, and he says that his poetic Marathi can compete with the sweetness of nectar. Through his *Jñāneśvarī*, he removes a linguistic barrier to salvation, which is now accessible to everyone.

Ekanātha (1548–1609 CE) is the next saint poet of great importance. Born Brāhmaṇ and trained in the Sanskritic lore, Ekanātha is attracted to the tradition of devotion and turns his attention to the use of Marathi to express his devotion and erudition. Just as Jñāneśvara brought the *Bhagavad Gītā* into Marathi, Ekanātha translated the *Bhāgavata Purāṇa* into Marathi. The Brāhmaṇs of his day were not generally in favor of translating Sanskrit scriptural works into Marathi, and Ekanātha was accused of sacrilege by translating the *Bhāgavata Purāṇa* into Marathi. We are told that Ekanātha had to face a Brāhmaṇ-tribunal at Varanasi. This tribunal ordered that Ekanātha's Marathi translation be thrown in the Gaṅgā. However a miracle happened, and the Marathi translation floated on the waters of the Gaṅgā instead of sinking. This miracle established Ekanātha's authenticity and the spiritual power of his Marathi works. In Ekanātha we see a Brāhmaṇ going in the direction of the vernacular and establishing not only its practical utility but also its legitimacy in the eyes of the very Brāhmaṇs who initially rejected it.

We find similar stories about the saint Tukārāma (1598–1649 CE). Tukārāma was born in a Śūdra caste and had no access to Sanskritic learning. Tukārāma says that he does not speak with his own power, but it is his god, Viṭṭhala, who makes him speak. He claims to be a lame man, who is made to walk by god's power. Tukārāma's assertion that God Viṭṭhala directly communicates with him, a Śūdra, in his own lowly language, brought him into conflicts with the local Brāhmaṇs. They also forced him to drown his Marathi devotional poems into the river Indrāyaṇī. However, again a miracle happened, and the books were saved from drowning, thus establishing Tukārāma's authenticity and his access to god.

Emboldened by his own religious experience, Tukārāma claims that he, a Śūdra, alone knows the true meaning of the Vedas, while the Brāhmaṇs simply carry the burden. He heavily criticizes the Brāhmaṇs for simply playing linguistic games and says that all the Vedas, *śāstra*s, and Purāṇas ultimately teach devotion to Viṭṭhala (Kṛṣṇa/Viṣṇu). Here is a Marathi devotional song by Tukārāma:

Viṭṭhala is our life and the place where the scriptures dwell.
In Viṭṭhala all spiritual powers are.
On Viṭṭhala our meditation rests.

Viṭṭhala is our family god.
Viṭṭhala is my fortune, my caste, and my mind.
Viṭṭhala is my merit and my goal.
I love the splendor of Viṭṭhala.

Viṭṭhala pervades all beings.
He lifts the seven subterranean worlds.
Viṭṭhala is spread over the three worlds.
Viṭṭhala dwells in the heart of the saints.

Viṭṭhala is the very essence of our life.
Viṭṭhala became young to give us his grace.
Viṭṭhala assumed a form for our love.
Viṭṭhala puts the world in motion.

Tukā says:
Viṭṭhala is our father, mother, and uncle.
Viṭṭhala is our brother and sister.
We have no affection for our family apart from him.
Now, there is no one else.

The themes of a vernacular text being thrown in river and the judgment of a devotee by orthodox Brāhmaṇs, and so on, are common to the received stories of North Indian saints, like Tulasīdāsa, Kabīr, and Nānak, and show a pan-Indian set of motifs indicating that the struggle of vernacular *bhakti* tradition with the orthodox Sanskritic traditions maintained by Brāhmaṇs were not a narrow regional phenomena but resonated in all the different regions and communities of India.

The linguistic tensions continued in Maharashtra in other arenas as well. Stories of the seventeenth-century King Śivājī (1627–80 CE) show some interesting issues. Born in a warrior family, Śivājī rebelled against the Muslim rulers in Maharashtra and succeeded in establishing his own independent kingdom. At this time, the Brāhmaṇs generally came to believe that there were no true Kṣatriyas left on earth any more, and while they continued to work for the local kings, they refused to accept them as genuine Kṣatriyas. Śivājī's spiritual *guru* is said to be the Brāhmaṇ saint Rāmadāsa (1608–81 CE). Rāmadāsa's poetic and philosophical works have been preserved mostly in Marathi. In 1676, Śivājī had his royal coronation performed and had him officially declared a Kṣatriya Hindu king. The famous Sanskrit *paṇḍita* Gāgābhaṭṭa of Varanasi performed his coronation. There are traditional stories about the tensions between Rāmadāsa and Gāgābhaṭṭa. Gāgābhaṭṭa, the stories say, did not want Śivājī to continue his association with Rāmadāsa and with Marathi. He promised to teach him Sanskrit, so that he can function fully in the image of a classical Kṣatriya king.

Importance of the divine name

In the process of making religious practice more accessible to the masses, a number of strategies seem to have come into existence. While the emphasis on knowing the true name of a thing or a divinity, and thus ritually gaining access to and control over it, is attested in the oldest Vedic literature, the devotional importance of remembering and reciting the name or names of god is attested in the epic and Purāṇic literature. Prayers in the form of concatenation of various names of a divinity are attested in the *Mahābhārata* and the Purāṇas. An early example of this is the popular *Viṣṇusahasranāma* (thousand names of

Viṣṇu) found in the *Mahābhārata*. Such concatenations of 108 or 1,008 names become available in later times for almost all different Hindu gods and goddesses. These prayers, along with a widespread practice of repeating a given name of a divinity or the sacred symbol like *oṃ* or repeating a particular salutational formula like *oṃ namaḥ śivāya*, offer devotional access to a wide range of people, who need not, and did not, know the Sanskrit language as such. Added to this are practices of naming one's children with the names of a divinity, wearing clothes with imprinted names of a divinity, and writing down the names of a divinity on different household materials.

The widespread belief in the power of the name of god may be illustrated with the *Rāmāyaṇa* story of the monkeys building a bridge from India to Sri Lanka. As the monkeys would drop huge boulders into the ocean, they began to sink. Then someone suggested that they should write the name of Rāma , the hero god, on each stone before it was dropped into the ocean. With this done, the stones floated on the ocean, and the bridge was finished in no time. When stones can float on the ocean, if inscribed with the name of god, a devoted person who constantly recites the name of god would certainly survive in the ocean of transmigration.

Multiple representations of language and scripture

We have already seen the process of linguistic performances of ancient Vedic sages being preserved as potent incantations by the later generations. The same process continued to work with most religious texts. For example, the *Bhagavad Gītā* was not just looked upon as a piece of philosophical literature, it was looked upon as a powerful *mantra* (chant), and there are several texts available which describe in detail the process of chanting the *Bhagavad Gītā* and the rewards for the chanting of the whole text, particular chapters, and particular verses and even just uttering the word "*gītā*." Manuscripts and printed books of works like the *Bhagavad Gītā* came to be worshiped as holy objects. The *Bhagavad Gītā* was at some point deified into a goddess, and prayers to "Mother, Goddess Gītā" were produced. In modern times, we find in India the so-called Gītā-*mandira*s (Gītā temples) where the *Bhagavad Gītā* is represented in all these forms, ranging from the image of the goddess, stone image of the book, the text inscribed on the walls and recited in its halls, and copies sold in the bookshop. The devotees are encouraged to access the *Bhagavad Gītā* in every possible way. The deification of texts was indeed not limited to the *Bhagavad Gītā*. In the Purāṇas, we already find the full deification of the four Vedas, each with a distinct iconography of its own, and the Vedas, thus deified and personified, appear as interlocutors in various conversations. This deification and personification of specific texts needs to be understood differently from the deification of speech into a goddess in the *Ṛg Veda* or representation of the goddess of speech in the form of the goddess Sarasvatī in classical times.

Language and scripture in modern Hinduism

The relation of language to religion in modern times is very complicated because of the variation one finds from region to region and from community to community. The rise of regional languages as languages of education and state business and the rise of linguistic nationalism in regions like Tamilnadu need to be confronted with the promotion of Hindi as the national language, the maintenance of English as the language of higher education and business, and the emotional support given to Sanskrit by religious groups like the Ārya Samāj and the political bodies like the Bharatiya Janata party and its sister organizations like the Rashtriya Svayamsevak Sangh and the Vishva Hindu Parishad. These differences are naturally reflected in the religious role given to languages by these various groups. The interaction of Sanskrit and the vernacular, including English for many, is the most interesting continuing religious phenomenon. While Sanskrit largely maintains its symbolic presence as holy chants, understanding of religious sentiment almost always takes place through one's vernacular.

When we come to modern times, the religious language appears in all its modern technological manifestations. The first major shift was from handwritten manuscripts to printing. This was then followed by the recording and broadcasting technologies. It started with the use of loudspeakers and microphones at religious performances. Religious songs and discourses are routinely broadcast from radio stations and from religious establishments. In the form of recorded cassettes and CDs, the religious songs and discourses can now be mass produced and distributed. If a priest is not available on a given day, the worshiper can now buy a recorded priestly voice telling him what to do and say. With the telecast of the *Rāmāyaṇa*, the *Mahābhārata*, and other stories about gods and goddesses, the religious language has made full penetration into every field of social activity and interaction. Finally, we are now in the age of the internet, where numerous web sites are providing access to different religious materials and numerous chat groups are offering worldwide discussions of issues deemed to be important for one's faith. From anywhere in the world, we can listen to the daily prayers recited in the Gaṇeśa temple (Siddhivināyaka temple) in Bombay, on line! The religious language keeps pace with changes in the material and the cultural environment of the religious community.

CHAPTER TWENTY-THREE

DARŚANA

John A. Grimes

THE TERM "DARŚANA"

Darśana, from the Sanskrit root *dṛś*, "to see," implies not only vision (which includes insight, intuition, and vision of the truth) but also the instrument of vision (such as viewpoint, worldview, doctrine, and philosophical system) (Grimes 1996: 109). In a word, *darśana* implies "sight" in all its myriad connotations, and the term, like most Sanskrit terms, is multisignificant, multivalent. Thus, besides expressing viewpoints or perspectives, the term also suggests the idea of right vision or realization (*mokṣa*). The former meaning customarily refers to the great Hindu philosophical systems (Ṣaḍdarśanas). Here, it is not so much a search for the truth as it is an exposition, elaboration, clarification, vindication, and conceptual fixation of what has been received. The latter meaning, on the other hand, refers to the person experiencing a vision or insight. In this case, it is direct, personal, and experiential. In other words, the "seeing" implied by the term "*darśana*" includes both conceptual knowledge and perceptual observation, critical exposition and intuitional experience, logical inquiry and spiritual insight, concrete and abstract, and gross and subtle. The English expression "I see" contains a hint of this multivalence in that it denotes both a direct vision as well as a correct understanding. It may be noted that the term "*darśana*" is also used, in certain contexts, to refer to the audience or "auspicious sight" of a revered, great, or holy person, deity, or place (Eck 1981b: 3).

Darśana, as a systematic elaboration of the truth, encompasses fundamental interpretations of reality more commonly known as the six classical philosophical systems of Nyāya, Vaiśeṣika, Sāṃkhya, Yoga, Mīmāṃsā, and Vedānta, declared to be based on the Veda, and, incidentally, the three heterodox systems of Cārvāka, Jainism, and Buddhism which were reactions to Vedic thought. In this technical sense, the term embraces the different streams of philosophical thought running parallel to one another and which were engaged in mutual dialogue, discussion, debate, criticism, and counter-criticism for the past two thousand years. However, it should also be noted that although this enumeration of the Darśanas—as enumerated in the doxographies—has been accepted and practiced for over one thousand years, the designation of the classical systems has not always been the same nor have the particulars of which systems are included therein. Thus, Nyāya was once the name for Mīmāṃsā, Ānvīkṣikī designated Nyāya, and so on (Sastri 1932: v–xxiii), and while the *Sarvadarśanasaṃgraha* elucidates sixteen philosophical systems, the *Sarvamatasaṃgraha* lists only twelve, the *Sarvasiddhāntasaṃgraha* ten, and so on (Halbfass 1988: 352).

Though Hindu culture does not have a univocal word for philosophy, *darśana* is widely considered to be the most appropriate Hindu terminological analogue to "philosophy" in a general sense and indicative of these traditional Hindu philosophical systems in a specific sense. According to Surendranath Dasgupta (1922–55, 1: 68n), historically, the first use of the word "*darśana*" in this sense of "true philosophical knowledge" may be found in the *Vaiśeṣikasūtra* (9.2.13) of Kaṇāda (sixth century BCE). Moreover, *darśana* reflects a genuinely Hindu understanding of not only philosophy but also theology. Other Sanskrit terms with varying corresponding precision to philosophy include *ānvīkṣikī*, *mata*, *nyāya*, *siddhānta*, *tantra*, *tarkaśāstra*, *tattvajñāna*, *vāda*, and *vidyā* (Halbfass 1988: 263–86).

Thus the word "*darśana*" is rich with meaning. Though there are many similarities between Hindu thought and Western philosophy, all that the term "*darśana*" denotes and connotes would only be partially recognized by Western philosophers. The Darśanas, as philosophical systems of thought, embody the cumulative reflection of Hindu wisdom through the ages and include epistemology, metaphysics, ethics, social customs, aesthetics, psychology, cosmology, physics, grammar, logic, speculations about language, exegesis of scriptural texts, psychophysical practices, dialectics, and even protests against orthodoxy. To study, understand, interpret, and continue the scholarship of the Hindu Darśanas, it is imperative that one realize that it holistically implies both thinking and living, theory and practice, an ancient, continuous, and seamless tradition. It has been able to combine, in an almost unique manner, conformity to tradition with an adventurous, inquiring mind.

COMMON CHARACTERISTICS

The various Hindu philosophical systems contain such a diversity of views, theories, and subschools that it is virtually impossible to single out characteristics that are common to all of them. This being acknowledged, there is an oft-quoted dictum, "unity in diversity," which is the Hindu paradigm par excellence. Thus, the various systems are subject, in varying degrees, to certain common factors. For instance, without a doubt every system has been influenced by the Vedas, either directly or indirectly. Some systems developed along the lines of a systematic interpretation of the Vedas, while others developed by refutation and rejection of Vedic thought. Whether this is a mere tipping of the hat, a traditional gesture of saluting an image without any further commitment, or whether one can find the latent seeds, if not the actual full-blown doctrine, a strong case can be made that it was from the seemingly bottomless font of the Veda that much of what eventually develops into Hindu philosophy had its initial stirrings. And yet, even today a mist still covers the whole Vedic period, which makes it very difficult to make out who said or did what, where, and at what time. This uncertainty too is part of Hindu philosophy.

Perhaps the most quoted common characteristic of all Darśanas is that they begin with spiritual dissatisfaction and culminate in a spiritual orientation. While the Cārvāka system alone is oriented towards pleasure as the attainment of the highest good in life, every other system investigates, in some sense or other, both the nature of the ultimate goal of life as well as the means thereto, be it salvation, liberation, or enlightenment. This acceptance of the ideal of liberation may play but a minor role in some systems, and it is true that many epistemological, logical, and even metaphysical doctrines were debated and decided on purely rational grounds that had little bearing upon the ideal of liberation, but, in one form or other, it does make its appearance.

Five basic concepts form the cornerstone of Hindu philosophical thought: the self or soul (*ātman*), religious duty (*dharma*), the accumulated effect of deeds in lives past, present, and future (*karma*), liberation (*mokṣa*), and the means thereto (*sādhana*). As previously noted, except for the Cārvākas, all Darśanas concern themselves with these five concepts, even if they have special meanings within a given system and are not treated in precisely the same manner. Of these, *karma* and its logical corollary of reincarnation is distinctly, illustratively Hindu. So too is the idea that dissatisfaction, suffering, and bondage are the offspring of human ignorance. The other concepts are not altogether absent in Western thought, important differences notwithstanding.

In Hindu thought, the various philosophical systems do not represent a historical growth, that is, that they did not develop in a purely linear fashion. All the important schools started almost simultaneously and developed through mutual criticisms over the centuries. The first systematizations of the schools were in the form of condensed aphorisms (*sūtra*) which emerged out of the presystematic Vedic and Upaniṣadic age. These foundational "threads" thus expressed in a sort of telegraphic language the gist of the system in a technical terminology which, being logical, ordered, and concise, was easy to memorize and enabled its founder to express precisely the content of the system. In an age when there were no written books, this was an important consideration. However, because the aphorisms are so Proteus-like, pithy, abstruse, and difficult to discern without any additional explanation, they admit of different interpretations, and thus a commentary (*bhāṣya*) literature arose which became the most important exposition of a system. Then, upon the commentaries were written subcommentaries (*vārttika*) and glosses (*ṭīkā*) whose function was to further elucidate and interpret both the basic texts and their primary explanations. However, unlike the original aphorisms and their direct commentaries, subcommentaries and glosses are free to go beyond the doctrines set in their parent texts and extrapolate, criticize, object, and clarify in ways that are not open to the conventions set for the foundational works. As well, there emerged a third type of philosophical works consisting of manuals, independent treatises, dialectical classics, and critiques. These either expound doctrines for the purpose of instructing those who belong to the tradition or for combating the criticisms leveled by those who are opposed to the tradition concerned. Thus, even though no new Darśanas were subsequently founded, independent thinking, new innovations, and original insights continued to develop. This innovation enabled Hindu philosophy to combine both tradition with insight and interpretation.

Every system follows a common technique in the elaboration of its doctrines. First is stated the opponent's or prima facie (*pūrvapakṣa*) view. This view is then criticized (*khaṇḍana*). Finally one establishes their own doctrine (*siddhānta*). The method of exposition of the Hindu philosophical systems is thus dialectical and critical. Not only does a system state its own position, but it also gives a short compendium and criticism of other rival systems.

Another common characteristic of the systems is that even though they virtually share a common vocabulary, the precise meaning and value placed upon any given term is of times unique within a particular philosophical system. For example, a word like *jīva* (individual human being) has as many different technical definitions as there are schools of thought (Grimes 1996: ix).

Another common characteristic of the Hindu philosophical systems is that very little can be said about their founding philosophers (*sūtrakāra*) and central commentators (*bhāṣyakāra*). Virtually nothing is known with any precision about their dates and places of birth, identity, or life's activities. The little information available is comprised of bits and pieces, speculations, and legends, derived either from hagiographies or from scant references in other works. This paucity of detail however should not be attributed to what is alleged against India, a lack of any sense of history. Traditionally, the reason the philosophers do not talk about themselves in their works appears to be their desire to let the truths about which they expound speak for themselves. As individual thinkers they claim to consider themselves to be insignificant before their thought, and even the most original among them disclaims any originality for the doctrines which they expound. They all declare that they are but the transmitters of a hoary tradition, a tradition which requires repeated refinement and exposition. Further, it has been said that there is an underlying assumption in the Hindu tradition that no individual can claim to have seen the truth for the first time, and thus all an individual can do is to state, explicate, and defend some eternal truth. Hence, there arose the tradition of authority, of expounding upon what has come before, and of one's affiliation with one of the Darśanas.

ORIGINS

According to the orthodox Hindu tradition, the origin of many of the various philosophical ideas that were to develop into the great philosophical traditions lies in the Vedas, a body of texts whose own origins are still obscure and which seemingly were compiled between 2000 and 400 BCE. The Vedas, India's ancient primary scriptures, conjure visions of Brāhmaṇ priests sitting around sacred fires chanting magical incantations, and curling skyward exotic fragrances. In the minds of the orthodox, the Vedas evoke antiquity, mystery, revelation, wisdom, and authority par excellence. To the skeptical, the Vedas represent superstition and a primeval bottomless bog which entangles, envelopes, and eventually kills all who associate with them.

For many, especially those within the orthodox Hindu community, the Veda is said to be the source of everything, that is, any and every doctrine or idea which has made an appearance within the fold of Hindu thought is declared to have its roots in the Veda. In regards to philosophy, for instance, there are those who declare that Vedic, especially Upaniṣadic, ideas led to the Vedānta philosophical systems; Vedic meditation and prayer led to the devotional schools; Vedic rituals led to Mīmāṃsā and *karma* theories; Vedic accounts of creation led to Sāṃkhya cosmology; Vedic religious experiences led to Yoga and Tantra; Vedic logic led to Nyāya; Vedic social customs led to the Dharmaśāstras; and protests against the Veda led to Cārvāka, Buddhism, and Jainism. There are many modern scholars who deny that the Veda is the source of most of what develops into Hindu philosophy. However, to a great degree, this disparency revolves around the precise definition that one applies to the Veda.

Ages must have passed between the time that the earliest Vedic hymns were heard and their final arrangement into collections. The very word "*saṃhitā*" (collection) itself presupposes that there was a time when the various *mantra*s were not "collected together." Further, besides collecting the various *mantra*s together in some sort of coherent fashion, incredible pains were taken to devise a mechanical linguistic device by which the sacred texts, which were, and will continue to be, handed down from time immemorial could be preserved in their pristine purity. Both of these efforts represented a vital and dramatic concern for learning, and both will appear once again in the formation of the philosophical systems.

The Vedas themselves contain countless themes ranging from hymns for deities to ritual sacrificial rules to myths, parables, prayers, ethical admonitions, music, magic, and so on. Running throughout, however, like a thread through a necklace, can be found a spirit of inquiry into "the one being" (*ekam sat*) that underlies the diversity of empirical phenomena. Speculative, philosophical questions were asked, such as: In the beginning was there being or nonbeing? How did the one become many? What does the person consist of? What is that by which, once known, all things are known. The Vedas also contain explicitly or implicitly such concepts as *ṛta*/*dharma* (moral law, cosmic order, truth), *karma* and rebirth, *ātman* and *brahman*, *prakṛti* (nature), and *māyā* (magical power/illusion). Although the terms employed did not have a precise technical or philosophical meaning in these early texts, many of the hymns display a remarkable sense of wonder, inquiry, and intellectual sophistication.

A more systematic speculation begins with the Upaniṣads. While the Vedic Saṃhitās present seminal philosophical ideas, the Upaniṣads display abstract and metaphysical speculations. Emerging from the Vedas, the Upaniṣads no longer focused centrally on sacrificial rites but pursued a direct, immediate, and life-transforming knowledge of *brahman*/*ātman*. The Upaniṣads answer the question, "Which is that one being?," by establishing the equation *brahman* is *ātman*. *Brahman*, that is, that which is greater than the greatest as well as that which bursts forth into the manifest universe, the one being is nothing other than *ātman*, identifiable as the innermost self in human beings but also in reality the innermost self in all beings.

The Upaniṣads mark a major turning point in the development of Hindu thought. They place meditation and mystical experience and the philosophical interpretation of its significance at the heart of the religious quest. An intellectual description of the self has shifted to an experiential one. Though there are passages of sophisticated philosophical analysis and argument in the Upaniṣads, in the end it is not intellectual conviction but lived realization that is the aim of Upaniṣadic teaching. Given their focus on the lived experience of meditation and on the disclosure of being it offers, it is no surprise that the Upaniṣads were used as a sourcebook and reference point not only by subsequent orthodox thinkers but also by heterodox dissidents such as the Buddhists.

PERIODS OF HINDU PHILOSOPHY

Before the first millennium CE there is no historiography in regards to Hindu philosophy. Chronologies are therefore notoriously difficult to establish. With this in mind, one may make a broad outline of Hindu philosophy with five major periods of development, though it should be borne in mind that the periods overlap and are not chronologically precise. The Vedic age or formative period (2500–800 BCE) was an age when the roots of Hindu philosophy were developing. The tone, if not the precise pattern, were developed here and to this day have played a major role in the development of the Hindu philosophical traditions. Besides the orthodox adherents, the intellectual climate of this time included skeptics, naturalists, determinists, indeterminists, materialists, and no-soul theorists. The second period is the Upaniṣadic age or the speculative period (800–400 BCE). The Upaniṣads mark the transition from an emphasis on ritualism (*karmakāṇḍa*) to philosophic thought (*jñānakāṇḍa*). Though not systematic treatises on philosophy, the Upaniṣad's mystical utterances formed the basic springs of much of Hindu philosophy. Herein are contained the great speculative themes regarding the nature of knowledge, the nature of *brahman* and *ātman*, the nature of the universe, world evolution and world appearance, and the soul and its destiny. The third period is the classical or aphoristic period (400 BCE to 400 CE) and marks the age when the basic philosophic teachings of most of the various Darśanas were condensed into aphorisms (*sūtra*) which helped to express precisely the content of the various systems in a technical vocabulary. Also the heterodox reform movements, Jainism and Buddhism, both flourished during this period. The fourth period is the commentary and independent treatise period (400–1400 CE). Because the *sūtra*s are (almost) unintelligible without a commentary, commentaries, subcommentaries, glosses, and independent treatises were written explaining, elucidating, and expanding upon the original teachings. The greatest names of Indian philosophy belong to this period. There was the great Buddhist propagator of Mādhyamika, Nāgārjuna, and the Buddhist logicians Asaṅga, Vasubandhu, and Dignāga; the Mīmāṃsākas Kumārila and Prabhākara; the Naiyāyikas Uddyotaka, Vācaspati Miśra, Udayana, and Gaṅgeśa Upādhyāya; the grammarian Bhartṛhari, and Abhinavagupta of Kashmir Śaivism; and the great Vedāntins Gauḍapāda, Śaṃkara, Rāmānuja, Madhva, and Madhusūdana Sarasvatī. Finally, the fifth period is the modern period (1800 to present) represented by contemporary philosophers and their interaction with the Hindu tradition in attempts to preserve and expand the tradition as well as to appropriate its past.

FUNDAMENTAL CATEGORIES

There are said to be eight fundamental categories common to all the Hindu philosophical systems (with the exception of the Cārvāka) (Ramachandran 1976: 1): valid means of knowledge (*pramāṇa*), truth and validity (*pramāṇyam*), error and invalidity (*apramāṇyam*), god/reality (*īśvara*), individuals (*jīva*), physical universe (*jagat*), liberation (*mokṣa*), and the means to liberation (*mokṣa sādhana*). The first three categories deal with epistemology and theories of knowledge. Collectively, they are called an inquiry into knowledge (*pramāṇavicāra*). The next three categories deal with metaphysics and an inquiry into reality. They are known as *tattvavicāra*. The last two categories deal with liberation and the practical teachings thereto. They concern the application of metaphysics to life itself, as it is lived in daily experience. These last two categories are known as *prayojanavicāra*. Thus, all the Hindu philosophical systems, being school oriented, concern themselves with how, what, and why to know.

Depending upon how one views philosophy, one can either find metaphysics upon epistemological grounds or one can find epistemology on metaphysical grounds. Method and material are interdependent. Any theory of knowledge presupposes certain declared and undeclared metaphysical assumptions, and any metaphysical theory is blind without a sound epistemological methodology. Method is barren without material, and material is blind without methodology. In Hindu philosophy, the general trend has been to base epistemology upon metaphysics for the simple reason that scripture (Veda) has been regarded as revealed wisdom which embodies a direct experience of reality. Thus, the nature of reality, as well as the possibility of knowledge, is revealed by scripture. The task left to epistemology was to denote the various sources of knowledge, the validity and truth of knowledge, and the problem of invalidity and error. With this ascertainment, epistemology could then declare the proper method by which reality may be known.

Epistemological theories appear to have originally developed so as to intellectually establish, and safeguard, the validity of the Vedic texts from the onslaught of skeptical attacks leveled against them. However, notwithstanding their original impetus, once this endeavor was commenced it seems to have taken on a life of its own. Epistemological doctrines gradually separated from the religious context. Concerns arose questioning how one knows? What is the nature and origins of knowledge? What are the instruments of knowledge? Theories arose to ensure the possibility of knowing perceptual, nonperceptual, and transcendental entities.

The common assumption of all the philosophical Hindu epistemological theories is that there are three factors involved in knowledge: the subject which knows (*pramāta*), the object which is known (*prameya*), and the process of knowing (*pramiti*). These three are known as the *tripuṭī*. The various schools differ in regards to not only what is known and who knows but also in regards to the means of knowing.

Hindu philosophy admits up to six possible means of knowledge: perception, inference, comparison, postulation, nonapprehension, and verbal testimony. According to each system, the number of *pramāṇa*s accepted as valid will depend upon the types of knowledge that are recognized. The Cārvāka school accepts perception (*pratyakṣa*) as the only means of valid knowledge; Buddhists and Vaiśeṣikas accept perception and inference (*anumāna*); Jainas, Sāṃkhya, Yoga, Viśiṣṭādvaita, and Dvaita Vedānta accept perception, inference, and testimony (*śabda*); Nyāya accepts perception, inference, testimony, and comparison (*upamāna*). The Prabhākara Mīmāṃsā school accepts perception, inference, testimony, comparison, and presumption (*arthāpatti*, which is the process of knowledge which makes something intelligible by assuming something else). For instance, if Anil is fat and Anil does not eat during the day, one can assume that Anil eats at night. The Bhāṭṭa Mīmāṃsā and Advaita accept perception, inference, verbal knowledge, comparison, presumption, and noncognition (*anupalabdhi*, which is the process of knowledge employed to cognize the absence of an object).

Perception (*pratyakṣa*, literally, "against the eye") is the foundation stone, without which no epistemological or metaphysical structure can be built. It is the most fundamental of the *pramāṇa*s with immediacy or directness as its distinguishing feature. Philosophy commences with the common, everyday view of the world and that view is built upon perception. All subsequent theories, therefore, either start from perception or else must offer a satisfactory account of perception. It is a basic fact that the world is perceived. Any philosophical account of the world must acknowledge this fact.

Perception is special because it gives immediate knowledge. No other *pramāṇa* does this. All the other *pramāṇa*s (except that which relates to the suprasensible) are dependent upon it in one way or another. As Gaṅgeśa said: "Perceptual cognition is the knowledge to which no other knowledge is instrumental." Further, Hindu philosophy recognizes two types of perception, determinate (*savikalpaka*) and indeterminate (*nirvikalpaka*). Advaita recognizes these as two distinct types of perceptual knowledge, while Nyāya, Vaiśeṣika, Sāṃkhya, and Mīmāṃsā hold that determinate and indeterminate perceptions are two distinct stages of development in the perception of a sense-object. They posit that indeterminate perception is the primary or undeveloped state of perceptual knowledge which is the immediate apprehension of the bare existence of an object at the first contact with the sense-organ. At this stage, there is no comprehension of quality or kind. On the other hand, determinate perception is the distinct apprehension of an object with its generic and specific attributes. It should also be noted that Viśiṣṭādvaita, Dvaita, and Jainism reject completely any possibility of indeterminate perceptual knowledge, while Buddhism rejects completely determinate perception.

Inference has been described as flawless reasoning from a mark to a certain conclusion on the basis of an invariable relation that subsists between them. Inference (*anumāna*) literally means "after-knowledge or knowledge that follows other knowledge." According to Hindu philosophy, there are three essential factors involved in inference: the reason (*hetu*), the conclusion (*sādhya*), and the relation of invariable concomitance between the two (*vyāpti*). For example, the presence of the mark (smoke) on the hill is the reason for reaching the conclusion that there is fire on the hill (because there is an invariable concomitance between smoke and fire). Nyāya presents the classical five-membered syllogism of Hindu philosophy: *pratijña*, the statement to be proved: hill has fire; *hetu*, the reason: because it has smoke; *udāharaṇa*, the universal proposition with example: whatever has smoke has fire (the kitchen); *upanaya*, the application: the hill has smoke which is invariably concomitant with fire; *nigamana*, the conclusion: therefore, the hill has fire.

The *vyāpti* is the relation of invariable concomitance between the reason and the conclusion. It is the vital element in inference. The method of ascertaining the soundness of *vyāpti* has been discussed in depth by Hindu logicians. According to the Nyāya school, the *vyāpti* is to be verified by means of positive and negative instances. There are other schools who posit that the method of agreement in presence is sufficient to establish the soundness of *vyāpti*.

Virtually every Hindu philosophical system has inquired about, and determined, the nature of language. In India, linguistic speculation is as old as the Vedas. And the orthodox philosophical systems continue this tradition unbroken up to the present day. Each system investigated and investigates in its epistemology such questions as the relation of a word to reality, the different modes of meaning, the process of linguistic knowledge, and the validity and falsity of words as knowledge. Further, with the exception of the Cārvāka school, each Hindu system accepted language (*śabda*) as an aid of one sort or another in arriving at knowledge. The Cārvākas, Vaiśeṣikas, and Buddhists held that perception and/or inferential reasoning exhausts knowledge about reality, and thus they denied words as knowledge (*śabda pramāṇa*) as an independent means of valid knowledge. But the Vaiśeṣikas and the Buddhists, unlike the Cārvākas, postulated a utility to religious discourse. Therefore, according to them, religious discourse has a use and can be determined as valid or invalid through the process of perception and/or inference. The remaining schools all postulated that the nature of reality transcends the compass of perception and reason. Thus, they presented testimony (authority, revelation) as the sole means of acquiring knowledge about that sphere which exists beyond the reach of perception and inference.

The nature of religious discourse and its relation to reality has been primarily determined by the metaphysical position proposed by each system. The Nyāya and Vaiśeṣika schools posit a total correspondence between language and reality. Whatever is real is knowable and, as well, describable in words. The early Buddhists, on the other hand, say that language distorts reality. And the grammarians hold that not only does language reveal reality but it also is reality. The Cārvākas go to the opposite extreme and claim that religious discourse is mere prattle, invented by deceptive priests to hoodwink and subjugate the masses. Finally, Advaita Vedānta calls it a methodological device by which a seeker after truth will be assisted in unveiling the ever-present, immediate reality. From realism to idealism, from pluralism to absolutism, and from empiricism to transcendentalism, most of the possible philosophic positions have been presented by the various Hindu philosophical systems.

The Hindu philosophical systems investigate, sometimes with a degree of repetition that becomes tiresome to others, such matters as the status of the finite individual; the distinction as well as the relation between the body, the mind, and the self; the types of entities which may be said to exist; the existence and nature of god; theories of causation; the relation of realism to idealism; the problem of whether universals or relations are basic; and the nature of, and the paths leading towards, liberation.

THE DOXOGRAPHIES

The relatively recent presentation of Hindu philosophy as a series of classical schools (seemingly static and complete) owes a considerable debt to the traditional Hindu Sanskrit doxographies (see Halbfass 1988). For it was in these doxographies, in that literature which summarizes and classifies the main schools or systems, that the term "*darśana*" gained its meaning as the familiar and characteristic word for philosophy. Most of the traditional Hindu doxographies use the word "*darśana*" in their title, in particular those two which are the best known as well as the most interesting and significant ones. The Jaina author Haribhadra (eighth century CE) was the earliest known philosopher to use the word "*darśana*" in the sense of systems of philosophy (*sarvadarśanavācyo'rthaḥ*) (*Ṣaḍdarśanasamuccaya* 1). The fact that Haribhadra chose the word "*darśana*" for the title of his doxography reveals that by the time of the eighth century, it had become a well-known designation for "philosophical" systems or doctrines. Further, Haribhadra uses the term "*darśana*" in two ways: to indicate "what is true and complete insight" (*ṣaḍdarśana*) and "to describe various philosophical views" (*darśanas*). Perhaps the most famous of the doxographies was the *Sarvadarśanasaṃgraha* (Summary of All Systems) by Mādhava-Vidyāraṇya (fourteenth century CE). It not only embraces the various systems but also distinguishes itself by its skillful utilization of sources. It begins by presenting the school of Materialism, criticizes it, and advances from school to school, theory by theory, until finally presents Śaṃkara's Advaita as the conclusion and crown of all philosophical systems. Other well-known doxographies include Śaṃkara's (falsely ascribed to?) *Sarvasiddhāntasaṃgraha*, Rāghavānanda's *Sarvamatasaṃgraha*, and Mādhava Sarasvatī's *Sarvadarśanakaumudī*.

Works such as these, whose titles indicate that they offer a survey of "six" or "all" systems, have an obvious tendency to schematize, stereotype, and distort the doctrines that they discuss. The enumeration of various "views" appears primarily for the sake of criticism and refutation. However, the various works offer differing degrees of openness and inclusiveness, and there is a thread running throughout that reveals a tendency to recognize other views as expressions of partial truths. As well, it should be noted that the various Hindu philosophical systems should not be interpreted as systems of "pure theory" for there are soteriological and practical elements always present, whether in their complete articulation or in their doxographic recapitulation. It is a given, and Hindu philosophers take it for granted and expound it explicitly, that the desire to know (pure theory) has to be motivated and guided by a goal or purpose and that in virtually every Hindu system, the ultimate goal of life is liberation.

What is striking is that these works differ in the number of systems that they discuss even if most of them are oriented around the number six. Further, there is neither a standard hierarchical arrangement nor a traditionally accepted list of doctrines to be covered. Any given hierarchical arrangement implies a soteriological gradation which assigns the followers of the lower doctrines an ethically, socially, and philosophically inferior status. Thus, while the doxographies may not be a very rigorous byproduct of the Hindu philosophical tradition, they did provide the paradigm for the modern presentations of Hindu philosophy.

HISTORY OF THE PHILOSOPHICAL SYSTEMS

A detailed history of Hindu philosophy has long been desired by the academic community. That no such history exists is chiefly due to the fact that the documents upon which it would have to be based are, in large part, nonexistent. The reasons for this are twofold. Brāhmaṇical tradition declares that the Vedas were authorless (*apauruṣeya*), produced by no human (or divine) agency. Thus they are ahistorical. Most of our understanding of the ancient and medieval periods has been largely derived from these surviving texts created by and for a literate and dominant group whose views were largely uncriticized. Indeed the only surviving fully articulated divergent views from the Vedic vision, a body of texts that predated known history, were those of Jainism (Jaini 1979), Buddhism (Harvey 1990), and Ājīvikism (Basham 1951). As well, there is no attention to chronology in classical Hindu philosophy, perhaps because, as has been suggested by many Hindu scholars, there was more concern with the progress of concepts than with the personalities who wrestled with them.

In light of this nonhistorical legacy, it is no wonder that a complete historical presentation of the Hindu philosophical systems does not exist. This lacunae of Hindu tradition's lack of any historiography of philosophy has been the subject of frequent comments, criticisms, and speculations. The roots of the philosophical systems are lost in the mists of time, and this gap has produced much scholastic frustration and lamentation. The Hindu tradition never developed individual historical presentations of the systems, chronologically arranged surveys of its philosophical doctrines, nor histories of the lives and works of its philosophers. All that is there are the completely impersonal doxographic surveys of the various philosophical traditions as well as the genealogies of teachers and disciples and their legendary hagiographies. Very little can be said with any precision about dates, places, and works.

Hindu philosophy has traditionally been classified in terms of six orthodox or "affirmative" (*āstika*) and three heterodox or "negating" (*nāstika*) schools. Pāṇini stated that an *āstika* is one who believes in a transcendent world and a *nāstika* is one who does not believe in it. In common parlance within India today, a "*nāstika*" means an "atheist." But in this philosophical context, the division into *āstika* and *nāstika* only means an acceptance of, or rejection of, the Vedic corpus as an authority. The *āstika* systems, which are termed "canonical," have this in common: they were created in order to reflect upon the Vedas and thus to achieve knowledge of reality. Their orthodoxy consists in the fact that they take the Vedas, the revealed scripture, as their points of departure or, at least in a minimalist exegesis, do not contradict them. The *nāstika* or heterodox systems would, on the contrary, not recognize the authority of the Vedas. Though it should be noted that this division is more political than intellectual, as there is very little Vedic content in some of the orthodox systems.

The *āstika* schools are Nyāya, Vaiśeṣika, Sāṃkhya, Yoga, Mīmāṃsā, and Vedānta, who all accept the authority of the Veda, and the *nāstika* schools are Cārvāka, Jainism, and Buddhism, who all deny the authority of the Veda. Thus, in some sense or other, the *āstika* schools all accept Vedic scripture (*śruti*) as a valid means of both empirical and transempirical knowledge, while the *nāstika* schools do not. The six orthodox systems have been coupled together in three pairs or allied systems (*samāna tantra*): Nyāya-Vaiśeṣika, Sāṃkhya-Yoga, and Mīmāṃsā-Vedānta.

Nyāya

Nyāya, which is famous for its acute analysis of discursive thought, is a philosophical system consisting of three main parts: an elaboration of a methodology for investigating the nature of things through valid means of knowledge (*pramāṇa*), the art of debate through syllogistic reasoning (logic), and metaphysical knowledge about nature, the soul, salvation, and god. The term "*nyāya*" means "logical reasoning," and this school is best known for developing the rules of logic and epistemology in Hindu thought. It is also known by other names such as Ānvīkṣikī (science of logic) and Tarkaśāstra (science of reasoning). Besides logic, Nyāya is famous for formulating an elaborate scheme of inference based on the syllogism. It is often described as logical realism because it accepts an extramental world and because it seeks to build its worldview through logical reasoning. Like its sister-system Vaiśeṣika, Nyāya is realistic with regard to things, properties, relations, and universals. As well, both are pluralistic and theistic admitting individual selves, external relations, and an atomistic cosmology.

Although logic was present in India before Nyāya became a philosophical school and was even regarded as an essential subsidiary to the study of the Veda, Gautama, also known as Akṣapāda and Dīrghatapas (*c.*400–100 BCE?), the author of the *Nyāyasūtra* and the founder of the Nyāya school, is credited with formulating the principles of Hindu logic and establishing it on a firm foundation. However, it should be noted that there is ample evidence that the *Nyāyasūtra* attributed to him appears to be no earlier than the first century CE (at least many interpolated parts of it) and is later than the *Vaiśeṣikasūtra* of its companion school. Gautama's ideas were then explained, amplified, systematized, and fashioned into a coherent system by Vātsyāyana (*c.*300–400 CE) in his *Nyāyasūtrabhāṣya*. Uddyotakara's (*c.*500–600 CE) *Nyāyavārttika* is devoted almost exclusively to logic and epistemology in an attempt to refute Dignāga's logic. The Nyāya school, almost from its inception, was in conflict with Buddhist logicians and their epistemological theories, and Uddyotakara was greatly influenced by and incorporated Dignāga's theories into the Nyāya system. As well, a subsequent Buddhist attack, this time from Dharmakīrti (600 CE), arguing that the Nyāya and Vaiśeṣika proofs for the existence of god (*īśvara*) were logically fallacious, resulted in Udayana (900–1000 CE) formulating the first systematic account of Nyāya theism.

The Nyāya system is an elaboration of sixteen philosophical topics (*padārtha*) as elucidated in the opening verse of the *Nyāyasūtra* which states that supreme bliss is attained by knowledge of the true nature of the sixteen categories: means of correct knowledge (*pramāṇa*), objects of correct knowledge (*prameya*), doubt (*saṃśaya*), purpose (*prayojana*), familiar example (*dṛṣṭānta*), established conclusion (*siddhānta*), members of a syllogism (*avayava*), hypothetical argument (*tarka*), decisive knowledge (*nirṇaya*), discussion for truth (*vāda*), controversy (*jalpa*), destructive arguments (*vitaṇḍā*), fallacies (*hetvābhāsa*), quibbling (*chala*), specious objections (*jāti*), and vulnerable points (*nigrahasthāna*). Nyāya teaches that ignorance is the root of all suffering and rebirth and that only complete knowledge of the true nature of things will bring deliverance (*apavarga*). Salvation is the supreme goal of life, and Nyāya employed logic and epistemology to not only to know reality but also to correct false, fallacious, and sentimental fallacies.

A new school of Nyāya known as Navya Nyāya (new logic) developed in the twelfth century. Unlike the earlier works which had concentrated on an elucidation of the categories as enumerated in the *Nyāyasūtra*, this neo-logical school put an emphasis on the valid means of knowledge (*pramāṇa*) and did not concern itself with metaphysics. The *Tattvacintāmaṇi* of Gaṅgeśa (1200 CE) is the major work of this school and the basis upon which all later developments derived. With it, the Navya Nyāya school developed not only a highly complex epistemology with its own technical language but also initiated a unique style of philosophical writing in India that is noted not only for its brevity but also for its precision.

Vaiśeṣika

The Vaiśeṣika school, founded by Kaṇāda (500–300 BCE?), the author of the *Vaiśeṣikasūtra*, emphasizes ontology and cooperates closely with its sister philosophical system, Nyāya, on matters of epistemology. It is a very old school of thought, and its name is derived from "*viśeṣa*" meaning "the characteristics that distinguish a particular thing from all other things." Thus, the Vaiśeṣika, like its sister-system, is a school of pluralistic realism basing its doctrines upon its key concept of *viśeṣa*, implying that the world exists independent of a thinking mind and consists of a plurality of reals which are all externally related. Praśastapāda (400 CE) wrote the earliest extant commentary on the *Vaiśeṣikasūtra* which is known as the *Padārthadharmasaṃgraha*. This work is not so much a commentary in the usual sense but more of an independent exposition of the Vaiśeṣika doctrines with the *sūtra* work as its basis.

The distinguishing doctrine of the school is that nature is atomic. An individual atom is said to be invisible, devoid of qualities, but possessing potentialities which manifest when it combines with others of the same type to form molecules of four of the elements (earth, water, fire, and air). The atoms are eternal and indivisible, and thus creation or recreation consists in the combination of all the separate atoms into the elements.

As a system of philosophy, the Vaiśeṣika teaches that knowledge of the nature of reality is obtained by knowing the special properties or essential differences which distinguish phenomena. It accepts the universe is extended in space and changing in time. The objective world of infinite variety is divided into six categories (*padārtha*): substance, regarded as the foundation of the universe (*dravya*); quality or attribute (*guṇa*); activity (*karma*); generality or that which characterizes all the members of a given class (*sāmānya*); particularity, unique feature, essence, distinguishing one member from another of the same class and that by means of which the individual atoms are distinguished (*viśeṣa*); inherence or relation, the relationship which exists between a substance and its qualities or between a whole and its parts (*samavāya*); and to these six was later added a seventh or nonexistence (*abhāva*). A category is that which can be known (*jñeya*), validly cognized (*prameya*), and named (*abhidheya*) exists objectively and has characteristics. The category of substance is then reduced to nine ultimate and eternal realities beyond which the mind cannot go and without which the objective world could not exist. The diversity of forms is nothing but a reflection of these nine basic realities, which, if realized, will enable one to attain the supreme goal of absolute freedom. These nine realities are: earth, water, fire, air, ether, time, space, soul, and mind. The first four of these are composed of ultimate elements or atoms (*paramāṇu*), which are the most unitary indivisible units, partless, and eternal. All material things are formed out of combinations of these atoms.

The Vaiśeṣika school, like many other schools of Hindu philosophy, propounds that all living beings, human and nonhuman, have souls that are different from the body, eternal, and ubiquitous. The supreme goal of life is liberation from the bondage of ignorance and *karma*. As well, the Vaiśeṣika system is well known for its attempts to prove the existence of the soul by a series of logical arguments.

Sāṃkhya

The Sāṃkhya school is one of the oldest, if not the oldest, systematic school of Hindu philosophy. Many of its ideas can be found in the *Ṛg Veda* and even more are scattered throughout the Upaniṣads, particularly in the *Kaṭha* (3.10, 5.7) and in the *Śvetāśvatara* (5.7.8, 5.7.12, 4.5.1.3). The supreme sage Kapila, who is alleged to be the founder of Sāṃkhya, is the author of the *Sāṃkhyasūtra* (*c.*500 BCE, now lost). The earliest extant authoritative book on the classical Sāṃkhya is the *Sāṃkhyakārikā* of Īśvarakṛṣṇa (300–400 CE?). It is an extremely influential Hindu philosophical text and a sort of codification of the Sāṃkhya teachings. It deals with the various patterns of enumeration and sets forth the purpose of the teaching, that is, liberation through discrimination between spirit (*puruṣa*) and nature (*prakṛti*). Sāṃkhya's remarkable influence on the development of the other philosophical schools, both orthodox and heterodox, has been oft-noted. In fact, most of Hindu culture, that is, philosophy, mythology, theology, law, medicine, art, *yoga*, Tantra, have all been influenced by the categories and basic ideas of Sāṃkhya. Some of its teachings, like those of the three qualities/attributes/constituents (*guṇa*), the dualism of consciousness and materiality (*puruṣa* and *prakṛti*), and its evolutionary theory of the twenty-four principles (*tattva*), have become an integral part of the Hindu tradition.

The term "*sāṃkhya*" means "number, enumeration, calculation, discriminative knowledge."

> As an adjective, the term refers to any enumerated set or grouping and can presumably be used in any inquiry in which enumeration or calculation is a prominent feature. . . . As a masculine noun, the term refers to someone who calculates, enumerates, or discriminates properly or correctly. As a neuter noun, the term comes to refer to a specific system of dualist philosophizing that proceeds by a method of enumerating the contents of experience and the world for the purpose of attaining radical liberation (*mokṣa, kaivalya*).
>
> (Larson 1987: 3)

Although the main outlines of the history of Sāṃkhya are reasonably clear, the details of the system are murky with three identifiable phases of the system's development seemingly embedded therein. A number of modern scholars have attempted (re)constructive efforts to make explicit that which seems to be implied therein.[1] These three identifiable phases are: ancient Sāṃkhya (1500 BCE) emphasizing enumeration, ascetic Sāṃkhya (600–700 BCE) emphasizing discrimination that leads to liberation, and philosophical Sāṃkhya (100 BCE) emphasizing technical dualistic philosophizing. These disparate and admittedly speculative and problematic outlines do, however, give a good general survey of the main subject matters which concern Sāṃkhya.

The central teachings of Sāṃkhya are that reality is twofold: spirit (*puruṣa*) of the nature of pure consciousness, many, pure, changeless, whose mere presence is responsible for the process of evolution; and matter (*prakṛti*) which is nonconscious, one, ever-changing, subtle, invisible, and therefore must be inferred from its creations, composed of the three qualities, and the ultimate cause of the universe though itself causeless. Nothing exists apart from these two principles, and matter is an object, selves are not. Selves can discriminate, matter cannot. Spirit has neither birth nor death, is nonactive, passive, a patient enjoyer, while matter is active, ever-changing, undergoing cycles of evolution and absorption. The supreme goal of life, according to Sāṃkhya, is for selves to know, to discriminate that the self has nothing to do with matter. This liberation is only phenomenal for the true self is always free. Bondage is but the activity of nature toward one not possessing discrimination, that is, knowledge of the distinction between *puruṣa* and *prakṛti*.

Sāṃkhya is known for its theory of evolution. Nature, primal matter (*prakṛti*), the principal source from which evolution starts, though one, is said to be a composite of three qualities (*guṇa*), the ultimate building blocks of the universe. Originally these three are invisible, in a state of equilibrium, and subsequently, by way of combination and perpetual recombination due to the proximity of spirit, they are in varying states of mutual preponderance. Nature, according to Sāṃkhya, is undergoing continuous transformations. It is the primary matrix out of which all differentiations arise and within which they return, undistinguishable. Of nature's three qualities, *sattva* represents luminosity and intelligence; *rajas* is energy, activity, that which represents the principle of discontinuity, change; and *tamas* is inertia, heaviness, coarseness, darkness, the principle of continuity. When the equilibrium of these three is disturbed, matter evolves in the following order: *prakṛti*, *mahat* or *buddhi* (intelligence), *ahaṃkāra* (egoism), *manas* (mind), five *jñānendriya*s (sense organs: hearing, touch, sight, taste, and smell), five *karmendriyas* (organs of action: tongue, hands, feet, organs of reproduction, and organs of excretion), five *tanmātras* (subtle elements of color, sound, smell, touch, and taste), and five *mahābhūtas* (gross elements: ether, air, fire, water, and earth). This emanation scheme may be seen as both an account of cosmic evolution and a logical-transcendental analysis of the various factors involved in experience.

Yoga

The technique of Yoga is ancient, complex, mysterious, and ambiguous. Various yogic spiritual practices are mentioned in a number of the major Upaniṣads as well as in Jaina and Buddhist texts. Etymologically, the word "*yoga*" derives from the Sanskrit root *yuj* "to bind together, to join, to unite." What is being conjoined is the individual self with the transcendental self; others say it is union with one's chosen deity (*Yogasūtra* 2.44); still others say it is the process of joining the breath, the syllable *oṃ*, and all this world in its manifoldness (*Maitrī Upaniṣad* 6.25). Further, *yoga* has been defined by Vyāsa as "enstasis" (*samādhih*). Patañjali defined *yoga* as the "cessation of the mind's fluctuations." The *Bhagavad Gītā* (2.48) defines *yoga* as "equanimity" (*samatva*). In its broadest sense, *yoga* is a technique for unifying consciousness as well as the resulting state (of ecstatic union with the object of contemplation) and refers to all of India's spiritual techniques, values, attitudes, and systems.

The Yoga system was first systematically expounded in the *Yogasūtra* of Patañjali (third century BCE). Even though there is a tradition which identifies them, scholars now generally agree that the author of the *Yogasūtra* is neither the grammarian Patañjali nor Patañjali who wrote a famous book on Āyurveda, the science of life and health. There is a commentary on the *Yogasūtra* by Vyāsa (500 CE) and another by King Bhoja (1000 CE). Vācaspati wrote a gloss on Vyāsa's commentary as did Vijñānabhikṣu, who represents a tendency to synthesize the views of Sāṃkhya, Yoga, and Vedānta.

The Yoga system stands in close relation to the Sāṃkhya system, adopting its metaphysics though it adds a twenty-sixth principle (the supreme lord, *īśvara*) to the Sāṃkhya list of twenty-five. As well, while Sāṃkhya is primarily intellectualistic and emphasizes metaphysical knowledge as the means to liberation, Yoga is voluntaristic and emphasizes the need for extreme self-control as the means to liberation.

The *Yogasūtra* is a short work of 196 aphorisms divided into four sections (*pāda*). The first section, "Contemplation" (*samādhi*), concerns the general nature of *yoga* and its technique. It defines *yoga* in its famous second aphorism as the "cessation of the mind's fluctuations" (*yogaś citta-vṛtti-nirodhah*). This chapter describes the fluctuations, modifications, and modulations of thought which disturb pure consciousness and then begins to describe means (practice/*abhyāsa* and detachment/*vairāgya*) by which they may be stilled. A method to achieve the goal of *yoga* is formulated by which the spirit (*puruṣa*) is isolated from nature (*prakṛti*) by means of mind control. The second chapter, "Spiritual Disciplines" (*sādhana*), begins by delineating the afflictions which disturb the mind and answers why one should practice *yoga*. It states the five external yogic practices of the eight-fold yogic path (*aṣṭāngamārga*): abstentions (*yama*) or nonviolence (*ahiṃsā*), truthfulness (*satya*), nonstealing (*asteya*), continence (*brahmacarya*), and nonpossession (*aparigraha*); observances (*niyama*) or purity (*śauca*), contentment (*santoṣa*), austerity (*tapas*), study (*svadhyāya*), and surrender to god (*īśvara praṇidhāna*); physical postures (*āsana*); breathing techniques (*prāṇāyāma*); and withdrawal from the objects of the sense organs (*pratyāhāra*). The third chapter, "Supernormal Powers" (*vibhūti*), delineates the last three limbs of the eight-fold *yoga*: concentration (*dhāraṇā*), meditation (*dhyāna*), and absorption (*samādhi*), and then speaks of the divine effects of yogic practices. Finally, chapter four, "The Nature of Liberation" (*kaivalya*), gives a general exposition of the study and practice of *yoga* leading to liberation.

Mīmāṃsā

The *Pūrva Mīmāṃsā* (First Investigation), also known as *Karma Mīmāṃsā* (Study of [Ritual] Action) of Jaimini (300–200 BCE?) concerns itself chiefly with the questions of the proper interpretation of the Vedic texts. The first four orthodox schools of Nyāya, Vaiśeṣika, Sāṃkhya, and Yoga are orthodox in name only, for they are neither dependent upon the Veda, nor profess to interpret the Veda, nor look to the Veda for justification of their doctrines. But Mīmāṃsā is a genuine Vedic tradition. Its basic assumption is that the scriptural texts are authoritative and faultless and have to be interpreted to explain away any apparent absurdities or contradictions. It is a system centered around investigating the nature of Vedic injunctions. This investigation led to the development of principles of scriptural interpretation and to theories of meaning. Jaimini, who composed the *Pūrvamīmāṃsāsūtra*, propounded that Vedic injunctions not only prescribe actions but also that these actions are the means to the attainment of desirable goals, including heaven. The earliest extant commentary upon Jaimini's work is the *Pūrvamīmāṃsāsūtrabhāṣya* of Śabara (200 CE). His commentary was interpreted by two great scholars, Prabhākara (700 CE) and Kumārila Bhāṭṭa (700 CE). Since there are differences between their two interpretations, two subschools arose named after the two scholars: the Prabhākara and the Bhāṭṭa.

Mīmāṃsā's central concern is "duty" (*dharma*), which is defined as the desired object (*artha*), whose desirability is testified only by the injunctive statements of the Vedas. The *Pūrvamīmāṃsāsūtra* commences with the aim of investigating and ascertaining the nature of religious duty (*dharma*). As religious duty is not a physical entity, it cannot be known through perception or any of the other means of valid knowledge which presupposes the work of perception. Thus Mīmāṃsā concludes that religious duty is knowable only through the scripture, and the essence of the scripture is injunctions and commandments which tell what ought to be done (*vidhi*) and what ought not to be done (*niṣedha*).

The Vedic scriptures were attacked by the Śramaṇas around 500 BCE, and the Mīmāṃsā school arose in order to reestablish the Vedic authority by resolving the apparent contradictions and other textual anomalies found in the Vedic texts. Thus was established the science of exegesis. The Mīmāṃsā philosophy of language was mainly concerned with the methodology of textual interpretation in order to give a cogent explanation of the scriptural texts of a prescriptive nature. It has to deal with apparent absurdities, inconsistencies, self-contradictions, ambiguities, and evolved rules of interpretation which were later accepted generally by all schools of thought and used freely in legal practice and commentarial literature. The Mīmāṃsā gave a semantic definition of a sentence, evolving the concepts of mutual expectancy, consistency, and contiguity as factors necessary for a sentence. In order to explain away apparent absurdities, it evolved the theory of metaphors.

The problems of interpretation led the Mīmāṃsā school to develop into a great philosophical school. Mīmāṃsā developed itself into a kind of philosophical discipline, incorporating into it a theory of knowledge, epistemology, and logic, theories of meaning and language, and a realistic metaphysics. With its emphasis on language and linguistics, the Mīmāṃsā has sometimes been called the *vākyaśāstra* (theory of speech).

Vedānta

The word "*vedānta*" means, quite literally, the "end of the Veda." Historically, the concluding portions of the Vedas (the Upaniṣads) were known as the Vedānta. By association, the philosophical schools which based their thought upon the Upaniṣads are also called Vedānta. Since Upaniṣadic thought is not comprised of any consistent system and seemingly propounds different views, it became necessary to systematize it. Bādarāyaṇa (*c.*400 BCE) attempted this systematization in the form of short aphorisms called *sūtras*. His work, the *Vedāntasūtra*, is also known as the *Brahmasūtra* because it is an exposition of, and inquiry into, *brahman*; as *Śarīrakasūtra* because it is concerned with the nature and destiny of the embodied soul; as *Bhikṣusūtra* because those competent to study it are renunciates; and as *Uttaramīmāṃsāsūtra* because it is an inquiry into the final sections of the Veda. Its first *sūtra* begins, "*athāto brahma jijñāsā*"—now, therefore, the inquiry into the absolute (*brahman*). Together with the *Dharmasūtra* of Jaimini, which is an inquiry into the duties (*dharma*) enjoined by the Vedas, these two investigations (*mīmāṃsā*) form a systematic inquiry into the contents and purport of the entire Veda, and thus these two *mīmāṃsā*s are orthodox schools par excellence.

There are numerous Vedāntic schools though all of them acknowledge three primary sourcebooks: the Upaniṣads, *Bhagavad Gītā*, and *Brahmasūtra*. Together these three are known as the triple canon (*prasthānatraya*) of Vedānta. These texts laid the basis for the development of the Vedānta philosophy. Unlike Jaimini who laid stress on the ritualistic portions of the Vedas, Bādarāyaṇa emphasized the philosophical portions, the Upaniṣads. Whereas the former put forth a path of ritual action (*karmakāṇḍa*), the latter recommends the path of wisdom (*jñānakāṇḍa*).

Though Vedānta is frequently referred to as one *darśana*, there are many different schools of Vedānta. Broadly speaking, the Vedānta schools may be divided into two main divisions with certain particular tendencies: non-dualistic with absolutistic tendencies, unqualified nondualism of Advaita Vedānta with Śaṃkara (*c.*650 CE) as its main proponent; and dualistic with theistic tendencies as expounded by Rāmānuja's (1027–1147 CE) qualified nondualism (Viśiṣṭādvaita) and Madhva's (1199–1276 CE) dualism (Dvaita). Other theistic Vedāntic *bhāṣyakāra*s include: Bhāskara (eighth century), Vallabha (1479–1531 CE), Nimbārka (eleventh century), and Caitanya (1485–1533 CE). No commentary on the *Brahmasūtra* survives before Śaṃkara's *bhāṣya* (*c.*650–700 CE), though there are stray references in various works to thinkers such as Bodhāyana, Upavarṣa, Bhartṛprapañca, Bhartṛhari, Āśmarathya, Auḍulomi, and Kārśakṛtsna.

All the Vedānta schools agree that the central teaching of the Upaniṣads is that *brahman* is the ultimate principle underlying the physical universe and individual souls. The chief difference among the Vedānta schools lies in the manner in which the world and individual souls can be said to be connected with *brahman*. There are certain passages in the

Upaniṣads which assert the nondifference of the world and individuals from *brahman*, and there are others which speak of their difference from *brahman*. These apparently contradictory passages have to be reconciled, and the mode of reconciliation adopted by each school represents its basic philosophical position.

According to some Vedāntic schools (Advaita), the Upaniṣadic texts teaching nondifference are primary, and those teaching difference are secondary, intended only to lead to the real teaching of nonduality. *Brahman* is the only reality, and the universe and individuals have no existence apart from *brahman*. In an oft-quoted verse, "*brahman* is real, the universe is nonreal, and individuals are not different from *brahman*." Further, *brahman*, which is the only reality, is beyond all determination, all attributes. It is only due to ignorance that the attributeless *brahman* appears as though endowed with attributes. Thus it follows that Advaita adheres to a doctrine that the *karmakāṇḍa* and the *jñānakāṇḍa* are independent of each other, while Viśiṣṭādvaita will defend the thesis that they jointly constitute a single work with Jaimini's coming first and Bādarāyaṇa's coming after it in logical order.

According to some theistic Vedānta schools (Viśiṣṭādvaita and Bhedābheda), the texts teaching difference and those teaching nondifference are equally important. The universe and individual souls are therefore different as well as nondifferent from *brahman*. In so far as the world and souls are imperfect, they are dependent and different from *brahman* who is perfect and independent. At the same time, they are nondifferent from *brahman* in the sense that they form the body and the attributes of *brahman*.

According to other theistic Vedāntic schools (Dvaita), the texts teaching difference convey the real teaching of the Upaniṣads. The universe and individual souls are absolutely different from *brahman*. However, this does not mean that they are independent realities. *Brahman* is the only independent reality, and the world and individuals, while separate from *brahman*, are dependent thereon. The Upaniṣadic texts which teach nondifference are intended only to emphasize the independent character of *brahman*.

Other

Kauṭilya's *Arthaśāstra* (*c*.321–296 BCE) systematized the science of political economy or material prosperity, which is one of the four Hindu goals of life. The work is mainly concerned with a human beings' subsistence, wealth, and property. It also covers theories of kingship and statecraft, concepts for the public good, relations between states, and the formation and implementation of policy.

A highly sophisticated philosophy of language developed at least as early as the fifth century BCE with the *Aṣṭādhyāyi* of the famous Pāṇini. This work has yet to be surpassed and produced a descriptive analytical grammar of Sanskrit, covering the analysis of phonemes, suffixes, sentences, rules of word combination, and the formation of verbal roots. From Pāṇini's beginnings, full-fledged linguistic philosophies were formulated by the leading thinker of the grammarian school, Bhartṛhari (400 CE), in his *Vākyapadīya* which analyzed language as a door leading to liberation. Maṇḍana Miśra (700 CE) continued this analysis in his *Sphoṭasiddhi* and *Vidhiviveka* developing his own variety of Advaita using the doctrine of *sphoṭa* (that from which meaning bursts forth).

The Śaiva schools are philosophical systems within the fold of Śaivism, religious sects that worship Lord Śiva as the supreme deity. Śaiva theology and philosophy developed primarily outside the Vedic-fold relying instead on the Tantras and Āgamas. There arose in India a number of Śaiva schools, including Vīraśaivism or Liṅgāyatism, which traces its origin to the five great teachers mentioned in the *Svāyambhuvāgama* (Revaṇasiddha, Marulasiddha, Ekorāma, Paṇḍitārādhya, and Vīśvārādhya) and Basava (1100 CE), who is the greatest expounder of the system; Śivādvaita of Śrīkaṇṭha (1200 CE), whose *bhāṣya* on the *Brahmasūtra* identifies *brahman* with Paramaśiva; Śaiva Siddhānta, a dualistic school which incorporated Tamil devotion with Kashmir Śaiva nondualism and whose most important philosophers include Appar, Jñānasaṃbandhar, Sundaramūrti, Māṇikkavācakar, Aruṇandiśivācārya, and Meykaṇḍa (1200 CE), whose *Śivajñānabodham* is the basic text of the school; and Kashmir Śaivism (also known as Trika, Spanda, and Pratyabhijña), a nondualistic philosophical system attributed to Lord Śiva himself and his *Śivasūtra*. It's most notable exponents include Somānanda (900–950 CE), Utpala (925–975 CE), Abhinavagupta (975–1025 CE), and Kṣemarāja (1000–50 CE). It recognizes the entire universe as a manifestation of divine conscious energy and explains how the formless, unmanifest supreme principle, Śiva, manifests as the entire universe.

Islamic philosophy in India has been represented by mystics known as Ṣūfīs, by the Mughal Emperor Jalāluddīn Akbar (1581 CE), and by various syncretistic religious leaders who attempted to harmonize Hindu and Muslim traditions (the most famous are Rāmānanda, Kabīr, Nānak, and Sāī Bābā).

Cārvāka

Cārvāka or Lokāyata is the Indian school of materialism/naturalism/humanism. Being an expression of "the person on the street or common sense" point of view, it has ancient origins even if it is not easy to trace the history of this school. It worked out it's philosophy in opposition to idealism, mystification, and all expressions of otherworldliness. There are Vedic references to heretics, nonconformists, skeptics, agnostics, and dialectical iconoclasts. As a philosophy it must have initially emerged as protests against the excessive ritualism and/or mysticism of the Vedic world. Subsequently, Upaniṣadic idealism, being unsuited to many a pleasure-seeker, must also have provided impetus for the doctrine. Further, in the post-Upaniṣadic age, political, religious, and social crises, exploitation and discontent, and the siren's lure of pleasure must have all contributed to the development of the Cārvāka school. It should also be noted that although this school is generally dismissed as unworthy of any real consideration because our chief sources of information about this school are given in the works of other schools only with the purpose to refute materialism, misrepresentations, exaggerations, and omissions have likely given us a caricature and not a true representation. As none of the foundational works of this system are extant, what we know of this school's philosophy comes primarily from Jayarāśi's *Tattvopaplavasiṃha* (600 CE) which appears to be a summary of Bṛhaspati's *Bṛhaspatisūtra* (now lost), from Mādhavācārya's *Sarvadarśanasaṃgraha*, and from stray references made in other works.

Cārvāka and Lokāyata are terms indicating a materialistic worldview. Bṛhaspati is generally stated as the traditional founder of the school. However, tradition is unclear about who this Bṛhaspati was and who or what the word "*cārvāka*" indicates. Either it is a proper name (of a seer mentioned in the *Mahābhārata*) or perhaps it indicates Bṛhaspati himself or a disciple of his. Etymologically, *cārvāka* is derived from the root *carva* "to eat," as in eat, drink, and be merry. The word may also be derived from "*cāru vāc*" meaning "sweet tongued." In a similar vein, the word "*lokāyata*" is interpreted as meaning "the philosophy for which the world is the basis," implying the common people's philosophy.

The central teachings of the Cārvāka may be summed up in Kṛṣṇapati Miśra's *Prabodhacandrodaya* (Act II): "Lokāyata is the only scripture; perception is the only valid means of knowledge; earth, water, fire, and air are the only elements; enjoyment is the only end of human existence; mind is only a product of matter; there is no other world; death means liberation," and in Mādhavācārya's *Sarvadarśanasaṃgraha* (chapter 1): "There is no heaven, no final liberation, nor any soul in another world; nor do the actions of the four castes, orders, and so on, produce any real effect. While life remains, let a person live happily, let him feed on *ghī* even though one runs into debt; once the physical body becomes ashes, can it ever return?." The Cārvāka is a useful and significant system in that it serves as a corrective whenever metaphysical flights of fancy, excesses, and extremes rear their heads.

Jainism and Buddhism

The heterodox (*nāstika*) schools of Jainism and Buddhism rejected both the Vedic authority and Upaniṣadic mysticism and encouraged human beings to use reasoning and spiritual austerity to find answers to the great philosophical questions. As well, they both recognized the rule of natural law in the universe. Especially in their early formative stages, both Jainism and Buddhism were opposed to any authoritarianism in arriving at conclusions, even that of a god. Both systems have origins reaching far back in history with the long line of Jaina teachers consisting of twenty-four *tīrthaṅkara*s (ford-makers) or Jinas (conquerors), the last of whom was Vardhamāna Mahāvīra (500 BCE), and Gautama the Buddha (*c.*563 BCE), within a tradition which declares that there have been countless Buddhas, each coming to turn the Dharma-wheel and reestablish the path to enlightenment. Within the Buddhist tradition, there is talk of six Buddhas of antiquity as well as Maitreya, the Buddha-to-come.

Mahāvīra taught the perfectibility of humans to be accomplished through a strictly moral and ascetic life. Central to Jaina teachings is the doctrine of *ahiṃsā* or noninjury, in thought, word, and deed, to all living beings. Also distinct and noteworthy are their doctrines of *anekāntavāda* or nonabsolutism (the thesis that things have infinite aspects that no one determination can exhaust) and a distinctive feature of Jaina logic known as the doctrine of standpoints or *naya* (the thesis that there are many partial perspectives from which reality can be determined, none of which is, taken by itself, wholly true, but each of which is partially so). This principle of standpoints is known as maybeism (*syādvāda*) with its sevenfold formulation: maybe it is; maybe it is not; maybe it is and is not; maybe it is indescribable; maybe it is and is indescribable; maybe it is not and is indescribable; and maybe it is and is not and is indescribable. The significance of this doctrine is that one's knowledge regarding anything is relative, a rather remarkably modern idea.

Buddha taught his four noble truths (suffering, inadequacy, the origination of suffering, the cessation of suffering, the path leading to the cessation of suffering); his eight-fold path to enlightenment (*nirvāṇa*); his doctrines of no-self (*anātman*), impermanence (*anitya*), and dependent-origination (*pratītyasamutpāda*). Out of the classical foundation laid by the Buddha developed the philosophical schools of the Theravāda and Mahāyāna traditions, most notably the Mādhyamika and Yogācāra traditions. Buddha, as a religious reformer, did not claim to be a divinely inspired prophet, a personal savior, or a deity incarnate in flesh. He declared himself to be a teacher, a supreme teacher, an awakened one who reveals a unique path to enlightenment.

MODERN DEVELOPMENTS

Much of the philosophical work done by modern philosophers, scholars, and writers is in the English language. The number of Sanskrit strongholds is dwindling, though there are still traditional Hindu scholars known as *paṇḍita*s or *śāstrī*s who are affiliated with schools of traditional learning, *āśrama*s, *pāṭhaśālā*s, and/or departments of Sanskrit at Indian universities at Varanasi, Calcutta, Pune, and other places. As well, one may take note of the recent dialogues arranged between Western-trained Indian professors of philosophy and traditional Hindu *paṇḍita*s. These include the Rege experiment at Pune; the meeting of Nyāya *paṇḍita*s at Varanasi, of Mīmāṃsā scholars at Tirupati, and of Kashmir Śaivism scholars at Srinagar (Klostermaier 1994: 385); and the work of such institutes as the Indian Council of Philosophical Research, the Rashtriya Sanskrit Samsthana, the Adyar Library, and the Tibetan Institute of Higher Studies.

In reviewing the works of modern Hindu philosophy, one comes across a number of divergent characterizations: those who write surveys or histories of Hindu philosophy; those who interpret one or more classical systems in comparison with either allied Hindu or Western doctrines; those who give a new interpretation or make a critical study of a classical system; those who treat modern philosophical problems in ways suggested by Western philosophy but as may be expounded by Hindu doctrines; and those who, with a thorough mastery of texts, meticulously and faithfully expound the classical systems (Murty 1985: 113).

Among the histories of Hindu philosophy written by modern Indian scholars may be noted those of Surendranath Dasgupta, Sarvepalli Radhakrishnan, Mysore Hiriyanna, Satischandra Chatterjee, Dhirendramohan Datta, and Jadunath Sinha, and, among Western scholars, those of Erich Frauwallner, Friedrich Max Müller, Karl Potter, and Klaus Klostermaier.

Second, there is the large body of work devoted to comparative philosophy. Under this rubric fall comparisons of such Hindu philosophers as Śaṃkara with Immanuel Kant, Johann Gottlieb Fichte, Georg W. F. Hegel, Martin Heidegger, and Jacques Derrida; of Rāmānuja with Hegel; of Bhartṛhari, Aurobindo, and Nāgārjuna with Derrida; of Buddhism with David Hume and Alfred North Whitehead; of Dignāga with the logical positivists; and of Neo-Nyāya logic with modern logic.

Third, there is a group of philosophers who deserve to be recognized for their original, creative work which is in continuity with Hindu tradition but not constrained by it. To this group belong, on the one hand, a number of major thinkers such as M. K. Gandhi, Rabindranath Tagore, Vivekānanda, Muhammed Iqbal, and Aurobindo, and, on the other, a number of brilliant academic philosophers, such as K. C. Bhattacharya, Sarvepalli Radhakrishnan, Kalidas Bhattacharya, R. D. Ranade, N. V. Bannerjee, R. Das, T. M. P. Mahadevan, T. R. V. Murti, P. T. Raju, Bimal Krishna Matilal, and J. N. Mohanty.

NOTES

1 Richard Garbe construes the old Sāṃkhya system of Kapila as primarily an ancient philosophy of nature; Surendranath Dasgupta reconstructs Sāṃkhya from the medieval text, Vijñānabhikṣu's *Sāṃkhyapravacanabhāṣya*; and K. C. Bhattacharya construes the Sāṃkhya system as a philosophy of the subject demanding imaginative introspection at every moment (Larson 1987: 46–47).

CHAPTER TWENTY-FOUR

KĀLA

Randy Kloetzli and Alf Hiltebeitel

There is no significant body of scholarship that systematically discusses and interprets the Hindu views of time in the way that Aristotelian scholarship has done in the West. Although Anindita Balslev (1983, 1993) has recently undertaken to fill this void and a variety of monographs address pieces of the puzzle, issues such as the relationship between time, motion, and soul remain unaddressed. Neither have the contributions of Hindu astrology to the understanding of time advanced much beyond the translations of some basic texts (*Yavanajātaka*, *Vṛddhayavanajātaka*, *Bṛhat Saṃhitā*, and *Bṛhad Jāṭaka*). However, there can be little doubt that the astrological sciences contributed significantly to concepts such as the moment (*kṣaṇa*, *nimeṣa*), destiny (*niyati*), and duration of life (*āyus*). Studies of time in Hindu myth and ritual are plentiful, but, with the exception of Madeline Biardeau (1981), narrowly focused. Nor have studies of time in India taken sufficient account of cross-cultural comparison, though again, and rather randomly, exceptions would include Michael Witzel (1984) on archaeoastronomy, Wilhelm Halbfass (1992) in Heidegger studies, and Romila Thapar (1991, 1996, 1997) on the vexing problem of "the supposed absence of history." A short chapter such as this will not provide the needed remedy. What it will attempt is to highlight these and other issues by exploring the richness of Hindu insights into the problem of time from multiple perspectives, including both non-Hindu Indian views as well as corresponding concerns within the Hellenistic world.

ONTOLOGICAL STATUS OF TIME

There are several distinct views within Hindu materials concerning the reality of time and its relationship to being. Generally cutting across Hindu and Buddhist philosophical debates are the concepts of *satkāryavāda* and *asatkāryavāda*: respectively, the theory of the preexistence of the effect or product in its cause, as typified by Sāṃkhya-Yoga and Advaita Vedānta, and the rejection of that theory by the Vaiśeṣika, maintaining that something new is produced, albeit out of preexisting eternal constituents. Also significant is the Mīmāṃsā concept of *apūrva*, which describes what is "unprecedented" or "not there before," in the outcome of a Vedic ritual, whose fruit is guaranteed but whose time of fruition is unforeseeable. Debate within the six systems, over against their heterodox counterparts, also generates the new position that the Veda is eternal.

Beginning with the most influential view: In Advaita Vedānta being is timeless, the "one without a second" (*ekamevādvaitīyam*). The veil of *māyā* covers the nondual *brahman* (unmanifest being) and projects the world of multiplicity and movement (Balslev 1993: 173). In some contexts it is even possible to state that "time does not exist." As Halbfass puts it, in Advaita, "time appears as fundamentally incompatible with reality in the true sense, that is, with the unbroken identity of *brahman*; accordingly, it is relegated to the status of *māyā*, cosmic illusion" (1992: 221).

In Sāṃkhya, time is part of the reality of change (*pariṇāma*), the internal modification of *prakṛti* or matter, and as such is part of manifest reality but is not a separate substance or *tattva*. The dynamic *prakṛti* in Sāṃkhya combines space, time, and matter in the same principle. In Sāṃkhya, involvement with time is therefore indirect; there is no event-in-time conception in this system. It is possible that Sāṃkhya indirectly supports a notion of "*kalpa*" as the interval between the entanglement of the soul (*puruṣa*) with *prakṛti* in its unmanifest (*avyakta*) state and its eventual severance or cutting (*kḷp*) from this entanglement, understood as liberation or *mokṣa*.

Vaiśeṣika has "a substantialist, realist ontology that . . . provides an extended critique of event-ontologies" (Halbfass 1992: 82, citing Potter 1971: 1). Its view is that time (*mahākāla*) is a substance and co-exists with being. Time is, however, "marginalized and superseded not by being presented as an appearance or illusion, but by being raised to the status of an eternal, 'timeless' substance," one among other basic world constituents (Halbfass 1992: 221). Vaiśeṣika includes a radical critique of the Buddhist (e.g. Sautrāntika) concept of "impermanence" as "momentariness": instead of "momentariness" being inherent to the very nature of reality, with the moment (*kṣaṇa*) analyzed in terms of lack of identity and givenness to destruction, Vaiśeṣika views momentary *karman* or acts as covering phases of several moments including destruction, and destruction itself as requiring explanation through *saṃyoga* (connection) and *vibhāga* (disjunction) rather than as being inherent (Halbfass 1992: 213–16).

According to the *Yogabhāṣya* of Vyāsa, the whole universe undergoes change in a single moment (*kṣaṇa*). Change occurs within what Yoga, like Sāṃkhya, understands as the internal modification (*pariṇāma*) of matter, and conventional usages of the "three times"—past, present, future—are thus inherent to "change" within matter and have no reality of their own (Balslev 1983: 48–53). Accordingly, in *Yogabhāṣya* 3.52, Vyāsa rejects the notion that time as such is a real entity (Halbfass 1992: 216, 216n66). Moments have objective reality, but the notion of a collection of moments, of a time continuum, is a mental construction (*buddhinirmāṇa*) (Balslev 1993: 173). Yoga's treatment of the moment, like the theory of momentariness—*kṣaṇikavāda*—as a systematic view within Buddhism, sees no continuity or fluidity in the perception of reality. Instead, the analysis is a psychological one in which the adept or *yogin* attempts to become aware of all the constituents of the perception of the moment, to inventory the contents of consciousness. For Yoga, this inventory is done to isolate the soul (*puruṣa*); for Buddhism, to eliminate attachment to all notions of soul (*anātman*). There is no *kāla* as a substratum in which events occur, let alone which is an agent in shaping or advancing the destiny of the soul. As developed within Buddhism, indeed, there is no soul. Taken to this extreme, there is a denial of time, motion, and soul.

All six orthodox Hindu philosophical schools, like the Buddhist and Jaina schools that they debate, agree to terms that effect a truncation of *bhakti*, "devotion" to one deity. If, for the six systems, there is at all a deity, he or she does not do much if anything with regard to time, motion, and the soul's salvation. For instance, as Halbfass says, "The Vaiśeṣika concept of time is only a faint . . . echo of the ancient mythology of time as a universal cosmic power and as the matrix of all entities. In classical Vaiśeṣika, time has been stripped of its dynamic and creative aspects" (1992: 213). One can understand correctly that Vaiśeṣika centers its truncation of this "ancient mythology" around the deity. But although one can turn to *Atharva Veda* 19.53–54 with their references to Time (Kāla) as the highest god and begetter of the worlds, a father who becomes his son Prajāpati, a solar horse drawing the wheel of beings, the notion of "an ancient time mythology" is itself simplistic since these hymns make of time more of a matrix for allusions than a myth or mythology. Indeed, it is more insightful to connect such a view in India, as elsewhere, with an "epic fatalism" than an "ancient mythology" (Hiltebeitel 1990: 33–35; Vassilkov 1999: 27–31), although one would have to debate as to its ancientness. One should appreciate, however, that, as Mikhail Bakhtin has argued, insights about temporality are often first achieved in narrative form and only "later 'transcribed' (often with considerable loss) into discursive philosophy" (Morson 1994: 87). As to the Vaiśeṣika system, it would be better to say that it differentiates itself not only from such a generality but from views that hierarchalize times, such as *Maitrāyaṇi Upaniṣad* 6.15: "There are, assuredly, two forms of Brahmā: Time and the Timeless. That which is prior to the sun is the Timeless (*a-kāla*), without parts (*a-kalā*). But that which begins with the sun is Time, which has parts" (Glucklich 1994: 39). Such hierarchizations of time in relation to the deity typify representations of the universe of *bhakti*, which are also articulated by erudite Brāhmaṇs—in the *Śvetāśvatara Upaniṣad*, the "proto-Sāṃkhya-Yoga" of the *Mahābhārata*, the epics more generally, the *Viṣṇu Purāṇa*, and so on—who transform older mythic temporalities into a "contemporary" rival theological-philosophical position. This view reverberates throughout the Hindu arts—music, dance, iconography (most famously in the dance of Śiva), architecture, literature, mythology, and so on—and is transposed with a little more fine-tuning into the oscillating temporalities of Tantra. Leaving its imagery for further discussion, it is enough to cite four formative expressions.

First, the *Śvetāśvatara Upaniṣad*, a text certainly no later than the six systems, begins with mention of time (*kāla*) as one of six rejected options as to what "it" is that accounts for the totality of the world (Olivelle 1998: 614). One quickly learns that the correct answer is the lord, who governs time (*Śvetāśvatara Upaniṣad* 3.2), past and future (3.15), the seasons (4.4), and day and night (4.18). The Upaniṣad then returns to time in its closing lesson: the lord is he who "always encompasses this whole world," at whose "command" the "work of creation . . . unfolds" sequentially into the five elements or "realities" (*tattva*), time itself, and the "subtle qualities (*guṇa*) of the body (*ātman*)," and who "carries on" after this "work is dissolved, as someone other than those realities. One sees him as the beginning, as the basis and cause of the joining (*saṃyoganimittahetuḥ*), as beyond the three times. . . . He, from whom the unfolding world has come forth, is higher than and different from the time-confined forms of the tree (*sa vṛkṣakālākṛtibhiḥ paro 'nyo*). . . . He is . . . the architect of time (*kālakāro*)" (*Śvetāśvatara Upaniṣad* 6.2–6, 16). Ontologically, the lord encompasses, originates, governs, and dissolves time while being other than and prior to its unfolding and rhythms, yet having an implicit temporal rhythm of his own. The *Bhagavad Gītā* makes such a double calibration explicit and more chronometrically specific in the lord's (that is, Kṛṣṇa's) disclosure that, beyond the cosmic rhythms of *yugas* and *kalpa*s, creations and dissolutions, "I am Time (*kālo 'smi*), cause of the destruction of the worlds, matured, and set out to gather in the worlds here" (11.32). *Mahābhārata* 12.335.80 then says, "And time (*kāla*), which [is computed by] the course of the stars, is the supreme Nārāyaṇa (*nārāyaṇaparaḥ kālo jyotiṣām ayanaṃ ca yat*)." And with a different kind of specificity, the *Viṣṇu Purāṇa* then adds time (*kālasvarūpa*) to the Sāṃkhyan schema—even though Sāṃkhya philosophy may not recognize time but prefer to speak only of the soul and manifest and unmanifest *prakṛti*—and speaks of time as one of the forms (*rūpa*) of Viṣṇu:

> These four—*pradhāna* (primary or crude matter), *puruṣa* (spirit), *vyakta* (visible substance), and *kāla* (time)—the wise consider to be the pure and supreme condition of Viṣṇu. . . . The deity as Time is without beginning, and his end is not known; and from him the revolutions of creation, continuance, and dissolution unintermittingly succeeds: for when, in the latter season, the equilibrium of the qualities (*pradhāna*) exists, and spirit (*pumān*) is detached from matter, then the form of Viṣṇu which is Time abides.
>
> (1.2.16, 1.2.26–27)

Meanwhile, of further importance for philosophically refining such a view, and for the importation of his language not only into *bhakti* but also Tantra, is Bhartṛhari. Though familiar with the Vaiśeṣika view of time as one of the world-constitutive substances, he "also mentions the view that this one time-substance is, by virtue of self-differentiation (*vibhaktena-ātmanā*), the cause of the 'origin, duration and destruction' (*utpatti, sthiti, vināśa*) of temporal beings," and is "the wire-puller [*sūtradhāraḥ*] of this world-machine"—*sūtradhāra* also means "stage manager." With its prior "power" (*śakti*) of "inherence" (*samavāya*), time differentiates and regulates the universe through its powers of "prevention" and "permission," that is, of withholding different entities from emerging and releasing others into actual existence, which it does "by activating . . . potentialities (*śakti*) that constitute the condition of the possibility of all" particulars. Reality (*sattā*) itself as the "eternal act" (*kriyānityā*) is thus "unleashed and manifested" in "lower universals" (*jāti*) that "develop their own drive towards concrete, temporal, individual existence." This view reverberates with theological and narrative allusions. Bhartṛhari also "refers explicitly to the relationship between language and time," for instance, in discussing the verbal and nominal senses of "being," and rejects a strictly cyclical view: "Ultimately, temporal occurrences are irreversible and nonrecurrent" (Halbfass 1992: 205–6).

TIME, MOTION, AND SOUL

In Hellenistic philosophy discussions of the relationship of motion and time are so elaborate that Simplicius (Cornford 1934) categorized them in the following manner: one eternal world with eternal motion; a continuous series of worlds coming into being in succession according to certain periods of time with uninterrupted everlasting motion; a discontinuous series of single worlds interrupted by states in which there is no time and with motion interrupted with intervals of motionlessness; and a single world only arising from the beginning of time with motion that has a beginning in time.

Motion, time, and soul are identical in Aristotelian philosophy. It is god who is the prime mover, the unmoved mover; all other motion is due to lesser souls in lesser heavens; motion is time. The motion of the outermost heaven—the *primum mobile*—is the basis for all of time. In a sense, the philosophy of Aristotle has yoked together the concepts of time, motion, and soul.

Hindu views on the relationship of time, motion, and soul are no less complex, although scholarship has not addressed these issues directly. As we shall see in the next section, the prevailing view would be a succession alternating motion and immobility and with time continuous or resumable as substance and/or divinity so long as there are souls left to be liberated. But certain epic and Purāṇic mythological passages could also be found to allow for all the possibilities mentioned by Simplicius and also for the notion that there are multiple worlds coexisting in multiple times. Yet other kinds of debate seem to be hidden behind myths and images. As Ariel Glucklich says, the relation between the "great chronological theories" of India and "the experience of time" "remains unclear and problematic" (1994: 41). If one considers that motion in Hinduism is articulated in thought, sound, and language, embodied in ritual, and perceived in images and that "whereas symbols can be *about* time, only images [can] exist *in* time" (Glucklich 1994: 38; emphasis in original), one can usefully identify six fundamental images that convey an identity between motion and time in Hinduism and relate the soul's bondage and liberation to the resultant complex. These are the loom, cooking, the horse or animal representing the motion of the universe or of the year, the chariot which in turn represents one of two images of the wheel, the churning of the ocean, and the flow and descent of the river Gaṅgā. The six images all lend themselves to a preponderant cyclicity, so it is worth noting that India also has the "arrow of time": for instance, "sensual pleasure is said to be [short-lived as] the measure of an arrow's flight" (*Mahābhārata* 12.284.32). Clearly, the arrow is played in a minor key. For the first two images, weaving and cooking, the relation between time in motion and the soul will be viewed, in part retrospectively, from the standpoint of Upaniṣadic and epic unfoldings. But the other four images resonate directly with the "classical" Greek and Hindu issues of time, motion, and soul. The six will be discussed as if they appeared sequentially from Vedic into classical Hinduism—an oversimplification, but, taken cumulatively and to some degree through the logic of their interrelations, a useful one, since it can be seen that in the background of each are "lived" images that can interrelate. It is also important to have a sense of the richness of these images and that they contain precise rather than vague imagery, reflecting ritualist expertise, debates, and scholastic disagreements of great energy.

The loom of acts and language

A number of Vedic passages employ the imagery of motion as weaving, most notably *Ṛg Veda* 10.130, which begins: "The sacrifice that is spread out with threads on all sides, drawn tight with a hundred-and-one divine acts, is woven by these fathers as they come near: 'Weave forward, weave backward,' they say as they sit by the loom that is stretched tight" (1). What was first woven, however, is the primal sacrifice, which was stretched and drawn warp and woof by man (the primal *puruṣa*) across the dome of the sky, while, to sacrifice him, the gods "made the melodies into shuttles for weaving." That was "the original model" consisting of meters, invocations, and chants, whereas what the fathers weave is "the copy." Yet, the poet asks, "What was the connection (*bandhu*) between them?" "The human sages, our fathers" (also "the seven divine sages") "harmonized with the original models. When the wise men looked back along the path of those who went before, they took up the reins like charioteers" (*Ṛg Veda* 10.130.2–6). On the contrary, those who sacrifice incorrectly, "using speech in a bad way, they weave on a weft of rags, without understanding" (*Ṛg Veda* 10.70.9), says a hymn to Vāc, divine speech. Words and acts of Vedic ritual are thus a weave of meters, melodies, chants, and invocations, with their "connections" harmonized through and across the generational "path" of time through space; and, as Brian Smith has shown, the meters and melodies are further "interwoven" with "strings of associations that join the two temporal orders" of the day and year with "the order of super-classes or *varṇa*s" (1994: 175). That the imagery relates this weave of time, motion, and social standing to the soul is then all but stated in two Upaniṣadic dialogues between the sage Yājñavalkya and the young (?) woman Gārgī Vācaknavī. First (at least in the order of the passages), Gārgī presses Yājñavalkya to tell her through eleven ascending steps how one thing is "woven back and forth" on another, from "this whole world" which, she says, is "woven back and forth on water," up to the worlds of *brahman* which, he tells her, are woven on those of Prajāpati. But when she asks on what the worlds of *brahman* are woven, he says it is one question too many and that if she pursues, her head will shatter (*Bṛhadāraṇyaka Upaniṣad* 3.6). Having presumably thought it over and found a better approach, Gārgī then demands to ask two arrow-like questions. First, "The things above the sky, the things below the earth, and the things between the earth and the sky, as well as all those things people here refer to as past, present, and future—on what, Yājñavalkya, are all these woven back and forth?" Yājñavalkya answers, "space" (*ākāśa*). Rather than start with worlds woven on water and then letting Yājñavalkya define the weave, she now starts with a weave of her own: that of the three worlds and the three times, and she gets an answer, "space," that Yājñavalkya had not included in his prior weave. Now she can shoot her second question: "Space," he soon responds, is woven on "the imperishable (*akṣara*) . . . at whose command seconds (*nimeṣāḥ*) and hours, days and nights, fortnights and months, seasons and years, stand apart. . . . Pitiful is the man, Gārgī, who departs from this world without knowing the imperishable" (*Bṛhadāraṇyaka Upaniṣad* 3.8). One point of note is that this is the only mention of a "second," "moment," or "blink" (*nimeṣa*) in the classical Upaniṣads, a measure which, as we have seen, is important in the Yoga system and in Buddhism, albeit that the more prominent term there is *kṣaṇa*. As we shall see, the "moment" is richly deployed in narrative modes that link *yoga* with *bhakti*. Second, the dialogical mode is itself temporal, implying time given to thought and to interpersonal maiuetics. Third, these dialogues would seem to give time a gendered quality. Finally, before dialogue, what really defines the weave of time is music, Vedic singing.

Cooking

Cooking like weaving is, to begin with, a Vedic ritual motion that moves with the time it defines to refine the selves or souls of beings, beginning with Brāhmaṇs. Thus *Śatapatha Brāhmaṇa* 11.5.7.1 says:

> Here is now the praise of the personal recitation (*svādhyāya*) of the Veda. The personal recitation and learning are sources of pleasure for the brahmin. He acquires

presence of mind, becomes independent, and acquires wealth day after day. He sleeps well. He is his own best physician. To him belong mastery of the senses, the power to find joy in a single object, the development of intelligence, glory, and cooking the world (*lokapakti*). As this intelligence grows, four duties come to incumb upon the brahmin: a Brāhmaṇic origin, behavior consonant with his status, glory, and cooking the world. As it cooks, the world enjoys the brahmin through the fulfillment of its four duties towards him: respect, generosity, nonoppression, and immunity.

(cited in Malamoud 1996: 23; slightly modified)

Svādhyāya is Vedic "individual recitation" or recitation "to oneself," as one of a Brāhmaṇ's five obligatory daily rites, the "sacrifice to *brahman*." According to the commentator Sāyaṇa, "The wise man wards off, by means of the *svādhyāya*, that suffering of the *ātman* that is re-death, *punarmṛtyu*" (Malamoud 1996: 268n1). The two elements of the phrase "cooking the world" also connote the "maturation" or "perfecting" of "people" or beings, but the metaphoric meaning is primary (Malamoud 1996: 23–24). Desire, consecration for sacrifice (*dīkṣā*), sweat, toil (*śrama*), creative fervor (*tapas*), painful over-heating, and exhaustion are for preparing food for gods who like their food cooked. These are bonds (*bandhu*) in a "course" or "way" (*adhvan*) that is defined by "ceaseless movement from one end of the sacrificial ground to the other," one that regulates an "effort" that mimes the "labour of the . . . Vedic seers, who so strongly desired the Universe, in the beginning, that they brought it into existence" (Malamoud 1996: 33). "Once consecrated, one prepares . . . [a] space for himself and one is born into a world one has made by oneself." That is, one cooks one's own world (Malamoud 1996: 45). The "metaphorical cooking of the sacrificer . . . precedes the actual cooking of the offering," the first being "the genuine oblation," the latter a "substitute" (Malamoud 1996: 45). Digestion, milk, sperm, gestation, marriage, cremation, and renunciation are also homologized to cooking. By cooking himself, the Brāhmaṇ can thus perfect a self for liberation while also cooking up the respect others have for him, the gifts he receives, his indomitability, and his immunity. Having woven such a world, he sleeps well. "This then, is 'cooking the world.' This world, cooked by the brahmin, is the 'created' world which he . . . [creates] and organizes around himself in the sacrifice." But "the world cooked by sacrificial activity" has no raw natural opposite.

Everything is already cooked such that all that remains is to re-cook it. This sacrificial fire fed by the brahmin does nothing other than redouble the activity of the sun . . .: "That (sun) cooks everything in this world" [*eṣá vā́ idáṃ sárvaṃ pacati*], by means of the days and the nights, the fortnights, months, seasons, and years. And this (Agni) cooks what has been cooked by that (sun): "he is the cooker of that which has been cooked," said Bhāradvāja.

(Malamoud 1996: 48, citing *Śatapatha Brāhmaṇa* 10.4.2.19)

If the sun is the measure of time and if the year and its units are the means by which the sun cooks, then it is but a short step to say that "time cooks" (*kālaḥ pacati*), a signature saying of the *Mahābhārata*. Similarly, the Tamil ritual of *poṅkal*—boiling to overflow a pot of sweetened milk at the high times of festivals but especially at the winter solstice—joins everyone, and especially women, in cooking the world.

The universe, time, or the year as an animal, especially a horse

The grandest of all the royal Vedic sacrifices, the *aśvamedha* or horse sacrifice, extended through a year in which the loosened horse could wander freely until it was escorted back to be sacrificed. During this time the king underwent *dīkṣā* (consecration), maintained celibacy, and listened to stories. The *bandhu*s between the horse, the year, and other temporal measures are emphasized at the beginning of the *Bṛhadāraṇyaka Upaniṣad*: "The head of the sacrificial horse, clearly, is the dawn—its sight is the sun; its breath is the wind; and its gaping mouth is the fire common to all men. The body (*ātman*) of the sacrificial horse is the year" (1.1.1). Through the sacrifice of the horse the king and the year are reinvigorated.

> The sun that shines up there, clearly, is the horse sacrifice; the year is its body (*ātman*). The fire that burns down here is the ritual fire; these worlds are its body. Now there are these two: the horse sacrifice and the ritual fire (*arka*). Yet they constitute in reality a single deity—they are simply death. [Whoever knows this] averts repeated death—death is unable to seize him, death becomes his very body (*ātman*), and he becomes one of these deities.
>
> (*Bṛhadāraṇyaka Upaniṣad* 1.2.7)

For Aristotle the universe is like an animal in that both have direction: up and down; front and back; right and left. Direction is the basis for the concept of proper place with fire rising up to the heavens and earth sinking down. The circular motion of the heavens, said to be right to left, is the basis for time (*De Caelo* 2.2, 4; *Physica* 4).

The chariot and its wheels

The universe is frequently represented as a chariot. The two wheels of the chariot can easily be considered to embody the two wheels of the universe—the wheel of the zodiac and the wheel of the equatorial plane. The interactions of these two produce the year and all the divisions of time. They produce all beings beginning with the beings of the zodiac, which in turn are intervals of time. Where the motion of the chariot becomes the stage for the instruction of the soul, as it does when Kṛṣṇa descends and accompanies Arjuna into battle as his instructor, we can see a close relationship between motion and time as well as between the cosmic and the individual soul.

Such images also combine. According to *Mahābhārata* 1.3.147–51, the year is a wheel of twelve spokes turned by six boys (the seasons) while two girls (night and day) weave black and white threads into "this colorful loom" in which the black threads are "creatures past" and the white ones creature "present." *Śvetāśvatara Upaniṣad* says of the "One alone . . . who governs all those causes, from 'time' to 'self.' We study it—as a wheel . . . [and] as a river" (1.3–5).

While the chariot and its wheels are images of time as motion, the wheel of astrology with its numerous divisions lends itself to images of moments and simultaneity (see pp. 573–75).

The churning of the ocean

Both Sanskrit epics relate the myth of a churning motion that gives rise to time and eternity. It relates how the gods and demons churned the cosmic ocean by means of the serpent Vāsuki wrapped around the cosmic mountain Mandara, thereby generating many things that can be considered components of time, the most valuable of which is the elixir of immortality. It is difficult not to see in this myth an equation of motion with time and even a sense that there are motions that are tantamount to various elements of time while there is also a perfect motion that is identifiable with immortality. There is not a single unmoved mover, but there may be a *primum mobile*. Churning implies two motions—a back and forth—and it is possible that this myth recognizes the two great motions of the heavens: the forward movement of the planets through the zodiac during the year, but the backward or precessional movement of these same bodies over the course of the great year. The precessional movement can be measured where the plane of the ecliptic intersects the equatorial plane. Or the two motions may be the waxing and waning of the moon, since it is at the lunar nodes that eclipses occur, possibly accounting for the association of the elixir of immortality produced by the churning with the eclipses (Rāhu and Ketu).

Themes of the elixir of immortality—or nondeath (*amṛta*)—are further associated with the moon, which is said to be filled with *amṛta* when it is full but to be consumed or stolen by two demons—or a two-headed demon—Rāhu and Ketu, interpreted variously as being visible in the waning phase, with the head of Rāhu consuming the elixir, or also in eclipses. Rāhu and Ketu are also understood as the head and tail of a dragon whose head and tail represent the eclipses. Such a dragon is physically a part of a number of instruments—including medieval Western instruments—which mechanically predict eclipses (Asprey & Company 1973; Hartner 1938; Peter Apianus, *Astronomicum Caesarem*). As a footnote, "*rāhu*s" and "*ketu*s" are terms employed by the astrological sciences to describe a variety of occultations. The notion of an elixir carries with it many hidden associations. It is something different from the year and the measures that are derived from the year(s). Like many of the images of time (and eternity), it is a liquid or a fluid, representing images of continuities rather than discontinuities.

The descent of the Gaṅgā

The imagery of waters—oceans, lakes, and rivers—and their relationship to time and eternity is vast and richly developed in India. The bases for this association are equally rich: part scientific, grounded in instruments such as the water clock; part poetic, in which that portion of the heavens below the equatorial plane is described as the waters and the portion above as the dry land or alternatively describing the circular motion of the heavens "as though caught in a whirlpool"; and part ontology, whereby the individual self caught in time is likened to a river that eventually loses its identity in the great ocean of eternity. That time can be understood as a river has already been indicated by *Śvetāśvatara Upaniṣad* 1.3–5, as cited earlier. The river is naturally suggestive of individuality, flow, continuity within change and direction—characteristics of time and the self. The most important rivers of Hinduism are in fact heavenly or celestial ones that descend to earth in various ways. In Vedic Brāhmaṇa literature, the Sarasvatī River evokes the Milky Way

(Witzel 1984). In the epics and Purāṇas, the Milky Way is the celestial Gaṅgā (*ākāśagaṅgā*), which is additionally brought down to earth. It nourishes and purifies the world, flowing through it and finally into the great ocean. In these texts the Gaṅgā is an image of motion. The descent of the Gaṅgā (*gaṅgāvataraṇa*) is a mytheme involving the descent of eternity into time, a replenishing of the world with time, with souls, and with the purifying agency to carry/move all souls to their respective heavens. In this image, we have an inversion of the Upaniṣadic image of the individual soul as a river that merges with the great ocean losing its identity or discovering its nonduality with the undifferentiated *brahman*. Here, eternity participates in motion and time to restore the world. In the case of texts such as the *Viṣṇu Purāṇa*, the descent of the Gaṅgā provides the bases for a cosmograph that is a "map of time" (see pp. 570–73). In the *Mahābhārata*, the heavenly Gaṅgā relates her celestial motions to dynastic time, framing the story by becoming the mother of Bhīṣma (the epic's authority on time) in the first book and receiving the Kaurava and Pāṇḍava heroes after their heavenly ascents in the final books (Hiltebeitel 2001a: 80–91, 271–77, 2001b). While the descent of the Gaṅgā is overwhelmingly a theme that relates motion to the transformation of eternity into time, even this theme was subject to the analysis of momentariness—particularly in Buddhist texts that offer elaborate visions of "Buddhas numerous as the sands of the Ganges" (Kloetzli 1983: 113–31).

THE DIVISIONS OR INTERVALS OF TIME

Hindu intervals of time seem straightforward on the face of it—moments, day, night, year—but a closer look reveals several things. First, each of the units of time has some significance for the destiny of the soul. Second, although the texts do not allow one to reconstruct the history of its construction, the elaborated classical chronometry is constructed at least in part of prior interval and time unit terminologies. *Mahābhārata* 12.224–25 may provide one of the earliest sequences to have many of the set pieces in place. Third, there are tensions between time as it is abstracted into this ostensibly cyclical classical chronometry and time as imaged in ritual, music, narrative, and everyday life. It is as if the abstracted chronometric time is constructed from ritual, musical, narrative, and experiential intervals and units only to provide a vast scaffolding within which to act otherwise, tap other beats (*tāla*), and tell other stories. Fourth, the complexity of philosophical speculation and layering of meaning coded in the ritual embodiments and mythological expressions of these intervals and units requires much interpretation, which remains a challenge. Images from one setting can be and are reworked with new insights in other settings. Fifth, other Indian traditions—notably, those of the Buddhists, Jainas, and Ājīvikas—invoke other temporal divisions with very different dramas and contours. Much remains to be done before Hindu moments, *yuga*s, and *kalpa*s, for instance, are fully understood, since the terminologies extend beyond their chronometric limits. First, we outline the conventional classical chronometry; then we unpack some of the terms of which it is constructed and indicate other terms and images that further complicate and enliven it.

Structured time has four main hierarchically defined rhythms, lesser ones encompassed by greater ones, with a fifth rhythm, the *manvantara*, not quite mathematically adjustable to the other four. Most immediate is calendrical time as it is defined up to the year. As noted, in *Bṛhadāraṇyaka Upaniṣad* 3.8.9, Gārgī traces such a skein—"the moments (*nimeṣa*) and hours (*muhūrta*), days and nights, fortnights and months, seasons and years"—in her dialogue with Yājñavalkya. Slightly more spun out, *Viṣṇu Purāṇa* 1.3 offers a chaste classical formulation:

> Fifteen twinklings of the eye (*nimeṣa*) make a *kāṣṭhā*; thirty *kāṣṭhā*s, one *kalā*; and thirty *kalā*s, one *muhūrta* [a forty-eight-minute 'hour' in terms of the Western minute]. Thirty *muhūrta*s constitute a day and night of mortals; thirty such days make a month, divided into two-half months [or fortnights]: six months form an *ayana* [the period of the sun's progress north or south of the ecliptic], and two *ayana*s compose a year. The southern *ayana* is a night, and the northern a day, of the gods. Twelve thousand divine years, each composed of [360] such days, constitute the period of four *yuga*s.

Other Purāṇas and the *Manusmṛti* offer slightly varied calculations (e.g. beginning with eighteen *nimeṣa*s to the *kāṣṭhā*) and also some additional intermediate units (Wilson 1961: 20–21). One appreciates that with the *ayana*s and the year, calculation shifts from human to divine measures, and that there is nothing like a decade or century to slow the rush from human years to divine millennia. The second rhythm of four *yuga*s, named after dice throws, then defines a theory of the "decline of the *dharma*." A Kṛta Yuga (perfect age) is followed by a Tretā Yuga, Dvāpara Yuga, and degenerate Kali Yuga ("age of discord," our time). Their respective lengths are 4,000, 3,000, 2,000, and 1,000 years, with each supplemented by dawns and twilights of one-tenth their totals. A four-*yuga* cycle or *mahāyuga* (great *yuga*) thus lasts 12,000 years. Even though this sum may initially have referred to human years, it is conventionally, as in the *Viṣṇu Purāṇa*, taken to refer to divine years that are 360 times as long as human ones. Thus a *mahāyuga* lasts 4,320,000 human years (360 × 12,000), and a Kali Yuga one-tenth that amount. Again shifting planes, the third major rhythm, that of the *kalpa*, is calculated not only in divine years but also days of Brahmā, one of the latter equaling a thousand *mahāyuga*s or 4,320 million human years. It is here that *manvantara*s or "intervals of the Manus" are calculated in at fourteen to the *kalpa*, which, when calculated in relation to *mahāyuga*s, makes a *manvantara* 71 and a fraction *mahāyuga*s. It is possible that the relation between the system of 14 *manvantara*s and the divine years represents the transmigratory paths of Brahmā in relation to the light/dark halves of the moon and the sun. Brahmā's days alternate with nights of equal duration, and when Brahmā has lived a life of a hundred years of 360 such days and nights, the universe has gone through 311,040 billion human years, a duration constituting its fourth major and outermost rhythm, which is sometimes said to pass in a "moment, wink, or blink" (*nimeṣa*) of Viṣṇu.

This chronology structures a nonsectarian Smārta vision of the universe in which the encompassing values are *yoga* and *bhakti*. A yogic supreme divinity, Viṣṇu or Śiva, undying and thus surpassing the life (or lives) of Brahmā(s), both transcends time and participates in its four rhythms, encompassing other values such as renunciation or *saṃnyāsa* (which is still temporally constrained by *kalpa*); *dharma* as "law" (reintroduced by the series of Manus), meditation or *tapas*, knowledge, sacrifice, and the gift (which are correlated with the successive *yuga*s); and the "momentariness" of the "wink, blink, or moment" upon which all of time turns and can be turned inside out. This reinforces the *bhakti* view that taken by themselves without devotion, these values—including the Buddhists' radical momentariness—are dysfunctional.

Working the chronometry backwards, this means that at the highest level of the *mahākalpa*, the deity as supreme *puruṣa* is a great *yogin* who interacts with time's ultimate rhythms through an oscillation between activity and concentration (*samādhi*). For such a deity time is "play" (*līlā*). Primal creation roughly follows the cosmogonic theory of evolution (*pariṇāma*) of the Sāṃkhya system, with the addition that this evolution results in the formation of a "cosmic egg," the Brahmāṇḍa or "egg of Brahmā." This is the spatial coefficient of a life of Brahmā, whose death brings a *mahākalpa* to its end at a *mahāpralaya* or "great dissolution," at which time the supreme deity, entering into *samādhi*, oversees the reversal of the creation process, devolving the egg back into primal matter and releasing souls from all spatiotemporal bondage in a vast collective liberation by resorption into himself. Interior to this rhythm, secondary periodic creations are carried out by Brahmā, whose cosmogonic activity—modeled on that of the earlier Vedic Prajāpati—is defined by sacrificial themes. Within the Brahmāṇḍa, Brahmā recreates the Vedic triple world of earth, atmosphere, and heaven (or heaven, earth, and underworld) as a world of *karma* and *saṃsāra*, defined by the values that pertain to the *yuga*s. There also emerge four worlds outside these but within the Brahmāṇḍa. These are neither destroyed during the "occasional (*naimittika*) *pralaya*s" that bring a triple world to an end nor created with the latter's recreation. They are reserved for beings who achieve heavenly destinies or release from *karma* and *saṃsāra* by renunciation, yet who must await the ultimate liberation that comes only with the "great dissolution." At this level, the *trimūrti* or "three forms" of the absolute *brahman*—a formulation of many meanderings but known already in the *Mahābhārata* (Brinkhaus 1999: 43)—cooperate, with Brahmā as creator, Viṣṇu as preserver, and Śiva as destroyer. Brahmā most typically creates the triple world by becoming the sacrificial boar (*yajñavarāha*) who retrieves the Vedas and the earth from the ocean. Śiva, taking the form of seven suns to ignite the "fire at the end of time" (*kālān-taka*), reduces the triple world to ashes. And Viṣṇu maintains the triple world around its sacrificial order during days of Brahmā, while during Brahmā's nights he sleeps as Nārāyaṇa on the serpent Śeṣa (remainder) or Ananta (endless), who, out of the ashes of the previous triple world, forms a couch for him on the cosmic ocean. Then with each *manvantara*, there are not only new Manus but also new Indras and other gods and a new group of the Seven Ṛṣis (the stars of the Big Dipper). Then within the still immense time of *yuga*s and *mahāyuga*s, what engages the deities is their *avatāra*s or "descents" into times of crisis and into one or another of the three worlds (i.e. not always the earth) to uphold the ever-imperiled *dharma*. The classical concept of *avatāra* is structured around Viṣṇu, for whom there develops a standard list of ten *avatāra*s, but the term is also used for "descents" of Śiva and the goddess, including, as we have seen, the goddess Gaṅgā, while lesser gods sometimes descend conjointly by their "portions" (*aṃśa*). Various attempts were made to correlate *avatāra*s with distinctive *yuga*s and the twilights between them and also with *kalpa*s. One thread that may reflect the early development of the *avatāra* doctrine in relation to time is the singular fact that one *avatāra*, Rāma Jāmadagnya (or Paraśurāma, as he is commonly known in post-epic texts, which are the first to acknowledge him as an *avatāra*), appears (as usually described) between the intervals of three successive *yuga*s: first in his own family drama between the Kṛta and Tretā Yugas, next in the *Rāmāyaṇa* and the life of Rāma in the interval between the Tretā and Dvāpara Yugas, and finally in the *Mahābhārata* where he figures prominently in the stories of Bhīṣma and Karṇa during the twilight between the Dvāpara and Kali Yugas (L. Thomas 1996). The most consistent association between *avatāra*s and the larger temporal structures, however, is that between Kṛṣṇa and the interval between the Dvāpara and Kali Yugas, the effect of which is to make Kṛṣṇa the incarnation whose descent launches "our own time." Ends and beginnings of *yuga*s (*yugānta*) being times of crises, we await the apocalyptic *avatāra* Kalkin, who will come at the end of this Kali Yuga and, with little to explain it, inaugurate another "age of perfection." Rāma Jāmadagnya and Kalkin have in common with the dwarf (Vāmana) *avatāra* that they are Brāhmaṇs who rectify dharmic disorder among the kings or Kṣatriyas of the triple world, and Rāma Jāmadagnya and Kalkin are in particular *fighting* Brāhmaṇs. Such are the conditions, then, under which humans experience the dizzying rhythms and moral purposes of their moments, days, and years.

Yet, as our preface to this skein has indicated, powerful as this cosmic drama is, and as frequently as it is invoked and evoked by its imagery, it is often no more than the curtain for other dramas. To begin with, no *bhakta*, *yogin*, *tāntrika*, *nātha*, or practitioner of any other discipline is waiting around for the death of Brahmā. Every practice is a shortcut. Tantric *yogin*s, for instance, are "time-trickers" (*kālavañcaka*), able to reverse time and gain back "lost time." Instead of the "blink" or "moment," they start from the "measure" (*mātra*) or elapsed time of a yogic inhalation and exhalation: ninety-six *mātra*s make a *ghaṭa*, sixty *ghaṭa*s a day and night, and so on, up to a *kalpa*, which is now a day of Viṣṇu—which is itself but a single *mātra* of Śiva, whose rhythms the *yogin* homologizes with his own (White 1996: 42–46). Furthermore, the terms and images are complicated and range beyond the skein itself.

Moment (kṣaṇa, nimeṣa)

The moment is most typically represented as a *kṣaṇa*, a "look" or "glance," or a *nimeṣa*, a "blink" or "twinkling of an eye"—in either case, an operation of the eye. The eye, of course, can equally be that of the deity or the individual. Moments can be seen to be innumerable, and some settings choose to view the forest rather than the trees. According to the *Spandakārikā* (Stanzas on Vibration) of the Spanda school of Kashmir Śaivism, *nimeṣa* can be taken as Śiva's "withdrawal," "contraction," or "involution" of himself as impeller of the cosmic process and as the opposite of the *unmeṣa* or "unfolding" or "expansion" of that process. The terms have to do with Śiva's power of reflective awareness which appears as a "subtle motion" of a "contracted (*nimeṣa*) state, corresponding to the withdrawal of previously emitted diversity," which is "itself" also "the expansion (*unmeṣa*) of the awareness of the unity of consciousness," while conversely "the expanded state (*unmeṣa*), indicative of forthcoming diversity, is itself the contraction (*nimeṣa*) of the awareness of the unity of consciousness" (Dyczkowski 1992: 63).

Dawns, twilights

Hymns to the beautiful goddess Uṣas, dawn, in the *Ṛg Veda* acknowledge the daybreak but also already recognize the destiny that is thereby announced: Uṣas, "born again and again dressed in the same color, causes the mortal to age and wears away his life span" (1.92.10). We return to this point below. The dawn is also one of two *saṃdhyā*s or "twilights" marking the beginning and end of a day or an age (*yuga*). As such, it is determinative of the destiny (*daiva*) or law (*dharma*) of that age.

Day and night

In the *Bṛhadāraṇyaka* and *Chāndogya Upaniṣad*s, days and nights are tied to the destiny of the soul as the model for transmigration following the burning of the corpse. The soul in these Upaniṣads has two possible courses upon dying. If, during the preceding lifetime, that individual had mastered the learning of the Upaniṣads and had realized the identity of the individual soul (*ātman*) with the absolute soul (*brahman*), then the soul departed along the path of the gods (*devayāna*). The *devayāna* proceeds as follows: On the burning of the corpse, the soul enters into the flame, thence into the day, thence into the bright half of the year, thence into the year, thence into the sun, thence into the moon, thence into lightning, and so finally into *brahman* (*Bṛhadāraṇyaka Upaniṣad* 6.2.2.15–16; *Chāndogya Upaniṣad* 4.15.5). In following the *pitṛyāna* and eventual rebirth, the soul enters the smoke rather than the flame, the night, the dark half of the month (waning of the moon), the dark half of the year (descending movement of the sun through the signs of the zodiac), the world of the fathers, the *ākāśa*, and finally into the moon "as long as a remnant (of good works) yet exists." Return from the moon results in rebirth according to a variety of principles.

Now, if this system of days and nights can provide a model for the transmigration of the soul, what can we infer from a system which states that Brahmā has a life of a hundred years each made up of three hundred and sixty days and three hundred and sixty nights? Does the cosmic deity Brahmā somehow transmigrate? What is the system of *avatāra*s? Days turn to years; years turn to *yuga*s and *kalpa*s, and *kalpa*s back to days as the individual soul and the cosmic soul interact in dramas of *yoga*, devotion, liberation, rebirth, and maintenance or support of the universe for the welfare of all beings.

The Hindu correlation of the *kalpa* with a day and night of Brahmā and the possibility that the intention is to integrate a system of *avatāra*s is even more suggestive when we recognize that certain Buddhist texts explicitly reject this relationship. There we read that there are no days and nights above the Kāmadhātu or "realm of desire" (i.e. in the world of Brahmā, Brahmaloka).

One may note that a Vaiṣṇava school, the Pāñcarātra (five-night or night of the five)—a term that has remained enigmatic—would seem to have had some of these intentions. Noteworthy for its speculations on time, it is possible that its name has been correctly explained as the night in which the five elements disappear, depending on the context, at the times of death, *mokṣa*, and the *mahāpralaya* (Katz 1989: 252, 261n23; Neevel 1977).

The year: the zodiacal circle, generation, and corruption

The year appears to occupy a special role in the Hindu tradition in a way that it does not in Jainism and Buddhism. All of time is measured in years. The *kalpa* embraces thousands of solar years (4,320,000,000). More to the point, the life of Brahmā is expressed in terms of years; its 100 years in duration complete a perfect symmetry with the duration of human life in the Kali Yuga, albeit the years of Brahmā are defined in terms of 360 days and nights each equal to one *kalpa*. The significance of the centrality of the year is underscored by the caution of a Buddhist text that the duration of life (*āyus*) "is incalculable" at the beginning of an age: "one cannot measure it by counting in thousands" of years (*Abhidharmakośa* 3.78; La Vallée Poussin 1988–90, 2: 470). For Buddhism, the *kalpa* (and some aspects of the duration of life) cannot be measured in years but only in terms of what are called innumerables (*asaṃkhyeya*). For Jainism, the cycle of time is divided into eras (*ara*s, "spokes," i.e. of the wheel of time), four of which are essentially *asaṃkhyeya* in duration, lasting 4, 3, 2, or 1 *sāgaropama*s, while the fifth and sixth—we are living in the fifth era—last 21,000 common years each. One *sāgaropama* is 8,400,000 × 1,014 years. Within the *asaṃkhyeya kalpa*s of Buddhism, duration of life starts as infinite, but Buddhas appear when length of life can be measured in years. For Jainism, years do not really begin until Mahāvīra whose birth is seventy-five years and eight-and-a half months before the start of the fifth age; otherwise time is measured in *sāgaropama*s.

A second fact that makes the Hindu understanding of the year unique is its interchangeability with the zodiac. We observe this in two ways. First, the year employed for the Purāṇic divisions is equal to 360 days. There is no doubt that choosing 360, rather than 365 or 366 or the Vedic year referred to below in the discussion of *yuga*s, is of significance. This corresponds to the divisions of the twelve signs of the zodiac into 30 degrees, thereby underscoring the identity or interchangeability of the year and the zodiac. The year is the sphere of the ecliptic containing the zodiac. It is the realm of form and the model in India for what Aristotle termed generation and corruption—the creation of the world and its dissolution; activity and meditation.

Another notable point is the equation of Prajāpati, the lord of creatures, with the year. In *Ṛg Veda* 1.10.121, the first existent being is called Prajāpati. Facing the chaos of the waters, he impregnates the waters and becomes manifest in them in the form of a golden egg or germ, from which the whole universe develops. He is called the one life or soul of the gods (*devānām āsuḥ*). Elsewhere, this same Prajāpati is identified with the year: "Prajāpati is the year, and he is composed of sixteen parts. Fifteen of his parts are the nights while his sixteenth part is constant. With each passing night he waxes and wanes" (*Bṛhadāraṇyaka Upaniṣad* 1.5.14). To the extent that Prajāpati is the lord of creatures, is the year, and is increased and diminished by his nights alone, he is the year understood as the zodiacal wheel of beings—the golden, luminous beings, the beings of the night.

While years are measured in terms of solar and other celestial movements, a main term for year, *varṣa*, refers to rain and to the rainy season. The combination could suggest the foundation for accentuating suns and rains at the *naimittika pralaya*, yet the latter measures a day rather than a year. *Varṣa* also denotes the divisions of the earth or "continents," suggesting a basis for according different measures of time—notably in terms of *yuga*s and life spans—to different "continents." Bhāratavarṣa or "India" is sometimes said to be the only "continent" where beings experience the Kali Yuga and its heightened corruptions but also, as a "world of acts" (*karmabhūmi*), to be the only one where salvation is possible (Dimmitt and van Buitenen 1978: 25, 28, 55).

Yuga and *kalpa*

If concepts such as dawn, day, and year have theological implications for the destiny of the soul, divisions such as the *yuga* and the *kalpa* have them even more so.

The term "*yuga*" refers to the union, joining, conjunction, or yoking together of two or more entities. The oldest Hindu astronomical texts concerned with Vedic ritual, about 200 BCE, recognize a *yuga* of five years that joins the solar and lunar calendars with sixty months of twenty-nine and 16/31 days each, plus intercalary months for a total of sixty-two months every five years (van Buitenen 1973–78, 3: 3–5). The *yuga* of the epics and the Purāṇas is more fluid and complex and, more than any other single interval of time, may be said to characterize the notion of time of classical Hinduism. Intermediary between yearly time and the *manvantara*s or *kalpa*s, *yuga*s, unlike the latter, are still "lived time."

We have noted that according to the *Śvetāśvatara Upaniṣad*, the lord as "architect of time" is "the basis and cause of the joining (*saṃyoga*)" of the intervals of time. Similarly, in the *Mahābhārata*, when Bhīṣma announces that the Pāṇḍava heroes have met the conditions to the full of spending their thirteenth year of exile incognito, he says, "The portions of time are joined together (*yujyante*) and so are the fortnights, months, lunar mansions (*nakṣatra*), and planets; even so the seasons are joined together (*yujyante*) and also the years. Thus with the divisions of time does the wheel of time (*kālacakra*) turn" (*Mahābhārata* 4.47.2). As "joints in time," *yuga*s are the first grand extension of what "connects" lived time with divine time, and their twilights are times of danger when things must be kept from going "out of joint." The *yuga*s of the epics and Purāṇas carry out this "yoking or joining" in terms of *dharma* and *adharma*; destiny and agency; divine agency (most notably via *avatāra*s) and human agency; divine and human duration of life (*āyus*); changes in human sexuality; kingship, with the well-developed notion in the *Mahābhārata* (12.70) that the king makes the *yuga*; and the emergence, important for understanding what these texts are saying about history, of barbarians (*mleccha*): in *Mahābhārata* 12.200.39–42, *mleccha*s did not exist in the Kṛta Yuga but proliferated (Greeks or Yavanas and Hūṇas are among the barbarians mentioned) in the Tretā and Dvāpara Yugas. But in the final analysis, the key for the Purāṇic *yuga* is that it is the intersection or union of the divine and the human. The *yuga*s may also incorporate a transformation of the hymn to *puruṣa* (*Ṛg Veda* 10.90), temporalizing the structures of this Vedic hymn with its thousands, quarters, and tenths and creating as it were a kind of "time-person" (*kālapuruṣa*).

Two prominent metaphors—the *dharma* bull and the *yuga*s as throws of the dice—are also latent with implications. The likening of *dharma* (generally law, but elsewhere motion) to a bull that after standing on all four legs in the Kṛta Yuga, loses one per *yuga* until he has but one left in the Kali Yuga, implies a self-evident tale of decline and imminent toppling, as well as a very patient and long-suffering bull. Indeed, standing on one leg would seem to imply immobilization or immobility, and it is worth noting that while this bull endures his dismemberment (recalling images of the sacrificial *puruṣa* and horse as they are linked with the creation and perpetuation of time), there seems always to be a "cow of plenty" or "cow of wishes" to help, in conjunction with the increasing baseness of human desires, to make the decline of the *yuga*s ever more and more palpably materialistic. As to the dice, the Sanskrit game of words that permits one to pass from "fate" or "what is divinely ordained" (*daiva*) to the game of dice (*dyūta*) has its fullest unfolding in the well-known story of Śiva, the lord of destructive time, playing dice with his wife Pārvatī and being drawn himself inside of the game's devolutionary vortex, a game that the poor man can almost never win, and into which, considering who is playing and what he is playing with (dice throws equivalent to *yuga*s, with their devolutionary 4, 3, 2, 1 ratio), draws the cosmos and us into it with him (Biardeau 1985: 13; Handelman and Shulman 1997: 45, 64–69). The *Ṛg Veda*'s "gambler's lament" (10.34), the dice match that closes the *rājasūya* sacrifice (rigged for the king to win), the pivotal gambling match in the *Mahābhārata*, and the story of Nala and Damayantī which the epic's heroes and heroine hear after losing the epic dice match, can all be read intertextually and with these themes in mind. The dice game is the tangible intrusion of the divine world into the human world, but a divine world whose deities not only play dice with the universe but whose rhythms are beyond at least Śiva's control.

As to *kalpa*s, while the term is most often associated with a division of time, it is also associated with ritual (according to a calendar) and sacrifice (a cutting or transition from one condition to another). This relationship is underscored by the statement of the *Śulbasūtra* (texts that provide the geometry for the construction of sacrificial altars): he who knows this *jyautiṣa*, the science of determining times, knows the sacrifices (Pingree 1981: 8).

As we have noted, there is a (relatively) simple use of the term "*kalpa*" in the *Yogabhāṣya* to indicate that it is the interval of time between the entanglement of the soul with *prakṛti* and its eventual disentanglement or enlightenment. No duration is assigned to this interval, and it is not integrated with other measures of time, such as day or night, year, and so on. We may infer that the beginning of the *kalpa* marks the beginning of time. This rather undeveloped sense of *kalpa* nevertheless carries a meaning that seems to carry throughout a broad spectrum of uses—if not all uses—of the concept, namely, that a *kalpa* is a disjunction reflecting a change in the status of the soul: if not to total liberation, at least to higher or lower orders of being.

The *kalpa* of the Purāṇas, however, incorporates a system of days/nights, human and divine years, *yuga*s, and *caturyuga*s, as well as actual astronomical measures of time (years). In turn it is subsumed by a system of days and nights; the days and nights of Brahmā. It is one of the noteworthy attributes of the Purāṇic *kalpa* that it incorporates astronomical time: the science of *siddhānta*. Indeed, the astronomical schools support the length of time assumed to be a Purāṇic *kalpa* (4,320,000,000 years). Other traditions see the *kalpa* not as a measurement of astronomy but as a construct of the mind. The Purāṇic understanding of the *kalpa*, therefore, may be taken as an affirmation of the reality of the world. The astronomical measurements of the *yuga*s and *kalpa*s are tied to calculations of the astronomical schools. One system dating from the fifth century

> assumes a true conjunction of the planets, their mandoccas, and their nodes at a sidereally fixed Aries 0^0 at the beginning and end of a Kalpa . . .; a later system simplifies the numbers by assuming a mean conjunction only of the seven planets at the beginning and end of a Mahāyuga. Both systems assume a mean conjunction or near conjunction of the seven planets at a sidereally fixed Aries 0^0 at the beginning of the current Kaliyuga, which is either midnight of 17/18 [February -3101 Julian] or 6 AM of 18 February -3101 Julian at Laṅkā and Ujjayinī.
>
> (Pingree 1978: 555)

The numerology of the Purāṇic *kalpa* is a product of the numerology of thousands. As a corollary, the duration of the life of Brahmā is also a product of the numerology of thousands. But other traditions state that the duration of life cannot be just a product of thousands. Multiples of thousands (possibly a shorthand for the astronomical sciences) produce large, but ultimately finite, calculations. Buddhism, on the other hand, recognizes time as divided into four *kalpa*s of innumerables (*asaṃkhyeyakalpa*). One of these *kalpa*s is said to last as long as it takes to reduce a great mountain to dust by rubbing it with a silken garment. "It is as if, O priest, there were a mountain consisting of a great rock, a league in height, without break, cleft, or hollow, and every hundred years a man were to come and rub it once with a silken garment; that mountain consisting of a great rock, O priest, would more quickly wear away and come to an end than a world-cycle" (*Saṃyutta Nikāya* 15.5.6). Similar examples from the *Mahābhārata* are cited by Hopkins (1903: 45–46): for example, "A particle of sand removed daily from the Himālaya till all the mountain is reduced to a plain"; or in a discourse on Time by a sage to the demon Vṛtra:

> The period for which a particular creation exists is measured by many thousands of lakes . . ., O Daitya! Conceive a lake that is one *Yojana* in width, one *Krosa* in depth, and five hundred *Yojana*s in length. Imagine many thousand such lakes. Seek then to dry up . . . [such] lakes by taking from them, only once a day, as much water as may be taken up with the end of a single hair. The number of days that would pass in drying them up completely by this process represents the period that is occupied by the life of one creation from . . . [the] first start to the time of its destruction (*Mahābhārata* 12.271.30–32; Ganguli 1970, 9.2: 324).

These measures of the duration of a *kalpa* are not a function of the astronomical sciences but a function of the divisions which the mind can imagine. They seem to embrace all the divisions of time down to the moment as the most minuscule without any special reliance on astronomical time and may be related to Plotinus' understanding of intellect as characterized by an infinity which is nevertheless limited (*Enneads* 6.6).

Other divisions of cosmic time within the Indian religious traditions are equally imaginative and should be taken into account when trying to understand the images and time divisions of the epics and the Purāṇas. Jainas, for instance, do not recognize *kalpa*s as divisions of time but speak of *kalpa* heavens; and Ājīvikas, like the *Mahābhārata* passage just quoted, speak of vast measures of time in terms of "lakes"—three hundred thousand of them.

THE COSMOS IS A MAP OF TIME; TIME IS THE BODY OF THE DEITY

Hindu cosmographs combine themes of the descent of time and of the celestial Gaṅgā with stereographic projections of the cosmos onto the equatorial plane resulting in cosmographs that may be understood as maps of time. In the process, these cosmographs combine scientific principles such as stereographic projection, a tangible and concrete understanding of *darśana* or "view" as a designation for philosophical or theological school, and even iconic representation with intricate mythological themes. In the case of the Purāṇic cosmograph, the descent of time occurs by the swallowing of the cosmic ocean by Agastya (the southern pole star Canopus) and then by the saving of the souls of the four ancestral generations of a solar line king, Bhagīratha, who effects the descent of the Gaṅgā (*gaṅgāvataraṇa*) to rescue these "fathers," beginning with the 60,000 sons of King Sāgara, "Ocean." It is further stated that the Gaṅgā flows from the foot of Viṣṇu near the north polar star, with the eye of Viṣṇu possibly identified with the south polar star. These associations would make the entire cosmos—and all the divisions of time—identical with the body of the deity (Kloetzli 1985).

There are other special qualities associated with the descent of time, notably, the appearance or birth of certain beings instrumental in the attainment of salvation, the propagation of the teaching or the righting of the *dharma*. Within Buddhism, the appearance of Buddhas is restricted to the period when the duration of human life is declining from eighty thousand to one hundred years.

The twenty-four *tīrthaṅkara*s of Jainism, of whom Mahāvīra is the last, appear during the decline of the ages (*ara*) from a happy age of infinite duration to an age of mixed happiness and suffering where time is measured in years. *Tīrthaṅkara*s do not appear during cycles when ages are improving and becoming of greater duration. Similarly, Hindu *avatāra*s appear in the twilights between *yuga*s as the duration of life is declining. As the most prominent *avatāra* of Viṣṇu, Kṛṣṇa describes this role in *Bhagavad Gītā* 4.7–8 as that of coming into being from age (*yuga*) to age whenever *dharma* languishes and *adharma* increases. We should simply note that the linkage between the appearance of beings and the descent of time, including its descent from a state of rest to one of motion, is found as far away as the writings of Empedocles.

It is to be noted that Raghunātha Śiromaṇi (fifteenth-sixteenth century), in rethinking the Vaiśeṣika notion of space and time, concluded that these were not separate categories but were identified with god, who, like space and time, is characterized as an all-pervading substance (Balslev 1983: 34–35). The sense of a permanent and enduring time as the body of the deity can present a world that exists for the benefit of all beings—this, in contrast to dramas of salvation that focus on the destiny of the individual soul and the illusory or mirage-like character of reality external to the individual soul. In such a world, time has significance for the collective of beings (sometimes called the *bhūtagaṇa* or *bhūtagrāma*, the "host or village of living beings").

One such map could be Viṣṇu's form as the celestial Gangetic porpoise (*śiśumāra*, literally, "child-killer"): "The form of the mighty Hari which is present in heaven, consisting of the constellations, is that of a porpoise, with Dhruva (the pole star) situated in the tail. As Dhruva revolves, it causes the moon, sun, and stars to turn round also" (*Viṣṇu Purāṇa* 2.9.1–2). Viṣṇu "upholds" this form under the names Nārāyaṇa and Janārdana (the tormentor of beings).

Some other maps of time may be called implicit or relate implicit to explicit maps, especially as they embody gender in relation to time and motion. The *puruṣa* hymn begins with "the male," who provides the spatiotemporal coordinates in the first four verses of the hymn. But nothing unfolds in time or space until we learn in verse 5 of Virāj, "wide dominion," probably the feminine principle and in principle the incipient earth: "From him Virāj was born, and from Virāj came *puruṣa*" (*Ṛg Veda* 10.90). *Puruṣa* seems to be man the vertical but to require Virāj to embody the horizontal. Similarly, among the dualities that "existed not" when there was only "that one," *tad ekam*, male and female are implied by the very fact that *tad ekam* is explicitly neuter (*Ṛg Veda* 10.129). One can trace such conundrums into the elaborate mappings of time found in the Śaivite schools of Kashmir Śaivism and Śaiva Siddhānta, with their "pulsating" or "oscillating" universe of emission from and reabsorption into Śiva. Here, *kāla*, "time," is one of the primary eleven *tattva*s ("such-nesses" or constituent units of manifest being) of *māyā* that *precede* the Sāṃkhya *tattva*s that, beginning with *prakṛti*, continue this "evolution." For the Spanda school of Kashmir Śaivism, *māyā*, the "arising of mental representation" that "is rooted in the embodied subject," is a *tattva* of Śakti who is ontologically one with Śiva: she is "the formation and activity of finite particulars in its infinite expanse," and he is "the essence or foundation" and transcendental "own nature" of phenomenal existence and all its manifestations within that expanse. Time therein is "essentially . . . (the sense of) division between the notions of past and future, etc., and consists of progressive differentiation . . . that divides off (moments, one from another)" (Dyczkowski 1992: 49–58, 125). For Śaiva Siddhānta, on the other hand, *māyā* is real and impure and ontologically separate from Śiva, governing "oscillations" between the pure Śiva and the impure world (R. Davis 1991: 42–47). In Kashmir Śaiva texts of the Krama school, "the supreme principle is the Goddess" who, within the "Wheel of [the] Twelve Kālīs," is "the Abode of the Center (of reality)" in the "form of the pulsation of consciousness," her "pulse" marking "an outward, forward movement . . . and an inward retraction" as the

> basis of the four-fold sequence . . . of arising . . ., manifestation . . ., the assimilation of time (*kālagrāsa*), and repose in one's essential nature. . . . Thus the Supreme Goddess has two aspects. One is self-established and tranquil. It is where "the repose of the Supreme Light spontaneously finds rest." As such She is the "cessation of destruction" (*samhārasamhāra*), the ultimate end of all sequences and processes, change and time. This aspect is never involved in the recurrent pulse of the cosmic process. The other aspect is the form of the Goddess as the Primordial Power (*ādyāśakti*) which generates, sustains and withdraws its manifestations, at one with Herself, and so pulsates with its rhythm. This is said to be that state in which consciousness is swollen like a seed about to generate its sprout.
>
> (Dyczkowski 1992: 56)

These lightly mythologized maps of cosmic time reverberate with numerous myths in which the gendering of time—especially as feminine (see Kristeva 1986: 190–93)—is embodied in narrative and icon. The Vedic goddesses Uṣas (dawn) and Rātri (night) are early examples, as is the correlation between the seasons and a woman's period through the word "*ṛtu*" for both. More classically, *Devī Māhātmya* 1.78 says of the goddess, "You are the night of time (*kālarātri*), the great night (*mahārātri*), and the terrible night of delusion (*moharātriśca dāruṇā*)"—that is, probably incrementally, the nights of the *naimittika pralaya* and *mahāpralaya* and the dark night of the soul. Kālarātri, personifying death, makes several appearances in the *Mahābhārata*. In one, Draupadī is herself Kālarātri or the "night of time" of Kīcaka, a rogue whose lustful thoughts of a nighttime tryst with her become his undoing. Most memorably, the "dark" (*kālī*) Kālarātri appears during the night raid upon the sleeping warriors that brings the Mahābhārata war to its ghastly conclusion with the slaughter of Draupadī's children. Draupadī makes time and her period work to the advantage of her five husbands, the Pāṇḍavas, by asking an insoluble question at the epic dice match. As the destructive "night of time," Kālī herself is by name either "time" or "the dark one," with both meanings interrelated and given full play in both Sanskrit and vernacular traditions. For instance, Velā, with such early meanings as "limit, boundary, time" in the *Śatapatha Brāhmaṇa* and "flood-tide" in *Maitrī Upaniṣad*, also means "the last hour, hour of death." As both "limit, frontier, terminus" and "time limit, period, hour," Velā is the Sanskrit form given in the *Bhaviṣya Purāṇa* to the heroine known better as Belā in the Hindi oral epic, *Ālhā*. This epic, known as "the *Mahābhārata* of the Kali Yuga" for its account of the end of "Rājpūt age" and the rise of the Delhi Sulṭānate, regards Belā as an incarnation of Draupadī and, like Draupadī, a "form of Kālī." Belā defines *Ālhā*'s time limit and provokes its age-ending battle when she announces she has only seven days to become a *satī* (Hiltebeitel 1999b). Then there is Sandhyā, the first *satī* according to the *Śiva Purāṇa*, whose name means "twilight." A beautiful girl with pretty eyebrows, she was mentally raped by her father Brahmā and her brothers, some of the great *ṛṣi*s, and had to be reborn as the chaste Arundhatī and marry one of these former brothers, Vasiṣṭha. Newlywed couples go out at dawn to sanctify their bonds of matrimony by observing this couple (Hiltebeitel 1999a).

The feminine also remains central to the rhythms of time in the mythologies of the major male deities. From a Śaiva standpoint, the male (the deity as supreme *puruṣa*) and the female (the goddess as *māyā*, *prakṛti*, or *śakti*) are reunited at the *mahāpralaya*, one representation of their fusion being that of Śiva as Ardhanārīśvara (the lord who is half female). Their nonprocreative union represents the unitive experience of the bliss of *brahman*. Primal creation would then lead somehow to Satī (being herself), Śiva's first "dark" (*kālī*) wife whose primal self-immolation at the sacrifice performed by her father Dakṣa purifies her to be reborn as Śiva's second wife, the usually light or golden Pārvatī, the "mountain lady" (Hiltebeitel 1999a) with whom Śiva plays dice with the ages. In more typically Vaiṣṇava terms, time in its four structured rhythms (see p. 562) is configured around the earth, who is a goddess and the most concretized of the five "elements" into which *prakṛti*, primal matter, evolves through the formation of a cosmic egg. Time not only oscillates and devolves but also fills the world with its mixtures of human conflict and calm, grief and joy, suffering and happiness, and bad and good fortune.

ASTROLOGY

The horoscopic sciences are common to the Hellenistic world and incorporated without significant change in India. Hindu systems of astrology do incorporate the system of lunar mansions (*nakṣatra*) not found elsewhere. They also place a greater emphasis on the eclipses associated with the lunar nodes. The resources and contributions of Hindu astrology remain to be mined. Nevertheless, several ideas relevant to the discussion of time can be seen to derive from Hindu astrology.

Time and destiny

The relationship between time and destiny is disputed. Both extremes find expression as well as a variety of middle grounds. For Sāṃkhya, time plays no role in the attainment of liberation. For the Ājīvikas action plays no role, while time determines all things and all conditions (Basham 1951). Certain passages in the *Mahābhārata* (12.215–21) equate time and destiny or fortune (*śrī*). For the Purāṇic vision, time as the form of the deity moves beings toward their destiny, their souls having been prepared by their karmic effort.

Destiny (*niyati*), of course, is fixed at the moment of birth. Thus a use of the moment or instant can be seen to go hand in hand with astrology. Two moments are of particular significance: the moment of birth and the dawn. The astrological sciences of India recognize the configurations of the planets within the houses of the zodiac at the moment of birth as determinative of the destiny of the native (the person for whom the horoscope is cast).

The configurations at dawn are determinative of the rulership of the earth or the destiny of the world. The rays of light from the dawn (prior to sunrise) come from unseen entities. As such, they may be thought of as bodiless or *videha*. The influence of those bodiless beings who rise helically and are therefore never seen is also a topic of astrological speculation. In Mahāyāna Buddhist traditions, the moment of death and the rays of light issued from the body of the cosmic Buddha fix (*niyati*) beings in their spiritual destiny (Kloetzli 1983).

The fundamental fact of destiny determined by birth horoscopes (geotaxy) is that of duration of life (*āyus*). It is fixed at the moment of birth based on the configurations of the planets within the zodiac. A secondary feature of horoscopes is whether the native will become a king. Horoscopy may also be said to deal with the production of beings: the beings of the zodiac (gods) and the destiny of beings beneath the zodiac (humans). This is the two-sidedness of the *kālapuruṣa*. We can see that for the classical Hindu view, the *āyus* is established for all beings born in a particular age or *yuga*, which defines the combinations of time that produce the conditions of the horoscope: destiny or fortune. Our destiny or fortune is that of the Kali Yuga, when the teachings of *bhakti* are appropriate to the weakened sensibilities of beings and the duration of human life is at its lowest point: one hundred years.

In the law of *karma* and with regard to *mokṣa*, Hinduism also recognizes the agency of both time and self, with the self being primary. Time as destiny determines the character of the age, but in the *karma* realms, actions of individuals prepare their future, and time in the form of the days, nights, and destructions at the end of the *kalpa*s move beings to higher or lower destinies.

Astrology and the wheel

The astrological sciences emphasize different understandings of the wheel from those mentioned so far. The horoscope is a diagram of all factors influencing destiny—from birth to death and even some factors following death, for example, liberation or rebirth. The wheel can serve as a model not only for the horoscope but also for those systems that present all divisions of time organized as a wheel of time. This includes the *kālacakra* or "wheel of time" traditions within Hinduism and Buddhism. An adaptation of the horoscopic wheel can also be used to array the linkage of all events from birth to death as a chain of dependent co-origination. This characteristically Buddhist formulation is intended to show the simultaneous arising of all ideas in a moment of thought.

Because the horoscope is a diagram of all factors influencing destiny, the wheel of time (*kālacakra*) can present all the moments of time as in a snapshot. While focusing on the moment as determinative or fateful or predictive of fortune, it can present images of totality, the coexistence of all conditions, as well as be the basis for the predictive sciences. These touchstones of astrology—the moment, destiny, the duration of life—underscore the tension between motion and time, durative and momentary notions of time, and fluid and static images of time.

Thus the wheel alone, in particular without the chariot or charioteer, can intuitively represent lack of motion or simultaneity (as especially in certain Buddhist usages) as readily as it can represent motion. As perhaps a reflex, while Kṛṣṇa discourses at considerable length in the *Bhagavad Gītā* and tells Arjuna in the epiphany that what is about to be has already happened because he, Kṛṣṇa, is Time itself and that Arjuna thus cannot change a thing about anyone's destiny except maybe his own, before Kṛṣṇa takes up the reins and sets the "chariot of the soul" of Arjuna in motion, it is as if everything else stands still.

HINDUISM AND CYCLICAL TIME

Although much has been written by way of viewing Hindu time as cyclical, often as a pessimistic vision of eternal recurrence and as founded on a "terror of history" (Eliade 1957, 1959a), the characterization of Hinduism as embracing a cyclical view of time presents a lopsided picture. Nor can one sustain the corollary notion that Hinduism does without linear time—a notion popularized by colonialist historiography in its judgment that India is a land "without history." There are, however, some good reasons to recognize cyclicity as an important element within Hindu views of time. First and foremost is the Upaniṣadic doctrine of reincarnation. This doctrine is not just a theoretical formulation in India (as it is with the Pythagoreans and with Empedocles) but is deeply embedded in the Hindu (as well as the Buddhist and Jaina) view of life. Repeated death and rebirth certainly involves a notion of cyclical time, but it is more correctly associated with a notion of conditioned existence (characterized by time), sexuality (a condition of being in time), life stages, duality, and so on, which can be brought to an end through the attainment of liberation or *mokṣa*. Time is without end, but time can be brought to an end and endless temporality is a condition from which escape or liberation is the ultimate goal.

As with much else in India, the logic and the imagery can—and do—become even more complex in the imagery of *avatāra*s. These incarnations or descents of the deity (as we have seen, mainly Viṣṇu but also other deities) suggest a transmigration of divinity. Does this transmigration come to an end in messianic figures such as Kalkin, the tenth and only future incarnation of Viṣṇu? Brahmā, often represented by the gander or *haṃsa*, a symbol of the soul, also seems to transmigrate through time but on some other plane, as if ultimately transmigrating between universes, befitting the notion that his days and nights add up to the life of one universe. Perhaps Viṣṇu and some others descend into and ascend out of time while Brahmā passes through it in its totality (or totalities).

Moreover, even though the most elaborate systems with regard to temporal speculation involve the cyclical creation and dissolution of the earth/universe and are thus regarded as a cyclical representation of time, the overall drama of these cosmologies is to accomplish the salvation, the liberation or beatitude, of all beings. Much remains to be done to clearly articulate the vision contained in these speculations on time, but this much is clear. Time exists for the benefit of all beings. One would thus do well to see it linked with notions not only of play (*līlā*) and mysterious divine power (*māyā*, *śakti*) but also of grace, compassion, and the gift. Time is fundamentally a drama of movement, possibly an epic narration, the embodiment of beings acting towards the maintenance of the world for the benefit/salvation of all beings.

Furthermore, interior to such a drama, Purāṇic texts also trace historical time back through *manvantara*s and *yuga*s via three major "time markers" in their royal genealogical lists (*vaṃśānucarita*). First, a deluge during the reign of the seventh Manu ends the period of cosmological origins and marks the beginning of the Solar and Lunar dynasties, whose first kings were this Manu's sons. Second, the Mahābhārata war ends the period for which Purāṇic authorship "constructs a record of what was perceived as the lineages of ruling clans" (Thapar 1991: 1). Relying on shorter royal genealogical lists in the two Sanskrit epics themselves, where they relate the ancestry of the main heroes, Purāṇic authors see in the full *Rāmāyaṇa-Mahābhārata* sequence a narrative through which such genealogical lists bring the Solar and Lunar dynasties to a cataclysmic end or profound rupture with the decimation of the Kṣatriya class. Finally, the emergence of Magadha as the beginning of the monarchical metropolitan state presents Purāṇic authors with a third marker to and through which these genealogies may be further traced into the "futures" of Purāṇically contemporary royal dynasties whose history is unquestionable but whose Kṣatriya status is considered low and dubious or is even denied. In these sections, the narrative changes from past tense to future tense in order to present the material as prophesy. Thapar remarks that "the brahmanical imprint" here "is apparent. As a projection of the decline of an earlier aristocracy and the moving in of upstarts, no statement could be more explicit" (Thapar 1991: 29, cf. 1978: 332–36, 1984: 138–47, 1992: 158–60, 1997; Hiltebeitel 1999b).

The Lunar and Solar *vaṃśas* must thus be studied as a double "dynastification" (Henige 1975) of the past: one that was purposefully constructed by the epic and Purāṇic poets from Vedic and heterodox bits and pieces to imagine a "Hindu" past that had, for the present at least, temporarily exhausted itself. Following on their descriptions of "epic age" exterminations, Purāṇic authors prophesy that the Solar and Lunar *vaṃśas* will each have one descendant "endowed with great yogic powers" who will stay in a village called Kalāpa, from which the pair "will revive the Kṣatriya race when the kṛta age will start again after the present kali age comes to an end and that some kṣatriyas exist on the earth like seed even in the kali age" (Kane 1968–77, 2.1: 380–82, 3: 873).

As we have noted, some astronomers calculate the beginning of the Kali Yuga to 3102–01 BCE, providing a "linear" reference point for the dating of inscriptions. Also, although the use of regnal years goes back to the reign of Aśoka (Thapar 1997: 569), it is not to be forgotten that Hindu culture also fostered a concept of eras (*saṃvatsara* or *varṣa*, also words for "year") as measures of historical time. The primary era used for recording the passage of years and calculating Hindu history is the Kṛta or Mālava era, better known as Vikrama era from the eighth century, which begins in 58–57 BCE and is named after Vikramāditya, supposedly to celebrate his victory after driving the barbarian Śakas from Ujjain. Following D. C. Sircar (1969), the name "Vikramāditya" is probably based on Candragupta II Vikramāditya (376–413 CE), called Śakāri or foe of the Śakas. Candragupta II's triumphs over the Śakas were probably transposed back upon a fictional Vikramāditya, who is credited with founding the era, which may itself have Scytho-Parthian origins in eastern Iran. It would thus seem to retrospectively project a founding "Hindu" imperial history back from the period of the imperial Guptas into one when India first encountered imperial designs primarily from outsiders, like the Persian Darius, Alexander, Seleucus Nicator, and Kaniṣka, and non-Hindu insiders like the Buddhist Aśoka (Sircar 1969). Similarly, the Śaka era, linked with the name of Śālivāhana, seems actually to mark the beginning of Kuṣāṇa rule in 78 CE. Śālivāhana is probably a personification of the Sātavāhanas, who were based in Pratiṣṭhāna on the Godāvarī River near Aurangabad in Maharashtra, but with origins in Āndhra and north Kanara. He seems to draw his profile from the first Śālivāhana dynast Simuka-Sātavāhana (mid-first century BCE) and from the later Gautamīputra Śātakarṇi (*c.*106–30 CE), who defeated a branch of Śakas. In some sources Vikramāditya and his era represent North India and Sanskrit,

Śālivāhana and his era, South India and Prakrit; in some the two become foes, in others they are even identified. Each becomes a "national hero of Indian folklore" (Sircar 1969: 120, *passim*). The threads that connect their mythologies through empire and era are sure reasons to reject notions of an original "real" Vikramāditya as a forgotten little king of Mālava. As Sircar (1969: 159) shows, Hindu usages regarding eras are built over time upon the consensus of "successors and subordinates" within imperial traditions. Eras point to recognition of linear time as associated with royal authority and were used not only in inscriptions but also in some annals and no doubt also for other official documents (Thapar 1997).

NARRATIVE TIME

From Salman Rushdie's *Haroun and the Sea of Stories* (1990) to Somadeva's eleventh-century *Kathāsaritsāgara* and long before that, there have been special things about storytelling in India. For the combination of antiquity, volume, and ingenuity, there is nothing like it—so much so that the folklorist Theodor Benfey (1801–91) could imagine India as the "home of story-telling and of tale-types" (Claus and Korom 1991: 57). Much that is formative in these oceanic storytelling traditions is anchored in the *Mahābhārata* and the *Rāmāyaṇa*, the two Sanskrit epics. Yet scholarship on these epics has positioned itself over another abyss: are the epic stories history or myth, real or false? The only way anyone has seen to bridge this impasse is to speak of "mythified" historical "kernels" (about which no one agrees) and long-ago heroes who have been "divinized." But this euhemerizing solution only imposes modern time-constructions (historicizing Western ones and Hindu nationalist ones converge here) on literatures and their audiences for which such constructions, until the last century or so, would have been entirely alien. We shall argue that to be attentive to what the epics do so formatively with and about time, another possibility must be considered: fiction.

But first, while both epics have many common concerns with time and Rāma even leaves the world by entering the Sarayu River with his brothers after he has been visited by Time (Kāla) (*Rāmāyaṇa* 7.95), it is the *Mahābhārata* that formulates a "doctrine of time" (*kālavāda*). Conjuring up notions of "editing" and "blending" to dismiss passages in which *kālavāda*, as we would rather see it, goes part and parcel with the epic's teachings on *bhakti* and the law of *karma*, Yaroslav Vassilkov (1999) tries to isolate an earlier *kālavāda* strand from "interpolations" that advance such teachings and to discover an "heroic fatalism" prior to the text that would come from an early phase of the epic's development. But more wisely, he sees that the *kālavāda* is "constitutive for the epic, being the quintessence of the epic *Weltanschauung*" (Vassilkov 1999: 26), and, as earlier above, not a holdover from some prior "ancient time mythology." The epic's *kālavāda* includes frequent references to the "wheel of time," to time's "revolving" (*paryāya*). The idea that those about to die are "already slain" and the theme that time "swallows" beings with its "gaping mouth" are not only combined in the *Bhagavad Gītā* but also found elsewhere in the text (Vassilkov 1999: 22–28). Not only does "time cook"; there is an "ocean of time" (*kālasāgara*) (*Mahābhārata* 12.28.43). The whole world is *kālātmaka* or "has time as its self" (*Mahābhārata* 13.1.45). Time is "the supreme lord" (*parameśvara*). Caught in "time's noose," always "bewildered" and "impelled by the law of time" (*coditāḥ kāladharmaṇā*), heroes and heroines should act knowing that although one cannot counter time, fortune does have its favorable moments (Vassilkov 1999: 24), and that sometimes, perhaps quite mysteriously, one can also play for time and that the openings for such play may be *given* by a god who "is time himself" or by an author who is a "preacher of time" (*kālavādin*) (Vassilkov 1999: 18–19):

> As if sporting, Janārdana [the "tormentor of beings," Kṛṣṇa], the soul of beings, keeps the earth, atmosphere, and heaven running. . . . By his self's *yoga*, the lord Keśava tirelessly keeps the wheel of time, the wheel of the universe, and the wheel of the *yuga*s revolving (*kālacakraṃ jagaccakraṃ yugacakraṃ . . . parivartate*). I tell you truly, the lord alone is ruler of time and death and of the mobile and the immobile. Yet ruling the whole universe, the great *yogin* Hari undertakes to perform acts like a powerless peasant (*kīnāśa iva durbalaḥ*).
>
> (*Mahābhārata* 5.66.10–14)

It is pointless to overlook such "devotional" passages in favor of a supposedly prior "heroic" *kālavāda*. That the epic occasionally attributes *kālavāda* to demons and condemns it and makes of Vṛtra, for instance, "a renowned calculator of time" (*kālasaṃkhyana-saṃkhyāta*) (*Mahābhārata* 12.270.23) is for the poets but another example of pointing up the dysfunctionality of any teaching truncated from the truths (including the chronicities) of *bhakti*.

Now for several reasons, the *Mahābhārata*'s use of the frame story is of special significance for understanding its "doctrine of time" and Hindu chronicities more generally. First, the epic is one of the first texts (its dating relative to the *Rāmāyaṇa* remains uncertain) to explore framing and its narrative possibilities in relation to themes of temporality. Second, the frame story is probably the leading device through which the text supports its vast and complex meditation on time. Third, the epic "takes time" in order to do interesting things with it and say provocative things about it, such as those mentioned earlier. Indeed, it is the first text to iterate, and reiterate, the four rhythms of time dealt with earlier, which, we can now see, are not only a curtain lifted over the main story or parameters of a *kālavāda* but also rhythms that can enframe each other, be collapsed to simultaneity, or make joins between the temporal experiences that the text itself offers. Indeed, this is so not only of these four rhythms but also of a "theoretical time" of explicit chronological statements about them in which the heroic events take place; a "narrative time" in which "complex manipulation of narrative techniques . . . move the plot forward, and fashion a literary duration"—and not only forward but also back and forth in time and into simultaneous meanwhiles; and a "performative time" in which one experiences the duration of the text as something meant to approximate oral recitation (quotes from Glucklich 1994: 45–51, with some different emphases). Fourth, it forms part of a cultural "reading" experience that relocates its temporalities into images that people live with. Thus as A. K. Ramanujan says, "No Hindu ever reads the *Mahābhārata* for the first time" (1991a: 419)—he says this of both epics (1991b: 46). Ramanujan argues that one "reads" rather than "hears" the *Mahābhārata* in such a close and detailed way because it "is a *structured* work" and, "in a largely oral tradition, one learns one's major literary works as one learns a language" (1991a: 21; emphasis in original). Recounting his own youthful experiences, he begins with a hearing, but one from a text-conversant *paṇḍita* who recounted *Mahābhārata* stories in a tailor shop, implying a prior reading. Also recalled are the "professional bards who 'did the Harikathā

Kālakṣepam,' redeeming the time with holy tales (and not always holy ones). . . . They sang songs in several languages, told folktales, sometimes danced, quoted Sanskrit tags as well as the daily newspaper, and made the *Mahābhārata* entertaining, didactic and relevant to the listener's present" (Ramanujan 1991a: 419). He finds the epic's "central structuring principle" to be "a certain kind of repetition" (Ramanujan 1991a: 421) that includes such framing devices as textual circularities and concentricities, nested relations between episodes and between episodes and "inset" stories like "Nala and Damayantī" (422–41). Ramanujan sees similar patterns of "rhythmic recurrence" in the *Rāmāyaṇa* (1991b: 40).

The frame story has been noticed at its possible inception in the Brāhmaṇas by Michael Witzel (1986) and in its great unfolding in the *Mahābhārata* by C. Z. Minkowski (1989). As both authors note, this narrative device may have its origins in India. And as both observe, it is likely that the frame story relates to the special attention given in India to the structured embeddedness of Brāhmaṇic ritual, one feature of which is that the *intervals* of certain rites—notably, the year-long *aśvamedha*—were a time designated for the telling of stories. Rituals that embox other rituals around a central rite could thus also enframe stories that enframe other stories. And this could be done in reverse, as narratives could enframe rituals. As Witzel (1987a: 413–14) shows, this is one way to think about how a story about rituals in the Brāhmaṇas also emboxes other stories. More complexly, the *Mahābhārata* makes the technique "self-referential" and turns it into one of literary composition: "An epic frame story is more than embedded: it is a story about the telling of another story" (Minkowski 1989: 402). The *Mahābhārata* is artfully designed as a story about a ritual—a collective *sattra* sacrifice performed by the *ṛṣis* of the Naimiṣa Forest—in whose intervals is told the story about another *sattra*—the snake sacrifice of King Janmejaya, a royal descendent of the epic's Brāhmaṇ author Vyāsa and its royal hero Arjuna—in whose intervals is told the story *of* (that is, in both senses, the story *by* and *about*) the author Vyāsa that is also his story about the heroes, a story that embeds many other stories and centers upon an emboxed narrative of a great "sacrifice of battle." More than this, the *Mahābhārata*, which never makes the author its direct narrator, makes *his* own story into a further outermost frame for the whole. The *Mahābhārata* poets construct Vyāsa's authorship not only in relation to similar functions of the deity (like Kṛṣṇa, he is an incarnation of a portion of Nārāyaṇa; one "is time," the other "preaches" it) but also in relation to a disciplic function and a bardic function. We never hear Vyāsa tell the tale himself; rather it is disseminated to us through two interlaced narrations, each said to be of Vyāsa's "entire thought": one (*Mahābhārata* 1.55.2) by his Brāhmaṇ disciple Vaiśampāyana at the snake sacrifice, in Vyāsa's presence, which we may call the outer frame; and the other (1.1.23) in the Naimiṣa Forest by a non-Brāhmaṇ bard named Ugraśravas (terrible to hear), which we may call the outermore frame. The first is a linear historical frame (the main story of a dynasty through six generations), in which the author is present not only to sire the first generation (with the births of the fathers of the two rival sets of cousins) but also to hear his story told to Janmejaya six generations later. The second is the cosmological frame, in which the story is told to the celestial *ṛṣis* who are, among other things, stars in the Naimiṣa Forest, which probably derives its name from *nimeṣa*—the blink, wink, moment, or twinkle—and seems to be the night sky (Hiltebeitel 1998). And the third is an enigmatic, ever-receding authorial frame that allows the author to move *literally* in and out of the spatiotemporal constraints and possibilities of his text.

One finds something similar, though less complex, in the *Rāmāyaṇa* (1.4, 7.84–86): Rāma hears the *Rāmāyaṇa* from his own twin sons, who have been taught to sing it by its author, the poet Vālmīki; they sing it, at Vālmīki's command and in his presence, during intervals of Rāma's own *aśvamedha* sacrifice, until Rāma recognizes them and realizes that he misses their mother, whom he had banished while she was pregnant with them because of a rumor of her infidelity (it will be too late for a reconciliation). Moreover, the entire story is previewed to Vālmīki by the sage Nārada, and part of it is told by Hanumān to Sītā when he finds her in captivity. Later authors redeploy the frame device in the Purāṇas and refined *kāvya* literature, story anthologies like the *Kathāsaritsāgara* and the *Yogavāsiṣṭha*, which enframes itself with a story of Rāma and about which Wendy Doniger O'Flaherty (1984: 127–32) makes the important point that some of these texts also enframe philosophical argument as their own metacommentary. Frame stories are of special significance for what many Hindu texts do with time and what they impart in ways of thinking about it. If we add that authors and their audiences are not only often *like* gods but also often *are* gods, a comment on the Hindu cultural sense of time mirrors such features: "Time is like a museum with endless corridors and alcoves. You, the viewer, are walking through the museum in the dark, holding a light to each scene as you pass it. God is the curator of the museum, and only He knows all that is in it. One lifetime represents an alcove" (Hall 1959: 30, citing a colleague). Or better, one kind of alcove, and then there are the corridors.

It is here that we come back to the impasse between myth and history and the need to consider the birth within pre-novelistic genres of a third category, fiction—as is being done with comparable literatures: for instance, the *Iliad* (Finkelberg 1998), Indian Buddhist Mahāyāna literature (Lopez 1993), biblical narrative (Alter 1981), Dante (Gellrich 1985). Frank Kermode presents a suggestive angle:

> We have to distinguish between myths and fictions. Fictions can degenerate into myths whenever they are not consciously held to be fictive. . . . Myth operates within the diagrams of ritual, which presupposes total and adequate explanations of things as they are and were; it is a sequence of radically unchangeable gestures. Fictions are for finding things out, and they change as the needs of sense-making change. Myths are the agents of stability, fictions the agents of change.
>
> (1967: 39)

In arguing against Northrop Frye's "archetypal" or "mythic" readings of literature, Kermode says, "We must avoid the regress into myth which has deceived poet, historian, and critic" (1967: 43). To be sure, Hindu epic poets made use of history and myth (in Kermode's sense) among their sources, and what they composed has since been taken to be one or the other or some combination of the two. Perhaps this was even the poets' goal. But what they also did while composing was explore the possibilities of fiction.

Comparison here is thus with the novel, a genre that, according to Paul Ricoeur, has "constituted for at least three centuries now a prodigious workshop for experiments in the domains of composition and the expression of time" (1985: 8). We may say something similar of the genre of "epic" in classical post-Vedic India, for among the many novelties explored by the epic poets, salient among them was the diversity of chronicities. However, whereas in the West, epic was anterior to the novel and something of an archaic foil to its novelties, in India epic (or what we call "epic" for lack of a better word) was what was new (we have no evidence to the contrary) and what was old and anterior was Veda. The epic genre thus allowed its poets to construct what Bakhtin (1981) calls a new "chronotope" ("literally, 'time space' ") (84), a "rule-generating force" (100) by which "spatial and temporal indicators are fused into one carefully thought-out, concrete whole. Time, as it were, thickens, takes on flesh, becomes artistically visible; likewise, space becomes charged and responsive to the movements of time, plot and history" (Bakhtin 1981: 84). Yet it is ironic that Bakhtin's well-known contrast between epic and novel cannot be well applied to the Hindu epics, which are as much like his "novel" as the Western epic that defines his contrast: "Outside his destiny, the epic and tragic hero is nothing; he is, therefore, a function of the plot fate assigns him; he cannot become the hero of another destiny or another plot" (1981: 36). Quoting this passage, Gary Morson writes, "By contrast, the life led by a novelistic hero does not exhaust his identity. He could have been different. We sense that, in potential, he has more lives than one" (1994: 112). These are ways that Hindu audiences experience a hero or heroine's epic life, with other lives both behind and before them and multiple possibilities for different lives within the lives the epics give them.

What the epic poets did, then, was construct a new chronotope: one with which to explore not only the joins and intersections between the four rhythms of time but also within which to give narrative form to all six of the images of time (pp. 563–68). Like the "workshop" that produced the modern novel, the epic poets achieved this by their "configuration and refiguration" of primarily Vedic images into an "empire of conventions" that would "grow in proportion to the representative ambition" of authors from the epics through the Purāṇas (cf. Ricoeur 1985: 13). To describe this new chronotope is to describe its "grid of conventions" (Alter 1981: 47), to get a sense of the chronicities they bring to life and the devices used to convey that sense (cf. Morson 1994: 4). For the purposes of this chapter, however, it will suffice to indicate five of the most important conventions and devices. The important point to be kept in mind is the innovative play with which the epic poets explored these conventions and devices while creating them.

Foreshadowing, backshadowing, and sideshadowing

These three devices are discussed by Morson, who shows how what he calls sideshadowing, a term of his own coinage, is introduced into the fiction of Feodor Mikhailovich Dostoevsky and Leo Nikolayevich Tolstoy in their resolve "to offer an alternative to prevailing deterministic and otherwise closed views of time" (1994: 6). Foreshadowing, common enough to many literatures, involves prefiguration and "backward causality"; "an effect of . . . [a] future catastrophe [is] visible in temporal advance" (Morson 1994: 48). The most obvious such device in the Hindu epics is the use of omens, through which "the future leaves its mark on the present" (Morson 1994: 63). For doomed characters like Karṇa and Rāvaṇa, omens signify a certain grandeur: "since omens do not happen to everyone, they create a sense of exceptionality and importance for those to whom they are directed" (Morson 1994: 71). Both epics are also full of other foreshadowings: in the names given to characters before significant moments; in themes; in inset stories through which heroes hear about things that pertain to what is about to happen to them (as also about what just happened to them); in what Ramanujan (1991a: 422–41) calls "autonomous complexes" of action that recur in different personages; and in recurrent ethical reflection on the nature and outcome of such action complexes, including both mental and physical acts. Foreshadowing gives the epics an oracular quality: certain characters—authors, gods, some *ṛṣi*s—know from the start what will happen, which audiences and readers come to understand too, but over a duration. In such a context, when foreshadowing takes center stage, time looks to be foreordained, fated, as when Kṛṣṇa tells Arjuna that the heroes on both sides "are already slain" before the battle begins; or when the *ṛṣi*s rejoice at the abduction of Sītā.

Backshadowing, on the other hand, is "foreshadowing after the fact," treating the past "as if it had inevitably to lead to the present we know and as if signs of our present should have been visible to our predecessors"; "in effect, the present, as the future of the past, was already immanent in the past" in "a more or less straight line" (Morson 1994: 13, 234). This "he should have known better" convention is used nowhere more strikingly than when the bard Saṃjaya, narrator of the *Mahābhārata*'s war books and gifted by Vyāsa with the "divine eye," rushes back from the battlefield at the beginning of each war book to announce to the blind Kaurava king Dhṛtarāṣṭra the death of the Kaurava general of that book and for the rest of the book then narrates the several days of battle that led up to that general's killing. Dhṛtarāṣṭra is precisely the blind king who should have known better, who will hear over and over from the author Vyāsa and from Saṃjaya, Vyāsa's appointed bard, why he "should not grieve" for what could never have been otherwise, and the antidote to which is *kālavāda*, the "doctrine of time."

Over and against these more-or-less linear chronicities and the foreordained worlds they imply, "sideshadowing projects—from the 'side'—the shadow of an alternative present" (Morson 1994: 11) that is filled with possibilities. "Its most fundamental lesson is: to understand a moment is to grasp not only what did happen but also what else might have happened. Hypothetical histories shadow actual ones. . . . Sideshadowing invites us into this peculiar *middle realm*" (Morson 1994: 119; emphasis in original). Thus the same god who can tell Arjuna that he is time and that the heroes gathered for war "are already slain" can precede this by telling him in the same *Bhagavad Gītā* (2.28, 10.20):

> The beginnings of things are unmanifest;
> manifest are their middles, son of Bharata,
> unmanifest again their ends.
> Why mourn about this?
>
> I am the beginning and the middle
> of beings, and the very end too.

The palpable tension between contingency and determinism opens the field of narrative possibilities. At every point we are given the possibility of many stories. The main stories are told in their own midst, one before it ends, the other perhaps before it has even happened (Hiltebeitel 2001a: 284–322). No story is ever the whole story. Every version has another version. Every outcome has multiple fatalities behind it. The stories that heroes and heroines hear are sideshadows of their own. Mysteries are left unsolved, questions (*praśna*) unanswered (most notably in the case of Draupadī). Characters are filled not only with griefs and doubts but also haunted by shadows (Vyāsa will always have before him the shadow of his liberated son Śuka) and rumors (most famously Rāma). Nothing ever really begins (as Duryodhana says of Karṇa, "the origins of rivers and heroes are obscure"; *Mahābhārata* 1.127.11) or ends. Thus J. A. B. van Buitenen can say, "The epic is a series of precisely stated problems imprecisely and therefore inconclusively resolved, with every resolution raising a new problem, until the very end, when the question remains: whose is heaven and whose is hell?" (1973–78, 2: 29). "Vortex times" follows one upon another: "As catastrophe approaches, *time speeds up*. Crises appear more and more rapidly until a moment of *apparently infinite temporal density is reached*" (Morson 1994: 165; emphasis in original). Yet, as with Tolstoy's novels, "continuation [is] always possible." There are loose threads left at the end of each crisis, each *Mahābhārata parvan* (join) or *Rāmāyaṇa kāṇḍa* ("joint" of a reed or cane), and often at the ends of the epics' shorter sections: the *adhyāya*s (readings) of the *Mahābhārata* or the *sarga*s (streams, cantos) of the *Rāmāyaṇa*. Each epic has also its epilogue. Moreover, within stories there is the Vedic convention of the ritual "interval" which the epic poets fictionalize into a narrative convention through which to tell the epics themselves. Through a design of deferral, apocalypses can coincide with the contingent and unfinalizable.

Moments

Closely related to what the epic poets do with the convention of the interval (*antara*) is what they make of the "moment": the "moment" that is also a "wink, blink, or twinkle" or a "glance." On such moments their stories turn, most notably when gods, the authors themselves, or other new *bhakti* sages like Nārada and Mārkaṇḍeya intervene—"appear" and "disappear"—in some "nick of time" or to bring about a "sudden or unexpected reversal of circumstances"—what Aristotle calls a "peripeteia" (cf. Ricoeur 1985: 23)—often by telling a story. *Antara*, *nimeṣa*, and *kṣaṇa* are what Bakhtin calls "link-words," like "suddenly" or "at just that moment." They "provide . . . an opening for sheer chance, which has its own specific logic . . . of *random contingency* . . ., which is to say, chance *simultaneity* . . . and *chance rupture* . . ., that is, a logic of random *disjunctions* in time": "Should there be no chance simultaneity or chance disjunctions in time, there would be no plot at all, and nothing to write a novel about" (Baktin 1981: 92; emphasis in original). In such a world, a hero's choice—for instance Arjuna's dilemma—can be momentous (cf. Morson 1994: 22). Moreover, as we have seen, in making a poetic convention of the term "*nimeṣa*," the poets of the *Mahābhārata* link the coming and goings of gods and sages with the epic's outermore frame and the turning world of the stars.

Yoga and bhakti

As we have noted earlier, within Hinduism it is the Yoga system that inventories the moment (*kṣaṇa*). The *Mahābhārata* fuses this emphasis with *bhakti*, making its author and main deity masters of *yoga*. By this means the author, like the deity, can envision the "whole story" as a divine plan and also intervene within it. Vālmīki also envisions the *Rāmāyaṇa* through yogic meditation, fuses this with knowledge of a divine plan, and, to a lesser degree, intervenes in his text. But there is no corresponding degree of play upon the notion of the "moment."

Fictional authors and bards

In each of the Sanskrit epics, a Brāhmaṇ author is among the first heroes of his own composition. While creating his new poem, he tells "old stories" (*purāṇa*) and "just so stories" (*itihāsa*) along the way, and in each case bards (*kuśīlava*, *sūta*) are among those who disseminate the poem. Thus Rāma's sons Kuśa and Lava are the first *kuśīlava*s, and Ugraśravas, son of Lomaharṣaṇa, after he has heard the *Mahābhārata* at Janamejaya's snake sacrifice, relays it to the *ṛṣi*s of the Naimiṣa Forest. However these epics were composed, we may say that both the authors and the bards are fictional characters within them. Yet it may be that those who did compose the epics gave hints of that process in describing the relations between poets, bards, other transmitters, and audiences. Regarding time, Vyāsa is said to have rested after the arduous process of composing the *Mahābhārata* in three years (1.56.32). Both epics portray their poets, unlike their bards, as being concerned with the longevity of their poems. The epics give us no reason to think of the stories going through a *prior* "bardic" transmission such as many scholars like to imagine. The transmission is in each case the reverse: from Brāhmaṇs to bards. Unlike the Brāhmaṇ authors, the bards also do not get much chance to intervene in the stories. Yet the authors can change the course of events.

With this, we face the literary question of how they "treat" their characters on two intersecting planes: "the real time of the creative process and the fictive time of the characters—two distinct ontological realms . . . [that] somehow take place together," to borrow Morson's (1994: 100) description of works of Fyodor Dostoevsky. Authors can *save* their characters from untimely deaths, as when Vyāsa appears from nowhere to lift Yudhiṣṭhira and Saṃjaya right out of the fray of battle (*Mahābhārata* 7.158.51–62, 9.28.35–39). Authors can *prompt* their characters, as when Vyāsa appears similarly to tell the Pāṇḍavas about Draupadī's *svayaṃvara* or "self-choice" marriage ceremony or when, at Vālmīki's command, Kuśa and Lava tell Rāma the *Rāmāyaṇa*, leading him not only to recognize his sons but also to attempt what will result in his wrenching final loss of Sītā. As is obvious from the last example, authors can also *be cruel* to their characters: something that becomes most evident when Vyāsa foreshadows the further cruelties of his story by beginning his genealogical intervention in the Kaurava line by horrifying, with his ugliness, the two princesses he is called upon to impregnate and then cursing their sons to be born blind (Dhṛtarāṣṭra) and pale (Pāṇḍu) after the first princess closes her eyes and the second blanches at his grim appearance (cf. Morson 1994: 79, on Tolstoy's cruelty to Anna Karenina).

But there is also the sense that in bringing characters to life, they become big enough to surprise the authors, even to "contend [with them] on . . . [almost] equal terms" (Morson 1994: 41). It is as if Rāma and Yudhiṣṭhira are so dear to these authors that they put off getting rid of them to the very last moment. In the *Mahābhārata* there is even the convention of having characters argue with god. As Morson says, "characters are sensed as major when they manifest a palpable unfinalizability" (1994: 93). Satyajit Ray once said that he would love to have filmed a *Mahābhārata* but could not figure out how to deal with eighteen major characters (American Film Institute, *c.*1980). As Morson says of Dostoevsky's heroes, "*It is as if each major character could be the organizing point for the novel*" (1994: 94; emphasis in original). Indian dramas and novels on epic themes bear out the same point.

Open textuality, enplotment, and reenplotment

"A work may be closed with respect to its configuration and open with respect to the breakthrough it is capable of effecting on the reader's world. Reading . . . is precisely the act that brings about the transition between the effect of closure from the first perspective and the effect of openness for the second" (Ricoeur 1985: 5). More than this, what of a text that works out ways to remain open, to effect openness? The *Mahābhārata*, as we have seen, is such a closure-resisting text. Moreover, it is a text of mixed genres that many have called "encyclopedic." While making reference to numerous genres—Veda, Upaniṣad, *saṃvāda* (dialogue), Purāṇa, *śāstra*, and so on—it also *is* each of those genres. The *Rāmāyaṇa* has such features too, but to a lesser degree, and is somewhat more closed off around the image of Rāma's and Sītā's "perfection." But even here, that perfection is repeatedly open to questions raised by the narrative itself. As Glucklich observes, "The time of the narrative is structured as a rhythmic progression between the fixity of dharma and the consequences of *adharma*" (1994: 48). This is true for both epics, and in terms not only of character and plot but also in the juxtaposition of an "eternal *dharma*" (*sanātanadharma*) with flexible notions of *kalivarjya* (*dharma*s or "laws or duties" specific to the Kali Yuga) and *āpad-dharma* (*dharma*s for times of distress) (Glucklich 1994: 39). Indeed, each of these temporalities is an invention of the epic poets. In creating such open textualities and temporalities, the epic poets opened the way to "multiple Rāmāyaṇas" (Richman 1991) and "multiple Mahābhāratas." Hindu audiences and readers love to ask "what if" questions of these texts. Popular editions of the Hindi *Rāmāyaṇa*, for instance, are printed with appendices of such questions (*praśna*), questions that open new stories (Hess 2001). Then, too, both epics are reenplotted in medieval vernacular oral epics in which their heroes and heroines take on new lives to work out the "unfinished business" of their prior ones (Hiltebeitel 1999b).

With Ricoeur, one may thus posit a "first phase" when conventions grow in proportion to the reality they represent, but in the case of Hindu epic, this first phase was not one of realism, like that of the novel. The reality it represents is one open to mystery and enigma, but also one that uses plot and language no less to conceal than to reveal—to conceal, among other things, the social conditions and history—post-Vedic and surely post-Aśokan—under which the epics were composed. Yet as that latter reality recedes, the conventions still remain staples for the Purāṇic representation of other historical realities.

This can be seen most notably in the *Bhaviṣya Purāṇa*, the "Purāṇa of the future," which revises the epic conventions to serve the purposes of "prophesying" the course of medieval and even colonial history. Once Lomaharṣaṇa, this Purāṇa's bard, who is also the father of the *Mahābhārata*'s bard, finishes describing the last days of the Pāṇḍavas and tells us that their "portions" (*aṃśa*) will be reborn for "an increase of Kalidharma" into this Purāṇa's "translation" of *Ālhā*, the Hindi oral epic, Vyāsa, settled in the Naimiṣa Forest and "under the sway of the sleep of *yoga*" (*yoganidrā*), enters into "meditation beyond the three strands of matter." The *muni*s with him also enter a yogic state, and after twelve hundred years they arise and bathe, and it is the era-beginning time of Vikramāditya. Then, after further prophesied times lead on to the Purāṇa's Sanskritized *Ālhā*, which narrates how many of the *Mahābhārata*'s heroes and heroines take rebirth in late twelfth-century events of the fall of the Rājpūts to the Muslim forces of Shihābuddīn, the *muni*s are again present to hear the declining fortunes of various Rājpūt clans. Still in the Naimiṣa Forest, they hear the bard foretell events from the Delhi Sulṭānate that will lead to a century of "*mleccha*" rule, which prompts the bard to urge the *ṛṣi*s to accompany him quickly to an auspicious mountain city called Viśālā. In misery they leave Naimiṣa Forest, and at Viśālā they all meditate on Hari (Viṣṇu). After years in *samādhi*, they ascend to the "home of Brahmā" or Satyaloka. Vyāsa now says he has told about the "whole future heard by the exercise of *yoga*" and asks what else his audience wishes to hear. Manu (he of the current Manvantara), paying homage to Vyāsa as, among other things, "the witness" (*sākṣiṇ*), asks him to dispel his ignorance about the highest *brahman*. Vyāsa then unfolds an unusual Purāṇic cosmogony, with an account of the *kalpa*s that identifies Viṣṇu-Nārāyaṇa as the "living self" (*jīvātma*) of sixteen parts and the "self of time" (*kālātmā*), and in effect maps the *kalpa*s onto the body of Śiva, the more encompassing self of eighteen parts who is the "pacifier of living souls" (*jīvaśaṃkaraḥ*). Whereas units of time pertain to *brahman* "with qualities," the supreme *brahman* is above time and born from the imperishable. The "foot" of that supreme *brahman*, "whose undecaying nature is a subtle light," is obtainable by ten years of *samādhi*, which the *ṛṣi*s have just completed. So they now experience the "denseness" (*ghanakam*) of *brahman* as being-consciousness-bliss, and in what would pass as an instant (*kṣaṇa*) on earth, they experience a hundred thousand earthly years. But opening their eyes on the second day, they see further deterioration of human life on earth: people living like cattle, caste-mixture, *mleccha*s as heretics, heretics of many types (*jāti*), and propounders of many paths. Having seen all this "in the presence of Lomaharṣaṇa," the *ṛṣi*s pay him homage, and Vyāsa tells them to listen to him as he emerges from "the eternal Yoganidrā" to tell the "story of the *kalpas*," beginning with the depredations of Timiriliṅga (dark phallus) or Tamburlaine that lead on to the Mughal empire (Hiltebeitel 1999b: 286–93).

So it is that under the sun, time can keep on "cooking a world" in which men and women can also cook themselves: a world of multiple intersecting temporalities that remains open also to new ones. It is thus no surprise that even today, "India time" can be both x.5 hours different from almost everywhere else on earth and mean something like *mañana*.

REFERENCES CITED

INDIC WORKS

The texts are listed without particulars regarding editions, translations, commentaries, and so on, which are known to specialists. Nonspecialists may derive comfort from the thought that *mantras* should be *heard*, not *read*.

Abhidharmakośa (of Vasubandhu)
Agni Purāṇa
Aitareya Āraṇyaka
Aitareya Brāhmaṇa
Āpastamba Dharmasūtra
Arthaśāstra (of Kauṭilya)
Aṣṭādhyāyī (of Pāṇini)
Āśvalāyana Gṛhyasūtra
Atharva Veda Saṃhitā
Baudhāyana Dharmasūtra
Bhagavad Gītā
Bhagavadgītābhāṣya (of Śaṃkara)
Bhāgavata Purāṇa
Bhaktavijaya (of Mahīpati)
Bhaktirasāmṛtasindhu (of Rūpa Gosvāmī)
Bhaktisūtra (of Nārada)
Bhaviṣya Purāṇa
Bījak (of Kabīr)
Brahma Purāṇa
Brahmāṇḍa Purāṇa
Brahmasūtra (or Vedāntasūtra) (of Bādarāyaṇa)
Brahmasūtrabhāṣya (of Śaṃkara)
Bṛhadāraṇyaka Upaniṣad
Bṛhaddharma Purāṇa
Buddhacarita (of Aśvaghoṣa)
Caitanya Bhāgavata (of Vṛndāvana Dāsa)
Caitanya Caritāmṛta (of Kṛṣṇadāsa Kavirāja)
Caraka Saṃhitā (of Agniveśa)

Chāndogya Upaniṣad
Devī Māhātmya
Dīghanikāya
Gāthā (of Tukārāma)
Gauragaṇoddeśadīpikā (of Kavikarṇapūra)
Gautama Dharmasūtra
Gītā Govinda (of Jayadeva)
Gītābhāṣya (of Rāmānuja)
Harivaṃśa
Hiraṇyakeśi Dharmasūtra
Hiraṇyakeśi Gṛhyasūtra
Hitopadeśa
Īśānaśivagurudevapaddhati (of Īśānaśiva)
Jābāla Upaniṣad
Jaiminīya Brāhmaṇa
Jaiminīya Upaniṣad Brāhmaṇa
Jīvanmuktiviveka (of Mādhava-Vidyāraṇya)
Jñāneśvarī (of Jñāneśvara)
Kāmakalāvilāsa (of Puṇyānanda)
Kāmasūtra (of Vātsyāyana)
Kaṭha Upaniṣad
Kāṭhaka Saṃhitā
Kathāsaritsāgara (of Somadeva)
Kauṣītaki Brāhmaṇa
Kauṣītaki Brāhmaṇa Upaniṣad
Kauṣītaki Upaniṣad
Kena Upaniṣad
Kūrma Purāṇa
Mahābhārata
Mahābhārata Tātparya Nirṇaya (of Madhva)
Maitrāyaṇi Upaniṣad
Maitrī Upaniṣad
Mālinīvijayottara Tantra
Mantrārtharahasya (of Sundara)
Manusmṛti
Mārkaṇḍeya Purāṇa
Matsya Purāṇa
Muṇḍaka Upaniṣad
Nāmaliṅgānuśāsana (of Amarasiṃha)
Nareśvaraparīkṣa (of Sadyojoti)
Nāṭyaśāstra (of Bharata)
Netra Tantra
Netratantroddyota
Nītiśataka (of Bhartṛhari)
Nītivākyāmṛta (of Somadevasūri)
Nivṛtti (of Bhaktisiddhānta Sarasvatī)
Nyāyamañjarī (of Jayanta)
Nyāyasūtra (of Gautama Akṣapāda)
Nyāyasūtrabhāṣya (of Vātsyāyana Pakṣilasvāmin)
Padāvalī (of Mīrābāī)

Padāvalī (of Nāmadeva)
Padāvalī (of Raidāsa)
Pañcastava (of Kūrattāḻvān)
Pañcatantra (of Viṣṇuśarman)
Parāśarasmṛti
Pāraskara Gṛhyasūtra
Parātrīśikāvivaraṇa (of Abhinavagupta)
Pāśupatasūtra
Perumāḷ Tirumoḻi (of Kulacēkara Āḻvār)
Prabodhacandrodaya (of Kṛṣṇamiśra)
Praśna Upaniṣad
Pratyabhijñāhṛdaya (of Kṣemarāja)
Pūrva Mīmāṃsāsūtra (of Jaimini)
Raghuvaṃśa (of Kālidāsa)
Rājataraṅgiṇī (of Kalhana)
Rāmāyaṇa (of Vālmīki)
Rāmcaritmānas (of Tulasīdāsa)
Rauravottarāgama
Ṛg Veda Saṃhitā
Śābarabhāṣya (of Śabara)
Ṣaḍdarśanasamuccaya (of Haribhadrasūri)
Śaṃkaravijaya (of Anantānandagiri)
Sāṃkhyakārikā (of Īśvarakṛṣṇa)
Saṃyutta Nikāya
Śārīrakabhāṣya (of Śaṃkara)
Sarvadarśanasaṃgraha (of Mādhava-Vidyāraṇya)
Śatapatha Brāhmaṇa
Śaunakīya Atharva Veda
Śikṣāṣṭaka (of Caitanya)
Śiva Purāṇa
Śivasūtravimarśinī (of Kṣemarāja)
Smṛtimuktāphala (of Vaidyanātha Dīkṣita)
Somaśambhupaddhati (of Somaśambhu)
Spandanirṇaya (of Kṣemarāja)
Spandapradīpikā (of Bhagavadutpala)
Śrībhāṣya (of Rāmānuja)
Śrīkaṇṭhabhāṣya (of Śrīkaṇṭha)
Śrīvacanabhūṣaṇa (of Piḷḷai Lokācārya)
Strīdharmapaddhati (of Tryambakayajvan)
Sundarabāhu Stava (of Kūrattāḻvān)
Svacchanda Tantra
Śvetāśvatara Upaniṣad
Taittirīya Saṃhitā
Taittirīya Upaniṣad
Tantrāloka (of Abhinavagupta)
Tantrālokaviveka
Tantrasāra (of Abhinavagupta)
Tantrasārasaṃgraha (of Nārāyaṇa)
Tantravārttika (of Kumārila Bhaṭṭa)
Tattvaprakāśa (of Bhojadeva)

Tattvārthadīpanibandha (of Vallabha)
Tiruccantaviruttam (of Tirumaḻicai Āḻvār)
Tirumoḻi (of Periyāḻvār)
Tiruvāymoḻi (of Caṭakōpaṉ, aka Nammāḻvār)
Tripurārahasya
Vacana (of Basavaṇṇa)
Vaikhānasasmārtasūtra
Vaiśeṣikasūtra (of Kaṇāda)
Varadarāja Stava (of Kūrattāḻvān)
Varāha Purāṇa
Vasiṣṭha Dharmasūtra
Vāyu Purāṇa
Vedānta Parijāta Saurabha (of Nimbārka)
Vedāntasāra (of Sadānanda)
Vedārthasaṃgraha (of Rāmānuja)
Vijñānabhairava Tantra
Vinaya Patrikā (of Tulasīdāsa)
Vīramitrodaya (by Mitramiśra)
Viṣṇu Purāṇa
Vivekacūḍāmaṇi (of Śaṃkara)
Yājñavalkyasmṛti
Yajur Veda Saṃhitā
Yogasūtra (of Patañjali)
Yogasūtrabhāṣya (of Vyāsa)

NON-INDIC WORKS

Akbarnāma (of Abū al-Faẓl Allāmī)
Apocalypse (of Peter)
Astronomicum Caesarem (of Peter Apianus)
De Caelo (of Aristotle)
Enneads (of Plotinus)
Muntakhab-ut-Tawārīkh (of Badā'ūnī)
Physica (of Aristotle)
Prince, The (of Niccolò Machiavelli)
Ta'rīkh al-Hind (of al-Bīrūnī)

SECONDARY WORKS

Abbott, Justin E. and Narkar R. Godbole, trans. 1982 [1933]. *Stories of Indian Saints: Translation of Mahipati's Marathi Bhaktavijaya*. 2 volumes in 1 book. Delhi: Motilal Banarsidass.
Achaya, K. T. 1994. *Indian Food: A Historical Companion*. Delhi: Oxford University Press.
Achaya, K. T. 1998. *A Historical Dictionary of Indian Food*. Delhi: Oxford University Press.
Adriaensen, R., H. T. Bakker, and H. Isaacson. 1998. *The Skandapurāṇa*. Volume 1: *Adhyāyas 1–25*. Groningen: Egbert Forsten.
Agrawala, Vasudeva S. 1963. *Devī-Māhātmyam: The Glorification of the Great Goddess*. Varanasi: All-India Kashiraj Trust.

Aiyangar, K. V. Rangaswami, ed. 1942. *Kṛtyakalpataru of Bhaṭṭa Lakṣmīdhara*. Volume 8 of 14: *Tīrthavivecanakāṇḍa*. Baroda: Oriental Institute.

Aklujkar, Vidyut. 1999. "The Framing of the Shrew: Kaikeyī as Kalahā in the *Ānanda Rāmāyaṇa*." Paper Presented at "The Rāmāyaṇa Culture: Text, Performance, Gender, and Iconography" Conference, University of British Columbia, 19–20 February.

Allāmī, Abū al-Faẓl. 1972 [1907]. *The Akbarnāma of Abu-l-Faẓl* (trans. H. Beveridge). Volume 2 of 3. Delhi: Rare Books.

Allen, Charles, ed., with Michael Mason. 1975. *Plain Tales from the Raj: Images of British India in the Twentieth Century*. New York: St Martin.

Allen, Charles. 1977. *Raj: A Scrapbook of British India, 1877–1947*. New York: St Martin's Press.

Alley, Kelly D. 1998. "Idioms of Degeneracy: Assessing Gaṅgā's Purity and Pollution." In Lance E. Nelson, ed., *Purifying the Earthly Body of God: Religion and Ecology in Hindu India*, 297–330. Albany: State University of New York Press.

Alter, Robert. 1981. *The Art of biblical Narrative*. New York: Basic Books.

Ambedkar, B. R. 1948. *The Untouchables: Who Were They And Why They Became Untouchables?* New Delhi: Amrit Books.

Anand, I. M. S. 1990. " 'Bol, Bam!' The Pilgrimage to Vaidyanath Dham." *Sevartham* 15: 121–29.

Anantaramayya, Yeluripati. 1984. *Śrī Vāmana Purāṇam*. Tirupati: Tirumala-Tirupati Devasthanamulu.

Anantha Murthy, U. R. 1976 [1965]. *Samskara: A Rite for a Dead Man* (trans. A. K. Ramanujan). Delhi: Oxford University Press.

Apte, V. S. 1965 [1890]. *The Student's Sanskrit-English Dictionary*. Delhi: Motilal Banarsidass.

Asher, Catherine B. 1997. "Constructing Identities: 'Hindu,' 'Muslim,' and the Built Environment." Paper Presented at "What is Hinduism?" Symposium, University of Florida, Gainesville, 28–30 March.

Asprey & Company, with Harriet Wynter and the Collaboration of Various Museums and Private Collections. 1973. *The Clockwork of the Heavens. [Catalogue of] an Exhibition of Astronomical Clocks, Watches, and Allied Scientific Instruments*. London: Asprey.

Babb, Lawrence A. 1975. *The Divine Hierarchy: Popular Hinduism in Central India*. New York: Columbia University Press.

Babb, Lawrence A. 1986. *Redemptive Encounters: Three Modern Styles in the Hindu Tradition*. Berkeley: University of California Press.

Babb, Lawrence A. 1996. *Absent Lord: Ascetics and Kings in a Jain Ritual Culture*. Berkeley: University of California Press.

Babb, Lawrence A. and Susan S. Wadley, eds. 1995. *Media and the Transformation of Religion in South Asia*. Philadelphia: University of Pennsylvania Press.

al-Badā'ūnī ('Abdu-l-Qādir Ibn-i-Mulūk Shāh). 1976 [1884]. *Muntakhab-ut-Tawārīkh*. Volume 2 of 3 (trans. W. H. Lowe). Karachi: Karimsons.

Bailey, F. G. 1994. *The Witch-Hunt; or, The Triumph of Morality*. Ithaca: Cornell University Press.

Bailey, Greg. 1995. *Gaṇeśapurāṇa*. Part 1: *Upāsanākhaṇḍa*. Wiesbaden: Otto Harrassowitz.

Bakhtin, M. M. 1981 [1975]. *The Dialogic Imagination: Four Essays* (trans. Caryl Emerson and Michael Holquist; ed. Michael Holquist). Austin: University of Texas Press.

Balasubrahmanyam, V., trans. 1989. *The Hitopadesa*. Calcutta: M. P. Birla Foundation.

Balslev, Anindita Niyogi. 1983. *A Study of Time in Indian Philosophy*. Wiesbaden: Otto Harrassowitz.

Balslev, Anindita Niyogi. 1993. "Time and the Hindu Experience." In Anindita Niyogi Balslev and J. N. Mohanty, eds., *Religion and Time*, 163–81. Leiden: E. J. Brill.

Bandyopadhyaya, Saroja, comp. and ed. 1979. *Vaiṣṇava Padāvalī Ratnāvalī*. Calcutta: Natuna Sahitya Bhavana.

Barthwal, P. D. 1978. *Traditions of Indian Mysticism Based upon Nirguna School of Hindi Poetry*. New Delhi: Heritage.

Barz, Richard. 1976. *The Bhakti Sect of Vallabhācārya.* Faridabad: Thomson.

Basham, A. L. 1951. *History and Doctrines of the Ājīvikas: A Vanished Indian Religion.* London: Luzac.

Basham, A. L. 1954. *The Wonder that was India.* Volume 1 of 2: *A Survey of the Indian Sub-Continent Before the Coming of the Muslims.* London: Sidgwick and Jackson.

Basham, A. L. 1989. *The Origins and Development of Classical Hinduism* (ed. Kenneth G. Zysk). Boston: Beacon.

Basu, Tapan, Pradip Datta, Sumit Sarkar, Tanika Sarkar, and Sambuddha Sen. 1993. *Khaki Shorts and Saffron Flags: A Critique of the Hindu Right.* New Delhi: Orient Longman.

Bayly, C. A. 1983. *Rulers, Townsmen, and Bazaars: North Indian Society in the Age of British Expansion, 1770–1870.* Cambridge: Cambridge University Press.

Bayly, C. A. 1996. *Empire and Information: Intelligence Gathering and Social Communication in India, 1780–1870.* Cambridge: Cambridge University Press.

Bayly, Susan. 1999. *Caste, Society, and Politics in India from the Eighteenth Century to the Modern Age.* Cambridge: Cambridge University Press.

Beane, Wendell Charles. 1977. *Myth, Cult, and Symbol in Śākta Hinduism: A Study of the Indian Mother Goddess.* Leiden: E. J. Brill.

Beck, Brenda E. F. 1981. "The Goddess and the Demon: A Local South Indian Festival and Its Wider Context." In Madeline Biardeau, ed., *Autour de la déesse hindoue*, 83–136. Paris: École des Hautes Études en Sciences Sociales.

Beck, Brenda E. F., Peter J. Claus, Praphulladatta Goswami, and Jawaharlal Handoo, eds. 1987. *Folktales of India.* Chicago: University of Chicago Press.

Bedekar, V. M. 1969. "Principles of Mahābhārata Textual Criticism: The Need for a Restatement." *Purāṇam* 11, 2: 210–28.

Berger, Peter L. and Thomas Luckmann. 1966. *The Social Construction of Reality: A Treatise in the Sociology of Knowledge.* Garden City: Doubleday.

Bellah, Robert N. 1964. "Religious Evolution." *American Sociological Review* 29, 3: 358–74.

Bergaigne, Abel. 1963 [1878–97]. *La religion védique d'après les hymnes du Rig-Véda.* 4 volumes. Paris: Honoré Champion.

Bhaktivedānta Nārāyaṇa, Mahārāja, trans. and comm. 1994. *Śrī Śikṣāṣṭaka [of Caitanya] with Vivṛti by Śrīla Bhaktisiddhānta Prabhupāda.* Mathura: Gauḍiya Vedānta Publications.

Bhandarkar, R. G. 1982 [1913]. *Vaiṣṇavism, Śaivism, and Minor Religious Systems.* Poona: Bhandarkar Oriental Research Institute.

Bharati, Agehananda. 1963. "Pilgrimage in the Indian Tradition." *History of Religions* 3, 1: 135–67.

Bharati, Agehananda. 1970 [1967]. "Pilgrimage Sites and Indian Civilization." In Joseph W. Elder, ed., *Chapters in Indian Civilization: A Handbook of Readings to Accompany Lectures in Indian Civilization.* Volume 1 of 2: *Classical and Medieval India*, 83–126, 229–30. Dubuque: Kendall/Hunt.

Bharati, Agehananda. 1983. "India: South Asian Perspectives on Aggression." In Arnold P. Goldstein and Marshall H. Segall, eds., *Aggression in Global Perspective*, 237–60. New York: Pergamon.

Bhardwaj, Surinder Mohan. 1971. "Some Spatial and Social Aspects of the Mother Goddess Cult in Northwest India." Paper Presented at Third Punjab Studies Conference, University of Pennsylvania, Philadelphia, 6–8 May.

Bhardwaj, Surinder Mohan. 1973. *Hindu Places of Pilgrimage in India: A Study in Cultural Geography.* Berkeley: University of California Press.

Bhardwaj, Surinder Mohan. 1987. "Single Religion Shrines, Multireligion Pilgrimages." *The National Geographical Journal of India* 33, 4: 457–68.

Bhatia, B. M. 1991 [1963]. *Famines in India: A Study in Some Aspects of the Economic History of India with Special Reference to Food Problem, 1860–1990.* Delhi: Konark.

Bhatt, G. H. and U. P. Shah, general eds. 1960–75. *The Vālmīki-Ramāyāṇa: Critically Edited for the First Time.* 7 volumes. Baroda: Oriental Institute.

Bhatt, N. R., ed. 1982. *Mataṅgapārameśvarāgama (Kriyāpāda, Yogapāda, et Caryapāda) avec le commentaire de Bhaṭṭa Rāmakaṇṭha.* Pondicherry: Institut français de Pondichéry.

Bhattacharyya, Krishnachandra. 1956. *Studies in Philosophy* (ed. Gopinath Bhattacharyya). Volume 1 of 2. Calcutta: Progressive.

Bhattacharyya, Narendra Nath. 1973. *History of the Śākta Religion.* New Delhi: Munshiram Manoharlal.

Bhattacharyya, Narendra Nath. 1977 [1971]. *The Indian Mother Goddess.* New Delhi: Manohar.

Bhoosnurmath, S. S. and Armando Menezes, eds. and trans. 1970. *Śūnyasaṁpādane.* Volume 4 of 5. Dharwar: Karnatak University.

Biardeau, Madeline. 1968. "Some More Considerations about Textual Criticism." *Purāṇam* 10, 2: 115–23.

Biardeau, Madeleine. 1968–78. "Études de mythologie hindoue (I–V)." *Bulletin de l'École française d'Extrême-Orient* 54 (1968): 19–45; 55 (1969): 59–105; 58 (1971): 17–89; 63 (1976): 111–263; 65 (1978): 87–238.

Biardeau, Madeleine. 1976. "Le sacrifice dans l'hindouisme." In Madeleine Biardeau and Charles Malamoud, *Le sacrifice dans l'Inde ancienne*, 7–154. Paris: Presses Universitaires de France.

Biardeau, Madeleine. 1981 [1954–58]. *Études de mythologie hindoue.* Volume 1 of 2: *Cosmogonies purāṇiques.* Paris: École française d'Extrême-Orient.

Biardeau, Madeleine. 1985. "Nala et Damayantī, héros épiques." *Indo-Iranian Journal* 28, 1: 1–34.

Biardeau, Madeleine. 1989 [1981]. *Hinduism: The Anthropology of a Civilization* (trans. Richard Nice). Delhi: Oxford University Press.

Bigger, Thomas. 1998. *Balarāma im Mahābhārata: Seine Darstellung im Rahmen des Textes und seiner Entwicklung.* Wiesbaden: Otto Harrassowitz.

al-Bīrūnī, Abū Raiḥān Muḥammad ibn Aḥmad. 1971 [1888]. *Alberuni's India* (trans. Edward C. Sachau; ed. Ainslie Embree). New York: W. W. Norton.

Blackburn, Stuart. 1996. *Inside the Drama-House: Rāma Stories and Shadow Puppets in South India.* Berkeley: University of California Press.

Bloomfield, Maurice. 1908. *The Religion of the Veda: The Ancient Religion of India (from Rig-Veda to Upanishads).* New York: G. P. Putnam.

Blunt, E. A. H. 1931. *The Caste System of Northern India with Special Reference to the United Provinces of Agra and Oudh.* London: Oxford University Press.

Bodewitz, Henk W. 1999. "Hindu *Ahiṁsā* and Its Roots." In Jan E. M. Houben and Karel R. van Kooij, eds., *Violence Denied: Violence, Non-Violence, and the Rationalization of Violence in South Asian Cultural History*, 17–44. Leiden: E. J. Brill.

Bolon, Carol Radcliffe. 1988. "Two Chalukya Queens and their Commemorative Temples: Eighth Century Pattadakal." In Vidya Dehejia, ed., *Royal Patrons and Great Temple Art*, 61–76. Bombay: Marg.

Bongard-Levin, G. M. 1985 [1973]. *Mauryan India.* New Delhi: Sterling.

Bose, Manindra Mohan. 1930. *The Post-Caitanya Sahajiā Cult of Bengal.* Calcutta: University of Calcutta.

Breckenridge, Carol A. 1986. "Food, Politics, and Pilgrimage in South India, 1350–1650 AD." In R. S. Khare and M. S. A. Rao, eds., *Food, Society, and Culture: Aspects in South Asian Food Systems*, 21–53. Durham: Carolina Academic Press.

Briffault, Robert. 1929. "Sex in Religion." In V. F. Calverton and S. D. Schmalhausen, eds., *Sex in Civilization*, 31–52. Garden City: Garden City Publishing.

Brinkhaus, Horst. 1999. "Cyclical Determinism and the Development of the *Trimūrti*-Doctrine." In Mary Brockington and Peter Schreiner, eds., *Composing a Tradition: Concepts, Techniques, and Relationships*, 35–37. Zagreb: Croatian Academy of Sciences and Arts.

Brockington, John L. 1984. *Righteous Rāma: The Evolution of an Epic*. Delhi: Oxford University Press.
Brockington, John L. 1998. *The Sanskrit Epics*. Leiden: E. J. Brill.
Brooks, Charles. 1998. "The Blind Man Meets the Lame Man: ISKCON's Place in the Bengal Vaishnava Tradition of Caitanya Mahāprabhu." *Journal of Vaiṣṇava Studies* 6, 2: 5–30.
Brooks, Charles, with Steven J. Rosen. 1992. "Gauḍīya Vaiṣṇavism in the Modern World." In Steven J. Rosen, ed., *Vaiṣṇavism: Contemporary Scholars Discuss the Gauḍīya Tradition*, 149–66. New York: Folk Books.
Brooks, Douglas Renfrew. 1990. *The Secret of the Three Cities: An Introduction to Hindu Śākta Tantrism*. Chicago: University of Chicago Press.
Brooks, Douglas Renfrew. 1992. *Auspicious Wisdom: The Texts and Traditions of Śrīvidyā Śākta Tantrism in South India*. Albany: State University of New York Press.
Brown, C. MacKenzie. 1990. *The Triumph of the Goddess: The Canonical Models and Theological Visions of the Devī-Bhāgavata Purāṇa*. Albany: State University of New York Press.
Brown, Carolyn Henning. 1983. "The Gift of a Girl: Hierarchical Exchange in North Bihar." *Ethnology* 22, 1: 43–62.
Brubaker, Richard Lee. 1978. The Ambivalent Mistress: A Study of South Indian Village Goddesses and their Religious Meaning. PhD dissertation. Chicago: University of Chicago Library.
Bruner, Jerome S. 1996. *The Culture of Education*. Cambridge: Harvard University Press.
Brunner-Lachaux, Hélène, ed. and trans. 1963–98. *Somaśambhupaddhati*. 4 volumes. Pondicherry: Institut français de Pondichéry.
Brunner [-Lachaux], Hélène. 1974. "Un tantra du nord: *le Netra Tantra*." *Bulletin de l'École française d'Extrême-Orient* 61: 125–97.
Brunner [-Lachaux], Hélène. 1975. "Le *sādhaka*, personnage oublié du śivaïsme du sud." *Journal Asiatique* 263, 3–4: 411–43.
Bryant, Edwin. 2001. *The Quest for the Origins of Vedic Culture: The Indo-Aryan Migration Debate*. New York: Oxford University Press.
Bühler, Georg, trans. 1886. *The Laws of Manu: Translated with Extracts from Seven Commentaries*. Oxford: Clarendon.
Bühnemann, Gudrun. 1988. *Pūjā: A Study in Smārta Ritual*. Vienna: De Nobili Research Library.
Buitenen, J. A. B. van. 1957. "Dharma and Mokṣa." *Philosophy East and West* 7, 1–2: 33–40.
Buitenen, J. A. B. van. 1966. "On the Archaism of the *Bhāgavata Purāṇa*." In Milton Singer, ed., *Krishna: Myths, Rites, and Attitudes,* 23–40, 215–17. Honolulu: East-West Center Press.
Buitenen, J. A. B. van. 1968. *Rāmānuja on the Bhagavadgītā*. Delhi: Motilal Banarsidass.
Buitenen, J. A. B. van. 1972. "On the Structure of the Sabhāparvan of the Mahābhārata." In J. Ensink and P. Gaeffke, eds., *India Maior: Congratulatory Volume Presented to J. Gonda*, 68–84. Leiden: E. J. Brill.
Buitenen, J. A. B. van., ed. and trans. 1973–78. *The Mahābhārata*. 3 volumes. Chicago: University of Chicago Press.
Burghart, Richard. 1978. "Hierarchical Models of the Hindu Social System." *Man: The Journal of the Royal Anthropological Institute (ns)* 13, 4: 519–36.
Caldwell, Sarah. 1999. *Oh Terrifying Mother: Sexuality, Violence, and Worship of the Goddess Kāḷi*. Delhi: Oxford University Press.
Callewaert, Winand M. and Mukund Lath, trans. 1989. *The Hindi Padavalī of Nāmdev: A Critical Edition of Nāmdev's Hindi Songs*. Delhi: Motilal Banarsidass.
Callewaert, Winand M. and Peter G. Friedlander. 1992. *The Life and Works of Raidās*. New Delhi: Manohar.
Caracchi, Pinuccia, with Shukdev Singh. 1999. *Rāmānanda: e lo yoga dei sant*. Alessandria: Edizioni dell'Orso.
Carey, William and Joshua Marshman, eds. and trans. 1806–10. *The Ramayuna of Valmeeki*. 3 volumes. Serampore: Baptist Mission Press.

Carman, John and Vasudha Narayanan. 1989. *The Tamil Veda: Piḷḷāṉ's Interpretation of the Tiruvāymoḻi.* Chicago: University of Chicago Press.
Carstairs, G. Morris. 1957. *The Twice-Born: A Study of a Community of High-Caste Hindus.* London: Hogarth.
Cascaro, P. and R. Zimmerman. 1987. "Du Gange a Grand-Bassin, le pèlerinage de Mahâshivarâtrî à l'Île Maurice." In Jean Chelini and Henry Branthomme, eds., *Histoire des pèlerinages non chrétiens. Entre magique et sacré: le chemin des dieux*, 217–27. Paris: Hachette.
Case, Margaret H. 2000. *Seeing Krishna: The Religious World of a Brahman Family in Vrindaban.* New York: Oxford University Press.
Cassels, N. G. 1988. *Religion and Pilgrim Tax under the Company Raj.* New Delhi: Manohar.
Castoriadis, Cornelius. 1997 [1986–93]. *World in Fragments: Writings on Politics, Society, Psychoanalysis, and the Imagination* (ed. and trans. David Ames Curtis). Stanford: Stanford University Press.
Caughran, Neema. 1997. The Potter, the Brahm, and the Butcher's Ghost: Caste and Family Dynamics in North India. PhD dissertation. Syracuse: Syracuse University Library.
Chakrabarti, Dilip K. 1995. *The Archaeology of Ancient Indian Cities.* Delhi: Oxford University Press.
Chakrabarti, Dilip K. 1997. *Colonial Indology: Sociopolitics of the Ancient Indian Past.* New Delhi: Munshiram Manoharlal.
Chakrabarti, Kunal. 2001. *Religious Process: The Purāṇas and the Making of a Regional Tradition.* Delhi: Oxford University Press.
Champakalakshmi, R. 1996. "From Devotion and Dissent to Dominance: The Bhakti of the Tamil Āḻvārs and Nāyanārs." In R. Champakalakshmi and S. Gopal, eds., *Tradition, Dissent, and Ideology: Essays in Honour of Romila Thapar,* 135–63. Delhi: Oxford University Press.
Chandra, Lokesh. 1980. "Rāmāyaṇa: The Epic of Asia." In V. Raghavan, ed., *The Ramayana Tradition in Asia*, 648–52. New Delhi: Sahitya Akademi.
Chatterji, Bankimchandra. 1882. *Ānandamaṭh.* Calcutta: Radhanath Bandyopadhyay, Johnson Press.
Chatterji, Bankimchandra. 1986 [1884]. "Hindudharma." In *Baṅkim Racanābalī: Sāhitya Samagra* (comp. Vishnu Basu), 2 of 2: 776–79. Calcutta: Tuli-Kalam.
Chaturvedi, Parashuram, ed. 1966 [1964]. *Mīrāṃbāī kī padāvalī.* Allahabad: Hindi Sahitya Sammelan.
Chaudhuri, Nirad C. 1979. *Hinduism: A Religion to Live By.* Oxford: Oxford University Press.
Chitre, Dilip, trans. 1991. *Says Tuka: Selected Poetry of Tukaram.* New Delhi: Penguin.
Claus, Peter J. and Frank J. Korom. 1991. *Folkloristics and Indian Folklore.* Udupi: Regional Resources Centre for Folk Performing Arts.
Clooney, Francis X. 1990. *Thinking Ritually: Rediscovering the Pūrvamīmāṃsā of Jaimini.* Vienna: De Nobili Research Library.
Clooney, Francis X. 1993. "In search of Nammāḻvār: Reflections on the Meeting Point of Traditional and Contemporary Scholarship." *Journal of Vaiṣṇava Studies* 1, 2: 8–26.
Clooney, Francis X. 1996. *Seeing Through Texts: Doing Theology Among the Śrīvaiṣṇavas of South India.* Albany: State University of New York Press.
Clothey, Fred W. 1972. "Pilgrimage Centers in the Tamil Cultus of Murukan." *Journal of the American Academy of Religion* 40, 1: 79–95.
Coburn, Thomas B. 1980. "The Study of the Purāṇas and the Study of Religion." *Religious Studies* 16, 3: 341–52.
Coburn, Thomas B. 1984. *Devī-Māhātmya: The Crystallization of the Goddess Tradition.* Delhi: Motilal Banarsidass.
Coburn, Thomas B. 1991. *Encountering the Goddess: A Translation of the Devī-Māhātmya and a Study of Its Interpretation.* Albany: State University of New York Press.

Cohn, Bernard S. 1955. "The Changing Status of a Depressed Caste." In McKim Marriott, ed., *Village India: Studies in the Little Community*, 53–77. Chicago: University of Chicago Press.

Collins, Steven. 1988. "Monasticism: Utopias and Comparative Social Theory." *Religion* 18, 2: 101–35.

Cornford, F. M. 1934. "Innumerable Worlds in Presocratic Philosophy." *The Classical Quarterly* 28, 1: 1–16.

Cort, John E. 1993. "An Overview of the Jaina Purāṇas." In Wendy Doniger, ed., *Purāṇa Perennis: Reciprocity and Transformation in Hindu and Jaina Texts*, 185–206, 279–84, 308–15. Albany: State University of New York Press.

Courtright, Paul B. 1985. *Gaṇeśa: Lord of Obstacles, Lord of Beginnings*. New York: Oxford University Press.

Craven, Roy C. 1976. *A Concise History of Indian Art*. New York: Praeger.

Crawford, S. Cromwell. 1987 [1984]. *Ram Mohan Roy: Social, Political, and Religious Reform in 19th Century India*. New York: Paragon.

Creel, Austin B. 1977. *Dharma in Hindu Ethics*. Calcutta: Firma K. L. Mukhopadhyay.

Crooke, William. 1926 [1894]. *Religion & Folklore in Northern India*. London: Oxford University Press.

Crooke, William. 1971 [1897]. *The North-Western Provinces of India: Their History, Ethnology, and Administration*. Delhi: Indological Book House.

D'Sa, Francis X. 1980. *Śabdaprāmāṇyam in Śabara and Kumārila: Towards a Study of the Mīmāṃsā Experience of Language*. Vienna: De Nobili Research Library.

Dalmia, Vasudha. 1999 [1997]. *The Nationalization of Hindu Traditions: Bhāratendu Hariśchandra and Nineteenth-Century Banaras*. Delhi: Oxford University Press.

Damdinsuren, T. S. 1980. "Rāmāyaṇa in Mongolia." In V. Raghavan, ed., *The Ramayana Tradition in Asia*, 653–59. New Delhi: Sahitya Akademi.

Dandekar, R. N. 1985. "Gleanings from the *Śiva Purāṇa*." Paper Presented at Conference on the Purāṇas, University of Wisconsin, Madison, August.

Daniel, E. Valentine. 1984. *Fluid Signs: Being a Person the Tamil Way*. Berkeley: University of California Press.

Daniel, Sheryl B. 1983. "The Tool Box Approach of the Tamil to the Issues of Moral Responsibility and Human Destiny." In Charles F. Keyes and E. Valentine Daniel, eds., *Karma: An Anthropological Inquiry*, 27–62. Berkeley: University of California Press.

Daniélou, Alain. 1976. *Les quatre sens de la vie et la structure sociale de l'Inde traditionelle*. Paris: Buchet/Chastel.

Das, Bhagavan. 1956 [1937]. "Introduction." In Haridas Bhattacharyya, ed., *The Cultural Heritage of India*. Volume 4 of 6: *The Religions*, 3–28. Calcutta: Ramakrishna Mission Institute of Culture.

Das, Shyam, trans., and H. H. Goswami Srimat Vrajesh Kumarji Maharaj, ed. 1985. *Chaurasi Baithak: Eightyfour Seats of Shri Vallabhacarya*. Baroda: Shri Vallabha Publications.

Das, Veena. 1977. *Structure and Cognition: Aspects of Hindu Caste and Ritual*. Delhi: Oxford University Press.

Dasgupta, Shashibhushan. 1962 [1946]. *Obscure Religious Cults*. Calcutta: Firma K. L. Mukhopadhyay.

Dasgupta, Surendranath. 1922–55. *A History of Indian Philosophy*. 5 volumes. Cambridge: Cambridge University Press.

Dave, J. H. 1957–61. *Immortal India*. 4 volumes. Bombay: Bharatiya Vidya Bhavan.

Davis, Marvin. 1983. *Rank and Rivalry: The Politics of Inequality in Rural West Bengal*. Cambridge: Cambridge University Press.

Davis, Richard H. 1991. *Ritual in an Oscillating Universe: Worshipping Śiva in Medieval India*. Princeton: Princeton University Press.

Davis, Richard H. 1997. *Lives of Indian Images*. Princeton: Princeton University Press.

De, Sushil Kumar. 1961 [1942]. *Early History of the Vaisnava Faith and Movement in Bengal: From Sanskrit and Bengali Sources.* Calcutta: Firma K. L. Mukhopadhyay.

De Jong, J. W. 1983. "The Story of Rama in Tibet." In K. R. Srinivasa Iyengar, ed., *Asian Variations in Ramayana*, 163–82. New Delhi: Sahitya Akademi.

De Smet, Richard. 1977. "A Copernican Reversal: The Gītākāra's Reformulation of Karma." *Philosophy East and West* 27, 1: 53–63.

Dehejia, Vidya. 1990. *Art of the Imperial Cholas.* New York: Columbia University Press.

Deleury, G. A. 1960. *The Cult of Viṭhobā.* Poona: Deccan College.

Deleury, G. A. 1987. "L'Inde et la religion du pèlerinage." In Jean Chelini and Henry Branthomme, eds., *Histoire des pèlerinages non chrétiens. Entre magique et sacré: le chemin des dieux*, 195–216. Paris: Hachette.

Deliège, Robert. 1999 [1995]. *The Untouchables of India* (trans. Nora Scott). Oxford: Berg.

Derrett, J. Duncan M. 1973. *Dharmaśāstra and Juridical Literature.* Wiesbaden: Otto Harrassowitz.

Desai, Devangana. 1975. *Erotic Sculpture of India: A Socio-Cultural Study.* New Delhi: Tata McGraw-Hill.

Deussen, Paul. 1906. *The Philosophy of the Upanishads* (trans. A. S. Geden). Edinburgh: T. & T. Clark.

Deva, Krishna. 1975. "Bhūmija Temples." In Pramod Chandra, ed., *Studies in Indian Temple Architecture*, 90–113. New Delhi: American Institute of Indian Studies.

Devasenapathi, V. A. 1960. *Śaiva Siddhānta as Expounded in the Śivajñāna-Siddhiyār and Its Six Commentaries.* Madras: University of Madras.

Dhaky, M. A. 1975. "The Genesis and Development of Māru-Gurjara Temple Architecture." In Pramod Chandra, ed., *Studies in Indian Temple Architecture*, 114–65. New Delhi: American Institute of Indian Studies.

Dhavamony, Mariasusai. 1971. *Love of God According to Śaiva Siddhānta: A Study in the Mysticism and Theology of Śaivism.* Oxford: Clarendon.

Dimmitt, Cornelia and J. A. B. van Buitenen, eds. and trans. 1978. *Classical Hindu Mythology: A Reader in the Sanskrit Purāṇas.* Philadelphia: Temple University Press.

Dimock, Edward C., Jr. 1966. *The Place of the Hidden Moon: Erotic Mysticism in the Vaiṣṇava-Sahajiyā Cult of Bengal.* Chicago: University of Chicago Press.

Dimock, Edward C., Jr., trans. 1999. *Caitanya Caritāmṛta of Kṛṣṇadāsa Kavirāja* (ed. Tony K. Stewart). Cambridge: Harvard University, Department of Sanskrit and Indian Studies.

Dimock, Edward C., Jr. and Denise Levertov, trans. 1967. In *Praise of Krishna: Songs from the Bengali.* Garden City: Anchor Books.

Dirks, Nicholas B. 2001. *Castes of Mind: Colonialism and the Making of Modern India.* Princeton: Princeton University Press.

Doniger, Wendy, trans., with Brian K. Smith. 1991. *The Laws of Manu.* New York: Penguin.

Doniger, Wendy. 1993. "The Scrapbook of Undeserved Salvation: The *Kedāra Khaṇḍa* of the *Skanda Purāṇa*." In Wendy Doniger, ed., *Purāṇa Perennis: Reciprocity and Transformation in Hindu and Jaina Texts*, 59–81, 262–65, 304–5. Albany: State University of New York Press.

Douglas, Mary. 1966. *Purity and Danger: An Analysis of the Concepts of Pollution and Taboo.* London: Routledge & Kegan Paul.

Douglas, Mary. 1974. "Deciphering a Meal." In Clifford Geertz, ed., *Myth, Symbol, and Culture*, 61–81. New York: W. W. Norton.

Dube, S. C. 1967 [1955]. *Indian Village.* New York: Harper & Row.

Dubey, D. P. 1987. "Kumbha Mela: Origin and Historicity of India's Greatest Pilgrimage Fair." *The National Geographical Journal of India* 33, 4: 469–92.

Dubey, D. P. and Lallanji Gopal, eds. 1990. *Pilgrimage Studies: Text and Context.* Allahabad: Society of Pilgrimage Studies.

Dubois, Abbé J. A. 1897. *Hindu Manners, Customs, and Ceremonies* (trans. Henry K. Beauchamp). Oxford: Clarendon.

Dudbridge, Glen. 1970. *The Hsi-yu chi: A Study of Antecedents to the Sixteenth-Century Chinese Novel*. Cambridge: Cambridge University Press.

Dumarçay, Jacques. 1986. *The Temples of Java* (ed. and trans. Michael Smithies). Singapore: Oxford University Press.

Dumézil, Georges. 1958. *L'idéologie tripartie des indo-européens*. Brussels: Latomus.

Dumézil, Georges. 1968. *Myth et épopée*. Volume 1 of 3: *L'idéologie des trois fonctions dans les épopées des peuples indo-européens*. Paris: Gallimard.

Dumont, Louis. 1960 [1959]. "World Renunciation in Indian Religions" (trans. D. F. Pocock and R. G. Lienhardt). *Contributions to Indian Sociology* 4: 33–62.

Dumont, Louis. 1967 [1966]. *Homo hierarchicus: essai sur le système des castes*. Paris: Gallimard.

Dumont, Louis. 1970 [1966]. *Homo Hierarchicus: An Essay on the Caste System* (trans. Mark Sainsbury). Chicago: University of Chicago Press.

Dumont, Louis. 1980 [1966]. *Homo Hierarchicus: The Caste System and Its Implications* (trans. Mark Sainsbury, Louis Dumont, and Basia Gulati). Chicago: University of Chicago Press.

Dumont, Louis. 1986 [1957]. *A South Indian Subcaste: Social Organization and Religion of the Pramalai Kallar* (trans. M. Moffatt, L. and A. Morton, revised by the author and A. Stern). Delhi: Oxford University Press.

Dunham, John. 1985. "Manuscripts Used in the Critical Edition of the *Mahābhārata*: A Survey and Discussion." *Journal of South Asian Literature* 20, 1: 1–15.

Durkheim, Émile. 1947 [1912]. *The Elementary Forms of the Religious Life* (trans. Joseph Ward Swain). Glencoe: Free Press.

Durkheim, Émile and Marcel Mauss. 1963 [1903]. *Primitive Classification* (trans. Rodney Needham). Chicago: University of Chicago Press.

Dyczkowski, Mark S. G. 1987. *The Doctrine of Vibration: An Analysis of the Doctrines and Practices of Kashmir Shaivism*. Albany: State University of New York Press.

Dyczkowski, Mark S. G. 1988. *The Canon of the Śaivāgama and the Kubjikā Tantras of the Western Kaula Tradition*. Albany: State University of New York Press.

Dyczkowski, Mark. S. G., trans. 1992. *The Stanzas on Vibration: The Spandakārikā with Four Commentaries: The Spandasaṃdoha by Kṣemarāja; the Spandavṛtti by Kallaṭabhaṭṭa; the Spandavivṛti by Rājānaka Rāma; [and] the Spandapradīpikā by Bhagavadutpala*. Albany: State University of New York Press.

Eck, Diana L. 1981a. "India's *Tīrthas*: 'Crossings' in Sacred Geography." *History of Religions* 20, 4: 323–44.

Eck, Diana L. 1981b. *Darśan: Seeing the Divine Image in India*. Chambersburg: Anima.

Eck, Diana L. 1982. *Banaras: City of Light*. New York: Alfred A. Knopf.

Eck, Diana L. 1986. "Dakṣa's Sacrifice and the Śākta Pīṭhas." Paper Presented at American Academy of Religion Annual Meeting, Atlanta, Georgia, 22–25 November.

Edgerton, Franklin. 1939. "The Epic Triṣṭubh and Its Hypermetric Varieties." *Journal of the American Oriental Society* 59, 2: 159–74.

Edgerton, Franklin. 1942. "Dominant Ideas in the Formation of Indian Culture." *Journal of the American Oriental Society* 62, 3: 151–56.

Eggeling, Julius, trans. 1882. *The Satapatha Brâhmana: According to the Text of the Mâdhyandina School*. Volume 1 of 5: *Books 1 and 2*. Oxford: Clarendon.

Einoo, Shingo. 1993. "Changes in Hindu Ritual: With a Focus on the Morning Service." In Yasuhiko Nagano and Yasuke Ikari, eds., *From Vedic Altar to Village Shrine: Towards an Interface Between Indology and Anthropology*, 197–237. Osaka: National Museum of Ethnology.

Eliade, Mircea. 1957 [1951]. "Time and Eternity in Indian Thought." In Joseph Campbell, ed., *Man and Time: Papers from the Eranos Yearbooks*, 173–200. New York: Pantheon.

Eliade, Mircea. 1959a [1949]. *Cosmos and History: The Myth of the Eternal Return* (trans. Willard R. Trask). New York: Harper & Row.

Eliade, Mircea. 1959b [1957]. *The Sacred and the Profane: The Nature of Religion* (trans. Willard R. Trask). New York: Harcourt, Brace.

Eliade, Mircea. 1969 [1954]. *Yoga: Immortality and Freedom* (trans. Willard R. Trask). Princeton: Princeton University Press.

Entwistle, Alan W. 1987. *Braj: Centre of Krishna Pilgrimage*. Groningen: Egbert Forsten.

Erdosy, George. 1995a. "The Prelude to Urbanization: Ethnicity and the Rise of Late Vedic Chiefdoms." In F. R. Allchin, with contributions from George Erdosy, R. A. E. Coningham, D. K. Chakrabarti, and Bridget Allchin, *The Archaeology of Early Historic South Asia: The Emergence of Cities and States*, 75–98. Cambridge: Cambridge University Press.

Erdosy, George. 1995b. "City States of North India and Pakistan at the Time of the Buddha." In F. R. Allchin, with contributions from George Erdosy, R. A. E. Coningham, D. K. Chakrabarti, and Bridget Allchin, *The Archaeology of Early Historic South Asia: The Emergence of Cities and States*, 99–122. Cambridge: Cambridge University Press.

Erdosy, George, ed. 1995c. *The Indo-Aryans of Ancient South Asia: Language, Material Culture, and Ethnicity*. Berlin: Walter de Gruyter.

Erndl, Kathleen M. 1993. *Victory to the Mother: The Hindu Goddess of Northwest India in Myth, Ritual, and Symbol*. New York: Oxford University Press.

Eschmann, Anncharlott, Hermann Kulke, and Gaya Charan Tripathi, eds. 1978. *The Cult of Jagannath and the Regional Tradition of Orissa*. New Delhi: Manohar.

Farquhar, J. N. 1920. *An Outline of the Religious Literature of India*. London: Oxford University Press.

Filliozat, Jean. 1937. *Étude de démonologie indienne: le Kumāratantra de Rāvaṇa et les textes parallèles indiens, tibétains, chinois, cambodgien, et arabe*. Paris: Imprimerie Nationale.

Finkelberg, Margalit. 1998. *The Birth of Literary Fiction in Ancient Greece*. Oxford: Clarendon.

Fisher, Robert E. 1988. "Inspired Patron of Himalayan Art: Eighth Century Kashmir." In Vidya Dehejia, ed., *Royal Patrons and Great Temple Art*, 25–36. Bombay: Marg.

Fitzgerald, James L. 1985. "India's Fifth Veda: The *Mahābhārata*'s Presentation of Itself." *Journal of South Asian Literature* 20, 1: 125–40.

Fitzgerald, James L. 1998. "Some Storks and Eagles Eat Carrion; Herons and Ospreys Do Not: Kaṅkas and Kuraras (and Baḍas) in the *Mahābhārata*." *Journal of the American Oriental Society* 118, 2: 257–61.

Fitzgerald, James L. 2002a. "Making Yudhiṣṭhira the King: The Dialectics and Politics of Violence in the *Mahābhārata*." *Rocznik Orientalistyczny* 54, 1: 63–92.

Fitzgerald, James L. 2002b. "The Rāma Jāmadagnya 'Thread' of the *Mahābhārata:* A New Survey of Rāma Jāmadagnya in the Pune Text." In Mary Brockington, ed., *Stages and Transitions: Temporal and Historical Frameworks in Epic and Purāṇic Literature*, 89–132. Zagreb: Croatian Academy of Sciences and Arts.

Fitzgerald, James L., ed. and trans. 2004. *The Mahābhārata: Book 11, The Book of the Women; Book 12, The Book of Peace, Part 1*. Chicago: University of Chicago Press.

Fitzgerald, James L. forthcoming. *The Many Voices of the Mahābhārata*. [A Review Article of Alf Hiltebeitel's *Rethinking the Mahābhārata: A Reader's Guide to the Education of the Dharma King*.] *Journal of the American Oriental Society*.

Flood, Gavin. 1996. *An Introduction to Hinduism*. Cambridge: Cambridge University Press.

Flood, Gavin. 1997. "The Meaning and Context of the Puruṣārthas." In Julius Lipner, ed., *The Fruits of our Desiring: An Enquiry into the Ethics of the Bhagavadgītā for our Times*, 11–27. Calgary: Bayeux Arts.

Flood, Gavin. 2002. "The Purification of the Body in Tantric Ritual Representation." *Indo-Iranian Journal* 45, 1: 25–43.

Flood, Gavin, ed. 2003. *The Blackwell Companion to Hinduism*. Oxford: Blackwell.

Fonia, K. S. 1998 [1987]. *The Traveller's Guide to Uttarakhand*. Joshimath: Garuda Books.

Forrester, Duncan B. 1980. *Caste and Christianity: Attitudes and Policies on Caste of Anglo-Saxon Protestant Missions in India.* London: Curzon.

Forster, E. M. 1983 [1912–59, 1953]. *The Hill of Devi and Other Indian Writings*. London: Edward Arnold.

Fort, Andrew O. 1998. *Jīvanmukti in Transformation: Embodied Liberation in Advaita and Neo-Vedanta*. Albany: State University of New York Press.

Foulston, Lynn. 2002. *At the Feet of the Goddess: The Divine Feminine in Local Hindu Religion.* Brighton: Sussex Academic.

Fox, Richard G. 1969. *From Zamindar to Ballot Box: Community Change in a North Indian Market Town.* Ithaca: Cornell University Press.

Francisco, Juan R. 1980. "The Ramayana in the Philippines." In V. Raghavan, ed., *The Ramayana Tradition in Asia*, 155–77. New Delhi: Sahitya Akademi.

Frauwallner, Erich. 1956. *Geschichte der indischen Philosophie*. Volume 2 of 2: *Die naturphilosophischen Schulen und das Vaisesika-System; Das System der Jaina; Der Materialismus*. Salzburg: Otto Müller.

Frauwallner, Erich. 1984. *Nachgelassene Werke.* Volume 1 of 2: *Aufsätze, Beiträge, Skizzen* (ed. Ernst Steinkellner). Vienna: Österreichischen Akademie der Wissenschaften.

Freed, Stanley A. and Ruth S. Freed. 1964. "Spirit Possession as Illness in a North Indian Village." *Ethnology* 3, 2: 152–71.

Freeman, Rich. 1999. "Texts, Temples, and the Teaching of *Tantra* in Kerala." In Jackie Assayag, ed., *The Resources of History: Tradition, Narration, and Nation in South Asia*, 63–79. Pondicherry: Institut français de Pondichéry.

Frykenberg, Robert Eric. 1989. "The Emergence of Modern 'Hinduism' as a Concept and as an Institution: A Reappraisal with Special Reference to South India." In Günther D. Sontheimer and Hermann Kulke, eds., *Hinduism Reconsidered*, 29–49. New Delhi: Manohar.

Fuller, C. J. 1984. *Servants of the Goddess: The Priests of a South Indian Temple.* Cambridge: Cambridge University Press.

Fuller, C. J. 1992. *The Camphor Flame: Popular Hinduism and Society in India*. Princeton: Princeton University Press.

Furer-Haimendorf, Christopher von. 1943–48. *The Aboriginal Tribes of Hyderabad.* 3 volumes. London: Macmillian.

Gail, Adalbert. 1977. *Paraśurāma, Brahmane und Krieger: Untersuchung über Ursprung und Entwicklung eines Avatāra Viṣṇus und Bhakta Śivas in der indischen Literatur.* Wiesbaden: Otto Harrassowitz.

Galanter, Marc. 1984. *Competing Equalities: Law and the Backward Classes in India.* Berkeley: University of California Press.

Gandhi, M. K. 1946 [1930]. *The Gospel of Selfless Action or the Gita according to Gandhi* (trans. Mahadev Desai). Ahmedabad: Navajivan.

Gandhi, M. K. 1947. *India of My Dreams* (comp. R. K. Prabhu). Bombay: Hind Kitabs.

Gandhi, M. K. 1993 [1925–29]. *An Autobiography: The Story of My Experiments with Truth* (trans. Mahadev Desai). Boston: Beacon.

Ganguli, Kisari Mohan, trans., [and Pratap Chandra Roy, publisher]. 1970 [1884–96]. *The Mahabharata of Krishna-Dwaipayana Vyasa: Translated into English Prose from the Original Sanskrit Text.* 12 volumes. New Delhi: Munshiram Manoharlal.

Gaster, M. 1893. "Hebrew Visions of Hell and Paradise." *The Journal of the Royal Asiatic Society of Great Britain and Ireland (ns)* 25: 571–611.

Gellrich, Jesse M. 1985. *The Idea of the Book in the Middle Ages: Language Theory, Mythology, and Fiction*. Ithaca: Cornell University Press.

Gengnagel, Jörg. 1996. *Māyā, Puruṣa und Śiva: Die dualistische Tradition des Śivaismus nach Aghoraśivācāryas Tattvaprakāśavṛtti*. Wiesbaden: Otto Harrassowitz.

[Ghose], Sri Aurobindo. 1959 [1922]. *Essays on the Gita*. Pondicherry: Sri Aurobindo Ashram.

[Ghose], Sri Aurobindo. 1962 [1949]. *The Human Cycle*. In *The Human Cycle; The Idea of Human Unity; [and] War and Self-Determination*, 1–361. Pondicherry: Sri Aurobindo Ashram.

[Ghose], Sri Aurobindo. 1971 [1914–21]. *The Synthesis of Yoga*. Pondicherry: Sri Aurobindo Ashram.

Ghoshal, U. N. 1966 [1923]. *A History of Indian Political Ideas: The Ancient Period and the Period of Transition to the Middle Ages*. London: Oxford University Press.

Ghurye, G. S. 1964 [1953]. *Indian Sadhus*. Bombay: Popular Prakashan.

Glucklich, Ariel. 1988. *Religious Jurisprudence in the Dharmaśāstra*. New York: Macmillan.

Glucklich, Ariel. 1994. *The Sense of Adharma*. New York: Oxford University Press.

Godakumbura, C. E. 1980. "Rāmāyaṇa in Śrīlaṅkā and Laṅkā of the Rāmāyaṇa." In V. Raghavan, ed., *The Ramayana Tradition in Asia*, 430–54. New Delhi: Sahitya Akademi.

Gokhale, G. K. 1916 [1908]. *Speeches of the Honourable Mr. G. K. Gokhale*. Madras: G. A. Natesan.

Gold, Ann Grodzins. 1988. *Fruitful Journeys: The Ways of Rajasthani Pilgrims*. Berkeley: University of California Press.

Gold, Ann Grodzins. 2000. "From Demon Aunt to Gorgeous Bride: Women Portray Female Power in a North Indian Festival Cycle." In Julia Leslie and Mary McGee, eds., *Invented Identities: The Interplay of Gender, Religion, and Politics in India*, 203–30. Delhi: Oxford University Press.

Gold, Ann Grodzins and Bhoju Ram Gujar. 2002. *In the Time of Trees and Sorrows: Nature, Power, and Memory in Rajasthan*. Durham: Duke University Press.

Gold, Daniel. 1987a. "Celibacy." In Mircea Eliade, ed., *The Encyclopedia of Religion*, 3 of 16: 144–48. New York: Macmillan.

Gold, Daniel. 1987b. *The Lord as Guru: Hindi Sants in North Indian Tradition*. New York: Oxford University Press.

Goldman, Robert P. 1972. "Akṛtavraṇa vs. Śrīkṛṣṇa as Narrators of the Legend of the Bhārgava Rāma *à propos* Some Observations of Dr. V. S. Sukthankar." *Annals of the Bhandarkar Oriental Research Institute* 53: 161–73.

Goldman, Robert P. 1977. *Gods, Priests, and Warriors: The Bhṛgus of the Mahābhārata*. New York: Columbia University Press.

Goldman, Robert P. 1978. "Fathers, Sons, and Gurus: Oedipal Conflict in the Sanskrit Epics." *Journal of Indian Philosophy* 6, 4: 325–92.

Goldman, Robert P., trans. 1984. *The Rāmāyaṇa of Vālmīki: An Epic of Ancient India* (ed. Robert P. Goldman). Volume 1 of 5: *Bālakāṇḍa*. Princeton: Princeton University Press.

Goldman, Robert P., ed. 1984–96. *The Rāmāyaṇa of Vālmīki: An Epic of Ancient India*. 5 volumes. Princeton: Princeton University Press.

Goldman, Robert P. 1995. "Gods in Hiding: The Mahābhārata's Virāṭa Parvan and the Divinity of Indian Epic Heroes." In Satya Pal Narang, ed., *Modern Evaluation of the Mahābhārata: Prof. R. K. Sharma Felicitation Volume*, 73–100. Delhi: Nag.

Goldman, Robert P. 1997. "*Eṣa Dharmaḥ Sanātanaḥ*: Shifting Moral Values and the Indian Epics." In P. Bilimoria and J. N. Mohanty, eds., *Relativism, Suffering, and Beyond: Essays in Memory of Bimal K. Matilal*, 187–223. Delhi: Oxford University Press.

Goldman, Robert P. and Sally J. Sutherland Goldman. 1994. "Vālmīki's Hanumān: Characterization and Occluded Divinity in the *Rāmāyaṇa*." *Journal of Vaiṣṇava Studies* 2, 4: 31–54.

Goldman, Robert P. and Sally J. Sutherland Goldman, trans. 1996. *The Rāmāyaṇa of Vālmīki: An Epic of Ancient India* (ed. Robert P. Goldman). Volume 5 of 5: *Sundarakāṇḍa*. Princeton: Princeton University Press.

Goldman, Sally J. Sutherland. 2001. "The Voice of Sītā in Vālmīki's *Sundarakāṇḍa*." In Paula Richman, ed., *Questioning Ramayanas: A South Asian Tradition*, 223–38. Berkeley: University of California Press.

Gonda, J. 1954. *Aspects of Early Viṣṇuism*. Utrecht: N.V. A. Oosthoek's Uitgevers Mij.

Gonda, J., trans. 1965a. *The Savayajñas (Kauśikasūtras 60–68)*. Amsterdam: North-Holland.

Gonda, J. 1965b. *Change and Continuity in Indian Religion*. The Hague: Mouton.

Gonda, J. 1966. *Loka: World and Heaven in the Veda*. Amsterdam: North-Holland.

Gonda, J. 1976. *Triads in the Veda*. Amsterdam: North-Holland.

Gonda, J. 1980. "The Śatarudriya." In M. Nagatomi, B. K. Matilal, J. M. Masson, and E. C. Dimock, Jr., eds., *Sanskrit and Indian Studies: Essays in Honour of Daniel H. H. Ingalls*, 75–91. Dordrecht: D. Reidel.

González-Reimann, Luis. 2002. *The Mahābhārata and the Yugas: India's Great Epic Poem and the Hindu System of World Ages*. New York: Peter Lang.

Goodall, Dominic, ed. and trans. 1998. *Bhaṭṭa Rāmakaṇṭha's Commentary on the Kiraṇatantra*. Volume 1: *Chapters 1–6*. Pondicherry: Institut français de Pondichéry.

Gopalan, Gopalan V. 1978. "Vrat: Ceremonial Vows of Women in Gujarat, India." *Asian Folklore Studies* 37, 1: 101–29.

Gopinatha Rao, T. A. 1968 [1914–16]. *Elements of Hindu Iconography*. 2 volumes in 4 books. New York: Paragon.

Gottschalk, Peter. 2000. *Beyond Hindu and Muslim: Multiple Identity in Narratives from Village India*. New York: Oxford University Press.

Goudriaan, Teun. 1978. *Māyā Divine and Human: A Study of Magic and Its Religious Foundations in Sanskrit Texts, with Particular Attention to a Fragment on Viṣṇu's Māyā Preserved in Bali*. Delhi: Motilal Banarsidass.

Goudriaan, Teun. 1979. "Introduction: History and Philosophy." In Sanjukta Gupta, Dirk Jan Hoens, and Teun Goudriaan, *Hindu Tantrism*, 1–67. Leiden: E. J. Brill.

Goudriaan, Teun and Sanjukta Gupta. 1981. *Hindu Tantric and Śākta Literature*. Wiesbaden: Otto Harrassowitz.

Goudriaan, Teun and Christiaan Hooykaas. 1971. *Stuti and Stava (Bauddha, Śaiva, and Vaiṣṇava) of Balinese Brahman Priests*. Amsterdam: North-Holland.

Greenough, Paul R. 1982. *Prosperity and Misery in Modern Bengal: The Famine of 1943–1944*. New York: Oxford University Press.

Grimes, John. 1996 [1988]. *A Concise Dictionary of Indian Philosophy: Sanskrit Terms Defined in English*. Albany: State University of New York Press.

Grintser, Pavel A. 1974. *Drevneindijskij epos: genezis i tipologiya* [The Old Indian Epic: Genesis and Typology]. Moscow: Nauka. [Summarized by J. W. de Jong, "Recent Russian Publications on the Indian Epic," *The Adyar Library Bulletin* 39 (1976): 1–42.]

Grünendahl, Reinhold. 1993. "Zur Klassifizierung von Mahābhārata-Handschriften." In Reinhold Grünendahl, Jens-Uwe Hartmann, and Petra Kieffer-Pülz, eds., *Studien zur Indologie und Buddhismuskunde: Festgabe des Seminars für Indologie und Buddhismuskunde für Professor Dr. Heinz Bechert zum 60. Geburtstag am 26. Juni 1992*, 101–30. Bonn: Indica et Tibetica.

Gupta, Akhil. 1998. *Postcolonial Developments: Agriculture in the Making of Modern India*. Durham: Duke University Press.

Gupta, Anand Swarup, ed. 1971. *The Kūrma Purāṇa*. Varanasi: All-India Kashiraj Trust.

Gupta, Dipankar. 2000. *Interrogating Caste: Understanding Hierarchy and Difference in Indian Society*. New Delhi: Penguin.

Haberman, David L. 1988. *Acting as a Way of Salvation: A Study of Rāgānugā Bhakti Sādhana*. New York: Oxford University Press.

Haberman, David L. 1994. *Journey Through the Twelve Forests: An Encounter with Krishna*. New York: Oxford University Press.

Hacker, Paul. 1978a [1960]. "Zur Entwicklung der Avatāralehre." In Lambert Schmithausen, ed., *Kleine Schriften*, 404–27. Wiesbaden: Franz Steiner.

Hacker, Paul. 1978b [1970]. "Aspects of Neo-Hinduism as Contrasted with Surviving Traditional Hinduism." In Lambert Schmithausen, ed., *Kleine Schriften*, 580–608. Wiesbaden: Franz Steiner.

Halbfass, Wilhelm. 1986. "Review of Erich Frauwallner's *Nachgelassene Werke*." *Journal of the American Oriental Society* 106, 4: 857–58.

Halbfass, Wilhelm. 1988 [1981]. *India and Europe: An Essay in Understanding*. Albany: State University of New York Press.

Halbfass, Wilhelm. 1992. *On Being and What There Is: Classical Vaiśeṣika and the History of Indian Ontology*. Albany: State University of New York Press.

Halbfass, Wilhelm. 1994. "Menschsein und Lebensziele: Beobachtungen zu den *puruṣārthas*." In Francis X. D'Sa and Roque Mesquita, eds., *Hermeneutics of Encounter: Essays in Honour of Gerhard Oberhammer on the Occasion of his 65th Birthday*, 123–35. Vienna: De Nobili Research Library.

Hall, Edward T. 1959. *The Silent Language*. Garden City: Doubleday.

Han, U. Thein and U. Khin Zaw. 1980. "Rāmāyāṇa in Burmese Literature and Arts." In V. Raghavan, ed., *The Ramayana Tradition in Asia*, 301–14. New Delhi: Sahitya Akademi.

Handelman, Don and David Shulman. 1997. *God Inside Out: Śiva's Game of Dice*. New York: Oxford University Press.

Hara, Minoru. 1983. "Rama Stories in China and Japan: A Comparison." In K. R. Srinivasa Iyengar, ed., *Asian Variations in Ramayana*, 340–56. New Delhi: Sahitya Akademi.

Hara, Minoru 1997. "A Note on the *Gṛhasthāśrama*." In Siegfried Lienhard and Irma Piovano, eds., *Lex et Litterae: Studies in Honour of Professor Oscar Botto*, 221–35. Turin: Edizioni dell'Orso.

Hardgrave, Robert L., Jr. 1969. *The Nadars of Tamilnad: The Political Culture of a Community in Charge*. Berkeley: University of California Press.

Hardy, Friedhelm. 1979. "The Tamil Veda of a *Śūdra* Saint: The Śrīvaiṣṇava Interpretation of Nammāḻvār." In Gopal Krishna, ed., *Contributions to South Asian Studies 1*, 29–87. Delhi: Oxford University Press.

Hardy, Friedhelm. 1983. *Viraha-Bhakti: The Early History of Kṛṣṇa Devotion in South India*. Delhi: Oxford University Press.

Hardy, Friedhelm. 1994. *The Religious Culture of India: Power, Love, and Wisdom*. Cambridge: Cambridge University Press.

Hari Rao, V. N. 1967. *The Śrīrangam Temple: Art and Architecture*. Tirupati: Sri Venkateswara University.

Harle, James C. 1963. *Temple Gateways in South India: The Architecture and Iconography of the Cidambaram Gopuras*. Oxford: Bruno Cassirer.

Harman, William P. 1989. *The Sacred Marriage of a Hindu Goddess*. Bloomington: Indiana University Press.

Harris, Marvin. 1985. *Good to Eat: Riddles of Food and Culture*. New York: Simon and Schuster.

Hart, George L. III. 1975. *The Poems of Ancient Tamil: Their Milieu and their Sanskrit Counterparts*. Berkeley: University of California Press.

Hartner, Willy. 1938. "The Pseudoplanetary Nodes of the Moon's Orbit in Hindu and Islamic Iconographies." *Ars Islamica* 5: 113–54.

Harvey, Peter. 1990. *An Introduction to Buddhism: Teachings, History, and Practices*. Cambridge: Cambridge University Press.

Hastings, James, ed. 1908–26. *Encyclopaedia of Religion and Ethics*. 13 volumes. New York: Charles Scribner.

Hawkins, R. E., ed. 1986. *Encyclopedia of Indian Natural History: Centenary Publication of the Bombay Natural History Society, 1883–1983*. Delhi: Oxford University Press.

Hawley, John Stratton, with Srivatsa Goswami. 1981. *At Play with Krishna: Pilgrimage Dramas from Brindavan*. Princeton: Princeton University Press.

Hawley, John Stratton. 1984. *Sūr Dās: Poet, Singer, Saint*. Seattle: University of Washington Press.

Hawley, John Stratton and Mark Juergensmeyer, trans. 1988. *Songs of the Saints of India*. New York: Oxford University Press.

Hawley, John Stratton and Donna Marie Wulff, eds. 1996. *Devī: Goddesses of India*. Berkeley: University of California Press.

Hazra, R. C. 1962 [1937]. "The Purāṇas." In S. K. Dube, U. N. Ghoshal, A. D. Pusalker, and R. C. Hazra, eds., *The Cultural Heritage of India*. Volume 2 of 6: *Itihāsas, Purāṇas, Dharma, and other Śāstras*, 240–70. Calcutta: Ramakrishna Mission Institute of Culture.

Hazra, R. C. 1975 [1940]. *Studies in the Purāṇic Records on Hindu Rites and Customs*. Delhi: Motilal Banarsidass.

Heesterman, J. C. 1978. "Veda and Dharma." In Wendy Doniger O'Flaherty and J. Duncan M. Derrett, eds., *The Concept of Duty in South Asia*, 80–95. New Delhi: Vikas.

Heesterman, J. C. 1981. "Householder and Wanderer." *Contributions to Indian Sociology (ns)* 15, 1–2: 251–71.

Heesterman, J. C. 1983. "The Ritualist's Problem." Paper Presented at Association of Asian Studies Annual Meeting, San Francisco, California, 25–27 March.

Heesterman, J. C. 1985. *The Inner Conflict of Tradition: Essays in Indian Ritual, Kingship, and Society*. Chicago: University of Chicago Press.

Heesterman, J. C. 1987. "Vedism and Brahmanism." In Mircea Eliade, ed., *Encyclopedia of Religion*, 15 of 16: 217–42. New York: Macmillan.

Heesterman, J. C. 1993. *The Broken World of Sacrifice: An Essay in Ancient Indian Ritual*. Chicago: University of Chicago Press.

Heesterman, J. C. 1994. "Puruṣārtha: Ein religions-hermeneutischer Versuch." In Francis X. D'Sa and Roque Mesquita, eds., *Hermeneutics of Encounter: Essays in Honour of Gerhard Oberhammer on the Occasion of his 65th Birthday*, 137–51. Vienna: De Nobili Research Library.

Hein, Norvin J. 1993 [1983]. "[Hinduism]." In Robert K. C. Forman, general ed., *Religions of the World*, 83–150. New York: St Martin.

Hellman, Eva. 1993. Political Hinduism: The Challenge of the Viśva Hindu Pariṣad. Phd dissertation. Uppsala: Uppsala University Library.

Henige, David P. 1975. "Some Phantom Dynasties of Early and Medieval India: Epigraphic Evidence and the Abhorrence of a Vacuum." *Bulletin of the School of Oriental and African Studies* 38, 3: 529–49.

Henry, Victor. 1904. *Les littératures de l'Inde: Sanscrit, Pâli, Prâcrit*. Paris: Librarie Hachette.

Hess, Linda. 1999. "Rejecting Sita: Indian Responses to the Ideal Man's Cruel Treatment of His Ideal Wife." *Journal of the American Academy of Religion* 67, 1: 1–32.

Hess, Linda. 2001. "Lovers' Doubts: Questioning the Tulsi *Rāmāyaṇ*." In Paula Richman, ed., *Questioning Ramayanas: A South Asian Tradition*, 25–47. Berkeley: University of California Press.

Hess, Linda and Shukdeo Singh. 2002 [1983]. *The Bījak of Kabir*. New York: Oxford University Press.

Hiebert, Paul G. 1971. *Konduru: Structure and Integration in a South Indian Village*. Minneapolis: University of Minnesota Press.

Hiltebeitel, Alf. 1980. "Śiva, the Goddess, and the Disguises of the Pāṇḍavas and Draupadī." *History of Religions* 20, 1–2: 147–74.

Hiltebeitel, Alf. 1981. "Draupadī's Hair." In Madeline Biardeau, ed., *Autour de la déesse hindoue*, 179–214. Paris: École des Hautes Études en Sciences Sociales.

Hiltebeitel, Alf. 1988–91. *The Cult of Draupadī*. 2 volumes. Chicago: University of Chicago Press.

Hiltebeitel, Alf. 1990 [1976]. *The Ritual of Battle: Krishna in the Mahābhārata*. Albany: State University of New York Press.

Hiltebeitel, Alf. 1998. "Conventions of the Naimiṣa Forest." *Journal of Indian Philosophy* 26, 2: 161–71.

Hiltebeitel, Alf. 1999a. "Fathers of the Bride, Fathers of Satī: Myths, Rites, and Scholarly Practices." *Thamyris* 6, 1: 65–94.

Hiltebeitel, Alf. 1999b. *Rethinking India's Oral and Classical Epics: Draupadī among Rajputs, Muslims, and Dalits*. Chicago: University of Chicago Press.

Hiltebeitel, Alf. 1999c. "Reconsidering Bhṛguization." In Mary Brockington and Peter Schreiner, eds., *Composing a Tradition: Concepts, Techniques, and Relationships*, 155–68. Zagreb: Croatian Academy of Sciences and Arts.

Hiltebeitel, Alf. 2001a. *Rethinking the Mahābhārata: A Reader's Guide to the Education of the Dharma King*. Chicago: University of Chicago Press.

Hiltebeitel, Alf. 2001b. "Bhīṣma's Sources." In Klaus Karttunen and Petteri Koskikallio, eds., *Vidyārṇavavandanam: Essays in Honour of Asko Parpola*, 261–78. Helsinki: Finnish Oriental Society.

Hiltebeitel, Alf and Kathleen M. Erndl, eds. 2000. *Is the Goddess a Feminist? The Politics of South Asian Goddesses*. New York: New York University Press.

Holdrege, Barbara A. 1991. "Hindu Ethics." In John Carman and Mark Juergensmeyer, eds., *A Bibliographic Guide to the Comparative Study of Ethics*, 12–69. Cambridge: Cambridge University Press.

Holdrege, Barbara A. 1996. *Veda and Torah: Transcending the Textuality of Scripture*. Albany: State University of New York Press.

Holdrege, Barbara A. 1998. "Body Connections: Hindu Discourses of the Body and the Study of Religion." *International Journal of Hindu Studies* 2, 3: 341–86.

Holdrege, Barbara A. 1999. "What Have Brahmins to Do with Rabbis? Embodied Communities and Paradigms of Religious Tradition." *Shofar* 17, 3: 23–50.

Hopkins, Edward Washburn. 1895. *The Religions of India*. Boston: Ginn.

Hopkins, Edward Washburn. 1903. "Epic Chronology." *Journal of the American Oriental Society* 24, 1: 7–56.

Hopkins, Edward Washburn. 1906. "Modifications of the Karma Doctrine." *The Journal of the Royal Asiatic Society of Great Britain and Ireland (ns)* 38: 581–93.

Hopkins, Thomas J. 1966. "The Social Teaching of the *Bhāgavata Purāṇa*." In Milton Singer, ed., *Krishna: Myths, Rites, and Attitudes,* 3–22, 213–14. Honolulu: East-West Center Press.

Hopkins, Thomas J. 1971. *The Hindu Religious Tradition*. Encino: Dickenson.

Hopkins, Thomas J. 1989. "The Social and Religious Background for Transmission of Gaudiya Vaisnavism to the West." In David G. Bromley and Larry D. Shinn, eds., *Krishna Consciousness in the West*, 35–54. Lewisburg: Bucknell University Press.

Houben, Jan E. M. 1994. "Liberation and Natural Philosophy in Early Vaiśeṣika: Some Methodological Problems." *Asiatische Studien/Études Asiatiques* 48, 2: 711–48.

Housden, Roger. 1996. *Travels Through Sacred India*. London: Thorsons.

Hsüan-tsang. 1969 [1884]. *Si-yu-ki: Buddhist Records of the Western World* (trans. Samuel Beal). 2 volumes in 1 book. Delhi: Oriental Books Reprint.

Hudson, D. Dennis. 1995. "The *Śrīmad Bhāgavata Purāṇa* in Stone: The Text as an Eighth-Century Temple and Its Implications." *Journal of Vaiṣṇava Studies* 3, 3: 137–82.

Hulin, Michel, trans. 1980. *Mṛgendrāgama: sections de la doctrine et du yoga, avec la Vṛtti de Bhaṭṭanārāyaṇakaṇṭha et le Dīpikā d'Aghoraśivācārya*. Pondicherry: Institut français de Pondichéry.

Hume, Robert Ernest, trans. 1921. *The Thirteen Principal Upanishads*. London: Oxford University Press.

Humes, Cynthia. 1996. "Vindhyavāsinī: Local Goddess Yet Great Goddess." In John Stratton Hawley and Donna Marie Wulff, eds., *Devī: Goddesses of India*, 49–76. Berkeley: University of California Press.

Huntington, Susan L., with contributions by John C. Huntington. 1985. *The Art of Ancient India: Buddhist, Hindu, Jain*. New York: Weatherhill.

Hutton, J. H. 1946. *Caste in India: Its Nature, Function, and Origins*. Cambridge: Cambridge University Press.

Ikram, S. M. 1964 [1962]. *Muslim Civilization in India* (ed. Ainslie T. Embree). New York: Columbia University Press.

Inden, Ronald B. 1976. *Marriage and Rank in Bengali Culture: A History of Caste and Clan in Middle Period Bengal.* Berkeley: University of California Press.

Inden, Ronald B. 1978. "Ritual, Authority, and Cyclic Time in Hindu Kingship." In J. F. Richards, ed., *Kingship and Authority in South Asia*, 28–73. Madison: University of Wisconsin-Madison South Asian Studies.

Inden, Ronald B. 1990. *Imagining India*. Oxford: Basil Blackwell.

Inden, Ronald B. and Ralph W. Nicholas. 1977. *Kinship in Bengali Culture*. Chicago: University of Chicago Press.

Ingalls, Daniel H. H. 1957. "Dharma and Mokṣa." *Philosophy East and West* 7, 1–2: 41–48.

Inglis, Stephen R. 1995. "Suitable for Framing: The Work of a Modern Master." In Lawrence A. Babb and Susan S. Wadley, eds., *Media and the Transformation of Religion in South Asia*, 51–75. Philadelphia: University of Pennsylvania Press.

Ishwaran, K. 1992. *Speaking of Basava: Lingayat Religion and Culture in South Asia.* Boulder: Westview.

Iyengar, K. R. Srinivasa, ed. 1983. *Asian Variations in Ramayana*. New Delhi: Sahitya Akademi.

Iyer, S. Venkitasubramonia, trans. 1993 [1985]. *The Vāraha Purāṇa*. Part 2 of 2: [Skandhas 137–218]. Delhi: Motilal Banarsidass.

Jackson, Robert and Eleanor Nesbitt. 1993. *Hindu Children in Britain*. Stoke-on-Trent: Trentham.

Jacobi, Hermann. 1893. *Das Râmâyaṇa: Geschichte und Inhalt, nebst Concordanz der Gedbuckten Recensionen*. Bonn: Friedrich Cohen.

Jaffrelot, Christophe. 1996 [1993]. *The Hindu Nationalist Movement in India*. New York: Columbia University Press.

Jain, Madhu. 1988. "Ramayan: The Second Coming." *India Today* 31 August: 81.

Jaini, Padmanabh S. 1979. *The Jaina Path of Purification*. Berkeley: University of California Press.

Jaiswal, Suvira. 1981 [1967]. *The Origin and Development of Vaiṣṇavism: Vaiṣṇavism from 200 BC to AD 500*. New Delhi: Munshiram Manoharlal.

Jamison, Stephanie W. 1996. *Sacrificed Wife/Sacrificer's Wife: Women, Ritual, and Hospitality in Ancient India*. New York: Oxford University Press.

Jayakar, Pupul. 1990 [1980]. *The Earth Mother: Legends, Goddesses, and Ritual Arts of India*. San Francisco: Harper & Row.

Jha, Ganganatha. 1964 [1942]. *Pūrva-Mīmāṁsā in Its Sources*. Varanasi: Banaras Hindu University.

Jha, Makhan, ed. 1985. *Dimensions of Pilgrimage: An Anthropological Appraisal.* New Delhi: Inter-India.

Jha, Makhan, ed. 1991. *Social Anthropology of Pilgrimage*. New Delhi: Inter-India.

Johnson, W. J., trans. 1998. *The Sauptikaparvan of the Mahābhārata: The Massacre at Night*. Oxford: Oxford University Press.

Joshi, B. 1993. "Militants Attack Hindu Pilgrims." *India Abroad* 13 August: 8.

Journal of Vaiṣṇava Studies. 1997. Special Issue on "Kṛṣṇa and the Gopīs." 5, 4.

Kaelber, Walter O. 1989. *Tapta Mārga: Asceticism and Initiation in Vedic India*. Albany: State University of New York Press.

Kahrs, Eivind. 1998. *Indian Semantic Analysis: The "Nirvacana" Tradition*. Cambridge: Cambridge University Press.

Kakar, Sudhir. 1982. "The Lord of the Spirit World." In *Shamans, Mystics, and Doctors: A Psychological Inquiry into India and Its Healing Traditions*, 53–88, 281–82. Chicago: University of Chicago Press.

Kalyāṇa. 1957. Special Issue on "Tīrtha" 31, 1.

Kane, Pandurang Vaman. 1930–62. *History of Dharmaśāstra (Ancient and Mediæval Religious and Civil Law)*. 5 volumes in 7 books. Poona: Bhandarkar Oriental Research Institute.

Kane, Pandurang Vaman. 1968–77 [1930–62]. *History of Dharmaśāstra (Ancient and Mediæval Religious and Civil Law)*. 5 volumes in 8 books. Poona: Bhandarkar Oriental Research Institute.

Kangle, R. P. 1960–65. *The Kauṭilīya Arthaśāstra*. 3 parts. Bombay: University of Bombay.

Kapadia, Karin. 1994. "Impure Women, Virtuous Men: Religion, Resistance, and Gender." *South Asia Research* 14, 2: 184–95.

Kapadia, Karin. 1998 [1995]. *Siva and Her Sisters: Gender, Caste, and Class in Rural South India*. Boulder: Westview.

Karve, Irawati. 1965 [1953]. *Kinship Organization in India*. Bombay: Asia Publishing.

Karve, Irawati. 1968 [1961]. *Hindu Society: An Interpretation*. Poona: Deshmukh Prakashan.

Karve, Irawati. 1988 [1962]. "On the Road: A Maharastrian Pilgrimage" (trans. D. D. Karve and Franklin Southworth). In Eleanor Zelliot and Maxine Bernsten, eds., *The Experience of Hinduism: Essays on Religion in Maharashtra*, 142–73. Albany: State University of New York Press.

Kasulis, Thomas P. 1992. "Philosophy as Metapraxis." In Frank Reynolds and David Tracy, eds., *Discourse and Practice*, 169–95. Albany: State University of New York Press.

Katz, Ruth Cecily. 1989. *Arjuna in the Mahabharata: Where Krishna Is, There is Victory*. Columbia: University of South Carolina Press.

Kaufman, Michael T. 1999. "Obituary of Raghubir Singh." *The New York Times on the Web* 20 April.

Keislar, Allan Mott. 1998. Searching for the Bhuśuṇḍi-Rāmāyaṇa: One Text or Many?: The Adi-Rāmāyaṇa, the Bhuṣuṇḍī-Rāmāyaṇa, and the Rāmāyaṇa-Mahā-Mālā. PhD dissertation. Berkeley: University of California at Berkeley Library.

Keith, Arthur Berriedale. 1925. *The Religion and Philosophy of the Veda and Upanishads*. 2 volumes. Cambridge: Harvard University Press.

Kennedy, Vans. 1831. *Researches into the Nature and Affinity of Ancient and Hindu Mythology*. London: Longman, Rees, Orme, Brown, and Green.

Kermode, Frank. 1967. *The Sense of an Ending: Studies in the Theory of Fiction*. New York: Oxford University Press.

Kerr, Ian J. 2001. "Reworking a Popular Religious Practice: The Effects of Railways on Pilgrimage in 19th and 20th Century South Asia." In Ian J. Kerr ed., *Railways in Modern India*, 304–27. Delhi: Oxford University Press.

Khare, R. S. 1970. *The Changing Brahmans: Associations and Elites among the Kanya-Kubjas of North India*. Chicago: University of Chicago Press.

Khare, R. S. 1976a. *The Hindu Hearth and Home: Culinary Systems Old and New in North India*. New Delhi: Vikas.

Khare, R. S. 1976b. *Culture and Reality: Essays on the Hindu System of Managing Foods*. Simla: Indian Institute of Advanced Study.

Khare, R. S. 1984. *The Untouchable as Himself: Ideology, Identity, and Pragmatism among the Lucknow Chamars*. Cambridge: Cambridge University Press.

Khare, R. S. 1986a. "The Indian Meal: Aspects of Cultural Economy and Food Use." In R. S. Khare and M. S. A. Rao, eds., *Food, Society, and Culture: Aspects in South Asian Food Systems*, 159–83. Durham: Carolina Academic Press.

Khare, R. S. 1986b. "Hospitality, Charity, and Rationing: Three Channels of Food Distribution in India." In R. S. Khare and M. S. A. Rao, eds., *Food, Society, and Culture: Aspects in South Asian Food Systems*, 277–96. Durham: Carolina Academic Press.

Khare, R. S. 1992a. "Introduction." In R. S. Khare, ed., *The Eternal Food: Gastronomic Ideas and Experiences of Hindus and Buddhists*, 1–25. Albany: State University of New York Press.

Khare, R. S. 1992b. "Food with Saints: An Aspect of Hindu Gastrosemantics." In R. S. Khare, ed., *The Eternal Food: Gastronomic Ideas and Experiences of Hindus and Buddhists*, 27–52. Albany: State University of New York Press.

Khare, R. S. 1992c. "*Annambrahman*: Cultural Models, Meanings, and Aesthetics of Hindu Food." In R. S. Khare, ed., *The Eternal Food: Gastronomic Ideas and Experiences of Hindus and Buddhists*, 201–20. Albany: State University of New York Press.

Khare, R. S. 1996. "Dava, Daktar, and Dua: Anthropology of Practiced Medicine in India." *Social Science and Medicine* 43, 5: 837–48.

Khare, R. S. 1998. "The Issue of 'Right to Food' among the Hindus: Notes and Comments." *Contributions to Indian Sociology (ns)* 32, 2: 253–78.

Killingley, Dermot. 1977. Rammohun Roy's Interpretation of the Vedānta. PhD dissertation. London: University of London Library.

Killingley, Dermot. 1993. *Rammohun Roy in Hindu and Christian Tradition.* Newcastle upon Tyne: Grevatt & Grevatt.

Killingley, Dermot. 1997a. "*Mlecchas*, Yavanas, and Heathens: Interacting Xenologies in Early Nineteenth-Century Calcutta." In Eli Franco and Karin Preisendanz, eds., *Beyond Orientalism: The Work of Wilhelm Halbfass and Its Impact on Indian and Cross-Cultural Studies*, 123–40. Amsterdam: Rodopi.

Killingley, Dermot. 1997b. "Enjoying the World: Desire (*Kāma*) and the Bhagavadgītā." In Julius Lipner, ed., *The Fruits of our Desiring: An Enquiry into the Ethics of the Bhagavadgītā for our Times*, 67–79. Calgary: Bayeux Arts.

Kingsbury, Francis and Godfrey E. Phillips. 1921. *Hymns of the Tamil Śaivite Saints.* Calcutta: Association Press.

Kinsley, David R. 1978. "The Portrait of the Goddess in the *Devī-Māhātmya*." *Journal of the American Academy of Religion* 46, 4: 489–506.

Kinsley, David R. 1986. *Hindu Goddesses: Visions of the Divine Feminine in the Hindu Religious Tradition.* Berkeley: University of California Press.

Kinsley, David R. 1997. *Tantric Visions of the Divine Feminine: The Ten Mahāvidyās.* Berkeley: University of California Press.

Klass, Morton. 1991. *Singing with Sai Baba: The Politics of Revitalization in Trinidad.* Boulder: Westview.

Kloetzli, W. Randolph. 1983. *Buddhist Cosmology: From Single World System to Pure Land. Science and Theology in the Images of Motion and Light.* Delhi: Motilal Banarsidass.

Kloetzli, W. Randolph. 1985. "Maps of Time—Mythologies of Descent: Scientific Instruments and the Purāṇic Cosmograph." *History of Religions* 25, 2: 116–47.

Klostermaier, Klaus K. 1994 [1989]. *A Survey of Hinduism.* Albany: State University of New York Press.

Klostermaier, Klaus. 1998. "The Education of Human Emotions: Śrīla Prabhupāda as Spiritual Educator." *Journal of Vaiṣṇava Studies* 6, 2: 31–41.

Knipe, David. 1997. "Becoming a Veda in the Godavari Delta." In Dick van der Meij, ed., *India and Beyond: Aspects of Literature, Meaning, Ritual, and Thought. Essays in Honour of Frits Staal*, 306–32. London: Kegan Paul.

Kolff, Dirk H. A. 1990. *Naukar, Rajput, and Sepoy: The Ethnohistory of the Military Labour Market of Hindustan, 1450–1850.* Cambridge: Cambridge University Press.

Koller, John M. 1972. "*Dharma*: An Expression of Universal Order." *Philosophy East and West* 22, 2: 131–44.

Kopf, David. 1969. *British Orientalism and the Bengal Renaissance: The Dynamics of Indian Modernization, 1773–1835.* Berkeley: University of California Press.

Kopf, David. 1979. *The Brahmo Samaj and the Shaping of the Modern Indian Mind.* Princeton: Princeton University Press.

Kripananda, Swami. 1989. *Jnaneshwar's Gita: A Rendering of the Jnaneshwari*. Albany: State University of New York Press.

Krishnamacaryar Swami, U. V. 1992. *Ācāryavaipavam*. Chennai: Sri Vishistadvaitha Research Centre.

Krishnamoorty, K., ed. 1991. *A Critical Inventory of Rāmāyaṇa Studies in the World*. Volume 1 of 2: *Indian Languages and English*. New Delhi: Sahitya Akademi.

Kristeva, Julia. 1986 [1979]. "Women's Time" (trans. Alice Jardine and Harry Blake). In Toril Moi, ed., *The Kristeva Reader*, 187–213. New York: Columbia University Press.

Kulke Hermann and Dietmar Rothermund. 1998 [1986]. *A History of India*. London: Routledge.

Kumar, Pushpendra. 1974. *Śakti Cult in Ancient India (with Special Reference to the Purāṇic Literature)*. Varanasi: Bharatiya Publishing.

Kumar, Sehdev. 1984. *The Vision of Kabīr: Love Poems of a 15th Century Weaver-Sage*. Concord: Alpha & Omega.

Kurin, Richard. 1981. Person, Family, and Kin in Two Pakistani Communities. PhD dissertation. Chicago: University of Chicago Library.

Kurtz, Stanley N. 1992. *All the Mothers are One: Hindu India and the Cultural Reshaping of Psychoanalysis*. New York: Colmbia University Press.

La Vallée Poussin, Louis de. 1930. *L'Inde aux temps des Mauryas et des Barbares, Grecs, Scythes, Parthes, et Yue-tchi*. Paris: Boccard.

La Vallée Poussin, Louis de, trans. 1988–90 [1923–31]. *Abhidharmakośabhāṣyam* (trans. Leo Pruden). 4 volumes. Berkeley: Asian Humanities.

Lamb, Sarah. 2000. *White Saris and Sweet Mangoes: Aging, Gender, and Body in North India*. Berkeley: University of California Press.

Lanman, Charles Rockwell. 1884. *A Sanskrit Reader*. Volume 1 of 2. Cambridge: Harvard University Press.

Lapoint, Elwyn C. 1978. "The Epic of Guga: A North Indian Oral Tradition." In Sylvia Vatuk, ed., *American Studies in the Anthropology of India*, 281–308. New Delhi: Manohar.

Larson, Gerald James. 1972. "The *Trimūrti* of *Dharma* in Indian Thought: Paradox or Contradiction?" *Philosophy East and West* 22, 2: 145–53.

Larson, Gerald James. 1981. "The Song Celestial: Two Centuries of the *Bhagavad Gītā* in English." *Philosophy East and West* 31, 4: 513–41.

Larson, Gerald James. 1987. "Introduction to the Philosophy of Sāṃkhya." In Gerald J. Larson and Ram Shankar Bhattacharya, eds., *Sāṃkhya: A Dualist Tradition in Indian Philosophy*, 1–103. Princeton: Princeton University Press.

Larson, Gerald James. 1995. *India's Agony over Religion*. Albany: State University of New York Press.

Lassen, Christian. 1866–74 [1843–62]. *Indische Alterthumskunde*. 4 volumes. Leipzig: L. A. Kittler.

Lath, Mukund. 1990. "The Concept of *Ānṛśaṁsya* in the Mahābhārata." In R. N. Dandekar, ed., *The Mahābhārata Revisited*, 113–19. New Delhi: Sahitya Akademi.

Lefeber, Rosalind, trans. 1994. *The Rāmāyaṇa of Vālmīki: An Epic of Ancient India* (ed. Robert P. Goldman). Volume 4 of 5: *Kiṣkindhākāṇḍa*. Princeton: Princeton University Press.

Leslie, Julia, trans. 1989. *The Perfect Wife: The Orthodox Hindu Woman according to the Strīdharmapaddhati of Tryambakayajvan*. New York: Oxford University Press.

Leslie, Julia, ed. 1991. *Roles and Rituals for Hindu Women*. London: Pinter.

Lévi-Strauss, Claude. 1963 [1962]. *Totemism* (trans. Rodney Needham). Boston: Beacon.

Lévi-Strauss, Claude. 1965. "Le triangle culinaire." *L'arc* (Aix-en-Provence) 26: 19–29.

Lévi, Sylvain. 1966 [1898]. *La doctrine du sacrifice dans les Brâhmaṇas*. Paris: Presses Universitaires de France.

Levitt, Stephen Hillyer. 1976. "A Note on the Compound *Pañcalakṣaṇa* in Amarasiṇha's *Nāmaliṅgānuśāsana*." *Purāṇam* 18, 1: 5–38.

Lewis, I. M. 1971. *Ecstatic Religion: An Anthropological Study of Spirit Possession and Shamanism*. Harmondsworth: Penguin.

Lingat, Robert. 1973 [1967]. *The Classical Law of India* (trans. J. Duncan M. Derrett). Berkeley: University of California Press.

Lipner, Julius J. 1996. "Ancient Banyan: An Inquiry into the Meaning of 'Hinduness'." *Religious Studies* 32, 1: 109–26.

Lipner, Julius J. 1998a [1994]. *Hindus: Their Religious Beliefs and Practices.* London: Routledge.

Lipner, Julius J. 1998b. "Philosophy and World Religions." In Brian Davies, ed., *Philosophy of Religion: A Guide to the Subject*, 311–25. London: Cassell.

Lipner, Julius J. 2000. "A Hindu View of Life." In Joseph Runzo and Nancy M. Martin, eds., *The Meaning of Life in the World Religions*, 115–31. Oxford: Oneworld.

Lipner, Julius J. 2001. "A Remaking of Hinduism? or, Taking the Mickey Out of Vālmīki." In Hent de Vries and Samuel Weber, eds., *Religion and Media*, 320–38, 613–17. Stanford: Stanford University Press.

Lopez, Donald S., Jr. 1993. "The Institution of Fiction in Mahāyāna Buddhism." In Shlomo Biderman and Ben-Ami Scharfstein, eds., *Myths and Fictions*, 355–88. Leiden: E. J. Brill.

Lorenzen, David N. 1987. "Traditions of Non-Caste Hinduism: The Kabir Panth." *Contributions to Indian Sociology (ns)* 21, 2: 263–83.

Lorenzen, David N. 1991a [1972]. *The Kāpālikas and Kālāmukhas: Two Lost Śaivite Sects.* Berkeley: University of California Press.

Lorenzen, David N. 1991b. *Kabir Legends and Ananta-das's Kabir Parachai: With a Translation of the Kabir Parachai Prepared in Collaboration with Jagdish Kumar and Uma Thukral and with an Edition of the Niranjani Panthi Recension of this Work.* Albany: State University of New York Press.

Lorenzen, David N. 1996. *Praises to a Formless God: Nirguṇī Texts from North India.* Albany: State University of New York Press.

Lorenzen, David N. 1999a. "The Life of Kabīr in Legend." In Alan W. Entwistle and Carol Salomon, eds., *Studies in Early Modern Indo-Aryan Languages, Literature, and Culture,* 209–26. New Delhi: Manohar.

Lorenzen, David N. 1999b. "Who Invented Hinduism?" *Comparative Studies in Society and History: An International Quarterly* 41, 4: 630–59.

Lubin, Timothy. 2001. "Veda on Parade: Revivalist Ritual as Civic Spectacle." *Journal of the American Academy of Religion* 69, 2: 377–408.

Lüders, Heinrich. 1959. *Varuṇa* (ed. Ludwig Alsdorf). Volume 2 of 2: *Varuṇa und das Ṛta.* Göttingen: Vandenhoeck & Ruprecht.

Ludvik, Catherine. 1994. *Hanumān in the Rāmāyaṇa of Vālmīki and the Rāmacaritamānasa of Tulasī Dāsa.* Delhi: Motilal Banarsidass.

Lutgendorf, Philip. 1991a. *The Life of a Text: Performing the Rāmcaritmānas of Tulsidas.* Berkeley: University of California Press.

Lutgendorf, Philip. 1991b. "The 'Great Sacrifice' of Rāmāyaṇa Recitation: Ritual Performance of the *Rāmcaritmānas*." In Monika Thiel-Horstmann, ed., *Rāmāyaṇa and Rāmāyaṇas*, 185–205. Wiesbaden: Otto Harrassowitz.

Lutgendorf, Philip. 1995. "All in the (Raghu) Family: A Video Epic in Cultural Context." In Lawrence Babb and Susan S. Wadley, eds., *Media and the Transformation of Religion in South Asia,* 217–53. Philadelphia: University of Pennsylvania Press.

Lutgendorf, Philip. 1997. "Monkey in the Middle: The Status of Hanuman in Popular Hinduism." *Religion* 27, 4: 311–32.

Mackie, J. L. 1977. *Ethics: Inventing Right and Wrong.* Hammondsworth: Penguin.

Madan, T. N. 1981. "The Ideology of the Householder Among the Kashmiri Pandits." *Contributions to Indian Sociology (ns)* 15, 1–2: 223–49.

Madan, T. N. 1987. *Non-Renunciation: Themes and Interpretations of Hindu Culture.* Delhi: Oxford University Press.

Mahesh Yogi, Maharishi. 1969 [1967]. *Maharishi Mahesh Yogi on the Bhagavad-Gita: A New Translation and Commentary with Sanskrit Text, Chapters 1 to 6*. Harmondsworth: Penguin.

Mahony, William K. 1998. *The Artful Universe: An Introduction to the Vedic Religious Imagination*. Albany: State University of New York Press.

Majumdar, R. C. 1951. *History and Culture of Indian People*. Volume 1 of 12: *The Vedic Age*. London: George Allen & Unwin.

Majumdar, R. C. 1953. *Inscriptions of Kambuja*. Calcutta: Asiatic Society.

Malamoud, Charles. 1981. "On the Rhetoric and Semantics of Puruṣārtha." *Contributions to Indian Sociology (ns)* 15, 1–2: 33–54.

Malamoud, Charles. 1983 [1980]. "The Theology of Debt in Brahmanism" (trans. Ian Young). In Charles Malamoud, ed., *Debts and Debtors*, 21–40. New Delhi: Vikas.

Malamoud, Charles. 1996 [1989]. *Cooking the World: Ritual and Thought in Ancient India* (trans. David White). Delhi: Oxford University Press.

Malinar, Angelika. 1996. *Rājavidyā: Das königliche Wissen um Herrschaft und Verzicht. Studien zur Bhagavadgītā*. Wiesbaden: Otto Harrassowitz.

Manuel, Peter L. 1993. *Cassette Culture: Popular Music and Technology in North India*. Chicago: University of Chicago Press.

Marglin, Frédérique Apffel. 1981. "Kings and Wives: The Separation of Status and Royal Power." *Contributions to Indian Sociology (ns)* 15, 1–2: 156–81.

Marriott, McKim. 1955. "Little Communities in an Indigenous Civilization." In McKim Marriott, ed., *Village India: Studies in the Little Community*, 171–222. Chicago: University of Chicago Press.

Marriott, McKim. 1966. "The Feast of Love." In Milton Singer, ed., *Krishna: Myths, Rites, and Attitudes*, 200–12, 229–31. Honolulu: East-West Center Press.

Marriott, McKim. 1968. "Caste Ranking and Food Transactions: A Matrix Analysis." In Milton Singer and Bernard S. Cohn, eds., *Structure and Change in Indian Society*, 133–71. Chicago: Aldine.

Marriott, McKim. 1976. "Hindu Transactions: Diversity without Dualism." In Bruce Kapferer, ed., *Transaction and Meaning: Directions in the Anthropology of Exchange and Symbolic Behavior*, 109–42. Philadelphia: Institute for the Study of Human Issues.

Marriott, McKim. 1989. "Constructing an Indian Ethnosociology." *Contributions to Indian Sociology (ns)* 23, 1: 1–39.

Marriott, McKim and Ronald B. Inden. 1974. "Caste Systems." In *Encyclopaedia Britannica*, 3 of 24: 982–91. Chicago: Encyclopaedia Britannica.

Marshall, John, ed. 1931. *Mohenjo-Daro and the Indus Civilization: Being an Official Account of Archaeological Excavations at Mohenjo-daro Carried Out by the Government of India Between the Years 1922 and 1927*. 3 volumes. London: Oxford University Press.

Marvin, Brian D. 1996. The Life and Thought of Kedarnath Dutta Bhaktivinode: A Hindu Encounter with Modernity. PhD Dissertation. Toronto: University of Toronto Library.

Marx, Karl. 1948 [1867–85]. *Le Capital*. Volume 2 of 3. Paris: Éditions Sociales.

Mauss, Marcel. 1947. *Manuel d'ethnographie*. Paris: Payot.

Mayer, Adrian C. 1960. *Caste and Kinship in Central India: A Village and Its Region*. Berkeley: University of California Press.

McCormick, Thomas. 1997. "The Jaina Ascetic as Manifestation of the Sacred." In Robert H. Stoddard and Alan Morinis, eds., *Sacred Places, Sacred Spaces: The Geography of Pilgrimages*, 235–56. Baton Rouge: Louisiana State University, Department of Geography and Anthropology.

McDaniel, June. 2004. *Offering Flowers, Feeding Skulls: Popular Goddess Worship in West Bengal*. New York: Oxford University Press.

McDermott, Rachel Fell. 2001a. *Mother of My Heart, Daughter of My Dreams: Kālī and Umā in the Devotional Poetry of Bengal*. New York: Oxford University Press.

McDermott, Rachel Fell. 2001b. *Singing to the Goddess: Poems to Kālī and Umā from Bengal.* New York: Oxford University Press.

McGee, Mary. 1991. "Desired Fruits: Motive and Intention in the Votive Rites of Hindu Women." In Julia Leslie, ed., *Roles and Rituals for Hindu Women*, 71–88. London: Pinter.

McGilvray, Dennis B. 1998. *Symbolic Heat: Gender, Health, and Worship among the Tamils of South India and Sri Lanka.* Middletown: Grantha.

McKean, Lise. 1996a. "Bhārat Mātā: Mother India and Her Militant Matriots." In John Stratton Hawley and Donna Marie Wulff, eds., *Devī: Goddesses of India*, 250–80. Berkeley: University of California Press.

McKean, Lise. 1996b. *Divine Enterprise: Gurus and the Hindu Nationalist Movement.* Chicago: University of Chicago Press.

McLean, Malcolm. 1998. *Devoted to the Goddess: The Life and Work of Ramprasad.* Albany: State University of New York Press.

McLeod, H. W. 1997. *Sikhism.* London: Penguin.

Meenakshi, K. 1996. "The Siddhas of Tamil Nadu: A Voice of Dissent." In R. Champakalakshmi and S. Gopal, eds., *Tradition, Dissent, and Ideology: Essays in Honour of Romila Thapar,* 111–34. Delhi: Oxford University Press.

Michael, R. Blake. 1992. *The Origins of Vīraśaiva Sects: A Typological Analysis of Ritual and Associational Patterns in the Śūnyasaṃpādae.* Delhi: Motilal Banarsidass.

Michaël, Tara, ed. and trans. 1975. *Le joyau du Śiva-yoga: Śivayogaratna de Jñānaprakāśa.* Pondicherry: Institut français de Pondichéry.

Michell, George. 1977. *The Hindu Temple: An Introduction to Its Meaning and Forms.* London: Paul Elek.

Mill, James. 1817. *The History of British India.* 8 volumes. London: James Madden.

Miller, Barbara Stoler, ed. and trans. 1977. *Love Song of the Dark Lord: Jayadeva's Gītāgovinda.* New York: Columbia University Press.

Mines, Diane Paul. 1989. "Hindu Periods of Death 'Impurity'." *Contributions to Indian Sociology (ns)* 23, 1: 103–30.

Mines, Diane Paul. 1997. "Making the Past Past: Objects and the Spatialization of Time in Tamilnadu." *Anthropological Quarterly* 70, 4: 173–86.

Minkowski, C. Z. 1989. "Janamejaya's *Sattra* and Ritual Structure." *Journal of the American Oriental Society* 109, 3: 401–20.

Minkowski, Christopher. 1991. "Snakes, *Sattras*, and the *Mahābhārata*." In Arvind Sharma, ed., *Essays on the Mahābhārata*, 384–400. Leiden: E. J. Brill.

Moffatt, Michael. 1979. *An Untouchable Community in South India: Structure and Consensus.* Princeton: Princeton University Press.

Mokashi, D. B. 1987 [1964]. *Palkhi: An Indian Pilgrimage* (trans. Philip C. Engblom). Albany: State University of New York Press.

Moreno, Manuel and McKim Marriott. 1989. "Humoral Transactions in Two Tamil Cults: Murukan and Mariyamman." *Contributions to Indian Sociology (ns)* 23, 1: 149–67.

Morinis, E. Alan. 1984. *Pilgrimage in the Hindu Tradition: A Case Study of West Bengal.* Delhi: Oxford University Press.

Morson, Gary Saul. 1994. *Narrative and Freedom: The Shadows of Time.* New Haven: Yale University Press.

Muir, J., comp. and trans. 1967 [1868]. *Original Sanskrit Texts on the Origin and History of the People of India, their Religion and Institutions.* 5 volumes. Amsterdam: Oriental.

Muir, Ramsay, ed. 1923 [1915]. *The Making of British India, 1756–1858: Described in a Series of Dispatches, Treaties, Statutes, and Other Documents.* Manchester: Manchester University Press.

Mukherjee, Prabhat. 1977. *History of the Jagannath Temple in the 19th Century.* Calcutta: Firma K. L. Mukhopadhyay.

Mukta, Parita. 1994. *Upholding the Common Life: The Community of Mirabai*. Delhi: Oxford University Press.

Müller, Friedrich Max. 1926 [1859]. *A History of Ancient Sanskrit Literature, so far as it Illustrates the Primitive Religion of the Brahmans*. New Delhi: Oxford and IBH.

Müller, Friedrich Max. 1867. *Chips from a German Workshop*. Volume 1 of 5: *Essays on the Science of Religion*. London: Longmans, Green.

Mumme, Patricia Y. 1988. *The Śrīvaiṣṇava Theological Dispute: Maṇavāḷamāmuni and Vedānta Deśika*. Madras: New Era.

Mumme, Patricia Y. 1991. "*Rāmāyaṇa* Exegesis in Teṉkalai Śrīvaiṣṇavism." In Paula Richman, ed., *Many Rāmāyaṇas: The Diversity of a Narrative Tradition in South Asia*, 202–16. Berkeley: University of California Press.

Murti, T. R. V. 1952 [1936]. "The Spirit of Philosophy." In S. Radhakrishnan and J. H. Muirhead, eds., *Contemporary Indian Philosophy*, 457–71. London: George Allen & Unwin.

Murty, K. Satchidananda. 1985. *Philosophy in India: Traditions, Teaching, and Research*. Delhi: Motilal Banarsidass.

Nandimath, S. C. 1979 [1942]. *A Handbook of Vīraśaivism*. Delhi: Motilal Banarsidass.

Narasimhachar, D. L. 1939. "The Jaina Rāmāyaṇas." *The Indian Historical Quarterly* 15, 4: 575–94.

Narayanan, Vasudha. 1987. *The Way and the Goal: Expressions of Devotion in the Early Śrī Vaiṣṇava Tradition*. Washington: Institute for Vaishnava Studies.

Narayanan, Vasudha. 1992. "Creating the South Indian 'Hindu' Experience in the United States." In Raymond Brady Williams, ed., *A Sacred Thread: Modern Transmission of Hindu Traditions in India and Abroad*, 147–76, 319–22. Chambersburg: Anima.

Narayanan, Vasudha. 1995. "Tiruveṅkaṭam in the Fifteenth Century." *Journal of Vaiṣṇava Studies* 3, 3: 91–108.

Narayanan, Vasudha. 2002 [1996]. "The Hindu Tradition." In Willard G. Oxtoby, ed., *World Religions: Eastern Traditions*, 12–125. Toronto: Oxford University Press.

Narayana Rao, Velcheru, trans., assisted by Gene H. Roghair. 1990. *Śiva's Warriors: The Basava Purāṇa of Pālkuriki Somanātha*. Princeton: Princeton University Press.

Narayana Rao, Velcheru. 1993. "Purāṇa as Brahmanic Ideology." In Wendy Doniger, ed., *Purāṇa Perennis: Reciprocity and Transformation in Hindu and Jaina Texts*, 85–100, 265–66. Albany: State University of New York Press.

Narayana Rao, Velcheru. 1995. "Review of Philip Lutgendorf's *The Life of a Text: Performing the Rāmcaritmānas of Tulsidas*." *Journal of Asian Studies* 54, 2: 600–603.

Nayar, Nancy. 1997. "After the Āḻvārs: Kṛṣṇa and the *Gopīs* in the Śrīvaiṣṇava Tradition." *Journal of Vaiṣṇava Studies* 5, 4: 201–22.

Neevel, Walter G., Jr. 1977. Yāmuna's Vedānta and Pāñcarātra: Integrating the Classical and the Popular. PhD dissertation. Cambridge: Harvard University Library.

Nehru, Jawaharlal. 1946. *The Discovery of India*. Calcutta: Signet.

Nelson, Lance. 1993. "Theism for the Masses, Non-Dualism for the Monastic Elite: A Fresh Look at Śaṃkara's Trans-Theistic Spirituality." In William M. Shea, ed., *The Struggle Over the Past: Fundamentalism in the Modern World*, 61–77. Lanham: University Press of America.

Nelson, Lance E. 1996. "Living Liberation in Śaṅkara and Classical Advaita: Sharing the Holy Waiting of God." In Andrew O. Fort and Patricia Y. Mumme, eds., *Living Liberation in Hindu Thought*, 17–62. Albany: State University of New York Press.

Neufeldt, Ronald W. 1980. *F. Max Müller and the Ṛg-Veda: A Study of Its Role in His Work and Thought*. Calcutta: Minerva.

Neufeldt, Ronald W., ed. 1986. *Karma and Rebirth: Post Classical Developments*. Albany: State University of New York Press.

Nicholas, Ralph W. 1995. "The Effectiveness of the Hindu Sacrament (*Saṃskāra*): Caste, Marriage, and Divorce in Bengali Culture." In Lindsey Harlan and Paul B. Courtright, eds., *From the*

Margins of Hindu Marriage: Essays on Gender, Religion, and Culture, 137–59. New York: Oxford University Press.

Nihom, Max. 1994. *Studies in Indian and Indo-Indonesian Tantrism: The Kuñjarakarṇadharmakathana and the Yogatantra*. Vienna: De Nobili Research Library.

Nikhilananda, Swami, trans. 1963. *The Upanishads: Katha, Iśa, Kena, Mundaka, Śvetāśvatara, Praśna, Māndukya, Aitareya, Brihadāranyaka, Taittiriya, and Chhāndogya*. London: George Allen & Unwin.

Nilakanta Sastri, K. A. 1963. *Development of Religion in South India*. Madras: Orient Longmans.

Nilsson, Usha S. 1969. *Mira Bai*. New Delhi: Sahitya Akademi.

Norman, K. R., trans. 1971. *The Elder's Verses*. Volume 2 of 2: *Therīgāthā*. London: Luzac.

Nye, James H. 1985. "Upapurāṇa and Mahapurāṇa: Appendix and Appendee?" Paper Presented at Conference on the Purāṇas, University of Wisconsin, Madison, August.

Obeyesekere, Gananath. 1980. "The Rebirth Eschatology and Its Transformations: A Contribution to the Sociology of Early Buddhism." In Wendy Doniger O'Flaherty, ed., *Karma and Rebirth in Classical Indian Tradition*, 137–64. Berkeley: University of California Press.

Obeyesekere, Gananath. 1990. *The Work of Culture: Symbolic Transformation in Psychoanalysis and Anthropology*. Chicago: University of Chicago Press.

O'Connell, Joseph T. 1973. "The Word 'Hindu' in Gauḍīya Vaiṣṇava Texts." *Journal of the American Oriental Society* 93, 3: 340–44.

O'Flaherty, Wendy Doniger. 1971. "The Origin of Heresy in Hindu Mythology." *History of Religions* 10, 4: 271–333.

O'Flaherty, Wendy Doniger. 1973. *Asceticism and Eroticism in the Mythology of Śiva*. London: Oxford University Press.

O'Flaherty, Wendy Doniger. 1976. *The Origins of Evil in Hindu Mythology*. Berkeley: University of California Press.

O'Flaherty, Wendy Doniger. 1980a. *Women, Androgynes, and Other Mythical Beasts*. Chicago: University of Chicago Press.

O'Flaherty, Wendy Doniger, ed. 1980b. "Introduction." In Wendy Doniger O'Flaherty, ed., *Karma and Rebirth in Classical Indian Traditions*, ix–xxv. Berkeley: University of California Press.

O'Flaherty, Wendy Doniger, ed. 1980c. "Karma and Rebirth in the Vedas and Purāṇas." In Wendy Doniger O'Flaherty, ed., *Karma and Rebirth in Classical Indian Traditions*, 3–37. Berkeley: University of California Press.

O'Flaherty, Wendy Doniger, ed. 1980d. *Karma and Rebirth in Classical Indian Traditions*. Berkeley: University of California Press.

O'Flaherty, Wendy Doniger. 1981 [1973]. *Śiva: The Erotic Ascetic*. New York: Oxford University Press.

O'Flaherty, Wendy Doniger. 1982. "The Shifting Balance of Power in the Marriage of Śiva and Pārvatī." In John S. Hawley and Donna M. Wulff, eds., *The Divine Consort: Rādhā and the Goddesses of India*, 129–43, 342–43. Berkeley: University of California Press.

O'Flaherty, Wendy Doniger. 1984. *Dreams, Illusion, and Other Realities*. Chicago: University of Chicago Press.

O'Flaherty, Wendy Doniger. 1985. *Tales of Sex and Violence: Folklore, Sacrifice, and Danger in the Jaiminīya Brāhmaṇa*. Chicago: University of Chicago Press.

Oldenberg, Hermann. 1915. *Die Lehre der Upanishaden und die Anfänge des Buddhismus*. Göttingen: Vandenhoeck & Ruprecht.

Olivelle, Patrick. 1978. "The Integration of Renunciation by Orthodox Hinduism." *Journal of the Oriental Institute* 28, 1: 27–36.

Olivelle, Patrick. 1981. "Contributions to the Semantic History of Saṃnyāsa." *Journal of the American Oriental Society* 101, 3: 265–74.

Olivelle, Patrick. 1984. "Renouncer and Renunciation in the *Dharmaśāstras*." In Richard W. Lariviere, ed., *Studies in Dharmaśāstra*, 81–152. Calcutta: Firma K. L. Mukhopadhyay.

Olivelle, Patrick. 1986–87. *Renunciation in Hinduism: A Medieval Debate.* 2 volumes. Vienna: De Nobili Research Library.

Olivelle, Patrick, trans. 1992. *Saṃnyāsa Upaniṣads: Hindu Scriptures on Asceticism and Renunciation.* New York: Oxford University Press.

Olivelle, Patrick. 1993. *The Āśrama System: The History and Hermeneutics of a Religious Institution.* New York: Oxford University Press.

Olivelle, Patrick. 1995. "Deconstruction of the Body in Indian Asceticism." In Vincent L. Wimbush and Richard Valantasis, eds., *Asceticism*, 188–210. New York: Oxford University Press.

Olivelle, Patrick, trans. 1996. *Upaniṣads.* Oxford: Oxford University Press.

Olivelle, Patrick, trans. 1998. *The Early Upaniṣads.* New York: Oxford University Press.

Olivelle, Patrick, trans. 1999. *Dharmasūtras: The Law Codes of Āpastamba, Gautama, Baudhāyana, and Vasiṣṭha.* Oxford: Oxford University Press.

Olivelle, Patrick. 2000. "From the Ṛg-Veda to Aśoka: A Brief History of Dharma." Paper Presented at University of California, Santa Barbara, Department of Religious Studies, 31 May.

Orenstein, Henry. 1965. "The Structure of Hindu Caste Values: A Preliminary Study of Hierarchy and Ritual Defilement." *Ethnology: An International Journal of Cultural and Social Anthropology* 4, 1: 1–15.

Orenstein, Henry. 1968. "Toward a Grammar of Defilement in Hindu Sacred Law." In Milton Singer and Bernard S. Cohn, eds., *Structure and Change in Indian Society*, 115–31. Chicago: Aldine.

Orenstein, Henry. 1970. "Logical Congruence in Hindu Sacred Law: Another Interpretation." *Contributions to Indian Sociology (ns)* 4: 22–35.

Organ, Troy Wilson. 1970. *The Hindu Quest for the Perfection of Man.* Athens: Ohio University Press.

Organ, Troy Wilson. 1974. *Hinduism: Its Historical Development.* Woodbury: Barron's Educational Series.

Orr, Leslie C. 1994. "Women of Medieval South India in Hindu Temple Ritual: Text and Practice." *The Annual Review of Women in World Religions* 3: 107–41.

Orr, Leslie C. 2001. "Women in the Temple, the Palace, and the Family: The Construction of Women's Identities in Pre-Colonial Tamilnāḍu." In Kenneth R. Hall, ed., *Structure and Society in Early South India: Essays in Honour of Noboru Karashima*, 198–234. Delhi: Oxford University Press.

Orr, W. G. 1947. *A Sixteenth-Century Indian Mystic: Dadu and His Followers.* London: Lutterworth.

Owens, Raymond Lee and Ashis Nandy. 1977. *The New Vaisyas.* Bombay: Allied.

Padoux, André. 1987. "Hindu Tantrism." In Mircea Eliade, ed., *The Encyclopedia of Religion*, 14 of 16: 274–80. New York: Macmillan.

Padoux, André. 1990 [1963]. *Vāc: The Concept of the Word in Selected Hindu Tantras* (trans. Jacques Gontier). Albany: State University of New York Press.

Padoux, André, trans. 1994. *Le cœur de la yoginī: Yoginīhṛdaya, avec le commentaire Dīpikā d'Amṛtānanda.* Paris: Boccard.

Pandey, Raj Bali. 1996 [1949]. *Hindu Saṁskāras: Socio-Religious Study of the Hindu Sacraments.* Delhi: Motilal Banarsidass.

Paranjoti, V. 1954 [1938]. *Saiva Siddhānta.* London: Luzac.

Parpola, Asko. 1994. *Deciphering the Indus Script.* Cambridge: Cambridge University Press.

Parpola, Asko. 1997. [*Significance of 108 Within Hindu Religious Culture.*] San Diego: http://www.acusd.edu/theo/risa-l/archive/msg00056.html.

Parry, Jonathan P. 1979. *Caste and Kinship in Kangra.* London: Routledge & Kegan Paul.

Parry, Jonathan P. 1980. "Ghosts, Greed, and Sin: The Occupational Identity of the Benares Funeral Priests." *Man: The Journal of the Royal Anthropological Institute (ns)* 15, 1: 88–111.

Parry, Jonathan P. 1994. *Death in Banaras.* Cambridge: Cambridge University Press.

Parsons, Talcott. 1949 [1937]. *The Structure of Social Action: A Study in Social Theory with Special Reference to a Group of Recent European Writers.* New York: Free Press.

Patton, Laurie and Edwin Bryant, eds. 2004. *The Indo-Aryan Controversy: Evidence and Inference in Indian History*. London: Taylor and Francis.

Payne, Ernest A. 1933. *The Śāktas: An Introductory and Comparative Study*. Calcutta: YMCA Publishing.

Peirce, Charles Saunders. 1934. *Collected Papers of Charles Saunders Peirce* (eds. Charles Hartshorne and Paul Weiss). Volume 5 of 8: *Pragmatism and Pragmaticism*. Cambridge: Harvard University Press.

Peterson, Indira Viswanathan. 1989. *Poems to Śiva: The Hymns of the Tamil Saints*. Princeton: Princeton University Press.

Pfaffenberger, Bryan. 1982. *Caste in Tamil Culture: The Religious Foundations of Sudra Domination in Tamil Sri Lanka*. Syracuse: Syracuse University Maxwell School of Citizenship and Public Affairs.

Pingree, David. 1978. "History of Mathematical Astronomy in India." In Charles Coulton Gillispie, ed., *Dictionary of Scientific Biography*. Volume 15, Supplement 1: *Topical Essays*, 533–633. New York: Charles Scribner.

Pingree, David. 1981. *Jyotiḥśāstra: Astral and Mathematical Literature*. Wiesbaden: Otto Harrassowitz.

Pintchman, Tracy. 1994. *The Rise of the Goddess in the Hindu Tradition*. Albany: State University of New York Press.

Pinto, Desiderio. 1989. "The Mystery of the Nizamuddin Dargah: The Accounts of Pilgrims." In Christian W. Troll, ed., *Muslim Shrines in India: Their Character, History, and Significance*, 112–24. Delhi: Oxford University Press.

Planalp, Jack M. 1956. Religious Life and Values in a North Indian Village. PhD dissertation. Ithaca: Cornell University Library.

Pocock, David F. 1972. *Kanbi and Patidar: A Study of the Patidar Community of Gujarat*. Oxford: Clarendon.

Poddar, Hanuman Prasad. 1989 [1940]. *Śrīrāmcaritmānas*. Gorakhpur: Gita Press.

Pollock, Sheldon. 1990. "From Discourse of Ritual to Discourse of Power in Sanskrit Culture." In Barbara A. Holdrege, ed., *Ritual and Power*, *Journal of Ritual Studies* 4, 2: 315–45.

Pollock, Sheldon, trans. 1991. *The Rāmāyaṇa of Vālmīki: An Epic of Ancient India* (ed. Robert P. Goldman). Volume 3 of 5: *Araṇyakāṇḍa*. Princeton: Princeton University Press.

Pollock, Sheldon. 1993. "Rāmāyaṇa and Political Imagination in India." *The Journal of Asian Studies* 52, 2: 261–97.

Potter, Karl H. 1963. *Presuppositions of India's Philosophies*. Englewood Cliffs: Prentice-Hall.

Potter, Karl H. 1971. "Introduction to the Philosophy of Nyāya-Vaiśeṣika." In Karl H. Potter, ed., *Indian Metaphysics and Epistemology: The Tradition of Nyāya-Vaiśeṣika up to Gaṅgeśa*, 1–208. Princeton: Princeton University Press.

Pou, Saveros, trans. 1977. *Rāmakerti: XVIe–XVIIe siècles*. Paris: École française d'Extrême-Orient.

Pou, Saveros, trans. 1982. *Rāmakerti II: deuxième version du Rāmāyaṇa khmer*. Paris: École française d'Extrême-Orient.

Powell, Anton, ed. 1995. *The Greek World*. London: Routledge.

Prakash, Om. 1961. *Food and Drinks in Ancient India: From Earliest Times to c.1200 AD*. Delhi: M. R. Manohar Lal.

Prinja, Nawal K., ed. 1996. *Explaining Hindu Dharma: A Guide for Teachers*. Norwich: Religious and Moral Education Press.

Radhakrishnan, Sarvepalli. 1931 [1927]. *Indian Philosophy*. Volume 2 of 2. New York: Macmillan.

Radhakrishnan, Sarvepalli. 1932. *An Idealist View of Life*. London: George Allen & Unwin.

Radhakrishnan, Sarvepalli. 1947. *Religion and Society*. London: George Allen & Unwin.

Radhakrishnan, Sarvepalli, ed. and trans. 1953. *The Principal Upaniṣads*. London: George Allen & Unwin.

Radhakrishnan, Sarvepalli. 1958 [1933]. *East and West in Religion*. London: George Allen & Unwin.

Radhakrishnan, Sarvepalli, ed. and trans. 1960 [1948]. *The Bhagavadgītā*. London: George Allen & Unwin.

Radhakrishnan, Sarvepalli. 1980 [1927]. *The Hindu View of Life*. London: Unwin Paperbacks.

Radhakrishnan, Sarvepalli and Charles A. Moore, eds. 1957. *A Sourcebook in Indian Philosophy*. Princeton: Princeton University Press.

Raghavan, V. 1961. *Some Old Lost Rāma Plays*. Annamalainagar: Annamalai University.

Raheja, Gloria Goodwin. 1988. *The Poison in the Gift: Ritual, Prestation, and the Dominant Caste in a North Indian Village*. Chicago: University of Chicago Press.

Rajan, Chandra, trans. 1993. *The Pañcatantra* [by] *Viṣṇu Śarma*. New Delhi: Penguin.

Ramachandra Dikshitar, V. R. 1951. *The Purāṇa Index*. Volume 1 of 3. Madras: Madras University.

Ramachandran, T. P. 1976. *Dvaita Vedānta*. New Delhi: Arnold-Heinemann.

Raman, K. V. 1975. *Srī Varadarājaswāmi Temple—Kāñchi: A Study of Its History, Art, and Architecture*. New Delhi: Abhinav.

Ramanujadasar, R. Ramaswami. 1984. *Śrīvaiṣṇavam*. Chennai: Alvarkal Amuta Nilaiyam.

Ramanujan, A. K., trans. 1973. *Speaking of Śiva*. Harmondsworth: Penguin.

Ramanujan, A. K. 1989. "Is There an Indian Way of Thinking? An Informal Essay." *Contributions to Indian Sociology (ns)* 23, 1: 41–58.

Ramanujan, A. K. 1991a. "Repetition in the *Mahābhārata*." In Arvind Sharma, ed., *Essays on the Mahābhārata*, 419–43. Leiden: E. J. Brill.

Ramanujan, A. K. 1991b. "Three Hundred *Rāmāyaṇas*: Five Examples and Three Thoughts on Translation." In Paula Richman, ed., *Many Rāmāyaṇas. The Diversity of a Narrative Tradition in South Asia*, 22–49. Berkeley: University of California Press.

Ramanujan, A. K. 1992. "Food for Thought: Toward an Anthology of Food Images." In R. S. Khare, ed., *The Eternal Food: Gastronomic Ideas and Experiences of Hindus and Buddhists*, 121–50. Albany: State University of New York Press.

Ramanujan, A. K., trans. 1993a [1981]. *Hymns for the Drowning: Poems for Viṣṇu by Nammāḻvār*. Harmondsworth: Penguin.

Ramanujan, A. K. 1993b. "On Folk Mythologies and Folk Purāṇas." In Wendy Doniger, ed., *Purāṇa Perennis: Reciprocity and Transformation in Hindu and Jaina Texts*, 101–20, 266–67. Albany: State University of New York Press.

Ramanujan, A. K. and Norman Cutler. 1983. "From Classicism to Bhakti." In Bardwell L. Smith, ed., *Essays on Gupta Culture*, 177–214. Delhi: Motilal Banarsidass.

Rao, K. L. Seshagiri. 1987. "Karma in Hindu Thought–I." In S. S. Rama Rao Pappu, ed., *The Dimensions of Karma*, 23–36. Delhi: Chanakya.

Raychaudhuri, Tapan. 1988. *Europe Reconsidered: Perceptions of the West in Nineteenth Century Bengal*. Delhi: Oxford University Press.

Redfield, Robert and Milton B. Singer. 1954–55. "The Cultural Role of Cities." *Economic Development and Cultural Change* 3, 1: 53–73.

Richman, Paula, ed. 1991. *Many Rāmāyaṇas: The Diversity of a Narrative Tradition in South Asia*. Berkeley: University of California Press.

Ricoeur, Paul. 1985 [1984]. *Time and Narrative* (trans. Kathleen McLaughlin and David Pellauer). Volume 2 of 3. Chicago: University of Chicago Press.

Rinschede, Gisbert. 1999. *Religionsgeographie*. Braunschweig: Westermann.

Risley, Herbert. 1915. *The People of India*. London: W. Thacker.

Rizvi, S. A. A. 1987. *The Wonder That Was India*. Volume 2 of 2: *A Survey of the History and Culture of the Indian Sub-Continent from the Coming of the Muslims to the British Conquest, 1200–1700*. London: Sidgwick & Jackson.

Rocher, Ludo. 1983. "Reflections on One Hundred and Fifty Years of Purāṇa Studies." *Purāṇam* 25, 1: 64–76.

Rocher, Ludo. 1986. *The Purāṇas*. Wiesbaden: Otto Harrassowitz.

Ronan, Colin A., ed. 1978. *The Shorter Science and Civilisation in China: An Abridgement of Joseph Needham's Original Text.* Volume 1 of 5: *Volumes I and II of the Major Series.* Cambridge: Cambridge University Press.

Rossi, Barbara, with contributions by Roy C. Craven, Jr., and Stuart Carey Welch. 1998. *From the Ocean of Painting: India's Popular Paintings, 1598 to the Present.* New York: Oxford University Press.

Rowe, William L. 1968. "The New Cauhāns: A Caste Mobility Movement in North India." In James Silverberg, ed., *Social Mobility in the Caste System in India*, 66–77. The Hague: Mouton.

Ruben, Walter. 1968. *Die Entwicklung von Staat und Recht im alten Indien.* Berlin: Akademie.

Rushdie, Salman. 1990. *Haroun and the Sea of Stories.* New York: Viking Penguin.

Sahai, Sachchidanand. 1976. *The Rāmāyana in Laos: A Study in the Gvāy Dvóraḥbī.* Delhi: B. R. Publishing.

Said, Edward. 1978. *Orientalism.* New York: Penguin.

Salomon, Richard. 1979. "*Tīrtha-pratyāmnāyāḥ*: Ranking of Hindu Pilgrimage Sites in Classical Sanskrit Texts." *Zeitschrift der Deutschen Morgenländischen Gesellschaft* 129, 1: 102–28.

Salomon, Richard, ed. and trans. 1985. *The Bridge to the Three Holy Cities: The Sāmānya-Praghaṭṭaka of Nārāyaṇa Bhaṭṭa's Tristhalīsetu.* Delhi: Motilal Banarsidass.

Sanderson, Alexis. 1985. "Purity and Power Among the Brahmanas of Kashmir." In Michael Carrithers, Steven Collins, and Steven Lukas, eds., *The Category of the Person: Anthropology, Philosophy, History*, 190–216. Cambridge: Cambridge University Press.

Sanderson, Alexis. 1986. "Maṇḍala and Āgamic Identity in the Trika of Kashmir." In André Padoux, ed., *Mantras et diagrammes rituels dans l'hindouisme*, 169–207. Paris: Centre National de la Recherche Scientifique.

Sanderson, Alexis. 1988. "Śaivism and the Tantric Traditions." In Stewart Sutherland, Leslie Houlden, Peter Clarke, and Friedhelm Hardy, eds., *The World's Religions*, 660–704. London: Routledge.

Sanderson, Alexis. 1992. "The Doctrine of the Mālinīvijayottaratantra." In Teun Goudriaan, ed., *Ritual and Speculation in Early Tantrism: Studies in Honour of André Padoux*, 283–312. Albany: State University of New York Press.

Sanderson, Alexis. 1995. "Meaning in Tantric Ritual." In Anne-Marie Blondeau and Kristofer Schipper, eds., *Essais sur le rituel III*, 15–95. Louvain: Peeters.

Sanderson, Alexis. n.d. "Śaivism: Its Development and Impact." Unpublished Typescript.

Saraswati, Baidyanath. 1977. *Brahmanic Ritual Traditions in the Crucible of Time.* Simla: Indian Institute of Advanced Study.

Sarkar, H. B. 1983. "The Ramayana in South-East Asia: A General Survey." In K. R. Srinivasa Iyengar, ed., *Asian Variations in Ramayana*, 206–20. New Delhi: Sahitya Akademi.

Sarkar, Jadunath, annot. and trans. 1901. *The India of Aurangzib (Topography, Statistics, and Roads) Compared with the India of Akbar; with Extracts from the Khulasatu-t-tawarikh and the Chahar Gulshan.* Calcutta: Bose Brothers.

Sastri, Kuppuswami S. 1932. *A Primer of Indian Logic: According to Annambhaṭṭa's Tarkasaṁgraha.* Madras: Kuppuswami Sastri Research Institute.

Savarkar, Vinayak Damodar. 1964 [1938]. "Essentials of Hindutva." In Vinayak Damodar Savarkar, *Samagra Savarkar Wangmaya: Writings of Swatantrya Veer V. D. Savarkar.* Volume 6 of 6: *Hindu Rashtra Darshan*, 1–91. Poona: Maharashtra Prantik Hindusabha.

Sawai, Yoshitsugu. 1986. "Śaṅkara's Theory of Saṃnyāsa." *Journal of Indian Philosophy* 14, 4: 371–87.

Sax, William. 1991a. "Ritual and Performance in the Pāṇḍavalīlā of Garhwal." In Arvind Sharma, ed., *Essays on the Mahābhārata*, 274–95. Leiden: E. J. Brill.

Sax, William S. 1991b. *Mountain Goddess: Gender and Politics in a Himalayan Pilgrimage.* New York: Oxford University Press.

Scharfe, Hartmut. 1979. "Kauṭalya on Conflicts within the Ruling Class." *Indologica Taurinensia: Official Organ of the International Association of Sanskrit Studies* 7: 387–91.

Scharfe, Hartmut. 1980. "Gedanken zum *mātsya-nyāya*." *Studien zur Indologie und Iranistik* 5–6: 195–98.

Schechner, Richard. 1985. *Between Theater and Anthropology*. Philadelphia: University of Pennsylvania Press.

Schmidt, Hanns-Peter. 1968. "The Origin of *Ahiṃsā*." In *Mélanges d'indianisme à la mémoire de Louis Renou*, 625–55. Paris: Boccard.

Schmidt, Hanns-Peter. 1987. *Some Women's Rites and Rights in the Veda*. Poona: Bhandarkar Oriental Research Institute.

Schmidt, Hanns-Peter. 1997. "Ahiṃsā and Rebirth." In Michael Witzel, ed., *Inside the Texts, Beyond the Texts: New Approaches to the Study of the Vedas*, 207–34. Cambridge: Harvard University, Department of Sanskrit and Indian Studies.

Schomer, Karine and W. H. McLeod, eds. 1987. *The Sants: Studies in a Devotional Tradition of India*. Berkeley: University of California Press.

Schreiner, Peter, ed. 1997. *Nārāyaṇīya-Studien*. Wiesbaden: Otto Harrassowitz.

Schwartzberg, Joseph E., ed. 1978. *A Historical Atlas of South Asia*. Chicago: University of Chicago Press.

Selwyn, Tom. 1981. "Adharma." *Contributions to Indian Sociology (ns)* 15, 1–2: 381–401.

Sen, Amiya P. 1998. "Bhakti Paradigms, Syncretism, and Social Restructuring in *Kaliyuga*: A Reappraisal of Some Aspects of Bengali Religious Culture." *Studies in History (ns)* 14, 1: 89–126.

Sen, Sukumar. 1983. *The Great Goddesses in Indic Tradition*. Calcutta: Papyrus.

Seshadrisarma, Janamanci. 1931. *Śrī Rāmāvatāra Tattvamu*. Volume 1 of 11. Madras: V. Ramaswamy Sastrulu.

Shah, A. M. and I. P. Desai. 1988. *Division and Hierarchy: An Overview of Caste in Gujarat*. Delhi: Hindustan Publishing.

Shah, A. M. and R. G. Shroff. 1959. "The Vahīvancā Bāroṭs of Gujarat: A Caste of Genealogists and Mythographers." In Milton Singer, ed., *Traditional India: Structure and Change*, 40–70. Philadelphia: American Folklore Society.

Sharma, Arvind. 1982. *The Puruṣārthas: A Study in Hindu Axiology*. East Lansing: Michigan State University, Asian Studies Center.

Sharma, Arvind, ed. 2003. *The Study of Hinduism*. Columbia: University of South Carolina Press.

Sharma, Har Dutt. 1939. *Contributions to the History of Brāhmaṇical Asceticism (Saṃnyāsa)*. Poona: Oriental Book.

Sharma, Krishna. 1987. *Bhakti and the Bhakti Movement: A New Perspective. A Study in the History of Ideas*. New Delhi: Munshiram Manoharlal.

Sharma, Ursula. 1973. "Theodicy and the Doctrine of Karma." *Man: The Journal of the Royal Anthropological Institute (ns)* 8, 3: 347–64.

Shāstrī, Haraprasād. 1910. "Causes of the Dismemberment of the Maurya Empire." *Journal and Proceedings of the Asiatic Society of Bengal (ns)* 6: 259–62.

Shulman, David Dean. 1980. *Tamil Temple Myths: Sacrifice and Divine Marriage in the South Indian Śaiva Tradition*. Princeton: Princeton University Press.

Shulman, David Dean. 1985. *The King and the Clown in South Indian Myth and Poetry*. Princeton: Princeton University Press.

Shulman, David Dean. 1992. "Devana and Daiva." In A. W. van den Hoek, D. H. A. Kloff, and M. S. Oort, eds., *Ritual, State, and History in South Asia: Essays in Honour of J. C. Heesterman*, 350–65. Leiden: E. J. Brill.

Shulman, David Dean. 1993. "Remaking a Purāṇa: The Rescue of Gajendra in Potana's Telugu *Mahābhāgavatamu*." In Wendy Doniger, ed., *Purāṇa Perennis: Reciprocity and Transformation in Hindu and Jaina Texts*, 121–57, 267–73. Albany: State University of New York Press.

Siegel, Lee. 1983. *Fires of Love—Waters of Peace: Passion and Renunciation in Indian Culture.* Honolulu: University of Hawaii Press.

Silburn, Lilian, trans. 1975. *Hymnes aux Kālī: la roue des énergies divines.* Paris: Institut de Civilisation Indienne.

Silverberg, James, ed. 1968. *Social Mobility in the Caste System in India.* The Hague: Mouton.

Simson, Georg von. 1984. "The Mythic Background of the Mahābhārata." *Indologica Taurinensia: Official Organ of the International Association of Sanskrit Studies* 12: 191–223.

Simson, Georg von. 1994. "Die zeitmythische Struktur des Mahābhārata." In Reinhard Sternemann, ed., *Bopp-Symposium 1992 der Humboldt-Universität zu Berlin: Akten der Konferenz vom 24.3–26.3.1992 aus Anlaß von Franz Bopps zweihundertjährigem Geburtstag am 14.9.1991,* 230–47. Heidelberg: C. Winter.

Singh, K. S. and Birendranath Datta, eds. 1993. *Rama-Katha in Tribal and Folk Traditions of India.* Calcutta: Seagull.

Singh, K. Suresh. 1975. *The Indian Famine 1967: A Study in Crisis and Change.* New Delhi: People's Publishing.

Singh, Khushwant. 1966. *A History of the Sikhs.* Volume 2 of 2: *1839–1964.* Princeton: Princeton University Press.

Singh, Rana P. B. 1987. "The Pilgrimage Maṇḍala of Vārāṇasī (Kāśī): A Study in Sacred Geography." *The National Geographical Journal of India* 33, 4: 493–524.

Singh, Shukdev, ed. 1972. *Bījak.* Allahabad: Nilabh Prakashan.

Sircar, D. C. 1967a. "Śakti Cult in Western India." In D. C. Sircar, ed., *The Śakti Cult and Tārā,* 87–91. Calcutta: University of Calcutta.

Sircar, D. C., ed. 1967b. *The Śakti Cult and Tārā.* Calcutta: University of Calcutta.

Sircar, D. C. 1969 [1966]. *Ancient Malwa and the Vikramāditya Tradition.* New Delhi: Munshiram Manoharlal.

Sircar, D. C., ed. 1973 [1948]. *The Śākta Pīṭhas.* Delhi: Motilal Banarsidass.

Smith, Brian K. 1989. *Reflections on Resemblance, Ritual, and Religion.* New York: Oxford University Press.

Smith, Brian K. 1994. *Classifying the Universe: The Ancient Indian Varṇa System and the Origins of Caste.* New York: Oxford University Press.

Smith, David. 1996. *The Dance of Śiva: Religion, Art, and Poetry in South India.* Cambridge: Cambridge University Press.

Smith, David. 2003. *Hinduism and Modernity.* Oxford: Blackwell.

Smith, Frederick M. 1987. *The Vedic Sacrifice in Transition: A Translation and Study of the Trikāṇḍamaṇḍana of Bhāskara Miśra.* Poona: Bhandarkar Oriental Research Institute.

Smith, Frederick M. 1991. "Indra's Curse, Varuṇa's Noose, and the Suppression of the Woman in the Vedic *Śrauta* Ritual." In Julia Leslie, ed., *Roles and Rituals for Hindu Women,* 17–45. London: Pinter.

Smith, Frederick M. 2000. "Indra Goes West: Report on a Vedic Soma Sacrifice in London in July 1996." *History of Religions* 40, 3: 247–67.

Smith, Frederick M. 2001. "The Recent History of Vedic Ritual in Maharashtra." In Klaus Karttunen and Petteri Koskikallio, eds., *Vidyārṇavavandanam: Essays in Honour of Asko Parpola,* 443–63. Helsinki: Finnish Oriental Society.

Smith, H. Daniel. 1995. "Impact of 'God Posters' on Hindus and their Devotional Traditions." In Lawrence A. Babb and Susan S. Wadley, eds., *Media and the Transformation of Religion in South Asia,* 24–50. Philadelphia: University of Pennsylvania Press.

Smith, John D. 1999. "Winged Words Revisited: Diction and Meaning in Indian Epic." *Bulletin of the School of Oriental and African Studies* 62, 2: 267–305.

Smith, John D. 1999–2001. *Electronic Text of the Mahābhārata.* Cambridge: http://bombay.oriental.cam.ac.uk/john/mahabharata/statement.html.

Smith, Mary Carroll. 1992. *The Warrior Code of India's Sacred Song*. New York: Garland.
Smith, Wilfred Cantwell. 1962. *The Meaning and End of Religion: A New Approach to the Religious Traditions of Mankind*. New York: Macmillan.
Smith, W. L. 1988. *Rāmāyaṇa Traditions in Eastern India: Assam, Bengal, Orissa*. Stockholm: University of Stockholm, Department of Indology.
Sopher, David E., ed. 1980. *An Exploration of India: Geographical Perspectives on Society and Culture*. Ithaca: Cornell University Press.
Sprockhoff, Joachim Friedrich. 1976. *Saṃnyāsa: Quellenstudien zur Askese im Hinduismus*. Volume 1 of 2: *Untersuchungen über die Saṃnyāsa-Upaniṣads*. Wiesbaden: Franz Steiner.
Srinivas, M. N. 1955. "The Social System of a Mysore Village." In McKim Marriott, ed., *Village India: Studies in the Little Community*, 1–35. Chicago: University of Chicago Press.
Srinivas, M. N. 1959. "The Dominant Caste in Rampura." *American Anthropologist* 61, 1: 1–16.
Srinivas, M. N. 1962. "A Note on Sanskritzation and Westernization." In M. N. Srinivas, *Caste in Modern India and Other Essays*, 42–62. Bombay: Asia Publishing.
Srinivas, M. N. 1965 [1952]. *Religion and Society among the Coorgs of South India*. Oxford: Clarendon.
Srinivas, M. N. 1976. *The Remembered Village*. Berkeley: University of California Press.
Srinivas, Smriti. 2001. *Landscapes of Urban Memory: The Sacred and the Civic in India's High-Tech City*. Minneapolis: University of Minnesota Press.
Staal, Frits. 1980. "Ritual Syntax." In M. Nagatomi, B. K. Matilal, J. M. Masson, and E. C. Dimock, Jr., eds., *Sanskrit and Indian Studies: Essays in Honour of Daniel H. H. Ingalls*, 119–42. Boston: D. Reidel.
Stablein, Marilyn. 1978. "Textual and Contextual Patterns of Tibetan Buddhist Pilgrimage in India." *The Tibet Society Bulletin* 12: 7–38.
Stanley, John M. 1977. "Special Time, Special Power: The Fluidity of Power in a Popular Hindu Festival." *The Journal of Asian Studies* 37, 1: 27–43.
Stanner, W. E. H. 1963 [1959–63]. *On Aboriginal Religion*. Sydney: University of Sydney.
Stcherbatsky, Th. 1978 [1968–69]. "History of Materialism in India" (trans. H. C. Gupta). In Debiprasad Chattopadhyaya, ed., *Studies in the History of Indian Philosophy II*, 32–41. Calcutta: K. P. Bagchi.
Stein, Burton. 1961. "The State, the Temple, and Agricultural Development: A Study in Medieval South India." *The Economic Weekly: A Journal of Current Economic and Political Affairs* 13, 4–6: 179–87.
Stein, Burton. 1980. *Peasant, State, and Society in Medieval South India*. Delhi: Oxford University Press.
Stevenson, H. N. C. 1954. "Status Evaluation in the Hindu Caste System." *The Journal of the Royal Anthropological Institute of Great Britain and Ireland* 84, 1–2: 45–65.
Stietencron, Heinrich von. 1986 [1985]. "Hinduism and Christianity." In Hans Küng, Josef van Ess, Heinrich von Stietencron, and Heinz Bechert, *Christianity and the World Religions: Paths of Dialogue with Islam, Hinduism, and Buddhism* (trans. Peter Heinegg), 133–286. Garden City: Doubleday.
Stietencron, Heinrich von. 1989. "Hinduism: On the Proper Use of a Deceptive Term." In Günther D. Sontheimer and Hermann Kulke, eds., *Hinduism Reconsidered*, 11–27. New Delhi: Manohar.
Stietencron, Heinrich von, K.-P. Gietz, A. Malinar, A. Kollmann, P. Schreiner, and M. Brockington, eds. 1992. *Epic and Purāṇic Bibliography (up to 1985): Annotated and with Indices*. 2 volumes. Wiesbaden: Otto Harrassowitz.
Stork, Hélène. 1991. "Mothering Rituals in Tamilnadu: Some Magico-Religious Beliefs." In Julia Leslie, ed., *Roles and Rituals for Hindu Women*, 89–105. London: Pinter.
Sukthankar, V. S. 1933. "Prolegomena." In V. S. Sukthankar, S. K. Belvalkar, and P. L. Vaidya, general editors, and others, *The Mahābhārata for the First Time Critically Edited*. Volume 1 of 19: *The Adiparvan*, i–cx. Poona: Bhandarkar Oriental Research Institute.
Sukthankar, V. S. 1936. "Epic Studies. VI: The Bhṛgus and the Bhārata. A Text-Historical Study." *Annals of the Bhandarkar Oriental Research Institute* 18: 1–76.

Sukthankar, V. S., S. K. Belvalkar, and P. L. Vaidya, general editors, and others, eds. 1933–66. *The Mahābhārata for the First Time Critically Edited.* 19 volumes. Poona: Bhandarkar Oriental Research Institute.

Sutherland, Sally J. M. 1989. "Sītā and Draupadī: Aggressive Behavior and Female Role-Models in the Sanskrit Epics." *Journal of the American Oriental Society* 109, 1: 63–67.

Sutherland, Sally J. M. 1992. "Seduction, Counter Seduction, and Sexual Role Models: Bedroom Politics and the Indian Epics." *Journal of Indian Philosophy* 20, 2: 243–51.

Sutton, Nicholas. 2002. *Religious Doctrines in the Mahābhārata.* Delhi: Motilal Banarsidass.

Sutton, Nick. 1997. "Aśoka and Yudhiṣṭhira: A Historical Setting for the Ideological Tensions of the *Mahābhārata.*" *Religion* 27, 4: 333–41.

Sweeney, P. L. Amin. 1972. *The Rāmāyaṇa and the Malaysian Shadow-Play.* Kuala Lumpur: Pener bit Universiti Kebangsaan Malaysia.

Sweeney, Amin. 1980. "The Malaysian Rāmāyaṇa in Performance." In V. Raghavan, ed., *The Ramayana Tradition in Asia*, 122–37. New Delhi: Sahitya Akademi.

Sweetman, B. W. H. 2000. Mapping Hinduism: "Hinduism" and the Study of Indian Religions, 1630–1776. PhD dissertation. Cambridge: University of Cambridge Library.

Tagare, G. V., trans. 1993 [1976]. *The Bhāgavata Purāṇa.* Part 2 of 5: [*Skandhas 4–6*]. Delhi: Motilal Banarsidass.

Tagore, Rabindranath. 1913. *Sādhanā: The Realisation of Life.* New York: Macmilllan.

Tagore, Rabindranath. 1931. *The Religion of Man.* New York: Macmillan.

Tambiah, S. J. 1973. "From Varna to Caste through Mixed Unions." In Jack Goody, ed., *The Character of Kinship*, 191–229. Cambridge: Cambridge University Press.

Tambiah, S. J. 1976. *World Conqueror and World Renouncer: A Study of Buddhism and Polity in Thailand against a Historical Background.* Cambridge: Cambridge University Press.

Tambs-Lyche, Harald. 1997. *Power, Profit, and Poetry: Traditional Society in Kathiawar, Western India.* New Delhi: Manohar.

Tawney, C. H., trans. 1968 [1880–84]. *The Ocean of Story Being C. H. Tawney's Translation of Somadeva's Kathā Sarit Sāgara (or Ocean of Streams of Story)* (ed. N. M. Penzer). 10 volumes. Delhi: Motilal Banarsidass.

Thapar, Romila. 1973 [1961]. *Aśoka and the Decline of the Mauryas.* Oxford: Oxford University Press.

Thapar, Romila. 1978. *Ancient Indian Social History: Some Interpretations.* New Delhi: Orient Longman.

Thapar, Romila. 1981. "The Householder and the Renouncer in the Brahmanical and Buddhist Traditions." *Contributions to Indian Sociology (ns)* 15, 1–2: 273–98.

Thapar, Romila. 1984. *From Lineage to State: Social Formation in the Mid-first-Millennium BC in the Ganga Valley.* Delhi: Oxford University Press.

Thapar, Romila. 1985. "Syndicated Moksha?" *Seminar* 313: 14–22.

Thapar, Romila. 1991. "Genealogical Patterns as Perceptions of the Past." *Studies in History* 7, 1: 1–36.

Thapar, Romila. 1992. *Interpreting Early India.* Delhi: Oxford University Press.

Thapar, Romila. 1996. *Time as a Metaphor of History: Early India.* Delhi: Oxford University Press.

Thapar, Romila. 1997. "Linear Time in Historical Texts of Early India." In Dick van der Meij, ed., *India and Beyond: Aspects of Literature, Meaning, Ritual, and Thought. Essays in Honour of Frits Staal*, 562–73. London: Kegan Paul.

Thiel-Horstmann, Monika. 1983. *Crossing the Ocean of Existence: Braj Bhāṣā Religious Poetry from Rajasthan. A Reader.* Wiesbaden: Otto Harrassowitz.

Thiel-Horstmann, Monika, ed. 1991. *Rāmāyaṇa and Rāmāyaṇas.* Wiesbaden: Otto Harrassowitz.

Thiruvengadathan, A. 1985. "The Cunaiyadal—Brahmanubhava Equation." In *Sri Andal: Her Contribution to Literature, Philosophy, Religion, and Art*, 88–99. Madras: Sri Ramanuja Vedānta Centre.

Thite, G. U. 1996. "On the Fictitious Ritual in the Veda." *Annals of the Bhandarkar Oriental Research Institute* 77: 253–57.

Thomas, Edward J. 1927. *The Life of Buddha as Legend and History*. London: Kegan Paul, Trench, Trubner.

Thomas, Lynn. 1994. "The Identity of the Destroyer in the Mahābhārata." *Numen: International Review for the History of Religions* 41, 3: 255–72.

Thomas, Lynn. 1996. "Paraśurāma and Time." In Julia Leslie, ed., *Myth and Mythmaking*, 63–86. London: Curzon.

Tilak, Bal Gangadhar. 1935–36 [1915]. *Śrīmad Bhagavadgītā Rahasya or Karma-Yoga-Śāstra, including an External Examination of the Gītā, the Original Sanskrit Stanzas, their English Translation, Commentaries on the Stanzas, and a Comparison of Eastern with Western Doctrines, etc.* (trans. Bhalchandra Sitaram Sukthankar). 2 volumes. Poona: Tilak Brothers.

Tokunaga, Muneo. 1996. *Machine-Readable Text of the Mahaabhaarata: Based on the Poona Critical Edition*. Kyoto: ftp://ccftp.kyoto-su.ac.jp/pub/doc/sanskrit/mahabharata.

Toomey, Paul M. 1986. "Food from the Mouth of Krishna: Socio-Religious Aspects of Sacred Food in Two Krishnaite Sects." In R. S. Khare and M. S. A. Rao, eds., *Food, Society, and Culture: Aspects in South Asian Food Systems*, 55–83. Durham: Carolina Academic Press.

Tull, Herman W. 1989. *The Vedic Origins of Karma: Cosmos as Man in Ancient Indian Myth and Ritual*. Albany: State University of New York Press.

Tully, Mark. 1991. *No Full Stops in India*. London: Viking Penguin.

Turner, Victor and Edith Turner. 1978. *Image and Pilgrimage in Christian Culture: Anthropological Perspectives*. New York: Columbia University Press.

Uberoi, J. P. S. 1996. *Religion, Civil Society, and the State: A Study of Sikhism*. Delhi: Oxford University Press.

van der Veer, Peter. 1988. *Gods on Earth: The Management of Religious Experience and Identity in a North Indian Pilgrimage Centre*. London: Athlone.

van der Veer, Peter. 1994. *Religious Nationalism: Hindus and Muslims in India*. Berkeley: University of California Press.

Varenne, Jean. 1982. *Cosmogonies védiques*. Milan: Archè.

Vassilkov, Yaroslav. 1995. "The Mahābhārata's Typological Definition Reconsidered." *Indo-Iranian Journal* 38, 3: 249–56.

Vassilkov, Yaroslav. 1999. "*Kālavāda* (the Doctrine of Cyclical Time) in the Mahābhārata and the Concept of Heroic Didactics." In Mary Brockington and Peter Schreiner, eds., *Composing a Tradition: Concepts, Techniques, and Relationships*, 17–33. Zagrab: Croatian Academy of Sciences and Arts.

Vasudev, Shefalee. 2002. "Pilgrim's Progress." *India Today* 22 April: 46–48.

Vaudeville, Charlotte. 1974. *Kabīr*. Oxford: Clarendon.

Vaudeville, Charlotte. 1986 [1965]. *Bārahmāsā in Indian Literatures: Songs of the Twelve Months in Indo-Aryan Literatures*. Delhi: Motilal Banarsidass.

Venkataraman, B. 1976. *Temple Art Under the Chola Queens*. Faridabad: Thomson.

Vidyarthi, L. P. 1961. *The Sacred Complex in Hindu Gaya*. Bombay: Asia Publishing.

Vincentnathan, Lynn. 1993. "Untouchable Concepts of Person and Society." *Contributions to Indian Sociology (ns)* 27, 1: 53–82.

Viraraghavacharya, T. K. T. 1997 [1953]. *History of Tirupati: The Thiruvengadam Temples*. Volume 3 of 3. Tirupati: Tirumala Tirupati Devasthanams.

Wadley, Susan Snow. 1975. *Shakti: Power in the Conceptual Structure of Karimpur Religion*. Chicago: University of Chicago, Department of Anthropology.

Wadley, Susan S. 1980. "Hindu Women's Family and Household Rites in a North Indian Village." In Nancy Auer Falk and Rita M. Gross, eds., *Unspoken Worlds: Women's Religious Lives in Non-Western Cultures*, 94–109. San Francisco: Harper & Row.

Wadley, Susan S. 1983. "The Rains of Estrangement: Understanding the Hindu Yearly Cycle." *Contributions to Indian Sociology (ns)* 17, 1: 51–85.

Wadley, Susan S. 1994. *Struggling with Destiny in Karimpur, 1925–1984*. Berkeley: University of California Press.

Wadley, Susan S. 2000. "From Sacred Cow Dung to Cow 'Shit': Globalization and Local Religious Practices in Rural North India." *Journal of the Japanese Association for South Asian Studies* 12: 1–28.

Wadley, Susan S. and Bruce W. Derr. 1989. "Eating Sins in Karimpur." *Contributions to Indian Sociology (ns)* 23, 1: 131–48.

Wagle, N. K. 1989. "Hindu-Muslim Interactions in Medieval Maharasthra." In Günther D. Sontheimer and Hermann Kulke, eds., *Hinduism Reconsidered*, 51–66. New Delhi: Manohar.

Wasson, R. Gordon, with the assistance of Wendy Doniger O'Flaherty. 1968. *Soma: Divine Mushroom of Immortality*. New York: Harcourt Brace Jovanovich.

Weber, Albrecht. 1872 [1870]. "On the Râmâyaṇa" (trans. D. C. Boyd). *The Indian Antiquary: A Journal of Oriental Research* 1: 120–27, 172–82, 239–53.

Weber, Max. 1946 [1904]. "Class, Status, Party." In H. H. Gerth and C. Wright Mills, eds. and trans., *From Max Weber: Essays in Sociology*, 180–95. New York: Oxford University Press.

Weber, Max. 1958 [1921]. *The Religion of India* (trans. Hans H. Gerth and Don Martindale). Glencoe: Free Press.

Wheeler, J. Talboys. 1867–81. *The History of India from the Earliest Ages*. 3 volumes in 4 books. London: N. Trübner.

White, David Gordon. 1992. "You Are What You Eat: The Anomalous Status of Dog-Cookers in Hindu Mythology." In R. S. Khare, ed., *The Eternal Food: Gastronomic Ideas and Experiences of Hindus and Buddhists*, 53–93. Albany: State University of New York Press.

White, David Gordon. 1996. *The Alchemical Body: Siddha Traditions in Medieval India*. Chicago: University of Chicago Press.

White, David Gordon. 1998. "Transformations in the Art of Love: Kāmakalā Practices in Hindu Tantric and Kaula Traditions." *History of Religions* 38, 2: 172–98.

Whitehead, Henry. 1921. *The Village Gods of South India*. London: Oxford University Press.

Whitney, William Dwight. 1873. *Oriental and Linguistic Studies*. Volume 1 of 2: *The Veda; the Avesta; the Science of Language*. New York: Scribner, Armstrong.

Widengren, Geo. 1965 [1961]. *Mani and Manichaeism* (trans. Charles Kessler). London: Weidenfeld and Nicolson.

Wilhelm, Friedrich. 1978. "The Concept of Dharma in *Artha* and *Kāma* Literature." In Wendy Doniger O'Flaherty and J. Duncan M. Derrett, eds., *The Concept of Duty in South Asia*, 66–79. New Delhi: Vikas.

Wilson, Horace Hayman. 1839. "Essays on the Puránas." *The Journal of the Royal Asiatic Society of Great Britain and Ireland (ns)* 5: 61–72.

Wilson, Horace Hayman. 1846 [1828, 1932]. *Sketch of the Religious Sects of the Hindus*. Calcutta: Bishop's College Press.

Wilson, Horace Hayman., trans. 1961 [1840]. *The Vishńu Puráńa: A System of Hindu Mythology and Tradition*. Calcutta: Punthi Pustak.

Winternitz, Maurice. 1963–83 [1904–20]. *A History of Indian Literature* (trans. V. Srinivasa Sarma [volumes 1 and 2]; Subhadra Jha [volume 3]). 3 volumes in 4 books. Delhi: Motilal Banarsidass.

Wiser, William Henricks. 1958 [1936]. *The Hindu Jajmani System: A Socio-economic System Interrelating Members of a Hindu Village Community in Services*. Lucknow: Lucknow Publishing.

Witzel, Michael. 1984. "Sur le chemin du ciel." *Bulletin des Études Indiennes* 2: 213–79.

Witzel, Michael. 1986. "JB Pulpūlanī: The Structure of a Brāhmaṇa Tale." In *Dr. B. R. Sharma Felicitation Volume*, 189–216. Tirupati: Kendriya Sanskrit Vidyapeetha.

Witzel, Michael. 1987a. "On the Origin of the Literary Device of the 'Frame Story' in Old Indian Literature." In Harry Falk, ed., *Hinduismus und Buddhismus: Festschrift für Ulrich Schneider*, 380–414. Freiburg: Hedwig Falk.

Witzel, Michael. 1987b. "On the Localisation of Vedic Texts and Schools (Materials on Vedic Śakhas, 7)." In Gilbert Pollet, ed., *India and the Ancient World: History, Trade, and Culture Before AD 650*, 173–213. Leuven: Departement Oriëntalistiek.

Witzel, Michael. 1989. "Tracing the Vedic Dialects." In Colette Caillat, ed., *Dialectes dans les littératures indo-aryennes*, 97–265. Paris: Boccard.

Witzel, Michael. 1995. "Ṛgvedic History: Poets, Chieftains, and Polities." In George Erdosy, ed., *The Indo-Aryans of Ancient South Asia: Language, Material Culture, and Ethnicity,* 307–52. Berlin: Walter de Gruyter.

Wolpert, Stanley. 1993 [1977]. *A New History of India*. New York: Oxford University Press.

Woodroffe, John. 1963 [1913]. *Introduction to Tantra Śāstra*. Madras: Ganesh.

Woodroffe, John. 1969 [1918]. *Śakti and Śākta: Essays and Addresses*. Madras: Ganesh.

Woodroffe, John. 1974 [1921]. *The World as Power*. Madras: Ganesh.

Younger, Paul. 1995. *The Home of Dancing Śivaṉ: The Traditions of the Hindu Temple in Citamapram*. New York: Oxford University Press.

Zelliot, Eleanor. 1981. "Chokhamela and Eknath: Two *Bhakti* Modes of Legitimacy for Modern Change." In Jayant Lele, ed., *Tradition and Modernity in Bhakti Movements,* 136–56. Leiden: E. J. Brill.

Zelliot, Eleanor. 1995. "Chokhāmeḷā: Piety and Protest." In David N. Lorenzen, ed., *Bhakti Religion in North India: Community Identity and Political Action*, 212–20. Albany: State University of New York Press.

Zelliot, Eleanor and Maxine Berntsen, eds. 1988. *The Experience of Hinduism: Essays on Religion in Maharashtra.* Albany: State University of New York Press.

Zimmermann, Francis. 1987 [1982]. *The Jungle and the Aroma of Meats: An Ecological Theme in Hindu Medicine*. Berkeley: University of California Press.

Zvelebil, Kamil V. 1973. *The Poets of the Powers.* London: Rider.

Zvelebil, Kamil V. 1975 [1974]. *Tamil Literature*. Leiden: E. J. Brill.

INDEX

Abbott, J. E. 198, 410
Abhidharmakośa (of Vasubandhu) 263
Abhinavagupta of Kashmir Śaivism 121, 129, 135–36, 138, 536, 549
ācāra (rules of conduct) 223
Ācāryavaipavam 170, 183
Achaya, K. T. 408, 411, 415, 423–24
action: *karma*, separating from "knowledge" (*jñāna*) 388; as *kriyā* 136
Ādhyātmarāmāyaṇa 90
Adhyayana festival 472–75
Ādi Granth 204
Ādiparāśakti, temple of 450
Adriaensen, R. 112, 113, 114
Advaita Vedānta school 22–23, 144, 304, 537, 539; perception in 538; by Śaṃkara 241, 547; view of time 554
"advantage-disadvantage" (*artha-anartha*) in social variables 362
aesthetic theory of *rasa* (flavor) 280
Āgamas 288, 470; dedicated to Śiva, Śakti Devī, and Viṣṇu 470
Agastya 63
Aghoraśiva 127
Agni 216; as fire god 42; as guardian of *dharmas* 216
agnicayana 273
agnihotra (daily fire sacrifice) 41, 220
Agni Purāṇa 107–8; *tīrthas* in 485
Agnivarcas Bhāradvāja 98
Agrawala, V. 143
ahaṃkāra (egoism) 544
āhavanīya fire 40
ahiṃsā ideal of "harmlessness" 54, 60; doctrine of noninjury 550; as pivotal principle of *dharma* 245
āhitāgni (household keeper of the fire) 40
air as component of *varṇa* 365–66
Aitareya Āraṇyaka 509–10
Aitareya Brāhmaṇa 272, 316, 330, 489
Aitareya Upaniṣad 39, 46
aitihāsika (legendary school) 44
Aiyangar, K. V. R. 486
Ājīvikism 540
Akālī Sikhs 499
Akanāṉūru 279
Akbar 499
Akkā Mahādevī 143, 280
Aklujkar, V. 86
Akṛtavraṇa Kāśyapa 98
"*akṣara*" as syllable 511
Aḻakiyamaṇavāḷa Perumāḷ 172
Alā'uddīn Khaljī 500
ālaya see temples
Alexander 576
al-Hind 10
Allāh 478
Allāmī, Abū al-Faẓl 496
Allen, C. 424
Alley, K. D. 476
all-India goddess network 481
All-India Kashiraj Trust 111–12
Alter, R. 580
Āḻvārs of Tamilnadu 105, 195–97, 199, 279, 457, 461; poetry of 170; poets writing in Tamil 167; Vaiṣṇava saints as Tamil poets 524, 526; among the *varṇadharmīs* 196
Amarasiṃha 99
Amaruśataka 266
Ambedkar, B. R. 378, 380
America: Hindu temples, building plans for 477; Śrīvaiṣṇavism 174
Anand, I. M. S. 483
Ānandamaṭh (by Bankimchandra Chatterji) 18
Ānandarāmāyaṇa 90
Anaṅgaraṅga (of Kalyāṇamalla) 265
ancestors (*pitṛ*) 338

sacrifice: act at center of Vedic tradition 311; autonomy of *yajamāna* 391; communal performance of 321; contemporary "Hinduization" of 42; denigration of 320; format as an act of social cooperation, traditional 320; fourfold division of labor of the 39; internalization of 46; performance, details of 40–45; ritual and *dharma* 219; *yajña* as action that is not binding 278
sacrificer: death and rebirth in sacrifice 317; fate after death 318
sacrificial offerings (*lājāhoma*) 350
sacrificial order (*adhiyajña*) 215
Sadānanda 294
Sadāśiva 126
Ṣaḍdarśanasamuccaya (of Haribhadrasūri) 539
sādhanabhakti 280
*sādhana*s (spiritual practice) 142; of different philosophical schools 293
sādhāraṇadharma (ordinary *dharma*) 238; dichotomy within 244; specific norms of *varṇāśramadharma* and common norms of 244
Sadyojyoti 127, 137
Sagar, Ramanand 92, 437
saguṇa bhakti 185, 195
saguṇa and *nirguṇa* visions of god 198
Sahadeva 57
Sahajiyā form of Vaiṣṇavism 180, 280
Said, E. 14
Saiddhāntikas 123
Śaiva Purāṇa 299
Śaiva Siddhānta 27, 127–28, 290, 297, 299–300; Āgama in 125; ascetics in 126; church of 139; emotional devotionalism (*bhakti*) 127; initiations 127; philosophy of 293; ritual of 128; southern 127, 132–35; Tantras 135; time in 571–72; the *Tirumuṟai* 134; traditions of the right (*dakṣina*) 126
Śaiva Tantrism 126, 281
Śaiva traditions 119, 123; esoteric 121; formation of 122; *guru* lineage 121; in Kerala 119; nondualistic 139
Śaivism 123, 129, 140, 296, 304, 416; community of South India 451; cults of possession and exorcism 132; early and Purāṇic 122; of Kashmir, monistic 137; non-Purāṇic 123–25; non-Saiddhāntika 126, 128–30; popular 130–32; schools 299–300, 548, 549; Tantras 125–27; temple ritual 135–37; temples in the United States 484; theology 137–38; *tīrtha*s 482; tradition 120–22
Śaivite Nāyanārs *see* Nāyanārs
Sajjana Toṣaṇī 180
Śaka era 576
Śākta systems 3, 119, 140, 295, 300; antecedents 145–47; definition 140–42; *dīkṣā* (initiation) 294; doctrines 290; general concepts 143–45; goddess and experience 159–61; idea of *māyā* 144; sacred geography 156–58; *sādhana* 294; scholarship 142–43; texts 120, 141, 143; theology, thrust of 145; traditions, scholarship 142–43; *see also* Śāktism
Śākta Tantrism 143, 154–56; schools of 154
śakti 4; Śiva's consort and power 119
*śaktipīṭha*s 156–58, 296, 304, 416; Sircar's enumeration of 482; theory and practice of 158
Śāktism 142; antecedents to 145–47; Bengali, varieties of 141; broad historical survey 142; defining 140–42; "dependent" 141; different forms 141; "independent" 141; studies of specific goddesses 142; study of specific localities and contexts 142; *see also* Śākta systems
Śālivāhana 576
Salomon, R. 486
salvation: five steps in the project of 168; principal ways of 296; in Upaniṣad 277
salvation myths: artistic representations of important 293; features of 293; Vedic 297
śama (restraining of the outgoing mental propensities) 294
samādhāna (contentment) 294
samādhi (trance) 295
Sāma Jātaka 90, 93
Samavai, Queen 451
samāvartana (taking leave of teacher and returning home) 348
Sāma Veda Saṃhitā 38, 41, 214
Sambo-ekotoba (of Minamotono Tamenori) 93
saṃhitāpāṭha (words combined in euphonic combination) 39
Saṃhitās 31, 215, 288, 310, 368, 512; in Vaiṣṇava Tantric tradition or Pāñcarātra 125; *see also* Vedas
saṃkalpa (declaration of intent) 274–75
Śaṃkara 50, 113, 241–42, 266, 287, 291–92, 294, 299, 372, 384, 398, 482, 536; AdvaitaVedānta 238; commentary on *Bhagavad Gītā* 241, 251; commentary on the *Brahmasūtra* 123; distinction between renouncers 400; *Śaṃkarabhāṣya* on *Bhagavad Gītā* 241, 251
saṃkara (mixture) 55
Saṃkarṣana 164
Saṃkarṣana-Balarāma 162

Tibet 263; Buddhist pilgrimage around Mount Kailāsa 478; texts of *Rāmāyaṇa* in 93
Tilak, B. G. 248, 301
time (*kāla*) 555; as animal 560; astrology 573–75; as body of the deity 570–73; continuum as mental construction (*buddhinirmāṇa*) 554; and cooking 558–59; cosmos as a map of time 570–73; day and night 565–66; descent of Gaṅgā 561–62; and destiny 573–74; division or intervals of 562–70; doctrine of (*kālavāda*) 577; foreshadowing, devices of 581–83; hierarchizations in relation to the deity 555; Hinduism and cyclical 575–77; Hindu views of 553; as loom of acts and language 557–58; moment 565; motion, and soul 556–62; narrative time 577–86; ontological status of 553–56; rhythms in mythologies 572–73; structured, four main hierarchically defined rhythms 562; studies in Hindu myth and ritual 553; and system of *avatārs* 566; year and zodiacal circle 566–67; *yuga* and *kalpa* 567–70
Timirliṅga (dark phallus) or Tamburlaine 586
Tipū Sulṭān Fath 'Alī Khān 497
tīrtha (sacred places) 478, 481, 501; classification 481–84; and contemporary politics 500–501; development overseas 483–84; and economics, politics and society 495–501; in Hindu world, place and symbol 479–80; history of holy place (Sthalapurāṇa) 461; interreligious contestation 498–500; meaning "ford" or "crossing place" 479; pilgrimage studies 486–88; regional empires, role of some 496–98; sources for the study of 484–88; symbolic importance 495–96; toponyms in the Purāṇas 485; tourism 494–95; as traditionally acknowledged and attractive pilgrimage centers or 5; *yātrā* to 485–95
Tīrthacintāmaṇi (of Vācaspati Miśra) 485
Tīrthakalpataru (of Bhaṭṭa Lakṣmīdhara) 485
"tīrtham" holy water 480
tīrthaṅkaras (ford-makers) 498, 550
Tirthaprakāśa (of Mitra Miśra) 485
Tīrtha-pratyāmnāyāḥ 486
Tīrthavivecanakāṇḍa (of Bhaṭṭa Lakṣmīdhara) 486
tīrthyātrā (a trip to a "place of crossing") 435
Tirucempāvai 134
Tirukkuṛal (of Tiruvaḷḷuvar) 253
Tirumaḷicai Āḻvār 458
Tirumūlar 27
Tirumuṟai, the 27, 134
Tirupati temple 496, 498; trust 484; Veṅkateśvara at 449, 469
Tiruppaḷḷyeḻucci 469
Tiruvāymoḻi (of Nammāḻvār) 168, 173, 196, 279; songs of 171; Vaṭakkutiruvīttipiḷḷai's comment on 183
titikṣā (forbearance) 294
Tokunaga, M. 69
Toomey, P. M. 416
tourism in *tīrthas*, modern 494–95
transcendental bliss (*niḥśreyas*) 250
transitions from one stage of life (*āśrama*) to another 338
trayīvidyā (triple knowledge) 147
Tretā Yuga 100, 194, 563–64
triad of goals or values of man 250
Trika tradition 126, 129; pantheon 130
triple canon (*prasthānatraya*) of Vedānta 547
Tripurārahasya 300
Tripurasundarī 155
Tristhalīsetu (of Nārāyaṇa Bhaṭṭa) 485, 486
trivarga (group of three) 4, 238, 251–52; of "principal human concerns" (*puruṣārtha*) 362
Troeltsch, E. 402
Tübingen Purāṇa Project 113
Tukārāma 37, 198, 527
Tull, H. W. 4
Tully, M. 88
Tulasīdāsa 84, 88, 91, 201, 204, 528; *Rāmcaritmanas* 167, 175, 200; social conservatism 201; socioreligious ideology conservative 200; and *varṇadharmībhakti* 200; *Vinaya Patrikā* 201
Turner, V. 486, 488
"twice-born" (*dvija*) *varṇas* 230, 359; ascetics (*Manusmṛti*) 362; Brāhmaṇs, Kṣatriyas, and Vaiśyas 229; Hindu male 383; ritual status of being 26

Uberoi, J. P. S. 363, 378
udāharaṇa (the universal proposition with example) 538
Udāsī *mahants* (abbots) 499
Udayana 536
Uddālaka 49
udgātṛ priest 41
Udyana account of Nyāya theism 542
ultimate elements or atoms (*paramāṇu*) 543
Umā Saṃhitā 298
universal norms: of *sādhāraṇadharma* or *sāmānyadharma* 244–45